Devotional
COMMENTARY

Devotional COMMENTARY

Lawrence O. Richards

Run So That You May Win
ivictor.com

Victor is an imprint of
Cook Communications Ministries, Colorado Springs, Colorado 80918
Cook Communications, Paris, Ontario
Kingsway Communications, Eastbourne, England

DEVOTIONAL COMMENTARY

Formerly published as *The 365-Day Devotional Commentary*
Printed in the United States of America

Cover Design: iDesign Etc.

Library of Congress Cataloguing-in-Publication Data applied for.

7 8 9 10 11 12 13 14 15 Printing/Year 08 07 06 05 04 03 02

CONTENTS

The Home Bible Study Library

Welcome to this volume of the Home Bible Study Library, a series designed especially for *you*. As a serious Christian, you're a student of God's Word. You're eager to study the Bible in greater depth, but without the technical language and academic approach of seminary textbooks. What you want are resource books that will help you go deeper into God's Word. You want resource books that will provide practical help as you minister as a Sunday school teacher, youth leader, Bible study leader, or simply as a learner. You want resource books that will bring Scripture alive and help you know the Lord better and better.

That's why we've published the Home Bible Study Library. Its four volumes are written in clear, easy-to-understand language by Dr. Larry Richards, a former seminary professor who has written over 200 books and study Bibles. Each book in this Home Bible Study Library guides you to better understand and apply God's Word, taking you to the heart of those issues that are close to the heart of God. While your Home Bible Study Library relies on the latest and best scholarship to illumine the text, each of its volumes speaks directly and movingly to ordinary men and women.

Each volume in this series has its own distinctive emphasis and makes its own unique contribution to your understanding of God's Word.

Bible Teacher's Commentary helps you think through the entire Bible, following each author's train of thought. It also gives suggestions for communicating key truths and passages to children, youth, and adults.

Devotional Commentary takes you through the entire Bible in a year, enriching your daily walk with God and helping you see the personal significance of both Old and New Testament passages.

Bible Reader's Companion features chapter-by-chapter coverage of the Bible, providing fascinating archaeological and cultural insights that enrich your understanding as you read the Scriptures. It also defines key terms and helps you trace key themes and doctrines through God's Word.

New Testament Life and Times takes you into the world of the first century A.D., bringing the teachings of Jesus and the letters of Paul alive in a fresh, vital way.

Together these four volumes in the Home Bible Study Library offer you a unique education in God's Word. Studying them will help you understand the Bible from cover to cover, deepen your personal relationship with God, and show you how to communicate to others what God is teaching you.

Devotional Commentary

I've heard it again and again: "I just can't get anything out of reading the Bible, especially the Old Testament." To far too many believers, God's Word seems about as vital and exciting as a history textbook.

But Scripture isn't a textbook. Scripture is God's living Word, speaking His message to you and me today. When we come to the Bible listening actively to hear God's voice speaking to us personally, the Bible truly comes alive.

That's why I wrote the *Devotional Commentary,* a year-long adventure designed to take you through the Bible from start to finish. My goal is to help you discover in every passage of Scripture some of the very personal messages God's Spirit communicates to Jesus' people. In the most surprising places you'll discover words of comfort, words of challenge, good news that will encourage you in difficult times, and penetrating insights that will purify and cleanse your life.

I've had more letters from people using this commentary than from readers of any of the over 200 books I've written. Many tell me that they've used it in their devotions not just for one year, but for three or four or even five.

I pray that God will use this book to help you experience His Word as a warm, personal message to you each and every day.

Lawrence O. Richards

HOW TO USE THE *DEVOTIONAL COMMENTARY*

Here are four flexible ways to use this Commentary to enrich your own life and your ministry to others. (1) You can refer to the Commentary for personal application when preparing a talk or lesson, or when reading the Bible on your own. (2) You can cover the Bible in a single year following any of two different 1-year reading plans! (3) You can follow one of the special reading programs that explore Personal Relationship with God or provide a Bible Overview. (4) You can use the Christian Year readings, perhaps with your whole family, to have a very special 40 Days of Lent, 10 Days at Christmas, or 7 Days at Easter.

However you may use this Commentary, our prayer is that using it will enrich your understanding of Scripture as God's very personal Word to *you*, and help you to hear His living voice today.

TWO DIFFERENT 1-YEAR READING PLANS

PLAN A:
Adventure Reading Plan: Genesis to Revelation

Begin with Genesis, and day-by-day trace the unfolding story of God's plan for humankind. Live the adventure with Abraham, Moses, and the Exodus generation. Observe the rise and fall of the Hebrew kingdoms. Probe the Wisdom literature of the Old Testament, and listen to the voices of the Prophets. Then see the fulfillment of the promise in Jesus, listen to His teaching, and accompany Him on His journey to the cross. Share the joy of Resurrection as the vibrant young church reaches out to a lost world. Finally ponder the lessons taught in the Epistles: lessons that have guided Christ's church for nearly 2,000 years.

PLAN B:
Variety Reading Plan: Alternate OT and NT readings

Keep your reading of Scripture fresh by balancing readings from the Old and New Testaments. Plan "B" readings follow the chart (below), and keep your devotional reading stimulating and invigorating. Each week or two you'll explore a different facet of God's Word: sampling the Prophets, tracing narrative history, journeying with Jesus, listening to the teaching of the Apostles, worshiping with the psalmist. In the span of a single year you'll read the entire Bible, yet each month will be filled with exhilarating variety and unexpected insights.

Or use this unique Devotional Commentary in one of several other ways.

January
Genesis
Luke
Song of Songs

February
Psalms 1–84
1 Corinthians
2 Corinthians

March
Joshua
Judges
Ruth
Hebrews
Job
James

April
Matthew
Jeremiah
1 Thessalonians
Philippians

May

Psalms 85–150
Daniel
Revelation
1 John
2 John
3 John
Nahum
Ezra

June

Nehemiah
Esther
Ephesians
Philemon
Hosea
Joel
Amos
Jonah
Micah
Zechariah
Galatians
Jude

July

Mark
Proverbs
1 Kings
2 Kings
Titus
Colossians

August

Exodus
Leviticus
Numbers
1 Timothy
2 Timothy
Ecclesiastes
Lamentations

September

1 Chronicles
2 Chronicles
1 Peter
2 Peter
Ezekiel
Obadiah
2 Thessalonians
Habakkuk

October

Romans
1 Samuel
2 Samuel
Haggai
Malachi
Zephaniah

November

Deuteronomy
John

December

Acts
Isaiah

SPECIAL READING PROGRAMS

A special 30-day reading program will help you explore either your own personal relationship with God or provide a Bible Overview. If you're not ready to commit to a one-year reading plan, try one of these 30-day programs and find out how to meet God in His Word, and listen for His personal message to you.

30-DAY BIBLE OVERVIEW

Day	*Passage*	*Day*	*Passage*
1	*Gen. 1–2*	16	*1 Kings 12–14*
2	*Gen. 3–4*	17	*Ezek. 8–11*
3	*Gen. 12–14*	18	*Hab.*
4	*Gen. 15–17*	19	*2 Chron. 34–36*
5	*Ex. 1–4*	20	*Jer. 31–34*
6	*Ex. 20–23*	21	*Matt. 1–2*
7	*Lev. 16–20*	22	*Matt. 6–7*
8	*Num. 11–14*	23	*Matt. 8–9*
9	*Deut. 5–7*	24	*Matt. 24–25*
10	*Josh. 6–8*	25	*Matt. 26–28*
11	*Jud. 1–3*	26	*Acts 3–4*
12	*1 Sam. 16–19*	27	*Rom. 2–3*
13	*2 Sam. 6–10*	28	*Rom. 4*
14	*1 Kings 1–4*	29	*1 Cor. 15*
15	*1 Kings 5–8*	30	*Rev. 20–21*

30-DAY PERSONAL RELATIONSHIP

Day	*Passage*	*Day*	*Passage*
1	*Gen. 15–17*	16	*John 17*
2	*Ex. 1–4*	17	*Rom. 4*
3	*Deut. 5–7*	18	*Rom. 8*
4	*Deut. 28*	19	*Rom. 12*
5	*1 Sam. 16–17*	20	*Rom. 13*
6	*Ps. 23*	21	*Rom. 14*
7	*2 Sam. 11–13*	22	*1 Cor. 13*
8	*Ps. 51*	23	*2 Cor. 8–9*
9	*Job 1–14*	24	*Eph. 1*
10	*Ps. 37*	25	*Eph. 2*
11	*Luke 5–6*	26	*Eph. 3–4*
12	*Luke 11*	27	*Eph. 5*
13	*John 10*	28	*1 John 1*
14	*John 15*	29	*1 John 2–3*
15	*John 16*	30	*1 John 4–5*

TEN DAYS AT CHRISTMAS

Day	*Passage*	*Day*	*Passage*
1	*Isa. 7*	6	*Mark 4–5*
2	*Isa. 9*	7	*Mark 6–7*
3	*Luke 2*	8	*Mark 8–10*
4	*Mark 1*	9	*Mark 11–12*
5	*Mark 2–3*	10	*Mark 14–16*

SEVEN DAYS AT EASTER

Day	*Passage*	*Day*	*Passage*
1	*Luke 22–23*	5	*1 Cor. 15*
2	*Luke 24*	6	*1 Thes. 3–5*
3	*Rom. 5*	7	*Rev. 21–22*
4	*Rom. 6–7*		

FORTY DAYS OF LENT

Day	*Passage*	*Day*	*Passage*
1	*Isa. 53*	21	*John 20–21*
2	*John 1:1-18*	22	*Heb. 1*
3	*John 1:19–2:24*	23	*Heb. 2–3*
4	*John 3*	24	*Heb. 4–5*
5	*John 4*	25	*Heb. 6*
6	*John 5*	26	*Heb. 7–8*
7	*John 6*	27	*Heb. 9*
8	*John 7*	28	*Heb. 10*
9	*John 8*	29	*Heb. 11*
10	*John 9*	30	*Heb. 12*
11	*John 10*	31	*Heb. 13*
12	*John 11*	32	*Rev. 1*
13	*John 12*	33	*Rev. 5*
14	*John 13*	34	*Rev. 14*
15	*John 14*	35	*1 Thes. 4*
16	*John 15*	36	*Rev. 19*
17	*John 16*	37	*Rev. 20*
18	*John 17*	38	*Isa. 65:19-66*
19	*John 18*	39	*Rev. 21*
20	*John 19*	40	*Rev. 22*

Genesis

INTRODUCTION

Genesis is the first of five books written by Moses during the Exodus period, about 1450–1400 B.C. Using as sources direct revelation from God and the written and oral traditions of his people, Moses surveyed history from the Creation to his own day.

The Book of Genesis is divided into two parts. Genesis 1–11 tells of God's dealings with the whole human race from Creation to the time of Abraham, about 2100 B.C. Genesis 12 introduces a vital theme. God makes a covenant with one man and with his descendants. God will work through this man, Abraham, and his family, Israel, to reveal himself to humanity and ultimately to provide a salvation available to all.

OUTLINE OF CONTENTS

I. God's Dealings with the Human Race .... Gen. 1–11
   A. Creation .... Gen. 1–2
   B. The Fall .... Gen. 3–5
   C. The Flood and aftermath .... Gen. 6–11
II. God's Dealings with Abraham's Family .... Gen. 12–50
   A. Abraham .... Gen. 12–25
   B. Isaac .... Gen. 22–27
   C. Jacob and Esau .... Gen. 25–36
   D. Joseph .... Gen. 37–50

READING GUIDE (14 Days)

If hurried, you may read only the "core passage" in your Bible and the Devotional in each chapter of this Commentary.

Reading	*Chapters*	*Core passage*
1	1–2	1:26-27
2	3–5	3:8-19
3	6–8	6:9-22
4	9–11	9:8-17
5	12–14	12:1-9
6	15–17	15:1-19
7	18–21	18:16-33
8	22:1–25:18	22:1-19
9	25:19–28:22	27:1-33
10	29–32	32:1-21
11	33–36	35:1-15
12	37–41	39:1-23
13	42–46	46:1-27
14	47–50	50:1-21

Genesis

JANUARY 1 *Reading 1*
THE CROWN OF CREATION
Genesis 1–2

"God saw all that He had made, and it was very good" (Gen. 1:31).

Each day's work of Creation closes with the divine evaluation, "it was good." Only the work of the sixth day, on which the Lord created humanity, earned ultimate approval—"very good."

Overview

God created the heavens and the earth (1:1). The orderly process described here moves from formation of a unique setting for life (vv. 3-19), to populating earth with animal life (vv. 20-25), to the creation of beings in God's own image (vv. 26-27). Man, the crown of the completed Creation, is destined for dominion (vv. 28-31). Genesis 2 returns to examine more closely these beings intended to be the crown of God's Creation.

Understanding the Text

Create Gen. 1:1. The Hebrew word *bara'* does not mean to "make something out of nothing." It means to begin or originate a sequence of events. Genesis affirms that God is the cause of all that exists. God, not chance, originated all life and uniquely shaped human beings. Contemplating God as Creator is a source of great comfort.

"Formless and empty" Gen. 1:2. The Second Law of Thermodynamics states that, left alone, any system will decay. Yet our earth contains life-forms that are highly organized and complex, far from the "formless and empty" state this universal law of nature predicts.

In Russia Dr. Boris P. Dotsenko, then head of the nuclear physics department in the Institute of Physics in Kiev, began to think seriously about the nature of the universe. "It suddenly dawned on me," he wrote later, "that there must be a very powerful *organizing* force counteracting the disorganizing tendency within nature, keeping the universe controlled and in order. This force could not be material; otherwise it too would become disordered. I concluded that this power must be both omnipotent and omniscient. There must be a God—one God—controlling everything" (Larry Richards, *It Couldn't Just Happen* [Fort Worth: Sweet, 1989], p. 17).

Later, in Canada for further studies, Dr. Dotsenko picked up a Bible. There he met the God he had decided *must* exist, and became a Christian.

"The first day" Gen. 1:5. Christians debate the implications of "day" in Genesis 1. Some believe "day" is used loosely to indicate an age. Others, noting the "morning and evening" mentioned in the text, conclude a 24-hour day is intended. Even here there is debate. Were the 24-hour days consecutive? Or might they have been separated by millions of years?

Scripture does little to satisfy our scientific curiosity. Why? Perhaps because it is "by faith we understand that the universe was formed at God's command, so that what is seen was not made out of what was visible" (Heb. 11:3). Even if the details were known, those without faith would scoff and still hold fast to their fancies.

But there is another reason as well.

Genesis calls us to look beyond the material to the immaterial—beyond the Creation to the Creator. Nothing should distract us from the reflection of God that we see in what He has made.

"Let there be" Gen. 1:3, 6, 9, etc. All but one of God's creative acts was accomplished by the simple expedient of speaking the word. The psalmist picks up this theme and cries, "He spoke, and it came to be; He commanded, and it stood firm" (Ps. 33:9). The echoes of God's speech still are heard in the creation that then sprang into being. Psalm 19 says that "the heavens declare the glory of God; the skies proclaim the work of His hands." It adds that "there is no speech or language where their voice is not heard" (vv. 1-3).

Creation's witness to the existence of God is a cornerstone of Paul's argument that human beings have wandered far from God. In Romans 1:20-21 Paul says that "since the Creation of the world God's invisible qualities—His eternal power and divine nature—have been clearly seen, being understood from what has been made, so that men are without excuse." They are without excuse because "although they knew God, they neither glorified Him nor gave thanks to Him."

What a reminder for you and me. As we walk by the seashore, gaze in wonder at the stars, or smell the fragrance of a flower, we are to sense God speaking to us through His creation. And, seeing Him, we are to worship and give thanks.

"Let them rule" Gen. 1:26. The concept of dominion stated here is not a "right to use" but an "obligation to guard and protect." Modern man's responsibility for earth's ecological well-being is stated here in Genesis, long before "advances" in modern science threatened the balance of nature.

"Fruitful and multiply" Gen. 1:28. The Bible maintains a positive, healthy attitude toward human sexuality. Sexual intercourse was not, as some have wrongly taught, the "apple" Adam and Eve were forbidden to taste! Here we find evidence, long before the Fall, that God has always intended human beings to enjoy and to use their sexual capacities.

"Good" Gen. 1:10, 12, etc. The Hebrew word used here has a wide range of meanings, from attractive and pleasing to beneficial and useful. God created our universe for a purpose. As it was originally constituted, the universe and all in it were ideally suited to display God's glory and to accomplish His purposes. The tragedy of sin, introduced in Genesis 3, has warped original Creation. Even so, the beauty and value God invested in it can still be seen.

"Let Us" Gen. 1:26. Some suggest the plural word, *Elohim,* used here of God, is a "plural of majesty." As human royalty at times speaks of "we" when "I" is intended, so God is said to refer to Himself as plural. Christians, however, see in this earliest expression evidence that Scripture's one God exists in the three Persons fully unveiled only in the New Testament.

"A Garden in the east" Gen. 2:8. The Genesis description of Eden is significant. God not only designed Eden for beauty (v. 9), but also to occupy the time and the talents of the beings God intended to place in charge. The Garden reflects the fact that man truly does bear God's image. Like God, Adam could accomplish meaningful work (v. 15). Like God, Adam had a capacity to create (v. 19). Like God, Adam also had freedom of moral choice (v. 16). God did not plant the "tree of the knowledge of good and evil" to trap Adam, but to give him the opportunity to choose that which was right and good, even as God chooses to do good.

"Suitable helper" Gen. 2:20. The phrase does not imply inferiority, for the same Hebrew word (*'ezer*) is used to identify God as man's helper in Psalm 33:20 and several other passages. Surely God is not inferior to man because He offers us help!

Actually "suitable helper" teaches the full equality of women with men. It indicates that in Eve, in contrast with all in the animal kingdom, Adam found a being who fully shared his nature and thus could relate to Adam physically, intellectually, and spiritually.

"From the rib" Gen. 2:22-25. The Jewish rabbis early noted that the mode of wom-

an's creation is significant. If Eve had been made of the original clay, Adam might have viewed her as a secondary and inferior creation. By shaping Eve from Adam's own substance, God affirmed the full identity of men and women as persons who bear the divine image. Adam saw the implications immediately and accepted them fully. Eve was welcomed as "bone of my bones, and flesh of my flesh."

What a lesson here for Christians to take to heart!

▶DEVOTIONAL
The Image and Likeness of God (Gen. 1:26-27)

One of the most stunning expressions found in Scripture lies here in Genesis 1. "Let Us," God says, "make man in Our image, in Our likeness." And the text continues, "So God created man in His own image, in the image of God He created him; male and female He created them."

The two Hebrew words used here to define the human essence are *selem*, meaning "image" or "representation," and *demut*, which implies comparison. When linked they make a decisive theological statement. The essence of human nature can only be understood by comparison with God Himself. We can never understand man by referring back to some supposed emergence from prehistoric beasts. In a totally unique creative act, God gave Adam not only physical life but also personhood—his own capacity to think, to feel, to evaluate, to love, to choose, as a self-aware individual.

The Genesis account itself emphasizes human uniqueness. All other aspects of Creation were called into being by God's spoken word. Yet for man God stooped to personally fashion a physical body, and then gently, lovingly infused that body with life. In order that there should be no mistaking God's intent, God fashioned Eve from one of Adam's ribs. Genesis is clear. Adam and Eve share the same substance. They participate alike in the image and likeness given to beings alone.

This account does more than explain man's origins. It has the power to shape our most basic attitudes toward ourselves and others.

Consider. If I am made in the image of God, then I must have worth and value as an individual. It's irrelevant to compare myself with others if my essential being can be understood by comparison with God! Knowing God made me in His image, I learn to love and to value myself.

Have you ever noticed how we handle things we value? We wear the new watch or pin proudly. When we lay it aside, we do so carefully, putting it in a drawer where it won't be damaged or harmed. If you and I grasp the value of being created in God's image and likeness, we will come to appreciate ourselves too. We'll refuse to be degraded by others, and we will reject temptations that would harm us physically or spiritually. Because we bear the image and likeness of the Creator, we are too significant to mar.

Consider. If others are made in the image and likeness of God, they must have worth and value as individuals, whatever weaknesses they display. When I understand that every human being shares the image-likeness of God, I will treat others with respect. I learn to overlook failures and to communicate love. I realize that the existence of God's image-likeness, however distorted by sin, means that the other person can respond, as I have, to the love of God displayed in Jesus Christ. So I reach out to him or her in love.

Consider. If men and women truly share the image and likeness of God, each must have a worth and value that is independent of sex, race, or social status. When I truly understand that every human being shares with me God's image and likeness, I begin to set aside the prejudices that drive so much of human behavior. I learn to see women as people and appreciate all they have to contribute in the family, the workplace, and the church. I become color-blind, and set aside categories like black and white, rich and poor, and begin to treat each person I meet with respect and affection.

When this happens, I have learned the lesson of Genesis 1:26-27, and begun to understand how precious others are to the God who made them, and who made me.

Personal Application

"Lord, help me to look at others with new eyes. Enable me to see each person as You do, and in practical ways to communicate respect and love."

Quotable
"Remember that sharing means more than cutting a piece of cake in two equal slices. It involves your whole attitude toward the other person. Remember all the ways you are equal persons in God's estimation; then equalize your life to fit His opinion, not that of society around you."
—Pat Gundry

JANUARY 2 *Reading 2*
THE ENTRANCE OF SIN
Genesis 3–5

"I was afraid because I was naked; so I hid" (Gen. 3:10).

One of the great mysteries that puzzles philosophers is solved in Genesis 3. Sin is no unexplained remnant of humanity's supposed rise from beastiality, but a heritage flowing from Adam's fall. Yet the focus in these two chapters is not on the fact of sin, but on its consequences.

Overview
Eve succumbed to temptation and induced Adam to disobey God (3:1-6). Overcome by guilt and shame, the pair ran from the Creator God who loved them (vv. 7-10). God found them and explained the consequences of their act (vv. 11-20). God Himself offered history's first sacrifice (v. 21) and led them from the Garden (vv. 22-24). Adam and Eve lived to see sin's consequences in their own family as Cain killed his brother Abel (4:1-16). Lamech, Cain's descendant, represents the sinful society that emerged (vv. 17-26).

Here lies the foundation of the Christian doctrine of "total depravity." Man is not as bad as he can be. But mankind, separated from God, is *as bad off* as it can be.

Understanding the Text
"He said to the woman" Gen. 3:1-6. Satan's approach to Eve is a classic model of the reasoning that leads us into sin. God's command not to eat of one tree in the Garden (2:17) established a standard. Satan attacked this standard in three ways.

Satan questioned the existence of the standard: "Did God really say?" (3:1)

Satan cast doubt on God's motives for establishing the standard: "God knows that when you eat . . . you will be like God" (v. 5).

Satan denied the consequences of violating the standard: "You will not surely die" (v. 4).

Yesterday I saw a debate over pornography on CNN's "Crossfire," and saw Satan's arguments marshalled once again. An ACLU lawyer ridiculed the idea that even gross pornography is wrong. He claimed censorship of pornography would deny readers their rights and pleasures. And he claimed that no harm would come through filling the mind with pornographic images.

Our only protection against evil is the belief which Eve abandoned. We must affirm what God has said. We must be convinced that His standards are not intended to deny us pleasures but to protect us from harm. And we must realize that tragic consequences will follow violating God's standards of right and wrong.

"Die" Gen. 3:4. In the Bible "death" is an all-encompassing term. It describes the end of biological life. But it also describes man's psychological, social, and spiritual state. When God warned Adam not to eat the forbidden fruit, He explained, "When you eat of it you will surely die."

Adam's sin brought "death" in all four of its meanings. Biologically the process of aging began when Adam sinned; a process that led to the death of the first pair and to the physical death which stalks every human being now. Psychologically Adam and Eve were stricken with guilt and shame, expressed here in their sense of nakedness (3:7). Socially Adam and Eve were set at odds, blaming each other for their act. The harmony they had known was broken by strife (vv. 11-13). Spiritually Adam and Eve were alienated from God, and this created a sense of fear. The God of love had suddenly become an object of terror (vv. 8-10).

No human being is as bad as he or she might be. But all human beings, the victims of sin's legacy of physical, pyschological, social, and spiritual death, are *as bad off* as they could be.

We're familiar with all these aspects of what the Bible calls "death." Each is a witness—a billboard—announcing loudly that sin is a reality with which we *must* deal.

"They sewed fig leaves together" Gen. 3:7. The phrase portrays man's first, futile effort to deal with sin. Adam and Eve tried to cover themselves. Yet they knew their attempt to deal with sin was a failure. How do we know? When Adam and Eve heard God nearby, "they hid from the LORD God among the trees of the Garden" (v. 8). Try as we may to deal with sin by our own efforts, deep down we human beings retain a sense of guilt and shame that witnesses to our lost condition. There never has been, and never will be, a human being saved by his or her own works.

*"God made garments of skin for Adam and his wife" Gen. 3:21.*This simple statement is filled with symbolic significance. It is referred to as "history's first sacrifice." God Himself took the life of an animal to cover the nakedness of Adam and Eve.

Note that God made the garments. We cannot deal with sin. God Himself must act.

Note that blood was shed. Here, as in Mosaic Law's system of sacrifices, several lessons are taught. Sin merits death. Yet God will accept the death of a substitute. There was no merit in the blood of bulls and goats slain on ancient altars. Animal sacrifice was God's visual aid, preparing humanity to recognize in the death of Christ on Calvary a substitutionary sacrifice that *does* take away sins.

"God banished him from the Garden" Gen. 3:23. Driving out Adam and Eve was an act of grace, not of punishment. The first pair was banished lest they "take also from the tree of life and eat, and live forever." It would have been horrible beyond imagination for Adam and Eve to have lived on through the millenniums, forced to witness the wars, the injustice, the suffering that flowed from their original act of sin. How appropriate Isaiah's words might have been, engraved over the forbidden entrance to Eden: "The righteous are taken away to be spared from evil. Those who walk uprightly enter into peace; they find rest as they lie in death" (Isa. 57:1-2).

"Cain was very angry" Gen. 4:1-16. Adam and Eve could not avoid observing this evidence of the spiritual death they unleashed on their descendants. When God accepted the sacrifice of Abel and rejected Cain's offering, Cain was filled with anger. Cain lured his brother "out to the field," where he attacked and killed him!

What a heartrending experience for Adam and Eve! One dearly loved son killed by another. And they knew that ultimately the fault was theirs! Adam and Eve had themselves introduced into history the sin that expressed itself in Cain's hostility and murderous act.

The story of Cain and Abel raises several questions. Why did God reject Cain's offering? The rabbis concluded that Cain offered God rotting fruit. A better explanation is that Abel, in making a blood sacrifice, followed a prescription that God had given Adam and Eve when He first clothed them in skins. In offering produce Cain suggested that his best was good enough to offer God. God's reminder, "If you do what is right" (v. 7), supports this interpretation. Cain knew the right way to approach God, but was unwilling to do so.

Why did Cain kill Abel? Anyone who sins and refuses to accept responsibility is likely to seek a scapegoat and be hostile toward that person. The truly good person is most likely to attract the hostility of the wicked, for his or her very goodness reminds the wicked of their sin.

Where did Cain get his wife? If Adam and Eve were the only humans, and Cain and Abel their only children, where could Cain obtain a wife? The answer, of course, is that Cain and Abel were *not* Adam and Eve's only children. Genesis 5:4 says they "had other sons and daughters." Cain and Abel are the only two mentioned in Genesis 4 simply because the story is about them! We can assume from 5:4 that a rather large community of Adam's children, and perhaps even his children's children, existed before Cain attacked his brother.

All these questions, however, divert us from the emphasis the writer of Genesis intends. The death that God announced would follow disobedience has struck not only Adam and Eve, but has been inherited by their children! Sin has corrupted the race of man, and we all live with the tragic consequences of Adam's fall.

"I have killed a man for wounding me" Gen. 4:23. Genesis 4 continues to trace the consequences of sin. A descendant of Cain named Lamech violated the divine order for society by marrying two women. He then justified murder, explaining that the man he killed had wounded him. One woman was no longer viewed as a man's partner, but women had become subservient, objects for a man to use. Injustice was rationalized, and murder was viewed by the proud as fair recompense for insult. In this passage we see society itself being torn from its moral foundations.

There is more than a touch of irony here. Genesis 4:19-22 describes achievements of Lamech's sons. One gained control over the animal kingdom (v. 20). Another introduced those aesthetics we humans associate with "culture" (v. 21). Another learned to wrest metals from the earth and shape them to man's use (v. 22). Is there any invention, are there any heights, that humanity cannot achieve?

Today we live in an amazing world. We send men to the moon, unmanned probes to distant planets. We focus radiation to destroy cancer cells, and flood the market with medicines that prolong life. We fill the airwaves with music, hurtle along highways in machines that are complex beyond our ability to understand. Yet despite all our achievements in the material universe, our society remains marred by suffering and sin. Cigarette companies responsible for the early deaths of 380,000 persons a year freely promote their product. The drunk and drug-impaired crash those complex machines into other human beings. Major free-world corporations help terrorist nations to construct chemical warfare plants. Child abuse and murder, wars and rumors of wars, fill the pages of our newspapers. Yes, man can achieve wonders in the material world. But humanity is spiritually dead, unable to overcome the pull of sin or to avoid its awful consequences. Again, we are not as bad as we might be. But, without God, we remain as bad off as we could be.

All this is taught and demonstrated in Genesis 3 and 4.

▶ DEVOTIONAL
"Because You Ate"
(Gen. 3:8-19)

The dialogue between God and Adam lies at the heart of these tragic chapters. God found Adam and questioned him. Adam's words revealed the fact that this was truly the story of a Fall, despite the claim of some that eating the forbidden fruit was a step upward.

Adam was now afraid of the God whose image he bore (v. 10). Adam was aware of his guilt and felt shame (v. 10). Adam refused to face reality and attempted to shift blame for his act to Eve (v. 12). Eve too would not accept responsibility (v. 13). God then announced consequences that must follow the choices made by each actor in the Genesis 3 drama.

It's important to see the consequences not as some arbitrary punishment but as a necessity required by the moral nature of the universe God created. The serpent that loaned his body as a vehicle to Satan lost his beauty (v. 14). Stripped of illusion, sin is always ugly and degrading. Satan won the hostility rather than the allegiance of the human race (v. 15). Unlike the angels who fell, mankind will not willingly form ranks behind Satan in his mad warfare against God. Satan also is destined to be crushed by One to be born of the fallen race (v. 15). In a moral universe, it is impossible for evil to triumph.

The consequences to Eve were physical, psychological, and social (v. 16). Some understand "increase your pains in childbearing" to indicate a more frequent menstrual cycle. "Your desire will be for your husband" indicates a new psychological dependence that will replace Eve's original sense of strong personal identity. And "he will rule over you" introduces for the first time the idea of hierarchy: that in a sinful universe human beings will struggle to gain dominance over one another, and that women will be forced by society into subservient and depersonalizing roles. Here the cause is not the morality of the universe, but the distortion caused by sin itself. When Adam and Eve abandoned submission to God's will to assert their own independent wills, conflict became inevitable.

Adam too would suffer, this time from the distortion sin caused in nature (vv. 17-19). Work became toil, and life a struggle against nature.

In all these things we see further evidence of the ruin sin brings. Yet we also sense a note of hope. What Adam did, Christ has and will repair. When Jesus comes, nature itself will be liberated (Rom. 8:18-21). But you and I can experience liberation even now! No, not from the physical changes caused by the first sin. But we can be liberated in our relationships. We can be liberated from competition in our homes and churches, and through mutual submission to God's will regain the harmony that reigned before the Fall. We can be liberated from the desire to establish our own superiority by dominating others. In Christ we can be liberated too from blaming, from hatred, and from doing injustice.

The dark picture drawn here as sin's consequences are defined reminds us of what once was before the Fall. That image of what man has lost informs us of the kind of persons we are called to be in Christ, and of the bright future Christ promises to the people of God.

Personal Application

What indications of the Fall do you see in your own relationships with others? Be encouraged! Christ died to deliver you from just these consequences of sin.

Quotable

"We are establishing an all-time world record in the production of material things. What we lack is a righteous and dynamic faith. Without it, all else avails us little. The lack cannot be compensated for by politicians, however able; or by diplomats, however astute; or by scientists, however inventive; or by bombs, however powerful."—John Foster Dulles

JANUARY 3 *Reading 3*
THE CLEANSING FLOOD
Genesis 6–8

> *"I will wipe mankind . . . from the face of the earth" (Gen. 6:7).*

The bright promise of God's original Creation had been blighted by human sin. Now Genesis introduced a theme which echoes throughout Scripture. God is moral judge of His universe. God will not shrink from His responsibility. God will surely punish those who sin.

Overview

Freed from restraint, men dedicated themselves to evil, and a saddened God determined to cleanse the earth (6:1-8). Noah, earth's sole righteous man, obeyed God's command to construct a gigantic ship (vv. 9-22). After Noah's family and breeding stock entered this ark, God caused a Flood which wiped out all other people and animals (7:1-24). A year later Noah's family emerged on a cleansed earth (8:1-20). After Noah worshiped, God promised not to destroy all life again—until the day of final judgment (vv. 20-22).

Understanding the Text

"Nephilim" Gen. 6:4. The meaning of the term is uncertain. Some take it to mean giants, produced by a union of fallen angels ("sons of God" being His direct creations) and human women. While verses 1-2 and 4 are obscure, the thrust of the passage is clear. Human wickedness reached new heights until "every inclination of the thoughts of [man's] heart was only evil all the time" (v. 5).

"Grief and pain" Gen. 6:6. Note the text does *not* say "anger and outrage"! God takes no pleasure in punishing those who sin. Instead He is deeply pained—by the hurt His creations cause one another and by the necessity of punishing persons made in His own image.

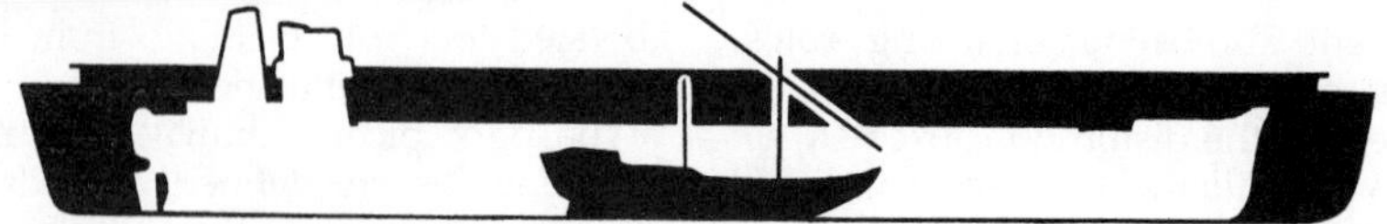

"A righteous man" Gen. 6:9. When applied to human beings in the Old Testament, "righteous" and "blameless" never imply being without sin. Instead they are used to portray persons who respond to God wholeheartedly and who honestly seek to please Him. Only Noah merited this description.

"450 feet long" Gen. 6:15. The ark was a massive ship even by modern standards (see illustration). It was intended to carry breeding pairs of various animal kinds and provisions for them, as well as to bear Noah and his family. Many different models of the ark have been designed, but the text gives us insufficient information to accurately portray the giant boat. The illustration on this page gives some sense of the size of the ark in relation to ancient and modern vessels.

"Everything . . . that had the breath of life in its nostrils died" Gen. 7:22. Many debate whether the Genesis Flood was local or universal. Certainly the text suggests a cataclysm, with subterranean and atmospheric waters surging on an earth wracked with earthquakes. The statement that "all the high mountains under the entire heavens were covered" has been taken by one side as evidence that the Flood was local, for there is not enough water on earth to top such peaks as Everest, Ararat, and McKinley. The same statement is taken by the other side as evidence *for* a universal Flood. The pressure of the waters may have caused earth's then unstable surface to thrust up modern peaks and to depress seabeds.

Yet this debate obscures the point the text emphasizes. Three times Genesis 7 repeats it. "Every living thing that moved on the earth perished" (v. 21). "Everything on dry land . . . died" (v. 22). "Every living thing on the face of the earth was wiped out" (v. 23).

The Flood is not fodder for geological debate, but history's great affirmation that God is mankind's judge—and that God *will* judge sin. The tossing seas on which Noah's ark floated are a reminder to keep before the eyes of those who scoff and follow their own evil desires. Peter calls on such persons to look back—and then to look ahead. "They deliberately forget that. . . . the world of that time was deluged and destroyed. By the same word the present heavens and earth are reserved for fire, being kept for the day of judgment and destruction of ungodly men" (2 Peter 3:5-7).

The Genesis Flood is history's grim reminder that sin merits divine judgment, and that sinners will be judged.

"Never again" Gen. 8:21. After a year in the ark (cf. 7:11; 8:13), Noah emerged to worship the Lord. At that time God made a solemn commitment never again to destroy all living creatures "as long as the earth endures" (v. 22). Complete and cleansing judgment is now reserved for history's end.

▶ DEVOTIONAL
Blameless among the People of His Time
(Gen. 6:9-22)

Noah is one of the most impressive men of the Bible. He lived in a totally corrupt society. Yet he himself was committed to godliness and succeeded in living a blameless life. Even more impressive is the fact that when told by God to build a giant ship in a time when rain was unknown (2:6), Noah immediately set out to do so!

Noah and his sons cut and shaped ton upon ton of beams to form a keel and skeleton. They sawed uncounted thousands of planks for siding. They planted, gathered, and stored crops to serve as food for themselves and the animals God would bring when His time was right. And all the time they must have suffered the ridicule of their neighbors, who came to listen to and scoff at mad Noah's predictions of water about to fall from the sky and destroy them all.

How long did Noah and his sons labor? Genesis 6:3 tells us. When God made His decision to judge, mankind was given 120 years. It was during that time Noah and his sons accomplished their herculean tasks. And during all that time Noah bore the jokes made at his expense. He ignored the loud whispers he was intended to hear. And he kept on working, surrounded by the tittering laughter of his neighbors. Despite it all, Noah remained faithful. He had heard God speak. And Noah "did everything just as God commanded him."

Chris, the teenage son of our pastor, Richard Schmidt, can understand the pressure on Noah. In the locker room he was ridiculed for his determination to remain sexually pure. "It's what I believe," he said, "and it's what I'm going to do."

Probably you can understand too. There are so many in our modern world who laugh at people who have heard God's voice and try to do "everything just as God commanded." Imagine! Noah knew just that pressure, from *everyone*, and for 120 years! Yet Noah remained faithful. And you and I can remain faithful too.

Peter gives us a special insight into what Noah's faithfulness meant. Yes, Noah's faithfulness to God's word meant deliverance for himself and his family. But 1 Peter 3:19-20 suggests that by the agency of the Holy Spirit Christ Himself spoke through Noah in the long decades that "God waited patiently" for Noah to finish his assigned task.

How important our faithfulness is. As we like Noah bear up under the pressure brought on us, Christ by His Holy Spirit speaks through us to the very persons who laugh and doubt. And this time, they may respond!

Personal Application

Our faithfulness when others jeer speaks more powerfully than the words of the most gifted preacher the world has ever known.

Quotable

"Sin is first pleasing, then it grows easy, then delightful, then frequent, then habitual, then confirmed; then the man is impenitent, then he is obstinate, then he is resolved never to repent. And then he is ruined."—Bishop Leighton

---

JANUARY 4 *Reading 4*
NEVER AGAIN
Genesis 9–11

> *"I now establish My covenant with you and your descendants after you, and with every living creature" (Gen. 9:9-10).*

Noah and his sons carried the seed of sin with them into the new world. But now God introduced another theme which, with that of Creation, sin, and judgment, echoes through the Old Testament. It is the theme of promise; of a divine commitment to human beings made despite what we are rather than because of what we are.

Overview

God permitted man to prey on the animal kingdom, but not on other human beings (9:1-7). He made the rainbow a sign of His promise never again to cut off all life by a flood (vv. 8-17). Yet the act of Noah's son Ham shows that sin was still imbedded in human nature (vv. 18-29). The roots of ancient nations are traced (chap. 10), and the origin of differing languages explained (11:1-9). A genealogy draws attention to a man who will be pivotal in God's grand plan of redemption—Abraham (vv. 10-32).

Understanding the Text

"I will surely demand an accounting" Gen. 9:1-6. In this brief but critical paragraph, God makes society responsible for individual behavior. Men are responsible to enforce God's prohibition against murder. The words "whoever sheds the blood of man, by man shall his blood be shed" supports proponents of capital punishment by commanding society to execute murderers. The rationale, "For in the image of God has God made man," is stated. Human life is of such ultimate value

that no lesser penalty for taking life can signify how important each individual truly is.

The same paragraph lays the foundation for human government. Lesser powers (such as making regulations that promote well-being) are implied in the "accounting" God requires of us for punishing murderers.

Covenant Gen. 9:9. This vitally important Old Testament word indicates a formal, legally binding commitment. God's promise to never again destroy all life with a flood was not lightly made.

"Saw his father's nakedness" Gen. 9:22. Here the NIV interprets. The Hebrew original reads "uncovered his father's nakedness." Just what this phrase suggests is uncertain, but the seriousness with which Genesis treats the event indicates that Ham did more than catch a glimpse of an uncovered body. The delicacy with which Shem and Japheth treated their father (vv. 23-24) is a reminder to us of the modesty with which Scripture treats sexual matters.

"Cursed be Canaan" Gen. 9:24-27. The "curse" uttered here did not cause Canaan's future condition, but predicted it. Old Testament curses and blessings are often predictive, though pagan peoples considered curses magical utterances which could cause harm to enemies.

There is no suggestion here that Canaan participated in his ancestor Ham's act. Yet the moral flaw seen in Ham developed through the centuries into the gross immorality practiced by the Canaanites, who practiced ritual prostitution by both sexes as a part of their religion.

Let's open our lives totally to the cleansing power of God. He can remove even the small flaws that might otherwise be magnified in the lives of our children.

"This is the account" Gen. 10:1-32. Genesis uses both language and land areas to identify ancient peoples. While exact identification is difficult now, many of these names of peoples and nations have been found on ancient inscriptions.

"Settled there" Gen. 11:1-4. Most agree that the tower built at Babel was a ziggurat, a stepped structure which in ancient times was often topped by a temple. Perhaps the words "reaches to the heavens" implies the early institution of idolatrous worship. Yet the text suggests a different sin. The tower was to be a symbol of racial unity, so man should "not be scattered over the face of the whole earth" (v. 4). But God had specifically told Noah and his sons to "fill the earth" (9:1-7). It may have seemed like a little thing. Yet it was important to God's plan for man to multiply. Here too is a lesson for us. All that God says to us is important. We need to be sensitive to every command.

"Confuse their language" Gen. 11:5-9. What an indication of God's sense of humor. Can you imagine the next morning, one of the workers saying, "Hand me another brick, will you?" And his friend hearing, "Xpul Kodlyeme kakkadoke, seppulvista?" And can't you see the people, milling about in search of others they can talk with and understand? Soon the speakers of different languages found each other, and each group drifted away to settle in its own territory. In this gentle way "the LORD scattered them over all the earth."

God often responds this way to our disobedience. He sends no lightning bolt, causes no great suffering. Instead He gently and sometimes humorously changes the direction of our lives.

It's hot in Dallas in the summer. One young couple, feeling a call to the ministry, enrolled in the seminary I attended. They arrived in August, and were greeted by a heat wave in which temperatures reached 112 degrees. After two days, the young man's "call" melted away, and they left town. How God must have chuckled. Like the confusion of tongues, His heat wave had "scattered" a couple who were not where they were supposed to be.

Perhaps you can look back too and see gentle ways God has redirected your life. How gracious God is. How good God is not to break out in anger every time we wander from His intended path.

"Became the father" Gen. 11:10-32. Genealogy was vitally important to the Hebrews. In Hebrew genealogies "became the father" often means "was an ancestor of."

Also, Hebrew genealogies often skip generations, just naming significant ancestors. There is no way to tell from genealogies like this how many generations or how long a time passed from the first person named in a list to the last. Instead the genealogy points us to the truly important persons in Bible history, here preparing us to meet Abraham.

▶ DEVOTIONAL

The Sign of the Covenant (Gen. 9:8-17)

The covenant is a key to grasping what the Old Testament teaches about the character of our God. In Old Testament times a covenant (Heb. *brit)* was a formal contract, intended to make an agreement legally binding. In international affairs a covenant was a treaty. In a nation's life it served as a constitution. In business a covenant was a contract. In personal relationships it was a commitment.

Most covenants in ancient times were two-party agreements. That is, each person or group involved specified what he or she would do to carry out the agreement. If one side failed to perform, the agreement was broken, and the other side was no longer obligated.

But look at God's covenant with Noah. *It is pure promise!* God made no conditions. There are no "ifs." Instead God simply said, "I now make a commitment to you and your descendants. Never again. Never again will there be a flood to destroy the earth." Whatever humanity may do, God remains committed to this promise made to Noah.

The text tells us that the rainbow is to serve as a reminder to God of this specific covenant promise. But the rainbow means something else to us. Rather than a reminder of a specific promise, the rainbow is a reminder of the character of God and the nature of our relationship with Him. The rainbow reminds us that God comes to us with promises, not demands; that God in grace makes commitments to us that do not depend on our performance. We may fail God, but God will never fail us.

Only in Jesus do we fully understand. Only in Christ's promise of eternal life to all who trust Him do we grasp the full wonder of God's grace. Yet we sense something of it here in Genesis. And each time we see a rainbow, we are reminded. The God who promised to never again destroy all life with a flood is the God of promise, the God of grace. The commitments that He makes to us in Christ are promises that will never fail.

Personal Application

The next time you see a rainbow, let it remind you of God's amazing grace.

Quotable

"God did not make the first human because He needed company, but because He wanted someone to whom He could show His generosity. God did not tell us to follow Him because He needed our help, but because He knew that loving Him would make us whole."—Irenaeus

JANUARY 5 *Reading 5*
LEAVING FOR CANAAN
Genesis 12–14

> *"So Abram left, as the* LORD *had told him" (Gen. 12:4).*

The focus in Genesis now shifts from the race as a whole to a single man, Abram. The rest of the Old Testament is about Abram and his descendants. Abram is both a historical figure and an exemplar. We are to see in his faith response to God the key to a personal relationship with the Lord, which all are invited to experience in Jesus. Looking into Abram's life provides insights for us that can transform our own walk with God.

Overview

Abram was given six promises, and then traveled to Canaan (12:1-9). His early adventures revealed both Abram's personal weaknesses (vv. 10-20) and his great strengths of character and faith (13:1–14:24).

Understanding the Text

"I will" Gen. 12:1-3, 7. The theme of gracious promise continues, as God told Abram what He would do. There is no hint of conditions here. Abraham had demonstrated his faith by obeying God's command to leave his homeland (12:1). Now God was free to shower unconditional gifts on His servant.

Some of the six promises to Abram have been kept. Others have implications that extend into the future. The six are:

I will make you a nation (12:2).	Abram fathered the great Hebrew and Arab peoples.
I will bless you (12:2).	Abram lived a full, rich life.
I will make your name great (12:2).	Jews, Christians, and Muslims honor Abraham as founder of their faiths.
You will be a blessing (12:2).	The Scripture and the Saviour came through Abraham.
I will bless those who bless you, curse those who curse you (12:3)	Nations have risen and fallen in accord with their treatment of the Jewish people.
To your offspring I will give this land (12:7).	This promise is viewed as the Jews' title deed to Israel.

As God made great commitments to Abram, so He makes commitments to all who exhibit Abram's trust in the Lord.

Ur of the Chaldeans Gen. 11:28. Excavations at Ur reveal that Abram chose to leave a wealthy city, then at the height of its power and influence. Gold sculptures and inlaid harps reflect Ur's culture. Mighty city walls and public buildings reflect its strength. Records of business transactions reveal its prosperity. Let's not suppose that Abram was some poor wanderer living in a tent when he heard God's voice. He was a wealthy man, living in a city with almost modern sanitation and with houses constructed to cool hot summer air.

Yet the text says "so Abram left" (12:4). He did not know where he was going. But even at 75 years of age Abram was willing to go to a land God said "I will show you" (v. 1).

In a sense our relationship with God follows this same pattern. God calls us to abandon our concern with what the world holds dear, and set out on a personal journey of faith. Our guide on this journey is God's own Word. What sustains us is the conviction that each day God will show us our next step. Like Abram, Christians who view life as a journey of faith can never settle down or call earth's cities "home." In the words of Hebrews 11:16, we are "longing for a better country -a heavenly one." We know that God has "prepared a city" for us, and that the heavenly city is our true and only home.

"Abram went down to Egypt" Gen. 12:10. God had led Abram to Canaan. But when a famine struck that land, Abram went to Egypt to live. There is no hint here of divine guidance. What we sense is Abram's fear and doubt as the drought in Canaan grew severe.

We need to remember that difficulties do not release us from obedience. Sometimes God wants us to remain where we are and trust Him through the dry times in our lives. We need a more direct word from God than circumstances can provide to show us His will.

"Say you are my sister" Gen. 12:11-20. Abram had faith. Yet like all of us, Abram too was flawed by sin. On the border of Egypt Abram asked Sarai to pass herself off as his sister. Fear motivated Abram to lie and, even more awful, to put his wife Sarai at risk. God delivered Abram in spite of these actions. And from Scripture's totally honest portrayal of Abram's weakness, we learn several important lessons.

* Even those with great faith can fail. Let's not be shocked at our own or at others' weaknesses.

* Personal failures affect others. What we do and are always has its impact on those around us.

* Only God can redeem our failures. Never let guilt or shame turn you away from God. He is the only One who can help.

* God does not abandon us when our weaknesses betray us. God can and will intervene for us when we turn to Him.

"Lot went with him" Gen. 13:1-18. Genesis 13 and 14 display Abram's great character strengths, even as 12:10-20 display his weaknesses.

The first strength is shown in his relationship with his nephew, Lot. When the herds of each man increased so much they had to part company, the older Abram gave Lot his choice of the land. By rights first choice belonged to the elder. That Abram did not demand his rights showed a noncontentious spirit that has great value in God's sight (2 Tim. 2:24).

Lot chose "the whole" of the well-watered plains, leaving his uncle only drier hill country. The choice was selfish. It may have appeared "good business." But these plains were dominated by Sodom and Gomorrah, which had a population already noted for wickedness. Later, when God judged Sodom and Gomorrah, all of Lot's wealth would be destroyed along with the two cities (Gen. 19:15). Abram's selflessness assured his future. Lot's selfishness assured his doom.

God rewarded Abram with a reminder. All he could see in every direction from his position atop the hills was given to him and to his offspring—forever. Lot's momentary possession of the richest land paled to insignificance when compared to the covenant promise made by Abram's God.

"They carried off Lot" Gen. 14:1-16. Archeologists have traced the route taken by military forces traveling from the north into Palestine. Many armies marched south to attack the cities of Syria-Palestine even in the centuries before the events described here.

A consortium of four kings attacked and defeated Sodom and Gomorrah, and carried off all their goods and food as booty. In early biblical times most warfare involved raiding for booty rather than an attempt to invade and control additional area. Lot and his goods were carried away with those of the other residents of Sodom. When Abram heard, he mustered his own small force and pursued. Attacking at night, Abram routed the larger enemy force and freed not only Lot but also the others.

Here Abram displayed the traits of loyalty and courage.

Melchizedek, king of Salem Gen. 14:18-20. Biblical names often have great significance. *Melchizedek* means "king of righteousness," and *Salem* means "peace." The text says this king was a "priest of the Most High God," one of the descriptive names the Old Testament uses in speaking of the Lord.

Even though Abram must have been aware of his own significance as one called by God and given unique promises, Abram accepted the blessing offered by Melchizedek. This act speaks of Abram's humility, for in Old Testament times the greater person blessed the lesser, and to offer a blessing involved an implicit claim of superiority. In this we see another of Abram's strengths: he remained humble despite his special relationship with God.

The New Testament treats Melchizedek as a theophany, a visible representation of God as a human being. Only Jesus, with a human nature supplied by a human mother, has a claim to be God enfleshed.

The Book of Hebrews sees Melchizedek as the model for Jesus' unique priesthood. The Old Testament is silent both about Melchizedek's origin and demise. With typical rabbinical insight, the author of Hebrews argues that Christ, whose origin is in eternity and who will now never die, is a Priest "in the order of" this person rather than in the line of levitical priests established by Moses.

"I will accept nothing belonging to you" Gen. 14:21-24. When the king of Sodom offered Abram the booty he had won back from the invading kings, Abram refused. His reason is clearly stated. He would accept nothing, lest people later say that the men of Sodom had made Abram rich. In this Abram had in view the glory due to God. Abram wanted only that which came so unmistakably from God's hand that others would be forced to say, "God has blessed His servant."

This is yet another of Abram's great strengths. He now was ready to depend fully on the Lord, and to give God the glory for any blessings he might receive.

We can appreciate these strengths in Abram's character and turn to him as a model of unselfishness, loyalty, courage, humility, dependence on God, and readiness to publicly give God glory for what He does in our lives.

▶ DEVOTIONAL
As the Lord Told Him (Gen. 12:1-9)

More than one commentator has suggested that God's promises to Abram were conditional promises. They say that the condition was obedience to God's call to leave Ur. After all, if Abram had not left, none of the things God promised could have come true.

This view distorts both the biblical text and a vital truth about the spiritual life. God's promises are not activated by our obedience. Our obedience is activated by the promises of God.

Sometimes you and I make the mistake of thinking that God is like the electrical wiring in our houses. There is tremendous power in those electrical wires. And you and I are the ones who cause the power to work! We activate the power by flipping a light switch, turning on a TV, or pushing in the control knob on our clothes washer. God too has tremendous power. And some Christians assume that they can turn that power on and off by what *they* do. If they flip the right switch, God acts. If they turn the dial to the right channel or push the control into the right setting, God will come through on call. But this is not what happens in our lives at all!

What happens is that faith establishes a relationship with God, the ultimate source of power. Faith maintains that relationship. It is an active trust in God and His promises that causes us to obey.

We see it so clearly in Abram's life. Because Abram believed God's promises, he abandoned Ur and its wealth to live a nomadic life in a new land. The promise of God activated Abram's obedience. His obedience did not activate the promises.

Later, in the land, Abram took his eye off the promises and became afraid. He feared the famine, and he feared what might happen if the Egyptians saw and wanted his beautiful wife. Because Abram forgot the promises, he disobeyed. *Yet even then God was faithful to His commitment!* He got Abram out of the mess his departure from Canaan and his lies had created, and brought Abram safely back to the Promised Land.

There Abram again fixed his gaze on the promises. He was unselfish in his relationship with Lot because he believed God had granted him the whole land. He was loyal and courageous because he believed God's promise to bless him. He was humble because he knew that with God on his side he had nothing to prove. He was unwilling to take the wealth offered by the king of Sodom because he wanted all to see clearly that God alone was the source of all the good that he received.

It was the promise, and faith in the promise, that freed Abram not only to obey God, but also to become the unselfish, loyal, courageous, humble, and straightforward kind of person we can all admire.

It must be this way with you and me too. We can keep on thinking that we must do this or do that to merit God's favor—and wonder why, when we push the right buttons, the power doesn't flow. Or we can simply keep our eyes fixed on God and on His promises to us, and let His overflowing grace enable us to obey.

Personal Application

"Lord, as I keep my heart fixed on You and Your promises to me, make me the kind of individual that Abram became."

Quotable

"Often, actually very often, God allows His greatest servants, those who are far advanced in grace, to make the most humiliating mistakes. This humbles them in their own eyes and in the eyes of their fellowmen. It prevents them from seeing and taking pride in the graces God bestows on them or in the good deeds they do, so that, as the Holy Spirit declares: 'No flesh should glory in the sight of God.' "—Louis-Marie Grignion De Montfort

JANUARY 6 *Reading 6*
KNOW FOR A CERTAINTY
Genesis 15–17

"Do not be afraid, Abram. I am your shield, your very great reward" (Gen. 15:1).

Faith is far more than mere hope that something unlikely may happen. It is a deep, internal certainty, rooted in our trust of what God has said. We return to the life of Abram, where we gain vital insights that can enrich our personal faith in God.

Overview
Childless Abram believed God's promise that he would have a son, but asked how he could *know* (15:1-8). God entered into a binding covenant with His servant so he might "know for certain" (vv. 9-13). Yet on Sarai's urging, .Abram fathered a son with her maid, Hagar, leading to family conflict (16:1-16). Fourteen years later God renewed the promise and changed Abram's name. The 100-year-old Abraham trusted God to give him a child through Sarah, and on God's command circumcised his household as a sign of faith in the covenant promises (17:1-27).

Understanding the Text
"I am your reward" Gen. 15:1. The bumper sticker on my van says "Fishing isn't a matter of life and death—it's more important than that." Here Abram was reminded that really, a relationship with God is what life is all about. God Himself was Abram's shield and reward. All Abram had or hoped for was centered in the person of his God.

God is all we have too, and all our hopes are centered in Him. Faith in God's promises helps keep us focused on the Lord.

"Abram believed God" Gen. 15:2-6. Despite the fact that he was growing older and was still childless, Abram believed God's promise of countless offspring. The Bible says God "credited it [his faith] to him as righteousness." We cannot offer God a sinless life. We have all fallen short, and will fall short again. All we can do is trust God and have confidence in His promise. In grace God accepts our faith—and writes "righteous" beside our name.

"How can I know?" Gen. 15:7-21 Abram did believe, but he wanted to *know*. God was not upset. Rather, God had Abram prepare the most binding of all forms of ancient covenants, the "covenant of blood." Hebrews 6:17-18 tells us that God took this action "because [He] wanted to make the unchanging nature of His purpose very clear to the heirs of what was promised." So He "confirmed it [His promise] with an oath. God did this so that, by two unchangeable things in which it is impossible for God to lie, we who have fled to take hold of the hope offered to us may be greatly encouraged." We believe. Because God is totally committed to us, we also *know*.

"Know for certain" Gen. 15:13. God knows and is in full control of the future. On this basis we, like Abram, need have no doubts when the Lord reveals His intentions to us. Abram knew on the basis of God's word alone. We know, not only because God is the One who speaks to us, but because we can look back, as Abram could not, on fulfilled prophecy. The 400 years in Egypt, the slavery imposed on Abram's descendants, the punishment of Egypt, and the Exodus deliverance are history today. Everything happened just as God said it would.

We do believe. And we do know.

"Perhaps I can build a family" Gen. 16:1-16. In biblical times, bearing children was viewed by women as giving meaning to their lives. Abram had believed God's promise, but as the years passed and no children came, Sarai became impatient. Finally she urged Abram to impregnate her maid, Hagar.

According to the customs of those times this was not an immoral act. It was a recognized way to provide a childless wife with children she would then call her own. But in this case, Sarai—and Abram—made a tragic mistake. The error is expressed in Sarai's thought, "Perhaps *I* can build a family."

How foolish, when God had said *He* would build Abram's family! And how foolish of us when we try to do God's work in our own strength, or insist on imposing our timing rather than wait for the Lord to act.

"She despises me" Gen. 16:5. Sarai's venture in self-effort turned out badly. Hagar did become pregnant. But Hagar then had, and showed, contempt for her mistress! Since she was pregnant by Abram, it was clear that the couple's childlessness was Sarai's fault.

Sarai hadn't expected this result when she ventured out on her own. That's our problem too. When we try to do things in our own way or in our own strength, things don't turn out as we intend. The conflict that then dominated Abram's tents reminds us to wait on God rather than going ahead without His guidance or direction.

Sarai reacted to Hagar's contempt with predictable hostility. Again, according to ancient custom, Sarai had full authority over her servant. She used it to mistreat Hagar. Hagar finally ran away, returning only when God promised that He would bless the child she carried.

And so, when Abram was 86, his son Ishmael was born, only to become the ancestor of those Arab nations which live, even today, in perpetual hostility toward the descendants of Sarah, the Jews.

"Your name will be Abraham" Gen. 17:1-22. Names were especially important in biblical times. They were intended to make a statement about the character or essential identity of the person or thing named. Abram's name meant "father," and he was childless! What a burden that name must have been.

Now God appeared to him, and told him he was to be called "Abraham," which means "father of many" or "father of a multitude"! Imagine, if you will, the snickers as, the morning after his conversation with God, the 100-year-old man announced to all his servants that, from now on, they were to call him "Abraham"!

Abraham's assumption of his apparently ridiculous name was another measure of his faith. Abraham was willing, as Noah had been, to be "a fool for God."

If you or I ever feel foolish when trying to please God, let's remember that name, Abraham. And let's remember too that Abraham was vindicated. Today he is honored by all as the spiritual father of a multitude beyond our capacity to count.

"He laughed" Gen. 17:17. Abraham's first reaction to the divine statement that his wife Sarah would bear a child was laughter. It seemed so incredible.

But God stated again, "Your wife Sarah will bear you a son, and you will call him Isaac." And Abraham believed.

You and I are seldom asked to believe the incredible. Or to follow a course of action that involves great risk. But when we are, we can remember that God's incredible promise to Abraham and Sarah was fulfilled. What God says He will do, He can do. And what God tells us to do, He is able to do through us.

"Every male among you shall be circumcised" Gen. 17:10-14. Circumcision is a sign of the covenant that God made with Abraham and his descendants through Isaac. It was intended to demonstrate faith. Those Jews who in the coming millenniums considered their relationship with God through Abraham important would have themselves and their sons circumcised.

Christians have no single practice that is analogous to circumcision. But there are ways in which we can show that relationship with God is important to us. Our faithfulness at church. Our consistency in reading God's Word. Our commitment to prayer. Our willingness to share the Good News of Jesus with others. Our generosity in giving. Our attempts to put what we learn from God into practice. None of these is the reality. None in itself establishes or maintains our relationship with the Lord. But each, like circumcision, is a sign. Each is a way we can express the fact that our relationship with God truly is important to us.

▶ DEVOTIONAL
Faith That Knows
(Gen. 15:1-19)

Abram did believe God. Genesis 15:6 assures us, "Abram believed the LORD." Yet he yearned for an inner certainty. This yearning led Abram to ask, "O Sovereign

LORD, how can I know?" (v. 8) When you and I, believers though we be, long for certainty, we can turn to this passage. God will speak to us, as He spoke to Abram.

God told Abram to bring animals and birds and cut the animals into halves in preparation for the most binding of all ancient covenants, the "covenant of blood." In this covenant the participants pledged their very lives. They symbolized this commitment by walking between the halves of sacrificial animals.

When all was ready for the covenant ceremony to take place, God caused Abram to fall into a deep sleep. Then God passed between the divided halves—alone.

There could be no clearer proof. God pledged His very life that He would fulfill His covenant promises. The fact that only God walked the path between the divided carcasses meant that God would fulfill His commitment—whatever Abram or his offspring might do! Since Abram did not walk that path, nothing he might do could make God's obligation null or void! Abram now "knew for certain."

We have this same certainty. Centuries later Jesus took another lonely walk—to Calvary's cross. There He made a New Covenant, and sealed it by His own blood. He died there for us. His death is God's pledge—God's pledge of His very life—that the forgiveness promised us in the Gospel truly is ours. We believe. And we also know for certain that we have been saved by Christ's blood.

Despite this evidence we may at times still be troubled by doubts and fears. God told Abram that his descendants would be "enslaved and mistreated" in the future (v. 13). Possession of God's promise was no guarantee God's people could avoid hurt. Faith is no title deed to a life of ease. When such things happen, we need to remember what God told Abram. "I am your very great reward."

God did not say, "A good life on earth is your reward." He said, "I am."

We need to remember this when troubles come. Our relationship with God through Jesus guarantees us only one thing. God loves us, and He is present with us at even the darkest of times. So let's not waver when hard times come, as though something strange were happening. God's people have often been enslaved and mistreated. But in it all, we believe and we know. God remains our shield. And He Himself is our reward.

Personal Application

Choose one verse from these three chapters to memorize as a barrier against doubt.

Quotable

"Without weakening in his faith, [Abraham] faced the fact that his body was as good as dead—since he was about a hundred years old—and that Sarah's womb was also dead. Yet he did not waver through unbelief, regarding the promise of God, but was strengthened in his faith and gave glory to God, being fully persuaded that God had power to do what He had promised."—Romans 4:19-21

JANUARY 7 *Reading 7*
SPIRITUAL UPS AND DOWNS
Genesis 18–21

"May the Lord not be angry, but let me speak just once more" (Gen. 18:32).

Abraham hesitated to pray for any righteous persons in wicked Sodom, concerned that God would be angry. Yet shortly after, Abraham again lied about his relationship with Sarah. Like Abraham, we sometimes fail to understand God's priorities. Abraham's spiritual ups and downs make those priorities very clear for you and me.

Overview

Angelic visitors announced Sarah would give birth within a year (18:1-15). They also revealed God was about to destroy Sodom and Gomorrah. Hesitantly Abraham interceded (vv. 16-33). God destroyed the cities, but delivered Lot (19:1-29). Fear again moved Abraham to lie about his relationship with Sarah (20:1-18). Isaac, the promised child, was born at last (21:1-7), and Ishmael, Abraham's son by Hagar, was sent away (vv. 8-21).

Understanding the Text

Abraham's hospitality Gen. 18:1-8. In Middle Eastern countries a great emphasis was placed on showing hospitality to strangers. This is illustrated in Abraham's welcome of three men who appeared near his tent, in his invitation to them to eat, and in his haste to personally bring them food. Looking back on this incident, the writer of the New Testament Book of Hebrews exhorts Christians, "Do not forget to entertain strangers, for by so doing some people have entertained angels without knowing it" (Heb. 13:2).

"The LORD said" Gen. 18:9-15. Some believe one of the three visitors Abraham entertained was a theophany, a pre-incarnate visitation by God the Son. We shouldn't suppose that angels look like human beings in their true state. However, when angels visited Abraham and others they often took on human form. There is no record of angels appearing as women. In each biblical incident angels appeared to be men.

The word *angel* in both Hebrew and Greek means "messenger." Whether the spokesman was actually the Lord or not, he spoke with God's authority. The Lord was about to fulfill His promise. Within the year Abraham and Sarah would have a child.

"Sarah laughed" Gen. 18:12. The same Hebrew word used to describe Abraham's earlier reaction (17:17) is used to describe Sarah's response. Sarah need not have been afraid, and tried to lie. God expects initial incredulity. It is impossible and unnecessary to hide our feelings from God.

"Then Abraham approached" Gen. 18:16-33. Before the visitors left, the Angel of the Lord told Abraham God was about to destroy the cities of Sodom and Gomorrah because "their sin [is] so grievous." At first Abraham simply stood there, stunned. Then he approached to intercede for any righteous who might be found in the cities.

This is one of Abraham's spiritual "highs"—a moment when his heart was truly in tune with God. We can learn much from this incident (see DEVOTIONAL). For now, note just one thing. Abraham was fearful and hesitant to press his request that God spare the cities for the sake of 50 good persons. Then for 45, then 40, then 30, then 20, and finally for 10. Abraham need not have worried. God was even more concerned than Abraham, and in fact spared the only "good" person to be found there: Lot.

God cares deeply for all people. He is never upset when we plead with Him for others. Prayers of intercession are especially welcome, for in offering such prayers our priorities match God's own.

"Bring them out to us" Gen. 19:1-29. Only two of the angels proceeded to Sodom. They were offered hospitality by Lot, Abraham's nephew. The men of the city demonstrated the extent of their wickedness, demanding that Lot send out his guests to become the victims of homosexual rape! When Lot refused, the Sodomites were determined to break into his home. Only the angels' intervention, in striking the men with blindness, prevented them.

Lot's offer to send out his virgin daughters shocks us today (v. 8). It should. Yet the incident shows how deeply the responsibility of a host to his guests was felt in the ancient world.

Lot's offer should not distract our attention from the sin of Sodom and from the implications of homosexuality for a society. The Bible identifies all homosexual acts as sin, labeling them detestable, degrading, sinful, shameful, indecent, and perverse (cf. Lev. 18:22; Rom. 1:22-28). Any society which condones, and then actually promotes such sin, as Sodom did, rushes headlong toward judgment.

"Thought he was joking" Gen. 19:14. Told by the angels to flee the city, Lot hurried to warn the two young men engaged to his daughters. The text calls them "sons-in-law" because the dowrys had been paid and the marriage contracts settled, though the weddings had not taken place. Lot's words of warning were taken as a joke. Lot had lived in Sodom too long without

speaking out to be taken seriously now.

It is one thing to love the sinner, as we are often urged to do. It is another to ignore the sin. Sodom reminds us that we are to confront sins in our society, exposing them for what they are, while retaining a deep and loving concern for the sinner. If we wish to warn others that God has determined a day in which He will judge the living and the dead, we cannot remain quiet on moral issues. Unlike Lot, who compromised when he settled down in the wicked city, we must speak out.

"The LORD rained down burning sulfur on Sodom" Gen. 19:24. The ruins of the wicked cities were once thought to lie under the southern end of the Dead Sea. Recently ash-covered remains of five cities have been discovered on the plains just south of its slowly receding waters. Archeologists believe that an earthquake ignited bitumen deposits in the area, creating the inferno described in verses 23-26. Sin is no laughing matter. And divine judgment is no joke.

"Lot and his two daughters" Gen. 19:30-38. The incident reported here reemphasizes a theme. Lot, in choosing to settle in a wicked city, not only compromised his own principles but also subjected his daughters to evil influences. As ever in the Old Testament, sins are shown to have lasting impact. Centuries later the Moabites and Ammonites, descendants of the children Lot's daughters conceived, became enemies of Abraham's offspring.

"She is my sister" Gen. 20:1-18. Again Abraham, fearful that someone might kill him to obtain his wife, told Sarah to lie about their relationship. Again God intervened. Just a short time before, Abraham had been afraid to pray for any righteous persons who might be in Sodom. Now Abraham was *not* afraid to abandon trust in the Lord and to lie! Abraham's spiritual "high" was followed by this spiritual "low."

When I attended the University of Michigan I worked full-time at a nearby mental hospital. I worked on the male receiving ward, where I conducted nightly Bible studies for any patients who wanted to attend. Some of the psychiatrists on the staff were opposed, and I prayed intently for my little ministry. Finally the issue was settled in a staff meeting, when the chief psychiatrist told his reluctant staff, "He probably should be speaking to *you!*"

The victory was followed by a strange spiritual low. With the conflict over, I lost all motivation to continue the class, and had to struggle with myself to keep on going.

Yet notice. Even though Abraham had clearly been in the wrong, God did not disown Abraham. Instead the Lord spoke to Abimelech, the ruler to whom Abraham had lied, and identified Abraham as His prophet. And, in response to Abraham's prayers, God blessed the wronged king.

Our spiritual highs often are followed by spiritual lows. When this happens God is as gentle with us as He was with Abraham. God does not disown us, for our relationship with Him rests on faith and not on our works.

In time God restored Abraham and Sarah, even as He restored my motivation to minister to the men on my ward. He will restore you from your spiritual lows too.

"God has brought me laughter" Gen. 21:1-7. Scripture now invites us to see the fulfillment of God's promise to Abraham. Sarah bore his son Isaac. Despite the years of anguish, Sarah at last knew joy.

Sarah's next words are significant for us. "Everyone who hears about this will laugh with me." Why are these words significant? Because they imply that Sarah's experience is a model of our own. We too may have years of waiting, years without laughter. Yet in the end we will be able to testify with Sarah, "God has brought *me* laughter too."

"Get rid of that slave woman and her son" Gen. 21:8-13. Sarah's demand that Abraham exile Hagar and Ishmael was against custom. Abraham considered it an immoral act. Also, Abraham cared for his son Ishmael. It took a direct command of God to move Abraham to take the required step.

Why was it necessary to expel Ishmael? God intended that the covenant promise given to Abraham should be transmitted through Isaac. Ishmael must be expelled so there would be no doubt about whose was the covenant line.

But God softened the blow. God promised Abraham He would make Ishmael into a great nation too, "Because he is your offspring."

God has a purpose in the separations we experience. What a comfort when they take place, to realize that our loved ones are precious to God, and that He is committed to be with them even though we cannot.

"God opened her eyes" Gen. 21:14-21. This has been a favorite passage of mine for years. Hagar and Ishmael, undoubtedly shaken and heartbroken, stumbled away into the desert. When their water ran out, Hagar gave up.

Then, when everything was darkest, God spoke to her. He told her not to fear, and "opened her eyes and she saw a well of water." God didn't create a new source of water. He simply opened her eyes to see what was already present. When we are in despair God very seldom needs to create something new to deliver us. Most often He simply opens our eyes to see the spiritual and other resources that are all around us.

"The Eternal God" Gen. 21:22-34. The section ends with the report of a treaty defining a harmonious relationship between Abraham and the ruler he had earlier wronged. More significantly, Abraham's relationship with the Lord is fully restored as well, and he "called upon the name of the LORD."

How significant the name given God here—the "Eternal God." God is ours, forever. He is with us, forever. Nothing in the present, the past, or the future can change the fact that He is God, and that we are His.

▶ DEVOTIONAL
God's Heartbeat
(Gen. 18:16-33)

When the Lord told Abraham He was about to judge wicked Sodom, Abraham was deeply concerned. He did not question the Lord's right to judge the wicked. He was concerned that the righteous would suffer an undeserved fate along with them.

Abraham's concern moved him to plead with God. This is the Bible's first recorded prayer of intercession, and teaches us two important lessons.

First, Abraham was a little fearful that he might overstep in making repeated requests. Sometimes we may feel that our repeated pleadings for others might somehow "bother" the Lord. The Lord's responsiveness to Abraham shows that He is not only willing to listen, but will respond to our prayers of intercession too.

Second, Abraham's fearfulness stemmed from a misunderstanding of God. Abraham was concerned that God might actually "sweep away" the city "and not spare" the righteous in it. Abraham gradually reduced the number he thought the city should be spared for from 50 to 10. Abraham left it at 10. But as the story is continued in chapter 19, we learn that there was only 1 person who might be considered even slightly good in the cities—and God brought that 1 person to safety. He even spared Lot's 2 undeserving daughters!

Abraham's mistake was to think that he could possibly care more for other persons that God does! Abraham was finally willing to see nine righteous die so the wicked might be punished. But God was unwilling to see even one suffer unjustly.

When we pray for others, let's remember that God cares for them far more than we possibly can. We can plead for others without fear of wearying God. God will do everything possible to answer our prayers of intercession.

Personal Application

Ask God to burden you to pray for others with some special need.

Quotable

"God did not make the first human being because He needed company, but because He wanted someone to whom He could show His generosity and love."—Irenaeus

JANUARY 8 *Reading 8*
"HERE I AM"
Genesis 22:1–25:18

"Because you have done this and have not withheld your son, your only son, I will surely bless you" (Gen. 22:16-17).

Abraham's faith was demonstrated when he left Ur, and when at an advanced age he believed God's promise of a son. The depth of Abraham's faith was demonstrated not only in one final test, but also in the impact Abraham had on those who knew him best.

Overview

Abraham's faith was tested when he was told to sacrifice Isaac (22:1-19). Abraham buried his wife Sarah (23:1-20), and sent his chief servant to obtain a wife for Isaac (24:1-66). After many more years Abraham died, and was buried by his two best-loved sons, Isaac and Ishmael (25:1-18).

Understanding the Text

"Here I am" Gen. 22:1. In the Old Testament, to "hear" God implies that a person not only understands what the Lord says but also will obey. Similarly, for God to "hear" prayers implies that He intends to answer them. This fact underlies Abraham's response when, some years after Isaac's birth, God spoke to Abraham again. In saying "Here I am," Abraham indicated his readiness to respond to what the Lord was about to say.

Abraham had no idea how great a test his faith was about to undergo (see DEVOTIONAL). But Abraham's readiness to respond is a model for us all.

Some years ago I led a Bible study group in Phoenix, Arizona. Barbara was a new Christian, excited and eager to grow in her faith. One of our group had become involved in an adulterous relationship with a leader in her church. We had confronted her and tried to help, but rather than break off the relationship, she stopped coming to Bible study. This person kept calling Barbara, offering excuses and attempting to justify her actions. One evening Barbara told how uncomfortable this made her, but shared that she didn't know what to do. I explained the Bible's guidelines on church discipline, which we had followed, and what to do when a person would not repent. I remember Barbara's enthusiastic response. "I can't wait for her to call again, so I can tell her what I have to do."

Barbara, a young Christian, had discovered a secret Abraham also knew. Our role is to say, "Here I am," when God speaks to us—and then do just as He says.

"She died" Gen. 23:1-20. This chapter is one of the most important in Genesis to students of ancient Middle Eastern culture. It contains a fascinating report of the polite bargaining that went on as Abraham negotiated with a Hittite for property on which to bury Sarah. Everyone in that day understood the Hittite's offer to "give" Abraham the field was simply politeness. In return, Abraham would have to make him a "gift" of whatever value the two would set on the property.

The price was high, partly because selling Abraham land would give him rights in the Hittite community which he would not otherwise have.

For us, the significance of the story is not found in its portrayal of customs, but in the grief experienced by Abraham as he laid his companion of so many decades to rest.

"He said to the chief servant in his household" Gen. 24:1-67. The chapter contains one of the true romances recorded in the Old Testament. Rebekah, a young and very beautiful girl, was asked to marry a wealthy suitor, sight unseen. A servant told her about him and brought her rich gifts. She herself was permitted to choose—and decided to go.

Those fond of allegory make Rebekah the church, make Isaac Christ, and make the unnamed servant the Holy Spirit, who comes from heaven to woo Jesus' bride. Perhaps. But there is more value in a careful examination of literal content of the text.

The servant is identified as Abraham's "chief servant." Earlier a man named Eliezer of Damascus was Abraham's chief servant who, according to custom in those days, would have inherited Abraham's wealth if his master remained childless (cf. 15:2-3). If this is Eliezer, all hope of gaining Abraham's wealth has now been lost. The significance of the "chief servant" has dwindled so much that the writer does not even bother to record his name!

Yet as this chief servant went about fulfilling his mission, we see that he had obtained something far more important than Abraham's wealth. He had "caught" Abraham's faith! He prayed and experienced God's answer to prayer (24:12-17). He recognized God's leading (v. 26). And he praised God for His kindness and faithfulness to Abraham (v. 27).

We stand amazed at the faith Abraham displayed in his readiness to offer his only son to God. Yet perhaps even more amazing is the fact that Abraham's faith in God had won his "chief servant," who knew him best of all, to a similar deep and selfless trust in God.

The truest test of our faith is not in how we behave in crisis. The truest test is whether we are able to influence those who know us best by the quality of our lives.

"His sons Isaac and Ishmael buried him" Gen. 25:1-18. I appreciate this verse so much. It tells me Ishmael came to understand his father's earlier rejection, and that the two were reconciled. God truly did bless Abraham, as He had promised.

How wonderful that Abraham's God is our God. How wonderful that God is committed to bless us too.

▶ DEVOTIONAL
"God Himself Will Provide" (Gen. 22:1-19)

The story is surely one of the best known in the Old Testament. God told Abraham to offer his son Isaac as a sacrifice. Abraham set out to obey. Just as Abraham was about to kill his son, God stopped him, and pointed to a ram whose horns had become tangled in a nearby thicket. God commended Abraham for his obedience, and reconfirmed His earlier promises to His servant.

This outline cannot do justice to the story or to its implications for our lives. For that we must carefully observe phrases in the text.

"Early the next morning" (v. 3). Think of it. Abraham was not only willing to obey, he seems to have been eager! No dawdling till noon, when it was too hot to travel. No excuse that, after siesta, it was too late to begin. Somehow we sense that to Abraham this seemed like an adventure, and Abraham was eager to discover how God would resolve his dilemma.

We often hesitate when we sense that God wants us to undertake something difficult. We need Abraham's spirit of adventure: his conviction that God will work things out, and consequent eagerness to see just how.

"We will worship and then we will come back to you" (v. 5). The New Testament comments on this verse, saying that

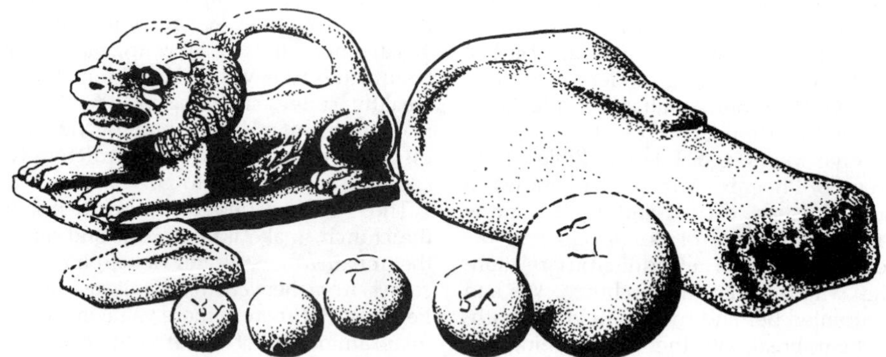

Coins had not yet been invented in Abraham's day. The "shekel" in Genesis 23:16 is a unit of weight, determined by stones like these piled on a balance scale. The familiar coin of New Testament times took its name from the unit of weight.

"Abraham reasoned that God could raise the dead" (Heb. 11:19). God had promised Abraham would have offspring through Isaac. Abraham was totally convinced God would keep this promise. Abraham was so certain that he said confidently, "We will return." Yes, Abraham fully intended to sacrifice Isaac, as he had been commanded. That "we will return" tells us that Abraham also *knew* that, somehow, his son would survive. Even if God had to raise Isaac from the dead, He would do so to keep His promises.

Lord, give us this kind of confidence in Your promises! With this kind of faith, obedience is made easy.

"Your only son" (v. 12). Isaac was not Abraham's only child. Yet Isaac was the only son who counted—the only one who could inherit the covenant and be counted in the covenant line. And, with Ishmael sent away, Isaac was the only son Abraham had left.

The phrase is a poignant one, for it suggests the pain God Himself must have felt in contemplating the day that His only Son, Jesus, would complete the sacrifice Abraham only began.

"Now I know" (v. 12). The old saying is accurate. Talk *is* cheap. Many who claim to be Christians talk a good faith. But the test of a real faith is obedience to God. Abraham had proved beyond the shadow of a doubt that he did trust God.

"Because you have done this . . . I will surely bless you" (vv. 16-17). Let's not misunderstand. The ultimate cause of blessing was God's covenant promise. But the proximate cause—the means God used to bring Abraham to the place where he could be blessed—was Abraham's obedience.

God intends to bless you and me. He is committed to do so. Yet only an obedient walk enables us to appropriate that blessing. It's as if rain is falling just over the hill. We smell its freshness, are eager to feel the renewing drops. And there's a path marked "Obedience" leading directly to it.

God's blessings do fall in refreshing showers. But only those who take the path marked "Obedience" experience them.

Personal Application

If there is anything God wants you to do that you have hesitated to do, let Abraham's experience encourage you to set out now.

Quotable

"Do little things as if they were great, because of the majesty of the Lord Jesus Christ, who dwells in thee; and do great things as if they were little, because of His omnipotence."—Blaise Pascal

JANUARY 9 *Reading 9*
RUSHING AHEAD OF GOD
Genesis 25:19–28:22

> *"Look, I am about to die. . . . What good is the birthright to me?" (Gen. 25:32)*

Unlike his twin Esau, Jacob placed a high value on God's covenant promise. But Jacob showed little spiritual sensitivity as he schemed and lied unnecessarily to obtain what God was already committed to give him. In rushing ahead of God rather than waiting on the Lord, Jacob brought pain and alienation to his family.

Overview

Before the birth of her twin sons God told Rebekah, Isaac's wife, that the older twin would serve the younger (25:19-26). Esau, the older, sold his birthright—his right to inherit the covenant God made with Abraham—to his younger brother Jacob (vv. 27-34). Isaac's experience shows how vital the birthright is (26:1-35). Years later Jacob and his mother schemed to steal Esau's blessing, through which the birthright would be transmitted (27:1-40). This antagonized Esau and forced Jacob to flee (27:41–28:9). At Bethel Jacob had his first direct personal experience with the God of the covenant, and committed himself to serve the Lord (vv. 10-22).

Understanding the Text

Isaac. Less is told of Isaac than any other patriarch. He is significant primarily as the bridge between his father Abraham and his son Jacob, whose name was later changed to Israel. Personally Isaac seems to have been a rather indecisive and passive person, without great spiritual insight. These traits are seen in his flight from conflict with Abimelech, and in his preference of Esau because he "had a taste for wild game" (25:28). Even though Isaac was overshadowed by both his father and his son, Isaac experienced God's grace, and at the end faith triumphed over personal preference as he acknowledged God's choice of Jacob over Esau and confirmed transmission of the covenant promises to his younger son.

"The older will serve the younger" Gen. 25:19-26. Romans 9 emphasizes the importance of God's statement to Rebekah before her twin sons were born. God's choice of Jacob, the younger, to inherit His covenant promise was made before the boys were born. This showed that the choice did not depend on what either did. God is free to choose as He wills. The fact that Esau proved to be uninterested in spiritual things shows how wise God's choices are.

"What good is the birthright?" Gen. 25:27-34 The firstborn son had the right to inherit most of his father's property and also any intangible possessions, such as title or position. Here the "birthright" that Esau sold so lightly included his natural right as eldest to the covenant promise of God. Archeological finds have shown that in patriarchal times the eldest son could and sometimes did sell his birthright. In selling his birthright to Jacob for a bowl of stew, Esau showed how unimportant he considered God's promises to be. The word "despise" here *(bazah)* means to "place little value on" something and actually implies contempt.

Jacob's character was flawed, yet he did value his relationship with God. God can work with people who see Him as important, despite their weaknesses. God could not work with Esau, for Esau had no place in his thinking for God.

"The LORD appeared to Isaac" Gen. 26:1-34. The story in this chapter might seem to be a digression. But it is vital in developing Moses' theme. Isaac possessed the covenant promises that Esau despised. What value did the covenant really have? First, God's guidance (vv. 1-6). The Lord appeared to Isaac and directed him to stay in Canaan rather than go to Egypt. He stayed in Canaan, on coastal land then occupied by the Philistines. Second, God's protection (vv. 7-11). Even though Isaac showed the same lack of active faith that led Abraham to lie about his wife in fear that he might be killed for her, God protected Isaac and his family. The "Abimelech" here is *not* the person Abraham lied to a century or so earlier. Most believe the name is a title, like Pharaoh. In Hebrew the name means "my father is king."

Third, the covenant assured God's blessing (vv. 12-22). God made Isaac rich, multiplying his wealth. Fourth, God's intervention (vv. 23-35). When land and water rights disputes drove Isaac to move again and again, God spoke to him, urging him not to fear. The Philistines finally made a treaty with Isaac because "we saw clearly that the LORD was with you."

In each of these incidents we see—and Esau and Jacob would have observed—how important possession of God's covenant promise truly was. With the covenant came God's commitment to guide, to protect, to bless, and to intervene. Spiritual realities seem irrelevant to some. But in fact they are far more important than anything the materialist can touch, see, or feel.

Isaac's blessing Gen. 27:1-40. In ancient cultures blessings given by parents or by one in authority were viewed as having great power. The deathbed blessing was equivalent to a last will, by which a person transmitted his tangible and intangible possessions to the next generation. Thus Isaac's blessing was eagerly sought by Esau and jealously desired by Jacob.

Jacob and his mother panicked when Isaac announced he was about to give Esau his blessing. They plotted together to deceive Isaac and to steal the blessing by passing Jacob off as his older brother. They did succeed in deceiving a then sightless Isaac. But they alienated Esau so greatly that he determined to kill Jacob after Isaac died!

The tragic thing about this story is that their deceit was unnecessary! Before the boys' birth God had announced to Rebekah that He intended to exalt her younger son over the older (25:23). Panic drove Rebekah and Jacob to lie and cheat to obtain something that God had promised *He* would give them!

How foolish to run ahead of God. Our situation is never so bleak that we have to adopt wrong or sinful means in a desperate effort to achieve good ends!

"Esau then realized" Gen. 28:1-9. Esau was not a bad person. He was simply one of those human beings whose eyes are so filled with images of this world that they cannot glimpse spiritual realities. After Jacob was sent (fled) to Paddan Aram to find a bride among relatives, it finally dawned on Esau that his parents were less than delighted with his Canaanite wives. In an effort to please them, he found another wife from among Ishmael's descendants. How touching, and yet how tragic. Esau did do the best he could. Yet his choice of Canaanite wives had been a symptom of his spiritual insensitivity, not the cause of his rejection. We can find admirable traits in those who have no concern for God. Yet however they try, they will always fall short. Their self-effort itself shows how little they know of Abraham's God.

"I am the LORD" Gen. 28:10-22. Jacob had seen the importance of a relationship with God in his father Isaac's experience. He had been aware of the value of the spiritual. Now, however, Jacob himself had a personal experience with the Lord.

At Bethel (which means "house of God") the Lord confirmed transmission of the Abrahamic Covenant to Jacob (vv. 13-15; cf. 12:1-3, 7). Jacob's words, "If God will be with me" (28:20-22), are not a bargain struck with God. They are instead a faith response to God. Since God has committed Himself to Jacob and will surely carry out His promises, then Jacob will be committed to the Lord.

Jacob's words are significant to us in two ways. First, Jacob shows us the basic benefits of a personal relationship with God (vv. 20-21). God is with us. He watches over us on our life journey. He provides the basic necessities. He gives us others with whom we can have a family relationship. Second, Jacob shows us the basic response that is appropriate. We honor the Lord as God. We set aside times and places to worship Him. And we express our commitment by giving.

▶DEVOTIONAL
"And Indeed He Will Be Blessed" (Gen. 27:1-33)

This is one of those Bible stories in which we generally focus on one character, and ignore the others. In this tale of the trickster, we give our attention to Jacob and perhaps to his mother, Rebekah, who schemed with him. Sometimes we think about Esau, whose tears and anger are both so understandable. Seldom do we look at Isaac. Yet I suspect that Isaac is the one who learned most from the incident, and is the only one who acted with faith and nobility.

You see, Isaac had always favored his son Esau. Esau was the outdoorsman, the athlete. He was, if you will, the "jock"; the virile athletic type his dad had always wanted, and perhaps had always wanted to be. Jacob, a mama's boy, just wasn't the kind of son that a dad dreamed of! Jacob was the kind who'd rather play the piano than baseball; who'd rather go to some museum than hunt or fish. And so, because Isaac was so drawn to his older son, he was blind to Esau's weaknesses, and unable to see Jacob's strengths.

In fact, for some 40 years Isaac had been blind to the fact that Esau cared nothing for God, and that Jacob did at least value God's blessing.

Up to the very end Isaac persisted in his opinion. Up to the very end Isaac intended Esau to inherit the divine promise. And then Isaac was tricked into pronouncing his blessing on Jacob!

When he found out he had been tricked, Isaac might have been angry. He might have withdrawn the blessing and replaced it with a curse! Instead, Isaac finally realized that for all those years *he* had been wrong! He realized that God intended Jacob to have the blessing and that Jacob at least *cared* about covenant relationship with Isaac's God. Realizing all this, Isaac acted in faith and with nobility. He confirmed the blessing he had just uttered, telling Esau, "and indeed he will be blessed."

You and I need to be as open and noble as Isaac proved to be. How willing we need to be, especially in our own families, to examine our attitudes—toward our spouses, our parents, our children, our brothers and sisters. If we have judged others on superficial criteria, we need to be ready with Isaac to acknowledge our mistake.

As Isaac shows us, it's never too late to change.

Personal Application

It is especially important to be realistic about our children and to value each one for his or her special qualities. Lord, help us to be as open and noble as Isaac proved to be.

Quotable

I walked a mile with Pleasure
She chatted all the way,
But left me none the wiser
For all she had to say.

I walked a mile with Sorrow
And ne'er a word said she;
But, oh, the things I learned from her
When Sorrow walked with me!
—Robert Browning

JANUARY 10 *Reading 10*
THE DECEIVER DECEIVED
Genesis 29–32

"Your father has cheated me by changing my wages ten times" (Gen. 31:7).

Sometimes we must be put in the place of the cheated to realize why God calls us to live a truly godly life.

Overview

Jacob found his relatives, and married two sisters, Rachel and Leah (29:1-35). Jealousy and conflict marred Jacob's home, but his flocks increased (30:1-43). Finally Jacob took his family and herds and fled his uncle Laban, the deceitful father-in-law who "changed my wages ten times" (31:1-55). Free of his oppressive uncle at last, Jacob fearfully prepared to meet Esau. At this critical moment Jacob met and wrestled with God, and his name was changed to Israel (32:1-32).

Understanding the Text

"Laban had two daughters" Gen. 29:1–30:24. Jacob's marriage to two sisters, and acceptance of their servants as concubines (secondary wives), was not immoral by the standards of his culture. Yet the conflict in Jacob's home suggests how wise it is to adopt monogamous marriage, as God intended. Each major character in this passage is worthy of careful consideration.

Laban. Laban was willing to use his own daughters and anyone else to gain his own ends. In Laban, Jacob, who had acted the same way earlier, met his match!

Jacob. Jacob proved to be a hard worker. He served Laban seven years to win his wife, Rachel, only to be tricked by Laban, who substituted Leah on the wedding night. Married to both, Jacob knew no peace, for the two sisters became rivals for his affection. In their competition to produce children, Rachel and Leah even forced Jacob to add their two maids, Bilhah and Zilpah, to his roster of wives. The deceiver had been deceived, and found himself the focus of family strife! Earlier Jacob had sung, "I'll do it my way." Now he faced the music!

Leah. Unlovely and unloved, Leah tried desperately to win Jacob's affection by giving him sons. She was jealous of her beautiful sister Rachel, and even though Leah bore Jacob six sons, she was never able to find happiness.

Rachel. Beautiful and loved by Jacob, Rachel was miserable because she was childless. She urged Jacob to sleep with Bilhah, as in that culture the sons of a servant girl were considered to be children of her mistress.

Each person strived for something he or she did not have, rather than seeking contentment in God's gifts. Rachel could have been happy in Jacob's love, but was jealous of her sister's fertility. Leah could have found satisfaction in her sons, but yearned for Jacob's love. Laban could have valued people rather than wealth, and would have been loved by them all. Jacob could have taken a stand against his father-in-law and his wives, but allowed each of the others to bully or take advantage of him.

Yet, despite their flaws, God used each of these individuals to create a family that would become the channel of His blessing to the world. And, despite the dissatisfaction each felt, each truly was blessed. How we need to accept ourselves and our limitations. How we need to rejoice in what we have, rather than make ourselves and others miserable in pursuit of what we do not have.

Jacob's flocks Gen. 30:1-43. On the surface Jacob's use of striped sticks while the herds of Laban mated appears to be sympathetic magic. This concept, common to ancient and modern systems of magic, assumes that any object can influence another to look or be like it. Yet this was *not* magic. Certainly Jacob gave God the credit when the recessive genes present in the animals became dominant, and the herds produced a majority of the dark, spotted, or speckled animals which Laban agreed would belong to Jacob (cf. 31:4-13).

God works comfortably within nature, turning "natural" events to His purposes. God worked through the genetic codes already present in the herds Jacob supervised. He is at work in the natural circumstances of our lives as well.

"Does he not regard us as foreigners?" Gen. 31:1-21 By ancient custom Jacob had probably been adopted by Laban. Jacob, his wives, and his children were considered to "belong to" Laban, the patriarch of the family (cf. 31:43). Yet after 20 years Laban had so mistreated Jacob's family that his daughters were ready to follow Jacob to Canaan. They had no confidence that Laban would care for their children, for he treated his daughters like foreigners rather than family.

"I am sending this message" Gen. 32:1-21. Jacob fled from an oppressive uncle toward a brother whom he thought hated him. What an uncertain time in his life! Jacob did the best he could to prepare for the meeting. He sent a messenger, so his return would not be a surprise (vv. 1-8). He prayed, reminding God of His promises (vv. 9-12). And he sent rich gifts on ahead (vv. 13-21). This last act was not bribery, but reflects the custom of giving gifts to persons whose favor one wished to obtain. By giving such gifts Jacob implied that he saw his brother as his superior.

When we find ourselves in uncertain circumstances, we would be wise to follow Jacob's prescription. We need to rely on God, to do all we can, and to remain humble before others.

"Your name will no longer be Jacob, but Israel" Gen. 32:22-32. Jacob's old name meant "supplanter." His new name, Israel, meant "struggler with God." While the wrestling match described here is intended literally, it clearly has figurative significance. Jacob had struggled all his life, trying one scheme after another to make his way. But now Jacob struggled to gain God's blessing. With the blessing won, Jacob was given a new name to mark his internal transformation.

Like Jacob we need to stop struggling to make our way in our own strength, and struggle instead to rely wholly on God. As Jacob illustrates, this does not mean we sit back and do nothing. It does, however, mean a change of attitude. Our confidence is to rest in the Lord, not in ourselves.

▶DEVOTIONAL
"This Message"
(Gen. 32:1-21)

It may seem strange, but Jacob's evident fear of Esau is a mark of personal growth.

Psychologists label Jacob's early problem "egocentrism." By this they mean seeing things only from one's own perspective, being unaware of the perspective of others. In his early years Jacob schemed to steal his brother's birthright and blessing, unconcerned about how these acts might affect his brother and their relationship. Jacob and his mother actually

The household gods Rachel stole (31:22-55) probably looked like these statues, from about 1800 B.C. Rachel's theft was intended as insurance against the future. In that age possession of the household gods constituted a claim against the family estate.

seemed surprised at Esau's anger. They had never even thought of how Esau might react to being victimized!

Twenty years later, however, Jacob himself had been the victim of a scheme. Laban had been as unfair to him as he had been to Esau! Now Jacob had experienced many of the feelings Esau must have known, feelings experienced by all who are victims—frustration, helplessness, and anger.

At last Jacob could identify with his brother Esau, and understand how his own actions must have made Esau feel. And because he understood, Jacob was afraid. No one deserves to be treated as he had treated Esau, or as he himself had now been treated. Such treatment arouses anger and deserves punishment.

All too often we Christians also fall into the trap of egocentrism. We may speak or act self-righteously, completely unaware of how our tone affects others. We strive to reach some good goal, yet we often are ignorant of how our methods hurt others.

God made Jacob sensitive to the feelings of the brother he had victimized by making Jacob himself a victim. I suspect that sometimes God uses the same prescription in dealing with us. When we are hurt it is often a reflection of the way we hurt others, a not-so-gentle reminder that God has charged us with the duty of loving others as we love ourselves.

It would be wonderful if you and I could be naturally sensitive to others. But this is an attitude we must develop. The promise and the warning are both clear in Jacob's life. The promise is that even unlikely individuals like Jacob can become persons who understand and consider others. The warning is that if we live egocentristic lives, taking advantage of others, God may place us in positions where we experience the very pain we have caused others to suffer.

Personal Application

If we consider the feelings of others, we will make wiser as well as more godly choices.

Quotable

Lord, make me an instrument of Your peace.
Where there is hatred let me sow love.
Where there is injury, pardon.
Where there is doubt, faith.
Where there is despair, hope.
Where there is darkness, light; and
Where there is sadness, joy.
O Divine Master, grant that I may not so much seek to be consoled as to console;
To be understood as to understand;
To be loved as to love;
For it is in giving that we receive;
It is in pardoning that we are pardoned; and
It is in dying that we are born to eternal life.—St. Francis of Assisi

JANUARY 11 *Reading 11*
A PLACE TO SETTLE
Genesis 33–36

"I will build an altar to God, who answered me in the day of my distress and who has been with me wherever I have gone" (Gen. 35:3).

At last Jacob returned not only to Canaan, but home. His 20 frustrating years with Laban were over, and his feud with his brother Esau had been resolved. It was now, looking back, that Jacob realized how great a role God had played in his life.

Overview
Jacob and Esau met and were reconciled (33:1-20). The revenge Simeon and Levi took on the city of a man who raped their sister created new fears for Jacob (34:1-31). God told Jacob to return to Bethel and settle there (35:1-15). Rachel died, but Jacob found his father Isaac (vv. 16-29). The story of the twins closes with a genealogy of Esau and the Edomite nation he founded (36:1-43).

Understanding the Text
"I already have plenty" Gen. 33:1-20. The terrified Jacob was stunned when Esau welcomed him joyfully. Should we credit Esau with a generous and forgiving spirit? Not really.

Esau had always been a materialist, unable to see any benefit in the spiritual. This attitude was displayed years before when Esau "despised" God's covenant promise by trading his birthright for a bowl of stew (25:29-34). Esau had been furious at Jacob's theft of their father's blessing, but only because he wanted the family heritage of material wealth. When, after Jacob's flight, Esau actually did become rich, his anger faded. To Esau it seemed that Jacob had fled penniless, with nothing but some meaningless promise from an invisible God. The statement, "I have plenty," sums up Esau's view. Why be angry? Jacob had gotten nothing of real value. In earthly riches Esau had everything he had ever valued or desired!

How different for Jacob. Jacob expected his brother to be furious because the covenant promises of God were the most important thing in Jacob's life!

In a sense, God blessed both Esau and Jacob. Each brother received what he wanted most in life. But only Jacob's choice had eternal value.

Rape and revenge Gen. 34:1-31. Dinah's brothers were right to be "filled with grief and fury" when she was raped. Yet when the young man of Shechem asked permission to marry Dinah, he was acting honorably according to the customs of that time. Certainly the brothers of Dinah were wrong to take revenge on an entire city for the act of one of its citizens.

Jacob, whose fears had been relieved by reconciliation with Esau, now had a new worry. Would the other Canaanites attack his family because his sons had taken such bloody revenge?

Like Jacob's, our life is never completely free of stress. One anxiety is relieved only to be replaced by a new one. Jesus said, "In this world you will have trouble" (John 16:33). We need a peace that has a source beyond this world, a peace that is unshaken by what happens to us here.

Death and reunion Gen. 35:16-29. The text only touches on highlights of the next few years of Jacob's life. Rachel, who had wept over her childless state, died giving birth to Benjamin (vv. 16-20). Jacob's eldest son had an affair with one of his father's concubines (v. 22). Jacob and Esau buried their father and mourned together (vv. 27-29). Pain, anger, disappointment, reconciliation, and loss—all these are a heritage we share with Jacob as human beings. Only relationship with God and confidence in His promises can make this life, with its mingled joys and sorrows, meaningful.

"The account of Esau" Gen. 36:1-43. Genealogies were especially important to God's Old Testament people. They provided a sense of continuity, enabling each generation to understand its identity by tracing its roots. Genealogies enabled the Hebrew people to trace those roots back to Abraham, and thus validate their claim to be God's chosen people, inheritors of His

promise to that patriarch. But why trace the line of Esau so carefully? Esau is not in the promised line. He even turned his back on the promise, considering it of no value at all.

Perhaps the genealogy of Esau serves as an important reminder that those outside the household of God must not be ignored or written off as unimportant. Every individual has worth and value in God's sight, and is to be valued by us. The 91 strangers named in this genealogy are meaningless to us, but no person is unimportant to God.

▶ DEVOTIONAL

"Settle There, and Build an Altar" (Gen. 35:1-15)

Jacob's return to Bethel, the "house of God," was special. It was there God had first spoken to him. Now Bethel was to become a refuge.

Three things in the text establish Bethel as a refuge: The altar, which speaks of worship (vv. 3, 7); the repeated promise, which speaks of God's presence (vv. 9-13); and the stone pillar, which speaks of remembrance (vv. 14-15).

(1) Worship is essential if you and I are to find inner peace in a troubled world. Like Jacob, we need a time and place set aside especially to meet with God. We need to settle there—to be consistent in keeping a daily appointment with the Lord. Jacob told his family to "get rid of the foreign gods you have with you." In worship we clear our hearts and minds of everything that competes with God for our attention, and focus completely on Him.

Perhaps the best definition of worship is "expressing appreciation to God for who He by nature is." That is, we think about God's qualities, His attributes, His loving acts, and we praise Him for who and what He is. Our Bethel is daily worship. There we begin to experience the peace that Jacob found.

(2) God's presence is experienced as we hear His voice speaking to us. This is what Jacob experienced at Bethel (vv. 9, 11). This is what you and I experience today as we open the Scriptures and read, not for new information alone, but to hear and respond to what God has to say to us personally. In God's Word we hear His promises, sense His guidance, find His empowering. Our Bethel is Scripture, for in the Word we sense the presence of the One who met with Jacob at Bethel so long ago.

(3) Remembrance is the way we reenter the presence of God at any moment throughout the day. The stone pillar that Jacob erected at biblical Bethel is best understood as a *zikkaron*. In the Old Testament a *zikkaron* is any object or religious celebration intended to help a believer identify with God's active presence in history. Whenever Jacob saw the stone pillar, he was carried back in memory to the fellowship with God he experienced at that place.

The Bethel you and I create by worship and by reading Scripture serves as an anchor for our day. At any moment we can return in memory and find fresh strength.

How important that we apply to ourselves the words God spoke to Jacob: "Go up to Bethel: and settle there."

Personal Application

Select a time and place where you can meet daily with God.

Quotable

Give thanks to the Lord, call on His name;
make known among the nations what
He has done.
Sing to Him, sing praise to Him;
tell of all His wonderful acts.
Glory in His holy name;
let the hearts of those who seek the
Lord rejoice.
Look to the Lord and His strength; seek
His face always.
Remember the wonders He has done,
His miracles, and the judgments He
pronounced.—Psalm 105:1-5

JANUARY 12 *Reading 12*
JOSEPH
Genesis 37–41

"Will your mother and I and your brothers actually come and bow down to the ground before you?" (Gen. 37:10)

Few Bible characters are as admirable as Joseph. He suffered injustice after injustice, yet persevered. His faith was ultimately rewarded, and Joseph realized that God had used each painful experience to accomplish good.

Overview

Joseph, Jacob's favorite son, was hated by his jealous brothers and sold into slavery (37:1-36), even though Joseph's brothers were far less godly than he (38:1–39:23). God rewarded Joseph's faithfulness with an ability to interpret dreams (40:1-23), which catapulted Joseph from prison to political power in Egypt (41:1-57).

Understanding the Text

Joseph. Joseph's faithfulness enabled God to use him greatly. Joseph's rise to political power in Egypt laid the foundation for the family to move to that land. For some 400 years the Hebrew people stayed there, first as guests and later as slaves. During that span of time the small family of 70 persons grew into millions. In effect, Egypt served as a womb in which God grew the nation which was born through Moses' ministry. While war after war ravaged Canaan, God's people were safe in Egypt, free to multiply "greatly" (Ex. 1:7).

At the same time, the story of Joseph is the dramatic portrayal of a truly good man who overcame a series of tragedies. Joseph accepted the role of a slave and then of a prisoner, served his masters faithfully, and retained his trust in God. God used each tragedy to place Joseph where Pharaoh would hear of his gifts, invite Joseph to interpret his dreams, and then give Joseph great power and authority. On the one hand the story of Joseph is an inspiring account of a young man whose faith in God is finally rewarded. On the other, it is a reminder that God truly is capable of transforming the "all things" in our experience so that they "work good" (Rom. 8:28).

Dreams. Dreams are critical in the story of Joseph. In the Old Testament, dreams may be ordinary (as Job 7:14) or may be means through which God reveals information (as Num. 12:6). Frequently revelatory dreams are symbolic and require interpretation. In other ancient religions, books existed that purported to provide a key for interpreting dreams, just as there are dream books found in modern bookstores! But in Scripture symbolic dreams can only be interpreted by God Himself or a prophet whom He gifts. As Joseph told Pharaoh, "I cannot do it [interpret a dream], but God will give Pharaoh the answer he desires" (Gen. 41:16).

The role of the interpreter in most of Scripture's dream stories should warn us against seeking personal guidance through dreams, or taking our dreams as a direct word from the Lord.

"A young man of seventeen" Gen. 37:1-11. Life must have seemed exciting to Joseph at 17. He was his father's favorite. And he dreamed that he would have a great future! Filled with such visions, Joseph was not aware of how his father's and his own behavior affected his brothers. They were jealous, and when Joseph told them of his dreams, they were angry.

We can't fault a 17-year-old for a lack of wisdom. We can, however, note how important it is to be sensitive to others and to be aware of how what we do and say affects them.

"What will we gain?" Gen. 37:12-36 The brothers' jealousy and anger spilled over when Joseph was sent to find them and their flocks. Most wanted to kill Joseph. But Judah, showing himself one of the better of the brothers, saved Joseph's life by suggesting he be sold as a slave to a passing caravan of Midianite merchants.

None of the brothers except Reuben intended for Joseph to be returned to his father. Only Reuben seemed to care for the anguish the death of Joseph would surely cause their father (cf. vv. 31-35).

"Judah" Gen. 38:1-30. Judah applied the

moral standards of his culture in his relationship with Tamar, the wife of one of his dead sons, who pretended to be a prostitute. The story suggests just how superior Joseph truly was. Judah seems to have done what he thought was right out of fear (v. 11), and was quick to judge Tamar when he thought she had sinned (v. 24). Joseph, pressured by far greater temptations, did what was right out of respect for God (39:9), and when he was later reunited with the brothers who sold him into slavery, Joseph freely forgave them (cf. 45:4-8).

It's one thing to be "good" by the standards of our culture. It is something else again, out of love for God, to rise above those standards to be truly righteous. Placed side by side, the stories of Judah and Joseph remind us that God uses the person who is totally committed to Him. The Judahs do have roles in God's plan. But the Josephs find truly significant places!

"Sin against God" Gen. 39:9. Our system of law makes a distinction between victim and victimless crimes. The notion is that some crimes, such as assault or theft from a home, create victims. Other criminal acts, such as prostitution or homosexuality, theoretically have no victims. Each person involved is a consenting adult!

Joseph was urged to have sex with his master's wife. She'd keep the secret. Potiphar would never know. Who could possibly be hurt by a little fling? After all, as our movie rating systems suggest, these are the kinds of things "adults" both do and enjoy!

Joseph wasn't fooled. The "victimless" crime was in fact a "sin against God."

Satan eagerly sticks new labels on old sins, trying to confuse humanity and provide us with excuses to do what we know is wrong. It's important that our vision be as clear as Joseph's, and that we be as honest with ourselves as Joseph was with Potiphar's wife.

"Two officials" Gen. 40:1-23. The title of "cupbearer" and "baker" were given to two important officials in ancient Egypt. These discoveries by archeologists are two of many which mark Genesis 40–41 as amazingly accurate in its report of practices in Pharaoh's court. Even a list of convicts in a royal prison, many with Semetic names, has been recovered.

The Genesis report is history, not fiction. Joseph, whose life teaches us so many lessons about God, was a real human being, with whose tragedies and triumphs you and I can identify.

It's helpful to make a list of Joseph's experiences, and to imagine how he must have felt as each event occurred. It's even more helpful to think back over your own life. Have you had experiences that affected you as the events of Joseph's life affected him?

How good of God to include the stories of men and women like Joseph, to give us insight into what the Lord may be doing in our own lives.

Joseph's Life

Happy childhood	Gen. 37:1-3
Jealous brothers	Gen. 37:4-11
Mistreatment	Gen. 37:12-36
Faithful service	Gen. 39:1-6
Commitment to right	Gen. 39:7-10
Unfair treatment	Gen. 39:11-20
Hard work	Gen. 39:21-23
Helping others	Gen. 40:1-22
Forgotten by others	Gen. 40:23
Unique opportunity	Gen. 41:1-40
Recognition at last	Gen. 41:41-57
Success/achievement	Gen. 41–50
Forgiving his family	Gen. 45
Reunion at last	Gen. 46

"God will give Pharaoh the answer" Gen. 41:1-40. When Joseph was called from prison to interpret Pharaoh's dream, he might have been filled with self-importance. Instead Joseph was careful to give God all credit. Joseph's words, "I cannot do it . . . but God" (v. 16) are an absolutely accurate reflection of our own spiritual condition.

All too many Christian leaders have fallen because they forgot the truth that Joseph remembered. Successes fill us with self-confidence, and all too soon we begin to act as if the achievements for which we are known were our own doing. We need to remember—and to say aloud what Joseph did. Such a confession will point others to God. And such a confession will protect us from the spiritual pride that goes before a fall.

Egyptian wall paintings show high officials invested with the symbols of authority that Pharaoh gave to Joseph.

"In charge of the whole land" Gen. 41:41-57. Joseph was only 30 when he was made chief official of the land of Egypt. But from age 17 God had placed Joseph in positions where he could develop the needed skills. In Potiphar's household, and then prison, Joseph was schooled to be an administrator!

There is no telling how God intends to use our painful experiences to equip us for significant service in the future. But Genesis reminds us that we must deal with such experiences as Joseph did, remaining positive and making the best of the opportunities we are given. If we follow Joseph's example, God will be able to promote us too.

▶ DEVOTIONAL
"While Joseph Was There in Prison, the LORD Was with Him" (Gen. 39:1-23)

One of the most difficult experiences any of us has to handle is being treated unfairly.

Carmine spent untold hours as an adult helping his parents with their business. Yet recently they told Carmine he would be left out of their will in favor of a brother and sister who never helped or seemed to care.

Jackie still cries whenever she thinks of the crash that took the life of her 21-year-old son on his wedding night.

Don is bitter because he learned that his wife, who treats him and his sons so coldly, has had an affair.

Maria has been passed over for promotions in the law office where she works. Younger women who are more attractive than she, are given the promotions, even though she knows more and works harder than they do.

Gil, forced to bring a law suit by the persecution of an ex-boss trying to drive him from the field where they both work, is being unmercifully attacked by Christian friends for taking a Christian brother to court.

I know each of the five persons I've just described personally, though I've changed their names. I know how much pain each feels. What hurts each most is that what's happening to him or her just isn't fair.

Joseph would surely understand, for he was treated unfairly too. In this passage which relates Joseph's story, we find three principles that could help each one deal with the unfair things in his or her life.

(1) Maintain a clear conscience. Joseph resisted Potiphar's wife's attempts at seduction. When she lied and had him thrown into prison, Joseph's conscience was clear. He knew what happened had not been his fault.

We can't stop others from treating us unfairly. But by living good lives we can make sure that what happens to us is not a consequence of our own sin.

(2) Keep on doing your best. Prison was very different from the palatial estate Joseph had supervised for Potiphar. But even there Joseph did his best. As a result he was "made responsible for all that was done there."

By doing our best despite life's unfairness we demonstrate our innocence, and we prepare ourselves for whatever task God may have for us in the future.

(3) Practice God's presence. The Bible says that "while Joseph was there in the prison, the LORD was with him." God is with us too even when life seems most unfair and the future bleakest. We can survive and triumph by practicing God's presence. We do this by remembering He is with us, by prayer, by consciously rely-

ing on Him, and by doing our best, aware that we serve the Lord and not man.

God does not guarantee that we will never be treated unfairly. But God does guarantee us His presence. If we practice that presence, keep on doing our best, and maintain clear consciences, we will not only survive. Like Joseph, we will triumph.

Personal Application

How is life unfair to you? Are you responding as Joseph did?

Quotable

O, yet we trust that somehow good
 will be the final goal of ill,
 To pangs of nature, sins of will,
Defects of doubt, and taints of blood;

That nothing walks with aimless feet;
 That not one life shall be destroy'd
 Or cast as rubbish to the void,
When God hath made the pile complete;

That not a worm is cloven in vain;
 That not a moth with vain desire
 Is shrivell'd in a fruitless fire,
Or but subserves another's gain.

Behold, we know not anything;
 I can but trust that good shall fall
 At last—far off—at last, to all,
And every winter change to spring.
—Alfred Lord Tennyson

JANUARY 13 *Reading 13*
WAIT AND SEE
Genesis 42–46

> *"Now we must give an accounting for his blood" (Gen. 42:22).*

Twenty-two years had passed since Joseph's brothers sold him as a slave. When famine drove the brothers to Egypt, and they applied to Egypt's second most powerful man, they had no idea he was Joseph. Yet it's clear that none of them have forgotten what they did to Joseph. The question was, Had they changed?

Overview

When famine drove Joseph's half brothers to Egypt to purchase food, they failed to recognize him (42:1-38). On a second visit, bringing Joseph's full brother Benjamin, Joseph tested them (43:1–44:34). Joseph finally revealed himself to his stunned family (45:1-28). The clan moved to Egypt, where Jacob was reunited with the son he thought was dead (46:1-34).

Understanding the Text

"You are spies" Gen. 42:1-17. When the brothers appeared in Egypt to buy grain, Joseph accused them of being spies. This, and the other things that Joseph did to his brothers, should be understood as tests. Twenty-two years earlier, when Joseph was only 17, his half brothers had sold him as a slave. Joseph wanted to know if the Lord had worked any change in their characters. The tests that Joseph devised showed that God had!

"Surely we are being punished because of our brother" Gen. 42:18-38. The brothers were shaken by their brief imprisonment and by the suspicions voiced by Egypt's ruler. The conviction that they were being punished shows they had never forgotten Joseph's pleading as they cruelly sold him into slavery. For over two decades they had lived with that memory.

People sin lightly, as if doing wrong were no great matter. But once committed, sin's memory snaps at our heels, burdening us with guilt and shame.

Note too Reuben's statement, "Now we must give an accounting." It sums up the Old Testament view of sin as (1) a violation of a known standard (2) for which one is accountable (3) and which merits punishment.

"Deeply moved" Gen. 43:1-43. This chapter is deeply emotional. We sense Jacob's anguish at the thought of danger to Rachel's other son, Benjamin. We sense the brothers' terror as they faced a return to Egypt, where they were convinced the ruler in-

tended to "seize us as slaves and take our donkeys" (v. 18). Only the prospect of starvation in Canaan forced Jacob to send Benjamin, and compelled the brothers to take the road to Egypt once again.

Joseph too was torn by emotion. He could hardly control himself at the sight of his brother, and word of his father. Yet Joseph controlled his emotions not out of necessity but out of wisdom. The test of his brothers was not complete. Joseph still needed to know their hearts.

All too often we act from emotion rather than wisdom. It is especially important in dealing with our children to do what is best for them, rather than what our heart tells us.

"Do not let me see the misery that would come upon my father" Gen. 44:1-34. The final test Joseph devised placed unbearable stress on his brothers—but it revealed what Joseph needed to know. How significant it is that Judah is the one who makes the plea recorded in verses 18-34. Years before Judah had been against murdering Joseph, but had been more than willing to sell him as a slave and bring home evidence that Joseph had been killed by a wild beast (cf. 37:26-31). Now Judah offers to become a slave himself in place of young Benjamin, motivated by thought of the anguish that the loss of Benjamin would cause his father!

God had worked a real change in the heart of this man who was so calloused just 20 years before.

It may seem strange, but realization that we have sinned often launches personal transformation. Guilt is not intended to drive us from God but to Him. Even a person who has something as terrible to look back on as Judah did need not despair. God is the God who forgives sin and who transforms the sinner!

Judah's reaction here offers hope to all who are burdened with memories of past sins. Our past need *not* determine our future! We can confess our sins to God and, like Judah, we can be changed.

"Joseph is still alive! In fact, he is ruler of all Egypt" Gen. 45:1–46:34. A stunned Jacob heard the news and realized that before he died he would actually see the lost son he loved so dearly. Emotionally this is the climax of the story of Joseph.

In the flow of Genesis, it is not. The historic significance of Joseph is that through his rise from slavery to power, God made it possible for his little family to move to Egypt where they could multiply and become a great people. Yet the joy that echoes in the brothers' excited announcement of the news that Joseph lived serves as an important reminder.

In working out His grand master plan for the ages, God never forgets the individual. He remembers each one of us and truly cares about our joys and our sorrows. I confess that I get tears in my eyes as I read Genesis 45:26-28. I suspect that God, figuratively speaking, had tears in His eyes as He witnessed that scene. Ultimately, God's most important works are not those He does in shaping history's flow, but those He does in the hearts of human beings. Transforming a Judah. Bringing a Jacob unexpected joy.

▶ DEVOTIONAL
Beersheba
(Gen. 46:1-27)

Beersheba lies in southern Canaan. It is a pleasant place, some 974 feet above sea level. Further south, however, one can look down on the Negev and the wilderness of Zin, deserts through which an ancient highway wound its way toward Egypt. In a sense, Beersheba lies on Canaan's border. To go further south is to leave the Promised Land behind.

I suspect this is why Jacob stopped at Beersheba to build an altar and offer sacrifices to God. Jacob was so eager to see Joseph again. The dry and devastated land of Canaan was no longer livable. Yet Jacob stopped at Beersheba.

I appreciate Jacob's wisdom. Many decades before, Abraham, driven by another famine, had hurried on past Beersheba in his rush to reach Egypt (12:10-20)—even though God had placed him in Canaan. Jacob wasn't about to leave the land in which God placed him, despite strong motives, without stopping at Beersheba to pray.

Genesis 46 tells us that there God spoke to Jacob in a vision, and told him not to be afraid to go down to Egypt. There God gave Jacob confirmation that he was doing the right thing.

I suspect that this part of the Joseph story provides a model for our own decision-making. We carefully consider our options. We note reasons to do one thing rather than another. On the basis of our information and our desires we "set out." And this is right. God has given us minds with which to consider and desires that move us toward one goal or another. Our decision-making as Christians should not be mystical, but just as practical and reasoned as was Jacob's decision to bring his family to Egypt.

But, as we set out, we need to be sure we stop at Beersheba. We need to be sensitive to God's leading and ask the Lord to confirm or to correct us in the direction we've chosen to move.

The 70 members of Jacob's family who were united in Egypt could be sure that they were where God wanted them to be. Jacob had stopped at Beersheba.

How good it is, as we make important decisions in our lives, to stop at Beersheba and indicate our willingness to continue or turn back at God's direction. When we stop at Beersheba, we will have the confidence that, whatever happens, we are living in the center of God's will.

Personal Application

Make decisions carefully. But make it a practice as you act on them to stop at Beersheba.

Quotable

"Gethsemane teaches us that the kingdom of God is entered only through a denial of one's own will and the affirmation of the will of God. Therefore, the cross must stand central to an understanding of the kingdom. Since the essence of the kingdom is our obedience to the absolute will of God, we understand it only as we bring our own will to the foot of the cross. No self-will can live unchallenged in God's kingdom."—Dennis Corrigan

JANUARY 14 *Reading 14*

"GOD WILL BE WITH YOU"

Genesis 47–50

> *"I am about to die, but God will be with you and take you back to the land of your fathers" (Gen. 48:21).*

Genesis ends with Jacob's family settled in Egypt. Yet the passing of the patriarchs marks the beginning, not the end, of what God will do for and through the descendants of Abraham, Isaac, and Jacob. It is the same with us. The passing of one generation is not the end. As we trust in God, we can say to our children, "God will be with you." We can rely on God to work out His purpose in their lives.

Overview

The family arrived and was settled on prime Egyptian land (47:1-31). Jacob counted Joseph's 2 sons as his own (48:1-22), and blessed all 13 before he died (49:1-33). Joseph buried his father, reaffirmed his forgiveness of his brothers, and obtained a promise that when God brought their offspring back to Canaan, Joseph's bones would be returned to his homeland (50:1-26).

Understanding the Text

"Egypt and Canaan" Gen. 47:1-31. Canaan depended on rainfall for the moisture needed to raise crops. Egypt, however, depended on the Nile River, which overflowed annually and enriched the farmlands lying along its banks. Times of famine are reported in ancient Egyptian records, yet the Nile generally made Egypt famine-proof. Egyptian reliefs and records depict peoples from Syria-Palestine asking permission to stay in Egypt in famine, and coming to Egypt to buy food.

"The land became Pharaoh's" Gen. 47:20. Ancient inscriptions confirm that Egypt was considered to belong to Pharaoh, and that 20 percent of the crop was to be his. Records also show that temple lands did *not* belong to Pharaoh, which meant that Egypt's rulers were often troubled by too-independent religious hierarchies. No independent Egyptian records tell the story

of Joseph or explain how Pharaoh's ownership was established.

"Your two sons . . . will be reckoned as mine" Gen. 48:1-22. It is sometimes confusing. The "12 tribes of Israel" are frequently mentioned in the Old Testament. Yet if we compare lists, there are actually 13 tribal groups! Levi is not included in some lists, because this tribe provided priests and worship leaders. On other lists, such as the one in Revelation 7:5-8, Levi is included and Dan is left out.

What happened is that Jacob "adopted" the two sons of Joseph. These two sons, Manasseh and Ephraim, became heads of tribal groups, and the name "Joseph" was dropped.

It's helpful for us to remember this if someone else is given credit for what we have done while our name remains unmentioned. Genesis reminds us that it isn't recognition that is important. It's contribution.

Joseph's name may not appear in Scripture's lists of Israelite tribes. But we know—and God knows—that he made a greater contribution than any of the other brothers!

Jacob's blessing Gen. 49:1-28. The concept of blessing is a powerful one in the Old Testament. In giving a blessing, a superior, such as a father, verbally conferred a gift or endowment to another person. This was not magic, for the Old Testament makes it clear that all blessing is from God (14:19; Num. 22; Deut. 10:8). Only a person who was in a close personal relationship with God could act as a channel through which God blessed others.

In Genesis 49, Jacob, enabled by God, looks ahead and in his blessing makes oft-obscure predictions about the future of each family group, based in part on the character of each of his sons (v. 28).

What is more important to us, however, is a phrase found in the blessing given Joseph. That phrase is, "Because of your father's God, who helps you, because of the Almighty, who blesses you . . . your father's blessings are greater than the blessings of the ancient mountains" (vv. 25-26).

The deep faith in God that Joseph displayed blessed his sons, and remained a vital influence even on distant generations. If we want to be a blessing to our children's children, there is no surer way than for us to live as close to God as Joseph did. When we are faithful and obedient, our "blessings are greater."

"The scepter will not depart from Judah" Gen. 49:10. Jesus came from the tribe of Judah. This blessing, which predicts a ruler to emerge from Judah's line, is one of the earliest and clearest of the Old Testament's messianic prophecies.

"A full forty days" Gen. 50:1-14. The text again provides an accurate picture of cultural backgrounds. Israelite burial took place as soon after death as possible, with no attempt made to preserve the body. In Egypt, however, a lengthy process of removing viscera and treating the body with preservatives was followed. Jacob was embalmed after the Egyptian pattern because he had asked his sons to bury him in Canaan, too long a journey to take with a corrupting corpse.

Why would Jacob want to be buried in Canaan? Jacob's request was an affirmation of faith. God had promised that his descendants would inherit Canaan. In choosing to be buried with his father and grandfather in Canaan, Jacob affirmed his conviction that his descendants would return and God's promises would be fulfilled.

"God will surely come to your aid" Gen. 50:22-26. When death finally visited Joseph, he too took the opportunity to affirm his faith in God's covenant. He had the family promise that, when God did bring the Hebrews out of Egypt and give them the Promised Land, his body would be carried home.

The deaths of Joseph and Jacob remind us that the funerals of believers, while darkened by grief, are also bright with hope. Neither Joseph nor Jacob viewed death as the end. Each looked beyond his own time on earth and found comfort in what God would do in the future. This is also the case with us. Because of Jesus we understand even better than they. Death's sting still hurts. But we know that the death of the body is our induction into a full experience of eternal life.

▶ DEVOTIONAL
What If?
(Gen. 50:1-21)

I remember how strange I felt that afternoon. I slipped into our living room, edged past my dad, and headed for my room.

Usually it wasn't like that. Usually I hurried home, ran to Dad, and asked if we were going fishing that afternoon.

Not that day. That day I'd gone to school clutching a coin Dad gave me to buy new shoelaces. I went into Eli Bassett's store. But I never made it past the candy counter. At school I tried to eat the candy, but it didn't taste right, and I threw it away. That afternoon I told my dad I had lost the money.

Somehow knowing that I had done wrong distorted my relationship with my dad. I didn't feel comfortable with him that afternoon. Not at all.

So I really can understand Joseph's brothers. They remembered the wrong they had done, and it made them uncomfortable. What if Joseph held a grudge? What if Joseph intended to pay them back? What if?

Joseph must have understood too. The text says that "he reassured them and spoke kindly to them." Joseph even made his commitment to them unmistakably clear: "I will provide for you and your children."

What was it that freed Joseph to forgive so freely? Perspective. Joseph realized his brothers had intended to harm him. But he also understood that God had used his siblings to achieve a good and important end. In looking beyond the act to consider God, Joseph was able to see his brothers' sins in a fresh perspective. Sensing the good hand of God even in the evil others did freed Joseph from anger and from any desire to take revenge.

It's strange, isn't it? The brothers suffered more from their earlier sins than the man they had sinned against! Just as a child I suffered more from misusing the money Dad gave me to buy shoelaces than he did. I suffered more because my act made me feel guilty, and awareness of guilt created what seemed to me an uncrossable gulf in my relationship with my dad.

When someone we know sins against us, we need to adopt Joseph's view of things. We need to realize that God can and will use even our hurts for good. We need to understand that sin hurts the sinner, perhaps even more than it hurts the person sinned against.

We can react with anger when we are hurt. We can strike out or use silence as a weapon to express our pain. Or we can take Joseph's course and "speak comfortably" to the person who sins against us. This doesn't mean that we ignore the sin. After all, Joseph said, "You intended to harm me." But Joseph went on to "speak comfortably" to his brothers, to reassure them of forgiveness and express again his commitment to them.

When we take Joseph's course, making plain our willingness to forgive and our continuing commitment to care for the one who has hurt us, then the pain of sinner and sinned against can be healed.

And we will have walked in a path marked out not only by Joseph, but by Jesus as well.

Personal Application

If you sense your alienation from someone who has hurt or sinned against you, why not try Joseph's approach?

Quotable

"Of the seven deadly sins, anger is possibly the most fun. To lick your wounds, to smack your lips over grievances long past, to roll over your tongue the prospect of bitter confrontations still to come, to savor to the last toothsome morsel both the pain you are given and the pain you are giving back; in many ways it is a feast fit for a king. The chief drawback is that what you are wolfing down is yourself. The skeleton at the feast is you."—Frederick Beuchner

---

The Variety Reading Plan continues with LUKE

Exodus

INTRODUCTION

Exodus means "going out." The book tells the story of the Israelites' release from bondage in Egypt about 1450 B.C.

Exodus tells how God, faithful to the covenant promises made to Abraham, Isaac, and Jacob, performed miracles to shatter the bonds holding His people. The fast-paced adventure moves quickly to Sinai. Here Exodus lingers, and in careful detail explores the Law that God gave His people to live by. This code was intended to teach the Israelites how to love God and how to love one another.

Exodus also introduces Moses, that towering Old Testament character who is revered in Judaism as the lawgiver, and whose faithfulness to God serves as a model for modern Christian laymen and leaders.

Most significant, however, is what Exodus reveals about God. God uses His power to redeem His people. God demands holiness from those who claim relationship with Him. And God provides a way for sinners to approach Him and be transformed.

OUTLINE OF CONTENTS

I. The Story of Deliverance .... Ex. 1–19
  A. Moses' call .... Ex. 1–4
  B. Miracles .... Ex. 5–13
  C. On to Sinai .... Ex. 14–19
II. God's Design for a Holy Community .... Ex. 20–40
  A. Laws for living .... Ex. 20–23
  B. Provision for worship .... Ex. 24–40

READING GUIDE (9 Days)

If hurried, you may read only the "core passage" in your Bible, and the Devotional in each chapter of this Commentary.

Reading	*Chapters*	*Core passage*
15	1–4	3
16	5–11	5:22–6:27
17	12:1–15:21	15:1-16
18	15:22–19:25	19:3-6
19	20–23	20:1-21
20	24–27	24:1-8
21	28–30	29:15-30
22	31–34	32–33
23	35–40	37

Exodus

JANUARY 15 *Reading 15*
GOD REVEALED TO MOSES
Exodus 1–4

> *"This is My name forever, the name by which I am to be remembered from generation to generation" (Ex. 3:15).*

In these chapters we meet Moses. But most important, in these chapters we meet God, and learn His most personal name, I AM.

Overview

The Israelites multiplied in Egypt, but were enslaved (1:1-22). Moses was found and adopted by a princess (2:1-10), but as an adult he identified with his people and was forced to flee (vv. 11-25). When Moses was 80 years old, God revealed Himself to Moses as I AM. Bearing the divine name, Moses was sent to Pharaoh to win Israel's freedom (3:1-22). Equipped with miraculous signs, a reluctant Moses returned to his people (4:1-31).

Understanding the Text

"The Israelites . . . multiplied greatly" Ex. 1:1-7. A family of 70 persons entered Egypt. Based on the number of men of military age reported in Numbers 1:46, there must have been between 2 and 3 million Israelites at the time of the Exodus!

"Multiplied greatly" suggests God's reason for Israel's sojourn in Egypt. Canaan served as a land bridge between Egypt and great northern empires. Armies marched across it and fought in its hills and valleys. If the Israelites had remained in Canaan, they could never have grown the population base needed to establish a nation.

"They put slave masters over them" Ex. 1:8-22. Initially the Israelites enjoyed a favored position in Egypt. They were settled in "the best part of the land" and many were employed by Pharaoh himself (cf. Gen. 47:5-6). Some time after Joseph's death, however, the Israelites were enslaved. This passage emphasizes the terrible conditions under which God's people were forced to live. Words and phrases like "oppress," "forced labor," "worked ruthlessly," and "lives bitter with hard labor" are used. The ultimate oppression is seen in Pharaoh's command that Hebrew boy babies be thrown into the Nile to drown!

The Israelites' situation in Egypt is intended to mirror the spiritual condition of the human race. As Israel was in bondage to Egypt, so all humanity is in bondage to sin. Only the miracle-working power of God, which forced Israel's release, can break the bonds forged by sin and make us truly free.

Moses Ex. 2:10. Moses is the dominant figure in Exodus and the next three Old Testament books. He was 80 years old when God commissioned him to deliver the Israelites, and he led God's people for 40 years. We can learn much from Moses' life, and will do so as we read Exodus, Leviticus, Numbers, and Deuteronomy. The New Testament says Moses was "faithful as a servant in all God's house" (Heb. 3:5). We can discover much about faithfulness in such revealing stories about Moses as are told in Exodus 32–33, Numbers 12, 16, and 21.

"He became her son" Ex. 2:1-10. This simple phrase reminds us that Moses, found by a princess, was adopted into Egypt's royal family. As the princess' son, Moses may

even have had a claim to Egypt's throne! Stephen repeated an accurate oral tradition when he said that "Moses was educated in all the wisdom of the Egyptians and was powerful in speech and action" (Acts 7:22).

Despite his advantages, Moses identified with his oppressed people and their God. Hebrews 11:24-25 says that "by faith Moses, when he had grown up, refused to be known as the son of Pharaoh's daughter. He chose to be mistreated along with the people of God rather than to enjoy the pleasures of sin for a short time."

This surely is one source of Moses' greatness. His priorities were not shaped by wealth or privilege. He truly cared about God and about God's people.

"He killed the Egyptian" Ex. 2:11-24. Despite Moses' concern for his people, he apparently wavered until he was 40 years old. Then when Moses saw an Egyptian beating a Hebrew he first glanced "this way and that and seeing no one" he then killed the Egyptian (v. 12). Moses was unready to take a public stand with the Hebrews, or to lead a slave uprising.

We can sympathize with Moses. How can anyone represent an oppressed people to their oppressors? Still, when even righteous anger is expressed in hostile acts, little is accomplished.

"Who am I?" Ex. 3:1-22 When God spoke to Moses from a bush that burned without being consumed, the 80-year-old seemed a very different person from the angry firebrand of age 40. Four decades of life in the desert had humbled Moses. The one-time prince of Egypt who dreamed great dreams had learned his limitations. When God said, "I am sending you to Pharaoh," Moses replied, "Who am I, that I should go to Pharaoh and bring the Israelites out of Egypt?"

The rest of the passage, which reports Moses' dialogue with the Lord, shows how hesitant Moses was. Moses brought up difficulty after difficulty—a pattern that continues into Exodus 4 despite God's repeated promises to be with Moses and bring him success.

Again we can identify with Moses. As we grow older, and discover our limitations, the dreams of youth fade away. We won't be famous. Or rich. Or find the cure for cancer. Or become a well-known evangelist. As our early self-image shrinks, we find ourselves less willing to risk. Instead of opportunities we see problems. Instead of trying, we think of all the reasons why we are sure to fail.

This is what happened to Moses. Even promises from God weren't quite enough to change a view that had developed over 40 years of failure. Yet in a sense it was Moses' awareness of his weaknesses that made him suitable for God's purpose! Moses had finally realized that there was nothing *he* could do. Now all Moses needed to learn was that God can do anything!

It's the same with you and me. It's healthy to acknowledge our weaknesses. But we need not dwell on them. What we really need to do is to fix our eyes on the Lord, and remember that there is nothing too hard for Him. Any task God may call you or me to do is a task that He can accomplish through us.

"What is that in your hand?" Ex. 4:1-9 Moses continued to object, focusing on his weaknesses rather than on God's strength. Finally the Lord gave him three miraculous signs to serve as evidence to the Israelites that God truly had sent Moses.

The signs weren't spectacular. And God chose simple things—the shepherd's staff Moses carried. His own hand. Water from the river.

But what strikes me as special is the phrase "in your hand." God took what Moses already had and transformed it.

We may not perform miracles. But God still takes what we have at hand and uses it to convince others that He is real.

"I will harden his heart" Ex. 4:18-23. Earlier God had given Moses repeated promises. Now He gives Moses a warning. Why? Sometimes human beings misunderstand the promises of God. We assume that God will make our lives easy and remove all the obstacles in our path. But God's promises *never* imply that! Instead the promises of God express His commitment to be with us and help us when the obstacles are greatest! It is only in facing, and living through, pain and tragedy that we experience God's faithfulness.

"The Lord *. . . was about to kill him" Ex. 4:24-26.* This puzzling event teaches an important lesson. Centuries before, God had commanded that male descendants of Abraham should be circumcised as a sign of their membership in the covenant community (Gen. 17:9-14). Moses had not yet circumcised his own sons. It seems likely Zipporah, his wife, had objected, for when Moses was taken deathly ill she apparently knew the reason, and acted immediately to circumcise her two boys. Her subsequent anger (Ex. 4:25) suggests she had been against the rite.

But why was it so important that Moses' sons be circumcised? Because Moses was to be a leader. A spiritual leader in any era must himself be obedient to God.

If we are to be used by God, we must first be responsive to Him.

"And they believed" Ex. 4:27-31. The Israelites welcomed Moses and believed his promise of deliverance. It must have been encouraging to Moses. But this early response, as is often the case, would soon turn into angry accusations as things didn't work out as the people of God expected.

Faith that counts is faith that persists, even when things seem to go wrong.

▶DEVOTIONAL
God Reveals Himself
(Ex. 3)

When Moses held back, fearful, on the doorstep of commitment, God told Moses His name.

In biblical times names had meaning. They were intended to convey something of the identity, the essence, of the thing or person named. So when God told Moses the name by which He was to be known "forever"—the name "by which I am to be remembered from generation to generation" (v. 15)—that revelation was significant.

The name the Lord revealed was "I AM." We know it as Jehovah or Yahweh. Wherever most English versions have Lord, the Hebrew reads "I AM."

That name is constructed on the Hebrew verb "to be," and is best taken to mean "The God Who Is Always Present." God, who was with Abraham centuries before, was present with Moses and the Exodus generation. God, who delivered them then, would be present with every coming generation as well! In the past, in the present, and in the future, GOD IS! He who was with Moses is with you and me even today.

These Exodus chapters help us see why this name of God is so important. When Moses hesitated to respond to the Lord, God gave him a series of promises. Note each of these in the text.

"I will be with you" (v. 12).

"The elders of Israel will listen to you" (v. 18).

"I will stretch out My hand . . . and [perform] wonders" (v. 20).

"I will help you speak and teach you what to say" (4:12).

How could Moses know that God would keep His promises? The name told him. God is the great I AM. Because He is always present with His people, God is able to fulfill in our present every promise He made in our past.

When God told Moses "this is My name forever," God was speaking to you and me as well as to His prophet. God truly is The One Who Is Always Present. He is with you today. He will be with you tomorrow. And because God IS, every promise He has made us in Christ will surely be fulfilled.

Personal Application

Is there a time or situation in which you need to hold on to the fact that God IS, and that He is present with you?

Quotable

"If I could give you information on my life it would be to show how a woman of very ordinary ability has been led by God in strange and unaccustomed paths to do in His service what He has done in her. And if I could tell you all, you would see how God has done all, and I nothing. I have worked hard, very hard, that is all; and I have never refused God anything."—Florence Nightingale

JANUARY 16 *Reading 16*
GOD REVEALS HIS POWER
Exodus 5–11

"Who is the LORD, that I should obey Him and let Israel go? I do not know the LORD and I will not let Israel go" (Ex. 5:2).

In ancient times a nation's gods were credited with its successes. The more powerful the nation, the greater its gods seemed to be. But in these chapters the God of Israelite slaves—our God!—is shown to be far more powerful than the gods of the greatest nation then on earth.

Definition of Key Terms

Miracles. The Hebrew words used to describe the plagues God brought on Egypt mean "wonder" and "miraculous sign." Most of the 10 plagues were natural disasters that had occurred at some time in Egypt. However, three things unmistakably marked them off as miraculous: (1) Their intensity. The disasters were far greater than normal. (2) Their timing. The disasters came and left at Moses' command. (3) Their subject. Several of the disasters occurred only in Egyptian districts, leaving areas occupied by the Israelites untouched. Whether God used natural forces to bring the judgments or not, the Egyptians who suffered under them were forced to acknowledge the power of Israel's God.

Overview

Pharaoh rejected Moses' demand and increased the work required of his Israelite slaves (5:1-21). God promised to act to redeem His people (v. 22–7:5). God's power was unleashed in a series of nine miracles which struck Egypt, devastating that land (v. 6–10:29). The final, decisive plague took the life of every firstborn male in Egypt (11:1-10).

Understanding the Text

Pharaoh's hard heart. These chapters speak often of the "hard" condition of Pharaoh's heart. The image suggests stubborn resistance to God. The biblical text speaks of Pharaoh hardening his heart (8:15), of God hardening Pharaoh's heart (7:3), and of his heart hardening (vv. 14, 22). To understand, we need simply to ask, What did God *do* to harden Pharaoh's heart?

The answer is that God revealed His power more and more fully. God hardened Pharaoh's heart in the same way that the hot sun hardens bricks. God did not harden Pharaoh's heart against Pharaoh's will. If Pharaoh's heart had been like wax rather than clay, it would have softened rather than hardened when God revealed Himself more fully.

If our hearts are like wax, we will respond to God as He speaks to us. If our hearts are like clay, we will be as Pharaoh. The more God speaks to us, the harder we will become until finally God is forced to break us.

"Make the work harder" Ex. 5:1-21. Moses' request that Pharaoh release Israel for a temporary pilgrimage was scornfully rejected by Pharaoh, who ridiculed the God of slaves (v. 2). He ordered that the slaves' quota of bricks be maintained, but that they be forced to gather the straw that earlier had been provided. Chopped straw was added to the mud used in making brick. The chemicals in the straw created a harder, longer-lasting brick.

The response stunned the Israelites and Moses. They had expected an easy victory because God was on their side! When no easy victory occurred, the people became angry with Moses and Aaron (v. 21).

We have to guard against unrealistic expectations. Psalm 37:7 says, "Do not fret when men succeed in their ways, when they carry out their wicked schemes." Rather than panic when this occurs, we are to "be still before the LORD, and wait patiently for Him" (v. 7).

"Their secret arts" Ex. 6:28–7:24. When Moses showed Pharaoh the authenticating signs God had given him, Egyptian magicians duplicated them. Some suggest the Egyptian magicians used trickery. Snake charmers even today cause cobras to become stiff by pressing on a nerve in their necks. They then throw them on the ground to arouse them. Others believe that the "secret arts" of Egypt's magicians was actual magic, performed with demonic aid. In this case the confrontation be-

tween Moses and Egypt's magicians was a true test of supernatural resources.

It doesn't really matter. Soon God began to perform such powerful acts that even Egypt's magicians told Pharaoh, "This is the finger of God" (8:19).

Today too human beings attempt to duplicate God's works. Hospitals promise cures for substance abuse. Psychiatrists offer freedom to the guilt-ridden. In certain cases they even seem to succeed! Yet true release from every dependency, and life-transforming forgiveness, remain a work of God. Pharaoh was unwilling to see the difference between what his magicians could do and what God could do. We need to be aware of that difference, and depend on the "finger of God."

The devastating plagues the Lord caused were a judgment on Egypt's gods (Ex. 9:27, 34), some of which are shown here. God's plagues were directed against the Nile god, whose waters killed rather than sustained life (7:14-24); the goddess of birth, Heqt, whose symbolic frogs became rotting heaps of death (8:1-15); and the sun god, Ra, whose impotence was shown as God imposed three days of absolute darkness (10:21-29).

The Ten Plagues

The Nile turned to blood	7:14-24
Frogs infest the land	8:1-15
Gnats fill Egypt	8:16-19
Flies swarm Egyptian districts	8:20-32
Anthrax devastates Egypt's cattle	9:1-7
Boils fester on all Egyptians	9:8-12
Hail crushes Egyptian crops	9:13-35
Locusts devour all vegetation	10:1-20
Darkness falls on Egyptians	10:21-29
Firstborn males of Egypt die	11:1-10

"I will deal differently with the land of Goshen" Ex. 8:22. A distinctive feature of several of the plagues is that they fell only on districts occupied by the Egyptians. Hebrew districts were immune. This clearly demonstrated the miraculous nature of the plagues. It also made it clear to the Israelites that they truly were God's special people.

"Those . . . who feared the word of the LORD hurried to bring their slaves and their livestock inside" Ex. 9:20. The verse reminds us that the Egyptians did not, as some have suggested, suffer innocently for the sin of Pharaoh. They participated, as taskmasters and in other ways, in the oppression of Israel. No one who sees evil and stands silent is guiltless.

Even so, God published Moses' decrees of judgment so that those who came to respect the God of slaves could protect their possessions. God is good to the guilty, gracious to all those who respond to His word.

"This time I have sinned" Ex. 9:27. When I last talked with Charlie he was lying in a hospital bed with two broken legs. He'd been lying drunk in a Brooklyn gutter and been run over by a truck. Charlie was like

Pharaoh. When things went against him, he vocally turned to God. But as soon as the trouble disappeared, there he was, back in the gutter again.

Pharaoh was a deathbed convert. When he was in trouble, he asked for prayer. But when each plague was lifted, Pharaoh went back to his old ways.

It's worthwhile to underline what Pharaoh said in each confrontation with Moses, and note that each expression of repentance was worthless. How do we know? We understand what was in his heart by observing what he *did* when each plague was removed.

Talk is still cheap. Words of repentance, without a change in life, are as empty as Pharaoh's promises.

"Every firstborn son in Egypt will die" Ex. 11:1-10. In the biblical world the firstborn son was special. He was expected to guide the family in the next generation, and he was the one through whom the family name would be preserved. Inheritance laws reflect the importance of the firstborn son: he received at least twice the portion of the other sons in the family.

Thus the death of every firstborn in Egypt was a stunning loss. Only this final, devastating plague would at last force Pharaoh to release his slaves.

We might view the plagues on Egypt as a series of increasingly painful punishments. If Pharaoh had relented at any stage, he could have avoided the more serious troubles that followed. Because Pharaoh remained hard, however, the ultimate penalty was finally imposed.

God's judgments are often gracious in exactly this way. They become more severe only as we continue to resist Him. When we sense the disciplining hand of God, it's wise to surrender immediately. Why should God have to strike what is dearest to us before we respond?

▶ DEVOTIONAL
God's Mighty Hand
(Ex. 5:22–6:27)

When Pharaoh increased the burden on the Israelites, Moses was as upset as the people. But his response in the situation was more spiritual. He didn't blame others. Instead Moses went to God to express his anger and his confusion.

We can sense both emotions in Moses' prayer. "O Lord, why have You brought trouble upon this people? Is this why You sent me? Ever since I went to Pharaoh to speak in Your name, he has brought trouble upon this people, and You have not rescued Your people at all."

It is wrong to blame others when things go wrong. It is not wrong to speak freely to the Lord. In expressing his emotions, Moses showed that he was willing to be totally honest with himself and with the Lord. And in coming to God, Moses acknowledged the Lord's sovereignty and power. Moses did not question whether God could rescue Israel. He cried out in frustration, questioning, "Why not yet?"

You and I, who believe in God, will feel the same anger and frustration that Moses knew at times. Such feelings need not suggest a lack of trust. But they do raise the question of timing. Why not yet?

God gives Moses his answer in 6:1-8. God will deliver with "mighty acts of judgment" so that "you will know that I am the LORD your God."

When our victories are easy, it's all too likely we will lose sight of God. But when all is so dark and hopeless that we are about to give up, and then deliverance suddenly appears, we know what happened is of the Lord. Often God delays deliverance, not because He wants us to go on suffering, but because He wants us to recognize His hand when He acts.

Personal Application

How does Moses' experience speak to your own frustrations and anger?

Quotable

"You will hear men say that people 'in olden times' believed in miracles 'because they didn't know the laws of Nature.' A moment's thought shows this to be nonsense. If events were not known to be contrary to the laws of nature how could they suggest the presence of the supernatural? How could they be surprising unless they were seen to be exceptions to the rules? And how can anything be seen to be an exception till the rules are known? If there ever were men who did not know the laws of nature *at all*, they would have no idea of a miracle and feel no particular interest in one if it were performed. Belief in miracles, far from depending on an ignorance of the laws of nature, is only possible in so far as those laws are known."—C.S. Lewis

JANUARY 17 *Reading 17*
GOD'S VICTORY
Exodus 12:1–15:21

"Do not be afraid. Stand firm and you will see the deliverance the L*ORD will bring you today" Ex. 14:13.*

The great celebration of Passover calls every Jewish family together to participate in an annual reminder of the deliverance God brought their forefathers in Egypt. The story told in these chapters portrays God's final victory over the gods of Egypt, Israel's passage through the Red Sea, and Israel's song of praise.

Definition of Key Terms

Passover. Passover is (1) a historic event, and (2) an annual Jewish festival commemorating the event. On the first Passover, a lamb, which had been taken into the home for three days, was killed and its blood was sprinkled outside on the doorposts. The meat was roasted and the lamb was eaten by the family the night God took the lives of Egypt's firstborn.

The highlight of the annual festival is a commemorative meal shared by members of a Jewish household. Eating this meal was to be "a lasting ordinance for you and your descendants" (Ex. 12:24). The purpose of the meal is to enable all generations to participate in what God did for their forefathers. In a real way, that first Passover won freedom from slavery not just for one generation of Jews, but for all generations to follow.

Deuteronomy 16:2, 5-7 establishes Passover as a national as well as a family celebration, to be marked by an entire week of sacrifice and public rejoicing.

The meal that Jesus shared with His disciples the evening before His crucifixion was Passover (cf. Matt. 26; Mark 14; Luke 22; John 13:1).

The writers of the epistles see the Passover lamb as a symbol of Jesus, who was "sacrificed for us" and whose blood frees us from bondage to sin and death (cf. John 1:29; 1 Cor. 5:7).

Overview

Lambs' blood on the Israelites' doorframes protected them the night God took the life of every firstborn in Egypt (12:1-30). The next morning God's people left the land of their captivity (vv. 31-51). Israel's firstborn were set aside for God in honor of the Exodus deliverance (13:1-16). Israel passed safely through the Red Sea (v. 17–14:31), and Miriam led the women in singing a song of praise to God for His commitment to His people (15:1-21). Yet within three days the Israelites questioned God's commitment to them (vv. 22-27).

Understanding the Text

"For the generations to come you shall celebrate it" Ex. 12:1-30. Passover is the first of several annual religious festivals ordained by God. Passover is Israel's celebration of freedom: a yearly reminder of the God who exercised His power to tear a slave people from the grip of oppressive masters.

It's not enough to think now and then of what God has done for us. We need to set aside regular times to remember. Celebrating God's work in and for us is as important now as celebrating Passover was for the Jewish people.

"Unleavened bread" Ex. 12:17. This is bread which has not had an opportunity to rise. No leaven or other fermenting agent is permitted in unleavened bread.

Modern Jews use the cracker-like matzos during the week-long Passover festival. The bread, like the Passover meal, serves as a reminder, for the Israelites left Egypt in such a hurry that there was no time to let bread rise.

"Hurry and leave" Ex. 12:31-51. When Pharaoh realized that all Egypt's firstborn had been struck dead, he urged the Hebrews to leave. The general population was so eager to have them depart that they

"loaned" Israel whatever gold or silver or clothing they asked for.

There would be nothing to spend such wealth on in the desert. But later the people of Israel donated much of this wealth to be used in making the tabernacle, Israel's portable house of worship.

"Consecrate to Me every firstborn male" Ex. 13:1. The celebration of freedom is closely linked with a fresh sense of Israel's obligation. Because God spared Israel's firstborn, all future firstborn would belong to Him!

You and I are given a freedom won at the cost of Christ's blood. It is appropriate that, since He gave Himself for us, we should give ourselves to Him.

When we remember what God has done for us, we are motivated to ask what we can do for God. It is important never to invert this order. We try to please God in order to obligate Him to us. Instead we are already obligated to Him for our salvation! Good can express love for the God who has saved us, but can never serve as a bribe to win God's favor.

"A pillar of fire" Ex. 14:1-31. God supernaturally guided Israel through the appearance of a cloudy-fiery pillar that either moved ahead of them or stood waiting over the camp. The Israelites had a clear, visible, and unmistakable indication of what God wanted them to do.

Despite such a clear indication, the Israelites were terrified when the pillar led them into what appeared to be a trap on the edge of a large body of water. (No one is sure what that body of water was, as the Hebrew reads *yom suph*, generally understood as "reed sea.")

Desperate circumstances led Moses to reassure Israel. He called on them to stand firm and watch to see what the Lord would do. We may find ourselves in desperate circumstances at times. When we do, we too need to stand firm, and expect God to act.

Moses' faith was not displaced. The waters which parted to let Israel through rolled over the Egyptian army, killing every soldier. Circumstances need not create fear, or even make us waver. Certainly no circumstances should cause panic as long as we have sought and tried to follow God's leading. He remains able to make us a path through the sea.

"Who among the gods is like You, O LORD?" Ex. 15:11 The deliverance stimulated Moses to write a song. The song, which reviewed what God had done, was intended as a teaching tool and instrument of praise. Music can serve us in much the same way. The tune of a familiar hymn, or its words recalled during a difficult day, remind us of God's presence and His power.

▶ DEVOTIONAL
Celebrate with Song
(Ex. 15:1-16)

Our nine-year-old, Sarah, is already picking up the tunes and words of popular music. We have to be careful about the artists she listens to and the words she hears. Somehow thoughts set to music find their way easily into the heart and mind.

That's one reason why we're so pleased Sarah is in the children's choir at church. She sings the music she's learning there around our house, and the words of Christian songs too are finding a home in her heart.

The song that Moses wrote, recorded here in this passage, picks up three aspects of the kind of music we should choose to hear.

Moses' song celebrates what God has done. We see this theme in verses 1-10. Like a warrior, majestic in his power, God acted to hurl Pharaoh's chariots and army into the sea.

Moses' song celebrates who God is. We see this in verse 11. God is majestic in holiness, awesome in glory, working wonders.

Moses' song celebrates what God will do for His believing people. This God who has worked so powerfully in the past will "lead the people You have redeemed." He will continue to use His power until "You bring them in and plant them on the mountain of Your inheritance."

You and I can decide to fill our homes and our thoughts with tunes that celebrate what God has done, who He is, and what He will surely do for us. This is one of the most important things we can do for our children as well as for our own spiritual growth and peace of mind.

Personal Application
Check out the Christian music available in your local Christian bookstore.

Quotable
"If anyone would tell you the shortest, surest way to all happiness and all perfection, he must tell you to make a rule to yourself to thank and praise God for everything that happens to you. It is certain that whatever seeming calamity happens to you, if you thank and praise God for it, you turn it into a blessing. If you could work miracles, therefore, you could not do more for yourself than by this thankful spirit. It heals and turns all that it touches into happiness."—William Law

JANUARY 18 *Reading 18*
GOD'S INTENTIONS
Exodus 15:22–19:25

> *"Although the whole earth is Mine, you will be for Me a kingdom of priests and a holy nation" (Ex. 19:5-6).*

The Israelites' discontent and quarreling on the journey toward Sinai demonstrates how far this people was from the holy nation God intended them to become.

Overview
Israel grumbled (15:22-27) and, though God provided meat and manna (16:1-36), the people tested God (17:1-7). Yet God gave a military victory (vv. 8-16), and Moses shared responsibility for settling disputes (18:1-27). They arrived at Sinai, where God displayed His holiness and announced His intention to make this unresponsive people a holy nation (19:1-25).

Understanding the Text
"The people grumbled against Moses" Ex. 15:22-25. The euphoria of the Egyptian defeat quickly disappeared when, three days into the desert, only bitter, alkaline water was found. Moses prayed to God, who showed him how to make the water sweet.

The incident established a pattern that was repeated on the journey to Sinai. (1) Something causes dissatisfaction. (2) The people mutter against Moses and God. (3) God responds graciously and provides what the people need or want. (4) Rather than being thankful, the people become more dissatisfied and more rebellious (see also 16:1-12; 17:1-7).

Some time ago "permissive" child-rearing was popular. The theory was, let the child do what he wants, and his natural beauty will unfold as the petals of a flower. The only problem was that permissive child-rearing produced selfish, unproductive, and dissatisfied adults, just as the permissiveness that God displayed during the three-month journey to Sinai allowed the Israelites to become more dissatisfied and more rebellious. Grace without responsibility, like love without discipline, doesn't promote holiness.

The behavior of the Israelites on the journey to Sinai shows us why God found it necessary to introduce the Law. The Law, with its clear standards, served to make the Israelites responsible for their actions, and provided God with a basis on which He could discipline when His people did wrong.

Today God does deal with us in grace. But He is too wise and too loving to give us everything we want or think we need. God continues to discipline Christians, not to punish but to guide us. Hebrews 12:10 says He "disciplines us for our good, that we may share in His holiness."

"If you pay attention" Ex. 15:26-27. The principle of reward for obedience introduced here is valid in every age. But the specific promise—that obedience would preserve from disease—was made to Israel rather than you and me. Paul's experience (2 Cor 12:1-10) shows us that Christians are *not* guaranteed healing and that God can use physical illness to accomplish spiritual purposes in our lives.

"Manna and quail" Ex. 16:1-36. Some suggest that manna was really the excretion of a desert plant, the tamarisk tree, which drops to the ground and hardens into a sweet substance. Manna, however, was the product of a miracle. Enough was produced to feed millions; it was available everywhere the people went for some 40 years; it appeared only six days a week. And, unlike the product of the tamarisk, manna bred worms when kept overnight, melted, was white in color, and could be made into cakes.

In Scripture, manna serves as a symbol of God's provision. The Lord knows our basic needs and He acts to meet them.

"Each one gathered as much as he needed" Ex. 16:18. It is significant that manna did not appear in the pot, but on the ground, where people had to gather it. God provides, but He expects us to work for what we get.

It's significant that manna appeared daily. Jesus taught His disciples to petition God for their "daily" bread. God meets our needs day by day, so that we will continue to depend on Him. If God put $10 million in our bank accounts, we would have "lifelong" bread, and would have no need to look to the Lord daily. Jesus wants His disciples to remain dependent on God, so we will seek Him daily and nurture our relationship with the Lord daily.

"Put the LORD to the test" Ex. 17:1-7. God's presence was visible to Israel in the cloudy-fiery pillar that led them, and in the manna that appeared daily. Yet when the people camped where there was no water, they accused Moses of trying to kill them and were "almost ready to stone" him.

God provided water. But Moses gave the name Massah ("testing") to that place because the people questioned whether God was with them or not.

When troubles come, it's natural to wonder where God is. But we must guard against the unbelief displayed by Israel at Massah. How? By making it a practice to rehearse all the good things God has done and is doing for us. Rather than focus on the problem, we need to focus our attention on the Lord.

"Now I know" Ex. 18:1-12. Jethro, Moses' father-in-law, came to Sinai to meet Moses. When Moses told him what the Lord had done in Egypt, and how the Lord had saved Israel on their journey to Sinai, Jethro praised God and said, "Now I know that the LORD is greater than all other gods."

Sitting with friends or relatives and simply telling what God has done in our lives is still the best way to share the Lord with others.

"If . . . God so commands" Ex. 18:13-27. Jethro advised Moses to distribute responsibility for settling any disputes that arose. But Jethro was careful to recognize God's lordship when giving his advice. He expected Moses to check with the Lord to confirm the wisdom of what he said.

We need to have this attitude when giving or receiving advice. However wise we feel our advice may be, it's important to urge others to bring that advice to God before acting on it. And when we are given advice, no matter how good, we need to seek confirmation from God before we act.

"You cannot handle it alone" Ex. 18:17-27. This chapter is often cited as evidence for "organization" in the church. It's better to see it as a word to workaholics.

One of the most popular speakers on Christian radio in the '80s is a workaholic, bringing home not briefcases but boxes of work to do on weekends and holidays. He urges listeners to give priority to their families, but his ministry has crowded his own family out of his life. Like Moses, he needs to be reminded that there are "capable men" who "fear God" and are "trustworthy" nearby. Delegating responsibility today as in Old Testament times is not only wise, it is right.

"In front of the mountain" Ex. 19:1-25. God's display of power at Mount Sinai is later described as a "consuming fire on top of the mountain" (24:17). It was intended to inspire awe and fear, and to communicate something of the holiness of Israel's God. Only Moses would go up into the thunder and constantly flashing lightning that shrouded the mountaintop.

Hebrews 12:18 describes the mountain as "burning with fire . . . [a vision of] darkness, gloom, and storm." It was so terrifying that even Moses said, "I am trembling with fear" (v. 21).

While Christians come directly to God through a loving Christ, something important about the nature of God was communicated at Sinai. Hebrews reminds us that we are to "worship God acceptably with reverence and awe, for our God is a consuming fire" (vv. 28-29).

▶ DEVOTIONAL
My Treasured Possession (Ex. 19:3-6)

It's all too easy in reading these chapters to focus on the obvious flaws in Israel's character. The people were ungrateful. They were rebellious. They were mean-spirited and hostile. They were selfish and petty. Perhaps a good way to sum it up is that they were the kind of folks who, if you had them as neighbors, would make you want to put your house up for sale. Yesterday.

Yet God delivered this people from Egypt and "brought you to Myself" (v. 4). God even says that He chose this people, "out of all nations," to be His treasured possession.

The Hebrew word here is significant. *Segullah* means "valued property," "personal possession," or "private treasure." God looked over the whole earth, and selected Israel to "be for Me a kingdom of priests and a holy nation" (v. 6).

These few verses remind us of wonderful things about our God. Like the diamond miner who picks up a rough and dull stone and shouts with delight, God delights in unlovely people. He knows what precious gems, through His shaping and polishing, sinners can become.

It's hard for you and me to have this delight in unlovely people. We tend to see only the rough spots, the dull and lifeless form. When we find ourselves placed next to people who are like members of the Exodus generation, we want to get up and move.

What we need to do is ask God to share His perspective with us. We need to see in the least lovely, someone who can be God's own treasured possession. Someone whom God can transform and make beautiful. Someone who can join God's kingdom of priests and become a holy citizen of the holy nation He intends to create.

Personal Application

The first step in developing God's perspective is to pray daily for unlovely others.

Quotable

Since I dislike you, how can I then fulfill
the law of love? Your speech, your
ways, your very image in my eye,
These all revolt me . . . (and it is
little help that I am sure you care no
whit the more for me!)

Thus battle head and heart, the one reverberant with pique,
The other incandescent in the light
of love. But both, I think, must surely
be of God, and so an acrid lesson says
That head must love whom heart insists it
cannot like.
God help me try!—Samuel J. Miller

JANUARY 19 *Reading 19*
GOD REVEALS HIS LAW
Exodus 20–23

"Worship the Lord *your God, and His blessing will be upon you" (Ex. 23:25).*

The rabbis identify 613 laws in Moses' writings. The 10 basic commandments are stated in Exodus 20. The principles expressed in the Ten Commandments are valid for all persons of all times, for they reflect the moral nature of God.

Definition of Key Terms
Ten Commandments. Protestants, Catholics, and Jews agree there are Ten Commandments. But they do not agree on which 10! Protestants take 20:3 as the first commandment. Catholics group verses 3-6 as the first commandment, and divide verse 17 into 2. Jews understand verse 2 as the first, and also group verses 3-6.

Four characteristics. Four characteristics of the Ten Commandments should be noted. (1) Each is stated as an absolute. Other ancient law codes generally listed acts and their consequences—if you do this, then this will happen. We are to follow God's commandments because they are right, not through fear of punishment. (2) Eight of the 10 are stated as negatives, but each implies a positive. Do not steal clearly calls us to respect others' property rights. (3) Each is addressed to "you" in the second person singular. God spoke not to all Israel, but to each individual member of the believing community. We cannot guarantee others will obey God's commands. But we each can be responsible for ourself. (4) Each commandment is relational. The first four show us how to live harmoniously with God. The last six show us how to live harmoniously with other people. We cannot violate God's commandments without harming our relationship with Him and with others.

Overview
God gave Moses 10 basic commandments revealing how to express love for God (20:1-11) and for other persons (vv. 12-21). Specific laws dealing with altars (vv. 22-26), servants (21:2-11), personal injury (vv. 12-36), and property (22:1-15) followed. Moses also identified heinous sins (vv. 16-31), commanded compassion (23:1-9), rest for land, man, and beast (vv. 10-13), and established three religious festivals (vv. 14-19). God promised to make His people prosper if they worshiped Him only and obeyed His laws (vv. 20-33).

Understanding the Text
"He shall go free" Ex. 21:2-11. Old Testament laws protected individual slaves far more than other law codes of the era, and called for a Hebrew slave to serve no more than six years. Only by a person's own free choice could he be bound to a master for life.

This Old Testament law teaches us that each individual is to be respected, whatever his or her social position. Even the weakest were not to be oppressed, but rather were to be protected.

"Held responsible" Ex. 21:12-36. The commandment said, "You shall not murder." Here the text cites a number of specific examples showing that "You shall not murder" implies, "You shall respect the life and well-being of others." Persons who intentionally harm others, or even cause others harm by their carelessness, are to be held responsible. Even leaving a pit one digs uncovered, should a person or animal fall into it, creates responsibility (vv. 33-34).

More than one doctor who has stopped to help a person injured in an auto accident has later been sued for malpractice. Today many states protect such a person with "Good Samaritan" laws. Yet it's easy to see why so many today feel, "I don't want to get involved." That saying does reflect the spirit of our times. But it does not reflect the Spirit of our God.

"Eye for eye" Ex. 23:24. People who cause another serious injury are to be held responsible. But the famous *lex talona*—the law demanding an eye for an eye, a tooth for a tooth—is seriously misunderstood. In the biblical world feuds were an ever-present possibility. The principle of an eye for an eye, a tooth for a tooth, *limits* the penalty a person can impose! An injured

party, or his angry and bitter family, might well try to extract a life for an eye, or a limb for a tooth! God's Law fixes responsibility, but at the same time does not permit escalation of a dispute.

"Restitution" Ex. 22:1-15. In Scripture, theft or other crimes of property are crimes against the victim. In our legal system, they are crimes against the state. Thus in our legal system the criminal is punished by the state and sent to jail. In the Old Testament legal system social harmony must be restored between the criminal and his victim, and so the criminal pays restitution.

These laws remind us that when we've hurt or harmed others, it's not enough to say "I'm sorry." We have no right to ask forgiveness until the injury has been undone and restitution made.

Forgiveness is free. But it is not cheap.

Unyielding and compassionate Ex. 22:16-31. The laws in this passage seem almost contradictory. Several bluntly demand the death penalty—for sorcery, beastiality, and idolatry. Others call for the utmost compassion to be shown the widow and the orphan. The needy are to be loaned money at no interest. Anyone who takes a garment as a pledge of repayment must return it at night, so the borrower can use it as a blanket.

Are the "harsh" laws of the Old Testament contradictory to the God of "compassion" revealed in other laws and in Jesus? Not at all. Some sins so corrupt a society and lead to so much suffering that it is necessary to take a firm and unyielding position.

What's important is to maintain our sense of balance. Unyieldingness without compassion is wrong, but so is a compassion that fails to require responsibility.

Some years ago no one questioned the concept of a medical quarantine. People with a contagious disease were restricted to their homes or to sanatoriums. This "violation of the sick person's rights" was accepted by all as necessary protection for the society. Yet today people with AIDS, a disease which is always fatal, are treated so carefully that no politician or public health official dares even mention the possibility of quarantine.

While Old Testament Law guards the rights of individuals, it never does so at the expense of the community. And it holds individuals responsible for their sins.

Liberty and justice for all Ex. 23:1-9. This guarantee in the U.S. Constitution is firmly established in Old Testament Law. Note a few of the principles stated here.

"When you give testimony, don't pervert justice by siding with the crowd."

"Do not show favoritism to a poor man in his lawsuit."

"Do not deny justice to your poor people in their lawsuits."

"Have nothing to do with a false charge."

Only by treating everyone the same, by being absolutely fair to rich and poor alike, to the famous and unknown, can we reflect the justice as well as the mercy of our God.

"The seventh day" Ex. 23:10-13. The only Ten Commandment not repeated in the New Testament as a principle for Christians to live by is the command to keep the seventh day holy. Still, there is much to learn from Old Testament Sabbath laws. One of the lessons is found in these verses. The Sabbath was established for man's benefit, not for God's, so that believers "may be refreshed."

We don't do God a favor by setting aside a day for worship and rest. We do ourselves a favor.

"Worship the LORD your God" Ex. 23:20-33. How does the emphasis on worship fit into these chapters on Law? Very simply. Worship is not simply going to church and singing hymns. Worship is putting our faith into practice by loving God and following His commandments.

When God gave Moses these laws to share with Israel, He identified them with worship and with success. When we put God first and honor Him with obedience, God gives us a full life.

▶ DEVOTIONAL
God Spoke All These Words (Ex. 20:1-21)

The Ten Commandments are more than laws that Israel was responsible to follow.

They express basic principles that human beings of all times are to live by. We can translate each one into a positive guideline by noting that each calls us to show respect for God and for others in simple yet vital ways. Here are the 10 as principles to live by.

1. You shall have no other gods before Me (20:3).	Respect God as your one and only Lord.
2. You shall not make an idol (20:4-6).	Respect God's nature and do not trivialize Him.
3. You shall not misuse the name of the Lord (20:7).	Show respect for God as real and present always.
4. Remember the Sabbath Day by keeping it holy (20:8-11).	Show respect for God by setting aside time to worship Him.
5. Honor your father and mother (20:12).	Show respect to your parents.
6. You shall not murder (20:13).	Show respect for the sanctity of human life.
7. You shall not commit adultery (20:14).	Show respect for marriage and members of the opposite sex.
8. You shall not steal (20:15).	Show respect for the property of others.
9. You shall not give false testimony against your neighbor (20:17).	Show respect for the truth and for the reputation of others.
10. You shall not covet (20:17).	Show ultimate respect for holiness by guarding your motives as well as your actions.

No clearer or more significant guidelines for living have ever been incorporated in any code of law. If we live by them, we will surely please God, and our entire life will become an act of acceptable worship.

Personal Application

Respect for God and others is revealed primarily in the choices we make daily.

Quotable

"Who speaks for God? He does quite nicely for Himself. Through His holy and infallible Word—and the quiet obedience of His servants."—Chuck Colson

---

JANUARY 20 *Reading 20*
FREEDOM AS A SYMBOL
Exodus 24–27

> *"Then have them build a sanctuary for Me, and I will dwell among them" (Ex. 25:8).*

Someone has observed that it took God 6 days to create the world—and 40 days to give Moses the blueprint for the tabernacle. Much has been written on the symbolic meaning of the tabernacle's design and materials. But the central theme is this: the portable worship center served as a visible reminder that God dwells among His people.

Overview

The Israelites committed themselves to keeping God's Law (24:1-8). Moses was instructed to build a portable house of worship, the tabernacle, which would serve as a symbol of God's presence with Israel (vv. 9-18). The instructions covered materials (25:1-9), furnishings (vv. 10-40), the design of the tent (26:1-37), its courtyard and its altar (27:1-21).

Understanding the Text

"Everything the LORD has said we will do" Ex. 24:1-8. God did not simply impose His Law on Israel. Moses carefully explained what God expected of people who would live in personal relationship with Him (Ex. 20–23; 24:3). Israel's ratification of the Law

marks a change in relationship with God. The people committed themselves to keep God's commands, and were then fully responsible for their acts.

The event also tells us something about God. He carefully, graciously, and thoroughly explained what relationship with Him involved before asking for commitment.

"Moses alone is to approach the Lord*" Ex. 24:1-18.* The chapter conveys a powerful sense of the special relationship Moses had with the Lord. Moses alone approached the Lord. Moses told the people God's words and laws. Moses wrote down everything the Lord said. Moses supervised the sacrifices to be made to the Lord. Moses called the people of God to full commitment. Moses not only came to the Lord on the mountain, but "stayed there" in God's presence.

It's amazing to realize that today you and I share privileges then accorded only to Moses. Through Jesus, God invites us to approach Him freely (Heb. 4:16). We too can share the Word of God with others (cf. Acts 8:4). Rather than writing down the Word of God, our hearts are tablets on which God Himself writes (2 Cor. 3:3). We join with others in offering God spiritual sacrifices (Rom. 12:2). We have been commissioned as God's ambassadors, to reconcile others to our Lord (2 Cor. 5:18-20). In Jesus, God has not only invited us to come to Him, but to abide with and in Him always (John 15:4, 7).

Moses was a great man. But you and I have even greater privileges.

"Make a sanctuary for Me" Ex. 25:1–27:40. The Old Testament emphasizes the importance of the tabernacle, a portable tent, in Israel's worship. Exodus takes seven chapters (25–31) to list tabernacle specifications, and then devotes six more to its construction (35–40). The New Testament touches on some of the symbolism, saying that the tabernacle design and use was intended to reflect heavenly realities (cf. Heb. 9–10).

Books have been written on the symbolic meaning of the tabernacle furnishings, and of the materials used. Gold is said to represent God's glory; silver, redemption;

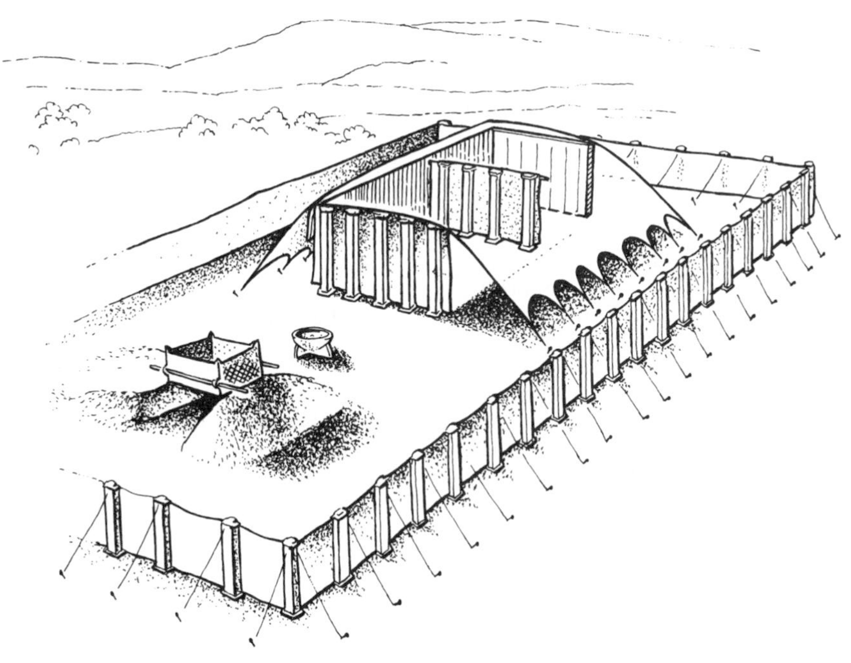

and bronze, judgment; while the color blue represents heaven; purple, royalty; and scarlet, sacrifice. However, because the Old Testament does not interpret the symbols, we can't be sure what the materials really signify.

Several significant realities reflected in the tabernacle are: (1) The tabernacle was a visible reminder that God *is* with His people. (2) The tabernacle had only one door, for there is only one way to approach God (John 14:6). (3) The altar just inside the door of the courtyard showed that a sinner could only approach God by sacrifice. (4) The curtain between the holy front room of the tabernacle and the "holy of holies" inner room was a reminder that human beings did not then have free access to God. When Jesus died, the curtain in the Jerusalem temple was torn from top to bottom, a sign of the free access to God we now enjoy (cf. Heb. 10:8-10).

"Each man whose heart prompts him to give" Ex. 25:2. Relationship with God in Old Testament times was far from formal and legalistic. Then as now, true obedience and real worship was a matter of the heart. How significant that all the materials used to construct the tabernacle were provided by people moved by love for God to give spontaneously.

God still wants our gifts and service to be expressions of love that are given freely, not acts motivated by fear or a sense of obligation (see 2 Chron. 29:5; 1 Cor. 9:17; 2 Cor. 9:7; 1 Peter 5:2).

"Make the tabernacle" Ex. 26:1-37. Moses was told to make the tabernacle and its furnishings "exactly like the pattern I will show you" (25:9). Chapter 26 shows us how detailed God's instructions were.

We may be bored reading passages filled with such "trivia." Yet they remind us that God is the God of details. What a comfort this is, for it reassures us that God is concerned with every aspect of our lives.

"Build an altar" Ex. 27:1-8. A bronze altar was placed just inside the one door that opened into the courtyard around the tabernacle proper. This altar was intended for one purpose—as a site for sacrifice.

The flow of Exodus helps us see why the altar was so important. God had freed Israel from slavery. He brought them to Sinai and gave His people a Law to live by. While Law did provide clear standards, it also made those who broke it guilty. And guilt drives a wedge between God and people! Immediately God acted to provide a way for sinners to approach and worship Him. He had Moses construct a tabernacle that symbolized His presence. And there, at its entrance, the Lord had Moses place an altar for sacrifices. Israel would sin, but blood would cover the offerer's sin and permit him to approach God.

The reality symbolized by the altar is Christ's death on Calvary. Because of Christ's blood, our sin is gone, and we come to God freely, knowing that forgiveness is ours.

God never intended sin to forever isolate human beings from Him.

▶ DEVOTIONAL
Intelligent Commitment (Ex. 24:1-8)

Looking back, Carol realized what had happened. Deep inside she had seemed to hear a voice telling her not to marry Stan. But she had wanted him so much.

Ten years later, after a devastating divorce that left her with two preschoolers, Carol was struggling with her pain but growing as a Christian. Then, when it was too late, she realized that the inner voice she heard had been the Holy Spirit, warning her. "But you know," she says, "back then I didn't even realize there *was* a Holy Spirit."

Today Carol teaches a class of divorced women in her local Methodist church. And she's amazed at how little most of them know about the Bible or life in Christ.

I can't help thinking of Carol and the many other true believers like her when I read these verses. God took such care to have Moses explain exactly what commitment to the Lord would involve. Moses "told the people all the LORD's words and laws" (v. 3). He then wrote down everything the Lord had said (v. 4). The next morning he got up and "took the Book of the Covenant and read it to the people" (v. 7).

God invited commitment. But He

wanted to make sure that the Israelites understood just what life with Him would involve.

It's true, of course, that people can put their trust in Christ without a deep understanding of the Gospel or of the Bible. But unless we go on to hear all God's words, to read them over, and the next day to listen again, we will fall far short of that intelligent commitment God desires. Intelligent commitment, featuring a growing understanding of God's will, would have protected Carol and will guard you and me.

Personal Application
Intelligent commitment means to know and to do the Word of God.

Quotable
"Therefore with mind entire, faith firm, courage undaunted, love thorough, let us be ready for whatever God wills; faithfully keeping His commandments, having innocence in simplicity, peaceableness in love, modesty in lowliness, diligence in ministering, mercifulness in helping the poor, firmness in standing for truth, and sternness in keeping of discipline."—Bede the Venerable

JANUARY 21 *Reading 21*
THE PRIESTHOOD
Exodus 28–30

> *"I will consecrate . . . Aaron and his sons to serve Me as priests" (Ex. 29:44).*

Only the priests in Israel were qualified to make the sacrifices required from those who approached God. The New Testament teaching that every believer is a priest (1 Peter 2:9) makes these chapters dealing with Israel's priesthood especially significant.

Definition of Key Terms
Priesthood. Only men from Aaron's family were permitted to serve as priests. Their function was to present sacrifices to God, to seek God's guidance for the nation or individuals, to instruct the people in God's Law, to serve as judges in certain cases, and to serve as guardians of the covenant and of Israel's sanctuary and sacred treasures.

The priests thus were mediators between God and the nation Israel. They represented the people to God by offering sacrifices and incense, by leading worship, and by praying for divine guidance. They also represented God to the people, for the priests instructed Israel in God's Law, were channels through which God communicated His will, and served as living reminders that God forgives sinning people.

Today each Christian is a priest with direct access to God. Each of us can represent others to the Lord in prayer. Each of us can be a channel through whom God's love and grace reach lost men and women.

The high priest. The Old Testament high priest had one duty that set him apart from other members of the priesthood. He and he alone entered the holy of holies on the annual Day of Atonement, carrying sacrificial blood which God promised would cover all the sins of His people (cf. Lev. 16).

The New Testament presents Jesus as the true High Priest, who entered heaven itself with His own blood. As our High Priest, Jesus made the one sacrifice of Himself which won all who believe an eternal salvation (Heb. 10:10-14).

Overview
Special garments were prepared for the high priest (28:1-43). Aaron and his sons were to be ordained in an impressive ceremony that lasted seven days (29:1-46). Sacred duties were described, and formulas for sacred oils and incense were recorded (30:1-38).

Understanding the Text
"Make garments for Aaron" Ex. 28:1-44. As high priest, Aaron was provided with distinctive clothing to "give him dignity and honor." Each item Aaron wore also had symbolic significance.

The ephod Ex. 28:6-14. This vestlike outer jacket featured two stones, mounted one on each shoulder. The name of each Israelite tribe was engraved on one of these stones. Whenever Aaron entered the tabernacle, he represented all the people of God.

Today Jesus, our High Priest, represents the church before God's throne. The New Testament says "we have One who speaks to the Father in our defense—Jesus Christ the righteous" (1 John 2:1).

The breastpiece Ex. 28:15-30. This pouch was attached to the ephod with chains of gold. Twelve precious stones were mounted on it, each with the name of a single tribe. The text says that "whenever Aaron enters the holy place, he will bear the names of the sons of Israel over his heart." The symbolism is powerful. Here each tribe, rather than being engraved with others on a stone shoulder tab, is symbolized individually by an expensive gem. Each is worn over the heart. Jesus does more than represent us in heaven. He carries each individual in His heart. Each of us is known and loved. Each of us is precious to our Saviour.

The Urim and Thummim Ex. 28:30. The breastpiece was a pouch called the "breastpiece of decision." It contained two items called Urim and Thummim, which were used by the high priest to discern the will of God.

No one knows just how they were used. Perhaps one represented no and the other yes, and they were drawn blindly by the high priest when inquiries were addressed to God. We do know, however, that God used them to communicate His will to Israel.

Today our High Priest has sent us His Holy Spirit. We do not know exactly how the Spirit guides or communicates His will to us. But we do know that, when we honestly seek God's guidance, the Holy Spirit leads us into His will.

Robe, tunic, and turban Ex. 28:21-42. The clothing worn by the high priest was made of the finest material and beautifully worked. We not only need to bring God our best. When we serve God faithfully, He gives us *His* best.

"Incense . . . every morning" Ex. 30:1-10. Revelation treats incense as a symbol of the prayers of God's saints (Rev. 8:3-4). Aaron "must" burn fragrant incense on a golden altar within the tabernacle "every morning." The image reminds us that daily prayer is a "must" for Christians, not only for our own spiritual benefit but because it is a vital ingredient in worship of God.

"Atonement money" Ex. 30:11-16. A half-shekel tax to be collected from each Hebrew male was used for upkeep of the tabernacle. The tax is described as an atonement, or ransom. In the Old Testament all atonement is associated with sacrifice. This is true here as well, for the "service of the tent of tabernacle" implies

payment for the sacrificial animals that were required for daily, Sabbath, and special festival offerings.

Note that each Israelite paid the same small amount. Rich and poor had the same access to God through sacrifices offered by the priests.

"A bronze basin . . . for washing" Ex. 30:17-21. Water in the Old Testament speaks of purification. Priests were never to approach the tabernacle without first washing in the bronze basin.

"Take the following" Ex. 30:22-38. The fragrant oils and spices used on worship were compounded according to special formulas. In Old Testament Law, a clear distinction was maintained between the secular and sacred, and sacred things were never to be used for any secular purpose. Anything one sets apart to God is to be fully dedicated to Him.

▶ DEVOTIONAL
Over His Heart
(Ex. 29:15-30)

James Dobson suggests in his book *Hide or Seek* that we must decisively reject the values of a society which dismisses the plain girl and the less intelligent man as having no worth or value. In a society that places so much emphasis on looks, intelligence, athletic achievement, and wealth, the majority grows up with a sense of personal inferiority and even of worthlessness. A low self-image, Dobson says, is the painful product of a society that devalues the individual.

But this is society's view—not God's. The difference is reflected in God's design of the high priest's breastpiece. God specified a different precious stone to represent each tribe in Israel. Each stone bore the name of one person, the forefather who represents the tribe. Each stone was attached with gold filigree to a pouch worn over the heart of the high priest. Each name was carried there, over his heart, into the very presence of the Lord.

God views each of us as an individual. Each of us is different, yet each is a precious gem to the Lord. And each of us is close to the heart of Jesus, God's High Priest.

Most of us will be unable to leave our children wealth or riches. But each of us does have an important gift we *can* give. We can give each of our children a sense of his worth, value, and specialness that reflects God's values, not the values of our society.

First, however, each of us needs to accept the gift God offers us in the symbolism of the jewels worn over the high priest's heart. The gift of realizing that *we* are special. Whatever our parents or our society may have implied, we have infinite worth and value to God. We are jewels. And He carries our names close to His heart.

Personal Application

Let any rings or jewels you wear remind you of the high priest's breastpiece, and of how precious you are in God's sight.

Quotable

"If individuals live only seventy years, then a state, or a nation, or a civilization, which may last for a thousand years, is more important than an individual. But if Christianity is true, then the individual is not only more important but incomparably more important, for he is everlasting and the life of a state or civilization, compared with his, is only a moment."—C.S. Lewis

JANUARY 22 *Reading 22*
GOD REVEALS HIS ANGER
Exodus 31–34

"My presence will go with you, and I will give you rest" (Ex. 33:14).

Aaron responded to popular demand and made an idol for the people to worship. Israel was about to discover that punishment as well as divine enablement is a work of God.

Overview

God enabled Israel's craftsmen (31:1-11), and emphasized the Sabbath obligation (vv. 12-18). Yet as Moses met with God on Mount Sinai, Aaron cast an idol (32:1-6), arousing God's anger and bringing swift discipline (v. 7–33:6). Moses was shown God's goodness (vv. 7-23) and was given new stone tablets on which God Himself had written His commandments (34:1-35).

Understanding the Text

"Filled him with the Spirit of God" Ex. 31:1-11. It's a mistake to suppose that all spiritual gifts are listed in Romans 12 and 1 Corinthians 12. Every special ability God gives can contribute to worship and enrich the lives of others. The person with "skill, ability, and knowledge in all kinds of crafts," as well as the preacher and evangelist, exercises a spiritual gift, and is to rely on the Spirit of God.

"Between Me and the Israelites" Ex. 31:12-18. Is the Sabbath for Christians? The text clearly states that the Sabbath is a sign of God's covenant with Israel. From the beginning Christians have met on Sunday, not the seventh day of the week. While the Sabbath commemorates Creation (v. 17), the first day of the week commemorates Jesus' resurrection (Matt. 28:1; Acts 20:7). What links the two is that each is a day of rest and worship. And each serves as a weekly reminder to believers of their personal relationship with God.

The golden calf Ex. 32:1–33:6. Calf and bull figures cast in metal often served as idols in Syria-Palestine. The figures represented the virile power of the god. In some cases the bull or calf seems to have been viewed as a throne on which an invisible deity stood or was seated.

Making such a figure was an overt rejection of God. Even worse, in saying, "These are your gods, O Israel, who brought you up out of Egypt," the people credited pagan deities with the saving work the Lord had performed!

How could such a thing happen in the very shadow of Sinai, where thunder and lightning testified to the presence of the Living God? Our only explanation is that sin so corrupts human beings that anyone is capable of ignoring evidence of God's existence. Even "proof" cannot change the heart or mind of an individual who is determined not to believe.

"Aaron answered them" Ex. 32:2. Aaron and Moses provide us with contrasting insights into spiritual leadership. When the people demanded that Aaron make them gods, Aaron did what they said (vv. 2-3). Leaders are supposed to do what God requires, not what people demand. Aaron went even further. He "saw" their reaction to the golden calf (v. 5). He then took the initiative and constructed an altar. Like a modern politician who relies on polls to discover what people want, and then promises it to them, Aaron sensed where the Israelites were going and hurried to get out in front!

At times each of us is tempted to take Aaron's "easy way out." Going along with the crowd may appear to be a way to avoid uncomfortable conflict. It isn't. It's a way to become guilty of our own and of others' "great sin" (v. 21).

"The Lord said to Moses" Ex. 32:9-14. While Aaron was weakly surrendering to the shouts of the Israelites, Moses was courageously pleading with God. The Lord told Moses what had happened in the valley, expressed His anger, and threatened to destroy Israel. He would establish His covenant with Moses alone.

Moses' appeal reflects two concerns: destroying Israel would cause the Egyptians to misunderstand God's motives in delivering the Israelites; and God must remain faithful to the promises He made to Abraham, Isaac, and Jacob.

"Whoever is for the L*ORD" Ex. 32:25-35.* When Moses saw Israel's idolatrous worship for himself, his reaction was much like God's. He was so angry and upset he broke the stone tablets on which God had inscribed the Law (v. 19). Then Moses called those who were "for the LORD" to come to him.

When Moses took a stand, he found that he wasn't alone. It's the same today. Teens, and adults as well, often feel alone in their commitment to what is right. "I'm the only guy in my class who's still a virgin," one 17-year-old complained. Yet when he took a stand for what he believed and stood up to the ridicule directed at him in the locker room, he found that he wasn't alone after all! Others who had been afraid to speak out came and told him they agreed.

Moses took that public stand. His courage moved the Levites, who had not participated in the others' sin but who had stood by silently, to join him openly.

When conscience convinces us that something is wrong, we need to follow Moses' lead and take an open stand. And if someone else takes the role of Moses, let's be ready, as the Levites were, to "rally to him."

"Brother and friend and neighbor" Ex. 32:27. Moses told the Levites to pass through the camp and kill those who had engaged in pagan worship. The incident points up a vital Old Testament principle. Believers are responsible to maintain holiness in the community of faith, even when this means standing against those who are near and dear to us. God must come first. No relationship can have priority over our commitment to the Lord.

"When the time comes for Me to punish, I will punish" Ex. 32:30–33:6. God forgives. But God also punishes. For the first time Israel, which had ratified the Law covenant and promised to obey God, realized that there is a penalty for disobedience!

Stripping off ornaments (33:6) was a sign of mourning and repentance in the ancient world. At last Israel was impressed with the seriousness of sin.

Christians are likely to make one of two errors in reacting to personal sins. One error is to be so stricken with guilt and fearful of punishment that we fail to appropriate the forgiveness promised us in Jesus. If this is our tendency, we will punish ourselves unnecessarily. The other error is to so emphasize the love of God that we ignore His holiness, and act as if sins are nothing at all. If this is our tendency, when the time comes for God to punish, He will!

"My Presence will go with you" Ex. 33:7-23. The Israelites couldn't see what transpired within the tent of meeting when Moses met with the Lord. But these verses do tell us.

Moses sought to learn God's ways and know Him better (vv. 12-13).

Moses appropriated God's promises and affirmed his dependence on the Lord (vv. 14-17).

Moses expressed his yearning to see God more clearly (v. 18).

These are helpful guidelines for our own times of private prayer. When we meet with God face-to-face, we too should focus on being taught His ways, on appropriating His promises, and on knowing Him more intimately.

"He passed in front of Moses" Ex. 34:1-9. On Sinai again, Moses chiseled out new stone tablets. God Himself wrote His Law on them. God did show Moses His goodness, summed up in one of the Old Testament's most famous confessions:

> The LORD, the LORD, the compassionate and gracious God, slow to anger, abounding in love and faithfulness, maintaining love to thousands, and forgiving wickedness, rebellion and sin. Yet He does not leave the guilty unpunished; He punishes the children and their children for the sin of the fathers to the third and fourth generation (vv. 6-7).

The second half of this confession is important. God's compassion and love must be seen against the background of His obligation to punish sin. The God who "does not leave the guilty unpunished" is first of all the God who displays overwhelming compassion and grace.

Some have questioned God's fairness in punishing children for the sins of the fathers. It's best to understand this and similar expressions as a revelation of reality. The fact is that sin affects not just the sinner but his descendants. Research has shown that those who abuse their children were typically abused when they were young. The pattern established by the parents is repeated in the children.

In this way sins of the fathers do bring punishment on their children, for the children tend to commit the same sins.

"A veil over his face" Ex. 34:29-34. Being in God's presence caused Moses' face to shine radiantly. No visible change may occur when you or I spend time with God. But regular meetings with the Lord do make a real difference!

▶ DEVOTIONAL
Face-to-Face
(Ex. 32–33)

It's clear from Exodus 32 that while the Israelites were in awe of Moses, they had little respect for his brother Aaron. As high priest, Aaron had an official religious position. But position alone is never enough to command respect.

Many qualities made Moses a strong spiritual leader. He was courageous. He sought to please God rather than men. He was willing to take a stand. He rallied support. He both prayed for sinners, and yet was willing to confront them. But the secret of Moses' greatness is found in the "tent of meeting," where Moses met the Lord face-to-face.

The text tells us that "whenever Moses went out to the tent, all the people rose and stood at the entrances to their tents, watching Moses until he entered the tent." No one knew what went on within the tent, though the pillar of cloud came down to stand by the tent door when Moses was inside. Yet the very fact that Moses met there with God instilled awe, and the evidence of God's presence caused the people to worship the Lord.

You and I have constant opportunities to influence others. These others include our own children, our neighbors, and coworkers as well as members of our church. Like Aaron, we may have a position, such as "parent," that implies authority. But the only way we will truly influence others is to follow the path of Moses and meet God regularly face-to-face. Our impact on their lives will be directly proportionate to the time we spend face-to-face with God.

Others won't know what happens in our private time with the Lord. But the aura of God's presence will go with us. Being with God changes us—and the change God works in us is the key to our ability to influence others to worship and obey Him.

Personal Application
Spiritual power is only a prayer life away.

Quotable
"I don't say anything to God. I just sit and look at Him and let Him look at me."—Old Peasant of Ars

JANUARY 23 *Reading 23*
SYMBOLS OF GOD
Exodus 35–40

> *"The people are bringing more than enough for doing the work the* LORD *commanded to be done" (Ex. 36:5).*

The importance of the tabernacle and its furnishings is seen in the fact that Exodus 35–40 repeats, often word for word, the description of Israel's worship center in Exodus 25–30. For nearly 500 years Israel worshiped at this portable tent, which with its furnishings symbolized basic truths about personal relationship with God.

Definition of Key Terms
Symbols. In Scripture a symbol is an object, person, practice, or saying which represents an underlying spiritual reality. While some symbols are unclear, others are powerful and obvious representations of spiritual truths. For instance, the blood spilled on Jewish altars both taught the grim truth that "the wages of sin is

death," and conveyed the glorious promise that God would accept a substitute. The full meaning of that symbol is only grasped in Jesus' death on Calvary. But the realities symbolized by sacrifice could be discerned in Old Testament as well as New Testament times.

The tabernacle and its furnishings, the writer of Hebrews says, are "a copy and shadow of what is in heaven" (8:5). That is, the tabernacle and its furnishings are symbols of spiritual realities. In reading these chapters we want to look not for the obscure, but for obvious representations of spiritual truths.

Overview

Materials were gathered and the tent church was constructed (35:1–36:38). Symbolically significant furnishings were prepared (37:1-29), as was the tabernacle courtyard with its altar and laver (38:1-31). Garments were woven for the priests (39:1-31). After Moses inspected the work (vv. 32-43), the tabernacle was set up and dedicated (40:1-33). It was then filled with "the glory of the LORD" (vv. 34-38).

Understanding the Text

"From what you have" Ex. 35:1-29. The materials used in constructing the tabernacle were contributed by the people. Completing any work of God in this world calls for giving by God's people.

"The ability to teach others" Ex. 35:30–36:21. Bezalel and Oholiab symbolize the mature Christian. God gave them the ability to *do* and, with it, the ability to teach.

Spiritually, the two qualities go together, as head and tail of a single coin. The believer must live God's Word in order to teach faith in a life-changing way, for Scripture is about life. Only when faith and actions go together can we teach others the true meaning of relationship with God.

If you and I are doers of the Word, our very way of life will teach others about Him.

"All the skilled men . . . made the tabernacle" Ex. 36:8-28. The central symbolic meaning of the tabernacle was as a visible sign of God's presence with His people. Note here the use of only the best and most

expensive materials in its construction. God deserves—and requires—the best we can provide.

The ark Ex. 37:1-9. The Old Testament has 22 ways of referring to the ark, including "the ark of the testimony" (25:22), "the ark of the covenant of God" (Jud. 20:27), "the ark of the LORD" (1 Sam. 4:6), and "the ark of the Sovereign LORD" (1 Kings 2:26). The ark, a gold-overlaid wooden box, was the focal point within the tabernacle where God's presence rested. Once a year the high priest was to sprinkle blood on the solid gold cover of the ark as atonement for all Israel's sins. This cover, where the blood was sprinkled, was the specific place where God could and did meet with man.

The ark, with its cover, which was called the "mercy seat," reminds us that human beings can meet with God only because the blood of His perfect sacrifice, Jesus, has been poured out.

The golden table Ex. 37:10-16. Loaves of bread were kept on this gold-overlaid table, on which were also solid-gold dishes and bowls. Commentators disagree over the symbolic meaning. The table and its contents represent God's provision of every need of those who approach Him. The bread also is taken to symbolize Jesus, the Bread of Life (cf. John 6).

The golden lampstand Ex. 37:17-24. This object, called a "menorah" by the Jews, was a seven-branched oil lamp that provided the only light inside the windowless tabernacle. The light-giving candlestick is a symbol of the divine illumination provided for those who approach God. The candlestick is also taken as a symbol of Christ, the Light of the world (cf. John 9).

The golden altar Ex. 37:25-29. The golden altar inside the tabernacle was a smaller version of the bronze altar that stood outside. Incense was burned on the inner altar; sacrificial animals were consumed on the one outside. The incense represents the prayers and worship of those who have gained access to God by the sacrifices offered without. The incense is also taken to symbolize the perfect life Jesus lived in our world (cf. John 17).

"They made the courtyard" Ex. 38:1-31. The curtains that formed the court which surrounded the tabernacle were some seven and a half feet high! No one could see over the fabric walls to glimpse the beauty of the tabernacle. Yet the curtains that formed the court were also made of the finest material. *Any* contact with God's dwelling was intended to impress with His beauty.

You and I come into daily contact with non-Christians, who may never have caught a glimpse of God. When we do we serve as curtains that surround the holy place. Our task is to impress them with the beauty of the Lord by reflecting Him in our character.

"Sacred garments for Aaron" Ex. 39:1-31. The clothing of the high priest also had symbolic significance. As believer-priests the lifestyle we adopt is to clothe us in beauty and reflect the motto engraved on a golden plate that was attached to the turban of Israel's high priest: "HOLY TO THE LORD."

"Moses did everything just as the Lord commanded him" Ex. 40:1-33. Moses was responsible to supervise and inspect the work of the people. But he himself always remained subject to the word of God. We can only trust leaders who are themselves willing to submit to the Word of God.

"The glory of the Lord filled the tabernacle" Ex. 40:34-38. The presence of God invaded the completed tabernacle and was visible to the Israelites.

▶ DEVOTIONAL
Living Symbols
(Ex. 37)

Methodist missionary Larry Rankins, of ALFALIT, tells of a group of Indians in Mexico who kept strictly to themselves, avoiding the whites who ridiculed and downgraded them. Then, aided by ALFALIT, this group of Indians was not only taught to read, but given help to build a bridge across a dangerous river that separated them from town. During a testimony time near the end of the project, one of the older Indians rose, and told how his people had felt worthless and ashamed before the superior whites. Now, not only able to read but also able to design and build their own bridge, they realized that they were a people who could stand tall and be proud.

God had used the bridge the Indians had built as a symbol—a symbol that they had personal worth and value. What a foundation for the ministry of the Gospel. For its Good News is that each human being has so much value in God's sight that Jesus, God's Son, gave His own life to redeem him or her.

God still uses symbols, and the symbol that most frequently serves as a bridge between God and the lost is a human symbol—the believer. If we look closely at Moses' description of the symbolic articles in the tabernacle, we learn three things about the people who serve God as symbols.

Human symbols are intended to be

beautiful. The luster of gold reflected every gleam of light on the articles within the tabernacle. We best represent God when His beauty is seen in our lives and in our attitudes toward others. First Timothy 1:5 says that the goal of teaching Christian doctrine is "love, which comes from a pure heart and a good conscience and a sincere faith." When we truly love others as Jesus did, His beauty shines through our lives.

Human symbols are intended to be complex. Note the complex detail worked into the gold lampstand. Ours is no cookie-cutter religion, turning out production-line Christians. Each believer is a "one of a kind" original. Each of us has different gifts, different personalities, different ways of serving and glorifying God. We need to appreciate each others' differences, for often it is in the way another Christian differs from us that we discover a fresh spiritual insight.

Human symbols are costly. The most expensive metal then known, gold, completely covered the tabernacle furnishings. Yet a redeemed human being is most costly of all, for we have been purchased at the price of Jesus Christ's own life.

Personal Application

Others do see Christians as representatives of God. We are symbols whether we choose to be or not.

Quotable

"Heretics are to be converted by an example of humility and other virtues far more readily than by any external display or verbal battles. So let us arm ourselves with devout prayers and set off showing signs of genuine humility and go barefoot to combat Goliath."—Dominic

---

The Variety Reading Plan continues with LEVITICUS

Leviticus

INTRODUCTION

About 2100 B.C. God selected a man, Abraham, and gave him special promises. The Lord would be Abraham's God, and the God of Abraham's descendants. God also told Abraham that his offspring would be enslaved in Egypt for some 400 years.

What God predicted happened. A group of Abraham's descendants, just 70 in number, settled in Egypt. There the family, called "Israelites" after Abraham's grandson Israel, multiplied rapidly. In time the dominant Egyptians made slaves of the Israelites. Crushed by oppression, the Israelites cried out to the God of their fathers.

About 1450 B.C. the Lord used Moses, an Israelite who had been adopted into Egypt's royal family, to free His people. The story of the miracles God performed for His people is told in Exodus. That book also relates the people's journey to Sinai, where God gave the Israelites a Law to live by and a tabernacle which symbolized His presence with them.

Leviticus focuses on the relationship of God with this chosen people. This book contains special instructions which God gave to Moses during the year the Israelites camped before Mount Sinai. These instructions show how God's chosen people can stay in intimate, continuing fellowship with the living God.

Leviticus is essentially a book about worship, a book about intimacy. Today you and I can apply many of the principles seen in the practices established for Israel to deepen our own personal relationship with the one true God.

OUTLINE OF CONTENTS

I. Worship as Sacrifice and Offering .... Lev. 1–7
II. Worship as Dedicated Service .... Lev. 8–10
III. Worship as Separation .... Lev. 11–15
IV. Worship as Assurance of Salvation .... Lev. 16–17
V. Worship as a Life of Holiness .... Lev. 18–22
VI. Worship as Personal Commitment .... Lev. 23–27

READING GUIDE (6 Days)

If hurried, you may read only the "core passage" in your Bible, and the Devotional in each chapter of this Commentary.

Reading	*Chapters*	*Core passage*
24	1–7	4:1–5:13
25	8–10	9
26	11–15	11
27	16–17	16
28	18–22	19:1-18
29	23–27	25:8-55

Leviticus

JANUARY 24 *Reading 24*
RULES FOR SACRIFICES
Leviticus 1–7

> *"If a member of the community sins unintentionally and does what is forbidden in any of the LORD's commands, he is guilty" (Lev. 4:27).*

Sacrifice and offering symbolize the worship of a people who fall short, who find forgiveness and, finding it, enjoy fellowship with the Lord. In these chapters a variety of sacrifices and offerings speak of that relationship.

Definition of Key Terms

Sacrifices. Animal sacrifice was an element in Old Testament worship before God gave the Law to Moses. God Himself made history's first sacrifice, killing two animals to provide clothing for Adam and Eve after they sinned (cf. Gen. 3:21).

The sacrifices described in Leviticus 1–7 go beyond sacrifice for sin. The burnt offering symbolized complete dedication, and the fellowship offering symbolized intimate relationship. Each sacrifice called for the worshiper to lay his hands on the head of his offering, identifying himself with it in surrender of life to God.

What a healthy reminder for us. Jesus gave His life that we might be forgiven. But, as His people now, we should not live the life He redeemed for ourselves. Instead we should gladly commit ourselves to live for the Lord in dedication and holiness.

Overview

God gave Moses detailed instructions for the community on burnt offerings (1:1-17), grain offerings (2:1-16), fellowship offerings (3:1-17), sin offerings (4:1–5:13), and guilt offerings (v. 14–6:7) (see chart on page 72). God then gave Moses instructions for the priests who made these offerings (v. 8–7:21). Israel was not to eat animal fat or blood (vv. 22-27), and was to give parts of sacrificed animals to the priests (vv. 28-38).

Understanding the Text

"Bring as your offering" Lev. 1:1-17. The whole burnt offering was a voluntary sacrifice. It symbolized the commitment of the worshiper to God. It is an expression of thanks, an indication of the worshiper's desire for fellowship with the Lord.

The shedding of blood speaks of atonement—of a covering for sin. But one thing set this offering apart. The entire animal, not just part of it, was to be consumed by fire.

For you and me too, dedication is voluntary. Salvation is ours when we accept Christ, the one Sacrifice of whom the entire Old Testament system speaks. But we have responded to Jesus fully only when we decide to dedicate our lives to the Lord too. Paul was probably thinking of the Old Testament whole burnt offering when he wrote in Romans 12:1, "I urge you, brothers, in view of God's mercy, to offer your bodies as living sacrifices, holy and pleasing to God—which is your spiritual worship."

"His offering is to be of fine flour" Lev. 2:1-16. The grain offering was to be ground fine, not whole or coarse. And it was to be mixed with olive oil, crushed from the fruit of that tree with great stones.

This offering, which was to be prepared by the worshiper, symbolizes the work of our hands. Atonement was by animal sacrifice, reminding us that nothing a person can do is sufficient to pay for his sins. Blood must be shed, a life surrendered. The grain offering reminds us that once atonement is made, what we do does count. We can use our redeemed life to work for Christ and His kingdom.

"A fellowship offering" Lev. 3:1-17. The Hebrew word is *shalom,* "peace." The basic sense of this powerful Hebrew term is "wholeness" or "well-being." The fellowship offering is a celebration of the inner harmony and peace experienced by a person who is right with God. As such it was an expression of thankfulness and joy (cf. 7:12-13).

The family of the worshiper ate parts of the sacrificed animal together. The symbolism is powerful, picturing the family as guests at God's table. To be served food in the Middle East was an honor and a mark of friendship. By serving food the host became obligated to protect his guests. Thus the fellowship offering reminds us how complete God's welcome is. We find wholeness and well-being in the presence of our God. And He fully commits Himself to those who approach Him with faith.

"He must bring to the LORD" Lev. 4:1–5:13.

SACRIFICES AND OFFERINGS
Leviticus 1:1–6:7

Offering	**Scripture**	**Procedure**	**Disposal**	**Symbolism**
Whole burnt (animal)	Lev. 1:3-17; 6:8-13 Num. 28:1-8	Lay hands on head of sac. Kill it on N. of altar.	Blood poured on altar, rest of animal burned.	Total commitment of the worshiper to the Lord.
Cereal (grain, cakes)	Lev. 2; 6:14-23	Food prep. by offerer, brought to priest.	Handful is burned, rest goes to the priests.	Gift of personal talents to enrich commitment.
Fellowship* (animal)	Lev. 3; 7:11-16	Lay hands on head of sac. Kill it at door of tabernacle.	Blood poured on altar, part burned, part to priests, part eaten by offerer's family.	Communal meal as guests of God, thus under His protection.
Sin (animal)	Lev. 4:1-25; 6:24-30; 12:6-8; 14:12-14; 16:10-11	Lay hands on head of sac. Kill it on N. of altar.	Blood on horns and base of altar. Parts burned. Parts to priest.	Confession of sin and identification with sacrificial animal that dies in place of sinner.
Guilt (animal)	Lev. 5:14–6:7; 14:12-18	Lay hands on head of sac. Must make restitution and pay a penalty.	Blood poured on ground. Parts to the priests.	Confession of sin and restoration of relationship with God/others whom worshiper has harmed.

*Thank offerings (Lev. 7:12; 22:29), votive offerings (Lev. 7:16-17; Num. 6:17-20), and freewill offerings (Lev. 7:16; 22:8; Num. 15:3) are types of fellowship offerings.

The sin offering is not voluntary. Whoever sins—an anointed priest, the whole community, a leader, or an ordinary member of the community—the same procedure must be followed.

It must have been difficult for some to bring the sin offering because as a public act this offering served as an open admission of sin. Leviticus 5:5-6 makes God's requirement very clear. "When anyone is guilty in any of these ways, he must confess in what way he has sinned and, as a penalty for the sin he has committed, he must bring to the LORD a female lamb or goat from the flock as a sin offering; and the priest shall make atonement for him for his sin."

It seems particularly difficult for Christian leaders to follow the principle expressed here. Even unintentional sins, with which this passage deals, are not to be hidden but are to be dealt with openly. Sometimes Christians worry that if others see their faults, they will doubt the Gospel. And so these Christians put on masks, pretend they've done no wrong, make excuses, and generally refuse to deal even with the unintentional ways they may have fallen short or hurt others.

This chapter, with its repeated affirmation, "They *must* bring," reminds us that dealing with personal sin is not an option in the believing community. It is a basic requirement for a healthy relationship with God.

"He is guilty" Lev. 5:14–6:7. The guilt offering picks up the theme of the sin offering. If a person violates any of the Lord's commandments "even though he does not know it, he is guilty and will be held responsible."

The guilt offering serves as a penalty for wrongdoing. On the one hand, God is to be repaid for misuse of any holy thing. For instance, a person who used the Lord's tithe to meet current expenses violated that "holy thing." The money used was to be repaid, plus an additional fifth, and as a penalty an animal was to be brought as a guilt offering.

On the other hand, if someone sinned against another person, he or she was to make full restitution, plus an additional fifth, and then as a penalty bring an animal as a guilt offering.

The guilt offering reminds us that we are responsible for our actions and for the harm we may do others, even when the harm is unintentional.

"Give Aaron and his sons this command" Lev. 6:8–7:21. Moses gave the priests specific instructions on how each offering was to be made.

"Say to the Israelites" Lev. 7:22-36. Two elements of the sacrificial system are emphasized in these words to the whole community. No one was to eat the fat or blood of animals (see Lev. 17). And the people are to be sure that the priests receive their share.

"These, then, are the regulations" Lev. 7:37-38. People centuries later have argued about who invented a sacred history to justify these practices. These two verses tell us unequivocably that it was Moses.

How? The verses are in the form of an ancient Mesopotamian colophon, a form used in the second millennium B.C. with which Moses would have been familiar. This form was not used centuries later, when some have suggested the biblical documents were actually written. These verses are as clear an indication of Mosaic authorship and date as is the copyright page of a modern book that bears the date and place of publication.

▶ DEVOTIONAL
"I Didn't Mean To"
(Lev. 4:1–5:13)

"Be careful; you might hurt somebody," Sue warned nine-year-old Sarah, who was running through our house with Maximillian, our schnauzer pup.

Sure enough, next time around, Sarah barreled into her mother, hurting Sue's back.

"Sarah!" Mom cried. "That hurt me."

Sarah's answer? "I didn't mean to."

That excuse, "I didn't mean to," has sneaked into a lot of popular theology. Right now one of my friends has experienced serious persecution from a well-known Christian leader whose excuse is, "I didn't mean to hurt him." His theory is if the acts which caused harm were not performed as a conscious, intentional violation of God's known will, no sin was involved. And, therefore, he is not responsible for the damage he's done to a brother's career.

Brenda, a very immature Christian in one of our Bible study groups, carried it even further. She argued that if a young person took contraceptives on a date, he or she was planning to have sex, and that was a sin. But if "it just happened," without planning, it wasn't sin! That's "I didn't mean to do it" theology carried to absurdity!

This passage of Leviticus calls on us to reevaluate our view of sin and of responsibility. Again and again the text says, If anyone "sins unintentionally and does what is forbidden in any of the law's commands," he is guilty.

We are fully responsible for our actions, for our unintentional violations of God's Law, and for any unintentional hurts we inflict on others. In God's sight, these are sins.

Why does God make such a point in this passage of unintentional sins? First, because God wants us to accept responsibility for what we do. We can't be close to God or to others if we keep on excusing sinful acts by whining, "But I didn't mean to do it." Second, God makes a point of these sins because, when we confess them and make right the harm we've done, God is ready to forgive.

It's hard for Sarah, just nine, to realize that she needs to accept responsibility and say, "I'm sorry. I won't run in the house anymore." She'd rather make that excuse, "I didn't mean to do it." Actually, we know she didn't *mean* to hurt her mom. But mean to or not, she did cause harm. Learning to be responsible for such acts is essential if Sarah is to grow up to be a mature and loving person, and learn to think ahead how to avoid causing hurt.

It's hard for grown-ups too. We often say honestly, "I didn't mean to do that to you." But what we learn from this passage is that, "I didn't mean to" is no excuse.

So let's accept responsibility for our actions. Let's practice confessing our unintentional sins and faults. And let's grow to that new level of spiritual maturity which follows.

Personal Application

When are you most likely to think or say, "But I didn't mean to"? How else might you respond in that situation?

Quotable

"What is the essence of religious ritual in the Bible? It is a means of communication between God and man, a drama on a stage watched by human and divine spectators. Old Testament rituals express religious truths visually as opposed to verbally. They are the ancient equivalent of television."—Gordon J. Wenham

JANUARY 25 *Reading 25*
WORSHIP AS SERVICE
Leviticus 8–10

> *"Moses said to the assembly, 'This is what the* Lord *has commanded to be done' " (Lev. 8:5).*

These chapters describe the initiation of Aaron and his sons into Israel's priesthood. Each underlines in a significant way that, while offering the Lord dedicated service is one way in which we can worship, our ministry must be performed in full accord with God's commands.

Overview

Aaron and his sons were ordained in an impressive, seven-day ceremony (8:1-36). They officiated at sacrifices offered "in the prescribed way" (9:1-24). Nadab and Abihu died for offering "unauthorized fire," and Moses emphasized the importance of serving God exactly as He had prescribed (10:1-20).

Understanding the Text

"Your ordination will last seven days" Lev. 8:1-36. An impressive ordination ceremony served to emphasize the importance of the Old Testament priesthood and the awesomeness of the priests' privilege. The men, their garments, and everything they

would use in serving the Lord were set apart wholly for God's service.

During the priests' ordination service Moses took the blood of a ram and placed some of it on the lobe of the priests' right ear, the thumb of the right hand, and the big toe of the right foot (vv. 22-23). Those who serve God must be ready to hear His voice, to devote every effort to God's service, and to walk in the Lord's ways.

The pattern holds true for believer-priests today. If we are to worship God with our service, we must listen to Him, work to achieve His ends, and maintain personal holiness by obedience.

"The Lord . . . consumed the burnt offering" Lev. 9:1-24. The priests began their ministry by offering a series of sacrifices, first for themselves, and then for the people.

The sequence of these sacrifices is significant. First was the sin offering (vv. 3, 8, 15). Second was the burnt offering (vv. 3, 12, 16). Third was the fellowship or peace offering (vv. 4, 18). The sin offering speaks of atonement, by which the offerer's sins are covered. The burnt offering speaks of personal, voluntary dedication of oneself to God. The fellowship offering speaks of wholeness and thanksgiving.

This same sequence is followed in our experience with the Lord. We must first trust the Saviour who died for our sins. Then we can dedicate our lives to His service. And only then, in personal relationship with Jesus and through commitment to Him, will we find joy and inner peace.

The concluding verses, which tell of fire from the Lord which consumed the sacrifices, indicates that God was pleased with and accepted the offerings of priests and people. No wonder the people "shouted for joy and fell facedown" when they saw the heavenly flames.

The Alliance Church in Salem, Oregon makes it a practice to place "Appreciation Cards" in the pews. Members are encouraged to write notes to people who have ministered to them that week, or have helped them in any way. Christians too feel joy and are moved to worship when we see evidence that God has accepted our service and used us to enrich the lives of others.

"Unauthorized fire" Lev. 10:1-7. We can't determine the motives of Nadab or Abihu in making the offering that led to their deaths. We do know that they violated God's clear command concerning how He was to be served. "Unauthorized fire" suggests one violation. Incense was to be burned only on coals taken from the altar of sacrifice (cf. 16:2). Moreover, only Aaron was to offer incense within the tabernacle (Ex. 30:1-10).

Whatever their motive, the actions of Nadab and Abihu showed utter contempt for God's careful and detailed instructions on priestly service. Immediately fire flared out from the Lord and consumed them, "and they died before the Lord."

God explained this punishment. "Among those who approach Me I will show Myself holy; in the sight of all the people I will be honored."

Those who claim to serve God must honor Him by serving in the way God has prescribed. It is particularly important that those who claim to represent God be obedient to Him. To some extent, God has placed His glory and honor in our hands.

"You . . . are not to drink wine or other fermented drink" Lev. 10:8-11. In the Old Testament, wine is frequently associated with joy and celebration. Fermented wine was drunk at feasts (1 Sam. 25:18), given as a gift (2 Sam. 16:1), and even poured on offerings to God (Ex. 29:40; Lev. 23:13; Num. 15:7).

While wine is often symbolic of rejoicing, drunkenness and abuse of alcohol are sternly rebuked. The priests are warned never to drink wine when they go into the tabernacle to serve the Lord. Why? Because the priests were responsible to "distinguish between the holy and the profane" and "to teach the Israelites all the decrees of the Lord." One who serves God and who is called to teach simply cannot risk any impairment of his or her faculties by drink or, in modern times, by drugs.

"Would the Lord have been pleased?" Lev. 10:12-20 Aaron and his other two sons continued to minister at the tabernacle after Nadab and Abihu were killed. However they may have felt, they and they alone could offer the required sacrifices. Moses

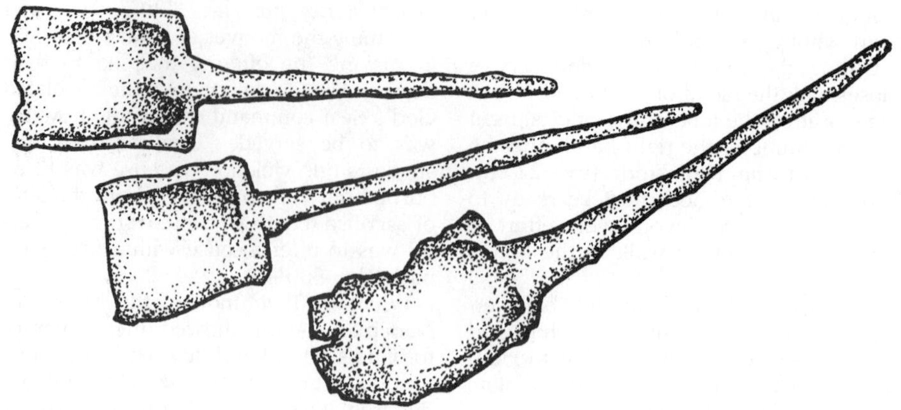

The censers in which the incense was burned were small, shovel-like instruments. Many censers, like those shown here, have been recovered from worship centers throughout the Middle East.

had commanded them not to mourn in the normal way Israelites behaved when death struck (v. 6).

Later that day Aaron and his sons did not eat their share of the sin offering as Moses has prescribed. Moses was angry, but Aaron explained: Would God have been pleased if he had exercised his privilege as a priest to feast on the sin offering, considering that day's tragic disobedience and its consequences?

▶DEVOTIONAL
Jesus Is Lord
(Lev. 9)

It's one of those theological issues people like to debate. Can you accept Jesus as Saviour without taking Him as Lord?

One side argues that all God requires is true belief that Jesus died for our sins. The other side argues that since Jesus is Lord, to truly believe in Him one must accept Him as both Saviour and Lord.

Building an analogy on Leviticus 9 helps us resolve the question. Note the sequence and the character of the sacrifices offered for both the priests and the people. A sin offering was sacrificed first. This sacrifice was to cover the sins of the offerer. As Leviticus 4–5 repeatedly says, the person approaching God must bring this offering if he is to be accepted. The burnt offering was sacrificed next. This sacrifice symbolized the total commitment of the worshiper to God, and was a voluntary offering. It represents that full personal commitment expected from a Christian who consciously commits himself or herself to Jesus as Lord. Third, the fellowship offering was sacrificed. This offering speaks of the wholeness and inner harmony experienced by a person who lives in intimate fellowship with the Lord.

The pattern suggests several realities to apply to the lordship debate. First, we *must* approach God through Jesus, our sin offering. Belief in Him as Saviour is the foundation of our salvation. Second, we *may*, once saved, voluntarily commit ourselves to Jesus as Lord. Third, following full commitment we will experience the peace that God makes available to His own.

This analogy seems to take sides with those who say you *can* accept Jesus as Saviour without committing yourself to Him as Lord. But the sequence is always linked! Christian experience is a series of steps toward intimacy. God never intends any believer, once saved, to stop short of full commitment and fellowship.

What an encouragement this is. Yes, it is exciting to know Jesus as Saviour. But salvation is the beginning, not the end, of our journey toward God. Only as you and I keep on walking toward Him, taking daily steps of commitment and obedience, will we discover the fullness of the joy that knowing Jesus promises.

Personal Application

Think of the Christian faith as a journey toward intimacy. How far along are you on the journey? What do you need to do to take your next step?

Quotable

"Aspire to God with short but frequent outpourings of the heart; admire His bounty; invoke His aid; cast yourself in spirit at the foot of His cross; adore His goodness; treat with Him of your salvation; give Him your whole soul a thousand times a day."—Francis de Sales

JANUARY 26 *Reading 26*
WORSHIP AS SEPARATION
Leviticus 11–15

"You must distinguish between the unclean and the clean" (Lev. 11:47).

A number of Old Testament laws seem to have as their main purpose establishing a unique lifestyle for God's people. The Israelites were reminded constantly of their relationship with the Lord and their difference from all other peoples on earth.

Definition of Key Terms

Clean and unclean. The Hebrew word *taher* means "to be or become clean, pure." *Tame'* means "to be or become unclean, defiled." In Leviticus, as in Numbers and Ezekiel, these words have a ritual or ceremonial association. "Clean" persons were permitted to participate fully in Israel's rites of worship. Persons who were temporarily "unclean" were not allowed to join the community in worship or to eat meat that had been sacrificed to the Lord. In some cases a person was physically isolated from others while he or she was unclean. Only later, in the Prophets, does the Bible employ "clean" and "unclean" to describe a person's moral condition.

In these chapters, clean and unclean are not "good" or "bad" in any moral sense, nor are they intrinsically "right" or "wrong," even though ignoring any of God's laws would be sin for Israel. In Leviticus, cleanness regulations showed God's people that the Lord was intimately involved in their everyday lives—He was concerned with what they ate, with their sicknesses, with birth and death, and with practices that promoted public health. In a very real way these regulations did set Israel apart, and demonstrated that the nation was to be separated unto the Lord.

Separation. The basic idea is to remove something from something else, and thus make a distinction between them. The relationship of separation to the many laws found in this section is defined in Leviticus 20:24-25, where God explained, "I am the LORD your God, who has set you apart from the nations. You must therefore make a distinction between clean and unclean animals and between unclean and clean birds." The sometimes peculiar practices described in these chapters of Leviticus were intended to constantly remind God's people that they were different from all other nations because of their personal relationship with the Lord.

Overview

Laws were intended to set the Israelites apart from other peoples, regulate their diet (11:1-47), and cleanse them from ritual impurity (12:1-8). To guard Israel's health, those with infectious skin diseases were isolated (13:1-46), and mildewed clothing was burned (vv. 47-59). A ritual of cleansing was provided for those who recovered from a skin disease (14:1-32), while recurrent mildew in a house required that it be abandoned (vv. 33-57). Various bodily discharges that made persons ritually unclean called for cleansing (15:1-33).

Understanding the Text

"These are the ones you may eat" Lev. 11:1-47. Three theories have been advanced to explain these dietary regulations. (1) They were intended to help Israel avoid pagan sacrificial rites. (2) They were intended to guide Israel to comparatively healthy sources of food, and to help Israel avoid animals more likely to transmit disease. (3) They were intended to help Israel maintain its separation from other nations

CLEAN AND UNCLEAN FOODS

	Animals	*Water creatures*	*Birds*	*Insects*
Clean	cud-chewing, split hoof— sheep, ox, goat, etc.	fins, scales	pigeon, chicken, etc.	jointed legs— grasshoppers, locusts, etc.
Unclean	all others— camel, horse, zebra, etc.	all others— eels, rays, sharks, etc.	birds of prey, carrion eaters— eagles, hawks, vultures, etc.	all swarming, creeping insects— bees, ants, cockroaches, etc.

by keeping the Jews constantly aware of their obligation to follow every command of God.

Christians are not required to follow Old Testament dietary laws (cf. Acts 10:9-22; Gal. 2:11-16). Our separation is to be internal, and cannot be defined by what we eat or by any other morally neutral practices. Yet we are to be aware at all times, as was Israel, that we are a people set apart to God. He is intimately concerned with everything that happens in our daily lives.

"The woman who gives birth" Lev. 12:1-8. The uncleanness is not caused by the child, but by the discharge of blood and fluids associated with childbirth (see 15:1-33).

Here the purification rites call for an animal sacrifice as well as washing with water. Note that the poor (12:8) are not required to bring a lamb, but only two doves or young pigeons. This was Mary's offering when she fulfilled these rites after Jesus' birth. Christ was not only born a true human being, He was born into a family living on the verge of poverty.

"An infectious skin disease" Lev. 13:1-46. Older versions translate *sara'at* as "leprosy." The word actually means any disease of the skin, and was extended to indicate mildew or rot which appeared on clothing or the walls of a building.

When any rash or swelling appeared on a person's skin, he or she was responsible to show it to the priest, in case it might become an infectious skin disease. If it were, the infected individual remained unclean and "must live alone; he must live outside the camp."

This regulation reminds us that even an animal sacrificed to God must be without blemish. Symbolically it speaks of the purity of life that Christ died to provide for us. Ephesians 5:25-27 tells us that Christ loved the church and gave Himself up for her "to make her holy, cleansing her by the washing with water through the Word, and to present her to Himself as a radiant church, without stain or wrinkle or any other blemish, but holy and blameless."

While laws concerning infectious skin disease had a similar symbolic message for Israel, these laws also served a practical public health purpose. Isolation protected God's own from many plagues that devastated other ancient peoples.

"The time of his ceremonial cleansing" Lev. 14:1-57. Cleansing regulations also contributed to Israel's public health. Before a person who had recovered from an infectious skin disease could return to the community, he was to shave off his hair and thoroughly wash his clothes and his body. In addition the person was to bring sin, burnt, and guilt offerings.

Note that the officiating priest was to smear sacrificial blood on the right ear, thumb, and big toe of the worshiper, just as was done in ordaining priests. The layman as well as the minister is to hear and respond to God's voice, to commit himself to active service, and to walk in God's ways.

"It must be torn down" Lev. 14:33-57. A house in which mildew keeps on recurring must be abandoned. There is no similar regulation for a human being. For you and me, God always holds out welcoming arms. All we need do is turn from our sin, confess it, and God will "forgive us our

sins and purify us from all unrighteousness" (1 John 1:9).

"When any man has a bodily discharge" Lev. 15:1-33. Any sort of bodily discharge made an Israelite ritually unclean. Anything an unclean person touched, as well as his clothing, also became unclean. Persons and clothing had to be washed in water, and were unclean "till evening." Evening is specified, as the Hebrews considered evening the end of one day and the beginning of the next.

Again these regulations had public health value. But they had at least one other implication.

Pagan religions typically coupled worship of deities with sexual intercourse, and often involved male and female cult prostitutes. But in Israel, a discharge of male semen made both the man and woman ritually unclean (cf. vv. 2, 16, 32). And no ritually unclean person was permitted to take part in the worship of the Lord! In this way God made it clear He is concerned with moral purity. Worship of the Lord was to be uncorrupted by perverted pagan practices.

▶ DEVOTIONAL
Separation Today
(Lev. 11)

When I was a new Christian I became involved in a little Baptist church that took an approach to Christian faith that was similar to Israel's separation laws. We had lists of things that a Christian did and did not do; things that set us apart from others. Teens carried red-covered Bibles to high school. None of us went to movies, smoked, danced, drank alcohol, or uttered a cuss word. We all came to church two times on Sunday and on Wednesday nights as well.

Despite what some may think, it wasn't a burden for me to live by those rules. I followed them joyfully, for in that same church I found warmth, acceptance, nurture, enthusiasm, commitment, fervent prayer, and an honest caring for one another as well as for the eternal destiny of our neighbors.

It was only later that I came to realize the truth. Our very real "separation" wasn't defined by the do's and don'ts at all. What really made us different and set us apart as a true community of God's people on earth was the warmth, the caring, and the commitment that we shared as we met to love Jesus and each other.

The death of Jesus canceled the regulations that governed Israel, and made them irrelevant for us today. But God's people are still supposed to be different, set apart from all others. And the difference God truly cares about is a difference marked by the love, the caring, and the commitment that I experienced in that first church I joined, so long ago.

Personal Application

Separation to God is a matter of the heart. Let what makes you different from others be something truly important.

Quotable

"We should not eat their bread because we may be led thereby to drink their wine. We should not drink their wine because we may be led thereby to intermarry with them, and this will only lead us to worship their gods."—The Talmud

JANUARY 27 *Reading 27*
WORSHIP AS ASSURANCE
Leviticus 16–17

"He will make atonement . . . because of the uncleanness and rebellion of the Israelites, whatever their sins have been" (Lev. 16:16).

Sin offerings dealt only with unintentional sins. On the Day of Atonement a sacrifice was offered which assured the Israelites that they could be forgiven for all their sins.

Definition of Key Terms

Atonement. The Hebrew word means "to cover or conceal." In Israel's sacrifices of atonement, God covered the sins of His people so that He could have fellowship with them.

Blood. Blood played a vital role in Old Testament sacrifices. It represented the biological life of man and of animals. In the Bible God's forgiveness of sin is consistently linked with the shedding of blood.

Overview

God gave the priests and the Israelites instructions for the Day of Atonement (16:1-34). Rules for the presentation of sacrifices were given (17:1-9), and the eating of meat without draining the blood was forbidden (vv. 10-16).

Understanding the Text

"His own sin offering" Lev. 16:1-6. Israel's high priest was required to sacrifice a bull for his own sin on the Day of Atonement. Only then could he sacrifice for the sins of his people. Each of us needs to approach God humbly, for we have all sinned.

The fact that Israel's high priest was to make a public sacrifice to atone for his own failings shows that each of us is also to remain humble before others.

A ram for a scapegoat Lev. 16:7-22. Two goats were selected for the Day of Atonement. One was sacrificed, and its blood was sprinkled on the altar. The other was set apart "to *azazel.*" The Hebrew word occurs only here, and its meaning is debated. The most likely explanation is that *azazel* is a technical theological term meaning "complete removal."

In the Day of Atonement ceremony, after the sacrifices were complete, the high priest laid both hands on the head of the scapegoat, symbolically transferring the sins of Israel to it. It was then driven out into the wilderness, symbolizing "complete removal" of "all their sins" from the covenant community.

This acting out of sin's removal was intended to convey to Israel a sense of assurance that their sins truly were gone. Israel was forgiven and accepted by the Lord.

"All their sins" Lev. 16:18-22. The Hebrew language distinguishes between the sins of those who try but fall short, and sins committed consciously and willfully. The first are inadvertent expressions of human frailty. The second are purposeful sins, described by Hebrew words that mean "wickedness" and "rebellion."

The sacrifices described in Leviticus 1–7 made no provision for forgiveness of willful sins. Only unintentional sins could be dealt with by personal sin offerings.

But on the Day of Atonement, God forgave all sins, including sins of wickedness and rebellion.

God wants us to know that, whatever we have done, He is ready to forgive. There is nothing we can do to merit salvation. But on history's ultimate Day of Atonement Jesus died on Calvary, paying the price for us, whatever we may have done.

"Atonement is to be made once a year" Lev. 16:24-34. The sacrifice of the Day of Atonement was to be repeated yearly. Hebrews 10:3-4 points out that the repetition of this sacrifice served as "an annual reminder of sins, because it is impossible for the blood of bulls and goats to take away sins." The sacrifice did cover Israel's sins. But if it had been truly efficacious, only one sacrifice would have been required.

How good to know that "we have been made holy through the sacrifice of the body of Jesus Christ once for all" (v. 10).

Christ offered for all time one sacrifice

for sins, and "by one sacrifice He has made perfect forever those who are being made holy" (v. 14).

Sacrifices outside the camp Lev. 17:1-9. All sacrifices made by the Israelites were to be offered at the tabernacle. This rule set Israel apart from other nations, whose people offered sacrifices to pagan gods at many different shrines. It reminds us of Jesus' saying, "I am the way and the truth and the life. No one comes to the Father except through Me" (John 14:6). If we are to come to God, we must approach Him in the one way He has ordained.

"The life of the creature is in the blood" Lev. 17:10-16. God reserved the blood of animals, the source and symbol of biological life, for sacrifice. Verse 11 says, "I have given it to you to make atonement for yourselves on the altar; it is the blood that makes atonement for one's life."

Because blood represents life itself, and was used in Israel's religion to make atonement for sin, blood was a sacred fluid. No Jew was to eat blood. The blood of wild game was to be drained on the ground and covered with earth. Eating any animal not drained of blood when it was killed made a person unclean.

The sacred nature of blood is reflected frequently in the New Testament, where the blood of Jesus stands for the life He gave for us. Ephesians 1:7 says that "we have redemption through His blood, the forgiveness of sins, in accordance with the riches of God's grace" (Eph. 1:7).

▶DEVOTIONAL

He Has Removed Our Sins from Us (Lev. 16)

I don't know how she got my phone number. But she called my Phoenix home daily from Toronto, Canada.

She was one of those folks who are tormented by uncertainty. Was she really forgiven? Did she really believe? Had God accepted her? After each conversation she seemed relieved, reassured. But the next day, the phone would ring again, as she shared her inner torment.

The ceremony described in Leviticus 16 reminds us that God doesn't intend you or me to doubt. He wants us to know that we are forgiven. He wants us to worship Him in the full assurance of faith.

What conveys assurance? The image of the scapegoat. The picture of the high priest, symbolically transferring "all the wickedness and rebellion of the Israelites—all of their sins"—to the goat. And the picture of that goat being led out into the wilderness, never to be seen in the community of Israel again.

David understood the message, and wrote in one of his psalms, "As far as the east is from the west, so far has He removed our transgressions from us" (Ps. 103:12).

Call up that image next time you feel uncertain about your relationship with God. Imagine all your sins. Close your eyes, and sense your sins being carried away, not by Israel's scapegoat, but by Jesus Himself. Then let assurance of forgiveness bring you inner peace.

Your sins *are* gone. As far as the east is from the west. So you truly are free. Free to worship God and to give Him thanks.

Personal Application

How does knowing that you are forgiven affect your feelings about God? About yourself? About your past sins and failures?

Quotable

"What could you want that forgiveness cannot give? Do you want peace? Forgiveness offers it. Do you want happiness, a quiet mind, certainty of purpose, and a sense of worth and beauty that transcends the world? Do you want care and safety, the warmth of sure protection always? Do you want quietness that cannot be disturbed, a gentleness that can never be hurt, a deep abiding comfort, and a rest so perfect it can never be upset?

"All this forgiveness offers you, and more. It sparkles in your eyes as you awake, and gives you joy with which to meet the day. It soothes your forehead while you sleep, and rests upon your eyelids so you see no dreams of fear and evil, malice and attack. And when you wake again, it offers you another day of happiness and peace."—Gerald Jampolsky, M.D.

JANUARY 28 *Reading 28*
A LIFE OF HOLINESS
Leviticus 18–22

"Keep My decrees and laws, for the man who obeys them will live by them. I am the LORD" (Lev. 18:5).

Worship is honoring God. We honor the Lord by praising Him. But we also honor the Lord by keeping His decrees and laws, and choosing to live holy lives.

Definition of Key Terms
Decree. The Hebrew word translated "decree" in these chapters means "to engrave." It suggests rules chiseled in stone, and thus unchangeable.

Law, statute. The Hebrew word is *mishpat.* It indicates a judicial decision, made by a competent authority, which thus serves as a precedent set to guide future judges.

The laws given in this section do not cover every possible violation of the principles found in the Ten Commandments. They serve as examples to guide Israel as future generations face new situations.

Overview
God expects His people to lead moral lives. Now Israel was taught that holiness calls for sexual purity (18:1-30), social responsibility (19:1-18), and rejection of pagan practices (vv. 19-37). Violation of moral laws requires punishment (20:1-27). An even higher standard of moral and ceremonial purity was set for Israel's priests (21:1–22:33).

Understanding the Text
"Sexual relations" Lev. 18:1-18. All societies studied by anthropologists have rules against incest. Most speculate that the rules are rooted in genetics: close relatives tend to produce a high percentage of defective children. But this passage extends incest beyond blood relationships to, for instance, the wife of one's father's brother.

The more likely reason why incest is destructive as well as wrong is that it creates destructive emotions that warp the very structure of the family, which is the basic unit in society. When the family is threatened, the whole nation is in danger.

These laws remind us of an important truth. God's laws define right and wrong. But they are not arbitrary. Those who obey find that God's laws lead us to healthy, happy lives. Those who violate God's laws find that disobedience leads to disaster.

"Do not defile yourselves" Lev. 18:19-30. The passage identifies several practices as "detestable" and defiling. Chief among them are homosexuality and bestiality—having sex with animals. It's impossible for one who takes Scripture seriously to dismiss contemporary homosexuality as merely an "alternative lifestyle." Homosexual acts are sin. God's decrees remain firmly engraved on the moral fabric of our universe.

"Children . . . sacrificed to Molech" Lev. 18:21. The topic is picked up again in 20:1-5, which condemns the practice in the strongest terms. Why? Hebrew scholars believe the root *mlk* should be translated "sacrificed as a votive offering" rather than as the proper name, Molech. Near the ruins of ancient Carthage a person can go today to a garden where the remains of thousands of children are buried. Most are infants, but their ages range to four years old. Each was burned alive as a votive offering to the goddess Tanat. There was something the parents wanted, and to obtain that favor from the goddess they offered her their child.

It reminds me of a friend, a Christian, who has had two abortions. She can't see anything wrong with what she did. "It's like drowning puppies," she says. But the reason she did not have the children was, simply, that it wasn't convenient. There was something else she wanted, and so she sacrificed her unborn children.

I suppose there are cases where, if the mother's life is endangered, abortions are justified. But to have an abortion just because giving birth is inconvenient is an act too similar to that of those parents of long ago, who traded the lives of their children to a pagan god or goddess in hopes of improved health, a better job, or wealth.

In God's eyes, there is *nothing* that equals the value of a human life.

"Do not" Lev. 19:1-18. What is implied in the Ten Commandments? They are restated here, some with implications spelled out. Here are verses to compare with each.

Commandment	*Verses*
I, II	4
III	12
IV, V	3
VI	16
VII	29
VIII, IX	11-16
X	18

"Different kinds" Lev. 19:19-37. Many of the rulings in this passage, such as not to mate different kinds of animals, or wear clothing woven of two kinds of material, reflect the principle of separation. Many practices in Israel were simply intended to remind God's people of their difference from others.

"Love him as yourself" Lev. 19:33-34. Israel had experienced mistreatment in Egypt. God encourages His people to remember how they felt there, and "when an alien lives with you," to treat him as one of their own.

Some people respond to mistreatment by becoming bitter and hostile to others. Any mistreatment you and I receive should make us more sensitive. Remembering how we have been hurt, we are to take special care not to hurt others.

"Put him to death" Lev. 20:1-27. Other ancient law codes frequently impose the death penalty for crimes against property. In contrast, Old Testament Law reserves capital punishment for crimes against persons and against public welfare.

In a holy community certain standards must be enforced. Each of the crimes listed here is more serious than it might appear. For instance, to "curse" a mother or father was not simply to swear at them. "Curse" here implies an attempt to harm by the use of magic. In Israel recourse to any supernatural power other than God was forbidden (cf. v. 27). An attempt to use such powers against one's parents was an especially heinous crime.

"To the priests" Lev. 21:1–22:33. The whole community of Israel was holy and was to live by the moral and ritual standards God had ordained.

But the priests were set apart to the Lord from within this holy community. Thus the standards by which they lived were even higher.

As believer-priests, Christians are called to live by the highest standards of holiness. Only by relying on God's Holy Spirit can we meet and surpass the righteous requirements of Old Testament Law (Rom. 8:4).

▶ DEVOTIONAL
The Nature of Holiness (Lev. 19:1-18)

Moses introduced this passage by quoting God: "Be holy because I, the LORD your God, am holy."

For most Christians, "holiness" is a rather mystical and somewhat puzzling term. We're willing to be holy, but we don't quite know what holiness is. We know that God is holy. We realize that we are to be holy, as He is. But *how* are we to be like Him?

The laws in Leviticus 19 are an expression of God's holy character. If we want an insight into the nature of holiness, all we need to do is to meditate on some of these verses, and consider what they tell us about God. For instance:

* "Do not reap to the very edges of your field or gather the gleanings of your harvest. . . . Leave them for the poor" (vv. 9-10).

* "Do not show partiality to the poor or favoritism to the great, but judge your neighbor fairly" (v. 15).

* "Do not do anything that endangers your neighbor's life" (v. 16).

* "Do not seek revenge or bear a grudge against one of your people, but love your neighbor as yourself" (v. 18).

What do we learn? Perhaps the surprising fact that holiness and love are identical twins!

The truest expression of holiness is showing love for others in simple, practical ways. Caring for the poor. Being fair to well-to-do and needy alike. Doing nothing that might harm another. Loving others as ourselves.

It is this kind of life God calls us to live daily. And this, the simple and practical living out of love, is holiness.

Personal Application

Using the criteria established in this passage, who is the "holiest" person you know?

Quotable

"At last I have found my calling! My calling is love."—Therese de Lisieux

JANUARY 29 *Reading 29*

WORSHIP AS COMMITMENT

Leviticus 23–27

> *"Follow My decrees and be careful to obey My laws, and you will live safely in the land" (Lev. 25:18).*

Believers demonstrate commitment to the Lord by the decisions they make. These last chapters of Leviticus survey a number of decisions the Israelites would face when they entered the Promised Land, and reflect choices you and I face today.

Overview

Commitment to the Lord was to be expressed by setting aside time to worship (23:1-44), by daily and crisis obedience (24:1-23), by demonstrating concern for the land (25:1-7) and compassion for the poor (vv. 8-55). To encourage commitment, God rewarded obedience (26:1-13) and punished disobedience (vv. 14-46). Beyond this, each person could voluntarily dedicate himself and his possessions to the Lord (27:1-34).

Understanding the Text

"The appointed feasts of the Lord" Lev. 23:1-44. Six annual festivals were to be kept by the Israelites. No work was to be done on any of these days. They were to be dedicated to worship and celebration.

The religious holidays were vivid reminders of the nature of Israel's relationship with the Lord. Several of them reenacted experiences Israel had with the Lord. These were intended to affirm each new generation's identity as a people redeemed, guided, protected, and provided for by the Lord. No wonder that most of the feasts were occasions for joy and rejoicing.

Israel's religious calendar set a pattern we Christians follow. At Christmas we remember the incarnation of the Son of God. On Good Friday we meditate on Christ's death for us. Each Easter we rejoice in His resurrection, which guarantees our own.

We can choose to focus on the spiritual meaning of our holidays, and so make them times of celebration and spiritual renewal.

"The Israelites did as the Lord commanded Moses" Lev. 24:1-23. This chapter describes two situations in which our commitment to God is to be expressed as obedience.

Verses 1-9 emphasize "continually," a "lasting ordinance," and "regularly." They speak of repeated patterns in each believer's life. We are to make sure that the ordinary things in our daily lives are in harmony with God's will.

Verses 10-23 describe a crisis. A young man of mixed parentage "blasphemed the name of the Lord with a curse." The implication is that he used God's name in a magical incantation intended to harm an enemy (cf. v. 10). Here was a situation very out of the ordinary! So the people wisely sought a ruling from God. When the ruling was given, the people obeyed and stoned the blasphemer to death.

When we face a crisis situation, we too need to wait until the will of the Lord is made clear, and then act on it.

Both habitual obedience to God's known will and seeking God's direction in crisis are ways we demonstrate a commitment to obedience that God welcomes as acceptable worship.

"The land itself must observe a Sabbath"

ISRAEL'S RELIGIOUS HOLIDAYS

Month	*Date*	*Holiday*	*Meaning*
1st Nisan (March–April)	14	Passover	In eating the Passover meal the family reenacted the night God killed Egypt's firstborn and won Israel's freedom. *We are a redeemed people.*
	15–21	Unleavened Bread	In eating bread made without yeast, the family shared the experience of that first generation. *We are people on a pilgrimage.*
	16	Firstfruits	In presenting the first sheaves of ripe barley to the Lord, Israel praised Him for the prospect of plenty. *We look to the Lord with hope and confidence.*
3rd Sivan (May–June)	6	Pentecost	In this joyful celebration, marked by many sacrifices, God is praised for a rich harvest. *We see God's hand in the gifts He has given us.*
7th Tishri (Sept.–October)	1	Trumpets	A day of rest marks the first day of the civil New Year. *God renews our life daily.*
	10	Day of Atonement	In the solemn rites of this day God reaffirmed the forgiveness offered to His sinning people. *God covers sin, and so can accept us sinners.*
	15–21	Tabernacles	Families live outdoors in lean-tos, reenacting the journey to the Promised Land. *God is with His forgiven people to meet our every need.*

Lev. 25:1-7. In Eden God had told Adam to "work it [the Garden] and take care of it." Now the Israelites are told to rest the land every seventh year, and not plant any crops. The principle is clear. Human beings are still responsible for earth's ecology. Acid rain isn't just a political football bounced between Canada and the U.S. It's a reflection of man's unwillingness to live responsibly in the world God has committed to his care.

"If you follow My decrees" Lev. 26:1-46. It's so easy to misunderstand. We often think of punishment as a penalty, when it is really encouragement. This chapter reminds Israel that God uses two means to encourage obedience.

The first means is reward (vv. 1-13). God promises to bless Israel if they follow His decrees "and are careful to obey My commands." Each blessing should make us thankful, and motivate us to keep walking in God's ways.

The second means is punishment (vv. 14-46). Punishment would follow "if you will not listen to Me and carry out all these commands." Yet even punishment is intended to encourage rather than create despair. How? First, punishment serves as a reminder that God remains involved in His people's lives even when we sin! If we did evil and prospered, we'd have proof that God has deserted us! Second, punishment shows that God is faithful to His word. The Lord promised to discipline Israel when they disobeyed. He would surely keep His word and bless them if they turned back to Him. Third, punishment makes people aware of their need for God. Only people aware of a need for the Lord are likely to turn to Him.

You and I need to see those infrequent times when God punishes us as encouragement. As Proverbs 3:11-12 says, "My son, do not despise the LORD's discipline and do not resent His rebuke, because the LORD disciplines those He loves, as a father the son he delights in."

"A special vow" Lev. 27:1-34. The Law set a minimum amount that the Israelites were to contribute to support ministers (vv. 30-33). But each individual had the privilege of making a special vow to the Lord. The person making a vow might give anything he possessed—himself, one of his family, an animal, his house, his family land, or a field he had purchased. In effect, the person making the vow paid the value of the dedicated thing into the tabernacle or temple treasury.

Why then doesn't the chapter simply

speak of giving various amounts of money rather than specify persons, animals, houses, and land? To teach us that everything important to us—every relationship and every possession—is to be held in trust and, when required, made available to the Lord. Money is impersonal. Only when it represents something that is near and dear to us does a gift we give to God have significance to us—or to Him.

▶ DEVOTIONAL
This Year of Jubilee
(Lev. 25:8-55)

It was to be a year for rejoicing, the Year of Jubilee. It was to be a year when every poor family won the lottery, and every rich man rejoiced for him.

When Israel entered Palestine, each family was to be given its own land to cultivate. That land, and the crops it produced, was to support the family and be the source of its wealth. God said that such land must not "be sold permanently." No family was to be thrust into poverty; each was to have and keep its own capital.

But what would happen if a family did have reverses and became poor? First, others who could were to help out, by lending money without interest or selling food at no profit (vv. 35-37). Second, if desperate, a man might sell the right to harvest crops the family land would produce, but not sell the land itself (vv. 13-29). Third, if destitute, a person might even sell himself, but such a person could not be treated as a slave (vv. 39-53).

But, when the 50th year came, the Year of Jubilee, everything was to be set right. Any debt the poor owed was canceled. Any land the family had sold was reclaimed. And anyone who lived in servitude was freed. No wonder "jubilee" has come to mean "jubilation," and "rejoicing."

God truly does care about the poor. Through these unusual provisions of Old Testament Law, God showed His people how they could express concern for the poor too.

Yet the Year of Jubilee that we read of here was never celebrated in Israel. Not once. When each 50th year came, the rich tightened their grip on their wealth. And the poor continued in their poverty. God's people had the opportunity to fulfill a dream. But again and again they turned away.

Today, when we read the ageless code that so beautifully displays God's concern for the poor and the oppressed, we too are called to dream of a just and moral society. A community of faith in which people have priority, and concern for those less fortunate is a mark of the godly.

Personal Application

What elements in this chapter's plan for dealing with poverty can Christians adopt today?

Quotable

"It is not the Christian man's part to think in this wise: what have I to do with this fellow? . . . Remember only those things which Christ hath done for thee, which should be recompensed, not in Himself, but in thy neighbour. Only see of what things he hath need, and what thou art able to do for him. Think this thing only, he is my brother in our Lord, co-heir in Christ, a member of the same body, redeemed with one blood, a fellow in the common faith, called unto the very same grace and felicity of the life to come."—Erasmus of Rotterdam

---

The Variety Reading Plan continues with NUMBERS

Numbers

INTRODUCTION

This fourth book of the Old Testament picks up the story of Israel's origins. The descendants of Abraham, God's man of faith, have been freed from slavery in Egypt. They have been guided to Sinai, where they were given a complex Law to live by and a tabernacle at which to worship. Now the Israelites are about to set out from Sinai on a pilgrimage to the Holy Land. Because of disobedience, that journey, which could have ended in rest for God's people within a few short months, was extended to some 38 years. On it, the generation that began Israel's pilgrimage died, to be replaced by a generation willing and eager to follow the Lord.

Numbers takes its name from the censuses which it records. The book is half narrative and half legislation. Its focus is the Promised Land toward which Israel journeys. Its stories and its laws are filled with lessons that we can apply on our own earthly pilgrimages toward heaven.

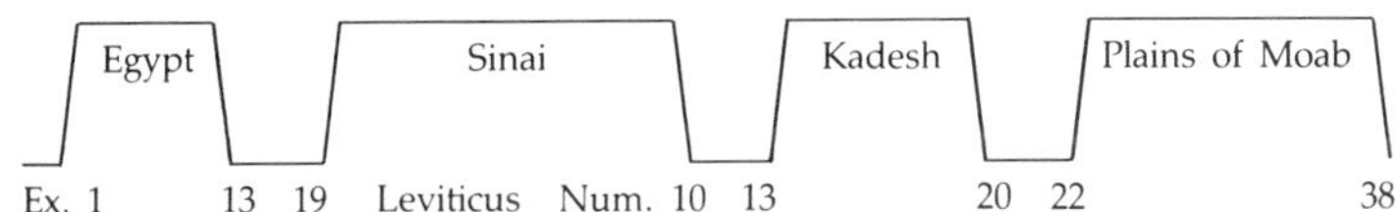

OUTLINE OF CONTENTS

READING GUIDE (6 Days)

If hurried, you may read only the "core passage" in your Bible and the Devotional in each chapter of this Commentary.

Reading	*Chapters*	*Core passage*
30	1–9	9
31	10–14	14
32	15–21	21
33	22–25	22:21-41
34	26–30	27:1-11
35	31–36	32

Numbers

JANUARY 30 *Reading 30*
READY FOR PILGRIMAGE
Numbers 1–9

> *"At the LORD's command the Israelites set out" (Num. 9:18).*

Pilgrimage demands each believer prepare for warfare and for worship. When God's people are on the march, they need to be ready for both.

Overview

After a year at Mount Sinai, the people spent 50 days preparing to journey on to Canaan. Moses took a census of fighting men (1:1-54), assigned campsites (2:1-34) and the travel tasks of the Levites (3:1–4:49). Three issues of ritual purity were decided (5:1–6:27), the tabernacle and Levites were purified (7:1–8:26), and the people celebrated Passover (9:1-23).

Understanding the Text

"Take a census" Num. 1:1-54. This first census reported in Numbers was to count men "able to serve in the army." The count included every able-bodied male over 20.

Each was "listed by name, one by one." The census found 603,550 able to serve.

It is fascinating to note the emphasis on individuals among the hundreds of thousands. When God's people are on pilgrimage, every person counts.

It's the same in the church today. No matter how many millions of believers there are, you and I are "listed by name" as members of God's army. The issue isn't whether or not we count. It's whether God can count on us.

Years later, after a new generation replaced the men and women now camped at Sinai, another army census was taken. The overall number was about the same, 601,730. But the number contributed by several of the tribes differed greatly.

Tribe	*Numbers 1*	*Numbers 26*
Reuben	46,500	43,730
Simeon	59,300	22,200
Gad	45,650	40,500
Judah	74,600	76,500
Issachar	54,400	64,300
Zebulun	57,400	60,500
Ephraim	40,500	32,500
Manasseh	32,200	52,700
Benjamin	35,400	45,600
Dan	62,700	64,400
Asher	41,500	53,400
Naphtali	53,400	45,400
	603,550	601,730

What does the decline of Simeon by some 37,000, and the increase of Manasseh by over 20,000, suggest? Simply that if we do not do our share, God's work will still be done. But someone else will win the blessing that might have been ours.

"Camp around the tent of meeting" Num. 2:1-34. In the 13th century B.C. Egyptian armies used the same square formation that the Lord introduced here. The royal tent was placed in the middle of the camp, surrounded by different army corps. The symbolism does not suggest that God is protected by His people; He is the protector. The organization of the camp proclaims to all that the Lord is Israel's Commander and King, the heart and center of the nation's life.

ORGANIZATION OF THE CAMP

	Dan 62,700	Asher 41,500	Naphtali 53,400	
Benjamin 35,400		Merarites 6,200		Judah 74,600
Manasseh 32,200	Gershonites 7,500	**Tabernacle**	Moses Aaron	Issachar 54,400
Ephraim 40,500		Kohathites 8,600		Zebulun 57,400
		W ◄——► E		
	Gad 45,650	Simeon 59,300	Reuben 46,500	

"I have taken the Levites from among the Israelites" Num. 3:12. The Levites were not counted among the fighting men. They were set aside to guard the tabernacle and to do the "heavy work" *('abad, 'abodah)* of taking it down, transporting, and erecting it.

These Hebrew words come from a root that means servant, or even slave. In Old Testament times the status of a servant depended on two things: how close he was to his master, and how significant his service was. The structure of the camp put the Levites closer to the Lord's tabernacle than any other tribe. And their work was to guard and transport the holiest objects in Israel's faith.

Doing God's "heavy work" is a privilege. It places us close to Him, and in serving Him we build for eternity.

The 22,000 Levites between 30 and 50 took the place of 23,273 "firstborn" that belonged to the Lord. God had claimed Israel's firstborn as His own when He slew the firstborn of Egypt.

How could there be only 22,273 firstborn in a community with over 600,000 men of military age? Some suggest that the 22,273 were born after the Exodus began, some 13 months earlier.

Why were only men between 30 and 50 counted? Possibly because God's "heavy work" calls for servants who are both mature and at the height of their strength.

"Send them outside . . . so they will not defile their camp" Num. 5:1-4. This is the first of three purity issues God raised in preparing Israel for pilgrimage. The camp was organized to prepare for war. But to journey safely, Israel had to depend on God and remain close to Him. Anyone who was defiled and might interrupt fellowship with God, as those with infectious skin disease, had to be put outside to keep from contaminating the community (see Lev. 11–15).

Application to our personal pilgrimage of faith is obvious. We are to cleanse our lives from impurities, as Israel was called to cleanse her camp.

"Wrongs another in any way" Num. 5:6-31. Ritual contamination by an infectious skin disease was visible. Moral failures were more difficult to ascertain. First, any person who wronged another "in any way" was guilty and "must" confess the wrong and make full restitution. We are each responsible to maintain a right relationship with God and with others in the faith community.

But what if another is unwilling to admit a wrong? The text describes a test to be given a wife whose husband suspects her of unfaithfulness. God promised to act through the rite to clear an innocent wife or to identify a guilty one. The rite reminds us that if we do not deal with sins ourselves, we, like the guilty wife, "will bear the consequences" of our sins.

"A special vow" Num. 6:1-21. The person who took a Nazarite vow took on many of the special obligations of Israel's priests. Priests could not drink wine before offer-

ing sacrifices (Lev. 10:9); the Nazarite could not use any product of the vine. The high priest could not mourn for his near relatives (21:2ff), nor could the Nazarite. On completing his vow, the Nazarite even offered the same sacrifices that Aaron did when he was ordained (cf. Lev. 8).

The presence of Nazarites reminded Israel that the whole community was holy, layman as well as Levite. Each believer could voluntarily commit himself or herself totally to the Lord.

"To bless the Israelites" Num. 6:22-27. With the community organized and purified, Aaron and his sons were able to pronounce one of the most beautiful of benedictions over Israel. The blessings described are ours too when we journey in purity with Jesus and His friends.

> The Lord bless you and keep you; the Lord make His face shine upon you and be gracious to you; the Lord turn His face toward you and give you peace.

Assured of God's presence and organized into a more disciplined force, Israel was ready for war. But first Israel had to be ready to worship.

"He . . . consecrated it and all its furnishings" Num. 7:1–8:26. Just before departing, the tabernacle, its furnishings, and the Levites who were to serve in it were all ritually cleansed by sacrificial blood and dedicated to the service of God.

The solemn ceremonies underlined the importance of holiness for anyone ready to set on life's spiritual pilgrimage.

▶ DEVOTIONAL
The Nature of Our Pilgrimage (Num. 9)

Israel's final act before setting out on the journey to Canaan was to celebrate the Passover. This annual festival of freedom recalled God's mighty acts in winning freedom for His people. It served to remind Israel of redemption from Egypt, for redemption had laid the foundation of Israel's existence. Redemption was each individual's charter deed to personal relationship with the Lord.

Even ceremonial uncleanness did not prevent a person from celebrating Passover. In fact, the ceremonially unclean were *commanded* to keep Passover. Why? Because personal relationship with God depends on the experience of salvation, not on living the good life.

But notice what follows this ceremonial reaffirmation of Israel's salvation. The writer of Numbers looks ahead and sums up the daily experience of Israel on pilgrimage. "Whenever the cloud [which indicated the visible presence of God with His people] lifted from above the tent, the Israelites set out; whenever the cloud settled, the Israelites encamped" (v. 17). A redeemed people can to look to the Lord for daily guidance.

It's the same for us today. Conversion is the beginning of our pilgrimage, not the end.

There may be warfare ahead. But God can and will guide us safely through life's trials. If we wish to travel safely, we must remember that God is with us, and look to Him daily for direction and guidance.

Personal Application

Organization speaks of discipline, and purity of moral commitment. Without both, our spiritual journey is sure to be marked by breakdowns and delay.

Quotable

Master, speak! Make me ready
When Thy voice is truly heard,
With obedience glad and steady
Still to follow every word.
I am listening, Lord, for Thee;
Master, speak, oh, speak to me!
—Frances Ridley Havergal

JANUARY 31 *Reading 31*
PERILS FOR PILGRIMS
Numbers 10–14

"How long will they refuse to believe in Me, in spite of all the miraculous signs I have performed among them?" (Num. 14:11)

Every defeat believers experience is ultimately rooted in unbelief. In these pivotal chapters of Numbers, we learn that a lack of trust in God may be expressed in different ways.

Definition of Key Terms

Unbelief. Unbelief here is not at all a failure to believe that God exists. As James reminds us, "Even the demons believe that—and shudder" (James 2:19). Rather unbelief is a failure to trust God, and is expressed in some failure to obey God's Word.

Overview

Signs of unbelief marred the journey to Canaan. Despite careful preparations (10:1-36), the Israelites complained of hardships (11:1-3), and displayed ingratitude (vv. 4-35). Even Miriam and Aaron were jealous of Moses' leadership (12:1-16). Israel camped on the border of Canaan, as a dozen men were sent to learn about conditions there (13:1-26). Most of the spies were terrified by the strength of Canaan's people (vv. 27-33). The people rebelled, flatly refusing to attack Canaan, and were sentenced to wander in the desert for 40 years, until all but two of the unbelieving Exodus generation were dead.

Understanding the Text

"You will be remembered by the LORD your God" Num. 10:1-10. Josephus says that the two silver trumpets that God instructed Moses to make were about 15 inches long. Two such trumpets were taken from the temple when Jerusalem was razed in A.D. 70, and are pictured on Titus' Arch of Triumph in Rome.

The trumpets were used to direct the tribes when on the march. The trumpets were also to be blown when Israel went into battle. God would "remember" His people then. Here "remember" does not mean think of, but to act on behalf of.

God remembers us on our pilgrimage too. As we will see, the real question is, Will we remember to act on His Word?

"You can be our eyes" Num. 10:11-36. Moses' request that his brother-in-law, Hobab, accompany Israel did not, as some have thought, show a lack of faith. The Midianites of that era were a nomadic people familiar with lands south of Canaan. Moses followed wherever the cloud God sent led him. Hobab provided information about the area toward which they were headed.

It's wise for Christians today to seek advice from other believers. It only becomes wrong if we permit human advice to take the place of divine guidance.

"The people complained about their hardships" Num. 11:1-3. The plains of Sinai are verdant compared to the desert of Et-Tih. The people felt oppressed by the desolation, and began to complain. God's cloud had led Israel into this desert. Yet after only three days, the people focused on their "hardships" rather than fixing their hopes on the good land toward which they were journeying.

God's fire burned only "some of the outskirts" of the camp. This fire was only a warning. Moses prayed, and the fire died down.

Unbelief is discouraged by every hardship. Faith focuses expectantly on the future.

"If only we had meat to eat" Num. 11:4-35. The people found a new cause of complaint: a monotonous diet! Numbers says "every family" was "wailing" at the door of its tent.

For a year now God had provided manna, a miraculous, perfectly balanced food that provided all the body requires for good health. Rather than be grateful, the people shouted their dissatisfaction.

God gave them what they wanted—meat to eat—but with it came a plague that killed thousands.

In 1 Timothy 6:8, the Apostle Paul portrays the attitude we believers are to adopt on our pilgrimage. "If we have food and clothing, we will be content with that." The person who truly trusts God is content with what He provides. A preoccupation with material things, whether diet or riches, is a subtle but real expression of unbelief.

What about the quail? Even in the early years of this century, great flocks of quail migrated across the Sinai peninsula. About 2 million of the low-flying birds were caught in the nets of Arabs living there. So the biblical story of low-flying quail has a modern corollary. Most important in Numbers, however, is the outcome. With the meat that Israel craved came a plague that killed thousands. For most of us, the abundance we sometimes crave would be spiritually disastrous. How much wiser to thank God for what we have than express unbelief by craving what we lack.

Moses too cried out. He felt crushed by the weight of leading an unresponsive people. God answered Moses by sharing His Spirit with 70 elders in Israel.

Not all discontent is ungodly. When our concerns are spiritual, or our needs are real, we should never hesitate to bring them to the Lord.

"Miriam and Aaron began to talk against Moses" Num. 12:1-16. Miriam, Moses' sister, was the leader of Israel's spirit-filled women and a prophetess (cf. Ex. 15:20). Aaron, Moses' brother, was high priest, Israel's supreme religious leader. Yet these two became jealous of Moses and challenged his prophetic role as the primary person through whom God spoke to His people.

God called the three to the entrance of the tabernacle. He affirmed Moses' primacy and struck Miriam with an infectious skin disease. Aaron was spared because the disease would have disqualified him from the high priesthood, and Israel needed him to make sacrifices of atonement.

The key to applying the passage lies in the description of Moses as "very humble" (v. 3). The Hebrew word, *'anaw,* describes Moses' attitude. It indicates an absence of pride or self-confidence, allowing complete dependence on God.

The story pinpoints a common peril for leaders through whom God has spoken. Such leaders are susceptible to those subtle expressions of unbelief, pride, and jealousy. In contrast, humility in leaders is a sign of continuing trust in God.

"Moses sent them to explore Canaan" Num. 13:1-25. Representatives of each tribe were sent to explore Canaan. Note that the Lord told Moses to send out the spies (vv. 1-24). Trying to learn as much as possible about where we're going is not an indication of unbelief.

"They reported to them and to the whole assembly" Num. 13:26-33. The spies agreed on their description of the land. It was rich and fertile. But it was populated by warlike peoples, living in walled cities. But the spies disagreed about what this meant to Israel. Ten were frightened, claiming, "We can't attack these people; they are stronger than we are." Two, Caleb and Joshua, disagreed. "We should go up and take possession of the land, for we can certainly do it."

Faith and unbelief are still displayed in how we interpret life's challenges. The problem is seldom in our assembly of the facts. It is in our interpretation of them. It is spiritual disaster to forget the most important fact of all; that God can lead us to triumph.

"We should choose a leader and go back to Egypt" Num. 14:1-46. The Israelites accepted the 10 spies' view and rebelled (vv. 1-4). Moses and Aaron "fell facedown" as an expression of horror at Israel's awful sin (v. 5). When they begged the people not to rebel against God, the "whole assembly talked about stoning them."

Moses and Aaron were saved only by an appearance of the visible glory of the Lord at the tabernacle.

In judgment God announced that every adult over 20, except for Caleb and Joshua, would die in the desert. For some 40 years the doomed generation would wander in circles near Kadesh Barnea until everyone had died.

As for the 10 spies who spread the bad report, they were struck down immediately by a plague (v. 37).

Direct disobedience is always rooted in unbelief and leads to the most severe judgments of all.

"Disobeying the LORD's command" Num.

14:39-45. After God's judgment was announced, the people decided they would attack Canaan after all. Moses rightly identified this as further disobedience.

Timing is important in a relationship with God. Acting too late is as much evidence of unbelief as original hesitation. Both lead to disaster and defeat.

▶ DEVOTIONAL
Afraid to Obey?
(Num. 14)

"Don't you think four years of God making me suffer is enough?"

The question came from a young woman in a Florida Sunday School class. Over several weeks her story had gradually been shared with the other women in the class. She had been engaged to a young man who made her pregnant, then broke the engagement to marry her best friend. Within a year that marriage broke up, and he returned to marry her. Now they were divorced too . . . but still living together.

Gently the teacher tried to explain. "Don't blame God for making you suffer. Most often suffering is a consequence of our own choices. If you want to avoid suffering, you have to make better choices."

This is a lesson that Israel failed to learn. Israel, like the 22-year-old in that Sunday School class, assumed that a person can believe in God and do whatever he or she chooses. Each heard God's voice of instruction, but each had decided not to obey. In making that decision, each displayed what Scripture calls "unbelief."

In Numbers 14 we sense the anger rebellious sins arouse, and also the grace still available to the sinner. God was angry enough with Israel to put the people "to death all at one time" (v. 15). Yet Moses reminded the Lord of His earlier revelation of Himself to Moses (cf. Ex. 34:6-7; Num. 14:17-18). God is "slow to anger, abounding in love and forgiving sin and rebellion." Yet God will "not leave the guilty unpunished."

In this passage, as in the life of the young woman in Sunday School, forgiveness and consequences are both displayed.

God did not strike Israel with death "all at one time." They lived long enough to see their children mature, and those children did gain the Promised Land. Yet as a consequence of their unbelief and rebellion they themselves could not enter the land. They suffered the very fate they feared, and died in the wilderness.

Unbelief still holds us back, blocking our obedience to the Lord. Sometimes our motive is fear. We want to obey God, but we are afraid to. Sometimes our motive is selfishness. We feel that if we obey God we won't get something we badly want. Whatever our motive, a failure to trust God enough to obey Him has consequences. Israel wandered in the wilderness. The young Florida divorcee suffers her uncertainties and pain.

How much wiser to simply put ourselves completely in God's hands, and to obey Him without holding back.

Personal Application

Be alert against the many forms that unbelief can take in your life.

Quotable

"See to it, brothers, that none of you has a sinful, unbelieving heart that turns away from the living God. But encourage one another daily, as long as it is called Today, so that none of you may be hardened by sin's deceitfulness. . . . As has just been said, 'Today, if you hear His voice, do not harden your hearts as you did in the rebellion.' "—Hebrews 3:12-15

FEBRUARY 1 *Reading 32*
PURITY FOR PILGRIMS
Numbers 15–21

"They are to be responsible" (Num. 18:3).

Repetition of earlier laws on sacrifice, and severe judgments that God inflicts on disobedient priests remind Israel that believers are called to be pure while on pilgrimage.

Overview
A review of sacrifices and offerings (15:1-31), execution of a Sabbath-breaker (vv. 32-36), and a new law (vv. 37-41) reminded Israel that God's people are to be holy. Swift judgment fell on disobedient Levites (16:1-50), as God reaffirmed Aaron's primacy (17:1-13) and emphasized again the responsibilities of priests and Levites (18:1-19), as well as the need for continual cleansing (19:1-22).

Trust was taught as the king of Arad was defeated (21:1-3), snakebite was cured merely by looking at a bronze serpent (vv. 4-9), and major Amorite powers were crushed in battle (vv. 10-35).

Understanding the Text
"Offerings made by fire" Num. 15:1-31. The travel narrative is interrupted here by rules governing a variety of offerings. Why? These chapters on ritual serve as a commentary on the preceding chapters. God's people had refused to believe and had disobeyed. These laws reminded them of God's original call to holiness.

Note too that the regulations were for "after you enter the land I am giving you." So these laws were also a promise that God would bring Israel home despite one generation's unbelief.

"The man must die" Num. 15:32-36. Verses 30-31 decree that anyone who "sins defiantly" must be "cut off from his people." A Sabbath-breaker, caught gathering fuel on that day, was stoned to death by the entire assembly. Israel needed to realize that deliberate sin corrupts the community and must be dealt with decisively.

"A blue cord on each tassel" Num. 15:38. Blue represents royalty and deity. It was the dominant color in the high priest's garments and the color of the cloth that wrapped the ark of the covenant. The blue thread in the tassels to be attached to the clothing of ordinary Hebrews reminded them that each believer was holy, a community called to be a royal priesthood.

"Isn't it enough for you that the God of Israel has separated you?" Num. 16:1-41 The Levites Korah, Dathan, and Abiram challenged the spiritual leadership of Moses and Aaron. They based the challenge on the very truth emphasized by the blue cord: the whole community is holy. Like others today, however, they emphasized one truth at the expense of others. The whole community was holy, but God had chosen Moses for leadership and Aaron's family for the priesthood. We need to be careful of those who base their views on one line of biblical teaching and ignore other truths intended to provide balance.

Psychologically, it's fascinating that this rebellion was led by Levites, for they enjoyed far greater spiritual privileges than the majority of the Israelites. Yet these Levites were upset that they could not serve as priests. Even today some with almost nothing are more thankful than those who have almost everything. It seems that when we have almost everything, the little we lack is most likely to create discontent.

This challenge to the leaders was yet another expression of unbelief. Korah and his coconspirators refused to acknowledge that God had spoken clearly, and often, through Moses.

Their sin too was met with immediate, spectacular judgment. Fire consumed those who dared to approach God with incense in violation of His law, while the earth opened to swallow Korah and the rest of his followers.

"You have killed the LORD's people" Num. 16:41-49. Accusation is yet another sign of unbelief. Again God acted in judgment, and a plague killed 14,700 Israelites.

This time the plague was stopped by an act of Aaron, who hurriedly offered incense and stood between the living and the dead.

This event initiated a series of events intended to underline the importance of Israel's priesthood, which alone could offer the sacrifices which cleansed Israel, and made holiness possible.

"You are to be responsible" Num. 17:1–18:32. To demonstrate His choice of Aaron, God miraculously caused Aaron's staff to sprout, bud, blossom, and produce fruit overnight. With the priesthood confirmed to Aaron's family, the text goes on to define their responsibilities. The priests are to care for the sanctuary, and offer the sacrifices necessary to cleanse a people so prone to sin (18:1-7).

In return, the priests are to receive a part of the sacrifices offered to God, and also to be given a 10th from the tithe given to the Levites by the other tribes.

Spiritual privileges bring both heavy responsibilities and great rewards.

"Water of cleansing" Num. 19:1-22. In Israel ritual uncleanness was contagious. If a person touched a dead body, he not only became unclean himself, but whatever he touched then became unclean. This meant that uncleanness had to be dealt with immediately, before the whole camp and the tabernacle itself could be contaminated. Thus the ashes of a sacrificed heifer were kept nearby, ready to be mixed with water and immediately sprinkled on anyone who had touched a dead body.

The rite was not magical, but reflected spiritual realities. Sin does contaminate and must be dealt with immediately. You and I too are to deal with our sins without delay. We are to confess our sins to God at once, make restitution, and rely on God's promise to forgive us and cleanse us from all unrighteousness (1 John 1:9).

"Just as [the Lord] commanded him" Num. 20:1-13. As the journey toward Canaan resumed, Israel reached the depths. Miriam died and was buried. When no water was found, opposition again arose. Moses became so upset that he failed to obey God completely, and struck rather than spoke to a rock from which God intended to produce water.

This failure to follow God's command, as much as Israel's open rebellion at Kadesh Barnea, was an expression of unbelief. As a result, God announced to Moses that he too would die before Israel entered the Promised Land.

No one is too important to God's work to avoid discipline. No one is so important that he or she need not bother to obey the Lord completely.

"Israel turned away from them" Num. 20:14-29. The dark days continued, as Israel retreated before a great Moabite army, and Aaron met his death.

Yet even in the gloom, a bright hope is expressed. The text says Aaron was "gathered to his people." This phrase is used in the Old Testament of the death of believers who have lived into old age. It expresses a firm belief that in death an individual is reunited with the loved ones who have gone on before.

When we suffer the loss of a loved one today, and everything seems dark, this phrase reminds us of the hope shared by God's people of all times. Death is not the end. It is a reunion. One day all who believe will join the happy company of the redeemed and enjoy fully God's gift of eternal life.

▶ DEVOTIONAL
Look, and Live
(Num. 21)

Often the sequence of events recorded in Scripture, as well as the events themselves, teach us important truths. This is certainly the case in Numbers 21, which contrasts so greatly with chapter 20. In the former chapter, Israel reached the low point on her journey toward Canaan. Even Moses was shown to be vulnerable to unbelief. Hopelessness, defeat, and death seemed to be all that God's people could look forward to.

But then the tenor of the Old Testament text shifts dramatically. Israel sought God's help and won a victory over the Canaanite king of Arad (vv. 1-3). What if that southern kingdom was tiny? It was a victory at last. When everything seems dark, every victory is important.

And then the people spoke against God and Moses again! This time the Lord sent an infestation of poisonous serpents. But again a new theme was introduced. Moses made a bronze serpent, raised it high on a pole, and promised that bitten individuals could simply look at the bronze snake and be cured. Individuals with faith looked. And they lived!

Even though the community is riddled with unbelief, there remains hope for individuals who are willing to trust God. Clearly, trust is an effective antidote for unbelief!

The next incident suggests that trust was now contagious, just as unbelief had been contagious before. The Israelites faced a major enemy in two neighboring Amorite kingdoms—and conquered them. God had said, "Do not be afraid of him, for I have handed him over to you, with his whole army and his land." This time the people believed, obeyed—and won!

This phase of the journey, which had begun in such despair, ended in joy. Israel was learning that a purified people, willing to trust God, would enjoy victory rather than defeat.

What a message for us to remember. No matter how flawed our past life, no matter how dark our present, we do have hope. We can determine now that the next steps we take on our pilgrimage will be steps of faith.

We can believe. We can obey. And, when we do, we can win!

Personal Application

Remember that both trust and unbelief are contagious. Be sure to give your loved ones the right "disease."

Quotable

Did we in our own strength confide,
Our striving would be losing,
Were not the right man on our side,
The man of God's own choosing.
Dost ask who that may be?
Christ Jesus it is He—Lord Sabaoth His name,
From age to age the same,
And He must win the battle.—Martin Luther

FEBRUARY 2 *Reading 33*
HOSTILITY TO PILGRIMS
Numbers 22–25

"Now come and put a curse on these people" (Num. 22:6).

In one way or another, believers on pilgrimage to God's Promised Land do threaten others. When opposition comes, it's good to remember that while some may curse us, God is committed to blessing us.

Overview

When Israel approached, the terrified Moabites and Midianites summoned Balaam, a pagan prophet, to curse God's people (22:1-8). Despite repeated warnings Balaam went to Moab (vv. 9-41). Three attempts to curse Israel failed, as God forced Balaam to bless Israel instead (23–24). The wily prophet suggested the Moabites seduce Israel into idolatry to force God Himself to curse His people (25:1-5). The plot failed when a godly priest intervened (vv. 6-18).

Understanding the Text

"Summon Balaam son of Beor" Num. 22:1-21. The approach of Israel terrified the Moabites and Midianites. Balaam was summoned to curse Israel. Here "curse" is a magic utterance believed to bind or limit another's powers.

Biblical passages invariably picture Balaam as a perverse character who loved money rather than God and was all too eager to curse Israel (cf. Deut. 23:4-5; 2 Peter 2:15; Jude 11; Rev. 2:14). The Old Testament says that Balaam was given "the fee for divination," and commonly would "resort to sorcery" (Num. 22:7; 24:1). These pagan practices are abominations forbidden in Israel (Deut. 18:10). Numbers 31:8-16 says that Balaam suggested Israel's enemies seduce God's people and lead them into idolatry, in hopes that God would then be forced to curse them. In view of all this, we can better understand Balaam's motives and his actions.

Balaam's constant reference to money should be seen as a subtle demand for a larger fee. His insistence that he would say only what God wanted him to say was not piety, but an effort to promote himself as God's appointed spokesman. While at first glance Balaam looked and sounded pious, piety was a front in his case intended to cover greed.

"Build me seven altars" Num. 23:1-6. Balaam followed a procedure laid out on a cuneiform tablet found in Babylon. That tablet prescribes, "At dawn, in the presence of Ea, Shamash and Marduk, you must set up seven altars, place seven incense burners of cypress and pour out the blood of seven sheep." The position of Balak "beside your offering," and Balaam's choice of a barren height to seek some revelation, also reflect common pagan practices.

Balaam was a pagan, following a pagan ritual, when God seized the initiative and spoke through him.

"Balaam uttered his oracle" Num. 23:7–24:9. The sacrifices were repeated three times, from three different heights. From each a different section of Israel's camp could be seen. Much to Balaam and Balak's frustration, each attempt to curse Israel was transformed by God into a blessing.

The first blessing (23:7-10) reflects on God's choice of Israel to be "a people who live apart and do not consider themselves one of the nations." How can Balaam curse a people whom God has not cursed?

How important this is for us to remember. We may experience hatred and even persecution on our Christian pilgrimage. But how can anyone harm a people God has not cursed? Paul reflects this reality in Romans 8:31 when he says, "If God is for us, who can be against us?"

The second blessing (Num. 23:18-24) focuses on God's presence among His people. "The LORD their God is with them; the shout of the King is among them." Therefore, "there is no sorcery against Jacob, no divination against Israel." What Balak fears will surely happen: Israel's army will be like a lion that "devours his prey and drinks the blood of his victims."

Today too it is God's presence that keeps us safe. Because of Him, it is our enemies who will ultimately know defeat.

The third blessing (24:3-9) predicts Israel's settlement in the land. Then it passes on to predict a day when a king "greater than Agag" will appear, and "their kingdom will be exalted." Saul, Israel's first king, did defeat Agag. Under the second king, David, Israel's kingdom was "exalted."

Our future too is certain and bright.

"In days to come" Num. 24:10-25. A furious Balak refused to pay Balaam, who argued that he could only say what God commanded. Balaam then volunteered additional oracles which portrayed the doom of Israel's enemies.

The Hebrew rendered "in days to come" is literally "in the latter days." That phrase may simply mean "in the future," but often indicates history's end. The clear direct reference of "a star will come out of Jacob; a scepter will rise out of Israel" is to David, with probable allusion to David's greater Son, Jesus. The Dead Sea Scrolls and many rabbis viewed the passage as messianic.

David did in fact crush Moab and Edom, as Balaam predicted. Other prophecies in these oracles have been fulfilled. The Amalakites (v. 20) were defeated by Saul and by David, and finally destroyed by Hezekiah (1 Chron. 4:43). The ships of Kittim most likely carried invading sea peoples, the Philistines, who defeated Israel's coastal tribes but ultimately came to ruin.

The point of these last prophecies, however they are interpreted, is to announce the ultimate defeat of all enemies of God's people. Believers do experience opposition as they move toward God's Promised Land. That opposition may cause real and serious harm. But "in the days to come" it is our enemies who will suffer defeat at God's hand.

"The people ate and bowed down before these gods" Num. 25:1-18. Numbers 31:16 says that Balaam advised the Moabites to corrupt Israel morally and spiritually. So Moabite women made themselves available on the edge of Israel's camp, and after seducing men "invited them to the sacrifices to their gods."

A death sentence was passed against those who had sinned, but apparently execution was delayed, and God sent a devastating plague. During this time one Israelite openly brought a Midianite woman into his tent. Phinehas, a priest, followed them into the Israelite's tent and killed them both with a single spear thrust. This act stopped the plague, but not until 24,000 had died.

The story contains two lessons for us. First, it's dangerous not to deal with sin immediately. If we are unwilling to deal with our sin, God will.

Second, Phinehas acted responsibly in killing the offending Israelite. As a priest he was responsible to maintain the purity of the camp. You and I too are responsible, if we see open and blatant sin in the community of faith, to take the initiative in dealing with it. Those who love God are to hate evil and stand against it.

▶ DEVOTIONAL
When Donkeys Speak
(Num. 22:21-41)

It was fascinating talking with the publicist one of my publishers had hired. I was in Los Angeles, visiting several radio stations for interviews on one of my books. Between stations the publicist spoke familiarly of a number of Christian "greats": men who have significant ministries, who are admired by many, and probably idolized by some.

"Take Jerry Falwell," she was saying. "He's one of the nicest, most gracious men I've ever worked with. When things went wrong, he never got upset. And after our trip, unlike some of the others, he thanked me for my help."

Then she went on to speak of another, very different, Christian superstar. This man was impatient, arrogant, and thoughtless. "Whatever they offer me," she said, "I'll never do any work with him again."

I remembered her as I read again the story of Balaam and skimmed several commentaries. Some writers are so impressed that God spoke through Balaam they assume that this proves Balaam was a true prophet, and even a pious man. One of God's own.

But such commentators fail to consider Balaam's donkey. You see, when Balaam set out for Moab, the text says God was "very angry" (v. 22). Balaam had kept on bugging God to go, despite the fact that he knew very well God had refused him permission. As Balaam approached an angel set to kill him, the donkey stopped and refused to go on. Balaam angrily beat the beast who resisted his will. And then the donkey spoke!

What irony. If the fact that God spoke through Balaam really proves he was a true prophet and a godly man, what does the fact that God spoke through a donkey prove? I suspect that being used as God's spokesman is evidence neither of personal piety or holiness—as several TV evangelists have demonstrated recently.

The story of Balaam finds its parallel in the New Testament. There Paul warns against the naive assumption that success in ministry or reputation indicates personal piety. He says, "If I speak in the tongues of men and of angels, but have not love, I am only a resounding gong or a clanging cymbal. If I have the gift of prophecy and can fathom all mysteries and all knowledge, and I have a faith that can move mountains, but have not love, I am nothing. If I give all I possess to the poor and surrender my body to the flames, but have not love, I gain nothing" (1 Cor. 13:1-3).

What is evidence of holiness? Paul answers, "Love." And says, "Love is patient, love is kind. It does not envy, it does not boast, it is not proud. It is not rude, it is not self-seeking, it is not easily angered, it keeps no record of wrongs. Love does not delight in evil but rejoices with the truth. It always protects, always trusts, always hopes, always perseveres" (vv. 4-7).

God can use anyone as His spokesman. Let's remember that it is love, not spectacular gifts, not "success" or reputation or even being used by God that is the mark of true spirituality and an intimate personal relationship with the Lord.

Personal Application

Being sensitive to God and obedient to Him is better than public recognition as one of His spokesmen.

Quotable

King Jesus
why did You choose
a lowly ass
to carry You
to ride in Your parade?
Had You no friend
who owned a horse

—a royal mount with spirit
fit for a king to ride?
Why choose an ass
small unassuming
beast of burden
trained to plow
not carry kings?

King Jesus
why did You choose
me
a lowly unimportant person
to bear You
in my world today?
I'm poor and unimportant
trained to work
not carry kings
—let alone the King of kings
and yet You've chosen me
to carry You in triumph
in this world's parade.
King Jesus
keep me small
so all may see
how great You are.
Keep me humble
so all may say
"Blessed is He who cometh
in the name of the Lord"
not "what a great ass He rides."
—Joseph Bayly

FEBRUARY 3 *Reading 34*
PROSPECTS FOR PILGRIMS
Numbers 26–30

> *"The land is to be allotted to them as an inheritance" (Num. 26:53).*

Purified again, the Israelites prepared to enter the Promised Land. The incidents and laws reported in these chapters serve as promises to God's people. Canaan was ahead, and victory was assured.

Overview
A military census revealed Israel's readiness to attack Canaan (26:1-65). Confidence that Israel will possess her heritage was shown by Zelophehad's daughters (27:1-11), by the commissioning of Joshua (vv. 12-23), and by a review of offerings to be made perpetually after the Conquest (28:1–29:40). Rules for personal vows, frequently made just before a war, were clarified (30:1-16).

Understanding the Text
"Not one of them" Num. 26:1-66. The census taken of those able to serve in the army established two important facts. The total number of men available was 601,730; just a few thousand less than 40 years before. And "not one of them was among those counted by Moses and Aaron the priest when they counted the Israelites in the Desert of Sinai" (v. 64). The old, disobedient generation was dead. Yet the community had suffered no loss of strength!

The obedient would inherit the land the disobedient despised.

"He died and left no sons" Num. 27:1-11. Moses was approached by five daughters of a man who had died and left no sons. Their request for property reflects the patriarchal structure of Israelite society. Only sons inherited, and the eldest son received twice as much as younger brothers.

First, the request reflected the daughters' faith that Israel would be successful and take Canaan. Only in victory would there be land for them to inherit.

This illustrates the way many Old Testament laws were developed. A new situation occurred, Moses brought the case to the Lord, and God's ruling became the precedent for determining similar cases.

"Commission him in their presence" Num. 27:12-23. The closer Israel came to Canaan, the nearer the time approached for Moses to die. Moses put aside any fears for himself and thought of what his death might mean to Israel. He prayed that God would "appoint a man over this community" to replace him.

The incident demonstrates Moses' stature as a truly godly man. The New Testament gives us a partial definition of Christlikeness when it says, "Each of you should look not only to your own interests, but also to the interests of others" (Phil. 2:4).

God responded to this prayer and told Moses to publicly commission Joshua to succeed him. Laying on of hands here is a symbol of transference of leadership.

It's good to know that, when people we depend on move on, God has others ready to fill their shoes.

"Present to Me at the appointed time . . . My offerings made by fire" Num. 28:1–29:40. The function of the next section, with its details concerning ritual offerings, seems out of place. Why here, rather than in a book like Leviticus?

These regulations function here as a divine promise. God specifies the animals which are to be offered to Him each day of the year, throughout Israel's occupation of its land. Adding them up, we see that each year the Israelites are to offer 113 bulls, 32 rams, and 1,086 lambs, plus over a ton of flour and a thousand measures of oil and wine. This is in addition to any freewill offerings or sin offerings made by the people.

The daily, week-after-week, and month-after-month listing of the offerings is a dual promise. Israel would surely occupy the land where the offerings were to be made. And that land would prove fertile, rich enough to support the Israelites and to provide generous offerings for the Lord.

"When a man makes a vow" Num. 30:1-16. Vows were voluntary pledges to give money or something else of value to the Lord. Once a person uttered such an oath, it was binding and could not be broken.

Vows often took the form of bargains: "If God does this, then I will . . . " (cf. Gen. 28:20-22; 1 Sam. 1:11). It was quite common for individuals to make vows just before a nation went to war (Jud. 11:30-31; 21:1-7). Now, just before Israel was about to invade Canaan, the laws concerning vows are clarified.

Briefly, any man making a vow was bound by it. Married or single women could also make vows but if, when first hearing of it, a husband or father wished, he could void the vow.

The passage introduces an important legal principle. If the husband or father does not say anything when first hearing of a wife or young daughter's vow, the vow is binding. Silence implies consent.

It's the same today. If you and I fail to speak out concerning something that is wrong but remain silent, our silence implies consent. And makes us a party to the wrong.

▶ DEVOTIONAL
The Prospect for Women (Num. 27:1-11)

"It's time to leave that church," Carol insisted. "I simply won't have my daughter brought up in an atmosphere where women are constantly put down."

What bothered Carol wasn't so much what church leaders said as what they did. Everything was done by men. There were no women ushers. Women never spoke from the pulpit—not even to give an announcement. Only men were allowed to serve Communion. Only men served on the church board.

Carol realized that her church had much to commend it. But the impression that women don't count, subtly conveyed by the church's practices, created a sense of oppression she could no longer stand.

The issue raised by Zelophehad's five daughters seems to mirror Carol's concern. Didn't Israel's patriarchal system discriminate against women? Weren't women second-class citizens in Israel too? Some might even argue that Israel's male-dominated culture is precedent for ruling women out of significant participation in churches today!

But were women discriminated against? On the surface, perhaps. However, when an Israelite girl married, her father provided her with a dowry. This marriage gift, frequently of clothing, jewelry, furniture, money, or even slave-girls, represented the daughter's share in the family estate. So women *were* valued and they did get their fair share! They simply received that share in a different way than through inheritance.

The story reminds us how important it is to understand the whole Old Testament way of life before we judge the fairness or unfairness of specific practices, and before we apply principles drawn from them to modern times.

What the story of Zelophehad's daughters actually reminds us of is that women *did* count in Israel. The significance of daughters was simply shown in a different way than that of sons. Yet each was valued. And each deserved a fair share of all the family possessed.

Perhaps what we should draw from this story is a challenge to reevaluate practices in our churches. The importance of women may not need to be affirmed in the same way that the importance of men is shown. But unless we do affirm women as full participants in the Christian commmunity, we violate their personhood, and deny the gifts that God has given to each and every one.

Personal Application

As we journey toward the Promised Land there's a place of service for every pilgrim.

Quotable

"Scripture ultimately proves that the Apostle Paul had high regard for the work and ministry of women. Scripture shows that local churches and other Christian ministries should eagerly endeavor to find fulfilling effective ministries for the godly women who serve them. Some of the tragic situations arising out of intense counseling between members of the opposite sex might well be avoided by allowing godly women to exercise their calling to counsel other women. . . . Many other facets of God's work often stand or fall on the availability of godly effective women to lead them."—H. Wayne House

FEBRUARY 4 *Reading 35*
PROMISES TO PILGRIMS
Numbers 31–36

> *"Take possession of the land and settle in it, for I have given you the land to possess" (Num. 33:53).*

Israel reached the border of the Promised Land. Everything in these last chapters can be taken as a firm promise that God will give His people victory and peace.

Overview

Israel crushed the Midianites (31:1-54), and 2½ of the 12 tribes were granted their lands (32:1-42). Moses reviewed Israel's journey (33:1-49). He charged the people to utterly destroy the Canaanites (vv. 50-56), fixed the boundaries of the Promised Land (34:1-29), and reminded Israel to set aside towns for the Levites and as cities of refuge (35:1-34). He also commanded that women who inherit land must marry within their own tribe (36:1-13).

Understanding the Text

"Take vengeance on the Midianites" Num. 31:1-24. The Midianites had not only opposed the Israelites, but had carried out Balaam's strategy and turned many Israelites to idolatry. The complete destruction of Midian was a divine judgment on this sin and on idolatry itself.

Often God uses human beings as instruments to punish sin.

"Not one is missing" Num. 31:25-54. The strength of the enemy is suggested by the 808,000 animals and 32,000 virgins taken as spoil. In Bible times girls married in their early teens, so the 32,000 represent a small percentage of the total population.

When roll was called by the Israelite commanders, they discovered that this total victory had been won without the loss of a single man! The victory over Midian was a preview and promise of the success God would bring His people if they continued to trust Him.

This time Israel responded appropriately. They donated all the gold they had acquired as a gift to the Lord. God's people had at last learned to be thankful.

"Let this land be given . . . as our possession" Num. 32:1-42. At first Moses took the request of the Reubenites and Gadites for the land of the Midianites as a failure to follow God wholeheartedly. The promise

of these tribes to join in the battle for Canaan showed they remained committed to the Lord. We need to measure others by their commitment to God, not whether they agree with us completely.

"Here are the stages" Num. 33:1-49. Commentators have come up with a variety of creative theories about the significance of the 42 stops mentioned here. Yet one thing is very clear. God had brought His people from Egypt to the very border of Canaan. Despite Israel's sins and failures, despite desolate and waterless wastes, despite enemy armies, God had been faithful. Looking back at each stage of the journey, Israel could see in what had happened a preview of the future. The God who had kept them safe would surely fight for them when they at last invaded the Promised Land.

Looking back can have similar value for us. Yes, we'll find many examples of personal failure. We'll recall times when life seemed desolate and empty. But we will also realize that God has brought us through those times, has guided, strengthened, and brought us safely to the present moment. Remembering God's faithfulness helps us to move ahead confidently as we take our next step toward the Promised Land.

"Drive out all the inhabitants of the land" Num. 33:50-56. Moses repeated God's command to expel all the Canaanites from the Promised Land. Too-intimate association with pagan peoples would corrupt Israel. God's people were to remain separate and pure.

The New Testament reflects this thought, with a significant modification. Paul notes that the only way we could avoid contact with pagans and their practices would be to "leave this world" (1 Cor. 5:10). So we are simply to avoid being "yoked together" with unbelievers (2 Cor. 6:14). We are to identify with our fellow believers, not with the unsaved. If our hearts belong to the Lord alone, and our most intimate values are shaped within a Christian community, then we will remain both separate and pure, able to represent Jesus to the people of this world.

"Give the Levites towns" Num. 35:1-5. Towns for the Levites were scattered through the territory of the other tribes. In this way the Levites, who with the priests were to teach God's Law to Israel, would be available.

We can't influence those with whom we have no contact.

"Cities of refuge" Num. 35:6-34. Old Testament Law makes a clear distinction between premeditated murder and accidental homicide. Specific situations are included as cases from which precedents can be drawn.

No national or local police force existed in Israel. The people of each community were responsible to enforce God's laws,

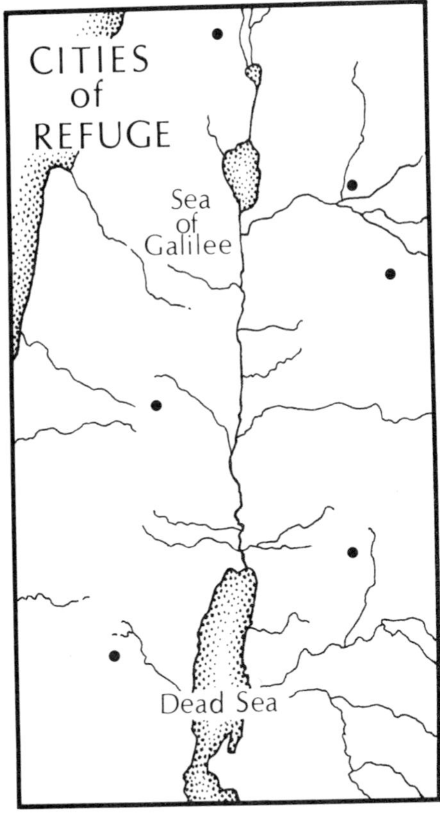

Cities of refuge were located so that anyone who killed another person accidentally would be within a day's journey of safety. God, who judges the guilty, is quick to safeguard the innocent.

after a jury of local elders determined the facts of each case. In the event of a killing, it was the responsibility of a near relative of the victim, called the "avenger of blood," to execute the murderer.

The law is very strict in its treatment of premeditated murder. "Bloodshed pollutes the land, and atonement cannot be made for the land on which blood has been shed, except by the blood of the one who shed it."

God would provide the land for His people. They were responsible to maintain its purity.

"Marry within the tribal clan" Num. 36:1-13. The Promised Land was to be divided among the tribes of Israel. Each tribe, and each family within the tribe, was to hold the plot of land it was given perpetually, as a permanent heritage from the Lord. While the daughters of Zelophehad were guaranteed land, they were told to marry within their tribe in order to preserve that tribe's heritage.

What God gives us is not to be lightly transferred to others.

▶ DEVOTIONAL
It's Their Choice
(Num. 32)

Many years ago I was best man at a friend's wedding. Jack was a young flier whom our pastor was convinced should go to the mission field as a Missionary Aviation Fellowship pilot. I remember how upset the pastor was when Jack announced he was getting married and staying with his airline. Pastor was convinced that Jack had chosen something less than God's best.

Moses would have understood our pastor's reaction. He was just as upset when the tribes of Reuben and Gad, and the half-tribe of Manasseh petitioned him to give them the Trans-Jordan region they had taken from the Midianites. The problem was that this territory lay outside Canaan, the land that God had promised to Abraham.

Was their request wise, or even right? The text gives no clear answer, though at first glance settling outside the Promised Land would seem to be an outright rejection of God's stated purpose and promises.

Yet two things suggest that the request was not motivated by a lack of commitment or of faith. The petitioning tribes promised to "cross over to fight" in the battle for Canaan. The Hebrew here is impressive. It actually says "hurrying before the Israelites" (v. 17). The tribes of Reuben and Gad demonstrated their commitment by their willingness to lead Israel into battle and bear the brunt of the attack. They showed their trust in God by a readiness to leave their families and herds unprotected while the fighting men went off to the war.

Moses accepted these conditions and granted Rueben, Gad, and the half-tribe of Manasseh vast lands east of the Jordan River. It is a good thing to remember when you or I are tempted to stand in judgment over another person's decision. Moses may not have liked the decision Reuben and Gad made. But, convinced of their commitment and trust in God, Moses granted them the freedom to make it.

You and I can't really say what God's best for another person is. And our view isn't really important. What counts is still his or her commitment to, and active trust in, God. Each person must have the freedom to follow where God leads.

Personal Application

The most important advice we can give another person is, Trust the Lord, and follow wherever He leads.

Quotable

"Every time we say, 'I believe in the Holy Spirit' we mean that we believe there is a living God able and willing to enter human personality and change it."—J.B. Phillips

---

The Variety Reading Plan continues with 1 TIMOTHY

Deuteronomy

INTRODUCTION

Deuteronomy is the fifth and last book written by Moses. Deuteronomy, placed historically about 1400 B.C., means "second (repeated) law." It is written in the form of a second-millennium-B.C. treaty between a ruler and his people.

The Israelites had been slaves in Egypt until God intervened about 1450 B.C. God set them free through a series of miracles and led them to Mount Sinai. There Moses, whom God had called to lead Israel, gave God's people a Law, a priesthood, a sacrificial system, and a portable place of worship. But when the Exodus generation approached Canaan, a land God had promised to Israel's ancestor Abraham, the Israelites rebelled. For 40 years Israel wandered in circles in the desert, until every adult member of that first, rebellious generation had died. In Deuteronomy Moses is speaking to their children—a new generation that is now ready to obey God and about to conquer the land God has promised to His people. This review of the divine Law is given to this new generation of Israelites to explain the nature of their relationship with the Lord. At the end of the book this new generation, knowing the nature of the relationship God intends to have with Israel, is challenged to commit itself fully to the Lord.

Deuteronomy reminds us that grace has always characterized God's relationships with human beings. God was motivated by love alone in choosing Israel. The Law showing Israel how to live in covenant relationship with Him is also an expression of love. Deuteronomy also teaches that love for God is the sole motive powerful enough to move human beings to respond obediently to the Lord. Deuteronomy, which is quoted some 80 times in the New Testament, has rightly been called the Old Testament's "gospel of love."

OUTLINE OF CONTENTS

READING GUIDE (10 Days)

If hurried, you may read only the "core passage" in your Bible and the Devotional in each chapter of this Commentary.

Reading	*Chapters*	*Core passage*
36	1–4	4:1-31
37	5–7	6:4-8
38	8–11	9:7–10:11
39	12:1–16:17	14:22–15:18
40	16:18–18:22	18:9-22
41	19:1–21:14	19
42	21:15–26:19	26
43	27–28	28:15-68
44	29–30	30:11-20
45	31–34	34

Deuteronomy

FEBRUARY 5 *Reading 36*
GOD'S MIGHTY ACTS
Deuteronomy 1–4

"These forty years the LORD your God has been with you, and you have not lacked anything" (Deut. 2:7).

Moses' review of the Exodus reminds a new generation that God is faithful despite human failure. But only if they are faithful to Him can God's people know success.

Overview

Moses reviewed each stage of Israel's journey from Sinai to their present camp just east of the Jordan River (1:1–3:29). Moses applied the lessons of history and challenged the new generation to obey and to worship God (4:1-49).

Understanding the Text

"It takes eleven days" Deut. 1:1-5. The three sermons of Moses that make up the bulk of Deuteronomy were delivered just over the Jordan from the Promised Land. The site was just an 11-day hike from Mount Horeb (Sinai) where God had given His people the Law. But that Law had been given 40 *years* earlier! What delay disobedience caused.

Deuteronomy 1–3 isolates crises that occurred on the journey, to explain Israel's years of frustrating delay.

God is committed to bring us to the place of blessing. But the length of time it takes you and me to arrive still depends on our willingness to obey.

"Hear the disputes" Deut. 1:9-18. Moses first mentioned problems, burdens, and disputes. These characterize all of us and reflect normal human weakness. Note that these did not delay Israel. Moses simply appointed judges and laid down guiding principles.

We're all subject to human weakness and to a variety of failings. This need not delay us on our spiritual journey. We are to judge ourselves and move on. God does not demand perfection, but He does expect us to deal honestly with our sins and failures.

"You rebelled against the command of the LORD" Deut. 1:19-46. Israel's tragic delay in arriving at the Promised Land was caused by conscious, willful disobedience of God's command. Moses identifies fear of the Canaanites as the immediate cause of the disobedience. That fear was rooted in a failure to trust God's love (v. 27) and His ability to help (v. 32).

Conscious disobedience is sure to delay our spiritual progress. However we may rationalize or explain rebellion, disobedience brings discipline and makes us vulnerable to disaster.

"He has watched over your journey" Deut. 2:1-15. This is one of the most touching statements in Moses' review of history. Despite Israel's rebellion and repeated sins, God "watched over your journey." The New Testament says, "If we are faithless, He will remain faithful, for He cannot disown Himself" (2 Tim. 2:13). God's commitment to us is rooted in His own character, not in anything we may do or fail to do.

Even when we rush headlong away from God, He continues to watch over us.

But Moses reminded Israel that the nation then wandered for 38 years until the

Rugged Mount Sinai (Horeb) is a symbol of the Law that God gave Israel through Moses. Today a monastery stands where Israel once camped. As Deuteronomy shows, despite the thunder that shook the mountain then, God's Law is rooted in and expresses His love.

entire rebellious generation perished (Deut. 2:14-15). God will watch over us. But He will also discipline us until tragedy roots out our tendency to rebel.

"Now begin to conquer" Deut. 2:16–3:20. When the old generation died out, God began to give the new generation a taste of success. In a series of increasingly difficult battles God gave Israel increasingly greater victories.

When you or I return to the Lord after a time of disobedience, our renewed trust is frequently developed by small, and then greater, spiritual victories. Each step of faith is rewarded as we relearn how to trust God completely.

"I pleaded with the Lord" Deut. 3:21-29. Moses is honest in reporting his own personal failure to trust God, though he does not go into detail here. The image of Moses pleading with God to be allowed to go over the Jordan and see the Promised Land is touching. Moses had been a faithful and godly leader. Yet his one act of disobedience was severely punished (cf. Num. 20). Why? Undoubtedly to remind us that no one is immune to divine discipline. No one can sin safely.

The text shows that God did, in a sense, grant Moses' request! The aged leader, then some 120 years old, begged to "go over and see the good land." Instead God led Moses to the top of Mount Pisgah and gave him a glimpse of Canaan.

The sight from this height across the Jordan is impressive. Rising from the fertile plain is a series of hills that gradually flow into an impressive range of mountains. The rich colors and shades reflect the complexity of Palestine, with its wide range of climates and soils which make the land capable of growing every kind of crop. Moses did not "go over" the Jordan. But he did "see the good land" to which he had successfully led God's people.

"Ask now about the former days" Deut. 4:32-40. Now Moses made it very clear why Israel needed to look back as well as to look ahead. In looking back at what God had done, the people would discover how great God is, and who they were to Him.

God alone had taken "one nation out of another nation, by testings, by miraculous signs and wonders, by war, by a mighty hand and an outstretched arm, or by great and awesome deeds." Who God is is defined by His acts in history.

Israel is defined by its relationship with God. Israel is a people whom God "loved" and "chose" and "brought . . . out of Egypt . . . to bring you into their land to give it to you for your inheritance." All this is understood by looking back. Appreciating who God is and seeing Israel's identity in Him would motivate Israel to obey and would bring God's people future blessing when taken "to heart."

It's the same with you and me today. We look back and realize what God has done in Jesus Christ. When we remember that His suffering and subsequent triumph were for us, and we realize how precious we are to God, our awakened love motivates us to serve our Lord.

▶DEVOTIONAL
Guaranteed Spiritual Success (Deut. 4:1-31)

I'm fascinated by those ads in airline magazines that promise salesmen quick and easy success. I've known one salesman, Ed, who listened daily to the tapes and regularly attended the seminars such ads market. But Ed wasn't exactly successful, and I remain suspicious about the promises those ads make. On the other hand, I'm positive that what Moses told Israel in Deuteronomy 4 can guarantee success in anyone's spiritual life.

What would you hear on one of Moses' tapes, or at one of his seminars? Probably something like this:

(1) "Keep the commands of the LORD your God" (v. 2). Absolutely safe guidelines to the good life!

(2) "Watch yourselves closely so that you do not forget the things your eyes have seen or let them slip from your heart" (v. 9). Review what God has done for you every day, and you'll stay motivated!

(3) "Teach them to your children and to their children after them" (v. 9). Share what God means to you. It will keep your faith fresh and make God real to your loved ones.

(4) "Watch yourselves very carefully, so that you do not become corrupt" (vv. 15-16). Don't get cocky. Anyone can slip and fall. Never give any idol—whether wealth, pleasure, power, love, or even good works—God's central place in your life.

Of course, I'm not sure Moses' tapes and seminars would sell. You see, people are always looking for an *easy* way to succeed. As far as spiritual success is concerned, there isn't any easy way.

So perhaps Moses would add one other step for us moderns. Like, "Work at your relationship with God."

Certainly Moses and the new generation of Israelites would say, with spiritually successful saints through the ages, "It's worth it!"

Personal Application

What disciplines have you developed to help you achieve spiritual success?

Quotable

"God calls us, not to success, but to faith—obedience and trust and service—and He bids us to be unconcerned with measuring the merits of our work the way the world does. We are to sow; He will reap as He pleases."—Charles Colson

---

FEBRUARY 6 *Reading 37*
LOVING GOD
Deuteronomy 5–7

> *"Love the LORD your God with all your heart and with all your soul and with all your strength" (Deut. 6:5).*

These chapters identify the fundamental principles of personal relationship with God. The rules which come later are merely illustrations of how these fundamental principles are to be applied by a people who love God.

Definition of Key Terms

Deuteronomy 6 calls on us to dedicate "heart," "soul," and "strength" to loving God. "Heart" in the Old Testament is the seat of both the mind and emotions. "Soul" is best understood here as one's "being." We are to love God with our whole self, not limit Him to smaller compartments of our lives. "Strength" suggests the will's direction of every capacity toward love. Use of three such powerful terms in a single verse makes it clear that relationship with God calls for wholehearted devotion. The implication of these chapters is that only a person truly devoted to God will obey Him.

Ten Commandments. Ten brief, basic rules showing human beings how to love God and other persons. For explanation of the Ten Commandments, see Exodus Reading 19.

Overview

The 10 basic commandments given at Sinai show how to love God and others (5:1-21). Keeping them promotes well-being (vv. 22-33). Love and reverence for God produce obedience, and are to be taught to future generations (6:1-25). God demands complete allegiance; competing faiths were to be driven from the land so that God could keep His covenant of love with Israel (7:1-26).

Understanding the Text

"It was not with our fathers . . . but with us" Deut. 5:1-21. The adults who stood before God at Mount Horeb (Sinai) and first heard the Ten Commandments were dead when Moses proclaimed them to this new generation. Yet Moses said God's covenant was "not with our fathers" but was "with all of us who are alive here today."

What did Moses mean? That God's Word has a powerful, present message for each listener. God's Word was first spoken centuries ago, but it is as fresh, vital, and compelling as if it had been just uttered today. In a real sense, God's Word *is* spoken today. The living God meets us in His Word. All He says there is said to us as well as to generations past.

You and I must never read the Bible as though it were merely a record of something that happened long ago. We are to read Scripture attentively, expecting God to speak to us in our today. As the writer of Hebrews says, "Today, if you hear His voice, do not harden your hearts" (Heb. 3:15). The Bible is God's voice. Through it He is speaking not only to our fathers, but to us!

"Hear . . . learn . . . and be sure to follow" Deut. 5:1. Each of these words is found in Moses' first words to the assembled Israelites (v. 1). The Ten Commandments state fundamental principles which are to be applied in our relationship with God and with others.

It's important not to confuse loving God and others with love feelings. Love is a choice. The person who loves God will hear God's Word, study to understand what that Word means, and then carefully apply it in daily life.

"That it might go well with them and their children forever" Deut. 5:22-33. Some act as if the moral standards revealed in the Ten Commandments are arbitrary and restrictive. They resent the "You shall nots" of Scripture, as if these were intended to spoil mankind's fun and make human life as miserable as possible.

Nothing could be further from the truth. God's laws are actually intended to promote human happiness. We humans are moral beings, created by God with a sense of right and wrong. Like a train that functions only when running on a track, human beings function in a healthy, happy way only when living morally good lives.

There is a special urgency in Moses' call to Israel to obey God. Israel enjoyed a covenant relationship with God. In this relationship God was committed not only to bless obedience, but also to punish disobedience.

Unbelievers as well as believers are better off living a morally good life. But God is actively involved in the life of believers. Because God cares so much about us, you and I are more likely to feel the immediate effect of our sins.

"When you eat and are satisfied" Deut. 6:10-25. Moses said "when" because he knew that God would surely bless His people. For Israel this meant inheriting "a land with large, flourishing cities you did not build, houses filled with all kinds of good things you did not provide, wells you did not dig, and vineyards and olive groves you did not plant." Still, such blessings are dangerous. When life is too easy, and we become satisfied, we tend to "forget the LORD."

Moses explained the way for believers to guard themselves when blessed. First, "fear the LORD your God." The word here means to treat Him with respect, remembering that He is able to discipline as well as to bless. Then, "keep the commands." The believer is to "do what is right and good." Finally, the believer is "in the future" to pass on faith to the next generation. This is the only way to guard ourselves and our children from empty, meaningless lives.

"You must destroy them totally" Deut. 7:1-6. The demand that Israel utterly destroy the

people who inhabited Canaan before her has troubled many. How does this command square with all the talk in Deuteronomy 6 of love? How do we understand it in view of God's revelation of love for all people in Jesus?

To answer we need to make several observations. First, archeology has confirmed Scripture's portrait of Canaanite culture as morally and religiously depraved. Some 600 years earlier God had told Abraham that He would not expel the people of the Promised Land then, because "the sin of the Amorites has not yet reached its full measure" (Gen. 15:16). Now that full measure of sinfulness had been reached, and Israel was to be God's instrument of punishment. It's important for us to remember that the God who loves human beings also hates evil. Any concept of God that fails to take His commitment to punish sin into account is essentially unscriptural.

Second, the command to destroy the Canaanites emphasized Israel's call to be a holy people. Intimate association with the Canaanites would (and did!) lead Israel into idolatry. Only by destroying the Canaanites who currently inhabited the Promised Land could Israel be safe from moral and spiritual corruption. It would be a strange parent indeed who would stand idly by and watch a much-loved child be infected with a deadly disease. God was protecting His children.

One other observation. Israel was *not* commanded to go beyond the borders of Canaan and wipe out the several racial groups represented in Palestine. God's first concern was for the well-being of His people.

Yes, God does care about everyone. But those who know and love Him are His first priority.

"It was because the LORD loved you" Deut. 7:7-26. Why did God choose Israel and decide to bless them? Why does God care so much for you and me today? The puzzle is resolved by stating an even greater mystery. Why? "It was because the LORD loved you."

God needs no reason other than love to bless us. Though there are many reasons why it is to our benefit to obey, we need no other reason than love for Him.

▶ DEVOTIONAL
"Communicating God's Love" (Deut. 6:4-8)

Loving God is so important. Surely a love for the Lord is the most important heritage we can pass on to our children.

When my oldest son was a seventh-grader in our local Christian grammar school, and I was a professor of Christian education at Wheaton College Graduate School, I did an experiment with his class to learn how boys and girls from Christian homes "caught" their parents' faith.

What I found was that most of the things parents did or did not do to pass on their faith made very little difference in their children's lives. The one thing that did make a difference is explained here, in words spoken by Moses millenniums ago.

Moses says that communicating faith begins with a parent's own love for God. A love "with all your heart and with all your soul and with all your strength" (v. 5). This kind of love opens us up to God, so that He can write His commandments on our hearts (v. 6). Why is this so important? Because as long as God's commandments seem only like demands engraved in stone, we will never be able to communicate either them or a love for God. It's only when God has written His laws on our hearts and they find expression in our lives that we are able to "impress" them on our children (v. 7). When God's love has made us sensitive to His commandments, so that He and they become such an integral part of our lives that we "talk about them when you sit at home and when you walk along the road, when you lie down and when you get up," then the God who is real to us will be real to our children too. Then our own love for God will find a home in the hearts of our boys and girls.

What makes the difference? Simply this. If God is real to you—if you love Him and follow Him faithfully—then God will be real to your children too.

Personal Application

Show your love for God daily by your commitment to doing His will.

Quotable

"Too often Christians regard the Law merely as a set of legalisms, and they view Jewish people as trying to follow the letter of the Law. On the other hand [they] then proclaim that the New Covenant describes how God works in grace to redeem His people and shower His love on them. In no way should such a compartmentalization exist between the Old and New Testaments. Deuteronomy describes how God blessed Israel and showered His love on them because of His grace and mercy. What the Lord expected from Israel in return was an outpouring of love. While some people misappropriated God's intentions and developed a legalistic substitute, a remnant in every generation always deeply loved, honored, and served the Lord their God."—Lewis Goldberg

FEBRUARY 7 *Reading 38*
REMEMBERING GOD
Deuteronomy 8–11

> *"Be careful that you do not forget the* L*ORD your God, failing to observe His commands, His laws and His decrees that I am giving you this day" (Deut. 8:11).*

Memory is a great gift. Our tomorrows may be shaped by how well we remember God's past deliverances and His judgments.

Definition of Key Terms

Remember. In the Old Testament "remember" is more than the mental act of thinking about something that has happened in the past. Its deepest meaning is to recall or pay attention to, and then to act on what has been remembered. In these chapters God called on Israel to remember what had happened on the journey to Canaan, in order to help them make better choices when they entered the Promised Land.

Overview

Israel was to remember the wilderness years, when God taught His people to depend on Him (8:1-20). Events on that journey revealed Israel's rebelliousness (9:1-29) and the faithfulness of the God who kept on calling His people to holiness (10:1-22). Looking back was to help Israel love God, to carefully observe His commandments, and so to experience His blessing (11:1-32).

Understanding the Text

"He humbled you" Deut. 8:1-9. The Hebrew root of "humble" means to be poor and thus dependent. During the wilderness years God let Israel hunger, then fed His people, to teach them to depend fully on Him.

When Jesus was challenged by Satan to turn stones into bread (Matt. 4; Luke 4), He quoted a verse from this passage: "Man does not live on bread alone but on every word that comes from the mouth of the LORD." Jesus knew what it means to depend completely on God and to be satisfied with what the Lord provides.

Before we assume that God intends to keep His people in poverty, note what the Lord provided for Israel. Food (v. 3), clothes that did not wear out (v. 4), and good health (v. 4). In the land they were about to possess God would give Israel agricultural and mineral wealth (vv. 7-9).

God may hold back material things to teach us to depend on Him. But Isaiah's promise still holds. "If you are willing and obedient, you will eat the best from the land" (Isa. 1:19).

"It is He who gives you the ability to produce wealth" Deut. 8:10-20. Pride and humility are contrasting attitudes. The humble person acknowledges his dependence on God. The proud individual credits his own "power and the strength of [his] hands" for his success. The curse of the proud is that in taking credit for abilities God has given, they forget the Lord. Moses warned that if Israel became proud, "You will surely be destroyed."

Paul portrayed the viewpoint you and I are to develop. "Who makes you different from anyone else? What do you have that you did not receive? And if you did receive it, why do you boast as though you did not?" (1 Cor. 4:7) If all that we have is ultimately a gift of God, we have nothing

This small metal calf was recovered by archeologists at a hilltop worship site in territory once occupied by the Israelite tribe of Dan. A calf or bull was a frequent motif in Canaanite worship. The animal either represented Baal, or was thought of as a throne on which the invisible deity sat. The bull symbolized virility in religions where ritual prostitution and sexual orgies played a major part. Israel's worship of a golden calf was a retreat to gross paganism.

to be proud about but much to be grateful for.

"Because of my righteousness" Deut. 9:1-29. How are we to interpret God's good gifts? Moses warned Israel not to assume that God's blessings were "because of your righteousness or your integrity." In fact, as the incident of the golden calf (vv. 7-21) and several other events (vv. 22-29) demonstrated, Israel had been "stiff-necked." This one graphic term sums up Scripture's portrait of sinful human nature. All mankind, like Israel, is unresponsive to God, disobedient, and actively rebellious.

Israel's occupation of the land is evidence of God's faithfulness to the covenant promises, not of Israel's righteousness.

God's love and faithfulness, not our good works, are the true explanation of any blessings He may shower on you or me today.

"At that time" Deut. 10:1-11. God's matchless grace is displayed in these verses. God forgave Israel's sin, provided new tablets on which His Law was inscribed, and told Moses to "lead the people on their way, so that they may enter and possess the land that I swore to their fathers to give them."

When remembering God, we must stand amazed at His forgiving grace.

"What does the LORD your God ask of you?" Deut. 10:12-22 In a brief review, Moses summed up the holy way of life God expected His people to live. Today too we are to "circumcise our hearts" (demonstrate inner commitment to God) by loving others and by worshiping and praising the Lord.

"Faithfully obey" Deut. 11:1-32. Note how intimately this chapter links remembering and responding. Again and again Moses reminded his listeners of what God had said and done. On this basis he called on Israel to "love the LORD your God and keep His requirements" (v. 1), to "observe therefore all the commands" (v. 8), to "faithfully obey the commands" (v. 13), to "be careful" to worship God only (v. 16), and to "carefully observe all these commands I am giving you to follow—to love the LORD your God, to walk in all His ways and to hold fast to Him" (v. 22).

Yet Moses did more than appeal to the past to show the value of obedience. He looked ahead as well, and linked the divine promise of future blessing to loving and serving God. In remembering God and how He had dealt with His people Moses was "setting before you today a blessing and a curse—the blessing if you obey the commands of the LORD your God . . . the curse if you disobey."

What God has done, He will do. For God is faithful and consistent.

▶ DEVOTIONAL
Remember Our Golden Calves (Deut. 9:7–10:11)

I really don't like to remember my sins. That flush of shame, that awareness of failure, aren't at all pleasant. Besides, as forgiven people, aren't our sins forgiven and the past forgotten?

While there's nothing spiritual about wallowing in guilt, every now and then we need to revisit sites where we have erected golden calves.

The golden calf that Israel made on the

plains of Sinai was the ultimate affront to God. God had delivered His people from slavery; Israel ignored Him and chose to worship an idol. God had fed and protected Israel; they decided to praise a creation of their own hands. In the most basic way the golden calf was a total rejection of God.

And yet, the Bible says, "At that time, the LORD said" (10:1). At that time, when Israel overtly rejected Him, God told Moses to return to the Mount, and there God gave Moses new tablets containing His Law (vv. 2-8). And at that time, God also said, "Go . . . and lead My people on their way, so that they may enter and possess the land that I swore to their fathers" (vv. 10-11).

Moses reminded Israel of the golden calf not to shame them, but to help them realize how great and how gracious God is.

This is why we need to revisit our golden calves now and then. To remember how forgiving, how loving, how gracious God has been to us. "At that time" in our lives, the time of our greatest failure, God came to us in Jesus. He lifted us up, took us in His arms, forgave us, and set us on our way again.

Revisiting our golden calves reminds us that not even our sins can cut us off from the love of God. Whenever we fail, God is able to pick us up and set us on the path of righteousness once again.

Personal Application

What event in your past makes you most grateful for God's forgiveness?

Quotable

"If we confess our sins, He is faithful and just and will forgive us our sins and purify us from all unrighteousness. If we claim we have not sinned, we make Him out to be a liar and His Word has no place in our lives. My dear children, I write this to you so that you will not sin. But if anybody does sin, we have One who speaks to the Father in our defense—Jesus Christ, the Righteous One. He is the atoning sacrifice for our sins, and not only for ours but also for the sins of the whole world."—1 John 1:9–2:2

FEBRUARY 8 *Reading 39*
WORSHIPING GOD
Deuteronomy 12:1–16:17

> *"You must not worship the LORD your God in their way" (Deut. 12:31).*

Worship is the way we express intimacy in our corporate and personal relationship with God. Because God is special, worship is to be special too.

Definition of Key Terms

Worship. Moderns tend to think of worship simply as singing hymns and praising God on Sundays. Hebrew and Greek words translated "worship," however, mean to "bow down" or "prostrate oneself." The image is one of showing utmost respect.

Broadly understood, any act by which we express deep respect for God is an act of worship. These chapters in Deuteronomy review some of the ways that Israel was to show respect for the Lord when they entered the Promised Land.

Overview

Worshiping Israel was to establish a central sanctuary (12:1-32), to reject idolatry (13:1-18) and pagan rites (14:1-2), honor dietary laws (vv. 3-21), faithfully pay tithes (vv. 22-29), and to forgive debts and release Hebrew slaves every seventh year (15:1-18). The Israelites were also to set firstborn animals apart to the Lord (vv. 19-23) and faithfully observe religious festivals (16:1-17).

Understanding the Text

"Seek the place the LORD your God will choose" Deut. 12:1-32. The people of Canaan had sacred sites scattered throughout the land. They offered sacrifices at these sites, held orgiastic rites, and practiced various kinds of magic intended to influence their gods. Israel's rites of worship, such as sacrifice, were to be held at

one place alone. The text promised that after Israel had taken the land, God would choose a particular site, and identify Himself with it ("put His Name" there). That site, not selected until the time of David, was Jerusalem.

Emphasis on a single worship center reflects a common Old Testament theme. There was only one entrance into Israel's tabernacle court, and one way to enter the tabernacle. Later the temple followed this plan. There was to be only one altar of sacrifice, one high priest, one mercy seat where sacrificial blood was poured out each year on the Day of Atonement.

The truth these things symbolized was expressed by Jesus, who told His disciples, "I am the way and the truth and the life. No one comes to the Father except through Me" (John 14:6). It may be popular these days to be broad-minded and say there are "many roads to God." But it is not biblical. Scripture supports that chorus: "One way, and only one."

"He tried to turn you away from the LORD your God" Deut. 13:1-18. Modern history shows how vulnerable people are to cults. How do we respond when someone knocks on our door with the message of Jehovah's Witnesses, the Mormons, Moonies, or some other cult? If anyone incites us to abandon the Lord for a cult, we will "not listen to [his] words" (v. 3). Rather we will remember that "it is the LORD your God you must follow, and Him you must revere" (v. 4).

God deserves our total allegiance. Worshiping Him as He has revealed Himself in Scripture is to be our first priority.

"Do not cut yourselves" Deut. 14:1-2. God's people are not to adopt the practices that reflect the attitude of the surrounding pagan peoples toward death.

"Do not eat any detestable thing" Deut. 14:3-21. Some have argued that Hebrew dietary laws prohibited the use of disease-carrying animals as food. The real explanation is more profound. God wanted to remind His people that He is involved in every aspect of their lives. In everything we do we can demonstrate respect for the Lord. Everything we do can thus be an act of worship.

"Bring all the tithes" Deut. 14:22-29. Israel's economy was to be agricultural, and her wealth was the land and its products. God, the Giver of the land, claimed a 10th of its bounty as His share of every crop. Showing respect for God by giving has been an integral part of worship from the very first.

"Do not be hard-hearted or tightfisted toward your poor brother" Deut. 15:1-18. The depth of a person's relationship with God is displayed in the way he or she treats others. This principle, woven throughout Scripture, is particularly evident in laws explaining how to treat the poor. Those in need are to be helped willingly. Every seventh year, the debt of all who have not been able to repay loans is to be forgiven. And any Hebrew who has been forced to sell himself into slavery is to be released.

Helping the poor is an act of worship which is especially pleasing to the Lord. The passage says, "Because of this the LORD your God will bless you in all your work and in everything you put your hand to" (v. 10), and again, "The LORD your God will bless you in everything you do" (v. 18).

"Observe the month" Deut. 16:1-17. When Israel conquered the land the people were to hold annual worship festivals, attended by all. The chart on the next page shows the religious calendar of Israel. For the meaning of each festival, see Reading 28, Leviticus.

▶ DEVOTIONAL
God's Share
(Deut. 14:22–15:18)

"Bring your tithes into the storehouse," Pastor L. used to preach. "Then you can give to others."

What he meant, of course, was that the local church ought to get the Christian's tithe. All other giving was over and above the 10 percent our pastor thought the local church deserved.

I understand his message. But I question his exegesis. Particularly when I read chapters like these in Deuteronomy. Here one thing links the tithe, which Israel was obligated to give, and generosity, which Israelites were urged to display. Why is that? Both required that giving and op-

tional giving were intended primarily to meet human need.

The regular tithe was delivered to the temple to be used to support the Levites and priests who served God there. Then, every third year, the tithe was stored locally so that "the Levites (who have no allotment or inheritance of their own) and the aliens, the fatherless and the widows who live in your towns may come and eat and be satisfied" (14:29). Both the giving God required and optional contributions He encouraged went to meet human needs.

If you were to look at my income tax forms for the past few years, you'd see an interesting pattern. Our local church receives regular support. But a greater percent of our giving is directed to ministries like Prison Fellowship, which minister directly to the powerless in our society. And some goes to nondeductible and even "secular" causes.

Certainly at the very least this important passage in Deuteronomy gives us fresh insight into the loving heart of our God. And perhaps cause to stop and evaluate the way we worship Him with our giving.

Personal Application
In what ways do you show your reverence for God on weekdays?

Quotable
"Piety cannot consist of specific acts only, such as prayer or ritual observance, but is bound up with all actions, concomitant with all doings, accompanying and shaping all life's business. Man's responsibility to God is the scaffold on which he stands as daily he goes on building life. His every deed, every incident of mind, takes place on this scaffold, so that unremittingly man is at work either building up or tearing down his life, his home, his hope of God."—Abraham Heschel

FEBRUARY 9 *Reading 40*
SERVING GOD
Deuteronomy 16:18–18:22

"Be sure to appoint over you the king the LORD your God chooses" (Deut. 17:15).

It is a very special calling to serve God as a leader of His people. When we are called by God to be a leader, He will guide our paths.

Definition of Key Terms

Prophet. The prophet in Israel was God's spokesperson, a man or woman commissioned to deliver messages from God. The role of prophet was not hereditary. God called and commissioned individuals as He chose, from any of Israel's tribes.

Though prophets foretold events that were to take place in the distant future, the prophet's primary ministry was to the people of his or her own generation. The prophet provided divine guidance for special situations, at times to individuals, but usually to those who ruled God's people.

Deuteronomy 18 is the key biblical passage dealing with the Old Testament prophet. It gives the criteria to be used by Israel in recognizing a spokesman for God. The true prophet will be an Israelite (v. 18). The true prophet will speak in the name of the Lord, not another god (v. 20). And what the true prophet predicts will take place or come true (v. 22).

Overview

A variety of leaders were to serve Israel under God, the nation's King (16:18–18:22). These included local judges (16:18-20), a supreme court composed of priests (17:8-13), a king (vv. 14-20), and the entire priesthood (18:1-8). When Israel required special guidance, God would provide it through prophets (vv. 14-22).

Understanding the Text

"Appoint judges . . . in every town" Deut. 16:18-20. There was no national police force in ancient Israel. Elders of good reputation in each community were to serve as judges. The judges were to determine the facts in legal cases and then apply Moses' Law to fix any penalties.

This first paragraph about those who serve God and His people rightly focuses on the character of the judges. We see the same thing in New Testament guidelines for selection of Christian leaders (1 Tim. 3; Titus 1). Character is more important than gift as equipment for spiritual leadership.

Character was important because judges must show no partiality and accept no "bribe." The word translated "bribe" can also be translated "gift." This injunction reflects the ancient and modern Middle Eastern practice of giving gifts to those from whom a person expects favors. The gift is not spoken of as a bribe, but the giver feels that he has a special relationship that merits favors from the person who receives it.

No "special relationship" was to exist in the covenant community. The judge's sole commitment is to be to justice.

"Purge the evil from among you" Deut. 16:21–17:7. Some wonder why "religious" laws are inserted here, in a section dealing with human leadership. The reason? God is Israel's Sovereign, the Ruler from whom human leaders derive their authority. If Israel should abandon God, the whole structure of authority would crumble. So Israel was not to set up any symbols of pagan worship, such as an Asherah pole or *massebot* (sacred stone). Israel was to honor God by bringing only the best to Him in sacrifice.

Complete commitment to God is so vital that any Israelite proven to have worshiped pagan gods or goddesses was to be stoned to death.

"Cases . . . too difficult for you to judge" Deut. 17:8-13. Priests at the central sanctuary were expected to have an in-depth understanding of the divine Law. Thus they were to serve as an authoritative supreme court and decide cases local elders could not resolve. The priest's decision was final, and had to be accepted. However, the decision had to be carefully explained and be rooted in the Law (v. 11).

We need to respect our leaders too. But leaders remain obligated to make decisions based on the Word of God, and are responsible to explain the biblical principles on which those decisions are based.

"Let us set a king over us" Deut. 17:14-20. It would be several hundred years after entering Canaan before Israel petitioned for a king. Then that request would be wrong, for two reasons. First, God was Himself Israel's King. The request for a human king reflected a lack of trust in God. Second, Israel was intended to be different from all other nations. The motive, to "be like the nations around us," implied abandonment of Israel's calling.

Yet this passage has a special and wonderful message for us. God used even rejection for His glory and mankind's good. When God's own Son entered the human race, He was born of Israel's royal line. Jesus, both God and man, has been exalted as King of kings and Lord of lords.

God's ability to weave Israel's failures into His plan should encourage us. Each of us will sin at times, as Israel did. When we do, let's remember God's grace. Let's ask Him to forgive us. And remember that God remains able to transform failure into good.

"He is to read it all the days of his life" Deut. 17:18-20. Israel's request for a king would reveal a spiritual flaw in God's people. God would still rule His people through that human king. But the king must be fully committed to God.

Four special rules for rulers are given. The king was to be "from among your own brothers." Only one of God's covenant people could rule the covenant community. The king was not to "acquire great numbers of horses." He had to depend on God rather than on military might. The king was not to "take many wives." In biblical times marriages between royal houses typically sealed treaties between nations. Taking many wives implied this practice, which would (and in Solomon's case did!) introduce paganism into the royal house itself. The king was not to "accumulate large amounts of gold and silver." The king was to rule for the benefit of his people, not for self-aggrandizement.

These rules have direct application to spiritual leaders today. Spiritual leaders must be true believers, must rely fully on God, must be completely committed to God, and must care more about the people they serve than any personal gain.

▶ DEVOTIONAL
God Surely Will Guide (Deut. 18:9-22)

When Karen came to Ron, an elder in our church, she was frustrated. She had an important decision to make. And her friends all gave her conflicting advice. So Karen decided to come to church and ask Ron to tell her what to do.

No specific "thou shalt" or "thou shalt not" applied. So Ron showed her several Bible passages with principles that might apply. Finally he told her to pray and ask Jesus what she should do.

Angrily Karen burst out, "But you're the elder. You're supposed to *tell* me what to do."

All of us have times when we feel a need for special guidance—for someone to tell us what to do. In the ancient world people commonly turned to sorcery or divination, or cast spells, in a search for supernatural guidance. Some moderns do the same thing, turning to palm readers, spiritists, or astrology. In this passage Israel is bluntly informed that such practices are "detestable." God's people are not to engage in any of them (vv. 9-14).

Then immediately, God made a promise. Yes, situations will arise which are not covered by Scripture. Yes, there *will* be times when people need special, supernatural guidance. But, God said, then "I will raise up for you a prophet."

God made a commitment. He Himself would provide any special guidance His people might need through prophets. Israel would never need to look to any source but God.

Karen was furious when Ron wouldn't tell her what to do. Ron explained that God has given His Holy Spirit to each believer. Karen needed to pray about her situation and let God Himself guide her. "I'm not God," Ron explained. "I don't know God's best for you, but He does. And if you listen, God will show you what to do."

Karen stayed angry for two days. But finally she decided to do what Ron said. Later she came back, excited. God *had* guided her, and she had found a solution neither she nor any of her friends had thought of. Ron, as a good servant of Jesus Christ, had helped another person learn that she truly could depend on God.

Personal Application

God has given you His Spirit too. You can look directly to God for guidance today.

Quotable

"Trust in the LORD with all your heart and lean not on your own understanding; in all your ways acknowledge Him, and He will make your paths straight."—Proverbs 3:5-6

FEBRUARY 10 *Reading 41*

HONORING GOD

Deuteronomy 19:1–21:14

"Make its people an offer of peace" (Deut. 20:10).

Human life is precious to God. Even in cases where the taking of life is permissible—in executing a murderer and in war—God's people are to honor the Lord by showing respect for life.

Definition of Key Terms

Murder. Hebrew makes a distinction between personal killings *(rasa')* and the general act of taking life *(harag).* Murder and manslaughter are *rasa',* while a judicial execution or killing in warfare is *harag.* A number of additional words are also used in describing slaughter in war.

It is important to understand that the commandment, "Thou shalt not kill," takes a stand against *rasa',* a personal rather than judicial or military killing.

Deuteronomy 19 deals with *rasa',* and chapter 20 deals indirectly with *harag.* Whether intentional or unintentional, *rasa'* is sin. But only intentional personal killings—what we would call first-degree or premeditated murder—merits the death penalty. As these chapters teach, imposing the death penalty on a murderer is not wrong, but required. One circumstance even required Israel to engage in wars of extermination.

Old Testament laws do not deal with all the issues raised by those who decry the death sentence, or those who take a pacifist stand on war. Yet these laws do make important distinctions we need to understand to discuss such issues intelligently. These laws do show that Israel was to honor God by showing unusual respect for human life.

Overview

Detailed regulations required Israel to honor God by respecting human life. Cities of refuge had to be established to protect those who committed accidental homicide (19:1-14). Strict rules of evidence governed all criminal cases (vv. 15-21), just as strict rules had to be followed in making war (20:1-20). Unsolved murder called for cleansing (21:1-9). Women captives were to be treated with unusual care and respect (vv. 10-14).

Understanding the Text

"Build roads to them" Deut. 19:1-3. Old Testament Law called for the establishment of cities where a person who killed another accidentally might be safe. The phrase "build roads to them" is significant. God wanted nothing to hinder or delay any person's flight to safety.

You and I are responsible to see justice done in our society. But we are also responsible to "build roads" that will guard the innocent.

"In a rage" Deut. 19:4-13. In Israel a near relative of a murder victim was responsible to execute the killer. Understandably such a person, a son or brother or father, might be angry enough to kill without waiting to check circumstances. The cities of refuge were established so that a person who killed another accidentally might be safe while the killing was investigated. If it truly was an accident, as in the illustration provided in verse 5, the killer could remain in the city of refuge until the current high priest died, and then return home. But if investigation showed the killing was intentional, then the elders of the city of refuge were to "hand him over to the avenger of blood to die. Show him no pity."

This law reflects the precious nature of human life. No amount of money, no possible penalty, can replace the life that has been taken. The death penalty affirms to the entire community the supreme value God places on a single human life.

"Do not move your neighbor's boundary stone" Deut. 19:14. The boundaries of family land were marked by stones in biblical times. Why is this law placed here in a discussion of life and death issues? Possibly because of the connection between a family's means of support—its land—and life itself.

The command not to murder establishes the significance of human life. It stands forever as a barrier to any act which in any way, directly or indirectly, might threaten the well-being of another human being. Christians today need to take a stand for laws that promote justice, as well as to call for the punishment of wrongdoers.

"One witness is not enough to convict" Deut. 19:15-21. In any criminal matter two or three witnesses were required to establish guilt. The judges were also to carefully examine the witnesses. Justice is so important that a lying witness must pay the penalty not of lying, but the penalty established for the crime about which he or she lied. Strict justice is required, that "the rest of the people will hear of this and be afraid, and never again will such an evil thing be done among you."

The surest way to promote crime is to fail to punish criminals.

"When you go to war" Deut. 20:1-9. Early Israel had no standing army. Instead a militia of citizens reported when the nation was threatened or went to war.

Biblical law granted humanitarian exemptions, and anyone who was afraid was sent home "so that his brothers will not become disheartened." These exemptions reflected a belief in God which Israel's priests were to proclaim before every battle. Victory did not depend on the size of Israel's army, but on God. "The LORD your God is the one who goes with you to fight for you."

Whenever you or I feel small and powerless, this is an important principle to remember. Neither our strength, nor that of the foe, is at issue. The issue is whether or not the Lord goes with us.

"When you march" Deut. 20:10-18. The passage makes an important distinction. When Israel went to war against an enemy outside the boundaries of Canaan, its armies were to invite surrender. Only if the enemy city resisted was the army free to kill and plunder. However, within Canaan, Israel was commanded to "completely destroy" foreign settlements. The reason is clearly stated. "Otherwise, they will teach you to follow all the detestable things they do in worshiping their gods, and you will sin against the LORD your God."

"Do not destroy its trees" Deut. 20:19. No parallel exists in the rules of war of other ancient nations. Only Israel was to preserve fruit trees when attacking a walled city. This law does more than reflect God's concern for all people. It shows that to Israel the ideal state was one of peace, not war. The Assyrians and Babylonians and other ancient world powers thrived on war and thought nothing of the devastation they caused. Only in Israel was peace to be the nation's first concern.

"If . . . it is not known who killed him" Deut. 21:1-9. The whole covenant community was responsible to enforce God's Laws. If a killer was unknown, the elders of the nearest town were to break the neck of an animal representing the killer, symbolizing their willingness to carry out the penalty God required. They then publicly announced ignorance of the killer's identity before priests, who represented the Law itself. This ceremony purged the land of guilt for shedding "innocent blood."

The ceremony portrays again the fact that in Old Testament Law the whole community of faith was responsible for the conduct of individual members.

"You may take her as your wife" Deut. 21:10-14. Ancient armies were noted for rape and pillage. But God's Law replaced rape with marriage. A change of clothing and cutting off of the captive woman's hair symbolized separation from her nation and adoption into Israel. She was then given time to mourn the loss of relatives, and when taken became a wife, not a

slave (v. 13). If for any reason a divorce took place, the woman was to be given her freedom rather than treated as a slave. Rules of warfare in other ancient nations recovered by archeologists show much more brutal treatment of captive women.

▶ DEVOTIONAL
Road Builders
(Deut. 19)

"I heard this rumor about you," my caller said. "And I just wanted to check it out for myself."

I really appreciated his phone call. I'd heard the story was going around, and laughed at it. I'm far from faultless, but this tale was ridiculous. The only trouble was that people who heard it kept on repeating it as if it were true. Ultimately a lot of Christian brothers and sisters heard the story, believed it, and repeated it. Yet this caller was the first—and only—person who ever bothered to check out the facts with me personally.

After a while the story died out. It wasn't true in the first place. And God guarded my ministry, so the rumor hadn't really hurt me. But the incident reminds me how much more eager we Christians are to grab a hatchet and take off after someone suspected of wrong—like modern avengers of blood—than we are to pick up our hatchets to build roads so the innocent can find their way to a city of refuge. Yes, let's punish the guilty. But let's make sure that no one who is innocent suffers unjustly.

So what are we to do when we hear about a supposed fault or problem in a brother or sister's life? Deuteronomy 19 suggests several road-building principles.

First, delay before you repeat a rumor. An Old Testament city of refuge was first of all a place where a person could find temporary refuge while his case was being investigated.

Second, check the facts. It's not enough to remain silent. Confront the one who told you the rumor. Where did he get his information? How does he know it is reliable? If the rumor is being repeated without personal knowledge of the facts, confront the person who told you. It is sin to testify falsely against anyone.

Third, if the rumor persists, speak to the person who is accused. He or she has a right to know what is being said and a right to be heard.

In no way are Christians to clear the guilty or to ignore sin. But rumor, gossip, and false accusation are evils to be purged from the believing community.

Personal Application

"Do this so that innocent blood will not be shed in your land."—Deuteronomy 19:10

Quotable

"He that accuses all mankind of corruption ought to remember that he is sure to convict only one."—Edmund Burke

FEBRUARY 11 *Reading 42*
OBEYING GOD
Deuteronomy 21:15–26:19

> *"The LORD has declared this day that you are His people, His treasured possession as He promised, and that you are to keep all His commands" (Deut. 26:18).*

Old Testament Law touched on every aspect of the Israelites lifestyle, showing that God was intimately involved in all of the believer's life on earth. Many of the laws in this section are notable for the concern they express for individuals.

Definition of Key Terms

"If . . . then." Many of the laws here are causistic in form: they apply general moral principles by looking at specific cases. The cases then became precedents, and were used to guide rulings when similar cases came before Jewish courts.

Overview

Laws touching on many aspects of Israel's life in the land are grouped in this section. Included among miscellaneous rulings are blocks of laws dealing with family (21:15-

21), marriage (22:13-30), and religious ritual (26:1-19).

Understanding the Text

"A stubborn and rebellious son" Deut. 21:18-21. There is no record of parents turning a son over to local judges for execution. But the case establishes several important legal principles.

First, this case underlines the importance of a stable family, for the family was the basic religious and economic unit in Israel. Other laws also stress the importance of honoring parents (cf. Ex. 20:12; 21:15, 17; Lev. 20:9), as did Jesus (Mark 7:10).

Second, parents did not have absolute rights over their children. In Roman law the father could order the death of a son. In Israel a parent could only punish. Only the judges of the community, who were charged with determining a son's guilt or innocence, could order execution.

Third, both father and mother must agree to bringing charges against a son. The rights of the wife and mother, ignored in many other ancient law codes, were affirmed in Israel.

Family is basic to us too. While nothing we parents can do will guarantee that our children will make godly choices, moms and dads share responsibility for giving boys and girls discipline and guidance.

"You must not leave his body on the tree overnight" Deut. 21:22-23. In ancient societies the bodies of executed criminals were often hung in the open as an object lesson to others. In Israel exposure was limited to a single day, for "anyone who is hung on a tree is under God's curse." Paul applies this to Jesus in Galatians 3:13, to show that Jesus truly became accursed in order to free us from the curse of the Law (i.e., the Law's demand that sin be punished).

"Do not ignore it. Help him" Deut. 22:1-4. A person who finds another's lost property is obligated to return it or care for it until the owner can be found. In Exodus 23:4-5 the obligation to help is extended to enemies.

Jesus applied this principle to answer an "expert in the Law" who challenged him to define the "neighbor" that Old Testament Law requires a person to love as himself. In His story of the Good Samaritan, Jesus showed that our "neighbor" is anyone in need whom we have the ability to help.

"A woman must not wear men's clothing" Deut. 22:5. Both men and women wore similar robes in Old Testament times. But cut and decorations were different. The injunction here does not, as some have thought, prohibit women from wearing slacks. What it does is to affirm the value of both sexes, and call for male and female to affirm their sexual identity by their dress rather than dress to deny that identity.

"When you build a new house, make a parapet around your roof" Deut. 22:8. Houses in Israel had flat roofs. An outside stairway led up to the roof, which was used by family and friends as a gathering place for talk and for work. This law, an extension of the commandment not to kill, requires building a low wall around the rooftop area. God's "do not" here and in other Old Testament case law is transformed into an active "do" that captures its deepest meaning.

You and I too are to actively promote the welfare of others, rather than simply do them no harm.

"Proof of her virginity" Deut. 22:13-19. Traditionally this law has been taken to indicate blood on the marriage bed showing that a girl's hymen was broken. But *betulim* here may mean "adolescence" rather than "virginity." So it is better to understand the "evidence" as a cloth used during menstruation. The young bride's menstrual flow was proof that she was not pregnant when married, as well as evidence that she had reached marriageable age.

"Sleeping with another man's wife" Deut. 22:22-30. Several laws dealing with adultery, seduction, and rape underline the importance of sexual fidelity. The pagan nations around Israel maintained a casual attitude toward sex. Our modern "playboy" view of sex as innocent fun is hardly new!

Biblical laws remind us that God's people are called to purity. Sex is to be an important part of life, but of married life. Sex is to be sacred to believers, an expression of intimacy and caring that is appropriate only within the context of marriage.

"If a slave has taken refuge with you" Deut. 23:15. The Code of Hammurabi condemned a man who hid a runaway slave to death. In Israel a slave fleeing from a foreign owner was to be given refuge and not to be oppressed because he had been a slave.

The Scripture's view of the value of human beings and how that value is affirmed is dramatically different from the view held by other ancient societies.

You and I need to be careful how we "label" others. Race, creed, religion, education, position, wealth—all these are unimportant. What counts is that each person is precious to God and is to be respected by us.

"Do not charge your brother interest" Deut. 23:19-20. Archeologists have found documents from cultures contemporary with the Old Testament that state interest rates. Some laws limited the rates that could be charged, but 15th-century contracts found at Nuzi, in northern Assyria, record interest rates of 50 percent!

The principle here is clear. We are to help those in need, not oppress them further for our own profit. The slumlord who charges high rent for substandard housing is in clear violation of the principle underlying this Old Testament regulation.

"Her first husband . . . is not allowed to marry her again" Deut. 24:1-4. Divorce and remarriage were permitted in Israel, even though they involve failure to achieve God's ideal of lifelong, monogamous relationship. This particular law, however, sets one clear limit. A person who has been divorced, remarried, and divorced again cannot marry his or her first spouse a second time.

It's likely that the purpose of this law is to strengthen the second marriage by making it impossible for a remarried spouse to return to his or her first marriage partner.

Divorce is never God's ideal. And marriage is not to be treated so lightly that it becomes little more than a game of musical chairs. We are to do everything possible to maintain and strengthen marital commitment.

"Not even the upper one" Deut. 24:6. It was common in Israel for a lender to hold some object owned by a borrower as security for a loan. This law mentions millstones, used daily by every Israelite family to grind the grain for making bread, to establish another principle. Nothing could be done by a lender which would limit the borrower's ability to make a living or to maintain his own life.

Modern law applies this principle when it protects the family house and car when a person files for bankruptcy.

The law reminds us of God's concern for each individual. Every person has a right to the resources needed to make a living and to support a family. When we limit the opportunities of some in society, we in effect take away their upper millstone.

▶ DEVOTIONAL
Ways of Worship
(Deut. 26)

"Let's sing that chorus again!"

I can get very enthusiastic singing choruses. (I have a loud voice.) And I enjoy informality in worship services. Once I might even have argued that only the spontaneous and informal could accurately represent corporate worship. If I ever did argue that case, I now confess that I was wrong.

What convinces me is the frequent inclusion in the Old and New Testaments of worship liturgy: words and phrases that were repeated by worshipers. This chapter contains a liturgy used at the Festival of Firstfruits, and a liturgy used when delivering tithes to the local storehouse every third year. Each includes affirmations that remind the worshiper just why he or she is appearing before the Lord, and who the Lord is to him.

If you attend a church that is rich in liturgical expression, join in thoughtfully. Listen to the words of your liturgy as though hearing them for the first time. Declare them from your heart. For liturgy can and often does capture in succinct and powerful form the basic realities of our faith.

Personal Application
The Apostles' Creed is one of the most ancient of Christian affirmations. If you do not know it, why not memorize it now?

Quotable
"I believe in God the Father Almighty, maker of heaven and earth: and in Jesus Christ His only Son, our Lord; who was conceived by the Holy Spirit, born of the Virgin Mary, suffered under Pontius Pilate, was crucified, dead, and buried; He descended into hades; the third day He rose again from the dead; He ascended into heaven, and sitteth on the right hand of God, the Father Almighty; from thence He shall come to judge the quick and the dead. I believe in the Holy Spirit; the holy catholic church; the communion of saints, the forgiveness of sins; the resurrection of the body, and the life everlasting."—The Apostles' Creed, A.D. 140

FEBRUARY 12 *Reading 43*
DISOBEYING GOD
Deuteronomy 27–28

> *"Cursed is the man who does not uphold the words of this Law by carrying them out" (Deut. 27:26).*

A basic principle of the Law Covenant is that obedience brings blessing; disobedience, punishment. How important it is that we understand the tragic consequences of our failure to obey God.

Overview
Moses and the elders gave instructions for building an altar when they entered the Promised Land (27:1-8). Directions were given for giving blessings and curses from Mount Ebal (vv. 9-26). Blessings for obedience (28:1-14) and curses for disobedience (vv. 15-68) were given.

Understanding the Text
"Build there an altar to the LORD" Deut. 27:1-8. This command is the last of the covenant stipulations stating what the people must do. The laws in chapters 21–26 list practices to be followed faithfully by future generations. This chapter calls for a ceremony to be performed once: a ceremony in which God impressed on Israel the utter necessity of obedience. By that ceremony the people of Israel indicated their complete acceptance of God's Law and the consequences of disobedience.

The altar and sacrifices made on it confirmed the official acceptance of God's Laws by that generation.

You and I need to be sure that our chil-

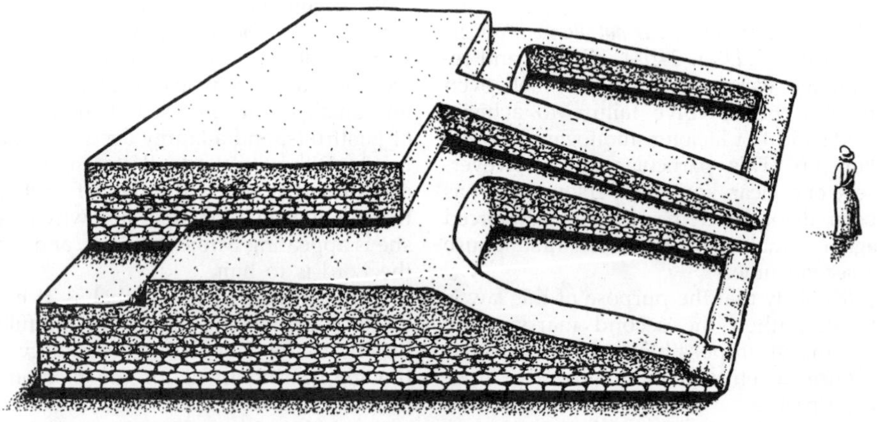

Remains of a massive altar have been found by archeologists on Mount Ebal. The illustration shows how the altar looked when it was first constructed.

CAUSE FOR CURSING

The sin	*Deut. 27*	*Parallel Passages*
Make idol	27:15	Deut. 4:16; 5:8; Ex. 20:23; Lev. 19:4; 26:1
Dishonor parents	27:16	Deut. 21:18-21; Ex. 21:15; Lev. 20:9
Move landmark	27:17	Deut. 19:14
Lead astray	27:18	Lev. 19:14
Withhold justice	27:19	Deut. 10:18; 24:17; Ex. 22:21; Lev. 19:33
Sex sin	27:20	Deut. 22:30; Lev. 18:6-8
Bestiality	27:21	Ex. 22:19; Lev. 18:23
Incest	27:22-23	Lev. 18:9-17; 20:14, 17
Murder	27:24-25	Ex. 21:12, 29; 23:7

dren understand the consequences of wrongdoing. When we have spelled out consequences, we have a clear basis on which to punish and correct.

"Cursed is the man" Deut. 27:9-26. Twelve violations sum up laws contained not only in Deuteronomy but also in earlier books of Moses. The chart on this page lists parallel passages.

The people were to shout "Amen!" to the recitation of each of these curses. There could be no confusion. Israel knew the Law and accepted responsibility for obeying it.

"If you fully obey" Deut. 28:1-14. The blessings promised to Israel for obedience focus on security and prosperity within the Promised Land. The Christian has no similar commitment from God. Rather we're told that God *has* "blessed us in the heavenly realms with every spiritual blessing in Christ" (Eph. 1:3).

Spiritual blessings assure us of God's loving presence in our lives, and that "in all things God works for the good of those who love Him, who have been called according to His purpose" (Rom. 8:28).

"If you do not obey" Deut. 28:15-68. Three groups of curses are found here. Verses 15-46 warn that if Israel disobeys, the nation will experience poverty rather than prosperity. Verses 47-57 warn that if Israel disobeys, the nation will live under constant threat of foreign invasion. Verses 58-68 warn that persistent disobedience will result in Israel being torn from her land and hurled among the nations. There God's people will find no rest, but only "an anxious mind, eyes weary with longing, and a despairing heart."

As many have pointed out, this chapter previews what actually did happen to Israel. First the Assyrians and Babylonians scattered God's people. Later Rome crushed those who had regathered in the Holy Land. Only today is there a sign of a regathering of scattered Israel in her ancient homeland.

When the prophets shouted out their warnings to rebellious Israel, they based many of their predictions on the divine program revealed in this critical Old Testament chapter. The fulfilled predictions of disaster remind us that no one can sin safely. God, directly or through the natural consequences following our actions, will punish sin.

▶ DEVOTIONAL
The "Now" Generation (Deut. 28:15-68)

A recent article in the St. Petersburg newspaper stated that while it takes an average of 8 to 10 years to experience the full destructive power of alcohol abuse, the person who starts taking crack cocaine will find his life ruined in six to eight *months!* Yet according to the paper, crack is epidemic in St. Petersburg, attracting users from every strata of society.

I'm not really surprised. We Americans have increasingly become a nation of people who demand instant gratification. We want our pleasures *now.* Tragically, few seem concerned whether getting them involves doing right or wrong, or whether the pleasures we demand will help or harm us in the long run.

Somehow, to many people, only the present seems important. The future, shaped by the consequences of present choices, seems too unreal to consider at all.

Perhaps this is why Deuteronomy gives four times as much space spelling out consequences of disobedience as describing blessings the obedient can expect. People have always tried desperately to ignore the future. We are not the first to pretend that sin is irrelevant and that today's choices will carry no consequences over into tomorrow.

I suspect that some would be a little upset with God for spending so much time painting such a dark picture. But actually, this passage reminds me of how gracious God is. He understands our human tendency to choose pleasure without considering tomorrow. By spelling out the dark consequences of wrong choices in terrible detail, God compels us to face reality.

No one can sin safely. No one can sin impudently. No one can escape the consequences of his acts for long.

Personal Application

Live a righteous life today, and tomorrow will take care of itself.

Quotable

"The wages of sin is death—thank God I quit before payday."—Reamer Loomis

FEBRUARY 13 *Reading 44*
CHOOSING GOD
Deuteronomy 29–30

> *"I set before you today life and prosperity, death and destruction" (Deut. 30:15).*

The most significant choice any human being can make is the choice between life and death; between loving and serving God, and ignoring Him.

Definition of Key Terms

Covenant. The Hebrew *brit* is a flexible term used of a variety of legally binding agreements. Between nations a *brit* is a treaty. Between individuals it can be a contract. God even used one familiar covenant form to confirm His promises to Abraham.

In ancient times *brit* was also used to describe the formal relationship between a ruler and his subjects. This passage of Deuteronomy follows the format used in the second millennium B.C. to state just such a relationship. It is in this "constitutional" sense that "covenant" is typically used in Deuteronomy, and especially here.

These two chapters are in essence a review of Deuteronomy 1–28. Israel had heard Moses' lengthy explanation of the relationship God, as King, intended to have with His people. Now, perhaps a few days later, Moses briefly reviewed the covenant that would serve as Israel's national constitution, and called on the people to commit themselves to it and to God.

Overview

Moses summarized God's covenant with Israel. He reviewed God's saving work (29:1-9) and His call to covenant relationship (vv. 10-15). Moses warned of curses on rebels (vv. 16-29) but stated God's intention to ultimately restore Israel (30:1-10). In view of this, Moses called for a firm commitment to the Lord (vv. 11-20).

Understanding the Text

"Your eyes have seen all that the LORD did" Deut. 29:2-9. Israel's relationship with God was initiated by saving acts. When the people were helpless, slaves in a foreign land, God performed "miraculous signs and great wonders" to free them. The most powerful motive the Israelites can have to commit themselves to God is to remember what He has already done for them.

It's the same with you and me. God doesn't ask for blind faith or commitment to the unknown. The God who calls for our commitment has acted in Jesus to save us from the power and the penalty of sin. We know His love through Jesus' death for us, and His power through Jesus' resurrection. Is it really safe to commit ourselves completely to God? In view of all He has done for us, we can answer with full assurance—yes!

"You are standing today in the presence of the Lord your God" Deut. 29:10-15. Hundreds of years earlier God had made a promise to Abraham, Isaac, and Jacob to be their God and the God of their children. He had confirmed the initial promise to Abraham in a legally binding covenant-making ceremony (cf. Gen. 15:8-16). This early covenant was still in force, stretching on through the centuries, giving each generation of Israelites a special relationship with God.

The Covenant of Law, proposed at Sinai, was God's way of showing the Israelites how each generation could experience the blessings of relationship with the God who was already committed to them.

The issue facing the Israelites who stood before Moses in that "today" was simple. Would they commit themselves to the God who was already committed to them?

The issue is very much the same for us today. God has executed His New Covenant of love in Jesus. Christ's death on the cross and His resurrection are proof of God's irrevocable commitment to you and me. The only question left, which each of us must face in our own "today," is, will we commit ourselves fully to Him?

"I will be safe, even though I persist in going my own way" Deut. 29:16-29. I was converted while in the Navy. I started a noon Bible study and began to put up Bible verses on the bulletin board near the office coffeepot. These stimulated a number of conversations and some debate. One of the big arguments my friends had against my new faith was, "Hey, if you're saved, you go to heaven no matter what, right? Then you can do whatever you want, and it's OK? That just can't be right."

I tried to explain that a person who knows Jesus loves God. It is love for God, not fear of Him, that keeps Christians from sinning. My cynical Navy buddies just couldn't accept that. If *they* knew they could get away with doing whatever they wanted to do, everyone figured he'd overdose on sin.

I suspect that, while my answer was right, I might deal with the question a little differently today. Perhaps as Moses dealt with Israel. We can't look at all God has done for us and decide that it means, "I will be safe, even though I persist in going my own way." Going our own way is *never* safe. It is a prescription for disaster.

For Israel, failure to commit to the God of the Covenant meant calamity. The land would become a burning waste; the people would stagger because of disease and foreign enemies. For us, a similar failure means life on a spiritual desert, with no sense of God's presence, no experience of divine guidance, no comfort or assurance, and the likelihood that our choices too will lead to disaster.

"Even if you have been banished . . . the Lord your God will gather you and bring you back" Deut. 30:1-10. A survey of Bible history shows that many generations of Israelites did turn from God to idolatry. The disasters Moses predicted happened, including exile from the Promised Land. But, as Moses made plain, God remained committed to His people. Disobedient generations experienced disaster, but their disobedience did not void God's promises to Abraham.

You and I can sin. But the door is always open for us to return to God. We can claim the promise made to Israel so long ago. "When you and your children return to the Lord your God and obey Him with all your heart . . . then the Lord your God will restore your fortunes" (vv. 2-3).

▶ DEVOTIONAL
"I Do"
(Deut. 30:11-20)

Perhaps the best analogy to the commitment God asks us to make to Him is the wedding ceremony. The wedding comes as the culmination of months (or better, years) of gradually coming to know another person. In time friendship blossoms into love, or initial attraction deepens into appreciation. Then each person realizes,

"I want to spend my life with this individual!" Then the two plan a wedding—a ceremony to announce to one and all that two people have decided to cleave only to each other, for better or for worse, in sickness and in health, till death do them part.

Yet it's fascinating. That ceremony, the culmination of so many young women's dreams, isn't an end but a beginning. It is the beginning of a lifetime of acting on the decision that the ceremony marked. It is the start of a lifetime of making choices shaped by the fact that at a particular point in time, two people stood side by side and committed themselves to one another. For then. And forever.

It's just this kind of ceremony that is in view in Deuteronomy 30. Moses calls on the new generation to make a life-shaping decision. Moses calls on Israel to make a commitment to God, to choose life with Him, and then to carry out that commitment the rest of their lives.

As Moses says, the life this commitment calls for "is not too difficult for you or beyond your reach." That life is spelled out in the word God has given us, a near word, in our mouths and in our hearts. Make and keep this commitment, Moses promised, and "you will live and increase, and the LORD your God will bless you." Hold back or turn away, and "you will certainly be destroyed."

We Christians need to realize that our initial relationship with Jesus is intended to grow and deepen to the point at which we too realize, "I want to commit my life to this Person who loves me." That realization may come in church, in response to a pastor's call. It may happen in the privacy of your own room, reading devotional literature like this book. When the realization does come, then you too have a decision to make. Will I commit myself fully to God, realizing that this decision will shape my choices for the rest of my life?

Perhaps Moses himself gives us the most compelling reason to make that commitment now. "This day," he says, "I call heaven and earth as witnesses against you that I have set before you life and death, blessings and curses. Now choose life, so that you and your children may live and that you may love the LORD your God, listen to His voice, and hold fast to Him. For the LORD is your life, and He will give you many years in the land He swore to give to your fathers, Abraham, Isaac and Jacob" (vv. 19-20).

Personal Application

If you have not made a specific commitment to love and obey God, why not make it now?

Quotable

"Most high, glorious God, enlighten the darkness of my heart and give me, Lord, a correct faith, a certain hope, a perfect charity, sense, and knowledge, so that I may carry out your holy and true command."—Francis of Assisi

---

FEBRUARY 14 *Reading 45*

MOSES' FAREWELL

Deuteronomy 31–34

"I am now a hundred and twenty years old and I am no longer able to lead you" (Deut. 31:2).

Each of us leaves a heritage behind when we reach the end of our lives. Moses left a glorious heritage: a generation prepared for victory, a Law for Israel to live by, and the memory of the God who keeps His promises.

Overview

God would be with Israel's new leader, Joshua (31:1-8). The Law was to be read to all Israel every seventh year (vv. 9-13), but God predicted future rebellion (vv. 14-30). Moses taught them a unique song, in the form of a judicial indictment, to encourage obedience (32:1-47). Just before his death (vv. 48-52), Moses blessed the tribes of Israel (33:1-29). An unknown author later added Moses' epitaph (34:1-12).

Understanding the Text

"I am now a hundred and twenty years old" Deut. 31:2. In Egypt, 110 was the symbolic

age of wise men. Like Moses, those who base their lives on relationship with God are wiser than this world's wisest.

It's fascinating to remember that Moses was 80 when he was first called to serve God. The last third of Moses' life was the most productive spiritually. Old age isn't the end for any of us, though persons who found great satisfaction in their jobs often feel this way. The time we once devoted to work can now be devoted to serving God and others.

"The LORD your God goes with you" Deut. 31:3-8. Moses presented Joshua as Israel's new leader and reminded the people that it was the Lord who had won past victories and who "goes before you."

It's only natural for us to depend on human leaders. But such dependence is misplaced. God, not Moses, was the key to past triumphs. Let's respect our leaders, but let's depend only on the Lord.

"Moses wrote down this Law and gave it to the priests" Deut. 31:9-13. It seems likely that what Moses delivered to the priests was the bulk of the Book of Deuteronomy. This book was to be read to the whole nation—"men, women and children, and the aliens living in your towns." The reading was to be done at the Feast of Tabernacles every seventh year, "as long as you live in the land."

All have a right to know and to understand what God says to us in the Scriptures.

"I know what they are disposed to do" Deut. 31:14-29. Despite commanding that the Law be faithfully and regularly taught to Israel, God told Moses that dark days were ahead. Israel would "soon" turn to idolatry and "break the covenant I made with them."

God knew "what they are disposed to do, even before I bring them into the land" (v. 21). The Hebrew word, *yeser,* ("purpose") here means a tendency, impulse, or disposition. The revelation of this tendency may come as a surprise, for under Joshua the Israelites obeyed God. In fact, their behavior was exemplary. But God, who knows the heart, saw the inner tendency toward sin despite outward obedience.

You and I need to be sensitive to our hearts. That tendency toward sin still exists within us. We can be in great danger even when there is no sign of faltering in our outward behavior. Jesus once explained His criticism of certain Pharisees who were extremely strict in their approach to God's Law: "These people honor Me with their lips," He said, "but their hearts are far from Me" (Mark 7:6). Only wholehearted love for God can guard us against our tendency toward sin.

"Moses recited the words of this song" Deut. 31:30–32:47. The Israelites were expected to memorize this lengthy "song," or poem. In cultures where reading and writing are less common, memorization of extremely long poems, legends, treaties, etc., is quite common.

This fascinating poem follows what is known today as the "RIB pattern." The Hebrew word, *rib,* means a controversy or a legal suit. The song was in effect God's indictment of Israel for breaking the covenant with Him as Sovereign.

What is striking is that the poem then went on to add material that is not found in ancient secular indictments! God assured Israel that though "they are a nation without sense" He would indeed have compassion on them (vv. 26-38). God would deliver Israel once again and free them from their enemies (vv. 39-43).

The *rib* pattern of the poem shows its ancient origin, for it fits comfortably into the culture existing in Moses' day. But the variation from that pattern is most important to us. Those who angered secular rulers perished. The statement which expressed the punishment due to covenant-breakers ended the indictment. But even when we sin and deserve judgment, punishment is not God's last word. His last word to us as to Israel is one of grace. We too can be restored.

We too can come back, and once again worship our God as a forgiven people.

"This is the blessing that Moses . . . pronounced" Deut. 33:1-29. The final blessing pronounced by a dying father was viewed as a will in the ancient Near East, and was legally binding. The blessing of Moses, Israel's spiritual father, contained elements of prophecy. The po-

etic blessings in these chapters are sometimes obscure but are based on traits of the tribal patriarchs and on God's revelation concerning their future. The blessings contain prayers, predictions, praise, and

GOD'S INDICTMENT OF ISRAEL

A statement of God's character	(vv. 1-4)
Implied accusation of Israel	(vv. 5-6)
Recalling God's acts for Israel	(vv. 7-14)
Specific charges against Israel	(vv. 15-18)
The sentence	(vv. 19-25)

commands. The emphasis of each blessing is shown below.

Reuben	A prayer for survival.
Judah	A prediction of victory.
Levi	A prayer for blessing, a call to faithfulness.
Benjamin	A promise of safety.
Ephraim	A promise of preeminence.
Manasseh	A prediction of strength.
Zebulun	A prediction of wealth.
Issachar	A prediction of wealth.
Gad	A promise of land.
Dan	A prediction of energy.
Napthali	A promise of blessing.
Asher	A prayer for strength and security.

The range of blessings predicted again shows that God desires the very best for His people. Yet, as this magnificent psalm of blessing concludes, we need to remember that the most important gift God can give is already ours—Himself. As Moses said, "the Eternal God is your refuge, and underneath are the everlasting arms."

▶DEVOTIONAL
Moses' Epitaph
(Deut. 34)

One of the unusual privileges I've had is to serve as chaplain to my family. Though ordained, I've not pastored a church. So most of the weddings I've performed, and all of the funerals, have been for family.

To date I've buried my mother, my dad, a stepmother, an uncle, and an aunt. Each time I've thought back over their lives, I've found something that made that person special. Each one of my relatives was very different from the others. But in each life God had done something beautiful. Something to remember that honored Him, and made the memory of our loved one more precious.

Then, after Moses' death, an unknown editor added an epitaph. He described the words God spoke to Moses (vv. 1-4), and the grief felt by Israel (vv. 5-8). He added a word about Joshua to show that life goes on (v. 9). And then he concluded with an epitaph intended to show what was special about Moses. "Since then, no prophet has risen in Israel like Moses, whom the LORD knew face to face, who did all those miraculous signs and wonders the LORD sent him to do in Egypt" (vv. 10-11).

Moses was special. And he deserved this epitaph as well as our awed respect. But what moves me most has been to realize, as one by one the members of my own family die, that every one of us is special.

When God enters a life, He takes at least one trait of ours and makes us beautiful.

Personal Application

What trait of yours will your family members remember with greatest joy?

Quotable

"Enjoy your life without comparing it with that of others."—Marques De Condorcet

The Variety Reading Plan continues with JOHN

Joshua

INTRODUCTION

The book takes its name from Joshua, who replaced Moses as Israel's leader. Moses had led the people of Israel out of Egypt to the border of the land God promised to give Abraham's descendants. Joshua commanded the forces that would conquer Canaan. The Book of Joshua tells the story of that Conquest and covers a period from about 1400 to 1375 B.C.

This is the first of several books that give Israel's national history from the time of Joshua to the Babylonian Conquest in 586 B.C. It is also a book with a message. Canaan is God's gift to His people. But that gift can only be claimed and held by obedience. Disobedience assures defeat.

Old Testament Overview
Israel as a Nation

PENTATEUCH	*HISTORY*	*PROPHETS*
I Origins	II Possession	III Dispersion
Genesis– Deuteronomy	Joshua–Judges 1–2 Samuel 1–2 Kings 1–2 Chronicles	Isaiah, other prophetic voices
To the land	In the land	From the land

OUTLINE OF CONTENTS

READING GUIDE (5 Days)

If hurried, you may read only the "core passage" in your Bible and the Devotional in each chapter of this Commentary.

Reading	*Chapters*	*Core passage*
46	1–5	2
47	6–8	6
48	9–12	10
49	13–21	19:49-51
50	22–24	24

Joshua

FEBRUARY 15 *Reading 46*
READYING FOR CONQUEST
Joshua 1–5

> *"Be strong and very courageous. Be careful to obey all the Law My servant Moses gave you; do not turn from it to the right or to the left, that you may be successful wherever you go" (Josh. 1:7).*

Sensing God's presence gave Joshua and the Israelites the courage they needed to move ahead. That same sense of "God with us" is the key to our spiritual victories today.

Background
When Israel invaded Canaan around 1400 B.C., the land was populated by a number of different peoples, organized in relatively small city-states. Yet many of the cities were protected by massive walls. The people were used to war, and some states maintained war chariots, the tanks of the ancient world. Though the city-states were independent, and had often warred with each other, cities in the north and south united to resist their common enemy, the Israelites.

Overview
God encouraged Joshua, Moses' successor (1:1-9). Joshua mobilized Israel to prepare militarily (v. 10–2:24) and spiritually (3:1–5:15) for the invasion of Canaan.

Understanding the Text
"As I was with Moses, so I will be with you" Josh. 1:5. Joshua had been the aide of Moses from the beginning. He led Israel's army from the first (cf. Ex. 17:9-13), a fact that has led some to suppose that Joshua had served as an officer in the Egyptian army. This is possible, as Egyptian texts listing soldiers with Semitic names have been recovered by archeologists. More important, Joshua was one of the original spies sent into Canaan some 40 years before. At that time only he and Caleb urged Israel to invade, sure that God could guarantee victory despite the military superiority of the Canaanites. Thus Joshua's credentials, both as a military and spiritual leader, were well established.

Perhaps, however, the greatest advantage Joshua had was to have served under Moses. He observed both that humble man's commitment to the Lord, and God's commitment to Moses. When God promised, "As I was with Moses, so I will be with you," those words must have brought great assurance.

Each of us needs a relationship with someone who can serve as a model. We each need to see in others both faithfulness to God, and God's faithfulness to them.

"Be strong and courageous" Josh. 1:1-9. Note particularly God's repeated words of exhortation and encouragement.

Exhortation	*Encouragement*
Be strong, courageous	I will be with you
Be careful to obey	I will give to you
Meditate on the Book of the Law	I will never leave
	I will never forsake
Be careful to do it	You will prosper, and succeed
Do not be terrified	God will be with you wherever you go
Do not be discouraged	

In just these few verses, Scripture sums

up the way to victory in any situation we may face.

"Get your supplies ready" Josh. 1:10-18. Joshua took immediate steps to prepare Israel militarily. His first step was to have the people check their supplies and organize for a river crossing. The people prepared too—by agreeing to obey Joshua as their commander.

The next step that Joshua took was to send spies to check out Jericho.

"Everyone's courage failed" Josh. 2:1-24. Jericho was a walled city that controlled passes leading up into Canaan's central highlands. Two spies who slipped into the city were sheltered by Rahab, a prostitute who very likely, as was quite common in those days, operated an inn. Rahab hid the spies and asked them to spare her life when Israel took the city.

The New Testament looks back on Rahab's act and commends her for this act of faith. James says, "Was not even Rahab the prostitute considered righteous for what she did when she gave lodging to the spies and sent them off in a different direction?" (2:25)

The incident shows us that in Old Testament times as well as today people of any nationality who trusted God could find salvation. It also reminds us that our past does not stand in the way of a personal relationship with God. It was not the good life Rahab had lived that saved her, but her active faith in Israel's God.

"The LORD will do amazing things among you" Josh. 3:1-17. The first element in Israel's spiritual preparation for the Conquest was clear evidence of God's continuing presence. This evidence was provided when the river waters ceased flowing as soon as the priests who carried the ark of the covenant set foot in the river.

Joshua displayed faith in announcing ahead of time that this would happen. When it happened as he said, Israel's confidence in both God and Joshua deepened.

God often gives us some special sign of His presence when we set about a difficult task. It's not wrong to ask God to encourage us with an answer to prayer, or some other sign of His presence.

"These stones are to be a memorial to the people of Israel forever" Josh. 4:1-24. The Hebrew word for "memorial" is *zikkaron.* This is a technical theological term for a thing, place, or repeated event intended to serve as a vivid reminder of some act of God on behalf of His people. For instance, the Passover festival was a *zikkaron.* Those who shared the Passover meal relived the experience of the Exodus generation. Each family sharing that meal realized that

Joshua commanded one man from each tribe to bring a large stone from the Jordan riverbed to Israel's campsite. The 12 stones were then heaped in a pile. That heap of stones served as a *zikkaron,* a permanent reminder to Israel that God parted the waters of the Jordan so His people could enter the land.

God had delivered *them,* not just their ancestors.

The heap that Joshua formed from the 12 stones taken from the Jordan River was to be a symbol to future generations. When "in the future" children ask, "What do these stones mean?" parents were to tell the story of how God caused the river to stop flowing. Touching and feeling these stones would help make history—and God—real to future generations.

Note Joshua's words of dedication when the heap of stones was set up at Gilgal. God had dried up the river as He earlier dried up the Red Sea, "so that all the peoples of the earth might know that the hand of the LORD is powerful and so that you might always fear the LORD your God" (v. 24).

"These were the ones Joshua circumcised" Josh. 5:1-9. Male circumcision is cutting off the flap of skin that covers the penis. During the years of wandering in the wilderness, the Israelites failed to circumcise their children, as they failed to obey other commands of the Lord. Now, before setting out on the Conquest, God told Joshua to have the Israelites perform this rite. Modern medicine has shown circumcision to have a number of health benefits. But in Israel it served a religious rather than public-health purpose. Circumcision was given the descendants of Abraham as a sign of their participation in the covenant of promise that had been given to him.

Among the promises given Abraham was a commitment to free Abraham's descendants from slavery and to give them "this land . . . the land of the Kenites, Kenizzites, Kadmonites, Hittites, Perizzites, Rephaites, Amorites, Canaanites, Girgashites and Jebusites" (Gen. 15:7-21). Circumcision, at this critical juncture in history, was an act of faith claiming God's ancient promises.

While the Book of Joshua stresses obedience, that obedience was rendered by those who had a faith relationship with God. Circumcision speaks of faith, not Law. Only the person with faith in God has any claim to His aid.

"The Israelites celebrated the Passover" Josh. 5:10. This was the final act of spiritual preparation: remembering God's provision.

When we put the sequence together we find a prescription for spiritual readiness: Sense God's presence. Set up reminders. Reaffirm faith. And celebrate what God has already done.

"The manna stopped" Josh. 5:10-12. From now on Israel would live by faith, not sight. The manna now ceased. No fiery pillar would lead. Daily, visible evidence of God's presence would be absent for the first time in the memory of many of the Israelites. Yet the people under Joshua would trust and obey God. Seen or unseen, God is with His people. We can trust Him to lead us to victory.

▶ DEVOTIONAL
When Knowing Isn't Enough (Josh. 2)

Rahab's confession was stunning. "The LORD your God is God in heaven above and on the earth below."

This pagan woman, a prostitute, had heard how the Lord dried up the water of the Red Sea. She'd heard of Israel's victory over kings east of the Jordan. And she had drawn a simple conclusion.

"The LORD your God is God."

What's even more striking is Rahab's report, "When we heard of it, our hearts sank and everyone's courage failed." All the people of Jericho had the same information. And all of them drew Rahab's conclusion. "The LORD your God is God."

The difference is that the people of Jericho decided to hold out anyway, while Rahab determined to commit herself to the God of the enemy.

I suspect that many today who are not believers share the conviction of the people of Jericho. They too know that "the Lord your God is God." But somehow they remain enemies. They erect walls, not of stone, but of good works, of excuses, of ridicule, of belief in evolution, or even of religion, and desperately try to hide behind them. They know. But knowledge alone cannot save.

Rahab teaches us the difference between knowing God as an intellectual act and knowing God personally. What Rahab did was to act on her knowledge that "God is." Rahab was willing to commit herself completely to God, sure that otherwise she had no hope.

How good to have made Rahab's choice. How good to have made our knowledge of God a stepping-stone to a decision to trust ourselves to Him. How good to know that we too are now safe.

Personal Application
How might the story of Rahab help a friend or relative who knows, but hasn't yet chosen to trust God?

Quotable
"God is more anxious to bestow His blessings on us than we are to receive them."
—St. Augustine

FEBRUARY 16 *Reading 47*
VICTORY, THEN DEFEAT
Joshua 6–8

> *"When the trumpets sounded, the people shouted, and at the sound of the trumpet, when the people gave a loud shout, the wall collapsed; so every man charged straight in, and they took the city" (Josh. 6:20).*

Obedience to an obviously foolish command brought Israel victory and taught a vital lesson. The key to winning is doing *everything* God's way.

Definition of Key Terms
Devoted. The Hebrew word is used of items which are dedicated to God, and thus cannot have any common or secular use. When the Israelites "devoted" an enemy city to God, they killed all its inhabitants and herds, and either burned all its wealth or brought it to the tabernacle as a gift to God. In this passage Jericho, the first of the pagan cities of Canaan to be attacked by the Israelites, was so devoted. This meant that no soldier was to take any loot for himself, a proscription which one man, Achan, defied with terrible consequences.

Overview
Israel obeyed God's command and successfully assaulted Jericho (6:1-27). But the sin of one soldier, Achan, caused defeat at Ai (7:1-21). Achan was executed (vv. 22-26). With the sin purged, Ai was taken (8:1-29). A solemn religious ceremony reminded Israel to keep God's Law (vv. 30-35).

Understanding the Text
"March around the city" Josh. 6:1-27. Jericho was a walled city. Excavations there reveal that its fortifications featured a stone base wall 11 feet high. At its top was a smooth stone slope, angling upward at 35 degrees for 35 feet, where it joined massive stone walls that towered even higher.

In ancient warfare such cities were surrounded and starved into submission, or were taken by assault. The attackers might try to weaken the stone walls with fire or by tunneling. Or they might simply heap up a mountain of earth to serve as a ramp. Each of these methods of assault took weeks or months, and the attacking force usually suffered heavy losses.

God's command to Joshua—to have the people march silently around Jericho for six days, and then after seven circuits on the seventh day to shout—was strange indeed. Yet Joshua followed His instructions to the letter. When the people did finally shout, the massive fortifications crumbled, and Israel won an easy victory.

The victory at Jericho was orchestrated to teach several lessons. Most important was that obedience, even when God's commands seem foolish, brings victory. The miraculous victory also confirmed Joshua's leadership. And it showed that God would surely fight for Israel in the battles ahead.

Each of us needs a Jericho at times. But Jericho victories are won only when obedience is complete.

"Joshua spared Rahab the prostitute" Josh. 6:25. Rahab's belief in Israel's God, shown when she hid two Israelite spies (Josh. 2), was rewarded. She and her family were spared when Jericho fell.

God still singles out believers when nations fall. See Ezekiel 18.

"They were routed by the men of Ai" Josh. 7:1-9. Ai, a small city above Jericho, defeated the 3,000 men Joshua set against it, killing 36 of the Israelites. The defeat panicked Joshua. As a good general, Joshua knew that a terrified army had little chance on the battlefield. Victory at Jericho had led to Joshua's "fame [being] spread through the land" (6:27). Joshua feared that news of the defeat at Ai would give heart to the Canaanites, and that they would unite and crush Israel.

Fear is never very far from any of us. Even when we have experienced God's blessing, as Joshua had, we're prone to forget if some setback comes. Looking back and remembering what God has done for us brings comfort. Looking ahead and worrying about what might happen is both foolish and useless.

"Israel has sinned" Josh. 7:10-21. When Israel was defeated at Ai, Joshua foolishly focused on the possible consequences. His prayer (vv. 7-9) clearly reveals his panic and worry about what might lie ahead. God's next words to Joshua put a new perspective on the situation. "Israel has sinned." Joshua was not to worry about possible *consequences* of defeat, but to look for the *cause* of defeat. Why Israel lost the battle was far more important than what the loss might mean in terms of enemy morale.

When we experience a setback, it's better for us too to look for the cause than to worry about consequences. If we examine ourselves and find no known sin, then we can advance with confidence. If we do find sin, even unintentional sin, we need to deal with it immediately.

In this case, Joshua apparently used the Urim and Thummim worn by the high priest to locate the man who had sinned. That man, Achan, then confessed to taking loot from Jericho even though he knew the city was devoted to God. The cause of the defeat was known. The sin then had to be dealt with.

"All Israel stoned him" Josh. 7:22-26. Some have expressed shock that Achan's theft merited the death penalty. But it was not for theft that Achan was stoned. His sin had caused Israel's defeat and the deaths of 36 men at the hands of the enemy. Achan was stoned because he "brought this disaster" on his people.

This event reminds us of an important reality. Anytime we sin we affect others. Like a stone tossed in a quiet pond, the ripples of human sins go on and on, disturbing not only our own peace but also the peace of others. Before we sin knowingly we should pause and consider how our act might affect others who love or depend on us.

But why was the family of Achan also stoned? Perhaps the best answer is seen in Achan's confession that he hid his plunder "inside my tent." The rest of the family shared his guilty secret, and thus became responsible as well.

"I have delivered into your hands the king of Ai, his people, his city and his land" Josh. 8:1-29. With the cause of Israel's defeat dealt with, God granted His people total victory over Ai. The city with its people were wiped out, fulfilling God's command to either drive out or destroy all the Canaanites, whose idolatry and other sins merited this punishment.

"Joshua built on Mount Ebal an altar" Josh. 8:30-35. After the victory at Ai Joshua fulfilled a command given by Moses (Deut. 27). He set the people on two opposing mountainsides, and after sacrificing to the Lord had them shout aloud the curses (disastrous consequences) of disobeying God's Law.

How powerfully that message was driven home to the men and women who had experienced defeat at Ai, had participated in stoning Achan, and had then seen defeat transformed into victory.

▶ DEVOTIONAL
Perspective
(Josh. 6)

Imagine yourself standing on the wall at Jericho. Put your hands on one of the massive stones in that wall, lean out, and look down from the dizzying height. Then look out and watch those crazy Israelites. For six days they've marched, without a word, around your city.

The first day, when you saw them coming, you and all your friends were terrified. You remembered all the stories about them and their God, and you trembled. When they didn't mount an assault, but just walked silently around your six-acre fortress, everyone was worried. You all sat up most of the night, talking, wondering what their plan was.

Then, the next day, they did the same thing. The third day they marched around Jericho you began to feel a little better. Maybe there wasn't a plan, after all. The fourth day, everyone felt relieved. You patted the walls, felt the solid rock, and began to feel safe. The fifth day, and the sixth, everyone was feeling bold. You began to shout insults. You laughed and ridiculed. Of course you were safe! How could anyone break through Jericho's walls? How could you all have been afraid of this band of barbarians, these desert wanderers who lived in tents, who had no idea at all how to attack a fortress like yours!

And so the fear you once felt turned to relief, and the relief to contempt. Those crazy Israelites. Let them march all they want. What can they do to you? Nothing! Nothing at all.

I suspect that Christians often look foolish to the people of the world. We march to a different drummer. We obey the commands of a hidden God. In a real sense we're outsiders, not insiders. It's not surprising if we seem a little ridiculous to the people of this world.

If you ever feel foolish for a stand you take as a Christian, remember that today is only the first day, or the third, or the sixth, of your march around Jericho. It's not until the seventh day comes, and this world crumbles like Jericho's walls, that those who have truly been foolish will be revealed.

Personal Application

No matter what others think, it is never foolish to obey God.

Quotable

"What else do worldlings think we are doing but playing about when we flee what they most desire on earth, and what they flee, we desire? We are like jesters and tumblers who, with heads down and feet in the air draw all eyes to themselves. . . . Ours is a joyous game, decent, grave, and admirable, delighting the gaze of those who watch from heaven."
—Bernard of Clairvaux

FEBRUARY 17 *Reading 48*
TOTAL VICTORY
Joshua 9–12

"So Joshua took the entire land" (Josh. 11:23).

The Bible says that Joshua waged war against Canaan's kings "for a long time" (11:18). God never said victory was easy. He only promises that victory is sure.

Definition of Key Terms

Destroyed. These chapters repeatedly speak of destroying completely, or totally destroying, Canaanite cities and all their inhabitants. The reasons for this policy need restating. (1) The Canaanites were a wicked people whose religion and morals were corrupt. The war and its devastation were a direct divine judgment on the Canaanites for their sins. (2) The Israelites were called to a holy lifestyle. Any Canaanites left in the land would (and did!) corrupt Israel religiously and morally. The destruction of the Canaanites was intended as protection for God's people.

Joshua's victories were complete, but he did not in fact exterminate all Canaanite peoples. Each Israelite tribe was to "mop up" any Canaanites left in the territory given to it. The failure of succeeding generations to carry out the divine policy of extermination led to the spiritual and national disasters that policy was intended to avoid.

One final note. The various peoples who settled in Canaan represented larger populations than existed in other lands. God's command to exterminate was limited to those living in Canaan, and did not involve extermination of an entire race.

Overview

The Gibeonites tricked Joshua into a peace treaty, which Israel honored (9:1-27). In a series of brilliant campaigns Joshua first crushed the southern (10:1-43) and then the northern (11:1-23) city-states of Canaan. The section concludes with a list of conquests (12:1-24).

Understanding the Text

"The men of Israel . . . did not inquire of the L*ORD" Josh. 9:1-27.* The story of how the Gibeonites, who lived just a few miles from the Israelite camp, tricked Joshua into making a treaty is especially instructive.

First, it reminds us of the importance of prayer. The Israelites examined the moldy bread and sour wine the Gibeonites presented as evidence that they lived outside of Canaan, and accepted their story without inquiring of the Lord. While you and I are to examine situations carefully before making decisions, we can't rely on the evidence of our senses alone. We need to make important decisions a matter for prayer.

Second, when the Israelites realized they had been tricked, they honored the "treaty of peace" they had made with the Gibeonites. Israel had made an oath and committed themselves. The fact that they were tricked did not invalidate the promise. We need to honor our word because we have given it. Whether others prove faithful or not, we are to be true to our commitments.

Finally, God redeemed Israel's mistake. The next chapter tells us that when other city-states in Canaan attacked the Gibeonites, Joshua came to the Gibeonites' aid and struck the exposed enemy armies. When we are faithful, God can use even our mistakes to accomplish His purposes.

"Five kings of the Amorites" Josh. 10:1-28. Five ethnically related kings of cities in Canaan's hill country joined forces to punish the Gibeonites for making peace with Israel. Joshua responded immediately to a plea for help and, after an all-night march, surprised the Amorite forces.

This was a great strategic victory, for the Amorite armies were caught in the open, outside the walls of their cities, where they could be more easily crushed.

God's intervention for Israel is seen in two circumstances. Hailstones killed many of the enemy. And the "sun stopped in the middle of the sky and delayed going down about a full day" so the slaughter of the Amorites could be completed.

"So Joshua subdued the whole region" Josh. 10:29-43. The defeat of the Amorite forces left their southern strongholds undefended. Joshua immediately turned his forces southward, and crushed the major cities in that region.

"They came out with all their troops . . . a huge army" Josh. 11:1-23. The northern city-states joined forces and gathered a huge army, which included a large chariot force. Josephus reports that this army had 300,000 foot soldiers, 10,000 cavalry, and 20,000 chariots!

The word "suddenly" describing Joshua's attack may intimate what happened. In biblical times chariots, often a decisive weapon in battle, were disassembled for transport over hills to the battlefield, and were reassembled there. It is possible that Joshua attacked the enemy before the chariots could be put back together and deployed.

Whatever element of tactics was involved, "the LORD gave them [the enemy] into the hand of Israel." We are to fight wisely, but the outcome of the battle is still entirely up to the Lord.

"Hamstring their horses and burn their chariots" Josh. 11:6. Why was Joshua told to destroy the captured war material of the enemy? Most likely because Israel was to depend on God, not on military strength. Because Joshua did depend on God, this command was obeyed.

"These are the kings of the land" Josh. 12:1-24. Most scholars believe that the Conquest, described so graphically in these chapters, actually took about seven years to accomplish. When total victory had finally been won, Joshua carefully listed the 31 Canaanite city-states that he defeated. Israel could look back on this impressive list and be encouraged. God, who had promised victory, had kept His word. Surely God could be trusted for victory in battles yet to come.

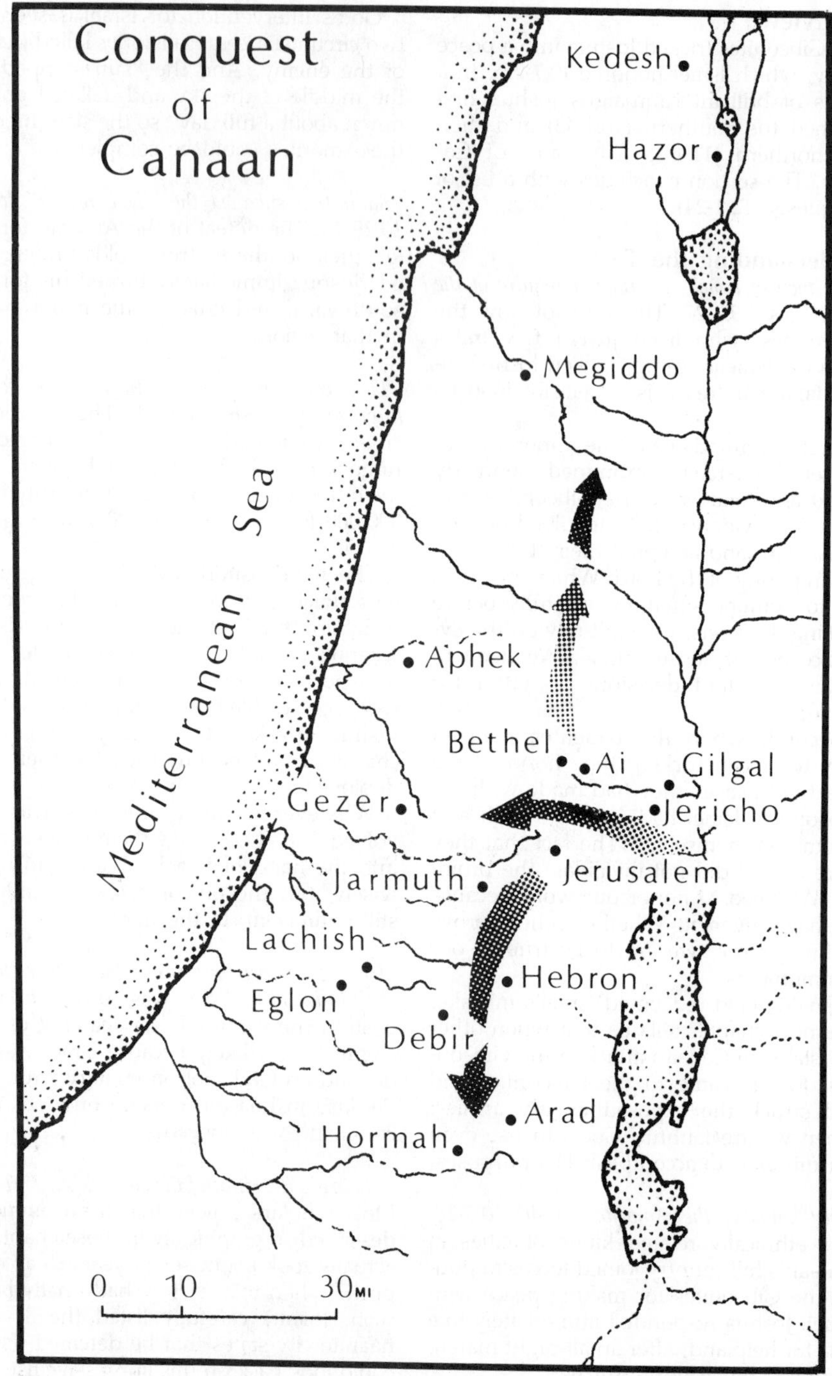

In a series of brilliant campaigns Joshua first conquered central Canaan, splitting the land in two. (1) He then turned south and subdued that region. (2) Finally he attacked and crushed major northern strongholds. (3) His divide-and-conquer strategy, his tactics of all-night marches and surprise attacks, are still studied in modern military academies.

▶ DEVOTIONAL
The All-Night March (Josh. 10)

I remember all too well how she used to sit there at the table, waiting for God to act. "I really want to serve God," she'd say. And I think she meant it. But even when opportunities came—an invitation to teach a Bible study, a call from a friend who asked her to visit—she'd wait. "I can't do anything on my own," she'd say. "I have to wait till God tells me to go. I have to wait till I see Him act."

Of course, my friend had never met Joshua. Or watched Joshua put his faith into action. If she had, she might have been surprised. Joshua wasn't the kind of person to wait around. Yes, he knew how important it was to listen for and to obey God's voice. But Joshua also knew that in most situations a person has to use ordinary judgment.

That's what happened when Joshua received word from Gibeon that a combined Amorite force was attacking their city. Joshua didn't say, "I'd better wait till God acts." He got his army together, commanded an all-night march, and the next morning took the enemy by surprise. And then God intervened, joining in the battle by hurling hailstones on the Amorites and by causing the sun to stand still. Joshua's all-night march had put him in the very place he needed to be for God to act.

Sometimes we're unrealistic in our expectations. We sit still and want God to act for us. The fact is that God usually acts only after we have demonstrated a faith like Joshua's. It's after that all-night march, when the battle is joined, that God acts.

So the next time you have an opportunity to serve—to teach a class, to counsel a friend—don't wait. Seize the opportunity. And expect God to act when you're actually serving. That's the place you need to be for God to work through you.

Personal Application

When opportunities to serve come, take them!

Quotable

"You can measure what you would do for the Lord by what you do."—T.C. Horton

FEBRUARY 18 *Reading 49*
ALLOTMENT OF THE LAND
Joshua 13–21

> *"Their inheritances were assigned by lot" (Josh. 14:2).*

The Bible says, "So the LORD gave Israel all the land He had sworn to give their forefathers" (21:43). The struggle may be long. But the fruit of victory is sweet.

Definition of Key Terms

Allotment. The land was distributed by casting lots. We would say "throwing dice." No chance was involved, for God Himself governed the fall of the lots (cf. Prov. 16:33). This method was also used within the tribes to determine each family's holdings. From this point on, each Israelite saw his family farm as a gift given him directly by the Lord. The family land was not to be sold, but to be treasured forever as a heritage from God.

In Psalm 16:6 David used the imagery of allotment to express appreciation for the role God had given him in life. As we contemplate God's goodness to us in Christ, David's words might well become our own. "The boundary lines have fallen for me in pleasant places; surely I have a delightful inheritance."

Overview

Joshua listed land occupied east of the Jordan (13:1-33). He carefully described territory occupied by the nine and a half remaining tribes in Canaan proper (14:1–19:51). Cities of refuge were established (20:1-9), and the Levites were given cities within the borders of the other tribes (21:1-45).

Understanding the Text

"Still very large areas of land to be taken over" Josh. 13:1. The power of the Canaanites

had been broken by the power of united Israel. But there were still pockets of resistance in each area allotted to the various tribes.

The Israelite population was not large enough to fill the whole land. Each tribe was responsible to take additional land as its population grew.

"I, however, followed the LORD my God wholeheartedly" Josh. 14:1-15. Among the lists of tribes and cities a very personal story is nestled. Caleb was 1 of the 12 spies who had scouted Canaan some 45 years earlier (cf. Num. 13–14). Only he and Joshua had urged Israel to trust God and invade Canaan then. Now, at 85, Caleb still actively trusted God. He asked for a parcel of land still occupied by an especially warlike people, the Anakites, and confidently said, "The LORD helping me, I will drive them out just as He said."

One of the gifts God gave me as a young Christian was the privilege of being in a church where the older men were models of just the kind of faith Caleb had. How fortunate we are to know the Calebs of today. Too often we tend to segregate older believers from our young. Yet the young people in our churches need to be exposed to godly older men and women.

"They . . . did not drive them out completely" Josh. 17:13. Despite victory, indications of future disaster appeared among the tribes of Israel.

There was disobedience. When the population of Manassah grew, the tribe subdued several Canaanite towns in its territory. But rather than drive these people out as God had commanded, the Manassites enslaved them.

There was a failure to trust. When challenged to take the extra land the tribal members claimed they needed, they responded, "All the Canaanites who live in the plain have iron chariots" (v. 16). Despite the unbroken record of military victories won with God's aid, iron chariots blocked this tribe's vision of God.

Past spiritual victories are no guarantee our faith will remain strong. We need to concentrate each day on obeying and trusting God.

"Flee to these designated cities" Josh. 20:1-9.

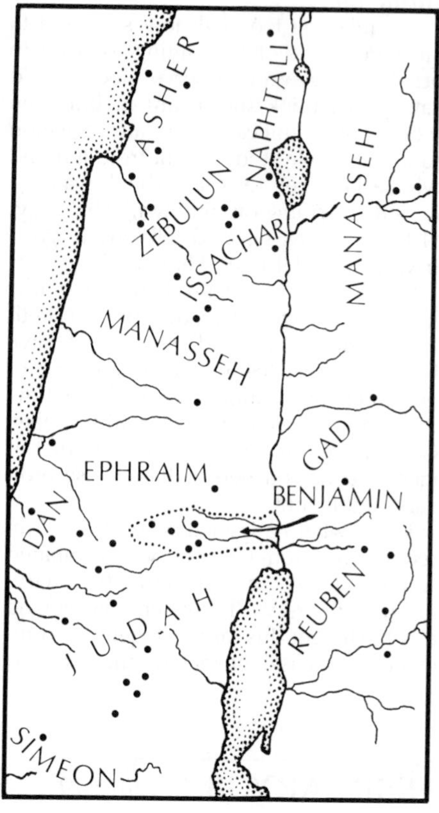

Joshua 20. The towns given priests and Levites were scattered through territories given the other Israelite tribes. The priests and Levites had been commissioned to teach God's Law. Every family in Israel was to be near to those who could instruct them in God's ways.

This is the third major passage on the cities of refuge, to which someone who killed another person accidentally might flee (cf. Num. 35; Deut. 19). A general principle of biblical interpretation is that anything repeated twice is very significant. Here we have a topic that is treated at length in three Old Testament passages. This clearly shows the importance God places on protecting the innocent when dealing with criminal matters.

We need to be careful that in our concern for justice we do not violate the rights of the innocent.

▶ DEVOTIONAL
Time to Let Go
(Josh. 19:49-51)

It's hard to imagine Joshua relaxing under an olive tree or tending vines on a terraced hillside behind his house. He's such an active and dynamic person. Neither generals nor spiritual leaders seem to be candidates for retirement.

Still, with the victories won and the land divided, Joshua settled down on his own inheritance. The Bible says he received the town of Timnath Serah, and "built up the town and settled there."

Actually, Joshua's retirement wasn't simply a well-merited reward for his decades of exemplary service. Joshua was retired for the benefit of Israel! Why?

When the people of Manasseh needed more land (Josh. 17), they hurried to Joshua and complained. Joshua told them, "Clear land for yourselves." The Manassites argued, fearful because the Canaanites had chariots of iron. They wanted Joshua to fight their battles for them. But Joshua wisely said, "Though the Canaanites have iron chariots and though they are strong, you can drive them out."

That last phrase is the key. "*You* can drive them out." It was time for Israel to stop depending on Joshua and to step out on their own. Manasseh, and all the other tribes, needed to trust God for themselves.

Joshua's wisdom in retiring is a lesson each of us needs to apply. We need to apply it as our children grow up, and especially when they leave home. We can encourage them. But we need to stop doing everything for them.

Counselors need to apply the lesson in their relationship with counselees. Spiritual leaders need to apply it in their relationship with a congregation, an organization, or with disciples. There comes a time when each of us needs to step down and tell those we have nurtured, "*You* can drive them out. It's time for me to retire. And time to learn what God can do for and through *you*."

Personal Application

In what relationships do you need to retire and let others be responsible for themselves?

Quotable

"When God contemplates some great work, He begins it by the hand of some poor, weak, human creature, to whom He afterwards gives aid, so that the enemies who seek to obstruct it are overcome."—Martin Luther

FEBRUARY 19 *Reading 50*
COMMITMENT
Joshua 22–24

> *"As for me and my household, we will serve the* Lord*" (Josh. 24:15).*

The first half of the Book of Joshua revealed what it took to conquer the land of Canaan. These chapters tell us what it will take to hold the Promised Land.

Definition of Key Terms

Serve. Joshua frequently called on Israel to serve God. The Hebrew word suggests a servant or slave. Its basic meaning is to perform tasks according to the will and direction of another. Serving God in Old Testament times did mean to worship Him. But it also meant to obey Him in all things.

Overview

The three eastern tribes erected an altar symbolizing solidarity with the Israelites in Canaan (22:1-34). Joshua addressed the leaders (23:1-16) and challenged the assembled tribes to serve God (24:1-27). Joshua died and was buried (vv. 28-33).

Understanding the Text

"You have not deserted your brothers" Josh. 22:1-9. Three tribal groups had asked for and received land east of the Jordan River. They had, however, promised Moses that their fighting men would join the other tribes for the war in Canaan. These tribes served faithfully, and were then sent home.

This concluding section of Joshua is filled with exhortations. The admonition given the eastern tribes is typical: "Be very careful . . . to love the LORD your God, to walk in all His ways, to obey His commands, to hold fast to Him and to serve Him with all your heart and with all your soul."

"An imposing altar there by the Jordan" Josh. 22:10-34. This story shows how easy it is to misunderstand another person's actions. When the returning tribes built an altar by the Jordan, their brothers interpreted it as an act of apostasy. God had commanded that sacrifices be made only on the altar that stood before the tabernacle. The Jordan altar seemed to the other tribes to be an act of rebellion against the Lord, and they were ready to go to war with their eastern brethren rather than risk divine punishment (vv. 19-20).

The eastern tribes explained to the delegation sent to them. They did not intend to use the Jordan altar for sacrifice. It was symbolic of the common racial and religious heritage they shared with the people west of the Jordan. By building the altar according to specifications given in the Law, the distinctive construction would provide evidence of the common heritage.

Both groups acted wisely in dealing with this issue. The western tribes decided to talk before acting. The easterners didn't take offense, but instead humbly explained what they had done.

It's good to remember the example of both groups when we become upset by something another person or group has done. Before we accuse, we need to go to the persons involved and talk about what has happened. And if anyone misunderstands an act of ours, rather than be upset, we need to be humble and willing to explain.

"Elders, leaders, judges and officials" Josh. 23:1-16. Joshua spoke separately to Israel's leaders, who would be most responsible to see that God's people continued to serve the Lord. Note the pattern of Joshua's remarks. He begins with a promise, moves on to exhortation, and then concludes with a reminder and warning.

The promise: God who had driven out the enemy would continue to push them out before them.

The exhortation: Be strong, be careful to obey God's Law, do not associate with pagan nations or their gods, and hold fast to the Lord.

The reminder: God has driven out the enemy, just as He has promised.

The warning: If you turn away from God, the Lord will no longer drive them out. What is more, "the LORD's anger will burn against you."

These four functions aptly sum up the responsibility and the ministry of most in spiritual leadership today—including parents. We are to live by and to communicate God's promises. We are to be faithful and to exhort faithfulness. We are to remember what God has done and to remind others. We are to be aware of and to warn others of the consequences of turning away from the Lord.

"The LORD drove out before us all the nations" Josh. 24:1-18. Joshua then spoke to all the people, and in essence made a case for commitment. He reviewed all that God had done. In one of the most famous of Old Testament affirmations of faith, Joshua expressed his own commitment: "As for me and my household, we will serve the LORD" (v. 15).

Joshua could make this commitment for himself. He could not make it for others. But Joshua could and did confront, making sure that each family in Israel realized that commitment was necessary.

The people recognized the validity of the case Joshua had made. The Lord *had* "brought us . . . up out of Egypt, from the land of slavery." And God had driven out the enemy. "We too will serve the LORD," the people said, "because He is our God."

"He is a holy God" Josh. 24:19-27. Joshua has made a case for commitment. Now he makes clear the cost of commitment.

A person who commits himself or herself to the Lord must make a *total* commitment. We can make no halfway covenant with the Lord.

Even when confronted with the cost of commitment, the people insisted that they would serve the Lord.

Verse 23 indicates two ways that complete commitment is demonstrated. (1) "Throw away the foreign gods that are among you." We are to keep nothing in our lives that might compete with God for our loyalty. (2) "Yield your hearts to the LORD, the God of Israel." We are to willingly surrender to the Lord everything we have and are.

"This stone will be a witness" Josh. 24:27. A witness is one who can testify to what he or she has seen and heard. At times inanimate objects were commissioned as witnesses to words of commitment (cf. Gen. 31:52; Deut. 31:21). Spoken words are binding. They are as permanent as the place in which they are spoken.

▶ DEVOTIONAL
The Present Time
(Josh. 24)

There's a wonderful epitaph for Joshua recorded here. "Israel served the LORD throughout the lifetime of Joshua and of the elders who outlived him."

Joshua made his case for commitment. Joshua clarified the price of commitment. Joshua provided an example of commitment. And throughout his lifetime the people of Israel faithfully served the Lord.

About this time someone is likely to object and point to what happened after Joshua died. It's true that after these few bright decades God's people deserted Him. For some 400 years during the Era of Judges, Israel knew cycles of brief revival and deepening apostasy. Yet what happened during those centuries had nothing to do with Joshua.

The New Testament puts it this way. "The present time is of the highest importance" (Rom. 13:11, PH). What that verse points out is that the only time you or I have is the present. We can't change the past. We can't control the future. But we can live for God in our today.

That's just what Joshua did. He served God as long as he lived. And, in his day, Israel served God.

You and I have no guarantee of what will happen to our children, our grandchildren, or our great grandchildren. Actually, that isn't our concern. We can't control the future. All you and I can do is follow Joshua's example of personal commitment and so influence those who are alive with us now.

Probably no one who reads this will be memorialized by some institution that lasts through the generations, as Luther was by the Lutheran Church, or as D.L. Moody was by the Moody Bible Institute. Probably we won't even be remembered two or three generations hence. Even if we were, that wouldn't be important. What is important is summed up in the epitaph Scripture gives to Joshua. All the days of his life, Israel served the Lord.

Joshua was faithful to God as long as he lived. As long as he lived, Joshua influenced the men and women of his day.

Personal Application

Touching just one life for God is the most significant thing any human being can achieve.

Quotable

"A holy life will produce the deepest impression. Lighthouses blow no horns; they only shine."—D.L. Moody

The Variety Reading Plan continues with JUDGES

Judges

INTRODUCTION

The Book of Judges spans the period between the death of Joshua, about 1375 B.C., to the crowning of Israel's first king, Saul, around 1040 B.C. The book traces the deterioration of Israel's faith and fortunes. It explains why the people of God failed to experience His blessing.

Judges takes its name from the charismatic leaders God raised up when Israel abandoned idolatry and turned to Him for help. The "judges" were national leaders in the fullest sense. Typically they functioned as military commanders, religious leaders, and governors of the tribes they served. This small book is usually valued for its stories of heroes like Deborah, Gideon, and Samson. But its message is more grim. The future is bleak for any nation that abandons God and the righteous way of life His Law describes.

OUTLINE OF CONTENTS

I. Causes of the Judges Era .... Jud. 1:1–3:6
II. Conditions During the Judges Era:.................. Jud. 3:7–16:31
Seven Cycles of Oppression/Deliverance
1. Othniel .... Jud. 3:7-11
2. Eglon .... Jud. 3:12-31
3. Deborah and Barak............................ Jud. 4:1–5:31
4. Gideon... Jud. 6:1–8:32
5. Tola and Jair .... Jud. 8:33–10:5
6. Jephthah .... Jud. 10:6–12:15
7. Samson .... Jud. 13:1–16:31
III. Human Consequences of the Judges Era .... Jud. 17:1–21:25

READING GUIDE (6 Days)

If hurried, you may read only the "core passage" in your Bible and the Devotional in each chapter of this Commentary.

Reading	*Chapters*	*Core passage*
51	1–3	2
52	4–5	5
53	6–8	6:25–7:21
54	9–12	11:29-40
55	13–16	16
56	17–21	19

Judges

FEBRUARY 20 *Reading 51*

SPIRITUAL DECLINE

Judges 1–3

> *"Another generation grew up, who knew neither the* Lord *nor what He had done for Israel" (Jud. 2:10).*

There is cause and effect in the spiritual as well as physical universe. The cause of the failure of the next generation to know God was rooted in the incomplete obedience of its parents.

Background

Centuries before, God had promised Abraham that his descendants would possess Canaan. Under Joshua these descendants, the Israelites, invaded the Promised Land. In an extended military campaign Joshua broke the power of the Canaanite city-states, and then distributed the land to Israelite tribes. But there were still pockets of resistance; areas occupied by the various ethnic groups that had settled Canaan long before. Each Hebrew tribe was responsible to drive out any Canaanites left as its population grew and its people needed more land. But there was one requirement. The Canaanites were to be exterminated or driven from the land, lest their religion corrupt God's chosen people.

The Book of Judges tells the tragic story of a people who have been blessed by God, but forfeit their future by incomplete obedience.

Overview

Judah boldly attacked Canaanites remaining in its territory (1:1-26). But other tribes failed to drive the Canaanites out (vv. 27-36). God refused further aid to His disobedient people (2:1-5). The next generations turned to idols and intermarried with the Canaanites, causing national decline. Even the judges God provided effect only temporary recommitment to the Lord (vv. 6-23).

Understanding the Text

"The Lord *was with the men of Judah" Jud. 1:1-26.* After Joshua's death the tribe of Judah demonstrated continuing faith in God. They boldly attacked the Canaanites still within their territory. The victories they won should have encouraged all Israel.

One of the most significant things we can do to strengthen our faith is read Christian biographies. While these are not published frequently today, the life stories of men and women of faith can challenge and encourage us. Relatively recent publications like *Through Gates of Splendor* and *Born Again,* as well as older classics about Hudson Taylor and George Müller, can deepen our awareness of what God is able to do through individuals.

If only the rest of the tribes of Israel had learned from Judah's experience, the next few hundred years of Israel's history might have been different.

"The Canaanites were determined" Jud. 1:27-36. The other tribes did not follow Judah's example. They hesitated to attack the Canaanites in their territory. The Canaanites were more determined to stay than Israel was to obey God and drive them out!

This hesitation to obey God led to direct disobedience. When Israel did become strong, rather than attack the Canaanites they simply enslaved them.

Any failure to obey is a step toward direct disobedience.

Archeology confirms the Old Testament picture of the Israelites confined in Canaan's hill country (Jud. 1:19). In the lowlands Canaanite chariot armies seemed too strong for the fearful Israelites to attack. Chariots like this one were the tanks of ancient warfare. By this era they were used to directly attack and smash formations of foot soldiers.

"They will be thorns in your sides and their gods will be a snare" Jud. 2:1-5. God confronted Israel with the sin of disobedience and pronounced judgment. He would withdraw His support. Now Israel would not be *able* to drive out the Canaanites.

In the spiritual life, "will not" all too soon becomes "cannot."

"Therefore the LORD was very angry" Jud. 2:6-23. The author of Judges now injects a summary that traces a sequence of events which was repeated throughout this era. Each element of the cycle can be seen in most of the stories of the judges found in this book.

The overall evaluation of the period is expressed powerfully in 2:19. "But when the judge died, the people returned to ways even more corrupt than those of their fathers, following other gods and serving and worshiping them. They refused to give up their evil practices and stubborn ways."

Each cycle saw the people of God pull farther away from the Lord, and subjected them to even harsher judgments.

The normal Christian life is intended to be an unbroken walk of fellowship with the Lord. Those who see Christian experience as a cycle of sin, confession, restoration, temporary obedience, and sin again, have missed the message of this Old Testament book. Each time we choose to venture into sin we are likely to go farther. God is always willing to take us back. But sin will ultimately harden our hearts against Him.

"Again the Israelites cried out to the LORD" Jud. 3:12-31. Judges 3 briefly outlines the story of two early judges. Note that each story incorporates all elements of the cycle outlined below.

SIN	3:7	3:12
SERVITUDE	3:8	3:13-14
SUPPLICATION	3:9	3:15
SALVATION	3:9-10	3:13-29
SILENCE	3:11	3:30

We can break cycles like this in our lives only by resisting the temptation to sin.

CYCLE OF EVENTS

SIN	2:11-13	The Israelites turn to Baal worship and immorality.
SERVITUDE	2:14-15	Foreign nations defeat, oppress Israel.
SUPPLICATION	2:15	Under oppression Israel confesses sin, prays.
SALVATION	2:16	God raised up judges to deliver His people.
SILENCE	2:18	During his life the judge keeps Israel more or less faithful to the Lord.

▶ DEVOTIONAL
Growing the Next Generation (Jud. 2)

Ever run into one of those sayings designed to make parents feel guilty? Like, "As the twig is bent, so grows the tree"? Or, "The apple never falls far from the tree"?

Personally, I don't buy the implication. Each person is responsible for his or her own choices. I can't take credit for the godly choices my grown-up children make. And I'm not responsible for their wrong or foolish choices either.

But this passage, like so many in these early books of the Old Testament, makes it clear that each generation does influence the next. Here the text tells us that "after that whole generation [which had fought with Joshua for Canaan] had been gathered to their fathers, another generation grew up, who knew neither the LORD nor what He had done for Israel" (v. 10). Somehow a whole generation had failed to communicate the reality of its experience with God to the next.

If you wonder why they failed, the answer is right there in chapter 1 of this Old Testament book. After Joshua's death, only Judah exhibited trust in God and took on the Canaanite enemy. The others hesitated, fearfully. And when, by sheer force of growing numbers, they overawed the Canaanites, rather than drive them out the Israelites enslaved them. The parents failed to trust God. They disobeyed God. And their children "knew neither the LORD nor what He had done for Israel."

You and I can't guarantee that our children will know the Lord or live for Him. But if we trust God enough to act on His Word, if we are obedient in our daily lives, our children will never be able to say of God, "I didn't know Him."

The reality of who God is is displayed in the faith moms and dads put into practice, and in their obedience to His Word.

Personal Application

There's nothing more important we can do for our children than love, trust, and obey the Lord.

Quotable

"There is just one way to bring up a child in the way he should go and that is to travel that way yourself."—Abraham Lincoln

---

FEBRUARY 21 *Reading 52*
DEBORAH
Judges 4–5

> *"So may all your enemies perish, O LORD! But may they who love You be like the sun when it rises in its strength" (Jud. 5:31).*

Women were not generally leaders in patriarchal Israel. But her sex did not disqualify Deborah, whose spiritual gifts were acknowledged by God's people.

Overview

Deborah, the prophetess-leader of Israel, told a hesitant Barak to raise an army (4:1-11). The Israelite victory (vv. 12-24) is celebrated in one of the most beautiful of ancient poems, Deborah's song (5:1-31).

Understanding the Text

Deborah. Deborah is identified as a prophetess. God used her as His spokesman, communicating special messages to His people. The text also says she was "leading [judging] Israel at that time." This was very unusual in a society that emphasized male leadership and female subordination. The text also says that Deborah served as a sort of supreme court and settled disputes that could not be decided locally. Any one of these roles would set off any individual as special, male or female. Possession of all three roles indicates that Deborah was a truly unusual woman, with great personal and spiritual gifts.

Deborah reminds us that society's stereotypes need not hold for God's people. God's choice of Deborah shows that He is free to work through any human being. That choice reminds us that a person's sex does not automatically qualify or disqualify him or her for significant ministry.

Barak. Barak himself is a fascinating study. Barak was hesitant and fearful, unwilling to face the enemy unless Deborah accompanied his army (4:8). This was despite the fact that Deborah had promised Barak victory in God's name. Dependence on God is desirable. Dependence on human beings, even those who may represent God, is not. Barak's mistake was to trust God to act only through Deborah, rather than trust God directly. We can appreciate and honor our spiritual leaders; but we must not exalt them to the extent that Barak exalted Deborah.

"Jabin, a king of Canaan, who reigned in Hazor" Jud. 4:1-11. Hazor had been destroyed by Joshua. But the strategic site was rebuilt, and a new Jabin (probably a dynastic name) controlled the lowlands and "cruelly oppressed" Israel. That oppression is described in 5:6-10. The Israelites feared to travel by roads, abandoned many villages, and lacked weapons. On the other hand, the Canaanites, under their skilled commander, Sisera, had 900 iron chariots.

A look at a map shows that the oppression affected only the northernmost of Israel's tribes, notably Naphtali and Zebulun. Deborah's location in Ephraim's highlands suggests that she was not directly affected.

We don't need to be directly affected by suffering to become involved. Paul says of the body of Christ, "If one part suffers, every part suffers with it" (1 Cor. 12:26).

"Sisera gathered together his nine hundred iron chariots and all the men . . . to the Kishon River" Jud. 4:11-16. In the dry season the Esdraelon Valley through which the Kishon trickled was ideal for chariot warfare: flat and hard, with room to maneuver. However, when wet, the valley turned to muck, making chariots a liability.

While Judges 4:15 simply says that "the LORD routed Sisera" and that "Sisera abandoned his chariot and fled on foot," Deborah's song explains. She describes how "the heavens poured, the clouds poured down water" (5:4).

Baal, worshiped by the Canaanites, was originally a god of thunder and thunderstorms. Here the Lord turns the storm against the worshipers of the storm god and uses rain to neutralize their military advantage! The victory over the Canaanites was a divine judgment on the religion of the Canaanites as well as on their treatment of God's people.

"Please give me some water" Jud. 4:17-23. Sisera's request for water may suggest more than thirst. Among nomadic peoples even the most deadly of enemies who was given food or drink came under the protection of his host. In the absence of her husband, Jael acted as hostess. She gave Sisera the drink he requested and hid him in her tent. She then violated custom and with a single blow drove a sharpened tent peg through his forehead.

We shouldn't be surprised at Jael's strength. Among nomadic Middle Eastern people women pitch the tents, so the tent peg and mallet would have been familiar tools.

Despite her violation of hospitality, Deborah blessed Jael. Unlike others, Jael came forward "to help the LORD, to help the LORD against the mighty" (5:23).

There are times when Christians too need to step forward, even when an act of conscience goes against community standards. Civil disobedience during the '60s—the civil rights movement—was one such time. I suspect that picketing abortion clinics in the '90s is another time when Christians need to be willing to come forward to "help the LORD against the mighty."

"Through the window" Jud. 5:28-31. The imagery and irony of this brief passage has led to its recognition as perhaps the most brilliant of all ancient poems.

"They destroyed him" Jud. 4:24. The victory over Sisera's army drained the strength of the Canaanites. The war wasn't over. But that battle was the turning point. The text says that after the battle the Israelites grew stronger, and finally they destroyed the Canaanite king and his kingdom. Judges 5:31 adds, "Then the land had peace for forty years."

Some Christians believe that turning to Jesus solves all problems automatically.

I've known one or two alcoholics who claimed that after their conversions they never wanted to touch another drop. But I've known many more who report that they have to struggle daily against the urge to take just one drink.

The victory over Sisera reminds us that we do have to battle the things in life that oppress us. We have to take a stand and claim the victory. But the first battle in which the enemy suffers a crushing defeat may well be a prelude to years of struggle. We, like the Israelites, need to grow stronger and stronger, and to recognize that it may take a long time to "destroy him."

▶DEVOTIONAL
Staying by the Campfire (Jud. 5)

Deborah's song is a victory shout. It vibrates with excitement and praise. It overflows with joy and enthusiasm. And no wonder. The battle with Sisera was the turning point for a whole generation. Twenty years of oppression were transformed into 40 years of peace. Deborah and Barak led an army of men whose proudest claim in years to come would be, "I was there, at the river Kishon." No wonder the victory poem is so electric, so vibrant and filled with joy.

Except for a few verses in the middle. Verses that describe the tribes who failed to answer the call to battle the Canaanites. The men of Ephraim came. The tribes of Zebulun and Issachar were there. But where was Reuben? Where were Gilead and Dan and Asher when "the people of Zebulun risked their very lives"?

"In the districts of Reuben," Deborah says, "there was much searching of heart. Why did you stay among the campfires to hear the whistling for the flocks?" (vv. 16-18) Why, when opportunity came to make history, did these people stay home, absorbed in the ordinary tasks of daily life? Sitting around the campfire. Caring for the sheep. As though nothing special were happening just over the mountain, where their brothers risked their very lives.

There's really no answer to that question. Was it a lack of vision? A failure to see the opportunity? Was it a lack of caring, a failure to be moved by the suffering of others?

Whatever the reason, these members of God's household failed to sense that the critical moment had arrived. They failed to act. And God won the victory without them.

And what a lesson for us today. God will win His victories with whoever volunteers. But how sad it would be for us if we were to stay by our campfire while history was made.

Personal Application

What opportunity is too great for you to miss today?

Quotable

"We will lie down for such a long time after death that it is worthwhile to keep standing while we are alive. Let us work now; one day we shall rest."—Agostina Pietrantoni

---

FEBRUARY 22 *Reading 53*
GIDEON
Judges 6–8

> *"Go in the strength you have and save Israel out of Midian's hand. Am I not sending you?" (Jud. 6:14)*

The hesitant hero of this story did ask God for reassuring signs. And God did graciously reassure him. Gideon's experience teaches an important lesson about "putting out the fleece." But not, perhaps, the lesson we expect.

Definition of Key Terms

Angel of the L*ORD*. Many believe the Old Testament Angel of the Lord is a theophany, an appearance of God in human form. It is important to distinguish between such Old Testament appearances and the Incarnation. In Jesus Christ, God the Son took on human nature and became a true human being. The Angel of the Lord simply looked like a human being.

Overview

Israel's southeastern tribes were severely oppressed by the Midianites when the

Angel of the Lord commissioned Gideon to deliver them (6:1-16). Gideon obeyed God and tore down a local altar to Baal (vv. 17-35), but asked for miraculous signs to confirm God's commitment to keep His promise (vv. 36-40). Gideon's army was reduced to 300 men (7:1-8). After further confirmation (vv. 9-14), Gideon attacked and routed the Midianites (vv. 15-25). Gideon's humility avoided intertribal war (8:1-5), but he decisively punished Israelite towns that refused aid when he was pursuing the Midianite kings (vv. 6-21). Later Gideon made a gold ephod which became an idol to Israel (vv. 22-35).

Understanding the Text

"The power of Midian was so oppressive" Jud. 6:1-6. The Midianites were a nomadic people who periodically invaded Israel to steal the harvest. These southwestern people led a coalition of Midianites and other races of the Syrian desert. When Israel originally conquered them, they had relied on donkeys for transportation (Num. 31:32-34). Here they are described riding camels, perhaps the first large-scale military use of these animals in history.

The Midianites penetrated deeply into southern and central Israel, stealing or ruining crops and forcing the Israelites to hide in caves.

"You have not listened to Me" Jud. 6:7-10. An unnamed prophet reminded the Israelites that God had been faithful in His commitment to them. The disaster came because the Israelites were not faithful to the Lord.

It's foolish to blame God for the evil consequences of our own sins.

Even so, God heard Israel's prayers (v. 6) and determined to save His disobedient people once again. How good to realize when we have sinned that God will hear us if we turn to Him.

"Where are all His wonders?" Jud. 6:11-14 When the Angel of the Lord appeared, Gideon was threshing grain in a winepress. The normal place for threshing was a windy hilltop, where the breeze would separate wheat and chaff. Gideon used a winepress, usually a walled area at the bottom of a hill, to thresh. The act illustrates how fearful the Israelites were that they might be seen by the Midianites and their crop stolen.

It's no wonder that Gideon, forced to look fearfully in every direction as he surreptitiously threshed his grain, responded with sarcasm when the angel told him, "The LORD is with you, mighty warrior." If Gideon was a mighty warrior, why was he hiding in a winepress? If God was really with Israel, where were the miracles of deliverance He performed for the fathers?

All too often our circumstances rob us of a sense of God's presence too. Yet often, as in Gideon's case, when we feel most deserted, or even most cynical, God has already begun to act.

God told Gideon, "Go in the strength you have." Each of us is to act in the strength we have, relying on the fact that God is truly with us even if we do not sense His presence.

"Gideon . . . did as the LORD told him" Jud. 6:15-29. Gideon's "offering" was the kind of gift normally given to a visitor, not a sacrifice such as would be made to God. When fire flared from a rock and burned up the food Gideon brought, he realized that his guest was the Angel of the Lord.

Though Gideon was perhaps too aware of his weakness (v. 15), he obeyed God's command and destroyed the local altar of Baal and the associated Asherah pole. This might well have taken Gideon's 10 men all night! One Baal altar found at Megiddo was 4½ feet high and 26 feet across, made of bricks cemented in mud!

Gideon's fear of the men of the town was a result of his accurate assessment of the situation. If he had acted in the daytime, the townspeople would surely have stopped him. God did not command Gideon to tear down the altar by daylight. Gideon's choice suggests wisdom, not cowardice.

It's not necessary to advertise our obedience. It's enough to obey.

"They called Gideon 'Jerub-Baal' " Jud. 6:30-35. The furious citizens were put off by the ridicule of Gideon's father, apparently an influential man. The name, when first given to Gideon, suggested Baal was at war with Gideon. Later, after the victory over Midian, the emphasis subtly shifts, and "Jerub-Baal" is used proudly in the

sense of "Baal fighter."

"If You will save Israel . . . as You have promised" Jud. 6:33-40. Gideon acted boldly and sent messengers to several tribes to recruit an army. His public actions were bold, but Gideon still experienced private doubts and fears.

Gideon's prayers about the fleece were not an effort to determine what God's will was. Gideon knew that. The requests were made for Gideon's own personal encouragement, and were made only after Gideon had already demonstrated his willingness to obey God.

"You have too many men" Jud. 7:1-8. Gideon needed that reassurance. In a series of steps God reduced Gideon's army from 32,000 to a mere 300. The reason is instructive. Victory won by 300 over thousands would make God's role clear.

Sometimes we are asked to undertake great tasks with few resources, that the glory might belong to God.

"If you are afraid to attack" Jud. 7:9-15. Gideon was given one last encouragement by the Lord, in the form of a dream reported by a Midianite as Gideon lay hidden near the enemy camp. The specification of "barley bread" is significant. Barley was the grain used by the poor to make bread. It symbolized downtrodden Israel.

In the ancient world, dreams were viewed as a channel by which the gods communicated with men. In this case, God did give the dream and its interpretation. God is not limited in the means He uses to communicate with us—or in the instruments He chooses.

"A sword for the LORD and for Gideon!" Jud. 7:16-25 Gideon's primary weapon in the battle was terror. The sudden appearance of flaming torches on the hillside, accompanied by a cacaphony of loud, harsh notes blown on 300 rams'-horn trumpets, threw the Midianite camp into such turmoil that in the confusion the enemy soldiers struck out at each other. The Midianite army fled, and the Israelites appeared and took up pursuit.

It's easy to join the fight when our side is obviously winning. It's harder to be 1 of 300 who take that first stand against an enemy. Yet without the first, bold 300, there could be no victories at all. Let's remember this when you or I are challenged to take a stand on any moral issue in our church or society.

"Their resentment . . . subsided" Jud. 8:1-3. Gideon's original call for volunteers had not gone to the tribe of Ephraim. Now this group, which did pursue the fleeing Midianites, criticized Gideon. Gideon did not try to explain. He did not take offense. Instead he very wisely gave the Ephraimites credit for what they had accomplished, and suggested humbly that they had done more than he himself had.

Let people who want credit have it. Those who most deserve credit, like Gideon, seldom find it important.

"The officials of Succoth" Jud. 8:4-17. The attitude of the officials of Succoth and Peniel, who not only refused to aid Gideon but even ridiculed him, called for repayment. These Israelites refused to join in the battle, and displayed contempt for the God who had called Gideon to lead Israel in a holy way.

"During Gideon's lifetime, the land enjoyed peace" Jud. 8:22-35. Gideon, still carrying the name "Baal-fighter," kept Israel from worshiping Baal during his lifetime. But Gideon showed two signs of weakness. One, he made a gold ephod (like a vest, worn by Israel's high priest), which in time was worshiped as an idol.

Two, though Gideon overtly refused an offer of kingship, he later named one of his children Abimelech. The Hebrew means "My father is king!" Later this son took his name too much to heart. After Gideon died, Abimelech killed all of his brothers, and for a time served as a petty king ruling over a tiny part of the land of Israel.

▶ DEVOTIONAL
Put Out Your Fleece? (Jud. 6:25–7:21)

How can you know the will of God for your life? Well, one way is *not* by "putting out the fleece." That act by Gideon has another meaning entirely. Gideon sought reassurance, not knowledge of God's will. God graciously answered Gideon's prayer, because Gideon had *already* demonstrated his readiness to obey.

There's a pattern in these chapters that is very important.

A fearful Gideon obeys God and tears down Baal's altar (6:25-32).

A Spirit-filled Gideon summons the Israelites to battle (6:33-35).

A very human Gideon asks God for reassurance, and is given it when he puts out the fleece (6:36-40).

An obedient Gideon sends home nearly all of the Israelite army (7:1-7).

A fearful and very human Gideon is reassured by the dream God gives a Midianite soldier (7:8-15).

A now-confident Gideon leads the attack on Midian.

Note that reassurance was given *after* Gideon had obeyed a command of the Lord, not before. Sometimes we mistakenly put out our fleece, or beg God for some sign, before we obey Him. Then we wait, miserable, when no sign is given. What the experience of Gideon tells us is that obedience precedes reassurance. God may graciously give us a sign of His presence. But such signs are given to those who have already demonstrated faith by beginning to do His will.

Personal Application

If you know what God's will is for you, don't wait for a sign before you obey.

Quotable

"The will of God is not always clear, especially with regard to the intricacies of daily conduct in our baffling world. But often the will of God is clear, and its main directions are always clear. A man ought not to expect light on God's will in life's intricacies of conduct if he is unwilling to follow a clear will in life's simplicities."—George A. Buttrick

FEBRUARY 23 *Reading 54*
ABIMELECH AND JEPHTHAH
Judges 9–12

> *"Then they got rid of the foreign gods among them and served the* Lord. *And He could bear Israel's misery no longer" (Jud. 10:16).*

Two disadvantaged young men remind us that environment determines no one's future. What counts are the choices each individual makes in life.

Overview

Abimelech, son of Gideon and a Canaanite woman of Shechem, killed his 70 brothers and set himself up as a petty king with the aid of his mother's people (9:1-21). Within three years the Shechemites rebelled, and Abimelech was killed (vv. 22-57). Jephthah (JEFF-thah), son of an Israelite father and a prostitute, was rejected by his family and clan, but was called back when the tribe was threatened by the Ammonites (11:1-12). When negotiation failed (vv. 13-28), Jephthah led Israel to victory (vv. 29-33). But the victory was won at great cost to Jephthah's daughter (vv. 34-40), and led to intertribal warfare (12:1-7).

Understanding the Text

"His mother's clan" Jud. 9:1-6. Identification of the Shechemites as "men of Hamor" (v. 28) and their worship of Baal-Berith indicate the population of this city was primarily Canaanite. Abimelech enlisted their aid by (1) reminding them he was their own flesh and blood, (2) by implying Gideon's 70 sons intended to rule over them, and (3) by implying a threat to their religion by using the name Jerub-Baal, "Baal fighter." The citizens of Shechem financed the ritual murder of Gideon's other sons with money from their temple treasury.

The story reveals the character of Abimelech. He was ambitious, manipulative, without conscience or scruples, quick to use religion, but with no personal faith or religious commitment. Abimelech, child of an Israelite and a Canaanite, rejected the Lord and chose the ways of his pagan forebearers.

"One day the trees went out to anoint a king"

Jud. 9:7-21. Gideon's youngest son, Jotham, escaped when his brothers were slaughtered. His parable about trees was pointed. Those trees which were beneficial to men refused the title. Only the thistle, which was useless, wanted the crown. But the thornbush was not only useless, it was dangerous, for its dry branches were quick to catch and spread fires. Jotham warned the citizens of Shechem. If they had not "acted honorably and in good faith" in making Abimelech king, "let fire come from Abimelech and consume you . . . and let fire come out from you . . . and consume Abimelech!"

Anyone who fails to act honorably and in good faith spreads around his own feet the fuel that will burst into flame and destroy him.

"God repaid the wickedness that Abimelech had done" Jud. 9:22-57. Abimelech's petty kingdom did not encompass all Israel. From the cities named, he appears to have ruled only in western Manasseh. Within three years this small kingdom fell apart, as the citizens of Shechem, near important trade routes, turned to banditry and thus defrauded Abimelech of taxes he might have collected from merchants and travelers (v. 25). Abimelech attacked and destroyed Shechem. He himself was killed attacking another rebellious city. Abimelech and his coconspirators in Shechem had destroyed each other, just as Jotham predicted.

Jotham's prediction required no supernatural source. Evil acts always have evil consequences for the perpetrators.

Abimelech and Jephthah. The story of Abimelech prepares us for the story of Jephthah. Each of these young men had a mixed parentage. Each may have been rejected by his brothers. But here the similarity ends. While Abimelech rejected the Lord, Jephthah trusted Him completely. While Abimelech murdered his brothers, Jephthah saved his family and tribe. The origins of each of these men may well have caused them pain. Each may have experienced unfair treatment. Yet it was the decision each made to reject or to seek personal relationship with God that was the determining factor in his life.

"He led Israel twenty-three years" Jud. 10:1-5; 12:8-15. These chapters briefly note five judges who ruled for various periods of time. The rule of many of the judges overlapped, as most had influence over only a few of the tribes and part of the land.

"Because the Israelites forsook the LORD and no longer served Him" Jud. 10:6-18. The depth of the apostasy preceding Jephthah is suggested by (1) the list of five nations whose gods Israel served along with the Canaanite Baals and Ashtoreths, (2) severe oppression from both the western Philistines and eastern Ammonites, and (3) God's expressed unwillingness to save His people though they repented (vv. 11-13). All this displays not only Israel's sin but also God's compassion. Even though the punishment was deserved, God "could bear Israel's misery no longer" (v. 16).

How comforting to remember when we fall that the Lord "does not treat us as our sins deserve or repay us according to our iniquities" (Ps. 103:10).

"Jephthah . . . as a mighty warrior" Jud. 11:1-11. After the death of his father Jephthah, the son of a prostitute, was driven away by his half brothers with the support of the elders of Gilead. As David would when forced to flee from Saul, Jephthah gathered a small force of adventurers who were in debt or otherwise outcasts. They quickly gained a military reputation. When asked to return and lead Israel's army, Jephthah negotiated with the elders and was promised the position of "head and commander"; that is, chief in peace as well as war.

Prejudice drove Jephthah from Gilead. Need brought him back. It's easy to forget another's past when we need their help. How much better to treat everyone graciously in the first place.

"Jephthah sent messengers" Jud. 11:12-28. Jephthah pointed out that the Ammonites had no claim on the land they planned to take, for it was Israel's by right of conquest and by right of 300 years of occupation. This message is revealing. First, it shows that Jephthah, despite his rejection by the Israelites, had a deep faith in Israel's God. Second, it shows the Israelites had a clear memory of what God had done to bring His people into the land.

The faith of this outcast in Israel's God surely shamed those of "pure blood," who knew as much as Jephthah about God, but who had rejected Him in favor of idols. Let's remember that the only basis you or I have for pride is that we actively love and serve God. Lineage, wealth, or social position are meaningless.

"Jephthah made a vow to the LORD" Jud. 11:29-40. Making a promise to do something special for God should He provide victory was not at all unusual in Israel. Jephthah, whom the text specifies was filled with the Spirit of the Lord, made such a vow before his war with the Ammonites. As Israelite houses of this era made room for animals as well as people, Jephthah undoubtedly had an animal sacrifice in mind when he made his vow.

"The men of Ephraim . . . crossed over" Jud. 12:1-7. On word of Jephthah's victory, Israelites west of the Jordan crossed over in force and threatened him. Their complaint that they had not been invited to fight was a lie (v. 3), and likely a disguised demand that they share in the spoil of victory. The threat to "burn down your house over your head" was simple blackmail.

Jephthah responded by calling out his forces and crushing the invaders.

▶ DEVOTIONAL
The Rest of the Story (Jud. 11:29-40)

The story of Jephthah's vow is a favorite of those who enjoy debate. One side insists that Jephthah actually killed his daughter as a blood sacrifice. The other argues that he did not. As is often true with difficult Bible passages, the debate obscures the rest of the story—and its point.

But did Jephthah actually sacrifice his daughter? Not at all. The law of vows (Lev. 27:1-8) permitted substitution. What Jephthah did was commit his daughter to lifelong celibate service at the tabernacle, as in Exodus 38:8; 1 Samuel 2:22. This is supported by the fact that (1) the text emphasizes her perpetual virginity, not her death (Jud. 11:37-39), (2) child sacrifice was condemned in the Law (Lev. 18:21; 20:2-5), (3) no priest would officiate at a human sacrifice, and (4) Jephthah's letter to the Ammonites shows he knew the Law, for it was the source of the history he quoted.

But what about the rest of the story? It's told in the simple words of the young teenage daughter. "My father, you have given your word to the LORD. Do to me just as you promised."

God had been faithful in giving Israel the victory. The little family of Jephthah and his only child, a daughter, must be just as faithful to Him, whatever the cost.

Personal Application

True faith is better expressed by quiet commitment than by erudite debate.

Quotable

"We should not attach much value to what we have given God, since we shall receive for the little we have bestowed upon Him much more in this life and in the next."—Theresa of Avila

FEBRUARY 24 *Reading 55*

SAMSON
Judges 13–16

"Samson led Israel for twenty years in the days of the Philistines" (Jud. 15:20).

This text does *not* conclude, "and the land had rest." Samson, for all his physical strength, lacked the inner strength needed to put his people ahead of his own raging desires.

Definition of Key Terms

Philistines. Great numbers of these people settled on Palestine's coastal plains about 1200 B.C. after an unsuccessful invasion of Egypt. Gradually they penetrated the hill country occupied by Israel, and intermingled with the Israelites. Israel was unable to resist the encroachment, in part because the Philistines had the secret of smelting iron and had weapons superior to anything Israel possessed. Samson conducted one-man war against the Philistines, but never marshalled his people to resist the invaders. The Philistines remained a dangerous enemy through the judgeship of Samuel and the reign of Saul, until crushed by David about a hundred years after the time of Samson.

Overview

Samson's birth was announced by the Angel of the Lord (13:1-24). He insisted on marrying a Philistine, but was deceived and humiliated at the wedding (14:1-15). Revenge escalated into open hostilities in which Samson personally killed a thousand men (15:1-20). But his passion for Delilah led Samson to reveal the secret of his strength (16:1-17). He was captured, blinded, and forced to grind grain for his enemy (vv. 16-22). Samson's strength returned and he died destroying a Philistine temple, killing thousands of his enemies (vv. 23-31).

Understanding the Text

"Teach us how to bring up the boy who is to be born" Jud. 13:1-25. Samson is one of the few in Scripture whose birth was preannounced to his parents. He shares this honor with Isaac, John the Baptist, and Jesus.

Samson's parents were godly Israelites who believed the prediction and asked God to show them how to bring up their son. This prayer was answered: Samson was to be brought up as a Nazarite—a person set completely apart to God (see Num. 6:1-8). Nazarites drank no wine, did not cut their hair, and were to follow certain other requirements.

It is striking that in this and other tales of the judges the author does not editorialize. He simply tells his story, without moralizing or comment. Yet the stories speak for themselves, particularly in Samson's case. Unlike Jephthah, Samson had loving and godly parents. Even as a teenager "the Spirit of the LORD began to stir him" (Jud. 13:25). Samson's many flaws can hardly be traced either to his parents or to God.

What a comfort to godly Christian parents whose children have not chosen to follow Jesus. Every tormented mom or dad, who looks back and wonders, "What did I do?" or "What did I fail to do?" can find comfort in the story of Samson. There was no failure on the part of Samson's parents. The flaws that later destroyed Samson were in Samson himself.

"Get her for me" Jud. 14:1-20. Samson's desire for a Philistine woman indicates his weakness. God's Law forbad intermarriage with pagan peoples (Deut. 7:3). Yet Samson was ruled by his desires. His passion for a woman, based merely on her looks, seemed more important to him than God's expressed will. So, despite his objections, Samson's father arranged for the marriage.

The comment that "this was from the LORD, who was seeking an occasion to confront the Philistines" is likely a gloss, or comment by a later editor. But the point is well taken. God is able to turn even our weaknesses to His purposes.

A confrontation was stimulated when Samson posed a riddle that the Philistines he challenged could answer only by threatening his bride. Samson's comment that he had not even explained it to his father or mother (Jud. 14:16) is interesting. As a Nazarite he was not supposed to touch a dead body. Yet he had taken honey from the body of a lion that he killed.

The incident is another indication of his parents' godly character, and Samson's own flaws.

"I have a right to get even" Jud. 15:1-20. When Samson learned that his father-in-law had given his bride to someone else, he captured a number of jackals (not foxes) and set them loose in Philistine grain fields with firebrands attached to their tails. Escalation followed. The Philistines burned Samson's bride and her father to death, and then demanded that the Israelites turn Samson over to them to be executed. The Israelites bound Samson, but after he was turned over Samson broke his bonds and, using the fresh jawbone of a donkey, "struck down a thousand men."

The text sheds light on several aspects of the period and the Samson story. First, the casual brutality of the Philistines is seen in their burning of Samson's bride and her father (v. 6). Second, the subservient attitude of the Israelites is shown in their failure to support Samson and in their fear of the Philistines, who "are rulers over us" (v. 11). Most revealing of all are Samson's references to his "right to get even" and to do to the Philistines "what they did to me" (vv. 3, 11). This is the same kind of thinking that characterized the Philistines (v. 10). Samson gave no thought to the oppression experienced by the people he led. His vendetta with the Philistines was personal. Samson hated the Philistines not for what they had done to his people but for what they had done to him personally.

Approaches to the gates of ancient cities were carefully constructed to prevent access. The gates themselves were massive, usually reinforced with metal. Samson not only tore off the gates of Gaza, which weighed many hundreds of pounds, but carried them to the "top of the hill that faces Hebron," 38 miles away!

God used Samson's selfishness to "begin the deliverance of Israel from the hands of the Philistines" (13:5). But Samson himself is revealed to be a shallow person, without the spiritual depth or concern for others that marks the truly godly.

"Each one of us will give you eleven hundred shekels of silver" Jud. 16:1-21. The combined payment of almost 150 pounds of silver was a vast sum for that day. Delilah was as eager to have the money as Samson was to have her! Neither of the major figures in this story merits admiration. Each shows very human weaknesses against which you and I must guard.

"He killed many more when he died" Jud. 16:23-31. Samson's last prayer suggests he had learned little during his lifetime, for his concern is still with revenge, this time "for my two eyes" (v. 28).

The temple to which Samson was brought probably was built on a plan common to such structures of that era. If so, most of the Philistines were gathered on the roof, which was supported by a number of pillars. The crowd, pressing forward to see the captive hero, would have made the whole structure unstable, so that when Samson pushed against the pillars, the temple collapsed. More died with Samson in that fall than Samson had killed during his lifetime.

What a difference between this epitaph and that of other judges, which commonly read, "And the land had peace." Samson brought death to Israel's enemies. But this morally weak strongman failed to make peace for his own people or for himself.

▶ DEVOTIONAL
Now, or Never?
(Jud. 16)

The story of Samson and Delilah is one of the best known in Scripture. Samson's passion for Delilah is legendary, as is her betrayal of him for money.

Yet as we read the story, we're reminded more of children than adults. Samson and Delilah each desperately wanted what he or she desired . . . now. Reading the story we're amazed that Samson kept going back to Delilah when what she said and did so clearly showed her intent to betray. But Samson's passion was so dominating that he cared nothing for the future. His only concern was that his desire be satisfied now.

We wonder at Samson's blindness. It's so much easier to see a fault in someone else than in ourselves. How often have we made choices because we want something now, without considering the future? How often have our choices been made simply on the basis of our will, without pausing to consider God's?

Samson reminds us that we grown-ups can't afford to adopt a child's perspective on life, and let ourselves be controlled by our passions and desires.

Personal Application

In the choice between now and never, never is often best.

Quotable

"Inordinate love of the flesh is cruelty, because under the appearance of pleasing the body we kill the soul."—Bernard of Clairvaux

---

FEBRUARY 25 *Reading 56*
RESULTS OF APOSTASY
Judges 17–21

> *"In those days Israel had no king; everyone did as he saw fit" (Jud. 21:25).*

History books seldom provide as much insight into a period as do stories of men and women who lived in it. In three brief slices of life, the author of Judges shows us how dark the era really was.

Background

The material in these last chapters of Judges is undated. It is not associated with any specific judge. It is instead "slice of life" material: cross sections taken from the period to reveal the religious, personal, and social consequences of Israel's failure to serve God. These stories illustrate the price ordinary people paid for the apostasy of the nation.

Overview

An Ephraimite named Micah used stolen silver to make an idol, and recruited a Levite to serve as family priest (17:1-13). The Levite and idol were taken by Danites seeking land. They set up a northern worship center which competed with the tabernacle during this era (18:1-31). When men of one Benjamite town gang raped and killed a Levite's concubine, civil war broke out between the other tribes, nearly wiping out Benjamin (19:1–21:25).

Understanding the Text

"Now I know that the LORD will be good to me" Jud. 17:1-13. The simple story of Micah and his idol portrays the religious consequences of the period. The clearest and most important of God's requirements had been distorted or lost.

Under God's Law (1) making idols was forbidden, (2) Aaron's descendants only were to serve as priests, (3) sacrifices were to be made only at the tabernacle, (4) and blessing was an outcome of obedience rather than ritual observance. Yet Micah violated each of these basic religious principles—and was convinced that his actions merited God's favor!

Perhaps even more revealing, Micah was able to find a Levite willing to serve as family priest. This despite the fact that Levites were commissioned by God to teach His Law in Israel.

This story is told first for a very simple reason. Loss of knowledge of God is the underlying cause of the crumbling of the whole society.

"They named it Dan" Jud. 18:1-31. The story continues as a group of Danites seeking resettlement passed by Micah's home. This group had abandoned the land allotted to the tribe under pressure from for-

eign powers. The Danites offered Micah's Levite a post as priest to the whole tribe. He gladly accepted, and the Danites took him and Micah's idols with them.

Moving north, the Danites attacked a "peaceful and unsuspecting" city and established themselves there. This story is significant. Dan became an important worship site, and after Solomon's kingdom was divided in 931 B.C., Dan was sanctified as an official worship center by the apostate Jeroboam I.

Dan's origin as a worship center is thus traced back to the theft of an idol, and the service of an unqualified priest. It maintained this character throughout its history.

When we build for the future, we need to lay a firm foundation of integrity.

"Such a thing has never been seen or done" Jud. 19:1-30. The story of the rape and murder of a Levite's concubine by Benjamites is intended to give insight into the moral situation in Israel. Not a single actor in this story, and certainly not the Levite, is displayed as a righteous person.

"We'll go up against it as the lot directs" Jud. 20:1-48. When the tribe of Benjamin refused to surrender the men who had raped and murdered the Levite's concubine, civil war broke out. Only some 600 men of Benjamin survived.

Under the Law, the tribe of Benjamin was responsible to turn the evildoers over for punishment. The Benjamites chose instead to protect them.

This final story sums up the author's analysis of the period. He began with religious decline, moved to moral failure, and now shows the impact of rejecting God on the society as a whole.

"The Israelites grieved for their brothers" Jud. 21:1-25. To preserve the tribe of Benjamin, the other tribes provided wives, by killing the men from a city which failed to respond to the call to war, and by inventing a religious fiction.

The tribes had taken an oath not to "give" wives to any Benjamite. So they decided to permit the men of Benjamin who needed wives to catch and carry off marriageable girls who participated in an annual religious festival.

Here we see Israel's tendency to bend rules. There is no suggestion in the text that the people appealed to God for guidance. Instead they relied on the kind of sophistry which passed over intent to emphasize the letter of the Law. Just this kind of thing was later criticized by Jesus when He condemned many of the Pharisees (cf. Mark 7:9-13).

▶ DEVOTIONAL
Moral Integrity
(Jud. 19)

Someone suggested that people who live in glass houses shouldn't throw stones. Jesus made the point by insisting that we should ignore the speck in another's eye until we've dealt with the beam in our own. There's something of this flavor in the story of the Levite's concubine.

The Levite was unwilling to stay the night in an alien (Canaanite) city. But when he stopped at a Benjamite city, the men of the town refused the couple hospitality (v. 18). Later they attempted to make him the victim of homosexual rape (v. 22). Instead the Levite pushed his concubine, a secondary wife, out the door. The Benjamites abused her all night and she died in the morning. Filled with moral outrage, the Levite cut up her body and sent pieces throughout the other tribes as a call to vengeance.

The irony, of course, lies in the fact that the Levite himself showed no concern for his concubine, either when he thrust her outside rather than defend her, or the next morning when he coldly addressed her dead body, saying, "Get up; let's go."

The story is ironic because Levites in Israel were supposed to serve God. They were, with the priests, the established guardians of the Law and of morality. When a guardian loses all moral sensibility, and abandons others or treats them as objects, society is truly lost.

The failure of the Levite is a warning to us. Yes, we do need to stand against injustice and sins in our society. We are to be stone throwers. And even "mote inspectors." But we can do this only from a position of personal moral integrity.

Personal Application

Our lives even more than our words must witness to righteousness.

Quotable

"We are full of words but empty of actions, and therefore are cursed by the Lord, since He Himself cursed the fig tree when He found no fruit but only leaves. It is useless for a man to flaunt his knowledge of the law if he undermines its teachings by his actions."—Anthony of Padua

The Variety Reading Plan continues with RUTH

Ruth

INTRODUCTION

The Book of Ruth tells the simple and beautiful story of Naomi, a Hebrew woman, and her Moabite daugher-in-law, Ruth. Set in the dark days of the Judges, the tale of Ruth and Naomi reminds us that even in the worst of times godly men and women live quiet lives of faith.

The book, probably written during Israel's early monarchy, is significant for two other reasons. It traces the lineage of David, one of Ruth's descendants. And it illustrates the Old Testament concept of the kinsman-redeemer who, moved by family loyalty, acts to save a helpless relative. One day God's Son, Jesus, born of this family line, would become true Man that He might be the Kinsman-redeemer of humankind.

OUTLINE OF CONTENTS

READING GUIDE (1 Day)

If hurried, you may read only the "core passage" in your Bible and the Devotional in this Commentary.

Reading	*Chapters*	*Core passage*
57	1–4	2–3

Ruth

FEBRUARY 26 *Reading 57*
RUTH'S STORY
Ruth 1–4

> *"Where you go I will go, and where you stay I will stay. Your people will be my people and your God my God" (Ruth 1:16).*

The simple, appealing story of this "woman of noble character" reminds us that however corrupt a society seems, godly individuals can still be found.

Definition of Key Terms

Kinsman-redeemer. The Hebrew word is *ga'al.* Its root means to "act as a kinsman" or to fulfill one's family obligations. In Old Testament Law this included (1) redeeming land sold by a poor relative, to keep it in the family (Lev. 25:25-28), (2) redeeming a relation from slavery (vv. 48-55), (3) avenging murder (Num. 35:10-28), and (4) marrying a childless relation's widow, in which case the first son would be considered that of the dead husband (Deut. 25:5-10). The Hebrew word powerfully expresses the sense of one's obligation to help family members whenever this is possible, and has great theological implications. In becoming true Man, a member of the human family, Jesus became our Kinsman-redeemer, accepting the responsibility of paying the price for our redemption. Hebrews 2:14-15 says, "Since the children have flesh and blood, He [Jesus] too shared in their humanity so that by His death He might destroy him who holds the power of death . . . and free those who all their lives were held in slavery by their fear of death."

Overview

A famine drove Naomi's family to Moab, where the men died (1:1-5). One daughter-in-law, Ruth, returned to Bethlehem with Naomi (vv. 6-22). Ruth gleaned in the field of Boaz, a close relative of Naomi's. His kindness (2:1-23) encouraged Naomi to have Ruth seek a kinsman-redeemer marriage (3:1-18). Boaz married Ruth, and their first son, Obed, became the grandfather of David, Israel's greatest king (4:1-22).

Understanding the Text

"Return home, my daughters" Ruth 1:1-15. In Moab the husband and two sons of Naomi all died, leaving her and her two daughters-in-law alone. The normal course in such a situation would be for the younger widows to remarry. According to custom, if there were a younger son in the husband's family he might take the widow as a wife. In this case the aged Naomi had no more sons, and thus no future to offer either of her daughters-in-law. Sending them away was intended as a kindness.

It's tragic when, like Naomi, we feel our best years are past, and that we have nothing left to offer to others. In her bereavement Naomi honestly felt this way. But one of her daughters-in-law disagreed.

"Don't urge me to leave you" Ruth 1:16-22. One daughter-in-law, Ruth, saw more in Naomi than did Naomi herself. Perhaps Ruth sensed a faith in Naomi that Naomi herself had lost sight of. At any rate, Ruth made a commitment—to Naomi, and to Naomi's God.

This reflects the process by which men and women today often find their personal relationship with God. Individuals are drawn to a Christian or to Christians, and through them come to know Christ. Barbara, a young mother, explained how she became a Christian. She'd heard me speak at a church, and found it interesting. So she came to our small group Bible study, and "found people who really loved me." At first Barbara felt a little strange, realizing she wasn't "a real Christian." But she was accepted and loved anyway, and within a few months she welcomed Christ as her personal Saviour.

When we share our lives with others, even when we're having troubles as Naomi was, something about the reality of our relationship with God shines through and draws others to the Lord.

"Don't go and glean in another field" Ruth 2:1-23. Mosaic Law commanded landowners to leave that part of the harvest which dropped to the ground or was not yet ripe for the poor to gather. The name given to working in another's field to gather the leftovers was "gleaning."

As Naomi and Ruth had no other means of support, Ruth went out to glean in a field near Bethlehem. The owner was Boaz, who had heard of Ruth and her loyalty to Naomi. He not only welcomed her to his fields, but even told his workers to leave extra on the ground for her.

Boaz's kindness and his obvious trust in God (v. 12) suggest that he was the kind of person God intended every Israelite to become when He gave Israel the Law. Boaz, more than any other in this story, reminds us that godly individuals can be found in even sinful societies.

But was Boaz unusual for this time? His warning to his workers not to touch (rape) Ruth, and his warning to her not to go and glean in another field, remind us that the story is set in the time of the judges when "everyone did as he saw fit" (Jud. 21:25). Boaz was an exception, a godly man, in a time when ungodliness was the rule.

How encouraging to us. No matter what others around us may do, you and I can still follow the Lord. We do not have to surrender to the evil influences in our society. And neither do our children!

"Is not Boaz . . . a kinsman of ours?" Ruth 3:1-18 The kind treatment Boaz extended to Ruth excited Naomi. As a relative, Boaz was in a position to play the role of kinsman-redeemer. This would involve marrying Ruth, working the family land which would have been inherited by Naomi's dead son, and giving Ruth a son who would carry on Naomi's husband's line. Suddenly it appeared to Naomi that she might have a future after all!

Naomi then instructed Ruth to go to Boaz's threshing floor at night, and to "uncover his feet and lie down." Ruth did as instructed. When Boaz awoke, she asked him to "spread the corner of your garment over me."

The exact meaning of this expression, and the meaning of uncovering Boaz's feet, are lost in antiquity. Some have thought the feet were uncovered so they might become cold and awaken Boaz. Boaz understood the request to be covered by his garment as a proposal of marriage. There is no suggestion of immorality in this part of the story, though in pagan religions threshing was possibly associated with fertility rites.

"I have also acquired Ruth . . . as my wife" Ruth 4:1-11. Because there was a closer relative in town, Boaz had to offer him the first chance to serve as kinsman-redeemer. Leviticus 25:48-55 suggests that the order of relationship moved from brothers, to uncles, to uncles' sons. It is impossible to tell the exact relationship of either Boaz or the other candidate.

When the other man heard that redeeming the family land involved marriage to Ruth, he refused. Taking both the land and Ruth would mean first paying off any debts on the land, supporting Ruth as his wife, and then giving the land away to any son she might bear. The cost seems to have been more than the other relative was willing to pay. But Boaz, who admired Ruth and wanted her as his wife, was willing to pay whatever it cost to have her.

Boaz's public announcement that he was exercising the right of the kinsman-redeemer and taking Ruth as his wife was all that was required in that day to constitute marriage. The story proper concludes here, with congratulations and best wishes offered by the city elders and other townsmen (Ruth 4:11-12).

"He will renew your life" Ruth 4:13-18. In time Ruth had a son, and in that son Naomi found comfort and hope. In a sense, because the child was considered the offspring of Naomi's own son, he was her grandson; an indication that life would go on and that Naomi would not be forgotten.

Yet most touching is the praise the women of Bethlehem heaped on Ruth. In an age where having sons was the most important thing in most women's lives, the women of Bethelem could praise "your daughter-in-law, who loves you and who is better to you than seven sons."

It was Ruth's love, as much as the child held tightly in Naomi's arms, that had renewed her life.

How great a gift we give others when we love them. Love is still able to lift a despondent person like Naomi and to renew her life.

▶ DEVOTIONAL
The Right Choice
(Ruth 2–3)

"It scared me," Carrie told the counselor. "I realized the guys I was dating were just like my first husband, who drank too much and beat me."

Counselors recognize the problem. Both guys and girls find themselves attracted to unhealthy relationships. They don't stop to analyze what they really want in marriage, or why they find the wrong kind of person so attractive. Yet there is probably no more significant choice any person can make than that of a mate. And there may be no more helpful book on choosing a spouse than Ruth.

Ruth's first impression of Boaz was his kindness. Even a cursory reading of Ruth 2 shows that Boaz was kind in word and action. He was generous, godly, and sensitive to Ruth's feelings (cf. vv. 15-16). While Naomi was impressed by Boaz's ability to provide a home and security, undoubtedly Boaz's personal qualities appealed to Ruth.

Boaz blessed Ruth for her interest in him, even though he was older than she. Ruth showed family loyalty in seeking out a kinsman-redeemer, and family loyalty was greatly valued in Israel. Boaz also knew Ruth was "a woman of noble character." The word "noble" here is a strong one, suggesting more than good character. Ruth was viewed as an ideal woman by the whole community, which had been impressed with her many qualities. So Ruth was attractive to Boaz not only for her youth and beauty but for the kind of person she was.

In this case both persons chose wisely—and the wisdom of their choice is reflected in the character of their great-grandson, David.

How much we Christians today need to pattern our choice of a mate on criterion like those used by Ruth and Boaz. The superficial things emphasized in modern romance—looks, style, wealth, and social skills—are no foundation for the lifelong commitment of marriage.

Personal Application

We need to be careful in establishing any long-term relationship.

Quotable

"There can be no true and faithful learning of Christ when we are not ready to *unlearn.* By heredity, by education, by tradition, we have established thoughts about life which are often great hindrances to living the truth. To learn of Christ requires a willingness to subject every value we hold to His inspection for criticism and correction."—Andrew Murray

---

The Variety Reading Plan continues with HEBREWS

1 Samuel

INTRODUCTION

First and 2 Samuel were originally a single book in the Hebrew canon. Together they give a complete history of the transition of Israel from a group of loosely related tribes ruled by judges to a united and powerful monarchy. The time spanned is roughly 120 years, from about 1050 to 931 B.C.

First Samuel traces the emergence of the monarchy through the stories of three men. Samuel served as Israel's last judge. He anointed Israel's first king, Saul. When Saul proved unwilling to obey God's commands, Samuel secretly anointed David to succeed him. David's rise to prominence after he killed Goliath and his persecution by Saul are reported in this book, which contains many familiar and favorite Bible stories.

OUTLINE OF CONTENTS

I. The Ministry of Samuel . . . . 1 Sam. 1–7
II. The Rule of Saul . . . . 1 Sam. 8–15
III. The Rise of David . . . . 1 Sam. 16–31

READING GUIDE (8 Days)

If hurried, you may read only the "core passage" in your Bible and the Devotional in each chapter of this Commentary.

Reading	*Chapters*	*Core passage*
58	1–3	1
59	4–7	6–7
60	8–12	10–11
61	13–15	15
62	16–17	17
63	18–20	18
64	21–25	24
65	26–31	27

1 Samuel

FEBRUARY 27 *Reading 58*
THE BEST GIFTS
1 Samuel 1–3

> *"All Israel . . . recognized that Samuel was attested as a prophet of the* Lord*" (1 Sam. 3:20).*

When you or I experience frustration or depression, there's help in the story of Hannah.

Background
Samuel was born in the days of the Judges. During most of his life his people were limited to Israel's hill country by the powerful Philistines on the sea coast, and by the Ammonites across the Jordan. These early chapters which tell of Samuel's childhood, focus on important formative influences on one who became Israel's last judge and most significant prophet since the time of Moses.

Overview
Hannah vowed to dedicate her son to the service of God if only He would enable her to give birth (1:1-20). When Samuel was weaned she fulfilled her vow (vv. 21-28), expressing her joy in one of Scripture's most beautiful prayers (2:1-11). Samuel grew up under the guidance of the priest, Eli, whose own sons were evil (vv. 12-26) and were judged by God (vv. 27-36). In contrast Samuel exhibited a readiness to listen to God (3:1-18), and was early recognized by Israel as a prophet (vv. 19-21).

Understanding the Text
"In bitterness of soul Hannah wept much and prayed to the Lord*" 1 Sam. 1:1-20.* Hannah was a childless woman in a society which viewed bearing sons as fulfillment. Her pain is the same felt by every person who feels himself or herself useless and a failure. In Hannah's case, the wound was kept open by the constant provocation of her husband's second wife, Peninnah, who had several children and took perverse pleasure in tormenting Hannah over her barrenness.

For years Hannah wept before the Lord when the family attended the religious festivals held regularly at Shiloh, where the tabernacle stood during much of the Judges era. Finally Hannah made a vow—a promise that if God gave her a son, she would give her son up and let him serve God at the tabernacle.

There are many lessons to be learned from this brief chapter. The biographies of many Christian leaders tell of mothers who even before they became pregnant gave their future children to the Lord. Many years after I was led to go into the ministry, my own mother told how she had made a similar dedication—and followed it up with a lifetime of prayers that my sister and I might both serve God. We owe so much to godly mothers who see their children as gifts from God intended to be given back to Him.

Another lesson is found in the costliness of the commitment Hannah made. Having a son was Hannah's heart's desire. Yet she was willing to give up that treasure should it be given to her. Often you and I must mentally surrender what we want most to God before we are ready to receive it.

Samuel, Hannah's son, grew up to become one of the greatest of Old Testament prophets, and surely the greatest of the judges. How proud Hannah must have been to realize as Samuel grew up "all

Israel . . . recognized that Samuel was attested as a prophet of the LORD." How wise it is to place our most precious possessions in God's hand. He is far more able than we to use them for His glory, and for our fulfillment.

"He will live there always" 1 Sam. 1:21-28. Hebrew children were typically weaned at three or even four years of age. So Hannah had Samuel for those precious infant and toddler years. Elkanah's response to his wife's announcement that she would present Samuel to the Lord is significant. According to the law of vows (Num. 30), a husband could void a wife's vow when he first heard of it. Here Elkanah confirms Hannah's vow: "Do what seems best to you."

Hannah needed a godly, understanding husband, for sons were economic assets in ancient Israel. How important that a husband and wife share a common commitment to God. God warns us not to marry out of the faith with no intent to deny us any pleasure. This rule is a wise and loving provision intended to give us unified, happy homes.

"My heart rejoices" 1 Sam. 2:1-10. We can imagine Hannah's anguish as she approached the tabernacle at Shiloh, hand in hand with little Samuel, knowing she must leave him there and return home alone. Yet when the gift had been given, Hannah suddenly found herself filled with joy! God's Holy Spirit had filled the emptiness she had feared.

There would be moments of loneliness ahead. Hannah surely missed her little son. But this song of praise, in which Hannah contemplated the greatness of God, is witness to the comfort she found in her faith. A comfort available to you and me as well.

We learn that God also comforted Hannah in a practical way. She saw her son at annual religious festivals. And God gave her three more sons and two daughters (v. 21). It's good to remember that we can never out-give the Lord.

"Eli's sons were wicked men" 1 Sam. 2:12-26. The priesthood in Israel was hereditary, a role to be filled only by descendants of Aaron. Thus Eli's sons served in the priesthood as their father had. But while Eli was godly, his two sons were "wicked men." They treated the Lord's offering "with contempt" by violating ritual regulations (vv. 12-17), and used their position to seduce women who came to worship (v. 22). The two sons ignored their father's rebuke. Despite their example Samuel chose to follow Eli's example, and "grew up in the presence of the LORD."

Samuel and Eli's sons all grew up next to Israel's place of worship. Yet only Samuel sensed the reality of God, and lived in His presence. Going to church can be a meaningless experience for us too unless we understand that we are coming together with other believers to experience the presence of God, and to worship Him.

"Why do you honor your sons more than Me?" 1 Sam. 2:27-36 The prophet who confronted Eli preannounced the death of his two sons "on the same day." He asked the aged priest this question. But we may wonder, what more could Eli have done?

The answer is grim. Eli surely knew the stories of other priests who had treated God's altar with contempt and been killed by the Lord (cf. Num. 16). At the very least Eli could have removed his sons from the priesthood. At the most he could have followed the ancient law that permitted parents whose sons were incorrigible to accuse them before the elders, with the penalty, if found guilty, being death (Deut. 21:18-21).

Eli's failure to act showed that he honored his sons more than he honored the God whom the sons treated with contempt.

There are times when parents have to take sides *against* their children. A mom or dad who constantly intervenes to help children avoid the consequences of wrong actions dooms them, as surely as Eli's failure to act against his sons made their deaths inevitable. The saying, "Blood is thicker than water," must be balanced by another. "Right is more important than relationship."

"Speak, for Your servant is listening" 1 Sam. 3:1-21. The word "listen" in Hebrew is very significant. To "hear" (the same word in Hebrew) implies not simply the

physical act, but also processing and responding to what is said. Thus when a psalmist asks God to "hear my prayer," he is begging God to act. And when Samuel told God, "Your servant is listening," he expressed his willingness to respond to everything God said.

Here the writer brings out the contrast between Samuel's attitude toward God and that of Eli's sons, who "did not listen" to their father's rebuke but kept on sinning. It was the willingness of Samuel to "listen" that made him suitable to be God's instrument in a critical period of sacred history.

There is nothing more significant for anyone who wishes to be used by God than to adopt Samuel's attitude of "speak, for Your servant is listening."

▶ DEVOTIONAL

Where to Seek Comfort (1 Sam. 1)

I find it easy to feel with Hannah, so despondent and depressed by what must have felt like total failure. I suspect all of us have down times. Times when life seems dark and empty, as if everything had gone wrong.

With Hannah it had gone even further. The pain was so great that her heart had become bitter. In her bitterness food lost all attraction, and she was unable to eat (v. 7).

In Hannah's case, the problem was resolved when she made her vow to God and the Lord answered her prayer. For some of us the answer doesn't come so quickly. Or perhaps at all. And so it's important to know where to seek comfort *during* the bitter times.

The answer is seen in the text's description of Elkanah, Hannah's husband. The Bible says that "he loved her." Rather than berate her for her failure to produce sons, Elkanah tried to comfort Hannah, saying, "Don't I mean more to you than ten sons?" It's clear that despite what Hannah suffered, her husband was a constant, present blessing.

This is where you and I are to find comfort while we wait for God to relieve our pain. No, not in a loving husband or wife. But in whatever present blessings God may give us. We need to focus on the good things, for in them we find evidence that God hasn't forsaken us after all. In them we find evidence that we are loved, even though we may feel despair.

Focusing on God's good gifts won't take the pain away immediately. But it can make the pain bearable. And in time, whether we receive what we long for or not, awareness of God's love will sustain us and lead us to experience joy.

Personal Application

God gives good gifts to all. All we need is the wisdom to recognize them, and the grace to appreciate them.

Quotable

"What is the command associated with being given the desires of our heart? 'Delight yourself.' The word 'delight' means to be soft and pliable. We might say be moldable and teachable. It means more than being happy or excited about God."—Earl D. Wilson

FEBRUARY 28 *Reading 59*
THE LOST ARK
1 Samuel 4–7

"A god has come into the camp" (1 Sam. 4:7).

We should never take the symbols of our faith for the reality. Yet to many, symbols are important.

Definition of Key Terms

The ark of the covenant. The ark was the holiest object in Israel's religion. This box-like, gold-covered object contained memorials of the Exodus—notably the stone tablets containing the Ten Commandments and a container of manna. Two cast angels were mounted on its lid, their wings touching over its center, where each year the high priest sprinkled sacrificial blood on the Day of Atonement. The ark, which symbolized the presence of God with His people, was to be kept in the inner room of the tabernacle. The act of Eli's sons in removing it showed both their contempt for God's command, and a superstitious awe of the ark as a symbol.

Archeologists have recovered many Philistine artifacts. These show a high level of material culture and artistic achievement. The Philistines far outclassed the Israelites in their skills, but were far inferior in their religion.

Overview

The Philistines killed Eli's two wicked sons in battle and captured the ark of the covenant (4:1-22). Plagues frightened the Philistines into returning the ark (5:1–6:21). Some 20 years later, Samuel led Israel back to God (7:1-6). God then helped the Israelites hand the Philistines a crushing defeat at Mizpah, and guarded them throughout Samuel's lifetime (vv. 7-17).

Understanding the Text

"A god has come into the camp" 1 Sam. 4:1-11. The Philistine reaction when the ark was brought into the Hebrew camp tells us much about their religion. They worshiped idols and supposed that Israel's God was an idol too. What is more significant, however, is Israel's reaction. God's people shouted for joy, for they too believed that the Lord Himself was identified with this material object.

We can value symbols of the holy. But we must never confuse them with God or rely on them as if they were God Himself. As Jesus taught us, "God is Spirit, and His worshipers must worship in spirit and in truth" (John 4:24).

"The glory has departed from Israel" 1 Sam. 4:12-22. In the battle, Eli's sons were killed and the ark captured. The loss of the ark was a disaster, but not because it was a "god." The ark was the one place where blood could be sprinkled on the Day of Atonement to cleanse Israel of sin. The true glory of God, displayed in His goodness and forgiving love, truly had departed from Israel. God's people now had no avenue of approach to the Lord to find forgiveness.

We may take pride in the beauty of our churches or cathedrals. Yet the true glory of God is not to be found in them, but in His love and His grace.

"He afflicted the people . . . with an outbreak of tumors" 1 Sam. 5:1–6:21. When the ark of God was placed in the temple of Dagon, a Philistine god, the idol fell before the ark. Even a symbol of God is greater than the gods of pagans.

Many believe that the "tumors" God sent were actually hemorrhoids. How fitting. The Philistines were not even allowed to sit comfortably in the presence of God's ark!

At last the Philistines decided that the God of Israel caused their discomfort and returned the ark. For 20 years it rested on the property of a man called Abinadab.

"Because they had looked into the ark of the L*ORD" 1 Sam. 6:19.* When 70 Israelites curiously looked into the ark, God struck them down. Why? Eli's two sons had shown contempt for God by ignoring rules for conducting worship. These men showed contempt for God by treating the ark, a holy thing, as if it were an ordinary object. While the symbol is not the reality, symbols of the holy are to be treated with respect.

"The Israelites . . . served the L*ORD only" 1 Sam. 7:1-6.* When Samuel grew to adulthood he was able to lead Israel back to the Lord. Samuel was recognized as a spokesman of God (3:20). When he promised that God would deliver His people from Philistine oppression, he was believed.

Sometimes only suffering will move us to turn to God. If that's what it takes, God will bless us with suffering.

"The L*ORD answered him" 1 Sam. 7:7-17.* When the Philistines attacked a religious convocation at Mizpah, Israel fought back as Samuel prayed. The Bible says that the Lord answered him. Samuel had listened to God all his life. Now God listened to him. Obeying God's Word lays a good foundation for prayer.

The text tells us that Samuel served as Israel's "judge" (ruler) all the days of his life. During this time Israelite strength grew, and they were at last able to push the Philistines out of the highlands.

▶DEVOTIONAL
Symbols and Reality
(1 Sam. 6–7)

The ark of God was His chosen symbol of His presence with Israel. It was not God. He did not inhabit it. But in a real way it stood for Him. As such, the symbol was to be treated with respect.

When the victorious Philistines carried the ark into the temple of their god, they saw it as a trophy. Placed there, the ark would symbolize the superiority of their deity to Israel's God. Instead the prostrate, broken idol of Dagon proved that the Lord alone is truly God.

When a plague of "tumors" broke out in the Philistine cities, the Philistines knew the cause. Israel's God was so holy that the Philistines could not even survive the presence of a symbol that represented Him.

When the ark was returned, God struck down 70 of His own people who curiously looked inside it, treating it as if it were a common object rather than something set apart and holy.

Each of these events helps us understand those who find significance today in Christian symbols. The stained glass, the churches, the organs, the crosses, the ritual, the Christmas crèches, even the roadside shrines, are not to be identified with God, as though He were present in them. Yet each can serve as a symbol of the holy. Each can remind believers of who God is, and in reminding, can invite them to worship.

You or I may not rely on symbols in our worship. We may not feel they are needed, or we may even feel that they hinder true worship. But the ark of God, which was holy in the Old Testament era, reminds us that God does speak to some through symbols. And when He does, the symbol is sanctified by His use.

Personal Application

We need to be sure that our religious symbols actually do direct our thoughts to God Himself.

Quotable

"Clearly nothing that the organized church can do by its services, by religious books, by radio and television will effect the needful change. Only as the individual translates his Christianity into terms of the way he does his daily work and the loving spirit he shows daily in his contact with others, can Christianity leaven the very heavy lump of modern life."—Leslie D. Weatherhead

MARCH 1 *Reading 60*
ISRAEL'S FIRST KING
1 Samuel 8–12

"Give us a king to lead us" (1 Sam. 8:6).

The story of Israel's transition to a monarchy reminds us that the root of our problems is often in ourselves.

Definition of Key Terms

King. In Old Testament times kings controlled all the functions of government—legislative, executive, and judicial. The people owed total allegiance to their ruler, and the ruler in turn protected his people by leading them in war as well as peace.

As originally conceived, Israel was a theocracy—a people whose King was God. In the Old Testament Law Covenant God committed Himself to fight Israel's battles and to cause the nation to prosper. In turn the people were to obey the laws enacted by their Monarch, and give their allegiance completely to Him.

The role of the king in Old Testament times, and the teaching of Scripture that God was Himself Israel's King, helps us to see why Israel's request for a human monarch was in fact a rejection of the Lord.

Anoint. The act of pouring oil on the head of a person. Anointing was a symbolic act consecrating persons whom God had chosen for a special role, such as priest or king.

Overview

Israel's request for a king implied rejection of God (8:1-22). Samuel anointed Saul privately (9:1–10:8), and later publicly introduced him as God's choice (vv. 9-27). After Saul led Israel to victory over the Ammonites (11:1-11), the people confirmed Saul as ruler (vv. 12-15). Samuel stepped down from political leadership, but warned Israel to obey God, and promised to pray constantly for them (12:1-25).

Understanding the Text

"Appoint a king to lead us, such as all the other nations have" 1 Sam. 8:1-22. Moses had predicted that one day Israel would have a king (cf. Gen. 49:10; Num. 24:17; Deut. 17:14-20). Yet the motive of the elders of Israel who asked Samuel to appoint a king was wrong.

God had held back the Philistines all of Samuel's long rule as judge (1 Sam. 7:13). But Samuel's sons, who he unwisely had appointed judges, accepted bribes. This, with Samuel's age, created uncertainty about the future. The need even seemed urgent when the Ammonites prepared to move against Israel (12:12). Rather than inquire of God what to do, the elders of Israel turned to pagan ways to deal with a leadership vacuum. They asked for a king "as all the other nations have." God pointed out to a visibly upset Samuel that the request was in fact a rejection of Him, for since the Exodus the Lord Himself had functioned as Israel's King.

Samuel warned Israel by showing the faults in the pagan system. Kings demand taxes, take the brightest and best to serve their administrations, and even transfer citizens' property to their attendants (8:10-18). But the people insisted. They desperately wanted to "be like all the other nations, with a king to lead us and to go out before us and fight our battles" (v. 20).

Like the ancient Israelites, modern Christians can be all too quick to turn to secular solutions. In times of uncertainty we often run to the world. Pastors struggling with church leadership sign up for seminars on management. Missionaries eager to reach a lost world look to statistics for principles of church growth. Parents desperate for guidance try pop psychology. While each of these may be of some help, each secular system has its drawbacks. But most tragic, each serves as a substitute for better ways that God has mapped out in His Word for believers.

Israel's insistence on a monarchy at this point in history stands as a warning to us. When we face uncertainty, let's seek God's answer, rather than adopt the world's solutions and be "like all the others."

"He will deliver My people from the hand of the Philistines" 1 Sam. 9:1–10:8. The text describes a series of events that makes it clear the Lord personally supervised the

choice of Saul. The loss of several donkeys launched Saul on a trip that led, step by step, to Samuel. God identified Saul as the one God intended to govern His people.

After Samuel anointed Saul to be king, Samuel made a series of predictions intended to convince that reluctant young man that God had indeed chosen him (10:2-7).

A question that has troubled believers is, Why did God choose Saul, in view of Saul's later failures? Did God intend to show the people the error of their ways by selecting a flawed leader? Not at all. The people had asked for a leader who would "go out before us and fight our battles." When God told Samuel to anoint Saul, the Lord told him, "He will deliver My people from the hand of the Philistines" (9:16). God gave Israel a king who would do just what the people asked!

We need to evaluate our prayers carefully. Is what we ask for what we really need? Is what we ask for what is truly best for us?

What Israel should have asked for is a king after God's own heart. One who would be responsive to God, and keep Israel close to the Lord. It is a measure of God's grace that when Saul's flaws were fully revealed, the Lord provided His people with just such a king in David.

"See the man the LORD has chosen" 1 Sam. 10:9-26. One of the means used in the Old Testament to determine God's will was casting lots. Another was the Urim and Thummim—most likely smooth stones indicating yes or no—carried by the high priest. Here some such means was used to indicate the Lord's choice of a tribe, clan, family, and finally individual.

Saul, possibly moved by an appealing modesty or perhaps by fear, was found hiding among the baggage. He was an imposing figure, "a head taller" than any other Israelite. Based on the average height of Israelites in that era, Saul was probably between 6'4" and 6'6" tall. Saul was presented to the people, most of whom were impressed by his height and shouted, "Long live the king!"

Like Israel, we're often impressed by externals. Samuel's invitation, "See the man," reminds us not to judge by appearances, but to look for character.

"Let us . . . reaffirm the kingship" 1 Sam. 11:1-15. The Ammonite attack on Jabesh Gilead may have been a direct challenge to Saul, who as a Benjamite might trace his lineage to this city (Jud. 21:9-16). Saul rallied Israel and led the people to victory.

The victory resolved any remaining doubts, and Saul was confirmed as king by all the people at Gilgal. Saul's gracious treatment of those who earlier refused to acknowledge him was notable (1 Sam. 11:12-13). So was Saul's humble attitude, as he gave credit for the victory to "the LORD [who] has rescued Israel" (v. 13).

"You have not cheated or oppressed us" 1 Sam. 12:1-5. Few political or spiritual leaders can conclude their careers as Samuel did. He led for love of the people and for love of God, not for personal gain or power.

"If both you and the king who reigns over you follow the LORD your God—good" 1 Sam. 12:6-25. Samuel turned over the reins of political power to Saul in the public gathering at Gilgal, though he continued as spiritual leader (cf. v. 23). The speech was dramatic. Samuel recounted how faithful God had been when Israel looked to Him as ruler, and made it plain that Israel's motive in seeking a king at that time was wrong. To underline this, God sent a destructive thunderstorm. As wheat harvest is the dry season in Israel, this was viewed as a miraculous sign, and led Israel to admit their request for a king was a sin.

Samuel's response is for us as well as for Israel. "Do not be afraid. You have done all this evil; yet do not turn away from the LORD." Sin is wrong, but God will not reject the person who turns from it and clings faithfully to Him.

▶ DEVOTIONAL
Fully Equipped
(1 Sam. 10–11)

Every child who goes to Sunday School is familiar with Saul's failure. He is the flawed king, the vindictive enemy of David, who again and again disobeyed God. It's no wonder that some question whether God deliberately chose a man who would fall short, as punishment for those who insisted on a king. Did God set Israel up? Was Saul God's choice only so He could later say, "I told you so"?

That question is answered clearly and firmly in the text. And the answer is no. In fact, God thoroughly prepared Saul—not for failure, but for success.

Notice. Saul was given signs to ensure that he realized he had been chosen by God (10:1-7). God immediately let Saul know that He was personally involved in Saul's choice and his life.

Saul was infused by the Spirit of God and, the text says, "God changed Saul's heart" (vv. 9-10). God worked within Saul to make him sensitive to the Lord.

Saul was suddenly able to prophesy, causing amazement in those who knew him (v. 11). God prepared Saul's acquaintances for Saul's new role.

Saul was publicly selected by God at Gilgal (vv. 20-24). God made it clear to the whole nation that Saul was His choice.

Saul was again filled by the Spirit when he called out the nation to fight the Ammonites (11:7). God gave Saul special enablement when the crisis came.

And Saul's victory was evidence of God's presence. The new king realized that "the LORD has rescued Israel" (v. 13).

What this shows is that God did nothing that might have caused Saul's later failures. Instead, the Lord did everything possible to equip Saul for success! As the New Testament affirms, "God cannot be tempted by evil, nor does He tempt anyone; but each one is tempted when, by his own evil desire, he is dragged away and enticed" (James 1:13-14).

What an important message for you and me. When God calls us to any task, He intends us to succeed! And He provides all the resources we need to achieve success. If we stay close to Him we will avoid the tragedy that later befell Saul, Israel's first king.

Personal Application

Because each of us does have flaws, it is vital that we stay close to the Lord.

Quotable

"With every thought from the Word that your understanding grasps, bow before God in dependence and trust. Believe with your whole heart that God can and will make it true. Ask for the Holy Spirit to make it work in your heart until the Word becomes the strength of your life."—Andrew Murray

---

MARCH 2 *Reading 61*
SAUL'S FLAWS
1 Samuel 13–15

> *"Because you have rejected the word of the LORD, He has rejected you as king" (1 Sam. 15:23).*

Too often success breeds pride. When that happens, there's a real danger that we will no longer rely on—or obey—the Lord.

Overview

Facing a powerful Philistine army, Saul panicked and officiated at a sacrifice rather than waiting for Samuel (13:1-15). Yet the poorly equipped Israelites (vv. 16-22) led by Jonathan, Saul's son, attacked (14:1-14) and routed the enemy (vv. 15-23). The intervention of the army saved Jonathan, who unknowingly violated Saul's command (vv. 24-52). Ironically, the man who was willing to execute his son for disobeying him unintentionally, knowingly disobeyed God, and was rejected by the Lord (15:1-35).

Understanding the Text

"Their situation was critical" 1 Sam. 13:1-7. The Philistines were the major enemy of Israel during this era. They controlled the coastlands. Archeologists have found evidence of Philistine outposts as far inland as the Jordan valley. When Saul's son attacked one of these outposts, the Philistines assembled a great army to put down the Hebrew uprising.

Earlier the men of Israel had responded to Saul's call and turned out to fight the Ammonites (11:7). Now they ran and hid, and some even left the country. Many in Saul's tiny standing army of 3,000 began to desert. In describing the Ammonite battle the text says Israel was moved by "terror [awe of, respect for] of the LORD." Now all they felt was fear of the Philistines.

The Old Testament rightly says that the "fear of the LORD is the beginning of knowledge" (Prov. 1:7). It's foolish to lose sight of the fact that God is more powerful than any human foe.

"You acted foolishly" 1 Sam. 13:8-15. Earlier Samuel had instructed Saul to meet him at Gilgal before any major engagement, and to wait there seven days (cf. 10:8). Waiting now became too much for Saul, who panicked as he saw more of his tiny force desert. Rather than wait for Samuel, Saul himself sacrificed to the Lord. Saul sinned in officiating at the sacrifice. Only priests were to serve the altar. By acting as he did, Saul disobeyed Samuel's command to wait and God's prohibition against any but Aaron's descendants offering sacrifices. Here "foolish" is a strong word, implying not a lack of understanding but a lack of moral character. Under pressure Saul showed that he was deeply flawed.

The text adds an ironic note. Saul later counted and found that he still had 600 men with him. This was twice as many as the 300 with which Gideon had earlier routed a similar enemy horde.

Weapons of iron 1 Sam. 13:16-22. It's true that Israel lacked weapons. The Philistine secret of working iron gave them unquestioned military superiority. But Gideon defeated his enemy with 300 pitchers, 300 torches, and 300 trumpets.

If only Saul had remembered what God had done, he might have been less fearful and more willing to obey.

"That will be our sign" 1 Sam. 14:1-14. The text introduces Jonathan, Saul's son, who attacked a Philistine frontline post after seeking and receiving a sign that "the LORD has given them into our hands." Jonathan and his armor-bearer were outnumbered too. But Jonathan, unlike Saul, trusted God completely and had no fear.

"Withdraw your hand" 1 Sam. 14:15-23. After Jonathan's victory, God threw the Philistine camp into a panic. Saul, hearing the commotion, called for a priest to use the ephod [not "ark"] to consult God. As the tumult across the valley increased, Saul couldn't wait, and told the priest to "withdraw your hand." That is, he said, "Don't bother," and rushed off to battle.

Despite Saul's behavior, the Lord helped Israel. The Philistines began to run away, and the Israelites who had hidden joined in the pursuit.

"None of the troops tasted food" 1 Sam. 14:24-45. Saul uttered a curse on any Israelite who should eat until the battle was over. Jonathan did not hear this vow and tasted some honey he found during the battle.

Saul's command was unwise. His troops pursued the Philistines some 18 miles (from Micmash to Aijalon)! Afterward they were so exhausted that they butchered cattle and ate the meat on the spot. This eating of meat before the blood had been drained was a serious violation of Old Testament Law.

When Saul was eager to go on and invade Philistine territory, the priest, whom Saul had rushed to consult earlier, insisted Saul ask God for guidance. But God gave no answer. (Many believe the priest carried a blank stone in the ephod as well as stones indicating yes and no.) Saul assumed that some sin was blocking the response. When lots were cast, Jonathan was chosen, and admitted violating his father's command. Though Saul's command had been unwise, when uttered as a curse it was binding, and disobedience was a sin.

When Saul proposed executing Jonathan, the army refused to let Saul harm him.

Again we sense irony. Saul was ready to kill his own son for disobeying his command. Yet Saul himself thought nothing of disobeying the Lord, Israel's God and true King.

"He fought valiantly" 1 Sam. 14:47-48. Most of the text is given to an analysis of Saul's flaws. Two verses sum up his strengths. Saul was a valiant soldier, who did defeat Israel's enemies.

To the biblical writer, who gives only two verses to chronicle Saul's victories, what counts is not Saul's prowess but his pride. Not his accomplishments, but his personal failings. It's the same today. The true measure of a man is not found in what he does, but in the kind of person that he is.

"I was afraid of the people and so I gave in to them" 1 Sam. 15:1-34. The final revealing incident describes Saul's attack on the Amalekites. This invasion was divine punishment, and the city attacked was to be "devoted" to God. That is, all the people and animals of the area were to be killed, and no booty taken.

Saul did attack. But he returned with vast herds and with a royal prisoner. God sent Samuel to confront the disobedient king. At first Saul insisted he had obeyed God. After all, the Amalekites had been destroyed. Finally Saul admitted that he had violated God's command, and confessed that he had done so because he "was afraid of the people."

What a commentary. Saul, the king, was ruled by fear. He had feared the Philistine army. Now he was afraid of his own people. If only Saul had feared God, respect for the Lord would have freed him from the burden of fearing mere men.

"Please honor me . . . before Israel" 1 Sam. 15:30. The verse is a fitting epitaph. A heartbroken and angry Samuel announced God's final rejection of Saul. This disobedient king would establish no dynasty in Israel. And all Saul could think of when Samuel turned away is how it would look to his people!

May God deliver us from caring more about what people think than what God thinks of us, and from the hypocrisy that such an attitude generates.

▶ DEVOTIONAL
Saul and You
(1 Sam. 15)

Some find reading about Saul frightening. Saul reminds them of their own weaknesses. Saul reflects their own flaws. And so they wonder. Perhaps like Saul they've gone too far. Might they too be rejected by God?

Yet the story of Saul isn't intended to frighten us. It's in our Bible to encourage us. And to teach us how to avoid the pitfall that trapped Israel's first, failed king.

Saul's basic problem was that he was unwilling to trust God, and so found it impossible to obey Him. Saul panicked when confronted by a massive Philistine force (1 Sam. 13). He forgot that God was able to deliver. Because he did not trust God to act in the deteriorating situation, Saul disobeyed the Lord.

By the time we read this last story, Saul is even afraid of his own people. Once again Saul's fear comes from a lack of trust, and is expressed as a failure to obey the Lord.

The one thing that ruined Saul's life and destroyed his future was his inability to trust God, expressed in his failure to obey. This is what's so encouraging about Saul's story. As we read it we come to understand the central issue in the spiritual life. Saul's story teaches us that the one thing we must do is to trust God, and that trust will free us to obey.

When you or I feel fear or sense panic, that's the time to pause and remember who our God is. To think about His greatness. To remember His power. To meditate on His love. When we keep our hearts fixed on who God is, we trust ourselves to Him. And we obey.

Personal Application

Trust in God frees us to obey. And obedience protects us from Saul's fate.

Quotable

"He that cannot obey, cannot command."—Benjamin Franklin

MARCH 3 *Reading 62*
SHEPHERD AND SAVIOUR
1 Samuel 16–17

"I come against you in the name of the LORD Almighty, the God of the armies of Israel" (1 Sam. 17:45).

When the obstacles we face seem overwhelming, it helps to remember the young shepherd boy, David, whose faith gave him courage to face the giant Goliath.

Biography: David
David was Israel's ideal king, a type of the Messiah whom the Old Testament predicts will one day rule not only the Holy Land but the whole earth. As Israel's king, David welded the 12 tribes into a powerful, united nation. He conquered Israel's enemies, and multiplied its territory 10 times. David also united the nation spiritually, making Jerusalem the religious as well as political capital. He reorganized Israel's worship and wrote many of the psalms used in public services.

Despite his many accomplishments, David is portrayed in Scripture as a very human individual. He was a man who truly loved God, yet a man who had serious weaknesses. What distinguishes David from Saul is David's humility and his willingness to confess his sins, not only to the Lord but also publicly (cf. Ps. 51). Like so many other famous men, David's children disappointed him, and David failed to deal wisely with them.

David is an important figure theologically. The Old Testament predicts that the Messiah, the promised Deliverer of humankind, would descend from David. Other prophecies show that this Person, David's greater Son, would also be the Son of God. Genealogies in the Gospels make it clear that Jesus Christ meets this requirement, and fulfills God's promise to David that the ultimate Ruler would come from his family line.

Overview
God sent Samuel to the house of Jesse, where the old prophet anointed David to become Israel's future king (16:1-13). David entered Saul's service as a musician (vv. 14-23). When the Philistines assembled to attack Israel, only David was willing to face their champion, the giant Goliath (17:1-37). In history's most famous duel, young David killed Goliath with his sling (vv. 38-58).

Understanding the Text
"Man looks at the outward appearance, but the LORD looks at the heart" 1 Sam. 16:1-12. God sent Samuel to the home of Jesse of Bethlehem to anoint one of his sons king in place of Saul, whom He had rejected. There Samuel was impressed by Jesse's oldest, who looked impressive but was not God's choice.

We see the wisdom of God's rejection of Eliab later, when Eliab not only cowered before Goliath with the rest of Israel, but angrily rebuked David for expressing his belief that God would help an Israelite defeat "this uncircumcised Philistine" (cf. 17:26-28).

It's significant that even Samuel, a wise man with much spiritual insight, was deceived by Eliab's physical appearance. It's not surprising that today we place too much importance on beauty when choosing a mate, and on TV image when selecting national leaders. God's rebuke of Samuel is one each of us needs to take seriously. Like God, we need to make choices based on what is in others' hearts. Lacking God's perfect knowledge, you and I need to go slowly in developing relationships. More than one life has been ruined by making a quick commitment without knowing enough about another's character.

"From that day on the Spirit of the LORD came upon David" 1 Sam. 16:13. The New Testament teaches that the Holy Spirit now lives in each believer, and is the Source of our spiritual growth and power (cf. 1 Cor. 3:16; 2 Cor. 3:18). But we should not read this New Testament meaning into the Old Testament phrase. In the Old Testament, the Spirit "coming upon" someone is a technical theological phrase. It means simply that God empowered the person spoken of for a specific task. In David's case the task was to be ruler of Israel, with all the military and other responsibilities rule would entail.

God provides the resources we need to accomplish any task He sets before us.

"An evil spirit from the LORD" 1 Sam. 16:14-23. Saul, having rejected God, was now subject to fits of rage and deep depressions. The Old Testament ascribes the cause of his irrational moments to an "evil spirit from Yahweh." Some take this to indicate a demon, one of Satan's followers, who was permitted to torment Saul (cf. Matt. 12:24). Others believe the phrase speaks of Saul's own spirit, "evil" in the sense of harmful or painful. Either interpretation affirms God's sovereignty, and suggests either punishment or a last effort to turn Saul back to God.

David was introduced to court life when he was recommended as a skilled harpist. David's playing quieted Saul during his bad times. David did not stay with the king permanently, but was allowed to return home at times when Saul was well (1 Sam. 17:15).

"I defy the ranks of Israel!" 1 Sam. 17:1-16 The armies of Israel and Philistia were drawn up opposite each other. A deep ravine cuts across the Elah valley, and apparently neither force was willing to risk attacking across it. So the giant Goliath came out daily for over a month and challenged Israel to send out a representative to fight him. Such duels before the main battle were not uncommon in ancient times. As Goliath was some 9′9″ (3 meters) tall, and carried a spear whose point was heavier than a modern shot put, the Israelites were too terrified to accept the challenge.

"Who is this uncircumcised Philistine?" 1 Sam. 17:17-31 In Old Testament times citizen soldiers had to provide their own supplies. So Jesse sent his youngest, David, to bring more food to his brothers. David was shocked that no one had been willing to fight Goliath, and openly expressed his surprise.

The question, "Who is this uncircumcised Philistine?" is dismissive. Since Goliath was not one of God's covenant people, he could expect no help from the Lord and thus should be defeated easily.

David's repeated questions about the reward offered to anyone who would defeat Goliath, and his bold statements, angered his older brother. But they had their desired effect. Saul heard about David's remarks, and called him to his tent.

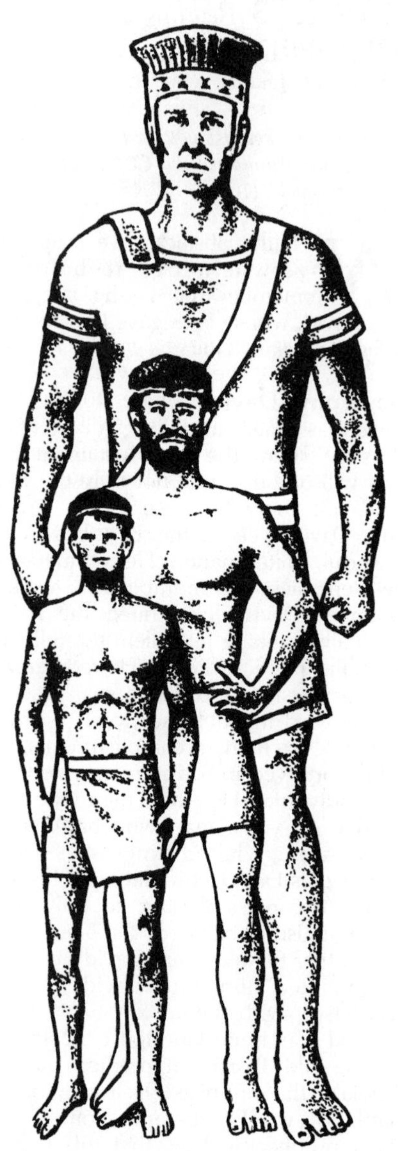

In Old Testament times the average Israelite was about 5′ tall. The picture shows a typical Israelite, Saul (who was a head taller than any of his people [cf. 1 Sam. 10:23]), and the giant Goliath.

"You are not able" 1 Sam. 17:32-37. Saul's

heart must have sunk when he saw David, a mere youth, and smaller than average at that. But David confidently related his exploits against wild animals who attacked his father's sheep, and his belief that the Lord would "deliver me from the hand of this Philistine." Perhaps Saul was impressed. At any rate, he gave David permission to fight.

God can still do more with one little person willing to try than with a whole army of hesitant soldiers.

"I come against you in the name of the LORD" 1 Sam. 17:38-54. We all know the outcome of that battle. With a single stone hurled from his sling David killed Goliath, serving ever since as the prime example of faith overcoming impossible odds.

"Whose son is that young man?" 1 Sam. 17:55-58 The question does not contradict the 1 Samuel 16 description of David in Saul's court. Saul knew who David was, but did not remember his lineage. David identified his father, who benefited from David's victory by being forever exempt from royal taxation (cf. 17:25).

▶ DEVOTIONAL
Giant Killers
(1 Sam. 17)
There have been too many sermons on the subject to belabor the point. The odds seemed impossible when David went out to meet Goliath. Yet, with faith in God and a simple shepherd's sling, David won.

Everyone has times when he or she faces a personal Goliath in some situation in which the odds seem impossible. A challenge that no one else is willing to take up. A struggle it seems impossible to win. When that happens, we, like David, have nowhere to turn but to God. We are to remember that we too can meet that personal giant in the name of the Lord Almighty, the God of hosts.

It was in God's name that David killed Goliath. It is with God's help that Christians through the ages have faced similar impossible odds—and won.

Personal Application
Learn to see your problems as "uncircumcised Philistines." Face them with courage and faith.

Quotable
"Difficulties are God's errands. When we are sent upon them we should esteem it a proof of God's confidence and as a compliment from Him."—Henry Ward Beecher

---

MARCH 4 *Reading 63*
DAVID IN SAUL'S COURT
1 Samuel 18–20

> *"When Saul saw how successful [David] was, he was afraid of him" (1 Sam. 18:15).*

Character is often revealed in how a person reacts to success. Especially the success of others!

Biography: Jonathan
Jonathan is one of the most attractive of Old Testament characters. Though heir to Saul's throne, Jonathan remained close to David and confronted his father for treating David unjustly. When Jonathan learned that Saul had made up his mind to kill David, Jonathan warned his brother-in-law. Aware that God intended to strip the throne from his father's house because of Saul's sins, Jonathan pledged to support David, and David promised to do good to Jonathan and his family. After Jonathan was killed in battle and David became king, David kept that promise. Jonathan's unselfish love for David continues to serve Christians as a model for friendship.

Overview
The success of David, now an officer in Saul's army, made the king jealous and fearful (18:1-19). Saul attempted to use his

daughter Michal's love for David to get him killed in battle, but David again succeeded and married into the royal family (vv. 20-30). David avoided several attempts on his life by Saul (19:1-24). When Prince Jonathan, David's friend, realized Saul was determined to kill his son-in-law, he helped David flee (20:1-42).

Understanding the Text

"Saul was afraid of David, because the LORD was with David but had left Saul" 1 Sam. 18:1-16. The defeat of Goliath won David high rank in Saul's army. David's military successes were so spectacular, and his popularity so great, that Saul became intensely jealous.

Earlier Saul had shown that he was more concerned with being honored by his people than with being faithful to God (15:30). David's popularity made Saul intensely jealous. When Saul realized that David's success was due to his relationship with the Lord—a relationship which Saul had forfeited—Saul also feared David. Terrified that David might supplant him as king, Saul himself twice tried to kill David (18:11).

When Saul offered David his eldest daughter, as he had pledged before the battle with Goliath, David realized this would place him in even greater danger and refused.

"She may be a snare to him" 1 Sam. 18:20-30. As David's popularity grew, Saul hesitated to attack him directly. Learning that Michal, his youngest daughter, was in love with David, Saul had court officials tell David that the king truly wanted him as a son-in-law. Saul waved the normal dowry, or bride price, which for a king's daughter would have been extremely high. Instead Saul said he would settle for trophies proving David had killed a hundred Philistines. Saul's whole purpose in this was to get David killed by Israel's enemy so that he could not be blamed. When David succeeded, Saul could do nothing but keep his promise. Yet this added evidence of God's blessing made Saul an even more determined enemy.

What is sometimes overlooked is Saul's cruel use of Michal. He cared nothing for the fact that she loved David, and thought nothing of the misery David's death would cause his youngest girl. Later, after David fled, Saul married Michal off to another. The brutal disregard of her father, as well as of others, undoubtedly contributed to the bitterness and anger she later exhibited toward David and toward God (cf. 2 Sam. 6:20-23).

Actions motivated by jealousy and anger always are harmful—to the individual and to everyone around him or her.

"Jonathan spoke well of David" 1 Sam. 19:1-7. A reconciliation affected by Jonathan was short-lived, despite Saul's promise not to put David to death. It's not uncommon in intimate relationships for a person who strikes out and hurts another to show remorse and promise, "I'll never do it again." But when a pattern develops, with repeated apologies followed by repeated fits of jealousy and rage, be warned.

"Michal let David down" 1 Sam. 19:9-17. At last Saul determined to murder David openly and have done with it. Michal got word of the plot and helped David escape. Recent research suggests that *teraphim,* the object Michal laid on David's bed and covered with blankets, does not necessarily mean "idol" in this context.

How significant that two of Saul's children took sides with David against their own father. We too need to act on what we believe is right, whatever the cost.

"Is Saul also among the prophets?" 1 Sam. 19:18-24 When Saul heard that David had gone to Samuel and that the two were together at Ramah, he sent men to capture David. However, when Saul's men approached Samuel, they were overcome by God's Spirit and "prophesied." Many believe that here "prophesy" is some form of ecstatic speech, perhaps a corollary to the New Testament gift of tongues.

Saul himself went to Ramah, and he too experienced the Spirit of the Lord coming on him. Remember the limited meaning in the Old Testament of the Spirit "coming upon" a person. This was no sign of spirituality, or even of faith. After all, the Spirit once enabled a donkey to speak to the pagan seer, Balaam (Num. 22).

"We have sworn friendship with each other in

the name of the L*ORD*" *1 Sam. 20:1-42.* In an angry confrontation with his father, Jonathan was at last convinced that Saul would never stop trying to kill David. Jonathan warned David, and the two pledged eternal friendship.

What an example these two are for Christians. Potential rivals for the same throne, each set aside personal interests out of the deep affection they had for each other. Jonathan risked his father's anger, and even his life, on behalf of David. Later David restored the fortunes of Jonathan's youngest son, despite the fact that Jonathan's line had a claim to the throne and might produce a rival. These two each display the attitude that Paul later exhorted all Christians to have. "Each of you should look not only to your own interests, but also to the interests of others" (Phil. 2:4).

▶ DEVOTIONAL
Dealing with Jealousy (1 Sam. 18)

Insecure people are likely to be threatened by the success of others. What David experienced isn't uncommon at all. Some husbands are threatened when their wives are promoted at work or earn a college degree. Bosses are frequently threatened by bright, competent employees. Others are threatened when a friend proves popular, or is attractive, or even dresses well. Like Saul, such insecure people are likely to express their jealousy as anger and strike out. Usually they strike with words intended to humiliate or belittle, or to rob another of credit.

In a way we should be sorry for the person who is so insecure that he or she has to cut others down in an effort to build himself up. But it still hurts when someone strikes out at us. So the question is, what can we do in a situation where we, like David, are innocent victims of another's vindictiveness? First Samuel 18 suggests three principles.

(1) Keep on trying to do well. David didn't let Saul's antagonism rob him of his enthusiasm for his work as an army officer or destroy his effectiveness.

(2) Stay close to the Lord. Part of Saul's antagonism was rooted in his awareness that the Lord was with David. David's success grew out of that relationship, as God blessed David's efforts. Staying close to the Lord when victimized by others will comfort us. And it will enable us to keep on living successfully.

(3) Maintain a humble demeanor. David wisely refused to become Saul's son-in-law when first offered the privilege. David was honestly humble. But he was also wise enough to realize that Saul was insincere in his offer. The best way to avoid traps others may set for us is to be honestly humble.

Later David set this principle aside and married a daughter of the king. God protected David, but the marriage did nothing to bring David to the throne. It only confirmed Saul's hostility toward David.

There is little we can do to change a person who is determined to be hostile toward us. But if we follow David's example, we can keep our own hearts pure, and limit the damage a hostile person may do.

Personal Application

It's usually wiser to avoid hostile individuals than battle them.

Quotable

"If people speak ill of you, live so that no one will believe them."—Plato

MARCH 5 *Reading 64*
DAVID THE FUGITIVE
1 Samuel 21–25

"Saul's son Jonathan went to David at Horesh and helped him find strength in God" (1 Sam. 23:16).

The fugitive years were some of the most important to David spiritually. Out of the painful experiences recorded in these chapters came some of David's most beautiful psalms.

Overview

In flight, David lied to obtain help from a family of priests at Nob (21:1-9). He escaped from Philistia only by pretending madness (vv. 10-15). David gathered some 400 fighting men and settled in a wilderness area (22:1-5). There he learned that Saul had murdered the priests who helped him (vv. 6-23). David's force saved a Judean city (23:1-6), but fled when Saul set out with an army to kill him (vv. 7-29). David spared Saul's life, and the king called off pursuit (24:1-27). The intelligent and beautiful Abigail prevented David from taking revenge on her foolish husband, and later became David's wife (25:1-44).

Understanding the Text

"David went to Nob, to Ahimelech the priest" 1 Sam. 21:1-9. David lied to Ahimelech, telling him that David was on a mission for Saul. The lie seemed innocent enough, as David was desperate for food and a weapon. David was soon to learn that even "little" lies can have tragic consequences.

Later Jesus commented on the fact that Ahimelech gave David some of the consecrated bread that was to be eaten only by priests (cf. Ex. 25:30; Lev. 24:5-9). Jesus commended Ahimelech, who realized that the moral obligation to help a person in need was more important than ritual regulations (Matt. 12:3-4; Mark 2:25-26).

David was wrong to ignore his moral obligation to be truthful with Ahimelech. But Ahimelech was right to give his moral obligation to David higher priority than a ritual obligation.

"David . . . went to Achish king of Gath" 1 Sam. 21:10-15. David was also given a weapon by Ahimelech the priest—the sword of Goliath. We can sense something of David's mental state when we're told that he went from there to Gath, the giant's hometown, where the weapon was sure to be recognized! It was recognized, and David escaped only by pretending to have gone insane.

We can probably account for both David's lie to Ahimelech and his flight to Gath by remembering that David was still very young. His life was in danger, and he was alone and helpless. Yet out of this experience of panic and uncertainty David forged an unshakable faith in God. The truths learned in this period sustained David all his life, and are reflected in Psalms 34 and 56.

Only a person who has known fear grasps the necessity of trust.

"You will surely die, Ahimelech" 1 Sam. 22:6-23. When Saul learned that Ahimelech had helped David, he accused the priest of conspiracy. Ahimelech answered reasonably. Everyone knew David was loyal—wasn't he the king's son-in-law, and captain of the king's bodyguard? The paranoid Saul may have been further enraged by this implied praise of David. On Saul's orders 85 priests and their entire families were murdered!

One son, Abiathar, escaped. When David heard what had happened he immediately confessed, "I am responsible for the death of your father's whole family." David could never have imagined that Saul would be so wicked as to kill the priests of Nob. But David realized that his lie had led to the tragedy.

There is no such thing as a "little" lie. Speaking or acting with intent to deceive others is wrong.

Without excusing David's sin, it's important to see again how his character contrasts with that of Saul. At an earlier time Saul had refused to admit a sin of his, even when he was obviously guilty, and he was confronted by Samuel! (15:13-20) David immediately accepted responsibility for the consequences of his lie, even though there is no hint that Abiathar blamed him.

If we remain as honest with ourselves, with God, and with others, we too will grow toward spiritual maturity, as David did.

"David and his men . . . kept moving from place to place" 1 Sam. 23:1-29. David used his growing force of men to aid the Israelite city of Keilah against the Philistines. Yet the people remained loyal to Saul, perhaps out of fear. This left David no place to go but into wilderness areas where he might hide from Saul's army. Saul's army was closing in when a rumor that the Philistines were attacking drew Saul away. Psalm 54 reflects David's fears and his faith in this critical situation.

Again we remember that it is when we find ourselves in desperate situations that we learn, "God is my help; the Lord is the One who sustains me" (Ps. 54:4).

"Jonathan . . . helped him find strength in God" 1 Sam. 23:16-18. This final meeting of the two friends reminds us how significant Jonathan was in the life of the younger David. Jonathan had saved his life. Now, when David seemed to have no future, Jonathan expressed his conviction that the Lord would one day make David king. Jonathan also expressed his own willingness to take second place. Jonathan would have made a great and godly ruler. But his role in life was to be a great and godly friend.

Few of us will achieve greatness in this life. But each of us can be the kind of friend who helps others find strength in God.

"You have treated me well, but I have treated you badly" 1 Sam. 24:1-22. David did not kill Saul when he had the opportunity, but spared his life. Later David stood at a distance and showed Saul a piece of his robe to prove that he could have killed the king. In calling himself "a dead dog" and a "flea" David used images to convey the idea that he was harmless, and no threat to Saul.

Saul, deeply moved, admitted he was wrong. He asked that David not kill his family when the Lord made David king. David promised and later kept his word.

Saul may have been sincere at that moment, but David knew that Saul was fickle and untrustworthy. Don't rely on what a person says or feels at the moment. Rely on what he or she does over a long period of time.

"Think it over and see what you can do" 1 Sam. 25:1-44. Abigail's wisdom in defusing David's anger over the insults of her husband Nabal provides a model we can follow (vv. 23-31). Notice that Abigail (1) admitted that Nabal had done wrong to David, (2) brought the provisions that Nabal had refused to provide, (3) and asked David's forgiveness.

Abigail also led David to consider the long-range consequences of acting in anger. David intended to become king. Killing some of his future subjects was hardly wise, for it would create fear and hostility. Why should David have the burden of needless bloodshed on his conscience?

If we want people we wrong to set aside their anger, we need to take the three steps taken by Abigail.

It's no wonder that when God struck down Abigail's husband a short time later, David wanted her for a wife.

▶DEVOTIONAL
Striking Back
(1 Sam. 24)

Maybe it's when that crazy driver cuts you off at a corner, making you jam on the brakes to avoid an accident. Maybe it's when the boss takes credit just one time too many for your work or ideas. Maybe it's when your abusive spouse belittles you in front of friends. But it happens to all of us sometime. We get tired of being a victim. And we want to strike back.

I suppose it's all right to be angry when people turn us into victims. God understands that rush of adrenaline, the flushed face, and the sudden feeling of fury. But no anger—even justified anger—gives us the right some people claim. The right to strike back. "Don't get mad," the world says. "Get even."

Once David himself might have felt that way. But when Saul unknowingly entered a cave where David and his men were hiding, David had grown spiritually. David's men were excited. "Look, David," they whispered. "Here's your chance! God's handed Saul over to you! You've got him now. Kill him!"

David's response teaches us how you and I as believers are to deal with those who victimize us. David did not allow his men to harm Saul. Later he told the king, "May the LORD avenge the wrongs you have done to me, but my hand will not touch you" (v. 12).

How do we deal with those who wrong us? First, we turn them over to the Lord, asking Him to avenge any wrongs they may have done to us. This is a positive action, and relieves us of the feeling of being victims. We have actually "taken them to court." Not a human court, but the highest court of all. Then we simply wait for God to judge.

At the same time, we make a personal commitment. David said, "My hand shall not touch you." For us this means we determine not to take revenge, or try to repay others for the wrong they do to us.

The choice David made isn't an easy one. When we're wronged, when we're angry, we want so much to strike back and hurt the person who hurt us. But the choice David made is the *right* choice. This is what counts with God and what should count with us too.

Personal Application

In what relationship do you need to apply the lesson of this incident?

Quotable

"Nothing is more to be feared than too long a peace. You are deceived if you think that a Christian can live without persecution. He suffers the greatest persecution of all who lives under none. A storm puts a man on his guard and obliges him to exert his utmost efforts to avoid shipwreck."—Jerome

MARCH 6 *Reading 65*
THE FUGITIVE YEARS END
1 Samuel 26–31

> *"One of these days I will be destroyed by the hand of Saul" (1 Sam. 27:1).*

Sometimes the pressure becomes so great that we try to run away. David finally became discouraged and fled to Philistia. As is often the case, the deepening darkness was a harbinger of a new dawn.

Background

Mercenaries. In ancient times bands of unemployed soldiers often hired out their services to foreign rulers. Later David himself had a guard of 600 men from Gath, who remained faithful to him when his own people rebelled (cf. 2 Sam. 15:16-22). When David fled from Saul into Philistine territory, the ruler of Gath treated him and his men as a mercenary force, and expected David to be loyal to the mercenary code of that day.

Overview

David and his followers settled in Philistine territory (27:1-12). As war approached, Saul desperately sought guidance, finally turning to a medium who consulted the dead (28:1-25). Meanwhile, David was saved from fighting against Israel when the Philistine rulers expelled his men from their army (29:1-11). David returned home to find his city burned and the wives and children of his men captured (30:1-6). They overtook the raiders and saved their families (vv. 7-31). Saul was killed in the Philistine war, and David's adventurous fugitive years ended at last (31:1-13).

Understanding the Text

"The LORD forbid that I should lay a hand on the LORD's anointed" 1 Sam. 26:1-25. Once again David had an opportunity to kill Saul, this time while he slept surrounded by his army. Instead David took the king's spear and water jug, and used these items to prove he had again spared his enemy. Saul promised to stop pursuing David, and admitted that David would "do great things and surely triumph."

The king might well have been sincere—for the moment. But sincere words are not sufficient evidence of reform. David knew by now that Saul was not worthy of trust. Despondent and afraid that "one of these days I will be destroyed," David decided to leave Israel.

We can give Saul the benefit of the doubt, and say that he was sincere when he made this promise. Sometimes you and I are sincere when we make commitments. But sincerity is not enough. Sincerity moves us to make commitments. But it takes integrity to keep them.

We must guard against thinking that our own sincerity is enough when we make promises to others. We must be men and women of integrity.

"David . . . went over to Achish . . . king of Gath" 1 Sam. 27:1-12. The Philistine ruler treated David as a mercenary leader, and gladly gave him a country town to live in. Achish expected David to live up to the mercenary code.

David, however, raided Israel's enemies, telling Achish that his raids were against Hebrew settlements. This deception was not to David's credit. But David's decision to leave Israel almost forced him to act deceptively. David intended to be king of Israel one day, and would never raid his own people. Yet David was in a position where he had to act as a subject of one of Israel's most bitter enemies.

David's experience teaches us an important lesson. One way to avoid deceit is to stay out of situations where lies will seem necessary.

"Find me a woman who is a medium" 1 Sam. 28:1-25. Saul was terrified by the size of the Philistine army that was drawn up against him. He received no answer when he went to God for guidance. So he ordered his retainers to locate a medium.

The Old Testament called for the death of those who used sorcery, divination, or other occult practices (Lev. 19:31; Deut. 18:10-11). Saul himself had tried to rid the land of occult practitioners. In his fear, he now turned to dark forces for aid.

The familiar story tells how stunned this "witch of Endor" was when the shadowy form of Samuel actually appeared. She may have been a channel for demonic expression, but she had no access to the spirits of the dead. Samuel told Saul clearly that it was too late for him. Israel would be defeated in the next battle with the Philistines, and Saul himself would be killed.

It is possible for a person to wander so far from God that there is no way back to the place of blessing. Yet to the king who lived in paranoid terror, seeing conspiracy everywhere, death would be a gift.

There are worse things than dying. One of them is living on after losing all sense of God's presence.

"I would be pleased to have you serve with me" 1 Sam. 29:1-11. As a vassal of Achish, David was obligated to have his fighting men join the Philistine army. What a dilemma this posed! The decision David had made when discouraged by Saul's constant harassment placed him in an impossible situation.

There is no record of David asking the Lord if he should move to Philistia. It's important for us to learn not to make hasty decisions when we are emotionally drained and that it is never wise to make significant choices without carefully seeking God's guidance.

In this case, God rescued David again. The other Philistine rulers refused to let David serve with Achish, and so Achish apologetically sent David back home.

Did David learn his lesson? Apparently. The next chapter tells us that he paused under the most intense pressure to consult the Lord before acting (cf. 30:7-8).

It is bad enough when you or I make serious mistakes. It is worse if we fail to learn from them.

"They had attacked Ziglag and burned it" 1 Sam. 30:1-31. Returning home, David found his village burned and the wives and children of his men captured. This was a devastating low point for David, as his own men were bitter enough to talk of stoning him.

Now David consulted the Lord and was guided by the Urim and Thummim to follow and attack the raiders. The families were rescued, and David even had extra spoil taken from the raiders to give as gifts to various communities in Judah. His generosity served David well. It helped the people of Judah forget his flight to Philistia, and later Judah was the first tribe to recognize David as king.

"Saul and three of his sons . . . died" 1 Sam. 31:1-13. Israel was defeated by the Philistines and Saul was killed. The text adds a touching note. The bodies of Saul and his

sons were taken by night from the walls of a Philistine city where they had been nailed for display. This was done by the men of Jabesh Gilead. In his first act as king, Saul had saved that city from the Ammonites. Its citizens now repaid his kindness.

During his long reign Saul had proved to be an effective military leader. And he was rightly honored by his people. If not for his one great flaw, the inability to trust and obey the Lord, Saul could have been a great king, and his godly son Jonathan a worthy successor.

With Saul's death, David's fugitive years were over.

▶ DEVOTIONAL
Moving to Philistia?
(1 Sam. 27)

My 31-year-old son is a "starving artist." No. Not one of the artists who contributes to the sales sponsored under that name. Paul is a very talented painter, totally committed to his art. And living on the wrong side of poverty.

Paul can understand the pressure that David felt after months and years of narrow escapes from Saul. He can understand why David, deeply discouraged, finally decided to move to Philistia. Often my son has wondered if he shouldn't just give up his art and take a job that promises more than a bare living. To him that would be as great a surrender as David's decision to move into Philistine territory. It would be a denial of who he is, and who he is called by God to be.

I can't judge what my son should do. It hurts me deeply to see his struggles and not be able to help. Sometimes I think it would be easier for him just to give up. To let his exceptional talent go, and try to make a better living in this world.

Then I remember David.

He gave up. But among the Philistines David found himself forced to deny who he was—the future king of Israel. David lived a double life there, and was again forced to lie just to survive.

There may be no guidance for my son in this period in David's life. But there are principles that you and I need to live by. When life is hard, let's guard against seeking the easy way out. All too often the "easy way" takes us into a situation in which we're forced to compromise who we are just to survive.

Personal Application

Circumstances are seldom the best guide to God's will.

Quotable

This stubborn, adolescent will of mine
Is making me a spiritual delinquent!
It drives me recklessly about on life's freeways,
At times endangering both myself and others along the way.
If I bring it daily unto God in prayer,
Surely He can curb these tendencies
With His understanding love
And gently bend it to His will and way
During this difficult period of growing up
Toward spiritual maturity.—Carolyn N. Rhea

The Variety Reading Plan continues with 2 SAMUEL

2 Samuel

INTRODUCTION

First and 2 Samuel were originally a single book in the Hebrew Bible. They tell the story of the historic transition of Israel from a group of scattered tribes ruled by judges to a united and powerful nation. The time spanned by the two books is roughly 120 years, from about 1050 to 931 B.C.

Second Samuel continues the story of David, once a fugitive but now king, first of Judah, and then of the whole Hebrew nation. This book about David reports his many accomplishments, but just as honestly relates his personal failures and family problems. Through this story we come to a greater appreciation of David as a human being, and to a much greater appreciation of David's gracious God.

OUTLINE OF CONTENTS

I. David's Triumphs .... 2 Sam. 1–10
II. David's Troubles .... 2 Sam. 11–20
III. Other Stories of David .... 2 Sam. 21–24

READING GUIDE (5 Days)

If hurried, you may read only the "core passage" in your Bible and the Devotional in each chapter of this Commentary.

Reading	*Chapters*	*Core passage*
66	1–5	3–4
67	6–10	7
68	11–14	13–14
69	15–20	15–16
70	21–24	24

2 Samuel

MARCH 7 *Reading 66*
DAVID BEGINS HIS REIGN
2 Samuel 1–5

> *"David was thirty years old when he became king, and he reigned forty years" (2 Sam. 5:4).*

Even with the fugitive years behind him, David's first years as ruler were filled with tension. Don't expect life to be without struggle despite victories along the way.

Overview

David lamented the death of Saul and Jonathan (1:1-27). His affirmation as king in Judah (2:1-7) led to lengthy civil war (v. 8–3:5). Abner, commander of the enemy army, decided to go over to David (vv. 6-21). David was innocent of two assassinations, of Abner and of Saul's son Ish-Bosheth (v. 22–4:12). Nevertheless these deaths ended the war, and David was at last confirmed as king over a united Israel (5:1-5). David captured Jerusalem and made it his capital (vv. 6-16). When the Philistines attacked, David handed them the first in a series of devastating defeats (vv. 17-25).

Understanding the Text

"Go, strike him down!" 2 Sam. 1:1-16 The account of Saul's death here differs from that in 1 Samuel 31. Why the conflict? This account reports what the Amalekite who brought Saul's crown to David said, not necessarily what happened. The Amalekite told his story, expecting some reward from David for killing his enemy. Instead David ordered him executed, for by his account he was guilty of murdering the Lord's anointed.

David's reaction showed proper respect for both God and Saul, and clearly indicated that despite his persecution by Saul, David had wished the monarch no personal harm.

"David took up this lament" 2 Sam. 1:17-27. David expressed the pain he felt at the death of Jonathan and Saul in a poem intended to honor them. The poem speaks of his love for "Jonathan my brother," and also honors Saul for his accomplishments.

Like David we need to be big enough to appreciate the good qualities of persons who may be personal enemies.

"The commander of Saul's army. . . . made [Ish-Bosheth son of Saul] king" 2 Sam. 2:8–3:5. The name Ish-Bosheth means "son of shame." His name was actually Esh-Baal, "Baal lives" (cf. 1 Chron. 8:33; 9:39). The biblical writer was unwilling to honor the name of the pagan deity, and substituted "shame."

Ish-Bosheth was actually a figurehead, even though acclaimed king by the northern tribes. The real power belonged to Abner, the army commander. In the civil war that followed, Abner killed a brother of David's commander, Joab. Gradually David's forces gained strength, while the northern armies grew weaker.

In this case it is possible to fix responsibility for the civil war on the ambition of one man, Abner. In view of the many lives lost and the disruption of the whole kingdom, Abner deserved the death he would soon receive at the hand of Joab. Abner's fate illustrates the principle of natural consequences stated by Jesus, when he said to Peter, "All who draw the sword will die by the sword" (Matt. 26:52).

"Abner was very angry" 2 Sam. 3:1-21. Abner's defection to David was precipitated by Ish-Bosheth's accusation that Abner had slept with one of Saul's concubines. Such an act would have had political implications in the ancient world, suggesting that Abner intended to claim Israel's throne. The army commander did not deny the accusation, but was furious at the implied charge of disloyalty (v. 8).

In his anger Abner determined to turn the kingdom over to David, and began negotiations to that end. Abner's words to the elders of Israel are significant. "For some time you have wanted to make David your king" (v. 17). Apparently only fear of Abner and the Benjamites, Saul's own tribe, had kept Israel's elders from acting before now (cf. vv. 19-21).

Fear often keeps people from doing what they believe is right. Had the elders of Israel feared God more than mere human beings the tragedy of civil war might have been avoided.

"Give me my wife Michal" 2 Sam. 3:13-16. Was it love or politics that led David to demand the return of Michal, the daughter of Saul? The chances are politics played a part, for his marriage to Saul's daughter strengthened David's claim to Saul's throne.

In any case, note that Michal was not asked if she wished to return to David or not. On David's demand she was taken away from her weeping second husband, Paltiel, and marched off to rejoin David. Michal had been used by her father (1 Sam. 18:20-25). Here she was apparently used by David. It's no wonder that later she became hardened and bitter.

We need to be especially careful not to use other people for our own ends. Human beings are to be valued, not used, and their interests are to be considered as well as our own.

"Wicked men have killed" 2 Sam. 3:22–4:12. Two assassinations cleared the way for David to become ruler of a united Israel; however, he had no part in either, for each was unjustified. Joab's main objective in killing Abner was revenge for his brother Asahel, whom Abner had killed in battle. Ish-Bosheth's assassins hoped to be rewarded for bringing David "good news!"

David quickly acted to show his people he had nothing to do with either death. He publicly mourned and honored Abner, and he executed the two men who assassinated Ish-Bosheth.

We may profit from the sinful acts of others. But we should never rejoice in them.

"They anointed David king over Israel" 2 Sam. 5:1-16. Seven years of civil war were over, and David began a 33-year reign over a United Hebrew Kingdom.

His choice of Jerusalem as capital was astute. The city, then occupied by a Canaanite people, lay on the border of the north and south. Its choice showed no favoritism to either section of David's country. The city was also relatively secure—so easily protected that the Canaanites scornfully predicted the lame and blind could hold it against any attacking force. They were wrong.

"The Philistines . . . went up in full force" 2 Sam. 5:17-25. During the long civil war Israel posed no threat to the Philistines. Now, however, they attacked, determined to kill or capture David. The Lord guided David to a decisive victory.

It is significant that David did not attack first. He had lived for a time near Gath, and had obligations to its ruler, Achish. When the Philistines attacked first, David was free to carry on warfare with them.

▶DEVOTIONAL
By Their Works
(2 Sam. 3–4)

Ever notice how easily people are swayed by words? "It'll be different when we're married," the abusive or jealous suitor pleads. "I'll never do it again if only you come back to me," is another popular pledge. "I'm not guilty of any such sin," is something we've learned to question, even when uttered by contemporary TV evangelists.

No. Words don't mean much. What really counts is what a person *does.*

It was the same in those turbulent years of internal strife when David was king in Judah, and Saul's son ruled in the north. "I'm no traitor!" Abner shouted at Ish-Bosheth (see 3:8-11), and then proceeded immediately to negotiate with David (v. 12).

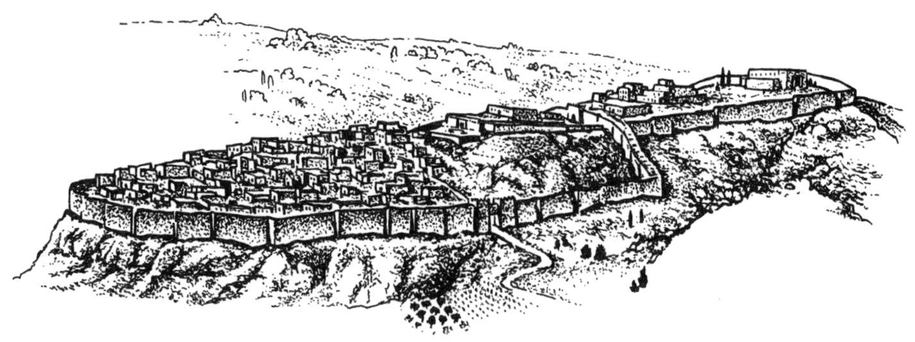

Archeologists believe the city of Jerusalem looked like this in the time of David and Solomon. The city probably had a population of 3,000–3,500.

Then Abner himself was deceived when Joab sent him a message in David's name. Abner returned to Hebron only to be murdered by David's army commander (vv. 22-28).

Back in Israel two more high army officers pretended to visit Ish-Bosheth in friendship, entered his house, and stabbed him in the stomach. The two then hurried to David, announcing a religious motive for their actions. "The LORD has avenged my lord the king" (4:1-8).

When there is turmoil in our lives, we can easily become confused. Especially if the people partly responsible glibly confuse issues with words. When that happens, we need to remember that words can be deceitful. The evidence we need to rely on is what a person does, not what he or she says.

Personal Application

In a trustworthy person, words and actions coincide.

Quotable

"Faith is a living and unshakable confidence, a belief in the grace of God so assured that a man would die a thousand deaths for its sake. This kind of confidence in God's grace, this sort of knowledge of it, makes us joyful, high-spirited and eager in our relations with God and with all mankind. That is what the Holy Spirit effects through faith. Hence the man of faith, without being driven, willingly and gladly seeks to do good to everyone, serve everyone, suffer all kinds of hardships, for the sake of the love and glory of the God who has shown him such grace. It is impossible, indeed to separate works from faith, just as it is impossible to separate heat and light from fire."—Martin Luther

MARCH 8 *Reading 67*

DAVID UNITES HIS KINGDOM

2 Samuel 6–10

"David went down and brought up the ark of God . . . to the City of David with rejoicing" (2 Sam. 6:12).

David's next actions indicate careful planning and political sensitivity. They also reveal another trait appropriate to exceptional people: a firm and joyous faith in God.

Background

Jerusalem. Moses predicted that God would choose a place in Canaan "for His name" (Deut. 16:2). That choice was made through David. From David's time on, Jerusalem was the very heart of the nation and of the Jewish faith. It remained the capital of Judah after Solomon's kingdom was divided. It was Jerusalem to which Jewish settlers returned after the Babylonian Captivity. Jerusalem was the focus of much of Christ's earthly ministry, and the city where He was condemned. Prophecy identifies Jerusalem as the place to which Jesus will return, and as the capital of the earthly kingdom which He will establish. There is no other site on earth as theologically significant as the City of David, Jerusalem.

Overview

David made Jerusalem the religious as well as political capital of Israel by bringing up the ark (6:1-23). God did not allow David to erect a temple (7:1-7). But God did promise David a permanent dynasty (vv. 8-17), moving David to praise the Lord (vv. 18-29). David defeated nearby enemies (8:1-14), created a national government (vv. 15-18), and showed kindness to Jonathan's only surviving son (9:1-13). In time David crushed all his enemies and extended Israel's domination from the Gulf of Aqaba in the south to the Euphrates River in the north (10:1-19).

Understanding the Text

"He and all his men set out . . . to bring up from there the ark of God" 2 Sam. 6:1-8. David's first attempt to bring the ark to Jerusalem ended in failure, caused by two violations of ritual law. The ark was Israel's most holy relic, a symbol of the living presence of God. Old Testament Law required that it be carried by members of a particular Levite family (Num. 3:27-32), and that it never be touched (4:15). When the cart on which the ark was placed tipped, and Uzzah reached out his hand to steady it, God struck Uzzah dead. David was both frightened and angry. Why had the God he so desired to honor acted in such a way?

This story has troubled many who read the Bible. God's action does seem unfair. Uzzah surely had intended no harm. Perhaps the answer lies in the casual way Saul had treated God for some four decades. He had never shown an interest in the ark, or even in obeying God. The sudden outburst against Uzzah reminded David and all of Israel that God truly is holy. And the Holy One of Israel is not to be treated casually!

"David . . . danced before the LORD with all his might" 2 Sam. 6:9-15. Before David attempted to move the ark again, he apparently consulted Scripture (cf. v. 13). This time David's joy was unrestrained, and he exchanged his royal robes for the kind of linen ephod worn by priests who served before the Lord. This clothing symbolized the fact that the king found his greatest fulfillment as a simple servant of God.

When you and I come before God, all our worldly accomplishments are meaningless. All that counts is a heart committed to love and serve the Lord.

"She despised him in her heart" 2 Sam. 6:16-23. Michal had been used by both her father and David (cf. 1 Sam. 18:20-25; 2 Sam. 3:13-16). It's no wonder she had become bitter. But Michal had permitted bitterness to gain such a grip on her life that she found no joy in the Lord. Instead of focusing on the ark and on the Lord, Michal focused on David's "disgraceful" refusal to maintain his royal dignity.

What a warning to us. Yes, others may misuse us. But if we permit ourselves to become so bitter that we cannot sense the presence of God, we will lose all perspective on life. Michal may have had a right to be bitter. But surely David, persecuted so long by her father, had a right to be bitter too. David triumphed over bitterness by keeping his focus on the Lord. Michal lost sight of God, and ended her life lonely and alone.

"The LORD Himself will establish a house for you" 2 Sam. 7:1-17. This significant Old Testament passage introduces the Davidic Covenant. This is the name given to promises which God made to David, which David recognized as an unbreakable divine commitment.

The heart of the covenant was God's announcement that He would "establish a house" for David. Here "house" is used in the sense of descendants. In the immediate future David's own son would erect a temple (v. 13). But as is common in biblical prophecy, the immediate future mirrors God's eschatological [end time] intent. Through David's line God would establish a kingdom that would "endure forever before Me."

The New Testament carefully traces the genealogy of Jesus Christ back to King David. Matthew especially shows how Jesus' birth fulfills Old Testament predictions about a coming King destined to rule eternally (cf. Matt. 1–2).

David did not understand all the implications of the divine commitment. But he realized that God was giving him a great gift when the Lord announced, "My love will never be taken away from him [David's descendants], as I took it away from Saul, whom I removed from before you" (2 Sam. 7:15). David's throne was secure, through his own lifetime, and beyond!

"David fought" 2 Sam. 8:1-14. David's next years were spent in battle with enemies to the north and east. God gave him success in every battle, and he was able to gain control of vital trade routes that passed through Damascus, establishing garrisons in Syria and across the Jordan in Edom. David's wars multiplied the territory Israel controlled many times over that held in the Judges era!

"I will surely show you kindness for the sake of your father Jonathan" 2 Sam. 8:15–9:13. The writer of 2 Samuel passes over David's vital work in setting up a national government (8:15-18), but gives extensive space to the story of David's kindness to Mephibosheth. The crippled son of David's old friend Jonathan is given his grandfather's extensive lands and a place in David's court at Jerusalem.

In most cases in which dynasties were replaced in ancient kingdoms, surviving members of the old king's family were slaughtered. David's unusual treatment of Mephibosheth is a better display of those strengths which won him the throne than his genius for bureaucratic invention.

Success does demand ability and hard work. But the secret of true greatness is found in godly character.

"I will show kindness" 2 Sam. 10:1-19. It would be wrong to portray David as a despotic aggressor. The story detailing the start of David's war with the Ammonites illustrates that many conflicts were actually forced on Israel.

David's unbroken string of military successes established Israel's dominance of the area during his lifetime.

▶ DEVOTIONAL
Precious Promises
(2 Sam. 7)

David had been eager to do something for God. When God turned down his offering, David must have been momentarily shaken. But then God went on. Rather than accept a gift from David, the Lord intended to give a gift *to* him!

How like God's dealings with us. We love Him, and want to give Him our very best. But whatever we do, we soon learn that God is the greatest Giver.

When David realized what great and precious promises God had made to him, he was stunned. "What more can David say to you?" the grateful king exclaimed.

And then David found something to say. David repeated God's promises, fixing them in his mind and heart. And then David simply praised God.

What a model for us. What can we say to God? What can we do for Him? Simply repeat His many promises to us, fixing them in our hearts and minds. And then lift our voices to praise the Lord.

Personal Application

The most appropriate thing we can give the God who gives us so much is praise.

Quotable

Thou that hast given so much to me,
Give one more thing—a grateful heart;
Not thankful when it pleaseth me,
As if Thy blessings had spare days;
But such a heart, whose pulse may be
Thy praise.—George Herbert

MARCH 9 *Reading 68*
DAVID'S PERSONAL FAILINGS
2 Samuel 11–14

"I have sinned against the LORD" (2 Sam. 12:13).

The biblical text reports David's triumphs. But it just as honestly relates his troubles. There is no attempt here, as in other ancient documents, to disguise the human failings of one who was admittedly Israel's greatest king.

Definition of Key Terms

Sin. Hebrew words distinguish between types of sin. Each implies existence of a standard that God has revealed. One Hebrew word pictures sin as falling short of the standard, another as twisting the standard, and a third as willful and rebellious refusal to live by the standard. Psalm 51, which records David's confession after his sin with Bathsheba, uses each of these Hebrew terms. David's passion, and his later failures with his family, remind us that all human beings are weak. These very personal stories of David also remind us that sin has tragic consequences. But most important, they teach us that God will provide the forgiveness each of us so often needs.

Biography: Bathsheba

A study of the text shows that Bathsheba was a victim not a seductress. What is even more terrible, she was the helpless victim of a man whom all Israel had come to know and trust as a godly leader. Yet as we trace the relationship of these two we see that Bathsheba was able to work through the anger she must have felt at being used, to forgive David, and to build a lasting and loving relationship. David's honest confession of his sin had freed Bathsheba as well as God to forgive.

As David was about to die he transferred his kingdom to Solomon, the fourth son Bathsheba bore him, in part to protect her and her children from harm (1 Kings 1:11-31). A Jewish tradition suggests that Solomon wrote Proverbs 31, his praise of the noble wife, in honor of his mother, Bathsheba.

Overview

David committed adultery with Bathsheba (11:1-13), and then arranged for the death in battle of her husband (vv. 14-27). When confronted by Nathan the prophet David confessed his sin (12:1-14), but despite David's prayers the child conceived in adultery died (vv. 15-31). David's weakness was reflected in his son Amnon, who raped a half sister (13:1-22). The girl's brother Absalom then killed Amnon (vv. 23-39). Absalom fled, but later this favorite son of David's was allowed to return to Jerusalem (14:1-33).

Understanding the Text

"David sent messengers to get her" 2 Sam. 11:1-5. The text carefully guards against the impression that Bathsheba intended to seduce David. Note that (1) David should have been at war, (2) he saw her bathing at an hour when everyone should have been asleep, (3) she was seen from the roof. This suggests her home was down the hill from David's palace, and she was probably bathing in an inner court. (4) She could hardly resist the royal messengers "sent to get her," and (5) the text says "he" slept with her. Nothing is said in the text to shift any blame from David to Bathsheba. There is no attempt to disguise David's guilt.

It is a tragedy when anyone sins. But if we should sin, we need to be completely honest about what happened. Excuses are no excuse.

"Uriah the Hittite" 2 Sam. 11:6-27. Uriah was most likely a mercenary soldier who

had joined David, and taken a name which means "Yahweh is my light." He appears in the text to have been an honorable and dedicated man. When he refused to join Bathsheba at their home (where David intended him to have sex with his wife to mask the fact that Bathsheba was already pregnant), David sent orders to General Joab to see that Uriah was killed in battle. David's first sin had led to one even worse—cover-up! When Uriah was killed in battle, David openly married Bathsheba.

"One sin leads to another" may seem to be a trite saying. But it is true. To be protected from ourselves, we need to guard our hearts against taking that first step away from God's standards.

"Why did you despise the word of the LORD by doing what is evil in His eyes?" 2 Sam. 12:1-13 David was confronted by the Prophet Nathan. In later years, prophets who spoke boldly to Israel's kings risked death. But David, despite his terrible sins, did love God. Rather than strike out at his accuser, David admitted that he had sinned.

Psalm 32 graphically portrays David's emotions after this great sin. When we are troubled by our misdeeds, only confession can provide relief. Listen to David's words, and see if they reflect experiences of your own.

> When I kept silent,
> my bones wasted away
> through my groaning all day long.
> For day and night
> Your hand was heavy upon me;
> my strength was sapped
> as in the heat of summer.
> Then I acknowledged my sin to You
> and did not cover up my iniquity.
> I said, "I will confess
> my transgressions to the LORD"—
> and You forgave
> the guilt of my sin.
> Psalm 32:3-5

David did more than confess his sin to Nathan and to God. David wrote Psalm 51, which was used in public worship. The superscription says "A psalm of David. When the Prophet Nathan came to him after David had committed adultery with Bathsheba."

We can confess private sins only to God. But public sins must be confessed to God and before God's people.

"The son born to you will die" 2 Sam. 12:14-31. David was forgiven, but the child born of the adulterous union was to die. That death actually illustrates the grace of God. Growing up, the child would have been a constant reminder to David and Bathsheba of their sin. Even worse, the child himself would have borne publicly the stigma of his parents' action. David put death itself in perspective when he said, "I will go to him, but he will not return to me" (v. 23). Death is not the end, even for a stillborn child. Life after death is a reality, and there are many situations in which to die is truly gain.

The death of any loved one hurts. But what comfort it is for believers to realize that death is not life's end, but entry into a full experience of that eternal life promised to us in the Lord.

"She . . . went away, weeping" 2 Sam. 13:1-19. Amnon's passion for Tamar changed to hatred after he deceived and raped her. People are more likely to hate someone they have wronged than someone who has wronged them. No one likes to be reminded of his or her faults, and the sight of someone we have wronged keeps our own failures before our eyes.

"A desolate woman" 2 Sam. 13:20-22. Note the contrast between this story of Amnon and Tamar and that of David and Bathsheba. In each case the woman was victimized. But David ultimately confessed his sin, while Amnon refused to confess and instead hated (perhaps blamed?) the innocent Tamar. Because David accepted responsibility for his sin, Bathsheba too found inner healing. Because Amnon would not accept responsibility, he was murdered and Tamar was unable to find peace.

There is only one healthy way to deal with sin. We must acknowlege our sins, accept responsibility for them, and trust God to forgive us and to undo the harm we have done to others.

"Strike Amnon down" 2 Sam. 13:23-39. Tamar's brother, Absalom, insisted Tamar

not mention the rape. For two years he pretended friendship with Amnon, whom he had come to hate. Then he conspired to have Amnon killed. Afterward, fearing the penalty the law established for murder, Absalom fled the country.

"Bring back the young man Absalom" 2 Sam. 14:1-33. General Joab devised a fable intended to give David a basis for restoring Absalom. The problem the fable set was a conflict of legal principles: murder deserved the death penalty, yet each family line in Israel must be preserved. When the case was presented to David, he reluctantly decided to protect the killer to preserve the family line. The woman who presented the case then argued that David should permit Absalom to return, suggesting it is godly to devise "ways so that a banished person may not remain estranged from him."

David did bring Absalom back to Israel, but could not bring himself to see his son for two more years.

The argument that Joab designed was specious in that David had other sons besides Absalom. The two cases were not parallel. David's delay in seeing Absalom suggests he was not comfortable with his decision. Yet God does devise ways to restore the banished: the way of forgiveness. By failing to forgive fully when Absalom was returned, David himself created a bitterness which found expression in rebellion and civil war.

▶ DEVOTIONAL
Furious Parenting
(2 Sam. 13–14)

Ken Schaeffer is a success as a parent. His son, also Ken, was valedictorian at a local high school and a National Merit scholar last year. His daughter, Cindy, was valedictorian of her class this year and also a National Merit scholar. Both Ken and Cindy are fine Christian young people. But while Ken is a success as a parent, he doesn't feel terribly successful otherwise. A fellow graduate of Dallas Seminary, Ken hasn't lasted in the pastorate, and he's never been able to make much money.

It may be surprising, but often the most successful people when judged by the world's standards have been terrible parents. And some of the "least successful" have raised children of whom anyone would be proud.

David, despite his achieving gold stars as Israel's greatest king, was a terrible parent. Some of his failures are highlighted in these chapters, and stand as examples you and I are to follow—if we want to ruin the lives of our offspring! What are David's prescriptions for parental failure?

Get mad, but don't discipline. When David heard what Amnon did to his half sister Tamar, the text says David was "furious" (13:21). But there's no hint that he even spoke to Amnon, much less disciplined him. Parents who fail to correct their children can expect greater troubles down the line.

Love your children too much. After Absalom fled, David "mourned for his son every day." David seems to have missed his son so much that he lost sight of what his son had done. Boys and girls who are loved so much that "anything goes" are heading for trouble.

Forgive, but not completely. David finally permitted Absalom to return to Jerusalem, but would not see him for two full years. If forgiveness is to be granted, it must be complete. Incomplete forgiveness, replete with little reminders of the past sins, creates bitterness and antagonism. When God forgives, He forgets. If we are to forgive a fault, we must do so completely.

David, a success in his career, was a failure as a parent. He was upset by what his children did, but did not discipline. He loved his children so much that he lost perspective. And he forgave incompletely. In his family life Israel's greatest king was one of history's greatest failures. While my friend Ken Schaeffer, in many ways a failure in his own eyes, is one of history's great success stories.

Personal Application

We need to give as much or more thought to our parenting as we do to our careers.

Quotable

"I think that what children in the United States desperately need is a moral purpose, and a lot of our children aren't getting that. They're getting parents who are very concerned about getting them into the right colleges, buying the best clothing for them, giving them an opportunity to live in neighborhoods where they'll lead fine and affluent lives and where they can be given the best toys, go on interesting vacations, and all sorts of things. . . . Parents work very hard these days; and they're acquiring things that they feel are important for their children. And yet vastly more important things are not happening. They're not spending time with their children, at least not very much."—Robert Coles

MARCH 10 *Reading 69*

ABSALOM'S REBELLION

2 Samuel 15–20

"Say, 'Absalom is king in Hebron' " (2 Sam. 15:10).

In difficult times we may even wonder if God has deserted us. Particularly if our conscience is not clear. Absalom's rebellion was just such a time for David.

Background

David ruled over Judah for seven years before the northern tribes acknowledged him as monarch. This rift between north and south was exploited by Absalom. His claim that he would support any northerner who came to Jerusalem with a complaint or legal case gradually won their support. After Absalom's rebellion was put down, the tension between the two sections again exploded briefly before being put down by Joab. Half a century later, after the death of Solomon in 931 B.C., sectional differences were still so intense that the kingdom broke into two parts. The northern splinter-kingdom, called Israel, existed until its destruction in 722 B.C. The southern splinter-kingdom, Judah, survived until 586 B.C.

Overview

Absalom gradually won allegiance of Israel's northern tribes and was proclaimed king (15:1-12). David fled Jerusalem with a few companions (v. 13–16:14). In Jerusalem one of David's secret supporters gave Absalom advice, enabling David to escape south (16:15–17:29). David raised troops there, and in the ensuing battle Absalom was killed (18:1-18). David set aside grief to honor his army (19:1-8), and returned to Jerusalem (vv. 9-43). Joab put down another brief northern rebellion and David's throne was secured (20:1-26).

Understanding the Text

"Absalom . . . stole the hearts of the men of Israel" 2 Sam. 15:1-12. Some commentators blame David's refusal to see Absalom for two years after his return from exile for making this handsome son bitter. But Absalom's plot follows a pattern established long before. Absalom had waited patiently to kill his brother Amnon (13:23). Now he labored patiently for four years to lay a foundation for his rebellion. Absalom's revolt was well-planned and premeditated. Absalom was not so much bitter as determined to have his father's throne.

It's popular these days to excuse a person's actions by blaming someone else for treating him or her unfairly. Yet in fact each of us is responsible for his own choices and actions.

"There will your servant be" 2 Sam. 15:13-23. David had served his country well. Yet most of his own people now rejected him. Their unfaithfulness is underlined by a mercenary captain who entered David's service only the day before, and yet was prepared to keep his oath of allegiance even if it should mean death.

There is nothing as painful as betrayal by a person we have every right to expect will be loyal.

"If He says, 'I am not pleased with you' " 2 Sam. 15:24-37. When the priests and Levites prepared to leave Jerusalem carrying God's ark, David sent them back. David's remarks reveal his own uncertainty. God might no longer be pleased with David, and the rebellion might be God's way of removing him from the throne. If so, David wanted the ark to remain a symbol of faith. And if God remained pleased with David, the king would surely return to the ark.

David may have been uncertain. But his

priorities remained clear. God was to be worshiped, not used in political campaigns.

David also remained a wise politician. He left behind several faithful men who would have gone with him, to provide him with information and to try to disrupt Absalom's plans.

"You man of blood, you scoundrel!" 2 Sam. 16:5-14 When Shimei reviled David he may have expressed David's own inmost doubts. David had not mistreated Saul's family, but he had indirectly caused many deaths. He surely had acted like a scoundrel in his affair with Bathsheba. The sins of his sons must also have weighed heavily on his heart. This may be reflected in David's refusal to let one of his supporters silence Shimei. After all, David suggested, he may be doing God's work (cf. v. 10).

David preferred to leave it all up to the Lord. God might very well transform those curses into blessing.

What others say about us matters very little. They may wish us ill. But if God is for us, what we will receive will be good.

"So I advise you" 2 Sam. 16:15–17:29. David's friend Hushai was able to disrupt Absalom's plans. The advice he gave permitted David to escape, while following the advice of Ahithophel would have guaranteed David's death.

Christians often receive conflicting advice from friends, relatives, or counselors. Often what we need is not more advice, but the wisdom from God to know what advice is best. How good to have the promise, "If any of you lacks wisdom, he should ask God, who gives generously to all without finding fault, and it will be given to him" (James 1:5).

"O my son Absalom" 2 Sam. 18:1–19:8. In the battle that followed Absalom was killed—against the king's express orders. Rather than rejoice in the triumph, David was brokenhearted with grief. Joab's rebuke reminded David of his duty, and the king went to receive the congratulations of those who had fought for him so loyally.

David's sorrow for Absalom's death was undoubtedly misplaced, but understandable. It's hard to acknowledge when our children's actions merit punishment. But like David we must at times put aside personal feelings and serve the public good.

"Amasa was not on his guard against the dagger in Joab's hand" 2 Sam. 20:1-13. Joab was a harsh man, but completely loyal to David. Like many loyal men, this commander of David's army acted at times without orders, or ignored orders if he thought his action was in the king's best interest. Earlier Joab had assassinated Abner, the Israelite military leader who was negotiating with David. In this battle Joab personally killed Absalom despite David's command that he be spared. Now Joab murdered Amasa, who had commanded Absalom's forces. While Joab might be commended for his loyalty, he merits no praise for his actions.

Many Christians seem to take Joab's course. They proclaim their loyalty to God, and they do try to serve Him. But they want to serve God their way, without submitting to His Word.

▶ DEVOTIONAL
In Flight
(2 Sam. 15–16)

We can sense David's mood as he fled Jerusalem with just a few retainers. Absalom, with a large army, was in pursuit. The situation seemed hopeless. And to top it all off, Shimei cursed David, shouting that God was just paying David what David deserved for his bloody past.

Everything had gone wrong. Besides, David's conscience wasn't clear. There were grounds to think that Shimei might be right. No wonder David seemed despondent and depressed as he gathered his cloak around him, and hurried over the Brook Kidron in the late evening shadows.

How did David really feel? And what can we do when we find ourselves feeling as he must have? The answer is in Psalm 3, which David penned "when he fled from his son Absalom."

First David looked around.

O LORD, how many are my foes!
How many rise up against me!
Many are saying of me,
"God will not deliver him" (Ps. 3:1-2).

Then David looked back.

But You are a shield around me, O
LORD,
my Glorious One, who lifts up my
head.
To the LORD I cry aloud,
and He answers me from His holy
hill (vv. 3-4).

Then David looked up.

I lie down and sleep;
I wake again, because the LORD sustains me.
I will not fear the tens of thousands
drawn up against me on every side.
Arise, O LORD!
Deliver me, O my God!
For You have struck all my enemies on
the jaw;
You have broken the teeth of the
wicked (vv. 5-7).

Then David looked ahead.

From the LORD comes deliverance.
May Your blessing be upon Your
people (v. 8).

Looking around, you and I see our difficulties realistically. But looking back, we remember that God has helped us in the past. Looking up, we find peace as we commit ourselves and our needs to the Lord. And looking ahead, we know we can expect good things from God.

Personal Application
When we face difficulties, we need to follow the simple pattern of looking—around, back, up, and ahead—with faith.

Quotable
"Be not miserable about what may happen tomorrow. The same everlasting Father, who cares for you today, will care for you tomorrow and every day. Either He will shield you from suffering, or He will give you unfailing strength to bear it."—Francis De Sales

MARCH 11 *Reading 70*
EVENTS OF DAVID'S REIGN
2 Samuel 21–24

"The LORD lives! Praise be my Rock! Exalted be God, the Rock, my Saviour!" (2 Sam. 22:47)

When you tell someone the story of your life, there are some things that just won't fit in a chronological report. Here in an appendix the writer of 2 Samuel relates more about David.

Overview
David permitted the Gibeonites to exact revenge for Saul's violation of an ancient treaty (21:1-14). The Philistine wars are summarized (vv. 15-22). David's song of praise for deliverance is recorded (22:1-51). After a report of David's last words (23:1-7) and a list of war heros (vv. 8-39), the book closes with an account of David's sin in taking a census of fighting men (24:1-25).

Understanding the Text
"It is because he put the Gibeonites to death" 2 Sam. 21:1-14. At the time of the Conquest, nearly 400 years before Saul's time, Israel had sworn in God's name not to harm the Gibeonites. Saul broke this treaty and ferociously attacked the Gibeonites, who still held land in Israel. When David learned that a famine which had struck Israel was God's punishment for breaking the oath sworn in His name, he asked the Gibeonites about reparations.

The Gibeonites demanded the death of seven of Saul's male descendants. David ordered they be executed and their bodies left unburied. Exposure of the dead body was considered a great disgrace in Israel.

Old Testament Law prohibits punishing any person for a parent's sins (Deut. 24:16). Because of this, and because 2 Samuel 21:1 fixes the blame on Saul and "his blood-stained house," it seems likely that the seven David executed had leading roles in the attempt to exterminate the Gibeonites.

Unpunished crime is a rebuke to any

nation. It was especially abhorrent to God, who used the famine to bring this terrible crime to David's attention.

"David sang to the LORD" 2 Sam. 22:1-51. The psalm traces David's rise from a fugitive to a conquering monarch, and praises God as the source of David's deliverance and his achievements. God protected David when he was in deadly danger (vv. 1-7), and David was in awe of His mighty power (vv. 8-16). God rescued righteous David from his enemies (vv. 17-25), and David acknowledged God's faithfulness to those who trust in Him (vv. 26-37). God raised David to power and international prominence (vv. 38-46), and David sang praises to the Lord for His unfailing kindness (vv. 47-51).

This song of praise, very similar to Psalm 18, reflects David's awareness that all he was and had become was a gracious gift of God. It was true, when the psalm was penned, that God's reward was "according to my righteousness." But this thought is no boast. David simply reflected on the fact that God is faithful in keeping his promise to bless those who keep "the ways of the LORD."

When I was a child I stood in the yard of my uncle's farm home and watched rain pour down on a field just across the road, while I remained perfectly dry. What David is saying is that by obedience we cross the road and find showers of blessing. God's blessings are always being poured out. Obedience puts us in the place where the blessings flow.

"The last words of David" 2 Sam. 23:1-7. David's last words praised God. More importantly, they show the basis on which David felt secure. "Has He not made with me an everlasting covenant, arranged and secured in every part? Will He not bring to fruition my salvation and grant me my every desire?"

Death found a confident David, resting in the promises God had made to him, certain of his own salvation and of a future after death.

The Bible picture's death as man's enemy, and fear of death as a stranglehold Satan has on mankind. David's confidence reminds us that for the believer death is not the end of existence, but the doorway to a glorious future.

"David's mighty men" 2 Sam. 23:8-39. It's likely that "the thirty" was an elite corps or special military unit, perhaps like our "green berets." Others assume these war heros served as leaders of David's legions. Whatever their role, they remind us that David did not win his victories alone.

No leader can do it all himself or herself. Every leader needs talented and able persons around him or her.

"Go and count Israel and Judah" 2 Sam. 24:1-17. While the chapter indicates that David committed a sin by taking a military census, the text does not indicate why David was wrong. Some suggest the census indicated self-confidence and a failure to rely on God. Others assume God commanded David not to take the census. The first-century Jewish historian Josephus says David failed to collect the half-shekel temple tax required of Hebrew males. Whatever the real reason, even General Joab knew David was wrong and argued against the census.

When David persisted, the Lord gave David a choice of punishments. David selected the most severe but shortest of the three.

It's unwise to insist on our own way against the conviction of others that what we intend is wrong.

"Burnt offerings that cost me nothing" 2 Sam. 24:18-25. The purchase of Araunah's threshing floor is theologically significant. This height near David's city of Jerusalem would be added to the city by Solomon, and become the site of the Jerusalem temple. The same mount is fixed by tradition as the place where Abraham came to offer up his son Isaac at God's command. Placed here, at the end of the book that records David's accomplishments, the purchase prepares us for the introduction of Solomon, who constructed the temple that David wanted so much to build.

The personal significance of the incident is found in David's response when Araunah offered to give him the land. "I insist on paying you for it. I will not sacrifice to the LORD my God burnt offerings that cost me nothing."

God is not honored by leaving Him

"tips" that we hardly miss. The God who loves us so much deserves costly offerings, whether of money or service.

▶ DEVOTIONAL
Who Done It?
(2 Sam. 24)

"The devil made me do it" is more than a saying. Sometimes Christians do blame the devil when caught up in some sin. Other times we may blame others. Or childhood trauma. Or any number of things. One of history's worst serial killers, Ted Bundy, blamed pornographic pictures he saw as a teen for the murders he committed across the country.

This chapter raises the question of blame by stating, "He [the Lord] incited David" to initiate the census (v. 1). In another account Satan is the one who incited David (1 Chron. 21:1). Yet in each of these chapters David accepts responsibility for the act and says, "I have sinned greatly in what I have done" (2 Sam. 24:10; see 1 Chron. 21:8).

Part of the answer is found in the Hebrew concept of causation. God is the ultimate cause of all that happens. Satan, as an independent being, while acting under the umbrella of God's permissive will, is an intermediate cause. But while God and Satan can be held responsible for their actions—God responsible for punishing Israel's sin, and Satan for attempting to harm God's people—David is ultimately responsible for his own choices as well. Neither God nor Satan *made* David count Israel.

You and I too are subject to many influences. Influence brought to bear by our friends or family. Influences from our childhood. Influences that appeal to our emotions, our baser passions, our desire to do good, etc. Even God the Holy Spirit influences the Christian, and undoubtedly Satan attempts to influence us too. Yet in the last analysis, no one can say, "The devil *made* me do it." Or, "My childhood *made* me do it." Without in any way arguing for the unrestricted distribution of pornography, we can say with confidence that Ted Bundy's early exposure to pornography did not *make* him commit his terrible crimes.

Our own will stands between our actions and the many influences that bear on each one of us. Ultimately when we fail we must say with David, "*I* have sinned greatly." The fault lies not with God, or with the devil, or with my childhood, but with me.

Why is it so important to face this truth and accept responsibility for our failures? Because to admit fault is the first necessary step we take on our journey toward God. When we accept the fact of our sin, we are preparing our hearts to seek, and to find, the forgiveness offered us in God.

Personal Application

There is no one further from God than the person who refuses to accept responsibliity for his sins.

Quotable

"The confession of evil works is the first beginning of good works."—St. Augustine

---

The Variety Reading Plan continues with HAGGAI

---

1 Kings

INTRODUCTION

First and 2 Kings composed one book in the Hebrew Bible. Together they relate the history of the Jewish kingdom from about 970 B.C. until 586 B.C. Half of 1 Kings is devoted to the prosperous reign of Solomon. The rest of the book tells of the division of that kingdom into northern (Israel) and southern (Judah) nations, and traces the history of each to about 852 B.C. The kings of each kingdom are evaluated according to whether they did right or wrong "in the eyes of the LORD." The impact of each rule for good or evil is explained.

Events emphasized in 1 Kings include the building and dedication of Solomon's temple (chaps. 5–9), the division of the kingdom (chaps. 12–14), the conflict between Elijah and Ahab (chaps. 17–19), and the rule of Ahab and Jezebel (chaps. 20–22).

OUTLINE OF CONTENTS

I. The Reign of Solomon ....1 Kings 1–11
- A. Solomon's ascension ....1 Kings 1–4
- B. Solomon's temple ....1 Kings 5–8
- C. An evaluation of Solomon ....1 Kings 9–11

II. The Divided Kingdom ....1 Kings 12–22
- A. The division ....1 Kings 12–14
- B. Various kings ....1 Kings 15–16
- C. Elijah and Ahab ....1 Kings 17–19
- D. Ahab's rule ....1 Kings 20–22

READING GUIDE (7 Days)

If hurried, you may read only the "core passage" in your Bible and the Devotional in each chapter of this Commentary.

Reading	*Chapters*	*Core passage*
71	1–4	1
72	5–8	8
73	9–11	11
74	12–14	13
75	15–16	15
76	17–19	19
77	20–22	21

1 Kings

MARCH 12 *Reading 71*
SOLOMON'S ASCENSION
1 Kings 1–4

> *"Now, O LORD my God, you have made Your servant king in place of my father David" (1 Kings 3:7).*

Solomon showed restraint in waiting for David to keep his promise and appoint him ruler. When we are sure of God's will, there is no need to plot and scheme.

Biography: Solomon

Solomon was the fourth son of David and Bathsheba. His selection by God to succeed his father (2 Sam. 12:24-25; 1 Chron. 22:9-10; 28:4-7) is a wonderful illustration of God's forgiving grace. The sin of the parents was washed away, and Solomon, child of the now-healed union, was lifted up to become king.

Solomon enjoyed a 40-year reign during which he held all the territory taken by his father. Wealth from trade and tribute poured into Israel during these years, and Solomon engaged in many expensive building projects. Solomon's wealth and his wisdom are both discussed in the first 11 chapters of 1 Kings.

Solomon's intellectual achievements include contribution of many proverbs to the Old Testament Book of Proverbs and, most believe, the Old Testament Books of Song of Songs and Ecclesiastes.

Overview

When David was old and feeble, Adonijah gathered supporters and attempted to make himself king (1:1-10). Nathan the prophet and Bathsheba appealed to David to keep a promise and appoint Solomon (vv. 11-27). Solomon was crowned (vv. 28-53), given advice by the dying David (2:1-12), and acted decisively to consolidate his power (vv. 13-46). Solomon's prayer for wisdom to lead the Lord's people was granted (3:1-15) and illustrated (vv. 16-28). Key men in Solomon's bureaucracy are listed (4:1-19), with an account of enough daily provisions to feed a court of 5,000 (vv. 20-28). The chapter concludes with a summary of Solomon's intellectual accomplishments (vv. 29-34).

Understanding the Text

"His father had never interfered with him" 1 Kings 1:1-10. David's failure to discipline Adonijah, as he had failed to discipline Absalom, bore similar fruit. David's promise to make Solomon king must have been well known. Yet with David old and feeble, Adonijah, David's oldest surviving son and the half brother of Solomon, plotted to make himself ruler.

Parents who fail to discipline their children share the blame when those children choose to do wrong.

"Nathan asked Bathsheba" 1 Kings 1:11-27. Nathan's appeal to Bathsheba suggests how deep a love now existed between David and the woman he had earlier betrayed. As favorite wife, Bathsheba won an immediate hearing, and her appeal was quickly followed by Nathan's appearance. There was no intrigue, but a straightforward appeal to David to keep his promise and make Solomon king.

David did keep that promise, and Solomon was acclaimed king.

"What's the meaning of all the noise?" 1 Kings 1:28-53 The sound of shouts and trumpets reached the crowd feasting with Adoni-

jah. When word came that Solomon was king, the guests all slipped away. People who are friends out of self-interest will desert us when troubles come.

Adonijah fled to the altar and grasped its "horns," the name given to handle-like projections on each of the top four corners. According to ancient custom a person who had killed another accidentally would be safe if grasping the altar horns. This act symbolized placing oneself under God's protection. Adonijah's action showed that he expected Solomon to execute him—something he intended to do to Solomon. People who plan evil tend to see evil in others.

Solomon assured Adonijah that as long as he proved to be a "worthy" person he would be safe. In context this implies renouncing all claim to the throne and supporting Solomon's right to it.

"Walk in His ways, and keep His decrees and commands" 1 Kings 2:1-11. Before David died, he exhorted his son to be faithful to God. Faith in God, with love for Him and dedication to obedience, is the most important heritage we can pass on to our children.

"I have one request to make of you" 1 Kings 2:13-25. Adonijah's request for the hand of Abishag, who had cared for David during his final illness, was politically motivated. In Old Testament times possession of a royal concubine was tantamount to laying claim on the throne (cf. 2 Sam. 3:7-8; 12:8; 16:21-22). Solomon realized that his older brother was still plotting to take his throne, and ordered his execution. The execution was not capricious. Adonijah had committed the crime of sedition.

Solomon also dealt with unresolved debts David had not been able to repay. Abiathar the priest, who supported Adonijah, was allowed to live in view of his years of loyal service to David. General Joab too had been loyal, but had often acted on his own, frequently to David's dismay (cf. 2 Sam. 3:22-27; 20). Joab's traitorous association with Adonijah gave Solomon a basis for ordering Joab's death. Solomon, however, saw his execution as retribution for those Joab had assassinated, thus removing potential guilt David incurred by permitting Joab's murders to go unpunished. Shimei, the troublemaker who had earlier cursed David but been allowed to live when David regained the throne, was warned not to leave Jerusalem. When he did, Shimei too was executed.

By these decisive and necessary acts Solomon gained firm control of his kingdom.

"Solomon showed his love for the LORD" 1 Kings 3:1-15. The "high places" mentioned here are local worship centers, generally on a hill in the countryside or on mounds in cities. The Canaanites too used "high places," and all too often in Israel's history worship at such locations injected pagan elements into Israel's faith. This is not implied here, as the text explains that Solomon and his people worshiped the Lord at them because "a temple had not yet been built."

Christians, like Solomon, may err in ignorance. God is gracious in such cases, as long as our love for Him is real and our motives are pure.

Solomon's love for God was demonstrated by his obedience to the Lord and by Solomon's request that God give him "a discerning heart to govern Your people and to distinguish between right and wrong."

The servant's heart that Solomon displayed pleased God, who throughout Scripture gives servanthood the highest priority (cf. Matt. 20:26-28).

"Cut the living child in two" 1 Kings 3:16-28. The story is told to illustrate Solomon's wisdom. But why this story, rather than some incident illustrating Solomon's knowledge of architecture, diplomatic skill, or brilliance in philosophical debate? This story is told because "wisdom" in the Old Testament sense is practical application of one's insights to life situations. Solomon had great insight into the jealousy motivating the woman whose child had died. He counted on his call for a sword to expose that jealousy and reveal the real mother, when there were no objective means available to determine who was telling the truth.

Solomon had asked for a "discerning heart to govern Your people." It was just this that God gave: wisdom for governing.

Let's not make the error of supposing a person who knows a lot is therefore wise. The wise person applies what he knows to make right and good decisions.

"Solomon's daily provisions" 1 Kings 4:20-28. Scholars have calculated the number of people in Solomon's court (his administration) based on the amount of food listed here. The best estimate lies between 4,000 and 5,000!

"And a breadth of understanding" 1 Kings 4:29-34. Solomon's wisdom is extolled, but so is his "breadth of understanding." Solomon is credited with thousands of proverbs and psalms, and with a careful study of botany and zoology. God gave Solomon far more than he requested. How great and good a God we have.

▶ DEVOTIONAL
Wise Enough to Wait (1 Kings 1)

I don't know about you, but I find it frustrating to sit in a doctor's waiting room. Waiting, when you feel the need to be doing something else, is never fun.

It's not fun to be in God's waiting room either. Waiting, when we feel we ought to be *doing* something. Waiting, while the pressure mounts and we know that *something* has got to happen.

The Bible is filled with stories of people under pressure who just couldn't wait. Jacob couldn't wait, but plotted to steal his brother's blessing (Gen. 27). Saul couldn't wait, but in desperation violated God's Word and Samuel's instructions by officiating at a burnt offering (1 Sam. 13). Yet Solomon, whose very life was threatened, seems to have waited quietly, confidently, as Adonijah attempted to steal the kingdom. Even at the last moment it was Bathsheba and Nathan the prophet, not Solomon, who begged David to act.

Bathsheba did urge David to act, sure that if Adonijah became king she and Solomon would "be treated as criminals." As evidence Bathsheba pointed out that Adonijah had given a feast and "invited all the king's sons" and others, but had excluded several of David's key advisers along with Bathsheba and Solomon. In the Middle East sharing a meal placed a person under the protection of the host. An invitation to Adonijah's feast was a promise of future safety should Adonijah become king. Not being invited meant that when Adonijah gained power he intended to execute that person.

In view of all this, Solomon's restraint is even more remarkable. We can explain it in only one way. Like his mother and Nathan the prophet, Solomon knew that God had promised he would succeed David on Israel's throne. And even then Solomon had the courage, and the wisdom, to wait on the Lord.

I don't like those times when God has me sitting in His waiting room. I'd rather be out doing something. Almost anything! Only by remembering that we, like Solomon, have been given great and precious promises by God can we find the courage, and the wisdom, to wait until God is ready to act.

Personal Application

When you must wait, wait on the Lord.

Quotable

"When his life's work was threatened, St. Ignatius Loyola was asked what he would do if Pope Paul IV dissolved or otherwise acted against the Society of Jesus, to which he had devoted his energies and gifts; and he replied: 'I would pray for fifteen minutes, then I would not think of it again.' "—Alan Paton

MARCH 13 *Reading 72*
SOLOMON'S TEMPLE
1 Kings 5–8

> *"The heavens, even the highest heaven, cannot contain You. How much less this temple I have built!" (1 Kings 8:27)*

Prayer is to reflect our understanding of who God is, and how God relates to human beings. Solomon's prayer at the dedication of the Jerusalem temple is a model of this element in prayer.

Background

The Jerusalem temple. Israel was to have only one place of worship, to demonstrate the unity of God and access to Him solely through sacrifice. That place was fixed in Jerusalem, at a temple Solomon constructed. Old Testament Law required that prescribed sacrifices for sin and worship be made only on the altar of the Jerusalem temple. God graciously "put His presence" there as a symbol of covenant love and a place for prayer and worship.

The temple Solomon built in Jerusalem lasted until the destruction of that city in 586 B.C. by the Babylonians. Later, when a group of captives returned from Babylon, a smaller temple was erected on the same site (Hag. 2:1-9). In the first century, this "second temple" was greatly expanded and beautified by Herod the Great, who took 46 years to reconstruct it. The second temple, where Jesus worshiped and taught, was destroyed by the Roman army in 70 A.D. The lack of a temple and altar today means that modern Judaism has no way to present the sacrifices for sin required under Old Testament Law. But the Prophet Ezekiel predicted that yet another temple will be built on the site in the days when the Messiah returns to rule the world (Ezek. 43:7).

Overview

Solomon organized his building effort (5:1-17). Construction of the Jerusalem temple began his fourth year (6:1-38). Solomon also constructed his own palace (7:1-12). The temple was furnished (vv. 13-51), and when all was ready Solomon brought the ark into the temple (8:1-21). He dedicated the magnificent edifice with prayer (vv. 22-61), sacrifice, and celebration (vv. 62-66).

Understanding the Text

"I intend . . . to build a temple for the Name of the LORD" 1 Kings 5:1-18. Solomon continued the friendship developed by David with Hiram, king of Tyre. That seaboard nation had lumber and skilled workers, but needed the grain that could be supplied by Israel. Solomon's commitment to build God's temple suited Hiram well.

It did, however, place a strain on Israel's resources. The text mentions "conscripted laborers." Solomon relied on the "corvee," a tax on time. The Israelite laborers gave four months of the year to Solomon's projects, and had eight months to work their own farms. This early corvee of workers for the temple was justified. Later, when Solomon became intent on many additional building projects, it became a drain on the overall economy and a source of bitter complaint.

"In the eleventh year . . . the temple was finished" 1 Kings 6:1-37. The illustration shows the finished temple, described in this chapter. It took seven years to complete. According to this chapter the whole interior was overlaid with pure gold.

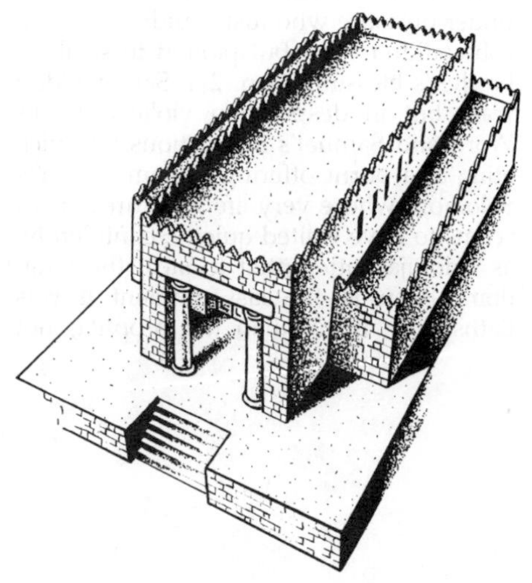

The Jerusalem Temple

"The construction of his palace" 1 Kings 7:1-12. Solomon's palace took 13 years to build. This is not because he viewed it as more important than the temple, or lavished more care on it. The palace complex had many buildings, a mix of public administrative centers and private dwellings. Also, David had spent his last years gathering resources for the temple, which considerably shortened the time it took for Solomon to complete the building.

It was God's decision to bless Solomon with great riches. We can hardly criticize how Solomon chose to use them. There is nothing wrong with being rich today—as long as, like Solomon, the rich person puts God's will first.

"A craftsman in bronze" 1 Kings 7:13-51. Here, as frequently in the Old Testament, "bronze" stands for every kind of metalwork. It is not possible to make accurate drawings of the temple furnishings from the description given here. What is clear is that no expense was spared. Solomon was committed to honor God by making His temple the most beautiful and expensive edifice possible.

"I have provided a place there for the ark" 1 Kings 8:1-21. The ark of the covenant was the most holy object in Israel's religion. It was there alone, on the top of this golden box, that sacrificial blood was spilt on the Day of Atonement, and "every sin" of Israel forgiven (Lev. 16). The ark was thus the one place on earth where the holy God met sinful men. The temple, as magnificent as it was, had meaning only because it housed the ark, on which God's presence rested.

All our magnificent cathedrals, all our mighty organs and stained glass windows, have meaning only if they serve as a place of meeting between God and a people who come to worship Him through Jesus Christ. And, if Jesus is there, present in the hearts of the congregation, a barn can serve just as sacredly as a church building.

▶ DEVOTIONAL
Prayer and God's Character (1 Kings 8)

"It's frustrating." Sue was talking about her class of adults and her difficulty in getting any of them to pray aloud. "They just don't seem to know much about prayer. And they sure aren't going to pray aloud when others are there."

I suppose it's even more frustrating for the women in her class. Wanting to pray. Feeling a need for prayer. But not feeling able to even try.

For anyone who feels a little like that—uncertain, hesitant—Solomon's prayer at the dedication of the temple can help. Solomon rooted his prayers in his understanding of what God was like. Knowing God, he knew something about how to pray.

Solomon knew that God is a faithful Person, who keeps His promise. So Solomon could claim the promises of God, and ask the Lord to keep them (vv. 23-26).

Solomon knew that God filled the universe, and yet bent to hear the prayer of a single individual. So Solomon could ask God to hear the prayers his people offered at the temple (vv. 27-30).

Solomon knew that God is moral Judge of His universe. So Solomon could ask God to punish the guilty and discharge the innocent (vv. 31-32).

Solomon knew that God forgives those who confess sin to Him. So Solomon could ask God to restore Israel's fortunes when His people repented (vv. 33-34).

Solomon knew that God is all-powerful, exercising sovereign control over all that happens on earth. So Solomon could ask God to intervene and act when His people faced disaster (vv. 35-40).

Solomon knew that God loves all humankind. So Solomon could ask God to bless even the foreigner who comes to Him in prayer (vv. 41-43).

Solomon knew that God is for His people. So Solomon could ask God to help them in wartime (vv. 44-45).

Solomon knew that God hates sin and yet loves the sinner (vv. 46-51). So Solomon could ask, no matter how great the sin or how terrible the discipline, that when God's people returned to Him the Lord would forgive and restore their fortunes.

And Solomon knew that God had singled out the people who were known by His name for endless love. So Solomon, and you and I, can be sure that God will hear and answer our prayers.

We may not need to make the specific requests that Solomon made. But like Solomon we can let what we have learned about God guide us in our prayers. We can pray confidently, knowing that God will act in accordance with who He is, and in accordance with the great love He has for you and me.

Personal Application
When you don't know what or how to pray, think about who God is, and let your thoughts of Him guide as you speak to Him.

Quotable
"If we ask anything according to His will, He hears us. And if we know that He hears us—whatever we ask—we know that we have what we asked of Him."
—1 John 5:14-15

MARCH 14 *Reading 73*
SOLOMON'S RULE
1 Kings 9–11

> *"King Solomon was greater in riches and wisdom than all the other kings of the earth" (1 Kings 10:23).*

Solomon's growing material prosperity was matched by spiritual decline. Solomon's experience is a warning to us today of the deceitfulness of success.

Overview
God appeared to Solomon again, with a promise and a warning (9:1-9). Some of Solomon's projects are listed (vv. 10-28), and his fame is illustrated by a visit from the queen of Sheba (10:1-13). Solomon's vast wealth is explained (vv. 14-29). Solomon's spiritual decline is traced to his passion for his foreign wives (11:1-13), and the resulting loss of most of his kingdom is predicted (vv. 14-43).

Understanding the Text
"If you walk before Me in integrity of heart and uprightness" 1 Kings 9:1-9. God appeared to Solomon 13 years after the temple was completed. The Lord reminded Solomon He had heard the king's prayer of dedication. Now, nearly 25 years into Solomon's 40-year reign, God renewed His promise to Solomon, but added a solemn warning. "If you or your sons turn away . . . and go off to serve other gods . . . then."

Why a second appearance now? Because, with Solomon's goals reached and his dreams fulfilled, Solomon was especially vulnerable. Success is often like this. As long as we are working, striving to reach a goal, we remain faithful to the Lord. But when we "have it made," we lose our sense of purpose and our dedication to the Lord. God's warning was especially gracious, coming at this critical time in Solomon's life. The great tragedy is that Solomon failed to heed what God said.

For some, retirement is a critical time. We've worked all our lives. Now it's time to relax and enjoy. Rather than use our time to serve God and others, some lose their sense of purpose and drift away from God.

That moment when we think we have succeeded can be the most dangerous for us spiritually.

"Here is the account" 1 Kings 9:10-27. The passage only hints at Solomon's magnificent achievements. For instance, Solomon's many impressive building programs, which have been partially explored by archeologists, are given only a word or two in verses 18-19. Yet these are among the most impressive in the ancient world.

Solomon's trading ventures are also mentioned only briefly (vv. 26-28). Yet he was the only king in Israel's long history to catch the vision of overseas trade and develop a fleet. His joint venture with Hiram of Tyre brought in vast wealth.

These merely hint at the great plans and visionary programs introduced by Solomon. Yet they remind us how exceptional Solomon truly was.

The same passage tells us that Solomon maintained the annual rituals that honored God (v. 25). Yet, as God reminded

Solomon, the Lord is concerned with "integrity of heart and uprightness" (v. 4). A wholehearted love for God, not faithful attendance at religious services, keeps us close to Him.

"The queen of Sheba heard about the fame of Solomon" 1 Kings 10:1-13. Solomon's wisdom is illustrated in this report of the visit of the queen of Sheba, modern Yemen. In ancient time Sheba was a trading center, linking Africa, India, and the Mediterranean lands. The questions she asked Solomon were *hidot,* in this context questions on issues involving practical and deeper theological truths.

The gifts the two exchanged likely were part of trade negotiations worked out during the visit. The queen left full of praise for Solomon and for God, who had given Israel such a wise ruler.

"King Solomon was greater in riches" 1 Kings 10:14-29. The passage continues with more about the splendor of the Solomonic era. It lists Solomon's personal annual income as 25 tons of gold! Like other kings of the ancient world, Solomon dedicated much of the gold to the temple, and used the rest in ostentatious display. Despite the record here of the sources of Solomon's wealth, some modern commentators have dismissed the biblical account as a product "of exuberant imagination." However, comparison with ancient inscriptions shows that ancient rulers did gather vast amounts of gold, and used it in the same way Solomon did.

Even more significant is the Egyptian record of gifts given by Pharaoh Osorkon of at least 383 tons of precious metals to Egypt's gods. Why is this significant? Because just five years before this gift, his father, Shishak, had attacked Jerusalem and "carried off the treasures of the temple of the LORD and the treasures of the royal palace" (14:26). Solomon did gather hundreds of tons of gold. And at least part of it was later given by Pharaoh Osorkon to Egypt's gods and goddesses.

The material things we give to God have no lasting significance to Him. What God yearns for is a fully yielded heart. This—and this alone—is His treasure.

"Solomon . . . loved many foreign women" 1 Kings 11:1-13. Old Testament Law forbad marriage to foreign women, and specifically prohibited accumulating large amounts of gold and silver as well as multiple marriages for kings (cf. Deut. 17:14-20). Solomon's marriages to foreign women, contracted to seal international treaties, were disastrous. Solomon not only permitted his wives to worship their old gods and goddesses, but began to worship with them.

Solomon's disobedience was judged severely. God determined to take most of the kingdom away from Solomon's offspring, but for David's sake reserved the tribe of Judah and Jerusalem for Solomon's descendants.

Solomon reminds us not to be overawed by others more intelligent than we are. The wise men of this world spin their theories, and may ridicule faith. But true wisdom is found in the simple person's complete trust in God and faithfulness to Him.

"The LORD raised up . . . an adversary" 1 Kings 11:14-43. Solomon's last years were marred by frustration. Enemies appeared to disrupt his plans and develop hostility toward Israel. Yet Solomon was unable to dispatch them. In Israel itself a gifted man named Jeroboam was promoted—but turned against Solomon when a prophet predicted that he, not Solomon's son, would rule the 10 northern tribes.

Solomon's success had depended on his relationship with God, not his intelligence. It's not our gifts but our God who brings us success.

▶ DEVOTIONAL
The End of Life
(1 Kings 11)

I remember the title of an old movie—*Will Success Spoil Rock Hunter?* Actually, that's all I remember about it. I suppose the movie itself is forgettable. But the title surely is not.

What *will* happen to you and me if we succeed? What if all our dreams come true? What if our hopes are all fulfilled? What if we achieve prosperity and "have it made"?

While few of us will know this kind of success, for most older people these days a time comes when we can stop striving.

The children have grown up and moved away. We're ready to retire. We have enough to live on, and reasonably good health. We can sit back now and relax. It's only later that we realize success has begun to spoil us, as it surely spoiled Solomon.

Solomon achieved. His plans were carried out. His dreams were fulfilled. His riches were beyond calculation. And then, with nothing more to do, he turned to his foreign wives and to their gods. As a result, Solomon's old age was a time of frustration and futility.

Most believe that Solomon wrote the Book of Ecclesiastes during the last, empty decade of his life. In this book Solomon looks back on all his accomplishments, looks honestly at his passions, and drearily concludes, "Meaningless! Meaningless! Everything is meaningless!"

And Solomon was right. As far as he went. In Eccelesiastes Solomon set out to find meaning in life "by wisdom" and "under the sun." The two phrases mean "by unaided human reason, not revelation," and "in the framework of the material universe." Solomon turned his back on God and lost touch with the Lord. Yet this wisest of men searched all human experience and concluded that, apart from God, everything is meaningless.

And so we return to that question, "Will success spoil you and me?" And the answer is, it can. It can. But only if, when we rest from our labors in this world, we also relax our commitment to the Lord. If we keep on putting God first in our lives, then success can and will be a blessing. For we will still seek the true meaning of life in our relationships with the Lord.

Personal Application

Retire from work, but not from serving God.

Quotable

"The heart is rich when it is content, and it is always content when its desires are fixed on God. *Nothing* can bring greater happiness than doing God's will for the love of God."—Miguel Febres Cordero-Munoz

MARCH 15 *Reading 74*
THE KINGDOM DIVIDES
1 Kings 12–14

"Only the tribe of Judah remained loyal to the house of David" (1 Kings 12:20).

The old saying suggests that "well begun is half done." It is just as true that "poorly begun is undone!"

Background

Israel. The Northern Kingdom of Israel was founded on an apostate religion. Not 1 of its 21 rulers did what was right in the eyes of the Lord. Gradually many true believers in the north drifted across the border to settle in Judah, illustrated by the growth of Judah's original 180,000 fighting men (12:21) to 400,000 fighting men just 18 years later (2 Chron. 13:3).

Decades later the Northern Kingdom was crushed by Assyria, and its people deported. This has given rise to the fable of "10 lost tribes." In fact, members of all 12 tribes of Israel were represented in Judah throughout the kingdom era, and no tribe has been "lost."

Many may turn from the Lord. But God will preserve His own.

Overview

Israel rebelled when Solomon's son Rehoboam threatened to raise already heavy taxes (12:1-19). The 10 northern tribes made Jeroboam king (vv. 20-24). Jeroboam set up a counterfeit religion (vv. 25-33), which was condemned by a prophet who came from Judah (13:1-34). The Prophet Ahijah announced God's judgment on the family of Jeroboam (14:1-20). Judah too abandoned God and suffered an Egyptian invasion (vv. 21-31).

Understanding the Text

"Rehoboam rejected the advice the elders gave him" 1 Kings 12:1-9. On Solomon's death his son Rehoboam took the throne. In Solomon's later years heavy taxes and an in-

creased corvee on labor caused resentment. The north made tax reduction a condition of recognizing Rehoboam's royal authority.

Rehoboam's pride was displayed in rejecting the conciliation advised by the elders, in favor of an arrogant demand for submission.

A leader who responds to the just complaints of others gains their loyalty. The leader who acts arrogantly deserves to lose support.

"Rehoboam . . . mustered the whole house of Judah" 1 Kings 12:20-24. When the north acclaimed Jeroboam as king, Rehoboam prepared for war. Only intervention by a prophet named Shemaiah headed off the conflict.

Shemaiah's advice is still appropriate for Christians, who too often find occasion to feud with other believers. "Do not go up to fight against your brothers."

"The king made two golden calves" 1 Kings 12:25-33. Jeroboam feared that if his people went up to Jerusalem to worship the Lord, as the Law required, they might in time seek political reunification. His fears led him to set up a system that counterfeited the Old Testament's revealed religion. Jeroboam chose two cities long associated with worship, Bethel and Dan, as worship centers. He appointed priests who were not of Aaron's line, changed the dates of religious festivals, and offered sacrifices on altars set up at Bethel and Dan.

This was a calculated abandonment of revealed religion. Yet it was intended to mimic the true. False religions often have elements in common with biblical faith. For instance, many of the world's "great" religions call for morality. Yet counterfeit faiths lack one essential ingredient—the presence and power of the one God, who has revealed Himself to us. Only God is able to forgive sinners and transform them so that they may live godly lives. Religion without the Lord is empty, as the religious system Jeroboam established was empty and useless.

"A man of God came from Judah to Bethel" 1 Kings 13:1-10. The day that Jeroboam dedicated the religious center at Bethel, a prophet appeared and announced that a future king of Judah, Josiah by name, would desecrate Jeroboam's altar by burning human bones on it. As proof, the altar would now split and ashes be poured out.

Jeroboam pointed at the prophet to order his death, but his hand and arm atrophied! Shaken, Jeroboam begged the prophet to pray for him, and his hand was restored.

Jeroboam knew that his acts displeased God. Yet this first king of divided Israel continued in his sinful course. "Even after this," the text tells us, "Jeroboam did not change his evil ways."

When God warns us, it is wise to change course!

"Abijah son of Jeroboam became ill" 1 Kings 14:1-19. Jeroboam's wife came to Ahijah the prophet in disguise. The prophet gave her a message of doom for Jeroboam. His son would die. And every male descendant of Jeroboam's would die a violent death.

The judgment was merited, for Jeroboam had set Israel on a course of apostasy and idolatry that would lead to national disaster.

Perhaps most significant are the words about Jeroboam's ill son. His death was intended as a blessing, for "he is the only one in the house of Jeroboam in whom the LORD . . . has found anything good" (v. 13).

Those of us who suffer the loss of a child, or of some other young person who is dear to us, often struggle to understand. Usually there is no explanation, and we are forced to keep on living by faith. Yet this passage reminds us that the death of godly persons is not always a tragedy. Sometimes it is intended as a blessing. The thought is echoed in Isaiah 57:1-2: "The righteous perish, and no one ponders it in his heart; devout men are taken away, and no one understands that the righteous are taken away to be spared from evil. Those who walk uprightly enter into peace; they find rest as they lie in death."

"Judah did evil in the eyes of the LORD" 1 Kings 14:21-31. Solomon's son Rehoboam permitted great apostasy in Judah, the Southern Kingdom. As a result, God

sent Shishak of Egypt to sack Jerusalem and steal the golden treasures Solomon had assembled (see 1 Kings 10). Life became hard in the divided kingdom, and incipient war flared up again and again between the Divided Hebrew kingdoms.

It's easy to gain momentum going downhill. It's much more difficult to stop and begin to go up again.

▶DEVOTIONAL

Don't Listen to Old Prophets (1 Kings 13)

One of my professors in seminary told the story of how, as a young and single pastor, one of the ladies in his congregation announced that God had told her he was to marry the lady's daughter.

In a way, his experience was like that of the young prophet God sent to Bethel to speak against Jeroboam's false religion. The passage tells us that after he completed his mission, and was on the way home, an old prophet who lived nearby stopped him. God had told the young man not to eat or drink in Israel. But the old prophet had a ready answer. God had told *him,* the old prophet, to tell his younger colleague that it was all right to stop over at his house and have a meal.

We don't know the old prophet's motive. Maybe he was lonely. Perhaps he was upset that God hadn't sent him to Jeroboam. Whatever the reason, the old prophet was lying. As the young prophet set out on his way back home, he was attacked and killed by a lion.

The incident carried an important message for Jeroboam. If God's word was so important that even a slight deviation brought death, how terrible Jeroboam's sin must be. As far as we know, Jeroboam remained unmoved. He even lived and ruled in Israel for another 22 years, perpetuating his own false cult.

The story has an important lesson for us as well. It's a lesson my professor had learned, and after being told many times by this lady of God's desire for him to marry her daughter, my prof taught the lesson to her. "When God tells *me* to marry your daughter," he said, "I'll do it."

The lesson? Just this. We don't have to listen to old prophets, who insist on telling us God's will for our lives. God will tell us that Himself. And only when He does are we to act.

Personal Application

God will show you what His will is. Be sensitive to Him, and beware of those who glibly tell you what you ought to do.

Quotable

"If you observe anything evil within yourself, correct it; if something good, preserve it; if something beautiful, foster it; if something sound, maintain it; if sickly, heal it. Read unwearingly the precepts of the Lord and, sufficiently instructed by them, you will know what to avoid and what to pursue."—Bernard of Clairvaux

---

MARCH 16 *Reading 75*

WARS AND REVIVAL

1 Kings 15–16

"Asa did what was right in the eyes of the LORD, as his father David had done" (1 Kings 15:11).

Corrupt leadership brings strife and suffering. Relief is found only in a return to the Lord.

Background

The following chart shows the years these chapters cover and the reigns of the kings.

Years	*In Judah*	*In Israel*
930	Rehoboam	Jeroboam
913	Abijah	
910	Asa	
909		Nadab
908		Baasha
886		Elah
885		Zimri
885		Omri/Tibni (Civil war)
880		Omri
874		Ahab

Definition of Key Terms

Father. "Father" in the Old Testament need not mean "male parent." In these books that deal with the monarchy, one ruler is often called the "father" of another. This may mean ancestor, as in 1 Kings 15:11 where David is called the "father" of his great-grandson, Asa. In some ancient literature "father" may simply mean "predecessor"; one who earlier occupied the same throne, even though there is no ancestral relationship. In addition, "my father" is frequently used as a term of respect for a mentor, as in 2 Kings 2:12.

Overview

The sinful direction set by Abijah of Judah (15:1-8) was reversed by his successor, godly King Asa (vv. 9-24). In Israel, Baasha wiped out the family of Jeroboam (vv. 25-31). His family was wiped out in turn by Zimri (v. 33–16:14), throwing the nation into civil war (vv. 15-20). Stability was reestablished by Omri (vv. 21-28), who was succeeded by his wicked but gifted son, Ahab (vv. 29-34).

Understanding the Text

"For David's sake" 1 Kings 15:1-8. Abijah, the son of Rehoboam, was one of Judah's forgettable kings. He ruled only three years, did evil, and died. The text makes it clear that he was tolerated as king only for the sake of David, who "had done what was right in the eyes of the LORD."

Typically only persons who do great evil or great good are remembered. The text reminds us that the blessings of those who do good overflow to bless future generations as well as their own.

"Asa's heart was fully committed to the LORD all his life" 1 Kings 15:9-24. The impact of Asa on Judah is seen most clearly by comparing what was happening in neighboring Israel. While Judah enjoyed relative peace and revival under Asa for some 40 years, Israel had a series of wicked rulers. During these years two of Israel's kings and their entire families were assassinated, and the land experienced a bloody civil war. There truly is great gain in godliness (cf. 1 Tim. 6:6).

Acts of Asa which show his commitment are listed. He expelled cult prostitutes, got rid of idols, and deposed the queen mother, his grandmother, because she worshiped a pagan goddess (1 Kings 15:11-13). Asa had many other achievements. Verse 23 says he constructed new cities in Judah, suggesting that he may have extended her borders. But all these are relegated to "the book of the annals of the kings of Judah." The truly significant accomplishments of Asa were religious. It was what he did for God that counts.

When the stories of our lives are written, our accomplishments too will pale compared to what we have done in service to our Lord.

"I am about to consume Baasha" 1 Kings 15:25–16:7. One of the best ways to learn is from other people's mistakes. But this also seems to be the most difficult way for most of us to gain understanding.

God rejected Jeroboam's line because of their commitment to evil, and announced that every male member of the family would be killed. Baasha was the instrument God used to carry out this judgment. Yet when Baasha had assassinated Nadab, Jeroboam's son, Baasha himself then "walked in the ways of Jeroboam and in his sin"!

Baasha had learned nothing from the destruction of Jeroboam's family. So, as the Prophet Jehu announced, Baasha and his house met the same fate.

My wife frequently detects Baasha's attitude in the teens she teaches in her high school English classes. A mention of a driver who recently killed two young people when driving drunk here in Florida brought only a smirk from most in her class until she challenged them to think what he faces as he goes to prison. And to realize that, once, he too had probably smirked at the idea that *he* might get into trouble driving drunk. "It can't happen to me" is the arrogant thought of those who simply will not learn from the mistakes of others.

As Baasha discovered, it *can* happen to me. He failed to learn from Jeroboam's and Nadab's mistakes. And it cost him his life.

"Omri became king" 1 Kings 16:21-28. The Bible says little about Omri other than to note that he established Samaria as the capital of the Northern Kingdom. Secular

sources say more. The Moabite stone, a monument found in 1898, tells us that Omri conquered Moab and imposed tribute. He rebuilt Israel's military strength, and from archeological finds we know he built at Samaria a large, attractive, and skillfully defensed city. A century later Assyrian annals still referred to Israel as the "land of Omri."

Again, all these accomplishments are dismissed in the biblical text. What is important about this king is that he too did evil. He formed an alliance with Phoenicia which was sealed by the marriage of his son, Ahab, to the Phoenician princess, Jezebel. This marriage led to the active promotion in Israel of a most virulent and wicked form of Baal worship.

Again we're reminded. Our impact on the material universe will fade away. But our impact on the spiritual universe, for good or evil, remains forever.

▶ DEVOTIONAL
The Stone Curtain
(1 Kings 15)

It's probably impossible for us not to classify people. "We" live in the suburbs. "They" live in the city. "We" are educated, well-dressed, and work hard. "They" are ignorant, sloppy, and lazy. "We" believe in God. "They" are pagans. "We" live good moral lives. "They" behave shamefully.

While such differences do exist, I suspect that the vast gap implied in "we"/"they" thinking does not. After all, "we" and "they" are both human beings. God loves "us" and He even loves "them."

Perhaps that's one reason why I find Asa such an attractive person. And why something that Baasha, king of Israel, did is so funny.

According to 2 Chronicles 15–16, Asa wasn't satisfied when revival came to Judah. He reached across the border to "them," the enemy, and invited all true Israelites to come up to Jerusalem and join in the celebration of the annual religious festivals called for in Moses' Law. Perhaps surprisingly, "they" came!

In fact, too many came! So many that Baasha, king of Israel, got worried. He quickly sent a force of soldiers up to Ramah, which controlled a mountain pass between the two nations, and began a fortification intended to "prevent anyone from leaving or entering the territory of Asa." It wasn't an "iron curtain." But it surely was a "stone curtain," constructed with the same intent as the Berlin wall. When Asa's "we" reached out with an invitation to come to God, too many of Baasha's "they" did just that!

So Asa bribed the Arameans (Syrians) to attack Israel. And when the Israelite troops withdrew from Ramah, Asa's people carted away the fortifications stone by stone.

What a lesson for us. The stone curtain people still erect between "us" and "them" doesn't protect God's folk. It protects Satan's territory! If we cart away the stones that wall us off from others, and share the good news of Jesus, we'll find hundreds of "them" eager to become "us" today.

Personal Application

Don't let "us"/"them" thinking cut you off from those who need Jesus.

Quotable

Longfellow could take a worthless sheet of paper, write a poem on it, and make it worth $6,000—that's genius.

Rockefeller could sign his name to a piece of paper and make it worth a million—that is wealth.

A painter can take a 50-cent piece of canvas, paint a picture on it and make it worth $10,000—that's art.

But . . . God can take a worthless sinful life, wash it in the blood of Christ, put His Spirit in it, and make it a blessing to humanity—that's salvation.—*The Compass*

MARCH 17 *Reading 76*
ELIJAH THE TISHBITE
1 Kings 17–19

"Then the word of the Lord *came to Elijah" (1 Kings 17:2).*

The utter humanity of Elijah has appealed to generations of believers. His story contains encouragement for Christians who ever find themselves depressed or discouraged.

Biography: Elijah

Elijah is undoubtedly one of the greatest of the Old Testament prophets. He appeared at a critical moment in Israel's history, when King Ahab, urged on by his Phoenician wife Jezebel, made a determined attempt to wipe out the worship of Yahweh in Israel. Through Elijah, the Lord entered the conflict and decisively defeated the pagan god, stimulating a popular return to the true faith.

But Elijah's confrontational role wore on the great prophet. Even in victory he recognized the superficiality of the popular revival, and felt depressed and alone. He was rested and reassured by God, and returned once again to represent the living God to an apostate king and nation.

Overview

Elijah announced a drought to Ahab (17:1). He then hid, first at Kerith (vv. 2-6), and then with a widow in Zarephath (vv. 7-24). After three years Elijah returned to confront the prophets of Baal on Mount Carmel (18:1-46). But after a decisive victory, Elijah inexplicably fled to Horeb (19:1-9). The Lord spoke to the despondent Elijah, gave him a task, and also a companion in Elisha (19:10-21).

Understanding the Text

"Neither dew nor rain in the next few years" 1 Kings 17:1. Baal was originally a god of storms, worshiped for his supposed ability to bring rain and make the land fertile. The drought announced by Elijah struck at the strength of the pagan deity that Ahab and Jezebel attempted to make dominant in Israel.

The drought displayed a major tenet of biblical faith: "The Lord, He is God!"

Archeologists can date pottery jars to within 25 years by their shape and decorations. These jars are from the time of Elijah, between 875–850 B.C. They remind us that Bible stories like that of the widow of Zarephath are not fairy tales, but are drawn from the lives of real people who used utensils like these nearly 3,000 years ago.

"First make a small cake of bread for me" 1 Kings 17:7-24. While hiding from Ahab, Elijah left Israel and went to Jezebel's homeland, Phoenicia! There he stayed with a penniless widow who first fed the prophet, and then herself and her son when Elijah promised that her near-empty jug of oil would not run dry, and her near-empty jar of flour would not run out. The widow's faith was rewarded. Instead of starving, the woman and her son were fed daily.

When the widow's son became ill and "stopped breathing," Elijah was there to ask God to restore him. The return of the boy to life was final, joyous proof to the widow. God truly did live and speak through Elijah.

When you and I are first called to faith in Christ it may seem that we, like the widow, are called on to give up something vital to us. For the widow, the demand was to surrender what little food she had left. But see what happened when she responded to the prophet's promise. Instead of less, she had more. Instead of giving, she gained. And ultimately that initial choice meant the restoration of her son to life.

Whatever you and I give up when we receive Christ, God gives us far more. And ultimately we have eternal life.

"Obadiah was a devout believer in the LORD" 1 Kings 18:1-15. After three years Elijah returned to Israel and met Obadiah, a high official in Ahab's government who was a secret believer. We assume he was a secret believer, for otherwise he would surely have been purged by Jezebel. Some might criticize Obadiah for compromising his faith. But our passage commends him as "devout." And we see that he used his position to save the lives of a hundred of God's prophets.

Obadiah reminds us not to judge others. We might not make the same choices they do, but each person is responsible to the Lord for the course he takes in life. Who is to say that Obadiah was not directed by God to make the choice he did?

"Bring the four hundred and fifty prophets of Baal and the four hundred prophets of Asherah" 1 Kings 18:16-40. The story of this confrontation on Carmel is one of the best-known stories in Scripture. Several things to note are:

**"who eat at Jezebel's table" (v. 19).* The queen supported the pagan "missionaries" she imported from her homeland to convert Israel to her faith. There was a concerted effort during this period to suppress worship of the Lord.

**"Elijah began to taunt them" (v. 27).* Pagan gods and goddesses were thought by their worshipers to be engaged in humanlike affairs, such as traveling, sleeping, and even doing business. Elijah's taunts ridiculed this humanistic view of deity.

*Ancient texts portray the Phoenician Baal as a bloodthirsty as well as lascivious god. His priests slashed themselves with knives in hopes the smell of blood might attract his attention.

**"repaired the altar of the LORD" (v. 30).* The "fallen down" condition of an altar dedicated to Yahweh shows how effective Ahab and Jezebel had been up to this time. But the spectacle of fire falling from heaven in answer to Elijah's prayer moved the people to turn on the pagan prophets and kill them.

"There is the sound of a heavy rain" 1 Kings 18:41-46. With the prophets of Baal executed and the Lord publicly acclaimed as God, Elijah sensed that God was ready to bring rain, and prayed to that end. The incident reminds us that God uses our prayers to accomplish His purposes. And that the believer who is close to the Lord will pray in harmony with His will.

▶ DEVOTIONAL
When Depression Strikes (1 Kings 19)

A book that I have suggests that "nearly everyone gets depressed. That basic feeling of emptiness, exhaustion, and meaninglessness is universal, crossing all borders of age, sex, and nationality."

The problem is, we sometimes don't understand our depression. As in Elijah's case, depression can strike when everything seems to be going extremely well. Even worse, we don't know what to do about our depression. Is it the mark of some deep spiritual flaw? Does depression indicate weak faith?

The story of Elijah's inexplicable bout of depression after the victory on Carmel encourages us. If a spiritual giant like Elijah can suffer from depression, maybe pygmies like you and I shouldn't expect too much of ourselves.

But even more, Elijah's experience shows us how God treated His prophet's depression and gives us clues to how we can help ourselves.

When Elijah became despondent and he ran from his ministry, God was not angry. Instead God actually provided food to sustain Elijah while he ran (vv. 6-9). It's easy to get down on ourselves when depression strikes. We need to remind ourselves that God is with us, bending to sustain us rather than to condemn.

When Elijah had rested, God gave His prophet a simple task to do (vv. 15-16). Depression often robs us of the will to act. It's important to get up in the morning, and set out to perform our daily tasks.

When Elijah doubted and complained, God reassured him. He was not alone, for God had reserved "seven thousand in Israel—all whose knees have not bowed down to Baal" (v. 18). Remembering that we're not alone in our experience can help.

Finally, God gave Elijah a friend and

companion to be with him (vv. 19-21). Having someone who cares is important, even if they don't know what to say or do to lift our mood.

Depression is a problem for many. And there are no easy answers. But we can lift some of the pressure on ourselves by recalling that God still loves us, by going about our work, remembering we're not alone, and by finding a friend who cares.

Personal Application

Let God's caring attitude toward Elijah guide you when others are depressed, and sustain you when you suffer depression.

Quotable

"He said not: Thou shalt not be troubled—thou shalt not be tempted—thou shalt not be distressed. But he said: Thou shalt not be overcome."—Julian of Norwich

MARCH 18 *Reading 77*
DARK DAYS OF AHAB
1 Kings 20–22

"There was never a man like Ahab, who sold himself to do evil in the eyes of the Lord*, urged on by Jezebel his wife" (1 Kings 21:25).*

Despite the strength of his wife's evil influence, God gave Ahab many chances to do right. Each of us is responsible for the choices we make and the opportunities we refuse.

Background

The 800s B.C. saw the rise of Assyria. In Syria-Palestine, Ben-Hadad II of Aram (Syria) led a coalition of kings determined to resist the Assyrians. Ben-Hadad seized the opportunity created by Israel's weakness after the three-year famine to invade Israel and force Ahab to join his anti-Assyria compact. Despite the defeats inflicted by Israel (1 Kings 20), Israel and Syria later did unite with seven other area states. In 853 B.C. at Qarqar the allies threw back the forces of Assyria's Shalmaneser III. This battle, not mentioned in Scripture, took place between the events reported in 1 Kings 20 and 22. First Kings 22 portrays Syria and Israel again at each other's throats, this time as Ahab set out to occupy Ramoth Gilead, which Ben-Hadad had ceded to him after his earlier defeats (cf. 20:34).

Against this background of international tension and strife, the biblical writer focused on the character of Ahab, king of Israel, and on Israel's gracious God.

Overview

God intervened to help Ahab repel two Syrian (Aramean) invasions (20:1-34), but Ahab was rebuked for sparing the Aramean ruler (vv. 35-43). When Jezebel arranged the death of Naboth so Ahab could have his vineyard, Elijah confronted the king and announced God's judgment (21:1-29). Micaiah the prophet accurately predicted Ahab's death in battle (22:1-40). In Judah, a devout Jehoshaphat succeeded his godly father, Asa (vv. 41-50).

Understanding the Text

"Meanwhile a prophet came to Ahab king of Israel" 1 Kings 20:1-30. Ahab, fully aware of Israel's desperately weak condition, was willing to surrender to Ben-Hadad of Aram. However, Ben-Hadad's progressively outrageous demands forced Ahab to resist.

When a prophet of God appeared and predicted victory, a sobered Ahab asked for—and followed!—God's instructions. Even the wicked may respond to God if desperate enough.

But why should the Lord intervene on behalf of wicked King Ahab? The text and context suggest three significant reasons. (1) At Carmel the people of Israel acknowledged God and killed the prophets of Baal. God kept covenant with them by fighting for His people. (2) In victory Ahab would "know that I am the Lord" (v. 13). There could be no future doubts in Ahab's mind that the Lord truly is God. (3) The Arameans challenged God's nature and power. Each victory revealed

God more clearly (v. 28).

Ahab's continuing commitment to evil despite God's gracious revelation of Himself tells us much about his character. Every expression of God's grace is intended to draw us to Him. Response to grace is up to us.

"Therefore it is your life for his life" 1 Kings 20:31-42. When desperate, Ahab was eager for God's help and direction. With the battles won, Ahab quickly reverted to his arrogant ways. The phrase, "You have set free a man I had determined should die," suggests that Ahab had been commanded to kill Ben-Hadad. When Ahab was rebuked he did not repent but became "sullen and angry."

"Deathbed conversions" are too often shallow and meaningless. When the danger is past, too many revert to their old attitudes and ways. It is not what we know about God that counts. What counts is how we respond to Him once we know.

"The LORD forbid that I should give you the inheritance of my fathers" 1 Kings 21:1-16. Old Testament Law forbad permanent sale of family land. The godly Israelite saw property allotted to the family in the time of Joshua as God's gift (cf. Josh. 13–19). Thus Naboth refused the king's offer to buy or trade his vineyard on religious grounds.

The king went home and sulked (vv. 3-4). Jezebel scornfully told him to "act as king" (v. 7), and promised to get him the vineyard. She then ordered, in Ahab's name, that Naboth be falsely accused and killed so Ahab could take his land.

Ahab did not order Naboth's death. But he was only too glad to profit from it. Undoubtedly Ahab would have been quick to adopt Jezebel's solution if only he had thought of it! "But *I* didn't do it" is an empty excuse if we profit from and condone the wrong actions of others.

"So you have found me, my enemy" 1 Kings 21:17-29. Elijah's response to Ahab's exclamation puts the king's remark in perspective. Elijah appeared only because "you have sold yourself to do evil." The king's enemy was not Elijah, but Ahab himself!

We really are our own worst enemies. But it is also true that when we choose to do right, we can be our own best friends!

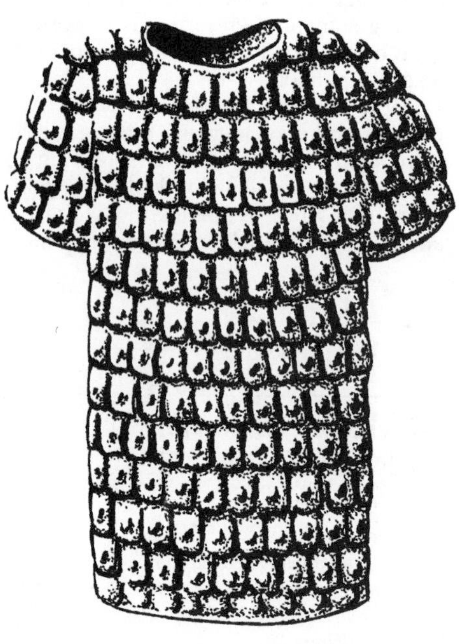

The armor Ahab wore when he was killed was probably made by attaching metal scales to a heavy shirt, as shown above. The person wearing scale armor was vulnerable to arrows which struck "between the sections" (1 Kings 22:34).

Ahab's repentance (v. 27) was sincere, but far too late. God could only delay the judgment destined for Ahab's line.

If even this most wicked of Israel's kings can find grace through repentance, think how much grace we can find when we repent.

"Attack and be victorious" 1 Kings 22:1-28. Ahab recognized the sarcasm in Micaiah's voice and demanded he tell the truth. That prophet then told the king he would be killed in the battle for Ramoth Gilead.

The lying spirit from the Lord troubles many. Two observations help. God is able to turn the evil done by Satan and his minions to accomplish good. The lying spirit may have had its own purpose in deceiving Ahab.

Perhaps most important, God did not deceive Ahab at all! Through Micaiah the Lord fully revealed what He intended. Ahab then chose to act on the lie told by his own prophets, and so rode to his doom.

God always reveals His truth to human beings. He is not responsible if men reject the truth in favor of lies.

"Jehoshaphat . . . king of Judah" 1 Kings 22:41-50. Despite his association here with Ahab, Jehoshaphat was a godly king. We are told more about him in 2 Chronicles 17–20.

▶ DEVOTIONAL
Jezebel's Theory of Leadership (1 Kings 21)

"Do it because I said so!" Mom shouted at Kara. That girl was so exasperating! It seemed to Mom that these days she had to shout just to get Kara's attention.

"You'll do the lawn before you go to practice, and that's that," Dad said grimly. "I don't care if you miss every practice and get kicked off the team. I'm your father, and what I say around here goes."

Oh, I know.

Teenagers can be irritating. Maybe Mom needs to yell at Kara. And maybe Dad is just putting his foot down because his son has put off a weekly chore. But some moms and dads who talk this way to their children have unwittingly adopted Jezebel's theory of authority.

We can deduce that theory from 1 Kings 21. Ahab wanted a vineyard? Well, Ahab was king, wasn't he? So King Ahab ought to get what he wanted. And he could use his royal power any way he wished to get it!

Actually Jezebel's theory is out of line with what the Bible teaches. Kings in biblical Israel were supposed to rule, under God, for the benefit of God's people. Kingship was never a right to command others for the king's benefit.

Sometimes Christian parents adopt Jezebel's theory of authority. They "act like a king" and command their children without taking time to listen and without enough concern for the child's needs. And they justify their ways just as Jezebel would. "I'm your dad. And I've got the right to tell you what to do."

Oh, yes. Sometimes Christian parents have to put their foot down. Maybe even yell a little. But Christian moms and dads can never forget that parenthood is a commission to servanthood. As Jesus said, "Whoever wants to become great among you must be your servant, and whoever wants to be first must be your slave—just as the Son of man did not come to be served, but to serve" (Matt. 20:26-28).

Personal Application

Servanthood means acting in another's best interests.

Quotable

"Meekness was the method that Jesus used with the apostles. He put up with their ignorance and roughness and even their infidelity. He treated sinners with a kindness and affection that caused some to be shocked, others to be scandalized, and still others to gain hope in God's mercy. Thus, He bade us to be gentle and humble of heart."—John Bosco

The Variety Reading Plan continues with 2 KINGS

2 Kings

INTRODUCTION

Second Kings picks up the history of the Divided Hebrew Kingdom where 1 Kings left off. The progressive decline of the Northern Kingdom was unbroken by any hint of revival, ending with its conquest by Assyria in 722 B.C. The Southern Kingdom, Judah, survived the Assyrian threat, but it too deteriorated spiritually and was finally crushed by the Babylonians in 586 B.C. Second Kings again features stories of God's prophets and their relationships with the rulers of the two kingdoms. Most prominent among the prophets are Elijah and Elisha, while godly kings responsible for Judah's preservation include Joash, Hezekiah, and Josiah.

OUTLINE OF CONTENTS

I. Elijah and Elisha ....2 Kings 1:1–8:15
II. Israel's Decline..................................2 Kings 8:16–17:41
III. Judah and Assyria ....2 Kings 18–23
IV. Judah and Babylon..................................2 Kings 24–25

READING GUIDE (6 Days)

If hurried, you may read only the "core passage" in your Bible and the Devotional in each chapter of this Commentary.

Reading	*Chapters*	*Core passage*
78	1–5	5
79	6–8	6:24–7:20
80	9–13	9–10
81	14–17	17
82	18–20	20
83	21–25	22–23

2 Kings

MARCH 19 *Reading 78*
THE MINISTRY OF ELISHA
2 Kings 1–5

> *"This is what the LORD says: 'I have this water' " (2 Kings 2:21).*

Where Elijah confronted kings and announced divine judgments, Elisha comforted God's people with healing. Both ministries are important in every age.

Biography: Elisha
Elisha's request for a "double portion" of Elijah's spirit reflects the custom in Israel of the oldest son and principle heir receiving double the amount set aside for other sons. God granted Elisha's request to become Elijah's "heir" and God's principle prophet in the Northern Kingdom. Elisha's ministry was one of encouragement. Elijah had confronted Ahab and Jezebel and thwarted their attempts to make Baal dominant in Israel. Elisha's ministries of mercy, and ministries dedicated to the protection of the nation, demonstrated the wisdom of serving God. Where Elijah emphasized God's holiness and justice, Elisha emphasized God's love.

Overview
Elijah announced God's judgment on Ahaziah, Ahab's son (1:1-18). He was then caught up into heaven, and Elisha took up his prophetic ministry (2:1-18). The tone of Elisha's ministry was set in the healing of poison waters (vv. 19-22), his prediction of victory over Moab (3:1-27), his provision of oil for a widow (4:1-7), restoration of the Shunammite's son (vv. 8-37), and two incidents of feeding the hungry (vv. 38-44). Elisha's international reputation brought a Syrian general, Naaman, to Israel where he was healed of leprosy and converted (5:1-27).

Understanding the Text
"Is it because there is no God in Israel?" 2 Kings 1:1-18 Elijah's ministry had been one of confrontation, demonstrating in decisive judgments the power and holiness of Israel's God. This demonstration was vital at a time when Ahab and Jezebel actively promoted Baal worship in Israel (see 1 Kings 17–22). The final miracle of Elijah, calling down fire on soldiers of Ahab's wicked son Ahaziah (cf. 2 Kings 1:10), was also intended to demonstrate to Israel that they must hold God in awe. Yet the God who is terrible in judgment is also merciful. When the captain of a third "fifty" begged for his life, he and his soldiers were spared.

Judgment is certain when leaders and people lose respect for God.

"When he struck the water, it divided to the right and to the left" 2 Kings 2:1-18. After long and harrowing service, in which Elijah almost single-handedly beat back the challenge mounted by the devotees of Baal, that prophet was taken up into heaven alive. His greatness is seen in Old Testament prophecy, which predicts Elijah's return before the final coming of the Messiah (cf. Mal. 4:5-6).

After Elijah was taken up, Elisha picked up the fallen cloak of his mentor. Returning to the Jordan he struck the waters as Elijah had. The fact that it parted for him also showed Elisha that his prayer was answered, and he was to take Elijah's place as Israel's premier prophet.

It's difficult when a significant leader dies. Yet God raises up leaders from the next generation to continue His work. The roster of human leaders constantly changes, but God remains the same. He is the One on whom we must always depend.

"In the name of the Lord" 2 Kings 2:19-25. Two miracles symbolize Elisha's ministry. Its comforting and compassionate nature are shown in the purifying of Jericho's waters. The act symbolized the blessing that could be Israel's through relationship with God the Healer.

The death of the youths (not children, as the KJV implies) who jeered Elisha symbolized that prophet's role as representative of the holy God. God yearns to bless His people. But God must be respected as Lord.

"How can I help you?" 2 Kings 4:1-44 Elisha's question to a widow whose sons were about to be sold as slaves to pay a debt, sums up the mission of this minister to Israel's common people. Elijah confronted kings. Elisha moved quietly among the people of the land. His ministry revealed what God would do for Israel if His people returned fully to Him.

Elisha's multiplication of the widow's oil showed God's ability to free His people from servitude (vv. 1-7).

Elisha's promise of a child to the Shunammite, and his subsequent restoration of the child to life, showed God's ability to preserve the lives of His people (vv. 8-37).

Elisha's purification of poisonous stew and his feeding of a hundred men with 20 small barley buns, showed God's ability to provide all that His people needed, and more (vv. 38-44).

Thus Elisha's ministry was primarily one of revealing the love of God. The last three foreshadow miracles performed by Jesus with the same intent. God walks among us to heal and sustain, not to harm or condemn. Through Elisha, as through Jesus, men and women discovered the overwhelming love of God.

"Gehazi hurried after Naaman" 2 Kings 5:19-27. Elisha refused any reward for healing the Syrian general, Naaman, of leprosy. His servant Gehazi, however, chased after Naaman, and accepted some 75 pounds of silver and other expensive gifts. In judgment Gehazi was cursed with Naaman's leprosy, and expelled from Elisha's presence.

Elisha had refused wealth, for he wanted Naaman to view his healing as a gift from God, not something he had purchased. Ministry freely offered and freely received is the purest, for it reflects the unique quality of grace that marks God's relationship with humankind.

▶ DEVOTIONAL
General Principles (2 Kings 5)

Preachers throughout the ages have seen it. The story of Naaman, a general in the Syrian army, mirrors many truths about the Gospel of Jesus Christ. Is it easy to see these truths? Why not see if you can draw some general principles about the Gospel and communicating the Gospel from the experience of General Naaman? Here are several elements found in this Bible story.

* Leprosy in Scripture is often a symbol of sin. Naaman was stricken with leprosy, and unable to help or heal himself.

* Naaman learned from a young Israelite girl that there was hope.

* Naaman was upset by what the prophet told him to do for healing. The prophet's instructions did not fit his preconceived notions.

* Naaman, after being urged by his servants, decided to try Elisha's prescription anyway.

* Naaman was completely cleansed, and realized that "there is no God in all the world" except the Lord.

* Naaman promised to worship the Lord only, and committed himself completely to Him.

And, oh, yes. After you translate these elements of the story into general principles, you might enjoy reading the story again to see if you can find even more.

Personal Application

Which of the "general principles" you found in this story are most helpful as you think of sharing Christ with others?

Quotable

"Elisha's is the type of ministry which may be ours. No one of us may be an Elijah, but everyone of us may be an Elisha. If possessed by God's Holy Spirit, we may perform deeds of mercy which will seem like miracles in other men's eyes. The character and career of Elisha are often disparaged in comparison with the more heroic figure of Elijah. Yet his beneficent life, less spectacular and more humane, is the inspired symbol of a ministry which lies within the reach of us all. Small kindnesses, small courtesies, small considerations, habitually practiced, give a greater charm to the character and often do more good in the world than great accomplishments."—Raymond Calkins

MARCH 20 *Reading 79*
ELISHA AND THE ARAMEANS
2 Kings 6–8

"Time and again Elisha warned the king, so that he was on his guard" (2 Kings 6:10).

In the most troubled of times there are still indications of God's power and presence. Even when enemies surround, faith remains aware that God is in charge.

Background

Hostilities between Aram and Israel extend into this period. Ben-Hadad II mounted a full-scale invasion and besieged Samaria. During these years there is no evidence of a true revival in Israel, despite the active ministry of Elisha. The enemy invasion, mention of a seven-year famine, and reduction of the people of Samaria to cannibalism, are all divine judgments on an unresponsive king and people (cf. esp. Lev. 26:29; Deut. 28:53-57). Elisha's ministry, so clear a testimony to the power and love of Israel's God, should have stimulated a return to the Lord. Yet despite familiarity with Elisha and God's acts through the prophet, the king and people continued to do evil.

Overview

Elisha continued to aid individuals (6:1-7), but also aided the nation. The prophet revealed the plans of the Arameans (Syrians) (vv. 8-23), and announced that God would lift the siege of starving Samaria (v. 24–7:20). Elisha's reputation aided the Shunammite woman (8:1-6). As the age of Elisha drew to a close the prophet anointed Hazael to be king of Aram (vv. 7-15), while in Judah Jehoram (vv. 16-24) and then Ahaziah (vv. 25-29) became king.

Understanding the Text

"It was borrowed!" 2 Kings 6:1-7 The loss of a borrowed axhead was a disaster, for under the law the person who borrowed it was to repay the lender. Elisha's miraculous intervention is an indication that God is concerned with the personal problems of individuals. God is never so busy taking care of the world that He has no time for you or me.

"O Lord, open his eyes" 2 Kings 6:8-17. When Ben-Hadad II realized his raids into Israel failed because the Prophet Elisha knew his plans ahead of time and gave warning, the king sent a force of soldiers to capture him. Here again is one of the Bible's most familiar stories, perhaps because it is so comforting.

When Elisha's servant saw the enemy army surrounding the city where they had slept, he was terrified. But when Elisha prayed, God let the servant see what Elisha knew was there: a protective army of flaming angels between them and the enemy.

We may not be able to see the guard God has set around us. But faith assures us it is there. Psalm 34:7 says, "The angel of the Lord encamps around those who fear Him, and He delivers them."

"Shall I kill them?" 2 Kings 6:18-23 Elisha then led the supernaturally "blinded" Syrians into Samaria itself. When the king excitedly asked if he should kill his enemies, Elisha had him prepare a feast for them, as honored guests. We're not told why this treatment temporarily stopped the raids on Israel (v. 23). Some suggest the kind treatment shamed Ben-Hadad. It seems more likely the Syrian king stopped

in frustration. Why raid an enemy you never seem to harm? At any rate, the incident illustrates the impact of following a course later outlined in Proverbs 25 and commanded by the Apostle Paul: "If your enemy is hungry, feed him; if he is thirsty, give him something to drink." The Christian is not to "be overcome by evil, but [to] overcome evil with good" (Rom. 12:20-21).

It's not only right to follow this principle. It works!

"Ben-Hadad . . . laid siege to Samaria" 2 Kings 6:24–7:2. A full-scale invasion of Israel brought Samaria to the brink of starvation. When the desperate king confronted Elisha, the prophet promised that the very next day bushels of grain would be sold at the gate of the city. The immediate reaction of one royal officer was, "Impossible."

This is an attitude we need to guard against. Nothing is impossible with God, as the rest of the story reminds us.

But we also need to learn from the unbelieving official. Elisha told him he would see what God did—but would not benefit from it. The next day that officer did see stores of food at Samaria's gate. But he was crushed to death in the rush of the starving mob eager to get to it.

Our unbelief will not keep God from working His miracles. All our unbelief will do is keep us from benefiting from them.

"This is a day of good news and we are keeping it to ourselves" 2 Kings 7:3-20. These words of four lepers who discovered that the Syrians had fled their camp, leaving all their supplies, are often quoted in sermons urging Christians to personal evangelism. Good news, the news that impending death has given way to the prospect of life, is too important to be kept from dying men and women.

But perhaps the role of the four lepers was even greater than appears on the surface. The Hebrew text says that they approached "the edge of the camp," meaning that they looked for a spot at the furthest edge of the Syrian encampment where they might creep in and possibly find food. One commentator suggests that the stealthy passage of the four lepers outside the enemy lines might have been vital to the miracle. Perhaps God "magnified their stumbling footsteps," so that they seemed like the approach of a great army, and so terrified the Arameans that "they got up and fled in the dusk" (v. 7).

Whether this theory is true or not, it is surely true that as you and I take our first hesitant steps toward sharing our faith, God will already be at work in the hearts of those we approach. The God who did the impossible and fed a starving city still does the impossible, turning hard hearts to Himself in our day.

"Hazael went to meet Elisha" 2 Kings 8:1-29. As Elisha's ministry drew to a close, he was told to anoint Hazael to succeed Ben-Hadad II. The prophet obeyed, even though he wept in anguish. Elisha knew Hazael's plot to kill and replace Ben-Hadad (cf. v. 11), and also knew that as king of Syria, Hazael would bring disaster on Israel.

As the era drew to a close, two kings ruled briefly in Judah, which was soon to be drawn deeply into sin by a ruler dedicated to evil.

▶ DEVOTIONAL
Angry with God?
(2 Kings 6:24–7:20)

Is it ever right to be angry with God? Perhaps. Even Moses was angry with God for burdening him with an intractable mob of Israelites (Ex. 17:4; Num. 11:11-15). But there was something very wrong when Jehoram's anger flared.

A lengthy siege had brought Samaria to the verge of starvation. Desperate, King Jehoram even put on sackcloth, a rough, abrasive garment signifying both grief and repentance. He did not, however, wear it openly, but under his royal garments. This was a grudging admission by Jehoram that perhaps his sins had contributed to the disaster. But it fell far short of an open and public call to repentance (cf. Jonah 3:6-10).

Then, walking the city walls one day, the king heard the plea of a woman who had resorted to cannibalism. He cried out in horror and rage, and his suppressed anger overflowed. "Bring me the head of Elisha," Jehoram ordered. If the king could not strike out at God, he would at least strike at God through His prophet!

Before the command could be carried out Jehoram changed his mind, and hurried to overtake the executioner. In the prophet's house the king revealed his bitterness. "This disaster is from the LORD," Jehoram said. And, "Why should I wait for the LORD any longer?"

Think for a moment about what the king's words and behavior reveal. Jehoram knew that God was behind the suffering of his people. Jehoram had donned sackcloth as a sign of personal repentance, and in the knowledge that Israel's only hope was that God would act.

Yet Jehoram's "repentance" was not real. His sins had been public, yet he hid the sackcloth that signified sorrow for sin and failed to call on his people to repent. Even the horror of cannibalism did not humble Jehoram, but made him angry! Self-righteously Jehoram blamed God for not accepting his grudging confession. In complaining, "Why should I wait on the LORD any longer?" Jehoram was saying, "I've pushed the right buttons, God. Now, blast You, why are You making me wait?"

Yes, godly men and women may be angry with God at times. But Jehoram's anger was of a different sort. He was angry with God when he himself was to blame, and angry that God would not accept his pouting, grudging, partial, "I'm sorry." The kind of anger Jehoram felt and finally expressed, grew from his own stubborn refusal to admit his sins and to bow in humility before the Lord.

Personal Application

Feeling angry at God may be a sign we need to check our personal relationship with Him.

Quotable

"God is not a cosmic bellboy for whom we can press a button to get things."—Harry Emerson Fosdick

MARCH 21 *Reading 80*

A NEW NORTHERN DYNASTY
2 Kings 9–13

"They blew the trumpet and shouted, 'Jehu is king!' " (2 Kings 9:13)

A new beginning is a God-given opportunity. We can take advantage of it, or miss our chance and slip back into old ways.

Background

During the years spanned in these chapters Judah and Israel were severely weakened. The Black Obelisk of Nimrud shows Israel's Jehu down on his knees before the Assyrian Shalmaneser, as retainers bring tribute. Soon Assyrian weakness led to resurgence of Aram, and during the rest of this period both nations were decimated in wars with Syria and unable to resist incursions by other peoples.

Overview

Jehu was anointed king of Israel (9:1-13). He killed Joram of Israel, Ahaziah of Judah (vv. 14-29), Queen-mother Jezebel (vv. 30-37), and the rest of Ahab's family (10:1-17). Jehu destroyed Baal worship in Israel (vv. 18-28) but maintained the state religion instituted by Jeroboam (vv. 29-36). In Judah, Athaliah killed her grandchildren and seized power (11:1). Seven years later a grandchild who escaped, Joash, was made king (vv. 2-21) and reigned 40 years (12:1-21). In Israel, Jehoahaz (13:1-9) and Jehoash (vv. 10-13) succeeded Jehu, and Elisha predicted three victories for Israel over Aram (vv. 14-25).

KING LIST

Date	*Judah*	*Israel*
852	Jehoram	Ahaziah
841	Ahaziah	Joram
841	Athaliah	Jehu
835	Joash	
814		Jehoahaz
798–782		Jehoash
796–767	Amaziah	

Understanding the Text

"You are to destroy the house of Ahab" 2 Kings 9:1-13. Jehu was selected by God

Jehu of Israel submits to Shalmaneser

to fulfill prophecy against the royal line of Ahab. Jehu was only too glad to accept the commission and anointing as Israel's next king.

Jehu exemplifies those who use religion to gain their own ends, without necessarily having a personal faith. Many are willing to "serve God" as long as God's will seems to match their own. The true test of commitment is submission to God's will when obedience seems to be against one's own self-interest.

"Throw him on that plot, in accordance with the word of the LORD" 2 Kings 9:14–10:17. Jehu enthusiastically set about the task of killing all members of Ahab's family and his important officials. He frequently referred to the Lord, and quoted prophecy foretelling the destruction of Ahab's house (9:25-26; 10:9-11). Yet his references to God were clearly self-serving. Jehu recalled a prophecy of Elijah which he overheard, and tossed the body of Ahab's son in Naboth's vineyard. But he ordered the burial of Jezebel, even though he knew dogs were prophesied to eat her flesh. In his public statements Jehu admitted he conspired against his master, but justified his acts against Ahab's family on religious grounds.

In fact, usurpers in the ancient Middle East commonly murdered all members of the preceding royal house. Even appeal to religion was not unusual, as in the case of the Hittite king Murshili II (mid-14th century B.C.). The ambitious man is quick to seize on any excuse likely to rouse public support.

Jehu was doing God's will. But Jehu was doing God's will for the wrong reason. Politicians today sometimes use God to appeal to certain voting blocks. We need to evaluate political use of religion very carefully, and even skeptically.

"Jehu destroyed Baal worship in Israel" 2 Kings 10:18-35. The worship of Baal had long been promoted by the royal house of Ahab. As Baalism was one of the power bases of the old regime, it was natural for Jehu to seek to stamp it out.

Why then was Jehu's call of all ministers to a great religious fesitival effective? Why weren't the devotees of Baal suspicious? It seems likely that as a high-ranking officer in Ahab's army Jehu had worshiped Baal with the royal house. As a person quick to use religion for his own ends, he may even have seemed especially devout! Only if Jehu had frequently participated in such worship could his announced intention to serving Baal "much" (v. 18) have been believed!

The text shows that even destruction of Baalism was not evidence of Jehu's personal commitment to the Lord. His ends achieved, Jehu dropped religious reform and continued the counterfeit state religion established by Jeroboam (vv. 28-31). As the text says, he was not "careful to keep the Law of the LORD."

Jehu had used God to gain the throne; now he had no use for God. Yet in fact he had a desperate need for God, who "began to reduce the size of Israel" and permitted the Arameans to overpower "the Israelites throughout their territory."

No one ever reaches the point where a relationship with God makes no difference in his or her life.

"Jehosheba . . . took Joash . . . and stole him away" 2 Kings 11:1-2. The story contrasts two women: Athaliah and Jehosheba. Athaliah, a daughter of Ahab and Jezebel, married Judah's king Jehoram. On hearing of the death of her son Ahaziah she killed her grandchildren to take the throne for herself. In contrast, Jehosheba risked her life to save the king's infant son.

The wicked take lives in the pursuit of ambition. The godly risk their lives for others in commitment to what is right.

"All the years of Jehoiada the priest" 2 Kings 11:4–12:21. The infant son of Ahaziah was raised in secret until age seven, when he was acclaimed king and Athaliah was killed. Joash served God until the priest who had raised him, Jehoiada, died. Under Jehoiada's tutelage Joash repaired the temple and reinstituted worship there. But after the death of the priest, the king abandoned God. Second Chronicles 24 tells us that Joash turned to Canaanite practices, and even ordered the death of a son of his old mentor Jehoiada who rebuked him.

We need godly people close to us to help us maintain our commitment to the Lord.

"Elisha's tomb" 2 Kings 13:12-25. The report of a man brought back to life when tossed into Elisha's tomb symbolizes the power of God to restore the nation as well as the individual. Nestled as it is in the report of Israel, crushed under Jehoahaz by the Arameans and finally resurgent as God enabled Jehoash to defeat them, the story serves as a parable for God's people. Even when all hope is lost, God is able to bring life and victory. How vital then that God's people return to Him.

▶ DEVOTIONAL
One Accord
(2 Kings 9–10)

It didn't take long for word of Jehu's attack on Ahab's family or of his frequent mention of the Lord to spread. The news excited an unusual man, who hurried to meet Jehu.

The man was Jehonadab [Jonadab] son of Recab. We know something about him from Jeremiah, who nearly 150 years later set bowls of wine before his descendants. They refused to touch it, saying their "forefather Jonadab" commanded them not to drink wine, and to live a nomadic rather than settled life. Apparently Jonadab, a rigorous and ascetic man, was repelled by the corruption in Israelite society and determined to lead a separated life. God commended the Recabites, for their faithfulness to Jonadab's commands shamed a Judah all too willing to disobey the commands of the Lord (cf. Jer. 35).

This Jonadab hurried to meet Jehu, undoubtedly to see if revival truly had come to Israel. When they met Jehu asked, "Are you in accord with me, as I am with you?" Jehu then invited the stern supporter of Yahweh to "come with me and see my zeal for the LORD" (2 Kings 10:15-16).

How Jonadab's hopes must have risen as he witnessed extermination of the rest of wicked Ahab's family, and then went into the temple of Baal with Jehu and saw him massacre every representative of that corrupt Canaanite faith.

But then, with Jehu's personal goals reached, his "zeal for the LORD" disappeared. He continued the cult of Jeroboam as Israel's state religion, and turned his attention to his real concern, ruling.

Nothing more is said of Jonadab. He disappeared until his descendants told Jeremiah the heritage left them by their ancestor. "Don't settle down," Jonadab told his sons. In other words, "Don't fix your hopes on the 'zeal' of politicians who use God for their own ends. Live your lives outside man's society."

What does the incident say to us? No,

not that we shouldn't have a part in our nation's political process. But surely that we must not fix our hopes on reforms to be accomplished here. Like the descendants of Jonadab, we Christians are strangers and pilgrims in a hostile world. We do what we can to influence it for good. But we always remember that God's purposes are not summed up in who wins the next election, and it is those overarching purposes with which we identify.

Personal Application

Be a good Republican or Democrat. But make being a good Christian your priority.

Quotable

"Let us not esteem worldly prosperity or adversity as things real or of any moment, but let us live elsewhere, and raise all our attention to Heaven; esteeming sin as the only true evil, and nothing truly good but virtue which unites us to God."—Gregory Nazianzen

MARCH 22 *Reading 81*
THE FALL OF THE NORTH
2 Kings 14–17

"The king of Assyria brought people from Babylon, Cuthah, Avva, Hamath and Sepharvaim and settled them in the towns of Samaria to replace the Israelites" (2 Kings 17:24).

The unbroken succession of wicked kings wore away the religious and moral foundations of Israel, and led inexorably to the fall of that nation to Assyria. One bad choice may not bring ruin. But a series of wicked choices surely will.

Background

Conditions in Israel deteriorated rapidly. Ruling houses were established by assassination or imposed on the people by Assyria. As history marched inexorably toward national disaster no one seemed to sense a need to turn back to God.

Overview

Amaziah of Judah was defeated and humiliated by Israel (14:1-22) before being succeeded by his son Azariah (Uzziah) (15:1-7). In Israel, Jeroboam II ruled 41 years (14:23-29). He was succeeded by a series of kings who ruled briefly (15:8-26), and under pressure from Assyria (vv. 27-31). In Judah the son of Jotham (vv. 32-38), Ahaz, bribed Assyria to invade Syria (16:1-20). The Northern Kingdom was crushed by Shalmaneser of Assyria, and the Israelites exiled from their land because "they forsook all the comands of the LORD their God and made for themselves . . . idols." Assyria resettled the northern territory with foreigners (17:1-41).

KING LIST

Date	*Judah*	*Israel*
793		Jeroboam II
792	Azariah	
753		Zechariah
752		Shallum
752		Menahem/Pekah
750	Jotham	
740		Pekahiah
732	Ahaz	Hoshea
722		EXILE
715	Hezekiah	

Understanding the Text

"Glory in your victory, but stay at home!" 2 Kings 14:1-22 Amaziah's victory over Edom fueled his ambition and he declared war on Jehoash of Israel. Second Chronicles 25 reports that he had trusted foreign gods, and the subsequent defeat was to teach Judah not to turn from the Lord.

Apparently Amaziah was captured and taken to Israel, but released after the death of Jehoash and sent back to Judah. Those in power there apparently resisted the king's return and assassinated him.

How much better for all of us to remain close to the Lord and be satisfied with what He gives us.

"Jeroboam . . . became king in Samaria" 2 Kings 14:23-29. The reign of Jeroboam II is dismissed in our text with a mere seven

verses. Yet Jeroboam II was undoubtedly Israel's most successful and notable ruler. The military power of Syria (Aram) had been destroyed by the Assyrians, and Jeroboam took advantage of this weakness. The territory Jeroboam captured rivaled that held in David and Solomon's day. He occupied Damascus and gained control of the trade routes which linked the ancient world, winning revenues which made Israel rich. But Israelite society was disrupted, as those with new wealth bought up farmlands and forced the dislocation of the population. Cities became overpopulated and poverty increased. Heavy taxes were laid on all, and the rich corrupted the justice system in their favor. Both Amos and Hosea ministered in Israel during Jeroboam II's time, and spoke out boldly against the era's injustice and corrupt religion.

In view of the political and sociological significance of the time of Jeroboam II, it's striking that the Bible says so little about him. Perhaps the answer is found in perspective. Compared with eternity, worldly accomplishments count for little. God saw fit to give Israel relief from oppression under Jeroboam II. But neither king nor people used this last opportunity to turn to the Lord.

"Azariah. . . . reigned in Jerusalem 52 years" 2 Kings 15:1-7. The revival of Israel's fortunes under Jeroboam II were matched by prosperity in Judah during Azariah (Uzziah's) long reign. As was the case with many of Israel's and Judah's kings, during this extended period Uzziah was co-regent with his father or his sons. According to 2 Chronicles 26 Uzziah's leprosy was a punishment for infringing on the rights of the priesthood. He lived in *beth ha-hophshith,* which may mean a "house of freedom," and indicate he was relieved of all duties.

It is no blessing to be set aside and unable to contribute. How important to remember that Christians, even if disabled, can labor in prayer for others. Through prayer we can have a significant part in the lives of others and in the work of Christ.

"Menahem gave him a thousand talents of silver" 2 Kings 15:17–16:20. The dominance of Assyria is increasingly shown in the stories of Israel's and Judah's kings after 750 B.C. Menahem paid Pul of Assyria 75,000 pounds of silver to prop up his claim to the throne. In essence Israel became a vassal state. Pekah lost northern Israel's lands and many of her people to Tiglath-Pileser. Ahaz of Judah bribed Tiglath-Pileser to invade his enemies, Syria and Israel. The Assyrian was of course delighted to do so.

Ahaz's association with the Assyrian was spiritually disastrous, for when the king went to Damascus to submit to the Assyrian monarch he was fascinated with a new-style altar, and had it copied for use in Jerusalem. The offerings made on it by Ahaz fall in the category of fellowship offerings (16:15-16; cf. Lev. 1–7).

Fellowship offerings symbolizing close relationship with God, made on a foreign altar in violation of Mosaic Law? It is easy to claim one has fellowship with God. But true fellowship with God is displayed by obedience to His Word.

"Shalmaneser king of Assyria came up to attack Hoshea" 2 Kings 17:1-41. The final destruction of Israel came when Hoshea refused to pay Assyrian tribute and sought help from Egypt. Samaria was captured after a three-year siege, and the Israelites were deported. Then foreigners were brought in by Assyria to resettle the land.

Israel, the Northern Kingdom, was no more. The question remains, would Judah, Israel's sister to the south, learn from Israel's destruction?

▶ DEVOTIONAL
Heaven and Hell
(2 Kings 17)

I know that many people are disturbed by the notion of hell. Heaven is one thing. But hell? A place of everlasting punishment?

While the story of Israel's decline includes no mention of eternal punishment, it does incorporate principles which bear on the question.

In earlier chapters of 2 Kings few editorial comments were made. Except for a formula which told whether a ruler did right or evil in God's eyes, the stories of Israel's and Judah's kings are told in simple, sparse prose, and readers are left to draw their own conclusions. But in this chapter the writer draws conclusions for us. The final disaster which befell Israel happened "because the Israelites had sinned against the LORD their God." They "worshiped other gods and followed the practices of the nations the LORD had driven out before them." "They rejected His decrees and the covenant" and "followed worthless idols and themselves became worthless." "They sacrificed their sons and daughters in the fire," "practiced divination and sorcery and sold themselves to do evil."

The principle the writer established echoes throughout Scripture. God holds man responsible for his sins. The nearly 200 years during which God withheld final judgment on Israel speaks of His grace. But the invasion of the Assyrians reminds us that judgment will surely come.

Heaven and hell? Yes. God's patience today in withholding judgment on our sins still reflects His patience. The Bible's warnings about hell remind us that despite God's grace judgment will surely come.

Personal Application

We, like history, need to testify to others of both God's grace and His commitment to judge sin.

Quotable

"A sentimental and hedonist generation tried to eliminate 'wrath' from its conception of God. Of course, if 'anger' and 'wrath' are taken to mean the emotional reaction of an irritated self-concern, there is no such thing in God. But if God is holy love, and I am in any degree given to uncleanness or selfishness, then there is, in that degree, stark antagonism in God against me."—William Temple

---

MARCH 23 *Reading 82*
ONE KINGDOM SURVIVES
2 Kings 18–20

> *"The LORD was with him; he was successful in whatever he undertook" (2 Kings 18:7).*

Hezekiah is praised as a king who trusted God and held fast to Him. One person who is fully committed to the Lord truly can make a difference in the fate of a nation!

Background

The material on Hezekiah is organized by theme rather than chronology. His healing (2 Kings 20) took place before the Assyrian invasion (2 Kings 18–19).

Hezekiah's first years of independent rule, from about 715 to 705 B.C., were spent in religious reforms. He then boldly rebelled against Assyria, which was weakened by internal strife. He attacked and defeated Assyria's vassal, Philistia, and set about strengthening Judah's defenses. In 701 B.C. a new ruler, Sennacherib, turned to the west to deal with the rebel coalition headed by Judah and supported by Egypt. The Assyrians swept along the seacoast and attacked Judah from the west, destroying the key fortified city of Lachish (see illustration). Sennacherib then prepared to attack Jerusalem. The dramatic story of how he was turned back is told in 2 Kings 19–20, and again in 2 Chronicles 32 and Isaiah 36–39. Sennacherib never returned to Judah. Twenty years later he was assassinated by two of his sons.

Overview

Hezekiah's godly character is praised (18:1-8). He rebelled against Assyria, leading to an invasion by Shalmaneser and destruction of many fortified cities (vv. 9-16). But when Hezekiah appealed to the Lord, Assyria was turned away from Jerusalem (v. 17–19:37), and the Southern Kingdom was preserved. The account of Hezekiah concludes with the story of an earlier healing and an unwise welcome of envoys from Babylon (20:1-21).

Understanding the Text

"Hezekiah trusted in the LORD, the God of Israel" 2 Kings 18:1-8. Hezekiah's commitment to God is seen here in his vigorous purification of the land of idolatrous practices. Second Chronicles 29–31 goes into

detail on the positive steps he took. He purified the temple, called Judah—and even invited the men of Israel—to a Passover celebration, and organized worship at the Jerusalem temple.

These religious reforms were given priority in the early years of Hezekiah's independent reign. Only when Hezekiah knew Judah was right with God did he set out to strengthen his nation politically. Hezekiah's successes against Philistia and Assyria rested on the firm foundation of relationship with God, for he realized that God alone could make him successful.

We too need to put God first. Our success in any endeavor must have as its foundation a right relationship with the living God.

"Has any god of any nation ever delivered his land from the hand of the king of Assyria?" 2 Kings 18:17-37 The ancients often measured gods by the military might of the land in which they were worshiped. By this criteria the gods of Assyria seemed supreme.

Pictorial reliefs of the siege of Lachish decorate Sennacherib's palace in Assyria. Assyrian records detail the spoil taken from Judah (cf. 2 Kings 18:14) and claim to have "shut Hezekiah up like a caged bird in Jerusalem." But the great king failed to take Judah's capital before rushing home.

The "field commander" (the title *rab shekka* probably indicates an administrative rather than military rank) spoke fluent Hebrew, and his shouted message was psychological warfare directed to the people of Judah rather than the king. The Assyrian call for surrender emphasized Judah's weakness, promised to resettle Judah's population in an even more fertile land, and ridiculed God's ability to save His people. It was true that Judah and Jerusalem were now weakened and vulnerable. But the Assyrian erred in equating the God of Judah with the idols worshiped by other peoples.

"So that all kingdoms on earth may know that You alone, O LORD, are God" 2 Kings 19:1-19. Hezekiah laid the Assyrian challenge before the Lord, and asked Him to act for His name's sake.

This is the firmest foundation for prayer. When our desire is to glorify God, and what we pray for will bring God glory, we can pray with utmost confidence.

"I have heard your prayer" 2 Kings 19:20-37. Isaiah the prophet was given God's answer to deliver to Hezekiah. Isaiah's response is in the form of a dirge poem, following a distinctive 3:2 pattern in Hebrew. Sennacherib had mocked God (18:21-24). Therefore God would "put My hook in your nose and My bit in your mouth" and drag the Assyrian back "the way you came" (19:25-28). Hezekiah was reminded that this was the year of Jubilee—the year to proclaim freedom (v. 29)—and so Sennacherib "will not enter this city or shoot an arrow here" for the Lord Himself would defend it (vv. 32-34).

That very night an angel of the Lord decimated the Assyrian army. In the morning the camp was filled with dead bodies! Sennacherib broke camp and returned home, never to return.

You and I can never predict the means God will use to deliver us when we put our trust in Him. We can, however, be sure that God can and will act.

"Hezekiah turned his face to the wall" 2 Kings 20:1-8. In turning his face to the wall Hezekiah dismissed Isaiah. He also focused entirely on the Lord, and put his hope in prayer.

The incident reported here happened some years before the Assyrian invasion, but after Hezekiah's religious reformation of Judah. Hezekiah's prayer reflects the feelings of many who find themselves suffering despite walking before God "faithfully and with wholehearted devotion." Doesn't the godly person deserve better at the hand of God?

God did hear Hezekiah's prayer, and considered his faithfulness. The king was promised healing and was also promised that God would defend Jerusalem from the king of Assyria.

"Hezekiah received the messengers" 2 Kings 20:12-21. Hezekiah's display of his treasures was unwise at best. The amount listed in Scripture included at least a ton of gold and, according to Assyrian records, nearly 30 tons of silver, which Assyria later carried away! Ultimately this treasure itself would be torn from fallen Assyria by Babylon, and Hezekiah's offspring would go into slavery.

Hezekiah's thankfulness for "peace and security in my lifetime" is sometimes criticized. Yet this lifetime is all we have, and God's challenge to us is to live it well. Future generations must meet the challenge of their own time. Hezekiah recognized this reality, and was rightly thankful that God would give his people peace as long as he lived.

▶ DEVOTIONAL
Thank You, Lord
(2 Kings 20)

There is more to the story of Hezekiah's answered prayer than meets the eye. God added 15 years to Hezekiah's life. But note that 21:1 says that "Manasseh was 12 years old when he became king." Manasseh, then, was born during the added years that God gave Hezekiah in answer to his prayer.

Who was Manasseh? Hezekiah's child grew up to become Judah's most wicked king, whose 55-year rule set the Southern Kingdom on the route to certain destruction. Yes, God answered Hezekiah's prayer, but it might have been better for Judah if He had not! The unstated lesson of Hezekiah's prayer is a surprising one. At times, rather than plead for healing, we should simply say, "Thank You, Lord," and rest in the firm conviction that whatever we receive from the hand of God is for the best.

Personal Application

Let every request we make be guarded by the phrase, "If it is for the best."

Quotable

"Indeed, one step taken in surrender to God is better than a journey across the ocean without it. . . . Perfectly to will what God wills, to want what He wants, is to have joy; but if one's will is not quite in unison with God's, there is no joy. May God help us to be in tune with Him."—Meister Eckhart

MARCH 24 *Reading 83*
JUDAH'S FALL
2 Kings 21–25

"I am going to bring such disaster on Jerusalem and Judah that the ears of everyone who hears of it will tingle" (2 Kings 21:12).

Manasseh's 55-year reign dragged Judah into detestable sins. Even a brief revival under Josiah could not reverse the plunge to judgment. The highway of sin leads to one destination only.

Background
Josiah's vigorous and successful reign took place during a time of Assyrian decline. In the 630s B.C. that great empire was weakened by internal strife. In 626 Babylon revolted, and in a stunningly quick rise made its bid to replace Assyria as the dominant world power. Nineveh fell in 612 B.C., and the final battle was fought in 605 at Carchemish. Josiah died in battle in 609 attempting to keep an Egyptian army under Pharaoh Neco from joining the Assyrians.

Despite the fact that Babylon then was dominant, Egypt consistently encouraged uprisings in the Palestinian states. Judah's kings were frequently led into rebelling against Babylon. In consequence, Judah suffered a series of Babylonian invasions and deportations. The final invasion came in 587, when Nebuchadnezzar laid siege to Jerusalem. In 586 the city was destroyed and its people deported to Babylon. The few Jews who remained murdered a Babylonian governor and garrison, and fled to Egypt. The Books of Jeremiah and Ezekiel graphically portray spiritual and political conditions during the last decades of the nation, and specify the sins for which Judah was judged.

Overview
Manasseh's 55-year rule set Judah firmly on the course of evil (21:1-25). His grandson, Josiah, led a bright but brief revival (22:1–23:30). Wicked kings then succeeded one another (v. 31–24:20), until Jerusalem fell to Nebuchadnezzar of Babylon and the people of Judah were carried into Captivity (25:1-30).

KING LIST

Years	*Judah's Rulers*
697–642	Manasseh
642–640	Amon
640–609	Josiah
609	Jehoahaz
609–598	Jehoiakim
598–597	Jehoiachin
597–586	Zedekiah
586	BABYLONIAN CAPTIVITY

Understanding the Text
"He has . . . led Judah into sin with his idols" 2 Kings 21:1-18. Manasseh's brutal, idolatrous reign led God to pronounce irrevocable judgment on Judah (cf. vv. 12-15).

What Manasseh's lengthy rule did was to impress a pattern on Judah's society. That pattern became so deeply ingrained that all Josiah's efforts at reform were unable to change it. Habakkuk, who ministered in Josiah's time, complained to God that Judah's society was marred with entrenched injustice despite restoration of temple worship (cf. Hab. 1:2-4).

A famous study traced the members of two New England families. One produced a long line of ministers, schoolteachers, and college professors. The other produced a series of criminals and murderers. In families, as in Manasseh's Judah, the lives we live can set the pattern for future generations.

"I have found the Book of the Law in the temple of the LORD" 2 Kings 22:1-20. Josiah's early religious commitment was shown in his efforts to repair the temple of the Lord. He was unguided, for apparently during the rule of Manasseh most copies of the Old Testament Scriptures were destroyed. Then a copy of the Law, which some take to be the entire five books of Moses, was found. A shaken Josiah realized how disobedient Judah had been.

Inquiries addressed to Huldah, a prophetess, brought back word that Judah's fate was sealed. But because Josiah had been humble and responsive to God, the disaster would come only after his death.

God is still looking for people who are shaken by society's abandonment of biblical principles of holiness and justice. When we are humble and responsive, God will bless us individually whatever may happen to our land.

Josiah's zeal was so great that he set out to rid Judah of all those practices against which God's Word spoke. The list of his actions suggests the extent of Judah's apostasy.

What we can appreciate about Josiah is his example of total commitment. We can ask nothing more than to be like Josiah, who "turned to the LORD . . . with all his heart and with all his soul and with all his strength" (23:25).

Josiah's 31-year reign over Judah did not change the direction of his nation. But Josiah's consistent efforts to serve the Lord won him the divine accolade. God does not require us to be successful. He does, however, call us to be totally committed.

"So Judah wbnt into captivity, away from her land" 2 Kings 25:1-26. Against the urging of Jeremiah and Ezekiel, who called for submission, Judah's last kings kept on rebelling against the Babylonians. The third time Babylonian forces appeared before Jerusalem, Nebuchadnezzar ordered the city and its temple to be razed, and the majority of its people taken into Captivity. The few who remained assassinated the Babylonian governor and his garrison, and fled to Egypt, leaving the land void of Abraham's descendants.

The Babylonian Captivity seems on the surface a great tragedy. Yet it proved to be an unusual blessing. In Babylon the Jews turned to the Scriptures to understand what had happened to them. They decisively rejected idolatry; after the Captivity the nation was never again drawn to the worship of false gods. And in Babylon the synagogue system of study and prayer was instituted; a system which has kept the focus of Israel on Scripture to the present day.

Even in the most terrible of judgments God remained true to His commitment to do His people good. Whatever happens to you or me, we can know that God is committed to us. He loves us, and He *will* do us good.

▶DEVOTIONAL
A Visit to Topheth (2 Kings 22–23)

One of the actions Josiah took in his zeal for the Lord was to desecrate Topheth, where sacrifices were made to "Molech." The reference to Topheth turns my thoughts to a modern horror which is very like the ancient practice.

What was a "topheth"? And what was a sacrifice made to "Molech"? A topheth was a district set aside for a class of sacrifices indicated by the Hebrew letters m-l-k. These were sacrifices in which children up to four years of age were presented as an offering made to a god or goddess from whom the offerer sought some benefit. Perhaps the benefit was a little more money. Perhaps better health. Perhaps a better job. Whatever it was, these parents seemingly thought nothing of bringing living children to the place of sacrifice and, as pounding drums drowned out anguished cries, burning them alive.

The modern horror? It's the practice of some of laying the lives of their unborn children on an abortionist's altar—with the same motives. A baby will cost too much money. A baby now will spoil the vacation we planned. A baby now will tie me to my house, just when I'm making progress on my job. A baby will be inconvenient—so I'll exchange the fetus nestled within me for what I hope will be a better quality of life for me.

But are the two practices really equivalent? In all honesty, we have to say they are. The infants of the ancients were individuals. Undeveloped, not yet adults, but separate and distinct persons from the parents on whom they had to depend. The fetus of today is also a separate and distinct person, with each cell marked off by a unique pattern of genes and chromosomes that are absolutely different from the pattern found in every cell of the mother's body. The unborn child is *not* part of the mother, but an individual in his or her own right. An individual moderns seem all too ready to treat with the same indifference as the ancients treated infants and toddlers.

So next time you hear some impassioned argument for the right of women to do what they want with their own bodies, don't be confused. What the pro-choice position asks is nothing less than the right to rebuild Topheth, where parents can offer up the lives of their children in the hope of a better life for themselves.

Personal Application

Each individual is precious in God's sight, however young or old he or she may be.

Quotable

My shining feet will never run on early morning lawn;
my feet were crushed before they had a chance to greet the dawn.
My fingers now will never stretch to touch the winning tape;
my race was done before I learned the smallest steps to take.
My growing height will never be recorded on a wall;
my growth was stopped when I was still unseen and very small.
My lips and tongue will never taste the good fruits of the earth;
for I myself was judged to be a fruit of little worth.
My eyes will never scan the sky for my high-flying kite;
for when still blind, destroyed were they in the black womb of night.
I'll never stand upon a hill, spring's winds in my hair;
autumn's winds of thought closed in on Motherhood's despair.
I'll never walk the shores of life or know the tides of time;
for I was coming but unloved, and that my only crime.
Nameless am I, a grain of sand, one of the countless dead;
but the deed that made me ashen grey floats on the seas of red.—Fay Clayton

---

The Variety Reading Plan continues with TITUS

1 Chronicles

INTRODUCTION

The two Books of Chronicles are a commentary on the history of the Hebrew kingdom, probably written about 450 B.C. The author focused on David's line, which ruled continuously in the kingdom of Judah. He developed the great themes of the Davidic promise, the significance of the temple and of wholehearted devotion to God. Together the Books of the Chronicles explain the fall of the Hebrew kingdoms, and offer hope to the struggling Jewish community in Judah. God is faithful to His promises, and Someone from David's line would one day restore the glory that had been lost.

OUTLINE OF CONTENTS

I. Names and Genealogies . . . . 1 Chron. 1:1–10:14
II. The Reign of David . . . . 1 Chron. 11:1–29:30

READING GUIDE (4 Days)

If hurried, you may read only the "core passage" in your Bible and the Devotional in each chapter of this Commentary.

Reading	*Chapters*	*Core passage*
84	1–10	2–3
85	11–16	11–12
86	17–21	17
87	22–29	28–29

1 Chronicles

MARCH 25 *Reading 84*
EVIDENCE FROM HISTORY
1 Chronicles 1–10

> *"All Israel was listed in the genealogies recorded in the book of the kings of Israel" (1 Chron. 9:1).*

History shows that God is faithful. As evidence, the author of Chronicles traces the lines of David and Abraham, each of whom received covenant promises from the Lord.

Background

Genealogies. The Hebrews maintained careful genealogical records. These were important, for God's covenant promises were made to the descendants of Abraham, Isaac, and Jacob (Israel). Each Jew's claim to relationship with God rested on his or her membership in the covenant community, as well as on personal faithfulness to the covenant code. The genealogical record was particularly important for priests and Levites, for only descendants of Levi—and in the case of priests, of Aaron—were qualified to serve God at the tabernacle or temple.

The genealogies recorded in Scripture use ancient records to trace family lines. These genealogies typically include representative ancestors rather than every individual in a line. For this reason most genealogies have "gaps," and it is impossible to use them to count the supposed number of years between, for instance, Adam and Abraham.

Overview

The author traced the lineage of David back to Adam (1:1–3:24), and of the sons of Israel, God's covenant people (4:1–8:40). The genealogies continue with a list of those who returned to Jerusalem from Babylon (9:1-34). Finally Saul's line is traced, with an account of his death and rejection as king (v. 35–10:14).

Understanding the Text

"These were the sons of David" 1 Chron. 1:1–3:24. The first genealogical list begins with Adam, and moves quickly to Abraham. It takes a quick look at the line of Ishmael, and then turns to look in detail at the line of Judah, the grandson of Isaac and son of Israel.

Judah's line is singled out for an important reason. This is the royal line, the family from which David came. The author not only shows that every king of Judah came from David's line, but also demonstrates that members of the Davidic line are still in Judah after the Exile!

How important this was. God had promised that there would never fail to be a descendant of David qualified to sit on Israel's throne (cf. 2 Sam. 7; 1 Chron. 17). The genealogies proved that God had been faithful to that promise. Thus the tiny community of Jews who had resettled in Palestine could rejoice. The God who had been faithful would continue to be faithful, and one day a Child of David's line would again take the throne and restore Israel's lost glory.

What a message for us today. God, who has been faithful, will be faithful. Like tiny Judah in 450 B.C., an insignificant district in a mighty Persian Empire, we too may struggle now. But we can look ahead to great things! The promised Descendant of David, Jesus Christ, has been born, and exalted to the throne of heaven. One day He will return and then we will reign with Him.

"All Israel was listed" 1 Chron. 4:1–9:1. As the genealogical lists continue, we sense again the author's purpose. In measured lists tribe after tribe is mentioned; family after family documented. God has been faithful not only to the royal line of David, but to every family in Israel.

"Saul and his sons, fallen" 1 Chron. 9:35–10:13. The account of Saul has a somewhat different purpose. It closes off the genealogical record which demonstrates God's faithfulness with a warning. Saul "died because he was unfaithful to the LORD." Even a member of the covenant community, even one exalted to be king over God's people, must submit to God and do His will. The faithless Saul was rejected, and "the LORD put him to death." Yet even the unfaithfulness of Saul could not thwart God's good purposes for His people. Saul was set aside, but the Lord "turned the kingdom over to David." David would be faithful to God. And God would give unique promises to him.

▶ DEVOTIONAL
Boring, Boring, Boring (1 Chron. 2–3)

First Chronicles seems to be the one place not to start reading the Bible. List upon list of names. Strange names, strung out one after the other. As more than one Christian has thought, "Boring, boring, boring."

Still, if you've ever felt unimportant or insignificant, these lists may have more meaning than you suppose. Think about it. Names. Each name representing an individual. Each name representing a person, most unknown to us, but every one known and remembered by God.

Most of the people on these lists are unknown to us because they play no great role in the sacred history. Few are heroes. Few performed great deeds. Most lived quiet, unexceptional lives. And yet not one name on these lists is lost. Not one name is misplaced.

When we stop to think about it, these "boring" lists of names are a reminder that God cares deeply for His own. It's not the great deeds we do, but the fact that we are His that counts. Insignificant? You? Never to God! There is no more chance of His misplacing you than there was of His losing a single thread in the line of His Old Testament saints.

Personal Application

However unimportant you may feel, you are vitally important to God.

Quotable

"God tells man who He is. God tells us He creates man in His image. So man is something wonderful."—Francis Schaeffer

---

MARCH 26 *Reading 85*
DAVID'S SUCCESS
1 Chronicles 11–16

> *"You will shepherd My people Israel, and you will become their ruler" (1 Chronicles 11:2).*

Our greatest accomplishments may not be those noted by historians. Here the Chronicler reminds us of things which are important to the Lord.

Background

The Chronicler left out three elements of David's story found in 1 Kings: the seven-year gap between David's rule in Judah and over all Israel, David's sin with Bathsheba, and the events surrounding Absalom's rebellion. The writer did not intend to gloss over David's faults but to focus on David's achievements, and reveal what was most important in David to the Lord.

Overview

As king of Israel, David established a new capital (11:1-9). Notable are David's ability to inspire loyalty (v. 10–12:40), to reawaken faith (13:1-14; 15:1-29), to make Israel secure (14:1-17), and to lead God's people in worship of the Lord (16:1-43).

Understanding the Text

"It was called the City of David" 1 Chron. 11:1-9. When David was recognized as

king by the entire nation, he selected a capital that lay on the border of the northern and southern sections, yet was part of neither's territory. A person who seeks to unite a people must be careful not to show favoritism to any one faction.

Parents should remember this principle. Because each child is unique, and because of age differences, we can't treat all our children alike. Yet we must guard against showing favoritism, and let each child know he or she is loved as an individual.

"Warriors who helped him in battle" 1 Chron. 12:1-40. David was notably successful in recruiting a committed fighting force, and in inspiring their loyalty.

One incident is particularly interesting. When David expressed a longing for water from a spring near his home in Bethlehem, three of his followers broke through the lines of Philistines garrisoned there to get it for him. David refused to drink the water, but poured it out "before the LORD" (i.e., as an offering to God). David's act was not rejection of the gift, but instead an expression of the value he placed on the lives of his men. It was right for men to risk their lives for the Lord, but not right to risk their lives to satisfy a longing of their leader.

David's concern for his men was one of the things which made him a great leader, and inspired loyalty in his followers.

"Do it in the prescribed way" 1 Chron. 13:1-14; 15:1-29. David's first attempt to bring the ark to Jerusalem failed because he loaded it on a cart rather than have it carried by Levites, as the Law prescribed. When David learned of this regulation, he understood why God had struck Uzzah, despite that individual's good intentions in trying to steady the ark. Israel, and David, were reminded that God is truly holy, and that all His commandments must be obeyed. As David launched his rule of a united Israel, God's Word alone could provide a foundation on which king and nation might stand.

"Shall I go and attack the Philistines?" 1 Chron. 14:1-17 The extent of Philistine domination is suggested in 11:18, which notes that they had established a garrison in Bethlehem. Bethlehem lies about seven miles east of Jerusalem. The Philistines, with their monopoly on iron weapons, had outposts deep in Israel's central highlands!

When David was made king, and given international recognition (cf. 14:1-2), the Philistines decided to invade in force. If they could kill or discredit David their domination of Israel would continue.

But why is this story found here, inter-

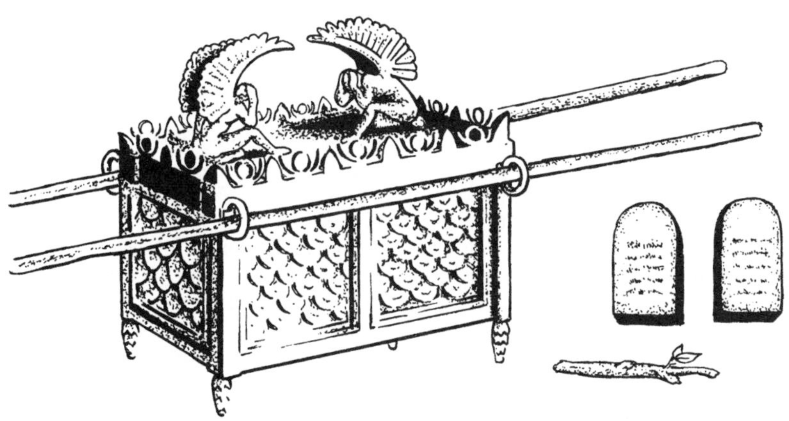

This gold-covered box was the most holy object in Israel's religion. It contained memorials of the Exodus journey—the stone tablets of the Law, a pot of manna, and Aaron's rod that budded. Most important, once a year on the Day of Atonement, the high priest poured sacrificial blood on its cover, to make an atonement for all the sins God's people had committed. In bringing the ark to Jerusalem, David made that city Israel's religious as well as political capital.

rupting the story of David's effort to bring the ark to Jerusalem? Very likely to show how well David had learned the lesson taught in Uzzah's death. In military affairs as in religion, it was vital to seek God's guidance. So, the text tells us, David "inquired of God" and, following the Lord's directions, defeated the Philistines.

David was able to make his people secure because he sought and did the will of God.

"He blessed the people in the name of the Lord" 1 Chron. 16:1-43. One of David's most important contributions to the life of Israel was his renewed emphasis on worship. This theme, developed later, is introduced here with the celebration held when the ark entered Jerusalem, and the psalm of thanks David wrote and gave to Asaph for use in public services.

As in all true worship, David's psalm celebrates the Lord, and honors Him for His many marvelous qualities.

If you or I ever feel uncertain about how to come to God in prayer, meditation on this or another of David's worship psalms can tune our hearts to sing God's praise.

▶ DEVOTIONAL
Inspiring Loyalty (1 Chron. 11–12)

One definition of a leader is, "He's a person who figures out where everyone is going, and gets out in front!" A better definition is, "A leader is someone who knows where he or she is going, and inspires others to come along."

The ability to inspire loyalty in others was one of David's greatest gifts. If you or I are to have a significant impact in our church or community, we need to follow David's lead and inspire loyalty in others. What does this extended passage on David's "mighty men" and his army teach us about inspiring loyalty?

Note first the quality of the men who joined David (11:1-47). The Hebrew word *gibborim,* frequently translated "mighty men," might be rendered "war heroes." Each of these men was an ancient "Rambo." But each, rather than run off on his own, joined David and served under him. To inspire loyalty, we need to appreciate others and give them opportunities to use their abilities.

We shouldn't be threatened if we work or minister with people who excel. David was generous in his appreciation for his war heroes, and gave them a significant role in his army. When we help others achieve, we earn their loyalty.

Note the steady increase of loyal men as "day after day men came to help David" (12:19-22). The men who came to join David did so not only because of his reputation, but to help David "against raiding bands" (v. 21). Even before David was made king, he fought against the enemies of God's people. To inspire loyalty we need to have a cause that motivates others to join us.

Note that literally thousands of Israelites finally "volunteered to serve in the ranks" of David's army, and to make him king (vv. 23-40). David's reputation, earned over many years of struggle, won over the whole nation.

If we want others to be loyal to us, we must first be committed to a cause. David had remained steadfast in his purpose, and won the respect of all people.

Personal Application

When God calls you to lead, seek others with ability, give them significant tasks, and be committed to your cause.

Quotable

"A great leader never sets himself above his followers except in carrying responsibilities."—Jules Ormont

MARCH 27 *Reading 86*
GOD'S PROMISE TO DAVID
1 Chronicles 17–21

"I declare to you that the LORD *will build a house for you" (1 Chron. 17:10).*

God's faithfulness to His promises to David provided a foundation of hope for the tiny, postexilic Judean community of 450 B.C. God's promises remain the basis of hope for us today.

Background

The Davidic Covenant. God made a series of promises to David through Nathan the prophet. David would defeat his enemies and bring Israel peace. An offspring of David would build the temple David dreamed of constructing. One day David's Offspring would be "set over My house and My [God's] kingdom forever; His throne will be established forever."

Some elements of the promises to David were fulfilled in his lifetime. David did defeat Israel's enemies, expand her territory, and win a reputation as Israel's greatest king. Other elements were fulfilled in Solomon, who succeeded David and built the Jerusalem temple. But those elements of the promise concerning an eternal kingdom relate to an "Offspring" to be born in the distant future. As New Testament genealogies show, this distant Offspring was Jesus Christ, who as the Son of God is destined to rule eternally.

The writer of the Book of Chronicles, intent on offering hope to his generation, reported the divine promise and in the next chapters showed that God was indeed faithful to His commitments in David's own lifetime. As the Chronicles continue, the author will show that the promised temple was built, and in 2 Chronicles will show that a descendant of David always sat on Judah's throne. God has been faithful, the Chronicler argues, so we can expect God to be faithful. One day a Descendant of David will restore the glory of Israel. He will live an endless life, and He will rule forever and ever.

Overview

David was not allowed to build a temple. But God promised to build David's "house" (17:1-15), stunning Israel's humble king (vv. 16-27). God's faithfulness to the promise is shown by David's victories (18:1–20:8). God used David's sin to lead him to the site of the future temple (21:1-30).

Understanding the Text

"I will raise up your offspring to succeed you" 1 Chron. 17:1-15. God does not ask us to do great things *for* Him. Instead He seeks to do great things *for* and *through* us. The Lord refused David permission to build Him a temple. Instead God told David what He would do.

What God intended to do *for* David was to make his name great and subdue all his enemies. David would have great success as a ruler (vv. 7-8, 10).

What God intended to do *through* David was to make His people secure (v. 9), and from David's family line raise up a Person who would rule God's kingdom forever (vv. 11-14).

This later prediction follows the "law of double fulfillment" which often governs interpretation of prophecy. The prophecy is fulfilled immediately, but that immediate fulfillment is a type of an ultimate fulfillment also intended. God did establish David's son Solomon as king, gave him a peaceful rule, and permitted him to build God's house. Yet in the distant future a far greater Offspring of David than Solomon would be born. That future Offspring will bring peace to the universe itself, and rule God's entire kingdom, not just for a few years but forever.

One of the lessons we learn from David is to submit to God so He can act for us. Only when we open our lives to the Lord and let Him act for us will God do great things through us.

"The LORD *gave David victory everywhere he went" 1 Chron. 18:1–20:8.* When David became king, Israel was a small nation surrounded by powerful enemies. These chapters recount the military victories which enabled David to expand his kingdom and control adjacent lands.

One incident reported in these chapters reveals David's conviction that his victories could be won only with the help of the Lord.

Deuteronomy 17:16 commanded that no king of Israel should obtain horses. This meant that Israel would have no cavalry and no chariot army, both important components of ancient armed forces. Chariots particularly were decisive weapons in many battles in the Middle East. Yet 2 Samuel 8:4 tells us that when David captured a thousand chariots from Hadadezer, he hamstrung all but a hundred chariot horses! This act, cutting the tendon in the horses' forelegs, lamed the animals and made them unfit for warfare.

David chose to obey God and rely completely on Him. He was not tempted to turn to the "super weapons" of the ancient world, for he knew that without God's help they would be useless—and with God's help chariots would be unnecessary.

What a lesson for us today. We need not rely on the weapons of this world. Without God's help, they are useless. And with God's help, we do not need them.

"A census of Israel" 1 Chron. 21:1-7. The Hebrew *shatan* means "adversary." It is possible that it should be rendered this way in 21:1. In that case, Satan was not involved but it was the appearance of adversaries preparing for war against Israel that prompted David to take a military census.

For some reason taking the census was wrong. Perhaps God had spoken against it. Perhaps it reflected a lack of trust in God. Whatever the reason, the act was sin, and God announced that He would punish David and Israel.

We are not only to act in harmony with God's Word, but also must examine our own motives. Romans reminds us, "Everything that does not come from faith is sin" (Rom. 14:23).

"Tell David to go up and build an altar to the LORD on the threshing floor of Araunah" 1 Chron. 21:8-30. David selected his penalty, but when he saw the death of so many, David begged the Lord to punish him personally. Instead God told David to build an altar on Araunah's threshing floor. This height just across from the present City of David was in fact the place where Abraham had come to offer up his son Isaac (Gen. 22). This was also the place which God had chosen for construction of the temple.

The incident is prophetic, in that where David built an altar and offered a prayer that turned away divine judgment, Solomon would build a temple that symbolized God's gracious presence with His people. There in the centuries to come Israel and Judah would also appeal to God. It was sin that brought David to the threshing floor to build an altar. Often sin would bring Judah to the temple built on that same threshing floor to seek forgiveness.

▶DEVOTIONAL
Claiming God's Promises (1 Chron. 17)

I suppose. "Claim God's promises" is one of the most frequent exhortations that Christians hear from the pulpit. Yet like much of religious jargon, that phrase may be puzzling to many. What does it mean to "claim God's promises"? And how does a person go about doing it?

David's response to the wonderful promises the Lord made to him is one of Scripture's clearest examples of claiming God's promises. David shows us how we too are to respond to promises from God, to claim His promises for ourselves. (1) David expressed wonder at God's goodness to him (vv. 16-19). (2) David praised God for His past acts on behalf of His people (vv. 20-22). (3) Finally David expressed confidence that God would "do as You promised." David says, "You, O LORD, have blessed it, and it will be blessed forever" (vv. 23-27).

How do we follow David's pattern? When we find a promise in God's Word, we are first to express our wonder at God's goodness to us. We should then praise God, thinking of all He has done for us in Christ, and in our lives to date. Then we need to express our confidence that God will keep the promise He has made—and then live obediently in the conviction that God will do all He has said.

If you and I claim God's promises by finding them, thanking God for them, believing them, and then acting on them—we will find out how completely faithful the Lord is to His Word.

Personal Application
When you find a promise in Scripture, claim it as your own.

Quotable
"Faith makes all evil good to us, and all good better; unbelief makes all good evil, and all evil worse. Faith laughs at the shaking of the spear; unbelief trembles at the shaking of a leaf; unbelief starves the soul; faith finds food in famine, and a table in the wilderness. In the greatest danger, faith says, 'I have a great God.' When outward strength is broken, faith rests on the promises. In the midst of sorrow, faith draws the sting out of every trouble, and takes out the bitterness from every affliction."—Robert Cecil

MARCH 28 *Reading 87*
DAVID'S PREPARATIONS
1 Chronicles 22–29

> *"My son Solomon is young and inexperienced, and the house to be built for the LORD should be of great magnificence and fame and splendor in the sight of all the nations. Therefore I will make preparations for it" (1 Chron. 22:5).*

Trusting the promise that his son would construct the temple he had yearned to build, David dedicated his last years to making preparations for a structure he would never see. We too are wise to prepare for a future beyond the span of our years here on earth.

Definition of Key Terms
Levites. The descendants of Levi were set aside during the Exodus to serve God. In that age their primary duty was to assist the priests and to take down, set up, and transport the tabernacle and its sacred objects. With a permanent temple about to be built, the Levites' duties had to be rethought. David gave much time to planning the duties of the Levites and organizing the tribe for temple service.

Overview
David made preparations for the temple Solomon was to build (22:1-13). He assembled materials (vv. 14-19), organized tasks for the Levites (23:1-32; 24:20-31) and serving priests (vv. 1-19), trained musicians (25:1-31), assigned guards ("gatekeepers") (26:1-19), and created other offices (vv. 20-32). David also reorganized the army (27:1-34). Near the end David charged Israel's officials to accept Solomon as king, and presented Solomon with detailed plans for the temple (28:1-21). David and others gave generously to the temple project, and David dedicated the gifts (29:1-20). David placed Solomon on his throne (vv. 21-25) and died (vv. 26-30).

Understanding the Text
"Devote your heart and your soul to seeking the LORD your God" 1 Chron. 22:1-19. David reminded Solomon of the promises God made to him, and exhorted his son to build the temple. But David was most concerned about Solomon's personal rather than public commitment to God. Solomon had to be devoted to the Lord and obedient, or his accomplishments would be meaningless.

The splendor of the temple Solomon was to construct, the activity of the Levites and priests carrying out their duties there, would all be empty if not motivated by love for the Lord.

"David separated them into divisions" 1 Chron. 24:1-19. Each division of priests served for two weeks at the temple, then returned to their home cities. This plan was in use in Jesus' time (see Luke 1:8).

"David . . . set apart some of the sons of Asaph, Heman and Jeduthun for the ministry of prophesying, accompanied by harps, lyres and cymbals" 1 Chron. 25:1-31. One of David's important contributions was to formally establish the role of music in worship. The "prophesying, accompanied" most probably indicates psalms set to music for public worship. Many of the psalms have musical notations in their superscriptions.

"The divisions of the gatekeepers" 1 Chron.

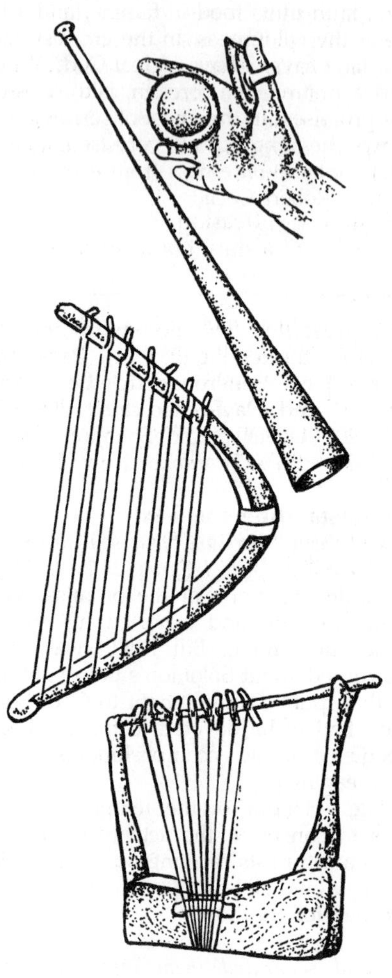

A variety of musical instruments were used in David's time. These were played at feasts and celebrations. They also made a vital contribution to public worship, which in Israel often was infused with a vibrant sense of joyous excitment. Harps, lyres, cymbals, and different kinds of horns provided accompaniment for recitation of many of the Bible's psalms.

26:1-19. The "gatekeepers" were armed Levites who occupied guard posts on the temple grounds. They not only were to keep order but also to protect the vast wealth to be assembled in temple treasure rooms.

"The army divisions" 1 Chron. 27:1-24. Israel, like other states, relied on citizen armies. Farmers and artisans became soldiers in time of national emergency, and then returned to their homes. David's innovation was to divide the citizen army into a dozen divisions of 24,000 men, each of which was on duty 1 month and off duty 11. The training provided during the duty month would keep Israel militarily strong and ready.

David's innovation was effective, and illustrates the modern doctrine of "peace through strength." Not once during Solomon's 40-year reign did Israel have to go to war. The military was ready—and unused.

"He has chosen" 1 Chron. 28:1-21. For a third time, the writer of Chronicles refers to the Davidic Covenant (cf. also 17:1-15; 22:1-19). God had chosen David and lifted him up to be king. God also chose Solomon to succeed David and to build His temple. All that had happened was rooted in God's sovereign choice.

But God's sovereign will does not rule out the exercise of man's free will. It is the responsibility of those God has chosen to acknowledge the Lord and serve Him wholeheartedly.

David's words to Solomon might well be addressed to you and me. God has chosen us in Christ, and through Christ granted us forgiveness and new life. So we are to acknowledge God "and serve Him with wholehearted devotion and with a willing mind, for the LORD searches every heart and understands every motive behind the thoughts" (v. 9). As David promised, if we seek God we will find Him. But if we reject God, we will never experience His blessing.

▶ DEVOTIONAL
Our Personal Treasures
(1 Chron. 28–29)

David's vision saw well beyond his time. David devoted his last years to planning a temple he knew he would not live to see. Then David took yet another step. He reported to an assembly of government officials, "I now give my personal treasures of gold and silver for the temple of my God" (29:3).

David's example moved others to give as freely and wholeheartedly. He offered a prayer of dedication (vv. 10-13), and then explained his philosophy of giving. That explanation, taken to heart, can make our own giving joyous and spontaneous. What, then, did David understand about giving?

David realized that "everything comes from You, and we have given You only what comes from Your hand." God is the greatest Giver of all. We take no risk in giving His own back to Him.

David realized that "our days on earth are like a shadow." The person who piles up treasures on earth is foolish. The only way to keep our personal treasures forever is to give them away, for then we will have reward in heaven.

David knew that God tests the heart and is pleased with integrity. God does not value the amount we give, but our intention. David gave "willingly and with honest intent." His giving was an expression of the reality of his love for the Lord.

If you and I adopt David's viewpoint on material wealth, it *will* make a difference in our giving. But most important of all, trust in God's ability to provide for us, and a perspective that values eternity more than time, will free us to experience giving as a joy and a true expression of our love for the Lord.

Personal Application

Giving is not a duty but a privilege.

Quotable

"The accumulation of vast wealth while so many are languishing in misery is a grave transgression of God's law, with the consequence that the greedy avaricious man is never at ease in his mind: he is in fact a most unhappy creature."—Pope John XXIII

The Variety Reading Plan continues with 2 CHRONICLES

2 Chronicles

INTRODUCTION

Second Chronicles continues the postexilic author's commentary on history. The author showed that God was faithful to His promise to David, whose descendants held the throne of Judah in an unbroken line. The author also evaluated each king by his dedication to God, expressed in his concern for the temple built by Solomon. None of these kings fulfilled God's promise of a ruler from David's line destined to establish a righteous, eternal kingdom. So the tiny Jewish community in Judah was to look ahead expectantly, and continue to serve the Lord until the promised Ruler came.

OUTLINE OF CONTENTS

READING GUIDE (7 Days)

If hurried, you may read only the "core passage" in your Bible and the Devotional in each chapter of this Commentary.

Reading	*Chapters*	*Core passage*
88	1–4	2
89	5–9	6
90	10–13	13
91	14–20	20
92	21–28	23–24
93	29–32	29
94	33–36	33

2 Chronicles

MARCH 29 *Reading 88*
SOLOMON'S TEMPLE
2 Chronicles 1–4

> *"Solomon gave orders to build a temple for the Name of the* Lord*" (2 Chron. 2:1).*

The temple Solomon built was not large, but in quality and workmanship it was the best he could create. We need not do great things for God. But whatever we offer Him should represent the best that we can do.

Definition of Key Terms

Temple. The Jerusalem temple, which housed the ark of the covenant, symbolized God's presence with His people. All the religious celebrations and all Israel's sacrifices were to be held there, in the presence of the Lord. Because the temple was fully identified with the public worship of God, the attitude of a king toward the temple was an accurate measure of his piety. A major feature of the revivals led by godly kings was always purification and/or repair of the temple, and revitalization of temple worship.

This fact is reflected in 2 Chronicles, which in each description of Judah's godly kings emphasizes the ruler's restoration of temple rites.

The emphasis on the temple in the Chronicles reflects conditions in the writer's day. A small group of Jews had ventured back to Judah from Babylon, intent on rebuilding the temple. After years of delay the temple was completed, but only after the Prophet Haggai reminded the Jews that the promised Messiah, the descendant of David destined to reestablish Israel, would come to God's house and fill it with glory (Hag. 2:6-9). Thus the temple must be ready, and God's people must worship there while awaiting the promised Offspring of David. The writer's purpose in the Chronicles, then, was to demonstrate God's faithfulness to His promises to David, and to encourage worship while waiting expectantly for God to keep the rest of the Davidic Covenant. The Jews must gather around God and His temple and wait.

Cherubim. The word seems to be a general term for various winged, supernatural beings who symbolize the holiness of God (cf. Ezek. 1:4-14; 10:1-22). We have no clear evidence to suggest how they were depicted on the inner walls of the Jerusalem temple.

Overview

Solomon pleased God by asking for wisdom to lead the Lord's people (1:1-17). He ordered construction of a temple dedicated to God (2:1-10), and obtained help from King Hiram of Tyre (vv. 11-18). The temple (3:1-17) and its golden decorations and furnishings (4:1-22) are described.

Understanding the Text

"Solomon son of David established himself firmly over his kingdom" 2 Chron. 1:1-13. Solomon had flaws. But 2 Chronicles focuses our attention on Solomon's concern for Israel's spiritual welfare, demonstrated in his building of the temple. In this and other ways Solomon foreshadowed the King yet to come from David's line. The similarity is emphasized when we first meet Solomon.

He had been appointed ruler, and immediately called all Israel together to worship the Lord. When invited by God to ask for a gift, he chose "wisdom and knowledge, that I may lead this people." The selfless request pleased God, who granted him wisdom, and added the riches and honor which Solomon had not requested.

The story emphasizes aspects of Christlikeness that are to characterize us as well. We too are to bring others to meet and worship the Lord. We too are to put others first, and seek gifts that enable us to serve.

"The king made silver and gold as common in Jerusalem as stones" 2 Chron. 1:14-17. First Kings devotes considerable space to descriptions of Solomon's wealth, wisdom, and commercial ventures. Second Chronicles hardly mentions these, but goes into great detail about Solomon's concern for the temple. To this commentator on history, the spiritual is far more important than material splendor.

The Chronicler's emphasis is a valid reminder that none of our worldly accomplishments are as significant as our spiritual achievements.

"The temple I am going to build will be great" 2 Chron. 2:1-18. The chapter lists some of the preparations Solomon made. The number of men involved, as well as the vast amounts of timber, stone, and precious metals, are impressive. Yet Solomon

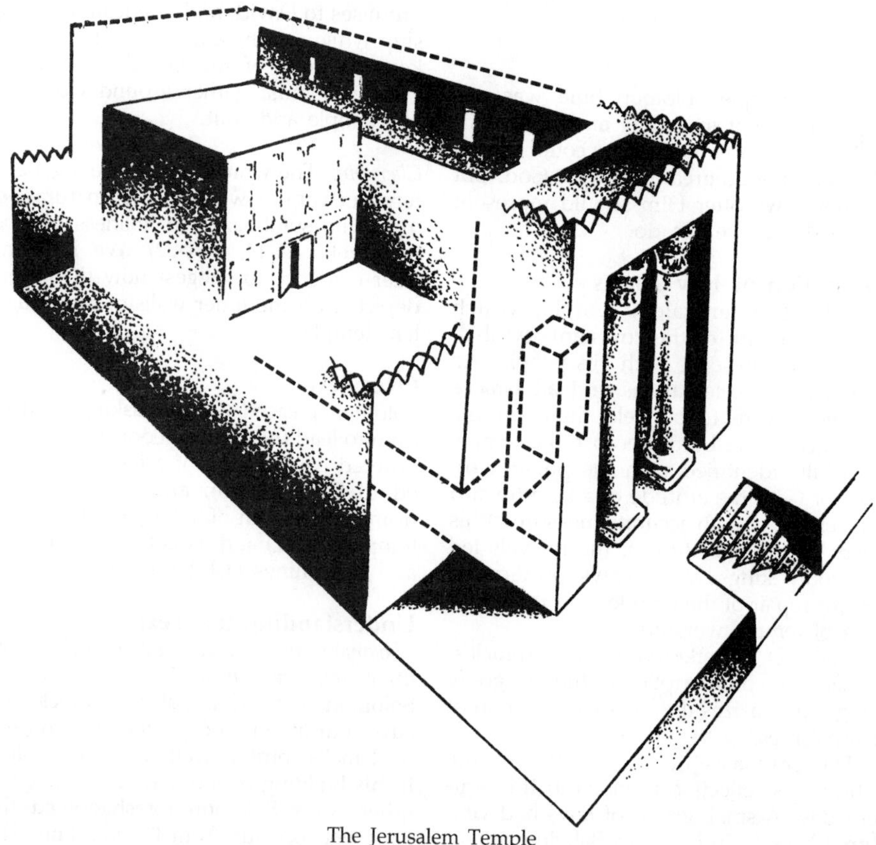

The Jerusalem Temple

The wonder of the Jerusalem temple was not in its size, but in the wealth and workmanship expended on it. The temple was long and narrow. At 90 feet long, 30 feet wide, and 40 feet high, it was about the size of a modern suburban house. The description given here in 2 Chronicles 3–4 does not provide enough details for an accurate portrayal, but the temple probably looked much like the drawing above.

clearly expressed a basic truth. The temple would be great "because our God is greater than all other gods."

It's true that God deserves our best. But it is important to remember that God Himself is our glory, not the monuments we erect to Him.

▶ DEVOTIONAL
Come Share
(2 Chron. 2)

The women who ran our Backyard Bible Clubs were concerned. A number of the clubs were held in neighborhood homes where the moms weren't Christians. Now some of those moms wanted to teach!

In some ways their doubts must have reflected Solomon's as he wrote to Hiram, king of Tyre. Though Tyre had maintained friendly relationships with David, the two nations were of diverse race and religion. Yet Solomon's letter not only offered to purchase lumber and hire workmen, but even requested a skilled metalworker to supervise his Hebrew artisans!

In effect Solomon invited Hiram to have a significant role in constructing a temple dedicated to Israel's God! Two things are striking about this passage. Solomon went to a Gentile to help him build God's temple. And that Gentile acknowledged God as no mere local deity, but the One "who made heaven and earth."

Israel had an exclusive relationship with the Lord, rooted in the Abrahamic Covenant and confirmed in history by God's acts on His people's behalf. Yet Isaiah spoke frequently of a day when Gentiles will flock to God, called by the bright light of Israel's Messiah (Isa. 11:10; 42:6; 49:6). The temple of Israel was to be a temple for all mankind. As Jeremiah 16:19 predicts:

> To You the nations will come
> from the ends of the earth and say,
> "Our fathers possessed nothing but false gods,
> worthless idols that did them no good."

That day of universal salvation is foreshadowed in the fact that God permitted the Gentile Hiram of Tyre to contribute so much to the Jerusalem temple. And the conversion of the Gentiles is foreshadowed by Hiram's recognition of God as Maker of heaven and earth.

Interestingly, the women who ran our Backyard Bible Clubs decided to make the hostesses "teacher's helpers." In that role several, like Hiram of old, came to know the Lord.

Personal Application

When others seem responsive to God, welcome them.

Quotable

"Take care not to frighten away by stern rigor poor sinners who are trying to lay bare the shocking state of their souls. Speak to them rather of the great mercy of God, and make easy for them what is at best a difficult task. Be especially gentle with those who from weakness of age or sex have not the courage to confess the ugly things they have done. Tell them whatever they have to say will be no news to you. Sometimes people are helped by your telling them about your own lamentable past."—Francis Xavier

MARCH 30 *Reading 89*
SOLOMON'S ACHIEVEMENTS
2 Chronicles 5–9

"May Your eyes be open toward this temple day and night, this place of which You said You would put Your Name there" (2 Chron. 6:20).

Solomon's early concern for God's glory, and the wisdom that attracted rulers of surrounding nations, serves as an example of the ministry of the Davidic Ruler yet to be born.

Background

Types. A "type" is an Old Testament person, event, or institution that corresponds in some significant way with a New Testament person, event, or institution. Solomon, as one who became king in accordance with God's promise to David, corresponds in some ways to THE Descendant of David, Jesus Christ, who will fulfill all elements of that promise and rule forever. The Chronicler selected those achievements of Solomon which exemplify the ministry of the coming Messiah. Specifically the Chronicler draws our attention to Solomon's concern for God's glory, shown in the dedication of the temple. He also draws our attention to the fact that Solomon's fame spread across the ancient world, and drew Gentiles to Israel. As Isaiah 60 says of the Messianic Age, "Nations will come to Your light, and kings to the brightness of Your dawn. . . . And all from Sheba will come, bearing gold and incense and proclaiming the praise of the LORD" (vv. 3, 6). In these things at least Solomon is a type, or example, of the Messiah that the Chronicler was sure would come.

Overview

Solomon's concern for God was shown in bringing the ark to the temple (5:1-14), in praising God for fulfilling His promise (5:1-11), in dedicating the temple with prayer (vv. 12-42) and sacrifice (7:1-10), and was confirmed by God's appearance to Solomon (vv. 11-22). The prominence of Solomon's kingdom (8:1-18), fame (9:1-12), and splendor (vv. 13-31), suggest the glories of a messianic kingdom to come.

Understanding the Text

"The priests then brought the ark of the LORD's covenant to its place in the inner sanctuary of the temple" 2 Chron. 5:1-14. When construction was complete, the temple furnishings were carried in by the priests. The occasion was one of great celebration. Every priest was consecrated in order to carry out the massive sacrifices. The most significant act was placing the ark of the covenant in the holy of holies, where it would remain, unseen except once each year by the high priest. The temple, bright with the beauty of the gold and craftsmanship lavished on it, was nothing apart from the presence of the ark within it. All its beauty was a tribute to that object which symbolized the forgiving presence of God.

Today God is present within the hearts of believers. No miracle of medical science can scan our hearts and detect the divine Spirit. But, like Solomon, we can lavish concern on providing the Lord with as beautiful and holy a residence as possible. Through the beauty of our lives others may sense the reality of the God within, who is the source of all our love and goodness.

"While the whole assembly of Israel was standing there" 2 Chron. 6:1-11. Like Solomon, the believer today speaks both to other human beings and to God. What do we say to others? Solomon's theme as he spoke to all Israel was simple. "God is faithful." God had promised David that Solomon would sit on his throne, and that Solomon would build a temple for the name of the Lord. What God said had now been fulfilled. So Solomon reminded Israel of the divine promise, and praises God for His faithfulness.

When we share our faith with others it's usually more effective to witness to God's faithfulness than to engage in a theological argument. We too can testify that God has kept His Word to us, and point others to the promises He makes to them in Christ.

"Then Solomon stood before the altar of the LORD" 2 Chron. 6:12-42. What do we learn from what Solomon said to the Lord? For one thing, we learn that there is no situa-

tion in which God's people cannot call on God to forgive, and to restore lost blessings.

"My eyes will be open and My ears attentive to the prayers offered in this place" 2 Chron. 7:1-16. Solomon dedicated the temple to the Lord, and in response fire fell from heaven and the glory of the Lord, as a visible cloud, filled it. This evidence that God chose to dwell in the temple moved an awestruck Israel to worship and praise.

This was undoubtedly what some have called a "mountaintop experience." It was a moment in time when God's people experienced His presence; when they felt especially close to the Lord and were, for the moment, wholly dedicated to Him.

The problem with mountaintop experiences is that sooner or later we find ourselves again in the valley. The emotion fades; the pressures of daily life intrude. All too often we even make unwise choices and wander from God's pathway. Then, suddenly, we realize we've lost that intense glow, that sense of dedication, that overpowering love for God, we felt on the mountaintop.

How do we recover after we've wandered deep into some dark valley? After God had revealed His glory to an ecstatic Israel, He gave this prescription to Solomon. "If My people, who are called by My name, will humble themselves and pray and seek My face and turn from their wicked ways, then will I hear from heaven and will forgive their sin and will heal their land."

There is a way back.

Humble yourself.

Pray and seek God's face.

Turn from wicked ways.

God promises to hear, to forgive, and to heal. God remains on the mountaintop, as His presence remained in the Jerusalem temple. However deep our valley, God invites us to turn, and climb back to Him.

"Pharaoh's daughter" 2 Chron. 8:1-11. In ancient times treaties were frequently sealed by the marriage of a royal daughter to a foreign king. However, Egypt resisted this custom. The fact that Solomon was given Pharaoh's daughter in marriage is strong evidence of the reputation, power, and glory of Israel and of Solomon himself.

"You have far exceeded the report I heard" 2 Chron. 8:12–9:30. The splendor of Solomon's kingdom and his worldwide reputation exemplifies the influence David's future, greater Son will have. The Chronicler emphasized Solomon's successes, but the story of the visit by the Queen of Sheba is particularly important. She represents all the Gentiles, who will come to Jerusalem in the Messiah's day to learn from the One who will fulfill all God's promises to David.

The story is significant for us too. We are to attract non-Christians to Jesus by the quality of our lives. The sour believer who grimly confronts every acquaintance with real or supposed sins is not the kind of witness God calls to the stand to testify to His goodness.

▶DEVOTIONAL
When to Pray
(2 Chron. 6)

The better we know God, the more comfortable we are in prayer.

This simple truth is illustrated in Solomon's prayer dedicating the Jerusalem temple. Solomon understood completely that God is transcendent. "The heavens, even the highest heavens, cannot contain You," Solomon cried. "How much less this temple I have built?" Yet Solomon also realized that God is present, here and now. "Will God really dwell on earth with men?" The wonderful and amazing answer is, "Yes!" And, in Solomon's day, the symbol of that vital, living presence of God with men was the temple God had chosen as the place to put His name.

But do we truly realize that God, who is too great to be contained in the vast universe, is with us always? Or do we at times forget His commitment to be "with men"? Certainly when we've sinned, or fallen short in some awful way and are overcome by shame, we're likely to feel far from God. And even to feel that He has left us too.

Perhaps that's why Solomon goes on in his prayer to list occasion after occasion when God's hand would lie heavy on Israel, and to ask that *then,* when Israel is furthest from God, He might hear "when a prayer or plea is made by any of Your people Israel."

What a reminder for us, as we read Solomon's long list of times when there is a need to pray but we may hesitate in fear or doubt. God has committed Himself to be "with men." Because God transcendent is also God present with us, we can come to Him even when we feel farthest away, and know that He hears our prayer.

Personal Application

God is never farther than a prayer away.

Quotable

"Come now, little man! Flee for a while from your tasks, hide yourself for a little space from the turmoil of your thoughts. Come, cast aside your burdensome cares, and put aside your laborious pursuits. For a little while give your time to God, and rest in Him for a little while. Enter into the inner chamber of your mind, shut out all things save God and whatever may aid you in seeking God; and having barred the door of your chamber, seek Him."—Anselm of Canterbury

MARCH 31 *Reading 90*

DAVID'S DESCENDANTS FALL

2 Chronicles 10–13

"He and all Israel with him abandoned the Law of the LORD" (2 Chron. 12:1).

God kept His promise to David. His descendants did rule on Judah's throne. But when David's descendants abandoned God, judgment followed. Even those covered by the promises of God cannot sin impudently.

Overview

Rehoboam's attitude caused the northern tribes to rebel and set up the rival kingdom of "Israel" (10:1-19). Those faithful to God left Israel to settle in Judah (11:1-23). When Rehoboam abandoned God's Law, the Lord permitted Egypt's Shishak to invade Judah (12:1-16). The next king of Judah, Abijah, defeated Israel in battle because he "relied on the LORD" (13:1-22).

Understanding the Text

"Be kind to these people" 2 Chron. 10:1-19. Rehoboam's arrogance was the immediate cause of Israel's rebellion. While the "turn of events" was "from the LORD," Rehoboam's foolishness serves as a healthy reminder. Use of authority, and the attitude of a person with authority, either wins or loses the allegiance of others.

Being kind to people is not only good leadership. It is the way Christians are called to live.

"So they obeyed the words of the LORD" 2 Chron. 11:1-4. The furious Rehoboam mustered an army to subdue the north. His plans for war were interrupted by the Prophet Shemaiah, who spoke not only to Rehoboam but to "all" in Benjamin and Judah. The text says "they" responded to the prophet's command not to fight against their brothers. Perhaps the king was one of the "they," but it seems likely it was the people rather than the king who responded to God's word.

There are times when we should *not* obey the law of the land. When human law conflicts with God's commands, we, like the men of Judah, are to obey God.

"Those from every tribe of Israel" 2 Chron. 11:5-17. In the north Jeroboam abandoned the ritual commands of the Old Testament and set up a counterfeit faith. He set up golden calves, ordained any who would serve as priests, and replaced the required religious festivals to be celebrated at Jerusalem with festivals of his own.

This apostasy forced the Levites and all "who set their hearts on seeking the LORD" to abandon the north and move into Judah. The strength of this movement is seen in the fact that Judah could muster only 180,000 soldiers when the kingdom divided, yet some 18 years later was able to field an army of 400,000!

How wise God was in commanding Judah not to fight their brothers. Fighting might well have hardened the hearts of those God intended to seek Him.

We too win many more to the Lord by loving them than by fighting them.

"You have abandoned Me" 2 Chron. 12:1-5. After a poor start, Rehoboam acted wisely as king, strengthening his kingdom. But with his defenses complete, the king and all Judah "abandoned the Law of the LORD." God abandoned Judah to be invaded by Egypt under Pharaoh Shishak. Shishak's description of his invasion is described in a temple inscription found in Karnak, Egypt. The Egyptian stripped the temple of the treasures David and Solomon had gathered, and Judah became a subject nation.

God is faithful to those who remain faithful to Him. He is also faithful to discipline His own when we abandon Him. The invasion was not intended to harm Judah. In fact, the vast wealth that was lost had been dedicated to God! In one sense it cost God to discipline His people.

Let's remember when we are disciplined that God's punishment is motivated by a love which cost Him far more than it can ever cost us.

"The leaders of Israel and the king humbled themselves" 2 Chron. 12:6-16. Two things are of note here. First, Judah is spoken of as "Israel." This is not a mistake in the text, though the Northern Kingdom rather than the south bore that name. The people of Judah *were* "Israel," in that all in the north who sought God had moved to Judah. The true, spiritual Israel of God lived in the south, and it was true Israel God now disciplined.

The second thing of note is that the king and people responded appropriately to discipline. They acknowledged the justice of God: they confessed that they deserved the punishment. The text says, "Because Rehoboam humbled himself, the LORD's anger turned from him."

Psalm 51:17 applies the lesson to you and me. "A broken and contrite heart, O God," the psalmist says, "You will not despise."

▶DEVOTIONAL
Gott Mit Uns
(2 Chron. 13)

You could find these words on the belt buckles of the Kaiser's German troops in WWI. You can find a similar slogan on our coinage: "In God We Trust." But when do words like these mean something? When do they become a door that opens for us God's intervention and help?

Perhaps Abijah, David's great-grandson, has the answer. Oh, Abijah was no spiritual giant. The Book of Kings tells us that Abijah, who became king after Rehoboam, "committed all the sins his father had done before him" and that "his heart was not fully devoted to the LORD" (1 Kings 15:3). Yet the Chronicler selects one incident in which Abijah's reliance on the Lord led to direct divine intervention.

Abijah was forced into a war with Jeroboam of Israel, though he had only half the troops. Yet Abijah shouted out a warning to the enemy! Judah, Abijah said, had been faithful to God. It had maintained the required services at the temple which God Himself had chosen, which was served by Levites and priests whom God had ordained. On the other hand, Israel came to battle carrying golden calves which they honored as gods, with priests God had neither called nor ordained.

Based on Judah's faithfulness in observing the requirements for worship which the north had forsaken, Abijah proclaimed "God is with us; He is our Leader. . . . Men of Israel, do not fight against the LORD, the God of your fathers, for you will not succeed" (v. 12).

Some might dismiss Abijah's words as mere psychological warfare. Others might criticize him for maintaining that worship rituals proved true devotion to the Lord. But the text tells us that God did deliver Judah. They were "victorious because they relied on the LORD, the God of their fathers."

What's fascinating is that, despite Abijah's failings and the sins of Judah, God did come to their aid! Abijah may have had more claim to divine favor than Israel, but nothing he or Judah had done really merited God's intervention. Still, when Judah relied on the Lord—and because they relied on the Lord—God did act.

It's the same for you and me today. We can't claim perfection. We fail God too often. We can't even claim to be better than folks who don't go to church. Going to church in itself scores no points with God. But when we are in need, we can do the one thing Abijah and Judah did which did win God's favor. We can abandon self-confidence, and rely completely on God.

It is trust, not being right, and not even being righteous, that brings God to our aid.

Personal Application

Rely on God to help, not because He owes you, but because of who He is.

Quotable

Lord,
I crawled across the barrenness
to You with my empty cup
Uncertain
in asking any small drop of refreshment.
If only I'd known You better
I'd have come running with a bucket.—
Nancy Spiegelberg

APRIL 1 *Reading 91*
TWO GODLY KINGS
2 Chronicles 14–20

> *"As for you, be strong and do not give up, for your work will be rewarded" (2 Chron. 15:7).*

The activities of two godly kings identify characteristics of spiritual revival we can apply to our personal lives, and to our churches. Mistakes of each king warn us away from spiritual dangers.

Overview

Asa relied on the Lord when Judah was invaded (14:1-15), and led his nation to swear fresh allegiance to the Lord (15:1-19). In old age Asa became autocratic and failed to rely on God (16:1-14). Jehoshaphat showed zeal for the Lord, and Judah became wealthy and powerful (17:1-19). His error was in allying himself with Israel's evil Ahab (18:1–19:3). Yet Jehoshaphat remained committed to God and worked to implement Moses' Law in Judah (vv. 4-11). He also relied on the Lord when invaded (20:1-17), and demonstrated faith by praising the Lord even before the subsequent victory (vv. 18-30). He lived and died a godly king (vv. 31-37).

Understanding the Text

"Seek the LORD *. . . and . . . obey His laws" 2 Chron. 14:1-7.* The chapter begins with a general evaluation of Asa and describes Judah's prosperity. Spiritual commitment is the foundation for national as well as personal well-being. Seeking the Lord is the first step in every revival.

"Help us, O LORD *our God, for we rely on You" 2 Chron. 14:9-15.* The second step in revival is seen in Asa's response to an invasion by the Cushites, or Ethiopians, then dominated by Egypt. He called on his people to rely on the Lord. Asa's active trust in God was well founded, as the Lord gave Judah a decisive military victory.

"Do not give up" 2 Chron. 15:1-19. Seeking God and relying on Him are only the first steps. As Azariah the prophet reminded Asa, we must be persistent in our commitment.

This quality was demonstrated in Asa's call to all Judah and the many Hebrews who had left apostate Israel and settled in the south. The nation gathered at Jerusalem in Asa's 15th year, and wholeheartedly agreed to actively and eagerly seek the Lord and to serve Him only. Revival may be stimulated by an individual, but comes only when God's own, as a people of God, achieve a shared commitment to the Lord.

Yet how important the leader and his or her full commitment is! This quality is shown by Asa, who deposed his grandmother as Queen Mother, a very significant role in ancient court life, because she went after idols rather than sought the Lord (vv. 11-18). If God is to use us to bring revival to His people, you and I must cleanse our lives of everything contrary to godliness.

"Because you relied on the king of Aram, and not on the LORD*" 2 Chron. 16:1-14.* Even a vital, spiritual revival is no guarantee of continuing godliness. We must be careful to keep our hearts fixed on God. Some 17

years after Asa stimulated revival in Judah, the king himself failed to seek or to rely on the Lord. Rather than trust God for victory when threatened by Israel, Asa paid the Arameans (Syrians) to attack them, not knowing that the Syrians would become an even greater threat in the future. When rebuked by a prophet, Asa imprisoned him. He began to oppress others, and even when he contracted a severe disease Asa failed to turn to the Lord.

What a warning for us. Just because we relied on the Lord in the past is no guarantee of the future. The only way to ensure continued blessings is to actively seek and trust God each new day.

"Only from the physicians" 2 Chron. 16:12. This criticism of Asa does not mean we should not go to a doctor when ill. Asa was not wrong to seek help from physicians. He was wrong to seek help "only" from physicians. We Christians rely on God, who often chooses to work through medicines and the medical profession.

"His heart was devoted to the ways of the Lord" 2 Chron. 17:1-6. Jehoshaphat too is introduced with a brief summary of his spiritual commitment. While not blameless, he too was a godly man concerned with the spiritual well-being of his people.

"They taught throughout Judah" 2 Chron. 17:7-19. The text introduces us to yet another characteristic of spiritual revival. Revival is rooted in a return to the Word of God. Jehoshaphat stimulated revival by organizing "Bible studies" in all the towns of Judah!

Once again building on solid spiritual foundations led to national prosperity and strength (vv. 10-19).

"He allied himself with Ahab" 2 Chron. 18:1–19:3. Jehoshaphat's error was to "help the wicked and love those who hate the Lord" (19:2). The believer who seeks revival is not to be unequally yoked with unbelievers.

While Jehoshaphat remained personally committed to God (cf. 18:6), his close association with the evil Ahab led to a disastrous military defeat. Later the Israelite princess he married to his son, Athaliah, would murder their descendants so she could take the throne for herself (22:10). The lesson is a vital one for us.

"Judge carefully, for with the Lord our God there is no injustice or partiality" 2 Chron. 19:4-11. Jehoshaphat saw to it that the Word was taught throughout Judah. But he did more. He established officials to administer the Law. That is, he saw to it that the Law was *lived* in Judah.

To maintain revival it's not enough to know the Word of God. We must put it into practice, as our rule and guide to daily life.

"Jehoshaphat resolved to inquire of the Lord" 2 Chron. 20:1-13. Again the text returns to the theme of relying on the Lord. When Judah was invaded, the king called on his people to actively seek God, and led his nation in prayer. "We have no power to face this," the king confessed. And so "our eyes are upon You."

Revival is kindled and maintained by a sense of our deep personal need for God's help always. Keeping our eyes on the Lord as sole source of help is a vital key to spiritual renewal.

"He did what was right" 2 Chron. 20:31-37. King Jehoshaphat was not without flaws. The text reminds us of this by telling of another time when he unwisely entered into a joint venture with Israel (vv. 35-37). And despite his efforts and his example, the people failed during his reign to set their hearts on God (v. 33). Yet he "did what was right in the eyes of the Lord."

This, the epitaph of all the godly kings of Judah, is an epitaph we might well desire for ourselves. We may accomplish less than we set out in life to do. But if we do what is right in the eyes of God, we have lived successfully and well.

▶ DEVOTIONAL
Praise before Victory
(2 Chron. 20)

I suppose we all know that it's appropriate to thank and praise God for His goodness even though we sometimes forget. This passage, however, points up an unexpected aspect of praise. We can praise before we experience His goodness. We can praise before we receive what we request.

Threatened by a massive invasion force, Jehoshaphat called on all of Judah to look to God. The king himself led in prayer, confessing Judah's lack of power and expressing total reliance on God. In response God spoke through the Prophet Jahaziel and promised victory. "The battle is not yours, but God's," the prophet proclaimed. "Stand firm and see the deliverance the LORD will give you. . . . Do not be afraid; do not be discouraged. Go out to face them tomorrow, and the LORD will be with you" (v. 17).

Immediately after receiving this word from God, the king and the people fell down to worship. And then in a "very loud voice" some of the Levites stood up and began to praise God.

The danger was still ahead. The invading army still threatened. But God's people began to praise Him before the promised victory was won!

The next day God did provide victory. Ancient armies were often composed of a variety of peoples, some hired as mercenaries and others engaged as allies. In this case God caused the various peoples who composed the invading force to annihilate each other before Judah's army even arrived! The praises that resounded over the slain enemy were so loud and heartfelt that the place was given a new name: Beracah, the "Valley of Praise."

One day when final victory is won, as we stand with Jesus in God's eternal kingdom, our shouts of praises too will be loud. Yet we too are called to praise now.

When we're afraid, we're called to praise.

When we're discouraged, we're called to praise.

When we face any enemy, we're called to praise.

And praise we can! For we too have the promises of God. You too can "go out and face [difficulties] tomorrow." You too can know that "the LORD will be with you."

And this, the assurance of God's presence with us, is cause for praise. Praise even before victory.

Personal Application

When discouraged or afraid, praise God that He most surely will be with you.

Quotable

"Relying on God has to begin all over again every day as if nothing had yet been done."—C.S. Lewis

APRIL 2 *Reading 92*
JEHORAM TO HEZEKIAH
2 Chronicles 21–28

> *"Although the LORD sent prophets to the people to bring them back to Him, and though they testified against them, they would not listen" (2 Chron. 24:19).*

The text of Chronicles highlights the righteous acts of Judah's kings. Yet it's clear that the spiritual condition of Judah after the time of Asa and Jehoshaphat did deteriorate. The flaws in Judah's kings serve as warnings for you and me.

Overview

The focus on Judah's kings continues, with reviews of the reigns of a series of morally and politically weak rulers: Jehoram (21:4-20), Ahaziah (22:1-9), Athaliah (v. 10–23:10), Joash (v. 11–24:27), Amaziah (25:1-28), Uzziah (26:1-23), Jotham (27:1-9), and Ahaz (28:1-27).

Understanding the Text

"He walked in the ways of the kings of Israel" 2 Chron. 21:1-20. Earlier kings showed that seeking and serving God was the path to national and personal blessing. Jehoram, who murdered his brothers and chose idols over the Lord, shows us that forsaking God leads to disaster. Though warned by the Prophet Elijah, Jehoram gave no thought to repentance. The resulting national disaster saw the rebellion of subject nations (vv. 8-10) and attacks by other hostile peoples (vv. 16-17). Jehoram himself died in agony of an "uncurable disease of the bowels" (vv. 18-19).

"His mother encouraged him in doing wrong"

2 Chron. 22:1-9. One source of Jehoram's evil was his marriage to Athaliah, a daughter of Ahab and Jezebel who was as committed to evil as her wicked mother. Athaliah dominated her 22-year-old son, who ruled only one year before being killed by Jehu, who exterminated the family of Ahab in Israel. Ahaziah's short life was so evil that he was accorded burial only because he was a descendant of godly Jehoshaphat, who was was still remembered with affection in Judah.

When we have parents and grandparents who set different courses in life, we can choose which example to follow. Ahaziah chose to be influenced by his mother. He did not have to choose her pathway.

"She proceeded to destroy the whole royal family" 2 Chron. 22:10-12. With her son dead, Athaliah decided to take the throne for herself. This broke tradition, but Athaliah was a determined as well as an evil woman. She killed all members of the royal family (except for a baby who was rescued and hidden away), and with no rival left, claimed royal power for herself. She held that power for some seven years, until the hidden child was revealed and crowned. Then she was killed by her own palace guards at the command of the high priest, Jehoiada.

Athaliah must have been an exceptional and forceful woman to have held the throne against all precedent. Yet how insecure any power gained and exercised by the wicked.

"Jehoiada the priest" 2 Chron. 23:1-21. The high priest, aware that God had promised to provide rulers for Judah from David's family line, protected the hidden prince, Joash. He also organized a rebellion against Athaliah. It is significant that his uprising included all the priests and all the Levites as well as all off-duty palace guards. Yet not one betrayed the conspiracy to Athaliah! Athaliah undoubtedly reigned by terror and murder. The leader who sets himself or herself up as the enemy of his or her people creates a fear and hostility that ultimately leads to an uprising in self-defense.

"After the death of Jehoiada. . . . they abandoned the temple of the LORD" 2 Chron. 24:1-27. Joash served God only as long as Jehoiada lived. The influence of this high priest is seen in that he chose wives for the king, the traditional role of a parent (vv. 2-3), and in the concern shown in Joash's early years for the temple. But when the positive influence of Jehoiada was withdrawn, Joash's personal character was revealed.

We can judge a person's character only after he or she has matured and begins to make his or her own choices. The choices Joash made led to disaster for him and defeat for his nation.

"But not wholeheartedly" 2 Chron. 25:1-26. The next king, Amaziah, did choose the Lord, but failed to follow Him wholeheartedly. His reliance on God was shown by dismissing a hundred thousand hired Israelite mercenaries when told to do so by a prophet. Because of his obedience, Judah won a great victory. But Amaziah inexplicably began to worship the gods of the nation he had defeated! Despite another prophet's warning, Amaziah went to war with Israel and suffered defeat.

Amaziah was taken and apparently kept captive in Israel. He was returned, possibly to create internal problems, as his son had been crowned king of Judah while he was captive. In the political infighting that followed Amaziah was forced to flee to Lachish, where he was killed.

A brief, early flare of faith is no substitute for lifelong commitment. Our only protection from potential disaster is consistent, daily commitment to the Lord.

"As long as he sought the LORD, God gave him success" 2 Chron. 26:1-23. Uzziah, who is also called Azariah, is yet another example of a king who was successful only as long as he remained committed to the Lord. He was a vigorous and active person who restored Judah to power (vv. 6-15), but when powerful was "unfaithful" to the Lord. Uzziah's contempt for the Lord is shown by his violation of laws governing temple ritual. The king was stricken with leprosy while in the temple, and lived in isolation the rest of his life (vv. 16-21), while royal business was conducted by his son, Jotham (v. 21).

"Jotham grew powerful because he walked steadfastly before the LORD *his God" 2 Chron. 27:1-9.* Jotham's 16-year reign was a time of blessing, marked by dominance over nearby nations. While the Lord blessed the nation on account of Jotham, "the people . . . continued their corrupt practices." True revival must touch the people of God as well as leaders.

"He . . . made cast idols for worshiping the Baals" 2 Chron. 28:1-27. The catalog of the sins of Ahaz is truly terrible, including the fiery sacrifice of his own sons. National disasters followed, as Judah was successfully invaded by the Syrians and the Israelites. Only intervention by the Prophet Oded kept the Israelites from taking thousands of the people of Judah to Israel as slaves.

These defeats did not turn Ahaz to God, but rather led him to beg Assyria for help against Syria and the Philistines. The Assyrians were only too happy for an excuse to expand westward—a movement which "gave [Ahaz] trouble instead of help."

The text says that "in his time of trouble King Ahaz became even more unfaithful to the LORD."

How true this always is. Under the pressure of troubles, human beings tend to reveal what is in their hearts. The believer is drawn closer to the Lord. The unbeliever turns against him in anger and frustration (see vv. 24-25).

▶ DEVOTIONAL
Borrowed Faith
(2 Chron. 23–24)

I was brought up in a Christian home, rich in love and acceptance. I went to church, lived a moral life, and believed in Jesus. It wasn't hard to do. After all, I was surrounded by people who believed; people who in simple, quiet ways, lived their faith.

Yet after two years in the Navy I realized that I had to make personal decisions of my own. Influenced by the teaching of Donald Grey Barnhouse, I began to study my Bible. I started and led a noon Bible study on my base. And I became active in a nearby local church.

I realized that at home I'd been living on borrowed faith. Out on my own, I learned that I had to develop and nurture a faith of my own.

This is a lesson that the life of Joash teaches as well. Joash was a good and godly king—as long as he was surrounded by people who believed, like the priest Jehoiada who raised him. It wasn't hard for him to live a good life, or even to "believe." But when Jehoiada died, Joash found that a borrowed faith is never enough.

When Joash began to make decisions on his own, he made wrong ones. He abandoned the temple of the Lord and worshiped idols. He and his people refused to listen to the prophets who warned them. Joash even killed the son of the man who had raised him, when that son confronted him concerning his sins. Ultimately, because king and people had forsaken the Lord, disaster came. Joash, who chose evil, was killed in his bed by officials who conspired against him.

The story of Joash underlines two important truths. First, we can't tell from a child or young person's early life what his future will hold. So, while we can rejoice in signs of early spiritual growth, we can't afford to become complacent. We need to keep on praying for our children, that as they mature they will develop their own personal and growing faith in God.

Second, we need to examine our own lives, to make sure we're not living on borrowed faith. For faith to be real, you and I need to take responsibility for our own choices—and to make sure that our choices are guided by a personal commitment to Jesus Christ as Lord.

Personal Application

How do your daily choices reflect your own personal commitment to God?

Quotable

Think not that faith by which the just
  shall live
Is a dead creed, a map correct of
  heaven,
Far less a feeling fond and fugitive,
A thoughtless gift withdrawn as
  soon as given:
It is an affirmation and an act
That bids eternal truth be present
  fact.—Hartley Coleridge

APRIL 3 *Reading 93*
WORSHIP BRINGS REVIVAL
2 Chronicles 29–32

> *"In the first month of the first year of his reign, he opened the doors of the temple of the LORD and repaired them" (2 Chron. 29:3).*

There is nothing as revitalizing for the believer as heartfelt worship of the Lord.

Background

During Hezekiah's reign the Assyrians crushed the Hebrew kingdom of Israel and deported its citizens. Sennacherib then invaded Judah, expecting to do the same. Divine intervention alone saved the Southern Kingdom, and Judah remained an independent nation for another 136 years.

In telling the story of these pivotal years in Judah's history, the author of 2 Chronicles emphasizes Hezekiah's concern for the worship of God, indicated by the attention he gave to the temple and to the Passover. The author's point is that the person or people who truly worship God find their faith renewed, and that God responds to a renewed faith by acting on behalf of His worshipers.

Overview

Hezekiah's emphasis of worship is seen in his rededication of the temple (29:1-36), his celebration of Passover (30:1-27), and reorganization of the priests and Levites who served God (31:1-21). The king's trust in God was rewarded as the Lord threw back Sennacherib's invading force (32:1-23). Later Hezekiah became proud, but repented and was restored (vv. 24-33).

Understanding the Text

"Now I intend to make a covenant with the LORD" 2 Chron. 29:1-11. Hezekiah was stimulated to restore the worship of the Lord to Judah by the realization that his nation's past troubles had come when his people turned their backs on God. Judah's only hope was to return to God in full commitment. This the king was determined to do personally and nationally.

The leader who wants to influence others must first be fully committed himself.

"The whole assembly bowed in worship" 2 Chron. 29:12-36. Hezekiah immediately set the priests and Levites to work purifying the temple and themselves. When this was done, "early the next morning" the king gathered his officials and went up to the temple to worship.

Hezekiah's action clearly demonstrated that worship was his first priority as king.

The immediate impact of this emphasis was internal. Those who worshiped found themselves singing praises "with gladness" and willingly bringing "sacrifices and thank offerings." Worship remains the key to joy for the believer. And worship remains the key to spontaneous giving.

A modern church which neglects worship will not touch the hearts of its members or overcome contemporary materialism.

"Come to . . . Jerusalem and celebrate the Passover" 2 Chron. 30:1–31:21. Hezekiah invited believers in hostile Israel to celebrate Passover with his own people. The invitation was accepted by many, who joined in the joyful worship.

The result is striking. The text tells us that after participating in the worship experience, the Israelites who were there went through the countryside destroying the pagan worship centers and altars in Judah and in their own tribal lands.

Worship still stimulates commitment. If we need encouragement to remain fully committed to God in our daily lives, we can find that encouragement in worshiping God with others.

It's one thing to share a spontaneous worship experience. It's another to maintain the spirit of worship. Hezekiah carefully organized the priests and Levites who were responsible for temple worship.

You and I need to be as disciplined. We need to set aside daily time for worship as well as to meet with others in a church that makes worship a priority.

If we do attend to worship, Scripture's commendation of Hezekiah will surely apply to us as well: "In everything that he undertook in the service of God's temple and in obedience to the Law and the commands, he sought his God and worked wholeheartedly. And so he prospered."

"Hezekiah . . . cried out in prayer" 2 Chron. 32:1-23. Worship deepens our awareness of who God is, and thus strengthens our trust in Him. When Judah was invaded by the Assyrians and Jerusalem was threatened, Hezekiah turned immediately to the Lord. And God answered.

The most important thing we can do to enrich our prayer lives and deepen our trust in God is to worship Him. When worship is a vital part of our relationship with the Lord, we too have great confidence in prayer when troubles come.

"Hezekiah's heart was proud" 2 Chron. 32:24-33. The author concluded with an account of Hezekiah's pride and repentance. Not even an enriched worship life will keep us sinless. We human beings are always vulnerable to our sinful natures. Yet the text reminds us that "Hezekiah repented of the pride of his heart, as did the people of Jerusalem." The closer our relationship with the Lord, the more responsive we will be to His rebuke.

▶ DEVOTIONAL
Kneel Down and Worship (2 Chron. 29)

The Hebrew words usually translated worship mean "to bow down" or "to prostrate oneself out of respect." The underlying thought is that of showing reverence; of a growing awareness of who God is, and the expression of our awe and our praise. David Mains views worship as "praising God for who He by nature is." That is, in worship we show our respect and appreciation by focusing our attention on one of His revealed attributes, and by thanking and praising Him for being this kind of Person.

This is the significance of the worship-based revival that Hezekiah led. Yes, that worship followed the ritual patterns that were established in Moses' Law. But we need only read the text to realize that Hezekiah's worship revival was a matter of the heart. Ritual served simply as a mode of expression.

For this worship, Hezekiah purified and consecrated himself, for God is holy (vv. 18-19).

For this worship, Hezekiah appointed a multitude of sacrifices, for God deserves our best (29:20-24).

For this worship, singers sang and trumpeters played, for God is the source of joy, and worship is to be joyful (vv. 25-28).

For this worship, Hezekiah and others brought rich gifts, for God has given us rich gifts, and we are privileged to return to Him some of what He gives (29:29-31).

And in this worship, Hezekiah and all Judah found a source of joy.

Whatever ways of worship we have today, if our worship is preceded by consecration, expressed joyfully and accompanied by gifts of our best, that worship will bring us joy and will deepen our trust in the Lord.

Personal Application

What place does worship have in your life and in your church?

Quotable

The Seven Modern Sins
Politics without principles.
Pleasures without conscience.
Wealth without work.
Knowledge without character.
Industry without morality.
Science without humanity.
Worship without sacrifice.—Canon Frederic Donaldson

APRIL 4 *Reading 94*
JUDAH'S LAST YEARS
2 Chronicles 33–36

"The Lord *spoke to Manasseh and his people, but they paid no attention" (2 Chron. 33:10).*

After Hezekiah, Judah fell into a sharp spiritual decline that sealed the Southern Kingdom's destiny. Despite a brief and superficial revival under Josiah, the nation rushed to judgment.

Overview

Manasseh plunged Judah into a half-century of apostasy (33:1-11). Manasseh's late conversion could not reverse the spiritual trend to evil (vv. 12-20), nor could the efforts of Josiah (34:1–35:27). Judah's last four kings merit only brief mention (36:1-14). Jerusalem fell, the people were exiled, but after 70 years a remnant returned to Judah to rebuild the temple (vv. 15-23).

The Topheth at Carthage

The remains of thousands of children burned as sacrifices have been found just outside ancient Carthage. The ashes, in votive jars, confirm the Bible's affirmation that pagans—and some kings of Israel and Judah!—did engage in the gruesome practice of child sacrifice.

Understanding the Text

"He did evil in the eyes of the Lord*" 2 Chron. 33:1-10.* Manasseh's 55 years were the darkest in Judah's spiritual history. He shut down the temple, except to use its courts for pagan worship centers, turned to the occult for guidance, and even used his own sons as burnt offerings.

"In his distress he sought the favor of the Lord *his God" 2 Chron. 33:11-20.* Manasseh was taken captive to Babylon, then a major city in the Assyrian Empire. There he had a conversion experience. Manasseh returned home eager to restore worship of the Lord to Judah.

Manasseh's experience foreshadowed that of Judah itself. Perhaps the author of Chronicles wants us to recognize the parallel. Babylonian Captivity, for Judah as for Manasseh, was intended by God for good. We too need to understand that our times of distress are not punishment but discipline. God permits them, and intends to do us good through them.

Manasseh's efforts to bring about spiritual renewal in Judah were too little too late. He was unable to undo the harm his rule had done to God's people. What a reason for turning to God early in our lives. Why wait to turn to God, and risk doing irreparable harm to those we love?

"I have found the Book of the Law in the temple of the Lord*" 2 Chron. 34:1-28.* Josiah, Judah's last godly king, ordered the temple repaired and cleansed. The workmen found the Book of the Law, possibly Deuteronomy, or perhaps the entire Pentateuch. It is not surprising the Law was lost: Manasseh's early hostility toward God undoubtedly was expressed by efforts to destroy Scripture.

When Josiah discovered just what God required of His people, and compared the life now lived in Judah, he was shocked. Judah was undoubtedly guilty and merited the just punishments detailed in that book.

Josiah's own immediate and humble response was honored by the Lord. The curses announced would not strike Judah during Josiah's lifetime; for that brief period Judah would still know peace (*shalom*, "well-being").

One godly person, who truly repents and seeks God, can affect the fate of an entire generation.

"He had everyone . . . pledge themselves" 2 Chron. 34:29-33. Josiah assembled all his people to hear the Word of God. Josiah then "had everyone" pledge to keep the Word. There is a vital distinction here. Josiah was eager to obey God. The text suggests that his spontaneous response was not mimicked by the people in general. Instead they obeyed the Word because the king "had" them do so. Note that it was only as long as Josiah lived that Judah followed the Lord (v. 33). The revival that took place in the heart of Josiah never reached the hearts of his people.

We can infect others with love for God. But we cannot command it.

"Josiah celebrated the Passover" 2 Chron. 35:1-19. Josiah's spectacular celebration of Passover expressed his own love for God (cf. v. 7). Some of his officials were also touched and "contributed voluntarily" to supply sacrificial animals.

Even when our love for God is unable to infect multitudes, some individuals will be touched, and will respond.

The emphasis on the worship seen here, as in stories of other godly kings, again reminds us that spiritual vitality calls for knowing, loving, and worshiping the Lord.

"He died. He was buried in the tombs of his fathers" 2 Chron. 35:20-27. Some have ridiculed the earlier prediction that Josiah would be "buried in peace" (34:28). How can this be reconciled with Josiah's death in battle? Very simply. During his entire reign Josiah and his kingdom knew God's blessing. Only after Josiah's burial would the blessing of peace be removed.

Yet there is another implication here. Death is not the end of blessing for the believer. It is the beginning of blessings beyond our power to imagine. In death as in life, Josiah found peace through personal relationship with God.

"He did evil" 2 Chron. 36:1-15. The last kings of Judah, with "all the leaders of the priests and the people became more and more unfaithful" to the Lord (v. 14). These people knew no peace, but only a terror and uncertainty that culminated in the fall of Jerusalem, and the survivors' exile to Babylon.

"He has appointed me to build a temple" 2 Chron. 36:15-23. The author of Chronicles, writing after the exiles' return, continued to emphasize worship. God did not forsake His people, but brought them back. And the focus of the decree which freed them was again the temple, which God moved Cyrus, the ruler of Persia, to order rebuilt.

The promises given to David had not yet been fulfilled. But if God's people, who were called by His name, remained faithful in worship, the promised Messiah would surely come.

▶DEVOTIONAL
Beyond Redemption?
(2 Chron. 33)

Everyone who followed the Ted Bundy case, or has read news stories on other serial killers, would be both repelled and fascinated by Manasseh. The text describes him as "despicable." His reported acts suggest he was far worse than that!

Spiritually Manasseh was cold and hardened. The Lord spoke to him, but Manasseh "paid no attention." Emotionally he was hardened. He could burn children alive without feeling any remorse.

Then came a distressful period of imprisonment in Babylon. And in his distress Manasseh sought "the LORD his God."

That simple phrase reminds us of a most wonderful truth. The Lord *is* the God of all humanity—of the righteous and even of the wicked. Manasseh, certainly one of the most wicked men who ever lived, turned to God and God, in truly amazing grace, chose to be "his God."

What a lesson to remember when we come in contact with the hardened, the wicked, and the evil. Our God is their God too! If they will only turn to Him, God will be their God. He will forgive them for Jesus' sake. And, as He did with Manasseh, He will transform their lives.

Personal Application
Like godly Josiah, wicked Manasseh sought the Lord with tears. God has made His choice: He is the God of Josiah and the God of Manasseh as well.

Quotable
"Some leaders say we are in a great revival right now. If we are. . . . I ask where are the tears? What's happening to the intense spirit of conviction that always marks such things? Why are the converts coming in trickles instead of waves upon waves? . . . We are not in revival, although we may be closer to its possibility than we realize."—David Mains

---

The Variety Reading Plan continues with 1 PETER

Ezra

INTRODUCTION

During the 70 years of Exile most of the Jews settled into a comfortable life in Babylon and other Eastern cities. Then in 539 B.C. Cyrus the Persian issued a decree permitting any Jew to return to his ancient homeland, to rebuild the temple of the Lord. Only a few responded. This enthusiastic group of settlers laid the temple foundation, but local enemies delayed its completion for 18 years. The first six chapters of Ezra tell the story of these pioneers and their struggle to finish the temple of the Lord.

In 458 B.C. another group of exiles, led by Ezra the priest, returned to Jerusalem. Ezra was a reformer, who taught God's Law in Judea and called God's people to rededicate their lives to the Lord. This book, written by Ezra, tells the story of these two groups of exiles who resettled the Promised Land.

OUTLINE OF CONTENTS

READING GUIDE (2 Days)

If hurried, you may read only the "core passage" in your Bible and the Devotional in each chapter of this Commentary.

Reading	*Chapters*	*Core passage*
95	1–6	6
96	7–10	9:1–10:4

Ezra

APRIL 5 *Reading 95*
THE EXILES RETURN
Ezra 1–6

> *"Everyone whose heart God had moved—prepared to go up and build the house of the* Lord *in Jerusalem" (Ezra 1:5).*

The enthusiasm of those who returned to Judah was tested by hardship and by opposition from local peoples. Despite a long delay, the Jerusalem temple was rebuilt and God was again worshiped at the site He had chosen.

Background

Timeline. This time line relates events reported in Ezra with other postexilic events.

Decree of Cyrus (Ezra 1:1-4)	538 B.C.
The first return (Ezra 1:5–2:70)	539 B.C.
Temple construction begins	536 B.C.
Opposition & Delay	
Ministry of Haggai	520 B.C.
Ministry of Zechariah	520 B.C.
Temple completed	515 B.C.
Events of Esther	483–473 B.C.?
Decree of Artaxerxes (Ezra 7:11ff)	458 B.C.
Return under Ezra	458 B.C.
Decree of Artaxerxes (Ezra 4:17ff)	446 B.C.
Decree of Artaxerxes (Neh. 2:1-8)	444 B.C.

Overview

A decree of Cyrus permitted the Jews to return to Judah and rebuild the Jerusalem temple (1:1-11). Ezra listed the returning families (2:1-70). They rebuilt the altar (3:1-6) and laid the temple foundation (vv. 7-13). Ezra quoted letters documenting opposition to the Jews (4:1–5:17) and the decree of Darius authorizing the temple completion (6:1-12). The task was completed (vv. 13-18) and Passover celebrated once again (vv. 19-22).

Understanding the Text

"In order to fulfill the word of the Lord*" Ezra 1:1-4.* Jeremiah had predicted the Captivity would last 70 years (Jer. 25:11-12; 29:10). Isaiah, writing in the time of Hezekiah, had named Cyrus as the ruler who would fulfill God's will (Isa. 45:1-5). The very year this Persian conqueror supplanted the Babylonian kings, he did issue a decree permitting the Jews to return home. The decree also authorized reconstruction of the Jerusalem temple!

Josephus says that Cyrus read Isaiah's prediction and was moved to fulfill it. It's more likely this decree was one of many similar orders issued by Cyrus, who reversed the Babylonian policy of deportation, and permitted all captive peoples to return home.

The prophecy of Isaiah, and the action of Cyrus, remind us that God is sovereign. He controls the fate of nations, and all history moves toward ends which He alone has determined. The One we worship truly is God.

"Everyone whose heart God moved" Ezra 1:5–2:70. While some 50,000 Jews turned their hearts toward home, many more thousands chose to remain in Babylon. The Captivity had not been harsh: recovered records show that Jews, who were settled in an attractive district by the Kebar canal, were successfully involved in

trade and business in the enemy capital. Why go back to face hardship, when life was easy in Babylon? Only those whom God moved to complete commitment would make the difficult choice.

Those who stayed were comfortable. But they missed out on so much. The names of the returnees are enshrined in Scripture. And only those who returned witnessed the restoration of God's temple and worshiped there.

How important to keep our hearts open to the Lord, so that if He calls us to a special place of service we will be willing to respond.

"With praise and thanksgiving they sang to the Lord*" Ezra 3:1-13.* Those who returned to Judah found a desolate land. Thorns and thistles choked once-fertile fields, while Jerusalem was a heap of ruins. How hearts must have fallen as the enormity of the task before the returnees was driven home.

Yet as soon as the people settled in their towns, they reassembled at Jerusalem. There they rebuilt the altar, roughed out the foundations for the new temple, and praised God.

The greater our difficulties, the more important it is to put God first. When we do we, like those in ancient Judea, find our hearts also filled with joy and praise.

"The enemies of Judah" Ezra 4:1–5:17. Judah was a tiny area within a larger administrative district of the Persian Empire. Neighbors in what had once been Israel at first offered to help build the temple. The offer was rejected: they were not members of the covenant people descended from Abraham, Isaac, and Jacob. The rebuff hardened local antagonism, which developed into active opposition. This opposition, with the difficulty faced by the returnees in scratching a living from ruined fields, halted construction of the temple.

The letters in these chapters are written in Aramaic, the diplomatic language of that age, rather than in Hebrew. Ezra clearly quotes material available to him in the Jerusalem archives.

Note too that the letters do not all date from the early return. What Ezra has done is to draw evidence from material written over a span of many years to document the fact that God's people faced serious opposition.

We too can expect opposition at times. Hostility from outsiders is no sign that God has abandoned us, but may in fact suggest that we are doing exactly what God wants!

"A decree concerning the temple of God" Ezra 6:1-12. In the end King Darius confirmed the order of his predecessor, Cyrus. Not only was the temple to be rebuilt, but the very officials who had opposed it were ordered to pay all construction expenses from the royal treasury!

The God of the Old Testament truly is sovereign. Men may plot against His people, but God's plans will be carried out.

"Then the people of Israel . . . celebrated the dedication of the house of God with joy" Ezra 6:13-22. There had been years of struggle and discouragement. But at last the temple was finished. By showing his ability to "change the attitude" of the ruler of the empire that supplanted ancient Assyria, God had "filled them with joy."

God is still at work, even in the lives of our enemies. The wait may be long, but God can still change attitudes, and fill us with joy too.

▶ DEVOTIONAL
Where Will the Money Come From? (Ezra 6)

I suppose it's one of our most common worries. We need to build an addition on the church. But where will the money come from? I'd like to go to seminary. But where will the money come from? I wish I could help that missionary. But where will the money come from? I feel God wants me to go into nursing. But where will the money come from?

The same question was surely asked in ancient Judah as the people considered finishing the temple. The Prophet Haggai described the desperate conditions of that time: "You have planted much, but have harvested little. . . . You earn wages, only to put them in a purse with holes in it" (Hag. 1:5-6). How could a destitute people, struggling to make ends meet, ever raise the funds necessary to complete God's temple?

In his message urging Judah to give priority to God's temple, the prophet makes this statement. " 'The silver is Mine and the gold is Mine,' declares the LORD Almighty" (2:8).

How the people of Judah must have struggled. They were convinced they must complete the temple. But where would the money come from?

And then the decree of Darius, in response to the challenge raised by Judah's enemies, arrived. There, with the permission to rebuild, were the words, "The costs are to be paid by the royal treasury" (Ezra 6:4). The endless wealth of one of the world's mightiest empires was suddenly made available to God's poverty-stricken people.

The incident teaches us an important lesson. "Where will the money come from?" is an important question. But not knowing should never deter us from acting if we are sure of God's will. The message from God that Haggai shared so long ago is still true. The silver is the Lord's. And the gold is the Lord's. When we commit ourselves to do His will, the Lord will provide.

Personal Application

Lack of funds cannot keep us from doing God's will.

Quotable

"In building, we need not act as the people of the world do. They first procure the money and then begin to build, but we must do just the opposite. We will begin to build and then expect to receive what is necessary from Divine Providence. The Lord God will not be outdone in generosity."—Alphonsus Liguori

---

APRIL 6 *Reading 96*
A SECOND GROUP RETURNS
Ezra 7–10

> *"Ezra had devoted himself to the study and observance of the Law of the LORD, and to teaching its decrees and laws in Israel" (Ezra 7:10).*

Some 80 years after the first group returned, Ezra led a smaller contingent home. Ezra's return was significant. This man who was dedicated to God's Law called the people of Judah back to their original commitment to God.

Background

An exciting revolution took place in Babylon. The Jewish people, shaken by the loss of their land and temple, turned to Scripture in a desperate search for hope. They met together weekly to pray and to discuss the Scriptures—and thus the synagogue was born. Some men devoted themselves to study, to do, and to teach God's Word—and the scribal movement was born. From the Babylonian Captivity onward the Jews, cleansed at last of idolatry, would be a people of the Book.

Ezra is the most famous representative of this group of scribes, and perhaps its founder. His ministry in Judah is a beautiful illustration of the purpose of Jewish scholarship, and of the important role generations of rabbis played in encouraging faithfulness to the Lord.

Overview

Ezra's journey from Babylon was summarized (7:1-10). Ezra recorded his commission from Artaxerxes (vv. 11-28), listed his companions (8:1-14), and gave details of the journey (vv. 15-36). In Judah, Ezra's prayer confessing Judah's intermarriage with foreigners (9:1-15) brought repentance, and the foreign wives were divorced (10:1-44).

Understanding the Text

"This Ezra came up from Babylon" Ezra 7:1-10. Ezra had had no opportunity to minister as a priest in Babylon. The temple rested in a faraway land. Though Ezra was uniquely equipped by his lineage to serve God as a priest, his circumstances made this impossible. But Ezra did have the Scriptures, and determined to serve God by studying them.

Ezra's problem, and his solution, have application to us today. For instance, some churches limit women to certain roles, even when they are equipped for other ministries. Ezra reminds us that a person who is determined to serve the Lord will find a way—and possibly have an even greater impact in that role than in the role he or she is denied!

"Now I decree" Ezra 7:11-28. The Persian ruler Artaxerxes I issued this decree in 458 B.C., and Ezra began the 900-mile journey the first of Nisan (March/April).

The decree explains the purpose of the expedition: Ezra was to bring offerings from the Jews in Babylon to the temple, and offerings from the king himself. Levites and priests who accompanied Ezra were exempted from taxes. Most significant, Ezra was authorized to see that God's Law served officially as the "law of the land," and to appoint judges to administer that law. Ezra's authority in Jewish affairs was thus absolute: "Whoever does not obey the law of your God and the law of the king must surely be punished by death, banishment, confiscation of property, or imprisonment."

Judah was no longer an independent kingdom. But under the enlightened rule of Persia, God's Old Testament Law would be better enforced than under many of Judah's own kings!

"I was ashamed to ask the king for soldiers" Ezra 8:15-36. It's clear that Ezra had represented the Lord as all-powerful to the rulers of Persia. How could he then ask to be protected on the long, dangerous journey by a guard of soldiers?

Rather than turn to the king, Ezra turned to God. He called his company to join him in prayer and fasting.

Ezra acted in what some might call a foolish way. He had announced that his God helps "everyone who looks to Him." Now Ezra had to "put up, or shut up."

Sometimes we hesitate to make claims about what God can do. What if we make some claim, and God doesn't come through? Ezra reminds us that God *can* and *will* care for His own. Speaking out about who God is and what He can do for those who love Him is not foolishness, but faith.

"While Ezra was praying and confessing" Ezra 10:1-44. On arriving, Ezra discovered that

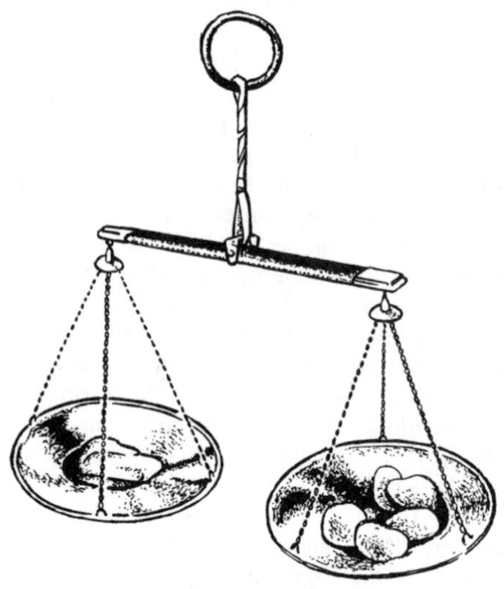

Balance Scales

Ezra 8:24-30 records the weights of gifts donated for transport to God's house. Many archeological finds demonstrate how carefully royal archivists weighed and recorded gold, silver, and commodities.

many in Judah had married foreign wives and had children by them, in clear violation of Old Testament Law. Ezra's anguished confession moved the people of Judah. Soon a large crowd was weeping and praying with him. As the spirit of conviction spread, all Judah assembled in Jerusalem. Ezra confronted them with God's prohibition against such marriages. The people confessed their sin, set up an investigating commission, and forced all who had married foreign wives to "send away all these women and their children."

The event suggests a number of lessons for you and me. First, we are more likely to move others to confession by taking sin to heart, and weeping over it, than by being judgmental. Second, while it may have been painful to break up families, it was necessary. God's people were to retain their racial purity. Third, the pain of separation could have been avoided by keeping God's Law in the first place. If the men named had not married foreign wives, no breakup of families would have followed.

Let's remember, when we are moved

by sympathy for those who suffer pain as a consequence of some sin, that the pain could have been avoided.

▶ DEVOTIONAL
Pointing the Finger
(Ezra 9:1–10:4)

It's tempting, when someone we know sins, to come down hard on him. After all, we're to discipline erring brothers, aren't we? The more blatant the sin, the more justified we feel confronting or criticizing.

Yet Ezra reminds us that it's not appropriate to point the finger of judgment. What is appropriate when others sin is tears. Not tears for them. Tears that *we* have let God down. Tears that we, the people of God, have failed.

When Ezra arrived in Judah, he learned that many Jews had taken foreign wives. This was a clear violation of Old Testament Law, and Ezra was appalled. But rather than strike out angrily at those who had sinned, Ezra identified himself with the sinners and confessed to the Lord. He did not speak of "their" guilt, but of "our guilt" (9:7). He did not condemn "their" disregard for God's laws, but cried out that "we have disregarded the commands" (v. 10). Rather than stand self-righteously in judgment, Ezra cried, "Not one of us can stand in Your presence" (v. 15). Ezra's heart was broken by the sin he found, and he accepted partial responsibility for the failure of men he had never even met.

We can't read Ezra's prayer of confession in this chapter without sensing the depth of this godly man's sense of anguish and shame. He was deeply hurt by the sins of his people: hurt for them, and for God. The reality of Ezra's hurt, expressed openly in weeping, prayer, and confession, moved the men and women of Judah to confess as well—and to purge the sin from their lives.

So next time you or I see sin in the body of Christ, let's not point the finger. Let's realize that if the church was what God called it to be, and if we were the Christians God called us to be, our brother or sister might not have fallen. Rather than judge, we need to let our hearts be broken, that through confession of our responsibility for one another God might purge the church as He did Judah in Ezra's time.

Personal Application

We are to grieve over other's sins as well as over our own.

Quotable

"The world doth scoff at what I now say, namely that a man may weep for his neighbor's sin as for his own, or even more than for his own, for it seems to be contrary to nature. But the love which brings this about is not of this world."—Angela of Foligno

---

The Variety Reading Plan continues with NEHEMIAH

Nehemiah

INTRODUCTION

This book continues the story of the Jews who came back to Judah after the Babylonian Captivity. Nehemiah, an important official in the Persian Empire, asked for the post of governor of tiny Judah in order to rebuild Jerusalem's walls. He arrived for his first term in that office in 444 B.C., almost 100 years after the first group of exiles returned. He succeeded despite much opposition and, with the aid of Ezra, also carried out spiritual reforms. Nehemiah serves today as a model leader and model man of prayer.

OUTLINE OF CONTENTS

I. Nehemiah Rebuilds Jerusalem's Walls . . . . Neh. 1:1–7:3
II. Nehemiah Institutes Reforms . . . . Neh. 7:4–10:39
III. Nehemiah Repopulates Jerusalem . . . . Neh. 11–13

READING GUIDE (3 Days)

If hurried, you may read only the "core passage" in your Bible and the Devotional in each chapter of this Commentary.

Reading	*Chapters*	*Core passage*
97	1–3	1:1–2:6
98	4–7	5
99	8–13	13

Nehemiah

APRIL 7 *Reading 97*
NEHEMIAH'S MISSION
Nehemiah 1–3

> *"Send me to the city in Judah where my fathers are buried so I can rebuild it" (Neh. 2:5).*

Nehemiah's concern for the state of the city of Jerusalem was in fact concern for the glory of God. The Holy City was in disrepair. Nehemiah's mission was to restore the city that God had chosen to represent His name.

Background

City walls. In the ancient world a city without walls was vulnerable to enemy attack, and thus insignificant. Only a walled city was considered respectable. This perception explains Nehemiah's grief when he heard that Jerusalem's walls were broken down and its gates burned, and also explains Nehemiah's references to the Jews' "troubles" and "disgrace." By rebuilding the walls of the city, Nehemiah would force the surrounding peoples to respect the Jews and to respect Israel's God.

Overview

Nehemiah was moved at a report of Jerusalem's ruined condition (1:1-4). After prayer (vv. 5-11), he begged King Artaxerxes to appoint him governor of Judah (2:1-10). In Judah he rallied local support (vv. 11-20) and set the people to work rebuilding the city walls (3:1-32).

Understanding the Text

"I mourned and fasted and prayed" Neh. 1:1-4. Nehemiah was secure in an important position in Susa, then the capital of the Persian Empire. Yet when he heard about conditions in Judah, he was brokenhearted.

Not every Christian can be a wall-builder. But each of us can have Nehemiah's concern for the welfare of fellow believers. First Corinthians 12 calls on us to view the church as a body, in which each believer is intimately linked with every other Christian. Thus the apostle writes, "If one part suffers, every part suffers with it" (v. 26).

Not every Christian can be a wall-builder. But each of us can pray. When we hear of others in need, the most important thing we can do for them may well be to follow Nehemiah's lead, and express our concern in heartfelt prayer.

And let's remember. Nehemiah's great ministry began with this prayer. If you or I wish to become spiritual leaders, we must begin where Nehemiah began. With prayer.

"The place . . . chosen as a dwelling for My Name" Neh. 1:5-11. Nehemiah's prayer acknowledged the sin which led to Jerusalem's destruction. Yet Nehemiah remembered that God had chosen Jerusalem as a "dwelling for My Name." The phrase means that God had chosen to identify Himself with the Holy City. Thus the glory of God was intimately linked with the condition of the city. The ruined condition of the city walls not only indicated hardships experienced by the Jews in Judah, but also cast a shadow that disguised the glory of God.

This is another important aspect of prayer. Prayer rightly expresses concern for brothers and sisters in need. But prayer is also to reflect concern for the glory of God. We urge God to act, not only that we may be blessed, but that He may be glorified.

First John observes that "if we ask anything according to [God's] will, He hears us" (5:14). Nehemiah gives us a simple way to check whether our prayers are in God's will. Does a prayer express concern for others? Does a prayer seek an answer which will glorify God? If the answer to these questions is yes, we can be confident that our prayer is in God's will.

"I was cupbearer to the king" Neh. 2:1-6. In ancient times the "cupbearer" had an important post in the administration of an empire. The holder of the office had direct access to the king, symbolized by the privilege of handing the ruler his cup at official banquets and functions. Thus Nehemiah was a very important person in Persia, whose services were highly valued by the king.

How fascinating that Nehemiah was willing to exchange the honor of this post for the relatively insignificant title of governor of tiny Judah! Yet Nehemiah did not look at it this way. To him the importance of the post depended on the importance of the person he served. In Susa he served the ruler of the mighty Persian Empire. But in tiny Judah, Nehemiah would serve God.

Let's remember this truth and grasp its meaning for us. The simplest Sunday School teacher is far more significant than a person on the President's staff, for the God he or she serves is far greater than any mere man.

"The king granted my requests" Neh. 2:7-10. Nehemiah attributed the king's permission to go to Judah and rebuild its walls to God's favor. We can thank others who help us. But when our requests have been preceded by earnest prayer we realize the help is evidence of God's grace.

"I also told them about the gracious hand of my God upon me and what the king had said" Neh. 2:11-20. When Nehemiah arrived, he surveyed the walls to discover how great the ruin was. Despite the heaps of shattered stone and burned timbers, Nehemiah then challenged the Jews to "come . . . rebuild the wall."

How did Nehemiah succeed in enlisting their aid? Rather than order, he encouraged. And he encouraged by (1) telling what God had already done, and (2) confidently predicting that "the God of heaven will give us success."

Effective spiritual leaders realistically evaluate difficulties. But they keep the attention of everyone on the Lord, seeking to build confidence in Him.

"The next section was repaired by the men of Tekoa" Neh. 3:1-32. Nehemiah showed effective leadership in his plan for rebuilding. Teams were formed and given specific responsibilities. The fact that each team is named here shows that Nehemiah was careful to give credit for accomplishments.

Effective leaders learn from Nehemiah to assign ministry teams specific missions, and to give them credit by name for all they accomplish.

▶DEVOTIONAL
Spiritually Prepared (Neh. 1:1–2:6)

One of the sermons I remember hearing when I was young was on Nehemiah 2:3-4. Our pastor pointed out that Nehemiah must have been a fast pray-er. The king asked him a question, "What is it you want?" And the text says, "Then I prayed to the God of heaven, and I answered the king." You can bet Nehemiah didn't keep the king waiting for an answer for two minutes while he slipped out to pray. What Nehemiah did was to aim a quick prayer toward heaven, and answer the king immediately.

As I remember, the point of the sermon was to encourage frequent, brief prayers offered during the day. Something like my wife's habit of asking God for a parking space when she drives to the mall. And her more significant prayer for protection as she watches five or six cars on our dangerous Highway 19 zoom through an intersection after the light has changed.

I think the point is well taken. Prayers can be brief, pointed, and frequent. But looking at Nehemiah we realize that the brief, pointed prayer is not really enough. Nehemiah himself says that "for some days I mourned and fasted and prayed" before seeking permission to go to Judah. Yes, standing there holding the king's cup, Nehemiah did offer a brief prayer.

But Nehemiah had prepared spiritually for that critical moment during the preceding days.

Brief prayers are important. But they can never be the whole of our prayer life. It is taking significant time alone with God that provides the spiritual preparation we need to meet the emergencies of our life.

Personal Application
A vital prayer life prepares us to meet emergencies successfully.

Quotable
"For me, prayer means launching out of the heart towards God; it means lifting up one's eyes, quite simply, to Heaven, a cry of grateful love from the crest of joy or the trough of despair; it's a vast, supernatural force which opens out my heart, and binds me close to Jesus."—Therese De Lisieux

APRIL 8 *Reading 98*
OPPOSITION TO REBUILDING
Nehemiah 4–7

"They were all trying to frighten us, thinking, 'Their hands will get too weak for the work and it will not be completed' " (Neh. 6:9).

Nehemiah faced serious opposition. The way he met various challenges serves as a model for us today.

Overview
Nehemiah faced ridicule (4:1-5) and the threat of attack from Judah's neighbors (vv. 6-23). He also found injustices in Judah that delayed the work (5:1-19). Nehemiah avoided traps set by enemies (6:1-14) and completed the wall (vv. 15-19). After checking genealogies, he repopulated Jerusalem (7:1-73).

Understanding the Text
"Can they bring the stones back to life?" Neh. 4:1-5 The stone in Judah is a soft limestone. When fired, all moisture evaporates and even massive stones crumble into dust. The very idea that Nehemiah might "bring the stones back to life from those heaps of rubble" amused the surrounding peoples. They openly ridiculed the Jews, and joked about their efforts.

Ridicule can be discouraging, especially when we undertake a difficult task. Nehemiah's response serves us as a guide for dealing with ridicule. He prayed that God would "turn their insults back on their own heads." Nehemiah did not argue or defend his calling. He knew that God could bring success, and that success alone can silence ridicule.

"We rebuilt the wall till all of it reached half its height" Neh. 4:6-23. As the wall gradually rose, the ridicule of the Jews' enemies turned to angry hostility. No one likes to be proven wrong!

Hostility soon turned to open opposition, as the neighboring peoples plotted an attack on Nehemiah's work force. Nehemiah met the threat by showing determination, and by preparedness.

He showed determination by arming his men. This evidence that the Jews were ready to defend themselves frustrated the enemy, who had planned a sneak attack on defenseless people. A show of determination in the face of an enemy often avoids conflict.

Nehemiah did not rest on that initial bloodless victory. From that time on half the people stood guard while the other half worked. Trumpet signals were established so the whole group could respond to an attack on any section of the wall. When we know enemies surround us, we need to plan in advance how to meet any attacks.

"A great outcry against their Jewish brothers" Neh. 5:1-19. The work was also threatened by injustice in Judah's society. The wealthy oppressed the poor, and rather than follow God's laws, they loaned money at high interest, then claimed lands and forced families into servitude in payment of the debt.

Nehemiah confronted the practice, and won agreement by the whole congregation to stop the usury and to return seized lands.

Note that Nehemiah was able to confront this internal sin because he himself was blameless. Unlike other governors, who lived by taxing their subjects, Nehemiah had paid all the expenses of his office himself!

Leaders need to be blameless if they are to exhort others with integrity. Parents too must be sure when correcting children that they are setting a good example. Nehemiah was able to accomplish all that he did not because he had secular authority, but because of the moral force of his example of full commitment to God.

"He had been hired to intimidate me" Neh. 6:1-14. Three more attempts were made by the Jews' enemies to halt work on the wall.

They attempted to isolate Nehemiah so they could harm him (vv. 1-4). Nehemiah refused to abandon his mission even for a brief time. We need to concentrate on the task God has given us, and resist those who would harm the work by distracting us.

They attempted to frighten Nehemiah by accusing the Jews of rebellion (vv. 5-9). It's not unusual for Christians to be misrepresented and falsely accused. All they can do in such cases is to assert, as Nehemiah did, that the accusations are not true, and to continue their work.

They attempted to intimidate Nehemiah into an act of unbelief (vv. 10-14). Nehemiah rejected the so-called prophecy of one Jew, who wanted Nehemiah to lock himself up inside the temple for self-protection. If Nehemiah had fallen into this trap, he would have displayed a lack of that faith in God that he was exhorting, and forfeited the confidence of his people. If we are calling on others to trust the Lord, we must surely display trust in Him ourselves.

Each effort of the enemy failed to distract Nehemiah from his mission. The result of Nehemiah's faithfulness was successful completion of his mission.

"So the wall was completed" Neh. 6:15-19. The impossible task was accomplished! The enemies of God's people "lost their self-confidence," and God was glorified. Even the enemies realized that the work had been done with the help of the Lord."

When you and I are called to any ministry we can approach it as Nehemiah did—with steadfast faith, and the knowledge that when we succeed, it will all be to the glory of God.

"The city was large and spacious" Neh. 7:1-73. Most of those who had resettled Judah lived in smaller towns, where there were fields to cultivate. Jerusalem had been largely unpopulated. Nehemiah, after carefully consulting the genealogical records to ensure each family's claim, settled 1/10th of the people in the city (cf. 11:1-2).

Once again the children of Abraham, Isaac, and Jacob not only lived on lands promised them by God, but also occupied the city God chose as a resting place for His name.

▶ DEVOTIONAL

Danger! Danger! Danger! (Neh. 5)

A favorite TV show of mine, long even off reruns, was "Space Family Robinson." One of the characters was a rotund robot, who each show would sense some approaching threat and cry out, "Danger! Danger! Danger!"

The danger might be a meteor storm or a space pirate or the breakup of a planet. But it was always a threat that the family met and overcame together.

Reading Nehemiah 5 reminds us that the greatest dangers to God's family aren't from without, but from within. Nehemiah easily met outsiders' ridicule, their threats, and their attempts at intimidation. What really threatened his mission was injustice in Judah itself!

Wealthy Jews took advantage of their neighbors' poverty to defraud them. These injustices created more poverty, hunger, and despair. How could the people of Judah unite to build Jerusalem's walls when so many were distracted by their deep personal needs?

It's the same today in Christ's church. The greatest hindrance to accomplishing the mission Christ has set for us is sin. When we ignore the needs of our brothers and sisters, when we put money ahead of ministry, when we are insensitive to others' hurts, we defraud our brothers and sisters of the love that can meet their needs and bind the body together in unity.

Only when we cleanse ourselves of sin, and practice Christian love within our fellowships, will the church be ready for mission.

Personal Application
Sins of Christians must be addressed if we are to have an impact on our world.

Quotable
"Sixteen years ago, I talked about the desperate needs in other parts of the world. Now I tell Christians, wherever they are, that they must 'refall' in love with Jesus. Christianity in the West today says we must have a bigger church and bigger car and a better suit. Once Christians fall out of love with that and fall in love with Jesus, I won't need to talk mission: they will become missionaries because they love Him."—Helen Roseveare

APRIL 9 *Reading 99*
NEHEMIAH'S REFORMS
Nehemiah 8–13

"Day after day, from the first day to the last, Ezra read from the Book of the Law of God" (Neh. 8:18).

Nehemiah had restored the walls of the city. He then turned to his most important task: restoring the relationship of the people of Judah with God.

Overview
Ezra read and explained God's Word to the people of Judah (8:1-18). The people confessed sins (9:1-38) and determined to give God priority (10:1-39). Nehemiah resettled Jerusalem (11:1–12:27), and the people joyfully dedicated its restored wall (vv. 27-47). Later, returning for a second term as governor, Nehemiah found the people had failed to live up to their commitments and initiated further reforms (13:1-31).

Understanding the Text
"Day after day . . . Ezra read from the Book of the Law of God" Neh. 8:13-18. A highlight of the eight-day Feast of Booths (Tabernacles) reported here was daily reading of the Old Testament. By spending one fourth of the day in reading (9:3), Ezra was probably able to cover the entire five Books of Moses. This reading of Scripture laid the foundation for the spiritual renewal that Nehemiah was so eager to stimulate.

Nehemiah 8:8 says Ezra read from the Book of the Law "making it clear and giving the meaning so that the people could understand." The biblical text recorded on ancient scrolls is in Hebrew. By Ezra's time ordinary people spoke Aramaic, a related but different language. Ezra had to translate as well as explain the text!

Scripture still has power to lift us out of any spiritual low.

"They stood in their places and confessed their

sins and the wickedness of their fathers" Neh. 9:1-38. The reading of Scripture provided the people of Judah with perspective. The history of their fathers was one of persistent rebellion, yet one shaped by continual expressions of God's grace. The Jews were now "slaves in the land You gave our forefathers" to Gentile kings, who "rule over our bodies and our cattle as they please." And this was "because of our sins" (vv. 36-37).

The perspective provided by Scripture produced a dual response. First, the people acknowledged that their present "great distress" was a consequence of their own and their fathers' failure to obey God. Second, the people determined to make a formal "binding agreement" to obey God from that time onward.

Scripture still speaks in the same voice. We are convicted of sin, and at the same time called to commitment. Conviction leads to conversion—if we too hear and respond.

"All these now join their brothers . . . and bind themselves" Neh. 10:1-39. The religious reforms stimulated by Ezra and Nehemiah touched the whole people. The reforms reveal areas in which Judah had fallen short. There was a general commitment to "follow the Law of God," but specific promises were made to avoid marriage with neighboring peoples, to keep the Sabbath holy, and to actively support temple worship.

The very concept of "reform" means that we identify weaknesses and commit ourselves to correct them. Self-examination is important for believers of every age. Self-examination, however, must always have correction as its goal. Without renewed recommitment, confession alone is unlikely to transform.

"To live in Jerusalem" Neh. 11:1–12:26. The agricultural lands that supported the small Jewish community after the Exile lay far from Jerusalem. The now-walled city had been sparsely occupied, especially as the people had failed to pay the tithes which would have supported the priests and Levites who were supposed to minister at the temple.

To support themselves, these worship leaders had been forced to move out to their villages and till their own fields.

The repopulation of Jerusalem, while necessary for its security, was religiously motivated. This is seen in the emphasis in the text on priests, Levites, and other temple officers (11:10–12:28). All these persons would have to be supported by the tithe pledged by the rest of the community. Such sacrifice could be motivated only by a pure desire to worship and honor God.

Sacrifice remains a significant measure of our commitment to and love for the Lord. The giving of many Christians goes beyond tipping God out of their excess, to tightening their belts in order to contribute more.

"The dedication of the wall" Neh. 12:27-47. The text emphasizes the fact that the dedication of Jerusalem's walls was an occasion to "celebrate joyfully." As two choirs marched in opposite directions to meet before the temple, the whole community rejoiced "because God had given them great joy."

There were two sources of this joy. The first was external and visible. The people of God had successfully rebuilt the walls. This visible accomplishment not only honored the Lord, whose city Jerusalem was, but also boosted Jewish morale. The Jews were no longer despised by their neighbors, who realized that the work had only been achieved "with the help of our God" (6:16). We do live in a material universe. Visible accomplishments not only impress others, and thus testify to the reality of God, but also serve as a testimony to us. We have a right to be joyful over visible as well as strictly spiritual achievements.

Yet the great well from which Judah's joy flowed was inner and spiritual. God's people had confessed their sins to Him, and had recommitted themselves to serve Him. There was a great sense of spiritual well-being. All sensed that they were again right with God.

For you and me too, the ultimate source of joy is to be found in our relationship with the Lord. When we are right with Him, visible signs of His presence become less important to us. When we are right with God, we can rejoice even when external things go wrong.

"I was not in Jerusalem" Neh. 13. After a

productive first term as governor of Judah, Nehemiah returned to serve the King of Persia. During his absence the people drifted back into their old practices of mixed marriage, doing business on the Sabbath, and failing to support those who conducted temple worship.

Nehemiah did return, and immediately set things right again. Nehemiah's whole life reminds us of an important spiritual principle. Leaders are called to encourage others to complete commitment to God, and to help them maintain that commitment. Today, as in Nehemiah's day, we need leaders who will help us serve God wholeheartedly.

▶ DEVOTIONAL
Remember Me for This (Neh. 13)

Here, in the last chapter of the book that bears Nehemiah's name, we find the clearest expression of this great Old Testament leader's heart. In his "remember me" statements, Nehemiah identifies those actions which he sees as his most significant service for the Lord.

What is striking about the list is that nowhere does Nehemiah say, "Remember me, O Lord, for rebuilding Jerusalem's walls." The one accomplishment which his contemporaries might have seen as most important, isn't even mentioned!

It's helpful for us to remember this in a day when so many take pride in buildings—in founding universities, in constructing beautiful churches, or in building great networks over which the Gospel can be heard. Certainly these are worthy endeavors, just as building the wall of Jerusalem was a worthy and holy endeavor. Yet what we see in Nehemiah 13 is that these are not the most *important* of spiritual endeavors.

For Nehemiah, what was most important was promoting the worship of God (v. 14). It was helping Judah honor God by keeping the Sabbath Day holy (v. 22). It was insisting that those who served the Lord remain pure (v. 30). What counted most to Nehemiah was his impact for God on the lives of the men and women of his own time.

What a blessing to see this in Nehemiah. You and I may never stand among the great builders of our times. But we can stand, with Nehemiah, as persons who encourage the men and women among whom we live to worship the Lord better, to honor Him more fully, and to remain pure.

If we do, when the day comes that God honors His servants, you and I will stand beside Nehemiah among the most significant people of God.

Personal Application

It is more important to touch one life for God than to build a great city.

Quotable

"I believe that the reason of life is for each of us to simply grow in love. I believe that this growth in love will contribute more than any other force to establish the kingdom of God on earth."—Leo Tolstoy

---

The Variety Reading Plan continues with ESTHER

Esther

INTRODUCTION

The Book of Esther is set in the Persian capital of Susa. It tells the story of a vicious plot against the Jewish people that was thwarted by Esther, a young Jewish girl married to the empire's ruler, Xerxes. This victory of the Jews over Gentile persecutors, which took place in the 470s B.C., is commemorated by the Feast of Purim, still celebrated in our own day.

The Book of Esther is unique for its failure to mention God. Yet its messages shine clearly through as the story unfolds. God did take providential care of His Old Testament people, even when they lived outside the Promised Land. And, God works through circumstance as well as through miracles.

OUTLINE OF CONTENTS

READING GUIDE (1 Day)

If hurried, you may read only the "core passage" in your Bible and the Devotional in this Commentary.

Reading	*Chapters*	*Core passage*
100	1–10	6–7

Esther

APRIL 10 *Reading 100*
DELIVERANCE OF THE JEWS
Esther 1–10

> *"If you remain silent at this time, relief and deliverance for the Jews will arise from another place" (Es. 4:14).*

The doctrine of providence holds that God quietly works through cause and effect in the natural world to supervise events. The Book of Esther shows how a series of "coincidences" combined to deliver the Jewish people from an early, organized effort to exterminate the race.

Background

The author of Esther is unknown. But the number of Persian loan words in the book, and the lack of similar Greek terms, indicates it was written early, between 450–300 B.C. The events described took place in the reign of Xerxes, best known as the invader whose attacks on Europe were thrown back by the Greeks at Marathon. The feast mentioned in Esther 1 is probably the same feast mentioned by Greek historians as one Xerxes called to plan his conquest of the West.

The author is careful to let the story carry his message. He points to no event as the handiwork of God, and fails to criticize any of the questionable acts of either Esther or Mordecai. Yet through the story we see that God, even though unmentioned, sovereignly works out the deliverance of His people.

Definition of Key Terms

Providence. Providence is a term theologians use to express the conviction that God works out His purposes through natural processes in the physical and social universe.

In this universe every effect can be traced back to a natural cause. In the world of cause and effect there is no hint of miracles, and no need to bring God up to explain what happens. In the natural universe the most one can point to is coincidence: "What a coincidence that Esther happened to be queen just when Haman tried to exterminate the Jews!" Or, "What a coincidence that the king couldn't sleep one night, and that the portion of the annals of his kingdom that were read to him recorded how Mordecai had uncovered a plot against his life." The believer can say that God arranged the coincidences—the unbeliever scoffs because each event can be traced back to natural causes that "fully explain" what happened without reference to God.

The story told in the Book of Esther illustrates divine providence by identifying "coincidences" which led to the deliverance of the Jewish people from a plot to exterminate them. Because this is a book about providence, God is not mentioned. Yet the string of coincidences, leading so naturally to the deliverance, is so striking that His activity is clearly implied.

The God of the Old Testament is God of the Covenant. God is committed to care for His chosen people, Israel. Against the background of the covenant relationship of God with the Jews, the story's "coincidences" testify to the fact of His providential care.

What you and I learn from Esther is that God is always at work in the lives of His people. The seeming "coincidences" that mark our lives are not simply products of cause and effect or of random change. The coincidences that mark our lives are ordained by God, and are intended for our good.

Overview

Esther was chosen as Xerxes' queen (1:1–2:23). Her uncle, Mordecai, aroused the hatred of a high royal officer, Haman. Haman determined to destroy Mordecai's whole race (3:1-15). Mordecai enlisted Esther's reluctant help (4:1–5:14). Coincidentally Xerxes honored Mordecai for a forgotten service (6:1-14). Esther revealed she was one of the race Haman plotted to exterminate, and Haman was hanged (7:1-10). The Jews gained the right to protect themselves from their enemies (8:1-17). Many enemies of the Jews were slain (9:1-16), and Purim, celebrating deliverance, was instituted (vv. 17-32). Mordecai gained high rank in Persia, and used it to help the Jewish people (10:1-3).

Understanding the Text

"The king and his nobles were pleased with this advice" Es. 1:1–2:18. The first "coincidence" in the book is that of Queen Vashti's rebellion against her royal husband. The author traces the reasoning of those who advised Xerxes to divorce his wife and choose a new queen. Vashti's willfulness, and the reasoning of Xerxes' advisers, cleared the way for Esther to become Queen of Persia.

God is able to use the free acts and the uncoerced reasoning of unbelievers to shape events.

"Two of the king's officers . . . conspired" Es. 2:19-23. Mordecai thwarted a plot against Xerxes' life. This act, though unrewarded at the time, was destined to loom large in the future.

Our own actions, and the responses of others to them, become elements in God's providential plan. Let's not worry if we are unrewarded at the time. Frequently God's purposes are long-range.

"They cast the pur *(that is the lot)" Es. 3:1-15.* Haman reacted to what he felt was Mordecai's insult by determining to exterminate the whole Jewish people. He turned to the occult to fix a day for the attack on the Jews. The lot fell, supposedly by chance, on a distant date, far enough off to give Mordecai and Esther time to counter his plot.

God is able to turn even evil practices to His good purpose.

"Who knows but that you have come to royal position for such a time as this?" Es. 4:1–5:14 Mordecai enlisted the aid of a reluctant Esther. It was clear to him that God had placed her in a strategic place to influence Xerxes in favor of the Jews. Even Esther's hesitancy, as she put off the confrontation and invited Xerxes and Haman to supper with her, played a part in God's timing of events.

"What honor and recognition has Mordecai received?" Es. 6 Unable to sleep that night, Xerxes had the annals of his kingdom read to him. The reader "just happened" to read the report of Mordecai's exposure of the plot against Xerxes' life, and the king realized Mordecai had not yet been rewarded.

The next day Haman was himself forced to walk through the streets of Susa, leading one of the king's horses on which Mordecai rode! Haman, furious and frustrated, sensed that his plot was going wrong.

"This vile Haman" Es. 7–8. That night at supper Queen Esther accused Haman of plotting against her and her people. The furious king ordered Haman's execution—on the very gallows he had erected intending to hang Mordecai! Mordecai was permitted to write a decree in the king's name granting the Jews permission to defend themselves if attacked. (The earlier decree was not reversed because by custom Persian laws once made could not be changed.)

"Mordecai the Jew was second in rank to King Xerxes" Es. 9–10. The Jews were successful in defending themselves against their enemies. Purim was instituted as a festival of deliverance. And Mordecai went on to achieve the second highest rank in Persia, which he used to aid his people.

The plot Haman had against the Jews had not only been thwarted but was turned around, so that its effect was to promote the welfare of God's people rather than to harm them!

▶ DEVOTIONAL
Look Back
(Es. 6–7)

It was only looking back that Esther and Mordecai could clearly see the hand of God in what had happened to them. It's like that for us too. We seldom sense God's hidden guidance or protection as events unfold. But when we look back, we see His hand more clearly.

My mother used to read a magazine called *Revelation,* edited by Donald Grey Barnhouse of Philadelphia. When I joined the Navy I went to a school in Norfolk, and then, because I had graduated high in my class, picked a duty station in Brooklyn, New York. It just happened that Dr. Barnhouse taught a Monday night Bible class in a Lutheran church in Manhattan. My mother, reading about it in *Revelation,* suggested I go see him. I began to go each Monday, and was stimulated to begin serious personal Bible study. I started a Bible study on my base, and soon sensed God's call to the ministry.

Coincidences? Mom reading a magazine. Me, stationed in a city where the editor came weekly to conduct a Bible class? Through that class being moved to personal study, and then called to the ministry? The humanist would say, "Yes, nothing but coincidence. A different set of coincidences and you could have been launched on an entirely different career." Yet, looking back, I clearly see the hand of God, working providentially to draw me closer to Him, and guide me into my life's work.

And there are so many more ways that, looking back, I can see the good hand of God, even in things that when I experienced them seemed like tragedies.

Perhaps this is the secret of discovering God's work in your own life. Look back. Examine the coincidences that set you on each new course. And realize that God was at work in each, even those which at the time brought pain.

You see, the doctrine of Providence tells us that God is at work in the life of each of His covenant people. God's activity may be hidden. But it is very real. Look back, and you'll see it in your life. Look back, and you'll find evidence of the constant love of your Lord.

Personal Application

God is at work on your behalf right now, through the coincidences of your life.

Quotable

"Trusting in Him who can go with me, and remain with you, and be everywhere for good, let us confidently hope that all will yet be well."—Abraham Lincoln

---

The Variety Reading Plan continues with EPHESIANS

Job

INTRODUCTION

Set in the second millennium B.C., when wealth was measured in cattle and the patriarch served as family priest, the epic of Job explores the relationship between human suffering and divine justice. Job, a righteous man, was crushed by sudden disasters. His three friends argued that God was punishing him for some hidden sin. Job resisted, but could find no alternate explanation for what had happened to him. In a lengthy poetic dialogue marked by the most difficult Hebrew in the Old Testament, Job and his friends struggled to understand the ways of God and the meaning of human suffering.

Though there are many examples of similar literature in the ancient East, Job is set off from them by its vision of God and its in-depth exploration of the issue of suffering. It is impossible to establish a date for the writing of this epic or to know its author.

OUTLINE OF CONTENTS

I. Disasters Strike Righteous Job . . . . Job 1–3
II. Job Dialogues with Three Friends . . . . Job 4–31
   A. Did God cause Job's suffering? . . . . Job 4–14
   B. Do the wicked really suffer? . . . . Job 15–21
   C. Had Job committed hidden sins? . . . . Job 22–31
III. Elihu Breaks the Impasse . . . . Job 32–37
IV. God Speaks Out . . . . Job 38–42

READING GUIDE (5 Days)

If hurried, you may read only the "core passage" in your Bible and the Devotional in each chapter of this Commentary.

Reading	*Chapters*	*Core passage*
101	1–14	1–2
102	15–21	21
103	22–27	25–27
104	28–37	33
105	38–42	42

Job

INTRODUCTION

[illegible]

OUTLINE OF CONTENTS

[illegible]

READING SCHEDULE

[illegible]

Job

APRIL 11 *Reading 101*
JOB'S ANGUISH
Job 1–14

> *"I have no peace, no quietness; I have no rest, but only turmoil" (Job 3:26).*

Job's inner anguish mirrors our own when we are struck by some unexpected tragedy and struggle to understand why.

Background

The Structure of the book. Job begins and ends with brief prose sections. The opening portrays God giving Satan permission to attack Job in an effort to make Job curse the Lord. Satan stripped Job of his possessions, family, and health, but failed the challenge as Job worshiped rather than cursed God.

The book then moves to an extended poetic exploration of God's role in human suffering. Job and his three friends believed God punishes sin. Job's friends concluded that Job had sinned. But Job was sure he had not knowingly done wrong. As the dialogues probed the question of suffering, Job found himself confronting not only his three friends but his own assumptions about God.

The dialogue ended in an impasse, which was broken by a younger listener, Elihu. He pointed out that God sometimes uses suffering to instruct, not to punish. Thus Job's suffering did not necessarily mean he had sinned, nor did it mean God is unjust.

God Himself then spoke, not to explain what He had done, but to point out that His nature is beyond human comprehension.

Job then repented and was commended by God. The Lord restored Job's health, doubled his wealth, and blessed him with a new family and lengthened life.

While the outline of this story is simple, the contents of the book are profound, probing as they do one of the most basic issues in human experience.

Overview

The setting is established: God permitted Satan to take Job's wealth, his family, and his health (1:1–2:10). Job shared his feelings with three friends (v. 11–3:26). In a cycle of attacks and defenses, each friend proclaimed God's justice, and suggested that Job deserved what had happened to him (4:1–5:27; 8:1-22; 11:1-20). Job defended himself against all of their charges (6:1–7:21; 9:1–10:22; 12:1–14:22).

Understanding the Text

"This man was blameless and upright" Job 1:1-5. The phrase does not mean Job was sinless. The Hebrew word for "blameless," *tamim,* indicates a person whose motives are pure and who lives a good moral life. Job's wealth may have impressed his neighbors. But his reverent awe for God and his decision to shun evil are keys to his character.

What shocks us is that terrible trouble could strike such a godly man. We feel that if Job is vulnerable, surely each of us is.

This is one of the important messages of Job. Relationship with God does not guarantee an easy life. Our relationship with God is more significant than that!

"Have you considered My servant Job?" Job 1:6–2:11 God is the One who drew Satan's attention to Job, and gave him permission to cause the devastating series of tragedies

that struck Job on a single day.

Satan contended that Job honored God only because God had given him material blessings. Satan claimed Job would "curse You to Your face" if God permitted Satan to take those blessings away.

Job did not act as Satan expected, but instead worshiped, acknowledging God's right to take what He had given (1:20-21).

Satan then claimed Job would curse God if his own life were threatened. So God permitted Satan to afflict Job with a painful and loathsome disease. Again Job refused to curse God, saying, "Shall we accept good from God, and not trouble?" (2:10)

At this point Satan passed from the scene, defeated, and is not mentioned again. But Job's suffering continued, showing us that God had His own purposes in permitting the satanic attack on Job.

One reason that God permits Christians to suffer is to display the reality of relationship with the Lord. Believers suffer when hurt, as other human beings do. But our continuing faith in God's goodness testifies to all that God does make a difference. God is glorified as Christians continue to hope in the Lord despite suffering. Like Christ, at this stage of the story Job has "entrusted himself to Him who judges justly" (1 Peter 2:23).

"Why did I not perish at birth?" Job 3:1-26 Three friends who visited Job were so shocked at his condition that they sat, silent, for seven days. At last Job opened the dialogue.

Job's earlier words had expressed his beliefs. Now he shared his feelings, and we discern an anguish so great that Job wished he had never been born.

It's not wrong for a gap to exist between what we believe and our emotions. Intellectually Job realized that God is free to act as He chooses. Emotionally Job was in the grip of anguish and fear.

When suffering strikes us, we often respond as Job did. We do trust in God. But our emotions are in turmoil, and we have "no peace, no quietness, no rest" (see v. 26). Such emotion is natural, for at best we human beings are finite, limited, and weak. How encouraging to realize through Job's experience that faith and fear can be present at the same time. Emotional turmoil is not evidence of a lack of faith, but rather an opportunity for us to affirm the reality of what we believe despite our feelings.

"Who, being innocent, has ever perished?" Job 4:1–5:27 Eliphaz, one of the three friends, was unable to respond to the powerful emotions Job had shared. Instead he brought up a point of theology. It's not the upright who are destroyed, but those who "plow evil" (4:7-8). Job must appeal to the God who corrects, and who can heal (5:17-18). If Job were right with God, the Lord would have protected him from disaster and Job would know peace (vv. 20-27).

Many of us, like Eliphaz, listen for concepts and not feelings. Eliphaz did not respond to Job's feelings or even acknowledge them. He might have said, "Job, I know you're hurting. I hear how devastating this is to you, and I do care." Instead Eliphaz jumped in with an oblique accusation, suggesting that Job's suffering must be his own fault.

When you or I respond to a person who is suffering with a theological statement, even with pious reassurance that "God must have a purpose in something so terrible," we miss our opportunity to minister. What a sufferer needs to know is that someone *cares.* An experience of the love of God through a caring friend is the first and greatest need of those who suffer.

"If only my anguish could be weighed" Job 6:1–7:21. Job tried again to share his feelings and his tormented thoughts. He felt cut off from God, and crushed by Him (6:8-10). As a despairing man Job had hoped for a sign of devotion from his friends, not accusations.

Job continued to focus on his feelings, speaking out "in the anguish of my spirit" and complaining in the "bitterness of my soul" (7:11). Life had lost all meaning for Job. He could not understand what he had done to God to deserve what had happened, or why, if he had sinned, God did not simply forgive him (vv. 17-21).

In this speech, part of which is directed to the Lord, Job expressed the doubts and uncertainties which tormented him even more than the loss and pain. Job's experience again helps us identify what happens within us when tragedy strikes. The very foundation of our existence—our conviction that God is good—is brought into question.

If we understand this we can accept our own doubts and uncertainty without feelings of guilt. And we can empathize with others who experience tragedy.

"How long will you say such things?" Job 8:1-22 Bildad was uncomfortable with Job's self-revelation. To protect himself from the flood of emotions, he too turned to theology. Bildad was unwilling to accept what Job felt because those emotions seemed to imply that the Almighty "pervert[s] what is right" (v. 3).

Bildad's solution? "Surely God does not reject a blameless man" (v. 20). If Job got right with God, the Lord would "yet fill your mouth with laughter and your lips with shouts of joy" (v. 21).

Bildad's error was a common one. He assumed that he knew so much about God he could speak for Him! "God doesn't reject the blameless" is transformed from a general truth to an unbreakable rule, binding God's own freedom of action. Bildad never once imagined that he might not know God well enough to explain the Lord's purposes in Job's life!

When you and I know others who suffer, we must avoid Bildad's error. We can't explain "why" because we are not wise enough to grasp God's purposes in another person's life. All we know for sure is that God loves all human beings, and that He does have a purpose in what happens to each one.

"I know that this is true" Job 9:1–10:21. Job was aware that what his friends had said was true. But this only made his torment greater. Job believed himself blameless (9:21), and thus had no explanation for what had happened to him. It was this that made his anguish so bitter! He couldn't even plead his case with God, for God had not brought any charges against him.

Again Job was forced to question the meaning of life itself. Why had he even been born? How much better it would have been if Job had died in infancy!

"Will no one rebuke you?" Job 11:1-20 Job's third friend was outraged by this talk. God must not be questioned!

But Zophar couldn't resist suggesting that Job must have sinned to suffer so, and that if Job would only "put away the sin that is in your hand" life would be brighter, for God would relieve his suffering.

Again, be warned. The person who assumes that he knows another individual's heart, much less understands all of God's ways, is almost certain to be wrong. To take such a position is spiritual pride, surely as great a sin as any we accuse others of committing.

"What you know, I also know" Job 12:1–14:22. Job responded with sarcasm. Job too knew the general truths about God that his friends had used against him. But Job also knew that in his case suffering could not be punishment for some known sin. Again Job addressed his complaint to God. Human beings are so weak. Why did God do this to him? Why not just permit Job to die and so avoid the brunt of what he experienced as the anger of God?

Again we sense the anguish that any believer experiences when his or her suffering cannot be explained. We know general truths about God. But we cannot know the specific reasons for what is happening to us. And suffering *feels like* God's anger, directed against us, rather than feeling like love.

How important to remember at such times that God does love us still.

▶ DEVOTIONAL
God's Hedge
(Job 1–2)

The doctor happened to look in on her as she lay in the labor room. What he saw brought a half dozen people on the run. My wife had suffered a massive placental separation, and only quick action by the doctor saved her and our daughter Joy.

There was only one problem. Joy had been without oxygen for several minutes. When she was born her face was blue, and the doctor warned that there might be brain damage.

There was. Today Joy, at 28, lives in a community for retarded adults in Arizona's Verde Valley. She will live there or in a similar facility all her life.

It's hard to express the bittersweet experience of bringing up a daughter who is strong and healthy, and yet suffers from irreversible retardation. Each visit is a reminder of what might have been, but can never be.

Yet at the same time each visit is a reminder that Joy is who God intended her to be. A young, strong, loving girl, who laughs and cries, rejoices and complains, who prays and sings and works up to her limited capabilities. Each visit is a reminder of Satan's complaint, recorded in Job 1:9. "Have You not put a hedge around him [Job]?" Haven't You protected him from me, so that I can't touch him or anything that he owns?

Satan's complaint portrays an important reality. God has put a hedge around every believer. He actively protects us from the dangers that threaten on every side. Only if God lowers the hedge—and that for His own purposes—can disaster strike.

When Joy was born, God lowered the hedge. I don't know why. But I believe He had His own good purpose. And I know that God raised the hedge again. God has protected our Joy, and given her as blessed a life as she could expect to live.

I can identify other times when God lowered the hedge around me. But each time the hedge has gone up again, and blessing has followed. Each time the hedge has gone down, I've become more aware of how often God's hedge has surrounded me and guarded me from harm.

Personal Application

When God lowers the hedge around you, consider the many more times you have had His protection.

Quotable

"How desperately people brush up their little faith in times of sorrow. It is quite easy to see that religious faith prospers because of, and not in spite of, the tribulations of this world. It is because this mortal life is felt as an irrelevancy to the main purpose in life that men achieve the courage to hope for immortality."—Reinhold Niebuhr

---

APRIL 12 *Reading 102*
DO THE WICKED PAY?
Job 15–21

> *"How often is the lamp of the wicked snuffed out? How often does calamity come upon them, the fate God allots in His anger?" (Job 21:17)*

Though Job's friends insisted differently, we all know, as Job knew, that every wicked man is not repayed in this life for his evil deeds.

Background

The fate of the wicked. Both Testaments describe God as a moral Judge who punishes the wicked and rewards the righteous. Job and his friends shared this view of God. But Job's friends assumed God must punish the wicked *in this life.* Thus it seemed to them that since Job was suffering so greatly, he must have sinned greatly.

Job knew he was innocent. And he had observed wicked people who prospered in this life. Their theology was nonsense, for it was contradicted by evidence they refused to even consider.

As the New Testament emphasizes, God does punish the wicked and reward the righteous. But not necessarily in this life. Yes, the books will be balanced. But this will take place only at history's end.

In this dialogue only Job seems to have eternity in view as he said, "I know that my Redeemer lives, and that in the end He will stand upon the earth. And after my skin has been destroyed, yet in my flesh I will see God" (19:25-26).

How tragic that some Christians adopt the simplistic view of Job's friends, and see all suffering as punishment for sin. God does permit innocent saints to suffer at times, and at times the wicked do prosper. The day of judgment, when all will be made clear, lies in the future. Until then we need to comfort, not accuse, our suffering brothers and sisters.

Overview

Eliphaz insisted that the wicked suffer terror and distress in this life, implying that Job must be wicked (15:1-35). Job replied that he had been upright, yet was assailed by God (16:1–17:16). Bildad picked up Eliphaz's theme, graphically describing the fate of the wicked (18:1-21). Job, upset by his friends' attacks, again shared feelings of abandonment (19:1-20). Yet he concluded with a magnificent affirmation of faith (vv. 23-27). Zophar added his own poem describing the ghastly fate of the wicked (20:1-29).

Job, after quoting his accusers, argued that in fact the wicked often prosper. The clichés his counselors used to imply Job is wicked were nonsence (21:1-34).

Understanding the Text

"Man, who is vile and corrupt" Job 15:1-35. Eliphaz was angry at Job for what he saw as arrogant self-defense. Eliphaz viewed man as sinful, while God acted as if bound by some fixed law, forced invariably to punish the rebel. There was no room in Eliphaz's theology for the notion that flawed human beings have value to God, or that God is moved by love rather than by a mechanical sense of justice which forces Him to react to each sin with appropriate, measured punishment.

Eliphaz's dialogue was filled with barbs hurled directly at Job. Again and again he brought up things that had happened to Job to illustrate punishments God directs against the wicked (cf. vv. 21; 1:17; 15:30, 34; 1:16; 15:28; 1:19; 15:29; 1:17).

Nothing causes us to rethink our concept of God like suffering. When suffering comes to us or to loved ones, we need to remember that our God is a God of love.

"Even now my witness is in heaven" Job 16:1–17:16. Job feared that he would die before his friends acknowledged his innocence. Thus he begged the earth not to cover his blood. Yet he was confident that witnesses in heaven knew he was right. Even though he felt devastated that "God assails me and tears me in His anger," he had hope that a heavenly friend and intercessor would testify to his righteousness and that he would be vindicated.

It's hard when friends wrongfully accuse us or misunderstand us. Then our hope, like Job's, is that ultimately we will be vindicated by the God who seems to attack us when we suffer.

"The lamp of the wicked is snuffed out" Job 18:1-21. Bildad continued the friends' effort to impose their views of God on Job. Once Job accepted their premise, that God only and always punishes the wicked, Job's defenses would crumble. He would doubt his own innocence, and no longer hold to what he considered his "integrity."

The image here is a powerful one. In Old Testament times a small lamp was kept burning in even the poorest homes all night long. A house with a snuffed-out lamp was an abandoned, empty house. Building on this image of desolation, Bildad described the calamities that befall the wicked.

We too are often tempted to use our theology—or a Bible verse—as a club to beat down the defenses of others. Surely Job's friends were wrong to attack Job in this way, rather than encouraging him with reminders of the love of God. Let's not err as they did in our use of God's Word.

"Those I love have turned against me" Job 19:19. Job's suffering, and his insistence that he had been wronged, had alienated not only his friends but even his loved ones.

Rather than treat Job with respect, even little children ridiculed him. His servants paid no attention to him, and his intimate friends detested him.

One of the most painful aspects of an illness or any other personal disaster is the impact it has on others' attitudes. The very time supportive love is most needed, friends and acquaintances back away.

It may be uncomfortable for us to spend time with persons like Job. But, as Job cried out, it is while people suffer that they have the greatest need for friends who will "have pity on me."

Again we're reminded that when another person is hurting is no time for theological discussion. What a hurting person needs is a hand to hold, a caring voice to listen to, and some evidence from friends that he or she is still loved and valued.

It is striking that Job, deserted by his friends, continued to have a strong faith in the God he felt has misused him. "I know that my Redeemer lives," Job affirmed. One day, long after this life was over, Job expected that "in my flesh I will see God."

▶ DEVOTIONAL
The Blessed Bad Guy
(Job 21)

Just now our newspaper is filled with reports of a battle between a man and his ex-wife over a multimillion dollar Lotto win. Scan the reports, and the impression grows that both these winners are "bad guys." From what each one says about the other—and I suspect both are right—each is a moral loser, selfish, and sinful.

It's just one more illustration of the bad guy striking it rich, while the poor, deserving Christian has to keep on struggling.

Of course, if Eliphaz or Bildad or Zophar read our local paper, they'd never see that article. All three were careful to reject any evidence that might call their theology into question.

That's what exasperated Job in the end, and led him to confront his friends. God always punishes the wicked? Honestly, "How often is the lamp of the wicked [really] snuffed out?" God crush the evil man? Be honest now! "Have you paid no attention" to the fact that the world over "the evil man is spared from the day of calamity"?

What Job finally shouted was, in effect, "Why don't you get *real!* Why don't you face facts? Why don't you consider what we all know, that sometimes bad guys actually are blessed? That the bad guys often hit the Lotto jackpot, while God's good guys struggle to make a living?"

Job's point was a good one. His friends preferred to distort reality in order to hold on to a flawed theology.

Later God would speak to Job's friends, and condemn them because "you have not spoken of Me what is right, as My servant Job has" (42:7). Job, who struggled to understand God despite confusing and even contradictory evidence, had "spoken of Me what is right." Job had been willing to challenge, not God, *but his beliefs about God.* Job's three friends took their beliefs for God Himself, and refused to reexamine them, even when clear evidence in their society called those beliefs into question.

This too is a lesson for you and me. Our trust is to be in God, not in our theology. Life constantly calls us to reexamine our beliefs about God, while holding firmly to the conviction that God exists, loves us, and is a rewarder of those who seek Him (Heb. 11:6). We can trust God completely. We should not have that same trust in our understanding of God's ways.

As Job's friends finally learned, the bad guy sometimes is blessed in this life, while the good guy suffers. When facts like these don't fit our theological pigeonholes, it's time to discard the holes and develop a better understanding of our Lord.

Personal Application

Don't be afraid to question your beliefs. God won't be upset. Really.

Quotable

"He permits His friends to suffer much in this world that instead He may crown them all the more gloriously in heaven, and make them more like His only begotten Son, who never ceased to do good and to suffer injury while He was on earth that He might teach us patience by His example."—Robert Bellarmine

APRIL 13 *Reading 103*
JOB'S CONDEMNATION
Job 22–27

"Is not your wickedness great? Are not your sins endless?" (Job 22:5)

Job's defense of himself and his disturbing questions about God's justice upset his friends. In their eyes such impious thoughts proved that Job must be numbered with the wicked.

Overview

Eliphaz was shocked at Job's apparent attack on God's justice (22:1-18), and urged Job to repent (vv. 19-30). Job complained bitterly that he was unable to meet with God or understand His purposes (23:1-17). Yet despite evidence to the contrary, Job remained convinced that God is a just Judge (24:1-25). Bildad affirmed the friends' belief that God is inaccessible to sinful man and so vindication is impossible (25:1-6). Job rejected this (26:1-4), and celebrated God's omnipotence (vv. 5-14). Taking his stand as a person falsely accused (27:1-12), Job affirmed his belief that God is just (vv. 13-23).

Understanding the Text

"Can a man be of benefit to God?" Job 22:1-18 Eliphaz was now convinced of Job's utter wickedness. How could Job even suggest that God might not immediately punish the wicked? Job could not possibly be vindicated by God, for the very fact that Job now suffered proved he had been a great sinner (cf. vv. 6-11). Job may have hidden his wickedness from men, but God saw what was happening even though He is veiled from our sight.

It is true that in his anguish Job had challenged his understanding of God's ways. But Eliphaz was wrong to take this as a rejection of God Himself. We too need to be careful not to take questioning for rejection, even when the questions seem as heretical to us as Job's questioning of God's justice did to Eliphaz.

"Submit to God and be at peace with Him" Job 22:19-30. Eliphaz was not without compassion. He still showed concern for his old friend, even though he was now convinced Job had always been a secret sinner. Eliphaz's solution was simple: Get right with God. If Job repented, "Then the Almighty will be your God." If Job repented, "You will pray to Him, and He will hear you."

How frustrating this advice must have been to Job, who knew that he *was* right with God! And how wrong Eliphaz was. Later Eliphaz himself would be forgiven only because God accepted the prayers of righteous Job on his behalf!

Eliphaz, who believed so firmly that God is a just Judge, missed one important point. If God truly is Judge, then human beings must leave judgment to the Lord. Eliphaz's complete misinterpretation of Job's suffering reminds us that we must withhold judgment when those around us go through trying times.

"If only I knew where to find Him" Job 23:1-17. Despite his anguish and doubts, Job wanted to find God, not run from Him! Job was convinced that God had been unfair to him, for, "My feet have closely followed His steps; I have kept to His way without turning aside." The blows that had struck Job had terrified him, and "made my heart faint." Yet despite his fear, Job actively searched for God.

Perhaps this is the greatest evidence of Job's godliness. Despite everything, Job wanted to draw close to God. Despite his fears, despite his conviction that God had not been fair, Job trusted God enough to want to know Him better, and was convinced that "when He has tested me, I will come forth as gold."

How wise Job was in this. Our one best response to trials is to draw closer to the Lord.

"God charges no one with wrongdoing" Job 24:1-25. In contrast to Eliphaz, who saw God bound by necessity to impose balanced punishment on sinners now, Job realized that God is free to act as He chooses. What Job did not understand was "Why does the Almighty not set times for judgment?" What principles does God follow in exacting punishment? Job agreed with his friends that God does judge. But experience proved that He does not always judge now.

It's important when questioning our beliefs to be clear about what we challenge. "God is Judge" is unmistakably affirmed in Scripture. How and when God judges may well be in doubt. To question the how and when of things isn't to challenge the basic truth. And, even if we find no answer to questions of how and when, there is no reason to discard the basic biblical truth.

"How then can a man be righteous before God?" Job 25:1-6 Bildad did not respond to Job, but made a significant statement. God was so pure that He can really have nothing to do with man, "who is but a maggot."

His statement was true, but distorted. Man is fallen, and in his sinful state "only a worm." Yet man was made in God's image, and God's grace reaches down to transform worms into the very image of God's own Son.

Job's view of himself as a righteous man, who has carefully obeyed God's laws and been committed to doing God's will, is in closer harmony with Scripture than the view of Job's friends that man is a maggot. God does not view us as worthless. And He does care when we honor Him by doing what is right.

"My tongue will utter no deceit. I will never admit that you are in the right" Job 26:1–27:23. Job's friends had spoken as if they took Job for a fool (26:1-4). Yet he knew fully the greatness of God (vv. 5-14). At the same time Job insisted that God had "denied me justice."

Job's friends believed he deserved all that had happened to him, and argued that Job's denials were an affront to the Lord. Job totally rejected this interpretation. To confess sin never committed would "deny my integrity." As long as he lived Job would "maintain my righteousness."

Job then eloquently affirmed God as a God of justice, the very theme that his friends had emphasized again and again. There is, however, a fascinating turn here. In Old Testament times, a person who falsely accused another of a crime was subject to the penalty for that crime. Job, the innocent, had been accused of wickedness by his friends. As God is a God of justice, wouldn't He impose on the friends the penalty for wickedness that they assumed was Job's due?

God does not hold guiltless the person who falsely accuses another, even when his or her motives may be the best.

▶DEVOTIONAL
Man, the Maggot
(Job 25–27)

There's something dreadfully wrong when the pregnant teen says, "I'm no good. I'm worthless. I'm no good at all."

There's something wrong when the drug addict shakes and quivers and mutters, "I'm nothin', man. Nothin'."

There's even something wrong when we open our hymnals and sing the familiar words, "Oh sacred head, now wounded . . . did He devote that sacred head for such a worm as I."

Oh, I know. We are sinners, every one. As Paul wrote in Romans, "I know that nothing good lives in me, that is, in my sinful nature" (Rom. 7:18). But this doctrine is very different from popular "maggot theology." Maggot theology says that because man is sinful, God doesn't really care what happens to us. Maggot theology insists that nothing a person can do can please God, or make any contribution to His glory. Maggot theology, exemplified by Eliphaz and Bildad, seeks to exalt God by demeaning man.

What's wrong with maggot theology? Just this. God made man in His own image, so every human being has worth and value in His sight. Because we are important to God, we human beings are intrinsically important! To view man as a maggot is to deny Scripture's revelation that man is the crown of creation.

Even more, to dismiss man as maggot is to trivialize the death of Christ. Jesus died to save individual human beings and to transform our race. If we were not vitally important in God's sight He would not have given up His Son for us.

Job did not accept maggot theology. Without understanding why, Job knew that it was important for him to maintain his integrity. Job could not have known about the contest in heaven, or that his stand made a contribution to the glory of God. Yet Job knew that *he* was important—so important that unfair treatment was wrong, and that denying himself would be as wrong as denying God Himself.

Today you and I need to realize that we truly are important to the Lord. He made us. Christ died for us. The way we live will either bring glory to God, or cause others to ridicule Him. Yes, we are sinners. But sinners or not, we are human beings, and every member of our race has value in the sight of our God.

Personal Application

Don't let a sense of sin destroy your awareness that you truly are important to God.

Quotable

"Our condition is most noble, being so beloved of the Most High God that He was willing to die for our sake, which He would not have done if man had not been a most noble creature and of great worth."—Angela of Foligno

APRIL 14 *Reading 104*
JOB'S INNOCENCE
Job 28–37

"Does He not see my ways and count my every step?" (Job 31:4)

Job's powerful defense portrays a practical piety that can serve you and me as a guide to godliness. And Elihu reminds us that suffering can be a gift.

Background

Elihu's contribution. Job and his friends had reached an impasse. They believed God punished the wicked. They believed that Job's torments were usually reserved for the wicked. The three friends concluded that Job had sinned. Job, who knew he had lived a godly life, believed that God was making him suffer unjustly. Elihu broke the impasse by showing that God may use suffering to correct or instruct. It was not necessary for Job's friends to condemn him without evidence, or for Job to despairingly conclude that God is unjust!

Elihu demonstrated that God may have purposes other than punishment in permitting human tragedies. Job still suffered. But he no longer had to feel that God was against him.

How important it is when we experience suffering to sense that God is bending near, definitely on our side.

Overview

The author inserted his own commentary on wisdom (28:1-28) before reporting Job's powerful affirmation of his innocence (29:1–31:29). Then a young listener, Elihu, spoke out (32:1-22). Both Job (33:1-33) and his friends (34:1-37) were wrong about God. The Lord is both just and considerate, and may use suffering redemptively as well as to punish (35:1–36:15). Moved by the thought that God cares enough to woo individuals "from the jaws of distress," Elihu concluded with a paeon of praise to God, who "does not oppress" (36:16–37:24).

Understanding the Text

"Where can wisdom be found?" Job 28:1-28 Many commentators believe this poem in praise of wisdom was penned by the author, not spoken by Job. If so, it reflects on the futility of the preceding argument of Job with his friends. Human beings can wrest precious metals from the earth, but only God has access to wisdom (cf. v. 23).

Archeologists have shown that many mining techniques utilizing vertical and horizontal shafts were used thousands of years before Christ. Man is able to find earth's hidden treasures, but wisdom, which lies in the realm of the spiritual, is beyond human reach. Yet God has revealed a way of wisdom that is simple and clear: "The fear of the LORD—that is wisdom, and to shun evil is understanding."

Like Job, you and I may not know the purposes God has in the things that happen to us. But we, also like Job, can choose to honor the Lord and live righteously. If we do, we will be wise as well as good.

"I dwelt as a king among his troops" Job 29:1-

25. Job recalled what life was like before he was stricken. He was honored, wealthy, treated with the utmost respect. Job fully expected life to go on this way for him, until he finally died of old age.

This is one of the most unsettling aspects of any tragedy—a death in the family, loss of employment, or a serious sickness. Hopes are shattered and our notion of what the future holds is mangled into uncertainty. At such times a person needs to sense God's supportive presence. No wonder Job suffered anguish. To Job, who felt that he was being punished, God had suddenly become both distant and unfair.

We can handle suffering if we are supported by a warm sense of God's presence and His love. Without this, suffering becomes unbearable.

"But now they mock me" Job 30:1-31. Job not only found himself suffering now, but found that everyone's attitude toward him had changed. Men mocked rather than honored him (vv. 1-15). God afflicted rather than blessed him (vv. 16-23). And no one helped or comforted as "the churning inside me never stops" (vv. 24-31).

Often those in the hospital feel their changed situation as intently as Job did his. A doctor friend of mine underwent surgery and extended follow-up treatment for cancer. He told me how awful it was for him, to go from being treated with the awe doctors are used to, to being told when to eat, when to sleep, when to roll over for another shot—all in a voice an adult might use with a young child.

How can we bear such attacks on our personhood? Only with loving support from others, and with the assurance that comes from knowing God still loves and values us.

"If I have walked in falsehood" Job 31:1-40. This chapter contains a "negative confession." Each "if" statement explains what Job did *not* do. Looking at them, we gain a clear picture of a virtuous life as lived by an Old Testament saint.

Studying this passage, you and I can learn how to "shun evil," which Job 28:28 calls true and godly wisdom.

"Elihu had waited before speaking" Job 32:1–33:7. In Old Testament times older persons were viewed with respect. In that culture it was expected years of experience would make a person wise. Out of respect for his elders Elihu, a young observer, had kept quiet until now. But he had become increasingly agitated as he saw flaws in the positions taken by both Job and his friends.

Elihu has been criticized by commentators for being wordy and redundant. Yet, as Elihu pointed out, sometimes even younger folk, who aren't used to organizing their thoughts as well as others, are given insights by the Spirit of God (33:1-4).

Elihu reminds us that God can speak to us through others—even our children! We are not to judge the validity of what a person says by his or her age, race, or background.

"You have said" Job 33:8–36:26. Unlike Job's friends, Elihu did not conclude that Job had sinned. Elihu did say that Job was wrong speaking of God as he had when defending himself, and frequently quoted Job's words (cf. 32:12; 33:1, 31; 34:5-7, 35-36; 35:16). Job had concentrated on God's justice. In so doing, he had overlooked God's love and compassion. Job had to try to see his suffering in the context of love, not of justice.

In view of God's love, suffering must be intended for good, perhaps to bring the wicked to repentance and blessing (36:5-15). Without making any judgment as to why God had permitted Job to suffer, Elihu suggested God's purpose was compassionate and redemptive.

We need to adopt Elihu's perspective when we experience suffering. We too need to filter our pain through a vision of God as loving rather than of God as Judge.

"Who can understand?" Job 36:27–37:24 Elihu was moved to conclude with praise of God's power and wisdom. How great God is! How His wisdom surpasses anything to which mere man can aspire!

No human being can hope to understand God's purposes, for He and they are "beyond our reach." We can only remember that "He does not oppress." Should suffering come, we must trust ourselves to God, remembering that He is truly concerned for all who know Him.

▶DEVOTIONAL
Shine on Me
(Job 33)

More Americans died in the Civil War than in all the other wars in which the United States has been involved, combined. Families lost husbands, fathers, and sons. Some 26 percent of the men in the South perished in the struggle, and by the end of the war many women and children there were literally starving. Those years, 1861–1865, were marked by intense suffering all over the United States.

Yet during the war the South, and particularly its army, was swept by revival, as many thousands came to know Christ. Against the background of suffering and spiritual renewal, a letter found on the body of a Confederate soldier shows how, in the darkest times, the light of God shines on us.

I asked for strength that I might achieve.
He made me weak that I might obey.
I asked for health that I might do greater things.
I was given grace that I might do better things.
I asked for riches that I might be happy.
I was given poverty that I might be wise.
I asked for power that I might have the praise of men.
I was given weakness that I might feel the need of God.
I asked for all things that I might enjoy life.
I was given life that I might enjoy all things.
I received nothing that I asked for.
All that I hoped for.
My prayer was answered.

Personal Application

Mine the silver of God's good gifts from the ore of your suffering.

Quotable

"God whispers to us in our pleasures, speaks in our conscience, but shouts in our pains: it is His megaphone to arouse a deaf world."—C.S. Lewis

APRIL 15 *Reading 105*
RESTORED BLESSINGS
Job 38–42

"The LORD blessed the latter part of Job's life more than the first" (Job 42:12).

The New Testament invites us to consider Job's experience, and realize that "the Lord is full of compassion and mercy" (James 5:11).

Overview

God challenged Job to consider His wisdom (38:1–39:30) and His power (40:1–41:34). Job repented (42:1-6). God restored and multiplied Job's blessings (vv. 7-16).

Understanding the Text

"On what were its footings set?" Job 38:1–39:30 God challenged Job to consider His wisdom, and realize how limited man's understanding is. On the surface God's theme seems to be His lordship over nature. He is Creator (38:4-15). He rules the inanimate universe (vv. 16-38). He rules the animate as well (38:39–39:30). In the passage God raised questions about the universe that puzzle even modern science! What is the foundation of matter, space, and time? (38:6) What patterns earth's climate? (vv. 22-30) How are instincts built into living creatures? (39:1-18) These and a myriad of other questions cannot be answered by human beings.

We need to realize the limits of our understanding and appreciate God's wisdom. It is futile to raise questions of "why?" when suffering comes. We must remember that God knows what He is doing, and put our trust in Him.

"Would you discredit My justice?" Job 40:6–41:34 God's next monologue is more

than an affirmation of His raw power. In the ancient world both "Behemoth" and "Leviathan" represented forces of evil in the world. Job was challenged to "look at every proud man and bring him low" (40:5-14). Job could not deal with wicked human beings! But God controls the very forces of evil represented by the two beasts (40:15-24; 41:1-34). In powerful symbolism God affirmed that He is moral Ruler of the universe. He can and does punish the wicked.

"I despise myself and repent in dust and ashes" Job 42:1-6. Before this revelation of God's wisdom and His rule of the moral order, Job could do nothing but repent. True, he had lived a blameless life. But he had been wrong to even think of God as unjust.

Repentance is not a negative in the Bible, even though people tend to think of it as somewhat shameful. To repent is to change one's mind or direction. Job now admitted that he had been wrong about God.

God is not upset when we are wrong about Him. This is why He is so careful to instruct us, so that we might know Him better. Through suffering Job had gained, not an answer to "why?" but a better understanding of God. Who can say that knowing God better isn't worth all the suffering Job—or you and I—may have to bear?

"As My servant Job has" Job 42:7-9. Job was commended by God for speaking "what is right." How could this be, when Job had been shown to be wrong, and repented?

The answer is found in Job's determination to face reality. Job's friends sounded pious, but they did not trust God enough to honestly examine evidence that He does not punish every wicked person here and now. They had *not* spoken of God "what is right," and were forgiven only through the agency of Job's prayers. Job did trust God enough to be honest with the facts as he knew them, even though these facts seemed to cast doubt on God's justice.

We needn't be afraid to struggle with hard questions in life, or in the Bible. God does have answers, whether or not we know what these answers are.

"Seven sons and three daughters" Job 42:10-17. God blessed Job throughout many added years of life. Every symbol of that blessing mentioned here is doubled—except the number of his children. Ten had died, and he was given 10 more.

Why? Because Job's first 10 children had not been lost, but would be with him in eternity. Along with such verses as 19:26, "After my skin has been destroyed, yet in my flesh I will see God," this clearly implies an early belief in resurrection.

It reminds us too that the blessings Job received are symbolic of the blessing we will surely know, if not here, when we are with Christ.

▶ DEVOTIONAL
Not an Answer, a Friend (Job 42)

When God finally spoke to Job, He did not explain why He permitted Job to suffer. This has left many puzzled, for the book seems to hold no answer to the questions it raises. Why do the innocent suffer? Why does tragedy strike the good man? There is no answer here.

But perhaps this is the point. The Book of Job portrays a God who is wise beyond our comprehension; a God who can and does judge wickedness. It also portrays a God who permitted Satan to torment Job, and who, after Satan's defeat, caused Job's suffering to continue. And it emphasizes the fact that Job was a righteous and blameless man. How does all this fit together?

As we read Job's words, we realize that he was a tormented man. Job was not only tormented by his losses and his pain, but an inner, gnawing uncertainty. We see it even in his very first speech, where Job said, "What I feared has come upon me; what I dreaded has happened to me" (3:25). Despite his personal commitment to the Lord, Job was uncertain about God's attitude toward him. When Job thought of God, it was with deep appreciation and respect, but also with an element of fear.

By the end of the book Job had suffered far more than he could have feared or even imagined. Yet Job had also met God. He had been rebuked, but he had also been commended. Job had even been told that his prayers for his three friends would be accepted. Suddenly Job realized something he had never quite accepted before. God *was* for him. God had observed his actions, and approved. Even when his pain was the greatest, his doubts almost overwhelming, and his words the most foolish, God cared. Through the experience of suffering Job had at last come to know that God was his Friend.

This, the certainty that despite our suffering God is our Friend, is perhaps the true message of Job. Christianity can offer no satisfactory intellectual answer to the mystery of innocent suffering. But, through Christ, God offers us the assurance that He is our Friend. With that assurance, we can face and be victorious in our pain.

Personal Application

When suffering comes, hold tight to the truth that God is your Friend.

Quotable

"In story times, when the foundation of existence is shaken, when the moment trembles in fearful expectation of what may happen, when every explanation is silent at the sight of the wild uproar, when a man's heart groans in despair, and 'in bitterness of soul' he cries to heaven, then Job still walks at the side of the race and guarantees that there is a victory, guarantees that even if the individual loses in the strife, there is still God, who will still make its outcome such that we may be able to bear it; yea, more glorious than any human expectation."—Sören Kierkegaard

The Variety Reading Plan continues with JAMES

Psalms

INTRODUCTION

Psalms is a collection of 150 religious poems which enrich the spiritual life of God's people. The Psalms touch on every human experience and on every aspect of the believer's personal relationship with God. In powerful images they guide us today to worship, to praise, to trust, and to hope in the Lord.

Hebrew poetry does not rely on rhyme or even rhythm for its power, but rather on parallelism, the matching or echoing of thoughts. Thus one line will reflect, contrast with, or reinforce the idea introduced in another, so that the original thought is enriched. This kind of poetry alone can be translated in all languages without loss of power or beauty.

Many technical terms are found in introductions to individual psalms. These reflect use of the psalms in Israel's public worship, and apparently indicate musical accompaniment, the type of psalm or occasion when used, etc.

The Psalms are organized in five "books." Each book was added to the official collection at a different date. Various types of psalms—of praise, worship, confession, imprecation, messianic hope, etc.—are found within each book in apparently random order. Superscriptions identify a number of authors of the psalms, including David (73), the sons of Korah (12), Asaph (12), and others.

As no other book of Scripture, Psalms guides us to focus our thoughts on the Lord, and enrich our private as well as public worship.

OUTLINE OF CONTENTS

I. Book I .... Psalms 1–41
II. Book II .... Psalms 42–72
III. Book III .... Psalms 73–89
IV. Book IV .... Psalms 90–106
V. Book V .... Psalms 107–150

READING GUIDE (21 Days)

If hurried, you may read only the "core passage" in your Bible and the Devotional in each chapter of this Commentary.

Reading	*Chapters*	*Core passage*
106	1–5	5
107	6–12	10
108	13–19	15
109	20–26	25
110	27–33	32
111	34–41	37
112	42–49	49
113	50–56	51

114	57–63	62
115	64–72	71
116	73–78	73
117	79–84	84
118	85–89	89
119	90–98	96
120	99–106	103
121	107–112	112
122	113–118	118
123	119	119:105-112
124	120–134	130
125	135–141	139
126	142–150	143

Psalms

APRIL 16 *Reading 106*
GOD'S GREAT MERCY
Psalms 1–5

> *"But I, by Your great mercy, will come into Your house; in reverence will I bow down toward Your holy temple" (Ps. 5:7).*

God's great mercy is reserved for those who delight in the Law of the Lord and refuse to walk in the way of the wicked.

Overview
There are two moral paths, each with its own destination (Ps. 1). Resistance to the Messiah, God's Son, is futile, for He is destined to rule earth (Ps. 2). David found peace when fleeing from his rebel son Absalom by remembering God (Pss. 3–4). David was confident that his merciful God would bless him even though he had to wait for his prayers to be answered (Ps. 5).

Understanding the Text
Psalm 1: "Two Moral Paths." There are only two moral paths a human being can take. This psalm graphically describes each.

"Walk . . . stand . . . sit" Ps. 1:1. Conformity to worldly morality has three stages. Walking "in the counsel of the wicked" is listening to their views. Standing "in the way of sinners" is acting as the wicked do. Sitting "in the seat of mockers" is adopting their hardened, immoral attitudes.

My wife and I have been shocked just this week to review some of the TV "comedy" shows that our nine-year-old Sarah wants to watch between 7 and 8 P.M. Their innuendos and often explicit statements clearly deny biblical morality, and we've had to declare such programs off-limits. The progression from walking, to standing, to sitting, reminds us that it's dangerous to take even that first step away from godly moral thought.

"He meditates" Ps. 1:2. Note again the importance of our thought life. If we fill our minds with and delight in God's Law, we prosper morally and spiritually. Today we say of computers, "garbage in, garbage out." Long ago God said this of the human mind. If you and I want to prosper spiritually we must guard our thoughts and our minds, and reject the "counsel of the wicked."

"The way of the wicked will perish" Ps. 1:6. In this life the ways of the wicked and godly exist side by side, competing for our allegiance. In the end, the two ways part—forever.

We must choose one of the two, and help our children choose, for there is no third way.

Psalm 2: "Messiah's Rule." The psalmist ridiculed those who resist the Lord and His Anointed One (2:1-6). The Anointed One speaks, announcing His commission from and relationship with God (vv. 7-9). The psalm concludes with a word of grace, calling for a submission which will bring blessing (vv. 10-12). Psalm 2 is frequently quoted in the New Testament (cf. Matt. 3:17; 17:5; Acts 4:25-28; 13:33; Heb. 1:5; 2 Peter 1:17; Rev. 19:15).

"An iron scepter" Ps. 2:9. The rod of iron

symbolizes complete authority. God's Messiah, Jesus, will enforce God's will despite human resistance.

"Be wise; be warned" Ps. 2:10-12. Each human has the opportunity offered rulers in this psalm. We can freely choose to serve the Lord, and find blessing. Or we can resist to the end, and be destroyed when His wrath flares up.

Jesus *is* Lord. Every human being must make a choice for Him—or against Him.

> Psalms 3–4: "Psalms in Flight." Each of these psalms reflects the thoughts and feelings of David as he fled Jerusalem during Absalom's rebellion (see 2 Sam. 15–18). The imagery is powerful as David reflected on his relationship with God, and found a peace which enabled him to sleep despite imminent danger.

"God will not deliver him" Psalm 3:1-2. Many who rebelled against David seemed to feel that God had abandoned him. Second Samuel tells us that Shimei accused the fleeing king of being a "man of blood" (16:7). Very likely David himself, remembering his sin with Bathsheba and other earlier failings, wondered if God was with him when the rebellion broke out.

Ancient warriors protected their bodies with shields made of layers of hardened skins, often studded with metal. David remembered how often God had shielded him from danger. Though David was fleeing for his life, the image of God as a shield (Ps. 3:3) brought inner peace and enabled the threatened king to rest.

Accusations are always hard to bear. When they are made by those who have been our friends, or by our own consciences, they are particularly painful. Add misfortune, when everything seems to be going wrong, and anyone might wonder if God were still with him or not.

Such experiences cause stress, rob us of sleep, and frequently make us so anxious that we become ineffective. We each need what David found in his situation—a way to relieve the stress and restore inner peace.

"You are" Ps. 3:3-4. What David did was to focus his thoughts on God, and to remember who God is. David had known God as a shield ("protector"), as his glory ("greatest value"), as one who lifted up his head ("source of strength"). Remembering who God had proven Himself to be in his life, David prayed to God with confidence.

When we consider who God is, and all He has done for us, we too find the freedom to come to God in prayer. When we cry out to God, we lift the burden from our back and place it on His.

"I lie down and sleep" Ps. 3:5-8. David found peace through prayer. He shifted his burden to God and, sure that the Lord would sustain him, was able to rest.

Prayer, addressed in confidence to a God whom we know loves us, is the secret of peace for you and me. This kind of prayer drains the tension from us. It frees us from fear even when thousands of enemies seem to surround us.

"Know that the Lord has set apart the godly" Ps. 4:1-3. The *selah* at the end of Psalm 3 means "pause, before going on." Here it seems to unite Psalms 3 and 4, leading most commentators to believe both psalms reflect on David's flight from Absalom.

David's enemies misjudged both David and God. Despite his flaws, David was honest in his devotion to God. And God was devoted to David. When we have this kind of relationship with God we can share David's confidence that "the LORD will hear when I call to Him."

"Who can show us any good?" Ps. 4:4-8 The defeatist looks at surrounding troubles, and despairs. David, however, looked up and found a source of joy in the knowledge that God's face was turned toward him. The image of God's face "shining on" a person means to look with favor; to look with the intent to do good.

So David found his good and his joy in God, not in an earthly abundance of "grain and new wine."

How much wiser David's course of seeking peace and joy in the Lord. Our fortunes on earth can change radically, as David's flight from Jerusalem shows. But God is unchanging. If we find our joy in the Lord, that joy will be with us always.

▶ DEVOTIONAL
Waiting
(Ps. 5)

I remember one summer when I was a child, how hard it was to wait for our summer vacation. The next day we were going up to Cedar Lake, to stay at Uncle Duane's cabin. As I sat on the front porch, waiting, I was sure that tomorrow would never come, that we'd never get in the car, never pull into the driveway set back from the lake, and never run down to the shore.

When we get older, waiting can be even more difficult. Usually the things we wait for are much more important. Waiting for a job. Waiting for a sickness to pass. Waiting for an answer to a life-changing question.

This psalm of David reminds us that he was familiar with waiting too. He waited for Saul to die so he could become king. Even after that, he waited years to be acknowledged by all Israel. How did David handle waiting, and still remain confident and hopeful? This psalm tells—and shows—you and me how to wait with confidence and expectant hope.

First, David expressed his emotions as well as his requests to God (vv. 1-3). He was persistent in "morning by morning" sharing his sighing and his needs.

Second, David remembered the character of God (vv. 4-8). God does not take pleasure in evil, and destroys the wicked. But David, by God's grace, was not numbered with the wicked. By God's grace David was one who worshiped the Lord, and who followed God's leading.

Third, David expected God to act in accord with His character (vv. 9-12). The wicked will be declared guilty. But God will act to protect those who love Him. "Surely, O LORD, You bless the righteous" is an affirmation of faith. Even though he had to wait, David knew—because of who God is—that blessing would surely come.

What a ground of expectation for us as we wait. We expect the best, because of who God is. God Himself and His character are the foundation of our hopes.

Personal Application

When waiting is most difficult, meditate on God's character, and be reassured.

Quotable

My life is but a weaving between my Lord and me,
I cannot choose the colors He worketh steadily.
Oft times He weaveth sorrow and I in foolish pride
Forget He sees the upper and I the underside.
The dark threads are as needful in the weaver's skillful hand
As the threads of gold and silver in the pattern He has planned.
Not till the loom is silent and the shuttle cease to fly
Shall God unroll the canvas and explain the reason why.—Author unknown

APRIL 17 *Reading 107*
TAKING REFUGE
Psalms 6–12

"O LORD my God, I take refuge in You; save and deliver me from all who pursue me" (Ps. 7:1).

When we sense our weakness, we hurry to take refuge in a majestic God who acts on behalf of those who love Him.

Overview

David, deeply aware of his weaknesses, took refuge in God (Pss. 6–7). God's creative work (Ps. 8) and His present rule (Ps. 9) gave the psalmist confidence. Victims can find refuge with God the King (Ps. 10), who dispenses justice from His heavenly throne (Ps. 11).

Understanding the Text

Psalm 6: The Cry of the Faint. In deep distress David experienced his own weakness, and cried to God for mercy.

"I am faint" Ps. 6. Many expressions in the Psalms remind us of our frailties. This psalm of David expresses our weakness graphically. David, aware that he had no strength left to face life's challenges, described his feelings of weakness. His bones were in agony, his soul in anguish. He was worn out from groaning; he flooded his bed with weeping and drenched his couch with tears. His eyes grew weak with sorrow.

These expressions may seem strange coming from a man who boldly faced the giant Goliath and fought fearlessly against Israel's enemies. But they remind us that there is nothing unmanly about tears, and nothing shameful in feeling helpless. They also remind us that we have complete freedom in our relationship with God to express our feelings to Him honestly.

David's words also help us understand why he is commended as a man after God's own heart. David was totally honest with himself and with the Lord. He was realistic about his weaknesses, and honest about his fears. Dishonesty—an attempt to maintain a "macho" image—keeps us from acknowledging our weaknesses. And keeps us from full dependence on the Lord.

Psalm 7: A Call for Judgment. God's sovereign rule is partly expressed in His judgments on mankind. David called on God to judge (punish) the wicked and to make the righteous secure.

"If there is guilt" Ps. 7:3-5. David did not fear to call on God to judge, for he himself had been careful to do what was right. It's dangerous to ask God to judge others if we are guilty of their sins!

"Arise, O LORD, in Your anger" Ps. 7:6. The Scriptures do teach the anger of God. But God's anger is unlike ours. (1) It is provoked by sin and injustice. (2) It is righteous, in that it never overreacts nor is vindictive. (3) It may be expressed in present judgments on sinners, but most often is reserved for the final judgment to take place at history's end.

David's call for God to arise in anger and judge is rightly motivated. David did not rejoice at the prospect of the wicked suffering. His concern was to "bring an end to the violence of the wicked and make the righteous secure."

We too can call on God to express His anger at the sins in our society. And we can work to implement just laws, intended not to punish so much as to end violence and make the righteous secure.

Psalm 8: God's Majestic Glory. God's glory is glimpsed in creation, but is most clearly revealed in the Lord's amazing decision to love and care for humankind.

"What is man?" Ps. 8:3-5 David was impressed at the glory revealed in creation (vv. 1-3). Yet what stunned him was the realization that God has chosen to be "mindful" of mankind. The word means to pay compassionate attention to.

Secular man scoffs at the notion that earth is any more than a tiny speck in a minor arm of 1 galaxy of 100 million stars in a universe estimated to hold 100 million galaxies! Yet David identified the greatest wonder: God bends down and pays close attention to this particular speck, for it is the home of humanity, and God has chosen to make human beings the focus of His loving care.

"You made him ruler" Ps. 8:6-8. It is to man's honor and glory that God has made us "ruler over the works of Your hands." This position implies creation in God's image, for God is ultimate Ruler of all things.

It's important to note the distinction between "rule" and "exploit." Too often people have taken authority as a right to use things or others for one's benefit. Here "rule" is actually "responsibility to care for" what God has created. Because God exercises loving care over us, permitting mankind to exercise loving care of the creation is a magnificent gift. It is what David here calls crowning "with glory and honor."

Psalm 9: In Praise of God's Reign. God is known by His justice. His rule was revealed in the fate of the wicked and David's enemies.

"You have upheld my right and my cause" Ps. 9:1-6. David praised God, for he saw the defeat suffered by his enemies as evidence that God is sitting on His throne, "judging righteously." Here David may be remembering the military victories won over surrounding nations, which enabled him to extend Israel's territory and influence.

"He will judge . . . in righteousness" Ps. 9:7-10. David celebrated the Lord, for he knew God not only reigns forever, but "will judge the world in righteousness; He will govern the peoples with justice."

Christianity is not, as has been suggested, a faith of "pie in the sky by and by." It is a faith rooted in the conviction that God rules, and will surely judge. The conviction that God rules enables a person who is oppressed or in trouble to find refuge and hope *now.*

Trust in God may not change our circumstances, but it changes us! The mere fact that we can experience peace despite persecution is the most convincing evidence that God is real.

"The LORD is known by His justice" Ps. 9:16. Those who do not know God by faith will learn of Him later, for God is and will be known by His justice. The moral order of the universe means that the wicked will fall into the pits they dig for others, and their own feet will be snared in the traps they have hidden. Hitler's Germany illustrates this. By treating others brutally, the Nazis became the cause of their own downfall and a vivid illustration of retributive justice.

Psalm 10: The Psalm of the Victim. Because God takes a hand in human affairs, the victim can commit himself to the Lord as King. See DEVOTIONAL.

Psalm 11: Righteousness Affirmed. The believer can take refuge in God, because God is righteous and will surely punish the wicked.

"The LORD is in His holy temple" Ps. 11:4. This phrase is no call to worship, but pictures God standing in the place of judgment. The psalmist identified the "holy temple" with God's "heavenly throne," and said that from it God examines the sons of men.

Because God hates the violence which the wicked perpetrate on the innocent, we can take refuge in Him. Even though the foundations of our society seem to crumble, we can be sure "upright men will see His face."

▶ DEVOTIONAL
Psalm of the Victim (Ps. 10)

The Greek philosopher Plato argued that it was better to have wrong done to us than to do wrong. Few today would agree with him. Being a victim seems somehow shameful, weak.

But in Psalm 10, the poet explained far better than Plato ever could why victims are more blessed than persecutors. If at any time you feel like a victim—misused by your boss, by a friend, family, or even by "the system," this is a psalm you might turn to. If you do you'll find no prescription for changing circumstances. What you'll find is a description of what happens *inside* the perpetrator, and inside the victim.

The perpetrator (vv. 1-11) is described by words like pride, arrogance, and boastfulness. His apparent success feeds these attitudes, and prosperity leads the victimizer to assume he is safe. Others are dismissed as weak, and God either fails to know or doesn't care.

On the other hand, the victim (vv. 12-15) experiences his helplessness. This leads him to commit himself to the Lord. In his suffering the victim has nowhere to turn but to God.

God, "King forever and ever" (vv. 16-18), hears the afflicted. The Hebrew concept of "listen" implies not only hearing but responding. God as Ruler of the universe will act to judge the wicked and to defend the oppressed.

This psalm of the victim recognizes the fact that injustices may exist for a time. But it reminds us that the people who persecute us do so out of a deadly pride and arrogance, and will surely be punished. On the other hand, being victimized brings us closer to the Lord.

How much better to be a victim who knows God, than a victimizer who scoffs at Him!

Personal Application

The next time you suffer as a victim, thank God that you are not the victimizer.

Quotable

Thrice blest is he to whom is given
The instinct that can tell
That God is on the field when He
Is most invisible.

Then learn to scorn the praise of men
And learn to lose with God,
For Jesus won the world through shame
And beckons thee His road.—F.W. Faber

APRIL 18 *Reading 108*
A TREASURY OF DAVID
Psalms 13–19

> *"But I trust in Your unfailing love; my heart rejoices in Your salvation" (Ps. 13:5).*

Seven psalms written by David help us sense the intimate life of prayer and praise which was the foundation of his greatness.

Overview

The believer trusts God (Ps. 13), but wicked men doubt His existence (Ps. 14). Righteous behavior (Ps. 15) and a dedicated heart (Pss. 16–17) bring blessing, for God Almighty saves His own from their enemies (Ps. 18). God declares His glory in creation and in His Word (Ps. 19).

Understanding the Text

Psalm 13: Benefits of Trust. The believer, like others, is vulnerable to despair—but can find peace through prayer.

"Sorrow in my heart" Ps. 13:1-6. David knew times of turmoil and uncertainty. The sense of impending disaster troubled him.

David turned to God and honestly expressed his feelings of impending doom (vv. 3-4). Then David remembered God's "unfailing love," and his emotions were transformed. The despair was replaced by rejoicing, and David found himself singing to the Lord (vv. 5-6).

This psalm reminds us that joy is just a prayer away from despair. We can bring our emotions as well as our needs to the Lord. As we focus on who the Lord is, our emotions will be transformed.

Psalm 14: The Fool and God. Evildoers never realize that the path they have chosen has brought them outside the circle of God's love.

"The fool" Ps. 14:1-3. The Hebrew word, *nabal,* is a term that describes a person whose heart is closed to God and whose life is characterized by gross immorality (cf. Jud. 19:23-24; 2 Sam. 13:12; Josh. 7:15). This powerful psalm reflects Paul's teaching in Romans 1. A person who will not acknowledge God becomes corrupt and does "vile" deeds. The psalm reminds us that no one who closes his heart to the Lord "does good, not even one."

"Will evildoers never learn?" Ps. 14:4-7 David seemed to shake his head in bemused amazement. Even in this life evildoers live with a sense of dread. How much better off are the poor whom they exploit, who have a refuge in the Lord. God will soon act and "restore the fortunes" of His people.

We should never envy those who exploit us. We have access to God, and will be blessed in the end.

Psalm 15: A Blameless Life. Only the person who lives a righteous life has fellowship with the Lord.

"Dwell in Your sanctuary" Ps. 15:1. In Old Testament times God's presence with Israel was symbolized in the temple. To "dwell in" that sanctuary pictures intimate fellowship with the Lord.

"He whose walk is blameless" Ps. 15:2-6. This simple description provides a good checklist against which to measure ourselves. And what a promise! "He who does these things will never be shaken."

Psalm 16: A Heart for God. This beautiful psalm looks beyond behavior to portray the inner life of a man whose heart is filled with God.

"You are my Lord" Ps. 16:1-2. David knew God not just as Lord, but as "my" Lord. Apart from this relationship, nothing he had was "good" (beneficial, of benefit). David then went on to consider those good things which were his through personal relationship with the Lord.

"The saints . . . in the land" Ps. 16:3-4. One good we receive is relationship with others who also know God as "my" Lord. Fellowship with other believers can be a delight.

"You have assigned me my portion" Ps. 16:5-6. The Hebrew says "allotted." This recalls the Conquest of Canaan, when the land was first divided among the tribes by lot. As God controlled the fall of the lot (like our dice), each family felt that it received its property directly from the hand of God. David used this imagery to convey his belief that God sovereignly gave him his own lot in life.

Each of us can have this joy. For God has placed each of us where we are, and will use us there.

"The LORD, who counsels me" Ps. 16:7-8. Each of us too can experience God's guidance. When we "set the LORD always before" us, keeping our eyes on Him, always following where He leads, we will "not be shaken."

"The path of life" Ps. 16:9-11. With the Lord as our Lord, we have security in this life and can look forward to an eternity of joy in God's presence.

Psalm 17: The Apple of God's Eye. Confident of God's great love, the believer chooses righteousness and looks ahead with confidence.

"My righteous plea" Ps. 17:1-5. Those who resolve not to sin can have great confidence in prayer.

"Show the wonder of Your great love" Ps. 17:6-9. We pray because we expect a God who loves us to act.

The "apple of the eye" is the pupil. The image may suggest God's eyes are constantly on the believer, watching over him. Or it may suggest that God protects the believer, who is as precious to Him as this window of the eye which makes sight possible.

"Like a hungry lion" Ps. 17:10-14. If David looked around, he saw enemies on every side. But when David looked up, he saw God, who "by Your hand" could "save me from such men."

It *does* make a vital difference whether you and I look around or look up. Looking around creates fear; looking up brings confidence.

"I will be satisfied" Ps. 17:15. David had awakening from sleep in mind, yet the verse possibly expresses his confident hope of resurrection.

Psalm 18: The Greatness of God. David's clear vision of God's awesome power and love remains a source of encouragement for believers today.

This long and beautiful psalm focuses our attention on those attributes of our God which are vital to remember when troubles come.

"I am saved" Ps. 18:1-6. David's prayers had been answered. God hears and responds to cries for help.

"He parted the heavens" Ps. 18:7-19. Our prayer-answering God is the "Most High." His past acts of intervention in the world reveal His awesome power.

"He has rewarded me" Ps. 18:20-29. David did not speak in pride, but in praise. God rewards those who seek to live righteous lives.

"Arms me with strength" Ps. 18:30-45. God is a source of constant strength to those who trust Him, and He gives victory to the righteous.

"The LORD lives!" Ps. 18:46-50 The God of history lives today, to save us from our enemies. We serve an all-powerful God who answers prayer, and who does intervene for us when we are in need.

Psalm 19: The Glory of God. God's glory is revealed in creation, which displays His power, and Scripture, which displays His moral purity.

"The heavens declare" Ps. 19:1-6. God speaks to every human being through creation. Every person has some truth about God, for the universe which displays "His eternal power and divine nature" (Rom. 1:20) shouts out to human beings without speech or language.

"The law of the LORD" Ps. 19:7-14. God's glory is more perfectly displayed in God's Word, which reveals His character and provides moral guidance.

The Word offers warning, and promises great reward for those who please God.

▶ DEVOTIONAL
Guidance from the Psalms (Ps. 15)

I was teaching a short, two-day course at Princeton Seminary's continuing education center, when I realized how much I did *not* want to come back the next summer.

Several months earlier I'd said that I would come to teach a two-week summer course. But as I flew east from my Phoenix home, I felt how much I missed my family. And I remembered about all the writing I had to do during those summer months. The thought of two weeks away during the next summer became almost unbearable.

So I decided, the last day of my short visit, that I'd tell the seminary that I just couldn't make it.

But that morning, my daily psalm "just happened" to be Psalm 15. As I read, one verse seemed to jump off the page and confront me. The blameless man "keeps his oath even when it hurts" (v. 4). I knew then that I had to return.

Usually when I read the Psalms it's for personal enrichment and/or worship. They lift up my thoughts and my heart to the Lord. But now and then God has a personal word of guidance for me in a psalm. And when God speaks, there's nothing to do but to listen and obey.

Personal Application

God can give us personal guidance through any passage of His Word. As we read, we need to listen carefully.

Quotable

"The great thing in this world is not so much where we stand as in what direction we are moving. To reach the port of heaven, we must sail sometimes with the wind and sometimes against it—but we must sail, and not drift, nor live at anchor."—Oliver Wendell Holmes

APRIL 19 *Reading 109*
THE GOOD HAND OF GOD
Psalms 20–26

"Your hand will lay hold on all your enemies; your right hand will seize your foes" (Ps. 21:8).

God has blessings for His own. We can claim these blessings now, as well as look forward to the time of Messiah's glory.

Overview
A prayer for blessing (Ps. 20) and a celebration of blessings received (Ps. 21) are followed by three psalms which span the career of the Messiah (Pss. 22–24). David reminds us that God guides and guards (Ps. 25), as His Word leads us to level ground (Ps. 26).

Understanding the Text

Psalm 20: A Prayer for Blessing. Here's a guide to extending our "best wishes" to another in prayer.

"May the Lord" Ps. 20:1. David's trust in God rather than chariots (v. 7) is expressed in his conviction that blessing comes from God. We who share David's belief will express our best wishes for others in prayers like his (cf. vv. 1-5).

Psalm 21: For Blessings Received. Remembering what God has done for us is a continual source of joy.

Notice the litany of blessings David lists:
"The victories won" (v. 1)
"Desires granted" (v. 2)
"Prayers answered" (v. 2)
"Presence welcomed" (v. 3)
"Crown given" (v. 3)
"Life—forever and ever" (v. 4)
"Glory bestowed" (v. 5)
"Joy in God's presence" (v. 6)
"Unfailing love" (v. 7)

David, knowing God's power and sure of his ultimate triumph, knew that these and other blessings were his forever (vv. 8-13).

You and I will do well to follow David's example and make a list of our own blessings from the Lord.

Psalm 22: The Suffering Messiah. Jesus the Messiah is unveiled in this poetic description of David's own experience.

"Why have You forsaken me?" Ps. 22:1-8 The opening words of this psalm, quoted by Jesus on the cross (Matt. 27:46), and the clear reflection of Isaiah 53 in Psalm 22:6-7, mark this psalm as a preview of Messiah's suffering and death.

"They have pierced my hands and my feet" Ps. 22:9-21. Other clear references to the cross are found in verses 16-18.

"All the ends of the earth will . . . turn to the Lord" Ps. 22:22-31. Out of Messiah's suffering will come praise for the Lord, and those who turn to the Lord will live forever.

Anyone who grasps the horror of crucifixion as a way of execution, or who senses what it must have meant for the holy Son of God to be made "sin for us" (2 Cor. 5:21) can see something of Jesus' emotions the day of His death. Yet by meditating on this psalm we enter much more deeply into the sufferings of Jesus on Calvary.

How good to read on, as we pass the 21st verse to find that what seemed a tragedy was in fact a triumph! Through Christ's suffering, "The poor will eat and be satisfied; they who seek the Lord will praise Him—may your hearts live forever!"

Psalm 23: Our Shepherd's Care. Even in the shadow of death David, the Messiah, and you and I, all find comfort in our Shepherd's care.

Psalm 24: Messiah's Coming Glory. At history's end the suffering Messiah will be revealed as the Lord Almighty, the King of Glory.

"The earth is the Lord's" Ps. 24:1-2. One basis for certainty that the Messiah will ultimately be vindicated is the fact that God is Sovereign. The earth, and everything in it, belongs to the Lord.

The shepherd was a familiar figure in Israel, and his love for his sheep was legendary. Day and night the shepherd watched over sheep which he knew individually, by name. The image of God as Shepherd, ever present with His people, remains Scripture's most comforting picture of the believer's relationship with his God.

"He who has clean hands" Ps. 24:3-6. Another basis for certainty is the Messiah's pure and sinless life. He will surely be blessed by the Lord.

This King of glory" Ps. 24:7-10. A final basis for certainty is the identity of the Messiah. He who comes is actually the Lord, the very King of glory!

Psalm 25: God's Guidance and Goodness. David had confidence that those who hope in the Lord will never be put to shame. (See DEVOTIONAL.)

Psalm 26: Level Ground. A godly life keeps the believer secure.

"I have led a blameless life" Ps. 26:1-8. The "blameless" life of Old Testament saints was not without sin. It was, however, characterized by a deep inner dedication to God that found expression in a godly way of life. This psalm beautifully describes the attitude which keeps believers of every age from sin.

It is marked by unwavering trust in God (v. 1), and by constant love for Him (v. 3). It is expressed by daily obedience to God's truth (v. 3), with rejection of the wicked as well as wickedness (vv. 4-5). And trust also finds expression in worship (v. 6) and praise (vv. 7-8).

Such dedication alone can produce that "blameless life" which the psalmist describes as "level ground."

Why level ground? Much of the Holy Land is steep and rocky, dangerous for travelers whose feet were shod not in modern climbing boots but in loose sandals. It was so easy to slip and fall, so easy to twist an ankle. But level ground was safe for the traveler. And so the image is clear: the one who loves the Lord enough to live a blameless life travels through this life safe and secure.

▶ DEVOTIONAL
Hope and Shame
(Ps. 25)

The ideas of "hope" and "shame" are often found together in the Old Testament.

"Hope" is a confident outlook, not because a person knows the future, but because the believer knows God and trusts in His character.

"Shame" is disgrace caused by a failure of some sort which exposes an individual to the ridicule of others. Thus the thought expressed in this psalm is that the one who puts his hope in God will never be exposed to ridicule, because God will never fail him!

What can we expect from God that will deliver us from shame?

First, we can expect God to show us His way, guiding and teaching us by His truth (vv. 4-5).

Second, we can expect God to forgive us, freeing us from the burden of our past and purifying us (vv. 6-7).

Because the Lord is good, He guides the humble into what is right (vv. 8-10). Because He is gracious, He forgives even great iniquity (v. 11).

What does the Lord have for those who experience His forgiveness, and go on to live in His will? There is a prosperity and sense of His presence (vv. 12-15) that remain with us despite loneliness, troubles, and even affliction (vv. 16-19). As we take refuge in the Lord, and live upright lives, we can face the future confidently. And without fear of being put to shame.

What a wonderful God we have!

Personal Application

God guides the forgiven man or woman into a life that is pleasing to Him—a life that never exposes one to shame.

Quotable

"Christianity has never been tried, the cliché runs. And of course it's true, but so is it true that Christianity has checked the movements of millions of men and women who but for the pull of dogma would know no vital brake upon their behavior. Sometimes the brake is effective, sometimes it is not. But that it should be there outweighs any concern over the excesses of Jimmy Swaggart or the ayatollah or the Mormon extremist or the Venezuelan savage—or the European relativist."—William F. Buckley, Jr.

APRIL 20 *Reading 110*
THE LORD IS
Psalms 27–33

> *"The LORD is my light and my salvation—whom shall I fear?" (Ps. 27:1)*

We now join David in psalms that praise God for who He is, and learn what His wonderful qualities mean to those who trust in Him.

Overview

To David God is a stronghold (Ps. 27), our strength and shield (Ps. 28). He is King forever (Ps. 29), a healer (Ps. 30), a rock and fortress (Ps. 31). He forgives sin (Ps. 32) and watches over all who hope in His unfailing love (Ps. 33).

Understanding the Text

Psalm 27: God our Stronghold. David focused our attention on the God who will never forsake us.

"The LORD is" Ps. 27:1. Faith is not an emotion; not something we create from within ourselves. What makes faith real and vital is not "how much" of it we have. What makes faith real and vital is its object. Even a little faith, reposed in God, can transform. Not because we "have" it, but because of who our faith is in.

As we come to this and the other psalms for today, we focus as David did on who the Lord is. When our trust and hope are fixed in Him, no matter how small our faith seems to be, God can and will come into our lives with a flood of strength and of joy.

"When evil men" Ps. 27:2-3. David devoted just 2 verses of the 14 in this psalm to the dangers which threatened him. The rest share his thoughts of God.

The proportion is about right. If we think on the Lord seven times as much as we worry, we too will find peace.

"To gaze upon the beauty of the LORD" Ps.

27:4-14. These verses are among the most powerful in the psalter, and several cry out for memorization. "Though my father and mother forsake me, the LORD will receive me" (v. 10), and "I am confident of this: I will see the goodness of the LORD in the land of the living" (v. 13), are promises you and I can claim.

Psalm 28: God, Our Strength and Shield. At times when God does not seem to answer our prayers, trust alone helps.

"Turn a deaf ear to me" Ps. 28:1-5. There are times when our prayers seem futile, launched toward a dull and silent heaven. God seems indifferent, willing to let us be dragged away with the wicked. Even at times like these, we are to remember that "the Lord is."

"The LORD is my strength and my shield" Ps. 28:6-9. How, when we cannot sense God's presence, can we say confidently with David that "He has heard my cry for mercy"? The answer is in who God is. He is the source of our strength and our protector.

As David remembered who God is, he said, "My heart trusts in Him, and I am helped." The circumstances had not changed, but suddenly David found his heart leaping with unexplainable joy.

What a wonderful gift from our wonderful God. Trust alone, anchored in our knowledge of who God is, helps.

Psalm 29: God, King Forever. It is appropriate to worship the Lord, who is enthroned as King forever.

"Ascribe to the LORD" Ps. 29:1-2. The Hebrew *yahab* is found only where "to the LORD" is part of the expression. It is a call to the purest kind of worship: giving praise to God for who He by nature is.

"The voice of the LORD" Ps. 29:3-9. The voice of the Lord is His power to create and to destroy by speaking a word. Human beings have to use physical tools to build up and tear down. God has merely to voice His thoughts, and it is done.

"The LORD sits enthroned" Ps. 29:10-11. The awesome power of God's voice affirms His sovereignty over all. The Lord is King, forever. It is doubly awesome that this God "gives strength to His people" and "blesses His people with strength."

Psalm 30: God, Our Healer. God can heal physically. And He will heal spiritually all who cry to Him for mercy.

"I will exalt You" Ps. 30:1-12. David praised God here for a physical healing. The phrase, "Going down into the pit," is a common Hebrew euphemism for death and burial.

While physical healing is primarily in view here, there is a clear spiritual application. God our Healer (v. 2) hears the cries of the penitent for mercy, and makes it possible for us to "give You thanks forever" (v. 12).

Here again is a verse affirming who God is that brings us great comfort. God is one whose "anger lasts only a moment, but His favor lasts a lifetime." Thus while "weeping may remain for a night," we can be sure that "rejoicing comes in the morning" (v. 5).

Psalm 31: Our Rock and Fortress. In powerful images David invited us to find shelter in God's presence.

"I have taken refuge" Ps. 31:1-5. As David fled from Saul, he found refuge in the rocky wilderness of Judah's hill country. There on some mountain height David and his men camped in relative security.

We can imagine David, seated by a campfire as his men watch the one or two approaches to his craggy fortress, sensing that for him, God is just such a "rock of refuge" (vv. 2, 4). David gladly committed himself into God's hands, and found rest.

"You saw my affliction" Ps. 31:6-18. David was pursued as an enemy by armies led by his father-in-law, King Saul. At times his situation seemed hopeless, and David was gripped by a despair that he expressed in verses 9-12. Yet, envisioning God as his fortress, David found grace to say, "I trust in You," and, "My times are in Your hands."

This is perhaps the greatest challenge we face when hard-pressed. We want relief now. We don't want to wait. We hate the pressure of our present need.

Yet our times as well as we ourselves are in God's hands. Until God acts, we must find grace to wait, holding tight to God as our refuge.

"Goodness . . . stored up" Ps. 31:19-24. God is good. Because of this we can be sure that He has goodness stored up for us who fear Him. For now, we are safe. In the future, we will be doubly blessed.

And so David concluded with a word of exhortation. "Be strong and take heart, all you who hope in the LORD" (v. 24).

Psalm 32: God Forgives. Old Testament saints as well as New experienced the joy, and the transforming power, of God's forgiveness. (See DEVOTIONAL.)

Psalm 33: God's Unfailing Love. Here is a bubbling spring of joy that will never run dry. God loves us—and has shown us love in so many ways.

"Sing joyfully" Ps. 33:1-3. Praise brings joy, for praise focuses our hearts on the Lord.

"His unfailing love" Ps. 33:4-19. What evidences of God's love are appropriate in David's—and our own—litany of praise?

* He is faithful, and His Word is true.
* He loves righteousness and justice.
* He created the starry hosts.
* His plans and purposes will come to pass.
* He considers from heaven all men do.
* He watches over those who fear Him, to protect them from disaster.

"We wait in hope" Ps. 33:20-22. Because of these proofs of God's unfailing love, we wait for Him in hope. And as we trust in Him, joy fills our hearts.

▶ DEVOTIONAL
The Call to Confession
(Ps. 32)

Owning up when we do something wrong really hurts. There's the shame. There's the fear that if we confess we'll be punished. There's the awful feeling that if we admit we've done wrong, we make ourselves vulnerable and lose some important part of ourselves.

Perhaps that's why Psalm 32 is so important. David, drawing from his own experience, shows us that while confessing to any sin may feel like loss, it is actually gain.

What does David have to share with us? After beginning with the affirmation that the forgiven man is blessed, David goes on to show us why.

Keeping silent is painful (vv. 3-4). Unconfessed sin lodges in our consciences and festers there. Like pus forming under a boil, unconfessed sin creates terrible pressure. Unconfessed sin seemed to sap David's strength; it felt like a heavy weight pressing down on him.

This is a first, important reason for confession. Unconfessed sin causes sickness in our souls.

Unacknowledged sin is unforgiven sin (v. 5). God is always ready and eager to forgive sin. But He cannot take away our sin until we release it to Him. This is what confession does: it brings our sin into the open; it holds sin up, fully exposed, to God. And then—wonder of wonders!—God does not punish, but forgives "the guilt of my sin"!

Forgiveness restores relationships (vv. 6-7). *Sin* makes us hide from God. Confession restores us to fellowship so that we can hide *in* God. With our sins forgiven, we are assured that God will protect us from trouble and "surround [us] with songs of deliverance."

Restored fellowship makes divine guidance possible again (vv. 8-10). God now is again able to instruct us in the way we should go because we again trust Him and are ready to respond to His leading. We are again sensitive to the Lord, so that He can now guide us gently rather than be forced to jerk us back onto His pathway as if we were some stubborn animal that can only be controlled with bit and bridle.

No wonder David, his restoration now complete, cried out in joy and gladness at this psalm's end.

What a message for each of us. Unconfessed sin distorts our relationship with the Lord. But when we acknowledge our sin, He not only forgives us, He restores us to intimate fellowship with Him. Once again He leads us in His ways.

Personal Application
If you are troubled with a sense of guilt, joy is only a prayer of confession away.

Quotable
This is the debt I pay
Just for one riotous day,
Years of regret and grief,
Sorrow without relief.

Pay it I will to the end—
Until the grave my friend,
Gives me a true release—
Gives me the clasp of peace.

Slight was the thing I bought,
Small was the debt I thought,
Poor was the loan at best—
God! But the interest!—Paul Laurence Dunbar

APRIL 21 *Reading 111*
TROUBLED TIMES
Psalms 34–41

> *"A righteous man may have many troubles, but the LORD delivers him from them all" (Ps. 34:19).*

When difficulties overwhelm, the believer can turn to God. The Lord will listen as we express our feelings. Most important, He will act.

Overview
David expressed praise for deliverance (Ps. 34), followed by two psalms of imprecations directed against enemies (Pss. 35–36). Yet we can celebrate trust (Ps. 37), even when we are disciplined (Ps. 38) or have lost perspective (Ps. 39). Whatever the situation, we can appeal to God for mercy in our times of need (Pss. 40–41).

Understanding the Text

Psalm 34: God's Unfailing Love. We are to praise God at all times, for in many ways we continually experience the unfailing love of our God.

"When he feigned insanity." The superscription gives us the setting of this psalm. David, giving in to despair, fled his homeland and went to the land of the Philistines. There he was recognized and escaped death only by pretending to be insane. Filled with relief, David's thoughts turned to the Lord, and as he journeyed back to Israel and his destiny, he saw fresh evidence of God's unfailing love.

"At all times" Ps. 34:1-3. There may be a hint of embarrassment here. David's flight to the land of the Philistines reveals fear, not faith. Let's remember God's love *before* we act foolishly, not after!

"He answered" Ps. 34:4-7. Even when we have acted foolishly, God does not abandon us. As David reported, "This poor man called, and the LORD heard him, He saved him out of all his troubles."

"Taste and see" Ps. 34:8-22. David invites us to experience God's goodness for ourselves. Let us commit ourselves to doing what is right. We may act foolishly at times, but if we are dedicated to pleasing Him, we can trust the Lord to deliver us.

Psalm 35: Against Enemies. This imprecatory psalm called down curses on David's enemies.

"Contend, O LORD" Ps. 35:1-28. Is it right for the believer to call on God to act against his or her enemies?

This and similar psalms grew out of the psalmist's conviction that he had a covenant relationship with the Lord. As God's servant, the believer is free to call on the Lord to deliver him, and to punish those who by acting against God's own have set themselves against the Lord as well.

There is another assumption in the imprecatory psalms. Those who seek to crush the godly are wicked. It is surely right for God to act against evil men.

In this context David rightly cried:

O LORD, You have seen this; be not
  silent.
Do not be far from me, O LORD.
Awake, and rise to my defense!

Contend for me, my God and Lord.
Vindicate me in Your righteousness, O
LORD my God;
do not let them gloat over me.

When God does act to vindicate the righteous, He displays His love—and His righteousness.

Psalm 36: A Word to the Wicked. David warned the wicked that a just God loves the upright in heart.

"An oracle . . . concerning the sinfulness of the wicked" Ps. 36:1-4. The Hebrew has *massa'*, a message of judgment delivered with an overwhelming sense of divine authority. David was completely convinced that evildoers, as defined in these verses, will be "thrown down" by the Lord (v. 12).

What characterizes the evil person? He does not respect God (v. 1) or even notice his own sin (v. 2). His words are deceitful (v. 3) and he is committed to a sinful course (v. 4).

"Your righteousness . . . Your justice" Ps. 36:5-12. God is faithful, righteous, and just. He cares for both man and beast, and gives refuge to high and low.

"Continue Your love to those who know You" Ps. 36:10-12. David's conviction that the wicked must fail rested squarely on his understanding of who God is. Because of who God is, David's heart assured him that the wicked will be judged. And God will continue to display love toward those who know Him.

Psalm 37: In Praise of Trust. What are the characteristics and the benefits of trust in the Lord? This, one of the best-loved of the psalms, explains. (See DEVOTIONAL.)

Psalm 38: A Prayer When Disciplined. Both Testaments tell us that the Lord disciplines those He loves. Here is a prayer for us when we are disciplined by the Lord.

"I am feeble and utterly crushed" Ps. 38:1-12. The New Testament says, "No discipline seems pleasant at the time, but painful" (Heb. 12:11). Reading David's description of his feelings, we sense how painful God's discipline was for him. David felt wounded, weak, crushed, filled with searing pain. Some may speak lightly of God's discipline. But anyone undergoing it knows how apt David's imagery is.

Yet consider. Rather than trying to hide, David came to God with his pain! And this is right. Like a little child who turns to Mommy for a hug after being spanked, we are to turn to God with arms held out. When we do, God, like any loving parent, will take us up in His arms and comfort us.

"You will answer" Ps. 38:13-22. Despite the fact that David realized he was being disciplined for sin, he was confident that God would answer his plea. How could David be so sure? He told us, "I confess my iniquity; I am troubled by my sin." David understood what 1 John 1:9 conveys to us as a promise: "If we confess our sins, He is faithful and just and will forgive us."

With his sin forgiven, David's prayer was sure to be answered:

O LORD, do not forsake me;
be not far from me, O my God.
Come quickly to help me,
O Lord my Saviour.

Psalm 39: A Prayer for Perspective. Frustrated by complaints he dared not utter, David begged God for perspective.

"I will put a muzzle on my mouth" Ps. 39:1-3. David was unwilling to say anything against the Lord in the presence of the wicked. Yet he was upset and angry that God had not answered his prayer for help (cf. v. 12). We may feel the same frustration with God at times. David leads us then to a surprising way to deal with such feelings.

"Show me, O LORD, my life's end" Ps. 39:4-6. David didn't ask to know the day of his death. He asked God to give him a sense of life's brevity. What happens to us here on earth lacks ultimate importance. We need to look beyond time, to eternity. If we can only sense the fact that "each

man's life is but a breath," we will gain perspective. The suffering that seems so terrible now lasts only for an instant. It is not unbearable after all.

"But now, Lord, what do I look for?" Ps. 39:7 With this perspective, David could bear the waiting. Even so, he hoped for God to help him in his brief "now."

How wonderful that God considers our brief moment of life important enough to bless us in our present; that during the present time we "may rejoice again" before departing our world.

> Psalm 40: The Celebration of Mercy. David remembered all that God had done for him, and found freedom to cry out for new mercies.

"He lifted me" Ps. 40:1-3. These words beautifully depict mercy. In the Old Testament "mercy" pictures a helpless individual, crying out for compassion to one who is able to give aid. The "slimy pit" graphically portrays man's helplessness. God's "lifting me out" is the intervention of God, and the "new song" of praise is the joy we find in realizing all the Lord has done.

"O LORD my God" Ps. 40:4-11. The greatest blessing of the man "who makes the LORD his trust" is a righteousness found not in sacrifice and offering, but in One who came to do God's will and so bring salvation.

Verses 6 and 7 are messianic, quoted in the great exposition of the meaning of Christ's sacrifice in Hebrews 10. In the One foreshadowed in David's words we find the righteousness, faithfulness, and salvation of our God.

"Do not withhold Your mercy from me" Ps. 40:11-17. It may seem strange, but it is the very fact that our sins overtake us, and our hearts fail, that qualifies us for mercy. Only one who senses his deep need will cry out to God for mercy. The man who shrugs off his sins, or persists in trying to dig himself out of sin's "slimy pit," will never look to God but will rely on his own supposed goodness.

What a privilege for us to stand, with David, and cry out:

> I am poor and needy;
> may the Lord think of me.
> You are my help and my deliverer;
> O my God, do not delay.

> Psalm 41: Psalm of the Merciful. In another psalm which has messianic overtones, David expressed his confidence that the Lord will show mercy to the merciful.

"He who has regard for the weak" Ps. 41:1-3. The merciful person is sensitive to those who are weak, and aids them. This quality, so richly displayed in God's character, is pleasing to Him in you and me. David is sure that God will deliver the merciful man when that man has need of God's mercy.

"O LORD, have mercy on me" Ps. 41:4-13. What a great blessing when we cry out to the Lord for aid to "know that You are pleased with me."

Ultimately the words of this psalm are those of the Messiah (cf. v. 9; Matt. 26:17-25). Yet we too can know God is pleased with us when we trust and seek to serve Him, and can appeal confidently for His mercy.

▶ DEVOTIONAL
The Joys of Trust (Ps. 37)

If you were to pick two psalms to memorize, the first would probably be the 23rd. But the second surely would be this great psalm in praise of trust.

No psalm has more comforting verses, more verses inviting lengthy meditation. No psalm has more verses that speak so directly to the human heart.

Because of this, it's almost sacrilege to analyze this psalm: to break its thoughts apart, to look for similarities and themes. And yet, how much this psalm tells us about the nature, and about the benefits, of trust.

If we seek to probe the nature of trust, we find in this psalm that trust is:

*Looking to God and doing good (v. 3).
*Delighting in the Lord (v. 4).
*Committing our way to the Lord (v. 5).
*Not fretting when the wicked succeed (v. 7).

*Refraining from anger and wrath (v. 8).
*Being satisfied with little (v. 16).
*Giving generously to others (v. 21).
*Turning from evil to do good (v. 27).
*Planting God's Law in our hearts (v. 31).
*Waiting for the Lord (v. 34).
*Keeping His way (v. 34).
*Taking refuge in the Lord (v. 40).

Trust is in fact a way of life, the way of life we choose when we commit ourselves to the Lord.

This same psalm reveals the outcome of trust. One who actively commits himself to the Lord can expect these benefits:

*To enjoy safe pastures (v. 3).
*To receive the desires of his heart (v. 4).
*To be vindicated (vv. 5-6).
*To inherit the land (vv. 9, 22, 34).
*To enjoy great peace (v. 11).
*To be upheld by God (v. 17).
*To gain an enduring inheritance (v. 18).
*To enjoy plenty in days of famine (v. 19).
*To be upheld by the Lord (v. 24).
*To always live securely (v. 27).
*To never be forsaken by God (v. 28).
*To not slip (v. 31).
*To see the wicked cut off (v. 34).
*To have a future (v. 37).
*To be helped and delivered by the Lord (v. 40).

The beauty of this psalm aside, its teaching is vital to our well-being. Only by an active trust in God, expressed in the choices made each day of our lives, can we experience the many benefits of a personal relationship with the Lord.

Personal Application

May we grasp the active nature of trust, and commit ourselves to faith's way of responding to God.

Quotable

"The African impala can jump to a height of over 10 feet and cover a distance of greater than 30 feet. Yet these magnificent creatures can be kept in an enclosure in any zoo with a 3-foot wall. The animals will not jump if they cannot see where their feet will fall.

"Faith is the ability to trust what we cannot see, and with faith we are freed from the flimsy enclosures of life that only fear allows to entrap us."—John Emmons

---

APRIL 22 *Reading 112*
OF THE SONS OF KORAH
Psalms 42–49

"My soul thirsts for God, for the living God" (Ps. 42:2).

Temple musicians, descendants of a rebel priest who died at God's hand, help us explore mysteries of our faith.

Background

Book II. Most believe this second collection of psalms was assembled during the time of Solomon. While containing other authors it, features works of David.

The sons of Korah. Korah rebelled during the Exodus and was killed (Num. 16). But his children were spared. One branch of his descendants became temple guardians (cf. 1 Chron. 9:17ff), while another branch served as temple singers and musicians (cf. 6:31, 33, 39, 44). These descendants of Korah contributed 12 works to the Book of Psalms, most of which may have been used in temple liturgy.

Overview

The sons of Korah probed deeply, to help us examine love for God (Ps. 42), divine vindication (Ps. 43), and the mystery of national defeat (Ps. 44). A wedding song conveys messianic truth (Ps. 45), while "God with us" is exalted as our fortress (Ps. 46). The last three psalms celebrate God's rule (Ps. 47), His eternal city (Ps. 48), and redemption from this transient world (Ps. 49).

Understanding the Text

Psalm 42: In Love with God. Love for God lifts the downcast spirit and revives hope.

"My soul pants for You" Ps. 42:1-5. The image is one of a lover separated for a time from his beloved. He can think of nothing but her, and misses her terribly.

This is the love-driven emotion of the temple musician, away for a time from Jerusalem, yearning to once again lead "the procession to the house of God." His only comfort is the hope that soon he will return to praise God there again.

"I will remember You" Ps. 42:6-11. The sense of separation is unbearable, yet the writer knows that the Lord "directs His love" to him. The separation hurts, yet the writer consoles himself that "I will yet praise Him, my Saviour and my God."

For this son of Korah, the temple symbolized God's presence, and he wished to be as close to God as possible. How wonderful that you and I can simply close our eyes, shut out the world, and be immediately in the presence of our Lord.

When your soul thirsts for God, go to Him. He is there, with you, only a thought away.

Psalm 43: A Plea for Vindication. In the end, God will prove that our faith has been well-placed.

"Vindicate me" Ps. 43:1. The psalmist envisioned God as Judge, taking his side in court against wicked men who had him in their power. The basis for his plea was that "You are God my stronghold."

"Why?" Ps. 43:2 Yet if God is ours, why must we suffer oppression? Why does He seem to reject us?

Such feelings are common when troubles come. We wonder why, and even question God's commitment to us. In fact, we can never understand the why. But the psalmist does have a solution.

"Send forth Your light and Your truth" Ps. 43:3-5. God's light and truth, images here for His Word, do not so much explain our troubles as lead us back to God Himself. "Then I will go to the altar of God," the psalmist said, and praise Him.

What we need most when hurting is not answers, or even relief. What we need is to come into God's presence, there to find hope and to offer praise.

Psalm 44: The Mystery of Defeat. History teaches that God gives victory when His people obey. Why, now that Israel remains faithful, has defeat come?

"We have heard" Ps. 44:1-8. Scripture testifies of the victories God won for Israel during the Conquest.

"But now" Ps. 44:9-22. Recent defeats puzzled the psalmist, for Israel had not forgotten God or violated His covenant. Why then did God not act?

"Awake, O Lord!" Ps. 44:23-26 Puzzled and pained, the psalmist begged God to "rise up and help us."

The psalm does present a puzzle, yet a common one. Why does God sometimes permit His most faithful servants to suffer? While Psalm 44 offers no specific answer, there may be a hint in verse 22. "For Your sake we face death all day long." Not all suffering is punishment. Some suffering may be the price we pay for remaining loyal to God in a hostile world. As Peter reminds us, to this we were called, "Because Christ suffered for you, leaving you an example, that you should follow in His steps" (1 Peter 2:21).

Psalm 45: A Wedding Psalm. The celebration of a royal wedding shifts focus to offer triumphant praise to the coming Messiah.

"At your right hand is the royal bride" Ps. 45:1-9. Many things in this world are shadows cast by realities to be found in the world to come. The joy of the wedding feast transports us to visions of the heavenly union awaiting God and Israel, Christ and His church.

The New Testament quotes verses 6-7, making it clear that this psalm truly is intended to transport us from earthly to heavenly celebration, enabling us to sense something of the joy we will know when our Lord returns (cf. Heb. 1:9).

Psalm 46: God Our Fortress. With God our refuge and strength, an ever-present help, we need never fear.

Psalm 47: Celebrating God's Rule. If

The stone ramparts of Israel's walled cities rose high above the ground. Massive and secure, designed to frustrate any attacker, they conveyed an image of security to all who lived nearby. One needed only look up from his fields and see the nearby fortress to feel safe. Psalm 46 repeats this image, to convey to us the peace we can find through our relationship with "our fortress," the Lord Almighty.

you belong to God, clap your hands in joy, for He is the great King of all the earth.

"The great King" Ps. 47:1-9. In ancient times "great King" was a unique title which was given only to world conquerors like Nebuchadnezzar or Cyrus. A ruler who added "great" to his title would be ridiculed, unless his might was overwhelming.

How right the psalmist is to title God the "great King." He subdued nations, and gave Israel her inheritance. He reigns over the nations even now. All the kings of this earth are subject to Him, and He is greatly exalted.

Remember this psalm the next time you feel discouraged or downhearted. Our God is the "great King." There is nothing that He cannot do, or will not do, for you and me.

Psalm 48: The Eternal City. Just beyond the earthly Jerusalem, the psalmist envisioned the citadels of the eternal city of God.

"The city of our God" Ps. 48:1-8. As the psalmist walked the walls of ancient Jerusalem he saw more than mighty stones. The city God had chosen represented all God's acts in history which revealed how precious Zion and Israel were to the Lord.

"Within Your temple, O God" Ps. 48:9-14. The setting for the rest of the psalm is within the temple, at worship. There the psalmist in his imagination walked the walls of God's eternal city, far more real and lasting, and far more splendid, than the solid rock of Jerusalem's ramparts.

The walls of the earthly city, unknown to the psalmist, were destined to be thrown down by conquering armies. But the eternal city remains, for "this God is our God forever and ever; He will be our guide even to the end."

▶ DEVOTIONAL
Sic Transit Gloria
(Ps. 49)

Successful Roman generals were sometimes granted a "triumph." They were permitted to parade their armies, with gangs of captives and wagons filled with loot, through the very streets of Rome.

But in the chariot of the general, standing just behind him, was an officer whose duty it was to whisper constantly in his ear, "You are but a man."

Psalm 49 serves much the same purpose. It is God's whisper in our ear, reminding us that no matter how much success we or others have, we are but men. All too soon we will die, and any worldly wealth or glory will pass away with us.

As the psalmist said, "Do not be overawed when a man grows rich, when the splendor of his house increases; for he will take nothing with him when he dies."

And, "Though while he lived he counted himself blessed . . . he will join the generation of his fathers, who will never see the light of life."

Why such a dreary psalm here, among others that lift our hearts and stimulate us to praise? Probably because this is not a dreary psalm at all, but one vibrant with hope.

Here, almost hidden among words of warning to the thoughtless who are captivated by the vision of glory or wealth in this world, is this promise: "God will redeem my soul from the grave; He will surely take me to Himself" (v. 15).

Our hope is not in riches, or in anything that this world has to offer. The glory of this world passes away, for we are but men, and all too soon we leave its changing scene. Our hope is in God, who redeems our souls from the grave, and surely takes us to Himself.

Personal Application

Enjoy this world. But don't become too attached to it.

Quotable

" 'Blessed are the poor in spirit' means: 'Blessed is the man who has realized his own utter helplessness, and who has put his whole trust in God.' If a man has realized his own utter helplessness, and has put his whole trust in God, there will enter into his life two things which are opposite sides of the same thing. He will become completely *detached from things,* for he will know that things have not got it in them to bring happiness or security; and he will become completely *attached to* God, for he will know that God alone can bring him help, and hope, and strength. The man who is poor in spirit is the man who has realized that things mean nothing, and that God means everything."—William Barclay

APRIL 23 *Reading 113*
FOR TROUBLED TIMES
Psalms 50–56

> *"Cast your cares on the LORD and He will sustain you; He will never let the righteous fall" (Ps. 55:22).*

Seven psalms of David teach us how to respond when we bring trouble on ourselves, and when others betray us.

Overview

Through Asaph God spoke to His people and to the wicked (Ps. 50). David modeled confession (Ps. 51), and in three psalms expressed his response to betrayal by others (Pss. 52–54). David then recorded a prayer for the distressed (Ps. 55) and for the afraid (Ps. 56).

Understanding the Text

Psalm 50: God as Judge. God speaks through this poem penned by a temple musician to His own people and to the wicked.

"The LORD, speaks and summons the earth" Ps. 50:1-6. An image from Israel's legal system pictures God, speaking from heaven, announcing His righteous judgments.

"O My people" Ps. 50:7-15. God's message to His own is simple. "Fulfill your vows to the Most High, and call upon Me in the day of trouble; I will deliver you, and you will honor Me." As we are faithful to the Lord, He will be faithful to us.

"But to the wicked" Ps. 50:16-22. The wicked should not misconstrue God's silence as indifference. God will condemn the righteous "to your face."

In a sense, the psalms of David that follow Asaph's prophetic poem illustrate its theme. In view of the fact that God is Judge, David shows us how we are to respond in various situations.

Psalm 51: Confession of Sin. David's confession after his affair with Bathsheba shows us how to respect God as Judge when we sin. (See DEVOTIONAL.)

Psalm 52: Betrayed by an Enemy. David took comfort in reviewing how different he was from his enemy.

"Doeg the Edomite" Ps. 52 superscription. When David fled for his life from Saul, he paused at Nob and took the sword of Goliath from the priests there (1 Sam. 21:1-9). Doeg, one of Saul's officials, saw him and later reported to Saul. The furious king

charged the priestly family with treason; Doeg himself executed 85 innocent priests and their families (22:6-19). When David heard this from the sole-surviving member of the family, he took responsibility, for he had seen Doeg there and knew he would surely tell Saul (v. 20). Yet David never suspected that the half-mad king ordered the execution of these men of God. Psalm 52 commemorates that day, and finds comfort in the fact that God will ultimately judge.

"You love evil" Ps. 52:1-7. Doeg's acts were a disgrace, an attempt to win Saul's favor at the price of others' lives. David says, "Surely God will bring you down to everlasting ruin."

"But I am like an olive tree" Ps. 52:8-9. The critical difference between Doeg and David was that "I trust in God's unfailing love." Because David, despite his mistake, honored God, his future was secure.

The one person the betrayer surely has betrayed is himself!

Psalm 53: The Fate of Fools. Evildoers never learn. God is watching, and will judge.

"The fool says in his heart" Ps. 53:1-5. The person whose heart is closed to God becomes morally corrupt (see Ps. 14). Yet God is observing him, and the dread in his own heart testifies against him.

"Oh, that salvation would come" Ps. 53:6. Despite the fact that David knew the fate awaiting evildoers, he yearned for God to act soon.

Psalm 54: Betrayal by Friends. Most painful of all is betrayal by those whom we have called our friends.

"The Ziphites": Ps. 54 superscription. The introduction to this psalm too gives us a historical setting. While fleeing Saul, David's band of men occupied southern Judah's hill country. There they even fought to save such cities as Keilah from marauding bands of Philistines (cf. 1 Sam. 23:1-18). Yet when David's company hid in the rugged range of hills known as Ziph, the Ziphites twice went to Saul and volunteered to betray his hiding place (vv. 19-25; 26:1-4).

"Save me, O God" Ps. 54:1-7. In an earlier psalm David described the wickedness of an enemy who betrayed him (Ps. 52). Here David said little against those fellow-countrymen who showed such ingratitude in betraying him twice! His only imprecation was, "Let evil recoil on those who slander me."

David wisely chose to focus on God Himself, His help, and the One who sustained him.

It's especially painful when a friend turns against us. When that happens we would be wise to follow David's lead. Don't dwell on the betrayal. Let God mete out any appropriate punishment. Released from any thoughts of hurt or revenge, David praised God, and remembered how the Lord "delivered me from all my troubles."

Psalm 55: Prayer When in Distress. David did feel betrayal—deeply. In this psalm he reminds us that however great our distress, we can cast our cares on the Lord and He will sustain us.

"My thoughts trouble me and I am distraught" Ps. 55:1-8. David again proved himself an emotional man, who freely expressed his feelings in prayer. When you or I are shaken or in despair, it helps to read a psalm like this one and pray along with David. Such psalms help us realize that when we are hurting God does care, and that we can come to the Lord as we are.

"Let death take my enemies by surprise" Ps. 55:9-15. David hardly wished the wicked well! Yet he was not being vindictive. The wicked are characterized by violence, strife, malice, and abuse. Such actions surely merit the judgment of God.

"But I call to God" Ps. 55:16-23. David's anguish and his anger both led him to the Lord. He could do nothing to alter God's timing. What he could do was to remember that God, "who is enthroned forever," will surely bring the wicked down. In view of this, David penned one of the most wonderful promises in Scrip-

ture. "Cast your cares on the LORD and He will sustain you" (v. 22).

Until God acts to destroy the wicked, He will surely sustain His own. He will never let the righteous fall.

Psalm 56: Prayer When Afraid. David saw fear not as an evil, but as an opportunity to trust.

"When the Philistines had seized him" Ps. 56 superscription. The setting for this psalm is David's flight to Gath. Depressed and certain that he would lose his life if he stayed in Israel, David went to the land of the Philistines. There he was recognized and seized. David pretended to be insane and was released (1 Sam. 21:10-15). The whole incident is electric with the fear that David experienced—fear that caused him to flee in the first place, fear when taken captive, certainly fear as he returned to his homeland still a fugitive.

"Be merciful to me" Ps. 56:1-13. David's sense of being surrounded by enemies was no paranoia. He was alone, and his enemies were all too real. Yet through this terrifying experience David came to see fear as a friend, rather than as an enemy.

How is fear a friend? Fear is a friend because it is only when we are afraid that we plumb the depths of trust. We cannot know what trust means unless we live through experiences in which the Lord is all we have to hold on to.

Through his experience of fear, David became able to share a great and wonderful discovery with us.

When I am afraid,
I will trust in You.
In God, whose Word I praise,
In God I trust; I will not be afraid.
What can mortal man do to me?

When trust releases us from our fear of others, we are truly free to "walk before God in the light of life."

▶ DEVOTIONAL
Night and Day
(Ps. 51)

Perhaps our most troubling times come when we are faced with the realization that we have sinned. How we deal with that sin makes all the difference in the world. It's like the difference between night and day. The difference between a crushing sense of guilt, and the buoyant realization that our heart is pure.

This well-known psalm celebrating God's forgiveness was written by David after he committed adultery with Bathsheba, and then arranged for the death of her husband in battle. The first half of the psalm portrays the dark side of our experience. The second half the bright newness God offers believers who confess their sins to Him.

Verses 1-9 feature words from the Old Testament's vocabulary of sin. David's usage draws together the entire Old Testament concept by using three major Hebrew terms. *Hata'* ("sin") is the failure to live up to God's established standard. *Pesha'* ("transgression") is conscious rebellion against that standard, while *'awon* ("iniquity") is deviation from or a twisting of the standard. Somehow the seeds of sin are rooted deeply in David's very nature, and have grown into a tangled, thorny thicket of willful and unintentional sins which have drawn the psalmist into acts that repel his better self.

There is a dark side to all our natures; a side expressed in acts of sin that cry out for forgiveness.

Yet David and you and I have hope. There is a bright side, revealed in verses 10-19. Aware of the darkness within him, David cried out, "Create in me a pure heart, O God, and renew a steadfast spirit within me." God, who spoke light into existence, can do a creative work in us and make our soiled hearts pure.

And when that happens? Then again there is joy in salvation. Then again we are able to "teach transgressors Your ways, and sinners will turn back to You."

From the purified heart pour forth hymns of praise, and from the humble acknowledgment of what we are comes something new; a life of holiness.

Personal Application

When we expose sin in confession, God makes our darkness light.

Quotable

"If only there were some evil people somewhere insidiously committing evil deeds, and it were necessary only to separate them from the rest of us and destroy them. But the line dividing good and evil cuts through the heart of every human being. And who is willing to destroy a piece of his own heart?"—Aleksandr Solzhenitsyn

APRIL 24 *Reading 114*
THE STEADFAST HEART
Psalms 57–63

> *"One thing God has spoken, two things have I heard: that You, O God, are strong, and that You, O Lord, are loving" (Ps. 62:11-12).*

These psalms of David trace the secret of his commitment to the Lord to an exalted vision of who God is.

Overview

Drawing from experience, David expressed his commitment to the Lord (Ps. 57). That commitment was rooted in his clear vision of God as Judge (Ps. 58), as fortress (Ps. 59), as his help (Ps. 60), shelter (Ps. 61), salvation (Ps. 62), and as his personal God (Ps. 63).

Understanding the Text

Psalm 57: The Steadfast Heart. David refused an opportunity to kill Saul, choosing instead to trust God to fulfill His purpose in David's life.

"When he had fled from Saul into the cave" Ps. 57 superscription. David was hiding in a cave when Saul entered that same cave to relieve himself. David's men saw it as a God-given opportunity for David to rid himself of an enemy and claim the throne God had promised to David (1 Sam. 24). But David refused to touch Saul, whom God had anointed king over Israel. Rather than an opportunity to kill Saul, David saw a God-given opportunity to do what was godly and right. This psalm conveys David's spiritual secret—the secret of his freedom to do what he knew was right.

"Be exalted, O God" Ps. 57:1-5. What does it mean to take refuge in the Lord? David shows us. It means to pray in the confidence that the Lord will fulfill "His purpose" for us, and that He will send "from heaven" and save us.

David chose to wait for God to act, sure that God would accomplish His purpose in David's life. David did not have to do wrong, for God would bring him to the Lord's intended goal. This was David's spiritual secret. He knew there was no need to do wrong, however great the pressure, for God would surely bless David and bring him to the throne in God's own time.

You and I too can have this kind of confidence in God. When pressures tempt us to seek relief by doing wrong, we can pray to a God who will never let His purpose in our lives fail.

"My heart is steadfast" Ps. 57:6-10. Despite David's many enemies, his heart was steadfast. David meant here that he maintained an unshakable trust in God.

It was many years after the event celebrated in this psalm that God did at last fulfill His purpose and place David on Israel's throne. Through all those years David maintained a steadfast trust in God's love, and in God's faithfulness.

That steadfast trust enabled David to sing praises even during the years of waiting and uncertainty.

"Be exalted, O God" Ps. 57:11. What a reminder. You and I exalt God, lifting Him up and displaying His beauty for all to see, by steadfast hearts.

Psalm 58: God Who Judges. David's heart was steadfast because he was convinced that "there is a God who judges the earth."

"Break the teeth in their mouths, O God" Ps. 58:1-11. In biblical imagery the teeth represent power to tear and to destroy. David was fully aware that this world is filled with wicked men who "devise injustice" and "mete out violence." Yet he knew

that there is a God who judges the earth. The day is coming when the wicked will be swept away. Then "the righteous will be glad when they are avenged."

Psalm 59: God My Strength. His life threatened, David cried to God and found strength in the image of God as his fortress.

"When Saul sent men . . . to kill him" Ps. 59 superscription. Saul acted openly against his son-in-law David by sending men to kill him in his own house (1 Sam. 19). David fled, weaponless and alone.

In this powerful psalm David envisioned his enemies as snarling scavenger dogs, prowling about and eager to devour him. Dogs were not pets in Old Testament times, and frequently represent the bestial aspect of wicked men (cf. Pss. 22:16; 68:23; Isa. 56:10-11; Jer. 15:3; Rev. 22:15).

Yet David found God a source of strength, and God's love a fortress in which he could take refuge.

A wonderful expression of David's faith is repeated twice. It is found after his vivid description of his enemies (v. 9), and after his confident prayer asking God to deal with those enemies for him (v. 17).

What wonderful verses to memorize and bring to mind when you feel endangered by the actions of others.

> O my Strength, I watch for You;
> You, O God, are my fortress,
> my loving God (vv. 9-10).

and

> O my Strength, I sing praise to You;
> You, O God, are my fortress,
> my loving God (v. 17).

Psalm 60: God My Help. David experienced God as his ally and his help.

"When he fought" Ps. 60 superscription. This is a victory psalm, sung after the war had been fought and won (cf. 1 Chron. 18–19). Against the background of the centuries of defeat that fractured Israel during the times of the Judges (vv. 1-3), David now celebrated what God had done to save and deliver a people who, under David, once again honored the Lord (vv. 4-8). The psalm ends with explicit recognition that future victories also depended on the Lord. "Give us aid against the enemy, for the help of man is worthless. With God we will gain the victory, and He will trample down our enemies" (vv. 9-12).

Psalm 61: God My Shelter. This brief psalm of praise was written after David received the throne.

"The rock that is higher than I" Ps. 61:1-2. David never lost the simple faith he had as a young shepherd. Despite the fact that he was now exalted as king over Israel, he never became proud. He remained a humble believer looking up to God and expressing his dependence on the Lord in prayer.

"You" Ps. 61:3-5. David knew and addressed God in personal terms. The im-

ages in these verses suggest how David felt about the Lord. David saw God as a refuge and strong tower: as One to whom he could flee in troubled times and find security. David saw God as a host: he was a vistor in God's tent. In the ancient East this meant he was under divine protection, with all his needs sure to be met by his gracious Host. And David saw God as sheltering wings: he was a baby chick, nestling for protection against its mother, and finding there not only security but also warmth.

It's fascinating to note the transition of the images. Each speaks of security. Yet God is first seen as a strong but impersonal power; then as welcoming Host; finally in utmost intimacy as a warm and protective parent. This transition may mirror our own experience with God. The better we come to know Him, the warmer and more personal the sense of our relationship with Him.

Psalm 62: God, My Salvation. Knowing God as Saviour enabled David to find rest. (See DEVOTIONAL.)

Psalm 63: God, My God. David's heart was steadfast, not simply because he knew who God is, but because he knew this God as *his* God.

"When he was in the desert" *Ps. 63 superscription.*The setting again is a time of trouble, as David with a small band of followers lived an outlaw's life in Judah's desert regions.

"O God, you are my God" Ps. 63:1-11. Awareness that God is "my God" is the foundation of a living faith. But to experience the full benefits of our faith we need to move beyond awareness to intimacy.

It is this that set David apart. He thirsted for God; he sought opportunities to worship at God's sanctuary (v. 2) and when alone (v. 6). His sense of God's love (v. 3) stimulated David to praise the Lord constantly (vv. 4-5, 7, 11).

If you and I wish to experience God in a deeply personal way as "my God," we need to follow David's lead. By taking every opportunity to turn our thoughts to Him and to praise Him, that same sense of God's living presence which sustained David will sustain you and me.

▶ DEVOTIONAL
Stressful, Restful Living (Ps. 62)

David lived a stress-filled life. His relationship with Saul was stormy, resulting in years of living as an outlaw in the land God had promised he would one day rule. As king, David knew constant warfare with surrounding nations. He was forced to invent and organize a national system of government. He knew great pressures at home, as his sons feuded with one another and one ultimately led half the nation in rebellion. Yet these years of stress were spiritually productive. David wrote many psalms, reorganized the Levites and priests to support strengthened national worship, and began planning for a temple to be built by his son, Solomon.

Today the shelves of our bookstores feature many books on stress. It seems that, in a fast-paced world which makes so many demands on our time, stress is a major concern. People are wound tight, emotionally and physically drained by the pressures of modern life. This makes Psalm 62 especially important for our times. In it David tells us the secret of stressful, *restful* living.

The secret is expressed in verse 1, and developed in the rest of the psalm. "My soul finds rest in God alone; my salvation comes from Him." In the Old Testament "salvation" indicates deliverance from earthly dangers or enemies. The word portrays God as One who acts on behalf of those who trust in Him. It was David's conviction that deliverance does come from God—that God can and will act in the material universe to save him—which brought his soul rest.

How powerful that conviction! No matter what the challenge, no matter how great the pressure, David was sure that God could and would perform some saving act. With this conviction David could not be shaken by events (vv. 2, 6). With this conviction, David was emotionally at rest no matter how great a force external pressures seemed to exert.

You and I too can find rest despite the stressful pace or pressures of our life. How? By following David's example, to "trust in Him at all times" and "pour out your hearts" to Him. This, with the conviction that "You, O God, are strong, and that You, O Lord, are loving," will give us rest.

Personal Application
Expect God to act in your life, and find rest in Him.

Quotable
"In time of trouble, say, 'First, He brought me here. It is by His will I am in this strait place; in that I will rest.' Next, 'He will keep me here in His love, and give me grace in this trial to behave as His child.' Then say, 'He will make the trial a blessing, teaching me lessons He intends me to learn, and working in me the grace He means to bestow.' And last, say, 'In His good time He can bring me out again. How and when, He knows.' Therefore, say, 'I am here (1) by God's appointment, (2) in His keeping, (3) under His training, (4) for His time.' "—Andrew Murray

APRIL 25 *Reading 115*
CONFIDENCE IN PRAYER
Psalms 64–72

> *"Praise be to the Lord, to God our Saviour, who daily bears our burdens. Our God is a God who saves; from the Sovereign* Lord *comes escape from death" (Ps. 68:19-20).*

The psalmists often express feelings of overwhelming need. Yet they also remind us that however great the need, our God is able to answer prayer.

Overview
This group of psalms is launched with a plea for protection (Ps. 64). God's ability to answer prayer is affirmed in psalms that review His righteous works (Ps. 65), His awesome works (Ps. 66), His rule (Ps. 67), and His saving works (Ps. 68). Two pleas (Pss. 69–70) are followed by a psalm expressing confidence in God (Ps. 71). Book II ends with a psalm by Solomon celebrating the ministry of the messianic King (Ps. 72).

Understanding the Text

Psalm 64: A Plea for Protection. David sought God's help against cunning enemies who plotted against him.

"I voice my complaint" Ps. 64:1-10. The Hebrew word translated "complaint" is better rendered "troubled thoughts." Those who plot against us and attack behind our backs are more dangerous than open enemies. David asked God to bring them to ruin, so all might see that God guards those who take refuge in Him.

When we are troubled, we too have a refuge in God, who is celebrated in the next four psalms.

Psalm 65: God's Righteous Works. David praised God as One who hears prayer, and whose righteousness is displayed in a creation He continues to care for.

"O You who hear prayer" Ps. 65:1-4. In Hebrew to "hear" prayer is to answer it. The God who has atoned for our sins and blessed us with good things does hear our prayers.

"Awesome deeds of righteousness" Ps. 65:5-13. We know that God does right by men, for He who created the world (vv. 5-8) continues to care for it, so that nature overflows with an abundance of all man needs to enjoy life.

Psalm 66: God's Awesome Works. These works, performed in man's behalf, assure David that the Lord will answer the prayers of those who fear Him.

"How awesome His works in man's behalf" Ps. 66:1-7. David called our attention to history, to "come and see" what God has done. In the past the Lord "turned the sea into dry land" for Israel's forefathers (vv. 5-7). Even more, the Lord had acted in

David's time. "He has preserved our lives and kept our feet from slipping" (vv. 8-9). God had also "refined us like silver," an image which speaks of the purification that comes through divine discipline (vv. 10-12). As a result of God's work in his life David now came to the Lord's temple a fully committed man (vv. 13-17).

The psalm's emphasis of commitment is important. As David said, "If I had cherished sin in my heart, the Lord would not have listened." When you and I try honestly to please God, we can be sure that He will answer our prayers (vv. 18-20).

Psalm 67: God's Just Rule. God rules His people justly, blessing those who praise Him.

"May the peoples praise You, O God" Ps. 67:1-7. In this psalm praise and blessing are two halves of a circle. Blessing causes us to praise God. And praise, our appropriate response to His gracious provision, maintains that intimate relationship with God which guarantees the blessing.

Today as we devote ourselves to praise, we can be sure that "God will bless us, and all the ends of the earth will fear Him."

Psalm 68: God's Saving Works. One of Scripture's most vibrant, triumphant psalms celebrates God's saving works and what they mean to His people.

"Sing to God" Ps. 68:1-6. The psalm opens with a triumphant shout; we can imagine it as a fanfare, played on a hundred trumpets.

Some commentators believe the psalm may have been sung when David triumphantly brought God's ark into Jerusalem and danced before the Lord (cf. 2 Sam. 6). Whether it was or not, the tone of this psalm is one of triumphant joy.

"When You went out" Ps. 68:7-18. God is praised for His triumphal march through history, in scenes that recall the Exodus, His appearance at Sinai, the thunderstorm that defeated Sisera in Deborah's time, and the rains which made the Promised Land a place of blessing.

"Who daily bears our burdens" Ps. 68:19-31. Relationship with Israel's saving God assured His people of victory (vv. 19-23). Israel marched in triumph, praising the Lord (vv. 24-27), who one day will see even the Gentiles bow before Him (vv. 28-31).

"Sing to God" Ps. 68:32-35. The psalm ends with another fanfare, joyfully trumpeting the power of the awesome God who "gives power and strength to His people."

Psalm 69: Plea of the Distressed. David represented the vulnerable man, a victim of slander, betrayal, and his own faults. In his distress the psalmist's only hope was that God would "rescue me from the mire."

"The floods engulf me" Ps. 69:1-5. Deep waters frequently represent overwhelming difficulties or troubles. Here David felt helpless before his enemies (v. 4) and his own sins (v. 5). "Folly" is not misjudgment, but sinful choice.

"Be disgraced because of me" Ps. 69:6-12. Humiliation of God's servant reflects on God and His people as a whole. The New Testament quote of verse 9 (John 2:17) reminds us that David was not speaking only of himself here. These words also reflect the humiliation of the despised and rejected Messiah.

"Answer me with Your sure salvation" Ps. 69:13-18. In distress the psalmist prayed to God for deliverance. He expected an answer, not because he deserved it, but as an expression "of the goodness of Your love."

"I am scorned" Ps. 69:19-21. In a series of powerful words David described his feelings: he was scorned, disgraced, shamed, helpless, alone. Again the words picture not only David's feelings, but also the experience of the Messiah. Dragged to Calvary Christ found no comforter, and was offered gall mixed with vinegar to drink (cf. Matt. 27:48-49).

"May they be blotted out" Ps. 69:22-28. Here David's natural feelings broke through, and he called down curses on his enemies. In contrast Jesus, from the cross,

prayed "Father, forgive them." Both expressions are appropriate. In Christ God offers forgiveness to all. Yet those who refuse to trust Messiah will "be blotted out of the Book of Life."

"The Lord hears the needy" Ps. 69:29-36. Even in his distress the psalmist praised God, sure that the Lord does hear and will not despise (reject the plea) of His captive people.

Praise rightly precedes deliverance as well as follows it. When we praise God for what He will do, we affirm our faith in Him. In praise we also find the courage we need to wait until God is ready to act for us.

Psalm 70: Plea of the Poor and Needy. When you or I recognize our need we turn to God, who alone is "my help and my deliverer."

Psalm 71: Confidence in the Lord. Memories of God's faithfulness bring the aged hope. (See DEVOTIONAL.)

Psalm 72: Ministry of the King. Solomon's vision of his own calling as king led him to celebrate the greater ministry of the coming Messiah.

Although this psalm is not quoted in the New Testament, its theme has been understood by both Jewish and Christian commentators as messianic. One day a coming King will "judge your people in righteousness" and "defend the afflicted." He will "rule from sea to sea" and "all kings" and "all nations will serve Him." He will rescue the weak and the needy "from oppression and violence, for precious is their blood in His sight." The ancient promises of God to Abraham will be fulfilled in Him, for "all nations will be blessed through Him, and they will call Him blessed" (cf. Gen. 12:1-4).

▶ DEVOTIONAL
Growing Old
(Ps. 71)

Most of us don't look forward to growing old. We expect old age to rob us of so much that's important. Our sight will begin to fail. Our hearing will fade. We'll lack the strength to do many of the things we now enjoy. Many of us will lose much of our sense of taste. Aches will come too, with an increased vulnerability to serious illness and pain. No wonder old age seems to loom like some dark threat on the horizon of our future.

Yet in this psalm David reminds us of something that several modern polls have revealed. Old age can be a time of blessing. Those polls have shown that no segment of our population is as content with their lot as those over 60!

Perhaps many of our older citizens find comfort and hope in their past experiences of God's grace. Listen to just a few of the verses in this towering psalm, and perhaps your view of old age may change.

> You have been my hope, O Sovereign
> Lord, my confidence since my
> youth.
> From birth I have relied on You (vv. 5-6).
>
> Since my youth, O God, You have
> taught me, and to this day I
> declare Your marvelous deeds.
> Even when I am old and gray,
> do not forsake me, O God,
> till I declare Your power to
> the next generation (vv. 17-18).
>
> Though You have made me see troubles, many and bitter,
> You will restore my life again;
> from the depths of the earth
> You will bring me up.
> You will increase my honor and
> and comfort me once again (vv. 20-21).

When we do grow old, we will have years of relying on the Lord and of experiencing His grace to sustain us. All God has taught us throughout our lives will so enrich us that we will be able to bless the next generation. If we learn to rely on the Lord in our troubles now, the years ahead can truly be golden. We will live those years in confidence, sure that beyond them God will restore our lives again, and then we will be forever young.

Personal Application

Today's experience of God's grace prepares us for whatever tomorrow may bring.

Quotable
"How completely satisfying to turn from our limitations to a God who has none. . . . For those out of Christ, time is a devouring beast; before the sons of the new creation, time crouches and purrs and licks their hands."—A.W. Tozer

APRIL 26 *Reading 116*
LESSONS FOR LIVING
Psalms 73–78

> *"I will remember the deeds of the* LORD*; yes, I will remember Your miracles of long ago. I will meditate on all Your works and consider all Your mighty deeds" (Ps. 77:11-12).*

Book III of the Psalms, a collection formalized at the time of the Exile, features the teaching psalms (*maskil*) of Asaph, a Levite who led a choir that praised God.

Overview
Asaph shared lessons for living in psalms which explore jealousy of prosperous wicked (Ps. 73), and puzzlement over the silence of God (Ps. 74). He proclaimed God as near (Ps. 75) and as known through His people (Ps. 76). And Asaph celebrated the Lord as a God of miracles (Ps. 77), of whom we learn through Israel's history (Ps. 78).

Understanding the Text

Psalm 73: Benefits of Faith. Asaph was overtaken by jealousy at the prosperity of the wicked. Only a change of perspective enabled him to grasp the benefits of faith. (See DEVOTIONAL.)

Psalm 74: The Silence of God. When disasters come God's people can only cry out to a God who has been silent.

"Why have You rejected us forever?" Ps. 74:1-2. The psalm posed a question that each of us is driven to ask at times. Why is God silent? Why hasn't He acted? Why does He seem to reject His people?

"Your foes" Ps. 74:3-8. In powerful images the poet described the ruin of the sanctuary in Jerusalem in 587 B.C. The defeat of Judah seemed to the psalmist to have been an attack on God Himself.

"We are given no miraculous signs" Ps. 74:9-11. Why, then, did God permit the enemy to mock Him? Why did God hold back, and not destroy them? Asaph questioned, but had no answer to offer. The silence of God was beyond explanation.

What are we to do when we too feel crushed, puzzled, and anguished because God permits us to suffer? Asaph had one suggestion only.

"But You, O God, are my King" Ps. 74:12-23. That suggestion is to affirm God as Sovereign, to remember His mighty acts in history, and to call on Him to defend His people and His cause.

We can never explain a present silence of God. But we can always remember that God has spoken in the past, and will speak again. Then, reassured by a fresh vision of how great our God is, we can continue—to wait.

Psalm 75: God Is Near. God, who will act in His own time to judge the earth, is near.

"Your Name is near" Ps. 75:1-10. God's name, standing here for His self-revelation, is "near" in two senses. (1) God is near now, for God upholds the moral pillars of the universe by raising some men up and bringing others down. His sovereignty is displayed in the fact that He chooses "the appointed time" for such judgments. (2) God is also near eschatologically, for a day is approaching when God will "cut off the horns [power] of all the wicked."

Psalm 76: Where God Is Known. The Lord is to be feared by those who see His works among His own people.

"His name is great in Israel" Ps. 76:1-3. The

people of Israel knew the true God, and exalted Him.

"You are" Ps. 76:4-10. The God Judah knew was characterized by majesty, power, and a righteousness expressed in His judgment of sinful men.

"Make vows . . . and fulfill them" Ps. 76:11-12. Asaph called on the people around Judah to submit and bring tribute (not "gifts") to God, who is to be feared.

This brief psalm reminds us that the God we know reveals Himself to others through us.

> Psalm 77: God of Miracles. When we are in distress, we too can remember that our God performs miracles.

"When I was in distress" Ps. 77:1-9. Asaph spoke of fervent, anguished, and continual prayer (vv. 1-3), which brought him no comfort at all (vv. 4-6). Sometimes prayer, the means by which we cast our burdens on God, actually increases the pressure we feel. When an answer to prayer is delayed we begin to wonder if God will ever show us favor again (vv. 7-9).

The theme fits the experience of the Jews who were taken captive to Babylon (cf. Ps. 74). The national disaster forced God's people to reevaluate their relationship with the Lord, and question the basis of their hope in Him.

Distress may force you and me to reexamine the foundations of our faith too. When this happens, our faith ultimately will be strengthened.

"To this I will appeal" Ps. 77:10-15. Asaph chose to remember "the deeds of the LORD," His "miracles of long ago." The key here is not simply that God is all-powerful, but that God has in the past used His power to redeem His people.

It is the same for us. When distress drives you and me to doubt, we are to recall what God has done for us in Christ. Jesus' resurrection demonstrates God's power. But it is the fact that the Son of God died and was raised, for *us,* that seals our confidence and hope.

"The waters saw You, O God" Ps. 77:16-20. In powerful images Asaph revisited the redemption of Israel through the waters of the Red Sea. We too can find our comfort and our hope in images, but images of Jesus on the cross, suffering for us, crying out to God to forgive His persecutors, promising paradise to the thief who believed in Him.

> Psalm 78: Memories. The message of God to Israel was engraved in the history of that people. Each act of God revealed more of the Lord; each event was a sermon directed to the people of today.

This psalm is a sermon intended to help Israel trust in God and forsake the stubborn ways of her forefathers (vv. 1-8). In the wilderness, God's people were judged when they willfully put the Lord to the test (vv. 9-31). Despite the fact that later generations forgot His miracles and were disloyal to His covenant, God was merciful to them (vv. 32-39). Despite the love displayed in the Exodus and Conquest (vv. 40-55), Israel continued to rebel against the Lord, and was justly punished (vv. 56-64). Then, despite Israel's faults, God chose David to shepherd His people (vv. 65-72).

The lesson of the psalm is clear. In David, Israel was granted a fresh start. God's people had to learn from their past, and follow David's example of faithfulness to the Lord if they hoped to avoid future disaster.

▶ DEVOTIONAL
What Good Is Faith, Anyway? (Ps. 73)

Probably you can understand Asaph's feelings. He'd tried all his life to be a good person. He'd tried to serve God. But all he'd gotten in return was sickness, hardships, and more troubles than he cared to name.

Of course, what really bothered Asaph was that he knew people with no faith at all who were healthy and strong, rich and carefree! No wonder Asaph was discouraged, and had begun to feel that "in vain have I kept my heart pure." What good is a faith that doesn't work in this world? What good is a faith that seems to bring more plagues and punishments on the believer than the world's wicked have to endure?

The psalm tells us that Asaph struggled with these thoughts in silence. And then, suddenly, one day in God's sanctuary, Asaph found his answer! Asaph realized that the troubles he experienced were gifts from God, and that the easy life granted the wicked was actually "slippery ground"!

What Asaph gained was a perspective that you and I need to keep constantly in mind. The easy life of the wicked is no reward, for it leads them away from any dependence on God! Why turn their thoughts to the Lord when they feel no need of His help? Yet, one day soon, they will be "swept away by terrors," for they will awaken to realize that this world is the dream, and eternity the reality.

And Asaph? Asaph, now ashamed of his earlier jealousy of the wicked, realized that the very trials he had hated had led him again and again to God in prayer. Only through his troubles had Asaph discovered God as "the strength of my heart and my portion forever."

Personal Application

The very difficulties that drive us to God are overwhelming evidence of His love.

Quotable

They took away what should have been my eyes,
(But I remembered Milton's Paradise).
They took away what should have been my ears,
(Beethoven came and wiped away my tears).
They took away what should have been my tongue,
(But I had walked with God when I was young).
He would not let them take away my soul—
Possessing that, I still possess the whole.—Helen Keller

APRIL 27 *Reading 117*
PRAYER FOR RENEWAL
Psalms 79–84

> *"Rescue the weak and needy; deliver them from the hand of the wicked" (Ps. 82:4).*

The anguish felt in Captivity and even after the return is expressed in psalms begging for renewal. They capture the emotions of oppressed believers throughout the ages who yearn for renewed evidence of God's favor.

Definition of Key Terms

The nations. In the Old Testament "nations" most often indicates pagan peoples. In the Psalms and Prophets "the nations" commonly represent peoples who are hostile to and who unjustly oppress God's chosen people.

Overview

Poems expressing captive Judah's anguish call for judgment on oppressors (Ps. 79), picture Judah as an uprooted vine (Ps. 80), and trace the national disaster to Israel's stubborn hearts (Ps. 81) and injustice (Ps. 82). Asaph begged God to judge pagan nations (Ps. 83), but Korah celebrated the blessing believers have even now through trust in God (Ps. 84).

Understanding the Text

Psalm 79: Against the Nations. Asaph reminded God of the violence done to Jerusalem by pagan nations and called on Him to pay them back.

"The nations have invaded" Ps. 79:1-4. The description of the ruin of Jerusalem best fits conditions of the Babylonian invasion.

"Pour out Your wrath" Ps. 79:5-8. Asaph begged God to judge the nations "that do not acknowledge You" and save his own desperate people. Asaph agreed that the disaster came because of the "sins of the fathers." But a new generation had arisen now, that appealed for mercy.

"For the glory of Your name" Ps. 79:9-11. Asaph argued that God should forgive His people and restore the nation for His

own glory. Ancient peoples measured the greatness of a deity by the power of the people who worshiped him. Judah's state held God up to ridicule.

"The reproach they have hurled at You" Ps. 79:12-13. Asaph called on God to pay back the nations, for in crushing Judah they had insulted the Lord.

This brief psalm has greater depth than at first appears. God should judge the nations because the land they invaded was His, the people destroyed were His, the glory tarnished by Judah's defeat was His, and the reproach was His. By punishing the nations God could display His forgiving grace and His mercy, reestablish His glory, mete out just punishment, and win the everlasting praise of His people.

Far more is involved in our own sin and discipline than we imagine. In a very real sense the loss involved is God's, not just our own! Yet this means that we can seek restoration confidently, knowing that God forgives and blesses not simply for love of us, but also for His own glory.

> Psalm 80. The Uprooted Vine. Asaph developed a common Old Testament image. Israel was a vine God had planted in Canaan, that now stood in desperate need of His care.

Three powerful images and three repeated appeals for restoration shape this psalm.

"O Shepherd of Israel" Ps. 80:1-3. God is able to save the people who are His sheep. Thus the psalmist appealed to God, "Make Your face shine upon us [i.e., look on us with favor], that we may be saved."

"O LORD God Almighty" Ps. 80:4-7. The Hebrew title means "God of Armies," and pictures a Sovereign Lord. God used His power to judge Israel; now the psalmist appealed to Him to use that same power to "restore us, O God Almighty; make Your face shine upon us, that we may be saved."

"O God Almighty!" Ps. 80:8-19 The Lord exercised His power in bringing His people out of Egypt and planting them in the soil of Canaan. He used it to break down the walls protecting His vineyard and expose it to destructive beasts. Asaph appealed to God to once again use His power to watch over His vine: to "restore us, O LORD God Almighty; make Your face shine upon us, that we may be saved."

> Psalm 81: Stubborn Hearts. History reveals both God's grace and Israel's stubborn, unresponsive heart.

Asaph had cried out to God for restoration. Yet in this psalm he explicitly recognized the fact that God is always willing to deliver and to bless. It was Israel's own failure to listen to the Lord and submit to Him that led to disaster. God, speaking through the psalmist, said, "If My people would but listen to Me, if Israel would follow My ways, how quickly would I subdue their enemies and turn My hand against their foes" (vv. 13-14).

We too can cry out to God when we are in distress. But we need to examine our lives, and see if our own unwillingness to obey is keeping God from giving us the blessing we so desperately desire.

> Psalm 82: Rise Up, O God. Asaph expressed his confidence that God would surely rise up and judge the nations.

The key to understanding this psalm lies in the meaning of the word "gods" in verses 1 and 6. The best interpretation views them as Israel's leaders, called "gods" because the Lord has delegated to them the responsibility of judging (cf. Ex. 21:6; 22:8, 28). These "sons of the Most High" were appointed to this high position to "defend the cause of the weak and fatherless"; and "maintain the rights of the poor and oppressed" (Ps. 82:3).

Privilege carries responsibility. The higher the privilege, the greater the responsibility. While God has given us great privileges, His is the ultimate responsibility. Thus Asaph was sure that God who holds men responsible will "rise up" and "judge the earth."

> Psalm 83: May They Perish. The psalm is an impassioned appeal to God to crush the nations that conspired against and attacked Israel.

Asaph felt justified in calling on God to punish the peoples who had wickedly attacked Isarel. The last verses pick up the emotion found in all the imprecatory psalms, and express one of the theological bases on which such appeals rest. "May they ever be ashamed and dismayed; may they perish in disgrace. Let them know that You, whose name is the LORD—that You alone are the Most High over all the earth" (vv. 17-18).

▶ DEVOTIONAL
Hidden Blessings
(Ps. 84)

Imagine yourself walking across a burning desert. You struggle through the soft sand, barely able to lift your feet on the shifting surface. The sun beats down on your head, burns through your shirt, drains your body of moisture so that your mouth feels like cotton and your tongue swells.

In a way, Psalms 78–83 describe Asaph's journey through a desert. God's people were weak and struggling. They were victims of enemies that had drained them and their land of every resource, and left them destitute and dying. It's no wonder that Asaph cried out again and again, appealing to God to restore the blessings once enjoyed by his people.

Now, suddenly, with Psalm 84, another psalmist reminds us that no matter how desperate our situation, any desert God's people may find themselves in has an oasis. In Old Testament times, God's people directed their feet upward. Approaching Jerusalem, buoyed up by the thought that they would soon appear before God in Zion, His people went "from strength to strength."

For you and me, the oasis is even more available. We need only to close our eyes to find ourselves in the very presence of the Lord. When our soul yearns for God, we can simply turn our thoughts to Him, and we are there, with Him.

Our days may be filled with troubles, and our hearts may ache, yet we can know the blessedness of those "whose strength is in You, who have set their hearts on pilgrimage." As pressures mount we can visit the Lord in our hearts, and be reminded that "no good thing does He withhold from those whose walk is blameless."

The peace, the quiet confidence, the strength we need, are all there, available in our desert places. As we draw on them we cry with the psalmist, "O LORD Almighty, blessed is the man who trusts in You."

Personal Application

The more difficult our days, the more we need to draw strength from God, and experience the blessing that is ours now through trust.

Quotable

"When I think upon my God, my heart is so full of joy that the notes dance and leap from my pen; and since God has given me a cheerful heart it will be pardoned me that I serve Him with a cheerful spirit."—Franz Josef Haydn

---

The Variety Reading Plan continues with 1 CORINTHIANS

APRIL 28 *Reading 118*
GOD'S FAITHFUL LOVE
Psalms 85–89

"Great is Your love toward me; You have delivered my soul from the depths of the grave" (Ps. 86:13).

Confidence that God loves us undergirds our faith. We trust Him, not only because He is able to help, but because He truly cares.

Overview

We experience God's love through a forgiveness (Ps. 85) that awakens commitment to Him (Ps. 86). God loves Zion (Ps. 87). And though we may experience despair (Ps. 88), we remain objects of His love and faithfulness forever (Ps. 89).

Understanding the Text

Psalm 85: You Forgave. In forgiveness God's love, faithfulness, righteousness, and peace all meet.

"You forgave the iniquity of Your people" Ps. 85:1-3. "Iniquity" is willful, rebellious sin. Even this God forgave, and covered His people's sins.

"Restore us" Ps. 85:4-7. As a forgiven people, God's own can expect renewed blessing as the Lord shows His unfailing love. God's promise of peace to the forgiven is contingent. Peace comes only to those who fear God and turn from "folly" (moral evil).

"Love and faithfulness meet" Ps. 85:10-13. How can we understand forgiveness? By seeing it as a place where God's love, faithfulness, and righteousness unite to bring peace. Because God loves us, He forgives. Because He is faithful to His covenant promises, He forgives. Because God is righteous, He pays the price in Christ that forgiveness requires. Where these three qualities unite in forgiveness, man is restored to that state of peace (well-being) which Adam and Eve first knew.

Viewing forgiveness as an expression of God's character and attitude toward man, we can be sure that "the LORD will indeed give what is good."

Psalm 86: The Undivided Heart. The forgiven man responds to God with gratitude, commitment, and trust.

"I am poor and needy" Ps. 86:1-4. The forgiven man acknowledges his need for mercy, and looks only to God for salvation and for joy.

"You are kind and forgiving" Ps. 86:5-10. The forgiven man recognizes the source of his blessing in God's character. Having experienced God's love, he prays freely to the One who alone can do marvelous deeds.

"Teach me Your way, O LORD" Ps. 86:11-13. The forgiven man focuses completely on God. With an undivided heart he seeks to learn and to walk in God's way. The forgiven man responds to God's great love with a wholehearted effort to glorify the Lord.

"You, O Lord, are a compassionate and gracious God" Ps. 86:14-17. Under attack by the arrogant, the forgiven man appeals to God for mercy, and confidently expects the Lord to provide signs of His goodness.

When you and I realize that we truly are forgiven, we too respond to the Lord with an undivided heart.

Psalm 87: Zion. The city of God reflects His glory.

"Zion" Ps. 87:1-7. The Zion of the Bible is first Jerusalem, the city God chose as the focal point of Old Testament worship; the location of His ultimate revelation of love in Christ Jesus. God chose Zion simply because of His love for this place from which His grace shines out on all men.

This psalm emphasizes the fact that Zion is not only a place, but also a people. To be born in Zion is to be one with the people of God, who gather round His revelation and rejoice in the Lord. The stunning emphasis of this psalm is that those who have been Israel's historic enemies, Rahab (Egypt), Babylon, and Philistia too, will one day know the Lord. It will be said of them as well as of Israel, "This one was born in Zion."

What an amazing reminder of God's grace, nestled here among psalms that celebrate forgiveness. And how we need to remember that those who seem God's most implacable enemies remain the objects of His forgiving love.

Psalm 88: In Distress. Those who know God well may still experience unremitting pain and grief.

"Day and night I cry out" Ps. 88:1-18. Most psalms which express despair or distress lead us from the depths to the heights. We share the psalmist's pain. But then our hearts are lifted as the psalmist turns his thoughts to the Lord. In affirming God's greatness or love the psalmist shows us where we can find peace.

This psalm is different. It speaks of an unrelenting darkness. Heman, its author, found himself "in the lowest pit, in the darkest depths." Though he called out to God "every day," there was no answer, and the psalmist felt rejected by the God on whom he depended. And this had been his lot "from my youth"! He had been afflicted, in terrors and despair, as long as he could remember.

What is the value of a psalm like this one? It reminds us that faith promises no 30-minute resolution of our problems, nor 30-second spiritual highs! There well may be days, weeks, or even years when all seems dark, and God remains silent. While faith frequently offers us inner peace in outward turmoil, some men and women with a true faith will find themselves living in unexpected, and unexplained, dark.

When that happens, we need not blame ourselves, as if the darkness were evidence of some personal spiritual lack. Psalm 88 reminds us that for some, who honestly trust and cry out to God, the answer is withheld and the darkness remains. When this happens, and we cannot say why, then we must believe that even the darkness is a gift, intended by God to be our "closest friend."

▶ DEVOTIONAL
Falling Out of Love
(Ps. 89)

We read about it all the time. Sometimes we even experience it. "I've just fallen out

In the Old Testament the throne is a symbol of not only human but divine rule. In the psalmist's exalted vision of God, His throne and the throne of the coming Messiah, "will endure before Me like the sun; and it will be established forever" (Ps. 89:36-37).

of love with my husband," the young wife writes to Ann Landers or complains to a counselor of "Can This Marriage Be Saved?" in the *Ladies Home Journal.* Or, perhaps the glow fades in our own marriage, and your spouse says, "I just don't love you anymore."

I suspect that many married couples in this land of ours, where divorce seems destined to strike 51 percent of those who marry for the first time, live with a conscious uncertainty about love. They aren't sure whether they are loved. Or even whether they really love their partner!

What reassurance we find in Psalm 89 that our relationship with God is different. There is no uncertainty here. God *does* love us. In fact, His love "stands firm forever." He is by nature a faithful Person: He will not take His love from us, and promises, "Nor will I ever betray My faithfulness." We can be comfortable in our relationship with God because He loves us with an unconditional, unchangeable love.

Psalm 89 is a long psalm. But it celebrates something basic in the nature of God, and vital to our relationship with Him. Because God's love stands firm forever, because faithfulness surrounds Him, we who walk in His presence are assured of blessing, of strength, and of a ready answer to our prayers.

Personal Application
Read the psalm thoughtfully. What evidence does it give that God is faithful forever? What does the fact of God's faithfulness mean to you?

Quotable
There is no place where earth's sorrows
Are more felt than up in heaven;
There is no place where earth's failings
Have such kindly judgment given.

For the love of God is broader
Than the measures of man's mind;
And the heart of the Eternal
Is most wonderfully kind. . . .

Pining souls! come nearer Jesus,
And O come, not doubting thus,
And with faith that trusts more bravely
His huge tenderness for us.

If our love were but more simple,
We should take Him at His word;
And our lives would all be sunshine,
In the sweetness of our Lord.—F.W. Faber

APRIL 29 *Reading 119*
OBSERVING RESTORATION
Psalms 90–98

> *"You make me glad by Your deeds, O Lord; I sing for joy at the works of Your hands" (Ps. 92:4).*

Book IV suggests a collection date near Judah's return from Exile. The first psalms remind us that every experience of God's blessing teaches us more about the character of our Lord, and deepens our appreciation of His great love.

Overview
A prayer of Moses for restoration (Ps. 90) is followed by psalms celebrating the joys of dwelling in God and proclaiming His love (Pss. 91–92). The following psalms hold God up as Ruler (Ps. 93) and Judge (Ps. 94). God is also celebrated for His voice (Ps. 95), His imminent coming (Ps. 96), His righteousness (Ps. 97) and His salvation (Ps. 98).

Understanding the Text
Psalm 90: A Prayer for Restoration. Moses reflected on the fragility of life, and appealed to God to "make us glad for as many days as You have afflicted us."

"From everlasting to everlasting" Ps. 90:1-6. God's eternal nature stands in awesome contrast to the brevity and fragility of human life. He is the only stable element in reality, beside whom the universe itself is young.

"Teach us to number our days" Ps. 90:7-15. The Exodus generation knew God's anger as their sins were exposed. Moses yearned for his people to learn the lesson taught by God's wrath, that the people might experience His compassion and be made "glad" for as many years as they had seen trouble.

How those who returned to their ruined homeland after decades of exile in Babylon must have identified with this psalm! How appropriate that it launches this book of psalms, which most view as liturgy used in public worship by the postexilic community.

Psalm 91: Dwelling in God. This psalm is the Old Testament's corollary to Jesus' call to the believer to "abide in Me."

"Rest in the shadow of the Almighty" Ps. 91:1-2. Safety is found in closeness to the Lord, represented here as "dwelling in the shadow of the Almighty."

"Surely He will save you" Ps. 91:3-13. Christ is the example of One who dwells in God's very shadow. When tempted, Jesus had no need to prove God's loving care by leaping from the temple's highest

point. He knew, without any need to test God, that the Lord had commanded "His angels concerning you to guard you in all your ways" (v. 11).

"I will rescue him" Ps. 91:14-16. These last, magnificent verses define what it means to dwell in God's shadow. It means to love Him, and to acknowledge His name. When you and I do love the Lord, and acknowledge Him in our daily lives, we can claim this promise: "He will call upon Me, and I will answer him; I will be with him in trouble, I will deliver him and honor him. With long life will I satisfy him and show him My salvation."

Psalm 92: Proclaiming God's Love. We too can exalt God, and sing for joy as we contemplate God's works and His thoughts.

"The righteous will flourish" Ps. 92:1-15. This too is a psalm with a promise. The "senseless man" cannot know God. But we who praise Him are filled with joy as we consider what He has done. With that joy comes assurance for the future. We have God's promise. Planted in the house of the Lord we will flourish forever, ever proclaiming and praising the Lord.

Psalm 93: God Reigns. God's throne was established in eternity. He is the one and only stable element in the universe.

Psalm 94: God Is Judge. God is moral Judge of His universe. The anxious person can find comfort in the love of a righteous God.

"O God who avenges, shine forth" Ps. 94:1-7. The oppressed believer cries out for God to judge, while the wicked man laughs at the notion God sees or cares.

"Take heed . . . you fools" Ps. 94:8-11. How senseless to suppose that a God who designed the ear cannot hear, and the eye cannot see! God does know—and will punish the wicked.

"Blessed is the man You discipline" Ps. 94:12-15. As Judge, God has given man His Law, in order to teach us His ways. The upright in heart follow it and are blessed.

"Your love, O LORD, supported me" Ps. 94:16-19. As Judge, God helps His own against the wicked, supporting them with love when they become anxious.

"He will repay" Ps. 94:20-23. As Judge, the God who is our present refuge will one day destroy the wicked and repay them for their sins.

If you or I become victims of the wicked, we too can celebrate God as Judge. He does see. He guides us with His Word, supports us with His love, and in the future God will repay.

Psalm 95: God's Voice. God is our King. We are to hear, and respond to His voice.

"Today, if you hear His voice" Ps. 95:1-11. The writer of Hebrews returns to this psalm two times, quoting or alluding to it in 3:7-11, 15, and 4:3, 5-11. The psalm recalls Israel's refusal during the Exodus to obey God and enter the Promised Land. That failure to obey led to 40 years of wandering in a wilderness until an entire generation died.

This psalm celebrates God as the great King. We acknowledge His lordship by responding when we hear His voice. Only by showing respect to God as King and Lord, and obeying His voice, can we find rest.

Psalm 96: God Approaches. This psalm is vibrant with shouts of joy as God approaches to "judge the world in righteousness." (See DEVOTIONAL.)

Psalm 97: God's Righteousness. The foundation of God's rule is justice and righteousness.

"Let those who love the LORD hate evil" Ps. 97:1-12. This psalm too is vibrant with a sense of awe at God's greatness. That greatness is displayed in a righteousness which establishes justice, punishes the wicked, and delivers the upright who hate evil.

If you and I live a righteous life, we are promised both light to guide us and joy to accompany us (vv. 11-12).

Psalm 98: God's Salvation. The whole universe joins the believer in singing praise to God for His salvation.

"Sing to the LORD" Ps. 98:1-3. The song of salvation celebrates the marvel of God's love, faithfulness, and righteousness, which bond together to win glory for "the ends of the earth."

"Shout for joy to the LORD, all the earth" Ps. 98:4-9. The phrase "all the earth" generally means all people of earth. But here it seems to have a different focus. The chorus is joined by the sea and all in it, the world and all living things in it, the rivers and mountains as well.

The psalm reminds us that nature too is warped from its original shape by Adam's sin (Gen. 3:17). Paul pictures the creation as "subjected to frustration" and waiting to be "liberated from its bondage to decay and brought into the glorious freedom of the children of God" (Rom. 8:20-21).

When God's salvation appears, you and I, and creation itself, will at last be set free.

▶ DEVOTIONAL
Line the Streets
(Ps. 96)

What would you do if you were walking through a dark alley, and suddenly met God?

This seems like a strange question. Yet it seemed the best way to express something I found some years ago when I did research on a class of children in a Christian school. I wanted to find out how eighth-graders in our local Christian school really felt about God, and how those feelings related to what they knew about Him. Briefly, a number of the boys and girls had a sense of warm, close, personal relationship with the Lord. But several felt uncertain, strained, and even distant. The immediate reaction of the first group, if they met God in a dark alley, would have been to run to Him with arms open, shouting out for joy. But the reaction of the second group would have been to draw back, and very possibly to slink away.

Remembering that research, I'm tempted to title Psalm 96 the Psalm of the Joyous Children. It is a shout of joy. It is a portrait of God's children lining the streets, with arms open, jumping up and down in excitement as the Lord approaches.

If our own relationship with the Lord is warm and close, this psalm will excite us too. The Lord is near! And we are lining the street, eager to meet Him and filled with a great joy.

Personal Application

Think of Christ's coming, and let the prospect fill your heart with joy.

Quotable

Let me hold lightly
Things of this earth;
Transient treasures,
What are they worth?
Moths can corrupt them,
Rust can decay;
All their bright beauty
Fades in a day.
Let me hold lightly
Temporal things,
I, who am deathless,
I, who wear wings!
—Martha Snell Nicholson

APRIL 30 *Reading 120*
WORSHIP THEMES
Psalms 99–106

> *"Praise the* LORD*! Give thanks to the* LORD*, for He is good; His love endures forever" (Ps. 106:1).*

Themes developed in worship psalms tend to focus on who God is, on what He has done, and on the wonder of His love for His people.

Overview
Israel worshiped the Lord as enthroned (Ps. 99), as God (Ps. 100), and as a God of love and justice (Ps. 101). One psalm foreshadows the Messiah's days and endless years (Ps. 102), while others celebrate God's great love (Ps. 103), His self-revelation in nature (Ps. 104), and particularly in history (Ps. 105) as a covenant-keeping God (Ps. 106).

Understanding the Text
Psalm 99: God Enthroned. God's absolute sovereignty is demonstrated in His gracious choice of Israel.

"The LORD *reigns" Ps. 99:1-9.* God has exercised His sovereignty in choosing Israel (vv. 1-3). That choice was just, as well as sovereign (vv. 4-5), for God's own keep His statutes (vv. 6-7). His justice is also displayed both in punishing Israel's misdeeds and in His forgiveness (vv. 8-9).

How important to remember that God does not use His power capriciously. He keeps His commitments, and does right.

Psalm 100: The Lord Is God. The one true God has revealed Himself in His personal name, Yahweh, "the LORD."

"Know that the LORD *is God" Ps. 100:1-5.* The personal name Yahweh was revealed to Moses. That name, which means "The One Who Is Always Present," was to be "My name forever, the name by which I am to be remembered from generation to generation" (Ex. 3:15). This psalm exults that it is Yahweh who is God. "He who made us, and we are His," is God. The Lord, who is good, and whose love endures forever, is ruler of the universe.

What a cause for thanksgiving. Because the Lord is God, we are safe and secure forever. For "His faithfulness continues through all generations."

Psalm 101: Love and Justice. David found a reason to praise, and a motive for godly living, in the love and the justice of God.

"I will be careful to lead a blameless life" Ps. 101:1-8. The psalm expresses David's commitment to the God whose love and justice he praised. That commitment was expressed in the psalmist's determination to live in a way that pleased God.

But note the motivation. David intended to lead a blameless life in view of the love and the justice of God. Because God loves us, we want to please Him. Because God is a God of justice, we can trust Him fully to reward those who do right, and to punish the wicked.

Our motivation too, when pure, is response to the love God has showered on us, and trust that His justice will guard and protect us as we live for Him.

Psalm 102: Messiah's Days and Years. Even in Old Testament times this psalm was known as messianic. It is a psalm which sensitizes us to the sufferings of the Saviour, and a future shaped by His ultimate exaltation.

"I am in distress" Ps. 102:1-11. In familiar terms this psalm evokes images of frailty and pain, rejection and despair. It was because of God's wrath against our sin, not the sufferer's, that the Father has "taken [Messiah] up and thrown Me aside."

"You will arise and have compassion" Ps. 102:12-17. In the Messiah, God's appointed time had come, and He Himself acted to have compassion on His people. Through that act "the LORD will rebuild Zion" when He appears "in His glory."

"Written for a future generation" Ps. 102:18-22. The benefits of the Messiah's act are not immediately visible. But they will be known in the future, when God declares His name openly and "the peoples and the kingdoms assemble to worship the LORD."

"Your years will never end" Ps. 102:23-28. Though death would cut short Messiah's days, His years will "go on through all generations." He is the One who laid the foundation of the earth. The universe will perish, but not Him, for "You remain the same, and Your years will never end." And, because of Messiah, "the children of Your servants will live in Your presence."

When we read such psalms and many of the prophets we realize how often God turned the eyes of His Old Testament people ahead, and how clearly He portrayed the coming Saviour. Most importantly, however, we ourselves are led to sense the wonder of a God who would enter our world and suffer here as a human being, in order to redeem a people who have no benefit to return to Him but our worship and our praise.

The Old Testament compares God's love to that of a father for his own children (Ps. 103:13). Only in the New Testament do we discover that God *is* a Father to individual believers. It is Father-love that has motivated God to do for us those wonderful things which Psalm 103 records.

Psalm 103: God's Great Love. David chronicled evidence of God's love in a psalm that is sure to move us to praise. (See DEVOTIONAL.)

Psalm 104. God in Nature. God's greatness is displayed in all the wonderful things which He has made. We are to meditate on creation's evidence of His glory, and praise the Lord.

"When You send Your Spirit, they are created" Ps. 104:1-35. This psalm parallels the Genesis Creation account. It is well to read it as a commentary on Genesis 1, not to explain how God created, but to celebrate the wonder of His works.

The parallels between this psalm and Genesis 1 are:

Day 1	Gen. 1:3-5	light	Ps. 104:2a
Day 2	Gen. 1:6-8	firmament	Ps. 104:2b-4
Day 3	Gen. 1:9-13	land, water	Ps. 104:5-13
		veg., trees	Ps. 104:14-18
Day 4	Gen. 1:14-19	hvnly. bodies	Ps. 104:19-24
Day 5	Gen. 1:20-23	sea creat.	Ps. 104:25-26
Day 6	Gen. 1:24-28	anmls., man	Ps. 104:21-24
	Gen. 1:29-31	food for all	Ps. 104:27-30

Psalm 105: God in History. God is known by what He has done in history for His people Israel.

This psalm praises the Lord for His "wonderful acts." The miracles and judgments of the Lord seen through the history of His dealings with Israel reveal Him as a covenant-keeping God, who keeps His promises and works miracles on behalf of His own.

Psalm 106: Covenant Love. In this dark counterpart to Psalm 105, the psalmist reviewed history's evidence of human failure. Against that background the wonder of God's covenant-keeping love shines bright and clear.

▶ DEVOTIONAL
Let Me Count the Ways (Ps. 103)

Elizabeth Barrett Browning wrote one of the English language's most powerful love poems. It begins:

> How do I love thee? Let me count the ways.
> I love thee to the depth and breadth and height
> My soul can reach, when feeling out of sight . . .

and it ends

> With my lost saints—I love thee with the breath,
> Smiles, tears, of all my life!—and, if God choose,
> I shall but love thee better after death.

Browning's powerful poem wasn't the first to count love's ways. The first was David, who a thousand years before Christ set down a list in Psalm 103 of ways in which God loves you and me. And his list is far more specific, far more extensive, and far more wonderful than Browning's.

How does God love us? He forgives our sins and heals our diseases (v. 3). He preserves our life and crowns us with love and compassion (v. 4). He satisfies our desires with good things (v. 5). He works justice for the oppressed (v. 6). He made known His ways to Moses and revealed Himself in history's mighty acts (v. 7).

And the list goes on.

He is compassionate and slow to anger (v. 8). He does not treat us as our sins deserve (v. 10).

And still there is more. Far too much to record in this brief meditation.

But if life ever seems hard and the future so bleak that you can see nothing but darkness ahead, turn in your Bible to this psalm that celebrates God's love. As you count with David the ways that God loves you, the darkness will break. And, with David, you will be lifted up to sing God's praise.

Personal Application

Jot down the number of this psalm on the inside back cover of your Bible, so you can find it at times when you feel down.

Quotable

"I believe that each individual is precious to God, and that a divine undefeatable purpose is being worked out in every life; a life that goes on after death. A thousand things happen to us which are not 'the will of God,' but nothing can happen to us which can defeat His purposes at last."— Leslie D. Weatherhead

---

MAY 1 *Reading 121*
GOD THE GLORIOUS
Psalms 107–112

> *"Be exalted, O God, above the heavens, and let Your glory be over all the earth" (Ps. 108:5).*

Book V begins here. The first six psalms focus on the glories of who God is and what He has done.

Overview

Six psalms lead us to praise the Lord as God of Rescue (Ps. 107), God of Victory (Ps. 108), God of Vindication (Ps. 109), God of Messiah's Triumph (Ps. 110), God of Wonders (Ps. 111), and God of the Good Man (Ps. 112).

Understanding the Text

Psalm 107: God of Rescue. The goodness of God is revealed through His rescue of the redeemed from four symbolic perils: destitution, imprisonment, sickness, and storm.

"Let the redeemed of the LORD say this" Ps. 107:1-3. The four perils that follow symbolize the actual experience of Judah during the Captivity. A generation recently

restored to the Jews' ancient homeland could identify with each situation, and realize afresh the wonder of God's redemption.

"Some wandered in desert wastelands" Ps. 107:4-9. The hungry, thirsty, and homeless of Judah cried to the Lord. God redeemed, and with unfailing love led them to a city where they could settle.

The pattern seen here is followed in each portrait of redemption. Calamity leaves God's people in desperate straits. They cry to God. He rescues them. Each calamity and rescue enriches our understanding of redemption, that we might praise God.

"Some sat in darkness and deepest gloom, prisoners" Ps. 107:10-16. They cried to the Lord, and with unfailing love He cut through the bars of iron.

"Some became fools through their rebellious ways" Ps.107:17-22. When they cried to the Lord, with unfailing love He healed their sickness and rescued them from the very brink of death.

"Others went out on the sea in ships" Ps. 107:23-32. In great peril from terrible storms they cried to the Lord. With unfailing love He calmed the storm and led them to their desired haven.

"Whoever is wise, let him heed" Ps. 107:33-43. The psalm concludes with a vision of God creating a fertile land from the wilderness in which the people might dwell. They rebelled and experienced oppression, but "He lifted the needy out of their affliction."

What does the psalm say to you and me? While the psalm draws on physical perils for its imagery, it symbolized that spiritual peril in which all human beings find themselves. Our God is a God of Rescue, for He redeems us from every danger. Freshly aware of the meaning of redemption, we too "give thanks to the LORD, for He is good; His love endures forever" (v. 1).

> Psalm 108: God of Victory. David rejoiced, for he was confident that "with God we will gain the victory, and He will trample down our enemies."

"My heart is steadfast" Ps. 108:1-5. David began this psalm, which is a prayer for help against Israel's enemies, with an expression of total confidence in the Lord. David's very petition was worship, for he knew that "great is Your love" and "Your faithfulness reaches to the skies."

What a reminder for us. Our requests too are to be made in complete confidence. Beginning each time of prayer with praise for who God is will help give us the steadfast heart from which David speaks here.

"God has spoken" Ps. 108:6-9. God has promised the victory that David now claimed. To toss the sandal represented Israel's domination of a humbled and submissive Moab.

David, even before the battle, so relied on the covenant commitment of God to be with Israel's armies, that he spoke as if the victories were already won. Has God made promises to us? If so, the answer to our prayer is as sure as if it were already given.

"With God we will gain the victory" Ps. 108:10-13. Underline each "will" of verse 13 in your Bible. And remember to pray with David-like confidence in God.

> *Psalm 109:* God of Vindication. God will vindicate the righteous and punish their accusers.

"Wicked and deceitful men" Ps. 109:1-31. Jesus tells us to pray for those who mistreat us and do good to our enemies. How does a psalm like this one, in which David pleaded with God to punish the wicked who oppressed him, fit with Jesus' contrasting emphasis?

We can hardly dismiss the imprecatory psalms by saying that in old times people were vindictive, or by contrasting the "God of the Old Testament" with the "God of Jesus." The fact is that both Testaments portray God as One who vindicates His own and punishes the wicked. Jesus often warned His listeners of eternal punishment, and 2 Thessalonians 1:6-7 says, "God is just: He will pay back trouble to those who trouble you and give relief to you who are troubled."

Yes, today you and I are to emphasize the grace of God, and display that grace in every dealing with others. But let's not forget that God is a God of justice as well as grace. The anger and antagonism David expressed toward the wicked who torment the righteous are but a dim reflection of the wrath God will unleash when the day of grace is past.

> Psalm 110: God of Messiah's Triumph. The coming Messiah of God is God (v. 1), destined to unite in His person the kingship promised to a descendant of David (vv. 2-3) and a new priesthood (v. 4), and destined also to judge the earth (v. 5).

Though only seven short verses, this is the most quoted of all Old Testament psalms. To understand its significance read Matthew 22:44; Mark 12:36; 16:19; Luke 20:42-43; Acts 2:34-35; 1 Corinthians 15:25; Ephesians 1:20-21; Colossians 3:1; Hebrews 1:3, 13; 5:6, 10; 6:20; 7:17, 21; 8:1; 10:12; 12:2; and 1 Peter 3:22.

The God we praise in this psalm is a God who, in Jesus Christ, will bring all His purposes to pass. He will redeem His own, He will judge the wicked of the world, and He will establish the endless kingdom of our God.

> Psalm 111: God of Wonders. We celebrate the wonder-working power of God, for His works have provided us with redemption.

"I will extol the LORD with all my heart" Ps. 111:1-10. Here is another psalm well worth memorizing. Its 10 short verses move us to praise as we see again that God has chosen to exercise His power to redeem and to care for you and me.

▶ DEVOTIONAL
God of the Good Man
(Ps. 112)

I was leading a retreat in Washington State, and asked each person in the very large circle to share one thing each really liked about himself or herself: one thing that marked him or her off as a good person.

I knew it would be hard for some. So many of us have been taught from childhood that we're only sinners saved by grace, that it somehow seems "wrong" to say or think anything good about ourselves. It was hard for the folks there in Washington. Only a few mentioned anything significant. Most choked out things like, "Well, I enjoy children," or "I dress nicely." But when we got to the pastor's wife, she said honestly, "I don't know anything good about myself."

How tragic. Because, you see, our God is not a God of sinners. He is a God *for sinners. But He is a God of sinners who are being made good!*

It is appropriate for David to speak of the blessedness of the "man who fears the LORD, who finds great delight in His commands." This is a man being transformed by his relationship with the Lord: a man who through that relationship has become good. He is generous and lends freely. He conducts his affairs with justice. He trusts in the Lord. He cares for the poor. And his righteousness, his good actions, "endures forever."

Why not take a moment before you read Psalm 112 to ask yourself the question I posed on that retreat. What are some things you like about yourself? What things mark you off as a good person? When you've made your list, then read in this psalm the blessings that God has in store for you.

He has made you good that He may bless you forever.

Personal Application

Be glad, but not proud, when you find good in your heart and life.

Quotable

"It is the highest and holiest of the paradoxes that the man who really knows he cannot pay his debt will be forever paying it."—G.K. Chesterton

MAY 2 *Reading 122*
PASSOVER PRAISE
Psalms 113–118

> *"The LORD remembers us and will bless us; He will bless the house of Israel, He will bless the house of Aaron, He will bless those who fear the LORD—small and great alike" (Ps. 115:12-13).*

This cycle of six psalms, known as the "Egyptian Hallel" (praise), was used at Passover. While only one psalm mentions Egypt, the theme of each fits the season during which Israel celebrated redemption from a condition of slavery.

Overview

Israel celebrated the Passover season with this cycle of six psalms. They affirmed God for raising up the oppressed (Ps. 113) and for deliverance from Egypt (Ps. 114). They offered the praise of the community (Ps. 115), the individual (Ps. 116), and all nations (Ps. 117). The cycle concluded with an exultant shout of praise that looked forward to Messiah (Ps. 118).

Understanding the Text

> Psalm 113: Raising the Poor. God is praised for stooping to lift the needy from the ash heap and seating them with princes.

"Praise the LORD" Ps. 113:1-3. Passover was truly a season of praise. Israel recalled all God had done for His people as each Jewish family reenacted the supper held the night death struck Egypt and passed by the blood-marked homes of God's own. At last Pharaoh acknowledged his sin, and released his slaves. Passover thus was a festival of freedom, a joyous celebration of God's salvation. No wonder this psalm begins, "Praise the LORD!" and called on Israel to praise Him "now and forevermore."

"Who is like the LORD our God?" Ps. 113:4-9 No wonder God is praised. The God of Israel, who is exalted over all nations and whose glory is above the heavens, stooped down to "lift the needy from the ash heap" and seat "them with princes."

We Christians too have a passover to celebrate. God in Christ became a man, and humbled Himself to accept death, that we whom faith marks with His blood might be lifted up beyond princes, to stand before the very throne of God. Praise Him indeed!

> Psalm 114: Out of Egypt. The very earth trembled as God's strong hand brought Israel out of slavery to freedom.

The verses of this psalm allude to God's historic acts of parting the Red Sea and Jordan River (v. 3), causing Sinai to quake (v. 4), and water to spring out of solid rock (v. 8). God's love motivated redemption; His power accomplished it. Then, as now, all His people could do was to watch in wonder as God did it all. And offer Him praise.

> Psalm 115: Israel's Praise. This psalm is a hymn sung by the whole community, rejoicing in its solidarity as a people of the Lord.

"To Your name be the glory" Ps. 113:1-11. Passover recalls events which set the God of Israel apart from the deities of all nations.

Pagans scoff because God cannot be seen, yet their idols of silver and gold are inanimate lumps. Grasping the vast difference between God and all the gods, the people of God cry out together:

> O house of Israel, trust in the LORD—
> He is their help and shield.
> O house of Aaron, trust in the LORD—
> He is their help and shield.
> You who fear Him, trust in the LORD—
> He is their help and shield.

"The LORD remembers us and will bless us" Ps. 115:12-18. Together the people of God affirmed that God will bless (vv. 12-13), and wish one another His blessing (vv. 14-15). Together they "extol the LORD, both now and forevermore."

Perhaps the thing we need to learn from this psalm is the benefit, the vital importance, of corporate worship. The whole psalm reveals a worshiping community that by its worship encourages all to trust God more deeply. We need the mutual support shared worship offers. We need the reminder that we are part of a vast company who know God, who have experienced His blessing, and who are confident that God will continue to bless.

No wonder the New Testament says, "Let us not give up meeting together, as some are in the habit of doing, but let us encourage one another—and all the more as you see the Day approaching" (Heb. 10:25).

Psalm 116: Personal Thanksgiving. Passover did not only commemorate the deliverance of the nation. It spoke of salvation of individuals as well. The true believer was sensitive to the personal nature of salvation, and cried out his thanks that "when I was in great need, He saved *me!*"

"I love the LORD" Ps. 116:1-7. The believer of every age has had a deep sense of need, and an awareness that God has somehow acted to meet that need. Faith that "the LORD is gracious and righteous, our God is full of compassion" has been expressed by calling on the name of the Lord, saying, "O LORD, save me!" And in every age, that cry has brought the soul rest.

It's no wonder that we love the Lord. We have felt His presence in our darkest hour, and know Him not simply as the Great Architect of the universe, or as uncaused cause, but our own gracious and loving Lord.

"How can I repay the LORD for all His goodness?" Ps. 116:8-19 When I tried to witness to other sailors after my conversion in the Navy, they were puzzled. How could salvation be free? After all, what beside fear of punishment could keep a person from doing whatever wrong he or she wanted to do?

The psalmist knew what every believer understands intuitively. God has delivered us from death, and His salvation has awakened love. All we ask, all we want to know, is how can we even begin to repay Him for His goodness.

This psalm says simply that we choose to be the slave of the One who has released us from slavery. We want only to serve the One who has served us. Our gratitude wells up, and with our life as well as our lips, we cry out, "Praise the LORD."

Psalm 117: God as Saviour: Passover is prophetic for all peoples, for it reveals a saving God.

Here the psalmist celebrates a truth of which the prophets often spoke. God is the Saviour not only of Israel, but of the world. In Christ the vision of this psalm has been fulfilled. All the nations, all peoples, praise and extol the Lord for the salvation Jesus has won.

▶ DEVOTIONAL
This Is the Day!
(Ps. 118)

Look back to see ahead. Turn to yesterday to see tomorrow.

It's almost a paradox. But it's true. When Israel looked back each Passover season at the redemption won for them from Egypt, they were in fact looking ahead, and viewing the ministry of the Messiah.

What will His coming mean? A shout of praise, that "His love endures forever" (vv. 2-4). Freedom found by taking refuge in the Lord (vv. 5-9). A fresh awareness of our desperate need, relieved by the fact that the Lord "has become my salvation" (vv. 10-14). Shouts of joy punctuating the realization that "I will not die but live" (vv. 15-18). Endless praise, as we enter the gates of heaven to give God thanks for our salvation (vv. 19-21). And in it all, the exaltation of Jesus who, rejected by the builders, became the cornerstone of God's plan of salvation (vv. 22-23).

Then comes the stunning realization that "this is the day that the LORD has made"—a day that spills over into eternity; a never-ending day throughout which we will give God thanks, exalting Him for He is "my God" and because "He is good; His love endures forever."

Today when you and I turn to look back, we see our tomorrow in the cross of Jesus, our Passover sacrifice. In the shadow of Calvary we sense the dawn of the day that the Lord has ordained for you and me. When we turn again after looking back at the cross, and look ahead, we can see just beyond the horizon of tomorrow the return of Christ.

What will that return mean? How clearly this majestic psalm tells us. For you and for me, Christ's return will mean freedom, shouts of joy, and endless days of praise.

Personal Application

When you look back to the cross, look intently until you see tomorrow.

Quotable

"I have written much about the need to come to terms with sin, about repentance and Christians' duty to change and live by God's ways. So perhaps it is a good time to remind ourselves that the relationship between man and God is always a two-way street. The corollary to man's repentance is God's grace, His loving forgiveness. Grace is what that singular moment in history at Golgotha is all about. For only through the power of Christ's resurrection can we find the forgiveness which makes life bearable."—Chuck Colson

MAY 3 *Reading 123*
DELIGHTS OF GOD'S LAW
Psalm 119

> *"Open my eyes that I may see wonderful things in Your Law" (Ps. 119:18).*

This, the longest psalm in the Bible, contains a series of eight-line meditations based on each of the 22 letters of the Hebrew alphabet. The psalm celebrates a revelation which brings delight, because each fresh word from God reveals not just information but its Author.

Definition of Key Terms

Some eight different Hebrew synonyms are used in referring to Scripture. These are:

Dabar ("word"), a general term for any form of divine revelation.

Torah ("law"), a teaching, indicating a single command, the Books of Moses, or all of Scripture.

Piqqudim ("precepts"), detailed instructions given by God as guardian of His people.

Huqqim ("statutes"), binding laws engraved on a permanent record.

Mispatim ("ordinances"), judgments made by God, containing God's judgments concerning man's rights and duties.

Miswot ("commandments"), orders given by competent authority.

'Edot ("testimonies"), vivid and unmistakable witnesses to man of God's will.

'Imra ("promise"), a term often translated "word," suggesting the trustworthiness of divine truth in any form.

Together these words form a clear picture of the Scriptures. They are God's authoritative Word, in which we can have complete confidence, and through which we learn to trust God and to live a life characterized by godliness.

Overview

Twenty-two brief meditations, each launched with a different letter of the Hebrew alphabet, delight the reader. They speak of the love revealed in words which unveil the Author and serve as light to guide the believer all his or her life.

Understanding the Text

Each of the 22 meditations found here has great value. What follows is only a sample of the richness available to us in the 119th Psalm.

"How can a young man keep his way pure?" Ps. 119:9-16 We tell Sarah, at nine, how important it is to keep her dental appliance in her mouth. Somehow she can't grasp the fact that it is either this, or wear metal during her teen years. Sarah is like the "young man" of this verse. She is too inexperienced to have gained wisdom, or be able to judge the future consequences

of present actions. How the young need a guide to life's good!

In a sense each of us is "young." None of us has the wisdom to make right moral choices on his own. And so in grace God gave us His Word to live by. He did not intend to restrict or limit us, but to guide us along paths that assure blessing.

We then are faced with a single basic choice. Will we or will we not "stray from Your commands"?

If we are to remain safely on that path, we need to hide God's Word in our hearts (v. 11), recount His laws (v. 13), rejoice in following His statutes (v. 14), meditate on his precepts (v. 15), and never neglect His Word (v. 16).

We tell Sarah, "Trust us. Keep your appliance in your mouth, and you'll have no regrets in the future." For Sarah too there is only one issue. Do what we say, no matter how little she wants to at various times.

Perhaps Psalm 119 can be viewed as the psalmist speaking to you and me as Sarah's mom and I speak to her. "Trust God," he said. "Concentrate on knowing and doing God's Word. If you do, you can be sure. Your future will be bright."

"Turn my eyes away from worthless things" Ps. 119:33-40. What a desperate need we have for perspective. For Sarah, our nine-year-old, everything she passes in the store or sees on TV awakens desire. She sees a colorful tote bag, and wants it. Never mind the fact that she has various bags at home, and has no need. She sees a delightful stuffed bear, and wants it. No matter that the attic has a box of stuffed animals given to her by adoring relatives.

When warned against asking for another thing, she says to me, "Buy this bathing suit, Daddy. You deserve it."

I tell her, "I don't need swim trunks. I already have some." She pouts, and can't understand when I tell her that even if I had a million dollars I wouldn't buy what I don't need. How hard it is, in a materialistic culture, not only to bring up a child, but even to tell the difference between our own "wants" and "needs."

And so the psalmist asked God to direct him "in the path of Your commands," and said, "for there I find delight." As I read on I realize how much I need the Word of God to give me perspective. I know that delight is found in the path of God's commands, not in possessions or pleasures. Yet I need His Word to:

> Turn my heart toward Your statutes
> and not toward selfish gain.
> Turn my eyes away from worthless things;
> renew my life according to Your Word.

I can't afford to lose the perspective on reality that can be found only in God's rich and wonderful Word.

"I have kept my feet from every evil path" Ps. 119:97-104. One thing you can't get away from is people. Whether they are your enemies or your friends, you and I are always surrounded by others. Young Sarah finds that both enemies and friends exert a terrible influence.

"But everyone has this kind of lunchbox," she complains. "The new one you bought me is junky." Or, "Why can't I have a notebook like Heather's?" Pouting, at times whining, always fearful she won't be accepted or liked if she doesn't have or do what the other kids have or do, Sarah at nine is learning about the tyranny of other's expectations.

We tell her that people will like her for herself, and that she doesn't need to follow the crowd. But that is hard for little ones, and even for most adults, to realize.

The psalmist, however, had made a commitment that guarded his heart against the tyranny of both enemies and friends. "I love Your Law," he said, and "I meditate on it all day long." God's commands made him "wiser than my enemies," and he cared little for their taunts. Through God's Word he had "more insight than all my teachers," and "more understanding than the elders."

The psalmist was able to stand back and evaluate the ways others followed, and to make his own choices, not just mimic them. "I meditate on Your statutes," he said. "I obey Your precepts." And we too, through that Word of God which becomes increasingly sweet as we know and obey it, find freedom from the expectations of others, and learn to "hate every wrong path."

▶ DEVOTIONAL
One Step at a Time
(Ps. 119:105-112)
One of the most helpful images in Psalm 119 is found in verse 105. "Your Word is a lamp to my feet and a light for my path."

In Bible times there were no powerful flashlights. The traveler carried a small oil lamp, whose flax wick gave off only a little light. There was enough to see by. Not enough to see what lay ahead down the path, but enough to take the next step without stumbling or falling.

What a reminder for us. The Word of God is a lamp to our path. It doesn't illuminate our future, but it does shine in our present. God's Word gives us the light we need to take our next step in life.

Personal Application
If we fill our minds and hearts with God's Word, we will have the light we need to know what we must do next.

Quotable
"I would distinguish between academic study and more general study of the Bible. At one level—and perhaps this is the most important level—I approach the Bible with a readiness and an expectation to hear the voice of God there. But there is no conflict between that more devotional use of the Bible and its academic study. I have sought to make available to my hearers, in a form they can assimilate, the results of my trying to enable them, like myself, to recognize and apply the voice of God in Holy Scripture."—F.F. Bruce

MAY 4 *Reading 124*
SONGS OF ASCENTS
Psalms 120–134

> *"I rejoiced with those who said to me, 'Let us go to the house of the LORD.' Our feet are standing in your gates, O Jerusalem" (Ps. 122:1-2).*

How do we feel when Sunday comes, and we approach the church where we worship? This group of psalms reminds us that worship is to be a joyful occasion, rich in meaning for the believer.

Overview
These 15 "songs of ascents," on a variety of themes, were probably chanted by Hebrew pilgrims as they approached Jerusalem to attend one of the Old Testament's annual worship festivals.

Understanding the Text

Psalm 120: The Homesick Soul. The first psalm of ascents pictures a burdened believer, far from his spiritual homeland. This land of strife is not his home: his homeland is a land of peace (*shalom:* well-being).

"I call on the LORD" Ps. 120:1-7. At stated times during the year each Hebrew was called to turn in his heart, if not possible to return physically, to Jerusalem, to join the believing community in worship at the temple of the Lord.

This psalm pictures a person living among the ungodly, who realized afresh at this time of year that he was a man of peace, who lived among those who were for war. How important for us to return to our roots, and with the community of faith look to and call on the Lord.

Psalm 121: Looking to God. There is no help in the hills on which the pagans worship. Our help comes from the Lord.

"The LORD watches over you" Ps. 121:5. What can we expect from the God who watches over us at all times? Simply that He will "keep you from all harm—He will watch over your life."

Psalm 122: Joy in Jerusalem. Arrival at Jerusalem, where God's people worshiped, was a cause of celebration.

Psalm 123: Dependence on God. God's people look to Him for mercy as a slave, dependent on another's kindness, looks expectantly to his or her master.

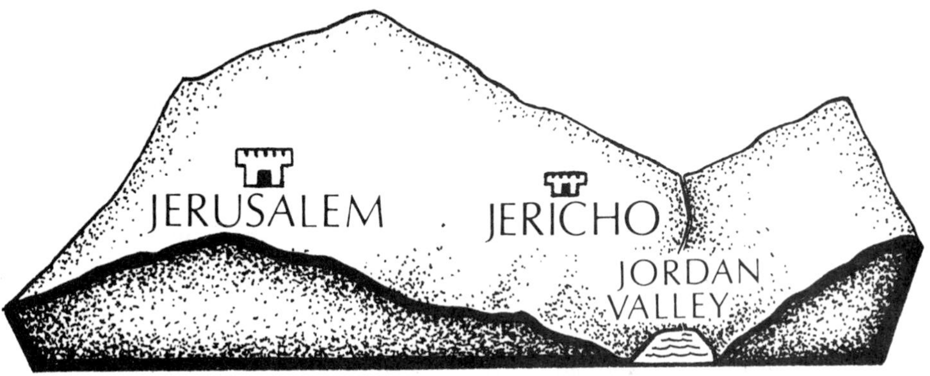

Jerusalem lies high in the mountains of central Palestine. From the time of David and Solomon, represented in this sketch, Jerusalem was unique—a site God chose through David as the one site on earth where a temple might be built, and sacrifices offered to the Lord.

"Have mercy on us, O Lord" Ps. 123:1-4. Mercy is a much-admired quality in the Old Testament. It is compassion and concern for a helpless person's plight, which finds expression in reaching out with help. The person who needs mercy is completely dependent on the willingness of another to help. How wonderful that as we depend on God, He does reach out to help us.

Psalm 124: God, Our Help. Only because God is on Israel's side has this people survived. So all Israel praises the Maker of heaven and earth, who has proven to be His people's help.

"If the Lord had not been on our side" Ps. 124:1-8. Modern nations have claimed to have God on their side. In World War I the belt buckles of German soldiers proclaimed, *"Gott Mit Uns,"* and U.S. currency announces, "In God We Trust." Yet only Israel had a valid basis for making this claim, for God's covenant promises were made to this people alone, not to modern nations. Even then, God was with His people to deliver them only when they were faithful to their own covenant responsibilities. You and I as individuals do experience God's grace. And we can determine to be faithful to the God who has been so good to us.

Psalm 125: A Song of Trust. God does good to those who are good. We can trust in Him, for He alone can never be moved.

Psalm 126: Great Things! Israel's restoration to her homeland after the Babylonian Captivity is just one of the "great things" the Lord had done for His chosen people.

"Those who sow in tears will reap with songs of joy" Ps. 126:1-6. Looking back, the psalmist could see that Israel's Captivity was a prelude to blessing. As you and I look back on the difficult times in our lives, we too will be able to sense the good hand of God at work.

Psalm 127: Our Heritage. The children God gives us are our "house," a heritage from the Lord who does not build houses but families.

"Sons are a heritage from the Lord" Ps. 127:1-5. The attitude of the Jewish people toward children is best expressed in this simple psalm which views them as a gift from God, and suggests that "the more, the merrier!"

Psalm 128: Fear of the Lord. The blessings of reverence toward God are celebrated here. We rejoice in the Lord. And we rejoice in His good gifts to us.

"May the Lord bless you" Ps. 128:1-6. Fear of the Lord, that Old Testament respect for God that motivates obedience, is the path of blessing for all of us. In most cases the blessing will be obvious: long life, prosperity, a large and happy family.

These are the things that the Jews of biblical times wished for one another as they gathered for worship. Peace and prosperity.

Not all of us who walk in God's way have this experience on earth. But every one of us who knows and serves the Lord is assured peace and prosperity in those "days of your life" which stretch on and on forever in eternity.

Psalm 129: Peace and Prosperity. Against the background of past troubles, the blessings of peace and prosperity seem doubly important.

Psalm 130: Redemption's Song. The man who stands amazed at God's willingness to forgive understands both his own sinfulness, and the extent of God's "unfailing love" and "full redemption." (See DEVOTIONAL.)

Psalm 131: Childlike Faith. David pictured faith as a young child, nestling against its mother, and contrasted this attitude with an arrogance which challenged God's Word.

Psalm 132: God's Covenant Oath. God's promise to David assured Israel of her destiny.

"The Lord swore an oath" Ps. 132:1-13. Jerusalem, the city of David, was ruled by an unbroken line of his Descendants. And one of his Descendants would yet be placed on Judah's throne, there to rule "forever and ever." In addition, God had chosen Zion as the location for His temple. So Israel's future was secure. God had said:

"This is My resting place forever and ever;
here I will sit enthroned,
for I have desired it—
I will bless her with abundant provisions;
her poor will I satisfy with food.
I will clothe her priests with salvation,
and her saints will ever sing for joy"
(vv. 13-16).

You and I too face a future that is totally secure. We can celebrate, for in Christ God's oath to David was fulfilled, and a new promise made to every person who puts his or her trust in the Lord.

Psalm 133: In Praise of Unity. Worship brings God's people together as a family. The oil "poured on the head, running down on the beard," speaks of celebration and happiness. We too find joy when we experience our unity with brothers and sisters in the family of God.

Psalm 134: In Praise of Ministry. What a privilege and joy to be servants of the Lord.

▶ DEVOTIONAL
"What Do You Mean, Nineteenth?" (Ps. 130)

Donald Grey Barnhouse used to picture a believer, burdened with a sense of guilt, appealing to God for forgiveness. The believer was ashamed, for he knew that he had committed the same sin many times before. "O Lord," he begged, "please forgive me again. I know I don't deserve it, as this is the nineteenth time I've committed this sin this month. But please, Lord, forgive me this nineteenth time." And, Dr. Barnhouse would say, the Lord looked up in surprise. "What do you mean, nineteenth?"

The point this great old expositor of God's Word was making is stated clearly in Psalm 130:3-4. "If You, O Lord, kept a record of sins, O Lord, who could stand? But with You there is forgiveness."

God keeps no record of our sins! When we confess, He forgives, and then our sins are gone.

What a blessing! Our past no longer is a weight we must carry with us always. Our past is gone, and we can look ahead with renewed hope. Through forgiveness we have been cleansed! Tomorrow will be different, and through Christ we will win victory over sins that in the past meant defeat.

Personal Application

Don't let a sense of shame keep you from enjoying God's forgiveness.

Quotable

Mother to Son

Well, son, I'll tell you:
Life for me ain't been no crystal stair.

It's had tacks in it,
And splinters,
And boards torn up,
And places with no carpet on the floor—
Bare.
But all the time
I'se been a-climbin' on,
And reachin' landin's,
And turnin' corners,
And sometimes goin' in the dark
Where there ain't been no light.
So boy, don't you turn back.
Don't you set down on the steps
'Cause you finds it's kinder hard.
Don't you fall now—
For I'se still goin', honey,
I'se still climbin',
And life for me ain't been no crystal stair.
—Langston Hughes

MAY 5 *Reading 125*
WORKS OF GOD'S HANDS
Psalms 135–141

> *"I praise You because I am fearfully and wonderfully made; Your works are wonderful, I know that full well" (Ps. 139:14).*

Praise and worship grow out of God's revelation of Himself to us. The more we know of what God has done and is doing, the more we respond to Him in worship.

Overview

The many and varied works of God for His people stimulate praise. The Lord is praised for works on behalf of Israel (Pss. 135–136). In contrast, the Babylonian captives were unable to sing the songs of Zion (Ps. 137). David praised God for the Lord's work in shaping his life (Pss. 138–139) and in preserving him from enemies (Pss. 140–141).

Understanding the Text

> Psalm 135: God Has Chosen Jacob. That choice, expressed in history by the Lord's defeat of Israel's enemies, moved the psalmist to call God's people to praise.

"Israel . . . His treasured possession" Ps. 135:1-7. The psalmist began by expressing his wonder that God should have chosen the Hebrew people to be His own. As the entire Old Testament testifies, this was a sovereign choice, not based on Israel's merits. God, "who does whatever pleases Him," selected Israel simply because He wanted to.

How good to know that God's choice of you and me is also an expression of His free will. God loves us because He wants to, not because we deserve to be loved.

"He struck down the firstborn of Egypt" Ps. 135:8-21. God's love counts. He, unlike the foolish pagan's idols, is able to act for us in the real world. No wonder Israel was moved to praise! God wrested Israel from slavery, struck down many nations, and gave His people their land as an inheritance.

> Psalm 136: His Love Endures. A mere six syllables in Hebrew compose the joyful response of the people as a worship leader chanted praise to God for His many wonderful works. We can capture that response in six English words: "for His love has no end!"

> Psalm 137: No Song to Sing. In Babylon, far from the inheritance promised by God, Israel was unable to sing songs of praise.

The preceding and following psalms show us that praise grows out of God's self-revelation. As we know Him through His works, our hearts respond.

In Babylon, far from their ancient homeland, the Jewish people felt crushed and isolated from God. Only when God acted again, to crush their oppressors and restore them to the Holy Land, would songs of joy again spring from their lips.

The psalm reminds us it is only when we see God at work, in history and in our present lives, that we know real joy. Jesus put it this way: "Ask and you will receive, and your joy will be complete" (John

16:24). Christ did not imply that receiving the thing we pray for will bring joy. His point was that in the answer to prayer we will sense God at work, and this—God active in our lives—gives us joy.

Psalm 138: His Purpose for Me. Each believer is also a work of God's hands, shaped for a purpose. We find joy, and are moved to worship as we trust Him to work in and through us.

"Exalted above all things" Ps. 138:1-3. David called us to focus thoughts of God on His "name" and His "Word." When we do, we learn to trust His qualities of love and faithfulness.

"When they hear" Ps. 138:4-5. The word uttered in the name of the Lord should stimulate even the kings of the earth to praise.

"You preserve my life" Ps. 138:6-9. David had a personal reason for praise. He had experienced God's love and faithfulness as the Lord preserved him in many troubles.

What David understood, and we need to appreciate, is that each of us is important to God. His love has led Him to make our lives meaningful by linking it to His eternal plan. We may not have a large part. We may not even know now what His purpose in us is. Yet God does have a purpose to fulfill in your life and mine. To Him, we do count!

We can say with David, "The LORD will fulfill His purpose for me; Your love, O LORD, endures forever—do not abandon the works of Your hands."

Psalm 139: You Know Me. In one of the most significant of his psalms, David probed the nature of his relationship with God, and traced that relationship back to the Lord's creation of his "inmost being." (See DEVOTIONAL.)

"You know me" Ps. 139:1-12. David was untroubled by the paradox of a transcendent God who is also imminent. He acknowledged God as One who fills the entire universe, yet saw the Lord as constantly, pervasively present with His servants. God was near, observing every act of David, conscious of his every thought. God is transcendent, far above the highest heaven. Yet God is also totally present in the saint's here and now, giving each of us His undivided attention.

"You created my inmost being" Ps. 139:13-16. David extended his wonder at God's concern for the individual to the past and the future. God has been with us, superintending our development from the womb. Furthermore God's care reaches on into the future: to "all the days ordained for me," which were written in God's book before even one of our days came to be.

How clearly this psalm teaches the significance of individual life: a significance underlined by God's careful attention to the individual from conception, through his fetal stage, into his childhood and beyond, encompassing every day of the individual's existence. God knows, even if many today deny, that life begins in the womb and extends on into eternity. How precious you are to God! And how precious the unborn.

"How precious to me are Your thoughts, O God" Ps. 139:17-24. David responded to the love he sensed in God's care with a desire to please the Lord. He wanted to understand the Lord's thoughts, to hate those who hated God, and to be cleansed of "any offensive way."

God does know us, even when we try to hide from Him. And when we consciously open our hearts, and become totally honest with God and ourselves, He tests our hearts, cleansing us from "offensive" ways.

Psalm 140: Justice for the Poor. David called on God to rescue him, sure that among His works is protecting the believer from men of violence, and securing justice for the poor.

Psalm 141: My Refuge. David sought help from God, first to live a righteous life, and then to be delivered from evildoers he expected God to judge.

▶ DEVOTIONAL
Darkness As Light
(Ps. 139)

I heard the story many years ago from a mom who used preschool lessons that I wrote. Her little girl came into the house, complaining, "I wish he'd leave me alone." Mom went outside, but found no one there.

A little later the three-year-old returned. "I wish he'd leave me alone." Again Mom looked, but no one was there.

When it happened a third time, Mom sat down with her daughter and asked: "Who?"

The answer was: Jesus! The three-year-old's Sunday School lesson was "Jesus Always Sees Me." The little girl had wanted to pick some forbidden flowers, and wished that Jesus would leave her alone so she could do it without being seen!

Sometimes we feel a little like that little girl. The idea that God is with us constantly, observing every act, aware of every thought, seems burdensome.

David, however, had a different perspective. We can never hide from God, for even darkness is light to the Lord. But David did not *want* to be hidden! The fact is that life itself is darkness to us! Only a God to whom darkness is as light can guide us safely from conception to eternity.

Even more, David realized that God is bending close to express His love, not to catch us in some sinful act. He stays close to guard us, and to guide us into His best. When we sense Him near and realize that what we feel is love we, with David, will invite Him, "Search me, O God, and know my heart; test me and know my anxious thoughts. See if there is any offensive way in me, and lead me in the way everlasting."

Personal Application

God knows us perfectly and loves us completely. We have no need to hide from Him.

Quotable

"In two ways the presence of God is an antidote against sin: first, because God sees us, and, secondly, because we see God."—Ignatius of Loyola

---

MAY 6 *Reading 126*
HALLELUJAH CHORUS
Psalms 142–150

> *"Praise Him for His acts of power; praise Him for His surpassing greatness" (Ps. 150:2).*

How great a contribution the Psalms make to our lives. In reading them we are led to praise the Lord.

Overview

Four psalms of David lift us from a desperate sense of need (Pss. 142–143) to confidence in God as our deliverer (Ps. 144) and then to praise (Ps. 145). The psalter ends (Pss. 146–150) with five beautiful praise psalms, each beginning and ending with the Hebrew shout, Hallelujah! which means "Praise the LORD!"

Understanding the Text

Psalm 142: In Desperate Need. The setting is the cave in which David hid from Saul's pursuing army. Troubled and discouraged, David cried out to God for rescue.

"Before Him I tell my trouble" Ps. 142:1-5. One of the most important lessons we learn from the Book of Psalms is that, like David, you and I can "pour out our complaints" to the Lord. We can tell Him every trouble, share every dark and distressed emotion. When no one else is concerned about us, we have in God One who truly cares.

God doesn't want you or me to clutch our fears or our pain to us. God wants us to share that fear or pain with Him, knowing that He will listen and does care.

"You are my refuge" Ps. 142:5-7. Sharing our fears or pain with the Lord reminds us of who God is. He not only listens, He is able to help! Our enemies may be too strong for us, but they are not too strong for the Lord. Our appeal is directed to the one Being in the universe who is able to help!

We come to the Lord with our fears and our pain. We come away in peace, with a renewed sense of hope. At last we can see ahead to a time when "the righteous will gather about me because of Your goodness to me."

Psalm 143: In Deep Distress. Once again fears drove David to the Lord. Again he was helped. He meditated on God's past works, and ultimately reached a clear understanding of how he must deal with his trials. (See DEVOTIONAL.)

Psalm 144: My Deliverer! God answered David's prayers and rescued him from his enemies. Here David celebrated the Lord as his deliverer.

"Praise be to the L*ORD, my rock" Ps. 144:1-4.* Wonder of wonders, God had again stooped to deliver a mere mortal, and David was awed by the fact. Echoing Psalm 8, David cried, "What is man that You care for him?"

We sense the joy David felt as he piled image on image, celebrating his loving God as *my* rock, *my* fortress, *my* stronghold, *my* deliverer, *my* shield. It is amazing that God should be all this for any human being. It is overwhelming that He should be all this for me!

"Part Your heavens, O L*ORD, and come down" Ps. 144:5-11.* These verses are not so much an appeal for God to act as they are celebration of a deliverance already experienced. In a sense David was reliving the rescue that lifted him from despair to joy.

"Then" Ps. 144:12-15. The outcome of deliverance is peace and prosperity. No wonder David cried, "Blessed are the people whose God is the LORD." God saves us from all our troubles, and He intends to bless.

Psalm 145: Praise His Name. This is an acrostic psalm: each line begins with a different letter of the Hebrew alphabet. We might name it, "Praising God from A through Z," as each letter brings to mind a different reason to praise the Lord.

Psalm 146: Praise the God of Jacob. This first of the five Hallelujah psalms that close the psalter focuses our attention on who Israel's God is, and what He does.

"Praise the L*ORD, O my soul" Ps. 146:1-4.* God is praised as our only real source of help and deliverance.

"The God of Jacob" Ps. 146:5-9. The name is rooted in history: this is the God who bound Himself by covenant oath to be the God of Israel. We celebrate Him, for this God is the Maker of all, faithful forever, sustainer of the oppressed, who frees the prisoner, heals the infirm, loves the righteous, watches over the alien, sustains the helpless, and frustrates the ways of the wicked.

All the psalmist knows about this God of Jacob thrills him, and moves him to sing praises!

"The L*ORD reigns forever" Ps. 146:10.* This is the capstone. The One we know and celebrate is Sovereign in this universe. In Him we are safe and secure.

Praise the Lord.

Psalm 147: Praise the Sustainer. The Hallelujah Chorus continues with praise to God for maintaining the universe He created, and caring for all who put their trust in His unfailing love.

Psalm 148: Praise Him, All Creation. Nature does more than reveal God's wisdom and power. All the splendor of Creation joins Israel in exalting God's name, and thus offers praise.

Psalm 149: Praise Him, All Saints. God's people, whom He created and whom He crowned with salvation, rejoice in the Lord and offer Him praise.

"In the assembly of the saints" Ps. 149:1-8. God's people have two callings, each of which are aspects of worship. First, God's people are called to sing His praises, and rejoice in the One who takes such delight in them (vv. 1-5). Second, God's people are to take a stand on this earth against evil (vv. 6-9). While in Old Testament

times Israel literally went to war against pagan peoples in their land, today we are to be engaged in spiritual warfare, doing all we can to uphold righteousness and do justice in our society.

Psalm 150: Praise the Lord. The final, jubilant psalm in this great Old Testament book pictures a people who gather before the Lord (v. 1) to praise His works and character (v. 2) with every resource they possessed (vv. 3-5), until all living things join in with shouts of joy (v. 6).

▶DEVOTIONAL
What Can I Do?
(Ps. 143)

No one likes to feel helpless. Almost any situation seems bearable if there is only something, anything, that we can do that might improve it. Despair and depression usually flood in only when we realize that we are helpless, unable to affect our situation, totally at the mercy of our circumstances.

I think David felt much like this when he penned Psalm 143. He cried out to God for mercy and relief (v. 1). He realized he had no right to expect God's help (v. 2). Yet his desperate situation filled him with dismay (vv. 3-4). David recalled what God had done and reaffirmed his trust in the Lord (vv. 5-8). But like you and me, David also seemed to cry out, "What can I *do?*"

The answer is simple and clear. We see it in David's words, "Show me the way I should go," and, "Teach me to do Your will" (vv. 8b, 10). We may be helpless to better our situations. But there is still something we can do! Each day, each hour, as we wait for God to deliver us, we can concentrate our attention on doing God's will for that day, for that hour.

What we can always do, no matter how helpless we may be to alter our situations, is to live each moment as servants of the Lord, ready always to respond as His "good Spirit" reveals an opportunity to serve Him.

What a sense of relief comes over us as we make David's discovery. We are not helpless after all. There *is* something we can do. The most important thing of all. We can do God's will.

Personal Application

When you can't change your situation, make it your priority simply to do each hour, each day, what God wills.

Quotable

"God is looking for people through whom He can bless the world. Say definitely: Here am I; I will give my life to this calling. Cultivate your faith in the simple truth: God hears prayer; God will do what I ask.

"Give yourself to others as completely as you give yourself to God. Open your eyes to sense the needs of a perishing world. Take up your position in Christ and in the power which His name and life and Spirit give you. And go on practicing definite prayer and intercession."—Andrew Murray

---

The Variety Reading Plan continues with DANIEL

Proverbs

INTRODUCTION

Proverbs is a collection of sayings that examines specific behaviors, asking whether each is wisdom or folly. The book's pithy observations state general principles that apply to all human beings, not just to believers. Many of the sayings in this book are ascribed to Solomon (970–930 B.C.), while Proverbs 25:1 indicates the collection was not edited and put in its final form prior to the time of Hezekiah (715–686 B.C.).

In thought, vocabulary, style, and themes the biblical proverbs are similar to Egyptian and Babylonian wisdom literature dating a millennium before Solomon, and to Phoenician writings from 14th century Ugarit. This not only supports the biblical dating of Proverbs to Solomon's time, but also suggests that the issues explored in Proverbs reflect a common interest of all peoples for advice on how to live wisely and well. Among the many topics given close attention in this book are wisdom and folly, wealth and poverty, righteousness and wickedness, generosity and stinginess, adultery, laziness, family, child-raising, and friendship. The proverbs themselves however, are not grouped by topic; thoughts on various subjects are scattered in apparently random order throughout the book.

Whether we simply read through Proverbs, or use a concordance to group its sayings by theme, we too are helped by the Bible's ancient words to the wise.

OUTLINE OF CONTENTS

READING GUIDE (5 Days)

If hurried, you may read only the passages related to the "core theme" in your Bible and the Devotional in each chapter of this Commentary.

Reading	*Chapters*	*Core theme*
127	1–9	Wisdom
128	10:1–22:16	Poverty
129	22:17–24:34	Responsibility
130	25–29	Anger
131	30–31	Wives

Proverbs

MAY 7 *Reading 127*
IN PRAISE OF WISDOM
Proverbs 1–9

> *"Wisdom will save you from the ways of wicked men, from men whose words are perverse" (Prov. 2:12).*

The wise person is not the individual of great intellectual achievement, but the person who makes appropriate choices in his or her daily life. To know what is right and to do it is wisdom for you and me, as it was for the ancient Hebrew.

Definition of Key Terms

Wisdom. The Hebrew root translated "wise" and "wisdom" (*H-K-M*) occurs over 300 times in the Old Testament. Together they portray a wise person as one who subjects himself to God and who applies divine guidelines when making everyday choices. In contrast, foolishness involves rejection of the divine guidelines, or another failure to apply them when making moral or other choices.

Several parts of the Old Testament are classified as "Wisdom literature." These include Job, Proverbs, Ecclesiastes, and Psalms 19, 37, 104, 107, 147–148. Wisdom literature does not state divine law, or record divine promises, but rather simply describes behavior that illustrates wise and foolish choices a person may make.

Overview

After summarizing the benefits of this book (1:1-7), these first chapters take the form of a father exhorting his son not to reject (vv. 8-33) but to embrace wisdom (2:1–4:27). He warned against adultery (5:1-23; 6:20–7:27) and folly (6:1-19), picturing wisdom and folly as two very different women (8:1–9:18).

Understanding the Text

"For attaining wisdom and discipline" Prov. 1:1-7. This introduction describes the purpose of the book, a major portion of which was written by Solomon. If we read carefully we can gain insights that will help us "acquire a disciplined and prudent life, doing what is right and just and fair."

"If sinners entice" Prov. 1:8-33. Parents of every era have worried about their children's choices. We may feel that we have more to worry about today, with drugs, violence, sex, and satanism so prevalent in our society. Yet each new generation has faced similar moral challenges, and parents have expressed their concern.

We can't help but identify with the themes mentioned by the father of Proverbs 1–9, who warned his son against "giving in" to peer pressure and getting in with the wrong crowd (vv. 10-19). Like him we warn our children to think beyond the moment and be wise. In the end those who ignore wisdom and make sinful moral choices will be overtaken by calamity. Then it will be too late: "They will eat the fruit of their ways." Only a person who listens to and follows the way of wisdom will "live in safety and be at ease, without fear of harm."

Perhaps we can sense in these words some of the desperation we may sometimes feel. Too many young people think, "That can't happen to me," and foolishly take that first experimental step that draws them inexorably into a way of life that leads to destruction. This father realized, as you and I do, that we can't make choices for our children. But we can point out the way of wisdom—and pray.

"You will understand what is right and just and fair—every good path" Prov. 2:1–4:27. Paying attention to wisdom has lasting benefits, which are expressed in these verses. Each of the benefits is rooted in the fact that God Himself "holds victory in store for the upright" and "is a shield to those whose walk is blameless" (2:6-7). While it is possible to view consequences of a good moral life as a natural outcome, Proverbs affirms a supernatural element. God observes our choices, and He Himself "guards the course of the just."

How do we achieve these benefits? Several sayings from Proverbs 3 and 4 are rightly famous, and merit memorization. Here are just four:

"Trust in the LORD with all your heart and lean not on your own understanding; in all your ways acknowledge Him, and He will make your paths straight" (3:5-6).

"Honor the LORD with your wealth, with the firstfruits of all your crops; then your barns will be filled to overflowing, and your vats will brim over with new wine" (vv. 9-10).

"Do not withhold good from those who deserve it, when it is in your power to act" (v. 27).

"Above all else, guard your heart, for it is the wellspring of life" (4:23).

What makes a parent's words authentic and compelling? Actually, it is his or her own life, the ability to *guide* another (4:11) along a path we ourselves have traveled. When we share truths that are authenticated by our own dedicated lives, our children will find it easier to "accept what I say" (v. 10).

"In the end she is bitter as gall" Prov. 5:1-23; 6:20-27. Adultery is dealt with at length, perhaps because the sex drive is so strong in the young; perhaps because sexual temptation so vividly contrasts the prospect of an immediate reward with delayed consequences. Wisdom demands that in making any choice we consider distant as well as immediate consequences. When it comes to sexual sins, the desire for immediate satisfaction often pushes aside any thought of the future. In our sexually oriented society, the warning of Proverbs against adultery is especially appropriate, not just for the young, but for each of us.

What are some of the points these passages make? While illicit sex seems to "drip honey," the long-range consequences are "bitter as gall" (5:1-14). God has provided us with marriage to satisfy our sexual needs: we are to be captivated by our spouse. The wise man focuses on developing his relationship with his wife, so that their love will be totally satisfying (vv. 15-20). God knows our ways, and has ordained that evil deeds ensnare the wicked (vv. 21-23). Immorality has consequences. As walking on hot coals scorches the feet, so committing adultery brings disgrace (6:20-35). A person controlled by his or her hormones is like a beast; an ox led to the slaughter or a deer stepping into a noose, "little knowing it will cost him his life" (7:1-26).

The thing that sets man above the animals is judgment: the ability to stand aside from instincts, and decide what to do on the basis of what is wise and what is right. The person who is drawn into sex sin acts like an animal, for he or she sets aside that human capacity and acts on the basis of passion alone. To commit adultery is not simply wrong, it is a denial of the Creator's gifts which set man above all other living creatures.

"Does not wisdom call out?" Prov. 8:1–9:14 These chapters picture wisdom and folly as two different women. The one quietly offering something more precious than all worldly riches and honor; the other raucously tempting those going by to pass through her doorway, only to tumble unexpectedly into the "depths of the grave."

The voice to which we respond as we live our daily lives demonstrates to all whether we are among the wise or among the foolish of men.

▶ DEVOTIONAL
The Beginning of Knowledge (Prov. 1–2)

One of those fascinating phrases that dot the Scriptures launches the Book of Proverbs. "The fear of the LORD is the beginning of knowledge." That phrase does not, of course, mean that it's smart to be scared of God. After all, Adam and Eve were scared of God after the first sin. They ran away and tried to hide, which wasn't smart at all! First off, they couldn't really hide from God. And second, only by running *to* God rather than away from Him could they have found relief from their guilt.

No, the "fear of the LORD" isn't being scared at all. What it means here, and in most Old Testament texts, is simply to have respect for God; to be fully aware and in awe of the fact that He is living and present.

This, the fact that we take God's existence and His presence into account when thinking about any issue or making any decision, is "fear of the LORD." And this, taking God's existence and presence into account, is the beginning of knowledge. If we take God into account, we look to Him for guidance. And we find it, for "the LORD gives wisdom, and from His mouth come knowledge and understanding" (2:6).

What a blessing to be among those who fear God and look to Him for wisdom.

But what a challenge to realize that we are responsible to live wisely. We are called not simply to know the will of God, but to let wisdom "enter your heart" so that we will "walk in the ways of good men and keep to the paths of the righteous" (vv. 10, 20).

Personal Application

God's wisdom is displayed in the way we live, not in what we say.

Quotable

"Wisdom is the right use of knowledge. To know is not to be wise. Many men know a great deal, and are all the greater fools for it. There is no fool so great as the knowing fool. But to know how to use knowledge is to have wisdom."—Charles H. Spurgeon

MAY 8 *Reading 128*
SOLOMON'S WISE SAYINGS
Proverbs 10:1–22:16

> *"The wisdom of the prudent is to give thought to their ways, but the folly of fools is deception" (Prov. 14:8).*

The pithy sayings of Proverbs apply to moderns as well as to the Israelite of the ancient East. Billy Graham once said he read a psalm each morning to enrich relationship with God, and a chapter of Proverbs each evening to guide his dealings with his fellowmen.

Background

On reading Proverbs. Either of two ways to read the Proverbs—straight through, or by drawing out sayings on a common topic—can be helpful. Either of these two ways is appropriate for devotional reading; each is illustrated in today's look at the sayings of Solomon. For your reading, choose the approach which feels most comfortable to you.

Overview

Each of these chapters contains sayings that share insights into a variety of practical matters. We can draw sayings on a given topic together to develop more complete pictures of such things as a righteous way of life, the values of discipline, or attitudes toward work, laziness, and poverty.

Understanding the Text

"The proverbs of Solomon" Prov. 10:1-32. This first chapter of Solomon's proverbs touches on many varied facts of life:

v. 1. The choices we make necessarily affect others, not just ourselves.

vv. 2-3. Wealth gained by wicked means can never provide security.

vv. 4-5. Hard work is rewarded—and so is laziness!

vv. 6-7. Goodness brings lasting blessing, wickedness does not.

v. 8. It's better to listen than to blither on without paying attention.

v. 9. The person with nothing to hide has nothing to fear.

v. 10. Any act that harms others is a first step on the road to ruin.

"The lot is cast into the lap, but its every decision is from the LORD" (Prov. 16:33) illustrates how Proverbs reveals a people's basic attitude toward life. The biblical universe is not ruled by chance, but all lies under the control of the sovereign God. We should read the Proverbs of the Bible with an eye to their underlying as well as obvious meanings.

v. 11. The spoken word can heal or harm others.

v. 12. Our basic character is revealed in the way we treat others.

v. 13. Punishment will overtake the man whose judgment is poor.

v. 14. Discretion calls for thinking before speaking.

vv. 15-16. Wealth provides a measure of security. But wealth unjustly gained provides only disaster.

v. 17. The teachable man is the best teacher.

v. 18. The problem with hatred is that it corrupts the one who hates.

vv. 19-21. Words are important. Be careful how you use them.

v. 22. God's blessing is the only true wealth. (This emphasis is suggested in the grammer of the Heb. construction.)

v. 23. What a person enjoys reveals his character.

vv. 24-25. The fears and insecurity experienced by the wicked are well-founded!

v. 26. How frustrating it is to work with a lazy person.

vv. 27-30. The confidence of the righteous is well-founded too!

vv. 31-32. The words of a righteous person are both wise and helpful.

"The plans of the righteous are just" Prov. 12:5. One topic which is given much attention by Solomon is righteousness. The righteous make just, not violent plans (v. 5; cf. 16:27, 30; 21:7), for they truly care about justice (17:23, 26; 18:5; 19:28). Because the righteous are concerned for those in need, the righteous are generous (12:10; 21:25-26). They hate falsehood and dishonesty (13:5), so in all they do the righteous are upright (11:3; 15:19; 21:8).

As a result the righteous are delivered from troubles that the wicked bring on themselves (11:8, 21; 12:21; 13:17; 22:5). They rightly feel secure (10:9, 25, 30; 12:3, 7; 14:11, 32), and have hope for the future (10:11, 16; 11:8, 19; 12:28; 16:31; 21:21). The righteous receive what they want; the wicked what they dread (10:24; 11:23). The righteous know joy (10:28; 12:20; 21:15) and are rewarded; the wicked get what they deserve (11:18, 31; 14:14).

The dividing line between the righteous and wicked is clear, no matter how a society may attempt to confuse it by calling the corrupt "adult," and by exploiting violence under the banner of "free speech."

God is never deceived, even though courts and lawmakers may be.

We who choose righteousness surely are and will be blessed. Those who reject it will receive what their actions deserve.

"He who spares the rod hates his son" Prov. 13:24. The Jewish people were noted for their love of children, and were among the best of parents in the ancient world. Such sayings as this lend no support to an abusive approach to child-rearing, but instead emphasize the necessity of discipline if boys and girls are to freely choose God's way as adults. Discipline was not harsh, but loving and purposeful: "Discipline your son, for in that there is hope" (19:18), and "folly is bound up in the heart of a child, but the rod of discipline will drive it far from him" (22:15).

Proverbs reminds us that we adults too are subject to discipline: God's. When God disciplines us, His motive too is loving. The wise person recognizes this and gladly responds, while the foolish man rebels and is punished (10:17; 12:1; 13:1, 18; 15:5, 12, 32; 17:10; 19:16, 25; 21:11).

"All hard work brings a profit, but mere talk leads only to poverty" Prov. 14:23. The proverbs of Solomon often contrast the benefits of hard work and the disaster courted by laziness. The one who works his land produces food, profit, wealth, and high status (10:4-5; 12:11, 24, 27; 13:4; 14:23; 22:29). Whatever his excuses (v. 13), the lazy man will soon lack even necessities (18:9; 20:4, 13).

▶ DEVOTIONAL
Blessed Are the Poor? (Selected Proverbs)

In general, the Proverbs seem to take a middle-class attitude and blame poverty on the poor. That view is reflected in such sayings as, "Lazy hands make a man poor" (10:4), "Do not love sleep, or you will grow poor" (20:13), "He who loves pleasure will become poor" (21:17), and, "Drunkards and gluttons become poor, and drowsiness clothes them in rags" (23:21).

At the same time, the Proverbs show that at times the poor are victims of powerful others. "A poor man's field may produce abundant food," 13:23 notes, "but injustice sweeps it away." The reality of injustice is shown in warnings against harming the powerless poor (18:23; 22:16). Indeed, the well-to-do are to offer help: "If a man shuts his ears to the cry of the poor, he too will cry out and not be answered" (21:13).

It's true that in society the rich are generally lionized and the poor ignored (14:20; 19:4, 6-7). It is also true that wealth protects the rich from dangers to which the poor are vulnerable (10:15; 18:11). Yet wealth is not an unmixed good, nor poverty an evil. After all, "A man's riches may ransom his life, but a poor man hears no threat" (13:8). No one bothers to kidnap a poor man!

Perhaps the most significant saying, however, is found in 19:17. "He who is kind to the poor lends to the LORD, and He will reward him for what he has done." What is so important about this proverb? It reflects the Old Testament's conviction that God has a special love for the poor. Society ignores, exploits, or abandons the poor. But God makes the poor an object of His special concern. When we are sensitive to the needs of the poor, we are close to God, for God Himself is on their side.

Personal Application

We are not to assign blame for poverty, but to help the poor.

Quotable

Advantages of Being Poor

1. The poor know they are in urgent need of redemption.

2. The poor know not only their dependence on God and on powerful people but also their interdependence with one another.

3. The poor rest their security not on things but on people.

4. The poor have no exaggerated sense of their own importance and no exaggerated need of privacy.

5. The poor expect little from competition and much from cooperation.

6. The poor can distinguish between necessities and luxuries.

7. The poor can wait, because they have acquired a kind of dogged patience born of acknowledged dependence.

8. The fears of the poor are more realistic and less exaggerated, because they already know that one can survive great suffering and want.

9. When the poor have the Gospel preached to them, it sounds like good news and not like a threat or a scolding.

10. The poor can respond to the call of the Gospel with a certain abandonment and uncomplicated totality because they have so little to lose and are ready for anything.—Monica Hellwig, as quoted by Philip Yancey

MAY 9 *Reading 129*
SAYINGS OF THE WISE
Proverbs 22:17–24:34

> *"My son, if your heart is wise, then my heart will be glad; my inmost being will rejoice when your lips speak what is right" (Prov. 23:15-16).*

Speaking directly to us, the wise of the ancient world recapture the style of chapters 1–9, of a father speaking with his hand resting on the shoulder of his son. As Proverbs 23:15-16 says, a good father rejoices when his son or daughter speaks what is right.

Overview

These "sayings of the wise" abandon the brief saying in favor of paragraph-length observations that convey the practical wisdom of the ancient world.

Understanding the Text

"Listen to the sayings of the wise" Prov. 22:17-21. Proverbs are valuable to us only if we listen carefully, take them to heart, and pass them on as well as practice them. They must also be understood not as gimmicks by which others are manipulated, but as ways to express our trust in the Lord in daily life.

This introductory paragraph helps us understand why the proverbs "work." While some simply provide penetrating insights into how human society works, many function only because God Himself supervises the consequences of the choices you and I make.

"Do not exploit the poor" Prov. 22:22-23. The warning not to exploit the poor "for the Lord will take up their case" illustrates the point made above. Living by the Proverbs does require faith. Many actually do become rich and seem to prosper at the expense of the poor. Only the conviction that God is a just Judge makes us sure that in the end "the Lord will take up their case and will plunder those who plunder them."

It takes faith to follow guidelines given in Proverbs, just as it takes faith to respond to any Word of God.

"Do not make friends with a hot-tempered man" Prov. 22:24-25. Never suppose that you can avoid being influenced by your friends. So don't choose as a friend someone with a major character flaw. This proverb warns, "You may learn his ways and get yourself ensnared."

"Do not be a man who . . . puts up security for debts" Prov. 22:26-27. Economic advice too is found in these proverbs. These verses simply mean: never cosign a loan unless you're ready and willing to pay it off yourself!

"When you sit to dine with a ruler" Prov. 23:1-3. The social climber is likely to find himself in a situation where he feels most uncomfortable!

"Do not wear yourself out to get rich" Prov. 23:4-5. The person who focuses his whole life on getting rich makes a bad bargain. Jesus made the same point when He called on us to store up treasures in heaven, where no moth or rust can corrupt and no thief break through and steal (Matt. 6:19-21).

Note again the relationship of this proverb to faith. Only the believer, who sees a reality beyond this present universe, is likely to show such restraint.

"Do not eat the food of a stingy man" Prov.

23:6-8. It doesn't really pay to wheedle favors from others by manipulating them with compliments. Anything not freely given creates hostility in the heart of the giver, and will not benefit us in the end.

"Do not move an ancient boundary stone" Prov. 23:10-11. In Israel, boundary stones marked the borders of each family's fields. To move the boundary stone was to steal a little bit of a neighbor's land. Why not? "Their Defender is strong; He will take up their case against you."

Again we see why the fear of the Lord is the beginning of wisdom. Only a person who takes God fully into account will view Him as the active Defender of the weak.

"Do not let your heart envy sinners" Prov. 23:17-18. Envy is a mix of resentment and admiration. If we do not secretly admire a sinner, and feel resentment that he has what we want, we will be free of one of life's most corrupting influences. How do we find such freedom? By being constantly aware of God. If we keep Him before us, we will not envy sinners and will have hope for the future.

"Do not join those who drink too much wine" Prov. 23:19-21. The partying lifestyle of the "beautiful people" of our day is not good for us—or for them!

"Do not gaze at wine when it is red" Prov. 23:29-35. The sober person who looks at a drunk sees the impact of alcoholism (v. 29). But the drunkard, fascinated by his wine, is unable to grasp the reality of his condition (vv. 30-33). Even when he staggers from side to side like a sailor on a stormy sea, he claims he is fine—and thinks only of where he can get his next drink (vv. 34-35).

"Do not envy wicked men" Prov. 24:1-4. The wicked are destructive influences; the wise are constructive. Sinners tear down, and trample beautiful things; the wise build, and furnish society with beauty.

"Do not gloat when your enemy falls" Prov. 24:17-18. Delight at an enemy's downfall is as great a sin as the one he is being punished for!

"An honest answer" Prov. 24:23-26. Total honesty is essential in every relationship, including honest confrontation of those who do wrong.

"A little sleep" Prov. 24:30-34. A look at the situation of the lazy man teaches an important lesson. It's dangerous to think, "Well, I'll just take it easy for a while." This soon becomes a lifestyle that guarantees poverty.

▶ DEVOTIONAL
Somebody Else
(Prov. 24:11-12)

I read a poem recently about Somebody Else. With tongue in cheek, the poet expressed admiration for this person who does so much for church and community. Why, every time anyone he knew was asked to help out, that person suggested Somebody Else do it. And, sure enough, Somebody Else did!

Proverbs 24:11-12 suggests, however, that you and I aren't to stand back and let Somebody Else take moral stands. "Rescue those being led away to death; hold back those staggering toward slaughter. If you say, 'But we knew nothing about this,' does not he who weighs the heart perceive it?"

We can plead ignorance.

But we remain responsible for what happens in our society.

I think the Rev. Donald E. Wildmon must have taken this proverb to heart. One night when he was trying to watch TV with his family, he had to ask his children to switch off a show on each of the major networks. After watching just a few minutes, each show portrayed some immoral or violent act he knew it was wrong to expose his family to.

That led him to visit the networks to express his concern and, when the networks failed to respond, to form an organization which now goes directly to advertisers. When a show approvingly portrays adultery, violence, or other immoral acts, Don Wildmon goes to the advertiser and asks if these are the values they want associated with their products. And if they do, he makes it clear that he is ready to exercise his right not to buy that product. Is this censorship? Not at all. Wildmon says, "I have as much right as any other individual in this society to try to shape society. I have as much right to try to influence people. I have as much right to create what I consider to be a decent, good, clean, wholesome, moral society."

In the words of Proverbs, when Wildmon saw our society "being led away to death" he refused to say he "knew nothing about this." Instead he accepted the responsibility that rests on all Christians to respond when evil threatens others. And he acted.

In acting as he has, Don Wildmon has set an example for us all.

Personal Application

The next time you see an injustice or a wrong, ask yourself: Is God's Somebody Else me?

Quotable

"One has to have an ethical base for a society. Where the prime force is impulse, there is the death of ethics. America used to have ethical laws based in Jerusalem. Now they are based in Sodom and Gomorrah, and civilizations rooted in Sodom and Gomorrah are destined to collapse."—Jesse Jackson

MAY 10 *Reading 130*
SAYINGS OF SOLOMON
Proverbs 25–29

> *"Fear of man will prove to be a snare, but whoever trusts in the* Lord *is kept safe" (Prov. 29:25).*

Though his observations are brief, this collection of Solomon's sayings gives us deep insights into personal relationships.

Background

In-depth study. So far we've noted two ways to study the Proverbs. One is to read through a chapter, and note specific verses that "jump out" at us. The other is to do a topical study, and compare all the proverbs on a particular subject.

In this unit we're looking at a third method for studying the Proverbs. I've called it "in-depth," though perhaps it might better be called "meditative." To use this approach we simply look at a proverb and think carefully about it. What does the proverb say? What does it imply? What is the background that gave rise to it? To what situations might it apply? In today's commentary I use this method to explore several proverbs selected from these sayings of Solomon.

Overview

These five chapters of brief sayings attributed to Solomon were added to Proverbs in the time of Hezekiah.

Understanding the Text

"If you argue your case with a neighbor" Prov. 25:8-10. What are we to do when we hear a rumor about someone, or see some suspicious act? Jump to conclusions? Run quickly to tell everyone we know?

This group of proverbs suggests that the worst thing to do is to spread a rumor, or even make an accusation based on something we've witnessed. After all, we don't know the whole story. We don't know the motive for the act we saw, or all the circumstances surrounding it. Solomon suggested that we withhold judgment, and not hurry off to "bring [our neighbor] hastily to court [i.e., accuse him]." We'll look mighty foolish if he has a good explanation!

Solomon suggested that we go to our neighbor and "argue our case" with him. This doesn't mean repeating what others have said in confidence: "Well, George said that you. . . . " To repeat what others say is betraying a confidence. Do this, and when others find out, you'll have a reputation that you'll never be able to live down!

On the one hand, Solomon's words are simply good advice. They make a lot of sense. On the other hand, they are rooted in a unique view of the godly society. In a godly society if you witness or hear something about another person, you can't just shrug your shoulders and say, "That's his business." You are accountable for the welfare of the other person, and for the purity of your community. To fulfill your responsibility you first go to the person involved. You share what you've seen or heard, and give him a chance to explain. In doing this you both show your concern for truth, and for the other person himself.

If he can explain, well and good. If confronting helps him to set things right, again well and good. If he will not respond, that's time enough to involve others and possibly the courts.

Solomon's point is that while you must do something, what you do had better be the right thing! And the right thing is not to gossip about what you've seen, or spread a rumor you've heard. The right thing is to go directly to the other person, to find out the truth, and to help.

"Faithful are the wounds of a friend" Prov. 27:5-6. What is friendship really all about? Today we can take courses on how to win friends and influence people. While those who teach tell us not to use the techniques they show us to manipulate others, all too often the goal we have in making friends is just this. We want to ingratiate ourselves; to use the relationship for some personal gain.

Solomon, in exploring friendship, makes a different proposal. To win friends *be* a friend. Truly care about the other person. Rather than use him or her, serve.

This view of friendship is behind each of Solomon's sayings. Why is open rebuke better than hidden love? Because such love is morally useless. It fails to tell its object his or her faults, and thus leaves him or her without information that might lead to reform. When we hesitate to rebuke a person our motive is not really love. It is fear that we might be rejected or attacked. We're not really concerned about the other person: we're concerned about ourselves!

Turning the saying around, Solomon invites us to evaluate our attitude to those who profess to be our friends. Do we prefer the flatterer? The person who has nothing but praise for us—while we're with him—may very well be an enemy. You can tell a true friend by his willingness to wound you when a wound is for your own good.

No, not everyone who hurts you is a friend. But we should be able to tell the difference between an insensitive clod who tells us something that is hurtful, and says, "Now this is for your own good," and the person who really cares and shows caring by telling us the truth in love.

Solomon's insights are just as valid today as they were 3,000 years ago. Friendship calls for honesty exercised in the best interests of another, and for appreciating such honesty from others, even when it hurts.

▶ DEVOTIONAL
Let It Out!
(Prov. 29:11)

I'm often amazed at the new treatments psychologists come up with. A few years ago one popular fad was, let it out! If you feel angry, let it out. Take this foam-rubber bat and hit something as hard as you can. If you feel hostile, say all those nasty things you're thinking. If you ventilate your feelings, the theory goes, you'll get rid of them. If you hold them in, they'll grow stronger.

Nice theory.

Of course, it doesn't really work. Solomon knew that 3,000 years ago, and said so when he wrote, "A fool gives full vent to his anger, but a wise man keeps himself under control" (v. 11). When we practice letting any sinful or negative feeling out, what happens is that we become less able to control it next time. Rather than "ventilating" the emotion and getting rid of it, we find it returns more often. And, like a muscle that we exercise over and over again, those feelings we "let out" become stronger too.

The reason is deeply rooted in the very nature of human beings. You and I are moral creatures. That means we are to stand in judgment of our own emotions. We are to choose *against* our emotions if those emotions are wrong. We are to be controlled, not by what we feel, but by what we know to be right. When a person chooses to "let out" his anger or hostility, he is not getting rid of it. He is permitting it to master him.

How wonderful that in Christ you and I have a better way to deal with our anger. We can choose to do what is right—and confess our sinful feelings to God and ask Him to change them, and us. When we do, God works His gradual transformation within us, until we become loving rather than angry women and men.

Personal Application
Do what you know is right, not what you feel.

Quotable
"There are many queer ideas about cross bearing. I recall a man once saying to me, 'I have a fierce temper, but I suppose that is my cross.'

" 'My friend,' I said to him (lovingly, I hope!), 'That is not your cross. It is your wife's cross, but it is your sin!' "—Alan Redpath

MAY 11 *Reading 131*
THE NOBLE WIFE
Proverbs 30–31

"Give her the reward she has earned, and let her works bring her praise at the city gate" (Prov. 31:31).

The last of the three sections in these two chapters puts to rest the notion that women had no significant role in ancient Hebrew society—and challenges those who today view women as somehow inferior to men.

Overview
Three authors contribute to these two chapters. Agur, humble, but a sharp observer of nature and humankind (30:1-33). King Lemuel, pen name for a man who shares his mother's thoughts on ruling (31:1-9). And the unnamed author of an acrostic poem in praise of a fine wife (vv. 10-31).

Understanding the Text
"I am the most ignorant of men" Prov. 30:1-4. Humility was a major trait of Agur. He had learned not to measure himself against other men, but against God. As a result he had no trace of false pride or arrogance. When we compare ourselves with the Lord, there's no room left for pride. If we learn nothing else from the Book of Proverbs, this single lesson would be enough.

"Two things I ask" Prov. 30:7-9. Humility had given Agur insight into himself. He realized how vulnerable mere human beings are. His second request, "Give me neither poverty nor riches, but give me only my daily bread," reflects this insight.

Agur's perspective was very different from that of the radio preacher who shouts, "God wants all His children to be rich!" What God in grace wants for most of us is to have enough—our daily bread. But not too much. Those with riches all too often feel no need of God. And those with nothing may steal for necessities. Agur, sensing his vulnerability, wanted to be put in neither position.

You or I may wonder what we would do if we inherited a lot of money and were suddenly impossibly rich. Agur reminds us to thank God for what we have. Why should we want to risk the dangers wealth brings?

"The way of a man with a maiden" Prov. 30:18-19. Agur made a variety of delightful observations, comparing human behavior with what he saw in nature. Here he expressed amazement at how eagles, serpents, and ships on the high seas found their way with no marked highway. Agur would never write an advice to the lovelorn column. He knew better! There are no highways for boy-girl relationships either. Yet somehow men and women find each other, marry, and produce the next generation. The way of a man with a maiden may be trackless, but despite the lack of beaten paths love too finds its way.

"It cannot bear up" Prov. 30:21-23. Agur, a man who disliked pride, noted four types who tend to be unbearably arrogant. The servant who becomes king (who, in the ancient world, probably assassinated the old king). The fool (here, *nabal,* the proud and wicked rebel) who is "full of food" and openly scoffs at any need for God. The "unloved woman" (old maid) who at

last finds a husband (surely not for her own qualities but most likely because of a large dowry). And the young servant girl who awakens the passion of her master, and replaces her mistress as his wife. In not one of these cases does the individual have reason for pride. In each case he or she has reason for shame!

You and I may take satisfaction in a position we've achieved by hard work and excellence. But how wicked to be proud of a position won without merit.

"It is . . . not for kings to drink wine" Prov. 31:1-9. These verses of advice by a king who wrote under the pen name of Lemuel reveal a very high view of royal responsibility. The king is servant to his people, called to protect the oppressed and judge fairly. Personal indulgence is "not for kings." They must spend their strength and vigor serving their people, not on chasing women or getting drunk.

These words of a mother remind us that we must view all authority in the context of servanthood. The man who is the "head of the house," like the king of these passages, is not to use his authority to exploit or "master" his wife, but to serve her and their children.

In Old Testament times women used simple machines like the distaff and spindle to make threads from wool or flax, then wove the threads into cloth they used to make the family clothing (v. 19). But, as verses 10-31 show, the wife of Old Testament times was far more than a menial who performed only simple, limited tasks while her husband took care of the important family business.

"A wife of noble character" Prov. 31:10-31. The Jewish rabbis suggested that these words were written by Solomon in honor of his mother, Bathsheba. This is unlikely. The woman here is an ordinary housewife. While it's true that the family is well-to-do, much credit for their prosperity is given to her!

The passage does not focus on the wife's personal relationships, but rather on what might be called her business sense. She gets up early, assigns the day's work to her servant girls (employees!), makes sure they have the resources needed to do their work, and supervises them during the day.

While the primary focus of her activities was the family needs, this Old Testament wife is also an entrepreneur. She markets the garments her staff produces: she sells linen garments and "supplies the merchants with sashes."

The passage also makes it clear that the wife is free to make use of the profits from her enterprise. She "considers a field and buys it." This is an investment. She's decided to diversify, and add wine making to her businesses! The wife's complete control of her earnings is illustrated by her generosity: "She opens her arms to the poor and extends her hands to the needy." In modern terms, she's set up a charitable foundation to distribute some of her profits to those less fortunate.

And what do the men in this society think of the activist wife? Why, "Her husband is respected at the city gate, where he takes his seat among the elders of the land." Rather than being a threat to his fragile male ego, the wife's accomplishments are a source of pride and add to his prestige!

What is so striking about the Proverbs 31 description is that it so powerfully contradicts the view of some Christians that a good wife must stay home, have babies, and keep busy with housework. Proverbs 31 shows us a woman of the Old Testament who is in fact a businesswoman, using her talents and abilities to the fullest, and performing the same kind of tasks that the men of that society performed.

The "noble wife" of the Old Testament is not the silent, subservient woman so many Christians imagine, but rather an assertive, accomplished woman, whose success has clothed her "with strength and dignity" and who is relied on to speak "with wisdom," for "faithful instruction is on her tongue."

▶ DEVOTIONAL

Give Her the Reward She Has Earned (Prov. 31:10-31)

I suppose it's all right to be upset with pastors now and then.

At any rate, I thought it was all right for my wife to be upset with ours. Graham is a lovely, friendly, and thoughtful young man, and we appreciate him. But as he himself is quick to admit, he's something of a chauvinist. Women belong at home. Or doing something female, like teaching grade school. The important decisions at home are to be made by the men. And all the decisions at church—frequently even all the talking about decisions—are for men only.

So one evening when we were at Graham's house for supper, my wife confronted him. Why aren't women first-class citizens at our church? Why are they automatically excluded from so many positions and activities?

Graham immediately jumped to the conclusion that Sue was lobbying for women preachers, and gave a somewhat stirring defense of the denomination's position. And missed the point entirely.

I suspect many in our churches miss the point entirely. The point is that women too are human beings. Women too have talents and abilities. Women too have spiritual gifts—gifts that go beyond teaching toddlers, changing diapers in the church nursery, and filling the Communion cups with grape juice. And of course, washing them afterward. Women, as members of the body of Christ, are essential to our spiritual growth and development. Yet in many churches women are given no significant role and permitted few significant ministries.

And it's a shame.

Particularly when the view so many have of women is based on a faulty image of the "biblical" bride. The little woman who stays at home, looks after the kids, and lets the man deal with the important issues of life.

Sometimes I wonder. Do you suppose it's possible that Proverbs 31 was written for our instruction? And that the words, "Give her the reward she has earned," is God's exhortation to husbands and church leaders of today?

Personal Application

God-given gifts and talents are to be used—whatever the sex of the person who possesses them.

Quotable

"God entrusted women with some of His most important tasks. He sent women with the Resurrection news to the rest of the disciples. Jesus accepted women into full discipleship. He commended Mary of Bethany for her efforts to sit at His feet and learn, rather than do the accepted thing and retire to the kitchen. To those who say women cannot fill positions of leadership, the Bible says women did. As the great evangelist D.L. Moody replied when someone asked him what a woman can do to serve Christ, 'What could they not do?' "—Patricia Gundry

---

The Variety Reading Plan continues with 1 KINGS

Ecclesiastes

INTRODUCTION

This book reports the efforts of "the Teacher," long believed to be Solomon, to find meaning in life apart from a personal relationship with God. His pessimistic conclusion: such a life is "meaningless," and will lead to despair. Only those who "fear God and keep His commandments" can live in hope.

OUTLINE OF CONTENTS

I. Prologue: Life Is Meaningless .... Ecc. 1:1-11
II. Proof: Meaninglessness Demonstrated .... Ecc. 1:12–6:12
III. Preferences: Making the Best of a Meaningless Life..... Ecc. 7:1–12:8
IV. Epilogue: Call to Fear God .... Ecc. 12:9-14

READING GUIDE (3 Days)

If hurried, you may read only the "core passage" in your Bible and the Devotional in each chapter of this Commentary.

Reading	*Chapters*	*Core passage*
132	1–4	2
133	5–8	7–8
134	9–12	11:7–12:14

Ecclesiastes

MAY 12 *Reading 132*
MEANINGLESS LIFE
Ecclesiastes 1–4

" 'Meaningless! Meaningless!' says the Teacher. 'Utterly meaningless! Everything is meaningless' " (Ecc. 1:2).

Many thoughtful non-Christians will find that this book reflects an all-too-familiar sense of despair. Life in this world has not changed fundamentally from the author's day. Apart from a personal relationship with God any life truly is meaningless.

Background

Ecclesiastes fits into a strain of ancient wisdom literature marked for its pessimism. Its sense of the futility of life is found in Egyptian works from about 2300–2100 B.C., as well as in Mesopotamian writings ranging from that date to the 7th century B.C. One work, the *Dialogue of Pessimism*, written about 1300 B.C., concludes that for man trapped in a meaningless universe only one "good" exists: "To have my neck broken and your neck broken and to be thrown into the river is good."

The writer of Ecclesiastes set the limits of his search for meaning. He would use his reason (to "explore by wisdom," 1:13) and he would use data he could gather by observation in this world ("under the sun"). While nature does provide evidence that God exists, He can be known as Redeemer only by special revelation. Thus the personal name of God, Yahweh, is not found in Ecclesiastes. Moreover, while the Teacher's conclusions are accurately recorded, and do follow what man can observe in society and the material universe, his conclusions do not correspond with revealed truth (cf. 3:20-21; 9:5).

What then is the value of the Book of Ecclesiastes? It serves an important pre-evangelism function, evoking images intended to make the reader sensitive to the futility of life apart from God. While the nonbeliever can enjoy the natural blessings which God graciously provides, he or she must always be troubled by an underlying sense of the ultimate meaninglessness of life.

Overview

The Teacher stated that life in this world is meaningless (1:1-11). To prove his point he examined wisdom (vv. 12-18), pleasures (2:1-16), hard work (vv. 17-26), religion (3:1-22), and life's unfairness (4:1-16).

Understanding the Text

"Meaningless! Meaningless!" Ecc. 1:1-11 The Hebrew word translated "meaningless" in the NIV and "vanity" in the *King James* is *hebel*. It's underlying meanings include futility, deceptiveness, unreliability, and brevity. Human life, if our 70 or so years on earth is all there is, is rendered empty. Short and insubstantial, life in this world can provide no permanent satisfaction.

It's hard for a young person, setting out with dreams of conquering the business or professional world, visions of pleasure, or even of marriage and family, to grasp how empty life will be even if he or she achieves those goals. This is perhaps one of the great values of this powerful Old Testament book: its dark outlook forces even the most optimistic individual to re-examine assumptions about the meaning of life.

What a blessing that this book is found

in a library of 66, with the others testifying to the fact that God did not create any individual life to flare up for a brief moment, and then to flicker out. Any time we are envious of this world's wealthy or famous, we can read Ecclesiastes and remember that the true meaning of our life is tied, not to time, but to eternity.

"The more knowledge, the more grief" Ecc. 1:12-18. In general, "wisdom" in Scripture is the ability to apply God's guidelines for moral living to practical issues, and thus to choose what is right. In this book, which rules out revelation *a priori,* wisdom remains practical. But here it is the ability to understand the practical implications of secular study and observation. The tragedy is that the pursuit of secular knowledge is a "chasing after the wind." Whatever we may achieve through science or philosophy offers no answer to the question of what makes individual life meaningful. In fact, the more one explores, the greater his or her sense of grief.

There is a vast difference between secular and spiritual knowledge. While the one can make our life on earth more comfortable, the other alone can give our life meaning and purpose.

It follows, as one of our pastors suggested at Sunday vespers, that we ought to concentrate on studying the Word of God. Only here will we find not only meaning but also lasting comfort and joy.

"I refused my heart no pleasure" Ecc. 2:1-11. Philosophers have categorized pleasures. Some are "pleasures of the flesh." The person who seeks pleasure in drugs, drink, or sex looks for it in bodily sensations. There are also "higher" pleasures. Among such pleasures tradition names the pleasure a person takes in his achievements, in accumulating wealth, or the pure intellectual pleasure of learning and displaying knowledge.

As pagan philosophers have taught, the problem with pleasures of the flesh is that a price must be paid. The drunk suffers hangovers and cirrhosis of the liver. The drug addict loses his grip on reality. But the Teacher makes a distinctive contribution. *All* pleasures are meaningless. As far as adding meaning to life, each is "chasing after wind."

"I hated all the things I had toiled for" Ecc. 2:17-26. The drive to achieve great things is incapable of providing life with meaning. In the end all that a person poured his effort and skill into, all that has taken such a toll in personal pain and grief, will be left to another who has not worked for it.

It's a lucky man (the sense here of references to God) who is satisfied with his work and his pleasures. In the last analysis, the "great man" who was driven to achieve is the miserable one.

"Yet they cannot fathom what God has done from beginning to end" Ecc. 3:1-22. While some have taken this chapter as an appeal to seek meaning through relationship with God, it seems best to understand it as a critique of natural religion. Nature does provide evidence that God exists. We see Him revealed in the regularity of His creation (vv. 1-8), and in man's universal assumption that there is more to life than food and drink (vv. 9-17). Yet God remains a mystery (v. 11), and there is no evidence from nature to support the conviction that human beings are different from animals (vv. 18-21). As man's religions can offer no certain knowledge about life after death, their practitioners must be satisfied with enjoying life in this world.

What a difference between man's religions and revealed religion. We alone can look beyond time, and *know* what eternity holds.

"I looked and saw all the oppression that was taking place under the sun" Ecc. 4:1-16. The existence of injustice contributes to the conclusion that, if this is all there is, life must be meaningless. Men so mistreat their fellows that death is preferable (vv. 1-3). The envy and competitiveness that motivate man's achievements destroy inner tranquility (vv. 4-6), while necessity alone bonds men together (vv. 7-12). Even possession of authority over others is fleeting and meaningless.

It's been popular in the past three decades to assume that somehow meaning is found in interpersonal relationships. But the one relationship that counts is ignored by secular man. Only a relationship with God, resting on His love for and commitment to us, can truly meet our needs.

▶DEVOTIONAL
Gotta Try It to Know
(Ecc. 2)

In his search for meaning the Teacher used two basic methods. Observe others. And, try it and see. When it came to pleasures—whether the pleasure of accomplishing some great building project, amassing great wealth, or a pleasure of the flesh—his approach was, "Try it and see."

We're often tempted to take this approach to life. "How can I tell unless I try it for myself?" The answer, of course, is that we know about lots of things that aren't beneficial without having to try them for ourselves. We wouldn't try jumping off a 10-story building to see if it's fun to fly. It might very well be. But the landing would be pretty hard.

How fortunate we are to have in Scripture a reliable guide to what is truly good for us, and what will hurt.

Rather than say with Qoheleth, "How can I tell unless I try," we say, "I know this isn't worth trying, for God's Word warns me away."

Personal Application

God is a better guide than experience.

Quotable

"Experience is the best of schoolmasters, only the school fees are heavy."—Thomas Carlyle

---

MAY 13 *Reading 133*
A MEANINGLESS LIFE
Ecclesiastes 5–8

> *"For who knows what is good for a man in life, during the few and meaningless days he passes through like a shadow?" (Ecc. 6:12)*

As we sense the despair that grips the Teacher's heart in his role as secular man, we realize afresh how great God's salvation is. Making the best of a meaningless life is secular man's fate. Our challenge is to make a meaningful life better!

Overview

In his role as secular man the Teacher showed life's meaninglessness by a further critique of religion (5:1-7), riches (vv. 8-20), and the brevity of life (6:1-12). His theme proven, the Teacher then suggested how to make the best of an essentially meaningless life (7:1–8:17).

Understanding the Text

"Let your words be few" Ecc. 5:1-7. In natural religion human beings seek to reach up to God from earth, and find Him distant and unreachable. This is the implication of the saying, "God is in heaven, you are on earth." God may know man, but man does not know God. Thus the religious person should let his words be few, stand in awe, and if he makes a vow to God, should fulfill it quickly lest the unknown God be angry.

In revealed religion, God is initiator. He reaches down from heaven to reveal Himself to man. This God is known on earth, and His will is known too.

How terrible it is to be driven by reason to acknowledge God's existence, but to know nothing about Him! How wonderful that in His Word and in Christ, our God has spoken to us of His love, compassion, and salvation.

"As he comes, so he departs" Ecc. 5:8-20. Several reasons are offered to show why wealth is incapable of providing life with meaning. A person may work hard—but his profits are eaten up in taxes (vv. 8-9). Even a rich man isn't satisfied with his wealth. He just wants more (v. 10). The more one earns the more he spends (v. 11). People with money lie awake worrying about keeping it (v. 12). Hoarded wealth is more likely to do harm than good—and when a man dies he can't take it with him (vv. 13-17). In short, the only value of wealth is as a narcotic, to keep a man so occupied with earthly pleasures that he doesn't realize how empty his life

really is (vv. 18-20).

When a Christian adopts materialistic values, he or she has chosen the empty, meaningless way of life of secular man. Christ died in part to free us from an unhealthy love of money.

"Even if he lives a thousand years" Ecc. 6:1-12. One of the most grievous evils identified by the Teacher is that, however long a man lives, it is not long enough. Even a person with wealth, possessions, and honor soon dies, with his appetites still unsatisfied.

In saying that "all man's efforts are for his mouth," the writer suggested that secular man is on a treadmill. He works to satisfy his physical needs and desires, yet however well-fed, he becomes hungry again, and however supplied with drink his thirst returns. In it all, his deepest need, the nameless desire for meaning, persists as an aching desire that no food or drink can quench. "Whatever exists has already been named." Life on earth is an endless repetition, a treadmill on which each new generation walks or runs until their "few and meaningless days" are over.

There is no meaning to be found in the life lived by secular man.

"Is better than" Ecc. 7:1–8:17. With the close of chapter 6, the author had finished presenting proof that life under the sun, without a personal relationship with God, is meaningless. But he continued his quest. Given the meaninglessness of life, what should a person do?

Solomon, unlike the authors of other ancient pessimistic wisdom literature, did not suggest suicide. Instead he suggested that a man examine his options, and choose the lesser of evils. We can trace the options he suggested in 7:1–12:8. In today's reading, here is the advice of the Teacher concerning choices open to secular man.

7:1-12. Even if life is meaningless, some things in life are better than others. For instance, sorrow is better than laughter—if only because it is more realistic! For the same reason, it's foolish to say that "the old days" were better than today!

Although these conclusions may not be obvious, it is obvious that some things are better than others. For instance, the end of a matter is better than the beginning. Patience is better than pride. The wise are better off than fools. Given this, the Teacher offers his advice.

7:13-14. Adopt a fatalistic attitude. What God has determined cannot be changed, and no one can know ahead of time whether God's future holds good times or bad for him.

7:15-22. Avoid extremes. Don't set out to be too righteous or too wicked, and ignore what other people may say about you.

7:23–8:1. Wisdom is better than stupidity. But wisdom has its limits. It will not enable a person to discover "the scheme of things," and it will not make a person righteous. In fact, wisdom forces one to the conclusion that while God may have made man upright, "men have gone in search of many schemes."

8:2-10. Adjust to the rules of your society. It is far better to fit in than to be a rebel. This thought underlies the Teacher's call to obey the king, and not rock the boat by challenging his authority.

8:11-14. Fear God as Judge. This is a difficult call, for one must take it on faith that in the end God will punish the wicked—despite the present prosperity of so many wicked men. In essence the Teacher suggested, don't take chances where God is concerned. Wisdom tells us He is there, even if we do not know anything else about Him.

8:15. Enjoy while you can. Take what pleasure is possible from this life, even though it is meaningless.

8:16-17. Finally the writer made a significant confession. Even the conclusions he had drawn rested on insufficient evidence! No one can really "comprehend what goes on under the sun." Human reason is incapable of drawing all the evidence together and reaching correct conclusions. Human reason cannot truly describe, or even comprehend, all of reality.

We conclude with this thought. The conclusions of secular man about the meaninglessness of life are faulty, simply because secular man does not have all the evidence, nor is he able to fit it together accurately. The best that secular man can do is guess about the true nature of the universe in which he lives. And his best guesses lead, inevitably, to the conclusion that life for the individual is empty and meaningless.

How wonderful that you and I do not have to guess! How wonderful that we know. We know the origin of our universe and its destiny. We know that we human beings have been created in the image of God, are loved by Him, and are destined to live forever! We know the saving power God has unleashed in this world through Jesus. And, because we know, we are freed from secular man's bondage to despair.

▶ DEVOTIONAL
"Better Than" Choices
(Ecc. 7–8)

Any set of beliefs that a person adopts is to be used as criteria to evaluate choices.

This may sound a little stuffy. But it expresses a vital truth. The Teacher of Ecclesiastes concluded that life was meaningless, and from that starting point went on to distinguish options in life which were better than others.

We Christians start with a different set of conclusions. We believe that life is meaningful. God loves us, and has chosen us, in Jesus' words, "to go and bear fruit" (John 15:16). Other New Testament passages put it a little differently, but the thought is the same. We have been chosen that we might "be for the praise of His glory" (Eph. 1:12). We are God's workmanship, "created in Christ Jesus to do good works" (2:10).

This is *not* a secular universe, formed by chance. It is a universe created by a personal God, who has chosen to love us—and chosen us to love and serve Him.

What options then are "better" if our set of beliefs about the world is formed by a belief in God and by experience of His love? Well, some of life's better things for the Christian include: Caring more about people than about things. Giving ourselves to serve rather than be served. Storing up treasure in heaven rather than on earth. Spending time with God's Word rather than TV sitcoms. Making time for our families rather than spending all our time and energy on our jobs. Depending on God rather than on ourselves, and expressing that dependence in prayer. And so on.

You can add to this list just as easily as I can.

You see, our problem isn't in knowing what "better than" choices are open to us as Christians. Our problem is in making those choices daily.

No, this isn't one of those "let's add on some more guilt" devotionals. It's just a reminder. The life of secular man really is meaningless. God's call to you and me to make "better than" choices is His invitation to discover something that secular man can never know.

A truly meaningful, and thus blessed, life.

Personal Application

The "better than" choices we make for Jesus' sake end up as blessings for us.

Quotable

"Wisdom is knowing what to do next, skill is knowing how to do it, and virtue is doing it."—David Starr Jordan

MAY 14 *Reading 134*
THE CONCLUSION
Ecclesiastes 9–12

"Fear God and keep His commandments, for this is the whole duty of man. For God will bring every deed into judgment, including every hidden thing, whether it is good or evil" (Ecc. 12:13-14).

Life truly is short. Unless we learn to live with eternity in view, our lives will also be meaningless.

Overview

The Teacher continued to explore the choices a secular man can make in view of life's essential meaninglessness. His advice: Enjoy life while you can (9:1-12), choose wisdom's ways (v. 13–10:20), prepare for the future (11:1-6), and enjoy your youth (v. 7–12:8). Finally, stepping out of his secular role, the Teacher advised: "Fear God and keep His commandments" (vv. 9-14).

Understanding the Text

"All share a common destiny" Ecc. 9:1-10. Death is the destiny that awaits all men. This, when life is viewed from a secular viewpoint, is all one can say. The dead have no "part in anything that happens under the sun." As far as one can tell apart from divine revelation "the dead know nothing; they have no further reward, and even the memory of them is forgotten."

If this life is all there is, then all one can do is enjoy and live this life to the full (chaps. 9–10).

It's important to remember that the writer was not serving as God's spokesman, but as spokesman for secular man. The text represents what man can discover about the most basic issues of life using only reason and data available to the senses. Such phrases as "the dead know nothing" are not revelations from God, but reasoned human conclusions.

"Wisdom is better" Ecc. 9:11–10:20. In this extended passage the Teacher expressed his preference for wisdom over folly. But there's a fly in the ointment! While wisdom is preferable, wisdom cannot guarantee anyone a better life!

Perfume jars like these were used in Old Testament times to hold sweet-smelling ointments. The image in Ecclesiastes 10:1 of dead flies spoiling the odor of perfume has given us the saying, "There's a fly in the ointment." We use it to mean that something has gone seriously wrong.

What is seriously wrong with wisdom? First, Solomon asked us to realize that nothing in this life can guarantee success (9:11-12). The swift do not always win the race. The largest army is not always victorious. Wisdom is no guarantee of wealth. In this world men are vulnerable, likely to be "trapped by evil times that fall unexpectedly upon them."

Chance is not the only factor that makes wisdom of uncertain benefit. Here is the writer's list:

9:13-16. Wisdom is often unrecognized. People pay more attention to rich fools than to poor wise men.

9:17–10:1. Wisdom can be thwarted, by those in authority (9:17), by moral deficiency (v. 18), and by mistaking spoiled advice for the real thing (10:1).

10:2-3. Folly, which is the opposite of wisdom and is associated with wickedness, competes with wisdom, and we are vulnerable.

10:4-7. When offended we are likely to react foolishly—and since so many fools hold high positions, we're likely to be offended!

Here the author drifted slightly and examined the consequences of folly:

10:8-11. Any foolish action has bad consequences for the actor, as illustrated by several sayings and proverbs.

10:12-14. Wise words are "gracious." The word means kind, appropriate, helpful. But foolish words degenerate into even wilder thoughts and actions, including pronouncements about a future no one can know.

10:15. Fools are incompetent guides to life: A fool can't even find his way into town!

10:16-20. Folly in national life, as in the individual, leads to disaster.

"Sow your seed in the morning" Ecc. 11:1-6. While no one can control the future (v. 3), it is best to prepare for it as carefully as possible.

"Let him enjoy them all" Ecc. 11:7–12:6. It is best to enjoy each day as it comes, and especially while you are young.

The exhortation to "remember your Creator in the days of your youth" is not a call to monastic life, but an invitation to enjoy all the good things God has provided in this creation. All too soon old age—the "days of trouble"—will come, when we lose the capacity to enjoy things. Then the world becomes dark (v. 2), for the body stoops (v. 3), teeth wear out (v. 3), eyes dim (v. 3) and hearing fades (v. 4). Weakness brings fear (v. 5) and drains desire (v. 5). Then man, like a cut cord, a broken bowl, or a shattered pitcher, is useful no more, and "the dust returns to the ground it came from, and the spirit returns to God who gave it."

Man is born.

Man lives a brief and empty life.

Man dies, and returns to dust.

If this is all there is, then life truly is meaningless.

"Now all has been heard" Ecc. 12:9-14. It's comforting to suppose that the Teacher, who the text here and in other places suggests is Solomon, stepped out of his role as representative of secular man at the end of Ecclesiastes. Although even here he did not use the name Yahweh, he did speak of God's commandments, which at least implies some self-revelation.

If Solomon is in fact the Teacher, and he did step out of his secular role, his words are especially powerful. In the end, we must all turn to God to find hope and meaning.

When we not only look back to see God as Creator, but also look up to see Him as our Lord and ahead to see Him as mankind's Judge, then we discover not only who God is, but who we are as well. Then we realize that any life lived for the Lord will find its meaning in Him.

▶ DEVOTIONAL
Wise Too Late
(Ecc. 11:7–12:14)

Solomon, who most believe is the Teacher of Ecclesiastes, was a godly young man. But in middle age, like the Teacher, he turned aside from wholly following the Lord. First Kings 11 tells us that passion for his foreign wives led him astray, even to the extent of worshiping their gods.

During this extended period of his life Solomon lived as a secular man. He accrued vast wealth, undertook massive building projects, and denied himself no pleasures. But then having "had it all," Solomon saw how empty his life was. "Meaningless! Meaningless!" is a cry of anguish that surely fits the tragic experience of Israel's most splendid king.

How sad that Solomon, so wise in many ways, lost his spiritual moorings. If indeed Solomon is the one who urges us to "remember our Creator in the days of our youth," uttering these words must have been tragic for him indeed. There is no greater tragedy than to become wise and old at the same time, and to look back and realize one has lived a wasted life.

I know unsolicited advice is about as welcome as unexpected visitors who appear on the doorstep with luggage in hand. But at least Solomon's advice is cheap. Not to him, of course. He paid for everything he learned in becoming wise too late.

For us the advice is free.

Only if we fail to follow it will we pay the truly terrible cost.

Personal Application

Put God first today. Tomorrow will be too little, too late.

Quotable

"He belongs to you, but more than that, He longs to be in you, living and ruling in you, as the head lives and rules in the body. He wants His breath to be in your breath, His heart in your heart, and His soul in your soul, so that you may indeed, 'Glorify God and bear Him in your body, that the life of Jesus may be manifest in you.' "—Jean Eudes

The Variety Reading Plan continues with LAMENTATIONS

Song of Songs

INTRODUCTION

This book, taken by some as an allegory of the believer's relationship with God, is better understood in its plain sense as a lyric love poem. Its joyful and sometimes erotic portrayal of the relationship between a lover and his beloved reminds us that intimacy within marriage is a gift, given by the God who created human beings male and female.

OUTLINE OF CONTENTS

READING GUIDE (1 Day)

If hurried, you may read only the "core passage" in your Bible and the Devotional in this Commentary.

Reading	*Chapters*	*Core passage*
135	1–8	4:1–5:1

Song of Songs

MAY 15 *Reading 135*
CELEBRATION OF LOVE
Song of Songs 1–8

> *"I belong to my lover, and his desire is for me" (Song 7:10).*

This ancient love song reminds us to rejoice in God's gift of marital intimacy, and to welcome that gift without hesitation or shame.

Background
Debate concerning Song of Songs focuses on two questions: What is this poem really about? and, What is the role of Solomon?

Some have been uncomfortable with the erotic elements in this poem, and have sought to "sanctify" them with a typical or allegorical interpretation. Commentators have suggested the poem is actually about the relationship between God, as Lover, and His Old Testament or New Testament people as His beloved. It is best, however, to take the book in its plain sense as love poetry, celebrating the joys of desire and intimacy experienced by a man and woman who become husband and wife. In this view there is nothing vulgar or "unspiritual" in the experience of sex, which God created to deepen the bond of commitment in marriage.

The text identifies this love poem as "Solomon's." Many characteristics of the Hebrew text suggest an ancient origin, and there is no good reason to doubt that it does date from the 10th century B.C. Still, Solomon's role is not clear. Some believe that this love poem was not composed by him, but was dedicated to him on the occasion of one of his weddings.

However we understand Solomon's role, Song itself remains one of the world's most sensitive and beautiful poems; a joyous and moving celebration of married love.

Overview
This lyric poem captures the joy and passion of two people who fall in love (1:1–2:7), experience growing desire (v. 8–3:5), and marry (v. 6–5:1). They are separated for a time (v. 2–8:4) but then are united again (vv. 5-14).

Understanding the Text
"Let him kiss me with the kisses of his mouth" Song 1:1–2:7. Falling in love was as delightful for the ancients as for us. He sees her as the "most beautiful of women," while she thinks, "How handsome you are, my lover!" It's almost impossible not to think of the modern teenager, who breathlessly tells her friends how she was almost ready to faint when he touched her, when we read, "Strengthen me with raisins, refresh me with apples, for I am faint with love" (2:5).

There's something special about first love. For those of us who have been married for years, this section of Song reminds us—and helps us appreciate the mature love that has grown from those early, giddy feelings.

This poem alternates speakers, sharing the thoughts of the Beloved, the Lover, and a chorus of friends. The NIV identifies each speaker. If the version you are reading does not, you can write in each beside the following verses.

Beloved	*Lover*	*Chorus*
1:2		1:4b
1:4c	1:8	

Beloved	*Lover*	*Chorus*
1:12	1:15	
1:16	1:17	
2:1	2:2	
2:3	2:14	
2:16	4:1	
4:16	5:1	5:1c
5:2		5:9
5:10		6:1
6:2	6:4	6:13a
	6:13b	
7:9b		8:5a
8:5b		8:8
8:10	8:13	
8:14		

"I looked for the one my heart loves" Song 2:8–3:5. The old saying, absence makes the heart grow fonder, is reflected in the longing expressed in these verses.

"Let my lover come into his garden" Song 3:6–5:1. Many believe Solomon, seen approaching with a host of retainers in 3:6-11, met the bride-to-be while visiting his kingdom in disguise. On his return she discovered her lover was king of the land, who intended to take her to his royal palace.

The next major section describes the physical charms of the bride (4:1-15), and finally moves to the marriage bed (v. 16–5:1). There in delicate symbolism that is found often in ancient Near Eastern love poetry, the lover comes "into his garden" to "taste its choice fruits."

While the imagery is delicate and tasteful, its erotic intent is unmistakable. (See DEVOTIONAL.)

"Where has your lover gone, most beautiful of women?" Song 5:2–8:4 Again the lovers were separated. Each was restless, and thought of the other's charms. The memory of their intimacy had not reduced, but intensified their desire.

"I have become in his eyes like one bringing contentment" Song 8:5-14. Reunited, the couple retreated to enjoy their relationship, and they learned that a love that burns "like blazing fire" does in time become a comfortable intimacy "bringing contentment."

▶DEVOTIONAL
Recapturing Sexual Love (Song 4:1–5:1)

"Sex" has been a four-letter word for far too many years. *Playboy*, the movies, and increasingly TV, exploit our sexuality by portraying situations that titillate and arouse. We can pick up the telephone, dial a number, and listen as a stranger invites us to imagine joining her as she describes explicit sex acts. Even PG-13 films now strive not only for a quota of filthy language but also a quota of scenes advertising immorality.

What's happened is that the world has recognized the importance of sex, and set about so distorting sexuality that Christians have become somewhat embarrassed about being sexual creatures.

Reading Song of Songs, and especially these verses that so erotically and yet sensitively portray sexual love, reminds us that Hollywood didn't invent sex. God did. It reminds us that sex isn't "evil." Sex is a gift given to us by God. Our Creator, who made us male and female, designed our bodies for every sexual delight. And He sanctified sex by making foreplay and intercourse a bonding act, intended to unite one man and woman in a unique and exclusive relationship.

It's this that we Christians have to recapture. We need to cleanse from sex that slimy but tingly sense of sin with which it is associated in the modern world. We need to purify our marriages of any residue of shame. And we need not only announce to the world that sex in Christian marriage is a pure and fulfilling delight, but also commit ourselves to exploring that delight fully with our spouse.

It is perhaps here that Song of Songs makes its greatest contribution to our lives. It reminds us that sex-talk can be beautiful, and need not be dirty. And it reminds us that true spirituality does not rule out the full enjoyment of the sexual side of married life.

Personal Application

Recapturing sex from the world begins in the Christian home.

Quotable

"Sex is holy as well as wholesome . . . it is the means by which we may cooperate with God in bringing into the world children of His own destined for eternal life. Anyone, who has once understood that, will be quite as careful as any Puritan to avoid making jokes about sex; not because it is nasty, but because it is sacred. He would no more joke about sex than he would joke about the Holy Communion—and for exactly the same reasons. To joke about it is to treat with lightness something that deserves reverence."—William Temple

The Variety Reading Plan continues with PSALMS 1–84

Isaiah

INTRODUCTION

Isaiah ministered in the critical period from 739 B.C. to about 680 B.C., during which Assyria carried the Northern Kingdom, Israel, into captivity and threatened Judah. The South was temporarily saved due to revival under godly King Hezekiah. Yet the first half of the Book of Isaiah is dark with grim warnings of judgment, and names Babylon as the future oppressor of Judah. The second half of Isaiah throbs with hope, as the great prophet described the ultimate deliverance of God's people.

Three repeated themes are woven throughout this great prophetic book. (1) Isaiah gave us an exalted vision of God, enhanced by names which reflect His attributes or character. (2) Isaiah provided vivid images of history's end, and the bright future awaiting God's people at that time. And (3), Isaiah constantly referred to the Messiah, the promised Redeemer, whom he described both as a Servant and as history's sovereign Lord.

Isaiah's emphasis on the Messiah, and especially his description of the suffering Saviour in chapter 53, has led some to refer to this beautiful book as the "Gospel" of the Old Testament.

OUTLINE OF CONTENTS

I. Visions of Judgment .... Isa. 1–35
   A. Israel's Holy One .... Isa. 1–6
   B. Book of Immanuel .... Isa. 7–12
   C. Oracles of judgment .... Isa. 13–24
   D. Judgment and deliverance .... Isa. 25–35
II. Historical Interlude .... Isa. 36–39
III. Visions of Splendor .... Isa. 40–66
   A. Beyond the Exile .... Isa. 40–48
   B. Messiah: God's Servant .... Isa. 49–55
   C. Redemption .... Isa. 56–59
   D. Restoration .... Isa. 60–66

READING GUIDE (13 Days)

If hurried, you may read only the "core passage" in your Bible and the Devotional in each chapter of this Commentary.

Reading	*Chapters*	*Core passage*
136	1	1
137	2–6	2
138	7–12	11–12
139	13–23	14:12-15
140	24–27	26
141	28–32	29
142	33–35	33
143	36–39	38–39
144	40–48	44

(Page 408)

145	49–53	52:13–53:11
146	54–58	55
147	59–62	60
148	63–66	65

Isaiah

MAY 16 *Reading 136*
BEHIND THE SCENES
Isaiah 1

"Ah, sinful nation, a people loaded with guilt, a brood of evildoers, children given to corruption" (Isa. 1:4).

In spite of material prosperity and a superficial religiosity, Judah like Israel was in desperate need of a spiritual awakening.

Background

Isaiah's life. Isaiah was apparently a member of the royal family, and according to tradition a cousin of King Uzziah (Amaziah), Judah's 11th king. In the course of Isaiah's ministry he confronted the rebellious Ahaz, and worked closely with godly Hezekiah. He was warned early that he would minister to a people who would not listen until "the cities lie ruined" and "the LORD has sent everyone far away and the land is utterly forsaken" (6:11-12).

Yet Isaiah was also given a glimpse of the splendor that awaits God's people at history's end. Isaiah, more clearly than any other prophet, foresaw the coming and ministry of the Messiah. Isaiah, more fully than any other, described the blessing God intends to pour out on Jew and Gentile alike.

Tradition tells us that Isaiah was martyred during the reign of Manasseh, the apostate son of godly King Hezekiah. If so this towering Old Testament figure, of whose personal life we know so little beyond what his writings reveal, must have died in hope, sure that God would accomplish the good purposes that He had revealed to and through His servant.

Perhaps the most significant thing we know about Isaiah is found in chapter 6. There Isaiah accepted his commission from his holy God, and was told that he must spend his life speaking to a people who would hear, but never understand; who would see, but never perceive.

What a burden for anyone to bear! And yet, Isaiah was faithful, not just for a year or 2, but over a 50-year span! Isaiah's contemporaries would not hear the words Isaiah spoke. Yet his words echo through the centuries, and conjure up images for you and me today that help us know God better, and that deepen our awe of God's wisdom and His love.

When God calls you or me to minister, and others do not seem to hear, or reject our efforts, we can remember Isaiah. His years of rejection bore unexpected fruit. And our faithful service will too.

Isaiah's times. When Isaiah began his ministry in Judah, around 739 B.C., both Hebrew kingdoms were prosperous and powerful. Yet Isaiah, like his northern contemporaries, Amos and Hosea, was deeply concerned over evidence of spiritual deterioration. Prosperity saw the development in each kingdom of a wealthy class, which victimized the less fortunate. The court system, which relied on honest judges and truthful witnesses, was corrupted to serve the rich and powerful. Religion was increasingly a matter of ritual observance; less and less a matter of love for the Lord.

In the late 730s, the states of Syria and Palestine formed a reluctant coalition to resist Assyria, the great northern power that was putting more and more pressure on the western Mediterranean states. In 722 the Northern Kingdom, Israel, was crushed and its people were deported by the Assyrians. Only divine intervention, in response to Hezekiah's prayer, turned Assyria back from an intended attack on Jerusalem.

During Isaiah's life, then, Judah gradually declined from wealth and relative military strength to vulnerability. Isaiah's listeners' failure to heed his words, and their continued indifference to the Lord, sealed the fate the nation would experience when it was invaded, not by Assyria but by Babylon.

Isaiah's Judah was very much like 20th-century America. Both nations were marked by prosperity and power. Yet in each the fabric of society was strained by moral decline and materialism. The very existence of such forces in society testifies to the superficiality of religion, and no superficial religion can save a nation from disaster.

While the charges lodged by Isaiah against Judah speak to us today, so do his words of hope. They remind us that whatever may happen to any nation, God remains in full charge of history. The visions Isaiah shared of God, of the coming Saviour, and of the splendor to be unveiled at history's end, thrill our hearts, and lead us to worship our sovereign, loving God.

Overview

After establishing the setting of Isaiah's prophetic ministry (1:1), the prophet, speaking in God's name, launched a vigorous indictment of his society (vv. 2-31).

Understanding the Text

"The ox knows his master" Isa. 1:2-4. "Knows" here, as in other places, implies "responds to." Even a dumb animal recognizes and responds to its master's voice. But Judah did not respond to God. Isaiah identified the reason. This was a willful rather than ignorant failure to respond. Note the three descriptive terms: forsaken, spurned, and "turned their backs on."

We may be critical of things the pagans among us do in ignorance. But sins we commit are far worse! We know God's will, but fail to do it anyway!

"Why should you be beaten anymore?" Isa. 1:5-9 Isaiah's prophecies are not arranged in chronological sequence. These verses suggest chapter 1 should be placed after Assyria had deported Israel. In that invasion many thousands of citizens of Judah were also taken into captivity.

God's warning here is best understood as a cry of anguish. It hurts the Lord to discipline His people. Why, oh why, will we not respond, and free Him from the painful necessity of punishment?

"What are they to Me?" Isa. 1:10-17 There is no indication here that the people of Judah violated any ritual regulation. Their fault, a fault which kept God from listening to their prayers, was moral. No one who sins against his fellowmen can be confident of a hearing with God. (See DEVOTIONAL.)

"Though your sins are like scarlet" Isa. 1:18-20. God chose scarlet for a simple reason. This bright red color was the most "fast" color known. While other colors might be bleached out, scarlet could not.

How powerful the promise, then. Even if our sins, like scarlet, are impossible to remove, God will do it if only we will turn to Him, becoming "willing and obedient."

Sometimes Christians cannot forget their sins. The past seems fixed, forever coloring their outlook. How wonderful to realize that God can—and in Christ, has—purified us, so that in His sight we are "white as snow."

"Zion will be redeemed" Isa. 1:21-31. All things change. The faithful city fell, and became wicked. You and I may fall too. Yet God will not leave us in such a state, any more than He would leave the ancient city or its people. God said, "I will remove your impurities," and, "You will be called the City of Righteousness."

What a wonderful word of reassurance. You may have failed God. But He will not fail you. He will "remove your impurities" and you will be known for your righteousness!

▶DEVOTIONAL
Right Is Only Half the Story! (Isa. 1)

One comedian has a routine in which he pictures two Christians meeting for the first time. They question each other, gradually discovering that they are both Conservative, Fundamental, Seventh-Day, Separated, Predestinarian Baptists, Great Lakes District. Then the final question is asked. Organized 1912, or Reconstituted 1934? When one answers 1912, the other pushes him off a cliff, shouting, "Die, heretic!"

We might resent the routine a little. But it is funny. And it points up a flaw in some of our thinking about faith. A flaw Isaiah saw some 700 years before the birth of Christ.

In verses 10-17 the prophet described a religious people whose ritual seems to be according to the Law. These folks had religion down pat, and were absolutely "right." They went up to the temple for the required festivals. They offered the right sacrifices. They made long prayers. But God called all these things meaningless.

He went on through Isaiah to tell these religiously right people to "stop doing wrong, learn to do right! Seek justice, encourage the oppressed. Defend the cause of the fatherless, plead the case of the widow" (vv. 16-17). The point, of course, is that what demonstrates a real and vital faith is not that we are "right," but that our relationship with God has produced righteousness.

I suppose it's good to be concerned about being right. But being right is, at best, only half the issue. What God cares about most is, are we righteous?

Personal Application

To please God, pay more attention to doing right than to being right.

Quotable

Henry David Thoreau once went to jail rather than pay his poll tax to a state that supported slavery. His good friend Ralph Waldo Emerson hurried to visit him in jail and, peering through the bars, exclaimed: "Why, Henry, what are you doing in there?"

Thoreau replied, "No, Ralph, the question is, what are you doing out there?"

MAY 17 *Reading 137*
DESTINY'S CHILDREN
Isaiah 2–6

> *"The Law will go out from Zion, the word of the* Lord *from Jerusalem" (Isa. 2:3).*

All too often we sense a great gap between what is and what should be. In these opening chapters, Isaiah reminded his hearers and us that what God intends ultimately will be.

Overview

Isaiah stated God's intention for Jerusalem (2:1-5), then pronounced judgment on its inhabitants for failing to walk in His light (v. 6–4:1). Despite the failure of God's people, the Lord will make Jerusalem holy (vv. 2-6). Isaiah defined Judah's sin in his "song of the vineyard" (5:1-7) and announced judgment as a series of woes (vv. 8-30). The section ends with a Isaiah's call to serve as a prophet (6:1-13).

Understanding the Text

"Come, let us go up to the mountain of the Lord*" Isa. 2:1-5.* Isaiah shared a vision of the ideal. God intended Jerusalem to be glorious: a beacon, calling all nations to Him and His Law. If only the nations would turn to the Lord and His Law, God would bring peace to the world. This thought is expressed in one of the most famous of Old Testament images: "They will beat their swords into plowshares and their spears into pruning hooks."

In Isaiah's day the ideal had not been realized. International conditions were grim, and Judah was threatened by powerful enemies. Yet Isaiah cried, "Come, O house of Jacob, let us walk in the light of the Lord." That is, let us live as though the ideal were present now!

God calls you and me to live in exactly this same way. The kingdom of God hasn't yet been established on earth. "Do unto others as you would have them do unto you" is often perverted by the world to, "Do unto others before they can do unto you!" Yet we who know Jesus as

Saviour are to live now *as if* God's kingdom were firmly in place. We are to ignore the "realities" that drive others to compromise with God's will, and to "walk in the light of the LORD."

"Their land is full of idols" Isa. 2:6–4:1. Having described God's ideal for the Holy City and its people, Isaiah went on to describe the reality. Rather than walking in the light of the Lord, the people of Judah had embraced the ways of the pagans they were called to influence! They had arrogantly adopted pagan superstitions (2:6), materialism (v. 7a), confidence in military might (v. 7b), even idolatry (v. 8).

Isaiah now warned his fellow countrymen. God would act to judge this arrogant people: they will be "brought low" (vv. 10-22). (See DEVOTIONAL.) In that day everything would fall apart: there would be anarchy within a nation desperate for leadership and stability (3:1-12).

Two groups were singled out: the elders and leaders of Judah, and the "women of Zion." The thought seems to be that the women's passion for wealth and luxury was a driving force in the corruption of the society. When judgment came these women would lose everything, including any hope of marriage, due to the death of so many of Judah's men.

The passage reminds us that no people who refuse to walk in the light of the Lord can prosper. But there is a special word to individuals, in verse 10. God told Isaiah, "Tell the righteous it will be well with them, for they will enjoy the fruit of their deeds." Whatever happens to our society, you and I need not despair. Our calling is to live righteous lives, and expect God to care for us whatever may come.

"Those who are left" Isa. 4:2-6. God's ideal surely will be achieved. This is the thought with which Isaiah closed his lengthy sermon. After judgment has removed sinners and purified survivors, a cleansed and holy Jerusalem will serve as a shelter and shade for humanity.

But this will only be accomplished by the appearance of a person called "the Branch of the Lord." This term, "branch," is a frequent title of the Messiah, who is to come from David's family line and to accomplish the ultimate deliverance of the Jews and all humankind.

Again Isaiah's words serve as a reminder to us. God's ideal is more than we can accomplish in our own strength. But God Himself has acted in Christ to make it possible for you and me to walk in the light of the Lord. We are His new creation. All we can do is to honor the Lord by living righteous lives, however dark the ways of this present world.

"Woe to you" Isa. 5:8-30. A "woe" is an

The low vines of Palestine's grapes produced a crop associated in the Old Testament with joy and fulfillment. In one of Scripture's most powerful images Judah is likened to a vineyard, planned and planted by God, intended to bear fruit that would gladden the Lord's heart (5:1-7). But instead of the justice and righteousness God sought, His vineyard, Judah, produced injustice and bloodshed.

exclamation, a cry of grief or anguish, that is typically associated with divine judgment. This series of woes is announced for specific sins that are particularly grievous. These are: (1) creating large personal estates at the expense of poorer landholders (vv. 8-10); (2) hedonistic living that shows "no regard for the deeds of the LORD" (vv. 11-17); (3) making evil a life's work and scoffing at divine judgment (vv. 18-19); (4) calling evil good and good evil (v. 20); (5) relying on one's own counsel rather than revelation (v. 21); (6) failing to take governmental responsibilities soberly (vv. 22-23).

God's judgment will surely fall on such a people, for each action described shows that "they have rejected the Law of the LORD Almighty, and spurned the word of the Holy One of Israel."

These woes can be summed up by noting that the sins condemned involve a reconstitution of society. A desire for wealth and personal pleasure is expressed in societal values that replace the values revealed by God. The good traditional values are replaced by evil new values, and scoffed at by those who are wise in their own eyes. Even those who administer the nation's laws accept the new values, and so "acquit the guilty for a bribe."

It may be hard to live by God's values in our own society. But it was hard in Bible times too! Only a firm commitment to God and His ways can guard us against evil influences that press in on every side.

"I saw the Lord" Isa. 6:1-8. Scholars debate whether this chapter belongs with 2–5 or with 7–12. It seems best to place it here. Isaiah had bluntly warned Judah of impending judgment. The story of his call by God is included to prove his words are authoritative.

Isaiah's account emphasized the holiness of God (vv. 1-4), the prophet's awareness of his own sinfulness (v. 5), his cleansing (vv. 6-8), and his subsequent willingness to serve as God's messenger (v. 8).

In a sense Isaiah's call reflects our own experience. When you and I are forgiven, we too become responsible to serve as God's messengers to others in our society.

"How long?" Isa. 6:9-13 Isaiah's task was to communicate his message of judgment until it was fulfilled, and the doom he pronounced came. You and I are also to communicate our message until God's words are fulfilled. But the message we carry is the good news of salvation! Let's not become discouraged if others do not respond immediately. Let's keep on sharing, until the Gospel bears its fruit.

▶ DEVOTIONAL
Arrogance Brought Low (Isa. 2)

It's surprising how extensive the Old Testament's vocabulary of "arrogance" is. One Hebrew root, *zid,* pictures a self-important pride that leads to acts of rebellion. Another root, *ga'ah,* implies overwhelming self-confidence linked with insensitivity to others. A third, *gabah,* suggests a sense of self-importance.

What's wrong with being proud? Well, nothing. As long as our pride is simple satisfaction in our accomplishments, or honesty about our strengths and abilities.

But pride becomes arrogance when it grows beyond simple satisfaction to become a self-important disdain for others, or a bloated self-confidence that makes us feel we can step outside the moral rules that govern others and get away with it.

In fact, the feeling that we can "get away with" something that "other people" can't, lies at the heart of arrogance. The stockbroker who makes money with insider information, the adult who takes one more drink before driving, the teen who thinks that just trying crack or sex can't hurt, all fall into the category of the arrogant. And, in Isaiah's words, "The eyes of the arrogant man will be humbled and the pride of men brought low" by God (vv. 11, 17).

What's the antidote to arrogance? The same verses have the answer: "The LORD alone will be exalted in that day." We exalt the Lord when we accept our place as creatures who are totally dependent on His goodness and His grace. We exalt the Lord when we keep His commands, not just out of love but out of a conviction that God is wiser than we are. We exalt the Lord when we honor others as persons of worth and value because they too are His creatures and objects of His love. We exalt the Lord when we find joy in our accomplishments, and thank Him for the gifts that made them possible.

When you and I live humbly, exalting God rather than ourselves, we avoid the judgment earned by the arrogant.

Personal Application

With God in first place, we will never be in last!

Quotable

You know, Lord, how I serve You,
with great emotional fervor,
in the limelight.
You know how eagerly I speak for You,
at a women's club.
You know how I effervesce when I promote a fellowship group.
You know my genuine enthusiasm
at a Bible study.

But how would I react, I wonder
if You pointed to a basin of water,
and asked me to wash the calloused feet of a bent and wrinkled old woman,
day after day,
month after month,
in a room where nobody saw,
and nobody knew!—Ruth Harms Calkin

MAY 18 *Reading 138*

GOD'S SILVER LINING

Isaiah 7–12

"For to us a Child is born, to us a Son is given, and the government will be on His shoulders" (Isa. 9:6).

Dark clouds hung on the international horizon when Isaiah spoke the words recorded in these chapters. But three times the sun broke through, as Isaiah spoke of the coming Messiah who would set all things right.

Background

The international scene. The states of Syria-Palestine, led by Pekah of Israel (Samaria) and Rezin of Syria (Damascus) forged a coalition of kings to resist Assyria. Ahaz of Judah refused to join, and the two kings threatened to invade Judah. In desperation Ahaz sent envoys to offer the Assyrians a large bribe to attack Syria and Israel before the two local powers could attack him!

This strategy backfired. Assyria accepted the bribe, and overwhelmed Judah's enemies, but then invaded Judah as well!

Today's text describes a confrontation between Isaiah and Ahaz, as the prophet announced that God would protect Judah from Pekah and Rezin. Told to ask God for a sign, Ahaz refused. He would not trust God, but insisted on turning to Assyria, thus sealing the devastation of his homeland as well as the destruction of his enemies!

Isaiah's words in this situation are a healthy reminder for you and me when we find ourselves in difficult situations, and look about desperately for a way out. "Do not fear what they fear, and do not dread it. The LORD Almighty is the One you are to regard as holy, He is the One you are to fear, He is the One you are to dread, and He will be a sanctuary" (Isa. 8:12-14).

Overview

A reluctant Ahaz was given the sign of Immanuel (7:1-16), and told that Assyria, on whom he relied, would bring devastation to Judah (v. 17–8:22). Yet a Child identified as "Mighty God" would be born and reign on David's throne (9:1-7), but not before the wickedness of Israel, Judah, and Assyria have been punished (v. 8–10:19). The survivors of Judah would rely on the Lord (10:20-34), and Messiah will establish God's righteous kingdom worldwide (11:1–12:6).

Understanding the Text

"The virgin will be with Child and will give birth to a Son, and will call Him Immanuel" Isa. 7:1-16. "Immanuel" is a Hebrew construction that means "God with us." Actually, it is an unusual construction that makes the point: "WITH US is God!"

Isaiah would not have understood the

full significance of the name. Yet it, as well as other names given the Messiah in this section of Isaiah, made it clear that the promised Child was to be both human and divine. Thus Matthew referred to this prophecy when he described Jesus' conception not by any human father but by the Holy Spirit (Matt. 1:23).

The promise was a sign to Ahaz, in that it identified a period of time within which his enemies would no longer threaten him. From conception to birth is nine months; from birth to weaning to solid food was typically two to three years. So Ahaz was told that within three years the kings he feared would no longer be a threat. And the "whole house of Israel" was invited to watch David's line for a Virgin Birth, and told that the Child would be the promised Deliverer.

Each of the three great messianic visions in these chapters dates some 700 years before the birth of Christ! Cast against the background of Israel's and Judah's troubled times, they remind us that the Lord is in complete control of history. Whatever happens to us today, our future is secure, for tomorrow is in God's hand.

"The LORD will bring on you" Isa. 7:17–8:22. The Assyrian invasion of Israel and Judah reminds us that God can use even wicked people to accomplish His purposes. Yet the passage reminds us of something else. What makes us vulnerable to the wicked is our own sin. Isaiah portrayed his fellow countrymen consulting mediums and spiritualists rather than God, as abandoning the Law, and as people who when distressed curse God rather than seek forgiveness. Holding tight to the Lord is our only protection against "distress and darkness and fearful gloom" (8:19-22).

"To us a Child is born" Isa. 9:1-8. The Child to be born was a Son, given us as a gift by His Father. He is called "Mighty God" as well as Wonderful Counselor and Prince of Peace. The name "Everlasting Father" is more likely "Father [source] of Eternity." Each of these names makes it clear that the promised Messiah is no ordinary human being.

What no natural descendant of David could do—uphold the kingdom "with justice and righteousness from that time on and forever"—this miraculous Descendant who is God as well as man, will accomplish.

Names like these help us appreciate just who Jesus is. We sense the warmth of His love as we walk with Him through the Gospels. But Isaiah reminds us that our gentle Jesus is Father of Eternity, One whose elemental power has shaped and still upholds our universe.

"His anger is not turned away" Isa. 9:8–10:4. What makes a person angry, as well as what he loves, is a key to understanding his character. What makes God angry? Isaiah tells us, as he pronounced, "Woe to those who make unjust laws, to those who issue oppressive decrees, to deprive the poor of their rights and rob My oppressed people of justice, making widows their prey and robbing the fatherless" (10:1-2).

If these same things in our society make us angry, then our hearts are in tune with God.

"I will punish the king of Assyria" Isa. 10:5-19. Is it fair for God to punish Assyria, which He Himself chose to discipline His people? The answer again reveals the delicate balance that Scripture maintains between divine Sovereignty and human free will. God permitted the rise of Assyria so that nation might discipline His people. But Assyria chose to use the power given to it "to destroy" (v. 7). Assyria became proud, as though God were not the source of its might. Assyria is not being punished for having the power God gave it, but for its pride and misuse of God-given power.

God isn't to blame for the way any person or nation uses the wealth or power He grants. God gives us the freedom to choose how to use His gifts—but holds us responsible for our choices.

▶ DEVOTIONAL
We Live in Hope
(Isa. 11–12)

One of the best movies I've seen in several years is *Dead Poets' Society.* It tells the story of a teacher who challenges students at an exclusive private school to think for themselves—with tragic results. One young man finds the courage for the first time to do what he wants rather than what his father demands. He acts in a play. His angry father takes him out of the school, tells him he has to spend the next 10 years studying for a medical career, and forbids him to ever act again. That night, unable to face such a future, the young man takes his father's gun and commits suicide.

That's a strange thing about suicide. Most people who kill themselves do so because they feel hopeless. Most who kill themselves don't do so because of some terrible present lack. They have money, food, clothing, shelter, and friends now. It's just that looking ahead, they can't see any meaningful future.

Isaiah 11 and 12 remind us that it's just the opposite for true believers. The believer of Isaiah's day faced imminent danger from powerful foreign enemies. His society was marked by injustice; many may well have been homeless and hungry. Yet what Isaiah offered God's people was a vision of the future. A descendant of David (11:1) will appear, to establish righteousness on earth (vv. 2-5). In His day nature itself will be at peace (vv. 6-9). All the hostile world powers that have threatened Judah will rally to Israel's Messiah, and the Lord will "reach out His hand a second time to reclaim the remnant that is left of His people" (vv. 10-16). Then God's people will know the full meaning of salvation, and will together sing praises and give thanks (12:1-6).

Inspired by this vision of the future, the believer was filled with hope.

How strange it is. The suicide, who has everything needed for life on earth, kills himself because he can't face the future. Yet many a believer who has suffered persecution or lacked life's necessities has lived victoriously because his hope is fixed in God.

In Christ, the future is never truly bleak. Beyond whatever darkness we face, we know there lies a glorious tomorrow.

Personal Application

Rather than hope for some thing, hope in God.

Quotable

"No man ever sank under the burden of the day. It is when tomorrow's burden is added to the burden of today that the weight is more than a man can bear. Never load yourself so. If you find yourself so loaded, at least remember this: it is your own doing, not God's. He begs you to leave the future to Him, and mind the present."—George MacDonald

---

MAY 19 *Reading 139*
AGAINST THE WICKED
Isaiah 13–23

> *"How the oppressor has come to an end! How his fury has ended! The LORD has broken the rod of the wicked, the scepter of the rulers" (Isa. 14:4-5).*

These chapters of Isaiah take a new direction, and communicate a single message: God surely will act against the enemies of the righteous.

Background

Sovereignty. The NIV translates *'adonay yahweh* by "Sovereign Lord." The first Hebrew word is an intensive form of the word for "master," or "owner"; a form used only of God in the Old Testament. While the name itself, rendered "LORD God" in older versions, tells us little about the nature of God's sovereignty, these chapters of Isaiah reveal much. Little Judah was surrounded by powerful enemies, who frequently brought God's people into subjection. Yet the God of Israel was worshiped as Lord of the whole earth and Creator of the heavens. How could this vision of an all-powerful God be supported in view of the relative weakness of His people?

Isaiah's answer is found in this series of oracles—prophetic announcements of judgment—directed against Judah's enemies. God is in complete charge of the flow of history. The Lord will judge the wicked world powers that have oppressed His people. One by one they will fall. As the decades march on, the fall of Judah's enemies will provide evidence that God is God, and that the good He intends for His people will surely come to pass.

At times we may feel overwhelmed, reading through chapters of the Old Testament which seem to us obscure or even perhaps irrelevant. Yet these oracles against the nations were not irrelevant to his listeners—nor are they irrelevant to you and me. They remind us too that, though the wicked may at times seem to prosper, God is sovereign. People and nations pass away and history flows on, channeled by God's hidden power. In God's time history will empty into an eternity that He has planned from the beginning, and all God's people will be blessed.

Overview

Our sovereign God will overthrow all enemies of His people. Judgment will fall on Babylon (13:1–14:23), on Assyria and Philistia (vv. 24-32), Moab (15:1–16:14), Damascus (17:1-14), Ethiopia (Cush) (18:1-7), Egypt (19:1-25), Egypt and Ethiopia (20:1-6), Babylon, Edom, and Arabia (21:1-17). It will fall on contemporary Jerusalem (22:1-25), and on Tyre (23:1-18).

Understanding the Text

"An oracle concerning Babylon" Isa. 13:1–14:23. Why Babylon? In Isaiah's day Assyria, not Babylon, was supreme. In Isaiah's day the Medes, cast here as the agents of Babylon's downfall, were allies rather than enemies. How could Isaiah speak so certainly of events that happened, not in his own time, but over a century later?

Such questions have led some to insist that Isaiah could not have written this oracle. But such questions remind us of the sovereign power of God, who knows things that have not yet come to pass, and reveals them through His prophets.

Perhaps one of the most striking images is found in 13:19-22, which pictures a deserted Babylon, so much a specter that no Arab will pitch his tent there, a home for wild animals that will scurry among its ruins. For well over 2,000 years the site of ancient Babylon has been just such a specter. The night winds have howled through heaps of ancient mud bricks, and superstitious Arabs have avoided and feared Babylon's desolation.

What an image of worldly glory! It flourishes for a moment. And then as history rushes on, worldly glory crumbles. How empty the ambitions and the achievements of the world.

"Ar in Moab is ruined" Isa. 15:1–16:13. Moab had been an enemy of Israel from the days of the Exodus (cf. Num. 22–24). Isaiah announced that Moab would be devastated within three years (Isa. 16:14).

Nestled among the predictions of destruction is a beautiful passage that reminds us of an important truth. God's judgments are not vindictive, but are intended to bring blessing and peace. "The oppressor will come to an end, and destruction will cease; the aggressor will vanish from the land. In love a throne will be established; in faithfulness a man will sit on it—one from the house of David—one who in judging seeks justice and speeds the cause of righteousness" (vv. 4-5).

"The glory of Jacob will fade" Isa. 17:1-14. The coalition of Syria and Israel, formed to resist Assyria, was doomed to fail. Damascus, the capital of Syria, would fall, leaving Israel exposed to the brutal invader. But Isaiah did not see Israel's destruction as an unmixed evil. Stripped of national pride and glory, destitute, and starving, "Men will look to their Maker and turn their eyes to the Holy One of Israel" (v. 7). What we are likely to see as a disaster is often intended by God for some greater good.

"Stripped and barefoot" Isa. 20:1-6. In the 1960s when Arthur Blessett marched in U.S. cities carrying a gigantic wooden cross, he was frequently ridiculed. But Blessett felt called, and was willing to be thought a fool for Christ.

Isaiah must have felt something of a fool in the eighth century B.C., when he was told by God to wander the streets of Jerusalem stripped (to a loincloth) and barefoot for some three years. This relative of the royal family exposed himself to shame at God's command, to serve as an object lesson. Soon the sovereign God would execute judgment against Egypt and Cush (Ethiopia), and their people would suffer Isaiah's fate.

God is unlikely to ask you or me to walk about in diapers or drag a cross. But there will be times when we feel a little embarrassed or foolish at the thought of doing something we feel convicted is God's will. At such times let's take heart from the example of God's bolder servants, and put obedience first.

"O city of tumult and revelry" Isa. 22:1-25. Jerusalem rejoiced over its deliverance from the forces of Sennacherib in 701 B.C. Isaiah, however, was distressed. The goodness of God should have led the people of Judah to repent (vv. 12-13), not to party!

In this Isaiah reflected a thought expressed later by the Apostle Paul: "Do you show contempt for the riches of His kindness, tolerance and patience, not realizing that God's kindness leads you toward repentance?" (Rom. 2:4)

▶ DEVOTIONAL
Move Over, God
(Isa. 14:12-15)

The author of Ecclesiastes said it. "There is nothing new under the sun." He was right. Try as hard as one can, it's even impossible to invent a new sin!

I suspect that's one reason why so many commentators take Isaiah 14:12-15 not just as the description of some arrogant but petty Babylonian ruler, but as a description of Satan. Probably they're right in seeing at least a reflection of Satan here. The passage does describe what is perhaps the root of every sin. Some call it pride. What it really is, is the intention of the creature to "make myself like the Most High." It's the intention of the creature to sit on the throne of the universe, and have its own way.

If Satan is in view here, his intention was quite literal. He really did say in his heart, "Move over, God, I want Your throne." You and I aren't likely to express ourselves quite as blatantly. But all our sins do reflect the same attitude. What we feel and think is, *"I want. . . ."* and *"I will. . . ."*

What's wrong with that? It's just that there is room in the universe for only one God. Our attitude should be, "What You will" and our desires, "What You want."

It may seem strange, but that one little change in pronoun can help us avoid the judgment that these chapters assure us will overtake the wicked. If in our heart of hearts we replace the "I" with "You," a good and holy life will follow.

Personal Application

In the Christian life if not the alphabet, "U" always comes before "I."

Quotable

"Psychologist Bernard Rimland, at the Institute for Child Behavior Research in San Diego, has just published a simple test.

"Make a list of 10 persons whom you know the best. After each name write either H (for happy) or N (for unhappy). Then go down the list again, this time writing S (for selfish) and U (for unselfish) after each name. Once you have completed your list, draw a table . . . count each category, and place the numbers in the appropriate cell.

"When Rimland added up the cases of 1,988 people rated by 216 students in 6 college classes, he found that the happy/selfish category was almost empty (only 78 of the cases), while 827 fell into the happy/unselfish cell. Paradox: Selfish people are by definition devoted to bringing themselves happiness. Judged by others, however, they seem to succeed less often than people who work at bringing happiness to others.

"Conclusion: Do unto others as you would have them do unto you."—Cris Cox

MAY 20 *Reading 140*
RUIN TO RESURRECTION
Isaiah 24–27

"On this mountain the LORD Almighty will prepare a feast of rich food for all peoples" (Isa. 25:6).

The judgment of God on sin is part of His plan for the redemption of humanity. When sin is punished and the wicked wiped out, salvation will come and "the earth will give birth to her dead."

Background

Divine judgment. Some feel uncomfortable with the notion of divine judgment. Isaiah, however, was completely comfortable. In these chapters, which all commentators see as a unit, Isaiah examined the relationship of history, divine judgment, and God's ultimate intentions for humanity. The message of the passage is, first, that the disasters that overtake men and nations demonstrate God's determination to punish sin. But second, no human failure will prevent God from shaping the righteous society that His holiness demands. The God who judges sin and forgives those who trust Him will create a just moral society at history's end.

Overview

Isaiah predicted devastating judgments (24:1-23) which would bring about the triumph of God (25:1-12). For the righteous, God's triumph promises a resurrection (26:1-21). In His judgments God will destroy oppressors and restore the blessings of the oppressed (v. 20–27:13).

Understanding the Text

"Its people must bear their guilt" Isa. 24:1-23. Isaiah announced that the whole world will be punished. No class of people (v. 2) will escape, for earth's inhabitants have "broken the everlasting covenant" (v. 5). This is a reference to the covenant God made with humanity in Noah's time (Gen. 9:16), which made man responsible for maintaining a just society.

Though God's judgment will leave earth devastated (Isa. 24:6-13), the people of God will "acclaim the LORD's majesty" (vv. 14-16). With all evil human and spiritual powers judged, "the Lord Almighty will reign on Mount Zion and in Jerusalem, and before its elders, gloriously" (vv. 17-23).

What is striking here is the picture of the saints, praising God while everything around them crashes in ruins. Each believer must be affected by the kind of devastation described here. Yet faith gives the believer the ability to see the hand of God in what seems nothing but tragedy to others. Faith also gives us the strength to praise God and "acclaim the LORD's majesty" when every earthly hope is lost.

"You have been a refuge" Isa. 25:1-12. Isaiah explained the outcome of God's acts of judgment, and described the future of the blessed. What the future holds is praise for God, who has stilled "the song of the ruthless" (vv. 1-5). With the wicked destroyed, God prepares a "feast of rich food for all peoples." It is then that God will "swallow up death forever" and "wipe away the tears from all faces; He will remove the disgrace of His people from all the earth" (vv. 6-8).

While images of the future differ slightly between the Old Testament and the New Testament, there is no difference at all in the two Testament's description of who will enjoy it. The blessed of every age are those who can say, "Surely this is our God; we trusted in Him, and He saved us. This is the LORD, we trusted in Him; let us rejoice and be glad in His salvation."

How natural it is for you and me to join Isaiah in praise to the Lord, and share Isaiah's joy. We too know God as our Saviour. We trust in Him. We know that He will deliver us from the coming judgment. We will be at His side when the song of the ruthless is stilled.

"Your dead will live" Isa. 26:1-21. Not even death can thwart God's purposes. Isaiah looked ahead and saw a day when salvation's song will be sung in Jerusalem (vv. 1-7). Yet his own day was one of longing, not of fulfillment. "We wait for You," Isaiah sighed, and added, "My soul yearns for You in the night; in the morning my spirit longs for You." His yearning was

great, because, even "though grace is shown to the wicked, they do not learn righteousness" (vv. 8-10).

You and I may know Isaiah's frustration well. Yet we have the same promise that gave Isaiah hope. Isaiah looked ahead, and knew that "Your dead will live; their bodies will rise. You who dwell in the dust, wake up and shout for joy. Your dew is like the dew of the morning; the earth will give birth to her dead" (v. 19).

Even death cannot thwart God's purposes. We live in hope, because we know that if we should die before we see God's plan for this earth achieved, He will raise us from the dead to share His triumph!

"In that day" Isa. 27:1-13. The phrase "that day" typically indicates history's end, an eschatological period during which God draws the threads of all His purposes together. Someone has suggested that the phrase simply means, "in God's time."

Well, what is it that will happen "in God's time"? (1) The Lord will destroy evil spiritual powers, 27:1. (2) The Lord will restore and protect His Old Testament people (vv. 2-7). (3) This will be accomplished after God has atoned for their guilt, and by strict punishment weaned them from their hunger for idolatry (vv. 8-11). (4) This will happen when God recalls His people from exile, and the nation is regathered to "worship the LORD on the holy mountain in Jerusalem" (vv. 12-13).

History does maintain its purposeful flow, coursing as God directs. At history's end God will bring all things to the conclusion that He intends.

When will this happen? We cannot know. But it will happen.

"In that day."

In God's time.

▶ DEVOTIONAL
Waitin' for Justice
(Isa. 26)

We had just written (another) letter to our superintendent of schools. When our third-grader changed schools midyear, she was placed in a classroom where she suffered serious verbal abuse from other children, and received no support from her teacher.

The stress caused Sarah some serious stomach problems. It caused us serious upset too, because only after a number of complaints did we get Sarah transferred to another classroom. Even then her first teacher seemed to take it out on Sarah by threatening to fail her in one of her subjects.

What was frustrating was that, despite the fact Sarah had an A her first semester, and an A the first quarter in her new school, the teacher threatened to fail her for the year—and despite stated school policy we were not even allowed to check the grade book. I could go on and list other abuses, but the point I want to make is simple. All of us, even in the best of times, are victims now and then of injustice.

I know that our situation with Sarah is relatively insignificant. There are far greater injustices suffered by others. But the experience has made us more sensitive to the frustration experienced by the powerless.

This is what Isaiah felt as he cried, "Your name and renown are the desire of our hearts." He went on to complain that though grace is shown to the wicked, they do not learn righteousness, but keep on doing evil (vv. 8-10). How frustrating to try, but always to be kept waiting. How frustrating to struggle, but never seeming to dent injustice.

When something like this happens to us, we need to remember the hope that brought Isaiah comfort. All will be made right, in God's time. It may not be during our lifetime. But, "Your dead will live!"

Even death is not the end. Even death can't thwart the ultimate achievement of justice for all in this world. One day, in God's time, we'll hear His voice calling us. He'll cry out to those of us who dwell in the dust, and we will "wake up and shout for joy." For then we will have justice. Then we will have peace.

Personal Application

Fight injustice. Even if you lose, you will surely win in God's time.

Quotable

"In Germany, they first came for the Communists, and I didn't speak up because I wasn't a Communist; then they came for the Jews, and I didn't speak up because I wasn't a Jew. Then they came for the Trade Unionists, and I didn't speak up because I wasn't a Trade Unionist. Then they came for the Catholics, and I didn't speak up because I was a Protestant. Then they came for me—and by that time no one was left to speak up."—Martin Niemoller

MAY 21 *Reading 141*
THE ARM OF FLESH
Isaiah 28–32

> *"Woe to those . . . who trust in the multitude of their chariots and in the great strength of their horsemen, but do not look to the Holy One of Israel, or seek help from the* Lord*" (Isa. 31:1).*

In condemning Judah's failure to consult the Lord before rebelling against Assyria, these chapters of Isaiah serve as a warning to us as well. We are to look to God for guidance. And do His will.

Background

The messages in this section of Isaiah date from about 705 B.C. Sargon, one of Assyria's most successful rulers, had just died. The leaders of Judah saw this as an opportunity to rebel against Assyrian domination, and made a treaty with Egypt. The decision was foolish because while the Egyptian power once again extended to all its traditional territory, Egypt remained weak. It could offer no significant military help to any ally. The decision was also wrong because the leaders of Judah had failed to consult God. Thus an angry Isaiah interrupted the festival announced by Judah's leaders to celebrate their declaration of independence from Assyria. In graphic images and plain words Isaiah denounced Judah's leaders. Now they were tipsy with the drink served at their premature celebration. In acting without consulting God, they showed that even before they had one bowl of wine they had as little judgment as any drunk!

We need to visualize an angry Isaiah and drunken, dulled leaders as we read these chapters.

Overview

Isaiah condemned Judah's decision to rebel against Assyria and make a treaty with Egypt. That treaty was a covenant with death (28:1-29), and God's unresponsive people would suffer humiliation (29:1-24). Plans made without consulting God will fail (30:1–31:9), yet God's plan to establish a righteous kingdom will succeed (32:1-20). In His time God will arise. Jerusalem will again experience peace (33:1-24).

Understanding the Text

"The remnant of His people" Isa. 28:1-6. Isaiah repeated a warning given the Northern Kingdom, Israel, before Samaria's fall some 20 years before. The earlier warning came true. So would the warnings Isaiah was about to utter concerning Judah.

How much easier to learn the lessons of history, rather than learn by painful personal experiences! God's Word enables us to avoid disastrous mistakes by showing us what happens when the Lord's people fail to consider and do God's will.

Verses 5-6 remind us that human failure to obey God cannot thwart the accomplishment of His purposes. All that our disobedience does is rob us of blessings we would otherwise have experienced.

"Do and do, do and do" Isa. 28:7-22. Isaiah's words made no sense to the tipsy celebrants in Jerusalem. Unable to grasp Isaiah's message, the priests mumbled, "Who is he trying to teach?" while the prophets muttered, "To whom is he explaining his message?"

The repeated phrases, "Do and do, do and do, rule on rule, rule on rule," have been taken to (1) represent the mutterings of the drunks, who could only catch and repeat phrases Isaiah uttered, or (2) to represent the way young children are taught the basics in school, by rote and repetition. Another possible interpretation is (3) that these phrases represent the legalistic way in which Isaiah's hearers approached faith. They could not comprehend the invitation to peace through trust in God imbedded in Scripture. All they could see were the ritual rules.

Whichever is intended, the people of Isaiah's day would not understand God's message. So God determined "with foreign lips and strange tongues" to speak to this people (v. 11). The Assyrians would speak in a language God's people could not mistake—the language of sword, fire, devastation, and misery.

If we do not listen to God's quiet, loving voice, He remains capable of grabbing us by the shoulders, and shaking us until we pay attention!

"It will break in pieces like pottery" Isa. 30–31. Again and again these chapters stress the futility of relying on anything other than God. Perhaps the clearest expression of this is found in 31:3: "The Egyptians are men and not God; their horses are flesh and not spirit. When the LORD stretches out His hand, he who helps will stumble, he who is helped will fall; both will perish together."

We're so vulnerable to the attitude seen here in the people of Judah. We keep on putting our trust in things we can touch, see, and feel. The Persian poet Omar Khayyam put it this way:

Ah, take the cash,
And let the credit go.
Nor heed the rumble
of a distant drum.

You and I, however, are to listen for that distant drum, and ignore the cash! We know that the only things that are real, the only things that offer true security, are spiritual and not material.

If we keep this truth clearly in mind, and act on it, we will be safe from the sin that brought disaster on ancient Judah.

"This is the way; walk in it" Isa. 30:21. Modern airliners have a special guidance system for landings. If the plane strays either right or left of the flight path, a warning is sounded, and the pilot brings it back to the correct bearing.

God had this guidance system long before manned flight was dreamed of! If our relationship with the Lord is characterized by "repentance and rest" and "quietness and trust" (v. 15), then God will speak to our hearts when we stray to the left or right of His path for us. His Spirit will speak to our hearts, and tell us "this is the way; walk in it."

The Christian life *is* a supernatural life. We can't explain how God's Spirit guides us. But we can and do hear His voice.

"Till the spirit is poured upon us from on high" Isa. 32:1–33:24. Isaiah constantly contrasted the dark days of divine judgment with the brightness of the kingdom the Lord will establish afterward. The pattern is clearly seen in these chapters. Isaiah's fellow countrymen had doomed themselves to anguish and mourning. But God's plans to bless His people cannot be overturned by the wickedness of any number of generations. In a beautiful passage Isaiah said that the Promised Land will become a waste—but only

'till the Spirit is poured upon us from on high
and the desert becomes a fertile field,
and the fertile field seems like a forest.
Justice will dwell in the desert
and righteousness live in the fertile field.
The fruit of righteousness will be peace;
the effect of righteousness will be
quietness and confidence forever.

Isaiah 32:15-17

▶ DEVOTIONAL
I Don't Know
(Isa. 29)

It's frustrating to teach folks who simply won't learn. My wife once asked one of her 11th-graders a question about a short story they were studying. The story was called, "The Sculptor's Funeral." Her question was, "Who died?" The student she asked replied, "I don't know, I didn't read the story."

She asked the question again. "Well, read the title and tell me, who died?" And the irritated student answered, "I told you I didn't read the story! I don't know."

I expect Isaiah felt the same frustration as he tried to communicate God's message to his unwilling listeners in Judah. They were as dense as drunks. It was like giving a book to a person, only to have them hand it back and say, "I can't read." The words of Isaiah simply made no sense to the people of Judah.

Today we wonder, Why? Why didn't the people of Isaiah's day grasp his message? Why couldn't they see what seems so clear to you and me?

But the Lord explained (v. 13). The people of Judah had a superficial faith. In modern terms, verse 13 says: "They go to church. They sing hymns, and mouth the creeds. But while the preacher gives his sermon their thoughts are on other things. Their 'worship' isn't of Me. It's just doing things that others expect—showing up on Sunday, dressing right, supporting what to them is more of a 'club' than a community of faith."

When religion fails to focus on God, but deteriorates to a mere social convention, then the hearing of churchgoers is dulled. God speaks. But they can no more hear Him than can a man lying in the gutter in a drunken stupor (vv. 9-10).

How do we protect ourselves from this kind of dullness? Today, as then, it is a matter of the heart. Going to church isn't something we are to do because it's expected. We are to go to church to worship God, to learn more about Him, to express our love in worship, praise, and generous giving. When we come near to God with our whole heart, then you and I *will* hear God speak to us. And we will understand what He says.

Personal Application

Get your heart and not just your family ready for church next Sunday.

Quotable

"How rare it is to find a soul quiet enough to hear God speak."—François Fénelon

---

MAY 22 *Reading 142*
DAY OF VENGEANCE
Isaiah 33–35

> *"For the* Lord *has a day of vengeance, a year of retribution, to uphold Zion's cause" (Isa. 34:8).*

Beyond the troubles glory waits. What these chapters tell us is that faith enables believers to live safely even while the consuming fire burns.

Overview

God is a sure foundation for our times (33:1-9) and hope for our future (vv. 10-24). Isaiah contrasted the judgment that will devastate the nations, represented by Edom (34:1-17), with the joy awaiting the redeemed (35:1-10).

Understanding the Text

"Be our strength every morning" Isa. 33:1-9. God is a sure foundation for every time, "a rich store of salvation and wisdom and knowledge." But we must use a key to open that storehouse, to enjoy its bounty. The text says, "The fear of the Lord is the key to this treasure."

As we've seen, "fear" of God is a reverential awe that keeps us aware of Him at all times. Our awareness that God is, and that He is sovereign, gives us confidence even in the most uncertain of times.

"Who of us can dwell with the consuming fire?" Isa. 33:10-16 Isaiah pictured God, rising as a monarch from His throne to set out for war (v. 10). This terrified the sinners of Zion (v. 14), who despair of surviving the consuming fires of God's judgment, and they cried out, "Who of us can dwell with [survive] the consuming fire?"

They did not expect an answer. But Isaiah provided one. "He who walks righteously and speaks what is right, who rejects gain from extortion and keeps his hand from accepting bribes, who stops his ears against plots of murder and shuts his eyes against contemplating evil."

These words contain no promise that the believer will be immune to trouble in those times when God judges a nation. When the bombs fall, the believer and unbeliever alike will be without electricity and fresh water. No, to "dwell with the consuming fire" is to maintain a hope that contrasts with the despair of the wicked. The righteous take refuge in God, and have faith that no matter how grim life's circumstances, God will supply the necessities to maintain life (v. 16).

"Nothing there to be called a kingdom" Isa. 34:1-17. The contrast drawn here is between civilization and wilderness. Between nature tamed by man and fields returned to the wild. The nations that God would judge refused to respond to the Lord. Their lands would be returned to the birds and the beasts.

The scroll here is the prophecy found in the preceding verses. Everything God says will happen will come to pass. What God has ordained is certain.

It's striking that Scripture so often contrasts cultivated fields and wilderness when calling up visions of blessing and judgment. God really did create our earth to be the home of man.

"It will burst into bloom" Isa. 35:1-10. This brief chapter concludes the first book of Isaiah. These chapters have drawn dark pictures of divine judgment, with brief flashes of light. But this final chapter glows with warmth and hope. Some of the most beautiful and best known of Isaiah's images are found here.

For some 10 years I lived in Arizona, in desert country. Dry and parched for so much of the year, the desert literally burst into bloom with the fall rains. The dominant tans and browns suddenly disappeared and in their place was a warm green, decorated with a riot of delicate colors.

What a vision of the future God has in mind for earth, and for us. All that is dry and parched in our lives will soak in His rain. Then we too will rejoice and blossom, for our lives will reflect the glory of the Lord, the splendor of our God.

"Steady the knees that give way" Isa. 35:3-4. When you and I feel weak and overcome, we find strength in this thought: "Your God will come." While others shrink back in terror, we rejoice at the thought. He comes with retribution for them, but to save us.

"Then" (Isa. 35:5-10). The concluding words of Isaiah are so vivid that they speak for themselves. No comment can do them justice. The prophet shared what God's coming will mean for us, His people, in verses 5-10.

▶DEVOTIONAL

Upon the Burning of Our House (Isa. 33)

On July 10, 1660, the house of Puritan poet Anne Bradstreet burned to the ground, leaving her destitute of earthly possessions. She shares the pain she felt in a poignant poem bearing the title of this devotional.

> When by the ruins oft I past
> My sorrowing eyes aside did cast,
> And here and there the places spy
> Where oft I sat and long did lie:
> Here stood that trunk, and there that chest,
> There lay that store I counted best.
> My pleasant things in ashes lie,
> And them behold no more shall I.

Anne understood the pain that always accompanies the loss of familiar and precious possessions. Anne understood, and expressed, the pain felt by believers of every era who must live through a period when God arises to judge their societies.

But Anne also understood the secret of dwelling among the consuming fires that burn then. Her poem continues:

> Raise up thy thoughts above the sky
> That dunghill mists away may fly.
> Thou hast an house on high erect,
> Framed by that mighty Architect,
> With glory richly furnished.
> Stands permanent though this be fled.
> It's purchased and paid for too
> By Him who hath enough to do.
> A price so vast as is unknown
> Yet by His gift is made thine own;
> There's wealth enough, I need no more.
> Farewell my self, farewell my store.
> The world no longer let me love,
> My hope and treasure lies above.

The secret? To realize that the fires can burn only what is destined to pass away. And to remember that what God has purchased for His own stands permanent, though all in this world be fled.

Personal Application

Treasures in heaven free us from despair when we lose earthly possessions.

Quotable
"Beware of an overconcern for money, or position, or glory. Someday you will meet a man who cares for none of these things. Then you will know how poor you are."—Rudyard Kipling

MAY 23 *Reading 143*
GOD'S SOVEREIGNTY
Isaiah 36–39

"I will put My hook in your nose and My bit in your mouth, and I will make you return by the way you came" (Isa. 37:29).

We can have every confidence that the biblical vision of history's end will come to pass. The past demonstrates that God truly is in charge of events, despite the pretentions of this world's great men.

Background
Sennacherib's forces invaded Judah in 701 B.C. Assyrian annals report that he laid siege to 46 walled cities and forts, and "shut up Hezekiah in Jerusalem like a bird in its cage." Jerusalem seemed sure to fall. But, as these chapters relate, the Assyrian forces suddenly withdrew, and the city was saved.

Why are these historical chapters inserted here, between two collections of Isaiah's prophecies?

In the first 35 chapters of this greatest of Old Testament prophetic works, Isaiah proclaimed God's sovereignty. He announced that in God's time the Lord would deliver His people and will punish the pagan nations that had oppressed them. But God's time, identified as "that day" or "the day of the LORD," must have seemed distant and even unreal to many in Judah. It's easy to *say* God's dominion extends over this world as well as over the spiritual realm. But as long as expressions of that dominion are relegated to the distant future, there is no proof.

But there *was* proof that Isaiah spoke the truth; proof available in the prophet's own day! The Assyrians invaded Judah in overwhelming force. Yet when Hezekiah prayed, God through Isaiah promised to deliver Jerusalem—and did! The events reported in Isaiah 36–39 draw together the key themes of the first 35 chapters of Isaiah in such a way as to demonstrate the validity of each!

It is these themes and their demonstration that convey God's personal message to His people, today as well as in Isaiah's time.

Overview
Sennacherib's delegation called on Judah to surrender rather than trust in God (36:1-22). Isaiah predicted the invasion would be turned back, despite Assyrian threats (37:1-13). Hezekiah prayed (vv. 14-20), and was given specific promises, relayed by Isaiah (vv. 21-38). Hezekiah recovered from a near-fatal illness (38:1-22), but was rebuked for showing Babylonian envoys Judah's wealth (39:1-8).

Understanding the Text
"On what are you basing this confidence of yours?" Isa. 36:1-22 Sennacherib's field commander called for Jerusalem's surrender. Again and again he challenged Hezekiah, who lacked the trained men to serve as cavalry even if the Assyrians would supply the horses! Did they depend on Egypt? Or on God? None of the gods of other peoples were able to protect their lands against Assyria's military might. "How then can the LORD deliver Jerusalem from my hand?"

The attitude expressed by the Assyrian commander is that of scoffers through the ages. "God" may exist somewhere "out there." He may be important to us "bye and bye." But He is irrelevant now, for He is powerless to act in the material universe. To have confidence in God when facing overwhelming odds makes no sense to such people.

Many in Judah undoubtedly felt just this way. As we've seen, Isaiah's ministry was to a people who were "ever hearing, but never understanding" (6:9-10). All his talk about the sovereign power of God, all his promises of future redemption, all his words of warning seemed like nonsense to the majority.

"On what are you basing this confidence of yours?" As events unfolded, it became clear that Isaiah's and King Hezekiah's confidence was rightly placed—in God. These chapters remind us. There are no circumstances we can imagine which can limit God's power to save.

"Do not be afraid of what you have heard" Isa. 37:1-13. Hezekiah asked Isaiah for a word from God, and received it. But the Assyrians continued to bombard the king with threats and ridicule. Forty-six of Judah's forts had fallen to Assyria. Why should Jerusalem be different? "God" is a nice notion, a comforting concept. But the Assyrians possessed the greatest military force the world had known. No "god" had ever been able to resist Assyria's forces.

It's strange, but most Christians find it easier to withstand open hostility than ridicule. When people rage at our faith in God, we resist. But when people laugh at our beliefs, many believers crumble. Hezekiah responded in exactly the right way. Rather than crumble or feel shame, he went directly to God and said, "Lord, they're ridiculing *You.*"

This is the key that frees us to stand before any ridicule from our contemporaries. We need to realize that others are not scoffing at us, but at God. We need to turn to Him, seeing Him as "God over all the kingdoms of the earth," who "made heaven and earth." And we need to say, "Lord, they're insulting *You.*"

How does this enable us to stand? It reminds us of who our God is, and how foolish scoffers are. And it shifts responsibility to respond to ridicule away from us, to God Himself. Like Hezekiah, we can then wait patiently for Him to act.

"He will not . . . shoot an arrow here" Isa. 37:21-38. God's answer to Hezekiah's prayer was a specific promise. The vast Assyrian army was just a few miles away from Jerusalem. Yet not only would Sennacherib be barred from the city, his soldiers would not even be permitted to fire a single arrow over Jerusalem's walls!

Then God intervened, and the Assyrian army suffered a vast number of mysterious deaths in a single night. Greek historian Herodotus, writing hundreds of years later, reports a garbled account of the event that he learned while visiting Egypt.

Suddenly even the most dull of Judah's people must have realized it. God is not irrelevant at all! God *is* sovereign. Every word from His mouth is as certain to be fulfilled as if it had already come to pass (vv. 36-37).

"I have heard your prayer" Isa. 38:1-22. God is master of the fate of nations. But is this sovereign God concerned with the fate of individuals?

Isaiah now included a report of Hezekiah's struggle with a fatal illness. The heartbroken king begged God for added years of life, pleading that "I have walked before You faithfully and with wholehearted devotion." God answered this prayer, and promised Hezekiah 15 added years.

The story is placed here in part because it shows that God is concerned with each person. But more importantly, it shows that the plea of a righteous person can turn aside divine judgment, even after that judgment has been announced (cf. v. 1).

This has been one of the major themes of Isaiah 1–35. Despite Israel's sin, God had called again and again for spiritual renewal. Despite predictions of judgment, a heartfelt return to the Lord would bring blessing instead. Hezekiah, Judah's righteous king, showed the way for his whole land.

▶ DEVOTIONAL
A Tough Teacher
(Isa. 38–39)

Ray Rubinski, one of the teachers at Gulf High where my wife teaches 11th-grade English, stopped her in the hall one day. Sue was wearing a black skirt, white blouse, and rather severe black bow. "Sue," Ray said, only half-kidding, "I wish you wouldn't wear that outfit. It reminds me of the nuns who used to beat my hand with a ruler when I was a kid in Catholic school."

Some of the nuns in old-time parochial schools did have a reputation. I suppose some of them earned it. But if you want to meet a real tough teacher, get introduced to history. Her lessons can change your life. But if you fail to learn from history, you're really in trouble!

Hezekiah teaches us an important history lesson. He listened to Isaiah's words about God's sovereignty, and trusted the Lord to remove the Assyrian threat. God did. When Hezekiah became sick, he recalled what God had said through Isaiah about the Lord's willingness to restore the godly, even after judgment had been announced. So Hezekiah called on God, pleading his godly life. And the Lord did heal, even though He had earlier announced that Hezekiah would die.

But then Hezekiah slipped. Isaiah had also spoken of Babylon as an enemy of God's people. Yet when envoys from Babylon came to "congratulate" the king on his recovery, Hezekiah showed them every one of his royal treasures. A furious Isaiah announced that the day was coming when the Babylonians would carry Hezekiah's treasures and his descendants into Captivity.

What is the lesson in Hezekiah's personal history? Simply this. We need to take *all* of God's words to heart. We can't just believe the parts we like, and claim the promises we want fulfilled. We need to pay close attention to every message of the Word, for forgetting any words or choosing not to hear can cause us trouble indeed.

History is a good teacher. It provides proof that God is real, and is trustworthy. But history is a tough teacher too. If we fail to learn its lessons, we will surely experience its consequences in our lives.

Personal Application

Learn from Hezekiah to pay attention to *every* word of God.

Quotable

"There are four things that we ought to do with the Word of God—admit it as the Word of God, commit it to our hearts and minds, submit to it, and transmit it to the world."—William Wilberforce

MAY 24 *Reading 144*
COMFORT
Isaiah 40–48

> *"Announce this with shouts of joy and proclaim it. Send it out to the ends of the earth; say, 'The LORD has redeemed His servant Jacob' " (Isa. 48:20).*

Hope for us as for ancient Israel rests entirely on the incomparable nature of our God.

Background

The historical section in Isaiah 36–39 closes with the account of Isaiah's denunciation of Hezekiah for welcoming Babylon's envoys. These chapters serve to illustrate Isaiah 1–35. But they also serve as a bridge introducing us to Isaiah 40–66. For suddenly Isaiah seemed catapulted a hundred years ahead in time. The Babylonian invasion was past, and the Jews were captives in a strange land. Yet Isaiah spoke words of comfort, confidently describing the destruction of Babylon and the salvation of God's people. The nation will yet be redeemed, and God's purposes in His people will be fulfilled.

The theory that one or more different persons wrote the second half of Isaiah is rooted in the viewpoint of chapters 40–66. In the first half of Isaiah, Assyria is the main enemy, and the prophet's message is a grim oracle of judgment. In chapters 40–66 Babylon, which has conquered Judah, is about to be judged, and Cyrus, her Persian conqueror, is named. Rather than the darkness of impending judgment, these later chapters are bright with the confident hope of restoration.

Yet the idea that Isaiah wrote both sections poses no great problem for those who take a repeated message found in chapters 40–66 seriously. The God who spoke through Isaiah is fully able to "declare to us the things to come" and to "tell us what the future holds" (41:22-23; 45:21). Speaking by the Spirit of God Isaiah, like other ancient Hebrew prophets, was transported beyond his own time. His words of comfort and hope were rooted in the sure conviction of what God would do, not what He had already done.

Some of the most powerful and exalted passages in the entire Bible are found in these chapters of comfort. These passages can fill us too with hope. They remind us as they reminded ancient Israel of just how wonderful and how loving our God is.

Overview

Judah's sovereign Lord intends good for His people (40:1-31). God, not the idols worshiped by the nations, controls the future (41:1-29). Though Israel failed its national calling as God's servant, One from the nation will fulfill God's purpose (42:1-25) when the Creator acts to redeem His chosen people (43:1–44:25). As evidence, God will appoint one named Cyrus to restore Jerusalem (v. 26–45:25). Oppressive Babylon will be crushed, and God's word of blessing for Israel will be fulfilled (46:1–48:22).

Understanding the Text

"Here is your God" Isa. 40:1-31. The first time I traveled in the western America, I couldn't believe the sky. It seemed so big. I had to keep looking to the left and right to take it all in.

This is something like Isaiah's treatment here of God. He is so big, Isaiah has us look to the left and the right to try to take Him in. Looking left, Isaiah described a God "enthroned above the circle of the earth" to whom the nations seem "like a drop in a bucket" (vv. 6-26). Looking left, we are simply overwhelmed by the awesome greatness of God's power and mighty strength.

Then Isaiah has us look right, and we see the Creator stoop down to touch the individual, and give "strength to the weary." Because ours is a God who not only creates but who also cares, "Those who hope in the LORD will renew their strength. They will soar on wings like eagles; they will run and not grow weary, they will walk and not be faint" (vv. 27-31).

"Here is My servant, whom I uphold" Isa. 42:1-25. There are two "servants" in Isaiah. One is Israel (cf. vv. 8-10), which failed to accomplish God's purpose. The other, introduced here, is the Messiah. This Servant, who is to come from God's failed servant, "will bring forth justice; He will not falter or be discouraged till He establishes justice on earth" (v. 4).

As a "covenant for the people" this Servant will Himself be the foundation on which Israel will build its future—a future which includes salvation for the Gentiles as well as the descendants of Abraham (vv. 6-7).

In context Isaiah's message about the coming Servant of the Lord is intended for comfort and hope. But it is also a challenge. God's Old Testament people were called to do justice, and by holy living to be "a light for the Gentiles." In fact, every believer of every age is to be just this kind of servant of the Lord. We must do justice, live holy lives, and bring the light of a hope that releases "from the [spiritual] dungeon those who sit in darkness" (v. 7).

Jesus has fulfilled God's commission as "the" Servant of the Lord. Now you and I are called to be servants too.

"Fear not, for I have redeemed you" Isa. 43:1-28. Like other chapters in this section, Isaiah 43 is rich in verses that invite memorization. Here are a few from this chapter, crafted to comfort us.

> Fear not, for I have redeemed you; I have called you by name; you are Mine. When you pass through the waters, I will be with you; and when you pass through the rivers, they will not sweep over you. When you walk through the fire, you will not be burned; the flames will not set you ablaze (vv. 1-2).
>
> I, even I, am He who blots out your transgressions, for My own sake, and remembers your sins no more (v. 25).

"I will raise up Cyrus" Isa. 45:1-25. One of the basic sources of comfort for the believer is the conviction that God is in complete control of events.

The theme is illustrated by God's act in naming Cyrus, long before his birth, and announcing that Cyrus will be given a "title of honor, though you do not acknowledge Me" (vv. 1-7). Whether or not the great ones of our present world honor

God, He alone is the source of their existence and position.

The theme is demonstrated by Creation. The universe knows only one all-powerful Being, who "made the earth and created mankind upon it" (vv. 8-17). Surely the Creator has full power to mold those who are works of His hands into whatever form He chooses.

The theme is confirmed by God's unique self-existence. In a universe in which men worship idols, there is "none but Me" who is able to save, who utters a word "that will not be revoked," and who will ultimately receive the homage of all (vv. 18-25).

God is in control of world events—and of the days of our lives. Because He is, and because the Lord is "a righteous God and a Saviour" (v. 21), we face the future with confidence and hope.

"I foretold the former things long ago" Isa. 48:3-8. Some people will always try to drain religion of the supernatural. It was true in Isaiah's day, and it's true in our day as well. We can almost hear frustration in the prophet's voice as God spoke to Judah through him: "I foretold the former things long ago, My mouth announced them and I made them known; then suddenly I acted, and they came to pass. . . . You have heard these things; look at them all. Will you not admit them?"

There is no more compelling evidence for the supernatural origin and authority of the Scriptures than fulfilled prophecy. Time and time again the Bible records the prediction of some prophet—and hundreds or thousands of years later what is predicted is fulfilled in detail. Yet, time and time again, some struggle to find excuses not to admit what God has said and done.

The skeptic finds no comfort in Scripture because he or she will not believe in an all-powerful God who acts in the world of men. The believer rejoices and finds a firm foundation of his or her hope.

"Your peace would have been like a river" Isa. 48:17-22. The person who fails to trust God's Word completely forfeits more than comfort. He or she forfeits peace. God said through Isaiah, "I am the LORD your God, who teaches you what is best for you, who directs you in the way you should go." He added, "If only you had paid attention" then "your peace would have been like a river."

The person who abandons confidence in the Word of God will soon abandon God's commands as well. When that happens, he or she will discover that "there is no peace," says the Lord, "for the wicked."

Trust in God's Word is not simply an intellectual issue. It is one of the pivotal issues of faith and life.

▶ DEVOTIONAL
Bigger Than Me
(Isa. 44)

This chapter contains the Bible's classic exposé of idolatry. It pictures a workman forging an idol of metal or carving it from wood. And it ridicules the idol-maker, who sees no contradiction in burning half the wood of a tree he cut down to cook his food, and then praying to the remaining block of wood, "Save me; you are my god."

But the idol-maker is ridiculous. He wants someone or something to save him. But he chooses something he himself has made to serve as a god. "Give me a god," the idol-maker seems to say. "But don't give me a god bigger than me. Give me a god I can control: one I can make out of a tree I cut down; one I can shape to suit myself."

In biblical times evidence of idolatry lay all around. You could see and touch the metal or wooden figures of the gods. Today we like to think man has progressed beyond idolatry. But in fact, the very same attitude dominates the thinking of many in this "scientific" age.

No, we don't have metal or wooden figures. But we do have computers. We do have spaceships. We do have hydrogen bombs and rockets. We have many such works of our own hands, and all too often humanity says to these things man himself has created, "Save me. Save me. I'm counting on you to deliver me."

And then God's Word comes to our generation. He reminds us that our craftsmen too "are nothing but men." To have confidence in things that we have made is the essence of idolatry. It is to exchange hope in the living God for hope in dumb, silent works of our own hands.

Mankind does want gods. But gods that are under human control. When we meet the God of Scripture, we meet a God who is bigger than we. Then we abandon our attempts to control Him—and joyfully submit to the loving-kindness and the guidance of a living God.

Personal Application
An idol is anything less than God that you expect to save you.

Quotable
"The calves of Jeroboam still remain in the world, and will remain to the last day; not that any man now makes calves like Jeroboam's, but upon whatsoever a man depends or trusts—God set aside—this is the calves of Jeroboam, that is, other and strange gods, honored and worshiped instead of the only, true, living, and eternal God, who only can and will help and comfort in time of need. In like manner also, all such as rely and depend upon their art, wisdom, strength, sanctity, riches, honor, power, or anything else, under what title or name soever, on which the world builds, make and worship the calves of Jeroboam."—Martin Luther

MAY 25 *Reading 145*
GOD'S SERVANT
Isaiah 49–53

"It is too small a thing for you to be My servant to restore the tribes of Jacob and bring back those of Israel I have kept. I will also make you a light for the Gentiles, that you may bring My salvation to the ends of the earth" (Isa. 49:6).

The portrait of Jesus found in these chapters of Isaiah is unmistakable. The description of His vicarious suffering is one of Scripture's clearest explanations of the meaning of Jesus' death.

Overview
The commission of the failed servant nation (49:1-4) is taken up by an Individual who will redeem and restore Israel (vv. 5-26). Equipped by Yahweh, this Servant will rely fully on the Lord (50:1-11). God will redeem Israel, as He cared for her in the past (51:1–52:12). But this will be accomplished only by the Suffering Servant's death (v. 13–53:12).

Understanding the Text
"I have labored to no purpose" Isa. 49:4. The image in Hebrew is striking, if somewhat indelicate. As God's servant Israel is compared to a distended and supposedly pregnant woman. She struggles in labor, but instead of a child, produces nothing but gas!

What an image of futility. God chose Israel, intending to display His splendor through her. Israel had failed completely in her role as a servant. Yet, as Isaiah developed the servant theme, we see that even so God will display His splendor in His Old Testament people. That splendor will not be seen in what they have done, but in what the Lord has done for them!

It's the same with you and me. Our efforts to earn salvation are useless. Yet God has chosen to display His splendor and beauty in us. His splendor is not seen in what we do, but what God does for us in Jesus Christ.

"Can a mother forget the baby at her breast?" Isa. 49:5-26 The Servant of God will redeem Israel, and also will lead Gentiles to submit to the Lord.

While the emphasis in Isaiah 1–35 is on judgment, here the emphasis is clearly on the deep love God feels for both Gentile and Jew. Through His servant God will give the gift of salvation to all. Love has caused God to engrave His plans for the redeemed on the very "palms of My hands" (49:16).

This reference may not be to the nail prints Jesus bears today in His hands. Yet what a reminder. God was willing to pay the price of His deep love. We sense that love as we read Isaiah's words:

> Can a mother forget the baby at her breast and have no compassion on the child she has borne?
> Though she may forget, I will not forget you (Isa. 49:15).

"The Sovereign LORD helps me" Isa. 50:1-11. According to Isaiah, one thing alone would enable God's Servant to succeed where Israel failed. Where Israel rebelled, this Servant would be totally obedient.

The words of this passage awaken a deeper appreciation of Jesus and the life He lived on earth. He committed Himself to help His fellowman by obeying God completely. Only by relying on the Lord—by opening His ears and not being rebellious—was He able to win our salvation.

Isaiah's major passages dealing with the Servant of the Lord are called Servant Songs. They speak primarily of Jesus and the life He lived here on earth. But they apply quite directly to you and me. We who have been redeemed are called to be God's servants, as Jesus was (cf. Matt. 20:26-28). This passage tells us much about our own servant lifestyle.

We are to sustain the weary (v. 4a). To do this we must listen closely to the Lord (v. 4b), and obey rather than rebel against what He says (v. 5). The path of obedience is difficult, often exposing us to ridicule and even persecution (v. 6a). But we, like Jesus, must remain committed, and trust the Lord to vindicate us in the end (vv. 7-8).

"Look to Abraham, your father" Isa. 51:1–52:12. The past is always intended to give us comfort. We can look back on times of pain, and on tragedy. But we can also find evidence of God's love.

History is in fact designed to give God's people hope when things seem most desperate. Isaiah paused in his look ahead to the day of God's Servant, to direct the thoughts of his hearers back to their roots. The saints (51:1) were urged to remember Abraham. God kept His promise to Abraham and from one childless man He produced a vast people (v. 2). Surely the Lord will "comfort Zion and will look with compassion on all her ruins."

You and I have roots too. Ours grip that historic moment when Christ died, only to be raised again. God who promised Jesus' resurrection, and who has kept His promise to give us new life in Him, will surely bless us as well.

Christians do debate the meaning of the promises in Old Testament books like Isaiah. Are they intended literally, to be fulfilled in the Jewish people when Christ returns? Or are they intended spiritually, images of the blessings that are ours now in our Lord? Whatever our interpretation, we can agree on the application of passages like this one. What God has done in the past—His utter faithfulness to His promises—gives us hope for tomorrow. Joy is destined for Zion's people, and when the Lord returns they will:

> Burst into songs of joy together, you ruins of Jerusalem, for the LORD has comforted His people, He has redeemed Jerusalem (Isa. 52:9).

For ancient Jew and modern Christian both, "How beautiful on the mountains are the feet of those who bring good news, who proclaim peace, who bring good tidings, who proclaim salvation, who say to Zion, 'Your God reigns!' " (Isa. 52:7)

"He was crushed for our iniquities" Isa. 52:13–53:12. Just how clear is it that these verses speak of Jesus Christ? When I was in the Navy one of my friends was a Jewish sailor named Gershom Magin. I remember one day asking him to listen to me read a passage of Scripture, and challenging him to tell me if it was from the Old Testament or New Testament, and who it was about. I then read Isaiah 53. Immediately Magin said, "That's in the New Testament. And it's about Jesus."

Gershom couldn't believe it when I showed him that the passage was in the Old Testament, and that it was written about Israel's Messiah. The description was just too powerful and too clear for there to be any doubt that the prophet is speaking about the Saviour, dying on a cross some 700 years after his own time.

▶DEVOTIONAL
Holy of Holies
(Isa. 52:13–53:11)

There's something awe-inspiring about holy places.

Moses was told to take off his shoes; he was standing on holy ground. The Jerusalem temple was holy; only by passing the altar of sacrifice could one approach. And then, inside the temple, beyond its outer room, was the holiest place of all—the holy of holies. There only the high priest might go, and then only once a year, bearing the blood of a sacrifice offered for his own sin and for the sin of the people. No one rushes boldly, thoughtlessly, into any truly holy place.

It is with just this same sense of awe that we must open the Old Testament to Isaiah 52:13–53:12. This is holy ground: the Great Architect's blueprint of history's ultimate holy of holies. Here we see with total clarity the plan and the purpose of God in Christ's sufferings—and here we sense the anguish Jesus knew.

Read the verses. See the Servant of God, so battered and disfigured He hardly seems human anymore. Live with Him as He is despised and rejected by men. Watch Him take up our iniquities and be pierced for our transgressions. See the blood flow as His life is crushed from Him, as from a sin offering. And realize that He chose this fate, that by His wounds we might be healed.

Why did Jesus die? The answer is here, in the Old Testament's holy of holies. He died to pay for our iniquities, that we might be saved.

Reading these ancient words we can only bow our heads and worship. They bring us into the very presence of our God. They themselves have become holy ground.

Personal Application
Read this passage with reverence and awe.

Quotable
"The whole life of Christ was a continual passion; others die martyrs but Christ was born a martyr. He found a Golgotha even in Bethlehem, where He was born; for to His tenderness then the straws were almost as sharp as the thorns after, and the manger as uneasy at first as His cross at the last. His birth and His death were but one continual act, and His Christmas Day and His Good Friday are but the evening and morning of one and the same day."—John Donne

---

MAY 26 *Reading 146*
RIGHTEOUSNESS
Isaiah 54–58

"Let the wicked forsake his way and the evil man his thoughts. Let him turn to the LORD, and He will have mercy on him, and to our God, for He will freely pardon" (Isa. 55:7).

God has determined good for all who love Him. How important to commit ourselves to righteous living, that we might share in all the blessings that lie ahead.

Overview
God will restore Zion (54:1-17). He invited all to share in that coming celebration (55:1-13). These blessings are for the righteous (56:1-8) rather than the wicked (v. 9–57:13); for the contrite (vv. 14-21), whose faith is a matter of doing justice rather than keeping ritual fasts (58:1-14).

Understanding the Text
"I will have compassion on you" Isa. 54:1-17. The work of Messiah (Isa. 53) is finished. Now the Lord, as "your Redeemer," announces that "with everlasting kindness I will have compassion on you."

The strongest image here is that of God as Zion's (Jerusalem's) husband. The bride has been unfaithful, and "for a brief moment" abandoned by her angry husband. Yet God's marriage covenant is an unbreakable commitment. "My unfailing love for you will not be shaken," He says, and goes on to describe the glory to be experienced when the Lord and His people are fully reconciled (vv. 11-17).

The husband-wife image here reminds us of Hosea, who obeyed God's command and wed a woman who was, or became, a prostitute. Hosea kept on loving his wife, as God kept on loving His unfaithful people (cf. Hosea 1; 3).

Sometimes we assume that adultery is "grounds for divorce." What Isaiah and Hosea suggest is that adultery is grounds for forgiveness. The marriage commitment is forever. Only if one partner simply refuses to confess sin and be reconciled is divorce an option. Anyone who has lived with an unfaithful spouse can understand the pain God experiences when we are unfaithful to Him. And understand how much it costs Him to keep on loving anyway.

"You who have no money" Isa. 55:1-7. It is impossible for us to "buy" salvation. And so, with the price of salvation already paid by God's Suffering Servant (Isa. 53 again!), God invites us to "buy" what we need "without money and without cost."

But the passage says even more. God has laid out a great feast—for the wicked! His invitation is not to the spiritually bankrupt: it is to those who owe an unpayable debt.

God's timeless invitation still stands. How important it is to remember this truth not just for ourselves, but whenever we meet a person whom we might write off as beyond redemption. It is the evil to whom this invitation is addressed:

> Seek the LORD while He may be found; call on Him while He is near. Let the wicked forsake his way and the evil man his thoughts. Let him turn to the LORD, and He will have mercy on him, and to our God, for He will freely pardon (Isa. 55:6-7).

"My salvation is close at hand" Isa. 56:1-2. The belief that God is about to intervene in this world is a powerful motivation for doing what is right. The New Testament says, "We know that when He appears, we shall be like Him, for we shall see Him as He is. Everyone who has this hope in Him purifies himself, just as He is pure" (1 John 3:2-3).

Meditating on Jesus' return, and praying for that day to arrive soon, spurs us on to live godly and righteous lives.

"The eunuchs who keep My Sabbaths" Isa. 56:3-8. The Law in Deuteronomy 23:1-8 banned eunuchs and certain foreigners from taking part in Israel's worship. Isaiah consoled each group, promising to give them "within My temple and its walls a memorial and a name better than sons and daughters."

Everyone that has felt excluded by others, who knows the uncertainty and self-doubt exclusion produces, can appreciate the impact of these words of comfort. Even "outsiders" will have a special and secure place when God's kingdom appears in its fullness.

"They find rest" Isa. 57:1-2. These two verses give us an important perspective on life and death. In general the Bible views death as an enemy, and sees long life as a blessing and gift from God. Yet death holds no terror for the believer. In fact, there are times when life itself is a greater burden.

Here Isaiah observed that the premature death of a righteous man may well be a loving gift given by the Lord. What a powerful pair of verses to recall or to share when someone we know dies young. What assurance, here in the Old Testament, that upon dying those who walk uprightly "enter into peace; they find rest as they lie in death."

"Him who is contrite and lowly in spirit" Isa. 57:14-21. Two other passages help us understand what a contrite and lowly spirit is. The same Hebrew terms are found in Psalm 34:18 and Proverbs 29:23. These read:

> The LORD is close to the brokenhearted and saves those who are crushed in spirit,

and

> A man's pride brings him low, but a man of lowly spirit gains honor.

What God commends is a humble attitude, which even in adversity recognizes that the Lord is high and holy, and thus accepts life's trials while maintaining steadfast trust in God.

God is especially close to all who maintain this attitude, for God is very real to such persons.

"You have not seen it?" Isa. 58:1-12 The Old Testament gives four common reasons for fasting. To express grief (as 1 Sam. 31:13), to indicate honest repentance (1 Kings 21:27), to emphasize the solemn character of certain religious festivals (Lev. 16:29, 31), and in association with appeals to God in prayer (2 Sam. 12:16-22). Isaiah 58 seems to combine the third and fourth reasons. These people fasted in hopes of getting something from God—and were quite upset when God didn't appear to notice! (v. 3)

The passage makes it clear that these people wanted to relate to God on their terms—while God insists that human beings relate to Him on *His* terms. "Religion" was a price the people of Judah were willing to pay to gain God's favor. But they kept their religion and their daily life carefully isolated from one another. In God's sight, however, relationship with the Lord can never be separated from morality! The person who is in a position to have prayers answered is the individual who practices God's kind of "fasting."

God will answer prayer "if you do away with the yoke of oppression, with the pointing finger and malicious talk, and if you spend yourselves in behalf of the hungry and satisfy the needs of the oppressed" (vv. 9-10).

We have to be careful not to let our own faith in the Lord deteriorate into mere religion, and so mistake rituals we follow for a real and vital relationship with Christ. One of the surest ways to test the quality of our walk with the Lord is to examine the way we respond to others with needs. Are we committed "to loose the chains of injustice and untie the cords of the yoke, to set the oppressed free and break every yoke? Is it not to share your food with the hungry and to provide the poor wanderer with shelter—when you see the naked, to clothe him, and not to turn away from your own flesh and blood?" (vv. 6-7)

▶ DEVOTIONAL
It's Not Fair!
(Isa. 55)

Having raised five boys and girls, I've come to appreciate the power of the word "fair." You see, "It's not fair" is one of those magic phrases that children use to manipulate Mom and Dad.

It's not fair that he gets to stay up later than I do.

It's not fair that I have to get the dishes out of the dishwasher.

It's not fair that my teacher let her clean the board instead of me.

It's not fair that she has five throw pillows on her bed, and I only have four.

After a while, the complaint that "it's not fair," apparently intended to produce as much parental guilt as possible, is something moms and dads dread to hear!

Yet Isaiah 55 as a passage cries out, "It's not fair." And here these words are intended to delight. Just imagine someone comes up to you, and begins to talk as Isaiah does in this passage.

"You're thirsty and hungry? Well, for goodness sake, come on over here! What? You can't pay for what you need? That's all right. Here you can buy without money and without cost.

"Yes, I know it's not fair. You think you should pay for what you get. But you're hungry. So forget fairness. Come join the celebration."

And,

"Hold up there! I want to talk to you. You know, you've made a real mess of your life. You've made a determined start toward hell. Your ways are wicked and your thoughts are evil.

"No, wait a minute. Don't run off. This paper I'm holding isn't your execution order. It's a pardon. Yep, that's right. A full pardon.

"Oh, I know it's not fair. You deserve the most terrible punishment God can devise. But what God wants to give you is joy and peace and singing. He wants to give you a broad and beautiful land where even the trees of the field will clap their hands, and no thornbushes will grow.

"Why? Well, I can't really say. All I know is God's thoughts aren't our thoughts and His ways aren't our ways. We think that everything's got to be fair. God has this idea that fair won't work when it comes to our relationship with Him. And so instead of being fair, God has decided to be gracious and loving.

"Why? Beat's me.

"But I can tell you one thing. Three of the most wonderful words in any language are:

" 'It's not fair.' "

Personal Application

Don't use fairness as a measure of the way you deal with others. Use grace.

Quotable

We are the only Bible
The careless world will read,
We are the sinner's gospel,
We are the scoffer's creed,
We are the Lord's last message,
Given in deed and word.
What if the type is crooked?
What if the print is blurred?
—Annie Johnson Flint

MAY 27 *Reading 147*
DAWN OF A NEW AGE
Isaiah 59–62

> *"The sun will no more be your light by day, nor will the brightness of the moon shine on you, for the LORD will be your everlasting light, and your God will be your glory" (Isa. 60:19).*

We can catch only a glimpse of the future that God has in mind for His people. But what we can see is glorious.

Overview

Judah's sin was great, but a penitent people will be redeemed by the Lord (59:1-21). In that day Zion will be glorious (60:1-22), and her people blessed (61:1-11). Then at last the land and her people will be holy (62:1-12).

Understanding the Text

"Your iniquities have separated you from your God" Isa. 59:1-2. God firmly intends to bless His people. Yet Judah had not experienced blessing.

When something like this happens, some people are sure to blame God. Isaiah portrayed his contemporaries complaining that God's hearing was bad, or that His arm was a bit crippled so He couldn't produce miracles as He used to. But that wasn't the explanation. The fault wasn't in God but in people. Human sin is the barrier that separates us from God.

What the prophet meant is that sin is like a one-way mirror. Light passes through it from one side, but is reflected back by the other. Similarly sin is no barrier to judgment. That passes through easily. But sin is a barrier to blessing. No matter how hard we seek blessing, the prayers of sinners are reflected back, unanswered.

"Our offenses are many in Your sight" Isa. 59:9-16. The first step in dealing with personal sin is to acknowledge it. It is the same with national sin. We must come to grips with the reality of our situation, and turn to God without illusion.

The person who says, "Well, we're not as bad as some," is in as hopeless a situation as the worst of this world's sinners.

It's not pleasant to be as honest with ourselves as Isaiah was in 57:12-15a. But just this kind of brutal honesty is necessary preparation to receive the forgiveness and cleansing God is eager to extend.

"His own arm worked salvation" Isa. 59:17-20. The prophet pictured God, appalled that there is no one to intercede for those whom sin has ruined. He saw the Lord stand, and put on attributes associated with redemption as though they were parts of a warrior's armor.

What critical attributes are associated with redemption? (1) The breastpiece of "His own righteousness." God is committed to do the right thing as well as the loving thing. This is why the Suffering Servant of Isaiah 53 had to die: "to bear [pay for] the sins of many." (2) The "helmet of salvation." God has deliberately chosen to deliver those who have been ruined by sin. And (3) "garments of vengeance." Those who will not look to God in faith, fearing and revering God's name, must themselves bear the consequences of their evil deeds.

What will happen when God does arise, and come to Zion as His people's Redeemer? For those who do repent, God promises permanent possession of both His Spirit and His Word, "from this time on and forever."

"Your gates will always stand open" Isa. 60:11. In the ancient world the gates of a walled city were shut at night, to keep out robbers, or any enemy force that threatened the neighborhood. God's promise that Zion's gates will always stand open is symbolic of perpetual peace. When the Redeemer comes, nothing will threaten God's people.

The promise is made explicit later in the chapter. "No longer will violence be heard in your land," God says, "nor ruin or destruction within your borders, but you will call your walls Salvation and your gates Praise."

The rest of the passage uses images that are picked up in the Book of Revelation, and used there of the New Jerusalem, to be erected on a freshly created and holy earth (cf. Rev. 21).

What value do such passages, that describe a time at the extreme edge of God's future, have for you and me today? Perhaps most important, they tell us exactly where we are going, and what our future holds. However painful the present, we are assured that "your days of sorrow will end." No one can steal the future from us. We know for certain that in God's time "the Lord will be your everlasting light."

"The LORD has anointed me" Isa. 61:1-2. One day, some seven centuries after Isaiah, Jesus of Nazareth unrolled the scroll containing Isaiah's prophecy to this passage. There in His home synagogue Jesus read the prophet's words, identifying Himself as the One the Lord had anointed "to preach good news to the poor" and to "bind up the brokenhearted." But Jesus broke off His reading in midsentence. What He read identified His mission to "proclaim the year of the Lord's favor"—but there He stopped. Why? Because the next words read, "and the day of vengeance of our God."

Already some 2,000 years have stretched on since Christ's proclamation of the year of the Lord's favor. One day, the Bible says, Jesus will return "in blazing fire" to "punish those who do not know God and do not obey the Gospel" (2 Thes. 1:6-10). When Christ failed to read those words, He implicity recognized the fact that centuries would stretch out between His first coming and His return. These centuries are "the year of the LORD's favor." For one and for all, this is the time during which Jesus is seen hanging on the cross, or raised triumphantly, beckoning us to come to God by Him.

Soon the year of God's favor will end. Then Jesus will again be seen, this time in terrible splendor, come to execute the "day of vengeance of our God."

Each man and woman must take the Jesus of his or her choice. The Saviour, who died for the love of sinners. Or the Avenger, who punishes those who love sin.

▶ DEVOTIONAL
He Stole My Future
(Isa. 60)

She was so vital. Even though she had two children, she seemed fresh and young—as if she were just out of school. She was successful too. The aerobic workshop she taught was adopted by our local pro football team. And on top of everything, she had a husband who loved her.

Then she hurt her back.

When the pain wouldn't go away, she followed the advice of her doctor and had back surgery. In that surgery something terrible happened. Nerves were inadvertently cut. When she came out of surgery she learned that the pain would still be with her. And that she had lost bowel and bladder control. And lost the ability to even move about, except with a clumsy metal walker.

Desperately she went to the best hospitals in our state and to others. The doctors just shook their heads. There was nothing they could do. Not now. With the slip of the surgeon's knife, he stole her future.

All too many of us know what it is to have our future stolen. The things we've planned and looked forward to can be taken by a loved one's death. By a lost job. By an illness. By war, fire, or theft. There are no guarantees given to any of us for what tomorrow may hold.

But still, no one can really steal our future. Yes, people like that surgeon can steal tomorrow. But beyond tomorrow you and I have treasures that no one can touch. In the words of Isaiah, we look forward to a time when "the LORD will be your everlasting light, and your God will be your glory. Your sun will never set again, and your moon will wane no more; the LORD will be your everlasting light, and your days of sorrow will end."

How good to remember when someone or some event steals tomorrow, that beyond tomorrow, our eternal future remains secure.

Personal Application
When looking ahead, be sure to look far enough to be secure.

Quotable
"Pity is one of the noblest emotions available to human beings; self-pity is possibly the most ignoble. Pity is the capacity to enter into the pain of another in order to do something about it; self-pity is an incapacity, a crippling emotional disease that severely distorts our perception of reality. Pity is adrenaline for acts of mercy; self-pity is a narcotic that leaves its addicts wasted and derelict."—Eugene H. Peterson

MAY 28 *Reading 148*
ENDLESS PEACE
Isaiah 63–66

" 'As the new heavens and the new earth that I make will endure before Me,' declares the LORD, 'so will your name and descendants endure' " (Isa. 66:22).

Beyond the judgment at history's end lies endless peace and joy. Just as beyond the cross, peace awaits the person who comes to Jesus.

Overview
A vision of God's apocalyptic day of vengeance (63:1-6) moved Isaiah to desperate prayer for his people (v. 7–64:12). God replied. Sinners must be punished, but a remnant of Israel would survive (65:1-16). God will then create a new heaven and new earth (vv. 17-25). After the judgment, Zion will suddenly be repopulated (66:1-17), and all peoples will worship as brothers before God's throne (vv. 18-24).

Understanding the Text
"This is how You guided Your people" Isa. 63:7-19. Like the psalmists and the other prophets, Isaiah looked to history in an effort to understand God. In his prayer Isaiah recalled God's kindness in the past, and realized that Israel's rebellion caused God to turn against them. Yet the image of God as a tender and compassionate Redeemer persisted. Where was the God of love that His people had known? Why are enemies permitted to trample down God's inheritance and His holy place?

Similar conflicts between the God we know and present experience have troubled saints throughout the centuries. We can ask, "Why, O Lord?" But we need to remember at such times that revelation has priority over experience.

Our feelings and our experiences provide no certain knowledge of God. That is reserved for history and Scripture. Only if we hold fast to these two sources of certainty will we live in hope.

"How then can we be saved?" Isa. 64:1-12 Isaiah asked, "Why?" But in the case of ancient Israel, he knew the answer. Israel continued to sin against God, and evoked His anger.

Will reform help? Will God relent if His people repent? Isaiah's belief was, in Israel's case, no. "All of us have become like one who is unclean," Isaiah says, "and all our righteous acts are like filthy rags." God hid His face from (that is, turned away from) His people "and made us waste away because of our sins."

So what can a sinner do when he at last realizes that his best is less than nothing. That even his "righteous acts are like filthy rags"?

Isaiah went back to the beginning, to God's intention. God is "our Father." He is the source of Israel's existence as a people. As a potter, God shaped these descendants of Abraham. Isaiah's hope was that God would not abandon the work of His hands, and would not "remember our sins forever."

You and I give the same answer when asked, "How then can we be saved?" Nothing we can do can help us. Man's

Hebrew farmers hitched their robes up around their waists when trampling ripe grapes. Even so, the rich juices stained their legs and their garments. In one of Scripture's most vivid images, Isaiah 63:1-6 pictures God on the day of judgment, terrifying in His strength, trampling the world as the farmer stomps on ripe grapes, stained with the blood of the wicked.

most righteous acts are like filthy rags. But we too can go back to the beginning! We can realize that God created human beings in His image, to be loved and to love Him. Our hope is rooted in the belief that God will not abandon the works of His hands, but will act to redeem us despite our sins.

This is the very heart of the Gospel's glorious good news. God did act, in Jesus Christ, to redeem us. Gladly we abandon all pretense of righteousness, and then we accept the salvation that He has so graciously chosen to give us despite our sins.

"Behold, I will create" Isa. 65:17-25. After the judgment God will "create Jerusalem to be a delight and its people a joy." Set on a new earth that is spinning in new heavens, we will at last realize what original earth might have been had man not sinned.

The classic description so captivates man's yearning that it is repeated not only in Isaiah but also in the world's great literature.

"They will not toil in vain or bear children doomed to misfortune; for they will be a people blessed by the LORD, they and their descendants with them. Before they call I will answer; while they are still speaking I will hear. The wolf and the lamb will feed together, and the lion will eat straw like the ox, but dust will be the serpent's food. They will neither harm nor destroy in all My holy mountain," says the LORD (vv. 23-25).

"The new heavens and new earth that I make will endure" Isa. 66:1-24. Today everything changes. In our area one well-known financier is building himself a $15-million home. It has swimming pools, a bowling alley, and other features, all controlled by a complicated computer system. Even the "guest house" is larger than the homes in which most Americans live.

Ironically, he may never live in this private palace he's building for himself. He has been indicted for insider trading, fraud, and a number of other crimes.

What a contrast with God's New Jerusalem. The "house" God plans is designed to be inhabited by joyous people gathered from every nation and tongue. And the new heavens and earth God designs, will endure.

▶ DEVOTIONAL
That's the Gospel Truth (Isa. 65)

The concept of hell troubles many people. How could a good and loving God ever destine anyone to an eternity in what Revelation calls a "lake of fire"?

The fact is, God doesn't!

Chapter 64 contains Isaiah's plea for a salvation that must somehow be rooted in God, since man's best efforts are but filthy rags in the Lord's sight. In this chapter God responded to Isaiah's prayer. He told the prophet that He has always been eager to save. But obstinate Israel rejected His grace. Even so "descendants of Jacob, and from Judah" will "possess My mountains; My chosen people will inherit them." People who seek God *will* be saved, despite their sins.

But then God speaks of individuals who continue to "forsake the LORD and forget My holy mountain." Such persons are destined for the sword; they are marked for slaughter. But note. It is not that *God* chose their fate. God did everything He could to save them. He called to them, but they did not answer. He spoke, but they did not listen. Instead *they chose* what displeased God (65:12).

It's an important truth to grasp. And it is part of the Gospel. Yes, some will go away to eternal punishment. But it is not God who fixes a man's destiny. It is the man himself.

The only way a person can be condemned to hell is to condemn himself, by refusing to respond to God's revelation of His power and His love.

So if you know anyone who is worried that God might send him to hell, share the Good News. God won't send him to hell. The only person who can do that is the person himself. Instead, God is standing between human beings and eternal punishment, still calling, still speaking, still promising forgiveness. All anyone has to do is reach out and take salvation as a free gift.

And that is good news indeed.

Personal Application

Heaven or hell. It really is our choice.

Quotable

"Amos Gbaa from Liberia taught me quite a bit even though I was his tutor. Amos' job was to translate each section [of Scripture] and identify the parts that needed improvement. When he came to a sentence where I had used the word 'offer,' Amos had used the word 'gift.'

"I explained the importance of the distinction. The Gospel is not 'given' but 'offered.' The person hearing must make a choice.

"Amos said I was missing his point. 'In Liberia we do not make offers,' he said. 'We only give gifts. If I come to your house and say, Here is a pineapple from my field, that is not an offer. You had better accept it. If you don't, you would be giving me a terrible insult.'

"I thought about it more. With an offer, the buyer is completely free to decide for or against the product or to simply ignore it. The hearer of the Gospel, on the other hand, can accept it or reject it, but not ignore it, because it is a gift. Amos was right. God is giving you the gift of life through the Gospel."—Stan Nussbaum

---

The Variety Reading Plan concludes here

Jeremiah

INTRODUCTION

Jeremiah ministered in the four turbulent decades preceding the fall of Jerusalem on March 15–16, 597 B.C. These decades were marked by the sudden collapse of Assyria, and a subsequent power struggle between the emerging Babylonian Empire and a resurgent Egypt. Caught in the middle, tiny Judah vacillated, alternately rebelling and submitting to one, then another of the great powers. Near the beginning of Jeremiah's ministry, Josiah instituted a number of religious reforms. Despite the reformation, Jeremiah warned the nation that soon they would suffer invasion and exile. Boldly Jeremiah confronted Judah with the sins that cried out for divine judgment. But a hardened Judah refused to heed the prophet's warnings. Jeremiah himself suffered persecution, and was rejected by his fellow countrymen. Yet he lived to see his predictions of disaster fulfilled, and his tormentors silenced.

Despite his ministry of condemnation, Jeremiah also conveyed a message of hope. Judah would fall. But God would make a New Covenant with His faithless people. In a coming, though distant, day, Judah's sins would be forgiven and her people given a new heart. Jeremiah's powerful presentation of God's New Covenant promise makes this book bright with hope, despite its repeated theme of judgment.

OUTLINE OF CONTENTS

I. Jeremiah's Mission .... Jer. 1–10
II. The Broken Covenant .... Jer. 11–20
III. Judgment at Hand .... Jer. 21–29
IV. New Covenant Promises .... Jer. 30–38
V. Jerusalem Fallen .... Jer. 39–51
VI. Historical Appendix .... Jer. 52

READING GUIDE (10 Days)

If hurried, you may read only the "core passage" in your Bible and the Devotional in each chapter of this Commentary.

Reading	*Chapters*	*Core passage*
149	1	selected passages
150	2–6	3–4
151	7–10	9:17–10:16
152	11–15	15
153	16–20	19–20
154	21–29	29
155	30–33	31–32
156	34–39	38
157	40–45	45
158	46–52	50–51

Jeremiah

MAY 29 *Reading 149*

MAN WITH A MISSION
Jeremiah 1

> *"Before I formed you in the womb I knew you, before you were born I set you apart; I appointed you as a prophet to the nations" (Jer. 1:5).*

Jeremiah is often called the weeping prophet. He was called by God to suffer with a people destined for judgment, who persistently rejected the prophet and his message. We may yearn to be commissioned by the Lord for some vital ministry. But Jeremiah reminds us that the spiritually prominent have a price to pay.

Overview

Jeremiah was commissioned to communicate the word of the Lord at a critical time in Judah's history. This chapter reports his call, and provides the key to understanding both the pressures on God's servant and the promises that sustained him.

Understanding the Text

"Through the reign" Jer. 1:1-3. The first verses of Jeremiah specify the kings during whose reigns the prophet cried out to God's people. Jeremiah's call came during the reign of godly King Josiah, in 627 B.C., and the first 10 chapters of this book record messages given during the Josian revival. Chapters 21–39 record messages given during the reigns of evil rulers, Jehoiakim and Zedekiah. In 587 B.C. Jeremiah was imprisoned for treason, and chapters 40–52 report the culminating events of his life—and of Jerusalem's fall.

Here is a brief chronology of the tumultuous times during which this prophet lived and ministered.

686 Wicked Manasseh rules
648 Josiah born
642 Amon succeeds Manasseh
640 Josiah succeeds Amnon
633 Josiah turns to the Lord
Ashurbanipal of Assyria dies
628 Josiah begins reforms
Jeremiah begins ministry
626 Nabopolassar becomes king of Babylon
621 Book of Law found in the temple
612 Nineveh, Assyrian capital, taken by the Babylonians
609 Josiah killed in battle
Jehoahaz rules three months
Jehoiakim placed on throne by Egyptians
605 Egyptians defeated by Babylonians
Nebuchadnezzar becomes king of Babylon
First Jewish captives deported to Babylon. The group includes Daniel
601 Babylon invades Egypt, is thrown back
598 Jehoiachin becomes king in Judah, but is taken to Babylon in April of 597
597 Zedekiah becomes king in Judah
588 Babylonians begin siege of Jerusalem, on January 15th
586 Jerusalem falls on August 14th. The final deportation takes place
The Babylonian governor of Judah is assassinated October 7
The remaining Jews reject Jeremiah's counsel and flee to Egypt

During such times, the Word of God is most desperately needed. But that word, delivered by God's spokesman Jeremiah, was consistently rejected by Jewish people and their rulers, despite the fact that their world was crumbling around them.

We need to be especially sensitive to God's Word in our own times of stress, even if what we hear condemns our attitudes and challenges our values. Ultimately, God's Word is intended not to destroy but to heal.

"I formed you in the womb" Jer. 1:5. These words to Jeremiah remind us that God is deeply involved in the formation of every human being from conception. On the one hand this is a great comfort. God knew you and me as individuals before we were born. He knew us, loved us, and participated in every stage of our development. The gifts and talents you have were carefully nurtured, even as you developed in embryo. This means that you and I can be glad in who we are. We are the persons that God intended us to be. The abilities we have are His gifts, and He can use you and me to His glory.

On the other hand, this verse offers us a challenge. Many are confused by the rhetoric of moderns who place no value on the human fetus, dismissing the unborn as some insignificant part of a mother's body, as easily discarded as hair that is too long or a broken fingernail. God's words to Jeremiah, "I formed you in the womb," confront us with the fact that the unborn child is a separate, individual person, precious to God and with full rights as a separate human being. Perhaps Jeremiah's example of commitment to an unpopular cause, despite ridicule and abuse from his society, may encourage us to stand with God for, rather than against, the unborn.

"I am only a child" Jer. 1:6-8. When God called Jeremiah as a young man in his early 20s, he felt terribly vulnerable and inadequate. He surely had his reasons. Jeremiah grew up in a priestly family during the reign of Manasseh, who had murdered many pious men. He was young and untested, unsure of himself as any young person is likely to be. The thought that God viewed him as special, and had a special mission for him, was overwhelming.

It's appropriate when we approach any ministry to share Jeremiah's emotions. In ourselves we are inadequate, mere children. The person who approaches any spiritual service with an arrogant self-confidence is sure to fail. We need to grasp, as did Jeremiah, that no matter what natural gifts God has given us, we can do nothing in or by ourselves.

In this case, however, Jeremiah's protests indicate more than humility. The future prophet's objection was rebuked, as if he were using his sense of weakness as an excuse to refuse God's call. God responded, "You must go." Yet, even God's rebuke conveys a promise. Jeremiah was told not to be afraid, "For I am with you and will rescue you."

When God calls any person to a ministry, He commits Himself to be with that individual. God will be with you as you serve Him, despite your weaknesses, and despite any fears you may have.

"Over nations and kingdoms" Jer. 1:9-16. These verses provide a preview of the message that Jeremiah would deliver to Judah. It was an unpopular message, for it conveyed God's intention to bring a powerful new kingdom from the north down on His people and their land.

Jeremiah was told that as God's prophet he was "over" the kingdoms of this world. That is, they would behave as he announced they would.

Most often we think of ourselves as subject to the political powers of the nation in which we live. Jeremiah was reminded that real authority belongs to God—and that a person who proclaims the Word of God is greater than any worldly power. Ultimately the world will submit to God's authority, and will surely do what He has willed.

You and I too live in tension between the powers of this world and the Word of God. If we commit ourselves to do God's will and to live by His Word, we, like Jeremiah, will be "over nations and kingdoms."

"Get yourself ready!" Jer. 1:17-19 Jeremiah was about to set out on a great adventure. He had been called to live not by the values and beliefs of his society, but by God's Word. And he had been called to proclaim that Word, whatever the cost might be to him personally. Jeremiah now had to prepare himself: he had to make a

firm decision, and commit himself to God's way only.

You and I are challenged to make the same commitment. We are not to drift through life, believing in God but living like men and women of the world. We are to take a stand, as Jeremiah did. We are to make a firm decision to live by, and to witness to, the Word of God.

Again God's challenge is accompanied by a promise. A promise that you and I as well as Jeremiah can claim. "Today I have made you a fortified city. . . . They will fight against you but will not overcome you, for I am with you and will rescue you" (vv. 18-19).

▶DEVOTIONAL
The Price of Commitment (Selected passages)

If we glance ahead through the Book of Jeremiah, we learn something of the price that Jeremiah paid because of his complete commitment to God.

His message was so unpopular that some men actually conspired to take his life (cf. 11:18-20). Others attempted to neutralize Jeremiah's influence by slandering him. They said, "Let's attack him with our tongues and pay no attention to anything he says" (18:18). Still others simply ridiculed God's faithful prophet. This apparently hurt Jeremiah most of all, for he wrote:

> I am ridiculed all day long; everyone mocks me. . . . So the word of the LORD has brought me insult and reproach all day long (20:7-8).

Later in his life Jeremiah was imprisoned and his life threatened by Judah's rulers. He was accused of treason, and considered a national disgrace.

None of this was easy for the sensitive prophet. In one passage that captures the despair he often felt, Jeremiah cried out, "Cursed be the day I was born!" And he concluded his cry with this lament: "Why did I ever come out of the womb to see trouble and sorrow and to end my days in shame?" (vv. 14, 18)

But Jeremiah did not end his days in shame. His predictions of doom came true, and it was his enemies who were put to shame in the end.

Even so, what sustained Jeremiah through the difficult years was not the conviction that he was right, but a deep compassion for those to whom he spoke. Jeremiah warned of judgment—in hope that some would hear, repent, and be saved. "The LORD sent me to prophesy against this house and this city," one of his sermons affirmed. But his hope was that his listeners would "now reform your ways and your actions and obey the LORD your God. Then the LORD will relent and not bring the disaster He has pronounced against you" (26:12-13).

Yes, if we fully commit ourselves to the Lord there may very well be a price to pay. Yet because God's Word is true, we will be proven right in the end. And, until then, we will be sustained by the awareness that our faithfulness may be the means of bringing others with us to the Lord.

Personal Application

The rewards of commitment far exceed any cost.

Quotable

"I go out to preach with two propositions in mind. First, everyone ought to give his life to Christ. Second, whether or not anyone gives Him his life, I will give Him mine."—Jonathan Edwards

MAY 30 *Reading 150*
JUDAH'S SINFUL HEART
Jeremiah 2–6

"They are skilled in doing evil; they know not how to do good" (Jer. 4:22).

Judah's sins are spelled out, and the judgment due is defined. Jeremiah found his ministry bitter, for his anguished heart knew that the people of Judah would never listen or repent.

Overview

Judah had forsaken God in favor of pagan idols, despite His loving care (2:1-37). Even so, spiritually unfaithful Judah was urged to return (3:1-25), before judgment came from the north (4:1-31). Josiah's religious reformation had not touched Judah's heart (5:1-31), and the enemy was commissioned to punish the Holy City (6:1-16). Everyone listening to Jeremiah stood at a crossroads: the way he or she chose would determine his destiny (vv. 17-30).

Understanding the Text

"The devotion of your youth" Jer. 2:1-8. Last week my wife and I walked on the beach in the little Michigan town where we met. It was a very special time, as we remembered how that meeting had grown into love and the discovery that God intended us to wed. This is what looking back to first love is supposed to be like. Yes, our love has changed as we've lived together. But the change has been one of growth and maturity. We are closer now. Yet remembering that early love still has the power to make us smile, and look at each other with even deeper affection.

What a contrast we see here. God feels only pain when He looks back on His relationship with the people of Israel and Judah. The love of the bride who followed Him then has not simply faded. Despite all the blessings God poured out on His own (vv. 6-7), the people He loved had strayed far from Him, and "followed worthless idols."

Only a person who has been betrayed by a husband or wife he or she loved can understand the depth of God's pain—or the seriousness of Judah's sin.

We need to look back on those days when we first came to know the Lord, and remember our first love for God. We may not feel exactly the same as we did then, or express our love in just the same way. But if we have grown in our relationship with the Lord, looking back and remembering can bring us that same feeling of renewed intimacy that my wife and I experienced in Michigan. And if remembering brings us no joy, we may take it as a warning from God to check and see if we have strayed.

"My people have committed two sins" Jer. 2:10-37. This passage takes the form of a *rib,* or an indictment presented in court. God brought two serious charges against Judah.

God's people had forsaken Him, the "spring of living water." It was water alone that made the Holy Land produce crops. Thus water was the one necessity Judah required for prosperity. Despite the fact that God was the one utter necessity in the life of His people, they "long ago broke off Your yoke and tore off Your bonds; [they] said, 'I will not serve You' " (v. 20).

Judah's even more serious sin was to dig "their own cisterns, broken cisterns that cannot hold water." Cisterns were plastered underground pits where water was stored for use during the dry season. Here they represent the pagan gods to whom Judah turned. The twin choices to reject God and to turn to idolatry are inexplicable. No pagan nation ever changed its gods. Yet Judah abandoned the Lord. The closest thing to an explanation is given in verses 23-24. The people of Judah had behaved like a female camel in heat, in the grip of an uncontrollable urge. There is no rational explanation for anyone to reject God, much less to seek spiritual or other help elsewhere!

Perhaps this is the message of this lament. Human beings are not "rational" in making choices. Rather we often find ourselves in the grip of sin, which expresses itself as an instinctive rejection of the one true God, and in a hunger that leads men to turn anywhere in search of substitutes. Only the grace of God can preserve any of us from the power of indwelling sin. Only the grace of God can help us remember

His benefits, and honor the Lord as the one essential source of our well-being.

"You have the brazen look of a prostitute" Jer. 3:1-13. These early messages of Jeremiah were given during the religious revival promoted by godly King Josiah. This reform is described in 2 Chronicles 34–35. Josiah repaired the temple and reinstituted worship there. When the lost book of Old Testament Law was found, Josiah called for national repentance. He held a Passover service that the people joyfully participated in, and did all he could to stamp out idolatry by desecrating places of pagan worship. Yet, as this chapter shows us, all his efforts failed to touch the hearts of the people of Judah.

The failure is portrayed in Jeremiah's reference to a specific Old Testament law. A person who divorced his wife might remarry, but could never marry the first wife again if either of them had been married to another in the interim. Judah, like a faithless wife, had abandoned her Husband, God, and gone on to join herself not to just one but a series of lovers. Even so God was willing to take faithless Judah back! And Judah seemed to come back. But the people of Judah treated the whole thing lightly. It was as if their spiritual unfaithfulness didn't matter at all! Judah came back smirking, saying, "My Father, my friend from my youth." These were words that a young wife often spoke to an older husband. But they were not appropriate for Judah to speak, as if she were still an innocent and had not rejected the Lord and turned to idols! And so God said through Jeremiah, "You have the brazen look of a prostitute; you refuse to blush with shame."

God's grace is overwhelming. Even after we have been unfaithful to Him, He is willing to take us back. But we are to come as a penitent, deeply aware of our sin and bowed with shame. We are not to come brazenly, or lightly, as if our unfaithfulness to God had no significance at all.

"Yes, we will come to you" Jer. 3:14-25. Jeremiah's generation did not return to God. But the prophet looked ahead, and foresaw a day when God's people would turn to Him again. In these verses he described what repentance and true return involve. There is a decision to return to God (v. 22b). There is a fresh grasp of the futility of past ways (vv. 23-24). And there is an overwhelming sense of shame, as the greatness of past sins overwhelms (v. 25).

None of these marks of repentance were present in Judah. May they be found in our lives whenever we stray and then turn back again to the Lord.

"The whole land will be ruined" Jer. 4:1-31. Despite God's call to Judah to wash the evil from her heart, the people refused to heed. Jeremiah had no choice but to announce the judgment that must come because of "your own conduct and actions."

This is an important concept for us to grasp. God does not punish people without cause. It is our own actions, not God, that bring disaster on us.

And what a disaster awaited Judah. Through His prophet the Lord said, "The whole land will be ruined, though I will not destroy it completely. Therefore the earth will mourn and the heavens above grow dark, because I have spoken and will not relent."

"They have lied about the LORD" Jer. 5:1-17. The particular lie that Jeremiah drew attention to challenged God's justice and His power. Judah had been "utterly unfaithful" to God. Their spiritual adultery had been matched by their moral deterioration. They had abandoned morality, and acted like "well-fed, lusty stallions, each neighing for another man's wife" (v. 8). They had abandoned justice: Jeremiah could not find "one person who deals honestly and seeks the truth" (v. 1). Despite this, Judah complacently said, "No harm will come to us" (v. 12).

This is the lie that Jeremiah identified. They had said that God "will do nothing."

Let's never forget that God is the moral judge of humanity. He not only can, but will act to judge sin.

"Let us fear the LORD our God" Jer. 5:18-31. To fear God means to hold Him in awe: to take Him seriously. Here God reminded Judah of His greatness. He is the One who set the seas in their beds, and established the boundaries of the land. "Should

you not tremble in My presence?"

Today there are many in America who have no real awe of God. This is truly tragic. Yet the greatest tragedy of all is described by Jeremiah. "A horrible and shocking thing has happened in the land: The prophets prophesy lies, the priests rule by their own authority, and My people love it this way." There may be little we can do to affect the secular tone of modern life. But what is most important is to retain our own awe of God, and to take His presence and His power seriously. We must constantly say to ourselves what the people of Judah refused to utter: "Let us fear the LORD our God."

"This city must be punished" Jer. 6:1-15. Judah refused to listen to God's word. So now Jeremiah, using the authority God gave him over nations, commissioned Babylon to attack the Holy City. Because the word of the Lord was offensive to the people of Judah, the "city must be punished."

"Stand at the crossroads and look" Jer. 6:16-30. The invitation here is a call to consider. The "ancient paths" represent the ways laid down in God's Law. These are good ways, for when a person walks in them he or she "will find rest for your souls."

Jeremiah now outlined the consequence of the only other choice available. One must either walk in the ancient paths, or strike out to find a new path for himself. Yet the new paths offer no one rest. Instead, as we peer with Jeremiah down that alternate highway, we see in the distance clouds of dust raised by marching men. We see the sun glinting on the points of spears, and hear the thunder of hooves as cavalry approach in battle formation. And suddenly we are gripped by fear, for we realize that along that road judgment rushes to meet us.

How thankful we can be that we have chosen the good way, the ancient way, and that we walk in it.

▶ DEVOTIONAL
With Compassion
(Jer. 3–4)

It's easy to become self-righteous when looking at others' sins. We can become quite passionate about injustice and wickedness. And in the process we can sound more than a little judgmental.

Reading these two chapters that sum up Jeremiah's early preaching we do sense righteous indignation. The prophet was brutally frank. Israel and Judah were "faithless." God's sinning people were brazen and shameless. The idols they had worshiped were detestable, and the people wickedly harbored evil thoughts.

Yet despite the blunt confrontation which marks this prophet's style, he shouts out his angry words with a broken heart. Listen, as Jeremiah echoes God's own bitter pain.

> Oh, my anguish, my anguish!
>   I writhe in pain.
> Oh, the agony of my heart!
>   My heart pounds within me,
>   I cannot keep silent.
> For I have heard the sound
>   of the trumpet;
> I have heard the battle cry (4:19).

What moved the prophet was not only a concern for righteousness. He was moved by compassion for a people whose own wicked choices destined them for disaster. How both God and His prophet yearned for Judah to repent. There was no joy for either in being right. There was no surge of satisfaction at the thought of the judgment that must surely fall on the people of Judah for their sin. Instead there was anguish and pain.

There are times when we Christians must confront others over wicked acts. There are times we must take a firm stand against sin. But at such times we must carefully guard our hearts. There is no room then for even a hint of spiritual pride. There is no room for even a glint of gladness that the wicked will get theirs in God's time. Instead, we are to feel, as Jeremiah did, the pain that God knows—not only at the sin, but also at the necessity of judging the sinner.

If we have compassion even as we announce the coming judgment, others may sense in our words what God most wants to convey. His greatest desire is not to punish, but to redeem. Not to condemn, but save. Not to reject, but to welcome the sinner home, forgiven, for Jesus' sake.

Personal Application
Speak boldly to others. But always in love and with compassion, remembering that we too are vulnerable to sin.

Quotable
"As murder storywriters assume, and as most of us learn by experience, we have in us capacities for fury, fear, envy, greed, conceit, callousness, and hate which, given the right provocation, could make killers out of us all—baby-sitters or Bluebeards, professional thugs or amateur hit men. G.K. Chesterton's Father Brown explained his method of detection by saying, 'You see, it was I who killed all these people'—in the sense that he looked within himself to find the mentality that would produce the crime he was investigating, and did in fact discover it there. . . .

"Brown, though fictitious, states fact. When the fathomless wells of rage and hatred in the normal human heart are tapped, the results are fearful. 'There but for the grace of God go I.' Only restraining and renewing grace enables anyone to keep the commandments."—J.I. Packer

MAY 31 *Reading 151*
DEATH HAS CLIMBED IN
Jeremiah 7–10

> *"I did not just give them commands about burnt offerings and sacrifices, but I gave them this command: Obey Me" (Jer. 7:22-23).*

In a powerful image, Jeremiah warned his nation that death had "climbed in through our windows." We need to take Jeremiah's words seriously today, for some of the same attitudes which characterized ancient Judah are prevalent in "Christian" America.

Overview
Jeremiah's stunning "temple sermon" condemned Judah's superficial religion (7:1-19) and warned of coming slaughter (v. 20–8:4). Judgment must strike the tainted land; divine punishment was fixed and certain (v. 5–9:26). Yet after scorning Judah's idolatry (10:1-22), Jeremiah prayed that the suffering which was ahead would correct, not destroy (vv. 23-25).

Understanding the Text
"At the gate of the LORD's house" Jer. 7:1-2. Jeremiah 26 gives us another report of this sermon, and sets its date. Jeremiah spoke in the fall or winter of 609 B.C. Josiah, the godly reformer, had just been killed in battle. Jehoiakim had been set up as king by Egypt. The dream of independence that flourished under Josiah was dead. Yet Judah had one last source of confidence and hope: the temple of the Lord. Surely God would never desert the nation where the temple stood that He had designated "My resting place forever and ever" (Ps. 132:14). Jeremiah's sermon challenged this deeply held belief so forcefully that many shouted for his death!

What does Jeremiah's sermon say to us today? Simply that just because a nation has a superficial form of religion, its people have no guarantee of peace or prosperity. America can take no comfort in being a "churchgoing" nation. What Judah and our own country must be is a holy nation, not just a religious one.

"Do not trust in deceptive words" Jer. 7:3-11. Jeremiah's sermon condemned a distorted "temple theology." The people of Judah believed that because the temple of the Lord was enclosed in the walls of their Holy City, they were safe. Surely God would not act against His own house!

Jeremiah cut the ground out from under this popular belief. "Will you steal and murder, commit adultery and perjury, burn incense to Baal . . . and then come and stand before Me in this house, which bears My Name, and say, 'We are safe'?"

Today too some are confident that God will not permit disaster to strike America. Don't most of the missionaries in the world come from the U.S., and aren't they supported by Christians here? Doesn't every survey show that a large portion of our population believes in God? Modern popular theology often equates our nation or democracy with a temple of the Lord. How could God permit us to fall?

Yet when we look at the news we see constant reports of the very sins which destined Judah for destruction. Child abuse is a constant headline. Murder is commonplace. Just last week a young woman who had fought drug abuse on her block in St. Petersburg was shot in her own home. And officials of HUD, an agency supposedly dedicated to helping the poor, were shown to instead have fraudulently funneled millions of dollars to wealthy friends. We need to face the fact today that religiosity without holiness is completely worthless. The only thing such religion guarantees a people is divine judgment!

Tragically, the fallacy is also found within the church. The Jim Bakkers of TV and radio somehow assume that because they present the Gospel verbally, they will not be held responsible for moral and financial depravities. They are just as wrong as were the leaders in Jeremiah's time. We are to present the truth, yes. But truth without holiness is a mockery and an insult to God. And God will not be insulted.

"So do not pray for this people" Jer. 7:12-29. There comes a time when it is too late for a people to avoid judgment. God told Jeremiah that that was the case with Judah. We will see this theme—"Don't pray for this people"—repeated in future chapters.

How can we tell when a people have come to this sorry state? God told Jeremiah to look back—and then look around. Looking back Jeremiah was reminded that for generations the people of Judah had followed the "stubborn inclinations of their evil hearts." They "did not listen or pay attention" to the prophets. Now, as Jeremiah looked around, he realized that when he himself spoke, "They will not listen to you; when you call them, they will not answer."

It is persistent refusal to hear and respond to the Word of God that puts a people beyond the reach of prayer. Yet note that it took centuries, even generations of rejection, before God told Jeremiah to pray for Judah no longer. Neither our country, nor our friends, nor our families, have persisted in unbelief so long. We can, and must, keep on praying that the nation and people we love will respond to the Lord before it is too late.

"People will no longer call it Topheth" Jer. 7:30–8:3. The valley referred to here lay outside Jerusalem and was a sacred area where the Jews offered child sacrifice: "Something I did not command nor did it enter My mind" (7:31). God warned through Jeremiah that these "sacred" precincts will be desecrated by the bones of the people who worshiped pagan deities there. In that day at last the valley will be called by its right name: "the valley of slaughter."

One of Satan's favorite strategies is to give abominations deceptive names. In Jeremiah's time the place where innocents were slaughtered was called a "topheth"—a "sacred precinct." Today they are called "family planning clinics," and defense of the decision to kill the unborn is presented as a woman's "right to choose." Homosexuality is called an "alternative lifestyle," and TV and movies glamorize immorality as "adult." When God acts in judgment, all our abominable practices will be stripped of their deceptive names, and identified for what they are. Until then, you and I must stand for the truth, and speak the truth, even as Jeremiah did in his day.

"Get up" Jer. 8:4-17. Jeremiah introduced a lengthy passage on judgment with a peculiar question. Don't folks who fall down get up? Don't folks who turn aside (get lost) try to find their way back? (v. 4) The people of Judah had gone against nature itself, for having fallen into idolatry, they simply lay there. And having turned away from God, rather than looking for a way back they actually refused to return!

Jeremiah offered two explanations. The people themselves refused to repent; each "pursues his own course" (vv. 6-7). The scribes who were responsible to interpret the Word of God had "handled it falsely." The text suggested they twisted the Law to make it mean what they wanted. Many passages in Jeremiah suggest that their main deception was to make it seem that Judah could sin with impunity, rather than to affirm the necessity of holiness. The flaw in these spiritual leaders is their motivation: "All are greedy for gain;

prophets and priests alike, all practice deceit" (vv. 8-17). As a result, people and priests will perish.

"Since My people are crushed, I am crushed" Jer. 8:18–9:2. Jeremiah's own deep compassion for the sinning people of Judah reminds us that even the harshest words of judgment are to be uttered in love. But God's response reminds us that we are to avoid another danger. We are not to be so compassionate that we find ourselves on the side of those who deserve judgment!

Jeremiah was torn by these two opposing forces, and wished that he could simply "leave my people and go away from them; for they are all adulterers, a crowd of unfaithful people." But neither Jeremiah nor you and I can avoid this tension as we try to live godly, caring lives in our society. The most difficult challenge we face may well be to speak the truth in love, without compromising truth for love, or love for truth.

"Should I not punish them for this?" Jer. 9:4-16 Jeremiah was reminded that he lived "in the midst of deception." Even those whom he thought of as friends were secretly enemies. There were people who "speak cordially" to a neighbor, but in their hearts "set a trap for him."

Today's newspaper tells of a young woman who set up a "charity" to help victims of spina bifida. She collected over $250,000 . . . and kept all but about 6 percent to support her waterfront home and Mercedes! She is typical of those who use deceit to present themselves as "friends," while in fact attempting simply to use others for their own profit.

God reminded Jeremiah, "Should I not punish them for this?" The question is rhetorical. And the answer is, "Yes." God should, and will punish. He says, "I will lay waste to the towns of Judah, so that no one can live there." No one can sin and expect to prosper.

"Gather up your belongings to leave the land" Jer. 10:17-22. Jeremiah delivered God's relentless message. He would judge Judah. An enemy would appear from the north (Babylon) that would make Judah desolate and carry her people away captive.

One can talk and debate and argue about the meaning of various passages of Scripture. But some are unequivocably clear. This is one of those clear and final statements, which God uttered through Jeremiah to Judah. Enough talk! Pack your clothes! Judgment is coming, and will soon be here.

"It is not for man to direct his steps" Jer. 10:23-25. Jeremiah now submitted to the inevitable. God is sovereign. A man's life is not his own: he must live in the time and place and circumstances that God has decreed.

Yet while Jeremiah recognized the inevitability of the coming judgment, he had one request. He asked God to use Judah's defeat for her correction, rather than total destruction (v. 24). Let destruction be the fate of those nations that refuse to acknowledge Him and have devastated the Holy Land (v. 25).

▶ DEVOTIONAL
Death Climbs through Our Windows (Jer. 9:17–10:16)

Bringing up children is really tough today. I'm finding it much harder with our 9-year-old girl than with my "first" family of boys, now 31 and 27. Right now Sarah is enamoured with the "New Kids on the Block." She loves their songs, wants to buy teen magazines that tell about them, and thinks the group's scrawny 16-year-old is a "hunk."

She's also very fashion conscious. It's no use to bring home a schoolbag until she's seen what her classmates have. And not to have anything the others have is a total social disaster.

And it bothers me. Somehow I keep thinking of verses in these chapters of Jeremiah, and wondering how to apply them in our own home. God warned Judah that "the customs of the peoples are worthless" (10:3). Yes, I know the passage is talking about idolatry. But it says to me that the whole system of values adopted in any basically pagan society is worthless. And that God's people are not to fall prey to such "senseless" notions.

On the one hand, I have no doubts about our decision to block out several TV channels with a "parental control" code. But I'm troubled by an uncertainty about just how far to go in restricting our daughter in other ways.

What troubles me most is Jeremiah's observation that "death has climbed in through our windows and has entered our fortresses" (9:21). We can bar the smiling death's head that knocks at our door. It is the death that climbs in through our windows, when we're unaware, that spoils us—and our children.

I do know this. I can't rely on my wisdom today. All I can do is struggle to follow God's advice in Jeremiah 9:24, and strive daily to understand and know "Me, that I am the LORD, who exercises kindness, justice and righteousness on earth, for in these I delight."

Personal Application

We have a special need these days for divine wisdom to see through our society's deceit.

Quotable

"Adam's choice cost him Eden; Esau's, his birthright; Achan's, his life; Lot's, his home and herds; Absalom's, his father's throne; Saul's, his kingdom; the rich young ruler's, the companionship of Christ. Judas lost his apostleship; Demas his discipleship. Pilate, Agrippa, and Felix chose wrong and missed immortality. Ananias' choice fooled no one but himself. Caleb and Joshua chose well, while Jonah's first choice nearly shipwrecked himself and the crew.

"Ye older ones, what would your answer be as a father, a mother, as a Christian leader, if, concerning our young people, God would say to you today, 'Ask what I shall make of these young people'? Would your answer prove you know how to choose the things that matter most?"—Robert G. Lee

JUNE 1 *Reading 152*
THE BROKEN COVENANT
Jeremiah 11–15

> *"This is what the LORD says: 'Those destined for death, to death; those for the sword, to the sword; those for starvation, to starvation; those for captivity, to captivity' " (Jer. 15:2).*

Relationship with God is marked by commitment—on both sides. When we fall short of our commitment to God, He remains committed to us. But God's commitment includes punishment, in order that by discipline *He* might purify and restore.

Overview

Jeremiah announced Judah's punishment for breaking her covenant with God (11:1-17). Jeremiah's life was threatened, and God responded to the angry prophet's appeal (v. 18–12:17). Jeremiah delivered five symbolic warnings (13:1-27) to a people who "greatly love to wander" (14:1-15), and then graphically portrayed the coming disaster (v. 16–15:9). But the prophet, who bore God's name, would be kept safe (vv. 10-21).

Understanding the Text

"Proclaim all these words" Jer. 11:1-17. Most believe this sermon was delivered during the reign of Josiah, just after the lost Law of the Lord had been rediscovered in the temple. Despite Josiah's active efforts at reform, the Prophet Jeremiah was called to remind Judah of the terms of her ancient covenant with God. If the people obeyed wholeheartedly, God said, "I will fulfill the oath I swore to your forefathers, to give them a land flowing with milk and honey." But Jeremiah was also told to confront. God knew that the house of Judah had "broken the covenant I made with their forefathers," and that their towns were filled with pagan idols. Because of the broken covenant the Lord had "decreed disaster for you."

Two themes we've seen before are repeated here. "Consecrated meat" (v. 15) represents superficial public religion. No mere reform of ritual without complete moral and spiritual commitment could help. And again Jeremiah was told, "Do not pray for this people" (v. 14). For them it was too late.

It's not too late for us. But our commitment must be more than settling comfortably into some Sunday pew, and putting our dollars in the offering plate. Only complete moral and spiritual commitment are appropriate to our own covenant relationship with God in Christ.

"The men of Anathoth" Jer. 11:18-23. Jeremiah was shaken when God revealed a plot against his life by the men of Anathoth. The prophet was shocked: he never expected his preaching to provoke such a savage reaction. He said, "I was like a gentle lamb," meaning that he was totally naive.

It's better for us to be naive than to be cynical. And it's often better for us not to know the plots others may hatch against us. If we are as faithful as Jeremiah in doing God's will, we may rest assured. The God who protected Jeremiah will guard us as well.

"I would speak with you about your justice" Jer. 12:1-17. Jeremiah, as you and I often are, was in a "hurry-up" mode here. His query, "Why does the way of the wicked prosper?" really means, "Why don't You act to punish the wicked now?" In bloodthirsty terms, Jeremiah cried, "Drag them off like sheep to be butchered!"

In response God gave a full-orbed vision of what He intended. He knew the character of Judah well, and warned Jeremiah against trusting anyone—even in his own family (vv. 5-6). God would abandon this wicked people to become a prey to pagan nations (vv. 7-13). But He would "again have compassion" and restore His people in the end (vv. 14-17).

What is striking here is the pain God felt at the prospect of punishing Judah. The Lord cried out in anguish, "I will give the one I love into the hands of her enemies" (v. 7). God takes no pleasure in punishments. He disciplines because He must. And because, ultimately, discipline brings restoration to fellowship.

Any time you or I feel God's heavy hand of discipline, it's important to remember what the Lord told Jeremiah. We are still "the one I [God] love," even when we deserve and receive punishment. And divine discipline is not abandonment. The Lord will "again have compassion, and bring each of them back to their inheritance."

"The LORD's flock will be taken captive" Jer. 13:1-27. The chapter lists five different warnings given Judah through Jeremiah. The first was by a symbolic act: the prophet's linen "belt" was buried by a river representing the distant Euphrates (vv. 1-11). When it was dug up months later, it was rotted and ruined. This linen garment was most likely a thigh-length undershirt, worn next to the body. It symbolized the intimacy of the relationship God intended to have with Israel and Judah. But in Judah linen had come to represent luxury and pride. Only removal from the land, and symbolic burial in Babylon, would ruin Judah's pride and make the people responsive to God once again.

The second message was based on a popular saying associated with drunkenness: "Every wineskin should be filled with wine" (vv. 12-14). Here the "wineskin" was a *nebel,* a large earthen jar. Judah's people and leaders would be as foolish as drunkards, and God would smash and destroy them all.

The third warning was in plain words, condemning arrogance and announcing Captivity (vv. 15-17). The fourth called the king and queen mother to step down from their thrones and go into Captivity (vv. 18-19). The final warning was a denunciation of Judah's sins, and again in plain words announced the coming Exile (vv. 20-27). Here the Lord specified the reason for the coming disaster. This people are so accustomed to doing evil that they don't even know how to do good! (v. 23) They will be scattered like chaff because of their detestable moral and spiritual ways.

The only way to be good is to practice doing good. We become what we do. Modern men and women, as well as the people of Judah, can become so used to doing wrong that doing good is foreign to them.

"They greatly love to wander" Jer. 14:1-16. Jeremiah was again told not to pray for Judah. Because the people "do not restrain their feet" (from wandering) the Lord would "now remember their wickedness and punish them for their sins."

Jeremiah observed that the prophets of Judah had a different message. These recognized spiritual leaders kept preaching, "You will not see the sword or suffer famine." God's answer was that all promises of lasting peace were lies. Disaster had been determined, and even the most holy of Israel's saints could not avert it if they were present (15:1-2). The prophets spoke, but God "did not send them," and they were telling lies (14:14-15).

"Popular" preaching isn't something for spiritual leaders to strive for, or for you and me to seek out. Any popular message, of prosperity without perspiration, of blessing without battles, of success without suffering, of national greatness without social justice, or of divine approval without personal holiness, marks the speaker as one whom God has not sent, and the message as something less than God's own.

▶ DEVOTIONAL
Do Not Turn to Them
(Jer. 15)

It hurts to be out there, visible—and alone. It always has. I understand that pressure I mentioned in yesterday's devotional; pressure that's reflected in our nine-year-old's compulsion to be in style and just like the other kids in her class. Adults feel the same pressure. And Christian adults perhaps especially. Many Christians make a real effort to fit in, and not make too much of their Christian faith or convictions. Taking any stand, particularly if you seem to be the only one holding an unpopular position, is a painful proposition.

Jeremiah felt the pain. He took a stand, and announced God's message of judgment on his society. As a result he was isolated; "a man with whom the whole land strives and contends" and "everyone curses." And it hurt. He "sat alone," and as a result felt "unending pain." I don't suppose that any of us would choose to be in Jeremiah's place, despite the fact that later generations have honored him.

This chapter tells us, however, what motivated Jeremiah—and what sustained him. The motivation is explained in verse 16. "When your words came, I ate them; they were my joy and my heart's delight, for I bear Your name." The prophet took God's words into his heart. They became part of his very being. As he digested their meaning, he was filled with joy and delight. And the more he feasted on the words of God, the more he realized what it means to bear God's name.

This is our primary source of motivation as well. We are to feast on God's words: to "eat" them, digesting and applying their meaning. As we do we realize how wonderful it is to bear God's name, and we are moved to honor Him in all we do and say. Because we do bear God's name, we will often be moved to represent Him publicly by our words as well as by our way of life. And the more we "eat" and delight in God's words, the more clearly we will see those issues on which we must speak out.

But what sustains us if, as may happen, speaking out brings ridicule or social isolation? God promised Jeremiah, "I will make you a wall to this people, a fortified wall of bronze" (v. 20). No one and nothing could penetrate the wall of protection that God erected around His servant. But with that promise of protection came a warning. "Let this people turn to you, but you must not turn to them" (v. 19). Those who oppose us may very well find their way inside the wall, for God's Word is an open door inviting them to enter. But you and I must never step outside the wall, by abandoning our complete commitment to Scripture, in order to adopt the values, beliefs, or ways of a lost world.

Yes, often it does hurt if we take a stand for our faith and feel ourselves isolated from others. We all want to be popular and to fit in. Often we can, and without compromise. Yet when a conflict does come, let's remember that we bear God's name. Let's be guided by His words. And, as we seek to represent our Lord, let's be sustained by His words to Jeremiah: "I am with you to rescue and save you" (v. 20).

Personal Application

When we acknowledge the fact that we bear God's name, His Word will guide us concerning those things about which we must make a personal stand.

Quotable

"When I was fourteen, I heard Lyman Beecher preach on the Lordship of Jesus Christ. I went to my room, locked the door, then threw myself on the floor of my room. This was what I said. 'O God, I belong to Thee. Take what is Thine own. I gladly recognize Thy ownership of me. I now take Thee as my Lord and Master.' From that time to this I have never known a thing to be wrong without having an aversion to it. I have never seen anything to be right without having an attraction to it."— Wendell Phillips

JUNE 2 *Reading 153*
THE POTTER
Jeremiah 16–20

> *"Therefore I will teach them—this time I will teach them My power and might. Then they will know that My name is the* Lord*" (Jer. 16:21).*

There is no more powerful image in Scripture of God's sovereignty than that of the potter, shaping clay to form whatever vessel he decides. This passage reminds us that God is sovereign. Yet the exercise of His sovereign power is tempered by love—even in the case of complaining Jeremiah.

Overview

In view of the coming disaster, Jeremiah was forbidden to live a normal human life (16:1-21). Three causes of Judah's failure were identified (17:1-13), leading Jeremiah to cry out for personal healing (vv. 14-18). Judah was then challenged to put God first by honoring the Sabbath (vv. 19-27).

At the house of a potter God announced again the certain disaster He was preparing against Judah (18:1-23). Jeremiah smashed a clay jar to symbolize the devastation destined for Jerusalem (19:1-15). Pashhur had the prophet beaten (20:1-6), leading to another anguished complaint by a weary and bitter Jeremiah (vv. 7-18).

Understanding the Text

"You must not marry and have sons or daughters in this place" Jer. 16:1-21. God restricted Jeremiah. His prophet was not to live a normal life in the city destined for destruction. He was not to marry (vv. 1-4). He was not to mourn with others at funerals (vv. 5-7). He was not to celebrate at such festivities as weddings (vv. 8-9). Jeremiah was destined to be a perpetual outsider: a specter, who walked silently among members of his society but whose grim isolation from them was to be a reminder of the judgment bearing down on the land.

This strange behavior was intended to raise questions—and create opportunities for Jeremiah to announce God's Word.

We should see God's refusal to let Jeremiah marry as a grace-gift to His prophet, though it surely must have seemed a painful burden. But when the city population starved, and its young men were cut down by the invading army and its young women raped by its soldiers, Jeremiah would be spared the anguish of watching his own children suffer this fate. The popular saying is, "Every cloud has a silver lining." A more accurate expression is, "Every burden God asks us to bear carries a hidden blessing."

"Through your own fault you will lose the inheritance I gave you" Jer. 17:1-18. Again we're reminded. When judgment comes, don't blame God.

The Lord identified three faults that assured disaster. One: Sin was engraved on the tablets of Judah's hearts (vv. 1-4). The image of writing on the heart is a common one in Scripture (cf. 2 Cor. 3:2-3). It is a reference to innate character; to the very core of one's personality. There is not the slightest scratch on Judah's heart to indicate any response to God's Word. What is there, scored deep by bold slashes with a diamond (not "flint") point, is sin. Two: Judah had turned away from God to trust in mere man (Jer. 17:5-8). There is no remedy for sin but trust in God. Yet Judah would not put her confidence in the Lord. Three: The human heart is corrupt beyond any cure (vv. 9-13). Judah's heart constantly turned toward evil. Surely God could not be blamed for dooming a people of sinful character and corrupt heart, who refused to put their trust in Him.

Jeremiah wisely took this revelation personally, and cried out, "Heal me, O Lord" (vv. 14-18). Despite the fact that he had "not run away from being Your shepherd" to Judah, Jeremiah was fearful and uncertain. If only the people of Judah had responded as the prophet did now! If only they had cried out to God for healing. But instead they scoffed, and ridiculed Jeremiah saying, "Where is the word of the LORD?" Because disaster was not there, they could not see it ahead!

What a blessing that we have seen the coming judgment, and with Jeremiah cried out to God for spiritual healing. And what a joy to know that, because of Jesus Christ, healing is ours. God has erased the sin engraved on our hearts, and replaced it with His own Living Word. He has healed us from within, and taught us to trust not in man but in Him alone. A day of "double destruction" was hurtling down on Judah. But we wait for the redoubled blessings to be ours when Jesus comes.

"Keep the Sabbath Day holy" Jer. 17:19-27. Why, with all the many sins committed by the people of Judah, did God tell Jeremiah to focus his preaching on keeping the Sabbath Day holy? Surely the practice of idolatry in Judah was worse than the practice of carrying a load of firewood! Certainly the immorality Jeremiah had mentioned was more serious than doing a little work on God's day of rest!

It's best to see this message, with its promise of blessing for obedience (vv. 24-26), as a test case. If the people of Judah would put God first on the Sabbath, they would put Him first in their daily lives. The failure of Judah to honor God on the day set aside for that purpose revealed a reversal of all their values.

We too are to put God first on the day we worship Him, and in our private devotions as well. When we give the Lord priority in this, our other priorities will fall in line.

"At the potter's house" Jer. 18:1–19:15. The sermon on sovereignty that was stimulated at the house of a Jerusalem potter led to another outburst of fury against Jeremiah.

Rather than respond to God's invitation, an angry populace chose to "attack [Jeremiah] with our tongues" and "pay no attention to anything he says" (18:18). After years of such rejection, Jeremiah angrily cried out against his persecutors. Let their children be given "over to famine. . . . Their wives be made childless and widows . . . their men be put to death" (v. 21).

It is not for us to judge this vitriolic outburst. The fact is that the people of Judah merited—and would soon receive—just this fate. What we should remember, however, is that despite the most terrible provocations the Lord urged the people of Judah to return to Him again and again. When we suffer unjustly as Jeremiah surely did, it's hard not to remember "all their plots to kill me" and hope for just retribution.

In Jeremiah's time potters placed lumps of clay on a round platform, which they turned with their feet. Under their skilled hands, the clay took on whatever form they intended. As Jeremiah watched a potter at work, God told him to remind Judah that the nations are like clay in His hands! He can destroy, or restore. But the people of Judah rejected this explicit invitation to turn to the Lord. They said, "It is no use. We will continue with our own plans."

Yes, God is sovereign. But this truth is intended to bring hope! The heavenly Potter has sovereignly determined to bless all who turn wholeheartedly to Him.

Still at the potter's house, Jeremiah was told to purchase a clay jar and take it to the "sacred confines" (Topheth) where the rulers and people of Judah practiced pagan sacrifice. There Jeremiah smashed the jar, and announced in God's name, "I will ruin the plans of Judah and Jerusalem. I will make them fall by the sword before their enemies." Then Jeremiah returned to the city, and repeated his message of coming destruction.

In a sense, God answered His prophet's prayer. Jeremiah's persecutors, who were God's committed enemies too, would suffer just the fate the prophet desired.

"The priest, Pashhur" Jer. 20:1-6. This high temple official heard Jeremiah's preaching, and ordered him beaten and placed in stocks. When released, Jeremiah boldly predicted that Pashhur would see his friends die, the temple treasures he supervised taken away, and that he and his family would die in Exile.

It's no fun being persecuted for our faith. But it's better to be the persecuted than the persecutor!

▶ DEVOTIONAL
The Other Fellow's Shoes (Jer. 19–20)

In some ways, Jeremiah strikes me as something of a pill. Always looking grim. Always condemning. And, worst of all, always complaining.

We see each of these traits in chapters 19 and 20. Grim Jeremiah is undoubtedly a prophet of doom (chap. 19).

Granted that the people of Judah fully deserved the disaster about to strike, Jeremiah seemed at times to be a little too enthusiastic. He almost licked his chops over their fate! (cf. 18:19-22) Granted too that Jeremiah faced hard times. It was no fun to be publicly beaten and placed in the stocks for speaking God's word (20:1-6). But when we read Jeremiah's words of complaint to the Lord after this incident, we can almost hear the whine in his voice. And it grates on us.

"Lord, You tricked me into serving You. I didn't expect ridicule! But that's all I get" (vv. 7-8).

"Lord, I've tried not speaking. But then You give me this pain, and the only way I can get relief is to speak out again" (v. 9).

"Lord, everybody's whispering and plotting against me" (v. 10).

"Lord, at least let me see them get zapped" (vv. 11-12).

"Lord, I try praising You, and You have rescued me (v. 13). But I still curse the day I was born. And I'm still angry that people rejoiced over my birth (vv. 14-16). I wish," and here the whine becomes pronounced, "that someone had performed an abortion and murdered me in the womb (v. 17). Why did I ever come out of the womb to see trouble and sorrow and to end my days in shame?" (v. 18)

Now, I've known some whiners. And they're no fun to be around. In fact, before long we get so tired of their whining that we tune such people out, ignoring them and their feelings.

Yet two things impress me about the complaints of Jeremiah. First, everything he complained about was rooted in reality. He really did have a painful and difficult life. Compared to Jeremiah, my life has been a bed of roses. So perhaps I should listen more patiently, with more compassion, and realize that if I had been forced to walk in his shoes, I might have felt just as Jeremiah did. Perhaps too I can learn from Jeremiah. Despite all his complaints, despite the depression and despair that often gripped him, Jeremiah was totally faithful to God. He spoke God's word to others, even when he knew ahead of time that they would listen with hostility and make his life even more difficult. What are a few complaints compared to this!

But second, when Jeremiah complained, God listened! God didn't seem to become impatient, or angry, or even to ignore His prophet. And I can learn from this. People who hurt often will complain. And what they need most may very well be simply the sympathy and understanding of another person. A person willing to listen, and willing to admit, "Yes, it would be tough to walk in your shoes." A person willing to express a little admiration of people like Jeremiah, who have chosen, despite their problems, to commit their cause to the Lord (v. 12).

Personal Application

When you hurt, seek God's ear. When others hurt, be God's ear for them.

Quotable

If we knew the cares and trials,
  Knew the efforts all in vain,
And the bitter disappointment,
  Understood the loss and gain;
Would the grim, eternal roughness
  Seem, I wonder, just the same?
Should we help where now we hinder?
  Should we pity where now we blame?—Rudyard Kipling

JUNE 3 *Reading 154*
JUDGMENT DAY TODAY
Jeremiah 21–29

> *"Inquire now of the* Lord *for us because Nebuchadnezzar king of Babylon is attacking us" (Jer. 21:2).*

The scene now shifts to the final years of Judah's existence. Jeremiah's predictions were coming true: the land was under siege. These chapters report a series of incidents, in no special chronological order, from Judah's last frantic months of independence.

Overview

Zedekiah was refused divine aid against Babylon (21:1-14), and Jeremiah condemned Judah's evil kings (22:1-30). In the distant future Messiah will restore a scattered Israel (23:1-8), but the immediate future holds judgment, despite the lies of Judah's prophets (vv. 9-40). God would bless those who went into Captivity (24:1-10), and in 70 years restore Judah to her land (25:1-14). Later He would punish her pagan persecutors (vv. 15-38).

Jeremiah was viewed as a traitor and threatened with death (26:1-24). Yet he did not stop calling on Judah to submit to Babylon and God's will (27:1-22). His words are authenticated by the predicted death of the false prophet Hananiah (28:1-17), but a letter to Jewish captives already in Babylon sparks a new charge of treason against Jeremiah (29:1-32).

Understanding the Text

"Perhaps the Lord *will perform wonders for us" Jer. 21:1-14.* With the city under siege, King Zedekiah at last turned to Jeremiah and the Lord for help. Grimly the prophet repeated the message he had given faithfully for so many years. God would not fight for, but against, His people.

Jeremiah did offer one hope. Those who left the city of Jerusalem and surrendered to Nebuchadnezzar would survive. Those who stayed in the city to resist him would die. It was this call to surrender that aroused so much fury, and led to accusations of treason against Jeremiah. "My country, may she ever be right; but right or wrong, my country," was clearly the sentiment in Judah. This popular patriotic slogan is just as wrong today as it was then. In a conflict between right and country, or God and country, we must choose as Jeremiah did. We must take our stand for God and right.

"Does it make you a king to have more and more cedar?" Jer. 22:1-30 The king of this passage is Jehoiakim, who earned Jeremiah's rebuke by tyrannically forcing unpaid labor to expand his palace while the land groaned under tribute demanded by Egypt's Pharaoh Neco (cf. 2 Kings 23:34-35). This was a direct violation of Old Testament Law (cf. Lev. 19:13; Deut. 24:14-15), and marked Jehoiakim as a user, rather than a servant, of his people.

Jeremiah's question, quoted above, focuses our attention on the nature of all spiritual leadership. In his denunciation of Jehoiakim, he contrasted this wicked king with his godly father Josiah. Josiah was a true king: a true servant of his people. This description of Josiah might well serve as a motto and guide for anyone in a position of spiritual leadership:

> "He did what was right and just, so all went well with him. He defended the cause of the poor and needy, and so all went well. Is that not what it means to know Me?" declares the Lord (vv. 15-16).

"I will raise up to David a righteous Branch" Jer. 23:1-8. Wicked Jehoiakim, who abused his power, was to be carried away to Bab-

ylon and have the "burial of a donkey" (22:19), without honor or regret. Now the prophet drew the ultimate contrast. One day the deposed king will be replaced by another from David's royal line, a righteous Person who will "do what is just and right in the land," and provide a restored Judah with salvation and safety.

The Messiah, who we realize today is Jesus Christ, truly stands in contrast with Judah's flawed kings. In order to provide His people with salvation and safety, King Jesus willingly suffered a criminal's death. And, in dying, He demonstrated once and for all that what qualifies a person to rule—what marks a person off as a true leader—is the readiness to serve others at personal cost.

"They commit adultery and live a lie" Jer. 23:9-40. Once again contrast catapults us into a new but related topic. Judah was filled with prophets: professional religious leaders who claimed to be channels through whom God communicated His word. Unlike Josiah, who was committed to doing good, and unlike the Messiah, who was both righteous and just, these prophets were false prophets. Jeremiah said that these godless men "follow an evil course and use their power unjustly."

What was it that marked them off as false prophets? The same traits that mark off godly from ungodly ministers today. One: "They commit adultery and live a lie" (v. 14). Their personal lives do not display the moral purity that the ministry of the Word of God requires. Two: "They strengthen the hand of evildoers" (v. 14). There is no emphasis on holiness in their ministry: no call to complete commitment to God. Three: "They fill you with false hopes" (v. 16). They preach popular messages; messages that people want to hear. Their promises of peace, health, and prosperity are "visions from their own minds." Four: "The dreams they tell one another will make My people forget My name" (v. 27). They mouthed God's name when giving messages that were supposedly from Him. But because the messages are actually only dreams stolen from one another, the result is that their hearers know less and less about God, and thus "forget" His name.

We should not judge any modern preacher, or publicly tag any individual with the label "false prophet." Yet we should use these criteria to evaluate whom to listen to—and whom to support financially.

"For twenty-three years . . . I have spoken to you again and again" Jer. 25:1-38. The message of those 23 years was the same: "Turn . . . from your evil practices, and you can stay in the land." But Judah refused to listen to the words God spoke through His prophet.

Twenty-three years! We can appreciate the frustration of the prophet, as again and again he uttered warnings and invitations—and again and again was ignored or persecuted. Twenty-three years. We can understand more of God's grace, when we realize that it was really He who was ignored and rejected. And when, as the predicted invasion was taking place and Exile was certain, God added another note of promise. The Captivity was to last only for "seventy years." Then, "when the seventy years are fulfilled," Babylon will be repaid. Indeed, all the nations that were enemies of God's people will be punished.

Three themes are linked in this chapter. (1) God brings disaster on His own in order to discipline them. (2) Discipline is intended to restore God's own to right relationship. (3) If God is willing to so punish sin in His own, how will the rest of mankind escape judgment?

There is another significance to the prophecy of the 70 years. In Babylon the people of Judah would look back, and in anguish wonder if God had deserted them forever. There they would consider their desolated land and the ruins of the temple, and wonder if by their sin they had forfeited their ancient relationship entirely. Then they would recall Jeremiah's prediction, that after 70 years a remnant would return. And, in that prophecy, the exiles would find hope.

"This man should be sentenced to death" Jer. 26:1-24. This chapter jumps back, near the beginning of Jeremiah's public ministry. It gives details about the reaction to Jeremiah's "temple sermon," which is recorded in chapter 7. It is placed here to demonstrate the consistency of Judah's response

to Jeremiah's message, from the beginning on through the decades of rejection and frustration.

That initial reaction was intense, and the religious leaders were the first to call for Jeremiah's execution (26:7-12). At that time the royal officers and the people resisted, pointing out that speaking a message in the name of the Lord was not a capital offense (vv. 16-18). It would surely be dangerous to kill a prophet (v. 19).

Did Jeremiah's release after being threatened with death suggest any openness to God's word? Not at all. It only showed that God was guarding Jeremiah, for another prophet who preached the same message was executed by the reigning king, Jehoiakim (vv. 20-24).

Some ignore God's messages; some react with anger; some believe. Some messengers are protected by God; some are killed by God's enemies. The only guarantee anyone has when he takes the role of a Jeremiah is that God is sovereign, and that His Word must be heard.

"Serve the king of Babylon, and you will live" Jer. 27:1-22. The scene shifts back to the time of Zedekiah, with Babylonian invasion forces threatening the kingdom. Jeremiah announced that God the Creator had chosen to give Judah and the other nations of Syria-Palestine over to the Babylonians. If Zedekiah surrendered the nation to Nebuchadnezzar, he and his people would live.

At this time a number of Judah's best families had already been deported to Babylon, in 605 B.C. It was then 597 B.C., and within a year the Babylonian forces would be outside the city gates. There was no basis for hope, and yet Zedekiah would not listen to Jeremiah.

Revelation describes a similar irrational response at history's end. The earth itself will be rocked by disaster after disaster; so much so that the supernatural origin of the judgments will be plain to all. Observing this in a vision, John said that all mankind "hid in caves and among the rocks of the mountains. They called to the mountains and the rocks, 'Fall on us and hide us from the face of Him who sits on the throne and from the wrath of the Lamb! For the great day of their wrath has come, and who can stand?' " (Rev. 6:15-17) Even the certainty of judgment cannot turn a man from his sins. Only the message of God's saving love in Jesus can reach and melt the hardened human heart.

Jeremiah was called to proclaim judgment, and his generation was unmoved. You and I are called to share the Gospel's Good News, and this message is still "the power of God for the salvation of everyone who believes" (Rom. 1:16).

"I will break the yoke of the king of Babylon" Jer. 28:1-17. Jeremiah was constantly opposed by false prophets, who loudly proclaimed messages that contradicted his own. At the time Jeremiah was urging Zedekiah to surrender to the Babylonians, a false prophet named Hananiah announced that God would free Judah from Babylon's power and would bring back the captives already in that land. He then broke the wooden yoke Jeremiah wore to symbolize submission to Babylon. Jeremiah was then told to forge a yoke of iron. And to announce that because Hananiah claimed to speak in God's name when God had not sent him, that Hananiah would die before the year was out. Within two months, Hananiah was dead!

In Old Testament times prophets were authenticated as God's messengers by making predictions that would soon be fulfilled, or by performing some miraculous sign. That way there could be no mistake about who God's spokesmen really were. Despite the fact that Hananiah died as Jeremiah predicted, the people of Judah still refused to listen to him.

Today too there is an authenticating work of God that helps us recognize His spokesmen. This is a work of the Holy Spirit performed within believers. Jesus spoke of this work when He said, "I know My sheep, and My sheep know Me" (John 10:14-15). We need to authenticate modern teachings, first by the objective standard of the Word of God, and then by the subjective standard of the Spirit's inner voice.

▶DEVOTIONAL
Bad Good News
(Jer. 29)

It almost seems a contradiction in terms. "Bad" good news? But this is just what Jeremiah 29 is about.

Read the chapter, and you and I can see only good news. It contains a letter that Jeremiah wrote to instruct and encourage the Jews who had already been transported to Babylon. In it Jeremiah encouraged the captives to settle down, build houses, enjoy life, and prosper in that great world capital (vv. 4-9). Jeremiah also conveyed God's promise to bring His people back to their own land after 70 years. "I know the plans I have for you," God said through His prophet, "plans to prosper you and not to harm you, plans to give you hope and a future" (vv. 10-14). You can hardly imagine better news than that! You'd think the exiles would jump up and down with excitement, or at least settle back with a sigh of relief and thank God.

Instead, the leaders in exile sent a missive to Judah's ruling priest, demanding in God's name that Jeremiah be put in stocks and neck-irons! Jeremiah was a madman, who should be shut up once and for all!

To the exiles in Babylon the good news that Jeremiah conveyed seemed to be bad news. They didn't want to hear it! They wanted to come home, now.

The other day I listened to a "Crossfire" program on CNN. The debate was between a little-known media evangelist and a man promoting a book in which he labels every radio and TV preacher a crook. And the very worst charge that the author hurled against the evangelist was, "You believe that everyone who doesn't believe in Jesus is going to hell, don't you?"

What a case of "bad" good news. The Gospel message is that everyone deserves hell. Yet in love God sent Jesus to die for us, so that through faith in Him human beings might be forgiven and receive eternal life as a free gift.

Somehow that critic of evangelists turned the whole message around, and made it appear that God condemned people for not believing in His Son, ignoring the fact that all mankind is lost and condemned without Him.

Well, don't be too surprised if what happened to Jeremiah, and what happened on TV, happens to you sometime. People have an amazing capacity to twist God's good news and make it appear to be bad news. But if it does happen to you, don't let your critic succeed. Keep the focus on the "good" of the good news, and rejoice in what the Lord means to you.

Personal Application

Arguing with folks determined to make good news appear bad is about as productive as trying to make hay grow on the moon.

Quotable

"As Tennyson passed the cottage of an aged lady, he asked, 'What news this morning?' Replied the old lady, 'Lord Tennyson, I know only one piece of news—that Jesus Christ died for all mankind.' 'Madam,' said Tennyson, 'that is old news and new news and good news!' "—Howard A. Banks

JUNE 4 *Reading 155*
NEW COVENANT PROMISES
Jeremiah 30–33

> *"I will put My Law in their minds and write it on their hearts. I will be their God, and they will be My people. . . . For I will forgive their wickedness and will remember their sins no more" (Jer. 31:33-34).*

The key to understanding God's work in believers today is to understand the impact of the New Covenant, and to realize that this covenant was instituted in the death of Jesus Christ.

Overview

A collection of sermons focused on the restoration (30:1-11) and healing (vv. 12-24) of the Old Testament faith community. God's everlasting love guaranteed future blessedness despite present mourning (31:1-30). But to accomplish His purposes God had to make a New Covenant with His people (vv. 31-40). Jeremiah bought a field occupied by the enemy to demonstrate his personal confidence in God's promises of restoration (32:1-44), which he repeated despite being imprisoned (33:1-26).

Understanding the Text

"I will bring My people . . . back" Jer. 30:1-11. The messages in these chapters are unified by the theme of restoration. While they may be drawn from different periods of Jeremiah's ministry, they most likely are set, as the incidents in chapters 32 and 33, in Judah's last days, with Jerusalem about to fall.

These messages underline a peculiar characteristic of prophetic preaching. When God's people are prosperous and comfortable, the prophets thunder against their sins and predict judgment. Yet when judgment comes, and God's people tremble with fear, the same prophets comfort with promises of forgiveness and restoration. There is no conflict between the two themes. The predictions of punishment are intended to bring repentance and, if there is no repentance at the warning, the punishment itself will bring repentance later. What we do see is that God is always careful to communicate just the message His people need for their particular situation. One modern pulpiteer observed that his calling was to "afflict the comfortable, and comfort the afflicted." If you and I are too comfortable in this world, we need the stern words of God to remind us that we are to remain committed to justice and holiness. If we suffer, we need loving words of promise, that remind us of God's love and His commitment to do us good.

"I will restore you to health and heal your wounds" Jer. 30:12-24. Here the "wound" God speaks of is spiritual. His people are "beyond healing" because their "guilt is so great, and your sins so many."

Before God can restore the material prosperity of His people, He must restore their spiritual health. This is impossible for the people of Judah: their wound is "incurable" and "beyond healing." But God will devise a way, and then He will restore them to relationship with Him (v. 22) and to national prosperity.

The order here is important. God is eager to bless us. But first we must be healed within, and in right relationship with Him. As Jesus put it, our first concern is to seek the kingdom of God and His righteousness. Then "all these things will be given to you as well" (Matt. 6:33).

"I have loved you with an everlasting love" Jer. 31:1-14. If we search for any reason for God's promise of restoration in the people of Judah themselves, we'll be disappointed. Nothing in their character or actions was attractive. Nothing merited God's consideration. Instead the reason Jeremiah gave was simply that God had chosen to love His people "with an everlasting love." It is the overflow of His "loving-kindness," a term that speaks of God's compassionate commitment to His covenant promises, which lies at the root of His actions.

It is the same with us today. When God sent His Son into the world, it was to save His enemies! He saved us despite, not because of, what we are. "While we were still sinners, Christ died for us" (Rom. 5:8). Let's never fall into the error of thinking that God saved us, or will save another person, because we are "good" or "nice" or somehow deserve His favor.

And what a blessing this is! The nicest of us are flawed, and if we had to depend on our own works, would be uncertain about gaining God's gift. But since all depends on the love of God, we can be confident and sure. God's love is boundless, and as Jeremiah says, "everlasting." Only because we rely completely on the love of God can we say with confidence that we have been, are being, and surely will be "saved."

No wonder Jeremiah called on Judah to "sing with joy" and "make your praises heard." Trust in the love of God will turn our "mourning into gladness," and will give us "comfort and joy instead of sorrow."

"Mourning and great weeping" Jer. 31:15-30. The saying is quoted in Matthew's Gospel (2:17-18), and applied to the slaughter of innocent babes at Herod's order, in that king's futile attempt to kill the Christ Child. Yet here the reference clearly is to Rachel, the ancestress of the northern tribes, weeping over the deportation of Israel to Assyria in 722 B.C. Her tragic figure also weeps at Ramah, the very site where exiles were gathered before being deported to Babylon (Jer. 40:1). God told her to stop weeping, for He would restore her banished offspring, making them again a source of joy rather than grief.

The Matthew quote is not intended as direct fulfillment, but as an application. In both cases, God will overrule. Tragedy will give birth to blessing; grief will give birth to joy.

"I will make a New Covenant with the house of Israel" Jer. 31:31-40. A covenant was a formal, legal promise or commitment. Jeremiah predicted that a "time is coming" when God would make a New Covenant with Israel, to replace the "old" Mosaic Code under which the Jews lived. Note that God did not "make" that covenant in Jeremiah's time, but rather promised to replace the old with a new agreement at some future date.

The New Testament makes it clear that the promised "New Covenant" was formally instituted by the death of Christ. That covenant took the most binding of all Old Testament forms: it was a "covenant of blood," formalized by the offering of a blood sacrifice. How Jeremiah would have wondered, and bowed his head in awe, if he had known that the sacrifice necessary to keep the promises imbedded in the New Covenant would be the very Son of God.

Jeremiah did describe the nature of the New Covenant. It is "not like" the Mosaic Code, which recorded God's Laws in stone and failed to offer complete forgiveness. Through the New Covenant, God would "put My law in their minds and write it on their hearts." The New Covenant offers inner spiritual renewal and transformation. Through the New Covenant, God would "be their God," united by a bond which nothing in heaven or hell can break. And through the New Covenant, God would "forgive their wickedness" and "remember their sins no more."

Today you and I enjoy the spiritual benefits of this New Covenant through our faith in Jesus Christ. One day, according to Jeremiah, a restored Israel will dwell again in Judah and Jerusalem, secure in the ancient Promised Land. Then Israel too will recognize her Messiah, and the spiritual benefits you and I now enjoy will belong to this people whom God chose to love with an "everlasting love."

"Call to Me and I will answer you and tell you great and unsearchable things you do not know" Jer. 33:1-26. Jeremiah was in prison, held for his "treasonable" advice that Judah surrender to the Babylonians. God spoke to him again, and revealed the "unsearchable." Here is God's plan for the future of His people: a future no one could imagine then apart from divine revelation.

What is the outline of that future? Judah would be carried into Captivity (vv. 1-5). They would be brought back to the land, and its fortunes would be restored (vv. 6-13). The complete fulfillment of this promise awaits the appearance of a Descendant of David, who may rightly be called "the LORD Our Righteousness." Until that time comes, there will always be a descendant of David qualified to sit on Israel's throne (vv. 14-18). And, Jeremiah announced, this salvation intention of God is as firm as the Creation intention, which set the stars in their courses and established the rhythmic cycle of day and night (vv. 19-26). Of one thing we can be sure. God has not rejected His people Israel. And He will not reject us.

▶ DEVOTIONAL

Money Where Your Mouth Is (Jer. 31–32)

"I do! I do! I know you can!" The little fellow jumped up and down when the tightrope walker asked who believed he could carry a man on his shoulders as he walked his tightrope over Niagara Falls. But when told, "OK, brother. You're first," you couldn't see the little fellow for dust! It's an old story, but it surely illustrates the point. If you really believe something, you should be willing to display your faith by your actions.

This is what God asked Jeremiah to do. The prophet had boldly announced a future restoration and blessing of Jerusalem (chap. 31). Now he was told to buy a field, wrap the deed up carefully, and bury it where it could be found 70 years later when a remnant of Jews returned from Babylon. There was only one catch. The field Jeremiah was told to buy was outside of Jerusalem, occupied by the Babylonian army that was even then besieging the city walls! And Jeremiah was even told to pay full price, in silver, for what everyone then must have considered worthless land (32:6-15).

Jeremiah was stunned. After obeying the Lord, he voiced his surprise in prayer (vv. 16-25). God reminded His prophet, "I am the LORD, the God of all mankind. Is anything too hard for Me?" (v. 26)

What a word for us. We believe, but sometimes when led to what seems a risky or costly act, we hold back. Like the little boy who fled the tightrope walker when invited to take the first ride, we tend to flee when challenged to put our faith into action.

When the temptation to flee comes, how good to remember God's command to Jeremiah to buy a seemingly worthless field. That "foolish" act echoes down to our own day as evidence of the prophet's faith—and evidence of the wisdom of obeying even "foolish" and seemingly costly commands of God.

Personal Application

The answer to God's question, "Is anything too hard for Me?" is still "No!"

Quotable

"I was a free man in a worldly position; my father was a decurion, indeed, I bargained away my aristocratic status—I am neither ashamed nor sorry—for the benefit of others. In short, I am a slave in Christ to an outlandish nation because of the unspeakable glory of eternal life which is in Christ Jesus our Lord."—Patrick of Ireland

---

JUNE 5 *Reading 156*

UNDER SIEGE

Jeremiah 34–39

> *"You will see the king of Babylon with your own eyes. . . . And you will go to Babylon" (Jer. 34:3).*

Jerusalem was under siege. Jeremiah was imprisoned, the king powerless—and the people unrepentant.

Overview

Jeremiah warned Zedekiah to surrender (34:1-7). Judah's disobedience to God (vv. 8-22) was contrasted with the Recabites' obedience to an ancestor's command (35:1-19). Jehoiakim's destruction of an early Jeremiah scroll is recalled (36:1-32). Returning to Zedekiah's day, Jeremiah was imprisoned and thrown into a muddy cistern to die (37:1–38:13). The powerless Zedekiah questioned Jeremiah privately (vv. 14-28) just before the city was finally taken (39:1-18).

Understanding the Text

"Go to Zedekiah king of Judah" Jer. 34:1-7. In a final effort to spare the city God sent Jeremiah to Zedekiah. Only a few pockets of resistance to the invading Babylonians

remained in Judah (v. 7); it was clear that further resistance was hopeless. Yet even now if Zedekiah would surrender, God promised to spare his life and give him an honorable burial.

The incident reminds us of the two thieves on the cross. All hope of living is past. Death stares grimly from the doorstep. Even then, God gives sinners a chance to repent.

"Proclaim freedom for the slaves" Jer. 34:8-22. This passage suggests that Zedekiah did make some effort at reform. In hopes of winning God's favor he led his officials and Jerusalem's citizens to free their Hebrew slaves. Old Testament Law required that Hebrew slaves be freed after just a few years of service (Deut. 15:12-18). But the wealthy of Jerusalem violated this law and kept fellow Jews in perpetual servitude. This the people now pledged to correct, and released their Hebrew slaves. But when the feint of an Egyptian army caused a temporary lifting of the siege of Jerusalem (cf. Jer. 37:4-5), "they changed their minds and took back the slaves they had freed and enslaved them again."

In this they not only disobeyed the Lord, but also violated a most solemn "covenant of blood," made by walking between halves of a slain calf. This act symbolized the punishment they merited if they broke the covenant promise, made "before the LORD." Now God would impose just this penalty.

The problem with many "deathbed conversions" is that when death seems imminent, almost any promise will be made. But when the danger recedes, people revert to their old ways. The reality of repentance and faith can never be verified by mere words. True repentance and faith can only be displayed by a lifetime of obedience to God's commands.

"You have obeyed the command of your forefather Jonadab" Jer. 35:1-19. The Recabites were a family of nomadic tribesmen who had carefully followed the instructions of a forefather not to drink wine and not to live in houses or take up agriculture. God pointed out this obedience, and contrasted it with Judah's persistent refusal to obey One far greater than Jonadab, the Lord Himself. Judah would be punished for her refusal to obey God. As for the Recabites, they were rewarded with the promise that "Jonadab son of Recab will never fail to have a man to serve Me."

It is not emotional protestations of faith, or sudden deathbed conversions, that count with God. These may or may not be real. What pleases God is the believer's persistent, consistent life of simple obedience to His Word.

"The king burned the scroll containing the words that Baruch had written at Jeremiah's dictation" Jer. 36:1-32. The contrast between the Recabites and the people of Judah continued with this story from the time of Jehoiakim, about 15 years before the other incidents reported in these chapters. The Recabites had remembered the words of Jonadab: God caused His words through Jeremiah to be written in ink, an unforgettable testimony. What had happened? King Jehoiakim had actually burned the manuscript, a futile attempt to blot out the Word of God!

The attempt was futile indeed. Jeremiah simply dictated another copy—with added text—to his secretary Baruch, while the prophet and his scribe hid from Jeiakim.

And what did this attempt to blot out Scripture gain Jehoiakim? Complete rejection by God. He and his family would be set aside, and David's royal line would be traced through a brother, not the apostate king.

People still try to ignore or discredit the Word of God. But their efforts are just as futile as Jehoiakim's—and have the same consequence of rejection by the Lord.

"Please pray to the LORD our God for us" Jer. 37:1-10. Zedekiah completely ignored God's word (v. 2), but he wanted Jeremiah to pray for him! How typical of the unconverted. God doesn't merit their attention—unless they want something from Him.

God did respond to Zedekiah's request. He sent Jeremiah to tell the king that the withdrawal of the Babylonian forces to meet an Egyptian threat was temporary. The Babylonians would return, resume their attack, and burn Jerusalem down.

Yes, anyone can pray. But like Zedekiah, those who have ignored God all their lives might not like the answer they receive.

"You are deserting to the Babylonians" Jer. 37:11-21. During a break in the siege, Jeremiah tried to leave Jerusalem on business, but was stopped at the gate and accused of deserting to the Babylonians.

Jeremiah's constant urging of surrender clearly had antagonized "patriots." In their anger they and the king's officials had Jeremiah beaten and imprisoned. In the first of several private interviews with Zedekiah, Jeremiah again urged surrender. Rather than being returned to a prison where he was in danger of dying, Jeremiah was kept in the "courtyard of the guard" and fed daily.

The reaction of the "patriots" is typical. In the stress of the siege the people blamed Jeremiah, who had warned them for years of what must happen if they continued to disobey God. They struck out at him, rather than accepting responsibility for the situation.

Blaming others is one of the most useless and destructive of all possible responses in any situation. The only positive response is to look honestly at causes, to accept responsibility for our own role, then to take any appropriate action. In Judah the people still refused to accept responsibility for the actions that brought the Babylonians down on them. The people of Judah simply blamed Jeremiah, and directed their frustration and anger at him.

The same trait is common in spouse and child abusers, and in alcoholics. They refuse to accept responsibility for their actions, and instead blame their victims! Until a person accepts responsibility for his own acts, there is no hope of change. Such people will continue to victimize the innocent, just as the officials of Judah victimized righteous Jeremiah.

"This man should be put to death" Jer. 38:1-13. The compulsive anger of guilty men who deny their responsibility is further shown in the reaction of high officials to Jeremiah's continued preaching. The prophet again warned that only those who left Jerusalem would survive to go into Captivity. This additional "treasonous" preaching, which no doubt threatened the morale of the defenders, led to demands that Jeremiah be put to death. Zedekiah, unwilling to resist their pressure, shrugged and turned Jeremiah over to them.

Jeremiah was then placed in an empty city cistern, a giant water-storage pit. He sank deep into the muck, and was left there to die.

Don't ever think, if you are in a relationship with an abuser or alcoholic, that things will somehow get better. Even if you do what's right, as Jeremiah did, you

Jeremiah was placed in a cistern much like this one, and left to die.

can count on more intense persecution. Only when the abusing individual accepts responsibility for the sinfulness of his own acts is there any hope of change. Until then you can expect more hostility, more anger, and more abuse.

Jeremiah's situation, however, was not hopeless. God sent another official, named Ebed-Melech, to help him. Jeremiah was lifted out of the cistern, and returned to the courtyard of the guard.

A neighbor of ours, seriously abused by her husband, prayed desperately that God would send someone to counsel her. That day my wife met her at our community pool, and spent an hour sharing with her. Three weeks later the neighbor, feeling desperate again, uttered the same prayer. Again she "just happened" to meet my wife, who again spent several hours talking with her. God has an Ebed-Melech for you when you are desperate too. Pray, as our neighbor did, and ask God to send someone who can help.

"Then he put out Zedekiah's eyes" Jer. 39:1-10. Jerusalem fell, as Jeremiah had predicted. Zedekiah tried to flee, but was captured. His sons were slaughtered as he watched, and then his own eyes were gouged out, so that the last sight the king saw was the murder of his family. Then Zedekiah, and all but a few of the poorest in Judah, were taken into Captivity, as the smoke of burning Jerusalem rose behind them. The king had refused to heed the word of the Lord. The responsibility for what happened to him was his own.

The blinded, childless king, being dragged away in shackles, is a graphic reminder of a basic spiritual truth. Anyone can choose to ignore the Word of God. But no one can avoid the consequences of that choice.

"Go and tell Ebed-Melech" Jer. 39:11-18. The Babylonians cared for Jeremiah, whom they must have viewed as an asset. Given the choice, Jeremiah chose to remain with the little group of Jews left in the land rather than to accompany the captives to Babylon. After all, Ezekiel and Daniel were both in Babylon. The exiles would not be without guidance. But who would care for the poor remnant remaining in Judah?

Jeremiah's first mission was one of comfort. Ebed-Melech, who had earlier saved the prophet, was told that though the city must be destroyed, he would be saved, "because you trust in" the Lord. This man's rescue of Jeremiah had been an act of faith.

The incident encourages us. Just as there were consequences to Zedekiah's disobedience, so there were consequences to Ebed-Melech's act of faith. God does, as Hebrews says, "reward those who earnestly seek Him" (Heb. 11:6).

▶ DEVOTIONAL
Pity the Poor, Powerless King (Jer. 38)

TV found a winner when it decided to feature "Lifestyles of the Rich and Famous." Ah, how the average person envies them. Wealth! Power! What more could a human being want?

But Jeremiah gave a totally different notion of the "rich and famous" of his time. His portrait of Zedekiah, the King of Judah, takes us behind the scenes, and reveals a man more to be pitied than envied. For this king was powerless!

When officials demanded the death sentence for Jeremiah, Zedekiah shrugged and said, "He is in your hands. The king can do nothing to oppose you" (v. 5). After Jeremiah was rescued by the bold Ebed-Melech, Zedekiah went to Jeremiah alone, to ask what was to happen to him in the future (vv. 14-16). The king was told that if he surrendered he and his family would live (vv. 17-18). Zedekiah hesitated, and shared his fears. The Babylonians might hand him over to the Jews who had deserted to them, and he might be mistreated (v. 19). Again Jeremiah urged surrender (vv. 20-23), but the king only begged that Jeremiah not tell his officials what either of them had said, but simply to say that Jeremiah had begged for his life (vv. 24-28).

What a portrait of a king! Afraid of the future. Terrified of his own officials. Knowing what was right, but totally unable to do it, even if he wanted to. The most powerful man in Judah was the least free to act; the least able to do what was wise and right. Oh, yes, we should pity the poor, helpless king. And we should learn from him.

The greatest gift that God can give us is freedom—the freedom to do what we believe is right. Often the rich are too concerned for their wealth to do what they believe is right. They are captives of what they possess. Often the famous are too concerned about what others will think to do what they believe is right. They are captives of their fame. And often the powerful are too concerned about maintaining their position to act on what they believe is right. They are captives, not wielders, of their own power. Only those who care supremely about doing God's will are truly rich, for they alone are truly free.

Personal Application

Do God's will, and you will be greater—and happier—than any king.

Quotable

Whenever Richard Cory went down town,
We people on the pavement looked at him:
He was a gentleman from soul to crown,
Clean favored, and imperially slim.
And he was always quietly arrayed,
And he was always human when he talked;
But still he fluttered pulses when he said,
"Good morning," and he glittered when he walked.
And he was rich—yes, richer than a king
—And admirably schooled in every grace:
In fine, we thought that he was everything
To make us wish that we were in his place.
So on we worked, and waited for the light,
And went without the meat, and cursed the bread;
And Richard Cory, one calm summer night,
Went home and put a bullet through his head.—Edward Arlington Robinson

---

JUNE 6 *Reading 157*
FLIGHT TO EGYPT
Jeremiah 40–45

> *"You made a fatal mistake when you sent me to the LORD your God and said, 'Pray to the LORD our God' " (Jer. 42:19-20).*

Knowing the will of God obligates us to do it. Better not to ask God's will unless you intend to do it!

Overview

Brisk narrative chapters tell of the assassination of the Babylonian-appointed governor, Gedaliah (40:1–41:15), and the Jewish remnant's hasty flight to Egypt despite Jeremiah's warnings (v. 16–43:13). Now destruction faced the fleeing population, which persisted in idolatry (44:1-30). A footnote contains God's promise to, and rebuke of, Baruch (45:1-5).

Understanding the Text

"You people sinned against the LORD" Jer. 40:1-6. Jeremiah was found chained with other captives due to be sent to Babylon. We do not know whether or not the Babylonian commander truly believed what he said to Jeremiah when he set the prophet free (vv. 1-3). But his words show that the enemy was well acquainted with the prophet's message.

We never know how far our words carry when we witness to our faith in God or share His message with others.

"Gedaliah . . . took an oath to reassure them" Jer. 40:7–41:15. Gedaliah is one of Scripture's least-known but most attractive figures. When he was appointed to govern Judah, he took pains to reassure the remaining population. He promised to represent their interests to the Babylonians, and settled them on productive land where they would have food and ultimately prosper.

At first all went well. Reassured by Gedaliah's appointment, Jews who had fled to neighboring countries returned, and the initial harvest was abundant. When warned of a plot to assassinate him, Gedaliah brushed it aside, refusing to believe the worst of a person he thought of as honorable and a friend. In all this Gedaliah showed himself to be a truly good man. But Gedaliah was an exception, and good men do not prosper in the land of the wicked. He was murdered, along with the small garrison of Babylonian soldiers left in Judah.

Perhaps only the words of Isaiah provide insight when a person like Gedaliah dies before his time, and the wicked seem to prosper. "The righteous perish, and no one ponders it in his heart; devout men are taken away, and no one understands that the righteous are taken away to be spared from evil. Those who walk uprightly enter into peace; they find rest as they lie in death" (Isa. 57:1-2).

"Please hear our petition" Jer. 41:16–42:3. The murders terrified the Jewish population. Surely the Babylonians would avenge this terrorist act! All the remaining Jews, under discharged army officers led by Johanan son of Kareah, assembled and begged Jeremiah to ask God what they should do.

On the surface this step seems a pious and wise one. But, as noted earlier, it is dangerous to ask God for guidance unless we fully intend to do as He directs.

"May the LORD be a true and faithful witness against us if we do not act in accordance with everything [you] tell us" Jer. 42:4-22. After a 10-day delay, Jeremiah brought the anxious remnant God's answer. The message was unequivocable and clear. The Jews were to remain in the land; God would see to it that Nebuchadnezzar dealt kindly with them. They were definitely not to go to Egypt. If the people did try to flee to Egypt, "not one of them will survive or escape the disaster I will bring on them."

As the men of Jeremiah's day were about to discover, it's not what we don't know of God's will that may be our problem. Knowing God's will carries the obligation to do God's will. Failure to do what we know is right is far more serious than not understanding what the Lord requires.

"They entered Egypt in disobedience" Jer. 43:1-13. The people of Jeremiah's time had decided beforehand what they wanted God to say. When Jeremiah's message disagreed with their expectations, they accused Jeremiah of lying!

It seems like such an easy way out. You don't like what the Bible says? Well then, just decide not to believe it! You feel uncomfortable about this or that passage? Then just ignore it, or revise it to suit. A contemporary paraphrase by Shirley Maclaine, the *New Age Version,* renders Romans 3:23 as: "For all have experienced momentary lapses and have come up a tad shy of the Divine Entity's absolute idea, but hey, nobody's perfect. So don't worry. Be happy!"

Nice try, Shirley. But this admittedly more cheery phrasing does not change the truth affirmed in the original. "All have sinned and fall short of the glory of God."

One of the most exciting finds by archeologists in Jerusalem is the *bullae* (seal) used by Baruch, the scribe to whom Jeremiah dictated this Old Testament book. The seal, illustrated here, was used as an authenticating stamp and reads "to/from Baruch // son of Neriah // the scribe."

And it has no impact on the fact that "the wages of sin is death" (6:23). One can choose to deny, ignore, or reinterpret the Word of God. But nothing a person does can change the fact that what God says is true and binding.

"To this day they have not humbled themselves or shown reverence" Jer. 44:1-30. Rebelliously the leaders and remaining people of Judah announced that they were going to Egypt anyway. What's more, "We will burn incense to the Queen of Heaven and will pour out drink offerings to her just as we and our fathers . . . did in . . . the streets of Jerusalem."

This defiance of God and His Word was the final demonstration of the attitude which cost the people of Judah their kingdom. Now the remaining few trudged into Egypt, terrified of the Babylonians behind them, but blind to the destruction that God assured them lay ahead.

And so the remnant disappeared into the desert, as the focus of God's plans for His people shifted to highlight the captives in Babylon.

▶ DEVOTIONAL
Seeking Great Things (Jer. 45)

Baruch was a frustrated man. His confrontation with Jehoiakim over the words Jeremiah dictated to him had ruined his prospects! He saw a bright career going down the drain.

We know from the text of Jeremiah that Baruch was a member of a respected Jerusalemite family (36:4), and that his brother was an official in the royal court (51:59). He was trained as a scribe, very likely in order to serve in government. Everything about Baruch—background, education, connections—suggests that he could normally expect to gain a high-status, high-paying position in the local aristocracy.

And then somehow Baruch got mixed up with Jeremiah, was linked with that unpopular prophet in the mind of King Jehoiakim—and that was it! No high pay. No fancy chariot. No job with the king. Kaput! And so Baruch pouted, and complained, "Woe to me."

I suppose we can identify with Baruch to some extent. He had great plans for himself, and a real prospect of making it big. When his plans crashed down around him, he became despondent, "worn out with groaning" and finding "no rest." Life didn't seem worth living to Baruch unless he achieved his goals, and made it in the big city.

It was then God spoke to Baruch, and rebuked him. God was about to bring the whole society crashing down! "Should you then seek great things for yourself?"

Bluntly God told Baruch, "Seek them not." And then God made a promise. In the coming disaster the Lord would give Baruch something more precious than position—God would let Baruch "escape with your life."

Sometimes we need to be reminded, as Baruch was. We may not see the realization of our dreams. We may not reach the potential we think we have. We may never take our place among the rich and famous of this world. But compared to the gift that God has given us, the gift of life, these things mean little. "Seek them not," is still some of the best advice Scripture has for the godly. Instead of wanting what we do not have, let's be grateful for God's gift of life. And use our lives to serve Him.

Personal Application

Satisfaction is not found in getting what you want, but in wanting what you get.

Quotable

"Greatness after all, in spite of its name, appears to be not so much a certain size as a certain quality in human lives. It may be present in lives whose range is very small."—Phillips Brooks

JUNE 7 *Reading 158*
AGAINST ALIEN NATIONS
Jeremiah 46–52

"That day belongs to the LORD, the LORD Almighty—a day of vengeance, for vengeance on His foes" (Jer. 46:10).

If judgment truly begins at the house of God, as Hebrews suggests, how will God's enemies escape? In these chapters Jeremiah directed his message of impending judgment to the nations that had mistreated God's covenant people.

Overview

A collection of oracles condemning foreign enemies concludes the book. Jeremiah described judgment about to fall on Egypt (46:1-28), Philistia (47:1-7), Moab (48:1-47), Ammon (49:1-6), Edom (vv. 7-22), Damascus [Syria] and others (vv. 23-39), but especially on Babylon (50:1–51:64). The book concludes by recapping Jerusalem's fall (52:1-34).

Understanding the Text

"Concerning Egypt" Jer. 46:1-28. For over a thousand years Egypt had tried to extend its sphere of influence to include Canaan—and had often succeeded. Godly King Josiah fell in 605 B.C. fighting Pharaoh Neco, and Judah's last kings had been encouraged to rebel against Babylon by empty promises of Egyptian aid. Egypt had proven herself a brutal overlord and a deceptive ally. Thus Jeremiah portrayed Egypt as a warlike nation intent on conquest (vv. 1-9). But the day of battle belongs to the Lord. Pharaoh was only a "loudmouth" (v. 17): the sword will "devour till it is satisfied" (v. 10).

There is irony in verses 11 and 12. From the third millennium B.C. Egypt was renowned for her physicians, medicines, and books on healing. But now for Egypt herself "there is no healing."

While verse 28 makes it clear that Jeremiah is speaking of a contemporary defeat of Egypt by the Babylonians, the Lord intends events to convey a timeless message. God is in charge of history. The defeat of Egypt is evidence that the Lord can—and one day will—deliver His people and return them to their land (vv. 27-28).

History still witnesses to the moral nature of our universe and conveys a message of hope. Nations built on evil, as was Nazi Germany, carry the seeds of their own destruction. God values righteousness and peace, and one day will give His people both.

"Concerning the Philistines before Pharaoh attacked Gaza" Jer. 47:1-7. The chronological note is obscure but suggests that Jeremiah focused on current events. The Egyptians were about to crush the remnants of Judah's ancient enemies, so terrifying them that fathers would not even turn back to help their own children (v. 3).

Note that God used the agency of one of His people's enemies to bring ruin to another. You and I don't need to take revenge on those who mistreat or harm us. Such people have plenty of other enemies God can and will use to repay them!

"Concerning Moab" Jer. 48:1-47. The Moabites originally occupied the high plains east of the Jordan River. Moab had tried to seduce the Israelites into immorality and idolatry on their journey from Egypt (Num. 25:1-3), and the two peoples were generally hostile to each other after that time. The prophecies in this chapter seem to summarize the oracles other Old Testament prophets directed against this people (cf. Isa. 15–16; Ezek. 25:8-11; Amos 2:1-3; Zeph. 2:8-11).

The destruction described here is merited, for in her complacency (Jer. 48:11-15) and conceit (vv. 26-34) Moab "defied the LORD" (v. 42). Despite this the Lord lamented over Moab (v. 36), and in the future will "restore [her] fortunes" (v. 47).

One of the most significant features of biblical prophecies of judgment is that they typically conclude just like the oracle against Moab. Sins are exposed, judgment is decreed, and yet, always, God expresses His love and promises that after necessary discipline His people will be restored. Even foreign nations, with no claim to a covenant relationship with the Lord, are to be justly punished for their sins but, in the end, their fortunes too will be restored.

We can understand such promises made to Israel and Judah. After all, God by a formal, legal covenant committed Himself to bless Abraham's children. But He has no such obligation to foreign nations that not only fail to know Him, but are even enemies of His chosen people. Yet again and again we see that God intends to bless all peoples—not because He has to, but simply because He cares.

Theologians speak of a doctrine called "common grace." Somehow God has chosen to bless all human beings in many ways, whether they know and trust Him or not. Reading the oracle against Moab we sense, despite its theme of judgment, a strong current of very uncommon grace! God's love will leap over every obstacle. He will find a way to redeem His enemies as well as His own.

"Concerning" others Jer. 49:1-39. Several hostile peoples are dealt with in this chapter. Again the focus is on the contemporary historical setting rather than the "last days." Babylon, the agent God will use to discipline His people, will also strike the Jews' enemies. In one act God will both discipline His own people, and punish those historically hostile to them.

The message of these chapters must have been encouraging to the exiles once they were in Babylon. When they struggled to understand why, as we all do when tragedy strikes, the revelation of God's purpose to punish the nations as well as Judah would help His people sense the consistency and fairness of the Lord. God is a moral judge, who will punish all sin. Yes, He disciplines us. But He is evenhanded in His acts. He disciplines us. And He punishes those who are not His own. And, most wonderful of all, He offers pardon to all.

"Concerning Babylon and the land of the Babylonians" Jer. 50:1–51:64. Jeremiah's major oracle against foreign nations was reserved for Babylon. The spectacular rise of this Chaldean power would be matched by a sudden fall (50:1-20). God would call other nations against her, for "the LORD has opened His arsenal and brought out the weapons of His wrath" (vv. 21-27). The exiles of Judah would return triumphantly to their homeland (vv. 28-40) after God called up an army from the north to crush Judah's conqueror (vv. 41-46). Amid further descriptions of Babylon's doom (51:1-5, 11-19), the prophet added a warning to the people of Judah. Babylon was beyond healing. When the time came to return home, the people of Judah should "flee from Babylon."

This lengthy prophecy carries a postscript. Seraiah, an official who accompanied Zedekiah to Babylon in 594/3 B.C. (cf. v. 59), was to read these prophecies against Babylon to the captives already there, and then sink his copy in the river, to symbolize the impossibility of Babylon arising again.

"All this happened to Jerusalem and Judah" Jer. 52:1-34. Jeremiah had written in most passionate language about Judah's sins, and about impending judgment. But now, in a brief appendix, there is only a blunt, straightforward account of Jerusalem's fall. It is almost as if all emotion has been exhausted, all passion drained. There is hardly even a capacity to feel horror, for the terrible has become commonplace. Zedekiah rebelled. The Babylonians finally took the city from starving defenders. The king's children were executed and he was blinded. The temple was burned and its holy vessels cut up for transportation to Babylon. Key spiritual and military leaders left alive were executed. The few thousand survivors were then transported to Babylon.

It's left for us to read between the lines, if we wish. To feel the hunger and fear; the anguish of watching loved ones die. To sense the anger and hatred that surged—often against Jeremiah—as the futility of resistance became more and more clear. But all that was past now. It was over. And, in Babylon, the remnant of the people of Judah would be given a fresh start.

Judgment never is pleasant. But the historical accounts of Scripture remind us that judgment is sure.

▶ DEVOTIONAL
Babylon Must Fall
(Jer. 50–51)

The awesome specter of Babylon dominates many chapters of the historical and prophetic books of the Old Testament.

The impression made on God's people by this ancient kingdom is so great that the name has been transformed into a symbol. The symbol is seen most clearly in Revelation 17 and 18, where Babylon stands first for humanistic religion, and then for materialistic human society. All man's achievements, all that human beings strive and hope for in this world, is summed up in that one word, Babylon.

I'm not an exponent of allegorical interpretation of Scripture. Or of spiritualizing the Old Testament. Yet in these chapters describing the coming destruction of historic Babylon, something more than history is at stake. The prophet says, "Babylon must fall because of Israel's slain, just as the slain in all the earth have fallen because of Babylon" (Jer. 51:49). And somehow, in those words, I hear a message for me today. Babylon, with its worldly hopes and worldly ways, with its focus on wealth and power, with its pride in human achievement, is responsible for so much spiritual deadness. The excitement of hitching a ride to Babylon, of making it big in the Big City, has made God's priorities and His ways seem dull and even foolish to many. Yes, Babylon must fall, because so many are slain by her superficial attractiveness.

And the very first place Babylon must fall is from my heart.

Personal Application

Only a heart fixed on God will have no room for love of the world.

Quotable

"Worldliness is a spirit, a temperament, an attitude of the soul. It is a life without high callings, life devoid of lofty ideals. It is a gaze always horizontal and never vertical."—J. Henry Jowett

---

The Variety Reading Plan continues with 1 THESSALONIANS

Lamentations

INTRODUCTION

Five somber "dirge" or "funeral" poems express grief over the loss of the Jewish homeland and the destruction of Jerusalem. These poems, meditating on the tragedy and its causes, reflect a long literary tradition in the Middle East. They were clearly written by an eyewitness to Jerusalem's fall. Tradition identifies Jeremiah as the author.

The number of verses in each poem is divisible by 22 because these are acrostic poems; each verse or set of verses begins with a different letter of the 22-consonant Hebrew alphabet.

OUTLINE OF CONTENTS

READING GUIDE (1 Day)

If hurried, you may read only the "core passage" in your Bible and the Devotional in this Commentary.

Reading	*Chapters*	*Core passage*
159	1–5	3

Lamentations

JUNE 8 *Reading 159*
CRIES OF DESPAIR
Lamentations 1–5

> *"See, O LORD, how distressed I am! I am in torment within, and in my heart I am disturbed, for I have been most rebellious" (Lam. 1:20).*

A sense of despair over some great loss is no stranger to any human being. Yet reflection on our tragedies can offer us important insights, and do much to restore hope.

Overview

The author lamented the lost splendor of Jerusalem (1:1-22) and the pitiless destruction of its inhabitants (2:1-22). Understanding this to be a consequence of sin, the author dared hope in God (3:1-66). The punishment, though great, will end (4:1-22), and a humbled Judah may be restored (5:1-22).

Understanding the Text

"Like a widow is she" Lam. 1:1-11. This first poem personifies Jerusalem. The city is compared to a widow who has lost touch with all her children. She is not only alone but is ignored by old friends, and ridiculed by heartless neighbors. All she has is memories of better days. But for her, remembering is bitter. The memories only drive home her loneliness and cause her to weep bitter tears.

What a penetrating insight! Like Jerusalem, many human beings live selfish, sinful lives. Wealth or beauty or power makes them popular for a time. But, when these are lost, such people find themselves deserted and alone. How much better the humble, loving individual, who quietly serves God and others, and when widowed is surrounded by a loving family and caring friends.

"My sins have been bound into a yoke" Lam. 1:12-22. Have you ever noticed how so many people think of "freedom" as release from moral restraint, or the right to do whatever wrong thing they want? Jeremiah pointed out that Judah's insistence on following pagan gods and sinful passions was not freedom, but captivity! Each sin was like another branch, being tightly woven and bound together in the shape of a yoke that would rest on Judah's neck and become an unbearable weight.

Seeing Jerusalem's and Judah's suffering, the observer was to trace its cause to rebellion against the commands of her righteous God. If we take this message to heart, we will never make Judah's mistake and suppose that sin, which binds us for judgment, offers a way to be free.

Knowing that sin is the cause of our suffering may cause a "torment within" that matches all outward afflictions (v. 20). Yet acknowledging sin is a first, and necessary, step toward restoration.

"The Lord is like an enemy" Lam. 2:1-22. The author is right in adding "like" to his description. God had done to Jerusalem and Judah what an enemy might do.

God destroyed Judah's strongholds, and multiplied her mourning (v. 5). He destroyed her temple (vv. 6-7). He exiled her king and people (v. 9). And these acts caused utter anguish. Speaking as an eyewitness, the author said, "My eyes fail from weeping, I am in torment within, my heart is poured out on the ground because my people are destroyed, because children and infants faint in the streets of the city" (v. 11). In all of this the Lord had "done what He planned" and "fulfilled His word" (v. 17). He "summoned against me terrors on every side. In the day of the LORD's anger no one escaped or survived" (v. 22).

What a challenge for faith when God acts "like an enemy." It is then we must remember that despite whatever tragedy strikes us, God is not our enemy.

In the case of Judah, the cause of God's action can be traced back to persistent sin. In our times of suffering, we may not find such a clear-cut reason. Yet, even—and especially—if we are uncertain about the cause of our suffering, we can hold tight to the truth this phrase in Lamentations affirms. God may act like an enemy, but our enemy He is not!

"Why should any living man complain when punished for his sins?" Lam. 3:34-66 The author of Lamentations was a realist. He didn't try to explain away suffering, muttering that of course God wouldn't do anything as terrible as bring on the destruction that shattered Judah and Jerusalem. Too many today try to "protect" God by denying Him the power. "God was just as sad and surprised about what happened as you are," they say, in a futile attempt to comfort. Not the author of Lamentations. He simply, and with firm conviction, said, "The Lord has decreed it."

He said something else too. If tragedy is indeed punishment for known sins, then on what basis can a person complain? God is a moral judge: He ought then to punish sins!

If tragedy should strike, it's wise for us to acknowledge God's sovereign control of events, and then look first to ourselves. If we are aware of serious sin in our lives, then we can follow the prescription found in verses 40-42:

> Let us examine our ways and test
> them, and let us return to the LORD.
> Let us lift up our hearts and our hands
> to God in heaven, and say:
> "We have sinned and rebelled
> and You have not forgiven."

If unconfessed and unrepented sin was the cause of our suffering, we can expect God to hear this prayer. But even if sin was not the cause, we can remain confident that God will respond to us as He did to the author of Lamentations in verses 55-57:

> I called on Your name, O LORD,
> from the depths of the pit.
> You heard my plea: "Do not close Your
> ears to my cry for relief."
> You came near when I called You,
> and You said, "Do not fear."

"Your punishment will end" Lam. 4:1-22. We cannot really imagine the horrors of the siege of Jerusalem, graphically described here in verses such as 9-11. Yet the portrait is not intended to solicit sympathy. Instead the picture of suffering drives home the immensity of the sin which caused God to crush His own, dearly loved people. Any horror we feel should be horror of sin, and the source of our relief is the conviction that, for God's people, even sin-caused sufferings will end.

▶DEVOTIONAL
The Man Who Has Seen Affliction (Lam. 3)

It's not very impressive when a person who has known nothing but blessing tries to comfort a sufferer. How can the rich understand poverty? How can the child whose parents loved him understand the abused? How can the woman with a husband and children understand the widow's loss, or the divorcee's pain? It's far more meaningful when we hear words of comfort from a person we can identify with: from a fellow sufferer.

This is why the author's words in Lamentations 3 are so powerful. He immediately identified himself as "the man who has seen affliction." Here was someone who spoke about suffering from firsthand experience. To make sure we know he understood, he even went on to show how extreme his suffering had been. Then, when we realize that here is an authority, a person who can fully identify with us, he said, "Yet this I call to mind and therefore I have hope: because of the LORD's great love we are not consumed" (vv. 21-22).

The author of Lamentations would understand whatever suffering you or I are called to experience. And after listening to our complaint, he would speak bluntly to us, and say that God's "compassions never fail." He would remind us, "They are new every morning," and would invite us to praise the Lord, telling God, "great is Your faithfulness."

The author, as a "man who has seen affliction," would give us one more piece of advice. He would tell us to say to ourselves, as he did when the pain was greatest, "The LORD is my portion; therefore I will wait for Him."

As we wait in faith, we will be sustained by the conviction that sustained Jeremiah. We too know, despite everything, that "the Lord is good to those whose hope is in Him, to the one who seeks Him; it is good to wait quietly for the salvation of the LORD" (vv. 25-26).

Personal Application

Suffering saints through the ages counsel us to wait quietly for the salvation of the Lord.

Quotable

"When trouble, restless fears, anxious fretfulness, strive to overpower the soul, our safety is in saying, 'My God, I believe in Thy perfect goodness and wisdom and mercy. What Thou doest I cannot now understand; but I shall one day see it all plainly. Meanwhile I accept Thy will, whatever it may be, unquestioning, without reserve.' There would be no restless disturbance, no sense of utter discomfort and discomposure in our souls, if we were quite free from any—it may be almost unconscious—opposition to God's will. But we do struggle against it, we do resist; and so long as that resistance endures we cannot be at peace. Peace, and even joy, are quite compatible with a great deal of pain—even mental pain—but never with a condition of antagonism or resistance."—H.L. Sidney Lear

The Variety Reading Plan continues with 1 CHRONICLES

Ezekiel

INTRODUCTION

The Prophet Ezekiel ministered to the exiles in Babylon. His carefully dated prophecies fall between 593 B.C. and 585 B.C. In poetry and in prose rich in allegory, parable, proverb, and prophetic vision, Ezekiel echoed Jeremiah's call for submission to Babylon. Serving as a watchman, called to give warning of impending danger, the prophet uttered a series of dark predictions concerning Jerusalem's sin and fall. These ceased when that city fell in 586 B.C., and were replaced by promises of hope for the future. In the first half of the book the theme of Ezekiel's messages is seen in his review of the moral and religious history of Israel; in the second the theme of hope is expressed in visions of Israel's restoration and future worship.

Three additional themes with particular relevance to today are also woven throughout Ezekiel. These themes are the nature of God, the purpose of divine judgment, and each individual's personal responsibility for his or her own actions.

OUTLINE OF CONTENTS

READING GUIDE (9 Days)

If hurried, you may read only the "core passage" in your Bible and the Devotional in each chapter of this Commentary.

Reading	*Chapters*	*Core passage*
160	1–3	3
161	4–7	4
162	8–11	10–11
163	12–19	18
164	20–24	20
165	25–32	28:11-19
166	33–36	36
167	37–39	39
168	40–48	43–44

Ezekiel

JUNE 9 *Reading 160*
EZEKIEL'S CALL
Ezekiel 1–3

> *"You must speak My words to them, whether they listen or fail to listen, for they are rebellious. But you, son of man, listen to what I say to you. Do not rebel like that rebellious house; open your mouth and eat what I give you" (Ezek. 2:7-8).*

Ezekiel's call reminds us that any person who realizes who God is, is obligated by that knowledge to communicate His Word—whether others choose to listen or not.

Background
Ezekiel was a member of a priestly family deported to Babylon with the captives taken there in 597 B.C. He was 30 (1:1), the age when qualified descendants of Aaron were permitted to take their place as ministering priests, when God appeared to him in a vision and called him to serve as a prophet. The year was 593 B.C., and until the destruction of Jerusalem in 586 B.C. Ezekiel emphasized Judah's sin, warning of the coming destruction of the Holy City and its temple.

This message was as unpopular in Babylon as Jeremiah's words were back in Judah. The exiles hoped desperately for a return to their homeland; a hope that was encouraged by false prophets. Yet until the people of Judah acknowledged the full extent of their sin, and gave up all hope of divine reprieve, no spiritual healing or restoration could begin. In Judah, Jeremiah called on the nation to repent. In Babylon, Ezekiel emphasized the importance of individual repentance and recommitment. Like Jeremiah, Ezekiel would face resistance, and know discouragement. There was little glory in being a prophet whose words brought about little change. Yet like Jeremiah, Ezekiel remained faithful to God. And the words he spoke so long ago have great meaning for you and me today. May we, unlike the exiles among whom Ezekiel lived, hear—and respond.

Overview
Ezekiel saw the glory of God in a vision (1:1-28), and was told to speak God's words to His rebellious people (2:1-9). The reluctant Ezekiel ate a scroll containing God's words, and was again warned that the Israelites would not listen (3:1-15). Yet Ezekiel was to be a watchman, giving warning, and had to speak when God gave him a message to convey (vv. 16-27).

Understanding the Text
"The likeness of the glory of the LORD" Ezek. 1:1-28. Ezekiel's vision has fascinated biblical scholars. It was not unusual for prophets to have visions (cf. Isa. 6). But the content of this vision is unique, and the Hebrew describing it difficult to translate.

Briefly, Ezekiel described a great wheeled crystalline platform, resting on four upright living creatures. Each creature had four faces, representing God's creative work in human, wild and domestic animal, and bird kingdoms. The whole structure moved nimbly but noisily in any direction. Despite the wonder these details may create, the focus of the vision is One seated on a throne resting atop the crystalline platform (called an "expanse" in the NIV). This Person, clearly God, appeared humanoid, but His figure burned so brightly that Ezekiel could see no other details. Even the light surrounding Him, encompassed by rainbow-like radiance, was too overwhelming for Ezekiel to bear, and he fell facedown before the Lord.

Artists have toyed with representations of this vision. Scholars have struggled with the Hebrew, and argued alternate translations. Yet Ezekiel moved quickly in his description from the vehicle to its Rider. As awe-inspiring as his details of wheels within wheels and strange living creatures may be, the focus of Ezekiel's vision is God Himself. It is Ezekiel's glimpse of God—too glorious to be scrutinized or described—that caused the prophet to fall to the ground in the traditional posture of worship and praise.

There are times when our attention is drawn to spectacular settings—grand cathedrals, stained glass, crowds of thousands singing, beautifully staged TV shows—all may perhaps enhance our worship. But at times they may distract our attention from the Lord. The challenge you and I face is to look above these "platforms" for worship, and to view the intrinsic glory of the One they are intended to honor. For our worship to be meaningful, we need to see the Lord and, in awe of His splendor and love, fall down with Ezekiel before Him.

"Son of man, stand up on your feet, and I will speak to you" Ezek. 2:1-2. What a stunning verse! "Son of man" here simply means "human being." In Hebrew "son of" has the meaning, "sharing the nature of." Here the text emphasizes the fact that Ezekiel, a mere man, is accepted by God!

Not only was Ezekiel addressed, but he was told to "stand up." In the ancient East a person prostrated himself before even a human ruler or overlord. To be told to stand in such a person's presence was a mark of acceptance and honor. Here God is the One who told Ezekiel, "Stand up on your feet."

Finally, the apparition told Ezekiel, "I will speak to you." God not only pays attention to a mere man, and lifts him up, but communicates as well!

In this one verse we sense the wonder of God's love for all mankind. God comes to us, for we cannot find or approach Him. He calls to us, despite the fact that we corrupt and puny beings run from Him. He lifts us up, though we should only grovel at His feet. And He speaks to us, communicating His will, that we might participate in bringing righteousness to His universe.

It's good for us to fall down with Ezekiel before the holy God. But it is good too to remember that this God invites us to stand and, even though we are merely human beings, to serve Him as messengers to the rest of mankind.

"Do not be afraid of what they say or terrified by them" Ezek. 2:3-8. Even in biblical times words seemed fearful. It's not as though Ezekiel were in danger of execution. Or of being put in prison. What Ezekiel had to face was simply harsh and hostile words. Angry words, yes. Ridiculing words, yes. But just words.

It's like this in our day. Fear of witnessing to others isn't quite rational when we stop to think about it. We're not likely to be beaten for speaking about Jesus. We're not likely to be fired from our jobs or lose our homes or be imprisoned. The worst that's likely to happen is that someone may hurl a few hostile words at us, or talk about us behind our backs. And yet so many Christians are literally afraid to speak out.

God didn't ridicule Ezekiel's fears, and He doesn't ridicule ours. He simply told the prophet, whose society was far more hardened than our own, "Do not be afraid of what they say or be terrified by them." And then God reminded Ezekiel of the obligation which was his because of his own personal experience of the Lord: "You must speak My words."

How people respond to our sharing of the Gospel is irrelevant. God's command to speak is not.

"Eat this scroll" Ezek. 3:1-3. Eating the scroll symbolized digesting and applying the words of God. Only when we have taken God's words to heart can we share them with others.

"You are not being sent to a people of obscure speech and difficult language, but to the house of Israel" Ezek. 3:4-15. Ezekiel is the model of an unheralded missionary: a man who evangelizes in his own country. Yes, there's a need for foreign missionaries. But most Christians are called to minister

to people in their own society, whose language and customs are familiar.

The eager 20-year-old applying to the mission board for overseas service was asked how many people he had witnessed to during the preceding week. His answer was, "Well, none." How about the preceding month? Six months? Again, the answer was, "No one." The chairman of the interviewing board then asked him, "Young man, what makes you think being overseas will make you into a missionary, when you do no missionary work at home?"

▶ DEVOTIONAL
Watchman, Watchman
(Ezek. 3)

Some job descriptions are complicated, and others are relatively simple. To help Ezekiel understand the nature of his ministry, God gave him a title belonging to a person whose responsibilities were absolutely clear-cut. Ezekiel was to serve as a "watchman."

This post, though one with heavy responsibilities, required no special skills or training. In biblical times the watchman simply stood on the city walls and, if any danger approached, raised the alarm to warn the city's citizens. They then were responsible to rally to the city's defense.

Oh, I suppose a loud voice might be necessary. And the ability to stay awake nights. But beyond that, there wasn't much to the watchman's job at all.

How was Ezekiel to be like a watchman? Well, he was to warn the people of Judah of impending doom: to shout about the danger that approached. Then it was up to those who heard his cries to heed and deal with the danger. As God told Ezekiel, "If you do warn the wicked man and he does not turn from his wickedness or from his evil ways, he will die for his sin" (v. 19). No one could blame the watchman if the citizens, warned about the danger, plugged their ears, rolled over, and went back to sleep!

But the watchman, while his job was easy, carried a heavy responsibility. What if danger approached, and the watchman didn't cry out? In biblical times that watchman rightly forfeited his life!

And so the Lord told Ezekiel, if "you do not warn him or speak out to dissuade him from his evil ways in order to save his life, that wicked man will die for his sin, and I will hold you accountable for his blood" (v. 18).

Today it's helpful if we think of each Christian's "job description" in the same way. It takes no special qualification to serve our neighbors as a watchman. No seminary degree is required. Not even mastery of Scripture, or great spiritual depth. All that's called for is awareness that friends without Christ are in terrible peril—and a voice to lift to give them warning.

We can't guarantee that any individual will respond. But if we remain silent, we carry some responsibility for that other's fate.

Personal Application

A word of warning to another clears us of guilt, and may lead him or her to eternal life.

Quotable

"Jesus Christ didn't commit the Gospel to an advertising agency; He commissioned disciples. And He didn't command them to put up signs and pass out tracts; He said that they would be His witnesses."—Joe Bayly

JUNE 10 *Reading 161*
SWORD, FAMINE, PLAGUE
Ezekiel 4–7

> *"Because of all your detestable idols, I will do to you what I have never done before and will never do again" (Ezek. 5:9).*

There are times when the most severe of judgments is absolutely necessary. It was so in Ezekiel's day. As God's watchman, the prophet began his ministry by uttering dark and terrible words.

Background

It was not unknown for prophets to act out their messages. In Jerusalem, Jeremiah placed a yoke on his shoulders when calling for submission to Babylon. In Babylon, Ezekiel communicated a certainty of divine judgment by making the street in front of his house a stage, and performing strange acts there. How quickly the gossip would have spread, and members of the captive community would have come by to see and puzzle over the peculiar acts of their eccentric prophet. And, when everyone was talking and wondering what it all meant, Ezekiel would explain in blunt and powerful words. The drama drew the audience. The explanation must have aroused the utmost horror, as well as denial and disbelief.

Overview

Ezekiel publicly acted out the siege of Jerusalem (4:1-17) and shaved his head and beard to symbolize the city's fate (5:1-17). He prophesied against the mountains of

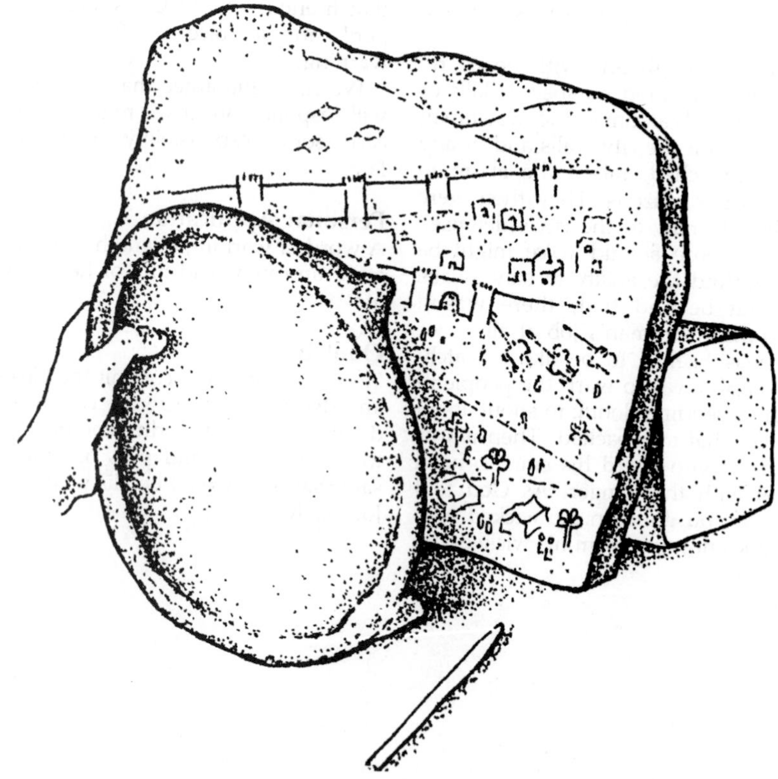

For over a year Ezekiel lay before a rough model of Jerusalem under siege, portraying the final Babylonian attack on the Holy City. It was unnecessary for Ezekiel to explain what his actions meant: the terrible meaning was plain to every observer.

Israel where pagan worship services were performed (6:1-14), and then announced plainly that judgment day was here: doom had burst forth (7:1-27).

Understanding the Text

"This will be a sign to the house of Israel" Ezek. 4:1-8. For some 400 days Ezekiel lay bound, first on one side and then the other before a model of Jerusalem under siege. Each of the 400 days represented a year during which Israel and Judah were to "bear their sin." If we calculate ahead from the dating Ezekiel uses, the first year of Jehoiachin's exile, the 400 years ended in 167 B.C.—the initial year of the Maccabean revolt, which won Judah limited independence from foreign powers.

"I will cut off the supply of food" Ezek. 4:9-17. Bread was commonly made of barley or wheat. Bread made by scraping together "wheat and barley, beans and lentils, millet and spelt" was "bread of affliction." That is, it was eaten only when a people were starving, mixing every scrap of food they could find. During the months Ezekiel was to act out the siege, he was allowed only eight ounces of this bread a day! This tiny ration, and Ezekiel's own deteriorating condition, spoke powerfully of famine and suffering, to be experienced as Jerusalem fell. The drama Ezekiel performed reminds us that when God judges a society even those who speak up against its sins suffer with the rest. There is no safe place anyone can hide when judgment comes. How much better to speak out before it is too late, and turn our own nation back toward righteousness.

"Shave your head and your beard" Ezek. 5:1-17. It was considered shameful in Old Testament times for a man to shave either head or beard. Ezekiel was told to bear the ridicule and reproach. His hair was divided into thirds, and disposed of in ways that illustrated the fate God intended for Jerusalem's inhabitants (vv. 11-12).

Again we sense the horror of sin, not so much by the listing of evils, but by descriptions of the punishments Judah would experience. As the desperate people of Jerusalem turned to cannibalism, eating even members of their own families, we sense a revulsion that captures something of God's feelings about the acts of sin which led to these terrible consequences.

If you and I fail to be horrified at sin itself, and draw back, God will horrify us with the punishment our sins bring!

"The mountains and hills" Ezek. 6:1-14. The mountains and hills are singled out in this prophecy because pagan worship sites were located in "high places." These locations would be the scene of slaughter, and the worship centers constructed there would be demolished.

The prophecy is not at all peculiar, in view of the fact that locations have always had symbolic significance to human beings. In our own nation we need only think of Bunker Hill, Valley Forge, and Gettysburg, to realize what great meaning is often attached to places. A place takes on an aura linked to the events that took place there.

This is something to consider when we think about our own homes. The mountains of Judah were associated with paganism and immorality. Do we guard our activities at home—and control our TV sets—so that in the minds of family members the place we live is associated forever with love, caring, hospitality, ministry, and righteousness?

"Violence has grown into a rod to punish wickedness" Ezek. 7:1-27. The symbolic messages acted out by Ezekiel now give way to an announcement in plain and terrible words. God was about to pour His wrath out on Judah. There would be no escape, for the sword would ravage outside, while plague and starvation stalked their victims within the Holy City. The warning Ezekiel gave is as valid for today as it was nearly 600 years before the birth of Christ. God will certainly "judge you according to your conduct and repay you for all your detestable practices" (v. 8).

▶ DEVOTIONAL
Symbolic Acts (Ezek. 4)

How in the world do we get through to people?

It's a question that's plagued prophets and preachers as well as ordinary believers from the beginning. Adam couldn't reach Cain—and Cain killed his brother Abel. Moses couldn't turn the Exodus generation, and they perished in the desert for their persistent disobedience. Isaiah and Micah and Jeremiah all called on the people of Judah to repent and change their ways. But their exhortations were ignored, and God's people skipped merrily along sin's highway—only to die by sword and famine and plague.

How *do* we get through? All too often words just aren't enough.

That's why Ezekiel acted out God's message to the exiles in Babylon. They wouldn't listen to words? Well, they did come to gawk at the gaunt prophet, lying bound beside toy Jerusalem. And to watch him wordlessly grind grains and cook his tiny daily portion of rough bread.

They may not have listened. They may not have repented. But at least Ezekiel got their attention. At last they heard what the earlier prophets had been shouting stridently for centuries.

That's why recently my wife and I signed a pledge card, and sent it to the offices of two large companies identified by an impressive coalition of Christian groups as sponsors of TV shows relying on excessive portrayals of sex and violence. That pledge card says that for the next year, we'll buy no more of their products. And, hopefully, millions of other Christians will sign, and carry out, that same pledge.

Oh, the boycott probably won't win any converts. It may not even bring about any restraint in TV-land. But it is a symbolic act; an act that sends a message a little louder than words. At the very least this act, multiplied by millions, may get someone's attention.

It may say what desperately needs to be said. That the moral boundaries of our society have been shrinking. That sins once publicly decried are now portrayed as normal behavior. And that unless Christians take a stand, and unless our voice is heard, God will surely act against our country too, to "judge you according to your conduct and repay you for all your detestable practices."

Personal Application

If Christians do not take a public stand for righteousness, who will?

Quotable

"We all like the twilight in spiritual and moral matters, not the intensity of black and white, not the clear lines of demarcation—saved and unsaved. We prefer things to be hazy, winsome, and indefinite, without the clear light. When the light does come difficulty is experienced, for when a man awakens he sees a great many things. We may feel complacent with a background of drab, but to be brought up against the white background of Jesus Christ is an immensely uncomfortable thing."—Oswald Chambers

JUNE 11 *Reading 162*
THE EMPTIED TEMPLE
Ezekiel 8–11

"Then the glory of the LORD departed from over the threshold of the temple and stopped above the cherubim" (Ezek. 10:18).

No church building, however spectacular, has any value at all unless God's presence is there. Churches, like Judah's temple, are vacant unless the Lord is honored, and His presence felt there.

Definition of Key Terms

The glory. The Hebrew word translated "glory" means "heavy" or "weighty." Figuratively it suggests impressiveness: the social weight of a rich man, or the symbols of a ruler's majesty, are both identified as "glory."

When the Old Testament speaks of the "glory of God" the term is typically linked with powerful images. God is seen in blazing splendor. Raw power and burning holiness are impressed on those permitted to glimpse His revelations of His essential nature.

But the "glory of God" is most of all associated with God's intrusions into our world of space and time. The fabric of the universe is torn, and for a moment God's elemental power is seen—as lightning flashing at Sinai, in the cloudy-fiery pillar that guided Israel in the wilderness, as an unknown brilliance settling down on the tabernacle as God took up unique residence among His Old Testament people (cf. Ex. 29:43). It is this, the unique presence of God which originally filled Solomon's temple and then located itself in the holy of holies, the temple's inner room (2 Chron. 7:1-3), that Ezekiel describes in these chapters.

There is a tragic significance in Ezekiel's vision of the glory of God leaving the temple. Those who had looked to that consecrated building for protection would from now on depend on what was merely an empty shell. With the glory of God withdrawn, the temple was nothing more than gilded stone, stripped of meaning and power.

Overview

Ezekiel saw a vision of idolatry in the Jerusalem temple itself (8:1-18). In the vision he witnessed the death of the idolaters (9:1-11) and the gradual withdrawal of God's glory from the temple (10:1-22). The people inhabiting Jerusalem would be punished (11:1-15), yet in the future the exiles' hearts would be changed, and they would be restored to their land (vv. 16-25).

Understanding the Text

"The elders of Judah were sitting before me" Ezek. 8:1-4. The vision reported in these chapters was given just 14 months after Ezekiel's call. In that time he had been recognized as a prophet, so that the elders of the exiled Jewish community came to consult with him. There is no indication they welcomed his words, or that they responded. But they knew that a prophet was among them.

As a new convert in the Navy, I began to talk to other sailors about the Lord. One day our commanding officer was holding a court martial, but couldn't find a Bible to swear in witnesses. Immediately one of the officers said, "Go see Richards. He'll have a Bible at his desk."

The earnest Christian, like Ezekiel, may not win converts immediately. But how quickly others realize that God has placed a spokesman among them!

"Do you see what they are doing?" Ezek. 8:5-18 While the elders of Judah were present Ezekiel was transported to Jerusalem in a vision, where he observed worship in the temple. The things he witnessed demonstrated the complete religious corruption of the people, and served as the basis of God's announcement that "I will deal with them in anger; I will not look on them with pity or spare them" (v. 18).

An idol and altar to a pagan deity had been erected within the temple court at the north gate (vv. 5-6). This gate led to the royal palace, and so suggests the active participation of the king in pagan rites.

Within one of the temple storerooms some 70 of Judah's elders were gathered to worship images of animals (vv. 7-13). This was not an official group, like the Sanhedrin. Yet it's very size, and the fact that it was composed of acknowledged leaders who also practiced idolatry in the privacy of their homes (v. 12), suggests how pervasive the apostasy in Judah had become.

Ezekiel also saw women "mourning for Tammuz" (vv. 14-15). Tammuz was a Summerian agricultural deity, who "died" with winter and "came alive" again each spring, and was the forerunner of a host of pagan nature gods. Both mourning and fertility rituals were associated with the worship of Tammuz.

Finally Ezekiel was shown 25 men in the temple's inner court worshiping the sun (vv. 16-18). What is so significant about this? First, their backs were to the temple. It was the practice in Judaism to pray toward the temple, the site of the Divine Presence. Second, being in the inner court marks these men off as priests and Levites, who alone would have had access to its confines! Not just the royal house, not just the elders, not just the women, but the very religious leaders of Judah were corrupt, practicing idolatry in Judah's only and most holy shrine.

Yet what strikes us most as we read the chapter is that as Ezekiel was carried toward the Holy City and its temple, he noted that "the glory of the God of Israel" was still there! (v. 4) Despite every provocation, God had not yet abandoned His people.

God is so gracious to us. He continues to exercise kindness long after we deserve punishment. Yet even as gracious a God as ours cannot be impudently treated with contempt forever. God will judge when human actions force Him to deal with our sins.

"Those who grieve and lament" Ezek. 9:1-11. Ezekiel saw a mark placed on all in Jerusalem who had a heart for God, and grieved over the spiritual condition in Judah. In his vision Ezekiel saw the rest of the population slaughtered. The bloodshed was so great that Ezekiel despaired of any surviving.

Two thoughts are of note here. First, the mark placed on true believers reminds us that God is able to care for His own even when there is devastation all around. Second, God told the destroying angels, "Begin at My sanctuary" (v. 6). Christianity is not to be used as a cloak for sin. Those who misuse religion for personal gain or merit will receive greater condemnation.

"The radiance of the glory of the LORD" Ezek. 10:1-22. In his vision Ezekiel saw the visible glory of the Lord, which rested as in his earlier vision on a vehicle propelled by guardian angels, here identified as cherubim. As Ezekiel watched, the glory of God rose from the temple and moved beyond its threshold, preparing to leave the city itself (cf. 11:23). As it departed, burning coals from its red-hot center were scattered over Jerusalem.

Hot coals, representing divine judgment, are frequently found in apocalyptic passages of Scripture that describe history's end (see Rev. 8–9). Utter devastation is a biblical mark of God's judgment, a reminder that a day of recompense awaits all who refuse to heed or to worship the Lord.

"Leaders of the people" Ezek. 11:1-12. The 25 men described in this chapter represent the aristocracy, which served as Judah's leaders. Comparison with Jeremiah 37 shows that even King Zedekiah lacked the power to overrule their political decisions.

While their comment in Ezekiel 11:3 is obscure, it's best to understand it as a consensus for war rather than peace, and an arrogant affirmation that they themselves are the worthy members of the nation (the "meat") and the exiles merely offal. They say this despite the fact that Jeremiah had faithfully spoken God's word in Jerusalem and counseled surrender to Babylon rather than resistance!

Through Ezekiel God announced that those Jews the leaders had wickedly slain were the true worthy members of the nation (v. 7). In Judah of that day, the "only good Jew was a dead Jew!" But, God told Ezekiel that since the leaders liked to think of themselves as Judah's "flesh," He would humor them. He would make Jerusalem a pot, and as the fires of judgment burned around her, they—the flesh within the caldron of judgment—could seethe in anguish!

A Robert Burns poem describes a woman sitting proudly in church, head held high, so all can see her new bonnet. Burns wryly observes that what the congregation noted was a louse, clinging to one of its bright ribbons. "O that God the gift would ge [give] us," the poem concludes, "to see ourselves as others see us."

Burns' poem stops just short of the point made by Ezekiel. The ultimate gift is to see ourselves as God sees us! Stripped of pretense, stripped of self-deceit and shared delusions, we, like the people of Jerusalem, need to realize the true nature of what we are, and what we do.

Like the leaders of Judah, some people today tell each other, "We are the flesh." They insist on protection for alternate lifestyles in the name of tolerance; they wrap media immorality in the mantle of free speech; and they accuse those calling for public standards of decency of censorship. And then arrogantly they tell one another, "We are the flesh."

What they fail to do is to see themselves as God sees them. And what they fail to realize is that they too will be placed in the caldron of divine judgment.

"As I was prophesying, Pelatiah . . . died" Ezek. 11:13. Ezekiel apparently described his visions out loud as he experienced them. As he spoke in Babylon Pelatiah, in Jerusalem, fell dead. The event unnerved Ezekiel, and he cried out, asking if the

remnant of Judah would be completely destroyed.

The death of Pelatiah served another purpose besides drawing out Ezekiel's anguished query. Later, when word arrived from Jerusalem that Pelatiah had died, the community in exile would realize it happened at the exact moment it was observed by the prophet. Ezekiel's message would thus be authenticated as a true vision from the Lord.

"I will . . . give them a heart of flesh" Ezek. 11:16-25. The heart of flesh is contrasted with a heart of stone. The one is responsive, the other unresponsive. The ultimate and only solution to Judah's problem was inner transformation. And God, whose supreme attribute is grace, would give the remnant of His people a new heart despite their centuries-old tradition of straying from His ways.

But all this lay in the distant future. Ezekiel was jolted back to his present by a final vision of the glory of God, going up from within the city, and hesitating above the mountains to the east, where the coming devastation of Jerusalem might be easily viewed.

▶ DEVOTIONAL
You Will Know
(Ezek. 10–11)

Devotionals are supposed to be warm and fuzzy. At least, I always thought so. There's supposed to be some positive bit of Scripture at the top, then a happy little story, followed by a one- or two-line prayer. We read them, feel good, and then can go on our way complacent because we've shared a little time with God and received our daily spiritual shot in the arm.

The trouble is, so much of Scripture just isn't warm and fuzzy. It doesn't even make us feel good, much less complacent. Look at these chapters of Ezekiel, for instance. Chapter 10 describes the glory of God, His vital presence, departing from the temple. And the people of Judah didn't even know! They went to the temple, worshiped at what was now just a heap of polished stones, and never realized that God wasn't around anymore.

Now, what kind of fodder is that for a devotional? Who wants to be warned to watch out for superficiality in religion? Who wants to be challenged to examine whether or not their own practices are merely going through motions that have no impact on their relationship with God at all?

The next chapter is even worse! Who wants to be told that what he or she thinks of himself, and what others think, is meaningless? Who wants to be reminded that what God thinks of him is all that counts? And who wants to be warned that, if her opinion is way off base, and she is unwilling to change, God's judgment will strip away all illusions and leave her crushed and exposed? Those words of threat and warning, "You will know [then] that I am the LORD," simply aren't the kind of words you expect to find in a devotional book!

No warm fuzzies in them! Only a certain gruesome chill.

Perhaps though it would be better if our devotionals featured fewer fuzzies and, like Scripture itself, called us to confront the truly critical issues of life. That's what these chapters of Ezekiel do. They confront us, and make demands. Is God real in your life? Is He really *there,* or are you fooling yourself going through empty rituals in great, empty rooms. And, are you honest with yourself? Do you see yourself as God does, and evaluate your acts by His standards of love and goodness?

Not many warm fuzzies in that, are there? Of course there might be something even more important. There might be a real meeting with God.

Personal Application

Use devotions to explore the whole counsel of God, and to expose yourself to God.

Quotable

"Some people want to see God with their eyes as they see a cow, and to love Him as they love their cow—for the milk and cheese and profit it brings them. This is how it is with people who love God for the sake of outward wealth or inward comfort. They do not rightly love God, when they love Him for their own advantage. Indeed, I tell you the truth, any object you have in your mind, however good, will be a barrier between you and the inmost Truth."—Meister Eckhart

JUNE 12 *Reading 163*
NO BASIS FOR HOPE
Ezekiel 12–19

" 'In your days, you rebellious house, I will fulfill whatever I say,' declares the Sovereign Lord" (Ezek. 12:25).

Maybe someday, but not now," and "Maybe somebody else, but not me," are still common reactions to warnings about the consequences of sin. This passage reminds moderns that such hopes are empty.

Background
The Jewish exiles expected an early return to their homeland. Optimism was fostered by false prophets, and encouraged by popular notions—that a God of love would never really judge; that the visions of Ezekiel would not come true; that if judgment did come it would strike a different generation.

In this section of Ezekiel the prophet dealt with the false hopes of God's still stubborn people. Through him the Lord announced that the judgments prophesied would strike the present generation. In an address on personal responsibility that is vitally relevant to us today, Ezekiel showed that individual choices affect individual destiny. It was too late for Judah as a nation, but the individual could still respond to God, and be safe.

Overview
Ezekiel acted out the imminent deportation of Jerusalem's population (12:1-20). Hope of delay was futile (vv. 21-28): the prophets who stimulated such hope lied (13:1-23), for purifying judgment (14:1-11) is inescapable (vv. 12-23). Two allegories show the justice of the coming judgment (15:1–16:63), while a third shows the futility of a military alliance against Babylon (17:1-24). Ezekiel then proclaimed that each person would live or die according to his own decision to obey or disobey God's word (18:1-32). The section concludes with a dirge poem for Judah's rulers (19:1-14).

Understanding the Text
"While they watch" Ezek. 12:1-16. Again Ezekiel acted out a prophecy. This time he played the role of an inhabitant of Jerusalem, packing his few belongings in the morning, and in the evening digging through the mud-brick wall of his house to crawl out with them and move to another location. In just this way the few survivors of Jerusalem's siege would crawl out of the ruined city on the way to Babylon.

But Ezekiel's actions had a more direct reference to the "prince among them." This is Zedekiah, called a prince because Judah's rightful king, Jehoiachin, was alive in Babylon. Zedekiah was to leave through a hole in the wall, his head covered (indicating a disguise), only to be snared by the Babylonians and brought to the land of the enemy, though "he will not see it."

Within a few short years, when the city of Jersualem fell, Zedekiah tried to make his escape. He fled toward the Jordan, but was caught by Nebuchadnezzar's forces. There his sons were slaughtered as he watched, and he was blinded. Zedekiah did go to the land of Babylon as a captive. But, in accord with Ezekiel's words, the eyeless king never saw the land of his exile.

The word of the Lord is sure. What God says is utterly trustworthy. How desperately the exiles needed to hear, and to believe. Even as today our generation needs to hear, and to believe, the words of Scripture.

"Tremble as you eat your food" Ezek. 12:17-20. Ezekiel was told to shudder as he ate and drank to portray the utter terror soon to be felt by the inhabitants of Jerusalem.

People who fail to fear the Word of the Lord will feel fear—when the things foretold in that Word come to pass.

"Every vision comes to nothing" Ezek. 12:21-28. Ezekiel now began to deal with the false hopes held by the captives in Babylon as well as by the Jews left in the homeland.

One basis for these rests on the observation that past warnings by God's prophets seem to have "come to nothing." Ezekiel did not bother to explain that judgment had been delayed by a gracious God, whose loving-kindness had been expressed in His long-suffering attitude toward an unrepentant people. Ezekiel simply said that the disasters foretold by the former prophets would be fulfilled "in your days."

This thought is reemphasized, for another popular saying is that prophetic visions of judgment are "for many years from now." It might be that God would do what He had said. But surely not now! Again God spoke through Ezekiel: "None of My words will be delayed any longer."

There's a carelessness here that is often reflected in the Christian church. When Christ taught His disciples about His return, He emphasized the importance of being ready (see esp. Matt. 25–26). The Lord might appear at any time, and so His servants are to actively go about His business, eager and excited at the prospect of His sudden return. It's to be this way for us: we're to be constantly aware that Jesus may come today—this morning, this afternoon!

Yet as the years pass, and we begin a career, marry, and plan for our children's college and for our retirement, the sense of imminence is somehow lost. Some, looking back over two millennium, dismiss the whole idea, saying "every vision comes to nothing." Others, more conservative, simply assume the return "is for many years from now." And so we settle down in this world, adopt its values, and lose sight of our calling as servants of a Master who may appear at any moment. A Master who expects to find His staff ready, actively involved in doing His business.

We do not know, as Ezekiel did, that this vision is for our generation. It may not be. I clearly remember my mother telling me, when I was a child of just five or six, that she expected the Lord to return in her lifetime. He did not. But I expect Him to return in mine.

And if He delays beyond the length of my years, not one thing will change. The vision of Jesus' return is still for each believer today. And the expectation that Christ might come at any moment remains one of the most purifying doctines in the Word of God.

"Foolish prophets who follow their own spirit" Ezek. 13:1-16. False prophets are a major theme addressed in Jeremiah and in Ezekiel. The emphasis reminds us to be very careful in our response to modern spiritual leaders. Ezekiel noted that such persons may be totally sincere: they "expect their words to be fulfilled!" He also observed that they tend to preach popular messages. People want to hear about peace? OK, the theme of today's sermon is peace, even though there is no peace (v. 10).

Sincerity without truth is as useless as a map of Kentucky when you're traveling through Texas. A good many people, totally sincere in what they believe, are on the highway to hell, and all too many totally sincere preachers are busy erecting signs along the roadway.

"They cover it with whitewash" Ezek. 13:10. What a powerful image. Build a flimsy wall, cover it with whitewash, and everything seems all right. But no matter how good it looks under all that trim, a flimsy wall remains flimsy.

The teachings of false prophets may look attractive. But however thick the coat of whitewash they are given, the teachings are still flimsy, and will be carried away in the torrent of God's judgment.

"I am against your magic charms" Ezek. 13:17-23. I suppose Shirley Maclaine is sincere in her "new age" writings and lectures. The crystal craze, the notion that there is power in pyramids, fascination with "channeling" and supposed contact with beings who lived long ago, all relate to the theme Ezekiel touched on here. Divination. Magic. Charms. Efforts to find and manipulate the supernatural while ignoring God.

Whatever the fad, Scripture has a simple message: God is "against the daughters of your people who prophesy out of their own imagination."

"They could save only themselves" Ezek. 14:12-23. Another argument raised by the exiles and by the population of Jerusalem against imminent judgment was rooted in Genesis 18. God heeded Abraham's prayer, and promised to spare Sodom if even five righteous men might be found in it. Surely God would not destroy a nation that must possess at least some godly men and women!

Ezekiel destroyed this notion—which by the way has remained popular in Judaism—by saying that even if several of sacred history's most righteous persons (Noah, Daniel, and Job) lived in Jerusalem, the city would perish even though they would be saved.

Similar thinking about our own country is just as erroneous. You've no doubt heard, or thought, something like . . . God will spare the United States because (a) We supply most of the world's missionaries, (b) We have the highest percent of churchgoers in the Western world, (c) We are a "Christian" nation, (d) Democracy is closer to the divine ideal than any other form of government, (e) Any other, similiar reason. Ezekiel suggested that such notions foster false hope. God deals with any nation as its deeds require. The righteousness of the few will in no way preserve the wicked.

"The wood of a vine" Ezek. 15:1-8. The Old Testament frequently portrays Israel and Judah as a vine (cf. Gen. 49:22; Ps. 80; Isa. 5:1-7; Hosea 10:1). The vine was prized for the fruit it bore, and so was an appropriate symbol of God's people as His prized possession.

But the vine was prized *only* for its fruit. The wood is stringy and twisted, and has no use in construction or value for fashioning furnishings. All a fruitless vine is good for is to be burned. Fruitless Judah, already charred by the flames of God's judgment, was totally worthless, and destined to be consumed.

"You prostitute, hear the word of the LORD" Ezek. 16:1-63. In an extended allegory the Lord compared His people to an unwanted girl-child, discarded at birth. God saved her life, nurtured her, and ultimately accepted her as His wife and showered her with presents. Then unfaithful Judah broke the covenant relationship by seeking out pagan gods to worship, and by turning to immorality. God would punish Judah for her spiritual adultery and prostitution, and for being "arrogant, overfed and unconcerned" with "the poor and needy." Yet when the time of punishment is past the Lord would again "establish My covenant with you" and make atonement for Judah's sins.

"The soul who sins . . . will die" Ezek. 18:1-32. In reading this chapter it's important to understand that "soul" is used in the common Hebrew sense of "person" or "individual." Also, death in this chapter is physical rather than spiritual. Ezekiel's message is that those who obey God will be spared in the coming devastation of Jerusalem, while God will use the Babylonian invasion to take the life of the wicked. Thus each individual's choices will determine his own fate. (See DEVOTIONAL.)

"His roar was heard no longer" Ezek. 19:1-14. The section ends with a dirge poem, a lament intended to express grief and sorrow. This poem is about the rightful kings of Judah, and particularly Jehoiachin, who was pulled into a cage with hooks and brought to Babylon. The Promised Land, once so fruitful, has become a desert, as shriveled as a vine torn from the earth and left, unrooted, on the burning sand.

Yes, judgment does come. It comes on individuals as well as nations. And when it does, even though judgment is deserved, we are free with Ezekiel to mourn over what was, and what might have been.

▶DEVOTIONAL
Who Done It?
(Ezek. 18)

A columnist recently made an acute observation about the gang of boys who raped and nearly killed a woman jogger in New York's Central Park. The columnist noted that already some psychiatrists had popped up, eager to explain away the attack, to call it an expression of frustration and anger by disadvantaged youths who had been forced by society to hate. What the columnist noted was that the boys involved, when asked "why?" at the time of their arrest, had just shrugged and said, "It was fun." No doubt, the columnist suggested wryly, by the time of the trial the teenagers would know enough to redefine their act, and blame society for victimizing them.

The argument that society is at fault when a person acts in a criminal way isn't new. Even back in Ezekiel's time, people were saying that if judgment came, it would be their father's fault, not theirs

(vv. 1-2). That's what "my teeth are crooked 'cause dad ate sour grapes" means. What happens to me, what I do, isn't my responsibility. My acts are determined by what others have done to me.

Ezekiel 18 confronts this still popular view, and flatly denies its validity. Yes, we may be influenced by others. But we remain responsible for our choices. What we choose to do is not determined by anyone else at all. When someone asks, "Who done it?" there's no use pointing the finger of responsibility at someone else, and crying, "It wasn't really me."

To drive home this point Ezekiel set up a number of cases. What about the good man who has a bad son? The dad's merits will not save the son from the consequences of his acts. What about the good son of an evil father? The dad's sins will not be held against the son. Each person is responsible for his own choices.

So the message is clear. Don't blame dear old Dad for what you do, even if Dad isn't such a dear. And don't blame society, even if society hasn't given you a fair shake. Most important, don't buy the notion that you haven't got a chance because of your past. You do have a chance. You can succeed. Because you can choose.

Personal Application

The freedom to choose is one of the many gifts that God has given to you.

Quotable

"The power of individual choice is the secret of human responsibility. I can choose which line I will go on, but I have no power to alter the destination of that line once I have taken it—yet I always have the power to get off one line on to the other."—Oswald Chambers

JUNE 13 *Reading 164*
DEFECTIVE LEADERSHIP
Ezekiel 20–24

"See how each of the princes of Israel who are in you uses his power to shed blood" (Ezek. 22:6).

Leaders carry heavy responsibility. They set the moral tone of a nation or community, and are accountable for the flaws and failures of the people they rule over.

Overview

Israel's history was one of rebellion (20:1-31), yet after punishment the nation would be restored (vv. 32-44). Ezekiel prophesied immediate judgment of fire (vv. 45-49) and sword (21:1-32), to descend on Jerusalem and her corrupt leaders (22:1-31). The people's sin was portrayed in a famous allegory (23:1-49), and even as the siege of Jerusalem began in faraway Judah, Ezekiel announced the event (24:1-15). When Ezekiel's wife died, he was told to "groan quietly," even as the people of Jerusalem would be struck dumb in their grief (vv. 16-27).

Understanding the Text

"Confront them with the detestable practices of their fathers" Ezek. 20:1-31. In July/August of 591 B.C. elders of the people came to "inquire of the LORD." The phrase means to consult the prophet about the outcome of plans they were considering.

God would not even listen to them, but told Ezekiel to lay out clearly the charges against them. So Ezekiel demonstrated from history that the people of Israel had always been rebellious. And charged that the present generation defiled itself in the same way "to this day" (v. 31).

The point of the passage was clear. It was time to repent, not to make plans! The elders of Judah formed committees and set up contingency plans, when what they should have been doing was calling the people of Judah to abandon idolatry and return to God.

You and I too must put first things first. It's fine to make careful plans for the future. But man's first priority is his personal relationship with the Lord. If that relationship is wrong, whatever plans we may make are irrelevant. It is futile to ask God for guidance, or pray about plans we're struggling to make, if serious sin has interrupted our fellowship with God.

At such times repentance is a first priority.

This was one of the most serious flaws in Judah's leaders. They seemed totally unaware of their own and of their people's spiritual condition. Insensitive leaders, out of touch with God, can only lead God's people to disaster.

"Afterward you will surely listen" Ezek. 20:32-49. God is as determined to pursue us as we ever are to escape Him! Judah would experience judgment. But there was no way that God would let His people stray permanently into idolatry and sin. (See DEVOTIONAL.)

"I will draw My sword from its scabbard" Ezek. 21:1-17. The Old Testament frequently pictures enemy nations as a rod of discipline. Here Babylon was pictured as a "sword." In Hebrew the word for sword indicates a "destroying instrument." Thus Ezekiel cried:

> A sword, a sword,
> sharpened and polished—
> sharpened for the slaughter,
> polished, and flashing like lightning
> (v. 9).

Judah had "despised the rod" of lighter punishments. Now she must bear the greater punishment inflicted by God's sword.

We see the same peculiar trait in some children. One child will respond to a stern glance or slight slap. Another will grimly endure a severe spanking, refusing to break or to give in. Stubborn Judah was like the strong-willed child, determined to have its own way despite correction. As a result, an anguished God must increase the intensity of the punishment. Judah must be taught to respond.

"Mark out two roads for the sword of the king of Babylon to take" Ezek. 21:18-32. Ezekiel was told to draw a map on the ground, marking clearly the route from Babylon to Syria-Palestine. There, above Damascus, the road forks, with one route leading to Judah, and the other along the highlands across the Jordan to the land of the Ammonites. Ezekiel was told that the king of Babylon, reaching that fork in the road, would call on his wise men to divine for a sign showing him which people to war on. God would see to it that the omens directed him to Judah!

The point Ezekiel made here was that the Babylonians did not have to invade Judah. God intervened to cause Nebuchadnezzar to select the Jews as his current victims.

But why? The spotlight is on Judah's leadership. The prince of Judah is "profane and wicked" (v. 25). In the coming judgment this exalted person will be stripped of the symbols of royalty, and they will not be restored "until He comes to whom it rightfully belongs" (v. 27).

"Each of the princes of Israel who are in you uses his power to shed blood" Ezek. 22:1-31. Again we see a recurring theme. Leaders are to serve God's flock, not fleece it! Those who use power to treat "father and mother with contempt" and to oppress the alien and mistreat the fatherless are users, not servants. The sins of the people of Jerusalem are listed (vv. 9-12), and rather than stand against such behavior the leaders conspire to profit from the situation (vv. 23-29). It is no wonder that God "will pour out My wrath on them and consume them with My fiery anger, bringing down on their own heads all they have done" (v. 31).

Any person who accepts the role of a spiritual leader takes on dreadful responsibility. He or she must purge himself of every selfish motive, and stand before the Lord "in the gap [of the wall] on behalf of the land." Spiritual leaders must be dedicated to standing before the Lord and to serving God's people. No other commitment can preserve us from straying—and from judgment.

"You will drink your sister's cup" Ezek. 23:1-49. In an extended allegory Israel and Judah were likened to two adulterous sisters. Judah had not learned from the punishment of Israel, and so would suffer the same terrible fate.

You and I can learn from both nations. They "have forgotten Me and thrust Me behind your back." We remember the Lord daily, and keep Him and His Word always before us.

"This very date" Ezek. 24:1-14. On January

15, 588 B.C., Nebuchadnezzar began the siege of Jerusalem. On that very date in Babylon Ezekiel announced what was happening in the homeland, and likened Jerusalem to a pot about to be brought to a boil, and the inhabitants to meat that is cooked until all the water is gone from the pot and even the remains are charred and useless. "The time has come for Me to act," God said: "I will not hold back."

God has fixed a date for the judgment of our world too. When that date comes, nothing can hold God back.

"I am about to take away from you the delight of your eyes" Ezek. 24:15-27. Before Ezekiel's wife died, the prophet was warned, and told to make no outward sign of mourning. He was only to groan quietly. When the devastation ended in Jerusalem, and death took the sons and daughters of the few survivors, they too would be too stunned and crushed to mourn.

Why should Ezekiel have to suffer the death of his wife? The best answer probably is, "Why not?" God's dearest saint is not immune from the anguish that is common to all men. God's most intimate friends often experience the darkest trials. During such times we sense our identity with the rest of humankind, and out of shared suffering often grows the most effective ministry. In our trials we, like Ezekiel, are often God's sign to others, pointing the way to comfort, and to Him.

▶ DEVOTIONAL
"It'll Never Happen!"
(Ezek. 20)

What is the most unlikely thing you can imagine? You walking on the moon? Being visited by little green men?

Well, those are pretty unlikely, I confess. In fact, they probably fit into the same category with something God scoffs at in this chapter. The category of "Never!" We find the category in verse 32: "What you have in mind will never happen." That "never happen" is one of the most comforting phrases in Scripture, especially for parents whose children seem to have abandoned the faith.

You see, the people of Judah wanted to abandon God. They wanted to adopt other ways and be "like the nations, like the peoples of the world." They were running away from God as fast as their legs could carry them. And despite this, God said, "What you have in mind will never happen." We might paraphrase this way: "You don't want to be My people, or live the good life I've chosen for you? Well, you can run—but I won't let you get away. Even though you reject Me, I won't reject you. You're Mine, and I'll never let you go."

God was determined to rescue His people from paganism in spite of themselves.

This passage is comforting to parents whose children make unwise choices. A son or daughter drifts away from God, adopts a doubtful morality, makes mistake after mistake, and suffers painful consequences. It's so easy then for parents to give in to despair. My child is lost. All hope is gone! But this passage tells us not to give up! Run away from God? "What you have in mind will never happen!" Abandon Mom's and Dad's values? "What you have in mind will never happen!" Make such a mess of life that there is no way back to God and goodness? "What you have in mind will never happen!"

Oh, there will be the pain of discipline until the wanderer turns back. The people of Judah were soon to discover just how painful the divine discipline could be. But to be abandoned? Never! God is a ferocious Lover. He never gives up, but fiercely pursues His loved ones until they return to Him.

And so if your children or mine make a bad turn along the road of life, let's not give up hope. What they had in mind when they turned away from the Lord will never happen! God doesn't let His loved ones get away.

Personal Application

Put your hope where your faith is. In God.

Quotable

I fled Him down the nights and down the days;
I fled Him, down the arches of the years;
I fled Him, down the labyrinthine ways
Of my own mind; and in the mist of tears
I hid from Him, and under running laughter.

Up vistaed hopes, I sped;
And shot, precipitated
Adown Titanic glooms of chasmed fears,
From those strong Feet that followed, followed after.
But with unhurrying chase,
And unperturbed pace,
Deliberate speed, majestic instancy,
They beat—and a Voice beat
More instant than the Feet—
"All things betray thee, who betrayest Me."
I pleaded, outlaw-wise,
By many a hearted casement, curtained red,
Trellised with intertwining charities;
(For though I knew His love Who followed,
Yet I was sore adread
Lest, having Him I might have nought beside).

. . . .

"Whom wilt thou find to love ignoble thee,
Save Me, save only Me?
All which I took from thee I did but take,
Not for thy harms,
But just that thou might'st seek it in
My arms. All which thy child's mistake
Fancies as lost, I have stored for thee
at home: Rise, clasp My hand, and come."—Francis Thompson

JUNE 14 *Reading 165*
AGAINST NATIONS
Ezekiel 25–32

> *"All the princes of the north and all the Sidonians are there; they went down with the slain in disgrace despite the terror caused by their power" (Ezek. 32:30).*

God is Ruler of the whole earth. Those who do not believe in Him, as well as we who do, are subject to His power. And we will be judged.

Background

This series of predictions against foreign nations was apparently given while the exiles in Babylon awaited word of Jerusalem's fate. Ezekiel had announced the commencement of that city's siege: now all the Jewish captives in Babylon could do was anxiously await word of what was happening in their homeland, some 700 miles away.

During that interim Ezekiel raised his voice against other nations who would become victims of Babylon. The implication for the Jewish captives was twofold. First, their God was God of the whole earth. He was not powerless against the nations that had historically troubled Judah, as Israel's and Judah's present subjection might imply. Second, God is Judge of the whole earth. National sins of aggression and atrocity, of treaty-breaking and arrogance, would be punished wherever they might be found! Judah and Jerusalem, about to fall to Babylon, were not being treated unfairly, but were being held accountable to a standard of righteousness that God requires of all humankind.

These chapters on the judgment of nations millenniums ago remind us, as they did the Jewish captives then, that countries are morally responsible to God for their international behavior. Nations that support terrorism, that break treaty commitments, that adopt policies of repression, and rely on force to coerce neighbors bring themselves inexorably under the judgment of a God who does act in history, and who will repay.

Overview

While awaiting word of Jerusalem, Ezekiel predicted the judgment to fall on pagan nations. He touched on the fate of states close to Judah (25:1-17), and focused in-depth on Tyre (26:1–28:26) and Egypt (29:1–32:32).

Understanding the Text

"Rejoicing with all the malice of your heart against the land of Israel" Ezek. 25:1-7. The Ammonites were one possible victim of the current Babylonian campaign, but were spared when Nebuchadnezzar turned west toward Judah (cf. 21:18-23). Their delight at Jerusalem's fall, however,

was rooted as much in malice against an ancient enemy as in relief. Now Ezekiel announced that their turn would soon come—as indeed it did.

The passage also reflects one element of God's promise to Abraham: those who bless his descendants will be blessed, and those who curse them will be cursed (cf. Gen. 12:3). The rise and fall of nations up to our own time suggests that God continues to bless those who welcome and support His covenant people.

"I will inflict punishment" Ezek. 25:8-17. The same thought is emphasized in prophecies against other nations close to Israel and Judah. Moab ridiculed Judah in her disaster (v. 8); Edom "took revenge on the house of Judah and became very guilty" (v. 12); Philistia "with ancient hostility sought to destroy Judah" (v. 15). In each case the nation not only was antagonistic to the Jews but had discounted her God. In each case, God said, "They will know that I am the LORD."

The capitalization of LORD in the English text tells us that the Hebrew reads YAHWEH. This unique personal name of God has great significance, and identifies Him as "The One Who Is Always Present." This is the name associated with God's great Exodus miracles, and with His later interventions in history on behalf of His people. It suggests a vision of God as living, active, present, and all-powerful.

The pagan nations around Judah, and indeed Judah herself, failed to see God in this way. But when judgment fell, then the true nature of God would be realized.

How wonderful that through Jesus you and I know God as living, active, present, and all-powerful in our own lives. With the eyes of faith we see constant evidence of His work in us and for us. Only those who forget who God really is, and behave as though He were not present, need punishment to remind them.

"O Tyre . . . I will bring many nations against you" Ezek. 26:1-21. Tyre lay only a hundred miles from Jerusalem, and on a clear day could be seen from its heights. The city was built half on the mainland, and half on an offshore island, and possessed two secure harbors. Tyre was a famous commercial center, and possessed a dominant fleet that was thought to make the sea-wrapped city impregnable. While other states in Syria-Palestine were being crushed by northern powers, Tyre retained her independence and prospered.

The prophecy against Tyre is complex, and has five major divisions. Chapter 26 describes the city's destruction. Chapter 27 is a lament, picturing Tyre as a trading-vessel loaded with goods that is suddenly wrecked. Chapter 28:1-10 is an oracle about the prince of Tyre, verses 11-19 a lament over the king of Tyre, and verses 20-26 a prophecy against nearby Sidon.

The date at the beginning of the prophecy (26:1) suggests Ezekiel spoke out against Tyre about a month after the fall of Jerusalem, with word possibly brought by traders from Tyre itself.

"I will make you a bare rock" Ezek. 26:14. This is one of the most quoted of Old Testament verses, referred to often by those who study Scripture's predictive prophecy. It reads, "I will make you a bare rock, and you will become a place to spread fishnets. You will never be rebuilt, for I the LORD have spoken, declares the Sovereign LORD."

Despite the scarcity of good natural harbors on the eastern Mediterranean coast, and despite the natural harbors at that site, Tyre has never been rebuilt. Where the grand city once stood a few fishermen still dry their nets. But the bare rock remains desolate and empty, as the waves roll endlessly against the shore.

"Merchant of peoples on many coasts" Ezek. 27:1-36. One of the most fascinating features of this chapter is the trade directory in verses 10-25a. The list of Tyre's trading partners, beginning with Tarshish in the west and moving east, is the most important existing document used by those who study commerce in the ancient Mediterranean world.

What a unique book our Bible is! People often say such things as, "The Bible is not a science textbook," as if it were all right to find our religion there, but everything else must be discounted. Yet Ezekiel's writings about Tyre describe in great and accurate detail Nebuchadnezzar's military campaign, and carefully and accurately reflect trading practices and trade goods of the era. The utter authenticity of such historic detail reminds us that the Bible is not a book of religious myth and mystery. It is a historical and accurate report of what God said and did in space and time. We can trust the Bible completely and in every detail, despite the attempts of some to challenge Scripture's accuracy and deny its character as a divinely inspired work.

"The king of Tyre" Ezek. 28:11-19. The shift in midchapter from addressing the ruler (*naged*) of Tyre to addressing the king (*melek*) of Tyre seems significant to many commentators. They believe that the focus of the prophecy shifts at this point from the human ruler of the contemporary city-state to Satan. This conviction is supported by the text's references to Eden (v. 13), to the subject's position as a "guardian cherub" (vv. 14, 16), and to the reference to his creation by God (v. 15). If this view is correct, what we have here is an analysis of Satan's fall, and a unique insight into the entry of evil into God's universe.

Again, if this view is correct, it suggests that even before man's creation earth was the focus of God's purposes in our universe. Satan, then a ranking cherub, strode the heavens above earth in a crystal Eden, all asparkle with glorious jewels. Though created "a model of perfection" and "blameless," pride corrupted this angelic being, and he was cast down to earth's surface. Untold ages later God refashioned the planet, and beneath original Eden planted a Garden, filled with frolicking beasts, where He placed Adam and Eve. There they were tempted by the deposed angel, and led by this now hostile foe of God and man to make the choice of sin.

Is this what we really have here, or are the words and phrases simply poetry, filled with symbols, not intended to be taken literally? Whichever view we hold, we can be sure that the sin of pride, that emphasis on the almighty "I," remains at the root of Satan's and man's fall. (See DEVOTIONAL.)

"Set your face against Pharaoh, king of Egypt . . . and against all Egypt" Ezek. 29:1–32:32. The last four chapters of this section, and indeed one twelfth of Ezekiel's words, are directed against Egypt. Why?

Historically tiny Judah was subject to the whims of the great world powers of that time, Babylon and Egypt. Less than a pawn in the game of international chess, Judah had been manipulated and betrayed by Egypt.

But as powerless as Judah seemed, the God of Judah is God of the whole earth. Now through Ezekiel the Lord announced that He would use His power to execute judgment on this manipulator of His people.

People with power tend to look down on the weak. What can the powerless person do against men of wealth and position? Nothing. But the God of the powerless is unimpressed by any human being. He can, and will, act.

Thus, Ezekiel said, Egypt would be destroyed, and her ruler would fall.

▶DEVOTIONAL
The Almighty "I" (Ezek. 28:11-19)

She was crying as she spoke with the late-night hostess of "TalkNet." She was 17 and pregnant. And things had been going so well. She was home with her dad again, after being sent off to boarding school. She had friends. She was having fun. Real fun. And then this!

She had to have an abortion, of course. Everything was going too well to spoil. Her question was, should she tell her dad? He'd tell her to get the abortion, but he might get mad and send her away again.

The talk show hostess gushed sympathy. That was really a hard decision. She had a regular therapist? Good. Why not talk it over with the therapist first, and ask him about telling her dad.

All I could mutter was, "Poor baby."

No, not the unborn child the caller had already determined to kill. Poor little 17-year-old.

Poor little girl, thinking only about her fun, and the pregnancy's threat to her good times. Never the slightest glimmer of an idea that the life she carried should be considered. Never a thought that possibly she should accept responsibility for the consequences of her fling at sex. Only the tears, only the terror, that she might lose the chance to keep on having fun.

Poor baby.

How fragile that universe we create, with ourselves as sole inhabitant and every other person just something to use for our amusement. How threatening when only "I" count, and then something comes along to threaten our self-indulgence.

Poor baby.

How is she ever to discover that God is the center of the real universe. How is she ever to realize that she is a Creature, whose true identity can only be found in putting Him first, and whose happiness depends on choosing to live by the standards He says are right and good.

I must confess I was upset by the talk show hostess. She clucked and cooed and sympathized, and never once even imagined that the pregnancy was a chance for this teen to consider another human being. The hostess, never in her wildest dreams, would suppose that putting self aside and acting responsibly might be the way this 17-year-old could find both her better self, and peace.

I know. I shouldn't have expected more. We live in a society where self is assumed to be the rightful center of each person's life. Why shouldn't the calling teen have thought only and always of herself? Doesn't everyone?

Poor baby.

Who will ever help her realize that the most insidious expression of Satan's original sin of pride is self-centeredness. That our greatest spiritual flaw, and most persistent enemy, is our own concentration on the almighty "I."

Personal Application

The old prescription still works: God first, others second, self last.

Quotable

ILLUSION

There's a heap o' joy in living,
  When we're living as we should;
And the greatest joy is giving,
  Where it does the greatest good;
And we come to this conclusion,
  As the more of life we see,
It is merely an illusion,
  When we live it selfishly.

It's the old, but truthful story,
  If we strive for great success,
And we win, it lacks the glory,
  If we won by selfishness,
For we find life's sweetest pleasure,
  After all is said and done,
When we give in fullest measure,
  Of the riches we have won.—Frank C. Nelson

JUNE 15 *Reading 166*
RESTORATION AHEAD
Ezekiel 33–36

> *"I will place over them . . . My servant David, and he will tend them . . . and be their shepherd" (Ezek. 34:23).*

Though Jerusalem was in ruins, God had not abandoned His people. However grim present circumstances may appear, there is always a future for the people of God.

Background

From chapter 33 on, the prophecies in the Book of Ezekiel look forward. Prior to that Ezekiel focused his listeners' attention on the history of sins that made Jerusalem's imminent fall certain. But with the city fallen and the homeland depopulated, the prophet was able to speak about the future. God would restore scattered Israel. Many wonderful promises in these four chapters underscore this glorious hope. Yet the fate of the individual still rests on his or her personal choice, to hear and obey God's Word, or to ignore and reject.

For us too, Scripture is filled with promising tomorrows that we can claim. But today as in ancient Babylon, the experience of God's blessing requires us to hear and to live by His Word.

Overview

Ezekiel began a new phase of his ministry by restating key truths: he was a watchman (33:1-11), and each individual was responsible to respond to God's Word (vv. 12-20). To avoid Jerusalem's fate, God's people must take His Word to heart (vv. 27-33). God would replace wicked leaders with the Messiah (34:1-24), and there would be peace (vv. 25-31). Edom would fall (35:1-15), but the mountains of Israel would be cleansed and repopulated by a people transformed by the Lord (36:1-38).

Understanding the Text

"I have made you a watchman" Ezek. 33:1-11. We see it even in nature. As the herd grazes, one male stands alert, head raised, sniffing the air. The watchbeast stands aloof from the crowd, and the welfare of the herd depends on how vigilant he is.

Ezekiel was a watchman for Israel. This was established in chapter 3, and the charge is repeated here. Ezekiel was faithful in warning the people of Judah before the city fell: he must continue to warn.

Ezekiel was required to be alert, to warn his people of spiritual dangers. The responsibility was heavy: Ezekiel would often be alone, standing apart from the crowd. But the very lives of his fellow Jews depended on his faithfulness.

Are we ready to pay the cost of being watchmen for our friends and neighbors? Are we prepared to share Jesus, warning others of the eternal cost of rejection, inviting them to accept the forgiveness and renewal Christ died to provide?

"He has done what is just and right; he will surely live" Ezek. 33:12-20. The message of personal responsibility was also found in the first half of Ezekiel, in chapter 18. There Ezekiel warned that responsiveness to God's word was the key to survival for those under siege in Jerusalem.

That siege was over now, and the bones of the wicked of Judah were scattered in Jerusalem's ruined streets. But the principle of personal responsibility had not been altered. In the future too, God will make a distinction between the good man who hears and obeys His Word, and the wicked man who turns his back on the Lord.

God's promises are for all His people. But they can be claimed only by those who trust—and obey.

"The people living in those ruins in the land of Israel" Ezek. 33:21-39. The few thousand Jews left in Judah had learned nothing from the recent devastation. Despite continued sinning (vv. 25-26), they supposed they had inherited Abraham's title to the land!

But God does not reserve His gifts for the wicked. What He reserves for them is punishment. The Book of Jeremiah tells how the remnant in Judah refused to accept God's guidance, and fled toward destruction in Egypt after the assassination of their Babylonian-appointed governor (cf. Jer. 40–44).

"A beautiful voice" Ezek. 33:30-33. Ezekiel had suddenly become popular among the exiles in Babylon! Everyone came to listen to him, and they were all full of compliments. Ezekiel heard, "Fine sermon, Ezekiel," everywhere he went. Folks just loved to come out every time Ezekiel held a meeting!

The trouble was, it was entertainment to the exiles (cf. v. 32). They listened and smiled and shouted, "Amen"—and probably had the gaunt preacher over for after-service dessert—all without taking his words to heart. "They hear your words," God told Ezekiel, "but do not put them into practice."

The true measure of a modern ministry isn't how popular a preacher becomes, or how many thousands come out to hear him.

The true measure of a modern ministry is hearing. Does the congregation then put God's words into practice?

"Prophesy against the shepherds of Israel" Ezek. 34:1-10. The term "shepherd" is often used in the Old Testament to designate Israel's kings and her spiritual leaders. Now Ezekiel looked back and identified the leadership flaws which contributed to Judah's recent disaster. The real purpose Ezekiel had in mind, however, was to create a background against which a coming Shepherd he was about to describe would stand out.

What flaws in Israel's and Judah's leaders brought the nation to disaster? The Hebrew kingdom's rulers had thought only of themselves rather than the flock (v. 2). They greedily exploited the flock for personal gain (v. 3). They refused to intervene on behalf of the weak and injured (v. 4). And they permitted the flock of God to be scattered throughout the nations (vv. 5-6). Because of these sins, God would "remove them from tending the flock so that the shepherds can no longer feed themselves" (v. 10).

James 3:1 warns against stepping presumptuously into a leadership role, "because you know that we who teach will be judged more strictly." Any person who views leadership as a position "above" others, rather than a position of service "under" them is not yet ready to be a spiritual leader.

"I Myself will tend My sheep and have them lie down" Ezek. 34:11-23. Human leaders have failed miserably to protect God's flock. In this powerful messianic passage God promises to intervene directly. He Himself will tend His sheep. God will "place over them one shepherd, My servant David." When the promised Descendant of David appeared, God's flock would at last have a Leader whose sole concern was their well-being.

How beautifully this thought is picked up by Jesus, who identified Himself as the Good Shepherd in John 10. In Christ, at long last, the people of God have a Shepherd who willingly "lays down His life for the sheep." Rather than grasp, this Shepherd gives. He is no hireling, but cares deeply for the sheep. His sacrifice of Himself proves once and for all that we are loved and secure. As we hear His voice, and follow Him, He will do us nothing but good.

"I will make a covenant of peace" Ezek. 34:25. Like Jeremiah, Ezekiel introduced the concept of a New Covenant which God will make with His people. In this chapter Ezekiel emphasized the material blessings associated with that covenant, while Jeremiah stressed the spiritual.

What material blessings are foreseen for that future time? The prophet emphasized a rescue of the Jews from the lands where they have been scattered. Then, in their ancient homeland, they will know a time of peace, safety, and prosperity.

This picture of the Jews restored to an abundantly fertile homeland is frequently found in prophetic images of a coming golden age (cf. Hosea 2:22; Joel 3:18; Amos 9:13-15; Zech. 8:12). All this is promised to Israel when at last David's promised Offspring appears as Ruler of every land.

Many understand such prophecies to teach a literal restoration of the Jewish people to the land of Israel at Christ's second coming. But there is a spiritual application too. When Christ reigns in a person's life, whatever the outward strife, there is peace within. Hidden in our hearts, beyond the reach of circumstance, there is a garden to which we can retreat, and there find rest.

▶ DEVOTIONAL
God's Holy Name
(Ezek. 36)

Looking around our little Phoenix congregation, I saw so many familiar faces. There was the young man who'd been so driven by sex that he lost his job and family, and almost his mind. There was the ex-hippy, who'd thought nothing of buying a record he wanted when his kids were without shoes. There, near the front, was the wife who'd been caught in adultery with a family friend, sitting by her husband. Everywhere I looked there were people I loved. People who brought honor to God's holy name.

Many people would be shocked at that last statement. But this is just the sort of thing Ezekiel was talking about in this 36th chapter of his book. Earlier, in chapter 6, Ezekiel prophesied "against" the mountains of Israel. Their high places, the sites selected for orgiastic pagan worship rituals, were to witness the destruction of God's rebellious people. Judah had dishonored the Lord, and He would proclaim His holiness by punishing them (36:16-21).

But now, Ezekiel prophesied "to" these same mountains. Their slopes will again be populated and fruitful (vv. 8-15). The mountains will observe the descendants of sinners, dancing and rejoicing in the Lord. And in that repopulation, God will affirm His holiness. As the Lord said through Ezekiel, "I will show Myself holy through you before their eyes" (v. 23).

How? What is it that the mountains and surrounding peoples will witness that demonstrates God's holiness? The next verses tell us, as the Lord continues to speak through His prophet. As for the returned exiles, God said, "I will give you a new heart and put a new spirit in you; I will remove from you your heart of stone and give you a heart of flesh. And I will put My Spirit in you and move you to follow My decrees and be careful to keep My laws" (vv. 26-27).

That's what I saw in church Sunday morning. People who were sinners. But people whom God had changed.

And the glory of God's holiness was revealed in their transformation.

Personal Application

Transformed sinners still bear witness to the holiness of God. And sinning saints remain a blot on His holy name.

Quotable

"God never asks us to do anything we can do. He asks us to live a life which we can never live and to do a work which we can never do. Yet, by His grace, we are living it and doing it. The life we live is the life of Christ lived in the power of God, and the work we do is the work of Christ carried on through us by His Spirit whom we obey."—Watchman Nee

JUNE 16 *Reading 167*
DRY BONES LIVE
Ezekiel 37–39

"I will attach tendons to you and make flesh come upon you and cover you with skin; I will put breath in you, and you will come to life. Then you will know that I am the Lord*" (Ezek. 37:6).*

People who find it hard to believe warnings of divine judgment also find it hard to believe God's good news.

Background

Prophetic overview. Biblical scholars tend to take one of two views of passages like the one we explore today. They either see the passage as a visionary's use of highly symbolic language to affirm some spiritual reality, or they see the passage as a literal, though often obscure, description of events which will actually take place in the future.

One who takes the first approach will see these chapters in Ezekiel as a symbolic affirmation of God's power over all the forces of evil throughout history, and an affirmation of His ultimate victory. In God's time evil will be put away, and only good will reign.

One who takes the second approach sees these chapters in Ezekiel as a preview of history. The timetable may be obscure, and the exact sequence of events uncertain, but what the prophet describes—a regathering of God's Old Testament people to Israel, invasion of the Holy Land, direct divine intervention, a national conversion of Israel, the rule of earth by a Descendant of David—all this is understood to lie ahead, perhaps just beyond the headlines of tomorrow's news.

Whichever view a person may hold today, there is no doubt that Ezekiel and the other Old Testament prophets expected a literal fulfillment of their visions of the future. Their belief was rooted in the conviction that the God of the covenant would be utterly faithful to His promises to Abraham, which included possession of a Jewish homeland as well as the spiritual blessing of intimate relationship with the Lord. And the prophets speak with a unified voice when describing the earthly future of God's Old Testament people. They may have misunderstood the meaning of what they foresaw. But each prophet, whether crying out about the destruction of Jerusalem, the fall of Nineveh, or the restoration of scattered Israel, expected his words to be literally fulfilled.

I don't want to come down too hard on the literalist side. But it is fascinating to note. Just 60 years ago if anyone had suggested that the Jewish people might have a nation of their own in Palestine, all would have scoffed. Yet today that nation is firmly established: struggling, yes, but there. The dry bones have begun to come back together. Perhaps even tendons and flesh have appeared. But again using Ezekiel's words, we might well say there is yet "no breath in them." Still a secular state, still relying on the arm of flesh rather than on God, Israel awaits the miracle that Ezekiel said would then surely come. And then the dry bones will live.

And we too will live. For these events, which the flow of history suggests may lie just beyond tomorrow, mean that Christ, David's Successor and Son, will appear. Then God's time for celebration by the redeemed of every age will at last have come.

Overview

The vision of a valley of dry bones emphasized God's power to revitalize and restore Israel and Judah (37:1-14). There will again be a united nation under a Davidic king (v. 28). But the restoration was linked with invasion by a great northern power (38:1-17), whose destruction by God Himself (v. 18–39:21) would precipitate lasting national conversion (vv. 22-29).

Understanding the Text

"These bones are the whole house of Israel" Ezek. 37:1-14. The text interprets Ezekiel's vision of dry bones that come together at his command, are fleshed out, and finally come to life. The bones in the vision represent Israel, whose people are scattered and hopeless among the nations. Though devoid of hope, God will "bring you back to the land of Israel" (reassemble the bones). The graves (representing the nations to which the Jews have been scattered) will be opened, permitting the return, and God's Spirit will be given to His people.

Whatever the prophetic meaning, the application to our lives is clear. All too often we too give up. We feel deadened, dried up. All seems bleak; we feel utterly doomed. When those emotions come, we need to remember the dry bones. God can take our dead and scattered hopes, pull them together, and breathe life into them again. Because we know the Lord, and because He loves us dearly, we do have hope and a future.

"They will never again be two nations" Ezek. 37:15-27. This powerful messianic prophecy again looks forward to a return of the Jews to their homeland, and establishment of a nation ruled by a Davidic King.

Once united under David and Solomon, the Hebrew nation split into Northern and Southern Kingdoms in 931 B.C. The population of the north (Israel) was deported by the Assyrians in 722 B.C., and scattered through many cities. The south (Judah) was crushed by the Babylonians, and its population taken in a series of deportations ending in 586 B.C. Now Ezekiel said that God intends to unite the scattered tribes of Israel, bring them back to the homeland, and establish a united kingdom to be ruled by a Descendant of David.

To date this has not happened. There have been partial returns, and a kind of semi-independence under the Maccabees. But no independent, united kingdom has emerged in the nearly 2,600 years since Ezekiel's time. In fact, the only known lineal descendant of David who yet lives is Jesus Christ! Thus this prophecy, which links a restoration of Israel to the land (v. 21), spiritual renewal (vv. 23-24), rule by a Descendant of David (v. 24), and a rebuilt sanctuary (v. 26), is one of the many that makes those who take a literal view of prophecy to believe that what is described here still lies ahead, and will be fulfilled when Jesus returns.

"Set your face against Gog, of the land of Magog" Ezek. 38:1-16. Now Ezekiel described an invasion force assembled from many nations about to strike a peaceful and unsuspecting Israel.

Several Hebrew phrases woven into the message fix the time. What Ezekiel foresaw will happen "after many days" (v. 8), "in future years" (v. 8). Another phrase, translated "in days to come" (v. 16) helps locate the prophecy in the end times, near history's end. Some see this as an attack to come just before the establishment of a Millennium of peace at Christ's return; others place it after the Millennium and identify it with a Satan-stimulated, final rebellion of humanity against God (cf. Rev. 19:17-21).

Etymologically "Gog" and "Magog"are impossible to identify, though many students of prophecy teach that these represent Russia. Of more significance is the fact that the enemy forces are drawn from nations at every point of the compass: the east (Persia), the southwest (Cush: Ethiopia), the west (Put: Libya, and the "islands of the sea"), the north (Gomer: Cimmerians?).

You and I may at times feel, "Everybody's against me." What Ezekiel is saying is that at history's end, "everybody" will be against God's people.

But the text shows something else. The Lord says to His enemies, "I will bring you against My land," and then adds, "so that the nations may know Me when I show Myself holy through you." God will use the evil intent of the wicked to bring them to a place where He can act openly against them.

What a reminder for you and me. Everybody may actually be against us. But God isn't against us. He has permitted our enemies to attack, only to put them in a position where they will be vulnerable to judgment. So the next time you feel a little persecuted, don't feel sorry for yourself. Feel sorry for your persecutors!

"In My zeal and fiery wrath" Ezek. 38:17–39:24. In a series of announcements (38:17-23; 39:1-16, 17-24) God told what He would do to the invading forces. He Himself would intervene and, with miracles that recall His acts for the Exodus generation, would utterly destroy the enemy. These acts will forever establish the Lord as God in the sight of both Israel and the nations (39:22).

But is God fair to establish His identity at the cost of so many human lives? The text answers us. In all that God has done, to Israel and to the nations, He has "dealt with them according to their uncleanness and their offenses" (v. 24).

▶ DEVOTIONAL
What to Forget
(Ezek. 39)

My wife tells our nine-year-old that God has a video recorder focused on her. One day, when we meet the Lord, He's going to show the tape, and give her her rewards. And, every once in a while when she does something especially nice, Sue tells her, "That's on your video tape."

I like her emphasis. So many mom's might turn this around, and when a child did something bad, shriek, "Now, that's going on your video tape!"

I couldn't help thinking of Sue's practice when I read Ezekiel 39. The passage so powerfully portrays God's hatred of sin and the judgment that sin merits. Reading it, we almost cringe at the thought of our own faults and the memory of our failings. But then we read God's summary, in the last paragraph. There, nestled in verses that express the compassion God will show when judgment is past, is a verse that says, "They will forget their shame and all the unfaithfulness they showed toward Me" (v. 26).

What a wonderful promise! Yes, we're weak. We stumble, and sometimes fall. And then what a burden of shame and guilt we bear. But God promises that when we see Him, when we truly "know that I am the LORD," no shred of memory of our sins will remain to mar our joy.

Personal Application

Forgiven means forgotten! Even now we can put our past behind us, and live in joy.

Quotable

"One day a Christian visited a minister in his home. As he sat in the study, he began to read one of the minister's books. Suddenly he cried, 'Glory! Praise the Lord.' The minister hurried into the study, asking, 'What's the matter?'

" 'Why, this book says that the sea is five miles deep! The Bible says my sins have been cast into the depth of the sea, and if it's that deep, I'm not afraid of their coming up again!'

"Nor do we need to bring them up!"—Walter B. Knight

JUNE 17 *Reading 168*
GOD'S GLORY RETURNS
Ezekiel 40–48

"The vision I saw was like the vision I had seen when He came to destroy the city and like the visions I had seen by the Kebar River, and I fell facedown. The glory of the L*ORD entered the temple" (Ezek. 43:3-4).*

The last chapters of Ezekiel describe the worship of a restored Israel, and a return of the glory of God. Here, Ezekiel looked ahead and assured the exiles, God's glory will return.

Background

Puzzling prophecy. This is one of the most difficult of all Old Testament prophecies. For those who spiritualize biblical prophecy, the problem lies in the multitude of details provided concerning the construction of the new temple. It's not just a question of what each detail might mean. The careful verbal blueprint reminds us of the instructions Moses was given for constructing the tabernacle—and those were intended to be literally carried out.

The main detailed specifications offer no problem for the literalist. Yet for the person who views Ezekiel's description here as a prediction of what will actually happen in the future, there are other difficulties. For instance, where do the scenes described here fit in Scripture's overall vision of Israel's future? And particularly, how does it relate to Revelation 21–22's similar description of the eternal state. And, what about the sacrifices to be offered on the future altar? Doesn't the New Testament teach that Christ's one sacrifice of Himself did away forever with the need for animal offerings? (cf. Heb. 7:18; 9:12, 25-28) Such questions can, of course, be answered. The sacrifices of the Mosaic era were intended to simply portray redemption. Apparently the sacrifices of Ezekiel's temple also serve as reminders of Christ's work. Since several of the feasts of the Old Testament era are not mentioned in Ezekiel, it seems that he describes a whole new system of worship, to be conducted in the very presence of the Messiah.

Though many delight to speculate on such issues when reading these chapters, our purpose is different. Rather than try to fit Ezekiel's final vision of the future into any prophetic scheme, we want to see what that vision suggests to us for our lives today. And there is something here for us to apply.

Overview

Ezekiel gave details of a new temple to be constructed in Jerusalem (40:1–42:20). God's glory will fill that structure (43:1-12), and commemorative sacrifices will be offered on its altar (vv. 13-27). Priests and Levites will again serve God (44:1-31) in sacred precincts (45:1-12). Israel will celebrate God's festivals (46:1-24) as a river flowing from the sanctuary waters the land (47:1-12), which once again has been allotted to Israel's tribes (v. 13–48:35).

Understanding the Text

"He took me to the land of Israel" Ezek. 40:1-5. In the year 573 B.C. Ezekiel saw the last vision reported in his book. In it he was transported to Israel, and told to communicate everything he saw to the house of Israel.

The very first thing that the prophet saw was a glorious temple. He was guided through it, and given every relevant dimension of what he saw.

One day these words may serve as a verbal blueprint to be followed by God's people. Many believe so. But to us today the immediate fixation on the temple reminds us that God is to have priority in our lives. As Ezekiel went on, his wondering gaze would shift to the king's palace, the city, the changed geography of Jerusalem, and ultimately to the land itself, once more divided among the 12 tribes of Israel. But the most wonderful sight of all, the most compelling, the thing that demanded his initial attention, was the temple. You and I may be blessed in many ways, and the sights we see around us may be glorious. But there is nothing more beautiful, nothing more worthy of our attention, than God Himself. If God is the center of our lives, as the temple is the focal point of future Israel, everything else will fall into place.

"I saw the glory of the God of Israel coming

from the east" Ezek. 43:1-12. This is the most significant element in Ezekiel's vision. In chapters 8–11 we have a report of Ezekiel's vision of the departure of God's glory. Now the prophet described a return. Once again the living, vital presence of the Lord Almighty would reside among His Old Testament people.

What is the significance of God's instruction to the prophet to "describe the temple . . . that they may be ashamed of their sins"? Simply that the description of future splendor will so powerfully demonstrate what Israel will become, that the very contrast would drive God's people toward holiness.

We find a similar thought in the New Testament. In 1 John 3 the apostle looked foward to Christ's coming, and announced that though we do not now know what we will be, we know that when Jesus returns we will be like Him. And, John said, "Everyone who has this hope in him purifies himself, just as He is pure" (v. 3). To know what God intends for us, to realize what we are becoming, is a powerful motivation for holy living.

This same theme is seen later in Ezekiel 45:9-12, a passage addressed to Israel's current "princes" (leaders). Ezekiel had just described the land to be set aside for the city of Jerusalem and its ruler, bordering on the temple itself. The rulers of the people would be the closest of all to the Lord. Thus God said through the prophet, "Give up your violence and oppression and do what is just and right." With a clear vision of what the future holds for us, the grip of selfish gain is relaxed, and we begin to act in harmony with who we truly are and will become in the Lord.

"I am to be the only inheritance the priests have" Ezek. 44:1-26. The duties of priests and Levites mimic their responsibilities in the Mosaic era. But after outlining their duties, the Lord added the verse above.

In past and future, Israel's priests were not given tribal land. They had no earthly inheritance. They were to belong to the Lord, and the Lord Himself was to be their inheritance.

What a blessing to be freed from the tyranny of possessions. How wonderful to focus only on God, to desire only to please Him, to know that while the material things we own are ours on loan, we do not possess them—and they do not possess us!

"You are to divide it equally among them" Ezek. 47:13–48:35. The prophecy of Ezekiel ends with God's people back in their land. There is an equal place set aside for each tribal group.

In the time of Joshua the territories allotted the tribes were unequal. Some clans were larger than others, and had need for more space. But now, at history's end, all such distinctions will be lost. None is greater, none smaller. And each has an equal place in the glorious kingdom of God.

There are many distinctions that people make between themselves and others now. Distinctions of wealth, of education, of position or prestige. We even make such distinctions in our churches, mentally ranking our fellow believers as up or down the spiritual ladder. That is a mistake. A mistake that will never be repeated in eternity. There too God's grace will be divided equally, for each of us will gladly stake a claim to fame on one thing, and one alone. We are sinners. Saved by grace.

▶ DEVOTIONAL
Worship the Lord
(Ezek. 43–44)

As Ezekiel wandered in his vision through the future temple, he was amazed at its size and beauty. The careful detail in which he recorded every measurement tells us that. But there is one verse that tells us more—about the temple, about Ezekiel, and about ourselves.

The verse, Ezekiel 44:4, describes the prophet coming to the front of the temple and there he said, "I looked and saw the glory of the LORD filling the temple of the LORD, and I fell facedown."

What do we learn about the temple? In his vision, Exekiel had been impressed by the temple. He had looked in wonder at the portico of the outer court. He'd wandered through the rooms set aside for the priests. But when he came around front, and caught a glimpse of the glory of the Lord, Ezekiel fell facedown, and worshiped.

You and I may be impressed by the

beauty of our churches. We may look in wonder at the crowds gathered there. We may be impressed by the qualifications of our ministers. But all such things are external; just the facade. What we need to do is figuratively come around to the front. We need to forget what we see looking at our faith from the back and side, and peer in the front door. When we do, everything else seems to disappear, for there, in the heart of the sanctuary, we too are able to see the glory of the Lord.

Many things about our churches are important. But the only thing that is truly essential is that when we come to worship we see and respond to God.

What do we learn about Ezekiel? That he was a searcher. He was impressed by the structure he examined. But he was not satisfied. Only when he was brought around to the front and saw the glory of the Lord did he fall down and worship. Ezekiel wanted God Himself, and finding Him worshiped.

What do we learn about ourselves? Like Ezekiel we can't be satisfied with the temple, however impressive it may be. Our destiny like Ezekiel's, the end of our quest, is realized when we see the Lord, and worship Him.

Personal Application

In church and in personal devotions, seek to meet and worship God.

Quotable

"Some people praise God for the good feelings it gives them; they praise Him because they think it makes everyone else feel good; they praise Him because they think that is simply what every good Christian should do. They do not focus their minds on God. The result is that their false praise drives out the true. Praise becomes mere pleasant-feeling babble.

"We need to speak directly to God, not to ourselves or our neighbors. As we look at Him, we will naturally praise Him for the real qualities we see. Our awkwardness will fade into the background as our attention is less and less on ourselves and more and more on Him."— Tim Stafford

---

The Variety Reading Plan continues with OBADIAH

Daniel

INTRODUCTION

Daniel contains the memoirs of a young Jewish captive taken to Babylon in 605 B.C. He with other youthful members of the Judean nobility were trained for posts as civil servants in Nebuchadnezzar's administration. The incidents and prophecies recorded in this little book span Daniel's 70-year career as a high government official.

The first half of the book tells stories of Daniel's relationship with the rulers of the Babylonian and Persian Empires. The second half reports prophetic visions given Daniel of the near and distant future.

The Book of Daniel contains many lessons for the believer. Daniel's life illustrates the power of prayer, and how to live by faith in a hostile society. Daniel's powerful images of the future continue to remind us that God is fully in control of history.

OUTLINE OF CONTENTS

I. Daniel's Political Career .... Dan. 1–6
II. Daniel's Prophetic Visions .... Dan. 7–12

READING GUIDE (4 Days)

If hurried, you may read only the "core passage" in your Bible and the Devotional in each chapter of this Commentary.

Reading	*Chapters*	*Core passage*
169	1–3	3
170	4–6	5
171	7–9	9
172	10–12	11

Daniel

JUNE 18 *Reading 169*
CAPTIVE'S COMMITMENT
Daniel 1–3

> *"But Daniel resolved not to defile himself with the royal food and wine, and he asked the chief official for permission not to defile himself in this way" (Dan. 1:8).*

The pressure to conform is intense in every society. But Christians today, like the teenage Daniel, are called on to express commitment to the Lord by taking a personal stand for what is right.

Background

Modern critics have supposed that Daniel was written in the Maccabean period, about 165 B.C. by someone who used Daniel's name to win acceptance for his writings. The underlying reason for this position is refusal to believe that anyone writing about 573 B.C., when at age 90 Daniel edited his memoirs, could with absolute accuracy have predicted the history of the Middle East. Yet Daniel's visions so clearly describe some 400 years of history that only two options exist: admit the supernatural origin of his revelations, or date the book after the events it describes.

Yet internal evidence shows that the writer knew intimately the inner workings of the Babylonian and Persian courts, and had information that was not available in the Maccabean era when the critics say Daniel must have been written! Such details as specific administrative titles, later changed, and Belshazzar's co-regency with his father, with many others, so perfectly fit the historical setting that fabrication can be ruled out. Also, Daniel is mentioned in Ezekiel 14:14, 20 and 28:3, admittedly an early book. And the Book of Daniel was itself accepted as Scripture by the Jews of the Maccabean era. The notion that the Jewish scribes, who so respected their holy books, could have been taken in by a contemporary fabrication, strains credulity.

It's good to know as we read this fascinating Old Testament book that any lessons we draw from Daniel's experience are rooted in the real-life experiences of a person like ourselves, rather than in the fictional activities of a mythical hero. And it is comforting to realize, as we explore the prophetic revelations of Daniel, that just as God's predictive Word came to pass in earlier days, His predictive Word concerning what lies ahead for us is as certain and as sure.

Overview

Daniel and three friends carefully followed Jewish dietary laws while in training for service in Babylon (1:1-16), and were blessed by God with wisdom (vv. 17-21). Daniel achieved high government rank by explaining Nebuchadnezzar's prophetic dream (2:1-49). God rescued Daniel's three companions, thrown into a blazing furnace for refusing to worship an idol erected by Nebuchadnezzar (3:1-30).

Understanding the Text

"Trained for . . . the king's service" Dan. 1:1-7. Young Daniel and at least three Jewish companions were registered in the royal academy, to be trained for three years. At the end of that time, they would be tested and given appropriate positions in the Babylonian administration.

On the surface it seems the four Hebrew youths were offered a great opportunity. But there is another way to look at it.

They were enrolled with young people from other conquered lands to be used. This was no act of benevolence by Nebuchadnezzar. It was just smart politics. Why let talent go to waste, when you have a gigantic empire to run? Take the brightest and best from every subject people, and use them.

Daniel and his friends, like the students from other nations, were totally aware of their minority status. An individual might attain power and wealth. But he would always be something less than the true Babylonian nobility.

People in a minority frequently try to adjust by adopting the views and ways of the majority. They conform and eagerly ape their masters. Or they may fight assimilation, becoming sullen and angry and rude. It's always painful to feel oneself an inferior—particularly if you know that you are being used. But Daniel and his friends show us a better way to respond when we feel we're being used because of our minority status.

"Daniel resolved not to defile himself with the royal food and wine" Dan. 1:8-10. The first step in adjusting to minority status is to determine what boundaries our commitment to God establishes. As a Jew, bound by the dietary laws of the Old Testament, Daniel knew he could not adopt the diet of the Babylonians.

Last evening I heard a teenage boy who called "Talk-Net." He was a member of a minority too—an 18-year-old who had not yet had sexual relations with a girl. His girlfriend had been urging him to have sex. He resisted, feeling that it wasn't right, and wanting to wait for marriage. But he was full of fears. What if his girl told other teens? What if it got around that he was "different." Adolescence was so important; he wanted so desperately to fit in. This time the "Talk-Net" host, a man, encouraged him to remain chaste and live by his own values. It would be a big mistake, the host said, to betray the one person he had to live with all his life—himself.

It was good advice. But still lacking. There must be an even stronger anchor for our moral choices than personal values. To stand firm under the intense pressures to conform that exist in any society is always hard. To succeed, a person needs what Daniel had: a strong sense of identity as one of God's people, and determination to live to please God rather than others.

"Please test your servants" Dan. 1:11-16. Some believers try to wall themselves off from social pressure by being obnoxious. If you develop an attitude of contempt toward "those people," and show that contempt in everything you do, most folks will let you alone.

Daniel took a very different route. While living by his own values, he was both friendly and respectful. Not at all defiant, he "asked permission" to choose his own diet. He was sensitive to the possible difficulties his stand might make for the Babylonian official over him, and proposed a test period of 10 days to allay that official's fears.

Daniel shows us that the believer can relate positively to the people of the world, even while rejecting the values of society. Because Daniel was this kind of person, he was able to testify about God to the most important persons in Babylon, including Nebuchadnezzar himself.

God does not want us to isolate ourselves from the people of this world. He simply wants to inoculate us against its values.

"God gave knowledge and understanding" Dan. 1:17-21. Here "knowledge" is accurate information and the skill required to apply that knowledge to solve practical problems of government, while "understanding" is the perceptive ability needed to sort out the false from the true and do so to make good decisions.

How striking that Daniel was gifted with the abilities needed to administer a great empire. God places His own in every strata of society. No group should be left without an internal witness to the power and grace of God.

When Nebuchadnezzar personally tested the graduates of his royal academy, Daniel and his friends were "ten times better" not only than the graduates, but than their instructors. The impression Daniel made in the secular arena laid a foundation for his later spiritual impact on the king.

"I have had a dream that troubles me and I want to know what it means" Dan. 2:1-10. The archives of Babylon contained many books on dream interpretation. It was popularly believed that dreams were an avenue through which the gods spoke to human beings. No wonder Nebuchadnezzar wanted to understand his troubling dream!

He also seems to have been suspicious of his own wise men. He insisted they tell him the dream before they interpreted it! It seemed a reasonable test. Since the professional class that gave the king advice claimed to be able to interpret the supernatural, they ought to demonstrate access to supernatural sources of information.

This morning the business news reported an astounding growth in astrology magazines, and described a new "upscale" product soon to enter that field. It's amazing how many people turn to astrology, never thinking, as Nebuchadnezzar did, that it might be wise to test the supposed supernatural abilities of any such advisers.

Only Daniel was able to report the dream and to interpret it. And he was careful to give God the glory, explaining to Nebuchadnezzar that he, Daniel, had no supernatural abilities but that "there is a God in heaven who reveals mysteries." If we truly want supernatural aid, why not appeal to God?

"He urged them to plead for mercy from the God of heaven" Dan. 2:11-23. Note two things about Daniel's approach to God. First, he enlisted others to pray with him for God's help. Yes, God does hear us when we pray. But gathering others to pray with and for us is an act of faith: we have faith that God hears all His children, and we have faith that when believers pray together God works powerfully through them. Second, note that when the answer to prayer came, Daniel devoted himself to praise even before he went to the king!

Daniel truly did put God first. This was undoubtedly the secret of his personal piety and his public achievements.

"Your dream and the visions that passed through your mind" Dan. 2:28-49. The giant image Nebuchadnezzar saw in his dream represented his own and succeeding Mesopotamian empires. These are the same empires seen in later visions of Daniel. Each of the empires is destined to be succeeded, until all are ultimately crushed and supplanted. In the end, "the God of heaven will set up a kingdom that will never be destroyed, nor will it be left to another people."

Daniel had demonstrated the ability that Nebuchadnezzar had required. Here was proof of contact with the supernatural. Here was evidence that there is a God in heaven. As a result Nebuchadnezzar promoted Daniel and gave his three Hebrew friends important posts. Most important, the experience was the beginning of what we might consider the conversion of Nebuchadnezzar himself.

God is at work even now in the most unlikely of unbelievers. The pagan king, author of a recovered poem expressing both his own arrogance and gratitude to his god for his advancement, had been given a dream by God. This had launched a course of events that impressed him with Daniel and with Daniel's God. Who knows what God may even now be doing within the heart of some "unlikely" person in your life?

"King Nebuchadnezzar made an image of gold" Dan. 3:1-30. Nebuchadnezzar's construction of a giant, gold-coated idol does not conflict with the report of his respect for Daniel's God. In that day the worship of several different deities was common, and the idea of exclusive devotion to a single God seemed strange. Thus the refusal of Shadrach, Meshach, and Abednego, Daniel's three Hebrew companions, to worship the king's idol, seemed totally unreasonable. Nebuchadnezzar took it as a personal affront, and when the three calmly refused to participate, the furious king ordered them thrown into a blazing clay furnace.

There the three were joined by a fourth Figure, and walked safely despite the flames. Nebuchadnezzar was impressed. Again this absolute autocrat had experienced the power of God, this time overruling his angry decision to execute the three Hebrews. The king quickly issued a command that no one say anything against the God of the three Hebrews. After all, what ruler aside from the Exodus Pharaoh would be foolish enough to ask for trouble! And he promoted the faithful three again.

Many have wondered where Daniel was when this great worship service took place. Some assume he was traveling, some that he was ill at home. More important is, why wasn't Daniel there? I suspect the reason is that Nebuchadnezzer already held Daniel in some awe, and would not have been surprised if he had refused to worship, or if he were rescued by a miracle. But here were three relative unknowns among the thousands of administrators in Nebuchadnezzar's empire. These three, like Daniel, were faithful exclusively to Judah's God, and their God acted to save their lives. By having this stand taken by the three rather than Daniel, the king's focus was shifted to God from God's servant, Daniel. God showed that He would act for anyone who was fully committed to Him.

What an important lesson for anyone on a journey toward faith to learn!

▶DEVOTIONAL
But Even If
(Dan. 3)

I like guarantees.

That's why, after checking on all the local services that promise to protect our home from underground termites, I went with Sears. Sears not only offered a competitive price, but promised to repair any damage caused by underground termites to the house or its contents—up to $250,000! Now that's a guarantee!

Of course, in our walk with the Lord no such guarantees are provided. Shadrach, Meshach, and Abednego understood that when they stood before a furious Nebuchadnezzar. "If we are thrown into the blazing furnace, the God we serve is able to save us from it, and He will rescue us from your hand, O king." God surely is able. And then they went on.

"But even if He does not, we want you to know, O king, that we will not serve your gods or worship the image of gold you have set up."

God can save us.

We believe He will.

"But even if He does not" we will serve the Lord and Him only.

What the three exhibited was a quality that you and I need in our own spiritual lives. Complete commitment. Commitment so complete that even if God does not exert His miracle-working power on our behalf, even then we will serve God and Him only.

I'm not sure, but I suspect the faith of the three Hebrews was almost as impressive to Nebuchadnezzar as the miracle. It is to me. And it reminds me that as much as I like guarantees, I must commit myself to God in every situation of life with absolutely no assurance that He will perform miracles on my behalf.

But then, you and I do have one guarantee, after all. Our God, who has power to do whatever He wills, is wise enough to do not what I want, but what is best.

And this is the best guarantee of all.

Personal Application

Be loyal to God and He will surely be loyal to you.

Quotable

"I will not mistrust Him, Meg, though I shall find myself weakening and on the verge of being overcome with fear. I shall remember how Saint Peter at a blast of wind began to sink because of his lack of faith, and I shall do as he did: call upon Christ and pray to Him for help. And then I trust He shall place His holy hand on me and in the stormy seas hold me up from drowning."—Thomas More

JUNE 19 *Reading 170*
TALES OF THREE RULERS
Daniel 4–6

"People must fear and reverence the God of Daniel. For He is the living God and He endures forever; His kingdom will not be destroyed, His dominion will never end. He rescues and He saves; He performs signs and wonders in the heavens and on the earth" (Dan. 6:26-27).

Throughout his life Daniel consistently witnessed to the power of God, and left an indelible impression on a series of world rulers. People around cannot help taking note of the truly committed individual.

Background
The Book of Daniel faithfully reflects the different customs of the Babylonian and Persian courts. Nebuchadnezzar of Babylon had absolute authority: His word was law. In Persia the ruler's word had the force of law, but once an official pronouncement was made, it could not be altered.

This difference sheds light on two elements of Daniel's story. Nebuchadnezzar's dream (Dan. 2) portrayed the succeeding empires as progressively inferior to that ruler's own. The inferiority is one of perspective: Nebuchadnezzar's absolute power (vv. 37-39) was gradually diluted in each succeeding world empire. To the ruler of Babylon even gradual movement from absolute autocracy would seem a mark of inferiority.

The change is also reflected in Daniel's story of his bout with the lions. Even though the Persian ruler wanted to save Daniel, he was helpless to change the tradition that bound him as well as others to his pronouncements. Thus Daniel's enemies were able to entrap and manipulate Darius, something impossible with Nebuchadnezzar.

Yet Nebuchadnezzar was as bound by his arrogance as Darius was by his treacherous officials. No one, however powerful they may seem, is truly free. Every human being is subject in the last analysis to his own character, to his circumstances and, certainly, to God.

Overview
Daniel interpreted a dream portending disaster to Nebuchadnezzar (4:1-27), and witnessed its fulfillment (vv. 28-37). As an old man Daniel interpreted a sign indicating the fall of the Babylonian Empire (5:1-30), and became a valued administrator of the Persian Empire which succeeded it (6:1-3). God thwarted the plan of Daniel's enemies and miraculously delivered him from a den of hungry lions (vv. 4-28).

Understanding the Text
"Until you acknowledge that the Most High is Sovereign" Dan. 4:1-27. Once again Nebuchadnezzar had an alarming dream and called Daniel to interpret. This time the dream was directed against him: It predicted that the king would become the victim of madness until he acknowledged the sovereignty of Daniel's God.

"The glory of my majesty" Dan. 4:28-37. God had twice shown Nebuchadnezzar His power, and the Babylonian ruler had been deeply impressed. However, he apparently thought of God as God of the Hebrews, and not a God sovereign over him. Arrogant people have this tendency. "Religion's all right for you," they'll say condescendingly. "Some people need God." Even those who think that God exists often fail to take the logical step of seeking a personal relationship with Him.

This was certainly the case with Nebuchadnezzar. He was too great a man to need God. Why, see all he'd accomplished!

The dream warned Nebuchadnezzar of his need to personally submit to the Lord. Daniel himself urged the king to repent, knowing that God's announcements of judgment are contingent. But within a year the king, his heart swelling with pride, was struck with madness.

Perhaps the greatest miracle here is that for "seven times," a period which typically indicates seven years, the throne of Babylon remained empty. Finally, after months or years of living like a beast in open fields, the king's sanity was restored, and he at last praised, honored, and glorified the Most High.

Many, perhaps rightly, view this as Nebuchadnezzar's conversion. At last the mighty ruler humbled himself, and took his place as a simple worshiper of the Lord of heaven and earth.

How often it takes just this—some disaster—to humble a person before he or she is ready to seek God. I suspect that Nebuchadnezzar would agree: If that's what it takes, the disaster is a blessing in disguise.

"King Belshazzar" Dan. 5:1. For many years Daniel's identification of "Belshazzar" as king was considered proof that the book was of late origin. Only a person ignorant of the history of the period would have "made up" such an individual.

But then archeologists discovered documents that showed Daniel, not the critics, was right! The text's report that Daniel was offered the third highest rank in government (v. 16) rings with authenticity, for Belshazzar was himself second, co-regent under his father Nabonidus!

How then can Nebuchadnezzar be called Belshazzar's "father" in the biblical text? One meaning of "father" is "predecessor." The term is often used in genealogies to indicate an individual who may be a distant ancestor. "Father" was also used in biblical times with the sense of "predecessor" on a royal throne. Even a supplanter like Jehu, who murdered the family of Ahab to set up his own dynasty, is called in Assyrian records a "son of Omri," the founder of the earlier royal line. A third consideration is that frequently a king like Belshazzar would marry a daughter of the founding line, and in this sense too be the "son" of the "father."

What impact does information like this have on our devotional use of the Bible? Perhaps little. But it does confirm our conviction that the Bible truly is the Word of God. And it reminds us that we not only can trust that Word, but that we must willingly subject ourselves to it.

"You . . . have not humbled yourself, though you knew all this" Dan. 5:1-30. When a hand appeared and wrote on the wall at a feast Belshazzar held the 15th of Tishri (in September, 539 B.C.), the king almost fainted with terror. The queen mother urged him to call Daniel, who had explained dreams for Nebuchadnezzar.

Daniel, now in his 80s, appeared and explained the mysterious words. The words were "numbered," "weighted," "divided," and indicated that the end of Belshazzar's rule had come (cf. vv. 26-27). Even though Belshazzar must have heard of Israel's God and of Nebuchadnezzar's conversion, the drunken king had brought the golden goblets dedicated for use at the Jerusalem temple to his table, to be used in toasts offered to pagan gods and goddesses.

Daniel's words tell it all. "You his son, O Belshazzar, have not humbled yourself, even though you knew all this." In setting himself against God, Belshazzar sealed his own doom and that of his kingdom. That very night, Babylon fell. Ugbaru, the commander of the Persian army that even then surrounded Babylon, diverted the waters of the river that flowed through Babylon. When the water level fell below that of the river gates, the invading force entered the city and captured the "impregnable" city in which Belshazzar had feasted.

"It pleased Darius" Dan. 6:1. The "Darius" of Daniel 6 is most likely a viceroy who ruled the empire while Cyrus, its conqueror, was away on a military campaign. Nothing is known of him from the secular sources now available, but 9:1 says that he was "made [appointed] ruler" suggesting that, despite his title, he was subject to another higher authority, even as the kings of Judah were subject during their last decades to the Babylonians.

Despite his advanced age, Daniel was appointed to an extremely high position in Darius' administration, and aroused the jealousy (and perhaps fear!) of other, less honest officials. These officials tricked Darius into issuing a religious decree they knew Daniel would not obey. They then accused Daniel, and despite Darius' best efforts, that ruler was forced to order Daniel thrown into a den of lions.

The deliverance of Daniel persuaded this ruler too of God's greatness, and he decreed that people "in every part of my kingdom" must "fear and reverence the God of Daniel."

I suspect that the royal command did little to create faith in Israel's God. After all, faith can't be commanded! What did create faith, at least in the king, was Daniel's faithfulness to the Lord. Despite the threat to life itself, Daniel continued to worship God openly. God's faithfulness to His loyal servant, like His faithfulness to us, nurtures budding faith in others.

You and I cannot command others to believe. But we can encourage them to believe—by an open, unashamed, and unpretentious witness to our Lord.

▶ DEVOTIONAL
Keep Your Gifts
(Dan. 5)

I love the picture this chapter brings to mind. There's Belshazzar, so scared that "his knees knocked together and his legs gave way" (v. 6). He stood there, trembling, in front of a suddenly sober mob of officials, trying desperately to look kingly. And in came Daniel, walking a little stiffly on his 80-year-old legs, but calm and dignified.

Struggling to keep his voice from squeaking, Belshazzar begged Daniel to interpret the miraculous writing that appeared on the wall. And then he promised, if Daniel could do this, "You will be clothed in purple and have a gold chain placed around your neck, and you will be made third highest ruler in the kingdom" (v. 16).

You have to hand it to ol' Daniel. He didn't laugh. He remained sober, accused Belshazzar of arrogance, and announced that his kingdom would fall to the Medes and Persians.

Daniel didn't even laugh. Can you imagine?

Daniel told the king to "keep your gifts for yourself and give your rewards to someone else." But the king insisted. And even when they brought out the promised gold chain and looped it over Daniel's neck, and draped his spare body in purple, the old prophet didn't laugh.

I'm afraid I might have in Daniel's place. It was so ridiculous. Here was Belshazzar, handing out rewards, and that very moment the level of the river that flowed through Babylon was falling! That very moment Persian troops were massing, ready to plunge through the shallows, under the river gates, and walk unopposed into impregnable Babylon. And pimply young Belshazzar, expecting Daniel to be impressed, was royally distributing largess that in the morning would be worth just about as much as, well, as Monopoly money is at the bank.

And Daniel didn't even laugh.

Probably we don't laugh enough. You see, the world is always holding out rewards, expecting us to be impressed. There's wealth. Status. Power. Acceptance. And all the time, just outside the gates, God is preparing to invade earth. When He does, and the kingdoms of this world become the kingdom of our God, all that earth has to offer will be worth—well, less than Monopoly cash.

So the next time some earthly reward is dangled in front of you, and your heart starts pounding with excitement, remember Daniel at Belshazzar's feast. Tell the world to keep its gifts for itself. Or, if others insist, and hand you some golden chain or a purple robe, chuckle inside, as Daniel must have done.

They can't bribe you.

You know that tomorrow, when this world crumbles as it must, its gold and robes will turn to dust.

Personal Application

Serve God, for His rewards only will last.

Quotable

"The eyes of this world see no further than this life, as mine see no further than this wall when the church door is shut. The eyes of the Christian see deep into Eternity."—John Vianney

JUNE 20 *Reading 171*
VISIONS OF THE FUTURE
Daniel 7–9

> *"I am going to tell you what will happen later in the time of wrath, because the vision concerns the appointed time of the end" (Dan. 8:19).*

Elements of Daniel's visions of the future have already been fulfilled. Others still await fulfillment.

Background

The last half of Daniel is filled with reports of prophetic visions that he was given by God. Most of these concern "the time of the end," either describing events that will take place then, or the sequence of events that lead up to history's conclusion.

In Old Testament prophecy "the whole earth" is best understood as "the entire region" impinging on and affecting life in the Holy Land. Thus the prophecies of Daniel focus on events in the Mediterranean world, including all of Asia Minor, Mesopotamia, and those powers such as Greece and Rome that exercised control over the area.

Many dismiss the final six chapters of Daniel as "apocalyptic literature," meaning that the imagery carries a powerful spiritual message, but that any truths it may express cannot be found in a literal interpretation. Yet it is clear that the visions of Daniel 7 and 8 are to be understood literally—and that the kingdoms described actually emerged in the hundreds of years that lay between Daniel's writing and the birth of Christ.

Thus it seems best to try to understand the visions and their interpretations literally, as portrayals, admittedly obscure at times, of what was the future when Daniel wrote. It's not possible to go into interpretive details in this commentary, for our focus is on devotional implications of the biblical text.

Yet even a casual reading of these chapters shows that the visions parallel Nebuchadnezzar's dream of a great image representing kingdoms to succeed his own. Even a casual knowledge of history makes it plain that the Medo-Persian, Greek, and Roman Empires match in each detail the predictive visions found in this amazing prophetic book.

Overview

Daniel's visions of four beasts (7:1-28) and of a ram and a goat (8:1-27) depict the future world powers. Daniel's great prayer of confession (9:1-19) precedes a revelation of God's "seventy-week" timetable for the completion of His purposes on earth (vv. 20-27).

Understanding the Text

"A stern-faced king, a master of intrigue" Dan. 8:23-25. These three verses illustrate both the difficulty of interpreting prophetic passages, and the care that must be taken.

Note that this ruler emerges during the time of the shaggy goat of Daniel 8, and is similar to, but different from, the king who emerges in the time of the fourth beast of Daniel 7. In fact, the goat of Daniel 8 corresponds to the winged leopard of Daniel 7: Each represents the kingdom won by Alexander the Great of Macedon and on his death divided between four of his generals.

Historically, commentators of every persuasion identify the hostile ruler of Daniel 8 with Antiochus Epiphanes, who attempted to stamp out the Jewish religion, desecrated the Jerusalem temple, slaughtered hundreds of Jews, and whose armies were ultimately defeated by Maccabean freedom fighters. Antiochus himself died of a disease strongly resembling stomach cancer, and thus as Daniel says was "destroyed, but not by human power."

What of the king of Daniel 7? Jesus in the New Testament speaks of him and his activities as still future (cf. Matt. 24). Emerging from the fourth beast—Rome, not Greece—his hostility, his actions, and his end will be like those of Antiochus. It is the likeness of the two rulers that makes Antiochus a fit model of an antichrist who will appear as history reaches its climax. Thus in Daniel's visions of the future, Antiochus corresponds to the Antichrist, but prophecies concerning the Antichrist were at most partially fulfilled in events which took place in Judea and

The Medo-Persian, Greek, and Roman Empires succeeded the Babylonian, just as Daniel foresaw. The final expression of the Roman kingdom, destined to be openly hostile to God and God's people and to be destroyed by the personal intervention of the Son of God, has not yet emerged (see Dan. 9).

Galilee some 165 years before Christ. The main focus of Daniel's visions remains the time of the end—a time that lies ahead for you and for me.

The point in all this is simple. We can expect the yet-unfulfilled predictions of Daniel to be fulfilled in the same way that the fulfilled portions have been—literally, historically, recognizably. Apocalyptic in nature or not, Daniel's visions concern events that will actually take place here on earth. Yet, while we expect a literal future fulfillment of Daniel's words, we realize that we do not yet have the necessary keys to unlock every mystery. We will recognize events when they happen. Many details will remain fuzzy until that time.

So once again we face the fact that our Bible is a truly trustworthy Book—a book whose supernatural origin and character can be demonstrated to all. Realizing this, we understand how important it is for us to treat Scripture with respect, studying it to hear His voice, and responding with obedience to the Spirit who gave, and who interprets, God's living Word.

"Seventy 'sevens' are decreed for your people and your Holy City" Dan. 9:20-27. Daniel's prophecies of the "seventy 'sevens' " is one of the most intently studied in the entire Scripture. Taking each "seven" as a cluster of 7 years, the prediction identifies 490 years, at the end of which God's program of the ages will be complete (v. 24). The countdown commenced with a decree

to rebuild Jerusalem. This was issued to Ezra by Artaxerxes in 458 B.C. But the seventy "sevens" are further broken up. A first group of 7 "sevens" (49 years) takes us to 409 B.C., and the repopulation of Jerusalem under Nehemiah and Ezra. The next group of 62 "sevens" takes us to A.D. 26, which according to some calculations marks the baptism of Jesus, Daniel's "anointing of the Most Holy" (One). Others calculate it to Christ's entry into Jerusalem on Palm Sunday.

There remains only one group of years until the end. Yet verse 26 says that after the 62, "the Anointed One will be cut off and will have nothing." Clearly there is a gap between the end of the 62 "sevens" and the last group of seven years—a gap that has stretched from the time of Christ up to our own day.

Many students of prophecy believe that one day God's countdown will resume. Then the last seven years of Daniel's prophecies, which most of the visions in the last three chapters concern, will also be fulfilled, and history will have come to God's intended—and predicted—end.

▶ DEVOTIONAL
Not Just "I'm Sorry"
(Dan. 9)

I see it all the time at home. Our little girl makes some remark or flounces off in disobedience. When it's over, we say, "I think it would be good to apologize." More than likely she sticks out her lower lip, whispers a grudging "sorry," and heads for her room.

I suspect that at times we're a little bit like Sarah when it comes to dealing with our sins. We just mutter our, "I'm sorry's" to God when we become aware of some failure, and hurry off to get on with our lives. But there was something very different about Daniel as he humbly and with a broken heart approached the Lord.

Daniel had been reading Jeremiah's prophecy that the Exile of Judah would last 70 years, and realized that the time was up! If Darius truly was a viceroy of Cyrus, it's probable that that very year Cyrus had issued his decree permitting Jews to return and rebuild their temple (cf. v. 17).

Why then did Daniel seem so broken as he prayed? His first words tell us: Daniel was suddenly awed at the thought of God's covenant love (v. 1). Against the background of God's love, Daniel sensed the utter depravity of his people. Israel and Judah were beneficiaries of God's grace, and recipients of His righteous laws. Yet they ignored His words and turned their backs on the prophets He sent them.

Deeply disturbed, Daniel identified with his people and their failings, and as a humbled sinner cried out to God. He recalled God's gracious acts (cf. v. 15), and understood how terrible it was that despite the Lord's goodness "we have sinned and done wrong."

Yet Daniel's prayer was more than a litany of failure. It was an appeal for even more grace! Daniel begged God to listen to the prayers of His people, and in grace to restore the land, the Holy City, and its temple.

What Daniel teaches us is that in our own prayers, of confession or of petition, we must not be like a child who sullenly says, "I'm sorry," even though not fully convinced her fault is all that bad. Instead we must measure our response to God against His grace, and deeply moved by how short we fall, come to Him in penitent humility.

Then, in His presence, with head and heart bowed, we like Daniel can appeal to God for even greater grace, crying, "We do not make requests of You because we are righteous, but because of Your great mercy."

Personal Application

Pride cancels out prayer; true humility wings it to the Lord.

Quotable ✓

"It was pride that caused the fall of Lucifer and Adam. If you should ask me what are the ways of God, I would tell you that the first is humility, the second is humility, and the third is still humility. Not that there are no other precepts to give but humility, but if humility does not precede all that we do, our efforts are fruitless."—Augustine of Hippo

JUNE 21 *Reading 172*
VISIONS OF THE END
Daniel 10–12

"He will exalt and magnify himself above every god and will say unheard-of things about the God of gods. He will be successful until the time of wrath is completed" (Dan. 11:36).

Among the great movements of peoples and armies described in this chapter, the character of God's opponents stands out.

Overview

Daniel's persistent prayer was answered (10:1-21). He gained further revelations concerning future tribulations under Antiochus (11:1-35) and Antichrist (vv. 40-45). Daniel's book concludes with a picture of the final Tribulation and triumph of God's Old Testament people (12:1-13).

Understanding the Text

"Since the first day . . . your words were heard" Dan. 10:1-12. After 21 days of fasting, the aged Daniel's prayer was answered by the appearance of an angelic messenger. Daniel was first complimented (vv. 10-11), and then encouraged. It had not taken 21 days for God to pay attention to Daniel's prayer, nor had He delayed His answer.

What a verse to hold on to when God seems to delay His answer to our prayers. As soon as our prayers are uttered, God does hear and answer. It may take time for that answer to arrive. But we need not doubt either the love of God, which moves Him to listen, or the power of God, which guarantees His ability to do whatever is best.

"The prince of the Persian kingdom" Dan. 10:13-21. The angel who spoke to Daniel provided a fascinating insight into the unseen world. His mention of Michael makes it clear that the "princes" of this text are also angels of significant status.

Even more can be deduced from the ability of the angelic "prince of Persia" to prevent the messenger from reaching Daniel until Michael intervened. The incident suggests, first, that angels are of different rank and power. Second, Satan's fallen angels are actively opposing the intent of God. Third, an invisible war between angelic armies even now is taking place on hidden battlefields. Fourth, what happens in that warfare can and does have an impact on events here on earth.

Yet the future is "written in the Book of Truth." All the efforts of Satan's minions will ultimately prove futile.

How does all this relate to you and me? It reminds us of what the Book of Hebrews says about the role of angels. They are "ministering spirits sent to serve those who will inherit salvation" (Heb. 1:14). The prize in God's invisible war with Satan is not just final victory. It is the good or harm done to persons whom God loves. And God's angels, a great host, actively minister to you and me, guarding us from the harm that God's great enemy and ours seeks to do.

"I tell you the truth" Dan. 11:1-35. Daniel had been granted a vision of a terrible future war, and begged God for more information. The angel messenger was sent to explain. The Hebrew word for "truth" is rooted in the concepts of faithfulness and reality. What the angel revealed would surely come to pass, and be worked out in Daniel's world of space and time.

In outline, the angel briefly related what would happen from that time to the death of Alexander (vv. 1-4), described wars that would be fought between the Ptolemies of the south and the Selucids of the north (vv. 5-20), and then focused on the terrible persecution of the Jews to be conducted by Antiochus Epiphanes in the 160s B.C. (vv. 21-35). All this is now past history.

But the scene then shifts, as it frequently does in prophecy, to an analogy of Antiochus. Even as Antiochus persecuted the Jews, his end-times counterpart, the Antichrist, will ravage the final generation of Jews (vv. 36-39). But his initial triumph will end in rage and frustration, and "he will come to his end, and no one will help him" (vv. 40-45).

"A time of distress such as has not happened" Dan. 12:1-13. The final chapter returns to the great end-time Tribulation (v. 1).

Though many elements of the prophecy are "sealed" (not to be known or understood beforehand), the angel did go on to give a specific timetable. From the time the Antichrist sets up an abominable image (cf. Matt. 24:15-27) in a yet-to-be built Jerusalem temple, only 1,290 days (3 1/2 years by the Jewish lunar calendar) remain until the end.

We play a little game in our family. While waiting to be served at a restaurant, we'll say, "How long till the food gets here?" Each of us makes a guess, and we watch closely to see who's right. Or we'll be driving, and guess just how many miles it is to our destination. We announce our numbers, and then, because the best we can do is guess, we wait and see who comes closest. There's no such hesitancy here. No guessing. Specific numbers are announced.

God knows His numbers exactly. He knows what, and when. We may not understand the sealed elements of Daniel's visions today. But we do know, from the very specificity of Scripture, that the future is known by God, and is securely in His hands.

"Multitudes who sleep in the dust of the earth will awake" Dan. 12:2. This verse is one of the Old Testament's clearest expressions of the hope of personal resurrection. The dead will rise, to meet their Maker and face judgment. Then some who awake will inherit "everlasting life," and others "shame and everlasting contempt."

It is a characteristic of the Old Testament to focus on the plans of God as they relate to this earth and the earthly future of His Old Testament people. Thus the Old Testament prophets seem preoccupied with the culmination of history, with great battles to be resolved by the appearance of the Messiah, and to the blessings of a peaceful existence here in a world ruled at last by Israel's God. On the other hand, the New Testament looks beyond this heaven and earth, and focuses our attention on an eternity in which individual believers experience personal transformation, and spend eternity with the Lord.

In a way, Scripture's visions of what will be are like a kaleidoscope. Each turn of that toy causes colored bits of glass to fall in a different way, constantly revealing complex new patterns. The view from one perspective may be different than the view from another. But each view is valid: Each shows another aspect of God's complex and variegated purposes, and impresses us anew with the wisdom and awesome complexity of God's eternal plan.

▶DEVOTIONAL
Successful, Until
(Dan. 11)

Put in a nutshell, the theme of this chapter is the struggle of exceptional men to excel, at the cost of world peace.

The theme is developed as God's angel messenger traces for Daniel the intense competition to exist between the generals who divided up the lands conquered by Alexander the Great. Their drive to excel and that of their successors was marked by a fierce competition for territory, wealth, and glory.

In describing the struggles of these ancient rulers, the biblical text gives us insights into the character of those whose goal in life is to "succeed," no matter what the cost.

Such men "stir up" their strength and courage to attack and compete with others. With "hearts bent on evil," they lie and scheme. Using flattery or force, they corrupt others to gain their personal ends.

The prime example of this kind of man is seen in verses 36-40. Driven by irresistible passions, this "king will do as he pleases," exalting himself "above every god." With no regard for deity or moral restraint, he "will exalt himself above them all."

It may seem strange, but something about such people seems to make for achievement. They are driven, yes. They use others, yes. They are amoral, yes. And these very traits give them an edge over those with less intense desires, greater consideration for others, and a habit of weighing choices morally. What troubles us is that while critical of such traits, all mankind seems to applaud their success. Most of history's dictators were men like these; most business barons whose concern was solely the bottom line were like this too. For all too many people, success and sin seem to be twins, always found in each other's company.

Of course, there's a footnote in Daniel 11's portrait. It's found in verse 36, and radically changes our evaluation of the man at the top. The verse says, "He will be successful until the time of wrath is completed."

Successful.

Until.

Yes, sin's methods work for the man who is driven to achieve. But they only work for a time. They only work "until."

Until God intervenes. Until the day of His wrath appears. Then, at the completion of that day, the driven man's success will crumble into dust, and all humankind will know that the truly successful person is that humble individual whose desire is to do God's will, rather than to impose his own.

Personal Application

Measure success not by what a man achieves, but by how he achieves it.

Quotable

"As church people, we sometimes assume that we are immune to the temptations of power. We don't make much money. Society gives us so little power that we think ambition—the drive to succeed, achieve and have prestige and influence over others—is a problem only for people in business or politics, not for people like us. We thus sometimes fail to see how we get caught up, for the very noblest of reasons, in the same ambitions that motivate everybody. Eventually, the people climbing to the top of the body of Christ can look just like those scrambling to the top of General Motors. Often you can't tell much difference between our leaders and those of the Gentiles."—William H. Willimon

The Variety Reading Plan continues with REVELATION

Hosea

INTRODUCTION

Hosea began his ministry near the end of the reign of Jeroboam II of Israel (793–753 B.C.). At that time Israel prospered economically, but was marked by injustice and spiritual decline. Hosea's message constitutes God's final warning to apostate Israel, and the prophet lived to see his predictions of judgment fulfilled when the kingdom fell to Assyria in 722 B.C.

The unique feature of Hosea is that prophet's relationship with his unfaithful wife. Gomer abandoned her husband to pursue adultery, even as Israel had broken her covenant with the Lord. But like God, Hosea had a genuine love for his bride. In the end he found her abandoned, rescued her, and took her back. Today as throughout Old Testament times, the Book of Hosea testifies to the unshakable love of God for His own.

OUTLINE OF CONTENTS

READING GUIDE (4 Days)

If hurried, you may read only the "core passage" in your Bible and the Devotional in each chapter of this Commentary.

Reading	*Chapters*	*Core passage*
173	1–3	3
174	4–6	6
175	7–10	10
176	11–14	11

Hosea

JUNE 22 *Reading 173*
AN ADULTEROUS PEOPLE
Hosea 1–3

> *"Go, take to yourself an adulterous wife and children of unfaithfulness, because the land is guilty of the vilest adultery in departing from the Lord" (Hosea 1:2).*

Christians today are to mimic at least one aspect of Hosea's life. We are to model the way we live with others on the way that God relates to us.

Background

From its inception by Jeroboam I in 731 B.C., the Northern Kingdom of Israel had practiced false religion. That ruler, sure reunion with Judah would follow if his people went regularly to Jerusalem to worship, as God's Law required, set up a counterfeit religious system in his own land. He established two national worship centers, at Bethel and Dan, and set up golden calves at both places, upon which Yahweh was supposed to ride. He ordained a non-Aaronic priesthood and reorganized the religious calendar.

Later Israel proved particularly vulnerable to a virulent form of Baal worship, actively promoted by King Ahab and his wife Jezebel. Even though this had been stamped out during the time of Elijah, Yahweh worship in Israel continued to be corrupt. Not only was the counterfeit system of Jeroboam I maintained, but elements of Baalism, including orgiastic rites and ritual prostitution, were practiced in the name of God. Israel had broken the covenant that bound her to the Lord; an act that was analogous to a woman breaking the marriage covenant.

It is this analogy that is developed in the Book of Hosea. In order to demonstrate to Israel the dynamics of her rejection of the Lord, God permitted the Prophet Hosea to marry a wife who became unfaithful. Hosea's visible suffering at the betrayal of a wife he sincerely loved enfleshed for God's people the Lord's own suffering at their betrayal of Him! But then, wonder of wonders, Hosea searched for and found his prostitute wife, purchased her out of the slavery into which she had fallen, and brought her home!

How Hosea's neighbors must have watched in awe. She deserved abandonment, yet an unquenchable love moved Hosea to restore her. Just as God's unquenchable love will move the Lord, after letting Israel taste the consequences of her spiritual adultery, to rescue Israel and also bring her home.

What a powerful reminder to us, first of all of the genuine character of God's love. But next, of the fact that Hosea was called by God to act out on earth the realities of heaven. Just so, you and I are to respond to others not as they deserve, but as God in grace has responded to us.

Like Hosea, each of us who knows Jesus is to be a living example of His unending love.

Overview

God commanded Hosea to marry a woman who would be unfaithful to him (1:1-11), even as Israel had been unfaithful to God (2:1-23). Showing genuine love for his wife, Hosea found her and brought her back, even as God will one day restore exiled Israel (3:1-5).

Understanding the Text

"During the reign of Jeroboam" Hosea 1:1. With Assyria and Syria temporarily weak,

the 40-year reign of Jeroboam was marked by military and economic resurgence in Israel. The king extended Israel's northern and eastern borders to occupy most of the territory held in David's day. Wealth flowed into Israel from trade, and local agriculture flourished. Everything seemed to be going so well!

Yet spiritually Israel's worship was corrupt, sprinkled with pagan practices. Society itself was corrupt, as the moral boundary stones too had been moved. Later Hosea cried, "There is no faithfulness, no love, no acknowledgment of God in the land. There is only cursing, lying and murder, stealing and adultery; they break all bounds" (4:2).

It is a tragic error to mistake GNP as a true measure of a nation's well-being. This happened during the reign of Jeroboam II when Hosea began to minister. And the prosperous, complacent people of Israel were deaf to Hosea's warning.

Yet there's a subtle message in this verse, which locates Hosea's ministry in the time of Jeroboam of Israel, but also the time of Ahaz and Hezekiah of Judah. That message? During Hezekiah's reign, some 30 years after Hosea began to preach, Assyria invaded and totally crushed the nation of Israel. The prophet lived to see his grim words of warning fulfilled.

In many ways America stands at the same crossroad. Too many of our society's moral boundary stones have been moved. There is too much violence, too much murder, too much stealing and adultery. And our strength can no more be measured in GNP and weapons systems than ancient Israel's. Spiritual and moral unfaithfulness remain precursors of certain national disaster.

"Go take to yourself an adulterous wife" Hosea 1:2-3. Scholars debate whether Gomer was perhaps a cult prostitute when Hosea married her. It seems unlikely, primarily because his marriage is intended by God to mimic the Lord's own experience with Israel. It seems almost certain that Gomer was chaste when they married, even as Israel was initially faithful to the Lord. Yet as time passed, she abandoned her husband to pursue other lovers.

I can't explain it. Two of my close friends, both fine Christian leaders, have been abandoned by their wives. In each case the wife has gone on afterward to a series of marriages or affairs, even as Gomer did in leaving Hosea. Why would a woman leave a husband who loved her, who provided for her, with whom she'd had children?

But then, why would anyone turn his or her back on relationship with God? Why abandon a God who loves us, who provides for us, who has sacrificed His own Son for us?

Perhaps the explanation has to be sought in the grip sin has on the human heart. We can't explain it. But each of us has to remain aware that deep within is the capacity to wander. Within each of us there lies a desire to go astray. When we think of Gomer—or when I think of my friends and their ex-wives—we need to acknowledge our own vulnerability.

And then we need to ask the Lord to help us stay ever so close to Him.

"Call him Jezreel" Hosea 1:4-9. The birth of each of Gomer's three children while she was with Hosea became an occasion for prophecy. With each birth, and through the names given each child, Hosea delivered a new message to his contemporaries.

"Jezreel" was the city where Jehu had slaughtered the family of King Ahab, and symbolized a similar destruction about to come on all Israel. *Lo-Ruhamah* means "not loved," or "not an object of compassion." God would soon cease to show favor to His people. *Lo-Ammi* means "not My people." The nation which had rejected God would soon be rejected itself. God would withdraw, not Himself, but His protection.

Each name confronts an unheeding Israel with the fact that sin has consequences. God would no longer intervene to protect His people from the natural consequences of their acts.

Today some suggest that AIDS is a punishment from God on those who practice homosexuality. Others express shock: God couldn't be so mean! Perhaps. But if AIDS is not a punishment, it surely is a consequence. Sin always has consequences. Some are just more easily identified than others. Jezreel is always just around the corner for those who practice sin. And "not loved" and "not My people" are the relational consequences for those who refuse to stay close to God but violate His precepts.

"Say of your brothers, 'My people' " Hosea 1:10–2:1. With the message of abandonment the Old Testament always includes a promise of restoration. Abandonment in the Old Testament is not rejection. It is much like a farmer, who leaves his fields to themselves for a time, letting the weeds that spring up when a field is untended flourish. In most Old Testament passages the word translated "abandon" actually means "withdraw."

If we persist in sinning, God may step back and permit us to experience the natural consequences of our wrong choices. But as Hosea said to Israel, God will surely step in again. He will purge His garden of corrupting weeds, and once again affirm "My people" and "My love."

"I will expose her lewdness" Hosea 2:2-13. In vivid poetic images Hosea now exposed the spiritual unfaithfulness of Israel, using the image of an adulterous wife. She is totally self-centered. She pursues lovers (other gods), but when they fail her she simply goes back to her husband, "for then I was better off than now" (v. 7). There is no sense of sin, no shame, no repentance. She simply comes back, as if she were doing her husband a favor by returning briefly before taking off again!

God announced through Hosea that He would force His wife Israel to face reality and to deal with her sins. Every material blessing would be taken away, and she would be stripped of prosperity.

Prosperity still insulates many people from spiritual realities. And it may be a blessing if all our "good things" are taken away.

"I will give her back her vineyards" Hosea 2:14-23. Again we see the extent of God's commitment to His own. Despite Israel's unfaithfulness, the Lord will one day restore His people. "I will betroth you to Me forever; I will betroth you in righteousness and justice, in love and compassion. I will betroth you in faithfulness, and you will acknowledge the LORD" (vv. 19-20).

If you've ever felt too guilty or ashamed to approach God, remember this verse. No matter what you have done in the past, God loves you. His goal is to make you holy, to make you His own. And God will succeed with you, and with His beloved of the Old Testament, Israel.

▶ DEVOTIONAL
As the Lord Loves
(Hosea 3)

Divorce is one of the most traumatic experiences a person can go through. Although I don't believe the statistics that supposedly indicate some 70 percent of the students in our local school system live with a single or remarried parent, I know that far too many adults and children know that terrible pain.

I'm sure that some divorces are not only justified, but necessary. Yet all too many are not necessary at all. Even when one spouse has an affair, the marriage doesn't have to end in divorce.

The pain of betrayal is intense. The hurt, the shame, the anger, all well up. Sometimes it all seems too much to bear—to keep on seeing "him" (or "her") every day. To imagine the spouse with the lover. For some, this is just too much to take.

Still, before a person files for divorce, it's important to consider Hosea. And to remember what God told him. "Go, show your love to your wife again, though she is . . . an adulteress." And then the Lord added, "Love her as the LORD loves the Israelites."

What a challenge! In our most intimate relationships, those relationships which have the capacity to cause us the deepest pain, we are to love as the Lord loves.

To love through the hurts. To love through the misunderstandings. To love through thoughtlessness, selfishness, and unconcern. Sometimes to love even through betrayal!

But however hard it may be, we Christians are called to love as the Lord loves.

I know that if we took this principle to heart, and practiced it in our homes, the divorce rate for Christians would drop. And despite the pain of such loving, the rewards would be great.

Personal Application

God's love won you. When you love as God loves, you win others.

Quotable
"If you truly want to help the soul of your neighbor, you should approach God first with all your heart. Ask Him simply to fill you with love, the greatest of all virtues; with it you can accomplish what you desire."—Vincent Ferrer

JUNE 23 *Reading 174*
ISRAEL INDICTED
Hosea 4–6

> *"The Lord has a charge to bring against you who live in the land" (Hosea 4:1).*

The Old Testament mirrors the heart of God. In the charges brought by Hosea, we can see those issues of justice and righteousness which we must deal with in our society today.

Overview
After preliminary charges (4:1-4), Hosea detailed the sins of priests (vv. 5-11) and people (vv. 12-19). He warned individuals (5:1-7) and the nation (vv. 8-15), but there was only superficial repentance (6:1-3). Thus God's indictment of His people goes on (vv. 4-11).

Understanding the Text
"A charge to bring" Hosea 4:1-3. After the first three autobiographical chapters, this chapter samples Hosea's preaching. This section, in the form of legal charges against Israel, begins with a general description of Hosea's society. The itemized charges are: there is no faithfulness, no love, no acknowledgment of God; instead there is cursing, lying, murder, stealing, adultery, and bloodshed.

Out of curiosity I picked up this morning's newspaper, and glanced at the headlines found in the section dedicated to our Florida county. Here are some of the stories that were featured:
* 13 mall stores robbed.
* Extra forces planned for Labor Day weekend to prevent drunk-driving accidents.
* Van window shattered by bullet.
* Armed robber arrested.
* Crack sweep nets four more.
* Teen charged with trying to run down boy with car.
* Ex-fire fighter charged with forgery.
* Man charged with DUI-manslaughter in 1988 accident.
* 18-year-old leader of a group of 15 charged with threatening three with bats and tire irons.
* Man 18, girl 14, charged with burglaries.

I didn't look closely at the stories. And I didn't include the more spectacular big-city headlines, like the one reporting the life sentence given a woman who turned her 13-year-old daughter over to a convicted rapist for a one-time sexual assault, to pay for the mother's crack cocaine.

In a way, the local stories are more frightening. They suggest that the corruption has spread further in our society than we might suspect. Perhaps we should listen closely to Hosea, for our own times are very much like the times in which Hosea ministered!

"I reject you as My priests; because you have ignored the law of your God" Hosea 4:4-11. The spiritual leaders of Israel were the first group to be indicted. They were to lead His people to godliness; instead they gave "themselves to prostitution, to old wine and new." They even relished "their wickedness."

The TV today showed a stooped Jim Bakker being led into a North Carolina courtroom. Yesterday damaging testimony against him was given by a former PTL staff member. Today his lawyer described him as "huddled up in a fetal position, lying on the floor of my office with his head under the sofa, saying that bad people were trying to hurt him."

The Lord needs to protect me from my first reaction, which is that he deserves whatever he gets. Instead I need to be crushed. Crushed and humbled that a spiritual leader of my own day could have "exchanged the glory" found in faithful service to God for contemptible things like millions of dollars, luxury homes and cars, and sexual trysts with church secretaries.

Jim Bakker's indictment is an indictment of us all.

"They are unfaithful to their God" Hosea 4:12-19. Hosea continued with an indictment of the whole population of Israel. They chased after idols and permitted their daughters to become cult prostitutes. Their very worship was corrupt. They used religious jargon in their speech (v. 15), but they loved their shameful ways.

It's fine to shout, "Praise the Lord." But unless our shouts of praise are matched by an equal enthusiasm for obeying the Lord, our religion too is meaningless.

"Hear this" Hosea 5:1-7. God brought charges against the priests, the people, and Israel's royal house, and convicted them. "This judgment is against you."

What did the "guilty" verdict mean? It meant that the divine sentence had been imposed, a sentence that involved the Lord's withdrawal from His people (v. 7). When troubles came, and Israel looked desperately for God to help her, He would not be found.

There is really no greater penalty. Without the Lord we are helpless before circumstances, enemies, and the consequences of our own foolish choices. If God were not here to turn to, there would be nothing at all we could do.

Let's consciously reject Israel's ways and attitudes whenever they crop up in our own lives. Let's hold tight to the hand God reaches out for us to grasp.

"He is not able to cure you" Hosea 5:8-14. Israel also renounced a national policy of reliance on God. Instead the nation relied on a treaty with Assyria to protect her against Syria. Assyria was only too happy to have this treaty as an excuse to march west. She gobbled up Syria—and then turned on her "ally" Israel.

When any nation rejects God, it is in danger. It takes a national revival—admission of guilt and passionate seeking of God (v. 15)—to make any society safe.

▶ DEVOTIONAL
Love Like a Morning Mist
(Hosea 6)

Some people are hopelessly optimistic.

"I know," they say. "I know I did wrong, and God has punished me for it. But all I have to do is come back to Him. If I just say, 'I'm sorry,' everything will be all right. Won't it?"

That's the kind of blithe optimism portrayed in verses 1-3. And it makes God shake His head in frustration. These people seem to think that some superficial turning to religion is what God wants. They seem to think that if they come to God and say "please," the Lord will be so delighted that He'll fall all over Himself to do them good.

But God wasn't interested in superficial religion then. And He isn't impressed by it today. God's judgments were intended to bring about a fundamental change in attitude, not a return to church! And so God said, "Your love is like a morning mist," and "I desire mercy, not sacrifice."

What do these two phrases tell us? First, that God isn't interested in fleeting emotions we may feel toward Him. He wants complete commitment. There's a vast difference between the "I love you's" breathlessly exchanged in the backseat of a car, and the "I do's" shared at a wedding!

Second, love for God is to be shown not in religious ceremonies but in daily life. Flowers are nice. But real love is better shown by helping with the dishes, changing dirty diapers, and "being there" when support and encouragement are needed. God isn't satisfied with a bouquet tossed His way on Sunday. He wants us to show our love for Him daily by doing His will. And so God seems to shake His head, and in frustration wonder aloud, "What can I do with you, Ephraim?" Despite the testimony of God's Law and the words of His prophets, Israel's concept of relationship with the Lord still remained shallow. And today we also tend to have a shallow concept of God.

God has no use for a "love" that is as fleeting and insubstantial as a morning mist.

Personal Application

Love God always, and you will always obey.

Quotable

"You wish to hear from me why, and how God is to be loved? My answer is:

the reason for loving God is God Himself, and the measure in which we should love Him is to love Him without measure."—Bernard of Clairvaux

JUNE 24 *Reading 175*
ISRAEL'S PUNISHMENT
Hosea 7–10

"My God will reject them because they have not obeyed Him; they will be wanderers among the nations" (Hosea 9:17).

Punishment must fit the crime. Here the various crimes that led to Israel's exile are described, along with predictions of that fast-approaching judgment.

Background

Exile. When Moses gave Israel her Law at the time of the Exodus, he included a catalog of the blessings that would be granted if God's people obeyed—and a catalog of punishments to be imposed if Israel rebelled and sinned.

Each catalog is found in Deuteronomy 28, with the "curses" for disobedience listed in verses 15-68. These curses, or punishments, are of increasing severity. The intent is that the people would turn back to God after light discipline. But if they persisted in sinning, increasingly heavy penalties would be imposed, each with the intent of bringing about repentance and renewal.

By Hosea's time Israel had experienced all the lesser consequences of their sin. All that remained for God to do was impose the penalty stated in verses 63-66. Reading those verses helps us understand the horror of the judgment about to befall Hosea's Israel—and helps us realize that God had done everything possible to avoid its necessity.

This judgment, exile from the land, was about to fall on a nation that had been warned for generations, by the written Word, by prophet messengers, and by persistent discipline.

How dangerous it is not to heed God's warnings. We should welcome warnings, for they are intended to spare us much pain.

Overview

Israel's disastrous domestic (7:1-7), foreign (vv. 8-16), and religious (8:1-14) practices demanded punishment. Israel would be taken captive (9:1-9), her glory fled away (vv. 10-17). Wicked Israel would be punished for her sin (10:1-15).

Understanding the Text

"The crimes of Samaria revealed" Hosea 7:1-7. National character is reflected in national leadership. In Samaria, the capital of Israel, the kings delighted in the wickedness of others—and became their victims. The image of the hot oven stands for the inflamed passions of those who conspired against Israel's rulers, approaching them with intrigue while intent on "devouring" them. The crimes are "revealed," for all in Israel would be aware of the fall of kings (v. 7).

But what specifically was Hosea talking about here? During Hosea's own lifetime four of Israel's rulers were assassinated and replaced by their killers! Zechariah by Shallum (2 Kings 15:10), Shallum by Menahem (v. 14), Pekahiah by Pekah (v. 25), and Pekah by Hoshea (v. 30). This ruinous domestic situation undermined any rule of law, and demonstrated the corrupt state of the nation.

I'm disturbed by the multitude of recent revelations of crime by our leaders in Washington. A Republican congressman was sentenced for perjury—for lying about seeking a loan from an individual who told him it was drug laundering money. A homosexual Democratic congressman admitted hiring a male prostitute, and later employing him on his staff. Respected high officials have been accused of using influence to obtain millions of HUD dollars for clients who then defrauded the government and, more reprehensible, the poor. So God's warnings in these chapters have a timely ring. "Whenever I would heal Israel," He said, "the sins of Ephraim are exposed and the crimes of Samaria are revealed." Our nation needs spiritual healing today. As each layer of bandages covering our wounds is unwound, more and more sins and crimes are revealed. We must face the fact that if national disaster is to be avoided, we Christians must repent—and pray.

"A flat cake not turned over" Hosea 7:8-16. My wife tells me I'm strange, but I like gooey pancakes. You know: pancakes that aren't quite cooked through, with raw dough inside.

Apparently God doesn't share my taste. The image in this verse, used to describe Israel, is that of a flat cake of bread cooked on one side by being plastered against the outside of a hot clay oven—but never turned over so it can cook on the other side. One side is done, the other is raw dough and, by implication, worthless.

What had made Israel worthless in God's sight? Hosea looked at the nation's mode of responding to danger. Like a frightened and senseless bird, scurrying first one way and then the other, Israel looked to first Egypt, then Assyria, for help (v. 11). But Israel never looked up, where the Most High resides (v. 16). Instead the people rejected His ways and spoke against Him (v. 13).

When we face danger, let's remember that we too have wings, and can fly. In looking up, and coming to God in prayer, we will find all the help we require.

"But Israel has rejected what is good" Hosea 8:1-14. It's fine to say, "O our God, we acknowledge You." But again Hosea confronted Israel with her hypocrisy.

First, a person who truly acknowledges God will not reject what is good. Morality and a genuine faith go hand in hand, and can never be separated.

Second, the chapter again and again points out the fact that Israel's religion was humanistic. That is, Israel's religious practices were not based on God's revelation of His will and His ways, but on the Israelites' own ideas of how to please God. They acknowledged God—but set up calf-idols at the worship centers dedicated to Him (vv. 4-6), in clear violation of His revealed will. Their multiplied "altars for sin offerings" have "become altars for sinning" (v. 11).

Humanistic religion always bears this same mark. Revelation is ignored, and God's express commands are pushed aside, to be replaced by the notions of men. People today too may cry, "O our God, we acknowledge You!" But unless that "worship" is in accord with biblical revelation, it is worse than meaningless.

"Ephraim will return to Egypt" Hosea 9:1-4. Here, as frequently in other passages, "Egypt" represents exile and slavery. But this time the Israelites would "eat unclean food in Assyria" (v. 3). They would go north, not south. Yet the experience would be the same.

If you or I were to be cut off from God, it would make no difference whether we settled in the north, the south, the east, or the west. Any place in which we were isolated from the Lord would be exile, and even the most comfortable of circumstances would be slavery.

"The prophet is considered a fool" Hosea 9:5-9. Rejection of God's message, and ridicule of His messengers, is an indication of hostility toward God Himself (v. 7b). The Israelites in Hosea's day did not like the message that "the days of punishment are coming, the days of reckoning are at hand" (v. 7).

There are parts of Scripture that you or I may not like, either. But this passage reminds us that the less we like a particular truth, the more we need to heed it! It's essential to guard against the repressed hostility that corrupted Israel's relationship with the Lord.

"Ephraim's glory will fly away like a bird" Hosea 9:10-17. It's so easy to assume that conditions are permanent. We get depressed when things go badly, and feel that things will never get better. And we tend to become complacent when things go well, assuming that the bad times are over for good.

Things were going well in the days of Jeroboam II when Hosea preached his message of judgment. People not only didn't like what Hosea said, they scoffed at him. How could prosperous and powerful Israel suffer such a fall? Yet within 30 years of Jeroboam II's death, while Hosea yet lived, everything that Israel counted on flew out the window! Her glory did "fly away like a bird," and God's word of judgment came absolutely true: "I will bereave them. . . . Woe to them. . . . I will drive them out of My house."

What has been, and what is, is no basis for confidence concerning what will be. We must expect our world to change—even to come falling down on our heads. We must place our confidence in God alone.

▶DEVOTIONAL
Sow Righteousness
(Hosea 10)

I like bumper stickers.

There are some I wouldn't want on my car. But I don't mind the one my wife attached to my van: "Fishing isn't a matter of life or death. It's more important than that." I don't even mind the one that says, "If you can read this, you're too close!" And I like many of the Christian bumper stickers I've seen—except when the person who has them plastered on his back bumper speeds up to cut me off as I put on my turn signal to change lanes on busy Highway 19.

It might have been good if in Hosea's time they had chariot stickers, or cart stickers, or donkey stickers. Hosea 10 suggests a few possibilities. How about "Idol is as idol does—nothing" (vv. 5-9). Or, "Don't look back. Your sin's catching up with you" (vv. 9-10). Or "Don't like the harvest? Then watch what you plant" (v. 15). Or maybe "We're strong enough to fail" (v. 13).

I don't suppose such stickers would have done much good. Some wag would have found a way to turn them around, like the stickers countering Campus Crusade's "I found it" campaign with bumper signs that proclaimed, "I lost it. Give it back!"

But there's one bumper sticker in Hosea 10 we all ought to place prominently, where we can see it daily. That one? "Sow for yourselves righteousness, reap the fruit of unfailing love" (v. 12).

Personal Application

It's not just a saying, it's a fact. We do reap what we sow.

Quotable

"Some people sow wild oats during the week and then slip into church on Sunday to pray for crop failure."—Rex Humbard

JUNE 25 *Reading 176*
ISRAEL TO BE RESTORED
Hosea 11–14

> *"I will heal their waywardness and love them freely, for My anger has turned away from them. I will be like the dew to Israel; he will blossom like a lily" (Hosea 14:4-5).*

There are few passages of Scripture that approach Hosea 11–14's emotional expressions of God's love. As we hear His cry, "How can I give you up, Ephraim?" we sense the depths of God's great love for you and me.

Overview

God's love is seen against the background of Israel's rebellion (11:1-7). In the last days God will restore Israel (vv. 8-11) despite her folly (v. 12–12:14). Israel fell into sin (13:1-16), but will return to God and be blessed (14:1-9).

Understanding the Text

"When Israel was a child" Hosea 11:1-7. Hosea now pictured God's relationship with Israel as that of a parent with a toddler. The child runs off; is brought back; runs off again, only to stumble and hurt its knee; is ministered to gently by its parent; and runs off again, completely unaware of the love shown by the parent whose guidance it ignores.

What an image: God, "bent down to feed them," and His people "determined to turn from Me."

Hundreds of years had passed, and Israel still had not learned. Israel's refusal to repent meant that "swords will flash in their cities."

How many people who have an image of the Lord as a loving God cannot grasp the fact that true love must seek the best for its object? A God of love will punish, even as a wise parent will punish a child who continually goes astray.

"How can I give you up?" Hosea 11:8-11 Unlike human beings, who are dominated by strong emotions when these emotions are aroused, the Lord is "God, and not man." Despite His justified anger against sinning Israel, He also felt compassion. God will be true to His love for Israel. One day He will roar like a lion calling back its cubs to the safety of the den.

"According to his ways" Hosea 11:12–12:14. It was not God who had brought the coming punishment on Israel. It was the people themselves. What had Israel done to bring judgment down on her?

God's people had "surrounded Me with lies" and been "unruly against God."

God's people had multiplied "lies and violence."

God's people had failed to "maintain love and justice."

God's people used "dishonest scales" and love "to defraud."

All this had bitterly provoked God to anger. "His Lord will leave upon him the guilt of his bloodshed and will repay him for his contempt."

The passage, however, leaves Israel and us an example to follow. The man Israel, then known by the name of Jacob, "as a man he struggled with God" (v. 3). The allusion is to Jacob's experience at Bethel, where he wrestled with the Angel of the Lord in a desperate struggle to obtain His blessing (cf. Gen. 32:25-29). Jacob did prevail, and won God's blessing. The forefather is thus held up as an example for contemporary Israel, to illustrate the intensity with which they must struggle to be blessed. What does that struggle involve? In Hosea's time or our own, to win the blessing of God we must "return to your God; maintain love and justice, and wait for your God always."

"I will come upon them like a lion" Hosea 13:1-16. Rather than struggle to obtain God's blessing, the people of Israel had thrown themselves eagerly into the pursuit of sin. Their craftsmen developed "cleverly fashioned idols," and they "offer[ed] human sacrifice." And this despite all God had done for them.

This people without gratitude, who had experienced God's kindness (vv. 4-7) would now experience Him in a different way. "I will come upon them like a lion," the Lord said (v. 7). "I will destroy you" (v. 9). "I will have no compassion" (v. 14).

Yet even when pronouncing judgment the Lord cannot resist a word of comfort. "I will ransom them from the power of the grave; I will redeem them from death" (v. 14).

If you should happen to feel the lash of God's discipline, remember this chapter of Hosea. The One who acts to destroy is also the One who ransoms. We can turn back to Him confidently, for He will welcome us home.

"Say to him" Hosea 14:1-3. Again and again the Old Testament shows us how to approach God after we have sinned. Here the prescription is repeated: Come asking forgiveness. Come trusting in Him only.

"I will heal their waywardness" Hosea 14:4. God tells us in advance how He will respond to such an appeal. He will deal with our waywardness and love us freely. He will do more than forgive. God will transform us, so that His anger may be permanently turned away.

"He will blossom like a lily" Hosea 14:5-9. Using images from agriculture, the Lord foresaw a time when Israel will again flourish in her land. Her idols put forever away, Israel will again enjoy the blessing of God.

The book closes with a question. "Who is wise? He will realize these things. Who is discerning? He will understand them. The ways of the LORD are right; the righteous walk in them, but the rebellious stumble in them."

▶DEVOTIONAL
Never Alone
(Hosea 11)

The man was bitter. Life had been unfair to him. He had been abused as a child. Not particularly gifted, he did poorly in school, and had difficulty finding a good job. Though a Christian now, married and with children, he often felt frustrated and angry.

A wise counselor opened the Bible to this chapter of Hosea. In verses 1-3 the hurting believer saw that though God's people hadn't been aware of it, all through their life as a nation God had been there. God had taken them by the arm, and they hadn't felt His touch. God led them gently, the leash woven of love. God's hand lifted burdens from their neck, and He Himself bent over to feed them.

The counseler showed him in verses 8 and 9 that God had felt every hurt, and that His heart had surged with compassion at Israel's suffering, even though it was deserved. And the counselor showed him in verse 11 that even the most vulnerable of beings will come, trembling, when God calls, only to be settled safely in his home.

And then the counselor asked the embittered Christian to close his eyes, and to relive those experiences that caused him so much pain. But this time he was to imagine God in each situation. He was to sense God beside him, and that the Lord was bringing him safely through. He was to sense God touching, and healing, every pain. He was to feel God lifting his burdens, and bending down to sustain him when he was ready to collapse in his weakness.

With eyes closed, the man did relive his experiences, and consciously invited the God of Hosea 11 to relive them with him. God had been there all the time! And as he became aware of that fact, and let himself feel God's loving touch, his bitterness was healed and his pain gave way to peace and joy.

Personal Application

The God of Hosea 11 has been with you all your life. Invite Him to heal your own memories, and cleanse you of bitterness and pain.

Quotable

"The happiest, sweetest, tenderest hearts are not those where there has been no sorrow, but those which have been overshadowed with grief, and where Christ's comfort was accepted. The very memory of the sorrow is a gentle benediction that broods over the household, like the silence that comes after prayer. There is a blessing sent from God in every burden of sorrow."—J.R. Miller

---

The Variety Reading Plan continues with JOEL

Joel

INTRODUCTION

Joel's vivid and passionate prophecy was stimulated by a terrible infestation of locusts that destroyed Judah's crops. Joel saw the disaster not only as a contemporary judgment, but as an event prefiguring a coming "Day of the LORD" at history's end.

In powerful words and images Joel portrayed the Sovereign God who will surely judge the sinful. God's people must repent from the heart to escape imminent disaster.

OUTLINE OF CONTENTS

READING GUIDE (1 Day)

If hurried, you may read only the "core passage" in your Bible and the Devotional in this Commentary.

Reading	*Chapters*	*Core passage*
177	1–3	2

Joel

JUNE 26 *Reading 177*
DAY OF THE LOCUST
Joel 1–3

> *"What the locust swarm has left the great locusts have eaten; what the great locusts have left the young locusts have eaten; what the young locusts have left other locusts have eaten" (Joel 1:4).*

Natural disasters in Israel and Judah were typically viewed in the Old Testament as God's judgments. Joel raised an important question for us to answer: what should our response to personal disasters be?

Background

Locusts. Throughout recorded history Africa and the Middle East have been plagued by swarms of these grasshopper-like flying insects. Even in the 1900s swarms so great that they blocked out the sun have been reported. When a flying swarm of millions upon millions of insects lands, they eat every green plant, leaving the land utterly desolate. Even worse, they often lay eggs before they move on, and just as new plants begin to sprout locust larvae attack the recovering vegetation. For a people like the ancient Israelites, whose livelihood depended on agriculture, a locust plague threatened existence itself. Just such an invasion of flying locusts, far worse than any in living memory (1:2-3), devastated Judah in Joel's day. The prophet interpreted that event as a divine judgment, and called on the people of Judah to repent. But even more, the utter devastation caused by the locusts stimulated a prophetic vision of devastation to be caused by invading armies at history's end, when the Day of the Lord finally comes.

Overview

A locust swarm that devastated Judah (1:1-12) moved Joel to utter a call for national repentance (vv. 13-20). The disaster prefigured the "Day of the LORD" (2:1-11), and made return to God urgent (vv. 12-17). Yet when that day comes God will save His people, and bless them afterward (vv. 18-32). God will judge hostile nations then (3:1-16), and Judah will know God's pardon (vv. 17-21).

Understanding the Text

"Has anything like this happened in your days?" Joel 1:1-4 It's typical of folks today to think that things "just happen." A personal tragedy is only "bad luck" that "could have happened to anyone."

The same attitude was all too typical among some in ancient Judah. But when an enormous swarm of locusts devastated Judah, the Prophet Joel cried out, "Think!"

This is the force of his question, "Has anything like this ever happened in your days or in the days of your forefathers?" Sometimes things happen that are so terrible we can't dismiss them as mere chance.

Underlying Joel's cry was the conviction that God is in control of events in this world. When disaster strikes, an appropriate response is not to shrug and say, "Bad luck," but to examine our hearts, and to see if perhaps God is crying out for our attention.

"Wake up, you drunkards, and weep!" Joel 1:5-12 There's nothing so frustrating to a parent as indifference. You try to reach your kids, you confront, discipline, even yell. And rather than repentance, or even rebellion, there's simply the shrug of a

shoulder and a muttered, "Oh, well."

That's what frustrated Joel and the Lord about Judah's response to the locust plague. They didn't cry out. They didn't make a fuss. They just sat around drinking their wine, shrugging their shoulders, and saying, "Oh, well."

How does God want us to respond when we are disciplined? First of all we need to wake up and weep! (v. 5) Discipline is designed to get our attention and to turn us back to the Lord, not just to make us hurt. Waking up and weeping is often the first indication that we've begun to pay attention to God's message.

The prophet added more verbs to portray an appropriate reaction to divine discipline. We mourn (v. 8). We feel a sense of despair and grief (v. 11). These emotions are not pleasant, but they are profitable. They show that we're taking events to heart. A godly sorrow, according to the New Testament, can lead us to repentance (2 Cor. 7:10).

"Put on sackcloth, O priests, and mourn" Joel 1:13-20. Joel called on the religious leaders of his day to serve as examples of how to respond to the national disaster. They were to first personally put on sackcloth—rough garments worn to indicate grief and sorrow—and spend the night in prayer (v. 13). Then they were to utter a call for a national day of prayer, when all would appeal to the Lord (v. 14). As terrible as the locust plague had been, it was only a preview of the terrors of the approaching Day of the Lord.

Clearly the clergy of Joel's day failed to interpret the locust plague correctly. They themselves did not repent and they called for no national return to the Lord.

What happens when the clergy are insensitive to the Lord? Just after the locust plague, God raised up another messenger, Joel, who was sensitive to Him! You and I needn't wait for clergy to take the lead when our own hearts are grieved, or when we feel a burden for our land. What we do need to do is take the situation to heart and express our own grief and sorrow to the Lord. Then, like Joel, we need to speak out!

"For the Day of the LORD is coming" Joel 2:1-11. The phrase, "Day of the LORD," is a technical term in biblical literature. It can be used to describe any time when God acts directly in history. But it's primary reference in prophecy is to events destined to take place in the years just preceding history's end.

Those years are both dark and bright. They are dark in that they introduce a time of worldwide tribulation, and especially a devastating invasion of Israel that causes intense suffering for the Jewish people. They are bright because they end with the surviving remnant of Israel restored to intimate relationship with God, and endlessly blessed by Him.

Here however Joel focuses our attention on the dark face of the Day of the Lord. He sees it as "a day of darkness and gloom, a day of clouds and blackness" (v. 2). An invading army, like the locust plague, would leave the land a waste and overrun every defense. Most awful of all, Joel pictured God on the side of the invaders (v. 11), using them as His instrument to punish His own people. No wonder Joel cried, "The Day of the LORD is great; it is dreadful. Who can endure it?" (v. 11)

All such Old Testament passages remind humankind that God has fixed a day for final judgment. And that judgment day is rapidly approaching. Yet no matter how vivid the images of its terrors, most humans remain indifferent. Most of us simply don't want to deal with uncomfortable things until we have to.

What Joel was telling Judah was that God's time for them was just around the corner of tomorrow. And the moment to deal with that very real and present danger had come! This is what the Gospel tells us too. Each individual must face God the Judge, and the time to make peace with God is now, not then! Why wait to welcome Christ into our lives and receive His forgiveness? Tomorrow may be too late.

"Even now . . . return to Me with all your heart" Joel 2:12-17. I don't know how she got my Phoenix, Arizona phone number. But I began to receive calls from her, from Toronto, Canada. She was tormented with the fear that God wouldn't accept her. What she had done seemed so terrible to her that she feared it was too late.

Joel's message to Judah was the same as

Jesus Christ's message to us today. It's not too late. "Even now" reminds us that as long as it is called "today," a person can turn to God and find pardon.

Joel, however, warned Judah that God is not interested in any superficial religious experience. It's not raising a hand, or walking down an aisle, or promising to give up drink. Joel said, "Rend your heart and not your garments" (v. 13). In biblical times people often tore their clothing to express grief or sorrow. Joel cried that any turning to the Lord must be heartfelt and real.

What can we expect if we truly turn to God? We can expect Him to act in character! He will welcome us, "For He is gracious and compassionate, slow to anger and abounding in love" (v. 13).

"The Lord will . . . take pity on His people" Joel 2:18-27. The generation that lives at history's end will repent at last. What is destined for them is an illustration of what you and I can expect when we turn to the Lord.

First, God will provide for us, meeting our basic needs (v. 19). Second, God will save us from our enemies (vv. 20-21). Third, He will pour out so many blessings that the hard times we have experienced will seem nothing in comparison—we will be fully repaid (v. 25). Seeing God's hand in all this, we will praise and bless the Lord, for we will know by experience that God is present, and that He is our God (vv. 26-27). (See DEVOTIONAL.)

"Afterward, I will pour out My Spirit" Joel 2:28-32. The primary focus of this promise is on the aftermath of the Day of the Lord. God will then bless all Israel, from child to adult, by pouring out His Spirit on everyone.

In Old Testament times the Spirit was given to equip a believer for some specific task or ministry. Now Joel foresaw a time when the Spirit will be poured out on all Israel and Judah. That event, after the judgments of the Day of the Lord, will be linked at history's end with various signs in the heavens and on earth.

But how, if Joel viewed the outpouring of the Spirit as something destined for Israel, and located it at history's end, could Peter explain events of the Day of Pentecost as "what was spoken by the Prophet Joel"? (Acts 2:16)

In the same way that the locust plague foreshadowed the ultimate Day of the Lord, so events at Pentecost foreshadowed the ultimate outpouring of the Spirit. Today you and I possess, with Jesus, the gift of the Holy Spirit. With and in Him we have a rich taste of the ultimate blessing to be given all by our loving God.

"I will gather all nations" Joel 3:1-16. The picture of the end given in Joel harmonizes with the picture found in other Old Testament prophets. God will stir up mankind's natural hostility toward Him and His people. Those who have been enemies of the Lord's chosen people will again invade. God will let them come, a great horde, and then, when they seem about to triumph, the Lord will judge the nations on every side.

"The mountains will drip new wine" Joel 3:17-21. The little Book of Joel closes with the promise of blessedness. The enemies of Israel and Judah will be punished, the people of God will again be holy, and God's pardoned people will live forever in His presence.

The journey we are on may be long and hard. But our destination is glorious.

▶DEVOTIONAL
The Years the Locusts Have Eaten (Joel 2)

For months she cried every night. Lying alone, her tears soaking the pillow, she sobbed out her "why?"

They'd been married for eight years, and she was three months pregnant with their daughter, when her husband just left. He couldn't stand being tied down anymore, he told her. And so he left her, with a two-and-a-half-year-old son and pregnant.

It was so hard, trying to deal with her loneliness, her doubts, her questions of, "What did I do?" and most terrible of all, "What will happen to me now?" She had to live with these questions not for days, or weeks, or even months, but for years.

Joel's warning to Judah of the coming Day of the Lord challenged God's people to repent and turn to God for healing. The chapter presupposes a people who have turned away from God, and who need to "return to Me with all your heart" (v. 12). There had been years of devastation. But Joel promised even God's rebellious people that the Lord has good in mind for them. Despite years of devastation, it is within the power of a loving God to "repay you for the years the locusts have eaten."

Today the young woman who cried herself to sleep so many nights is married again, to a husband who loves her. She loves her job teaching, and delights in the times she shares with her daughter, who is now nine. Life is good, and she's proven that God's promise to "repay you for the years the locusts have eaten" can be claimed even by those who never departed from Him, and whose suffering was something other than punishment for sin.

Personal Application

Hold on to God's promise to repay, no matter however long your suffering lasts.

Quotable

"My Good Shepherd, who has shown Your very gentle mercy to us unworthy sinners in various physical pains and sufferings, give grace and strength to me, Your little lamb, that in no tribulation or anguish or pain may I turn away from You."—Francis of Assisi

---

The Variety Reading Plan continues with AMOS

Amos

INTRODUCTION

Amos was a sheep rancher in Judah whom God sent to neighboring Israel, where he denounced the sins of that kingdom. His indictment of Israel charged the people with turning from God, exploiting the poor, and committing gross immorality.

The preaching of Amos was characterized by striking visions of coming judgment, and by a blunt portrayal of the social sins that made the prosperous era of Jeroboam II so corrupt. Through Amos' preaching we gain insight into God's concern for social justice, and into the responsibility of God's own to speak for the poor.

As other Old Testament prophetic works, the Book of Amos concludes on a note of promise. Sin must be punished. But afterward a chastened and purified Israel will be restored.

OUTLINE OF CONTENTS

I. Oracles of Judgment .... Amos 1–6
   A. Against the nations .... Amos 1:1–2:5
   B. Against Israel .... Amos 2:6–6:14
II. Visions of Judgment .... Amos 7:1–9:10
III. A Prediction of Renewal .... Amos 9:11-15

READING GUIDE (3 Days)

If hurried, you may read only the "core passage" in your Bible and the Devotional in each chapter of this Commentary.

Reading	*Chapters*	*Core passage*
178	1–2	2
179	3–6	5:1-17
180	7–9	8

Amos

JUNE 27 *Reading 178*
FOR THREE SINS
Amos 1–2

> *"They sell the righteous for silver, and the needy for a pair of sandals. They trample on the heads of the poor as upon the dust of the ground and deny justice to the oppressed" (Amos 2:6-7).*

This prophet, who spoke out against the corruption that festered in ancient Israel during an age of unparalleled prosperity, reminds us that justice, not wealth, is a measure of national health.

Background

The era of Jeroboam II in the eighth century B.C. was a time of unparalleled prosperity in both Israel and Judah. Together the two kingdoms recovered most of the territory held in the time of David's and Solomon's United Kingdom. Jeroboam not only extended his nation's territory, but also took control of ancient trade routes to the East, pouring vast wealth into Israel.

This wealth was not distributed equally, a fact which caused great social dislocation. Many were forced to leave family farms and move to the cities, where they struggled to exist. The newly rich used their wealth to create great estates, in violation of the biblical statute calling for families to hold their land in perpetuity. The wealthy controlled the court system, and within years the majority was figuratively ground into the dust, disdained by the rich who exploited them without compassion or concern.

At the same time, religion was popular, and many fine homes were constructed at Israel's major worship centers, Bethel and Dan. There a religion that mixed biblical and pagan rites was enthusiastically practiced—and strongly condemned by Amos and other prophets of the era.

It is against the background of a prosperous and complacent society, riddled with injustice and indifference to God, that Amos is to be understood.

Was Amos welcomed in Israel? Not at all. His brief months of ministry stirred up opposition and the prophet, his mission complete, apparently returned to Judah and his sheep. Yet Amos' written words remain an unmatched legacy: a call for justice that is as important for us to heed today as it was for indifferent Israel to heed so long ago.

Word Study

Justice. The biblical concept of justice finds one of its most powerful expressions in Amos. The prophet cried out urgently against those who "turn justice into bitterness" (5:7), and begged the people of Israel to "maintain justice in the courts" (v. 15). In sharp detail the prophet defined the injustice that marred Israel's society: "You hate the one who reproves in court and despise him who tells the truth. You trample on the poor and force him to give you grain. Therefore, though you have built stone mansions, you will not live in them; though you have planted lush vineyards, you will not drink their wine. For I know how many are your offenses and how great your sins. You oppress the righteous and take bribes and you deprive the poor of justice in the courts. Therefore the prudent man keeps quiet in such times, for the times are evil" (vv. 10-13).

But what *is* justice? The Hebrew words are *mishpat,* usually used when the text speaks of doing what is just, and *shapat,* which indicates the various functions of government. To do justice is to act in accord with one's rights and duties under law, and implies an objective code against which a person's acts can be measured.

In Israel, as for Christians today, that objective code was found in the Scriptures. God's revelation through Moses defined the Israelites' duty to God and to neighbor. This standard was more than a list of rules and regulations. It was a call to love God and others, with statutes that illustrated the practical implications of love in the social sphere. Even more significantly, the code was an expression of the loving nature of God Himself, who is committed to doing right by all in His creation. This law was an expression of God's own character; a model for all who yearned to be like the Lord.

Unredeemed human beings can never be completely just, as justice is ultimately a quality of God alone. Yet the concern we express for others is to demonstrate, in every social relationship and in every social institution, the spirit of love that infused the Hebrew Scriptures.

Justice, then, is showing love by doing what is right, as right is defined in God's revelation of Himself and of His will for mankind. It is just this that Israel in the age of Jeroboam II failed to do. There was no love, only selfishness. There was no concern for others, only a passion for personal comfort. There was no commitment to God's standards, only social conventions that openly favored the poor.

God still calls His people to do justice.. We are to show concern for the well-being of our fellow human beings, and to apply God's standards in our personal and national lives. Only by a commitment to justice can we hope to avoid the wrath that Amos announced must soon fall on Israel.

Overview

Amos of Judah traveled to Israel to announce an imminent outbreak of God's wrath on Israel's hostile neighbors (1:1–2:5), and on Israel herself (vv. 6-16).

Understanding the Text

"The words of Amos" Amos 1:1. Little is known of Amos beyond what is said in this verse. He was a resident of Tekoa, in the land of Judah. He identified himself as a *noqed,* a shepherd, who was given a vision and called by God to a prophet's ministry. This is not, however, a common word for shepherd. It suggests a wealthy rancher, even though Amos pictured himself actively caring for his flocks (cf. 7:15).

How appropriate that God should send Amos. Someone had to be sent to the prosperous of Israel, to charge them with injustice and selfishness. The fact that Amos himself was wealthy added weight to his words—and showed that a rich man can be truly righteous.

It's one thing for the poor to rail against the rich. It's something else again for a wealthy man to stand up and speak out against his own class. The man in rags who shouts on street corners is easily dismissed by the proper of society. But the man in a Brooks Brothers suit, the member of the club who stands up and confronts other members with the sinfulness of their behavior, can't be as easily dismissed.

Each of us, like Amos, belongs to a social class. While God may call us to condemn the sins of those in a different stratum of society, we are most likely to be heard—and to be right!—if we take a stand against the sins that characterize our own class.

"For three sins . . . even for four" Amos 1:3–2:5. The phrase, found in each oracle that Amos launched against one of Israel's hostile neighbors, means simply "for repeated sins." We can imagine Amos, climbing up on some prominent place, speaking to Israel's "beautiful people." He began his sermon by pointing to the northeast, toward Syria and Damascus. Loudly he proclaimed his news: for the repeated sins of this nation, so hostile to God's people, the Lord "will not turn back My wrath" (1:3).

Then, rotating slowly, Amos continued to denounce other nations in their turn. He spoke against Gaza and the land of the Philistines, against Tyre, against the Edomites and Ammonites, against Moab. How his listeners must have nodded and smiled! This was the kind of preaching they liked!

And then, when Amos had turned full circle, he pointed south and cried out,

"For three sins of Judah, even for four, I will not turn back My wrath" (v. 4). And at this, the crowd of Israelites must have broken out in loud cheering! At last their alienated brethren were going to get what they deserved.

I imagine the Israelites who first heard this sermon never suspected what Amos was leading up to. They never noticed that in drawing a circle around them, Amos had made Israel the bull's-eye!

Every time you and I rejoice over the troubles of someone who "deserves whatever he gets," we follow the example of those Israelites. We never stop to think that we too are guilty of faults and failings! In applauding the judgment of others, we condemn ourselves, for we agree that sins and failures should be judged.

"I will send fire upon Judah" Amos 2:4-5. Amos was from Judah, but he had no illusions about his fellow countrymen. He knew the mass of the people had "rejected the Law of the LORD and have not kept His decrees." He knew that many had "been led astray by false gods."

Before we condemn the sins of others, we need to be ready to confess our own. We cannot pronounce judgment, as if we were judges. All we can do is to confess the righteousness of God in condemning our sins, and thus take our place with those we warn. Amos did not come from a just society to criticize an unjust society. Amos came from a society he knew was sick with sin, to urge a nation terminally ill to face the fact that it was dying, and to turn to God for healing.

This is the attitude we need to adopt when sharing Christ with others. Not the "holier than thou" attitude of some. But the humble urgency of one who knows how desperately he himself needed the healing he received at Jesus' touch.

"Now, then, I will crush you" Amos 2:6-16. Amos then turned to Israel and held up a mirror so that the people could see themselves as God saw them. He began with a brief catalog of sins that revealed the injustice which marked Israelite society.

God is never indifferent to sin, wherever it may be found. Yet the sin that disturbs Him most is the sin found in those who claim to be His own.

▶ DEVOTIONAL
Where Cash Counts
(Amos 2)

Prosperity tends to drain the vitality of any people.

It happened to ancient Israel. It happened to Rome. It happened to the British Empire. And it's happening to America too.

Why? Because with prosperity comes a subtle change in the values held by citizens of a nation. This was the message of Amos to his contemporaries. Your values are turned upside down. Those distorted values doom you to judgment.

Amos identified the critical values which doom a people in his first charge against Israel. Materialism replaces humanitarianism. Selfishness shoves morality aside. And secular religion replaces the revealed faith. Note how each of these is described.

The people of Israel "sell the righteous for silver" (v. 6). Old Testament Law called on Israelites with money to spend it to redeem fellow countrymen who had become slaves (Lev. 25:39-52). In Amos' Israel cash counted with the rich, while poor people did not! This is the nature of materialism. A love for things replaces a love for people as the motivating drive in a person's life.

"Father and son use the same girl" (v. 7). Men selfishly "use" women rather than value them as persons. The drive to experience selfish pleasures stretches beyond the loosest bounds of morality. Traditional moral standards become objects of ridicule and are arrogantly shoved aside.

They "lie down beside every altar" (v. 8). They are religious, but practice a religion of ritual without reality. Old Testament Law commanded that garments taken as a pledge to guarantee repayment of a loan be returned at night, for such garments often served as the only blanket of the poor. Yet the people of Israel saw no conflict in being religious, and at the same time being disobedient to God and indifferent to the poor. Secular religion is a tool to oppress or a sop to conscience, while biblical faith is a call to commitment.

The point of Amos' first sermon, and this devotional, is really simple. We need to check our relationship by checking our values. Is profit more important to us than people? Are the standards we live by those of our society, or of our God? Is our faith a matter of Sunday attendance, or that plus week-long commitment to doing God's will?

The way we answer those questions, and the way our nation answers them, may well determine the future of our land.

Personal Application

The difference between God's people and the world's isn't just in what we believe, it's in what we value and in what we do.

Quotable

"If we have to choose between making men Christian and making the social order more Christian, we must choose the former. But there is no such antithesis. . . . There is no hope of establishing a more Christian social order except through the labor and sacrifice of those in whom the Spirit of Christ is active, and the first necessity for progress is more and better Christians taking full responsibility as citizens for the political, social and economic system under which they and their fellows live."—William Temple

JUNE 28 *Reading 179*

A JUST, MORAL SOCIETY

Amos 3–6

> *"You trample on the poor and force him to give you grain. Therefore, though you have built stone mansions, you will not live in them; though you have planted lush vineyards, you will not drink their wine" (Amos 5:11).*

The Old Testament's vision of a just, moral society was warped and twisted in Amos' day. Now as then, an immoral society must and will fall.

Overview

Israel's sins required punishment (3:1-15). Amos cried out against the pampered wives of the wealthy (4:1-3), corrupt worship (vv. 4-5), and indifference to God (vv. 6-13). The nation had to seek the Lord and do justice (5:1-15), or face the dark "Day of the LORD" (vv. 18-20). God hated Israel's corrupt religion (vv. 21-27), and would judge her for her complacency and pride (6:1-14).

Understanding the Text

"You only have I chosen" Amos 3:1-2. God would deal strictly with "the whole family I brought up out of Egypt," for He had established an intimate relationship with them alone. It is far worse for a people who know God to give themselves over to evil than for those who have had no personal contact with the Lord.

Today too relationship with God has responsibilities as well as privileges.

"Plunder and loot in their fortresses" Amos 3:3-14. In this passage Amos developed a simple theme: causes are related to effects. Thus people walk together because they have agreed to do so (v. 3), no bird falls into a trap unless one has been set (v. 5), and the sounding of a watchman's warning trumpet causes a city's citizens to tremble (v. 6). What cause then did God send His prophet to link with what effect?

Hostile nations were called to witness a strange thing. Normally a nation loots its enemy's fortresses. But Israel, which did "not know how to do right" plundered and looted "in their [own] fortresses" (v. 10). Because the society was corrupt and the rich unjustly looted the poor of their own land, "an enemy will overrun the land" (v. 11). The cause of the coming disaster was the injustice that was deeply entrenched in Israel's society.

Exercising his prophetic gift, Amos foresaw a day when Israel would be punished for her sins, when her worship centers would be razed, and the mansions of the rich would be left smoldering ruins (vv. 14-15).

Cause and effect operate in the moral as well as physical realm. This is the impact of Amos' teaching, and we need to take it to heart today. Any individual or nation that abandons justice as a guide to personal and social action in effect loots his or its own fortresses. One's only sure defense against disaster crumbles, and ruin will surely follow.

"You cows of Bashan" Amos 4:1-3. With pointed sarcasm Amos compared the sleek wives kept in luxury by their wealthy husbands with the fat cattle of a district famous for its cows. The charge that they "oppress the poor and crush the needy" implied that the wives' hunger for luxuries motivated their husbands to use any means to get the money needed to satisfy their demands. It's much like the modern fable of the young accountant driven to embezzle to keep the "love" of his girlfriend.

Yet Amos established an important principle here. The person who profits from an injustice is as guilty as the person who perpetrates it. One who benefits in any way from injustice is rightly subject to judgment.

Thus Amos pronounced God's judgment. The sleek wives of the wealthy would be dragged away into captivity, every luxury lost.

"Go to Bethel and sin" Amos 4:4-5. Amos pictured the wealthy of Israel, dressed in their Sabbath best, standing outside the sanctuary after a service, boasting to each other about their donations. What a modern scene! Oh, yes, you meet so many of "our kind" of people at services. And make such important business contacts. And of course it helps to be seen as an active supporter of the community by the "best people." This is part of the reason Amos struck out at Israel's worship. The well-to-do of Israel did "love to" (v. 5) boast about their offerings, using religion as a form of polite social competition. But the other reason for Amos' condemnation was that God never ordained worship centers at Bethel or Gilgal. In fact, Old Testament Law required He be worshiped only at the Jerusalem temple, and that sacrifices were to be made only on its altar.

If you and I truly want to worship God, our motives must be pure. And our worship must be in accord with God's revelation of His will.

"I gave you empty stomachs in every city" Amos 4:6-13. At first it seems a strange "gift." Especially as God went on to remind Israel through Amos that He withheld rain (v. 7), struck gardens with blight and mildew (v. 9), sent plagues (v. 10), and ordained defeats in battle (vv. 10-11).

We see the reason that these are a "gift" when we see their purpose. God sent these disasters in hopes that Israel would awaken to its sinful condition, and return to the Lord.

The old story tells about the city fella' who tried to drive an old mule. He shouted "Git up" and "Go." He ranted and raved. But the old mule never moved a muscle. Finally a farmer came over, picked up a two-by-four, and hit the mule on the head as hard as he could. The farmer then told the mule, "Git up," and sure enough, it got! Drawling, the farmer explained. "That mule will go, all right. But first you got to git his attention."

That's what Amos 4 is saying. God hit Israel with two-by-fours. But even then, the Lord couldn't get His people's attention. They were too intent on doing evil to pay any attention to His voice.

What a reminder for us. We can give God our full attention, and be responsive to His voice. Or God, in love, may hit us with some two-by-four to get our attention!

"Seek Me and live" Amos 5:1-16. The Bible makes a distinction between God hitting His own on the head with two-by-fours in order to get their attention and divine judgment. Sometimes when we think we are being punished, all God really is doing is shouting to us in a loud voice in an effort to help us hear what He has to say.

Amos now warned the people of Israel that God was about to actually judge them. Unless there was a radical change in their values and behavior (vv. 4-15, see DEVOTIONAL), the nation would be decimated (vv. 1-3) and every family would wail in mourning over the death of loved ones and of the nation itself (v. 16).

We need to learn to welcome any suffering that draws us closer to the Lord. Such pain is insignificant in comparison with its benefits—and in comparison with the judgment we might suffer if we stubbornly refused to turn to Him.

"Beds inlaid with ivory" Amos 6:1-7. Amos now returned to the lifestyle of Israel's complacent rich. They lounged on expensive couches and feasted daily on meat, entertaining each other with musical instruments and drinking wine by the bowlful. Yet it was not luxury itself that was wrong. What was wrong was that they "do not grieve over the ruin of Joseph." There was absolutely no concern for the poor; no sense of any obligation to use their wealth to aid those less fortunate.

Genesis 4 reports that after being confronted by God, Cain who had murdered his brother Abel, muttered, "Am I my brother's keeper?" God's Law had answered that question with a decisive yes! We are to love our neighbor as ourselves, and to display that love in practical ways. The complacent rich of Israel denied this fundamental principle by not only being indifferent to their poor neighbors, but also by exploiting them.

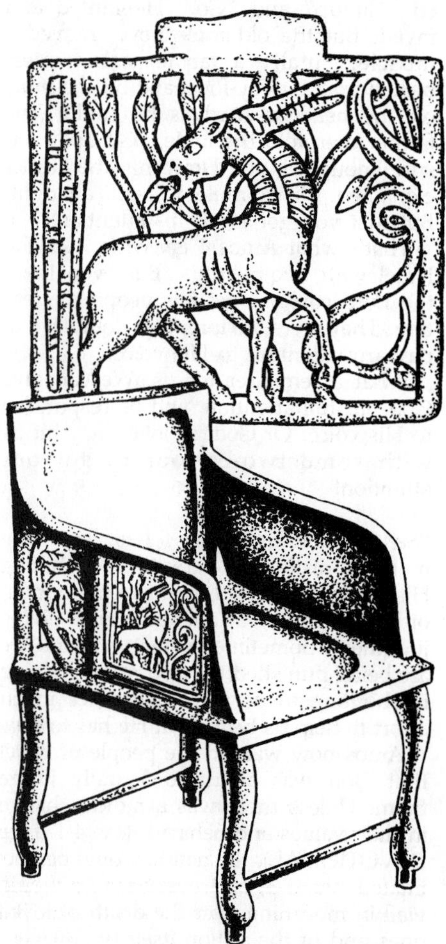

Archeologists have found pieces of ivory inlay in Samaria, the capital of Israel, from couches like those mentioned by Amos. While the poor of Israel starved, their rich exploiters continued to meet for daily banquets, indifferent to the suffering of their fellow citizens.

The angry prophet announced God's verdict. "You will be among the first to go into exile; your feasting and your lounging will end."

"I abhor the pride of Jacob" Amos 6:8-11. It's not wrong to feel good about our accomplishments. This is not the pride that Amos condemned. Rather Amos spoke against the arrogance of men and women who have prospered at the expense of the poor, and now gazed smugly about themselves at their lands, mansions, and luxuries.

Individuals who live in any society marked by institutionalized injustice should weep and repent, not look with pride at what they might possess.

"Do horses run on rocky crags?" Amos 6:12-14 The Hebrews, like other ancient peoples, loved riddles. So when concluding his indictment, Amos used such a saying. Do horses run on rocky crags, or do cattle plow there? The answer of course is, never. Horses would fall, and no crop could grow in such soil.

Israel, in turning justice into poison, had guaranteed her own downfall, and planted a crop destined to produce bitterness. There was no explaining such a choice. And there was no avoiding its tragic consequences. The Lord would "stir up a nation against you, O house of Israel," and that nation, Assyria, will "oppress you all the way."

Like Israel you and I are free to choose our own course. But we are not free to avoid the consequences of any choices we make. How important that we choose wisely, then, and willingly go God's way.

▶DEVOTIONAL
Seek Me, and Live
(Amos 5:1-17)

Amos 5 describes a people whose values are turned upside down. The chapter is a powerful call to God's people to establish the just, moral society the Lord yearned to see. It's a chapter relevant to us today, because like ancient Israel, prosperous America is confused about basic values.

What is necessary for any people or society to be truly just?

We are to seek God, and live (vv. 4-6). Note that the text emphasizes seek "Me." It's not religion that produces a just society, but personal relationship with the living God.

We are to lift up righteousness (vv. 7-10). The text pictures a people who "cast righteousness to the ground" rather than lift it up. Yet God, who established the natural laws that maintain the physical universe, is the source of just as sure moral standards. Israel's values were a reverse of the divine: the people "hate the one who reproves in court and despise him who tells the truth" (v. 10). No society that abandons biblical standards of righteousness or shows antagonism to them can build a just society.

We are to care for the poor. In Israel the poor were oppressed by such institutions as the courts, and by individuals, who extorted money from them. The slumlord is guilty, but so is any social system which denies the poor the rights accorded under law to the well-to-do. No society that exploits the economically deprived can be just or moral.

But what can you or I do about "society"? How can an individual have an impact on his or her world? Perhaps there is little we can do. But Amos showed us that we can do *something.*

Amos said, "Seek good" (v. 14). The verb is active, and you and I are to actively search for any good that we can do, and do it.

Amos said, "Hate evil, love good" (v. 15). Again the verbs are active. We are to be aware of what is warped in our society, and to really care. We are to hate evil and love so passionately that we act on our convictions, and take a stand.

Amos said, "Maintain justice in the courts" (v. 15). Again the verb is active, and the call is clear. There may be little we can do, but we are to do the little we can!

It's fascinating that Amos gave us no blueprint for social revolution. What he did do is to call on us to care. To care so deeply, so passionately, that we do whatever we can to hold up justice as a shining ideal.

Personal Application

Though there may be little you can do, do the little you can.

Quotable

"If you add little to little and do this often, soon the little will become great."—Hesiod

---

JUNE 29 *Reading 180*
VISIONS OF JUDGMENT
Amos 7–9

> *"Then the Lord said, 'Look, I am setting a plumb line among My people Israel: I will spare them no longer' " (Amos 7:8).*

Amos looked ahead, and he foresaw the certain judgment of a people who had refused for decades to heed God's call to repent.

Overview

Three visions of certain judgment (7:1-9) are interrupted by an account of Israel's reaction to Amos' preaching (vv. 10-17). The sinful kingdom, ripe for judgment (8:1-14) would surely be destroyed (9:1-10), yet one day Israel's prosperity will be restored (vv. 11-15).

Understanding the Text

"I will spare them no longer" Amos 7:1-9. In a vision Amos saw destructive judgments God was preparing to unleash on Israel. He successfully diverted the first two. But finally God refused to delay any longer.

The plumb line is a tool used by carpenters. It is simply a weight attached to a line, that is held against a wall or other construction to measure uprightness. Old Testament prophets frequently used the plumb line metaphorically as a tool used by God to measure the moral uprightness of a generation.

God's plumb line indicated that the judgment of Israel could no longer be delayed.

The New Testament helps us understand the principle of delayed judgment. It is an expression of God's kindness, tolerance, and patience. Yet the person or nation that persists in showing contempt for God's forebearance stores up wrath against "the day of God's wrath, when His righteous judgment will be revealed" (Rom. 2:4-6). Israel was not "getting away with" the wickedness entrenched in her society. Each failure to seize a new opportunity God gave His people to repent simply made the coming judgment more certain.

"The priest of Bethel" Amos 7:10-18. The attitude of the people of Israel toward Amos is illustrated in the reaction of Amaziah, who apparently functioned as high priest at the Bethel worship center. Amos was clearly challenging the social order. So the priest informed the king that Amos was "raising a conspiracy against you."

Amaziah then expelled Amos, commanding him not to prophesy because, "This is the king's sanctuary and the temple of the kingdom" (v. 13). What a revealing statement! The sanctuary did not belong to God, but the king, for religion in Israel was dedicated to maintaining the social status quo, not to challenging social evils!

Biblical faith is never a truly comfortable faith, for it calls us to constantly examine our lives and our society. Biblical faith is radical, in that it is never to be identified with a political theory, political party, or national ideology. Scripture calls us to stand outside our culture, and to judge it when it is wrong.

This the high priest of Israel's religion was unwilling to do. He willingly subordinated religion to politics, and when Amos stood up and announced God's judgment on Israel's sinful society, the high priest angrily demanded he leave town!

But it was not the radical Amos who was judged by this priest. The priest judged himself by his actions. And God announced that he would live to see the consequences of conformity (vv. 16-17).

As for unrepentant Israel, the people "will certainly go into exile, away from their native land."

"The time is ripe for My people Israel" Amos 8:1-14. My wife watches bananas set out on the kitchen counter carefully. She wants them just right—not too green, not too soft.

God through Amos announced that Israel had the "just right" stage: just right for judgment (see DEVOTIONAL). Israel had rejected justice. God will "never forget anything they have done" (v. 7). All will mourn in bitterness, and even if they should seek the world over for a word from God, "They will not find it" (v. 12).

"I saw the Lord standing by the altar" Amos 9:1-10. The altar and coals from the altar symbolize judgment in the Old Testament. A priest might take his stand at the altar to appease God by offering a sacrifice. But in this vision Amos saw God Himself at the altar. He stood there not to receive a sacrifice but to execute judgment.

The text makes this abundantly clear. God would kill the wicked with the sword. "Not one will get away, none will escape" (v. 1). God was committed to "hunt them down and seize them," for the Lord has fixed "His eyes upon them for evil and not for good" (v. 4).

This awesome picture of a God committed to execute judgment is an appropriate corrective to an overemphasis on the love of God. Yes, God is love. God eagerly desires to extend the benefits of salvation to all. But those who refuse to respond to a God of love must and will face Scripture's God of judgment and justice.

Those who live in a sinful kingdom may be completely sure that God "will destroy it" and that "all the sinners among My people will die by the sword" (v. 10).

"In that day I will restore" Amos 9:11-15. In a few brief verses Amos, as the other Old Testament prophets, added a word of hope. This unjust generation of God's people must fall. But God will restore the chosen race.

Amos specifically links that restoration to the appearance of a Ruler to come from David's family line. This is the meaning of

"I will restore David's fallen tent" (v. 11). When He appears, the Jews will be regathered to their land, and know an age of unparalleled prosperity. And how graphically Amos portrayed that time: "The reaper will be overtaken by the plowman and the planter by the one treading grapes" as "new wine" drips "from the mountains."

Israel rejected God, but God had not abandoned them. Calling Himself "the LORD your God," God promised, "I will plant Israel in their own land, never again to be uprooted from the land I have given them" (v. 15).

▶ DEVOTIONAL
Ripe for Judgment
(Amos 8)

One of the best marketing gimmicks I've heard about was thought up by the fellow whose crop of Yellow Delicious apples was ruined by hail. Every place a hailstone struck, a brown mark developed, making the apples almost worthless.

But the clever orchard owner found a way to turn his disaster around. He launched an advertising campaign warning customers to buy only apples with those brown spots that show they were tree-ripened!

Israel too bore distinctive spots. But there was no way the nature of those spots could be disguised. Such spots on any society mark it off as truly ripe, but ripe for judgment.

There is trampling on the poor.

There is indifference to true religion.

There is dishonesty in business.

There is exploitation of the weak and socially powerless.

Perhaps these marks are not yet visible on the surface of our society. But should you observe them, don't let yourself be fooled. They're not evidence of "tree-ripened" quality.

They are signs that our society too has become ripe for judgment.

Personal Application

Spots appearing in any society tell Christians it's time to repent, and pray.

Quotable

"Making an open stand against all the ungodliness and unrighteousness which overspreads our land as a flood is one of the noblest ways of confessing Christ in the face of His enemies."—John Wesley

---

The Variety Reading Plan continues with JONAH

Obadiah

INTRODUCTION

Obadiah is a prophecy of destruction, directed against Edom, a land across the Jordan River from Judah that was populated by descendants of Jacob's brother, Esau (Gen. 25). Obadiah said the Edomites collaborated with foreign invaders of Judah and mistreated Jerusalem's survivors; a charge which fits six different occasions in Judah's history! It is most likely that Obadiah predicted Edom's overthrow just after the Babylonian invasion of Judah in 586 B.C. Edom disappeared as an independent kingdom the latter half of the sixth century B.C., and its ruin is referred to in Malachi 1:3-4.

OUTLINE OF CONTENTS

I. The Demise of Edom .... Obad. 1-9
II. The Charge against Edom .... Obad. 10-14
III. The Day of the Lord .... Obad. 15-21

READING GUIDE (1 Day)

If hurried, you may read only the "core passage" in your Bible and the Devotional in this Commentary.

Reading	*Chapter*	*Core passage*
181	1	vv. 11-12

Obadiah

JUNE 30 *Reading 181*
JUDAH'S ENEMIES PERISH
Obadiah

> *"Because of the violence against your brother Jacob, you will be covered with shame; you will be destroyed forever" (Obad. 10).*

Those hostile to God's people take a great risk when they act against them.

Background

Names in Obadiah. The prophet used a number of different racial and geographic terms in this short book. The majority are synonyms used to identify either Edom or Judah. These names reflect the Hebrew custom of identifying peoples by their ancestors (thus "Esau" is another name for Edom and "Jacob" for Judah) or by place names (thus "Teman" also refers to Edom, and "Mount Zion" to Judah). If this is kept in mind the message of Obadiah will be much clearer.

Overview

Edom would be pillaged and her people slaughtered (vv. 1-9) as punishment for violence she directed against Judah (vv. 10-14). In the coming Day of the Lord all nations will judged and their lands occupied by God's own (vv. 15-21).

Understanding the Text

"The vision of Obadiah" Obad. 1. Nothing is known of Obadiah as a person. His name, however, means "servant of Yahweh." Obadiah did not think it was important even to identify himself, as most Hebrews did, by stating their father's or family name. Obadiah saw himself simply as God's servant. What was important was the message he had to deliver.

You and I want to adopt Obadiah's perspective. Oh, yes, we are important—important to a God who loves us for ourselves rather than for what we do for Him. But when we're given the mission of speaking for God, we must exalt the message. Obadiah would do nothing to detract from his message by drawing attention to himself.

"You who live in the clefts of the rocks" Obad. 2-4. Edomite population centers were built on a great ridge of mountainous land opposite the Dead Sea. These heights, ranging from 4,000 to 5,700 feet, made the land easily defensible, and it was in fact protected by a series of stone fortresses built to command the roads that wound up precipitous cliffs and traced the edges of terrifyingly deep gorges. These natural defenses contributed to the pride of Edom, reflected in their rhetorical question, "Who can bring me down to the ground?"

How dangerous a sense of security is! The Edomites felt untouchable. Arrogant, they struck out at Judah from behind the barriers they thought protected them. Undoubtedly if they had felt vulnerable they would never have risked trying to harm their neighbor.

God said to Edom, "I will bring you down." In this saying Obadiah reminded all of us that no one is ever beyond the reach of God. Every person is responsible for his actions, and every person is within reach of the disciplining hand of the Lord.

"Because of the violence against your brother Jacob" Obad. 10. The ancient covenant that God made with Abraham guaranteed that

God would bless those who blessed him and his descendants, and curse those who cursed him and his progeny. God recalled His promise, and announced through Obadiah that Edom would be "destroyed forever" because of just such an offense.

What a revelation of the nature of God's commitment to His word. If Obadiah did prophesy just after the fall of Jerusalem to the Babylonians, as many believe, the generation of Jews that were Edom's victims was an apostate generation. They willfully abandoned God to serve idols, and consciously rejected His word. They were themselves under the ban: themselves doomed to judgment. Even so God intended to keep His ancient promise. Those who cursed His people must be cursed. Edom must fall.

Remember this verse and its historical context next time you fail yourself and God and, burdened by a sense of shame, wonder if God can forgive you. God remains fully committed to every promise He has made to you in Christ, even as He remained fully committed to Judah despite far worse sins.

God keeps His word. You can trust Him to keep on loving you, keep on working with you, until at last you do reflect the very character of Christ.

"Look down on them in their calamity" Obad. 11-14. The text shows a fascinating progression in the behavior of Edom toward Judah. At first, as the invasion developed, the Edomites stood off, to watch and enjoy the discomfort of Judah (vv. 11-12). When it became clear that the people of Judah were losing, the Edomites became more brave. They marched through the gates of the ruined city to gather all the loot that might be left. They then became bolder still, and positioned troops along escape routes to "cut down their fugitives" and "hand over their survivors." It was a classic case of waiting till the fight was over, and then hurrying in to kick the loser.

Kicking a person who's down has always been popular, because it carries little risk. At least, little risk of the victim kicking back. What people need to remember, however, is that God takes the side of the oppressed.

So, if in your home, office, or your community, you're ever tempted to join the crowd that kicks one of life's underdogs, remember Edom. A victim may seem defenseless. But he or she has God on his side.

"For all nations" Obad. 15-21. Obadiah announced that the principles seen in his oracle against Edom have universal application. They do. One day God will openly act on behalf of the victims of every oppressive power. Even nations will answer to Him. When that happens every Esau will be destroyed, and Judah, the "loser," will occupy their territory.

There is no "ill-gotten gain." There is only "ill-gotten loss."

▶ DEVOTIONAL
Like One of Them
(Obad. 11-12)

I confess! I do like to read the comics when I get up in the morning. At least, I like to read three of them—Calvin and Hobbes, Sally Forth, and For Better or For Worse.

Last week—the first week of school—the little girl in Better threw her teddy bear on the school bus. She was assigned the painful task of writing a note of apology. In a later set of panels she aimed the bear carefully, and bopped her big brother squarely in the back of the head! Why? Because he was the one who encouraged her to toss the bear on the bus in the first place, and then laughed when she got caught and was punished.

I don't suppose cartoonist Lynn Johnston had been reading Obadiah. But she might have been. Obadiah 11 and 12 reads, "On the day you stood aloof while strangers carried off his wealth and foreigners entered his gates and cast lots for Jerusalem, you were like one of them. You should not look down on your brother in the day of his misfortune, nor rejoice over the people of Judah in the day of their destruction." In comic strip terms, "I didn't throw any bear!" And again in comic strip terms, "Na Naa Naaa! That bus driver got you good. Ha ha ha!" I suspect everyone suppressed a smile of satisfaction when the bear plopped on the brother's head. He sure deserved it!

That's what God said to Edom through Obadiah. And what He says to us. You can't stand around when you see your brother a victim, egg on the perpetrators, and be guiltless. If you don't step in with help, you are "like one of them."

Biblical faith doesn't let us stand on the sidelines when others are victimized. Even if the "others" aren't particular friends of ours. Even if they are our enemies.

Personal Application

Don't stand by when you see others in need. Help.

Quotable

"When a man does love his enemies, he knows that God has done a tremendous work in him, and everyone else knows it too."—Oswald Chambers

The Variety Reading Plan continues with 2 THESSALONIANS

Jonah

INTRODUCTION

Jonah is the narrative report of a prophet from Israel and his mission to Nineveh, capital of Assyria. Fearing that his nation's enemy might repent if warned of impending judgment, Jonah tried to flee. God dealt with His reluctant prophet, and Nineveh humbled itself and was saved, teaching Jonah and us a lesson about the compassion of God.

OUTLINE OF CONTENTS

I. Jonah's Flight .... Jonah 1
II. Jonah's Deliverance .... Jonah 2
III. Jonah's Preaching .... Jonah 3
IV. God's Rebuke .... Jonah 4

READING GUIDE (2 Days)

If hurried, you may read only the "core passage" in your Bible and the Devotional in each chapter of this Commentary.

Reading	*Chapters*	*Core passage*
182	1–2	1
183	3–4	4

Jonah

JULY 1 *Reading 182*
THE PATRIOTIC PROPHET
Jonah 1–2

> *"But Jonah ran away from the LORD and headed for Tarshish" (Jonah 1:3).*

Jonah had what he thought were good reasons to run from the Lord and from the mission God had given him. His story reminds us never to substitute "good reasons" for God's will!

Background

The patriotic prophet. Second Kings 14:25 identifies "Jonah son of Amittai" as a prophet who lived in the days of Jeroboam II of Israel, and who predicted that king's many victories. In the days of Jeroboam II the boundaries of the Northern Kingdom were extended almost to the borders achieved during the golden age of David and Solomon. As the prophet called to preannounce the king's victories, Jonah must have enjoyed great popularity, especially as life in Israel had been bleak before Jeroboam's vigorous rule. No doubt the prophet felt a great deal of personal satisfaction as well, as he watched his fellow countrymen begin to prosper in accord with the word of the Lord which he had been privileged to deliver.

God's command that Jonah go to preach against Nineveh, however, was something else again! Assyria had been, and still was, a threat to Israel's very existence! Jonah wanted no part of a ministry to that particular bunch of foreigners! All Jonah wanted to do was to keep on preaching his positive message of prosperity in his homeland.

Jonah's patriotic motivation, which is further explained in chapter 4, was so great that he determined to flee God's presence. It is at this point that Jonah's story begins.

Overview

Jonah was told to preach against Nineveh (1:1-2), but tried to flee to Tarshish (v. 3). Identified as the cause of a great storm that threatened his ship, Jonah was cast overboard (vv. 4-16), where he was swallowed by a great fish (v. 17). From inside the fish Jonah prayed, and was delivered (2:1-10).

Understanding the Text

"Go to the great city of Nineveh" Jonah 1:2. There is no indication that God explained the purpose of Jonah's mission to him. But chapter 4 indicates Jonah suspected. There Jonah said, "I knew that You are . . . a God who repents from sending calamity" (v. 2). Jonah suspected that if he went to Nineveh the city might repent of "its wickedness," and God would withhold the threatened destruction.

Jonah's explanation helps us understand the exact nature of the prophet's flight. He did not run from God because he failed to understand the Lord's purposes, but because he did understand them! Jonah simply didn't like those purposes.

God doesn't ask us to agree with what He plans. All He asks is that we acknowledge that He knows best—and obey.

"A ship bound for that port" Jonah 1:3. Most commentators believe that the port in question was Tartessus, in Spain. Looking at a map reveals its significance. Nineveh lay to the north. Tarshish was as far south on the Mediterranean as a vessel could go.

It's typical of young people who decide to abandon the faith and lifestyle of their parents to go as far in the opposite direction as they feel they can. If one of your children has taken the route to Tarshish, the story of Jonah is comforting. There was no way Jonah could get away from God. God will pursue our young people, even as He pursued His prophet.

"The LORD *sent a great wind" Jonah 1:4-6.* In the eighth century B.C. vessels that plied the Mediterranean stayed close to the coast, ready to run for shelter in case of a storm.

The storm that struck the ship terrified the sailors, and apparently made the landsman Jonah groggy. Jonah was aroused and urged to pray by the desperate seamen.

It's possible Jonah was unaware of how desperate the situation was, while the experienced sailors knew full well the extent of the danger.

"Who is responsible for making all this trouble for us?" Jonah 1:7-9 As the storm worsened, the sailors cast lots to find out who was responsible for the calamity. This was more than superstition. It reflected the sailors' awareness that such storms never struck during that particular season. It seemed clear to them that some supernatural cause was involved. The problem was, the sailors felt themselves innocent bystanders, caught in the conflict between some deity and someone on board the ship.

Jonah's disobedience had brought a shipload of innocents into grave danger. This illustrates a basic principle of all human life. Our lives and the lives of others are woven together. We cannot disobey God without in some way affecting others for ill. Nor can we obey God without affecting them for good.

"I know that it is my fault" Jonah 1:11-16. Jonah knew that he was responsible for the danger they were all in, and showed he was willing to accept that responsibility. He told the sailors to throw him overboard, and promised that then the storm would stop.

We can admire this in Jonah. So many who make mistakes are unwilling to ac-

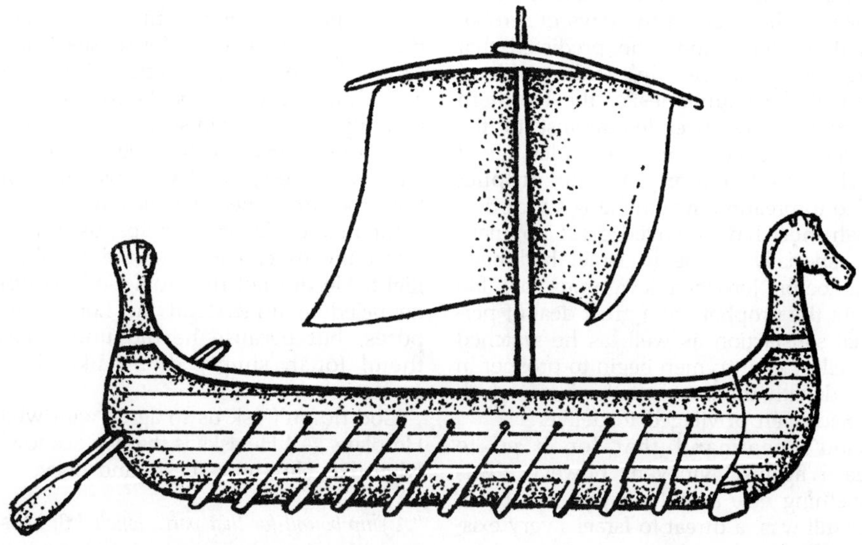

Archeologists have established the kind of fragile ship that sailed the Mediterranean in Jonah's time. The single-sailed cargo vessel might carry a few passengers, but most of the crew worked and slept on deck. Most ships in this era refused to put to sea during the Mediterranean's storm season, and the unexpected storm that struck Jonah's vessel was viewed as a divinely caused calamity (Jonah 1:7).

cept responsibility, and try desperately to avoid the consequences of their choices. Jonah was ready to accept those consequences, which he realized was necessary to save his shipmates.

But we can also admire the sailors. Despite Jonah's confession, they were unwilling to throw him overboard until every other hope was exhausted. Finally, begging God not to punish them for taking Jonah's life, they did as the prophet demanded and threw him over the side.

This too is an important reminder. It's easy to develop a "we/they" view of others, as though there were no moral or good persons in the world beyond the church. The sailors, all worshipers of other gods, and in terror for their own lives, still did all they could to save Jonah. We should appreciate such qualities in others. In fact, such qualities should make us all the more eager to share the good news of the salvation available to all in Jesus. (See DEVOTIONAL.)

"The LORD provided a great fish" Jonah 1:17. The Hebrew does not indicate a whale, despite the familiar *King James* rendering (Matt. 12:39-40). This makes all those stories of whaling men swallowed and later found alive (or dead) in a whale's stomach irrelevant. It's understandable that those determined to prove the reliability of the Bible would appeal to such evidence. But it is entirely unnecessary. Why? Because the text says that the Lord "provided" the great fish. This was no ordinary fish, but a Goliath among fish, prepared especially for the task of swallowing Jonah. Just as the appearance of the fish on the scene in time to swallow Jonah, and Jonah's survival in the stomach of the fish, were miraculous, so was the giant fish itself.

"I will look again toward Your holy temple" Jonah 2:4. Jonah 2 is a poem recapitulating Jonah's experience. He pictures for us the currents that swirled around him, and the clammy seaweed, some of which grows to a height of 50 feet or more, that wrapped around his head as he sank.

Near death, "I remembered You, LORD, and my praise rose to You, to Your holy temple."

These references to the temple recall Solomon's prayer at its dedication. In that prayer he asked God to restore any of his sinning people, "aware of his afflictions and pains, and spreading out his hands toward this temple" (2 Chron. 6:29, cf. vv. 26-27). Jonah's prayer was a tacit confession of his sin of disobedience, and a tacit commitment to be obedient. Then, rescued and rejoicing, Jonah openly affirmed, "What I have vowed I will make good."

How often we see it in the Old Testament. Whatever the sin, however great the disobedience, God is willing to accept the sinner who returns to Him. Upon confession the sinner is restored not only to fellowship, but in the case of Jonah, still entrusted with his original mission.

Your past failures, or mine, do not disqualify us from participation in the great purposes God is working out even now in our world. What a motive to surrender to Him, and once again be fully committed to doing His will.

▶ DEVOTIONAL
Make Me a BIG Blessing (Jonah 1)

Every once in a while I run across the notion that unless a Christian is really in close fellowship with the Lord, God can't use him or her to bless others.

Actually, that's not true, as the story of Jonah illustrates. Jonah was just about as far out of fellowship as a believer can get—running away from God—when that terrific storm hit his ship and frightened all aboard. And then look what happened. Jonah admitted he was responsible for the storm, got the sailors to throw him overboard, the storm stopped—and the sailors, convinced by all this of the power of Jonah's God, "greatly feared the LORD, and they offered a sacrifice to the LORD and made vows to Him" (v. 16). God used a disobedient Jonah to introduce Himself to a shipload of pagan sailors! And the pagan sailors believed.

Of course, Jonah wasn't around to enjoy his "success." He was drowning: sinking into the sea, his lungs bursting, sensing the clammy touch of the seaweed entwined around his head.

I think this is the message preachers should get across to Christians. Can God use a carnal or disobedient believer to accomplish His purposes? Of course! But—

will such a believer experience the blessing that usually comes with serving God? No. Like Jonah, the believer out of touch with God misses the blessing, for he's drowning in the sea of his own troubles and sorrows.

Oh, yes. There's one more thing to note. When Jonah was out of fellowship with the Lord, God used him to save a shipload. But when Jonah was back in fellowship, and went on to Nineveh, God used him to save a whole city.

Conclusions? I think I want to ask the Lord to make me a BIG blessing. He can use me more if I stay in fellowship with Him. And I'll sure enjoy it a lot more too.

Personal Application

Serve God wholeheartedly, and enjoy!

Quotable

"There is more joy in Jesus in 24 hours than there is in the world in 365 days. I have tried them both."—R.A. Torrey

JULY 2 *Reading 183*
GOD OF COMPASSION
Jonah 3–4

> *"Nineveh has more than a hundred and twenty thousand people who cannot tell their right hand from their left, and many cattle as well. Should I not be concerned about that great city?" (Jonah 4:11)*

God has compassion for all. We need to develop an attitude that mirrors His—not Jonah's!

Overview

When Jonah preached in Nineveh, the Assyrians repented (3:1-10). Jonah, upset and angry, asked God to let him die (4:1-4). Instead, God used a vine to teach Jonah a lesson in values (vv. 5-11).

Understanding the Text

"Then the word of the LORD came to Jonah a second time" Jonah 3:1. Jonah had willfully disobeyed God's call to preach in Nineveh. Now God gave him another chance.

We need to remember three things about second chances. God's will is going to be accomplished. God intended to warn Nineveh, and Nineveh would be warned, whether Jonah or some other person was God's agent. Jonah's disobedience merited discipline, not rejection! God gave His prophet a second chance. Usually He gives you and me many opportunities to respond to His guidance. It is much better to respond to God when His word first comes to us. Jonah would have avoided the terror of being thrown into the sea and being swallowed by the great fish if only he had been willing to do God's will when he first learned it.

Let's not count on second chances. But if we do fall into disobedience, Jonah's experience reminds us that we can still turn back to God and be used by Him.

"Now Nineveh was a very large city" Jonah 3:3-4. The size of Nineveh at this period has been established by archeologists as a maximum of 175,000. This compares to 30,000 in Samaria, the capital of Jonah's nation. The figures match well with the mention in Jonah 4:11 of 120,000. The reference to three days to go through Nineveh may mean it took Jonah three days to go through the fields and suburbs that surrounded Nineveh, rather than through the walled part of the city.

The point made in the text, however, is a simple one. Jonah's mission was to a metropolis: a city teaming with human beings. This emphasis helps us see why Jonah's mission was so important. Thousands of lives were at stake.

"The Ninevites believed God" Jonah 3:5-9. Amazingly, Jonah's warning of imminent destruction was taken to heart by all in Nineveh. The king abandoned his throne to publicly sit "in the dust" in the rough clothing which in that culture indicated sorrow and grief or repentance. He issued a decree that summoned all to fast, to call on God, and to "give up their evil ways and their violence."

Given the dating of Jonah to the time of Jeroboam II in Israel, the Assyrian Empire, of which Nineveh was the capital, was then seriously threatened by warlike northern tribes known as the Urartu, Mannai, and Madai. The enemy had pushed its borders to within a hundred miles of Nineveh, and the very existence of the ancient empire was threatened. A sense of weakness and of impending doom may have helped create openness to Jonah's message. Yet the spontaneous response of the whole population to a foreign prophet who wandered unannounced into the city with an unpopular message, underlines the fact that response to any word of God has supernatural roots.

God was working in the hearts of the pagans of Nineveh. When they heard, they believed.

We need to count on a similar work of God when we preach, teach, or share the Gospel conversationally. God may well have been at work preparing others to hear His Good News. His Spirit can bring that Good News home to their hearts in a compelling way, whatever the inadequacies of the messenger.

"He had compassion and did not bring upon them the destruction He had threatened" Jonah 3:10. One of the most clearly established principles in Old Testament prophecy is that most prophetic warnings of doom are contingent. They invariably come true—unless the people to whom they are addressed repent. We see this principle in earlier incidents, such as those recorded in 2 Samuel 12:14-23; 1 Kings 21:27-29; and 2 Kings 20:1-6. Repentance can cause God to relent.

This should not be misunderstood as a change of the divine mind. It's more like the red flashing lights and ringing bells that warn of a train's approach. Anyone on the tracks will be crushed. But a person who gets off the tracks will be safe.

When Jonah preached, he said in effect, "You people of Nineveh are about to be run over!" When the people of Nineveh repented, they in effect got off the tracks! The juggernaut of divine judgment rushed on—and passed them by!

What an object lesson for Israel. The prophets of God, not strangers but fellow countrymen, had shouted out warnings of impending doom for decades. Here, in the experience of Nineveh, a pagan nation, was an object lesson for God's own people. If only Israel would listen to the prophets and repent, God would relent in their case too.

The tragedy is that the people of Israel did not repent. The object lesson was wasted on them. The irony is that the very people that Jonah's preaching saved, the Assyrians, were the agents God used to bring judgment on an Israel too hardened to heed.

"Now, O Lord, take away my life" Jonah 4:1-4. When the city was not destroyed, Jonah was upset and angry. Like many of us, Jonah thought God should behave as he wanted Him to. More was involved in Jonah's case (see DEVOTIONAL), but isn't such a reaction all too typical?

We have it all figured out, and are sure that God should solve one problem this way, and another that. When He doesn't do it our way, we sulk or become angry. What we should do in such a case is thank God that He didn't do it our way!

Our notion of how things should be is limited by our lack of knowledge—and often by our lack of caring. God not only knows what is best, He loves always. Thanking God even when His decisions do not reflect our first choice is a sign of spiritual maturity. And common sense.

"Jonah was very happy about the vine" Jonah 4:5-6. Sullen and angry about Nineveh's repentance, Jonah settled down on a distant hill overlooking Nineveh, to wallow in self-pity and see what would happen to the city. As he sat under a typical desert lean-to shelter, a vine sprang from the ground, and grew large enough to provide shade. Jonah was happy for more than the shade. Such a little thing, and yet here was something green and living, and Jonah was comforted by its presence.

Often God provides some similar little thing to comfort us when the big things in life seem to have gone wrong. Jonah was right to be happy about the vine. And we are right to be happy about the little things that remind us of God's love. If we're wise, whenever suffering comes we will look actively for some such little thing, let it remind us of God's love, and let it bring us some happiness despite our sorrow.

"God provided a worm" Jonah 4:7-11. The end of the Book of Jonah at first appears strange. God took away the vine that gave Jonah that little bit of happiness, and when Jonah became even more despondent, God asked, "Do you have a right to be angry about the vine?" We can understand why Jonah answered, "Yes!"

But God had a reason. Jonah had "been concerned about this vine" that sprang up one night and died the next. Jonah had been happy that it was there beside him. But Jonah had cared nothing at all for the lives of the thousands upon thousands of people of Nineveh, to say nothing of the cattle there.

What a contrast with God, who is concerned about all His creation, and cared for the thousands of Nineveh. Even though they were idolaters, and the enemies of His own people, they were important to the Lord.

The challenge to Jonah was clear. Jonah, you cared about the vine. Why don't you care about other human beings? You were happy for the vine's existence, even though it was fleeting. Why aren't you happy about the life given to the thousands in Nineveh, rather than eager to see all those lives taken away?

There is a challenge here for us. What do we care about? What makes us happy? Is it the insignificant things of life? Or do we share God's values, and care about what is important to Him?

▶ DEVOTIONAL
Right, but Wrong
(Jonah 4)

Christians correctly tend to place emphasis on right doctrine. After all, we are to hold fast to what the Bible teaches. But the story of Jonah reminds us that we can be totally right, and very, very wrong.

Jonah 4 begins with a statement by Jonah of some of the rightest doctrine there is. "I knew," Jonah said, "that You are a gracious and compassionate God, slow to anger and abounding in love, a God who relents from sending calamity" (v. 2). That statement by Jonah is one of the Old Testament's central affirmations of faith; a characterization of God found first in Exodus 34:6-7, but repeated in Numbers 14:18; Nehemiah 9:17; Psalms 86:15; 103:8; 145:8; and Joel 2:13! And the phrase "gracious and compassionate" is found many, many more times in Old Testament descriptions of the Lord.

So Jonah's doctrine was about as pure as can be.

There was only one problem. Jonah said, "I knew . . . that is why I was so quick to flee to Tarshish" (Jonah 4:2). And that's why Jonah was angry now. Those rotten people of Nineveh went and repented! It would be just like God not to destroy them after all.

And again, Jonah was right. His doctrine was as pure as can be. It was just like God not to destroy Nineveh, and He did not.

In fact, it is because Jonah was right that he was so wrong. You see, the believer is not simply called to know about God. The believer is called to be like Him. We are not simply to know God is compassionate. Because God is compassionate, we are to be compassionate too. It's not enough for us to know that God cares for the pagan or the poor. We are to care for them too.

The doctrinally correct Jonah was about as far from harmony with God's heart as a believer can be!

What a reminder for you and for me. A person who is totally right about God intellectually can be totally wrong. Knowing about God is no substitute for being like Him in character, values, and concern for others.

Personal Application

Ask God for heart as well as head knowledge as you study His Word.

Quotable

"A man's heart is right when he wills what God wills."—Thomas Aquinas

---

The Variety Reading Plan continues with MICAH

Micah

INTRODUCTION

Micah was a contemporary of Isaiah and Amos. He joined them in warning Israel and Judah of impending judgment just before the great Assyrian invasion of 722 B.C. which resulted in captivity for the Northern Hebrew Kingdom. Micah showed the necessity of that judgment by picturing the injustice rife in each society, and a religion corrupted by idolatry.

While grim warnings of doom dominate this book, Micah foresaw a future restoration of God's people to their land. This will be accomplished by a Descendant of David, who was to be born in Bethlehem. The coming King will establish God's kingdom on earth, and will rule it in the strength and majesty of the Lord.

OUTLINE OF CONTENTS

I. Corrupt Kingdoms .... Micah 1–2
II. The Coming King .... Micah 3–5
III. The Kingdom of God .... Micah 6–7

READING GUIDE (3 Days)

If hurried, you may read only the "core passage" in your Bible and the Devotional in each chapter of this Commentary.

Reading	*Chapters*	*Core passage*
184	1–2	2
185	3–5	5
186	6–7	7

Micah

JULY 3 *Reading 184*
TWO CORRUPT KINGDOMS
Micah 1–2

> *"They covet fields and seize them, and houses, and take them. They defraud a man of his home, a fellowman of his inheritance" (Micah 2:2).*

Corruption in any society is a prelude to disaster. The people of Micah's day did not want to hear that message. But it is vital for any people to hear, and heed.

Background

Micah, a contemporary of Isaiah and Amos, ministered near the end of the critical eighth century B.C. Both Israel and Judah then experienced a resurgence of power and great material prosperity. For a few brief decades the great powers, Assyria to the north and Egypt to the south, were weak and indecisive. Under the aggressive leadership of Jeroboam II in Israel, and Hezekiah in Judah, the Hebrews extended their territory to include most of the land area held in the golden age of David and Solomon.

But prosperity was not universal. The newly rich in both kingdoms used their wealth to exploit the poor, and a time of great social dislocation resulted. Many families lost the land given their forefathers by God, and intended to be a family holding forever. The wealthy also controlled the courts, and fraud as well as bribery were tools used to perpetrate injustice. Many of the poor were forced to sell themselves and their families into slavery, and the rich disregarded the ancient Mosaic Law that required the release of a Hebrew slave after just seven years of service.

This aristocracy of wealth, which included the royal house and the leading priests, corrupted even the prophets, who proclaimed what their benefactors wanted to hear, rather than any uncomfortable words from God.

Religion too had suffered corruption. In Israel a non-Aaronic priesthood ministered at worship centers where bull-idols were supposed to represent God's throne. In both countries pagan rites and practices had become elements in what was thought to be worship of God. In neither nation was moral purity or social justice viewed as essential to religion, which for most people was simply a matter of ritual observance.

Each of the great eighth-century-B.C. prophets strongly condemned the sins of their society. Together they warned of impending doom, and urged God's people to repent. Yet each was aware that Israel and Judah were too caught up in materialism and selfishness to give a serious thought to God. Each spoke of a judgment day about to dawn.

The warnings of the great prophets went unheeded, and the catastrophe they predicted did come. During the lifetime of Micah and Isaiah a resurgent Assyria invaded the Holy Land. The kingdom of Israel was crushed, and its population dragged away into captivity, along with some 200,000 of the people of Judah. Judah, saved temporarily through the revival stimulated by godly King Hezekiah, survived for another 136 years. But there was no real change of heart in the Southern Kingdom, and Judah suffered the fate of Israel when crushed by the Babylonians in 586 B.C.

Despite constant grim reminders of the

sins that caused the destruction of the two corrupt kingdoms, each of the eighth-century prophets gave God's people reason to hope. A remnant would survive exile, and would return to the ancient Jewish homeland. Isaiah draws our attention to a Servant of the Lord who, by His suffering, would redeem God's people. Micah envisioned a coming King, a Descendant of David. Born in Bethlehem, this royal Person would rule a United Kingdom, and extend God's glory to the ends of the earth.

The tale of the two corrupt kingdoms is not a total tragedy. It is a tale that affirms the sovereignty of the God who will judge sin, but who then will establish His own kingdom on earth. A kingdom of justice, peace, and joy. A kingdom incorruptible, that will endure forever.

Overview

God would soon judge Samaria and Jerusalem for their sins (1:1-7). Micah wept and mourned at the prospect (vv. 8-9a), but only the day of judgment would humble God's people (vv. 9b-16). The oppressing classes would know ruin (2:1-5) despite the empty promises of false prophets (vv. 6-11). Yet one day God will regather His people (vv. 12-13).

Understanding the Text

"Samaria and Jerusalem" Micah 1:1. Capital cities named in the Bible often represent nations. Thus Nineveh represents Assyria, Damascus represents Syria, and here Samaria represents all of Israel, and Jerusalem the whole land of Judah.

There is, however, more implied in this simple literary device. The capital city was the residence of the royal family and the aristocracy: the ruling class that established policy and set the moral as well as political tone of the nation. In a real sense the capital city sums up the character of the nation it heads. This is why in biblical prophecy so many of the prophet's condemning words are directed against capital cities and their inhabitants.

Today we often hear doubts about whether the "private life" of a candidate for political office should be examined in his or her campaign. What a foolish question. Of course it should! The personal and social morality of the individuals who lead any government will have a dramatic impact, not only by the examples they set, but also on the legislation passed.

Micah's focus of his prophecy on Samaria and Jerusalem reminds us that we must examine the private lives and personal convictions of candidates for office. And must vote accordingly.

"The Lord from His Holy temple" Micah 1:2-7. Whenever the Old Testament pictures God speaking in or from His "holy temple," the image implies divine judgment.

Holiness is one of the most important of all biblical concepts. In the Old Testament the holy is that which is set apart to God, separated from everything that is common or profane. Holy objects such as the golden vessels used in the temple, holy ground, and especially holy people, were considered God's own and were to be for His use and service only.

God Himself is intrinsically holy. That holiness is displayed in two primary ways: in His own faithful commitment to what is good, and in His judgment of those who desert the way of holiness and turn away from their "set apart" condition.

Micah began his prophecy by showing Israel and Judah the God who is holy, and who stands in His holy temple. This God was about to exhibit His holiness by judging His wicked people. In the punishment for sin that Israel and Judah would experience, the holiness of God would be again displayed.

And so God said through Micah, "I will make Samaria a heap of rubble, a place for planting vineyards. I will pour her stones into the valley and lay bare her foundations. All her idols will be broken to pieces" (vv. 6-7).

What a reminder to you and me. We have been set apart to God too. We are to serve Him and to reveal His goodness through lives marked by this very quality. But if we turn away, and follow the path taken by Judah and Israel, God will still display His holiness in us. God will judge us, and in that judgment reveal His own holiness to all.

"Because of this I will weep and wail" Micah 1:8-9a. In biblical times individuals showed their humility before God, their

grief over and confession of sins, by loud weeping, wailing, howling, and moaning. They also stripped off their finer clothing, and wore only the oldest and most threadbare of garments.

Here Micah expressed his own reaction to his vision of coming judgment. He realized how wicked his nation was, and responded immediately by actions which showed his own sense of guilt and grief.

What a lesson. This man who uttered God's message of judgment identified with his sinning people.

It's all too easy for us to be judgmental in our relationship with those who fall short of God's standards of right and wrong. Yet Micah, rather than adopting a holier-than-thou attitude, was crushed by the enormity of the sins prevalent in his society. He was a member of that society, and therefore not guiltless himself. And so Micah, crushed by the realization that he in some way participated in the sins of his age, wept and moaned in grief and sorrow.

As godly persons, you and I are also to weep over the sins in our society. We are not guiltless, but bear some responsibility for all that happens in our nation and community. If we are to have an impact on our world, we must recognize that fact, humble ourselves as Micah humbled himself, and then set out to do all we can to effect change.

"Pass on in nakedness and shame" Micah 1:9b-16. Micah humbled himself at the vision of impending judgment. The people of Judah and Israel ignored the vision and rejected Micah's preaching. Yet soon they would be humbled—by events. Israel would be humbled as her survivors, their heads bowed in shame, stumbled in chains along the road to Assyria (v. 11). Judah would be humbled as the last fortress city protecting the route to Jerusalem, Lachish, fell to Sennacherib (v. 12).

People always have a choice. It is not a choice between arrogance and humility, between proud independence and submission to God. Oh, no. The choice is to submit to God when He speaks to us through His Word, or to submit bent over in shame as circumstances crush our pride. How wise to submit to God willingly, and let Him lift us up. How foolish to arrogantly resist God, and make Him crush us.

"Woe to those who plan iniquity" Micah 2:1-5. Micah here gave a clear picture of the exploitation of the poor by the rich. Good businessmen, the wealthy lay out their projects carefully. They were able to get the fields they coveted because they were willing to defraud, and "it is in their power to do it."

What the oppressors of the poor did not know was that even as they planned, God was making plans to overthrow them! And He most surely had the "power to do it"!

It's a healthy reminder. Those who seem to have power to oppress and work injustice in our society are blind to the plans God is even now laying against them. We may suffer injury now. But we know that God's day is coming, when the exploiters will say, "We are utterly ruined!"

"I will bring them together" Micah 2:12-13. Micah ended this first oracle on a positive note. The immediate future was dark with the gathering clouds of divine judgment. Yet those clouds would clear away, and God's scattered people would be brought back together again, to live in a kingdom that was no longer corrupt. Then their king, the Lord, will be "at their head."

▶DEVOTIONAL
Do Not My Words Do Good? (Micah 2)

I suspect that many a preacher has lost his pulpit because the congregation didn't like what he said to them.

It was something like this with Micah. And I can understand why. After all, Micah publicly lit into the well-to-do, who paid the bills then as now (vv. 1-5). You can't say "God is going to get you!" to the community elite and expect to be urged to keep preaching.

Even Micah's fellow prophets tried to rein him in. "Do not prophesy about these things," they told him (vv. 6-7). Let's have sermons that comfort, not confront. Let's have positive preaching, not negative.

Micah was incensed. You could hear him mutter, "If a liar and deceiver comes and says, 'I will prophesy for you plenty of wine and beer,' he would be just the prophet for this people!" They wanted someone who would just tell them what they wanted to hear, not what God wanted to say.

I've been impressed as I've worked with the prophets in preparing this book, that often God *doesn't* have comforting words to say. Often He confronts. Often He demands. Often He forces us to look at our lives, and to look at our society, with unclouded eyes. We don't want to hear that sinful societies cry out for judgment, and we don't want to face the injustice, the crime, the moral corruption, that mark our own nation today. And yet, God says to us through Micah, "Do not My words do good to him whose ways are upright?"

If we are committed to God and to His ways, won't His words do us good?

They did not do good to the people of the kingdoms to which Micah preached so long ago. They did no good, beause the people of Israel and Judah were unwilling to walk uprightly. They were unwilling to take God's words to heart, and to act on them. But if you and I do take God's uncomfortable words to heart, and act on them, those words will surely do us good. And do good to our nation.

Personal Application

Let God's uncomfortable words do you good. Listen to them carefully, and obey.

Quotable

I sought Him in the still, far place where flowers blow
  In sun-bathed soil;
I found Him where the thousand life-streams flow
  Through sin and toil.
I listened for His step within the still, deep-cloistered shrine
  Of secret thought;
I heard it o'er the world's heart tumult, still divine,
  The Voice I sought.
I thought, far off, alone, to feel His presence by my side,
  His joy to gain;
I felt His touch upon life's weary pulse beside
  A bed of pain.
So those who seek the Master following their own way—
  Or gain, or loss—
Will find Him where their dreams of self are laid away,
  And there—a cross.—Dorothy Clark Wilson

JULY 4 *Reading 185*
THE COMING KING
Micah 3–5

> *"But you, Bethlehem Ephrathah, though you are small among the clans of Judah, out of you will come for Me One who will be Ruler over Israel, whose origins are from of old, from ancient times" (Micah 5:2).*

Human leaders failed to lead Israel to righteousness. God would remedy man's failures by providing a Ruler of His own; One who will shepherd God's flock in the strength of the Lord.

Overview

Micah indicted Israel's rulers (3:1-4) and religious leaders (vv. 5-8), who had brought the nation to the edge of disaster (vv. 9-12). Yet ultimately Zion will be exalted (4:1-13) under a King (5:1-4) who will bring peace (vv. 5-6) and purity (vv. 7-13).

Understanding the Text

"Should you not know justice?" Micah 3:1-4 Micah began his second sermon by addressing the leaders of Israel. The challenge was appropriate. Surely those in government who have the responsibility of administering justice should be able to recognize what is fair and right.

But Micah pictured a group of leaders who "hate good and love evil." In vivid terms Micah pictured a nation whose citizens are cattle, to be treated like animals that are butchered and prepared for eating. The leaders exploited the people, and cared only about the personal profit they could wrest from the suffering masses.

Micah's charge may seem extreme, but it reflects a basic stance taken throughout Scripture. Leaders are called to serve others, never to exploit them. A youthful Solomon pleased God greatly when, rather than ask for personal wealth or glory, he requested "wisdom and knowledge, that I may lead this people" (2 Chron. 1:10). This is the attitude appropriate to any position of leadership, whether secular or spiritual.

Any opportunity we have to lead demands that we carefully examine our hearts. Are we motivated by a deep concern for the welfare of others? Or are we motivated by selfish concerns, by pride of position or a passion for power?

Exploitative leaders surrender their greatest resource. Micah said that when trouble comes "they will cry out to the LORD, but He will not answer them" (Micah 3:4). The leader whose motives and actions are pure can call on God, and expect Him to answer!

"If one feeds them, they proclaim 'peace' " Micah 3:5-7. Again Micah fixes our attention on motives. The prophets in Israel, charged with the responsibility of communicating God's message, were motivated by potential gain. If someone paid them, they were quick to say what their employer wanted to hear!

The consequences of approaching ministry in this way are the same as those of misusing secular leadership. "They will all cover their faces because there is no answer from God" (v. 7).

The most important thing that you or I can do is live in fellowship with the Lord. This keeps the channel open that permits us to speak to God, and God to speak to us.

"Hear this, you . . . who despise justice and distort all that is right" Micah 3:8-12. The spiritual consequences of flaws in leaders and prophets are great. But so are the material consequences. The aristocracy of Israel had created an unjust society. "Her leaders judge for a bribe, her priests teach for a price, and her prophets tell fortunes for money." As a result the nation itself could not count on God's help in time of need. An unjust society will be destroyed. As Micah said, "Zion will be plowed like a field, Jerusalem will become a heap of rubble, the temple hill a mound overgrown with thickets" (v. 12).

Don't count on God to help you if you're committed to a sinful lifestyle. Instead, count on God to bring disaster.

"In the last days" Micah 4:1-5. The sins of the nation's leaders had brought Israel to the verge of destruction. Even so, God's ultimate plan for Israel will be carried out. That plan is for all the peoples of the world to seek the God of Jacob. In the end, in God's time, the word of the Lord will flow from Jerusalem and become the living principle by which disputes are settled. War will be no more, and individuals will enjoy the produce of their fields and vines in lasting peace. Then Israel will "walk in the name of the LORD our God forever and ever" (v. 5).

Terrible things do happen in this world, caused by selfish and greedy men and women. But it was not meant to be like this. And it will not be like this. In God's time, life on this earth will become all that God originally intended it to be.

"I will assemble the exiles" Micah 4:6-13. The people of God will be scattered. But when God's time comes, they will be reassembled. The God who expels will restore. He who punishes will bless.

We need to remember this. However dark a present experience, bright daylight lies just ahead.

"But you, Bethlehem" Micah 5:1-5. Micah now uttered one of the Old Testament's most significant and clear messianic predictions. A Ruler is to appear who will bring the promised blessings to Israel. The Ruler will be born in Bethlehem, yet have "origins . . . from of old, from ancient times" (v. 2). This Ruler will shepherd His flock (Israel) in the strength of the Lord (v. 4). He will guarantee their security and peace, as His greatness reaches "the ends of the earth" (v. 4).

Like other messianic prophecies, this prediction makes no distinction between the first and second comings of Christ. He has been born, in Bethlehem, just as Micah predicted. He has not yet established that rule which will bring earth peace.

While Old Testament prophecy frequently fails to specify times, biblical prophecies have been fulfilled in a literal way. Jesus, as the Son of God, had origins "from ancient times." And Jesus was born in Bethlehem, just as Micah specified some 700 years earlier.

We seldom are able to grasp the full implications of biblical visions of the future. But we can be confident that what God states will happen does lie ahead. And we can look forward with excitement to seeing God's plan for our earth unfold.

His greatness will "reach to the ends of the earth" (v. 4). And we will see it!

"The remnant of Jacob will be in the midst of many peoples, like dew from the LORD" Micah 5:6-15. It may seem strange, but the exile of Israel and Judah served the best interests of God's people. It was a punishment. But it was a blessing too.

In tiny Palestine, the multiplication of the Jewish people would have been curtailed by the limited size of the land, and the powerful enemies that made the Holy Land a battlefield for so many millennia. But scattered throughout the world, the Jewish people grew to a vast number. How vast? Recent studies suggest that 1 of every 10 persons in the Roman Empire in New Testament times was a Jew! And that in the Parthian kingdom, which included much of the old Babylonian and Persian territories, that proportion may have been as great as 1 in every 5!

Life was not easy for the exiles. There was frequent conflict with the Gentiles who lived in the cities of the Roman and Eastern worlds. But God did preserve His people. There was always a remnant. And, in fact, there was a much greater "remnant" than had ever lived in the Holy Land even during its glory years!

What a thought for us to ponder. Even God's punishments are intended to bless. We are not to give up, but to remember that even through suffering God intends to do us good.

▶ DEVOTIONAL
King Jesus
(Micah 5)

"But what does it really mean, this promise of a coming King?"

The old Jewish man smiled, and unrolled a particular scroll till he came to what we identify as Micah 5.

"What does it mean? Well, first of all see, here, that the King we're talking about is God, the Ancient of Days. He'll come to us as our Messiah, born in Bethlehem of David's line (v. 2). It's because of who He is that He means what He does."

"So, sir, what does He mean?"

"First, He means that we are empty and unfulfilled without Him. See here. Till He comes and Bethlehem gives birth, we are an abandoned people. We need Him in order to find our very selves (v. 3).

"Second, He means security. Without Him we're at the mercy of circumstances and our enemies. But when He comes in the strength of the Lord, He will care for us as a shepherd cares for his flock. As God's sheep, we will be secure (v. 4).

"And third, son, He means peace. His greatness will reach to the ends of the earth, and His power will guarantee our safety. When He is present with us at last, His presence will itself bring us perfect peace."

The boy nodded slowly. Looking up toward the sky, he said, "I hope He comes soon."

Another young boy asked his father, "Dad, what does it mean to know Christ?" And his father opened his NIV to Micah 5.

"Look here," he said. "Remember that the Baby born in Bethlehem wasn't just any child. He was God, the Ancient of Days, come into our world. Only because Jesus is God can knowing mean what it does."

"So, Dad," the boy asked, "what does it mean?"

"First, it means that without Him we're all alone, with no one to help us, just like an abandoned baby.

"Second, it means that when we do know Him, we're not alone anymore. He's like a shepherd who loves and takes care of his sheep. And we're like sheep. We're helpless by ourselves. But safe when Jesus is taking care of us.

"And third, Son, it means that we never need to be afraid of things that are too big for us. Because Jesus' power reaches to every place on earth, we can have peace inside. Knowing Jesus means that we're God's own, safe forever from everything that might do us harm."

Nodding slowly, the boy looked up toward the sky. "I'm sure glad we know Him now, Dad. Aren't you?"

Personal Application
All that the coming Jesus would mean to God's Old Testament people, Jesus' presence means for us today.

Quotable
Beyond the war-clouds and the reddened ways,
I see the Promise of the Coming Days!
I see His Sun arise, new charged with grace
Earth's tears to dry and all her woes efface!
Christ lives! Christ loves! Christ rules!
No more shall Might,
Though leagued with all the Forces of the Night,
Ride over Right. No more shall Wrong
The world's gross agonies prolong.
Who waits His Time shall surely see
The triumph of His Constancy;—
When without let, or bar, or stay,
The coming of His Perfect Day
Shall sweep the Powers of Night away;—
And Faith, replumed for nobler flight,
And Hope, aglow with radiance bright,
And Love, in loveliness bedight,
Shall greet the morning light!—John Oxenham

JULY 5 *Reading 186*
GOD'S KINGDOM
Micah 6–7

"He has showed you, O man, what is good. And what does the LORD require of you? To act justly and to love mercy and to walk humbly with your God" (Micah 6:8).

One day God's kingdom will fill the earth. Until then we who know the Lord can live as citizens of that kingdom, our lives demonstrating our allegiance to King Jesus.

Background
God's kingdom. The biblical concept of a kingdom differs from the modern view. We tend to think of a kingdom as a location: a land with borders, within which a common language is spoken. In the Old Testament, a "kingdom" is a sphere within which the will of a king is supreme.

In one sense the entire universe is God's kingdom, for He is its Maker and ultimate authority. Yet ever since Satan's fall the universe has been a kingdom in rebellion against its rightful Ruler, just as ever since Adam's fall earth has been a rebellious planet.

Yet the Bible reveals the God who gently and lovingly seeks to win back earth's rebels. God spoke to Abraham, and gave Abraham promises broad enough to cover all his seed. God exercised His power to free Abraham's children, the Jewish people, from servitude in Egypt, and bring them to the land He had promised their forefathers. And God gave them a Law, to teach Israel the way of love—to show them how to live with Him as their King, by voluntarily submitting to His will.

Micah portrayed a people who had abandoned covenant life and refused to live with God as their King. Yet in this third sermon Micah reminded Israel and us of three great truths. God is still King, and God's people can still choose that simple lifestyle that is His will for His own. God is still King, and even in a rebellious society, an individual can maintain his citizenship in God's kingdom. And God will be King over the whole earth. Ultimately His sovereignty will be acknowledged by all, and the whole world will be the kingdom of our God.

Overview
Micah stated God's case against Israel (6:1-8) and announced God's sentence (vv. 9-16). He lamented the breakdown of covenant life (7:1-6), yet lived in hope (vv. 7-10) of God's ultimate victory (vv. 11-20).

Understanding the Text
"The LORD has a case against His people" Micah 6:1-5. Micah pictured the mountains of

Israel, those eternal witnesses to the historic story of redemption, as judges, who hear God state His case against Israel.

The question God asked Israel, "How have I burdened you?" (v. 3) might be paraphrased, "What have I done to make you fed up with obeying Me?" What had God done? Oh, all God had done was to be faithful to His covenant obligations as Israel's Ruler to protect His people. God redeemed Israel from the land of their slavery, provided a great leader in Moses, protected them from their enemies, and brought them safely through the wilderness to the Promised Land (vv. 4-5).

Whenever Israel, or you and I, stray from the Lord, we can't blame Him. God is utterly faithful to His people, fully committed to His covenant promises. If we become estranged from God, we can be sure of one thing. It wasn't God who moved away from us. It was we who moved away from Him!

"With what shall I come before the LORD?" Micah 6:6-7 What did this faithful God want from His people? Micah, taking the part of Israel, used irony to sum up what they had been willing to give Him: burnt offerings. Thousands of rams. Even, as the pagans, their own children. What a travesty. Israel had responded to God's love by practicing a religion of externals, a religion of ritual. It had even corrupted that religion by violating God's express will and offering child sacrifices.

God our King is no more satisfied today with mere religion than He was in Old Testament times. God has been faithful to us. He wants us to respond to Him from the heart, and to be faithful to what He as king has told us He desires.

"He has showed you, O man, what is good" Micah 6:8. When my father died, I chose this text for his funeral service. My dad had no special claim to fame. He was a rural mail carrier for over 30 years, a Justice of the Peace for another 10, and an enthusiastic fisherman. He had a dry sense of humor, twinkling eyes, a fine memory and speaking voice, and a quiet faith he seldom spoke about but never hid. Everyone who knew Dad respected him, but I suspect few thought of him as someone special.

That's why I chose this Micah text for his funeral. I've had the chance to meet and know some of the "greats" of our faith. And I appreciate them. But Dad represents to me the loyal citizen of God's kingdom, who, untainted by fame, responds to the Lord in the simplest and yet most beautiful of ways. What does God require? Religious rituals? Thousands of sacrifices? No, He's shown us what is good. What God our King asks is simply that in honor of Him we act justly, love mercy, and walk humbly with our God.

You and I may never make the list of Christian greats here on earth. But far more important than that is to be found on the role of those citizens of God's kingdom who respond wholeheartedly to the will of our King, and show it in a simple lifestyle of justice, mercy, and humility.

"I have begun to destroy you" Micah 6:9-16. The verdict was rendered in God's favor. He had been faithful as Israel's King. Israel has rebelled against His will. Justice and mercy are mocked in Israel, and humility was a joke (vv. 10-12). God is King, and such violations of His will will surely be punished.

The graphic description of Israel's punishment in these verses reminds us that God is a great King. Rebellion against Him must, and surely will be, put down.

"What misery is mine!" Micah 7:1-2 Micah now expressed, not the misery of Israel, but the misery of a godly individual in a corrupt society. His first cry was one of loneliness. He looked desperately for "the godly" with whom he might have fellowship. But the land was as barren of godly persons as a field that has been thoroughly harvested is barren of fruit to satisfy one's hunger.

Each of us has a basic need for fellowship with other believers. We need the mutual support. We need to know that we are not alone in our commitment to the Lord. If you want to grow in your relationship to God and as a Christian, perhaps your first priority should be to bond with Christian friends who share your commitment and desires.

"Do not trust a neighbor" Micah 7:3-6. A society in rebellion against God, as the soci-

ety Micah described here, corrupts relationships. Bonding can take place between the godly, because those who deal in justice, mercy, and humility can be trusted to care about others. But in a society where these qualities are lacking, the individual experiences isolation and alienation. The members of a corrupt society know they cannot trust themselves, and thus can trust no one else.

What an awful way to live: to "put no confidence in a friend" and "even with her who lies in your embrace be careful of your words." It is not only right to live as loyal citizens of God's kingdom.

It is the only way to live happily.

"Though I sit in darkness, the LORD will be my light" Micah 7:7-13. Micah had looked for godly people with whom to bond, and found none. He found only enemies, who gloated over the apparent failure of his predictions of doom to come true. And so Micah asked a question millions have asked through the ages. How does the godly person, who seeks to live as a citizen of God's kingdom while traveling through Satan's world, survive?

Micah said simply, "As for me, I watch in hope for the LORD, I wait for God my Saviour; my God will hear me" (v. 7). Though we sit in darkness now, we can see the light that is beginning to appear on history's far horizon. God is coming, and when He appears all the kingdoms of this world will become the kingdom of our God and of His Christ. What gives us hope despite present darkness is the certainty that God's day will dawn. As Micah said, looking forward to a restored Israel, "The day for building your walls will come" (v. 11).

"Shepherd your people with your staff" Micah 7:14-15. When God the King does come He will display His power. This is the significance of shepherding "with your staff." The staff was a sturdy stick carried by the shepherd. It not only aided him in walking over rough ground, but also served as a weapon to beat off wild animals that would attack his sheep. When God the King comes, He will protect His own. He will use His staff, parallel with "wonders" (miracles; acts of power like the plagues that struck ancient Egypt) in verse 15, to crush every enemy of His people.

It's good to remember that God *is* King. He merits our allegiance. But as sovereign Lord He has ultimate power. One day He will use it for His own, against all our enemies. How good it will be then to be good citizens of His kingdom, not rebels against His rule.

"They will turn in fear to the LORD our God" Micah 7:16-17. The display of God's power will convince even a hostile world that He is King. Deprived of their power, the nations will at last turn to Him.

▶ DEVOTIONAL
God Will Be God
(Micah 7)

It's not easy to say, when we feel as alone and helpless as Micah obviously did, "I watch in hope for the LORD" (v. 7).

Micah-like experiences aren't as unusual as they may seem. More than one Christian in our cities feels the same anguish Micah expressed. More than one feels alone (vv. 1-2). More than one feels surrounded by a violence and corruption with which he or she simply can't cope (vv. 3-6). The promise of our King's coming exists, but to many that day seems so far off. So unreal.

What keeps our hope alive in hopeless situations? Micah closed his book with a simple explanation. Our hope is kept alive by the simple fact that God is God. His nature, His character, is the firm ground on which our hope is built. It is because God is who He is that we know all will be well.

Who is He? Listen to Micah's words. "Who is a God like You, who pardons sin and forgives the transgression of the remnant of His inheritance? You do not stay angry forever but delight to show mercy. You will again have compassion on us; You will tread our sins underfoot and hurl all our iniquities into the depths of the sea. You will be true to Jacob, and show mercy to Abraham, as You pledged on oath to our fathers in days long ago" (vv. 18-20).

So when you're feeling down or defeated, read these words of Micah again and again. And remember, God will be God. And because He will be who He is, you and I can watch in hope for Him to act.

Personal Application
God's character is our guarantee of good things ahead.

Quotable
"If the Lord be with us, we have no cause of fear. His eye is upon us, His arm over us, His ear open to our prayer—His grace sufficient, His promise unchangeable."—John Newton

---

The Variety Reading Plan continues with ZECHARIAH

Nahum

INTRODUCTION

Nahum prophesied against Nineveh, the capital of Assyria, while that empire was still at the height of its power, in the mid-seventh century B.C. The prophet, a citizen of Judah, predicted the city's fall and vividly described the manner in which it was actually taken.

This brief book reminds us that God is the God of vengeance as well as love. Though God is gracious, He does not spare the wicked.

OUTLINE OF CONTENTS

READING GUIDE (1 Day)

If hurried, you may read only the "core passage" in your Bible and the Devotional in this Commentary.

Reading	*Chapters*	*Core passage*
187	1–3	1

Nahum

JULY 6 *Reading 187*
AGAINST NINEVEH
Nahum 1–3

> *"The LORD is a jealous and avenging God; the LORD takes vengeance and is filled with wrath. The LORD takes vengeance on His foes and maintains His wrath against His enemies" (Nahum 1:2).*

Any view of God that does not take into account His wrath is a distorted view. But rightly understood, even the doctrine of the wrath of God is a comfort to His saints.

Overview

God's wrath takes the form of a judicial judgment of sinners (1:1-14) that exempts His own (v. 15). The destruction of Nineveh (2:1–3:17), proud capital of wicked Assyria, demonstrates God's judicial vengeance (vv. 18-19).

Understanding the Text

"The LORD takes vengeance on His foes" Nahum 1:1-8. When we think about the wrath of God, or divine vengeance, it's helpful to remember that vengeance is directed against God's foes. Nahum described God as "slow to anger," but reminds us that He will "not leave the guilty unpunished."

God's wrath, or vengeance, is linked with a judicial act. It is the right thing for God to punish the wicked. In fact, it is just as right for Him to punish the wicked as it is for Him to care "for those who trust in Him."

Let's not make the mistake of thinking that vengeance somehow goes against God's character. As Nahum said, "The LORD is good" (v. 7). Yet "goodness" not only stands in contrast with evil, it stands against evil! If God were not willing to take vengeance on the wicked, and to treat them as objects of His wrath, God would not be good.

"One . . . who plots evil against the LORD" Nahum 1:9-15. The Ninevite who plotted evil against the Lord and counseled "wickedness" is identified in Nahum 3:18 as "the king of Assyria." It is likely that the specific reference is to Sennacherib, the most aggressive of Assyrian conquerors, who according to Assyrian records devastated some 47 fortified cities in Judah in 701 B.C.

An important principle is alluded to in this passage. God had used Assyria to afflict Judah (1:12). But the Assyrians remained responsible for their motives and actions. Assyria did not attack Judah as a conscious response to the known will of God. In fact, the Assyrian attack was evidence of plotting evil against God! We see that clearly in the ridicule directed against the Lord by the Assyrian field commander who called for Jerusalem's surrender (see Isa. 36). The principle this illustrates is: God can and does use the evil acts of wicked men to accomplish His own purposes. But God does not cause the wicked to do evil. Thus the wicked remain responsible for the evil they do.

So God declared through His prophet, "The LORD has given a command concerning you, Nineveh. . . . I will prepare your grave, for you are vile." This is to be the fate of all who plot and do evil (see DEVOTIONAL).

"The river gates are thrown open" Nahum 2:1–3:1. The rest of the Book of Nahum is

given over to four different descriptions of the fall of Nineveh. Undoubtedly the most significant is the description of the opening of river gates and subsequent flooding and fire in the city.

Nineveh was situated on three rivers, with a canal system that directed waters to its different districts. Once the suburbs of Nineveh were taken, these canal gates (as *bab-nari*, "gate of the river" may indicate) could be thrown open, and the city defenses flooded. As the walls of the palace collapsed, enemy soldiers swarmed into the city and plundered it.

What a destiny for the capital of an empire that had pillaged the world. All the treasures that had been assembled were taken. "She is pillaged, plundered, stripped!" (2:10) and all those who had struck terror into helpless victims were rendered helpless themselves. "Hearts melt, knees give way, bodies tremble, every face grows pale" (v. 10).

God was against Nineveh. In His wrath He had decreed her destruction and, therefore, her destruction was sure. Woe, then, "to the city of blood" (3:1).

"'I am against you,' declares the LORD" Nahum 3:2-17. Three additional descriptions of Nineveh's fall are contained in these verses (vv. 2-7, 8-11, 12-17). Together they are intended to drive home the horror of that day, and to portray as graphically as possible the implications of the wrath of God.

There is no vision of mercy here. Only visions of death and blood.

These are awesome images that bring home the reality of the wrath of God. Images that help us see that "God's vengeance" is no abstract theological concept, but a terror that hangs over the head of the wicked, whether they are aware of it or not.

"Who has not felt your endless cruelty?" Nahum 3:18-19 Again the prophet reminds us that the vengeance described in his book was decreed as a judicial act. All that came to the Assyrians was what they had earned by their own acts. The wrath of God is never capricious. Never a careless outbreak of anger.

God, the Judge, has determined a punishment that is just.

▶ DEVOTIONAL
Leaving the Guilty Unpunished (Nahum 1)

Seeing God as the God of vengeance, who is filled with wrath, is more than a little disquieting. But it's important if we are to have an adequate concept of God, and if we are to deal appropriately with crime in our society.

That's what's so impressive about this first chapter of Nahum. The prophet said, without qualification, "The LORD is good" (v. 7). But at the same time said, "The LORD is a jealous and avenging God; the LORD takes vengeance and is filled with wrath. The LORD takes vengeance on His foes" (v. 2).

What puts Nahum's vision of God in perspective is the fact of saying, "The LORD will not leave the guilty unpunished" (v. 3). Reading it, we realize that the wrath of God, and the vengeance of God, are judicial concepts. God the good must and will stand against evil. God the good must and will punish the guilty.

This is a lesson our society desperately needs to learn. Criminals should be charged and punished, not to "rehabilitate" them, or even to "get them off the streets." Crime should be punished because a state, like God, must take the side of what is righteous and good. And when a person does evil, it is good for society, as it is good for God, to take vengeance.

It's true that expressions of God's wrath never go astray, as human expressions of judicial wrath may and all too often do. Yet the principle is clear. Human beings are responsible for the wicked deeds they do. And it is right that those who do evil suffer punishment for their crimes.

Personal Application

Save your sympathy for the victim, not the criminal.

Quotable

"A modern society that outlaws the death penalty does not send a message of reverence for life, but a message of moral confusion. When we outlaw the death penalty, we tell the murderer that, no matter what he may do to innocent people in our custody and care, women, children, old people, his most treasured possession, his life, is secure. We guarantee it—in advance. Just as a nation that declares that nothing will make it go to war finds itself at the mercy of warlike regimes, so a society that will not put the worst of its criminals to death will find itself at the mercy of criminals who have no qualms about putting innocent people to death."—Patrick J. Buchanan

The Variety Reading Plan continues with EZRA

Habakkuk

INTRODUCTION

Habakkuk wrote in the time of godly King Josiah. The prophet was deeply troubled by the injustices prevailing in Judah's society despite a religious revival. God revealed His intention to use the Babylonians to punish Judah. The Lord went on to show the troubled prophet that the wicked only seem to succeed. Strengthened by his faith, Habakkuk knew God would sustain him in the coming turmoil.

Habakkuk has great value for Christians, for it teaches us that the "prosperity" of the wicked is an illusion, for the evil never truly succeed.

OUTLINE OF CONTENTS

READING GUIDE (1 Day)

If hurried, you may read only the "core passage" in your Bible and the Devotional in this Commentary.

Reading	*Chapters*	*Core passage*
188	1–3	2

Habakkuk

JULY 7 *Reading 188*
PERFECTED FAITH
Habakkuk 1–3

> *"The Sovereign* Lord *is my strength . . . He enables me to go on the heights" (Hab. 3:19).*

Faith grows fastest when challenged. What Habakkuk teaches us is that through our doubts and suffering, our faith can and will be perfected.

Overview

Habakkuk complained to God of injustice in Judah (1:1-4). He was told that the Lord was raising up the Babylonians to discipline His people (vv. 5-11). The prophet asked how God could permit the wicked to triumph (vv. 12-17), and was shown that despite appearances the evil man never really succeeds (2:1-20). God then showed Habakkuk the horrors of the coming invasion (3:1-16). Shaken, the prophet determined to trust God, and so reached the pinnacle of faith (vv. 18-19).

Understanding the Text

"Injustice" Hab. 1:2-4. Under Old Testament Law local elders met to settle disputes. There was no police force or national justice system. If local elders took bribes, or if witnesses lied, the law was "paralyzed, and justice never prevails." Habakkuk complained that the religious enthusiasm generated by Josiah's revival (see 2 Kings 23) had not touched the hearts of the majority. Because the majority was wicked, the righteous were hemmed in (outnumbered), so "justice is perverted."

In this morning's paper one article described how a witness against local drug pushers was being harassed and her family threatened. Our justice system does not distribute responsibility in the Old Testament way. Yet what the individual does remains the key to a just society.

Habakkuk, looking at the corruption in his society, wondered how God could permit Judah to continue in such a state. The answer, of course, is that God would not permit an unjust society to represent Him. There may well be a cost in taking a stand for justice. But there is an even greater cost if we fail to do so!

"I am raising up the Babylonians" Hab. 1:5-11. At the time God spoke to Habakkuk, about 621 B.C., the Babylonians (Chaldeans) were a subject people within the Assyrian Empire. In 625 B.C. Nabopolassar took the throne of Babylon and, within two decades, crushed the mighty Assyrians. This sudden and amazing overthrow of the dominant world power is referred to in verses 5-6, "I am going to do something in your days that you would not believe even if you were told. I am raising up the Babylonians."

There may be no obvious threat on the horizon capable of shattering an unjust society. The Book of Habakkuk reminds us how quickly God can raise up and bring down nations, to say nothing of individuals.

"Your eyes are too pure to look on evil" Hab. 1:12-13. As Habakkuk considered God's plan to use the Babylonians to punish Judah, he was even more deeply troubled.

You and I can hardly understand the terror caused by an invading army in ancient times. Verses 8-11 graphically portray ancient warfare, with swift cavalry attacks in the open, and earthen ramps

Babylonian war memorials show Jewish captives being taken to Babylon. God appointed them to execute judgment on His sinning people.

built up against the walls of besieged cities. The attacking armies were truly "bent on violence." Defeated foes were subject to torture, women and girls to rape, and even infants were speared or taken by the heels and swung against stone walls. The utter cruelty of the Babylonians repelled Habakkuk. But even more, he knew it must repel the Lord.

God is Israel's Holy One, too pure to even look on (i.e., "permit") evil. How then could God permit a people more wicked than His own to triumph over them.

We often may share Habakkuk's perplexity. We too see the wicked triumph, and we too wonder. How can God, our Holy One, permit such things to happen without acting in judgment? The answer, found in chapter 2, is surprising. God does not "look on" evil! God even now is actively judging those whose success causes us to doubt (see DEVOTIONAL).

"Write down the revelation and make it plain" Hab. 2:1-19. Habakkuk had set himself to wait for God's answer. When it came, the prophet was told to write it down and make it plain—for you and me! We can paraphrase the principles of God's present judgment of the wicked quite simply.

The wicked man never has enough (vv. 4-5). The wicked man is doomed to dissatisfaction. He is like a furnace, and each success like fuel added to a burning fire. The more he gains, the hotter the fire burns, and the more empty his life becomes! What a judgment this is: to win, and never be able to enjoy it.

The wicked are isolated (vv. 6-8). The wicked man makes his gains at the expense of others. This creates hostility, and makes the wicked man fearful. He knows he has earned the hatred of others, and so finds himself isolated and vulnerable. What a judgment this is: to look around, and know that others hate and fear you. To know that you are truly alone.

The wicked feel insecure (vv. 9-11). Driven by their insecurity the wicked concentrate on material gain. They count on wealth or power to set their "nest on high." The image is of a vulture, who nests on a mountain crag for safety. This is how the wicked live, desperately trying to erect barriers. What a judgment this is: to know that justice demands one's ruin, trying desperately to protect himself, but never able to feel safe and secure.

The wicked man's hopes will be dashed (vv. 12-14). The wicked man builds monuments to his achievements, even as Herod built cities to preserve his name and Hitler strove to create a "thousand-year Reich." Yet every such effort is in vain: they "exhaust themselves for nothing." God intends this world to be filled with knowledge of Him, not with monuments to murderers. What a judgment this is: to hope, and see every hope come to nothing.

The wicked will be repaid in kind (vv. 15-17). The actions of the wicked man arouse the antagonism of all around him. There will surely be a backlash. And what a judgment this is: violence, the tool he relied on in his quest for wealth and power, will be used against him, and he in his turn will be destroyed.

Never suppose that the wicked really succeed. An evil empire, or an evil person, may appear to prosper. But beyond the trappings of success, buried deep within the heart of the wicked, is a misery, an emptiness, a fear, that is the mark of the present judgment of the God too holy to look on evil.

"The LORD is in His holy temple" Hab. 2:20. Here and in other passages where God is pictured "in His holy temple," the image speaks of imminent judgment. Note that in Habakkuk's vision God announces He "is" in His holy temple. There is a great day coming, a day of final judgment. But never assume that God is powerless or inactive now. Habakkuk has shown us that God judges the wicked even as they seem to prosper.

Yet, seeing God in His holy temple, the prophet was confronted with the fact that judgment day for Judah—his own land—was at hand!

"God came from Teman" Hab. 3:1-15. At first Habakkuk welcomed the coming judgment. God would remember mercy even as He poured out His wrath. Perhaps, like Habakkuk, you and I take discipline lightly. *Let it come,* we think, never realizing the pain that may be necessary to purify us.

God quickly corrected His impatient servant. These verses describe three historic periods of judgment, not from the vantage point of a man, but from the vantage point of one who sees through the veil that isolates us from the spiritual universe. There he discovers an angry God, arrayed in holiness.

In his vision Habakkuk saw, not the plague that devastated the Exodus generation on the plains of Moab (Num. 25), but God Himself, burning in anger, His elemental power shaking the foundations of the earth, coming from Sinai to execute the judgment that Law required (Hab. 3:3-7).

In a second vision Habakkuk saw an enraged God sweeping earth clean by the Genesis Flood (vv. 8-10). In a third vision Habakkuk watched as God "in wrath" came as a mighty warrior to overthrow Egypt's armies and deliver His people from slavery (vv. 11-15).

Each of these visions was calculated to do just one thing. To show Habakkuk what it really means to experience disci-

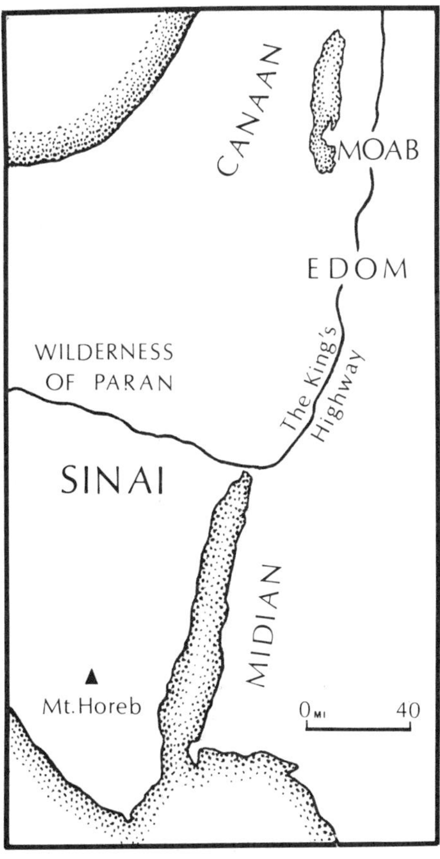

Sinai symbolizes not only God's Law but His holiness (Ex. 3:4-5; 18:16-24). The place locations mentioned in Habakkuk 3:3-7 tell us that Habakkuk saw the Lord, setting out from Sinai, coming to the plains of Moab to judge Israel for idolatry and immorality (Num. 25).

pline at the hand of the holy God.

"Decay crept into my bones, and my legs trembled" Hab. 3:16. At last Habakkuk understood. God had satisfied his doubts. Now God was ready to do a deeper work in Habakkuk's heart.

You see, belief is not simply an intellectual exercise. Faith is not built on intellect alone. The prophet finally realized that he would be among those who experienced the awful devastation of warfare. His fig trees would be shattered, his vines droop to the ground. At last the prophet realized that when the fields of Judah produced no food, he and his own would face starvation. Divine discipline meant all he knew, all he hoped for, all he possessed—would be taken away.

And then, as the prophet trembled at the prospect, a strange peace entered his heart. Though all these things must happen, "Yet I will rejoice in the LORD." In triumph the Prophet Habakkuk reached deep, and found a sustaining faith.

When a nation is judged for its sins, the righteous suffer with the wicked. Faith makes no man immune to the troubles that are common to mankind. But as Habakkuk caught sight of a mountain goat (not "deer") picking its way on a mountainside, unmindful of the danger of a fall, he realized a wonderful truth. Resting in God, the believer remains secure, whatever his circumstances.

Even in the dreadful days about to come, God would enable His servant Habakkuk to pick his way safely—like that mountain goat—despite the dizzying heights.

▶ DEVOTIONAL
Inside Out
(Hab. 2)

It isn't fair, of course. All too often the wicked do prosper. Sinners strike it rich while the godly struggle to make ends meet. The profane man, who scoffs at God, stays healthy, while a believer suffers a wrenching back injury or is stricken with cancer. The lazy employee, who lies about coworkers, gets the promotion, while the person who works hard and helps others is ignored.

Looked at from the outside, all these things seem unfair. And they are. Looked at from the outside, you or I might conclude that God is standing back, disinterested, letting people get away with anything they want. Or, even worse, we might conclude that God helps the wicked get ahead of the righteous.

But Habakkuk 2 reminds us, that's when we look at things from the outside. Such conclusions are based only on what we can observe: on what we can see. And so God invites us, in this fascinating chapter, to look at things from the inside.

When we do look to the inside, we discover that the wicked person who seems most successful is in fact the worst off! The wicked person is worse off because God is at work within, judging sin, and making the wicked man's every success meaningless.

What does Habakkuk 2 tell us is happening inside the person who succeeds in wicked ways? First, no such success can satisfy, but will only create more desire (vv. 4-5). Second, gains made at the expense of others isolate the "winner" from other people. Increasingly the wicked man finds himself alone, and lonely (vv. 6-8). Third, such gains create a sense of insecurity. A wicked man will try desperately to assure his safety, but the nagging awareness that he deserves punishment robs him of any sense of peace (vv. 9-11). Fourth, the hopes of the wicked are destined to be disappointed. God intends the earth to be filled with knowledge of Him, not monuments to murderers (vv. 12-14). Finally, the acts of the wicked create hostility. The harm a wicked person does others will create a backlash, and the violence he used will be directed against him. Wicked acts plant the seeds of their perpetrator's destruction (vv. 15-17).

I know.

There are times when it's hard not to envy the wicked man who prospers. But only if we look at such persons from the outside. Try looking at such men from the inside out. And then stop and think of all you have received in Christ. You have a life that's full, not empty. You have fellowship with Christian friends. You have the knowledge that you are secure in God's love. You have the certainty that all you hope for will indeed be yours. And you know that, if you are repaid in kind for the way you treat others, you will receive a blessing and not a curse.

Looking from the inside out, you and I discover the truth. Those the world thinks of as winners have lost.

And we have won.

Personal Application

Learn to evaluate from the inside out, and thank God for your many blessings.

Quotable

"God is not alone when discarded by man. But man is alone."—Abraham Heschel

The Variety Reading Plan continues with ROMANS

Zephaniah

INTRODUCTION

Zephaniah prophesied during the reign of Josiah of Judah (640–609 B.C.). Distressed by the shallowness of Judah's response to the godly king's reformation, Zephaniah announced that sweeping judgment was about to fall on Jerusalem as well as on pagan nations.

Zephaniah, the last of the preexilic prophets, summarized much of the judgment and salvation teaching of the earlier prophets. His emphasis fell on the darkest aspects of the Day of the Lord, within decades to be prefigured by Babylon's invasion of the Holy Land.

OUTLINE OF CONTENTS

I. Judgment of Judah .... Zeph. 1:1–2:3
II. Judgment of Gentiles .... Zeph. 2:4-15
III. Jerusalem's Destiny .... Zeph. 3

READING GUIDE (1 Day)

If hurried, you may read only the "core passage" in your Bible and the Devotional in this Commentary.

Reading	*Chapters*	*Core passage*
189	1–3	3

Zephaniah

JULY 8 *Reading 189*
GREAT DAY COMING
Zephaniah 1–3

> *"The great Day of the* Lord *is near—near and coming quickly. Listen! The cry on the Day of the* Lord *will be bitter" (Zeph. 1:14).*

Imagine history as a speeding train and the prophets as conductors, calling out the next station. Zephaniah's cry would be, "Last stop! We're coming into Judgment. Everybody off!"

Background

The age of Josiah. Josiah was Judah's last godly king. He took the throne following a half century of apostasy under Manasseh and Amon, and soon determined to lead his people back to the Lord. He attempted to purge the land of idolatry and reinstituted temple worship. Yet both Habakkuk and Zephaniah, who ministered in Josiah's time, viewed the reformation as superficial at best. Habakkuk portrayed the corruption of the legal system and society itself (Hab. 1:1-4), while Zephaniah cited evidence that Assyrian and Canaanite religions maintained a hold on the people (Zeph. 1:4-5). Prophets and priests were false to their calling (3:4), and political leaders still resorted to violence and perpetrated injustices (vv. 2-3). There were in Josiah's reforms outward indications of a return to God, but the lifestyle of the people gave no evidence of repentance or return.

It is against this background that Zephaniah cried out concerning the Day of the Lord, and emphasized its judgment aspects. The onrushing Day of the Lord "will be a day of wrath, a day of distress and anguish, a day of trouble and ruin, a day of darkness and gloom, a day of clouds and blackness" (1:15). For God's sinful people there can now be no escape.

Near the end of Josiah's reign the ancient world experienced great political upheaval. As Assyria engaged in a death struggle with a suddenly emergent Babylon, Judah won brief independence. Josiah became involved in trying to tip the balance of power between these two and Egypt, and was killed in battle in 609 B.C. Within a few years Judah was reduced to a subject state in the Babylonian Empire. Within three decades the Babylonians denuded the land of Judah of its people, and left Jerusalem, with its once beautiful temple, a heap of ruins.

When we read Zephaniah we find no unexpected revelation. All that Zephaniah said, earlier prophets had proclaimed over and over again. What we do sense, however, is a tone of finality. God had given His people opportunity after opportunity. Now, it was too late. Judgment was "near and coming quickly" (v. 14).

How desperately we need to respond to every word of divine warning. If we fail to respond, one day it will surely be too late.

Overview

Zephaniah predicted the "Day of the Lord," a dark day of judgment, due against Judah (1:1–2:3), Gentile nations (vv. 4-15), and against Jerusalem (3:1-8). Yet beyond the judgment lies a day of joy, in which God's scattered people will return and be restored to relationship with Him (vv. 9-20).

Understanding the Text

"Zephaniah" Zeph. 1:1. The prophet's name probably means "watchman for the

Lord." But what is interesting is that Zephaniah provided more genealogical information about himself than any other Old Testament prophet. He traced his ancestry back four generations, to "Hezekiah." Most commentators believe that this is King Hezekiah, the last godly king prior to Josiah.

Some see here simply Zephaniah's attempt to link himself with Judah's royal family. But the genealogy suggests something even more important. It reminds us that two whole generations, over 50 years, passed by during which Judah lacked godly leadership. The royal family faltered in its commitment to the Lord, and as a result the whole land turned eagerly to idolatry and sin.

You and I can no more afford to neglect the nurture of our children than could the kings of Judah. God may well bring a future generation back to Him, as He brought back Hezekiah's great grandsons, Josiah and Zephaniah. But how great the tragedy if son and grandson are lost.

"Those who turn back from following the LORD*" Zeph. 1:2-13.* These verses announce sweeping judgment, and express the reasons for God's anger. They also do more. They help us understand the futility of man's search for "freedom."

The people of Judah turned back from following the Lord. They thought obedience to Him was too restrictive. But what did they actually obtain?

They refused to worship the one true God, and found themselves worshiping a confusing host of pagan deities: Canaanite baals, the Assyrian "starry host," the Phoenician Molech. Some even added the Lord to this roster of gods, as if He were on a par with idols (vv. 4-5). The people of Judah still were bound by man's deep need for relationship with the supernatural.

They refused to obey God, and in seeking freedom adopted "foreign clothes" (v. 8). As today, the clothing one chose then indicated basic attitudes or orientations. The choice of foreign clothing suggests a rejection of Jewish identity and an effort to identify with Egyptian or Babylonian peoples (cf. Num. 15:38; Deut. 22:11-12). They were "free," but in their pursuit of freedom they lost their true selves.

They refused to obey God, and demanding freedom fell prey to superstition, such as the practice of refusing to step on the threshold of a house of pagan worship (Zeph. 1:8; cf. 1 Sam. 5:5).

They refused to obey God, and created a society in which each person was selfish, where violence and deceit were the norm (Zeph. 1:9).

They refused to obey God, and in asserting their freedom they lost all sense of spiritual reality, so that however great their need they never thought to seek the Lord, or ask Him what way they should go.

People today seem to have that same insistent desire for "freedom." God's ways seem restrictive, and so they "turn back from following the LORD." But always when human beings demand such freedom, they find themselves caught in a monstrous web. They become trapped, falling victim to counterfeit religions both humanistic and supernaturalistic, to superstition, to confusion, loss of identity, and finally loss of all touch with reality. They live in a world of illusion, not only lost, but subject to the wrath of the God who warns, "On that day I will punish" (vv. 8-13).

How glad we are to surrender such an illusory "freedom," and to choose to follow the Lord. We who follow Him gladly are free indeed.

"The great Day of the LORD*" Zeph. 1:14-18.* The "Day of the LORD" is a phrase used by Old Testament prophets to indicate events associated with God's direct involvement in human affairs to carry out some phase of His plan for humankind. While the "Day of the LORD" is most often an eschatological term used when describing history's end, any act of God can be identified with that day. Thus there is "the" eschatological Day of the Lord, and also "a" non-eschatological Day of the Lord.

What is important to note is that "a" Day of the Lord merits that identification because it bears marked likeness to "the" Day of the Lord.

This is what Zephaniah predicted here. "A" Day of the Lord was rushing down on Judah which, like "the" Day of the Lord, would be a day of wrath, distress, anguish, trouble, and ruin. The horrors of the imminent Babylonian invasion can be compared only to the horrors of the great day of divine judgment that will mark history's end.

This is an important reminder. God's final judgment day seems far off to most people. But for those who, like Judah, persist in sin, there is often "a" judgment day, as well as "the" judgment day! God is no less hostile to sin today than He was in our prophet's time. A Day of the Lord may be no farther from us than it was from Judah.

"You humble of the land" Zeph. 2:1-3. Zephaniah's warning concluded with an invitation. Before the time appointed for judgment comes, we can find shelter in the Lord. All it requires is humility.

What is humility? It is an attitude in stark contrast to that of those who demand the right to live their own lives. The humble gladly submit to God. The humble express their submission by seeking the Lord, and by doing what He commands. The humble are eager not for wealth, but for righteousness; not for high position, but to bow low before the Lord. There is shelter for the humble, even when the storm breaks around us.

There is hope for the humble. There is no hope for those who demand to be "free."

"I will destroy you" Zeph. 2:4-18. The coming Day of the Lord would not only devastate Judah but also the pagan peoples who have been hostile to the Lord. Afterward the remnant of God's own will at last be secure. Zephaniah said of their land, "It will belong to the remnant of the house of Judah; there they will find pasture. In the evening they will lie down in the houses of Ashkelon. The LORD their God will care for them; He will restore their fortunes" (v. 7).

"I have decided to assemble the nations" Zeph. 3:1-8. Now Zephaniah focused on Jerusalem, the capital city of Judah and its very heart. What he saw, despite the renewed activity on the temple mount which rose above Jerusalem's homes and businesses, was a city of oppressors, "rebellious and defiled" (vv. 1-5). The city had failed to respond to God's correction, and now must be punished.

God is never impressed by appearances. His concern today as in Zephaniah's time is with the heart.

▶ DEVOTIONAL
O Say Can You See
(Zeph. 3)

I've always been fascinated by the story. A British fleet stood off Baltimore, bombarding the fort that guarded its harbor. All through the night the guns roared. Through the clouds of acrid smoke explosions could be seen over the fort, as hollow powder-filled balls called bombs burst in the air. The darkness shrouded the stone walls of the fort, but the cacophony of sounds—the shrill whistling of shells, the booming of the cannon, the hollow thump of hit after hit—convinced every shipboard witness that the fort must fall, and Baltimore would be taken.

And then, as dawn's first light drove back the shadows, the witnesses saw an astounding sight. The fort still stood! And there, flying proudly above her ramparts, was the American flag.

Hurrying down below one witness seized a pen and dashed off lines that every citizen has heard a thousand times. "O say can you see," wrote Francis Scott Key, a prisoner that night on the British flagship, "through the dawn's early light, what so proudly we hailed at the twilight's last gleaming." The fort, and the flag, had survived.

What a picture of the scene we see in Zephaniah 3. The city of Jerusalem was under siege, being punished for her many sins (vv. 1-7). The Lord Himself was the assailing force, pouring out His wrath, striking the city in His fierce anger. The devastation seemed enough to consume the entire world in an awesome conflagration (v. 8).

And then, in the rest of the chapter, we make an amazing discovery. As that dreadful night of judgment comes to an end, and day dawns, we realize there are survivors! We see God's scattered people, purified, return to worship their God (vv. 9-10). We realize that the arrogance that characterized Jerusalem had been burned away, and the city now held only the meek and humble, who would do no wrong (vv. 11-13). And we hear a voice raised in song, tentative at first, but soon swelling in a glad chorus of joy as the people of the city realize that God, mighty to save, is with them, and will quiet them with His love (vv. 14-18). And suddenly we see the city itself begin to glow, as God gives His now holy people the honor and praise they thought that they had forfeited forever by their sin (vv. 19-20).

Just so we need to remind ourselves. When you or I suffer under the discipline of God, everything seems so dark. We feel crushed, unable to go on. Yet if we were only to look beyond, to tomorrow, we would catch a glimpse of the sight seen by Key, and by Zephaniah too.

O say can you see, just beyond the horizon of your dark today, the dawn of what God intends for you? Purified and restored, humbled enough to accept God's love, you too will be quieted with His love, and be given praise and honor in a peaceful land.

Personal Application

Look beyond your present circumstances, and fix your eyes on the good God will surely do you.

Quotable

"I bear my willing witness that I owe more to the fire, and the hammer, and the file, than to anything else in my Lord's workshop. I sometimes question whether I have ever learned anything except through the rod. When my schoolroom is darkened, I see most."—Charles H. Spurgeon

---

The Variety Reading Plan continues with DEUTERONOMY

Haggai

INTRODUCTION

Haggai was the first of the postexilic prophets. When a company of Jews returned from Babylon in 538 B.C., they laid the foundations of a new temple. But for the next 18 years members of the community concentrated on building their own houses, leaving the house of the Lord unfinished. Haggai urged the people to put God first, and finish the temple.

The people responded to Haggai, winning God's promise, "From this day on I will bless you." The project was resumed in 520 B.C., and the temple was finished in 515 B.C.

OUTLINE OF CONTENTS

I. The Call to Build .... Hag. 1
II. The Glory of the New Temple .... Hag. 2:1-9
III. Blessings for Judah .... Hag. 2:10-23

READING GUIDE (1 Day)

If hurried, you may read only the "core passage" in your Bible and the Devotional in this Commentary.

Reading	*Chapters*	*Core passage*
190	1–2	2

Haggai

JULY 9 *Reading 190*
PUTTING GOD FIRST
Haggai 1–2

> *"Is it a time for you yourselves to be living in your paneled houses, while this house remains a ruin?" (Hag. 1:4)*

The fall of Israel to Assyria, and of Judah to Babylon, illustrates what happens when people fail to put God first. The response of the postexilic community to Haggai's preaching illustrates what happens when people do put God first.

Background

The return. The Babylonians had taken the Jewish people into Captivity in a series of deportations between 605 and 586 B.C. It was not until the fall of Babylon and the ascension of Cyrus of Persia in 538 B.C. that a small contingent of some 50,000 returned to their devastated homeland. During the years of Exile once-fertile fields had become overgrown with weeds and briars, houses had fallen into ruin, while orchards and vineyards had died. The returnees faced a formidable task: they must reclaim the land, plant crops, and rebuild houses, for once-prosperous Judah was now a wild frontier.

In the grip of their first enthusiasm, a foundation for a new temple of God had been laid. But soon that enthusiasm was worn away under the pressures of survival. The focus of the community shifted from putting God first to putting their own many needs first.

For some 18 years they struggled to reestablish a viable society. But somehow they seemed unable to make progress. Every step forward seemed matched by two back. It was at this point that Haggai was sent by God to speak to the discouraged pioneers, to urge them to once again put God first.

Haggai is an encouraging book for believers today. It reminds us that blessings lie ahead for those who put God first.

Overview

On August 29, 520 B.C., Haggai urged Judah to finish the temple (1:1-11). The people obeyed God's voice and set to work (vv. 12-15). On October 17 Haggai promised the completed temple would be filled with glory (2:1-9), and on December 18 Haggai promised that from now on, God would bless (vv. 10-23).

Understanding the Text

"Give careful thought to your ways" Hag. 1:1-11. Haggai's initial message was blunt and practical. He reminded the community how they had struggled to survive the past 18 years. They had worked constantly, and yet seemed to have made no progress. He also reminded them that they had put aside rebuilding the temple in order to concentrate on meeting their own needs. And Haggai had just three questions for them:

Had it worked?

Were they really better off than they were before? Had setting God aside helped them get ahead?

The answer was no! They "expected much, but see, it turned out to be little."

The fact of the matter was that the prosperity of the postexilic community depended entirely on God. He was the One who controlled the reins; He was the One who could make them prosper. In setting God aside they abandoned the one essential for success.

Christians too might well be practical. Never mind for the moment whether it's right to set God aside for a time to concentrate on getting ahead. Just ask the question, "Will it work?" The answer today, as in Haggai's time, is no! Our God is a sovereign God, who is able to bless our efforts, or to withhold blessing. If we set God aside, and fail to give Him the priority He deserves, we abandon the one resource essential for our own success.

"They came and began to work on the house of the LORD Almighty, their God" Hag. 1:12-14. While the practical argument is compelling, it takes more than argument to cause a person to change his or her priorities. The text says that "the LORD stirred up the spirit" of the leaders and of the people (v. 14).

You and I may give others the best of reasons why they should trust the Lord or follow Him. And there are many good and practical reasons. Yet people will only respond if the Lord Himself stirs up their spirits within them.

Christian witnessing and Christian counseling both call for more than knowledge and more than skill in presenting good reasons for wise choices. Effective witness and counsel demands prayer that God will take our good reasons and good advice, open the heart of the hearer, and stir him or her up to respond.

"Be strong . . . and work" Hag. 2:1-4. As the work commenced it became clear that the new temple would be far less splendid than the first. So the people became discouraged. It hardly seemed worthwhile, when what they were doing fell so far short of what others had done.

You and I often fall into this trap. We compare our accomplishments or the tasks we are called to do with those of others. What we're doing seems so unimportant. So we become discouraged, and let our hands fall to our sides. God's first response to such an attitude is to give us a simple prescription. He says, "Be strong. . . . Be strong. . . . Be strong. . . . and work" (vv. 3-4).

Our calling is not to compare, but to be strong, and work at the task God gives us.

"I will fill this house with glory" Hag. 2:5-9. The dimensions of the new temple were far less than those of Solomon's. The new temple would also lack the expensive adornment of the earlier house of worship. Yet God not only promised to fill the new house with glory, but said that "the glory of this present house will be greater than the glory of the former house" (v. 9).

The ancient rabbis saw this as a messianic prophecy. The "desired of all nations [who] will come" (v. 7) they held to be the Messiah. The temple would be filled with glory not because of its material trappings but because of His presence.

How accurate this insight. Over half a millennium passed. But then Jesus of Nazareth did come, first as a Boy and then as an Adult, to the second temple. Herod had expanded and beautified the original structure. But the temple was glorious, not because of its ostentatious wealth, but because of the enfleshed presence of the God in whose honor it had been built.

There is a lesson here for us. What we do may seem unimportant when compared with what some accomplish. Yet as long as what we do is done for Christ, His presence floods the simplest task with glory.

"The silver is Mine and the gold is Mine" Hag. 2:8. The struggling community in Judah, hardly able to make ends meet, must have been discouraged by its poverty. How could it afford the high costs of construction, to say nothing of the costly equipment required for worship? Here God simply reminded His people, "The silver is Mine and the gold is Mine." The people of Judah were responsible to work. God was responsible to provide.

And God did! Ezra 6:8-12 tells us that when local opponents of the Jews complained, they were ordered by the Persian ruler to finance the entire project from tax revenues!

We need not know where our resources will come from. But we do need to be sure that what we do is in the will of God.

"From this day on I will bless you" Hag. 2:10-19. God promised to bless His obedient people. But He protected the little community, and us, from a common error.

Haggai was told to raise a question of

ritual purity with the priests. If a defiled person touched a holy object, would he be made holy? The answer was no. In fact, if a defiled person touched a holy object, that object became defiled!

God was about to pour out blessings on His people in Judea. They might conclude that it was because they once again worshiped at a temple. The questions and their answers showed that no one would be made holy by going up to the temple. God's blessing was to be poured out not because of the holiness of the people, but because of the grace of their God.

In choosing to put God first, the little community had placed itself on the one path that led to the blessing God was eager to bestow.

God's blessing today is evidence of His grace. We can never earn the good things He gives us. Yet our obedience does bring us to that shore of the river where His blessings flow.

"I will shake the heavens and the earth" Hag. 2:20-23. The book concludes with a word to Zerubbabel. This member of the royal family represented the Davidic line. The words mean that while the present generation will be blessed, a future generation will experience the full blessing promised by God. Then, at a future date, One from the house of David, the Messiah, will appear. He will shake the nations and establish the earthly kingdom of God.

▶ DEVOTIONAL
After Putting God First
(Hag. 2)

Haggai 1 invites us to look at the empty spaces in our lives, the disappointments and frustrations, and ask if this is what we want our lives to be. He then urges us to stop living selfishly, and put God first.

The little Jewish community in Judea in Haggai's day did just this—and decided to change their priorities. From then on, they would put the Lord first.

I suppose if this were all there were to this little book, it would be well worth reading. But actually, there's much more. Haggai 2 goes on to show us how life changes when we do put the Lord first in our lives.

What do we see there? First, we find significance in even little things. The rebuilt temple seemed small when compared to Solomon's spectacular structure. But then the Lord said, "I am with you," and we know that when we have put Him first, what we do is important indeed. In fact, we have the assurance that there is far more glory in the littlest thing we do for the Lord than in anything we have ever done before (vv. 1-9).

Second, we find repeated evidence of blessings we do not deserve. We discover that in putting God first, we have put ourselves in the center of that channel through which grace constantly flows.

There are material blessings, yes. But even more important, there is the knowledge that we are pleasing God, and fulfilling ourselves. And in this we find peace.

Personal Application

The only way to get ahead is to put God before us.

Quotable

"Do not wait to do a great thing. The opportunity may never come. But since little things are constantly claiming your attention, do them for a great motive—for the glory of God, and to do good to others."—F.B. Meyer

---

The Variety Reading Plan continues with MALACHI

Zechariah

INTRODUCTION

Zechariah ministered to the little group of Jews who returned to Judah after the Babylonian Captivity. His first prophecy is dated just two months after Haggai's call to finish rebuilding the Jerusalem temple (520 B.C.).

Zechariah too encouraged the temple builders. But he went beyond Haggai in calling for personal spiritual and social renewal. Only continuing commitment to the Lord and to justice would prevent further judgment.

Zechariah did predict that Judea would be dominated by Gentile powers for centuries. Yet he foresaw the appearance of the Messiah, who in God's time will establish a purified Jerusalem as capital of His glorious kingdom.

OUTLINE OF CONTENTS

I. Eight Night Visions ....Zech. 1–6
II. True Fasting ....Zech. 7–8
III. Messiah's Advent/Rejection ....Zech. 9–11
IV. Messiah's Return and Kingdom ....Zech. 12–14

READING GUIDE (3 Days)

If hurried, you may read only the "core passage" in your Bible and the Devotional in each chapter of this Commentary.

Reading	*Chapters*	*Core passage*
191	1–6	1
192	7–9	9
193	10–14	11

Zechariah

JULY 10 *Reading 191*
NIGHT VISIONS
Zechariah 1–6

"During the night I had a vision—and there before me was a man riding a red horse! He was standing among the myrtle trees in a ravine. Behind him were red, brown and white horses. I asked, 'What are these, my lord?' "(Zech. 1:8-9)

Much of Zechariah consists of visions which may seem hard to interpret. Yet each vision conveyed an important message to his community, and speaks to us today.

Background

There were only some 50,000 Jews in the tiny province of Judea. They had been permitted to return to their ancient homeland when Cyrus of Persia overthrew the Babylonian Empire. They had been in Judea for nearly 20 years when Zechariah began to minister, and were stirred by religious enthusiasm to complete the rebuilding of the Jerusalem temple. Despite their small numbers, they had great hopes. One day, according to God's promises, Jerusalem would be the center of the world, the capital of the Messiah destined to establish a worldwide kingdom of righteousness and peace.

Zechariah, in a series of night visions, encouraged this hope. But at the same time he warned the little community that there would be centuries of Gentile domination before that hope was realized.

Zechariah, whose name means "the Lord remembers," is rightly called the "prophet of hope." No Old Testament prophet spoke more clearly of the coming Messiah, or of His kingdom. Kenneth L. Barker, in the *Expositor's Bible Commentary* series, summarizes these twin themes. "Zechariah predicted Christ's first coming in lowliness (6:12), his humanity (6:12), his rejection and betrayal for thirty pieces of silver (11:12-13), his being struck by the sword of the Lord (13:7), his deity (3:4; 13:7), his priesthood (6:13), his kingship (6:13; 9:9; 14:9, 16), his reign and second coming in glory (14:4), his building of the Lord's temple (6:12-13), his reign (9:10, 14), and his establishment of enduring peace and prosperity (3:10; 9:9-10).

"As for the apocalyptic and eschatological aspect, Zechariah predicted the final siege of Jerusalem (12:1-3; 14:1-2), the initial victory of Israel's enemies (14:2), the Lord's defense of Jerusalem (14:3-4), the judgment of the nations (12:9; 14:3), the topographical changes in Israel (14:4-5), the celebration of the Feast of Tabernacles in the messianic Kingdom Age (14:16-19), and the ultimate holiness of Jerusalem and her people (14:20-21)."

Few Old Testament books, despite the obscurity of some of Zechariah's visions, contain a clearer picture of Christ's first coming or of events associated with that triumphant return that you and I look forward to today. Thus, for us too, Zechariah is the "prophet of hope." The power of our sovereign God guarantees a salvation and a restoration destined to come to you and me also through God's Messiah, Jesus Christ.

Overview

God called Zechariah (1:1-6), and gave him a series of eight visions concerning the restoration of Israel (vv. 7-17), the coming world powers (vv. 18-21), judgment of the nations (2:1-13), the coming Priest-King (3:1-10), present spiritual resources (4:1-14), the judgment of the guilty (5:1-4), cleansing from evil (vv. 5-11), God's final victory (6:1-8), and ultimately concerning Messiah's rule (vv. 9-15).

Understanding the Text

"Return to Me . . . and I will return to you" Zech. 1:1-4. Zechariah, who later became head of a priestly family that returned from Babylon (cf. Neh. 11:4), began his ministry with a lesson from history. God had urged earlier generations to turn to Him and away from their "evil ways and . . . evil practices." They had refused, and because they rejected the Lord, Israel and Judah had fallen. Zechariah warned his generation: "Do not be like your forefathers."

Note the association of turning to God and turning away from evil ways and evil practices. No one who had turned to the Lord would continue to practice evil.

But also note the lesson Zechariah drew from history. Evil ways and practices have consequences. Someone has said that experience is the best teacher. But how much easier for us it is to learn this lesson from the experience of others rather than from our own!

"How long will You withhold mercy?" Zech. 1:7-17 Though the first few verses of Zechariah look backward, the rest of the book looks ahead. We may be warned by lessons from the past. But we are motivated by bright prospects for the future. Zechariah's first vision offers just such a hope.

The riders of his vision had just scouted the nations, and found the world at peace. This itself was not good news, for the Gentile world powers had to be overthrown before Messiah's kingdom could be established. However, the Angel of the Lord told Zechariah that the Lord was "very angry" with the nations. He would overthrow them, and "return to Jerusalem with mercy."

This first vision does not answer the question, "How long?" In essence, the Lord was saying that "when" was not His people's concern. What He wanted them to know was that He would triumph.

You and I are to build our lives on the certainty of God's ultimate triumph, without being concerned about when. Christ may return in our lifetime. He may not. What gives us hope and motivates us to serve the Lord is not knowing when, but knowing that Christ's coming will surely take place.

In Zechariah 1:18-21 the four horns are world powers that will dominate Jerusalem, as in Daniel 7 and 8. The workman represents historic forces that operate to throw down each in turn, as history marches toward God's grand conclusion. This vision does deal with the prophet's question of "when?" It says, "Not soon, but certain!"

"I Myself will be a wall of fire around it" Zech. 2:1-13. The third vision was of a man surveying the city of Jerusalem. The angel explained it to Zechariah. God would crush the nations that had plundered His people. The Holy City will need no wall of stone then, for God Himself will be "a wall of fire" that guards a people who are "the apple of His eye."

The prophet was even told of a great movement toward God that would sweep "many nations" into His fold. But Judah and Jerusalem would be His special portion.

How amazing. When Zechariah spoke, Judea was a tiny district in one of 120 provinces in the vast Persian Empire. Yet one day Judah and her capital, Jerusalem, were destined to become the center of the world! What gave the exiles hope was not present blessings, for the Holy Land was then a barren and briar-filled waste. What gave the exiles hope was the vision of what the Holy Land would become.

We too may find little cause for pride or

confidence in our present situation. But when we look ahead, and remember God's promises, we will overflow with confidence! What gives us hope is the vision of what we will be—as Christ continues His work in us, and when He comes again.

"Men symbolic of things to come" Zech. 3:1-10. What must happen before the Holy City can experience the restoration Zechariah's visions promise? The prophet was given another vision, in which the angel calls the actors "symbolic of things to come." The vision was complicated, but its major thrust is clear. When Messiah comes, and renews the priesthood by taking up His own priestly ministry, God's people will at last be secure.

There are implications for us too in the symbolism. For any human being to know God's peace, he or she must be cleansed by God and clothed in His righteousness (vv. 1-5). Then, as we walk in His ways, we will have assured access to the Lord and the power to live holy lives (vv. 6-8).

"Seven channels to the light" Zech. 4:1-14. This fifth vision teaches dependence on God's Spirit, the resource who enables us to live holy lives while we await the Promised One's appearance. The vision was directed to Zerubbabel, the governor who was also of David's line. Even though, in that "day of small things," Judea seemed completely insignificant and powerless, the Lord reminded the governor that progress is made, "Not by might nor by power, but by My spirit" (v. 6).

This is one of those Old Testament verses that we would each do well to remember. In all we do, we are to rely not on our own might or power, but on the Spirit of God. If we serve in His strength, nothing that we do for the Lord will be a "small thing." God will use even the smallest in a great way.

"This is the curse that is going out over the whole land" Zech. 5:1-4. The scroll that Zechariah saw was a rolled-up book, on which were written God's commandments. These are called a curse because violation of the commands brings punishment. How is this a message of hope? Simply in that when the guilty are punished, the innocent in the community are safe. When those who do wrong go unpunished, soon no one is safe!

Modern society can only be safe when its laws are rooted in God's commands, and when those laws are enforced.

"It is a measuring basket" Zech. 5:5-11. The earlier visions were explained to Zechariah, or their symbolism was clear. Now we come to visions that are more obscure.

What is clear is that in this vision wickedness, personified as a woman, is carried away to Babylon.

What a reversal. Earlier the people of Judah had been carried off to Babylon because of their wickedness. Now evil itself is taken away from God's people and sent to Babylon.

We today have a similar choice. We can either hold on to wickedness, and suffer terrible consequences. Or we can let the Lord bind the evil in our hearts, and isolate us from its power. The Holy Spirit can do in our hearts what Zechariah predicted He will one day do for His people, Israel.

"The four spirits of heaven" Zech. 6:1-8. In his final vision Zechariah saw war chariots manned by heavenly warriors setting out in every direction. The pronouncement of rest (v. 8) suggests the final victory of God.

"The man whose name is the Branch" Zech. 6:9-15. The visions over, Zechariah was told to make a silver and gold crown and to crown Joshua, the high priest, who represented the "Branch," a common prophetic term for the coming Messiah. The crown is not a normal priest's headdress, but a royal crown.

The impact of this symbolic act is to affirm that the promises God has made to His people will be carried out—but only by the Messiah, who will unite in His own person the offices of Priest and King.

▶DEVOTIONAL
Not Soon, but Certain
(Zech. 1)

"Can we go to the mall tonight, Mom?" Nine-year-old Sarah desperately wants to get a special folder to keep her school journal in. She only has 15 or 20 folders now, but you know how that goes. It's the one she doesn't have that's special!

But what fascinates me is the sense of urgency. "Let's go find it. Now!"

Her mom has promised they'll look. But not now. Mom works all day, has to cart Sarah to music lessons, and had to go to school open house last night. Yes, they'll go look for that folder. But Mom won't make any commitments as to when. Sarah will have to be satisfied with a simple commitment. It may not be soon, but it is certain: They will look for her folder.

I understand why Sarah's not happy with the "not soon, but certain" answer. For a child, everything is urgent. Everything has to be "now"—except of course cleaning up her room, practicing the piano, or doing homework. Still, everything she wants has to be "now."

Zechariah 1 reminds us that God, like a good parent, tells us to be satisfied with "certain." Even to be satisfied with "not soon, but certain."

The prophet began by reminding his audience of the disasters that struck their forefathers because of disobedience (vv. 2-4). God's threatened judgment came. Not soon. But certain.

Then God gave Zechariah two visions. After seeing the first, the prophet begged God to tell him, "How long will You withhold mercy from Jerusalem?" God didn't answer at first, though He did make a binding promise. "I will return to Jerusalem with mercy." God's commitment to do good to His people is certain (vv. 7-17).

But then God gave Zechariah another vision; a vision of a series of world powers that would arise to dominate the Holy City, and would only gradually be worn away. This was God's answer to Zechariah's question about when. "Not soon."

Zechariah had to be satisfied with that. God had promised. The promises would be fulfilled. It would not be soon. But it was certain.

Sometimes you and I have to live with just this kind of answer to our prayers. "God, I'm hurting." "God, I need help." "God, work in my loved one's life." "God, meet our needs." When an answer is delayed, we grow so impatient. Like little Sarah, we want what we think we need now!

The next time you feel that kind of pressure, remember God's message to Zechariah. His word to us is often the same. "Not soon. But certain."

If we focus on the "not soon" we will be agitated and distressed. But if we focus on the "but certain," we will have peace.

Personal Application

Whatever your circumstance, God's commitment to do you good is certain and sure.

Quotable

"God in His unspeakable providence has arranged that some received the holy reward of their toils even before they set to work, others while actually working, others again when the work was done, and still others at the time of their death. Let the reader ask himself which one of them was made more humble."—John Climacus

JULY 11 *Reading 192*
JUSTICE, NOT FASTING
Zechariah 7–9

> *"These are the things you are to do: Speak the truth to each other, and render true and sound judgment in your courts; do not plot evil against your neighbor, and do not love to swear falsely" (Zech. 8:16-17).*

This passage deals with a repeated Old Testament theme. The measure of true religion is not in any outward observance, but in the quality of one's daily life.

Background

Fasting. Fasting in Old Testament times was never undertaken to lose weight. It always had a religious purpose. A fast might be undertaken by a person desperate for an answer to prayer, as in 2 Samuel 12:16-22 or Jeremiah 36:1-10. A fast often expressed deep grief and sorrow, as in 1 Samuel 31:13. Or fasting might indicate repentance, as in Joel 2:12-15. Fasting was also associated with the Day of Atonement. Fasting to show repentance is the only fast commanded in the Old Testament (Lev. 16:29, 31), and was intended to underline the solemn character of that high holy day.

Fasting in biblical times usually meant going without food only from sunrise to sunset. In Christ's time, especially religious Jews fasted each Monday and Thursday. One early church father encouraged Christians to fast too, but changed the days to Tuesday and Friday!

The New Testament describes two kinds of fasting: one, a public display intended to promote the notion that the fasting person is especially spiritual (cf. Matt. 6:16-18; Luke 18:12), and the other Spirit-led when seeking divine guidance or empowerment (cf. Matt. 4:1-2; Luke 4:1-3; Acts 13:2; 14:23).

Zechariah 7–8, which is Scripture's most direct discussion of fasting, suggests that we carefully examine our motives before undertaking a fast and makes it clear that God is far more concerned that His people live righteous and holy lives than with fasting.

Overview

When a delegation from Bethel asked about fasting (7:1-3), God rebuked them (vv. 4-7) and called for commitment to justice (vv. 8-14). Still, God promised Israel His favor (8:1-17). She will know joy in worship (vv. 18-23) and her enemies will be punished (9:1-8) when her King comes (vv. 9-13) and her Lord appears (vv. 14-17).

Understanding the Text

"Should I mourn and fast?" Zech. 7:1-3 The fasts the men of Bethel inquired about were fasts instituted by the exiles to commemorate events associated with the fall of Jerusalem, some 68 years earlier. The first generation of exiles felt that fall deeply, and undoubtedly had mourned with great sincerity. But now another generation, just 2 years away from finishing a new Jerusalem temple, wondered if there were any reason to keep the traditional fasts.

Note two things about the query. First, God had not commanded these fasts, so they were not binding. Yet it was right of the men of Bethel to raise the question with Jerusalem's spiritual leaders and seek God's guidance. However our religious traditions began, it is wise to seek God's guidance before changing them.

Second, the fasts had become mere tradition to the present generation. There is a difference between "tradition" and "mere tradition." What may be a vital form by which to express a real spiritual experience can seldom be passed to the next generation without becoming a mere tradition: form without the meaning or vitality. Each generation should have freedom to find ways to express its personal experience with the Lord.

"Was it really for Me that you fasted?" Zech. 7:4-7 God answered the question about fasting through the Prophet Zechariah. His answer was through a pointed question. Did the people really fast "for Me" all those years, or were they fasting for themselves?

In essence, God asked, "Were you sorry for your sins—or just sorry you got caught!" Was the motive for fasting one of guilt for the sins that caused the Exile? Or was the grief simply self-pity, a selfish expression of that very attitude which had led earlier generations to desert God in the first place?

What a question for us to ask ourselves when we experience the discipline of the Lord. We're sorry. We hurt. But does our heart ache over the sin, or just over the punishment? Have we shifted the focus of our concern to God, or are we still concerned only about ourselves?

"This is what the LORD Almighty says" Zech. 7:8-14. The men of Bethel had asked, "Should we fast?" God seemed to dismiss this question as unimportant, and responded, "Administer true justice; show mercy and compassion to one another. Do not oppress the widow or the fatherless, the alien or the poor. In your hearts do not think evil of each other" (vv. 9-10).

How often we become passionately concerned about unimportant issues! In Jesus' time the Pharisees were careful to tithe the leaves of tiny herbs grown by their doorsteps. But, Christ said, they neglected the weightier matters of the Law: justice, mercy, and faithfulness (Matt. 23:23). One of Satan's most effective ploys is to get believers to major on the minor. When the less significant dominates our thinking, we will ignore the truly central aspects of our faith.

Note that both Zechariah and Jesus focused on a lifestyle marked by justice, mercy, and compassion. If we are faithful in showing our commitment to the Lord by living holy and loving lives, the "little things" will fall into place.

Do you feel God wants you to fast? Then fast. But you know God wants you to do justice, show mercy, and care for the needy. Compared to these, fasting has at best a minor role in your spiritual life.

"I will return to Zion and dwell in Jerusalem" Zech. 8:1-15. When God said, "I am very jealous for Zion" He meant, "I have a passionate desire to do her good." The Hebrew word translated "jealous" is also rendered "zeal," and depicts a deep and abiding passion for its object.

What God said through His prophet to men concerned about fasting is this: "It's My love that motivates Me to do you good, not whether or not you fast."

What will God's love motivate Him to do for His Old Testament people? He will fill Jerusalem's streets with healthy, happy people (vv. 4-5). He will bring those who are dispersed back home (vv. 7-8). He will make the land productive (v. 12), and the people a blessing to all nations (v. 13).

We can have confidence that the Lord, in His love, will do the same for us. We may at times experience discipline. But we can claim for ourselves the promise that the Lord made to the little community in Judea: "Now I have determined to do good again to Jerusalem and Judah. Do not be afraid" (v. 15).

"These are the things you are to do" Zech. 8:16-17. How significant that this expression of God's will follows rather than precedes the promise of verse 15. Why is that significant? If "the things you are to do" had come first, we might have concluded that God blesses us because of what we do for Him. Since, however, "the things you are to do" follow the promise, we understand that our obedience is prompted by gratitude.

The legalist does what is right in an effort to win God's favor. The believer does what is right because he knows that he has already obtained God's favor through grace. We obey God because we love Him. We seek to please God because we understand all that He has done for us.

"The fasts . . . will become joyful and glad occasions and happy festivals" Zech. 8:18-23. The Jewish Talmud links each of these fasts with a specific event related to the fall of Jerusalem in 586 B.C. The fast of the fourth month commemorated the day the walls of the city were breached, of the fifth the day the temple was burned, of the seventh, the date Gedaliah was assassinated (cf. Jer. 41:2), of the tenth, the day the siege of the city was begun.

Why should these dates be celebrated joyfully, rather than remembered with sorrow? In part at least because these moments of intense anguish for the inhabitants of Jerusalem were at the same time occasions of divine purification. Out of the ruins of the city and temple came a spiritual revival that turned the Jewish people away from idolatry, back to Scripture and to God.

In the last analysis, every purifying judgment God imposes on His own, no matter how painful it may seem, will one day be remembered with joy. In God's time we will see its purpose, and will realize how the Lord used it to draw us closer to Him. Then, when joy floods in to force even the memory of anguish out, we will understand.

"I will defend My house against marauding forces" Zech. 9:1-8. When God spoke through Zechariah, Judah was an utterly insignificant district in a mighty Gentile empire. Weak and helpless, the Jews could look back over centuries of oppression by many foreign powers. As the theme of blessing was continued, God promised to deal with Judah's external enemies.

You and I too are subject to two kinds of hostile forces. There are the hostile forces within us—the pull toward sin, the fascination with temptations—and the forces outside—circumstances, a corrupt society, personal enemies, Satan himself. We are responsible to deal with only one: the enemy within. As we commit our hearts and even our desires to the Lord, we can be sure that He will defend us too and "never again will an oppressor overrun My people."

▶DEVOTIONAL
Gentle, but Oh So Tough
(Zech. 9)

For years Nicholson ran ads picturing a big, rough-looking workman with a beatific smile holding up one of their files. And the ads always said, "Tough, but Oh So Gentle."

This chapter reminds me of those ads. Of course Zechariah turned the ads around in order to introduce us to the Person who will fulfill all those wonderful promises God made to His people. Yet in just a few verses, he showed a gentle and tough side of the coming Messiah.

First there's the gentle side (v. 9).

The image is significant, for in the ancient East kings went to war riding horses. When they wished to signify peace, they traveled on a donkey.

We think, of course, of the triumphal entry of Jesus into Jerusalem, which Zechariah predicted here. Jesus came in peace, to bring peace. But the Jewish people wanted a conqueror, who would lead an uprising against Rome. Yet only through the covenant sealed by the blood of the Man of Peace could all who are captive to sin within have a prospect of peace.

But then Zechariah went on. The Man of Peace will appear again, this time as "the LORD . . . over them" (v. 14). Then He will sound the war trumpet, to shield His people and destroy all their enemies (v. 15). He will come again as the conqueror Israel yearned for, "save them on that day as the flock of His people."

Only then will all realize that that gentle King is also the Lord Almighty, the universe's sovereign Lord. Gentle, yes. But God, and as God mighty to save.

In a way, history is recapitulated in our experience with Jesus. We see Him first suffering and dying for our sins. We are moved by His love, we respond to His gentleness. Then, as we respond in faith, we discover His resurrection power. The suffering Saviour is also our resurrected Lord, and we kneel before Him in full surrender.

How important not to have a one-sided vision of Jesus. The Old Testament's quiet King is also Israel's overpowering God. Our gentle Jesus is Lord of all. We know Jesus well only when we are familiar with both aspects of His identity. We know Jesus well only when we know Him both as Saviour and as Lord.

Personal Application

If you know Jesus only as Saviour, don't miss knowing Him as Lord.

Quotable

"He only asks thee to yield thyself to Him, that He may work in thee to will and to do by His own mighty power. Thy part is to yield thyself, His part is to work; and never, never will He give thee any command which is not accompanied by ample power to obey it."—Hannah Whithall Smith

JULY 12 *Reading 193*
MESSIAH'S REIGN
Zechariah 10–14

"I will pour out on the house of David and the inhabitants of Jerusalem a spirit of grace and supplication. They will look on Me, the One they have pierced, and they will mourn for Him as one mourns for an only child" (Zech. 12:10).

There is no passage in the Old Testament that explores more thoroughly the relationship of the Messiah to God's plan for His Old Testament people. Nestled here we find vivid pictures of Christ in both His first and second comings.

Background

History's end. The Old Testament gives many dramatic visions of events to take place at history's end. The focus of these visions is invariably on this earth, and on the Holy Land. These passages universally portray a special role for the people of Israel, and repeat God's consistent commitment to restore Israel to a place of blessing. Students of prophecy who treat these passages in a literal way seek to put the different passages together, to gain as accurate a picture of God's end-time plan as possible. Other Christians tend to treat such passages in an allegorical or spiritual way, and thus study them for personal application today. Both schools see the prophets' messages as affirmations of God's sovereign control of history, of His total commitment to His people, and of the ultimate triumph of righteousness.

When coming to an extended passage like this one, we might take either approach. Or we might take a third.

One of the most exciting aspects of these Zechariah chapters is that they focus on the person and role of the Messiah. Here we have intimations of what Jesus would do in His first coming, and of what He will do at His return. So for devotional reading of these chapters, it may be most meaningful to look at specific messianic images—and see what these images have to say to us about who our Saviour is, and what He will do.

For a more traditional treatment of the picture of the future provided in Zechariah 10–14, see Victor Book's *Bible Knowledge Commentary* or *Teacher's Commentary.*

Overview

Zechariah portrayed God's future care of Judah (10:1-12), despite rejection of their Shepherd-King (11:1-17). When Jerusalem is besieged and then saved (12:1-9), Israel will first recognize and then mourn for "the One they have pierced" (vv. 10-14). Judah will be cleansed from sin by the stricken Shepherd (13:1-9), who will return to reign forever (14:1-21).

Understanding the Text

"From Judah will come the cornerstone" Zech. 10:4. The Jewish Targum viewed the Person identified in this verse as the Messiah, who was destined to come from Judah (cf. Gen. 49:10; Jer. 30:21). Here Messiah is pictured as the cornerstone, or foundation of the future. He is also the "tent peg," the chief support of the future state, and the "battle bow," or its war leader.

In essence Zechariah said that the future for Israel hinges on this one Person. How true this is for us. He is the foundation, the chief support, the only hope we have as well.

"I will not be your Shepherd" Zech. 11:4-14. In the Old and New Testaments the "Good Shepherd" stands for a godly ruler. Christ specifically took this title for Himself (cf. John 10). Here Zechariah portrayed not only rejection of the Messiah, but His betrayal for the sum of 30 pieces of silver.

The first overwhelming impression is simply this: Rejection of the Messiah brings diaster. The "dying die, and the perishing perish" (v. 9). It's the same today. Our destiny depends on whether we accept or reject Christ, the Good Shepherd whom God has chosen to care for His flock.

The 30 pieces of silver mentioned here are prophetic. This was the price that Judas received for betraying Jesus the night before He was crucified. In ancient Israel, 30 pieces of silver was the price of a slave (cf. Ex. 21:32). In later times it was used much like our "two cents."

Why do people reject Christ today? Essentially because they see Him as insignificant to them personally. They feel no need for personal salvation or for deliverance, and thus set no value on the Saviour's cross (see DEVOTIONAL).

Reference to the potter's field is also prophetic. After Christ was taken, Judas found no pleasure in the money and tried to return it. The priests refused to take it, and so Judas threw the coins on the floor. Since it was the "price of blood," the priests were unwilling to put it back in the temple treasury, and used it to buy a plot of land from a potter to be used for the burial of indigents, thus literally fulfilling the prediction of Zechariah.

How strange that the priests tried to distance themselves from the money—when they themselves paid the money in the first place. There is no way that we can ever separate ourselves from responsibility for our response to Jesus—no matter how hard we may try.

"They will look on Me, the One they have pierced" Zech. 12:10. This is an obvious reference to Christ, pierced by the nails on Calvary's cross. The Hebrew preposition is perhaps better taken as "look to" rather than "look on." The thought here is that at Christ's second coming, after God has "set out to destroy all the nations that attack Jerusalem" (v. 9), Israel will look to Jesus in faith (as Num. 21:9; Isa. 45:22).

"Strike the Shepherd" Zech. 13:7. This is another passage that the New Testament applies to Jesus (cf. Matt. 26:31-32). The Hebrew term "strike" clearly indicated the death of the Shepherd. The Babylonian Talmud, an ancient Jewish commentary, deals with the divergent images of the Messiah in His suffering and triumph by suggesting there are to be two Messiahs: a suffering Messiah, and a triumphant Messiah. Not until Christ's resurrection was it clear how one Person could die for the sins of the people, and later appear in power to rescue them.

"His feet will stand on the Mount of Olives" Zech. 14:1-21. After the Shepherd is stricken, he returns as "the Lord" to fight against Israel's enemies and stand physically on the earth. Again only New Testament events enable us to understand how this is possible. The Messiah is both man and God, both stricken and triumphant. When He returns He will stand on the mountains of Israel, and by His presence change their topography—and at the same time transform the whole land, until it at last is holy to the Lord.

▶ DEVOTIONAL
The Cost of Salvation (Zech. 11)

The 30 pieces of silver that Judas accepted to betray Jesus reflected the value placed on His life by that disciple. That price, predicted here in Zechariah, was the amount paid for a slave in Moses' day (cf. Ex. 21:32). In the first century, though it represented some 30 days of labor for a hired man, 30 pieces of silver was viewed by the well-to-do as an insignificant sum. The price tells us that, in the eyes of Christ's enemies, His life and death were totally unimportant.

What a contrast with the value implied in a story Jesus once told. Jesus told of a servant who owed his king "ten thousand talents." Translated, the sum represents millions of dollars. No person, by working, could earn such a sum in a thousand lifetimes. And yet, in the story, Jesus portrayed the king—who stands for God—forgiving the debt completely.

What's significant, of course, is that God forgives sinners solely on the basis of the death of His Son. The value that God places on Jesus' life and death is vastly greater than 30 pieces of silver. It is more than any human being could hope to earn, and yet it was not too great a price to pay for our salvation.

How important is Jesus to you and me? That depends on how aware we are of our sins. And of the greatness of the forgiveness that Jesus won for us at the cost of His own life. When we understand this, nothing else in the universe has any value at all compared to Him.

Personal Application

Value nothing more than Jesus. Make Him your all in all.

Quotable

"I no longer wish to find happiness in myself or in created and perishable things, but in Jesus my Saviour. He is my All, and I desire to belong wholly to Him. It is the most extreme folly and delusion to look elsewhere for any true happiness. Let us, then, vehemently and courageously renounce all other things and seek only Him."—Jean Eudes

The Variety Reading Plan continues with GALATIANS

Malachi

INTRODUCTION

Malachi is the last of the three postexilic prophets. He ministered to descendants of those who returned to Judea from the Babylonian Captivity. When Malachi wrote, priests and people had become lax in their worship at the rebuilt temple, which had been completed in 515 B.C. Through a series of sharp rhetorical questions Malachi challenged his generation to shrug off its spiritual lethargy, and stir up the fires of complete commitment to the Lord.

Malachi serves this same function for believers today. We too need to examine our hearts and our practices, and maintain that enthusiasm which is appropriate to a people of the living God.

OUTLINE OF CONTENTS

I. God's Favored Nation .... Mal. 1:1-5
II. Disrespectful Priests .... Mal. 1:6–2:9
III. Unfaithful People .... Mal. 2:10–3:12
IV. God's Promises .... Mal. 3:13–4:6

READING GUIDE (2 Days)

If hurried, you may read only the "core passage" in your Bible and the Devotional in each chapter of this Commentary.

Reading	*Chapters*	*Core passage*
194	1–2	2
195	3–4	3

Malachi

JULY 13 *Reading 194*
DISHONORING GOD
Malachi 1–2

> *" 'If I am a father, where is the honor due Me? If I am a master, where is the respect due me?' says the* Lord *Almighty" (Mal. 1:6).*

How can we honor God in our worship and in our daily lives? The pointed questions that Malachi asked his generation help us evaluate our own relationship with the Lord, and point to ways that we as His people can honor Him.

Background

Postexilic life. Some 50,000 Jews traveled from Babylon to Judea in 538 B.C. The Persian Cyrus had supplanted Babylonian rulers, and he decreed that captive peoples could return to their homelands. So a little group of Jewish pioneers, motivated by religious enthusiasm, set out for Judea. They were intent on rebuilding the temple of God and on building a faith-community in the land promised to Abraham's offspring.

The story, as told in Ezra and Nehemiah, and as reflected in the postexilic Prophets Haggai, Zechariah, and Malachi, is one of mixed triumph and tragedy. After the temple foundations were laid, the difficulties of reestablishing farms and homes on what was then a desolate frontier seemed overwhelming. Commitment to rebuild the temple waned as the exiles concentrated on meeting their own needs. Some 18 years later the Prophets Haggai and Zechariah rekindled the spiritual fires, and the temple was finished in 515 B.C. But again revival fires cooled.

About 80 years after the first group returned home, the scribe Ezra led another small contingent back to the Holy Land. God later supplied another godly leader in Nehemiah, who served as governor and rebuilt Jerusalem's walls. Each of these leaders, however, found a people less committed to God, with a lax lifestyle that revealed a marked lack of respect for the Lord.

Most commentators believe that Malachi, whose words condemned the same spiritual maladies, ministered sometime after the governorship of Nehemiah. If so, we can't help being amazed—and warned—by how quickly the Old Testament community drifted again from its commitment to the Lord.

Perhaps this is the major contribution of Malachi to our own lives. We see how vulnerable all of us are to spiritual drift. We're shown ways to find out if we ourselves are off course. And we are encouraged by the promise that as we remain true in our commitment to honor God always, we will be among those who make up God's most treasured possession.

Overview

God had loved His people (1:1-5). Yet His priests treated Him with contempt (v. 6–2:9), and His people wearied God with their unfaithfulness (vv. 10-17).

Understanding the Text

" 'I have loved you,' says the Lord*" Mal. 1:1-5.* The foundation of our relationship with the Lord is not our faith, but the fact of God's love. It is the unshakable conviction that God loves us and has shown His love for us in Christ, that creates faith, and keeps our love for the Lord growing.

How significant then that the people of Judah responded to God's affirmation of love with a cynical question: "Love? Oh yeah? How have You loved us?"

This is just the first of a series of seven such questions asked by the priests or people of Judah which revealed their spiritual lethargy. All talk of God, all occasions for worship, had become dreadfully boring to God's own. In modern terminology, worship had become a drag!

Unless you and I keep a clear focus on God's love, and return that love, our faith too will soon become meaningless. We will lose our sense of joy, and those things we have done to please God will seem like meaningless chores.

Keeping the "personal" in our personal relationship with God is our first and most important priority.

"I have loved Jacob, but Esau I have hated" Mal. 1:1-5. Here "Jacob" and "Esau" refer primarily to the peoples descended from the two brothers. God had demonstrated His love for the Jewish people ("Jacob") by restoring them to their homeland. But the Edomites ("Esau") had been displaced from their lands by the Nabateans, and the territory had become a "wasteland" inherited by "desert jackals." This was a divine judgment on a people who had from early times been hostile to God's chosen people, and merited punishment (cf. Ex. 17:8-16; Jud. 3:12-13; 1 Sam. 27:8; Obad.).

"I have loved" and "I have hated" is a way of expressing acceptance and rejection, and has two references. The saying describes God's rejection of any claim Esau might have had to inherit God's covenant promise to Abraham (Gen. 25:23; Rom. 9:13). And the saying contrasts what has happened to the Jewish people and the Edomites. Both the original choice of Jacob, and the subsequent experience of the Jewish people, display the love of God for His chosen race.

Today if anyone were foolish enough to challenge God, saying, "How have You loved us?" we would point to the Cross. And we would testify how Jesus has changed our lives. God's decision to sacrifice His Son, and the subsequent experience by Christians of the great salvation Jesus won for us, prove God's love beyond any shadow of doubt.

There may be times when you and I ask "why?" But we never need wonder whether God loves us. Grasping the extent of that love, we will say with the godly of Malachi's day, "Great is the LORD."

"How have we despised Your name?" Mal. 1:6-14 When God through Malachi confronted the priests of Judea for failing to honor Him, they responded blandly with another cynical question. The response was the same as a denial: "Despise Your name? Not us!"

Malachi went on to identify three ways these religious leaders showed contempt for the Lord.

First, they demonstrated disrespect by placing "defiled food on My altar" (vv. 6-7). Old Testament Law described in detail how sacrifices were to be offered (cf. Lev. 1–6). This was not mere ritual: careful observance of the rules governing sacrifices was a way to show respect for the Lord. The priests, however, disregarded the Law's regulations and so defiled the sacrifices (rendered them ritually unclean). It was as if our parents came over for dinner, and we served them a can of dog food.

Second, they demonstrated disrespect by offering disqualified sacrifices (Mal. 1:8-9, 13-14). Old Testament Law required that sacrificial animals be unblemished. These priests accepted diseased or crippled animals for sacrifice. Malachi said pointedly, "Try offering them to your governor! Would he be pleased with you?" Yet they dared to offer such beasts to God, who is no mere governor but the universe's great King!

Third, they disdained the privilege of leading in worship, finding it "a burden" and sniffing "at it contemptuously" (vv. 10-14). They had totally lost any sense of God's presence, and were merely going through the motions of worship.

What clear and simple—and yet overwhelming—tools for us to use in evaluating the quality of our own personal relationship with God. Are we careful to show respect for God in the way we worship, or are we careless in our church attendance and practice? Do we give Him our best, or does the Lord receive only our leftovers? Do we look forward to worshiping the Lord privately and with others, or has worship become boring and meaningless?

If we have fallen into the ways of the priests of Malachi's day, then we need to confess now. We need to focus again on God's love for us in Jesus, and ask the Lord to fan our love for the Lord into flames. Then we need to return to worship filled with a vital sense of Christ's living presence as we bow down to Him.

"If you do not set your heart to honor My name . . . I will send a curse" Mal. 2:1-9. The failure of the priesthood was critical, for "a priest ought to preserve knowledge, and from his mouth men should seek instruction" (v. 7). Any flaw in the priesthood was bound to affect the people they were called to serve. Malachi charged the priests of his day, "You have turned from the way and by your teaching have caused many to stumble" (v. 8). A priesthood that failed in its mission of serving God and instructing the people would surely be punished.

The warning is directly applicable to us. New Testament believers are called a "holy priesthood," serving under Jesus our High Priest (1 Peter 2:9). We too are charged with worshiping God and instructing others in His ways. Because our lives have such an impact on others, we must guard our commitment carefully. The higher the calling, the greater the responsibility. And ours is the highest calling of all!

"You have wearied the LORD with your words" Mal. 2:17. Most of us remember how small children pick up a phrase or saying, and repeat it again and again and again. After a time it seems as if you can't stand hearing it even one more time.

I have that problem with popular music. Right now a group called "New Kids on the Block" has captivated our nine-year-old. All I hear is snatches of their songs hummed or sung over and over again, or "Joe likes pizza," Joe this, and Joe that. I'm pretty sure I can't stand it much longer. But at least I've learned what it means to be "wearied with words."

Malachi portrays God as fed up too. He heard His people talking, and they were saying the same things over and over again. But God was not just annoyed by what they said. God was slandered! His own people claimed He was pleased with this or that person who complained, "Where is the God of justice?" In other words, "God's not being fair!"

Somehow the perspective of the people of Judea had become distorted, and neither the Lord nor His ways were understood.

How dangerous it is to suppose that we can judge what God does. How dangerous to suppose that we can relegislate morality, and pronounce "good" those who do what God says is wrong.

There's just this spirit loose in our land today, as moral issues are clouded by rhetoric and demands for the "right" to do wrong. As believers, we ourselves are bound by God's Word. We must stand with God in His identification of what is right and of what is wrong.

▶ DEVOTIONAL
Always Be True
(Mal. 2)

A children's song captures the meaning of the seventh commandment. "Always be true," it says. "Always be true to one you're married to."

Malachi too captured this meaning. "Judah has broken faith," the prophet proclaimed. Men had married pagan wives. Men had discarded older wives to marry younger, more sexually attractive girls. In many ways, but particularly in these, the people of Malachi's day showed that they totally misunderstood the concept of loyalty which lies at the root of every human relationship, and at the root of relationship with God Himself.

You see, God had long ago made a commitment to Abraham and his offspring. Those offspring had often proven rebellious and disobedient. Yet through the long centuries God remained faithful to His covenant commitment. God would love, endlessly, even if His people did not love Him in return.

That's what covenant means. Commitment. Loyalty. Always being true.

Marriage was intended by God to be a covenant relationship. It was to be a pact of loyalty, by which two of His people committed themselves to one another. Oh, there might be the unusual situation in which the hardness of one person ultimately made marriage impossible and divorce a necessity. But there could be no excuse for what was then going on in Judah. Men were obviously marrying to satisfy their passion, with no sense of the deeper meaning of marriage. They took foreign wives, who surely would not attract them by their character or faith! And they cast off older wives in a heated rush to find a younger bride, who would be no more to them than a sex object.

Where was the commitment so essential to covenant relationship? Where was loyalty? Gone! And, Malachi said, God is a witness on the side of the wife who is treated so shabbily. Malachi said God no longer pays attention to the offerings of such a husband, nor accepts them. Such divorce God hates, for it is an act of violence, tearing at and destroying the very heart of the abandoned wife.

Reading this passage I can't help thinking of one couple I know. He began an affair with a fellow worker, and then decided to leave his wife and two teenagers to marry her. He did leave. And I've counseled with both the wife and the teens, and seen the terrible damage his choice has done. Seeing their hurt, I understand why God hates such a divorce.

That husband has never faced the appalling nature of his betrayal, or acknowledged to any of the three he's harmed that his abandonment was a sin. The husband and his new wife go to church regularly. They sing in the choir. But I wonder if he ever senses the terrible fact that the Lord "no longer pays attention to [his] offerings or accepts them with pleasure from [his] hands"?

Personal Application

We are to model our relationships with others on God's covenant relationship with us.

Quotable

"There are more people who wish to be loved than there are willing to love."—S.R.N. Chamfort

JULY 14 *Reading 195*
GOD'S PRIZED POSSESSION
Malachi 3–4

> *" 'They will be Mine,' says the LORD Almighty, 'in the day when I make up My treasured possession. I will spare them, just as in compassion a man spares his son who serves him" (Mal. 3:17).*

The little Jewish community in Judea may have strayed from the Lord. But God kept careful track of individuals who loved and remembered Him. In the same way God maintains our names on His "scroll of remembrance."

Background

Tithing. Under Mosaic Law a tenth of all that the land produced belonged to the Lord. This tithe of flocks and produce was brought to the temple, where it was used to provide offerings and to support the priests and Levites who ministered there.

An additional tithe was to be set aside every third year, and retained locally, for the support of widows and orphans and others in need.

While the principle of the tithe can be seen before the Law was given (cf. Gen. 14:20), the concept underlying it is specific to the Old Testament Law. The Lord owned the Holy Land, in which His people were settled. As the One who gave them Canaan, God had a right to the "rent" due on the land His people worked.

Malachi challenged his generation, calling on them to "test" God in this. Begin paying the tithe, "and see if I will not throw open the floodgates of heaven and pour out so much blessing that you will not have room enough for it" (3:10).

While the tenth is not mentioned in the New Testament as a standard of giving (see 2 Cor. 8–9), certain basic principles are common to the teaching of each Testament. All we have comes from and belongs to God. We are but stewards of His possessions. We honor God by our giving, showing by our contributions to support modern ministries that the Lord is important to us. And showing too that we trust God enough not to rob Him of His share out of fear that we will not have enough.

Overview

Malachi predicted a day of purifying judgment (3:1-5). The Lord urged His people to show repentance by their tithes (vv. 6-12) and talk (vv. 13-15), and promised to bless individuals who fear Him (vv. 16-18). Malachi closed with a vivid image of the Day of the Lord (4:1-4), and a promise of Elijah's return (vv. 5-6).

Understanding the Text

"The Lord you are seeking will come to His temple" Mal. 3:1. These words were not a promise, but a threat. The people of little Judah complained about God. "Where is the God of justice?" they asked (2:17). Now Malachi warned them that the One they said they desired, will come.

We too look forward to the Day of the Lord and to Christ's second coming. But we need to ask ourselves a question that these folks never thought to ask. "Are we ready?"

There's nothing we can do to speed His coming. But we can and must prepare ourselves for His appearance.

In Judea in Malachi's time the people talked about Messiah's appearance. But they paid no attention to the commitment, the personal moral purity, and the zeal to do God's work, which would prepare them for that day.

It's certain that the One whom we desire will come. Let's make sure that when He appears, we will be filled with delight rather than regrets.

"He will sit as a refiner and purifier of silver"

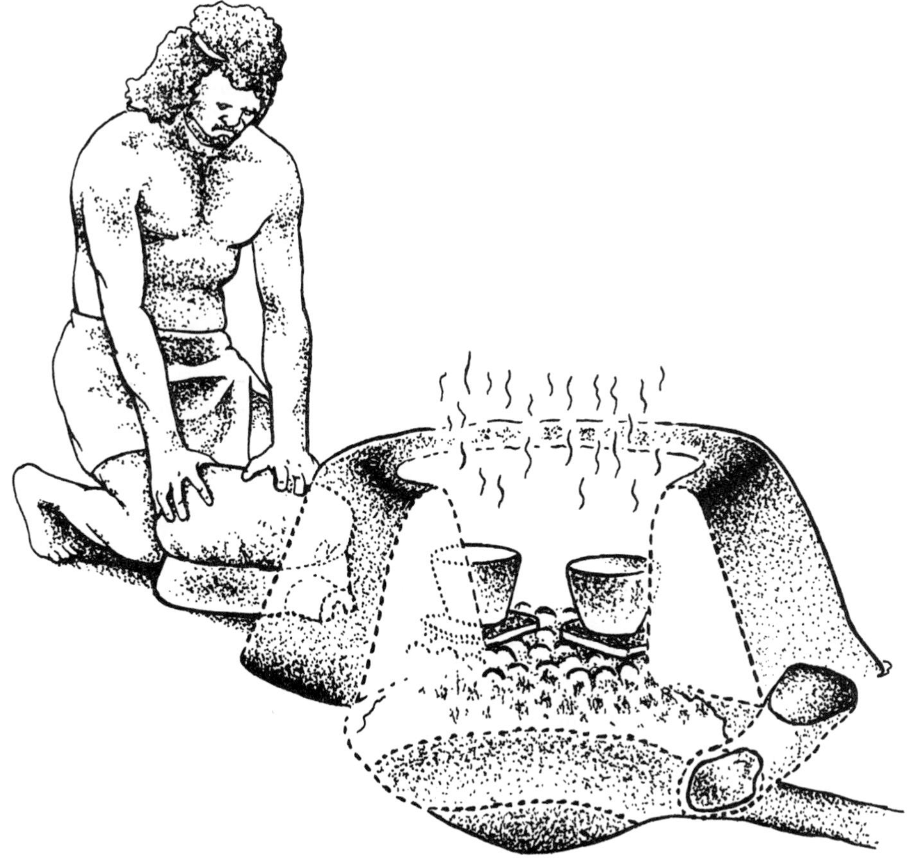

Mal. 3:2-5. Precious metals were placed in a crucible over hot fires. The ore melted, the impurities were skimmed off, and the unadulterated metal was poured into molds. "Launderer's soap" was a powerful chemical compound that was used to soak newly woven cloth. The bits of gummy matter that remained were dissolved, and the new cloth was thus brightened and purified.

Neither image suggests a pleasant experience. Each implies purification. As a result of God's painful purifying work, Malachi said that "the offerings of Judah and Jerusalem will be acceptable to the LORD."

Divine discipline today too may seem as uncomfortable as a refiner's fire or as distasteful as a powerful launderer's soap. So when undergoing discipline, you and I need to keep our eyes focused on the product. When God has purified and cleansed us, our offerings to Him—our worship, and our lives—will be acceptable once again.

"I will come near to you for judgment" Mal. 3:5. How much better not to need purifying, because we already live pure lives! Here Malachi listed some of the attitudes and actions that call for judgment. More importantly, he summed up their cause: these things are done by those who "do not fear Me."

If you and I maintain a reverential awe of God as well as love for Him, we need not worry about judgment. If we truly fear and love God, we will always do right by others.

"How do we rob You?" Mal. 3:6-12 It's possible for a believer to say in all honesty when he hears a call to turn back to God, "How am I to return?" This is because we are often unaware of straying from the Lord. Like Saul, we don't know that the Lord has departed from us (see 1 Sam. 16:14).

Malachi suggested a simple test. Go through your checkbook! Are you giving God a fair portion of what you earn? Or are you robbing God by selfishly using what He has given you without concern for others or for the ministry of the Gospel?

The question comes with a challenge. If you've been holding back because of fear that you won't have enough, God invites you to test Him. After all, the wealth of the universe is His. Shake off your fear, God says, and "see if I will not throw open the floodgates of heaven and pour out so much blessing that you will not have room enough for it."

God can be trusted. We need not hold back out of fear.

"You have said harsh things against Me" Mal. 3:13-18. It's not uncommon even for believers to wonder sometimes if faithfulness really pays. And as for unbelievers, they scoff loudly, preferring the ways of the arrogant rich to those of the humble.

But there are two defects in all such thinking. First, the whole idea that we worship God in order to "gain" something is flawed. We keep God's requirements because He is God, and we love Him. We do not obey God in order to be paid in the coin of earth's realm.

Second, the idea that God's blessings are material is also flawed. And so Malachi said of those who feared the Lord and talked about His name, "They will be Mine . . . in the day when I make up My treasured possession" and "I will spare them." The distinction between the righteous and the wicked can't be determined by this world's bottom line. The balance in our bank account has nothing to do with the treasure stored up for us in heaven.

Yes, at times we may wonder if it pays to serve God. When we do, we have God's Word that there is, and will be, a great distinction made between "those who serve God and those who do not" (v. 18).

"The sun of righteousness will rise with healing in its wings" Mal. 4:1-4. Malachi closed with another distinction between the righteous and the wicked. When the Day of the Lord comes it will "burn like a furnace" for "every evildoer," but will be like the warming and healing sun for those who revere God's name.

What a thought. When Jesus comes, He will seem beautiful to you and me. We will exult joyfully, and rush to be near Him. But the One we find so beautiful will strike terror into the hearts of those who have failed to bow the knee to Him.

How can we be sure that we will welcome Christ with delight? Malachi said, "Remember the Law of My servant Moses, the decrees and laws I gave him at Horeb for all Israel." If we do those things that we know please God, we will have no fears nor regrets at His coming.

"I will send you the Prophet Elijah" Mal. 4:5-6. The Old Testament closes with this promise. Jesus said that John the Baptist carried on an Elijah-like ministry. He preached repentance, and so turned hearts. But the people of Israel did not welcome their Messiah. They rejected Him, and turned Him over to the Romans to be crucified. Thus Malachi foretold another Elijah, destined to appear before Messiah returns and "that great and dreadful Day of the LORD['s judgment] dawns" (v. 5).

What a close to the Old Testament. The ancient issues are unchanged. God still struggles with men, calling His own to faith and obedience, warning the arrogant, and urging repentance. The history of God's people is replete with cycles of revival and sin, of restoration and judgment. Through it all one would think we, and all His people, must surely learn the lesson so clearly taught.

God does love us. He calls us to trust Him, and to display our trust in obedience. If we do, we can rest assured: there is blessing ahead. But for all who refuse to trust and turn to wickedness, the future holds only judgment.

It is coming. Just beyond tomorrow lies a great and terrible Day of the Lord.

▶DEVOTIONAL
The Eye of the Beholder (Mal. 3)

Every once in a while, about every day, I tell my wife she's beautiful. She usually smiles and says, "That's what you think."

She suspects that I'm biased, even though I keep telling her that I'm totally objective about her.

I must admit that in most cases, beauty is in the eye of the beholder. What seems beautiful to one person won't to another. It all depends on our perspective.

That's what Malachi said in this chapter of his little book. Our attitude depends on how we look at life. Malachi even identified three things that we need to look at from God's perspective.

The first is discipline (vv. 1-5). When some painful thing occurs, don't despair. Look at it as a purifying fire. See the beauty that exists within you, that God is so eager to display. God is willing to burn away your impurities, even though it hurts you. Don't think of the present experience. Look beyond it, and rejoice in what you will become.

The second is finances (vv. 6-12). Don't look at the little you have, and worry about how you'll make ends meet. This will only shut your heart to the Lord, and make you stingy in your giving. Instead remember that God possesses all the wealth in the universe. Trust Him enough to give freely, and expect Him to provide all that you need.

The third is blessings (vv. 14-18). Some media evangelists sound so much like the disgruntled of Malachi's day. They ask us to measure blessings by financial well-being, and so beg us to give to their ministry, promising that God will more than repay in good, hard cash.

But Malachi urged us to serve God not for profit, but out of love. Even so, we are abundantly repaid, not in cash here, but in blessings stored up for when Christ returns. Only in eternity will we see the distinction God makes between those who serve God and those who do not, so we should not expect large cash down payments now!

And don't expect those outside of Christ to see life as we do. Many Christians may not even share these perspectives. But you and I need to embrace the way of looking at life that Malachi adopted. We need to look beyond our pain, to look beyond limited resources, and to look beyond material rewards. When we see the beauty God seeks to create in us through discipline, the unlimited resources of our God, and the glory that awaits us in eternity, we will serve God with overflowing joy.

Personal Application

Be wise, and view life with spiritual eyes.

Quotable

God laid upon my back a grievous load,
A heavy cross to bear along the road.

I staggered on, and lo! one weary day,
An angry lion sprang across my way.
I prayed to God, and swift at His command,
The cross became a weapon in my hand.
It slew my raging enemy, and then
Became a cross upon my back again.
I reached a desert. O'er the burning track
I persevered—the cross upon my back.
No shade was there, and in the cruel sun
I sank at last, and thought my day was done.
But lo! The Lord works many a blest surprise,
The cross became a tree before my very eyes!
I slept—I woke—to feel the strength of ten,
I found the cross upon my back again.
And so through all my days from then to this,
The cross—my burden—has become my bliss.
Nor ever shall I lay my burden down.
For God some day will make my cross a crown.—Amos R. Wells

The Variety Reading Plan continues with ZEPHANIAH

Matthew

INTRODUCTION

The Gospel of Matthew launches the New Testament with a triumphant shout. The Messiah promised in the Old Testament has come! He is Jesus of Nazareth, whose death and resurrection offers forgiveness to all.

The hunger of the early church to know about the Lord led to the drawing of four portraits of Jesus by four different writers. This one is by Matthew, one of Christ's own disciples, who probably wrote before A.D. 70. Matthew quoted frequently from the Old Testament to show that Jesus is the Messiah promised there. Among his reports of what Jesus did, Matthew wove summaries of what Jesus taught: about God's kingdom (Matt. 5–7), about discipleship (Matt. 10), about God's plan (Matt. 13), about spiritual greatness (Matt. 18–20), about the future (Matt. 24–25).

Perhaps the greatest contribution of Matthew is to help us see Jesus as a Servant-King, and to help us sense our own calling to a servanthood like His. Reading this book we understand why Matthew was the Gospel most quoted by Christian writers of the first three centuries of our era.

OUTLINE OF CONTENTS

READING GUIDE (14 Days)

If hurried, you may read only the "core passage" in your Bible and the Devotional in each chapter of this Commentary.

Reading	*Chapters*	*Core passage*
196	1–2	1:18–2:6
197	3–4	4:1-11
198	5	5:21-48
199	6–7	6:5-13
200	8–9	9:1-13
201	10–11	10:16-31; 11:28-29
202	12–13	12:1-37
203	14–15	15:21-39
204	16–17	17:1-13
205	18	18:18-35
206	19–20	20:17-34
207	21–23	23
208	24–25	25:31-46
209	26–28	27:32-56

Matthew

JULY 15 *Reading 196*
LINEAGE OF THE KING
Matthew 1–2

> *"Where is the One who has been born King of the Jews? We saw His star in the east, and have come to worship Him" (Matt. 2:2).*

Matthew invites us to look beyond the scenes of history's most crucial birth. What he shows us is that Jesus had His origins in God's eternal plan, and that the Babe of Bethlehem embodies that plan's fulfillment.

Overview

Jesus' genealogy established His descent from Abraham and David (1:1-17). His virgin birth fulfilled Isaiah's prophecy (vv. 18-25). Other events (2:1-23) prove that Jesus is indeed the Messiah predicted by the Old Testament prophets.

Understanding the Text

"A record of the genealogy of Jesus Christ the Son of David, the Son of Abraham" Matt. 1:1. The Greek phrase, "a record of the genealogy," is found in the Septuagint only in Genesis 1 and 5. This indicates Matthew intended this phrase to mean "record of the origins." Thus the first verse launches us immediately into the central issue of the New Testament. Who is Jesus? What is His role in God's plan, and in our lives?

Matthew's answer is given in this two-chapter introduction, which demonstrates that Jesus is the "Anointed One" predicted in the Old Testament. That term, "Messiah" in Old Testament Hebrew and "Christ" in New Testament Greek, is Jesus' title. It means that He is the One through whom all God's promises will be fulfilled.

As the "Son of David" Jesus fulfilled the promise God gave David that a descendant of his would sit on Israel's throne, and rule a universal kingdom (cf. 2 Sam. 7:12-16; Isa. 9:6-7). Additional quotes from the prophets in these two chapters are from Old Testament passages that underline the theme of Messiah's rule (Jer. 23; Hosea 11; Micah 5). (See DEVOTIONAL.)

As "Son of Abraham" Jesus fulfilled the promise given the father of the Jewish race. He is the "Seed," through whom the entire human race would be blessed (Gen. 12:1-3; cf. Gal. 3:16).

Thus Matthew's very first words alert us. Jesus is the focus of all Scripture. He is the essence—the substance and the spirit of its message. He is both Lord and Saviour. Our response to Jesus determines our destiny.

"The father of" Matt. 1:2-17. Like other ancient genealogies, this one is organized to accomplish a specific purpose. While it is stylized, and does not include every ancestor, it is rooted in historical information that was available to Matthew in Old Testament documents and genealogical records maintained at the Jerusalem temple.

Even as late as the A.D. 90s, after the temple had been destroyed, when the Emperor Domitian ordered all descendants of David killed, the remaining few were located by referring to Jewish genealogical records.

The church historian Eusebius tells us that when the last two appeared before the Emperor, he looked at their calloused hands and let them live. What threat could mere farmers offer, whatever their line?

How fascinating. Jesus, born of poor parents, growing up in obscurity, working with His hands at the carpenter's trade, would likely have made just as slight an impression on the Roman ruler.

How difficult for us to judge greatness and humility if we look only at outward appearances. Jesus, the Son of God, the destined Ruler of the universe, King of an eternal kingdom, lived the most humble of lives, and died the most abject of deaths. As we read on in this Gospel we will see it over and over again. Jesus was a King, but a Servant-King. And as our King, Jesus calls us to a servant lifestyle like His own.

"Whose mother was Rahab" Matt. 1:5. Hebrew genealogies characteristically mentioned only male ancestors. Matthew departed from this pattern, and included four women, three of whom were Gentiles, and the fourth of whom he noted had been married to a Gentile (Bathsheba, who "had been Uriah's [a Hittite's] wife"). Furthermore, with the exception of Ruth, the women were hardly models of morality! Tamar, Rahab, and Bathsheba had all engaged in adultery, even though by the first century they were highly regarded by the Jewish people.

What point was Matthew making? We can perhaps suggest several. Perhaps Matthew was telling us that in the new era Christ introduced, women would have an increasingly important role alongside men. Very possibly Matthew was reminding us that Jesus has come to be the Saviour of the world, not just of the Jewish people. God introduced Gentile blood into the Saviour's line as a grand reminder that He values every human life, and sent His Son to redeem us all. And, perhaps, these particular women are there to remind us that human flaws do not cut us off from being recipients of God's grace. In fact, it is our flaws that led God to send His Son, that in a single grand redemptive act Jesus might cleanse not only our sins, but also those of the generations that preceded His birth.

"Joseph her husband was a righteous man" Matt. 1:18-25. Joseph is one of the most admirable characters in Scripture. Following Jewish custom, he had sealed the betrothal contract that was the first but binding stage in marriage. Many assume that Joseph was an older man, and that after the betrothal Mary stayed with her parents until she was old enough to conclude the marriage and move into Joseph's home. When Joseph learned that Mary was pregnant, he showed unusual compassion. Despite his feelings of hurt and betrayal, he "did not want to expose her to public disgrace."

Explaining this, Matthew called Joseph a "righteous" man. Why, in view of the fact that the Law's penalty for adultery is stoning, would this suggest righteousness? Some might feel it would have been more "righteous" to demand Mary be punished to the full extent of the Law!

The answer lies in the fact that "righteousness" in the Old Testament is conformity to God's heart as well as His Law. Even Saul realized that grace better displays righteousness than strict legality, for he once cried out to David, "You are more righteous than I. . . . You have treated me well, but I have treated you badly" (1 Sam. 24:17). Joseph took this principle to heart, and though he thought Mary had treated him badly, he determined to treat her well. Thus in a spiritual sense as well as the physical, Joseph was truly a "son of David" (Matt. 1:20).

The New Testament tells us little about Joseph beyond this. But how much these few words convey. He was a man like his ancestor, who had a heart for God and deep compassion for others. No matter how little known beyond our circle of family and friends you or I may be, we are spiritually great if Matthew's word about Joseph is true of us as well.

"The virgin will be with child" Matt. 1:20-25. The Hebrew term *'almâh* means "young woman," and while it is typically used of young unmarried women, it lacks the technical force of "virgin." However, there is no question about the Greek word Matthew chose here: *parthenos*. This is a young woman who has never had sexual relations with a man.

When the angel that appeared to Joseph in a dream quoted Isaiah 7:14 he definitively interpreted the prophet's meaning: it was Mary (a virgin) who bore Jesus as her Son.

The message, that Mary was pregnant by the Holy Spirit, was accepted by Joseph, as it has been by Christians throughout history. The name, "Immanuel," explains the implications. The Child conceived by the Holy Spirit is Himself God: God, come to be "with us," not simply as a presence, but as one of us. Why the name "Jesus"? The name means "deliverer" or "saviour," and expresses the purpose of His coming. God became one of us in order to "save His people from their sins."

Some who claim to be Christians do deny the Virgin Birth. Yet if Jesus was not both God and man, united through a miracle in Mary's womb, He was merely a man. And no mere man, doomed to struggle with his own sins, would be free to save us from ours. Without the Virgin Birth there is no biblical Christianity. With it, our destiny is secure. For with it, the Jesus on whom we rely is God, and as God He guarantees the salvation He won for us on Calvary.

"Where is the One who has been born King of the Jews?" Matt. 2:1-8 The familiar story of the magi, a name given a philosopher class in Persia, is told in order to further define who Jesus is. Alerted by the appearance of an unusual star, the magi traveled to Judea to honor One born to be King. Their arrival caused consternation, and Herod demanded to know where such a Person might be born. The answer was found in Micah 5:2: the promised Ruler was to be born in Bethlehem.

Herod's claim that if the Child were identified he would "go and worship Him" was a revealing lie! It was a lie, because the aging Herod, destined to live only a few more months, intended to kill the Infant. The determined king, who had ordered the execution of his own sons when he thought they threatened his throne, could not bear the thought of anyone but him ruling his domain. The phrase "go and worship" was revealing, because the word "worship" helps us realize that scholarly Jews in the first century understood the Old Testament to teach that the Messiah would be God as well as man (cf. Micah 5:4).

It's never enough to know who Jesus is. Those who acknowledge His supernatural birth, but fail to commit themselves to Him as Saviour, are very like Herod. They too are unwilling to acknowledge Jesus' right to the throne—this time the throne of their lives. Yet because of who Jesus is, we are to gladly bow, worshiping and welcoming Him, not only as Saviour but also as our Lord.

"They were overjoyed" Matt. 2:9-12. The magi serve as a positive model of response to Jesus, even as Herod serves as a negative model. These foreign visitors came joyfully to the house where the little family lived. There they worshiped the Babe, and "opened their treasures and presented Him with gifts."

The gifts recorded are the traditional gifts given to royalty—gold, incense, and myrrh. More significant, however, is the pattern we see here. They worshiped Jesus. They then opened their treasures. And then presented Him with gifts.

Too often we human beings worship our treasures. Money, or the things money can buy, become the focus of our lives. When we worship wealth we have no room for Jesus, or for others. We hug our treasures close to us, unwilling to part with them for any cause.

Worshiping Jesus frees us from materialism. Our "treasures" lose their grip on our hearts, and as we discover the joy of serving Christ, we willingly present our material treasures to Him as gifts.

"Take the Child and His mother and escape to Egypt" Matt. 2:13-17. Though the wise men never returned to direct the demented Herod to Jesus, Herod determined to see Him killed. To be sure he destroyed one Child, Herod ordered all male children under two in the neighborhood of Bethlehem killed.

The act underlines the cruelty of Herod, and also the futility of such cruelty. God had spoken to Joseph again in a dream and, no doubt using the gifts brought by the magi to finance the journey, Mary and Joseph escaped with the Christ Child to Egypt.

Matthew quoted here from Jeremiah 31:15, picturing the anguish of those who lost their children in Herod's purge. Yet Matthew 2:16-17 reminds us of a great truth. Even as the people of Jeremiah's day were told that after their suffering "they will return from the land of the enemy," so through the cross the infants who died will live again. "So," the Lord declared through Jeremiah, "there is hope for your future."

Jesus did live to die for us. Because of Him, even when we suffer painful tragedies, we too have hope for our future.

"He went and lived in a town called Nazareth" Matt. 2:19-23. After Herod died, an angel directed Joseph to return. The family settled in Nazareth, in Galilee, and there Jesus grew up and began His ministry.

This is the third occasion on which Joseph is given guidance by an angel appearing to him in a dream. How responsive Joseph was to the Lord. In each case the text says that "when he woke up" Joseph did what the angel of the Lord commanded. In verse 14 we read that "he got up, took the Child and His mother during the night and left for Egypt." Joseph was not only willing to obey, he did so without hesitation.

Mary is rightly honored as the mother of Jesus. She was a special young woman, highly honored by God. Yet what a human surrogate father Jesus had in Joseph! He was truly a special man, and his obedience was highly honoring to God. May you and I honor Him as much, and as well, by our readiness to obey.

▶ DEVOTIONAL
Behold Your King
(Matt. 1:18–2:6)

Babies are cute. They are not supposed to inspire awe.

Perhaps that's one reason why people find it so easy to trivialize Christmas. Baby Jesus, lying helpless in the manger, can be viewed with mild affection. Folks can smile down at Him, and then move on to the real business of the season—shopping, vacation, being with the family, sending cards that say "holiday greetings" and so are unlikely to offend with an overly religious message.

Despite what people may assume, Matthew wasn't interested in having us meet "Baby Jesus." We know, because over and over this Gospel writer quoted from the Old Testament. And the passages he selected and applied directly to Christ are passages that insist we see not an Infant but a King; not a Babe, but the Master of the universe.

Who is Jesus to Matthew? Matthew 1:23 identifies Him with a virgin-born Child predicted by Isaiah. What did Isaiah say about Him? He is "Immanuel," a name that in Hebrew means "With Us Is GOD!" Look at the Babe in the manger, not with mild affection, but in awe. For in this Child all the glory of God shines through.

Matthew also quoted from Micah 5, which predicted the birth in Bethlehem of a Ruler who would be the Shepherd of God's people Israel. Looking in Micah, we discover that "He will stand and shepherd His flock in the strength of the LORD." In fact, "in the majesty of the name of the LORD His God." His people will be secure, for His greatness will "reach to the ends of the earth." Why not, when His strength is the strength of God, and His majesty the name of the Lord, which He bears!

And when Christmas comes again, don't be concerned if the Supreme Court rules against local government displays of crèche and cradle. The plastic replicas, however cute, hardly represent the King of kings.

To catch the spirit of Christmas, read again Matthew's account— and the prophecies he quotes. And then bow down in awe.

Personal Application

The Christ we need to keep in Christmas is not the Babe so much as the King of kings.

Quotable

"Napoleon was right when he said, 'I know men, and I tell you, Jesus is more than a man. Comparison is impossible between Him and any other human being who ever lived, because He was the Son of God.' Emerson was right when he replied to those who asked him why he did not include Jesus among his Representative Men, 'Jesus was not just a man.' Arnold Toynbee was right when he said, 'As we stand and gaze with our eyes fixed upon the farther shore a simple figure rises from the flood and straightway fills the whole horizon of history. There is the Savior.' "—Billy Graham

JULY 16 *Reading 197*
THE KING'S PREPARATION
Matthew 3–4

"Jesus was led by the Spirit into the desert to be tempted by the devil" (Matt. 4:1).

Before Jesus began to preach, John the Baptist prepared Judea for His appearance. And God did a preparatory work in Christ's own life!

Biography: John the Baptist

John was Jesus' cousin, about six months older than Christ. He had been filled by the Spirit from his birth, being readied for his mission (Luke 1:14-17). We don't know how long John lived a hermit's life in the Judean wilderness (Matt. 3:4). But when Jesus was about 30, John appeared on the banks of the Jordan and began to preach.

John's appearance excited the Jewish population. Burdened by heavy taxes and ruled by an increasingly brutal Herod, there was an intense yearning for the Messiah to appear, a yearning attested in many first-century sources. John, austere and ascetic, burning with passion for God and holiness, seemed a likely candidate. His announcement that "the kingdom of heaven is near" stirred Jewish yearning into bright expectation.

John persistently denied that he was the Messiah (John 1:19-28). Instead he called for his listeners to confess their sins, repent, and prepare themselves spiritually for the true Messiah, whom God had revealed to him was even then living among them.

Matthew quotes from Isaiah 40 to define John's role. That passage launched the second half of the mighty Old Testament prophecy; a half in which the dominant theme shifts from judgment to joy. John's mission of preparation was to ready the people spiritually, for in a brief moment "the glory of the LORD [would] be revealed, and all mankind together will see it" (Isa. 40:5).

I suspect that when John denied being Messiah, many turned away. "Nothing but a messenger," they may well have thought. Yet this messenger readied hearts for Jesus, and thus for endless joy. There is no greater ministry any of us can have than John's. We cannot meet the deepest needs of others. But we can introduce them to Him who can meet every one.

Overview

John predicted Messiah's appearance, and preached baptism as a sign of repentance (3:1-12). Christ was baptized to identify Himself with John's righteous message (vv. 13-17). The Spirit then led Jesus into the wilderness, where He overcame temptation and demonstrated His commitment to God (4:1-11). Thus prepared, Jesus began to preach (vv. 12-17), called His first disciples (vv. 18-22), and demonstrated His God-given authority by miracles of healing (vv. 23-25).

Understanding the Text

"John the Baptist came, preaching . . . and saying, 'Repent' " Matt. 3:1-6. It's clear from Matthew and especially from Luke that John's preaching, like that of the Old Testament prophets, focused on the personal and social sins that marred society. John preached against materialism and selfishness (Luke 3:11), and against such widespread sins as overcharging (v. 13) and extortion (v. 14). Those who confessed their sins were warned to "produce fruit in keeping with repentance" (Matt. 3:8).

John's emphasis is important. In the first century the Jews took a bath in a *mikvah* in order to be ritually pure for worship. In contrast John called for an inner change of heart and mind (repentance), which is to produce a pure and holy life.

Repentance has always been a part of the Christian Gospel. Not "repentance" as being sorry for sin, or an effort at self-reform. In Scripture repentance is a change of heart and mind about God that bears fruit in a holy life. Without repentance there is no salvation, simply because whenever Jesus enters a life by faith, He does just such a transforming work in the human heart.

"Do this to fulfill all righteousness" Matt. 3:15. Many have debated why Jesus wanted to be baptized. John, His cousin, who knew Him well, was embarrassed to

baptize Jesus even before he knew that Jesus was the Messiah. John's baptism was for repentance—and John knew Jesus as a godly Jew who had no need to repent.

As a young sailor I went with my church youth group to a Billy Graham meeting in Madison Square Garden. When Billy called for those in the great hall who would dedicate their lives to the Lord to stand, the others in my youth group all stood. I remained seated. I had already dedicated myself to God, and it didn't seem right to just "go through the motions." The Lord knew where I stood with Him, and I was satisfied with that.

If I had understood these verses in Matthew better, I would have stood with them. Why? Because I would have realized that Jesus was baptized not because He needed to be, but in order to identify Himself with John's message! It was right for Jesus to take a stand with John. Just as it would have been right for me to identify myself with Billy's call to commitment.

It's an important principle for us to apply. We too need to be identified with what is right, and what is righteous. We too need to be willing to take a public stand.

John's Gospel tells us that it was only as Christ stood in the water beside His cousin, and the Spirit descended on Him as a dove, that John realized who Jesus is—the Messiah he had been commissioned to announce.

"Jesus was led by the Spirit into the desert to be tempted" Matt. 4:1. This verse emphasizes the importance of the temptation in preparing Jesus for His mission. The Spirit of God specifically led Christ into the wilderness "to be tempted."

Why was the temptation so important in Jesus' life? Because soon He would begin to preach, presenting not only the kingdom, but Himself as King. And as King, Christ must be Victor—not merely over the puny powers of nature or Satan, but over the pull of His human nature. Adam and Eve were unable to resist temptation, and all mankind fell. Christ now had to triumph over temptation, and in triumphing qualify Himself to lift all mankind up again.

Our temptations seem insignificant beside His: no cosmic issues are at stake. Yet Jesus' temptation does put ours in a special light. Temptations are not "bad." Nor are they intended to trip us up. God permits us to be tested, and sometimes even brings tests our way, in order that we might triumph over them. Each test passed victoriously strengthens us for the productive life God intends us to lead.

"Man does not live on bread alone" Matt. 4:2-4. Medical science has shown that after 30 to 40 days of fasting, hunger, which disappears the second or third day, returns. All the body's stored resources have been used, and the return of hunger is a sign that the body must have food again.

Jesus had fasted 40 days and "was hungry" when Satan approached our Lord and challenged Him to turn stones into bread. After all, as Satan suggested, that would be a minor miracle for the Son of God to perform!

Jesus answered by quoting a passage in Deuteronomy: "Man does not live on bread alone." Perhaps the most important word here is "man."

Think about it. Jesus did not respond to temptation by calling on His resources as Son of God, but instead met each one as "man." If Christ had met temptation by drawing on His deity, there would be no help for us in His example. But since Jesus met temptation as a man, using no more resources than are available to any human being, you and I have hope! We too can overcome our temptations. We can follow Jesus' example, draw on the resources He used, and triumph! (See DEVOTIONAL.)

This first temptation was directed against Jesus' physical nature. He was hungry. He wanted bread. Why not make bread? Christ quoted Deuteronomy 8:3, which calls on man to live by the Word of God.

The point of Christ's response is this: human beings are physical creatures. But we are more than animals. We have a spiritual nature that is to control the physical. God's will, not our physical needs or desires, is to govern our choices.

Today many people argue that if you want something, take it. If you feel an urge for sex, satisfy it. After all, it's "natural." Yes, it's natural for animals to satisfy their desires. But because we are more than animals, it is not "natural" for man to be driven by physical hungers. We are spiritual beings, and what is right and natural for us is to be driven by the living Word of our God.

"Throw Yourself down" Matt. 4:5-7. This temptation is a subtle one. Understanding it hinges on the nature of the "if" Satan used in speaking to Jesus.

Christ had been led by the Spirit into the wilderness. He had fasted 40 days, and was hungry and weak. And then, when He was weakest, Satan appeared! It would only be natural if Jesus, acting by choice in His humanity, had felt doubt. You or I surely would have. "God," we might have cried out, "if You really love me, why are You doing this to me now!"

Satan picked up on this doubt, and said, "If You are the Son of God." This is not the "if" we use in place of "since." It is the "if" of uncertainty. Satan was trying to nurture any kernel of doubt that might exist in Christ's human heart. And then Satan suggested a way to find out. "Jump off the pinnacle of the temple, and the Bible promises angels will catch You before You land. Then You'll know You have a special relationship with God."

The "pinnacle" was the corner of one of the great walls that surrounded the temple court, and fell off into the Kidron Valley far below. Jesus would not have been observed leaping into the valley. The test Satan proposed was not intended as a shortcut to popularity, but as reassurance of God's love. See Matthew 4:5-7.

Again Jesus quoted Deuteronomy, this time 6:16. Human beings are not to test God. They are to trust Him. God has shown His love throughout history, and has no need to prove it again to His own.

This is one temptation we are particularly susceptible to. When troubles come, we feel panic and uncertainty. We begin to doubt, and to wonder if God is with us or not. Jesus reminds us that the way to triumph in such situations is not to demand God prove His presence, but simply to trust the love He has demonstrated so clearly. For us, that ultimate demonstration is in Christ's death and resurrection. Surely He who has given His own Son to redeem us will never leave or forsake His own.

"All this I will give You" Matt. 4:8-10. Satan's third temptation was also subtle. He offered Christ immediate authority over all this world's kingdoms. Why would this be a temptation? Surely the Creator of the world could hardly be bribed with what He already possessed, and would one day claim.

I suspect that Satan's appeal was to Jesus' compassion. The world of that day as today reeked with injustice, and was deluged in the tears of human tragedy. Think of all the wars that would have been avoided were Jesus to rule today. Think of the sick who would be healed, the injustices corrected. It would surely be a good thing for Jesus to rule: good as far as you and I are concerned.

Jesus responded by refusing to pay the price. God, not Satan, is to be worshiped. God's will is to be our ultimate authority, and we are to bow to Him in all things. Even something "good" could not deter Jesus from obedience to the will of God. Even when that will would lead Him to a cross.

All too often we Christians are tempted by opportunities to do good. We may rush in, sure that God is pleased because our motives are so pure. But even the opportunity to do good can be one of Satan's traps. Like Jesus, we are to determine God's will for us, and to choose that will, even when God's will keeps us from doing something that seems good.

I am far more tempted by opportunities

to do good than to do evil. Recently I was invited to spend a number of weeks in South Africa, where some of my books seem to be making an impact on the church. Everything I could learn about the invitation marked it as an opportunity to do good, and I wanted to accept. Yet I was unsure, and after asking a number of friends to pray, finally decided that the Lord didn't want me to accept the invitation at that time. What a hard thing, this turning down opportunities to do good.

I suspect many of us, already overloaded with church duties, find it hard to resist the invitation to do one more thing. We need to make it a habit not to say yes lightly. We need to remember that we are to live our lives as Jesus did, by the will of God. And that sometimes God has other priorities for us than a "good" that may keep us overactive, even if we are active "for Him."

"From that time on Jesus began to preach" Matt. 4:12-17. With His victory won and His authority over inner, human frailties demonstrated, Jesus began His public ministry. He returned to Galilee, and made Capernaum the headquarters of His mission.

It's significant that the personal, inner issues were settled before public ministry began. God wants to do an inner work in our lives too, to qualify us for ministry with others

"Preaching the Good News . . . and healing every disease and sickness" Matt. 4:23-25. The miracles Jesus performed did authenticate His claim to be sent from God. But we need to note something important about those miracles. Jesus performed no miracle to ease His own hardships—not even the miracle of turning stones into bread. His miracles were performed for the benefit of others, and most frequently took the form of healing the sick and restoring the injured.

There's something appropriate about this kind of miracle. Jesus came offering inner healing to a lost humanity. And to demonstrate God's compassion, He healed their bodies as well.

It is still appropriate that those who share the Gospel with others have an equal concern for the social and physical ills that cause human beings so much pain. We demonstrate God's compassion today when we minister not just to men's souls, but to material needs as well.

▶DEVOTIONAL
Overcoming Temptation (Matt. 4:1-11)

I memorized the Bible verse. I quoted it to myself over and over again. I thought it surely would give me victory over the particular temptation that had me so defeated. But quote as much as I would, no victory came. I was just as vulnerable with my Bible verse as without it.

I suspect many of us have had this experience. We see Jesus recalling verses from the Old Testament and quoting them to Satan. Jesus was victorious. Why aren't we when we do the same thing?

The answer lies in the distinction between magic and faith. Magic is using an object or chant in a desperate attempt to ward off evil or control circumstances. Faith is a quiet confidence that what God says is true enough to act on. I had been using my Bible verse as a magic talisman, waving it desperately to repel temptation. But when we look at Matthew 4, we see that Jesus used Scripture in quite another way. He went into the Word, found a principle or truth, and said in effect, "I will now live by this truth."

Jesus saw the Word of God as truth, and determined to act on that truth. It was this exercise of faith that gave Him victory over His temptations. And it is just such an exercise of faith that will give us victory when we are tempted today.

Yes, let's look for the key to our victory in the Word of God. But let's not use the Bible in a pagan, magical way. Let's take God at His Word, act on what He says, and let God use our faith to give us the victory in Him.

Personal Application
Find victory by following Christ's example and living the Word of God.

Quotable
"The Bible tells only two temptation stories, the temptation of the first man and the temptation of Christ, that is, the temptation which led to man's fall, and the temptation which led to Satan's failure.

All other temptations in human history have to do with these two stories of temptation. Either we are tempted in Adam or we are tempted in Christ. Either the Adam in me is tempted—in which case I fall. Or the Christ in us is tempted—in which case Satan is bound to fall."—Dietrich Bonhoeffer

JULY 17 *Reading 198*
RIGHTEOUS KINGDOM
Matthew 5

> *"Do not think that I have come to abolish the Law or the Prophets; I have not come to abolish them but to fulfill them" (Matt. 5:17).*

Jesus spoke as King, with absolute authority in His kingdom. And Jesus spoke as God, not abolishing, but reinterpreting the meaning of biblical words whose implications had long been lost. As we listen closely, familiar Scriptures become fresh and new for us as well.

Background

Kingdom. In the ancient world a "kingdom" was the area ruled by a king. The definition is less simple than it seems. The ancient kingdom was not defined so much by territory, or by the language of the inhabitants, as by the ruler. Wherever a king's will was supreme, that was his kingdom. Wherever a king was free to act, and the populace obeyed, that was his kingdom.

Scripture presents God as King of the universe, in the sense that His will is sovereign. Yet many in this overarching kingdom of God are in rebellion. And so the fullest meaning of kingdom is not presently achieved in our universe.

The Old Testament particularly, but the New as well, speaks of a coming time when Christ will rule a kingdom that extends over the entire earth. Then the rebellious will be judged, and all will submit to His will. Then the universal kingdom and earthly kingdom will be one, and will be complete.

Scripture, however, also presents Jesus as King of a present spiritual kingdom. This kingdom exists alongside and within the present rebellious universal kingdom of God. Wherever human beings bow to Christ as Lord, and do His will, there the kingdom of Jesus has come. And there Christ, our King, acts in power to guide and protect His own.

We need to understand the nature of Christ's present kingdom, for the major thrust of what is known as the "Sermon on the Mount," reported in Matthew 5–7, is to teach us how to live as its citizens. These words are spoken to us, just as vital and filled with power as when Christ first uttered them nearly 2,000 years ago. As we take them to heart and apply them to our lives, we submit to Christ our King, and experience His blessed kingdom now.

Overview

Jesus announced blessings for citizens of His kingdom (5:1-12). He expects citizens of His kingdom to do good deeds (vv. 13-16), for He requires a righteousness that surpasses that of even the zealous Pharisees (vv. 17-20). Christ looked behind the acts the Law regulated to call for purity of heart (vv. 21-42) and that crowning expression of kingdom righteousness: a love like the Heavenly Father's for one's enemies (vv. 43-48).

Understanding the Text

"Blessed are the poor in spirit" Matt. 5:1-12. King Herod established many new cities during his 40-year reign. Each time he enlisted citizens by promising them many special benefits, including citizenship, a reduction of taxes, land, etc. This was a common practice in the Roman Empire during the age of Augustus, when many new cities were established.

But it is hard to imagine a ruler calling for citizens, and announcing that in his kingdom recruits will receive poverty of spirit, meekness, mourning, hunger, and thirst, and even persecution. Yet these are the blessings Jesus offers those who claim the citizenship He described.

What's more, King Jesus said that the poor in spirit, the meek, and mourning are blessed! He does not offer a change of condition, but blessing in and through settings that repel citizens of this world.

The Beatitudes will remain a mystery unless we realize that Jesus is speaking of the basic attitudes and values that produce spiritual fruit. It is not the person who claims to "have it made" spiritually who finds the kingdom, but the individual who recognizes how poor he is (v. 3). It is not the person who is satisfied with what the world offers, but the person who mourns and looks beyond its glitter, who finds comfort (v. 4). It is not the person who is arrogant, but the meek, who responds to God's voice, who inherits the earth (v. 5). It is not those who are satisfied with their own righteousness, but those who hunger and thirst for a righteousness they do not have who will be satisfied (v. 6).

To experience life in Jesus' kingdom, we need to reject the values and attitudes of this world and adopt the values portrayed here by our Lord.

"Let your light shine before men" Matt. 5:13-16. In biblical times every home had its lamp burning all night. The lamp did not give much light, but it testified to the fact that the house was inhabited. These lamps, small oil-filled bowls, were set high on pottery stands.

Jesus told His hearers that citizens in

The Beautitudes: Matthew 5:3-10

Jesus' Values		Countervalues
BLESSED ARE THOSE WHO . . .		**BLESSED ARE THOSE WHO ARE . . .**
(v. 3)	are poor in spirit	self-confident competent self-reliant
(v. 4)	mourn	pleasure-seeking hedonistic "the beautiful people"
(v. 5)	are meek	proud powerful important
(v. 6)	hunger for righteousness	satisfied "well adjusted" practical
(v. 7)	are merciful	self-righteous "able to take care of themselves"
(v. 8)	are pure in heart	"adult" sophisticated broad-minded
(v. 9)	are peacemakers	competitive aggressive
(v. 10)	are persecuted because of righteousness	adaptable popular "don't rock the boat"

His kingdom are to be like lamps, lights in the world. The good deeds performed by Jesus' people are to testify to the fact that this world, however dark it may be, still is inhabited by the King. When the good deeds of Christ's people are seen, men will grasp the source and praise "your Father in heaven."

Don't let anyone deny the role of good deeds in the Christian life. A Christian who does not perform good deeds is as useless to God and others as a lamp hidden under a bowl.

"I have not come to abolish them but to fulfill them" Matt. 5:17-20. Many have puzzled over Jesus' statement that He came to fulfill the Law and the Prophets. Christ speaks here as a Jew, dedicated as other rabbis of the first century to a single task: to explain the true meaning of God's words, and thus to "fulfill" them.

Yet Christ immediately sets Himself apart from other teachers. The Pharisees were zealous in keeping both the written and oral law. But in explaining the real meaning of God's Word, Christ was about to reveal a righteousness that "surpassed" any righteousness the Pharisees imagined they possessed through keeping the commandments.

As citizens of Jesus' kingdom, you and I are called to live a righteous life. But we must avoid the error of the Pharisees. We must not mistake true righteousness, or suppose that because we do certain things and refrain from others that we have reached spiritual heights. What we do is important, yes. But God is most concerned with what we are.

"You have heard that it was said . . . 'Do not murder' " Matt. 5:21-26. This is the first of six illustrations Jesus used to explain surpassing righteousness. All had heard the Old Testament Law that legislated against murder. The act of killing was wrong.

But Jesus went on to explain that God is not just concerned with murder. He noted the anger that flared up and led to murder! The truly righteous person is not one who just refrains from murder. He or she is one who does not respond to others with anger.

In this and in the following illustrations Jesus emphasized God's concern with the heart. Keeping the law about not murdering makes no one righteous. The truly righteous man is the one who does not become angry!

Actually, this kind of perfect righteousness is beyond us all. That's why we must become citizens of Jesus' kingdom. Only Christ's work in our hearts can transform us into the persons God calls us to be.

"Leave your gift there in front of the altar" Matt. 5:23-24. Is worshiping God important? Yes! But Jesus underlined the importance of the pure heart by saying that if we remember anyone has something against us, we are to go get that straightened out even if it means putting off worship!

But what's most important is the phrase, "If . . . your brother has something against you." We're not only responsible for our own anger, but for our brother's! If we've done anything to cause another to be upset, we must resolve that issue immediately, in order to preserve our brother from an anger that is inappropriate in the kingdom of God.

It perhaps seems too much! It seems hard enough to care for our own relationship with God. And the fact is, it is too much. But it is what our King expects. As we obey, He will do in us and in our relationships what we could never do alone.

This is the glory of living in Christ's kingdom. Jesus is Lord. And He can do in us and in others what we could never do by ourselves.

"Anyone who looks at a woman lustfully" Matt. 5:27-30. Again we see the shift in emphasis. Adultery is using another person as a sex object. Lust is viewing another person as a sex object. Christ wants us to realize that both the act and attitude are sinful. Righteousness calls for us to view all human beings as persons of worth and value. We are to serve others, not use them. Again Jesus calls us to view the Law as a revelation of the heart of God—and a revelation of the kind of person those who live in Jesus' kingdom will become as the King uses His power to transform them.

"Anyone who divorces his wife" Matt. 5:31-32. This follows the pattern of the others.

The Law permitted divorce, but Christ returned to God's ideal. While divorce might not be adultery technically, it is a violation of the covenant loyalty spouses owe to one another.

This is not a "no divorce" law, any more than the "no anger" and "no lust" principles are intended to be laws on the books of Christ's kingdom. It, like the others, is a reminder that what man needs is not rules to follow, but an inward renewal that makes us truly righteous. Only the truly righteous will find freedom from anger, freedom from lust, and freedom from the desire to divorce. In Jesus' kingdom alone, through the power of the King, a righteous life is possible.

"Do not swear at all" Matt. 5:33-37. It was common in first-century Judaism to make a distinction between binding and nonbinding promises. For instance, a person who swore by the temple altar was not bound by his oath, but if he swore by the gold on the altar, he was bound to fulfill his oath.

Jesus cut through the deceit involved and said, "Let your 'Yes' be 'Yes.' " Be the kind of person whose simple word is his or her bond.

"Do not resist an evil person" Matt. 5:38-42. The "eye for an eye" principle in the Old Testament established limits on the retribution a person might demand. If someone injured you and cost you the sight of an eye, you could not, for instance, justify taking his life. All you could claim was taking the sight of an eye.

Jesus now said, don't relate to others by what's "fair" at all! Rather than trying to get back at others who harm you, do good to them!

The passage has no direct application to the issue of pacifism. Rather, it applies directly to Jesus' challenge of values and attitudes, and describes the "surpassing righteousness" expected of those of us in Jesus' kingdom. We don't demand retribution. We do good, even to those who harm us.

The person who has learned to love even his or her enemies is a person who has lived long in the kingdom of Christ and a person who has known His transforming touch.

▶ DEVOTIONAL
Love Your WHOM?
(Matt. 5:21-48)

Jesus at first seems such a demanding King.

In this portion of His Sermon on the Mount Jesus made it clear that He expects citizens of His kingdom to do more than keep laws. He expects us to be the kind of people who never even want to break them!

In a series of illustrations He explained that His citizens aren't to get angry, much less strike out at another. We citizens aren't to lust, much less commit adultery. We're not to want a divorce, to plan to deceive, or even to want revenge when injured (vv. 21-42).

But then Jesus topped it off. Citizens of His kingdom are to "love your enemies and pray for those who persecute you" (v. 44). He explained that God is the kind of Person who "causes His sun to rise on the evil and the good, and sends rain on the righteous and the unrighteous" (v. 45). And we are to be "sons of your Father in heaven." It's really simple. We can sum up everything Jesus asks in a single phrase.

"Just be like God."

This would be impossible if it weren't for one thing. Jesus said, "Sons of your Father in heaven." You see, everyone in Jesus' kingdom is also family.

Through faith in Christ we enter a unique "your Father" relationship with God Himself. And God establishes a unique relationship with us. In Peter's words, God shares with us "His own indestructible heredity" (1 Peter 1:23, PH). Because God has poured His own life into us, it's not unreasonable at all to expect us to display a family resemblance.

I remember discovering as a teenager why I had the habit of cocking my head to one side when I rode in the car. Sitting in the backseat one day, I noticed that my dad held his head the same way, due to an old injury. From childhood I had been imitating him, without ever realizing it.

God isn't interested in the way we hold our heads. But He does want us to watch Him intently, see how He relates to us and to others, and so gradually become more and more like Him within.

As we live as faithful citizens of Jesus'

present kingdom, this is just what happens. We find to our amazement that we not only do good, we are becoming good! Transformed from within by the power of the King, we increasingly resemble our righteous and perfect God.

Personal Application

We are not to be satisfied with doing good, but must ask the King to help us be good.

Quotable

Make me, O Lord, Thy Spinning Wheel complete.
Thy Holy Word my Distaff make for me.
Make mine Affections thy Swift Flyers neat
And make my Soul Thy holy Spool to be.
My Conversation make to be Thy Reel
And Reel the yarn thereon spun of Thy Wheel.

Make me Thy Loom then, knit therein this Twine:
And make Thy Holy Spirit, Lord, wind quills:
Then weave the Web Thyself. The yarn is fine.
Thine Ordinances make my Fulling Mills.
Then dye the same in Heavenly Colors Choice.
All pinked with Varnished Flowers of Paradise.

Then clothe therewith mine Understanding, Will,
Affections, Judgment, Conscience, Memory,
My Words and Actions, that their shine may fill
My ways with glory and Thee glorify.
Then mine apparel shall display before Ye
That I am Clothed in Holy robes for glory.—Edward Taylor

JULY 18 *Reading 199*
PRAYER AND KINGDOM
Matthew 6–7

"Your Father, who sees what is done in secret, will reward you" (Matt. 6:6).

Prayer is an expression of intimate relationship with God. Here Jesus invites us to explore what prayer is—and what it can mean to you and me.

Definition of Key Terms

Hypocrite. The Greek word means "one acting a part," a character in a play. Some 16 of the 27 uses of this word in the New Testament are found in Matthew, which characterizes the hypocrite as a person (1) whose actions are intended to impress observers (6:1-3, 16-18), (2) whose focus is on the trappings rather than the heart issues of religion (15:1-21), and (3) whose spiritual-sounding talk hides corrupt motives. In Matthew 6 the hypocrite stands in contrast with the person of faith, whose relationship with God is "in secret."

Father. In these two chapters God is identified as "your Father" or "our Father" 10 times! The Old Testament speaks of God as Father, but in the sense of founder of Israel and Israel's religion (cf. Deut. 32:6). God cared for His people "as a father" would (1:31; Ps. 103:13), but the Old Testament stops short of suggesting an actual father/child relationship between God and believers. Here Christ introduced a new and stunning view of relationship with God. God is the Father of those who come to Him by Jesus Christ.

What does this new relationship mean to you and me? It means that we can trust God as Father (1) to reward us (Matt. 6:4, 6, 18), (2) to fully understand our needs (vv. 8, 32), (3) to forgive our sins and failures (v. 14), and (4) to give us good gifts when we ask Him (7:11).

Some of us have had human fathers who betrayed our trust. God is the ideal Father, whose every act is motivated by love. How beautifully these two chapters display God's unfailing Father-love.

Overview

Kingdom citizens have an "in-secret" relationship with God (6:1-5), knowing how

(vv. 6-8) and what (vv. 9-15) to pray. Such prayer has nothing to do with outward show (vv. 16-18). With our attention on heaven (vv. 19-24) and our trust in God as Father, we are freed to concentrate on kingdom living (vv. 25-34).

Because relationship with God is "in secret," we do not judge others (7:1-6), we consciously depend on our Father (vv. 7-12), and we choose His "narrow gate" (vv. 13-14). As we do, God's power is exhibited in our good lives (vv. 15-23) and obedience (vv. 24-29).

Understanding the Text

"Your Father, who sees what is done in secret" Matt. 6:1-6. Matthew 6 repeats the phrase "in secret" four times, and twice emphasizes the fact that God is "unseen." Why? Because Jesus wants us to understand our relationship with God as a deeply personal and intimate relationship, a bonding of our hearts to Him. Religion is not a matter of outward show.

Too many people attend church and make a show of being religious without having a personal, in-secret relationship with the Lord. Christ wants us to understand that in His kingdom, relationship with God must be real and personal, not like the "playacting" of the hypocrite, who does what he does to impress other human beings.

This emphasis in Matthew reminds us that we need to take time to nurture our in-secret relationship with the Lord. We need to "go into your room, close the door and pray to your Father, who is unseen." When we do nourish this relationship with the Lord, we can be sure that our "Father, who sees what is done in secret, will reward you."

"When you pray" Matt. 6:7-13. Jesus did not give His disciples what we call the Lord's Prayer to be repeated together when they gathered in church. He taught it as a model showing how each of us is to pray "in secret."

This does not mean, of course, that we should not use it in church. What it does mean is that we need to explore the pattern prayer to discern what it teaches you and me about developing a deeper "in-secret" relationship with our God. The challenge to explore the meaning is clear in Christ's contrast between it and pagans, who "babble" on and think that they will be heard "because of their many words" (v. 7). God wants us to understand the nature of prayer, and to make our prayer meaningful (see DEVOTIONAL).

"If you forgive men when they sin against you" Matt. 6:14-15. Some have been troubled by Jesus saying that God will forgive us "if you forgive men when they sin against you," but will not if we fail to forgive. Isn't the Gospel the Good News that God forgives our sins, not because of what we do, but because Jesus has died for us? (cf. Eph. 1:7; 4:32; Col. 1:14)

The conflict is apparent rather than real. The epistles describe a theological reality. Forgiveness is assured to all who truly trust in Christ. Here Jesus described a psychological reality. Forgiveness is experienced only by the forgiving.

Forgiveness is like a coin. A coin has two sides, heads and tails. It is impossible to have just one side of a coin. Forgiveness is like this. Its two sides are accepting and extending. We cannot grasp just one side of this coin. A humble person, who is aware of his own and others' frailties, will accept God's forgiveness. That attitude of humility which frees us to experience forgiveness is the very attitude that enables us to have compassion on others and to forgive them.

God does not not forgive the unforgiving because He is unwilling. Our own unforgiving attitude toward others keeps us from experiencing the forgiveness our Father is eager for us to know.

"When you fast, do not look somber" Matt. 6:16-18. Many Pharisees fasted twice a week as a religious duty. These were not 24-hour fasts, but 12-hour fasts, from dawn to dusk. Jesus did not criticize the practice of fasting. What He did criticize was those who advertised their fasts by putting streaks of dirt on their faces. What we do for God must be done for God. Whatever we do "to show men" is tainted.

"Do not worry about your life" Matt. 6:25-34. Jesus never suggested that it's wrong to be concerned about basic needs. He simply said it's unnecessary.

The pagan is gripped by anxiety because he faces an uncertain tomorrow. The Christian, who has a personal relationship with God as his Father, relies on One who not only knows, but also controls tomorrow. When we appreciate how much God loves us, we no longer feel pressure to "run after" even the necessities of life. This frees us to set right priorities, and "seek first His kingdom and His righteousness".

What a joy to worry about nothing except pleasing Jesus!

"Do not judge, or you too will be judged" Matt. 7:1-6. Here "judge" is not "to evaluate," but rather "to condemn" or "to be critical of." Because each Christian's relationship with God is "in secret," we have no basis for judging the motives or convictions of others, or even their failings and weaknesses. If we want to be critical, we are to be critical of ourselves!

There's a difference between this warning and Paul's call for the church to discipline sinners (1 Cor. 5:1-12). When a professing believer persists in behavior that the Bible clearly identifies as sin, we are to agree with Scripture and discipline. In this case we do not judge, but agree with the judgment of the Word of God.

What Jesus was talking about in Matthew is a spirit of criticism, or an arrogance that leads us to assume we have a right to judge the hearts of others. We do not. Just as the real nature of our own relationship with God is an "in-secret" kind of thing, so is the real nature of the relationship of others. Those who would live successfully in Christ's present kingdom must guard against that spirit of criticism and pride.

"Ask and it will be given to you" Matt. 7:7-12. Each of these images of prayer suggests persistence. Each also conveys a promise. Ask, it will be given. Seek, you will find. Knock, the door will be opened. What encourages us to be actively involved in prayer, and to claim these promises, is the certainty that God is our Father. As our Father, He is eager to give us good gifts.

"By their fruit you will recognize them" Matt. 7:15-23. Throughout Scripture, fruit is a symbol of God's transforming work within believers (cf. Isa. 5:1-7; John 15:1-11; Gal. 5:22-23). While our relationship with God is "in secret," the product of that relationship is highly visible!

Yet here Jesus spoke of recognizing false prophets by their bitter fruit. He did not suggest we go about pinching the fruit of believers to see how good it is!

Perhaps the reason is that good fruit takes time to ripen. The Christian's life will produce good fruit—but it will take time for that fruit to mature. Let's give others—and ourselves—the time needed for God's fruit to ripen rather than demand immediate evidence of His work in our lives.

"Everyone who hears these words of Mine and puts them into practice" Matt. 7:24-29. The clearest evidence of a vital relationship with God is that we hear God's words—and put them into practice. The person who truly loves Jesus will keep His commandments.

▶ DEVOTIONAL
How to Pray
(Matt. 6:5-13)

Anyone who plans to build a house would be wise to look at the blueprint first. In the same way, anyone who seeks to develop his or her "in-secret" relationship with God would be wise to study Jesus' "Lord's Prayer" carefully. It reveals the basic attitudes with which you and I are to come to God in prayer. Note how each petition teaches.

"Hallowed be Your name." We acknowledge God as He has revealed Himself. We express our respect for God, knowing Him to be living and active, sure that He is able to act in our lives.

"Your kingdom come." We acknowledge God as rightful King over all, and take our place as His subjects. We make a conscious choice to live as citizens of His kingdom, inviting it to come fully into our lives as well as into the world at large.

"Your will be done." We submit to God, choosing to obey His revealed Word, yet aware that we must also be sensitive to any personal guidance He may give us through His Holy Spirit.

"On earth as it is in heaven." We expect God's will for us to have an impact on what we do here on earth. We do not compartmentalize the "sacred" and "secular," but constantly look for ways to honor God in our work, our play, our everyday relationships with others.

"Give us today our daily bread." We trust God so much that we are secure in what He gives us each day, without being driven to pile up treasures on earth against tomorrow. We see each new day as an opportunity for some fresh experience of God's goodness to us.

"Forgive us our debts." We humble ourselves before God. We are deeply aware of our faults and failings, yet we rejoice that we are loved anyway. Further humbled by God's forgiving love, we have compassion on those who hurt or harm us. We take such hurts as an opportunity to demonstrate the reality of God's mercy by freely forgiving others.

"Lead us not into temptation." We rest in God. We know that He delivers us from evil and, while we seek no confrontation with the evil one, we know that should tests come, God will be present to deliver us.

When we approach "in-secret" prayer infused with these deep convictions, our personal relationship with the Lord is sure to deepen and grow.

Personal Application

Begin your prayer time with the Lord's Prayer, aware of the faith and dependence it expresses.

Quotable

MEDITATION ON THE LORD'S PRAYER

Lord, I cannot say "Our" . . .
 if my religion has no room for
 other people and their needs.
Lord, I cannot say "Father" . . .
 if I fail to resemble You in the way
  I live my daily life.
Lord, I cannot say "Who art in Heaven" . . .
 if my attention is focused only
  on earthly things.
Lord, I cannot say "Hallowed be Thy name" . . .
 if I who am called by Your name
  am not holy.
Lord, I cannot say "Thy Kingdom come" . . .
 if I fail to acknowledge Your
  sovereignty in my life.
Lord, I cannot say, "On earth as it is in Heaven" . . .
 unless I am truly ready to
  serve You here and now.
Lord, I cannot say "Give us this day our daily bread" . . .
 without doing an honest
  day's work, and without considering
  the needs of those less fortunate.
Lord, I cannot say "Forgive us our debts as we forgive our debtors" . . .
 if I harbor a grudge against my brother
  or sister.
Lord, I cannot say "Lead us not into temptation" . . .
 if I deliberately choose to remain
  in a situation where I am likely
  to be tempted.
Lord, I cannot say "Deliver us from evil" . . .
 if I am not prepared to take a stand
  against injustice in my society.
Lord, I cannot say "Thine is the Kingdom, the Power, and the Glory" . . .
 if I do not
  submit to Christ as King, if I fail to
  trust You to act in my life, or if in
  pride I seek my own glory.
Lord, I cannot say "Amen" . . .
 unless I can honestly say, "Come what
  may, this is my prayer."—Adapted from "Lamplighter," Speedway Christian Church, Indianapolis, Indiana

JULY 19 *Reading 200*
KINGLY POWER
Matthew 8–9

" 'But so that you may know that the Son of man has authority on earth to forgive sins. . . .' Then He said to the paralytic, 'Get up, take your mat and go home' " (Matt. 9:6).

Jesus had called for citizens to populate His kingdom. Now He displayed a royal power over all forces in natural and supernatural worlds.

Definition of Key Terms

Authority. The Greek word for "authority" is *exousia.* Its basic meaning is "freedom of action." A person with total authority has total freedom of action. No human being has total freedom of action. All of us are limited by others who act in ways that limit our freedom, as a slave is limited by his master, a soldier by his commander, a student by his teacher, or a citizen by his ruler. We are also limited by circumstances: our state of health, our financial condition, sex, size, etc.

Yet in Matthew 8–9 Jesus demonstrated an authority that is total! He is not limited by natural laws, by the sicknesses or sin that bind humanity, or by the demonic forces that attack us. His freedom to act is not even limited by death!

In the Sermon on the Mount (Matt. 5–7) Jesus laid down principles by which to live. His miracles of healing remind us that we can trust ourselves totally to Him, for He is Lord of all.

Overview

King Jesus, willing and able to heal (8:1-17), expects total allegiance (vv. 18-22). His authority to overcome nature (vv. 23-27), demons (vv. 28-34), and even human sin (9:1-13), shows that God was doing a new work among men (vv. 14-17). Jesus raised a dead girl (vv. 18-26) and continued to heal and cast out demons (vv. 27-34), providing a ministry model for workers in His kingdom (vv. 35-38).

Understanding the Text

"Lord, if You are willing, You can make me clean" Matt. 8:1-4. The old argument raised by skeptics states that if God has power to correct the evils that torment mankind, He must not be good, for He has not done so. On the other hand, if He does not have that power, He must not be God.

The argument breaks down as soon as we introduce the element of free will. A good and all-powerful God has given human beings freedom of choice, even though the choices men have made introduced pain and evil into our world.

The argument also breaks down when we read these chapters of Matthew's Gospel. Here we see a Jesus who is both good and all-powerful. Again and again Jesus exercised His power as God, and each time it was to help or heal a human being in need. Christ is willing. And He is able too.

*"I do not deserve to have You come under my roof" Matt. 8:5-8.*The centurion was a Roman army officer, not a Jew. Yet when one of his servants was stricken, he himself hurried to Jesus. Christ was willing to go with the centurion and heal his sick servant. But the Roman officer, one of the conquering race that dominated Judea and most of the world, humbly replied, "I am not worthy" (KJV).

What an example this is. At the feet of Jesus all human distinctions are lost, and every man becomes a supplicant no matter how high his worldly position.

At our local church we often serve Communion at the altar rail. Each person comes and kneels there, to receive the bread and wine. The wealthy and poor, the young and the old, the men and the women, the sick and the well, kneel together to worship and receive the elements that remind us of the price Jesus paid for our redemption. Kneeling there each of us is nothing more than a sinner saved by grace, yet nothing less than a citizen of Jesus' kingdom and a member of God's forever family.

In bowing before a mere Jew the Roman centurion affirmed a great truth. The most important rank a human being can carry is that of subject to the King of kings.

"I myself am a man under authority" Matt. 8:9-13. There is more in the story of the

centurion for us. He felt unworthy to entertain Jesus under his roof. But he also knew that Jesus' authority over sickness was not limited by distance.

When he said, "I myself am a man under authority," the centurion meant that his authority in the Roman army did not depend on him, but was granted him by his commanders in a chain leading ultimately to the Emperor himself. The centurion's orders were obeyed because the full weight of mighty Rome lay behind each command. In asking Jesus to "just say the word," and in affirming his faith that "my servant will be healed," the centurion confessed his belief that Christ too was one "under authority." When Jesus spoke, the full weight of God's sovereign power was available to enforce Christ's decree.

The centurion's faith was honored. Christ did speak the word, and the power of God, which neither distance nor evil forces can limit, flowed.

Let's remember the centurion's faith when we pray. Jesus has the power to meet any and every need.

"First let me go and bury my father" Matt. 8:18-22. The first flurry of healings stimulated great excitement. Many were eager to join the "Jesus Brigade," undoubtedly supposing that Christ would use His powers to break the grip of Rome and usher in the Messianic Age.

Two incidents cooled the early ardor. One "teacher of the Law" offered to follow Jesus wherever He went. Such persons were highly respected in first-century Judaism, and typically were relatively well off. When Christ answered that "the Son of man has no place to lay His head," the man's fervor faded away! A follower of Jesus must be willing to live as He did, and abandon hope of worldly gain.

Another man promised to follow, but "first" he must go and "bury my father." In Judaism the corpse was buried the very day of death. This man's father was not yet dead. What his words meant was, "First let me fulfill my obligation to stay with my father until he dies." Jesus' answer, "Follow Me, and let the dead bury their own dead," was clearly understood. No competing loyalty must outweigh our allegiance to Christ the King.

These words of Jesus are spoken to us

In Jesus' time some 300 small fishing boats like this one were operated on the Sea of Galilee. The preserved remains of one of these boats was recently found buried under the lake bottom, telling us how the boat was constructed and its inner frame designed. Jesus undoubtedly was in just this kind of boat when He stilled the storm that threatened Him and His disciples (vv. 23-27).

too. God gives us many material blessings, and many fulfilling relationships. But neither possessions nor relationships can be more important to us than serving Christ.

"Why are you so afraid?" Matt. 8:23-27 Those who were already committed followers of Jesus were privileged to see Him display His power over nature. A furious storm came up as the little company traveled by boat on the Sea of Galilee, terrifying even Christ's fishermen disciples. Christ's question after He had stilled the storm is one we can ask ourselves when we face trials or danger today: "Why are you so afraid?"

The question seems a foolish one if we look only at the tossing waves and hear only the shrieking winds. If we stop to realize that we are never alone, but Christ Himself is with us, the question is prudent indeed. Jesus has all power, and He can use it to deliver those who are His. Nothing can touch us that He does not permit. We have no need to go through life "so afraid."

"They pleaded with Him to leave their region" Matt. 8:28-34. Jesus' healing of two demon-possessed men in a Gentile district brought an unexpected reaction. It seems the demons Christ released went into a

herd of pigs, and "the whole herd rushed down the steep bank into the lake and died in the water." The local folk were terribly upset. Maybe two men were delivered from demonic possession. But their pigs were gone!

Wherever human beings place more value on possessions than people, Jesus will be unwelcome. Let's be sure that we never drive Him away by caring more for our "pigs" than for our fellow human beings.

"The Son of Man has authority on earth to forgive sins" Matt. 9:1-7. Christ had demonstrated His authority as King—over sickness, over nature, and even over evil spirits. But how could Christ demonstrate His authority over man's greatest antagonist, sin? The answer is contained in this story and the one that follows it.

When Jesus told a paralytic that his sins were forgiven, some "teachers of [biblical] Law" thought He was speaking blasphemy. After all, God alone can forgive sin. So Jesus proposed a test. It would be easy for anyone to say, "You're forgiven." After all, there's no way to prove forgiveness one way or another! But Jesus could prove that He spoke with God's own authority. He could tell the paralytic, "Get up and walk." Then everyone could see whether or not the paralyzed man walked.

This is exactly what Jesus did, and the Bible says that all who saw were "filled with awe." It adds "and they praised God, who had given such authority to men." Jesus' works proved that He did speak with God's own authority. His works in the physical realm were conclusive proof that His promise of forgiveness was valid indeed.

God still gives us physical proof of inner forgiveness—a truth we discover in the calling of Matthew (vv. 9-13). (See DEVOTIONAL.)

"Pour new wine into new wineskins" Matt. 9:14-17. Jesus puzzled nearly all who watched Him heal and listened to Him speak. Neither His actions nor His teachings seemed to fit the religion they knew so well. Even John's disciples were puzzled, and so asked Him questions about His practices.

Jesus responded with two illustrations from ordinary life. A person doesn't patch an old garment with new cloth. And a person doesn't pour new (unfermented) wine in an old wineskin.

In biblical times some containers for liquid were made of animal skins, typically scraped clean of flesh and then sewn tightly at the legs and other openings. Freshly squeezed grape juice was poured into a new skin, which would stretch as the wine fermented. Old skins lost the capacity to stretch, and would split if "new wine" were poured in them.

By these stories Jesus warned His listeners not to try to fit Him or His teachings in the categories in use in first-century Judaism. Jesus must be permitted to define a new way to think and to live in the kingdom He was even then about to establish.

You and I too have to be careful. It's so easy to force Jesus' teachings into our old ways of thinking. Jesus is Lord, and He alone has the right to define our way of life. Never try to make a teaching of Jesus fit one of our prejudices. Let's let Jesus' words reveal His own fresh, new way to face life's challenges.

"My daughter has just died" Matt. 9:18-26. The New Testament pictures death as the "last enemy" (1 Cor. 15:26). When Jesus went to the home of a ruler and spoke to his dead daughter, she revived. What a foretaste of the victory we will experience when Christ raises us from the dead, gives us resurrection bodies, and welcomes us to an eternity with Him.

"Nothing like this has ever been seen in Israel" Matt. 9:27-34. The evidence of King Jesus' authority that Matthew presents is summed up here, in the report of many more healings and exorcisms. The evidence was conclusive: all who saw it acknowledged that even in the wonder-working ages of Moses or Elijah, no comparable miracles had been performed. Even the Pharisees could not deny the miracle, but muttered, "Well, He must be doing them in Satan's power."

The evidence is in. And each person today too must determine for himself or herself whether to gladly submit to Jesus as Lord, or to reject Him and turn away.

"The harvest is plentiful but the workers are

few" Matt. 9:35-38 How do we display a decision to submit to Jesus as Lord? Very simply. We take the burden of continuing His mission on ourselves. We become the workers who, moved by compassion for the lost, go out as Jesus did "preaching the Good News of the kingdom and healing every disease and sickness."

Evangelicals have been accused of emphasizing evangelism and disregarding the physical and social needs of humanity. Let's remember that Jesus in compassion sought to heal the whole person. We are to preach and teach, yes. But we are to model our ministry on Christ's, and communicate the love of God as Jesus did by also feeding the hungry, caring for the sick, and doing justice to the oppressed.

▶ DEVOTIONAL
That You May Know (Matt. 9:1-13)

Some folks scoff at Christianity as "pie in the sky by and by." Others just shrug, and say they'll wait and find out after they die.

When Jesus was here He made sure no one had to wait to see. He told a paralytic, "Your sins are forgiven" (vv. 1-8). When some bystanders were upset by this claim, He offered proof. "So that you may know the Son of man has authority on earth to forgive sins." He told the paralyzed man, "Get up, take your mat and go home."

When the man stood up, and walked, the authority of Jesus was proved. The men of that day knew that Jesus could forgive sins.

But how about our day? The next story is for us. It's the story of a man named Matthew who sat at a tax booth (vv. 9-13). In the first century such men were scorned as sinners, and most did extort more money than was due. Jesus came to Matthew's booth and told him, "Follow Me." And Matthew got up and followed.

Matthew the tax collector. Matthew, whose friends were the outcasts of pious society, became a follower of Jesus.

This is the proof we see all around us of the fact that when Jesus says, "Your sins are forgiven," our sins truly are. Forgiveness makes just as dramatic a change in the moral life of the believer as Jesus' healing did in the frozen limbs of the paralytic.

A world that wants proof that Jesus saves can find it in the transformed lives of those who have accepted Him as Saviour.

Personal Application

Your life is to be presented to the world as evidence that Jesus saves.

Quotable

"Non-Christians first need to detect the reality of genuine Christian experience in our lives. Then they will be attracted by our words about Jesus Christ and what it means to know Him personally. After I have spoken to a group, students often approach me with personal questions: 'How does it work?' 'How can I have the kind of life you've been talking about?' 'Is there any hope for me?' It's always a privilege to sit down and explain how forgiveness, cleansing, and power can be individually ours in and through the Lord Jesus Christ."—Paul Little

JULY 20 *Reading 201*
DISCIPLES OF THE KING
Matthew 10–11

"I am sending you out like sheep among wolves. Therefore be as shrewd as snakes and as innocent as doves" (Matt. 10:16).

There is no greater challenge than to live our lives as disciples of Jesus, the Servant-King.

Definition of Key Terms

Disciple. In the first century an apprenticeship system was used to train spiritual leaders. Those in training attached themselves to a rabbi, and literally lived with him. Their goal was to both learn all their teacher knew, and to imitate his way of life.

Jesus used this then-familiar model to train His Twelve. Matthew 10 records special instructions Jesus gave them for a preaching mission, and further instructions that relate more to the period after His death and resurrection.

The word "disciple" is also used in a looser sense in the Gospels, to mean "believer" or "follower." But it is used in the narrower, technical sense of "leader-in-training" whenever applied to the Twelve.

Overview

Jesus commissioned the Twelve (10:1-4). He instructed them on an immediate preaching mission (vv. 5-16), and spoke of future challenges (vv. 17-31). Jesus explained what He expects of disciples (vv. 32-39) and the disciple's reward (vv. 40-42).

A demoralized John was encouraged (11:1-6) and praised (vv. 7-19) by Jesus, who damned the cities that refused to repent despite His miracles (vv. 20-24). Yet the weary who come to Jesus will find rest (vv. 25-30).

Understanding the Text

"He called His twelve disciples to Him and gave them authority" Matt. 10:1-4. We may be impressed at the authority Jesus gave His disciples. Driving out evil spirits and healing the sick sounds so impressive. But note that Jesus gave this authority only to the Twelve whom He had chosen and trained.

You and I may sometimes wish we had special spiritual powers. Let's remember that the only way to receive them is to serve our apprenticeship with Jesus as the Twelve did. We must stay close to Jesus, and learn from Him, before we can be trusted with spiritual authority.

This is one of four lists of the Twelve found in the New Testament (cf. Mark 3:16-19; Luke 6:13-16; Acts 1:13). Simon Peter is first on each list, and Andrew, James, and John always complete the first four. In each list, Judas Iscariot is last.

Each of the Twelve except Judas was a fully committed follower of Jesus. Yet there is no doubt that some were closer to Christ than others. Let's not only be disciples of Jesus, but be disciples who concentrate on remaining close to our Lord.

"Freely you have received, freely give" Matt. 10:5-10. At first Christ's ministry was directed to God's covenant people, the Jews.

This first mission of the disciples was also directed to Israel. What's most significant here, however, is Christ's directive to take no extra money, clothing, or traveling equipment. The disciples were to shun luxury. They were to depend on God to supply their needs through the hospitality of others. They were to give freely what they had themselves freely received.

If every Christian in ministry today were to adopt the attitudes commanded here—a contempt for material possessions, matched by a bold reliance on God alone—many who have exposed the Gospel to ridicule would today be ministering to the glory of God.

"Search for some worthy person there" Matt. 10:11-15. In New Testament times travelers seldom stayed at inns, but rather stayed with any householder who invited them. Hospitality was considered a great virtue among Jews, and few travelers had to sleep out overnight unless they wished to.

But Jesus encouraged His disciples to find some "worthy" person to stay with. The text defines a worthy person: it is one who "welcomes you," and who "listens to your words" (v. 14). Both are impor-

Most travel in the first century was on foot. From Matthew 10 and other written sources, as well as the finds of archeologists, we can reconstruct how the disciples must have looked as they set out by twos on their mission of preaching and healing.

tant. The disciples came as emissaries of Jesus, not ordinary travelers. The "worthy" are still identified by their response to the Master, not the disciple, and by their willingness to listen to His words.

"Be as shrewd as snakes and as innocent as doves" Matt. 10:16. Jesus' disciples were like sheep surrounded by a pack of wolves. They had no obvious defense against the hostility of the world. So they had to be both "shrewd" and "innocent."

In the Near East serpents were viewed as prudent beasts, who avoided danger. Hosea 7:11 pictures doves as "easily deceived and senseless." Yet the dove was also a harmless and innocent bird, while the serpent was seen as a dangerous and repelling beast. Somehow the believer is to walk a very fine line in carrying out Christ's mission to the world. Jesus' disciples were to be prudent without being dangerous, and innocent without being foolish.

How much we need Christ's help to deal wisely with the challenges of our Christian life.

"On My account you will be brought before governors and kings" Matt. 10:17-23. In these verses the focus of Christ's instruction seems to shift from the immediate, local mission, to the post-Resurrection mission to the whole world. Jesus warned of future hostility and suffering, but gave a very special promise.

In the first century those charged in court relied on orator-lawyers to plead their cases. Usually a person without this kind of expert help could expect the verdict to go against him! But Jesus told His own not to worry when arrested, for the Spirit of God would show them what to say when the time to speak in court came.

What a promise! Who speaks for us when we are persecuted or accused unjustly? God Himself is our Orator-Lawyer. We need never fear with the Holy Spirit handling our defense!

"So do not be afraid of them" Matt. 10:24-31. Jesus had bluntly warned His disciples that they must face danger and hostility (vv. 17-23). Now He told them not to fear.

Some fears—as of those proverbial things that go bump in the night—are imaginary. But sometimes disciples face very real dangers and truly hostile enemies. In this passage Jesus wasn't speaking about neurotic fear, but about the fear generated by very real perils. How do disciples deal with fear of real and present dangers?

First, we remember the men of Jesus' day were hostile to Him. Why should we who follow Jesus expect to have things better than our Lord? Second, we remember that one day all they do to us will be exposed to the light—and they will face judgment. Third, we remember that even if Christ's enemies kill our bodies, our essential selves do not perish, and we enter the realm of eternal life. Finally, we remember that nothing happens to us "apart from the will of your Father." Confidence in God's Father-love sustains us.

If you're an anxious kind of person, meditate for a time on these verses. Let the perspective of Jesus reshape your way of looking at life, and bring you peace.

"Whoever acknowledges Me before men" Matt. 10:32-42. What are the marks of Jesus' disciples, and their rewards? We can list the following.

A disciple of Jesus acknowledges Him before men (v. 32). A disciple of Jesus places loyalty to Christ above even the bonds of family (vv. 34-35). A disciple of Jesus takes up his cross and follows Jesus, a phrase which means subjecting one's will to God even as Jesus chose to subject Himself to the cross (v. 38). A disciple of Jesus surrenders all for the sake of his Lord (v. 37). (See Matt. 16 for "taking up the cross" and "losing oneself.")

So far it seems that the disciple's life is all "give up" and no "gain." But there are rewards! In the world of the New Testament a person's representative was treated as that person himself. As Jesus' disciples minister, some will welcome them as Christ's emissaries. Those who do so will gain rewards in the world to come—and the follower of Jesus will have the joy of knowing that it was through him or her that others were thus blessed. The Apostle Paul put it this way in his Letter to the Thessalonians: "For what is our hope, our joy, or the crown in which we will glory in the presence of our Lord Jesus when He comes? Is it not you? Indeed, you are our glory and joy" (1 Thes. 2:19).

You and I, with Paul, have the same joy in discipleship that Jesus had in fulfilling His mission. Jesus had the joy of knowing that because of His faithfulness, many would be saved. As others respond to our witness to Christ, we who share Christ's sufferings in discipleship will also experience this joy.

"Are you the One who was to come?" Matt. 11:2-6 John was imprisoned for over a year in the fortress of Machaerus, east of the Dead Sea. There he began to doubt. John had announced a Messiah who would bless but also judge (3:11-12). Jesus truly blessed the people by His healings and teachings. But where was the judgment of evil men, like Herod who had imprisoned John?

Jesus answered by quoting from Isaiah 35:5-6; 61:1, with possible reference to 26:19 and 29:18-19. Each of these passages speaks of blessings—and judgment! In essence Jesus was telling John, I am blessing now. In God's time, I will also judge.

We want to remember Christ's careful selection of the blessing sections of these verses. We too rightly emphasize the grace and love of God. After all, today is the day of blessing! Let's spread the Good News while we can. The day of judgment will come all too soon.

"There has not risen anyone greater than John the Baptist" Matt. 11:7-14. Jesus praised John as the greatest of the Old Testament prophets. Why? Because of all the prophets, John pointed most clearly to the Messiah. Many prophets spoke of Jesus' day. But John was privileged not only to announce that the Messiah was at hand, but also to point directly to Jesus and say, "I have seen and I testify that this is the Son of God" (John 1:34).

What did Jesus mean when He said that "he who is least in the kingdom of heaven is greater than [John]"? Simply that now, looking back on Jesus' cross, the simplest believer can point even more clearly to the Messiah, and more fully explain the meaning of His life, death, and resurrection for lost humankind.

What a stunning thought. When you or I point someone to Jesus as Saviour and Lord, we perform a ministry greater than that of any prophet of old.

"Woe to you, Korazin!" Matt. 11:16-24 John and Jesus both preached the kingdom of God and presented Israel with her King. But the people, like children bored with playing children's games (vv. 16-17), were satisfied with neither.

And so Jesus pronounced, "Woe," an expression communicating both grief and denunciation, on the cities where He had performed so many miracles. Even the most wicked pagan city would have responded if such wonders had been performed there. But God's own people refused to believe.

We have to be careful not to lose our own sensitivity to Jesus' voice. It's all too easy to let what we've been taught close our minds to fresh interpretations of Scripture, or to the guidance of God's Spirit.

"Come to Me, all you who are weary" Matt. 11:25-30. God reveals His Son to little children, but hides Him from "the wise and learned." Christ isn't teaching predestination here, but judgment. The little child responds trustingly to Jesus' word. The "wise and learned" stand back, evaluate, and rely on their own judgment. In the same way the person who is weary and burdened is ready to respond to Christ, while the individual who arrogantly rushes on in his own strength sees no need of the Lord.

▶DEVOTIONAL
Discipleship's Cost
(Matt. 10:16-31; 11:28-29)

Here it is again! A description of a job nobody wants.

I mean, who wants work as a sheep among wolves? (10:16) Who wants to be handed over to local councils to be flogged? (v. 18) Who wants family conflict? (v. 21) Who wants to be hated? (v. 22) Who wants to be persecuted? (v. 23)

It's fine to say things like, all this happened to Jesus first (vv. 24-25). And, hey, they can only kill your body, can't they? (v. 28) But no matter how you cut it, this business of being a disciple doesn't look all that attractive. Try putting this kind of ad in the paper, and see how many applicants you get.

But then, at the end of Matthew 11, Jesus added something that makes it all worthwhile. He invites us, "Take My yoke upon you and learn from Me" (11:29). The yoke, which rested on the shoulders of oxen hitched to a plow, was used to distribute the burden of work. The oxen pulled together, and neither was overwhelmed.

Being yoked to Jesus doesn't so much mean that we take on His burdens, but that He, pulling alongside us, takes on ours. Yes, it's tough to be a disciple. It's a challenging and disciplined life. Yet the disciple by the very fact of his commitment is yoked to Jesus. And in that relationship, with Jesus taking on most of the load, we find not added burdens but an amazing inner rest.

Despite all appearances, the disciple of Jesus knows the truth. Jesus' "yoke is easy and My burden is light."

Personal Application

The lightest load we try to carry alone is crushing.

Quotable

"I have read in Plato and Cicero sayings that are wise and very beautiful; but I never read in either of them: 'Come unto Me all ye that labour and are heavy laden.' "—St. Augustine

JULY 21 *Reading 202*
OPPOSITION TO THE KING
Matthew 12–13

> *"A wicked and adulterous generation asks for a miraculous sign! But none will be given it except the sign of the Prophet Jonah" (Matt. 12:39).*

As it became increasingly clear that one must choose for or against Jesus, opposition to Him and to His kingdom hardened. Today too some reject Christ not because they know so little about Him, but because they do not like the little they know!

Definition of Key Terms

Sabbath. The Sabbath Day was set aside as holy in Judaism. A person could do no work, but did worship, pray, and study the Scriptures. Over the years many rules of Sabbath observance had been propounded by the rabbis. These were intended to help the observant Jew keep from breaking the Sabbath inadvertently. But these rules, held by the Pharisees to be oral law given Moses on Mount Sinai and therefore just as binding as the written Law, were in fact only the notions of men. While Jesus was accused of being a

Sabbath-breaker, He in fact only violated human rules that were not binding at all.

It's all too easy to raise our applications or interpretations of Scripture to the status of Scripture itself. This is a tendency each individual, congregation, and denomination must guard carefully against.

Overview

Jesus' claim to be Lord of the Sabbath (12:1-14) and the Servant predicted by Isaiah (vv. 15-21) brought direct conflict with the Pharisees (vv. 22-37). Christ rejected their demand for a miraculous sign (vv. 36-45), but announced kinship with those who do God's will (vv. 46-50). In a series of parables told to puzzled crowds (13:1-35), and in another series told to His disciples (vv. 36-52), Jesus explained the unexpected aspects of His kingdom.

Understanding the Text

*"Your disciples are doing what is unlawful on the Sabbath" Matt. 12:1-13.*Two Sabbath incidents led to open conflict with the Pharisees. The first was provoked by Jesus' disciples, who plucked and ate grain on the Sabbath Day. In the first century grain was planted right to the edge of paths and trails. According to Old Testament Law a traveler might break off a stalk and eat as he walked along. The Pharisees objected because they classified this as "harvesting," one of the 39 kinds of work the sages prohibited on the Sabbath.

Christ answered in a familiar form of rabbinic argument. The Scripture says no layperson is to eat the temple showbread. But David ate, and was not condemned. If one wants to argue that David was special, all right: Jesus is more special. Again, the Law says not to work on the Sabbath. But the priests work then, offering sacrifices. If one wants to argue that the temple service is special, all right: Jesus is more special.

The argument makes a double point. The strict legalism of the Pharisees was not supported by the Old Testament. The written Law showed that God is more concerned with mercy than with sacrifice (i.e., with relationships than with rules and ritual). And, in the person of Jesus, the God who gave the Sabbath cleared the disciples: they were innocent of the crimes charged (vv. 7-8).

Shortly afterward Jesus entered a synagogue where there was a man with a withered hand. Looking for some crime to charge Jesus with, the Pharisees asked if it were right to heal (again "work") on the Sabbath. Jesus' reply was scornful. Even they would rescue an animal that had fallen in a pit on the Sabbath. Of course it is right to do good on the Sabbath. And then Jesus healed the man's hand.

What a revelation of the heart of Jesus—and of the Pharisees. These men who were so concerned over their rules cared nothing for the crippled man's suffering. They only wanted to use his injury to attack Jesus. In contrast, Jesus cared about the man, and willingly faced criticism to help him.

You and I are much closer to Jesus when we consider how we can meet others' needs than when trying to force others to live by our convictions.

"The Pharisees went out and plotted how they might kill Jesus" Matt. 12:14. Jesus' sayings and actions exposed the cold hearts of the Pharisees, and the emptiness of an approach to religion to which they had dedicated their entire lives. When so exposed, only two courses of action are open. One can humble himself, confess, and repent. Or with cold fury one can strike out at the person who threatens his very identity. The Pharisees chose to strike back, and determined to kill Jesus.

We must not be surprised when some are furious at the Gospel message. Like the Pharisees, many today have built their lives on a faulty foundation that they hold very dear.

"Jesus withdrew from that place" Matt. 12:15-21. Jesus responded to their hostility by simply leaving the area. Matthew explained by quoting a passage from one of Isaiah's "servant songs." Messiah "will not quarrel or cry out." He will be so gentle that He will not even snap a worthless reed flute, or discard a soot-filled candle wick.

You and I seldom win those who are deeply antagonistic. It's far better to leave them, as Jesus did, and go on healing the sick. Debate is never as effective as loving service. We win many more by showing compassion to those in need than by showing up those who want to argue.

"Could this be the Son of David?" Matt. 12:22-29 The Greek suggests the question should read, "This can't be the Son of David, can it?" There were doubts. But there was the growing awareness that Jesus might be the prophesied Messiah.

The Pharisees must have been driven to distraction when they learned the crowds were asking such a question. The zealous Pharisees were respected by all and viewed as prime examples of godly, spiritual men. If Jesus were accepted as the Messiah, this Man who showed up the spiritual void of the way they had chosen would surely rob them of all respect. In desperation the Pharisees began a whispering campaign. They couldn't argue that Jesus had performed no miracles. But they could plant doubt by suggesting He was in league with the devil.

When people can't do anything else to harm believers, they can lie about us. What is important is that our lives be so pure that everyone sees the lies are as ridiculous as the charge raised against Jesus.

"Blasphemy against the Spirit will not be forgiven" Matt. 12:30-32. What is the unforgivable sin? It is a denial of that which one knows God must be doing, even as it was clear that Christ performed His miracles by the Spirit of God. The sin is unforgivable because the person who commits it has so hardened himself that he willfully rejects what he knows to be true.

If you've ever worried that you might have committed this sin, relax. The very fact that you're concerned shows that your heart is not hardened like the hearts of the Pharisees.

"It finds the house unoccupied" Matt. 12:43-45. Self-reform is possible. Ben Franklin developed a list of desirable traits, and worked hard at developing them. But even if our bad habits are overcome, our lives are empty unless we invite Christ in, to empower us for godly living. The Pharisees were great at sweeping out. But their failure to welcome Jesus left them vulnerable to demons far worse than the ones they worked so hard to brush away.

Let's be careful to open our lives to

Parables of the Kingdom

The Parable	Expected Form	Unexpected Characteristic
1. Sower 13:3-9, 18-23	Messiah turns *Israel* and all *nations* to Himself	*Individuals* respond differently to the Word's invitation.
2. Wheat/tares 13:24-30, 37-43	The kingdom's righteous citizens *rule over* the world with the King.	The kingdom's citizens are *among* the men of the world, growing together till God's harvesttime.
3. Mustard seed 13:31-32	Kingdom *begins* in *majestic glory*.	Kingdom *begins in insignificance;* its greatness comes as a surprise.
4. Leaven 13:33	Only righteousness enters the kingdom; other "raw material" is excluded.	The kingdom is implanted in a different "raw material" and grows to fill the whole personality with righteousness.
5. Hidden treasure 13:44	Kingdom is *public* and for all.	Kingdom is *hidden* and for individual "purchase."
6. Priceless pearl 13:45-46	Kingdom *brings all valued things* to men.	Kingdom demands *abandonment* of all other values (cf. 6:33).
7. Dragnet 13:47-50	Kingdom begins with initial separation of righteous and unrighteous.	Kingdom ends with final separation of the unrighteous from the righteous.

Jesus, and let His love fill us with the compassion, mercy, and love these very religious opponents of Jesus lacked.

"He told them many things in parables" Matt. 13:1-35. A parable is a story that makes one central point, and relates every element in the story to this point. The parables in this chapter concern Jesus' kingdom, but are not obvious. In fact, Jesus said that He spoke in parables so that those who believed might understand—and those who did not believe would not understand (vv. 11-15).

What an illustration of God's grace. Those who showed that they would not hear the King were spared the revelation of further truth, for which they would have been held responsible. Those who were willing to respond were given truth in a form they alone would grasp.

This section of the Gospel closes with Christ's return to Nazareth, His hometown. He was famous now, known all over Galilee and Judea too for His miracles and teaching. Did the hometown folks roll out the red carpet, to welcome the returning hero?

No; instead they resented His fame. Wasn't He just the carpenter's Son? Weren't His brothers just ordinary folks? How did Jesus get off, putting on such airs?

Often the hardest people we have to minister to are those who know us well. Others are impressed. Our family and neighbors seem almost resentful. If this has happened to you, try not to be too upset. It happened to Jesus first.

Of course, there's also the rest of the story. Among those hometown folks who rejected Jesus were His own brothers (cf. John 7:3-5). Yet in Acts 1:14, on a list of those who were gathered in the Upper Room after Christ's resurrection, praying and waiting for the coming of the Spirit, we find "Mary the mother of Jesus, and his brothers."

Yes, it hurt to be misunderstood and rejected at home. But in the end, all the family did respond. All came to know Jesus as Saviour and as Lord. What an encouragement for you and me. We may be misunderstood at home, or even scorned. But a faithful, loving witness will bear fruit.

▶ DEVOTIONAL
Careless Words
(Matt. 12:1-37)

The Pharisees just didn't realize what they were saying until it was too late. They figured they had Jesus dead to rights when they criticized His disciples for picking wheat on the Sabbath. And then they rubbed their hands together in glee when they thought of tricking Him into healing a cripple on the Sabbath.

Then, oops! They realized all they'd done was expose their own failure to understand God's Word and their own cold hearts. They had accused the innocent (the disciples) and used the helpless (the man with the shriveled hand). They hadn't been thinking when they spoke.

That's the meaning of the "careless words" that Jesus speaks of in verse 36. It wasn't the mean, hateful accusations that the Pharisees hurled against Jesus that exposed them (vv. 22-32).

Actually, each person's heart can be read in his or her actions and words. Those things we say without thinking, like the Pharisees' challenges of Jesus, reveal the heart. In the Pharisees' case their words, so quickly uttered, revealed cold and uncaring hearts, totally unconcerned with the guilt or innocence of those they accused or with the suffering of the cripple they intended to use to trap Jesus.

What people say coming out of church or in public does not reveal their hearts. It's the words that slip out when they speak casually to their family, coworkers, or friends.

It's good every now and then to check on our own careless words. When we do, we'll be able to tell a lot about the quality of our personal relationship with Christ.

Personal Application

Careless words can reveal a loving heart as well as a hard one.

Quotable

"What will it mean in practice for me to put God first? This much at least. The 101 things I have to do each day and the 101 demands on me which I know I must try to meet will all be approached as ventures of loving service to Him, and I shall do the best I can in everything for His sake."— J.I. Packer

JULY 22 *Reading 203*
MORE MINISTRY
Matthew 14–15

"Great crowds came to Him, bringing the lame, the blind, the crippled, the dumb and many others, and laid them at His feet; and He healed them" (Matt. 15:30).

In His healings and in feeding the 5,000 and then the 4,000, Jesus met the physical needs of His people. But would they let Him meet their spiritual needs?

Biography: Herod

The Herod mentioned here is not Herod the Great, who died shortly after Christ was born. This is Herod Antipas, his son, who was only tetrarch of Galilee, though addressed by the courtesy title "king." This Herod had married his half brother's ex-wife, who was also his cousin, and was denounced by John the Baptist for incest. Herod imprisoned John the Baptist, but then vacillated. He wanted to kill John, but worried about the reaction of the people, and was himself in awe of the austere prophet. Herod and his wife Herodias remind us of Ahab and Jezebel. He, wicked but weak. His wife, wicked and brutally tough. In the end she saw to it that John, whom she hated, was killed. Later Herod's guilty conscience and superstition combined to convince him that the Miracle-worker, Jesus, was John the Baptist come back from the dead.

Overview

Events moved rapidly. John the Bapist was beheaded (14:1-11). Jesus miraculously fed 5,000 (vv. 12-21) and walked on water (vv. 22-36). But official hostility grew. Jesus openly condemned a delegation from Jerusalem (15:1-20). In contrast to the doubt in His homeland, a Canaanite woman believed (vv. 21-29). Back in Galilee Jesus fed another great crowd (vv. 29-39).

Understanding the Text

*"Because of his oaths and his dinner guests" Matt. 14:1-12.*Herod had political as well as personal reasons for wanting John dead. Yet he held back from executing the prophet—until he made a drunken promise in front of dinner guests.

The situation reminds us of an inner tug we all feel at times. We want to do something we know is wrong, but hold back. Until something pushes us over the edge. What provoked Herod to act against his better judgment? A foolish remark. And fear of what others might think.

Herod wasn't thinking clearly when he gave in to what clearly was peer pressure. He had other options. He might have rebuked his stepdaughter. He might have announced that the life of one of God's prophets was not his to give. But under the pressure of the moment he did what he knew was wrong.

That's the danger in peer pressure. Our concern for what others might think or say so clouds our thinking we can't come up with other options. We give in, and do what we know is wrong.

The story of Herod and John the Baptist reminds us that there is always one option open when others pressure us to do what we feel is wrong. We can say no and choose to act on our convictions. Only if we make this choice can we avoid the sense of guilt—and the judgment—that Herod later faced.

"When Jesus heard . . . He withdrew by boat privately to a solitary place" Matt. 14:13. The text tells us that after John the Baptist was beheaded, his followers came and told Jesus. It was then Jesus went privately to a "solitary place." We're not told why. But usually when the Gospels report that Jesus went to a "solitary place" it was to pray and commune with the Father.

What a comfort talking with God is when tragedy strikes. If Jesus needed to withdraw and spend time with His Father just then, we surely need such a retreat when we experience hurt.

"When Jesus landed and saw a large crowd, He had compassion on them and healed their sick" Matt. 14:14. Jesus tried to be alone, to meet His own need. But the crowds followed Him and were at hand when He landed! This time, as many others, Jesus set aside His own needs because He "had compassion" on the crowds.

The word "compassion" is a significant one. It indicates not only a deep emotional concern for others, but also an effort to meet others' needs. When the hurt others feel forces you or me to set aside our own concerns to meet their needs, we need not feel imposed on. We can rejoice. We are walking in the footsteps of our Lord.

"You give them something to eat" Matt. 14:15-21. The disciples showed a concern similar to that of Jesus when they encouraged Jesus to send the crowd off to buy food. But there was a great difference, one underlined by Jesus' suggestion that the disciples give the crowd food. The disciples felt for the crowd, but they could not meet their needs!

You and I often find ourselves in a similar situation. We feel deeply for others who suffer in destructive relationships, who struggle financially, who are in the grip of illnesses, or who are experiencing the consequences of their own unwise choices. Yet again and again it's driven home to us that there is really nothing, or so little, that we can do. That's undoubtedly how the disciples felt when they objected, "We have here only five loaves of bread and two fish" (v. 17).

What happened next is a great encouragement to us. Jesus took the little His disciples had, and miraculously multiplied it. Those five biscuit-sized loaves and two fish fed 5,000 men. Adding women and children, perhaps 20,000!

Jesus still performs miracles. If we have the compassion and the willingness to offer what we do have to others, Jesus can miraculously multiply our little to meet the needs of many.

"You of little faith . . . why did you doubt?" Matt. 14:22-35 This is undoubtedly one of the most familiar stories in the Gospels. The disciples saw Jesus walking on the waters of a stormy sea. Peter cried out, "Lord, if it's You . . . tell me to come to You on the water." Peter jumped out of the boat, and walked on the water toward Jesus. Then he took his eyes off the Lord and gazed at the frightening seas—and began to sink.

The story is the basis of hundreds of sermons, most reminding us to keep our eyes on Jesus not our circumstances.

But it's important to note something else. Peter here is an example both of faith and unbelief. He alone trusted Jesus enough to step over the side and venture out on the waves. If later he flinched at the fearful waves, it was only because he had faith enough to dare.

Faith isn't a static thing in any of our lives. It is constantly tested by our circumstances as we journey through life. We should not be surprised if those with great faith sometimes falter. And we should not be too hard on ourselves if, at times, fright leaves us sinking and in doubt. When times like this come, we need to remember Jesus' words to Peter: "Why did you doubt?" These words aren't a rebuke, but a reminder. When we, like Peter, retreat for a moment to "little faith," all we need do is ask, "Why doubt?" Jesus is here, with us, as He was there on the sea with Peter. The waves may crash all around us. But we will walk on them, not sink under them, if we keep our eyes fixed on our Lord.

"Some Pharisees and teachers of the Law . . . from Jerusalem" Matt. 15:1-9. The note "from Jerusalem" suggests that this may have been an official delegation of members of the Sanhedrin, the Jewish ruling council, come to interrogate Christ. They challenged Christ directly, charging Him with not teaching His disciples to "wash their hands" before they ate. This washing was not hygienic, but a matter of ritual "cleanness."

By the first century many detailed rules for washing before eating had been developed. One entire tractate of the Mishnah, the codification of Jewish practices organized by Rabbi Judah the Prince in the last half of the second century, discusses "hands." It tells just how they must be held when washing, the amount of water that must be used, etc., for a Jew to be ritually "clean" for eating.

Christ sharply attacked the delegation, not on this one issue, but on the approach to biblical religion that they represented. He pointed to one area where such rabbinic hair-splitting served to avoid a clear Old Testament command given by God, and said, "You nullify the Word of God for the sake of your tradition" (v. 6). Jesus condemned these men who came to judge

Him as hypocrites: They followed a pattern that Isaiah condemned long ago of honoring God with their lips, while their "hearts are far from Me."

If there is anything we learn from this incident, it is not to stand in judgment on others for their practices. Faith in Christ isn't a matter of externals. It is a matter of the heart. Convictions may differ in Christian traditions and communities. But what counts is this: Do we love God, and does what we do express that love? If our hearts are right, our practices are irrelevant.

"These are what make a man unclean" Matt. 15:10-20. In Old Testament religion to be "clean" meant to be in a state of ritual purity that permitted a person to approach and worship God. Such things as touching a dead body, having sex, or a body rash, made a person temporarily "unclean." This disqualified him or her from attending worship at the temple until a state of ritual purity had been restored. The Pharisees and teachers of the Law (rabbis, or sages) had multiplied the rules governing ritual purity, and treated them as though their rules had the force of Scripture.

Jesus directly attacked this whole way of thinking when He taught that "what goes into a man's mouth" (externals) cannot make him unclean. What really disqualifies a person for worship are those things which "come out of the heart." The list Matthew gave makes it clear that right living, not right ritual, is the key to a believer's close relationship with the Lord.

We need to make sure our own approach to faith mirrors the principle Jesus laid down here. Let's keep our lives free of those sins that flow from the heart, and not be concerned about the "do's" and "don'ts" that to some people are criteria of spirituality.

"Son of David, have mercy on me!" Matt. 15:21-28 This story puzzles many. But the clues to help us understand are right there in the text.

Jesus had temporarily withdrawn from Jewish territory. A Canaanite woman came and begged for mercy and healing for her daughter, addressing Jesus as "Son of David," His Jewish, messianic title. At first Christ ignored her pleading. Then He seemed to reject her appeal, saying, "I was sent only to the lost sheep of Israel. . . . It is not right to take the children's bread and toss it to their dogs."

In saying this Jesus reflected an important reality: no Gentile had a claim to Israel's blessings, for God's covenant promises were given to Abraham's seed. The woman did not argue or plead special need. She simply noted that the children and dogs both eat bread at the table. The difference is that the children eat until they are satisfied, and the dogs receive the crumbs that are left. This display of faith was rewarded. The daughter was healed "from that very hour."

The incident emphasizes the priority Jesus gave to the Jews in His earthly ministry. He was their Messiah: They had first rights to every blessing He offered. Even today many believe that Paul taught Christians should give Jewish evangelism priority when he spoke of the Gospel being "first for the Jew, then for the Gentiles" (Rom. 1:16).

Yet Jesus did heal, in response to the woman's faith. Faith in Christ is the great leveler. Through the one principle of faith both Jew and Gentile are welcomed into the one family of God. Today no one can claim God's favor exists beyond that claim established by faith.

But do note this. Jesus had just been examined by the skeptical and antagonistic men who represented Israel. And, unexpectedly, he found faith in a Canaanite woman—a descendant of those pagan peoples Israel had been charged to drive from the land. That's the exciting thing about faith. It crops up unexpectedly! Sometimes those who we think should believe hold back, and we become discouraged. And then, suddenly, faith appears in a person we would normally write off, and the revolutionizing power of God transforms his or her life. Then we thank God and, with fresh enthusiasm, continue to do His will.

▶DEVOTIONAL
Eat, but Don't Be Satisfied (Matt. 15:21-39)

Food plays a part in the two incidents reported here. A Canaanite woman begged for crumbs from the table of God's covenant people, and her strong faith was rewarded. Her daughter was healed "from that very hour."

Back home in Galilee Jesus was met by great crowds, who were amazed as He freely healed their lame, blind, crippled, and dumb. When they'd been with Him for three days without anything to eat, Jesus performed another miracle. He multiplied seven loaves and a few small fishes, and fed some 4,000 men "besides women and children."

And the text says, "They all ate and were satisfied." And the crowd went away.

What a contrast. The woman's daughter, healed "from that very hour," had her life changed forever. The Galilean crowd, satisfied with the meal, all left—and within a few hours would be hungry again.

It's wonderful that Christ in grace met the momentary physical need of the crowd. It's grand that He satisfied their hunger. But it's tragic that they then "were satisfied."

Yes. I know. All the text means is that they ate all they wanted; that they were full. Even so, it reminds me that so many people are satisfied if their material needs are met. If they have a place to live. Food to eat. A nice car. Money in the bank. How tragic that so many never feel the urgency that gripped the Canaanite woman and drove her to Jesus. Because in Jesus, and through faith in Him, we experience a spiritual transformation that makes life forever different, "from that very hour."

Personal Application

Expect more from your relationship with Jesus than meeting your material needs.

Quotable

"It is as easy for God to supply the greatest as the smallest wants, even as it was within His power to form a system or an atom, to create a blazing sun as the kindle of the firefly's lamp."—Thomas Guthrie

JULY 23 *Reading 204*
KING AND SON OF GOD
Matthew 16–17

> *" 'Who do you say I am?' Simon Peter answered, 'You are the Christ, the Son of the living God' " (Matt. 16:15-16).*

These chapters mark a turning point in Matthew's Gospel. From now on, Jesus spoke less of the kingdom, and more of the Cross.

Overview

Jesus rejected an official demand for a miraculous sign (16:1-12). Only His disciples acknowledged Him as Son of God (vv. 13-16). Jesus commended Peter (vv. 17-20), and began to instruct the disciples concerning the Cross (vv. 21-28). Christ's transfiguration displayed His glory to the disciples (17:1-13) before an unbelieving generation failed to see Christ's glory in an act of healing (vv. 14-22). Even then Jesus did not insist on His rights as the Son of God (vv. 23-27).

Understanding the Text

"The Pharisees and Sadducees came to Jesus and tested Him" Matt. 16:1-12. These two groups were at odds theologically and politically. Yet both saw Jesus as a threat. As both were represented on the Sanhedrin, this is very probably another official demand that Jesus prove His claims by a "sign from heaven."

It's amazing that this demand would be made, in view of the hundreds of healings and other miracles Christ had performed in Judea and Galilee. When I was in college I worked in a mental institution, and taught a Bible class there. One of the other attendants was a philosophy major at the University of Michigan like myself, and not a believer. I suggested that fulfilled prophecy provided the proof he said he needed of Scripture's supernatural origin, and he took up the challenge. After studying for several months he agreed. Fulfilled prophecy did prove Scripture's claims. But he still refused to accept Christ. He had not really been open or wanted to prove Christianity true. He had hoped to prove it false. Though all the evidence pointed in the opposite direction, he persisted in his unbelief.

Don't be surprised when some you witness to keep on in disbelief, even though they see answers to prayer and evidence of God at work in your life. Miracles didn't produce faith in Jesus' day.

All we can do is what Jesus did. Confront unbelief and keep on ministering to those whose minds are not yet made up.

"Who do people say the Son of man is?" Matt. 16:14 After years of ministry in Israel, Jesus sent His disciples to circulate among the crowds and listen to what people were saying about Him. They were full of praise of Jesus; all identified Him with some Old Testament great.

It was a clear case of damning with faint praise. It's as if you or I looked at a portrait by Rembrandt, and said, "Oh, it's a nice picture."

This is almost worse than the religious leaders' open hostility. And moderns take the same stand! "Oh, Jesus is all right. He was sure a good Man, and a wonderful Teacher. We've got a lot to learn from Jesus all right. Too bad He was crucified and died before His time."

People can respect Jesus as a good Person. But God calls us to acknowledge Jesus as Lord and Saviour. Anything short of worshiping Him as Son of God is rejecting Him completely.

"Who do you say I am?" Matt. 16:15-20 Jesus didn't send out His disciples because our Lord was curious about what the crowds thought. He sent them out to listen, so they would be forced to make a decisive personal decision.

It doesn't matter what others say about Jesus. It doesn't matter if our parents, or our friends, or our whole family are Christians or if they are not. Each one of us must answer for himself or herself the question that Jesus asked His followers then. "Who do you say that I am?"

If we say, with Peter, "You are the Christ, the Son of the living God," and thus trust ourselves to Him, we experience salvation and pass from death to life. If we side with the crowd, no matter how much we may approve of Jesus as a moral and spiritual Leader, we are lost.

There has been much debate about the meaning of Christ's words to Peter, "On this rock I will build My church." There has also been debate over the "keys of the kingdom of heaven" of which Jesus spoke. There is no grammatically compelling reason why Christ was not referring to Peter as the "rock." What is important is that Christ said "I will build" and "My church." Christ had been pouring His life into His disciples, including Peter, for years. Peter clearly was "first among equals" of the Twelve. Nothing Jesus said here suggests apostolic succession or that Peter was "pope." The church was then, is now, and always will be Christ's, and He its ultimate builder.

What about the "keys." The teachers of the Law in Jesus' time had "taken away the key to knowledge" (Luke 11:52) and bound the Jewish people to multiple rules that actually "hindered those who were entering [God's kingdom]." Peter, in preaching the first sermon to Jews (Acts 2) and Gentiles (Acts 10) used the key of knowledge of the Gospel and "loosed" those who had been bound, by directing them to Jesus.

"Jesus began to explain . . . that He must be killed and on the third day be raised to life" Matt. 16:21-27. Peter, commended just above, is now rebuked by Jesus. Peter didn't like the idea of Christ facing death by crucifixion. So he urged Jesus to avoid it! Jesus angrily pushed him away. Peter's attitude lacked the perspective of God.

Jesus went on to explain that every disciple must learn to look at his or her life from God's perspective. Each of us must "take up his cross and follow." Not that we will literally be crucified. Instead, each of us must, like Jesus, find and do the will of God for him or her. The believer's cross does not represent suffering, or death, but the plan and purpose of God for him or her.

Jesus went on to point out that God's purpose frequently seems negative to us rather than positive. It often seems to us that if we do the will of God, we will "lose our life." What we need to understand is that rather than losing our life, we will "save" it. Only in doing the will of God do we become our own better, purified selves.

So let's take up our cross. Daily. And

gladly. If you and I determine to do God's will each day, whatever the cost, we will each become what we most yearn to be.

"See the Son of man coming in His kingdom" Matt. 16:28–17:8. The promise Jesus made was not that some would live until Christ's second coming. It was that some who had believed in Him as Son of God would see the glory that was temporarily masked by His humanity.

The chapter division is unfortunate, for 17:1 tells us that just six days later Jesus took Peter, James, and John to a mountaintop where He was "transfigured before them" (v. 2). In the rays that blazed from His familiar form, in the bright cloud that enveloped them, and in the voice announcing Jesus as God's Son, Christ's essential glory was glimpsed.

It's significant to note that only those who knew Him as Son of God were given this vision, and then not all of the disciples shared it. Sometimes believers today go through life without ever an intuition of the surpassing glory of Jesus, while others seem to live in His presence. Let's take time to study and meditate on who Jesus is. As we do, Christ will show us His glory too.

"They could not heal him" Matt. 17:14-21. When Jesus returned to the valley, He found the nine disciples left behind had tried to heal an epileptic boy and failed.

Jesus healed the boy, and rebuked His disciples for their "little faith" (v. 20). The Greek word, *oligopistia,* is better understood as poor or defective faith. A number of failures of the disciples' faith are mentioned in this section of Matthew (14:26-31; 15:16, 23, 33; 16:5, 22; 17:4, 10-11). It was not the size of the faith, but a flaw in the faith that was to blame.

How do we know this? Because immediately Jesus said that "faith as small as a mustard seed" can move mountains! (v. 20)

What then was the flaw? Here the flaw was in the object of the disciples' faith: "Why couldn't we drive it out?" The disciples had begun to trust the power Jesus had earlier given them, and to think of it as their own. Actually any power they had, flowed from Jesus, and Him alone.

This is actually an encouraging story for

The first-century priesthood required the use of this silver coin to pay the half-shekel temple tax required annually of every Jewish male. Jesus reminded Peter that kings only collect taxes from strangers, not family (17:24-27). If Peter had remembered this, he would have realized that Jesus, God's Son, owed no temple tax to the Lord!

us. Often we hesitate to reach out to help others, dreadfully aware of our inadequacies. It's then we need to remember that our faith is in Jesus, not in our own strengths or resources. The flawed faith of the disciples serves as a reminder that even mustard-seed sized faith in Christ is enough to work miracles!

▶ DEVOTIONAL
No One Except Jesus
(Matt. 17:1-13)

The Christian mystics have an important contribution to make to each of our lives.

This is illustrated in the story of the Transfiguration—and in its immediate aftermath. Notice how the disciples fell down before the transformed Jesus, and how when they looked up they "saw no one except Jesus." What a mountaintop experience that was. They were deeply, completely, totally immersed in worship.

They started back down the hill and almost immediately they became sidetracked. "By the way, Jesus," you can almost hear one of them say, "I've always wondered about that Malachi 4 passage. Does it really mean what the teachers of the Law say: that Elijah must appear before the Messiah can?" The moment of worship had passed and was replaced by questions about the Bible and theology.

I know. The Bible and theology are important. I'm so convinced of that that I spend my life studying and teaching Scripture. But there are times when getting another answer from the Book, or asking another question, detracts from a person's spiritual life.

Just like asking that question about Elijah must have drawn some of the wonder from the memory of their worship, and diluted some of their awe of our Lord.

That's what the mystics have to teach us. That ultimately what is vital is not having all the answers, but worshiping Christ. Not knowing more, but knowing Him. Not study, but kneeling in awe before the One we meet in God's Word.

Personal Application

Study of God's Word will nurture your spiritual life—if it is accompanied by contemplation and adoration of Jesus.

Quotable

"If you desire to know how these things come about, ask grace, not instruction; desire, not understanding; the groaning of prayer, not diligent reading; the Spouse, not the teacher; God, not man; darkness, not clarity; not light, but the fire that totally inflames and carries us into God by ecstatic unctions and burning affections."—Bonaventura

JULY 24 *Reading 205*
KINGDOM GREATNESS
Matthew 18

> *"Unless you change . . . you will never enter the kingdom of heaven. Therefore, whoever humbles himself as this child is the greatest in the kingdom of heaven" (Matt. 18:3-4).*

The question about greatness is important. Today too Christians need to understand Christ's answer.

Overview

The mark of greatness in Christ's kingdom is a childlike responsiveness to the Lord (18:1-5) that guards others (vv. 6-9) by seeking the lost (vv. 10-14), seeking reconciliation (vv. 15-19), and forgiving freely as we have been forgiven (vv. 20-35).

Understanding the Text

"He called a little child and had him stand among them" Matt. 18:1-5. The significance of so many Gospel stories and sayings depends on what has happened just before them. Matthew 16 reported the failure of Israel to respond to Jesus, expressed in the open rejection of leaders and in the failure of the people to recognize Christ as Son of God. Now, in response to a question about greatness, Christ "called a little child." The child, unhesitating, came in response to Christ's call and "stood among them."

The key to greatness in God's kingdom is to respond just as unhesitatingly to the call of the King. You and I can "change and become like little children." We can hear and obey Jesus' voice. In the simple life of obedience we achieve what so many yearn for: greatness in God's sight.

What a tremendous blessing this is. Not many of us will become famous, or be remembered for notable achievements. Yet the simplest Christian can respond to God's voice, and in responding be truly great.

"If anyone causes one of these little ones who

believe in Me to sin" Matt. 18:6-9. Outsiders (the "world") will try to cause "one of these little ones who believe in Me to sin" (v. 6). Outsiders will actively try to cause Christ's disciples to stumble. It would be better for them to have drowned before doing so (vv. 6-7), or to lose the member of the body used to cause sin (vv. 8-9).

These words underline the importance of encouraging the attitude of "little oneness." It's difficult enough to maintain an attitude of childlike trust and responsiveness that is to characterize citizens of Jesus' kingdom. In fact, one of the most important missions of the church is to nurture this attitude in its members. We must remember that children aren't thrust out into the world alone. They are kept safe within the warm and loving context of the family. In the Christian family, the church, we can help each other become truly great.

Sometimes Christians hinder rather than help others respond to Jesus in simple faith. One question we need to constantly ask ourselves is: How can I help others love and respond to Jesus Christ?

If we're uncertain about the answer to that question, then the rest of Matthew 18 is particularly important. Here we are shown just how to help others live in a "little one" relationship with Christ and His church!

"If a man owns a hundred sheep" Matt. 18:10-14. The famous story reminds us that we human beings are very much like sheep. We are prone to go astray. Yet here Jesus pictured the shepherd hurrying off to find the one of his hundred sheep who was lost. Older versions beautifully capture the emotions of the shepherd who finds his lost sheep: he "brings it home rejoicing."

Nurturing "little oneness" in others means remembering that they too are likely to go astray, and that they too are precious. When one does go astray, we are to take the initiative and seek restoration. Perhaps most striking, when we find the straying little one we bring him or her home "rejoicing." There are no recriminations. No attempts to make the person who strayed feel guilt. There is simply joy that one lost has been found.

We need to remember and apply this principle in dealing with our children. Yes, they'll go astray at times. When they come back let's avoid recriminations. Showing our joy that they are home again will do more to prevent future straying than any punishment in the world!

"If your brother sins against you" Matt. 18:15-20. A new analogy is introduced, to stand alongside that of Christ's little ones as sheep. Jesus' people are family. And, as in any family, the children are sure to sin against one another. There will be jealousy. There will be competition. There will be lies. There will be hurts given and received. How do we handle the family spats that are so destructive of Christian "little oneness"?

Jesus gives a three-step procedure. Go to the person and show him his fault. If he listens (and here our forgiveness is implied, cf. v. 21), family harmony is restored. If he does not, bring along one or two others and try again. Finally, involve the whole church family. If the brother still refuses to listen, then "treat him as you would a pagan or tax collector." This phrase points to church discipline: not one member of the Christian community is to have fellowship with that individual.

How does this preserve "little oneness"? And who is the process designed to help? It helps everyone! It helps the person at fault, for the disciplinary process encourages confession and restoration. It helps the person hurt, for confession removes the obstacle to feeling close again. And it helps the congregation, which has shared in a process that affirms the importance of intimate, loving relationships as the context for our life together as little ones of Jesus. With that fellowship intact, we have a very special confidence in prayer (vv. 19-20).

I know. It's hard to go to someone and tell him what he did has hurt me. It's hard to confront. But Jesus commands it. And remember, responding to the voice of the King is the key to greatness in the kingdom of God.

"How many times shall I forgive my brother when he sins against me?" Matt. 18:21-22 Peter is such an attractive character. He's a leader. He's a risk taker. He's quick to speak up, eager to please, and always

very human in his strengths and weaknesses.

This time Peter displayed what he must have thought was a special dedication. "OK, Lord," he seemed to say. "I'm ready to try it. Why, I'll even forgive my brother if he sins against me seven times!"

Just how great a dedication this was is illustrated by rabbinic teaching of the time. The rabbis held that a person could be forgiven a repeated sin three times. But the fourth time, there was no forgiveness. Peter was saying he was willing to go further than anyone expected, in order to obey the Lord.

Many times we're like Peter. When you serve 25 church dinners, and no one even says, "Thanks," by the 26th you wonder. You begin to feel you're being taken advantage of, and it's not quite a labor of love anymore. When you forgive a person for repeated sins, as the offenses mount you become more and more upset. You feel that, if the person were really sorry, he or she wouldn't do it anymore. Yes, we're ready to do more than anyone has a right to expect. But there are limits.

Christ's call for "seventy-seven times" established a totally new principle. In the community of faith, there are to be no limits on mutual forgiveness. There are to be no limits on obedience! We are to continue to live as "little ones," responding to Jesus whatever others around us may say or do.

▶ DEVOTIONAL
Canceled Debts
(Matt. 18:18-35)

When our Lord called for brothers and sisters in God's family to extend unlimited forgiveness to each other (vv. 15-22), He didn't explain how this would help the repeat offender grow in holiness. That was left for the Apostle Paul to explain in 2 Corinthians 5.

What Jesus did do was give us the most compelling reason of all to forgive one an other. That reason is expressed in the story of a servant who owed a king a great debt. When the servant could not pay, the king "took pity on him, canceled the debt and let him go" (v. 27). Then the servant met a fellow servant, who owed him a paltry sum, and "had the man thrown into prison until he could pay the debt" (v. 30). The king was angered when he heard. It was hardly appropriate for one who had been forgiven so much to make such an issue of a debt which was so little.

The thrust of the story depends largely on the amounts of money Jesus mentioned. In the first century, a denarius was a silver coin representing one day's wages for a working man. A talent was a sum equal to 3,000 denarii, so the first servant's debt was the equivalent of 30,000,000 days' wages! If the first servant had labored every workday for 50 years, and given every cent earned to the king, it would have taken him some 2,725 lifetimes to pay his debt! Yet each of us has but a single lifetime to live. By any measure, the debt owed the king was unpayable, and the 100 denarii owed by the second servant was insignificant.

What a reminder when we find our hearts hardening toward a brother or sister after a few repeated hurts. God, the great King, has forgiven us an absolutely unpayable debt. He has forgiven our sins, simply because He took pity on us. In contemplating the forgiveness we have received from God, we find the grace we need to forgive one another.

Personal Application

Next time you find it hard to forgive, meditate on the forgiveness you have received from our Lord.

Quotable

"If you want to work for the kingdom of God, and to bring it, and to enter into it, there is just one condition to be first accepted. You must enter it as children, or not at all."—John Ruskin

JULY 25 *Reading 206*
MORE ON GREATNESS
Matthew 19–20

> *"Whoever wants to become great among you must be your servant, and whoever wants to be first must be your slave—just as the Son of man did not come to be served, but to serve, and to give His life as a ransom for many" (Matt. 20:26-28).*

The world has its own notions of how to achieve greatness in the spiritual realm. But each path the religious recommends is a detour away from the road taken by Jesus.

Overview

Jesus showed the fallacy in paths taken by the legalistic Pharisees (19:1-15) and a rich young man (vv. 16-30). He told a parable to show that greatness isn't a matter of working harder (20:1-16). True greatness is found in doing the will of God by serving others (vv. 17-26), and putting our own needs aside to meet theirs (vv. 27-34).

Understanding the Text

"Some Pharisees came to Him to test Him" Matt. 19:1-9. As in the earlier dispute of Jesus with the Pharisees over Sabbath-keeping, the real issue here was the Pharisees' approach to the Law, not the question they raised about divorce.

In the first century two Jewish schools of thought on divorce existed. One school held that divorce should be permitted only in the case of unfaithfulness. The other permitted divorce for any reason at all. What school did Jesus follow?

Jesus did not choose either, but pointed out that God's ideal was a lifelong partnership. Anything less than the ideal involved sin, for one aspect of sin is falling short of God's best.

The Pharisees objected. Why then did Moses permit divorce? Jesus said, "Because your hearts were hard." Understanding the hardness of human hearts, God knew that some marriages would be so destructive and marred by sin that He permitted divorce—even though it was not His ideal!

This answer utterly destroyed the Pharisees' reliance on Law, for it showed that God's Law was not the highest spiritual standard at all! The Law itself contained the proof. God's Law was a lowered standard, evidence of His grace in dealing with the human race.

This lesson was driven home in the next incident. Little children were brought to Jesus, who announced that "the kingdom of heaven belongs to such as these." In Judaism a child became responsible to keep the Law at 12 or 13. Not even the most strict Pharisee held the "little children" responsible to keep God's Law! What Jesus said showed that God relates to us in grace, not through Law. God's children respond to Jesus' voice, rather than live by rules of "do" and "don't do." No Pharisee could achieve greatness, no matter how zealous he was to keep the rules and regulations that were observed as a way of promoting spirituality and pleasing God.

What a lesson for us. Let's not boast of all we do and do not do for Christ's sake. Let us simply look into His Word, hear His voice, and respond. As little children, let's remember that our life with Him is rooted not in what we do for God, but in the grace God showers on us.

"What God has joined together, let man not separate" Matt. 19:6. Doesn't this verse mean that Christians today are not to divorce? Actually, no. Jesus was responding to an assumption hidden in the Pharisees' question. They debated divorce because they believed it was the right of an ecclesiastical court to decide who could and who could not divorce and remarry. In Deuteronomy 24 the Law simply said that, when a divorce takes place, the husband is to give the wife a "certificate of divorce." This written document was proof that she was unmarried, and could (and in most cases did) remarry. In the first century courts of sages, referred to in Scripture as "experts in the Law," sat in judgment on who could and could not divorce. At times they even forced husbands to grant their wives written bills of divorce. What Jesus meant when He said, "Let man not separate," was that no ecclesiastical court had the right to sit in judgment on a di-

vorce case. As the Old Testament decreed, this is a matter for the husband and wife alone to determine.

What a reminder to us today, for we too have a tendency to sit in judgment in this most painful and tragic of situations. We cannot condone divorce. But, with Jesus, we must confess that in some cases it is necessary. No pastor, board, or denominational court of inquiry has the right to say to one couple no, and to another yes. And no such ecclesiastical court has the right to authorize one person to remarry, and to deny remarriage to another.

The way of the Pharisee is unacceptable to God—whether in Jesus' day or in our own.

"What good thing must I do to get eternal life?" Matt. 19:16-22 The rich young man represents another approach people have taken in an effort to achieve spiritual greatness. When questioned, the young man showed that unlike many in his day he had consistently tried to do what is right in every human relationship.

But each of the commands quoted by Jesus (vv. 18-19) came from the "second tablet" of the Ten Commandments. That tablet sets standards for man's relationship with other men. What about the "first tablet," and those commands which deal with man's personal relationship with the Lord?

Jesus' answer, "Go sell your possessions and give to the poor. . . . Then come, follow Me" (v. 21), was designed to show the young man that his wealth came before God. That individual "went away sad," for he was wealthy. In a choice between God, in the person of the Son of God, and money, this young man chose money.

The first commandment of the Ten is, "You shall love the Lord your God." No matter how benevolent or just a person may be in his relationships with others, unless he or she loves God supremely, there can be no spiritual growth or achievement.

Let's remember this when the humanist praises good works, and assumes all that counts is being or doing good. The best person in the world who does not love God has broken the first and greatest commandment, for our supreme obligation is to love the Lord.

"Who then can be saved?" Matt. 19:23-26 When Jesus remarked that it is difficult for a rich man to enter the kingdom, the disciples were shocked. The ordinary man viewed the wealthy as blessed by God, for they had the opportunity to do good with their wealth and so gain merit with God. Jesus had a different perspective. The more we have, the more our possessions may possess us! The more we may consider how a choice affects our bottom line, rather than how that choice honors God. It is hard for a person with many resources tied up in this world to focus his or her attention on the next.

Thank God that He can do what we cannot. We can be saved for eternity. And we can be saved from slavery to our wealth so that we can instead become slaves of God.

"We have left everything to follow You" Matt. 19:27-30. Peter and the other disciples did not choose to follow Jesus for what they gained. But, like them, we sometimes wonder, "What will there be for us?"

Jesus' answer is reassuring. No one who follows Christ will lose! What we gain will be a hundred times as valuable as what we may be asked to give up (v. 29). All this . . . and eternal life too!

"He agreed to pay them a denarius" Matt. 20:1-15. This story of Jesus troubles many. It's obvious that the owner of the vineyard wasn't fair. Oh, he paid the first workers fairly: we know that a denarius was a day's wages in the first century. But we can understand why those who had worked all day for the agreed wage were upset when, at the end of the day, those who had labored just a few hours got as much as they did.

So what was Jesus saying? Simply this. Some people want to put relationship with God on a work-for-hire basis. "I'll work harder at being a good Christian than others. I'll go to more meetings. Serve on more committees. Be out every night of the week." And these folks often assume they'll be rewarded for being so busy.

The problem is, relationship with God is based on His generosity (v. 15). God relates to us in grace, not on the basis of works. The person who serves God out of love will, of course, be rewarded. But the person who serves actively because he thinks this is the way to make points with the Lord is doomed to disappointment. We don't advance spiritually by being busy.

This too is a lesson we need to learn. God calls us to love Him, and serve others. We can become so caught up in doing things for Him that we forget to simply love Him. And we forget to stop, listen to people, and try to respond to their needs. The person who is so active in church may very well be drying up spiritually, and spending his or her energies in an unproductive way.

"So the last will be first, and the first will be last" Matt. 20:16. This is the second repetition of this saying in our chapters (cf. 19:30). What does it mean? Simply that those who appear to be first in the spiritual lineup, based on their strict religion, their benevolence, or their active involvement in church affairs, won't be first when Judgment Day arrives. When we appear before the Judgment Seat of Christ to receive our rewards, those at the head of the line will be simple folk who have heard Christ's message about greatness, and have taken it to heart. Those who, as Jesus taught in Matthew 18, seek out and rejoice with the lost, seek harmony within the body of Christ, and are ready to forgive others because they themselves have been forgiven by God.

▶DEVOTIONAL
What Do You Want Me to Do? (Matt. 20:17-34)

Somehow, we can't seem to get it through our heads, can we? I suppose it's all right. Even Jesus' disciples took such a long time to comprehend the simple thing Jesus taught. You want to be great? Then serve.

James and John didn't understand. They asked their mother (or so the other disciples thought!) to lobby Jesus for the top positions in His kingdom. Jesus just shook His head, and told the two they didn't know what they were asking. High rank in the kingdom of Jesus calls for drinking His cup (vv. 22-23). And that cup, in Jesus' case, was death on the cross (vv. 17-19).

Jesus tried to explain. High position in the secular world means having authority: it means lording over people. Jesus on the other hand came to be a Servant and, like a slave, to put the good of another before His own (vv. 25-28). I suspect the disciples still didn't see what Jesus meant. Perhaps we wouldn't see it either, if it weren't for the incident with which this chapter ends.

Jesus led His disciples away from Jericho, up the road that led to Jerusalem and His crucifixion. How heavy His heart must have been, for He knew what lay ahead. As He left, two blind men, hearing from the crowd that Jesus was near, cried out urgently. The crowd tried to hush them. But the men shouted all the louder. And Jesus stopped. He called them to Him, and He asked, "What do you want Me to do for you?"

And at last we understand. Greatness in the kingdom of Jesus is stopping for the needs of others. It is setting aside for the moment our own hurts and concerns, to listen, and then to ask, "What do you want me to do for you?"

We may be little in the eyes of other men. But if we follow Christ's example of servanthood, we will be great in the eyes of God.

Personal Application

Begin each day asking God for an opportunity to serve.

Quotable

"Do all the good you can, by all the means you can, in all the ways you can, in all the places you can, at all the times you can, to all the people you can and as long as you can."—John Wesley

JULY 26 *Reading 207*
JESUS IN JERUSALEM
Matthew 21–23

" 'Love the Lord your God with all your heart and with all your soul and with all your mind.' This is the first and greatest commandment" (Matt. 22:37-38).

Jesus now entered His last week on earth. We see in the events which follow just how deep His love for His Father is.

Overview

Jesus entered Jerusalem hailed as the Messiah (21:1-11), angering temple leaders (vv. 12-17). Jesus condemned a fruitless fig tree symbolizing Israel (vv. 18-22), and told a series of stories which explain the fruitlessness of His people (v. 23–22:14). Jesus turned aside two verbal attacks (vv. 15-33) and silenced His critics (vv. 34-46).

Jesus then pronounced woes on the Pharisees and sages for their spiritual blindness (23:1-36), and lamented over the doomed city of Jerusalem (vv. 37-39).

Understanding the Text

"Your King comes to you, gentle and riding on a donkey" Matt. 21:1-11. A fervent desire for the Messiah burned underneath the surface of first-century Judaism, and found expression in a number of short-lived revolts led by pseudo messiahs. Taxes were heavy, and life was hard for the common people. When the crowds acclaimed Jesus, most undoubtedly hoped He would expel the Romans and set up a powerful, independent kingdom.

But Matthew reminded them of Zechariah's prophecy (9:9). This King came "riding on a donkey." In the ancient world kings rode horses when they went to war. A visit from a king on a donkey meant that he came in peace!

It's a helpful reminder for those of us who fear to surrender completely to Christ's lordship. He came in peace, to bring peace. Surrender to this King will quiet our inner conflicts, not increase them. Surrender to this King offers each of us the gift of perfect peace.

"Jesus entered the temple area" Matt. 21:12-17. Jesus' coming does not mean peace to everyone. Inside Jerusalem He entered the broad courtyard where merchants licensed by the high priest changed coins and sold animals for sacrifices, and drove them out. This infuriated the chief priests, who made a profit on the trade and, some early sources suggest, were not above extorting more than was fair. But they felt helpless to act against Him because the crowds shouted so enthusiastically for Him.

Not everyone is comfortable when Jesus enters today. There may be a conflict in us as there was in the first-century temple. But God's house is to be a "house of prayer." The Christian, who is the living temple of God, is to be completely dedicated to the Lord. Anything dishonest or unholy must be driven out of our lives.

"Found nothing on it except leaves" Matt. 21:18-22. As often happened, the disciples asked Jesus the wrong question when they saw how a fig tree He cursed withered in one day. Their question? "How did You do it?" Jesus in effect suggested the miracle was nothing special. With even a little faith the disciples themselves could perform miracles.

The question they should have asked was, "Why did You do it?" The answer to this question was, "Because the fig tree reminded Me so much of Israel!" Like the fig tree, God's people seemed to flourish. They were dedicated to God and practiced their religion zealously. But when that religion was carefully examined, there was nothing there but leaves. The tree produced no fruit!

In both Testaments fruit represents the moral product of intimate personal relationship with God. The New Testament summary describes fruit as "love, joy, peace, patience, kindness, goodness," etc. (Gal. 5:22-23). These inner qualities would be expressed socially as the justice and compassion so exhorted by the Old Testament prophets (see Isa. 5:1-7).

What is important to us is that this event introduces a series of stories that explain why the Jews of Jesus' day failed to produce fruit and alerts you and me to attitudes that will keep us from vital, fruit-producing lives.

"By what authority are You doing these things?" Matt. 21:23-27 It was clear from Christ's miracles that He was a spokesman authenticated by the Lord. Yet the religious leaders of the Jews refused to accept His authority. Instead, as successors of Moses (see 23:2), they claimed to be religious authorities.

Jesus' question about John the Baptist, however, revealed their hypocrisy. If they truly had divine authority, they would reveal the truth. Their failure to answer for fear of the crowds showed they really knew the Lord did not stand behind their pronouncements.

We too will be fruitless, unless we acknowledge the authority of Jesus in every area of our lives, and respond obediently to His Word.

"'I will, sir.' But he did not go" Matt. 21:28-32. Jesus' Parable of the Two Sons drives home an important point. It's not what we say that reveals our basic attitude toward God. It's what we do.

I know a number of people who talk religion and holiness very well. And I know that several of them are like the Pharisees, who say they are ready to obey God, but who do not put God's Word into daily practice. Religious words are the leaves some people use to disguise their fruitlessness.

*"Let's kill him and take his inheritance" Matt. 21:33-46.*This story focuses on motives. Why was it that the religious leaders of first-century Judaism refused to respond to Christ's revelation of His deity and messiahhood? Christ's analysis is, simply, that they wanted to "take His inheritance." They did not want to acknowledge His ownership of God's people, but were addicted to the thrill of running things their own way! And, oh, how the religious leaders hated Jesus for exposing their true motives (vv. 45-46).

All too often we have the same problem. Why don't we submit to Christ's lordship? Because we want to run our lives our own way! Never mind that Jesus has every claim to our total allegiance. Never mind that He will make wiser, better choices that are truly for our good. We want to be able to say, with the familiar song, "I Did It My Way."

What then is Jesus' prescription for fruitfulness? Three simple steps are given in these three parables. Acknowledge the authority of Jesus. Do what He tells you. Surrender your will to His.

If you and I put these steps into practice daily, we most surely will bear spiritual fruit.

"Everything is ready. Come to the wedding banquet" Matt. 22:1-14. One of the most compelling questions that can be asked about Jesus is, "Did He fail?" He came to God's chosen people, and they rejected and killed Him. What now?

The Parable of the Wedding Banquet answers the question. God's feast of salvation will have guests aplenty. Since those who were invited first saw fit to refuse, God's invitation has been extended to street corners and alleys of the whole world, and God gathers "all the people [His servants] can find." So surely the wedding hall will be "filled with guests."

But what does the note about an intruder "not wearing wedding clothes" mean? It was common practice for kings to clothe their dinner guests in fine robes. A person who had a right to join the feasting had been clothed by the king.

Many preachers have preached many sermons on this point. Unless we are clothed with righteousness by Jesus Himself we will not be welcome in heaven. And this is, of course, true.

Yet the larger point of Jesus' story must not be lost. God does not fail when any individual rejects the invitation to be saved. The failure is entirely that of an invited guest, who apart from faith in Christ can never enjoy the good things God has in store for us in eternity. And truly, the invitation is for all. Let's do our part in sharing that invitation with others, and not be discouraged if of the many we invite, few choose to respond (v. 14).

"Then the Pharisees went out and laid plans to trap Him in His words" Matt. 22:15-46. Jewish writings from the first through third centuries document the contemptuous view the sophisticated leaders in first-century Judea had for the "country bumpkin" people of Galilee. The Pharisees, who were Judeans, could not challenge Jesus' miracles. But they thought that, in

the verbal arena, they could surely show Him up!

The rest of the chapter traces four exchanges between Jesus and these men who spent their lives in study of the traditions of their faith.

Before looking at the first trap, note how the Pharisees used words. The very first thing they did was to try to disarm Christ by a compliment they did not at all mean: "We know you are a Man of integrity and that You teach the way of God in accordance with the truth" (v. 16). They tried to trap Jesus in His words, but their words revealed their deceitful hearts and in fact they trapped themselves! You and I can be sure that what we say is just as revealing about us!

Why did the Pharisees try to get Jesus to either endorse or reject paying taxes to Caesar? In the first century taxes created a heavy burden in the Jewish homeland, actually threatening the survival of some. No wonder this was an incendiary topic. If Jesus did endorse taxes, He must lose favor with the crowds. If He spoke against taxes, the Romans would surely deal harshly with Him!

We can appreciate the cleverness of Christ's reply. But it's more important to grasp the principle. We all have a dual citizenship—participants in human society, and at the same time in God's kingdom. We are to live as good citizens of each, honoring both God and our government.

"The Sadducees, who say there is no resurrection" Matt. 22:23-33. Again, what is striking is the obvious insincerity of those who challenged Christ. They believed there was no resurrection. Why ask a complicated hypothetical question about it?

I suppose the question had been useful in debates with the Pharisees, who did believe in resurrection. In form, the question is *reductio ad absurdum.* Try to reduce the other person's position to an absurdity (vv. 24-28).

Christ simply rejected the premise on which the argument rested—that there is such a thing as marriage in the resurrection. And then He went on to expose the Sadducees' basic unbelief. "You are in error because you do not know the Scriptures or the power of God."

Ultimately all our philosophy, all our careful logic, falls short. Our belief rests in confidence in the Scriptures, and assurance in the power of the God who reveals Himself to us in them.

"The greatest commandment in the Law" Matt. 22:34-40. What had led Pharisees and Sadducees astray? These were truly religious men, committed to their beliefs. Christ's answer to the last question asked Him exposed the flaw. All the Law and the Prophets spoke was intended to nurture love for God and love for one's neighbor. We pervert the Scriptures if we use them as did the various Jewish parties in the first century to build themselves up and cut their brothers down.

If we come to the Bible to discover how to better love God and others, we will avoid the attitudes which led to the corruption of first-century Judaism, and which were so strongly condemned by our Lord (see Matt. 23).

"Whose Son is He?" Matt. 22:41-46 Jesus then turned the tables and asked His adversaries questions about words. If the Messiah is David's Descendant, how is it that David acknowledges His superiority (i.e., "calls Him Lord")? In view of the fact that in Judaism the father is always viewed as superior to the son, there is only one ancestor. Under inspiration David affirmed His deity.

Why is it that "no one could say a word in reply"? It was not because no teacher had ever seen evidence in Scripture that the Messiah would be the Son of God. It was simply that these religious leaders did not want to acknowledge Christ's authority.

How often this is the issue today. It's not that people can't understand the Bible. It's just that people don't want to submit to its teachings. What a blessing it is to rid ourselves of such attitudes, and come to Scripture eagerly. What a blessing to love God, and bend every effort simply to please Him.

▶ DEVOTIONAL
Perfect Failures
(Matt. 23)

I suppose almost everyone knows that seven is the number of perfection in Scripture. The Creation was completed in seven days. Each week contains a cycle of seven days. Every seven years Israelites were to rest their fields and leave them unplanted. A seven-branched lamp in the temple represented the illuminating work of the Holy Spirit. And so on.

In view of this, it's fascinating to note that Jesus' final words on the Pharisees and teachers of the Law of His day are summed up in seven "woes." ("Woe" is an expression both of grief and denunciation.) I suppose the fact that there are seven of these "woe" statements indicates that the leaders were "perfect" failures.

So how do we keep from being perfect failures in our own spiritual lives? We avoid their seven deadly sins, each of which is associated with exalting ourselves over others rather than living humble, loving lives. The seven?

1. Shutting others out.
2. Making converts for our own sake and in our own image.
3. Making rules for others despite a lack of personal spiritual insight.
4. Majoring on minor religious issues while ignoring God's true priorities.
5. Being concerned with appearances rather than personal righteousness.
6. Covering sinful motives with deceitful talk and actions.
7. Professing responsiveness to God as a cloak to hostility.

Oh, yes. If you want a positive prescription, you might try a simple exercise. Just turn each of these seven around, and make your own list of seven qualities that make for spiritual success!

Personal Application

Be wary, for we too are vulnerable to the attitudes that ensnared the Pharisees.

Quotable

"Humility and self-contempt will obtain our wish far sooner than stubborn pride. Though God is so exalted, His eyes regard the lowly, both in heaven and earth, and we shall strive in vain to please Him in any other way than by abasing ourselves."—John of Avila

JULY 27 *Reading 208*
JESUS' PROPHECY
Matthew 24–25

> *"No one knows about that day or hour, not even the angels in heaven, nor the Son, but only the Father" (Matt. 24:36).*

Jesus did make specific predictions about the future. But He emphasized what His servants are to do until the future arrives!

Overview

Jesus answered His disciples' questions about the end of the age (24:1-28), the signs of His coming (vv. 29-35), and when these things will happen (vv. 36-44). He went on to emphasize the importance of being ready (vv. 45-51), emphasizing the importance of service in two parables (25:1-30). Ultimately Jesus will come again and establish His kingdom (vv. 31-46).

Understanding the Text

"Every one will be thrown down" Matt. 24:1-2. The Jerusalem temple was one of the wonders of the ancient world. Pagans as well as Jews traveled from all across the Roman Empire to see it. No wonder Jesus' disciples were stunned when Christ said that every stone of the magnificent edifice would be thrown down—a prediction fulfilled by Roman troops in A.D. 70, less than four decades after Christ's crucifixion.

As you and I think about the future, we need to do so with the attitude displayed by Christ. This world, with all its wonders, will come crashing down. Every material thing we hold dear will crumble into dust, or be destroyed with earth itself in blazing fires (cf. 2 Peter 3:10). We can appreciate all man's accomplishments. But we must fix our hopes on the world to come.

"What will be the sign . . . of the end of the age?" Matt. 24:3-29 Jesus answered the

three questions His disciples posed (v. 3), but in reverse order. First Jesus warned against mistaking the ordinary tragedies of war, pestilence, famine, and natural disasters as an indication the world is about to end. All these things are the stuff of which human history has always been woven, ever since Adam's fall. The world will not improve, nor will Christ's kingdom come through a gradual uplifting of our fallen race.

The course of human history is downward, not upward. Ultimately it will plunge into the abyss described by Daniel, when one known as the Antichrist desecrates the holy place and the world is plunged into the most dread Tribulation of all (vv. 15-21).

Many have tried to fit what Jesus taught here into a rigid sequence of prophetic events. There is no doubt that Christ's words are in fullest harmony with those of the Old Testament prophets, and that they "fit" the picture of history's end drawn in the older revelation. But there is a more important point made here.

Don't fix your heart on what this world offers. For this world is doomed.

This does not, of course, mean that you and I should not do all we can to promote interpersonal, societal, and international peace. It simply reminds us that mankind requires redemption. Apart from a transforming work of God, no lasting change can or will come.

And, tragically, most human beings will persist in rejecting Jesus and His claims.

"The Son of man will appear in the sky" Matt. 24:30-35. Jesus will return. How will He come? His first coming was quiet. He slipped unobtrusively into our world, a tiny Infant, and grew up in the guise of an ordinary Jewish man. His second coming will be spectacular: all the nations of earth will see Him appear in "power and great glory."

We need never wonder if Jesus has slipped in among us, unnoticed again. His next appearance will command the attention—and the respect—of all.

We need never be ashamed or embarrassed to witness of the unnoticed Jesus, whom our friends so successfully ignore today. They won't be able to ignore or overlook Him when He comes again.

"No one knows about that day or hour" Matt. 24:36-44. I can't imagine how many books and pamphlets have been written, promising to name the date of Christ's return. How could anyone be so foolish, when Jesus Himself said, "No one knows about that day or hour"?

Yet there's one positive characteristic in each writing. The authors expected Christ to come back in their own lifetimes.

Ever since the first century, Christians have looked forward to the return of Jesus. I well remember my mother, some 53 years ago as I write this—I was five then—telling me she expected the Lord to come in her lifetime. Today I expect Jesus to come in mine. He may not. But the important thing is that He could.

Why is it important? Because Jesus emphasized it. He said, "You also must be ready, because the Son of man will come at an hour when you do not expect Him."

If we recognize the perishability of this world, and expect Jesus to come at any moment, how our values and priorities will change! May God give each of us a deep sense of the imminence of Jesus' return.

"Who then is the faithful and wise servant?" Matt. 24:45-51 This parable is directed to leaders—those responsible for the care and supervision of others. Leaders are to be considerate and concerned with the others' well-being. The good servant, who treats others in this way, will be rewarded when Jesus comes back. But there are "wicked" servants in leadership who exploit and mistreat others. Ignoring the likelihood of the master's return, such servants shear rather than feed God's flock.

As I was writing this paragraph I stopped for a break, and switched on the TV. I saw a news flash. Jim Bakker has just been convicted of 24 counts of fraud: of lying to his TV partners about projects he knew could not be completed, and taking $3.7 million of their contributions for himself and his wife. Later Tammy Faye broke out into song, and told the assembled reporters that this earthly jury doesn't give the final verdict.

I wonder if she or Jim ever read this parable? Or its conclusion. In the most graphic and severe terms, Jesus speaks of punishment for those wicked servants of

God who "beat . . . fellow servants and . . . eat and drink with drunkards" (v. 49).

"Ten virgins who took their lamps and went out to meet the bridegroom" Matt. 25:1-13. Jewish marriage custom dictated that the bridegroom go to the house of the bride and escort her to his own house. The friends of the bride waited for him to come.

While many fanciful interpretations of this parable have been advanced, the basic point is clear. The bridegroom did not come when expected, but was delayed. And some of the young women waiting to join the bridal party didn't bring enough oil for their lamps, and the oil ran out.

In this set of illustrations about waiting for the delayed second coming of the Saviour, this parable makes a simple point. Expect Him at any moment. But be prepared for a long wait.

This is the perspective you and I are to adopt as we live our lives on earth. We are to look forward each morning to Jesus' return, and live as though He were to appear before evening. Yet we are to prepare for a lifetime here, ready to wait as long as it takes for Him to come.

"Entrusted his property to them" Matt. 25:14-30. This familiar parable too focuses on what we are to do while waiting for Christ to return. It makes the point that God has entrusted us with resources—of money, personal gifts, and abilities—and that He expects us to use those resources in His service.

Perhaps the greatest wonder here is that God trusts so much to us, and then gives us the freedom to use what He has given as we choose. God doesn't stand over us, barking out orders, dotting every i and crossing every t. Instead He steps back. He lets us have the pleasure of taking the initiative, the joy of achieving. He gives us freedom and support, and while He does hold us responsible, He wants us to succeed.

The servant who buried his talent in the ground portrays every Christian who has been afraid to risk stepping out for God, while the servants who made a profit represent each of us who has experienced joy in acting by faith to serve our God.

Like the other parables in this section, this one concludes with a grim picture of the punishment suitable to the failed servant. What we do in this life really does count. We truly must be about our Master's business.

▶DEVOTIONAL
Lord, When Did We See You? (Matt. 25:31-46)

Sometimes it's best to ignore theology when we read the Bible. Oh, I don't mean that theological questions shouldn't be asked. Or that we shouldn't try to answer them. I just mean that sometimes our earnest study gets in the way, so that we miss something simple that contains a great blessing.

Matthew 25:31-46 is a case in point: the story of the sheep and the goats. The meaning of the story is hotly debated. The "hungry and thirsty" Jesus called His brothers have been variously identified. They are the poor and oppressed, or the Jewish people in the Tribulation era, or the inhabitants of Christendom.

In the same way, the sheep and goat peoples have been taken in a variety of ways. Are they national groups, or individuals? If the passage is talking about salvation, is a "works righteousness" really intended?

While these are important questions, perhaps it's enough for our devotional reading to note one or two key facts. First, Christ identified Himself with "these brothers of Mine" who live on earth. What we do to meet the needs of others is not just done "for" Christ, but in a significant sense, to Him!

Second, as disciples of Jesus who do hunger or thirst, we can take comfort that Christ shares the experience with us. He does not watch: He participates.

Both the righteous, who help the brothers of Jesus, and the wicked, who do not, were surprised when the basis of their judgment was explained. Just as we may be surprised when Jesus returns to learn how deeply He was involved in our every experience.

Yet, if we tune our hearts and minds to what Jesus teaches here, a great and wonderful peace will come. We truly are not alone, whatever suffering we experience or need we have. Jesus is with us. In His presence we can find comfort and peace.

Personal Application
As you wait for Jesus to appear, remember that He is with you.

Quotable
"Receive every inward and outward trouble, every disappointment, pain, uneasiness, temptation, darkness, and desolation, with both thy hands, as a true opportunity and blessed occasion of dying to self, and entering into a fuller fellowship with thy self-dying, suffering Saviour. Look at no inward or outward trouble in any other view; reject every other thought about it; and then every kind of trial and duress will become the blessed day of thy prosperity."—William Law

JULY 28 *Reading 209*
THE CRUCIFIXION
Matthew 26–28

> *"When the centurion and those with him who were guarding Jesus saw the earthquake and all that had happened, they were terrified, and exclaimed, 'Surely He was the Son of God!' " (Matt. 27:54)*

With these last chapters of Matthew we enter the Christian's holy of holies. With a sense of deepest awe we witness again the death and the resurrection of our Lord.

Overview
Jesus predicted His imminent death (26:1-13) as Judas plotted with the chief priests to betray Him (vv. 14-16). During a final meal Jesus instituted Communion, and predicted Peter's denial (vv. 17-35). Jesus prayed in Gethsemane (vv. 36-46), where He was arrested (vv. 47-56) and taken before the Jewish high court (vv. 57-68). Peter did deny his Lord (vv. 69-75), and Judas hanged himself (27:1-10). Jesus was condemned by Pilate (vv. 11-26), mocked by His executioners (vv. 27-31), and crucified (vv. 32-56). He was buried (vv. 57-61) and His tomb placed under guard (vv. 62-66). But death is not the end! On the third day Jesus was raised from the dead (28:1-15), and later commissioned His disciples to "go and make disciples" (vv. 16-20).

Understanding the Text
"A woman came to Him with an alabaster jar of very expensive perfume" Matt. 26:1-13. This is one of Scripture's fascinating "little stories." As the high Jewish council plotted to arrest Jesus; as Judas mulled over the possibility of betraying Him; as Christ Himself spoke of imminent crucifixion; an unnamed woman slipped into the house in Bethany where Jesus was staying. Without saying a word she poured her perfume on His head and, so another Gospel tells us, washed His feet with her tears. And Jesus, calling what she did "a beautiful thing," promised that "wherever this gospel is preached . . . what she has done will also be told."

But why? What was so special here? Perhaps it's just that everyone around was caught up in the great events then unfolding. The city was astir with rumors after Jesus' triumphal entry. The priests and Judas were plotting. The disciples were excited by the possibility that Christ might soon set up His kingdom. But no one was sensitive to Jesus and the pain He then felt so deeply. No one, but the here unnamed woman, who wept with and for Him, and anointed Him with her greatest treasure.

You and I can become so busy. We can get caught up in our plans, in our dreams. Even when our bustling activity is religious—doing things for Jesus—we can be like the people who surrounded Jesus then. How much we need to pause, set aside our projects, and wait quietly to sense Christ's mood, and pour out our greatest treasures—worship and love.

"This is the blood of the covenant, which is poured out for many for the forgiveness of sins" Matt. 26:17-30. In these words Jesus summed up the significance of His death.

His death is God's guarantee that new promises to mankind have gone into effect. Through the death of Christ forgiveness of sins is made available to all human beings. And His resurrection is the guarantee that Jesus will come again, to escort us to our place in His "Father's kingdom" (v. 29).

As we share what different traditions call Communion, the Lord's Supper, or the Eucharist, we affirm our complete trust in His promises. We celebrate our forgiveness. And we anticipate Jesus' return.

"Yet not as I will, but as You will" Matt. 26:36-46. Throughout the Old as well as the New Testament, "cup" frequently stands for some distinct experience. Thus the "cup of His wrath" (Isa. 51:17) stands for the experience of divine judgment, and the "cup of salvation" (Ps. 116:13) stands for the psalmist's experience of salvation. Jesus' cup was not so much the physical torment He was about to experience as it was the awful prospect of taking on Himself the sin of humankind. At that prospect, He said, "My soul is overwhelmed with sorrow to the point of death" (v. 38).

The disciples could not understand, or even stay awake to share the awful loneliness with Him. Yet today we can watch, worship, and learn. Each of these is important. We watch, by meditating on Christ's sufferings, tuning our hearts to empathize. We worship, praising and thanking Him for the extravagant love He displayed. And we learn, growing in the conviction that like Jesus we must take whatever cup God offers us, and say with our Lord, "Not as I will, but as You will."

As the Resurrection proves, God's will is best.

"Legions of angels" Matt. 26:47-56. Looking at this part of Matthew's description, we're tempted to focus on the perfidy of Judas, or the bold defense of Jesus attempted by that "one of Jesus' companions" other Gospels name as Peter. But it's appropriate, in this account of Jesus' last hours, to focus instead on our Lord.

What is so impressive here is the fact that doing the will of the Father was not just a matter of surrender for Jesus, but also of resolve.

Jesus had just said, "Not as I will, but as You will." Yet as the crowds advanced to arrest Him, Jesus was fully aware that He did not have to go with them. Even then, He could have called on His Father for armies of angels! But He did not do so. His surrender was real, for it was expressed in the firm resolve that rejected every other option than that of God's will.

It's easy for you or me, moved by some emotion, to privately or publicly surrender to the Lord. We sing the old hymn, "I'll do what You want me to do, dear Lord," and hasten forward. And we mean it with our whole heart. Then. Yet even heartfelt surrender is meaningless unless it is expressed later in firm resolve. As Jesus showed such resolve, so we too are to live our lives.

"Tell us if You are the Christ, the Son of God" Matt. 26:57-68. Again our focus is on Christ. We could, of course, profitably study the Jewish court, which had already determined to condemn Jesus and struggled to find some charge to justify its intention. But instead we look at Jesus, silent until asked to confess His deity.

Confess it He did, and added that at the final judgment they would see Him again, seated "at the right hand of the Mighty One and coming on the clouds of heaven" (v. 64).

With this statement Jesus left every man with but a single choice. He must acknowledge Jesus as God—or reject Him. Christ is either who He said He was, or a madman.

The court had, of course, already made its decision. To them what Jesus claimed was blasphemy, and they exulted in the fact that under Jewish law blasphemy called for the death penalty (vv. 65-66). Today many Jewish scholars seek to distinguish the historical Jesus from the Christ of Christianity. The man Jesus, most argue, was a *Hasid,* a pious and charismatic Jew who emphasized an intimate and vital faith in Israel's God. Verses like these in Matthew must have been added after the church deified the young rabbi, whose early death was so tragic.

But it won't wash. Jesus still stands before the court of each man's mind, still claiming to be the Christ, the Son of God. And our eternal destiny hinges on whether our verdict is yes or no.

"He went outside and wept bitterly" Matt. 26:69-75. For a moment the scene seems to shift away from Jesus and onto Peter. But the shift is only apparent, not real. As Peter huddled close to the fires burning in the high priest's courtyard, cursing and denying that he was one of "that Man's" followers, we seem to see the saddened figure of Jesus seated earlier at the table, and hear His grief-laden voice tell Peter, "This very night . . . you will disown Me three times" (v. 34). We feel an overwhelming sense of Jesus' presence, even as Peter spoke. And suddenly, Peter felt it too! He realized what he had done, and "went outside and wept bitterly" (v. 75).

Jesus knew all along what Peter would do. And, all along, Jesus was willing to sacrifice Himself for men and women who, even with the best intentions, would fall short. All along, Jesus knew. And He knows now.

He knows when you and I disown Him by our words and actions. He observes sadly. And when like Peter we at last sense His presence again, it's all right to weep. Yet even as we do, we have the Cross to remind us that His love for us never faltered or failed.

"He went away and hanged himself" Matt. 27:1-10. Again the focus only seems to shift away from Jesus. This time we're shown Judas, suddenly filled with remorse, trying to return the 30 pieces of silver he'd taken for betraying the Lord. The priests were unfeeling when he cried, "I have betrayed innocent blood." Their only comment was, "That's your responsibility." And the priests, this time, were right.

As we read of the incident, the unseen figure of Jesus again dominates. For it must be that memories of Jesus now filled Judas' mind. In his mind's eye he saw Jesus, weary, refusing rest in order to help and heal. He heard Jesus speak of God as a loving Heavenly Father. He sensed the touch of Christ's hand on his arm, and remembered how the Lord reached out in compassion to cure the leper. All along Judas knew that Jesus was innocent, but now, when it was too late, a sense of His beauty and love overwhelm. Unable to rid himself of his images of Christ, crushed by a sense of guilt, yet unwilling to humble himself and ask forgiveness, Judas went out and hanged himself.

For the unsaved as well as the believer, Jesus remains history's one unforgettable Man. His image will either fill us with hope and love, or will stand as an unavoidable specter pointing silently to our guilt.

"He had Jesus flogged, and handed Him over to be crucified" Matt. 27:11-26. By all first-century accounts Pilate was a cruel man. He cared nothing for the beliefs or sensitivities of the people in the province he governed for some 10 years. And he undoubtedly enriched himself while serving as the Roman overseer of Judea.

Yet even Pilate was uncomfortable when Jesus was brought to him to be sentenced. Ultimately Pilate bowed to pressure brought by the Jewish leaders and the crowds, and condemned Christ to death. He didn't want to do it. But it was easier to surrender Jesus than to order His release and risk a riot.

Again we see the dominance of Jesus. He forces each individual who meets Him to stop, to face some crucial choice, and to decide.

Pilate tried to disguise his choice, telling the Jews, "It is your responsibility." It was not, of course. Only Pilate had the power to order Christ's crucifixion. And Pilate had the authority to release Him. Pilate tried to shift responsibility for his decision, but whatever he and the eager Jewish leaders said, Pilate remained responsible for his decision in the case of Jesus Christ.

So do we, each and every one. We can never shift responsibility for any decision we may make concerning Him. No one else will be condemned for us. And no one else's saving faith will save you or me.

As with Pilate, Jesus stands before us, and we, alone, must decide His case.

"The curtain of the temple was torn in two from top to bottom" Matt. 27:32-56. Crucifixions, though reserved for brigands and slaves, were not at all uncommon in the first-century Roman Empire. Yet this one was different. As a variety of spectators watched and listened (see DEVOTIONAL), Jesus cried out to His Father, the

skies darkened, and at the moment of His death the earth shook. Even the hardened Roman soldiers were terrified, exclaiming, "Surely He was the Son of God!"

Perhaps the most significant happening went almost unnoticed, for it must have been quickly repaired by the shocked priests and Levites who cared for the temple. There a thick, woven curtain was miraculously torn from top to bottom. That curtain isolated the holy of holies, the inner room where once a year the high priest entered to make atonement for Israel's sins.

The writer of Hebrews tells us that the curtain was symbolic, and showed that as yet no one had direct or immediate access to God. Sin still kept humanity from God's presence. So the tearing of that curtain announced a new era! The way into the holiest was now open! Through the death of Christ, forgiven sinners have direct and immediate access to Israel's God.

Yes, Christ's body was torn. But through the nails driven into His hands, and the spear thrust into His side, flowed the crimson lifeblood that, once spilled, bridged the ancient gap between God and man, and even now guarantees that we can come, boldly, to the very throne of grace to find help for every need.

"That deceiver said, 'After three days I will rise again' " Matt. 27:57-66. His friends buried Jesus with broken hearts. Only His enemies remembered His promise to rise again—and to them it was a threat, not a promise. They posted a guard to prevent the disciples from stealing the body to pretend resurrection had taken place. But they must have been uneasy when they went to bed at night.

What if Jesus had been telling the truth? What if Jesus were the Son of God!

That question was too awful to contemplate, and I suspect that not one of the leaders imagined Jesus would actually rise. In fact, even when He was raised from the dead, the leaders tried desperately to hide the fact (vv. 11-15).

But perhaps this is a question we should be asking our friends who suspend judgment on Jesus today. "I know you don't believe," we might say, "but what if Jesus really was raised from the dead? What if Jesus is the Son of God? What would it mean to you, if?"

And with those questions asked we can walk away, and wait. For Jesus was raised. He is alive. He is the Son of God. And He has sent His Holy Spirit into the world, to hold Jesus up before the minds and hearts of men, until each one gives his or her answer to just those questions today.

"I will be with you always" Matt. 28:16-20. Matthew closed with what is called "the Great Commission." We are to go to everyone, and make disciples. We are to baptize, and teach others to obey the words taught first by our Lord.

And we do not have to do it alone! That wonderful figure who so dominates the four Gospels, and especially the last few chapters of Matthew, still stands tall. The One who taught and healed with such authority, the One who died and was raised again, and so was "declared to be the Son of God with power," retains "all authority in heaven and on earth."

We meet Him in the Gospels.

And we now live with Him every day.

▶DEVOTIONAL
Standing By
(Matt. 27:32-56)

One of the most moving Bible studies I've ever experienced happened in our living room. It was near Easter, and I had our little group of friends turn in their Bibles to this passage. I gave each a drawing of this scene; a drawing that had three circles drawn at varying distances around the cross. Together we looked into the passage and found those who stood closest to the cross—the centurion, the soldiers, the thieves on the other crosses, the man who hurried up to offer Christ drugged vinegar. We filled in the second circle, and then the third. And then I asked each member of our group to select the one person he or she might most probably have been—to take that person's place—to witness the Crucifixion—and then to tell what he or she felt and thought as he or she witnessed the death of our Lord.

What an exercise for you and me, at any time of the year. Are we hardened, insulated against feelings by a protective shell, like the Roman soldiers? Are we trained, educated, competent, like the Roman centurion? Are we burdened with knowledge of our guilt, like the one thief on the cross, or bitter and angry like the other? Are we simply curious, like the man with the sponge of vinegar? Do our hearts break, as did that of Mary His mother and the other women? Are we cynical, like the priests and scribes?

Whatever our nature or present state, we can find a person with whom to identify in this chapter. We can stand with them, near the cross. We can watch the Saviour die. And, perhaps, as we do, we too can suddenly be filled with awe as the events unfold, and realize that—whoever we are, or whatever our condition—Jesus hangs there for us! And through His suffering, we can be healed.

Personal Application

Visit the cross often, and find there answers for your deepest needs.

Quotable

To God be the glory—great things He has done!
So loved He the world that He gave us His Son,
Who yielded His life an atonement for sin,
And opened the life-gate that all may go in.

Praise the Lord, praise the Lord,
Let the earth hear His voice!
Praise the Lord, praise the Lord,
Let the people rejoice!
O come to the Father through Jesus the Son,
And give Him the glory—great things He has done.—Fanny J. Crosby

The Variety Reading Plan continues with JEREMIAH

Mark

INTRODUCTION

According to very early tradition, this Gospel is based on the preaching and eyewitness stories told by the Apostle Peter. It was probably written between A.D. 65–70. The numerous explanations of Aramaic words and Hebrew practices suggest Mark wrote for Gentile readers. In the blunt, vigorous speech of the common man, Peter's interpreter, John Mark, portrayed Jesus as a Man of action, whose nature and mission can best be grasped by observing His works. Almost a third of this Gospel is devoted to the Crucifixion and events of the last week of Christ on earth.

OUTLINE OF CONTENTS

I. Prologue . . . . Mark 1:1-13
II. Early Galilean Ministry . . . . Mark 1:14–3:6
III. Later Galilean Ministry . . . . Mark 3:7–6:13
IV. Withdrawal from Galilee . . . . Mark 6:14–8:30
V. Journey to Jerusalem . . . . Mark 8:31–10:52
VI. Ministry in Jerusalem . . . . Mark 11–13
VII. Death and Resurrection . . . . Mark 14–16

READING GUIDE (9 Days)

If hurried, you may read only the "core passage" in your Bible and the Devotional in each chapter of this Commentary.

Reading	*Chapters*	*Core passage*
210	1	1:35-39
211	2–3	3:20-30
212	4–5	5:1-20
213	6–7	7:1-23
214	8–9	9:30-50
215	10–11	10:17-31
216	12–13	13
217	14	14:43-65
218	15–16	15:21-41

Mark

JULY 29 *Reading 210*
THE SON OF GOD
Mark 1

> *"A voice came from heaven: 'You are My Son, whom I love; with You I am well pleased' " (Mark 1:11).*

With almost no introduction, the author plunged into an account of events that proved his theme: Jesus is the Son of God.

Background

John Mark. A very early tradition, traced back to the Apostle John himself, identifies Mark as the writer of this Gospel. He apparently accompanied Peter when Peter was in Rome, and according to very early church historians, reflected Peter's preaching in his Gospel.

But John Mark himself has a fascinating story. He was the young son of an early Jerusalem convert, a woman to whose house Peter went after he was released from prison (Acts 12:12). Mark traveled briefly with Paul and Barnabas on their first missionary journey (13:5). But Mark deserted the missionary team (v. 13). Paul was so upset with him that when Barnabas insisted on taking Mark (who was also his cousin) on another journey, the two seasoned missionaries split up (15:36-41).

Yet later we meet Mark again, in Paul's epistles! There we see Paul's attitude had changed: Mark was not only to be welcomed by the churches the apostle had founded (Col. 4:10), but in prison Paul asked that Mark come to him "because he is helpful to me in my ministry" (2 Tim. 4:11).

What a lesson these few verses about Mark have for us today. First they warn us. Let's not be too quick to give up on young people. They can and will make mistakes. But with the kind of loving care and second chances that Barnabas fought to give Mark, they can grow and change.

Second, these verses encourage us. Like John Mark, you and I may at times go back on our commitment to the Lord or to ministry. How wonderful to realize that such failures do not disqualify us. John Mark not only went on to become a leader in the early church—God chose him to write one of the books of our Bible!

Whenever we open the Word of God to Mark's Gospel, we're reminded that God is willing to give us too yet another chance—and that if we take that chance, He will use us for His glory.

Overview

John the Baptist came in accordance with prophecy to announce Jesus' appearance (1:1-8). At Christ's baptism He was identified as the Son of God (vv. 9-13). He began His work by calling disciples (vv. 14-20), driving out evil spirits, and healing (vv. 21-34). Jesus found strength in prayer as He traveled throughout Galilee (vv. 35-39), demonstrating God's compassion by His healings (vv. 40-45).

Understanding the Text

"The Son of God" Mark 1:1. In Hebrew and in the Aramaic spoken by Jews in the first century, "son of" often represented descent or dependence. In one sense human beings and angels are "sons of" (beings created by) God.

Yet "son of" can have another meaning: a meaning that is rooted in identity. To say a person is a "son of man" means that he or she is a human being.

In what sense did Mark use "Son of

God" in his very first verse? Clearly in the most significant sense: Jesus is one with God. Jesus is God.

Mark did not argue this point. Instead he went on to demonstrate it, reporting a series of unique events and acts that made it clear just who Jesus is.

Perhaps this is one of the greatest values of Mark's brief Gospel. As we read, we are reminded again and again that the One whose adventures we share is the Son of God, come to live in our world; come to display in all He says and does the once-hidden character of our God. If we keep this in mind, we will often be awed by Jesus' display of the love and grace of God. And we will often be moved to pause and praise.

"So John came, baptizing" Mark 1:2-8. With no further introduction, Mark went into the exciting events that preceded Jesus' public appearance. In fulfillment of prophecy God sent a messenger to prepare the way for His Son. The messenger, John the Baptist, predicted One "more powerful than I" was to appear soon. He urged his listeners to prepare by repenting, and offered water baptism as a sign of repentance and appeal for forgiveness.

Yesterday a Christian sportsmanship award was given to a member of our church softball team. When the "Jim Smith Award" was given, the presenter had to choke back his tears. You see, Jim Smith had been his "John the Baptist." Some years earlier Jim had guided him to Christ and shown him how to live a Christian life.

You and I too can continue John the Baptist's ministry. Like Jim Smith, we can speak of the "more powerful One" who is about to appear again. We too can urge people to change their hearts and minds about God, and receive forgiveness. We can promise that those who do look to God's Son, Jesus, will not only be forgiven but will also receive God's gift of the Holy Spirit. We can understand our mission in life as Jim Smith and John the Baptist understood theirs—the mission of messengers sent to "prepare the way for the Lord" in the hearts and lives of our friends.

"You are My Son, whom I love" Mark 1:9-12. John said little about the baptism or temptation of Jesus. What he did say was clear evidence of Christ's deity. During the baptism, John saw the Spirit descend on Jesus like a dove, and heard a voice identify Christ as God's Son (v. 11). And, after being tempted by Satan, "angels attended Him."

Thus three lines of testimony identify Jesus as Son of God: the testimony of the Old Testament prophets, the testimony of God Himself, and the testimony of miraculous events.

It's encouraging to remember when we do undertake a John the Baptist-like ministry and point others to Jesus, that God still testifies to Christ's identity as we share Him. We have the external witness of Scripture. We have the internal witness of God's voice, speaking directly to the heart of the person we're witnessing to. And we have the miracle of God's transforming work in our own lives.

"They left their nets and followed Him" Mark 1:14-20. The other Gospels make it clear that Jesus and these fishermen had spent time together before the call described here. But notice what Mark emphasized in his story. When Jesus called Peter and Andrew, they left their nets "at once" (v. 18). "Without delay" He called John and James, and they responded so quickly that they "left their father . . . in the boat" (vv. 19-20).

The urgency we sense here permeates the Book of Mark. Jesus needed to reach as many as possible in the few short years of His ministry. And He needs now, as He needed then, disciples who feel the urgency too.

"He even gives orders to evil spirits, and they obey Him" Mark 1:21-34. Mark continued to demonstrate the truth of Jesus' deity. He taught with "authority." He cast out evil spirits, who knew and identified Him as "the Holy One of God." He healed all sorts of diseases. As the news spread over Galilee, it was increasingly clear that a unique Individual had appeared.

For some strange reason our day has seen a rise in interest in the occult. Horror books and films dwell on the demonic, and more than one serial killer has committed his or her crimes in the name of the devil. Many high schools even have small groups of Satan worshipers, perhaps in imitation of music groups that exploit the dark side of spirituality. Even in our little Florida county, the sheriff's office made it a point to ask teachers to report any indications of Satan worship by teens!

How good it is to remember that Jesus truly is the Son of God. All Satan's forces are helpless before Him.

"Filled with compassion, Jesus reached out His hand and touched the man" Mark 1:40-45. If we ever wondered whether the Gospel ministry should focus just on preaching salvation, or involve meeting a wide range of human needs, here's our answer. We follow Jesus' example.

Lepers in biblical times were not only diseased, but also were social outcasts. They were cut off from all normal contact with healthy persons, and suffered not only from their sickness but also from isolation and rejection. When one such person came to Jesus, the text says He was "filled with compassion." The Greek word indicates that Christ was deeply moved. But it indicates more. It suggests an empathy and emotional response that moves a person to action. In His action Jesus not only healed the leprosy, but He also touched the leper. Christ was sensitive to the need for healing, but also sensitive to the need of this rejected man for the touch of another human hand. Christ's love moved Him to meet the psychological as well as physical and spiritual need.

No human need should be ignored by those whose mission is to introduce others to Jesus Christ, for Christ's concern extends to every need a human being may have.

▶ DEVOTIONAL
Boring and Offensive (Mark 1:35-39)

That's what my wife called yesterday's sermon. "Boring and offensive." No, I wasn't preaching. And neither was our pastor. It was a guest preacher, who exhorted our congregation to greater involvement in social action. But in the process downplayed the importance of nurturing personal relationship with the Lord. "That," my wife later insisted, "is a perfect illustration of secular humanism." And she's totally down on that.

As usual, my wife's analysis was quite accurate. Yet the last incident in this chapter pictures Jesus' deep concern for the physical and psychological health of a leper! Isn't that social action?

Of course it is. And it tells us, as the preacher yesterday tried to, that you and I too are to have honest concern for social and psychological needs, as well as for the spiritual needs of others. The problem arises only when we isolate our relationship with God from our works. What bothered my wife was the fact that every kind of ministry has to be rooted in and grow out of our personal relationship with Jesus Christ. Ministry is no substitute for fellowship with God, just as good works are no alternative to salvation.

What we see in this story is that Jesus' own ministry of preaching and service was rooted in, and grew out of, His personal relationship with the Father.

That's what's so challenging. Jesus was so active. He was concerned about every need of the people of Galilee. He was constantly on the go; always in ministry. And yet even Jesus could not afford to neglect time alone with His Father. So what did Jesus do? He got up early. He went off to pray "while it was still dark" because He knew every daylight hour would be taken up serving others and preaching His Good News.

"That's why I have come," Jesus said, referring to His preaching. He had to get His work done. But in order to minister effectively, He had to have His time with God too.

That's really what was wrong with yesterday's sermon. It failed to remind us that whatever we do, it must flow from our relationship with Jesus, and that even the doing of good deeds must never be allowed to supplant time devoted to deepening our relationship with our Lord.

Personal Application

To be effective in any ministry, spend significant time in prayer first.

Quotable

"In fact, I have so much to do today that I shall spend the first three hours in prayer."—Martin Luther

JULY 30 *Reading 211*
LORD OF THE SABBATH
Mark 2–3

"The Son of man is Lord even of the Sabbath" Mark 2:28.

Jesus continued to act decisively despite opposition. In incident after incident Jesus demonstrated that He is the Son of God.

Background

Galilee. Most of the ministry reported in Mark took place in Galilee. In the first century Judea and Galilee were both predominantly Jewish districts. But the sophisticated men of Judea looked down on their coreligionists in Galilee as country bumpkins. Galileans were also viewed with contempt because they tended to be much less strict in their observance of multiple laws added by sages to the 613 statutes Jewish scholars had identified in the Old Testament. The Pharisees and "teachers of the Law" mentioned in Mark were almost certainly from Judea, come down to hear and evaluate the charismatic figure rumor held to be teaching and healing in Galilee.

The critical spirit of these experts in Old Testament and rabbinical law is clearly seen in these two chapters. Jesus, however, continued to act as boldly and spontaneously as before, even when His action brought Him into direct conflict with men the people generally respected as Judaism's spiritual leaders. In the conflict Christ not only claimed, but demonstrated, His lordship. As events make clear, one must either accept Jesus' claims, or reject them. There can be no compromise in our attitude toward the Son of God.

Overview

Jesus' claim to forgive sins (2:1-12), His association with sinners (vv. 13-17) and failure to fast (vv. 18-22) ignited opposition. Jesus' claim of lordship over the Sabbath then aroused the Pharisees' murderous hostility (v. 23–3:6). Yet crowds and His disciples still followed Jesus (vv. 7-19). Jesus denounced a charge that Satan was behind His miracles (vv. 20-30), and claimed relationship with all who do God's will (vv. 31-35).

Understanding the Text

"Why does this Fellow talk like that?" Mark 2:1-12 The phrase "this Fellow" showed the contempt the erudite delegation from Judea had for Jesus and other Galileans. But they clearly understood Jesus' pronouncement of forgiveness of a paralyzed man's sin as an act that implied a claim of Deity (v. 7).

The claim was proven when Jesus performed a healing miracle, after designating evidence of His power to forgive sins: the paralyzed man got up and walked out at Jesus' command.

Like many today, those religious leaders acknowledged the meaning of Christ's words. But they were unwilling to accept the evidence of His acts.

Yet this was Mark's thrust. Mark intended to prove by an accurate report of what Jesus did in Galilee, that He is, as He claimed, the very Son of God.

"When Jesus saw their faith" Mark 2:1-5. What was it that led to the wonderful exercise of Jesus' authority described in this story? It was "their" faith. It was the faith of a paralyzed man, joined with and strengthened by the faith of friends who cared enough to carry him to Jesus, and then to dig through a roof to reach Him.

Let's learn from this story the importance of mutual support. We each need others who will trust God with us, and will come to the Lord with us.

"Tax collectors and 'sinners' were eating with Him and His disciples" Mark 2:13-17. A basic tenet of the religious in the first century

The flat roofs of houses in Galilee were made of mud, daubed on layers of beams and branches, and then rolled flat and smooth. The Mark picture of "digging through" the roof in order to lower the man down to Jesus is totally accurate.

was that to remain "clean," they must isolate themselves from "sinners." If they had any contact with sinners, they would surely be contaminated! To see Christ eating with such people shocked the delegation of religious leaders come to Galilee to pass judgment on the young Prophet.

We need to take Jesus' example to heart today, and meditate on His answer. Jesus came to heal the spiritually sick, not to retreat to some spa where He could lie around with the righteous. Nor is our mission to the spiritually healthy, but to sinners who need to be called back to God.

Jesus lived, and teaches us to live, a dynamic kind of holiness. Our holiness is not attained by isolating ourselves from sinners, but by being constantly filled with love for God and for others.

"How is it that John's disciples and the disciples of the Pharisees are fasting, but Yours are not?" Mark 2:18-22 This kind of question is still asked often today. It's not a question of theology—why do you believe what you do? It's not even a question about morality—why do you live as you do? No, it's a question about a nonessential practice.

The Old Testament called for fasting on only one day each year—the solemn Day of Atonement (Lev. 16:31). Yet by the first century, the ultra-religious fasted twice a week, on Monday and Thursday. This was a 12- rather than 24-hour fast, from morning to evening. But it was something extra a person did in order to please God—or to appear especially pious. It was one of those "do's" or "don'ts" adopted to set a religious person apart from the "less spiritual."

Jesus spoke of new patches that never fit an old garment, and old wineskins that split if filled with unfermented grape juice. The revelation Jesus brought simply would not fit in the categories of first-century Jewish spirituality. In the same way, the quality of a modern believer's life in Christ cannot be squeezed into the categories some Christians use to measure behavior. So let's concentrate on celebrating Jesus, and loving others for His sake.

"What is unlawful on the Sabbath?" Mark 2:23–3:6 The Old Testament commanded the Jewish people to keep the Sabbath Day holy. But, aside from forbidding "work" on the Sabbath, and such things as buying and selling, no details of Sabbath-keeping are provided. Concerned lest anyone even inadvertently do what should not be done on the Sabbath, sages had over the centuries since the Babylonian Exile developed long lists explaining what one must not do. The restrictions were spelled out in detail. For instance, a person might spit on a rock on the Sabbath. But not on dry earth. The spittle might move some of the dirt, and thus "plow."

It was just this kind of detail that the Pharisees criticized when Jesus' disciples plucked grain to eat as they walked. Old Testament Law permitted a person walking along a path to eat what grew next to it. It was simply that the Pharisees classified plucking the grain as "harvesting," and thus "work" on the Sabbath.

Jesus' response dealt with the Pharisees' approach to the Law. Scripture itself tells of a time the high priest violated a direct divine command by giving David and his companions altar bread when they were hungry (v. 25). Why then should His disciples go hungry for a merely human statute?

When the same issue was raised another time, Jesus restored a cripple's hand, saying, as Lord of the Sabbath, that doing good is always right, even on the Sabbath.

Why did this make the Pharisees so furious? Because their entire claim to spiritual superiority was based on rigorous observation of just such man-made rules. And Christ dared to set such things aside as irrelevant!

The passage forces us to stop and evaluate. Do we measure spirituality by some list of do's and don'ts? Or do we take Jesus as our model, and concentrate not on our acts of piety, but on a spontaneous response to the needs of others for Christ's sake?

"Many people came to Him from Judea, Jerusalem, Idumea, and the regions across the Jordan" Mark 3:7-12. While the religious leaders were repelled by Jesus, great crowds gathered to Him from miles around. The excitement was not generated by what He taught as much as by the desire to experi-

ence or see some of His healings.

There's nothing really wrong with this. We all probably come to Jesus first out of a sense of personal need, and in hopes that He can meet that need. But later we must learn to love Him for His own sake, rather than for what He does for us.

"Designating them apostles" Mark 3:13-19. The word *apostle* means "one sent on a mission." In New Testament times an apostle represented the person who sent him, and was treated with the courtesy due to his sender. At the same time, the apostle was to accurately and faithfully reflect his sender.

The Twelve named here carried out that mission, even to the extent of driving out demons. What's important for us to note is that, even in the Gospel era, the Son of God carried on His work through representatives. Today you and I also have the privilege of representing Jesus to others. Let's rejoice that the effectiveness of our ministry does not depend on us, but on the Son of God who works actively through us.

What we undertake, He will do.

▶ DEVOTIONAL
Your Considered Opinion, Please (Mark 3:20-30)

It sounds so grim. So final.

The "unforgivable" sin.

The thing that a person does which places him beyond any hope of salvation.

I suppose it's no wonder that some folks torment themselves wondering whether they've committed this sin. But the one absolutely certain fact is, that no one who is worried could possibly have committed the sin Jesus was talking about in this passage.

Think about it.

A delegation of religious leaders had come down from Jerusalem to see this young upstart, Jesus, who was preaching and healing without a license from them. They stayed in Galilee for a few weeks, questioning Him and watching His healings. It was increasingly clear that Jesus wasn't someone they could control. And also that what He was teaching contradicted their approach to religion. In fact, He was a threat!

But it was also clear that He was performing real miracles. Healings were taking place. And evil spirits were being expelled, crying out that Jesus is the Son of God (v. 11).

So, what were the teachers of the Law from Jerusalem going to do? They had to either abandon their most deeply held beliefs (and their positions), or they had to find some basis for denouncing Christ and rejecting His claims. And this was what they did. They reached and announced their considered opinion: Jesus was in league with Satan! He was casting out demons because the prince of demons let Him.

This is the key to understanding the "unforgivable sin." It's looking at all the evidence provided by the Holy Spirit through Jesus' actions, carefully considering the options, and then choosing to see what Christ did as the work of Satan rather than God.

Why then did I say that anyone worried about committing the unforgivable sin today can be sure he or she hasn't? Simply because if you're anxious that Jesus won't save you, you obviously believe that He can. You may be worried about the quality of your own faith. But your considered opinion is that Jesus is the Saviour. You haven't rejected the Spirit's testimony about Jesus: you agree with it!

So what then should you do? Take heart. Jesus came, as Mark 2:17 reminds us, to call sinners. He is ready, willing, and eager to accept you into His family. And since you believe He can save you, all you need do is accept the gift of life He brings. Tell Him, "I accept" and, the transaction done, eternal salvation will be yours.

Personal Application

You and I meet the only qualification Scripture gives to applicants for salvation: we have sinned. And Christ died to forgive sinners.

Quotable

"A man who believes himself a sinner, who feels himself sinful, is already at the gates of the kingdom of heaven."—François Mauriac

JULY 31 *Reading 212*
PARABLES AND POWERS
Mark 4–5

"With many similar parables Jesus spoke the word to them, as much as they could understand" (Mark 4:33).

We may not completely understand the word pictures Jesus gives in these chapters of His kingdom. But there is no mistaking the power He exercises over every natural and supernatural force!

Background

The word translated "parable" is rooted in the Old Testament concept of a "riddle." There the riddle or parable may be any word play: a brief saying, a vivid image, a longer story. Each kind of "riddle" is intended both to display and to some extent hide information. In each, the hearer is expected to puzzle out the speaker's meaning.

There are many indications that the Hebrew people took great delight in riddles and parables, and enjoyed both telling and solving them. Yet in this passage Jesus had a deeper purpose in mind than to focus active and attentive listening. Jesus intended His parables to reveal secrets (Gk. *musterion,* "mysteries") about the kingdom which those "outside," who have refused to acknowledge Him as God's Son, will be unable to understand (4:11). He will not allow hardened individuals who have examined Christ's claims and come to the considered opinion that He is mad or in league with Satan to understand what God intends (v. 12).

What a reminder for us. The very first and essential issue we face when we come to Scripture is, What is our view of Jesus Christ? Our whole understanding of God's Word, as well as our salvation, hinges on how we answer that question. If we accept Him for who He is, God's Son and our Saviour, the Word of God will gradually be opened to us, and produce fruit in our lives.

Overview

The lengthy Parable of the Sower (4:1-9) was explained by Jesus (vv. 10-20), who went on to give other images of His kingdom (vv. 21-34). The divine power that will cause Jesus' kingdom to flower on earth was revealed, as Christ calmed a storm (vv. 35-41), cast out demons (5:1-20), healed (vv. 21-34), and even raised a dead child to life (vv. 35-43).

Understanding the Text

"A farmer went out to sow his seed" Mark 4:1-9. The first parable Jesus told is familiar, perhaps because He later interpreted it so that we understand its meaning. What the farmer sowed, scattering in carefully measured casts, was the Word of God. Even though some fell on ground in which it could not grow, the Word was sure to produce a crop.

Today over 1,500 radio stations, hundreds of local TV stations, and thousands of churches in the United States scatter God's Word to our population. Yet I've recently been impressed on how ineffective we are as communicators. My wife teaches 11th grade American Literature here in Florida. Many of our early American writers, steeped in the Puritan tradition, made allusions to the Bible in their poetry and stories. What Sue finds is that even in her honors classes, most teens are totally ignorant of the Bible. They read Huck Finn, but have no idea what Twain is referring to when he mentions "Moses and the Bullrushers." They have never heard of the Flood, and one teen expressed awed wonder as Sue explained the Virgin Birth, saying, "Did that really happen?"

The image Jesus used was that of a farmer, walking in his own field, rather than that of a king or emperor sitting in his palace and writing out decrees. What's the difference? The farmer owned only a small field, but worked it carefully. He himself walked where he scattered his seed. If communication of God's Word is to be effective, we need to scatter the Good News where we ourselves walk. For all their apparent power, Christian radio and TV fail to place the seed where it must be if it is to grow and produce fruit.

"Some people are like seed along the path" Mark 4:10-20. In this parable the "seed" has a dual meaning. It is about both the

word sown, and the soil on which the seed fell.

The parable suggests that we each have two responsibilities. We are to sow the word as we walk in our own fields. And we are to prepare our own hearts, so that when we hear the Word, it will grow and produce a crop in our lives.

"Don't you put it on its stand?" Mark 4:21-23 One of the most fascinating features of parables is that the same parable may be used to make different points in different contexts. In Mark 4 the riddle of the lamp on a stand has a different intent than in Matthew 5.

Here Jesus speaks of "the" lamp, not, as the NIV, "a" lamp. In Mark the reference is to Christ Himself. Though at the moment His true identity was hidden, God would surely disclose it, for His identity is "meant to be brought out into the open."

How was Christ's true identity, concealed during His life on earth, brought into the open? Paul said in Romans 1:4 that Jesus was "declared with power to be the Son of God by His resurrection from the dead." There is no question now about who Jesus is.

"Consider carefully what you hear" Mark 4:24-25. This is a basic principle of the spiritual life. We must appropriate what we learn, and use it. The more we apply truth the better able we are to understand and apply more.

On the other hand, if we fail to apply what we learn, we soon lose it and the capacity to learn more. There's a saying that sums up this teaching most effectively. Use it. Or lose it.

"The seed sprouts and grows" Mark 4:26-29. Christ's present kingdom has two dimensions: the human, and the divine. The Parable of the Sower emphasized each by speaking both of the ability of the Word to produce a crop and of the hearer as soil. Divine/human cooperation produced an abundant crop.

In verses 24-25 Jesus emphasized the importance of considering carefully what we hear. As we respond to His Word, more truth will be given to us. In this saying, it almost seems that spiritual growth is our responsibility alone. But here, in the next verses, Jesus looked at the supernatural element, and drew an analogy. A farmer sows seed, it takes root, and somehow "all by itself," the seed sprouts and grows. Miraculously, the soil produces a crop. Does the farmer understand the process, or control it? Not at all. He simply plants the seed and observes as the transformation takes place.

In the same way, the Word of God taken into our lives "sprouts and grows, though [we do] not know how." In some mysterious, supernatural way "all by itself the soil produces grain." We can't explain how God works in our lives. We can't even observe the process of transformation, though we will surely see its results. What we can and do know, however, is that God is at work in us as we welcome His transforming Word.

"It is like a mustard seed" Mark 4:30-32. The mustard seed is not the smallest of all seeds, but was the smallest seed then planted in the Middle East (v. 31).

The Jewish people, eager for the Messiah to come and save them from Roman domination, expected Him to appear in great power and immediate glory. Instead the Christ came as a simple Man of Galilee and, rather than assemble armies, taught and healed the sick. This was insignificant in many an eye. But while the origin of Jesus' kingdom might seem small, the kingdom is destined to dominate, even as this "largest of all garden plants" ultimately dominates the garden in which it is planted. One day Christ will come, and His kingdom will fill the whole earth.

"Many similar parables" Mark 4:33-34. There is a pattern in these parables. In speaking of His kingdom Jesus focused first on the present work of God within the believer, and concluded by speaking of a future, obvious work of God in the world.

For now, the kingdom's Word is sown, and produces fruit—very personal, subjective fruit. Yet kingdom power was openly displayed in Jesus' resurrection (vv. 1-23). For now, the kingdom's Word is heeded only by believers. Yet the kingdom is destined to dominate all when Christ returns (vv. 24-34). The greatest present evidence of Christ's royal authority is found in the lives of men and women who have heard and who respond to God's Word.

What a privilege today, to be living proof that Jesus lives; living testimony to the fact that soon He will return.

"A furious squall came up" Mark 4:35-41. We now come to a series of reports of miracles that Jesus performed. Why does Mark place these here, rather than somewhere else? Because Jesus had been speaking about God's hidden kingdom work in the lives of His people. While a transformed life is certainly evidence of God's work among us, it is not objective evidence. It is not the kind of clear, visible proof that so many seemed to require. So, in a series of miracle stories, Mark demonstrated to each reader the ultimate power that Jesus possesses. How wise we are to trust an all-powerful Jesus, even if His present work is experienced subjectively in human lives.

And what of this first miracle? It shows Jesus' authority over nature. Christ can stop the winds and still the waves with a word. Even natural laws, to which we humans must adjust, are subject to Jesus' will.

"Come out of this man, you evil spirit!" Mark 5:6-20 There are many helpful thoughts to develop from this passage. We might focus on the plight of the possessed man (vv. 1-5, see DEVOTIONAL). We might note the reaction of the people, who valued their pigs more than the tormented man's sanity (vv. 11-17). We might notice the witness of a man who had personal experience of Christ's power to change lives (vv. 19-20). Yet the main point of the story here is to affirm Jesus' power over all supernatural forces that are ranged against humankind.

As we commit ourselves to live as citizens of His kingdom, we can be confident of His protection.

"Power had gone out from Him" Mark 5:21-34. As Jesus was on the way to the home of a dying girl, He was touched by a woman with chronic bleeding. The search for a cure had cost her all she had, and drained her of hope. But when she heard about Jesus, she became convinced that if she could only touch His clothing she would be healed. And she was.

Again Mark selected a particular miracle to drive home his point. Christ, Ruler of the secret kingdom of God, has power over nature, over demonic powers, and over every illness. Knowing Jesus has such power gives us confidence to live by His Word, even if He should not choose to heal every believers' disease now.

"Little girl, I say to you, get up!" Mark 5:35-43 The final miracle demonstrated Christ's power over death itself. In a quiet display of His ultimate authority in the privacy of an inside room, Christ raised a dead girl to life again. Even man's greatest enemy must bow to the power of Jesus Christ.

In reporting these miracles, Mark did not intend us to expect repeats today. The present kingdom of God has a "secret," inner expression. One day, when Jesus comes again, all these powers will be openly displayed. Then, suffering and death will be no more. Until then, we live by faith in a King who can but who has chosen not to display His power openly. And yet faith has its rewards even now. In the fruit God's Word produces in us, the kingdom of Jesus flourishes today.

▶ DEVOTIONAL
It Goes with the Territory (Mark 5:1-20)

When Richard Rameirez, the Satan-worshiping "Night Stalker," and killer of at least 13 persons, was led away after hearing the jury's "guilty" verdict, he remarked, "Big deal. It goes with the territory."

That's what we note in the first five verses of Mark 5. Here is a demon-possessed man, living among the tombs and wandering the hills, night and day crying out and cutting himself with stones. Here is a tormented man, without friends and without hope. And Mark wants us to understand that this too "goes with the territory." Anyone in Satan's grip is sure not only to hurt others, but to suffer himself!

But then Jesus appeared, and released the demon-possessed man from his supernatural tormentors. And suddenly we find him, well again, clothed, and in his right mind (v. 15). What a contrast! And what a change, as the man returned to his home, joyously telling everyone how much the Lord had done for him.

Perhaps this is our key to understanding the real power of Jesus' present kingdom. God is doing something more important than marshalling armies, rebuilding a temple, and establishing His authority openly on this earth. He is working in the hearts and lives of those wandering in darkness, and releasing them from every torment that "goes with the territory" Satan controls.

For you and me, citizens of Jesus' kingdom who have sworn allegiance to Him, there is the experience of the grace of God that frees us to love others, and to serve a Lord who is committed to do us good.

Personal Application
Look for evidence of God's kingdom within your life and the lives of others.

Quotable
"And if thou be not in the kingdom of Christ, it is certain that thou belongest to the kingdom of Satan, which is this evil world."—Martin Luther

AUGUST 1 *Reading 213*
TRANSITION EVENTS
Mark 6–7

"They ran throughout that whole region and carried the sick on mats to wherever they heard He was" (Mark 6:55).

Now it was time for ordinary people, kings, and the religious elite all to make up their minds about who Jesus is.

Overview
As Jesus' ministry in Galilee drew to a close, Christ was resented in Nazareth (6:1-6). Though He gave power to His disciples (vv. 7-13), ordinary people still viewed Him as no more than a prophet (vv. 14-15), while Herod decided He was John the Baptist come back from the dead (vv. 16-29). Jesus displayed His power by feeding the 5,000 (vv. 30-44), walking on water (vv. 45-52), and healing (vv. 53-56). Jesus confronted the elite of Israel (7:1-23), and foreshadowed the universal Gospel by healing Gentiles who believed in Him (vv. 24-37).

Understanding the Text
"Isn't this Mary's Son and the Brother of James, Joses, Judas and Simon?" Mark 6:1-6 What a reminder of the secret nature of Jesus' present kingdom. Even Jesus went unrecognized and resented by the people in His hometown. They'd known Him all His life, perhaps had furniture He had shaped in their homes. All Galilee might be agog, talking excitedly about Jesus. But the folks at home weren't impressed. No sir! What's more, they resented Jesus: thought He was putting on airs, getting above Himself.

Don't be surprised if it's like this with you sometimes. You talk about your relationship with God in Jesus, and what He's done for you. And the people who know you best are the most likely to scoff or show resentment. When this happens, what we have to remember is that Christ does rule. Later Jesus' mother and brothers did come to faith (cf. Acts 1:14). If you live a Christlike life, and continue to share simply when the opportunity arises, the Lord can and will break down this most formidable barrier to belief: familiarity.

"He sent them out . . . and gave them authority" Mark 6:7-13. The unbelief of the folks at home did not limit Christ's power. It merely limited the ability of those who would not believe to experience it! How do we know? Shortly after, Jesus gave His disciples authority over evil spirits, and sent them out to preach. And they successfully exercised that power.

We might become sidetracked here by a debate over whether or not believers today can have authority over sickness and demons. But what's important is that Jesus' power is so great that it can be expressed through others, as well as in person.

You and I can minister to others, not because we have some special strength or ability, or even some special spiritual gift. You and I can minister because Jesus

Christ has chosen to work in and through those who believe in Him. The power to serve is His: the feet, hands, and mouth He uses belong to us.

If we surrender ourselves to Him, Christ will surely use us today to draw others into the hidden kingdom He rules.

"He is a prophet, like one of the prophets of long ago" Mark 6:14-15. Christ had ministered for many months, and perhaps even for years, in Galilee. Soon He would take His final journey up to Jerusalem to face crucifixion. It was appropriate at this time to ask what verdict concerning Jesus His fellow countrymen had reached.

The answer was disappointing. He was a prophet "like one of the prophets of long ago." For anyone else this would have been high praise. But not for Jesus, who was and is the Son of God. That verdict in fact constituted rejection both of Christ, and of the secret kingdom He offered. In each Gospel, this verdict marks a turning point. From this point on we see a shift in the emphasis of Jesus' message, and a growing emphasis on the Cross.

"John, the man I beheaded, has been raised from the dead" Mark 6:16-29. Herod Agrippa, the tetrarch of Galilee, is a fascinating model of a person whose hesitation pushes him over the edge of unbelief. Earlier Herod had arrested John but, in awe of the prophet, had failed to execute him despite the urging of his wife, Herodias. She hated John, who preached against her marriage on the grounds that Herodias had been married to Herod's half-brother, and the relationship was thus incestuous. At the time there were also political reasons why Herod wanted to be rid of John.

Yet Herod couldn't bring himself to kill John. He was both fascinated and repelled by John's teaching, and often heard him speak.

What doomed Herod was hesitation. He waited till, trapped by circumstances, he permitted John's execution.

In looking at the story in Matthew's Gospel, I suggested Herod was a victim of peer pressure. Here I suggest another factor was crucial: hesitation. If Herod had only made up his mind before he was trapped by circumstances. If only he had decided to repent, to divorce Herodias, and to release John. But he waited till it was too late.

Living in Jesus' kingdom calls for us to be decisive about moral issues. We must determine what is right, and do it. The longer a person waits to commit to what he or she knows is right, the greater the likelihood of a wrong choice.

"He gave thanks and broke the loaves" Mark 6:30-44. Here the familiar story has a special poignancy. Jesus had been rejected at home, misunderstood by His nation, and become the object of a king's superstitious dread. Yet Jesus continued to act with compassion, and displayed His power in the feeding of the 5,000.

But note. "Looking up to heaven" reminds us that no matter how misunderstood on earth, Jesus maintained a secure relationship with God the Father. No doubts, and no rejection by mere men could affect the channel through which Christ's power flowed.

It's the same with us. We may be misunderstood. We may be rejected by those closest to us. But as long as we maintain an intimate relationship with God, we have a source of unfailing strength. Christ's kingdom may be invisible. But it is very real. The power of the King still flows to and through His disciples today.

"Their hearts were hardened" Mark 6:45-56. The next miracle was witnessed only by Jesus' disciples. Their response showed that even those closest to Christ did not fully grasp who He is, or His power.

Jesus walked on the water, stilled the storm, and the next day went on healing all those in need. In these acts He not only showed Himself to be the Son of God, but also revealed how deeply God cares for man.

If you and I are to experience the fullness of life in Jesus' present, invisible kingdom, we need to remember: Jesus can; and Jesus cares. If we let our hearts become hardened through unbelief, we will miss the wonders that God has for us to experience here and now.

"The Pharisees and some of the teachers of the Law" Mark 7:1-23. The religious leaders of the Jews gathered, and again we sense how insensitive they were to the things

that concerned Jesus. They wanted to talk about ritual hand-washing. Jesus is dedicated to a heart relationship with the Lord (vv. 3-7). They were concerned with externals; Jesus was committed to cleansing the inner man (vv. 8-23).

Inward and outward religion comes into conflict whenever we place more stress on behavior than motive, and on symbolic actions than interpersonal relationships. Sunday go-to-meeting faces and well-pressed clothes have never been an adequate measure of participation in Christ's secret kingdom. (See DEVOTIONAL.)

"The woman was a Greek, born in Syrian Phoenicia" Mark 7:24-30. Up to this point Jesus' ministry has been concentrated in Jewish areas around Galilee. Chapters 6 and 7 report the failure of God's people to acknowledge Jesus as God's Son. His neighbors resented Him (6:1-8), the crowds saw Him only as a prophet (vv. 14-15), and Herod superstitiously thought Him John the Baptist back from the dead (v. 16). Even His disciples were hardened, failing to grasp the full extent of His power (vv. 51-52), while the Pharisees could think only of their rules and traditions.

So here Mark introduced a story about a Gentile woman who foreshadowed the future. God's Old Testament people had not welcomed the Son of God? Then the Gentiles will! God's covenant people must be approached first, but there is plenty on the table of His grace for all.

"He has done everything well" Mark 7:31-37. Mark's note on location places this event also in Gentile territory, without identifying the deaf and dumb man's nationality.

This too may be foreshadowing, for in the church founded on Christ's deity, Jew and Gentile would both find a place, and assume a new identity: Christian.

The last verse sums up not only this healing but all of Jesus' ministry to date. "He has done everything well." If some do not believe, it is because they, not Christ, are flawed.

▶ DEVOTIONAL
What's Wrong with Tradition? (Mark 7:1-23)

We all have our traditions. My wife puts up the Christmas tree December 1. It comes down on January 1. This is a simple, harmless tradition she has no intention of imposing on anyone else. But other kinds of traditions aren't quite so harmless.

Sue felt distinctly put down when told at a potluck by the pastor-emeritus of the church we attend, "We go around the table this way, not that!" It bothered him terribly that she didn't do what had been done there for years. And it bothered her that she was expected to be like everyone else!

Traditions often are experienced like this. They're not only the comfortable "way we do things," but are also a demand that others do it our way too. And in religion, tradition is especially unhealthy. Why? The passage suggests four reasons.

Our traditions can become a test of acceptability (vv. 1-5). Whenever we find ourselves measuring others by certain behaviors, rather than taking time to know them as persons, we've fallen victim to this danger.

Traditions can become a measure of spirituality if we're not careful (vv. 6-7). Whenever we're more concerned with fitting in with others' expectations than with pleasing God, we've fallen victim to a second danger.

Traditions can be used to set aside the commands of God (vv. 8-13). Whenever our group's interpretation of the Bible is more important to us than Scripture itself, we've fallen victim to this danger.

Tradition can shift our emphasis from personal piety and holiness to externals. Whenever we are more concerned with looking righteous than with being righteous, we have fallen victim to perhaps the most serious danger of tradition.

What does Jesus call for in place of tradition? He expects a radical reorientation of our perspective, from a concern with how things look, to a concern for what they really are.

If your heart for God, and my heart for God, are more important to us than either of our traditions, then and only then will we be free.

Personal Application

Let nothing distract your focus from your own heart, and the heart of others.

Quotable
"The Spirit of God is always the spirit of liberty; the spirit that is not of God is the spirit of bondage, the spirit of oppression and depression. The Spirit of God convicts vividly and tensely, but He is always the Spirit of liberty. God who made the birds never made birdcages; it is men who make birdcages, and after a while we become cramped and can do nothing but chirp and stand on one leg. When we get out into God's great free life, we discover that that is the way God means us to live 'the glorious liberty of the children of God.' "—Oswald Chambers

AUGUST 2 *Reading 214*
DISCIPLESHIP
Mark 8–9

"Jesus took Peter, James and John with Him and led them up a high mountain, where they were all alone. There He was transfigured before them" (Mark 9:2).

Disciples who remain committed to Jesus despite opposition may well suffer. But we are also privileged to witness expressions of Christ's power.

Overview
Now feeding the 4,000 (8:1-9), conflict with the Pharisees (vv. 10-21), and another healing (vv. 22-26) helped open the disciples' spiritual eyes to a deeper understanding of who Christ is (vv. 27-30). Jesus explained the requirements of discipleship (v. 31–9:1) and displayed His glory on the Mount of Transfiguration (vv. 2-13). In the valley Jesus cast out a demon (vv. 14-29), spoke of His coming death (vv. 30-32), and explained more of what it means to follow Him (vv. 33-50).

Understanding the Text
"The disciples picked up seven basketsful" Mark 8:1-13. Sometimes Christ's wonders have more impact on His followers than on outsiders. That is surely the case here. The 4,000 ate—and were satisfied. It was enough to be fed. But later the disciples picked up the leftovers, and gathered "seven basketfuls." Here the "basket" is a *spyris,* not as in the earlier feeding of the 5,000, a *kophinos.* The former is a very large basket: large enough to contain Paul as he was let down over the city walls of Damascus (Acts 9:25). The latter is like our "lunch bucket." What Jesus intended in this miracle was not only to show compassion for hungry crowds, but to build faith in His followers! What a response to the disciples' earlier complaint, "Where in this remote place can anyone get enough bread to feed them?" (v. 4)

At times even those of us most familiar with Christ will forget just how great His power is. And then, in grace, the Lord will act and remind us. When that happens let's not be satisfied, as the crowds were, with His meeting of the immediate need. Let's share the wonder the disciples must have felt as they gathered seven great baskets of leftovers that testified to the overflowing abundance of His grace and power.

"The yeast of the Pharisees and that of Herod" Mark 8:11-21. The Gospels describe Jesus' miracles as *dynameis,* "mighty acts." What the Pharisees now demanded were *semeia,* "signs" from heaven. These men who had refused to believe despite all Christ had done on earth insisted that God in heaven perform some obvious supernatural act to authenticate Jesus' claims.

Jesus' sigh expressed grief and disappointment at their unbelief. And later He warned His disciples against their "yeast." Here "yeast" is their dangerous and doubting attitude, which keeps asking for more and greater miracles as proof of Christ's deity and powers. We too need to be wary, for our life in Christ is to be lived by faith.

Christ continues to perform His "mighty acts" in our lives, as He transforms our hearts and relationships. Only unbelief can lie behind demands for "signs from heaven" as further proof of His love.

"When He had spit on the man's eyes and put

His hands on them" Mark 8:22-26. This is a unique story, not only in that Jesus adopted an unusual method of healing, but in that Jesus put His hands on the man twice while restoring his sight. Calvin commented, "He did so most probably for the purpose of proving, in the case of this man, that He had full liberty as to His method of proceeding, and was not restricted to a fixed rule."

This is a healthy reminder. God doesn't have to work in any set pattern, but is free to express His grace however He will.

Yet there seems to be more to Mark's placement of this story here. Just as the physical eyes of the blind man were opened gradually, and his first glimpses of the world were distorted, so the spiritual eyes of Jesus' disciples were opened gradually. In the events that follow we find their vision—and ours—becoming clearer still.

"Who do you say I am?" Mark 8:27-30 The crucial question is still the same today. What other people think and say about Jesus does not count. When God asks, "But what about you?" we must give the answer Peter blurted out. "You are the Christ." You are the Son of God.

"Peter took Him aside and began to rebuke Him" Mark 8:31-33. What an example of blurred vision! Peter recognized Jesus as the Christ, but when Jesus began to speak of suffering and death, Peter objected loudly!

Two things are important here. First, suffering was not inappropriate to the role of Christ—and it's not inappropriate for the Christian. If the Son of God suffered, we can expect God's other children to experience suffering too. Only a person with blurred spiritual vision could look at our suffering Saviour, and then expect the Christian life to be all roses and no thorns.

Second, to acknowledge Jesus as the Christ implies affirming Him as Lord. If Jesus is the Son of God, His will rather than ours must rule. Peter was completely out of line objecting to God's will for Jesus, even as at times we are out of line when we object to God's will for us!

We need clear spiritual vision. We need to get beyond the stage of seeing with distorted spiritual eyes.

"If anyone would come after Me" Mark 8:34-38. What are the requirements of discipleship? Stop making "self" the object of your life and actions, and instead choose to orient your life to God (v. 34). Surrender yourself, lose your life in service to Christ, and discover in serving the new and better person you will become (vv. 35-38). And take your stand daily on Jesus Christ and His words (v. 38).

"There He was transfigured before them" Mark 9:1-8. Earlier Jesus warned His disciples against the attitude of the Pharisees, who demanded a "sign from heaven." The believer is to live by faith, not propped up by a series of supernatural events.

But here we're reminded that sometimes some of us are given signs from heaven, not as aids to faith but as gifts of God's amazing grace.

Note that only three of the Twelve accompanied Jesus up to the Mount of Transfiguration. Not everyone experiences miracles. Yet even as here on earth Jesus was "transfigured before them," so God can and sometimes does perform wonders here today.

"Why couldn't we drive it out?" Mark 9:14-29 Mark's report of this incident is longer than either Matthew's or Luke's. It clearly depicts Christ's frustration with His disciples (v. 19), and the desperation of the father who believed, but doubted at the same time (v. 24).

I suspect that we are often like both father and disciples. We believe, but yet doubt. We act in Jesus' name, yet at times fail completely.

When the disciples asked why they had failed Jesus said, "This kind can come out only by prayer" (v. 29). Yet when Christ arrived He had not prayed, but said, "I command you, come out of him and never enter him again" (v. 25). Why then prayer?

I suspect because prayer serves to remind us of who God is, and our dependence on Him. "Why couldn't we cast him out?" the disciples had asked. But isn't any ministry performed by God through us, and not by us ourselves? When we pray we're reminded of who God is, and our faith is increased. Prayer is an antidote to unbelief, because it shifts our focus from what we can or cannot do to the Lord, who can do all things.

▶ DEVOTIONAL
Beneath the Cross
(Mark 9:30-50)

Easily confused? You bet! Jesus' disciples were. When Jesus told of His coming suffering and death, they just couldn't get it through their heads (vv. 30-32). The Christ? Suffer? But, Christ was destined to rule!

Only later, after the Resurrection, did Jesus' disciples begin to see that there's no real conflict between suffering and glory. That the Cross was a highway leading to an empty tomb. And the crown of thorns foreshadowed a crown of glory.

Sometimes we're confused too about the Christian life. We can't see how suffering fits. Doesn't God love us? Doesn't He want the best for us? And, if anyone suggests that suffering is best, for now, we may very well shake our heads and walk away.

Unless we take passages like Mark 9 more seriously. Here Jesus reminds us of the way of the disciple. A way that involves suffering, and the adoption of attitudes that seem foolish to selfish humankind. To become great, we become servants (vv. 33-35). To stand tall, we stoop to welcome a child (vv. 36-37). To protect truth, we give others the freedom to speak and serve as they wish (vv. 38-41). To experience God's kingdom now we dedicate ourselves to guard others from sin, even at the cost of foot or hand or eye (vv. 42-48). To worship we accept suffering (v. 49). To keep from becoming worthless to God, we nurture a spirit of self-sacrifice and devotion to God (v. 50). And, in living this kind of life, we expose ourselves to suffering, even as Jesus did when He chose the way of the Cross.

That's another reason to sit, from time to time, beneath the cross of Jesus. Not only to remind ourselves that Christ died for us. To keep from being confused. To remember that there is still no conflict of suffering with glory; that our highway to heaven may lead through valleys of pain.

Personal Application

Consider the Cross of Jesus, and remember all that it means for you and me.

Quotable

"Why should I start at the plough of my Lord, that maketh deep furrows on my soul? He is no idle husbandman, He purposeth a crop."—Samuel Rutherford

AUGUST 3 *Reading 215*
TO JERUSALEM
Mark 10–11

> *"Blessed is the coming kingdom of our father David!" (Mark 11:10)*

Christ was acclaimed entering Jerusalem. But many incidents revealed He was not esteemed for Himself.

Overview

Persistent unbelief is illustrated by the Pharisees (10:1-12) and a wealthy young man (vv. 17-31), whom Mark contrasted with little children (vv. 13-16). Jesus' prediction of His death (vv. 32-34) was ignored by His ambitious disciples (vv. 35-45), who had to be shown the nature of servanthood (vv. 46-52). Jesus was enthusiastically welcomed in Jerusalem (11:1-11), drove merchants from the temple (vv. 12-19), and on the way out of the city commented on the power of prayer (vv. 20-26). The next day He refused to explain His authority to hostile leaders (vv. 27-33).

Understanding the Text

"Some Pharisees came and tested Him" Mark 10:1-12. The intention of "testing," or better yet, "trapping" Jesus, reveals the continued hostility and unbelief of the religious elite. For comments on Jesus' teaching on divorce and remarriage, see Matthew 19:1-12, Reading 206.

"The kingdom of God belongs to such as these" Mark 10:13-18. Mark's report of this incident is especially powerful. He alone tells us that Jesus was "indignant" when His disciples pushed children away. He also

used an intense word to describe Christ's blessing of the children: *katalogein,* "to bless fervently."

Mark placed the incident here to contrast the dependence and receptivity of little children with the harsh legalism of the Pharisees, and the works-righteousness of the young man whose story is told next. Anyone who hopes to enter Christ's kingdom can do nothing but receive it as a gift, depending not on his own works, but on God alone.

At the same time, Jesus' indignation and His fervency in blessing the children remind us how important the young are to God. This is something I must constantly remind myself of. All too often I get caught up in work and ministry, and forget that the interests of little ones are vital to them—and that they are vital to God and to me.

Jesus gladly took time to bless little ones fervently. I need to make children one of my priorities too.

"What must I do to inherit eternal life?" Mark 10:17-23 Unlike little children, the wealthy young man was unwilling to receive or to be dependent. He wanted to "do" in order to earn a place in God's kingdom, and he relied on his wealth to help him.

No wonder it's so hard for people to enter and to live in Christ's kingdom. In our relationship with God we truly must abandon all that we've learned to rely on as adults, and return to childhood. Not earning but receiving is the key to entry. Not self-reliance but conscious dependence is the key to success. (See DEVOTIONAL.)

"We have left everything to follow You" Mark 10:28-31. What do we gain if we return to childhood and abandon all to depend completely on Jesus? The disciples asked, and Christ identified three things: (1) Here and now, a hundredfold more! In Christ our closest relationships are multiplied. We become members of a family of brothers and sisters, many of whom become closer than blood relatives. (2) Persecution. Like Christ, we too will suffer. (3) But suffering gives birth to glory, and in the age to come we will share with Jesus the full joy of eternal life.

I suppose each of us at times asks, "What will I get for what I must give up?" Jesus' answer is, "Gold in exchange for clay. Eternal life in exchange for a few fleeting years of selfish pleasure." We gain what we can never lose in exchange for what we could never keep.

"He took the Twelve aside and told them what was going to happen" Mark 10:32-34. This is the third time Jesus told the Twelve about His coming death (cf. 8:31; 9:31). Here the prediction was more detailed. But there's no indication that the disciples understood—or wanted to hear.

I once visited a friend whose brother, a missionary aviation fellowship pilot, had just been killed. I remember how uncomfortable I was. I wanted to help, but I didn't really know how, or what to say. Driven by my own discomfort, I must have seemed terribly unsupportive to my friend.

Jesus' words were intended to prepare the disciples for what was about to happen. Yet they were also an expression of His human need. We sense that need later when, in Gethsemane, He asked, "Could you not keep watch for one hour?" Even Jesus needed supportive and caring friends when He faced His cross.

Let's learn from the disciples' silence how not to listen to others. We need to set aside any discomfort we may feel, and listen carefully. We need to reach out a loving hand, to touch, to hug, and thus show that no one in Jesus' family need bear his or her cross alone.

"Let one of us sit at Your right and the other at Your left in Your glory" Mark 10:35-45. It's clear from Mark's use of "then" that this incident followed immediately after Jesus' prediction of His death. Something else is clear too. The disciples didn't really "hear" Jesus—because their thoughts were filled with plans for their own future.

James and John dreamed of high position in Christ's coming kingdom, and the others squabbled with them when they found out. They didn't hear Jesus because their thoughts were too filled with themselves.

All too often this is what happens to us. We're so busy with our own thoughts and dreams that we simply don't listen or care. It's no wonder Jesus went on to explain to His disciples that greatness in His kingdom isn't found in high position, but in servanthood. If you and I want to become truly great, we set aside thoughts of ourselves, and think first of others. "For even the Son of man did not come to be served, but to serve, and to give His life as a ransom for many" (v. 45).

"Have mercy on me!" Mark 10:46-52 In a simple act Jesus demonstrated the greatness that He taught. Despite the immediate prospect of His own suffering, He stopped to help a blind man the crowds uncaringly tried to quiet. When you and I learn to think of others despite our own hurts and concerns, we will be great indeed. For we will follow the example of our Lord.

"Jesus entered the temple" Mark 11:12-19. Both fig tree and temple symbolized first-century Judaism. The tree appeared to flourish, but had no fruit (vv. 12-14). The temple was spectacular, but was filled with avarice rather than prayer (vv. 15-17). When the hollowness of the religion was exposed, the religious leaders "began looking for a way to kill [Jesus]."

It is not anti-Semitic to be honest about the failures of first-century institutionalized religion. And it is not anti-Christian to be honest about the frequent fruitlessness of many churches today. Let's not measure spiritual reality by either flourishing activity, or by great buildings. Let's return to kingdom principles: dependence on Jesus, and servanthood toward all.

"Whatever you ask for in prayer" Mark 11:20-25. Fig trees do wither, because they are empty of spiritual power. Where do we find the power to follow kingdom principles? Jesus pointed His disciples to prayer.

But He also reminded them that faith in God has an essential corollary—a servant's heart. We must maintain both our dependence on God and our fellowship with others in His family. It is self-deceit to suppose that we have a healthy relationship with God if we harbor animosity rather than forgive.

"By what authority?" Mark 11:27-33 The ruling council or chief priests, sages, and lay elders claimed to speak with Moses' own authority (cf. Matt. 23:2). Yet when challenged by Christ to make an authoritative statement about John the Baptist, they held back. If they had possessed true spiritual authority, they would have spoken the truth—and lived it.

Jesus had no need to explain the source of His authority. His miracles, His teaching, His very lifestyle, all witnessed to the fact that He came from God.

It's to be like this with us too. Spiritual authority isn't rooted in ecclesiastical position, but in a relationship with God expressed in an authentic servant's life.

How could the crowds who cheered Jesus when He entered Jerusalem have cried for His death just three days later? They cried, "Blessed is the coming kingdom of our father David!" They wanted not the King, but the earthly glory they thought He would bring them. We need to contemplate Christ on the donkey, and welcome Him for who He is, not for what He might bring us (Mark 11:1-11).

▶ DEVOTIONAL
What's Wrong with Wealth? (Mark 10:17-31)

The disciples were shocked when Jesus spoke of wealth as a hindrance to entering His kingdom. In the first century the wealthy man was considered blessed. Only the wealthy would have time to study the Torah, the written and oral Word of God. Only the wealthy would have resources needed to do the good deeds that characterized the righteous.

This in part explains the shock of the young man who refused to abandon his wealth to follow Jesus. He depended on his money to help him find his way to eternal life. He was totally unwilling to abandon it and depend instead on Christ.

I suppose there is nothing really wrong with wealth. I have one or two Christian friends who are millionaires, and committed Christians too. But most of us aren't equipped to handle great amounts of cash and maintain our perspective. All too many of us, like the rich young man who came to Jesus, would discover that our money pulled against complete dependence on God, rather than encouraged it. And that the freedom to do anything and go anywhere that money brings, pulled against a disciplined search for God's will each day.

Sometimes I think I'd enjoy trying to be godly despite great wealth. I even suspect I might be able to use wealth wisely. But when I check my bank balance, I'm confronted with the fact that God doesn't trust me with any extra at all!

Then, if I remember, I think of the wealthy young ruler, and I thank God for this special expression of His grace. He has preserved me from a temptation that has caused many to fall.

Personal Application

Thank God for what He has chosen not to give you, as well as for what He provides.

Quotable

"Every time Jesus offers an opinion about riches, it is negative. Every time He teaches about the use of wealth, He counsels disciples to give it away. For people who take the Bible seriously, and who take Jesus most seriously of all, how seriously should we respond to these teachings about wealth? It may be time for more believers to consider the most obvious and least comfortable option: to obey them—to conform our lives to the commands of our Lord rather than the other way around."—Thomas Schmidt

AUGUST 4 *Reading 216*
LAST-WEEK TEACHINGS
Mark 12–13

> *"As He taught, Jesus said, 'Watch out for the teachers of the Law. . . . They devour widows' houses and for a show make lengthy prayers. Such men will be punished most severely' " (Mark 12:38-40).*

Confrontation is sometimes necessary. And at such times often blunt speech is required.

Overview

In the temple area, Jesus' Parable of the Tenants exposed the religious elite (12:1-12), who then failed to trap Him with questions about taxes (vv. 13-17) and the resurrection (vv. 18-27). Jesus named the greatest commandment (vv. 28-34), and to the delight of the crowd silenced His attackers (vv. 35-37). A poor widow's gift illustrated true piety (vv. 38-44). As Jesus left the temple, He predicted its fall and spoke of the end of the age (13:1-37).

Understanding the Text

"What then will the owner of the vineyard do?" Mark 12:1-9 The thrust of the allegory was clear to leaders and people. Isaiah had spoken of Israel as God's vineyard, prepared just as in Jesus' description (cf. Isa. 5:1-7; Mark 12:1). The situation was also familiar. In the first century most of Judea's best land was owned by absentee landlords, who leased it to tenant farmers for a percentage of the crop. Much prime land was owned by Herod and his cronies. The fury of such people, should the tenants dare defraud them, could be easily imagined!

Jesus' story identified the current religious leaders as rebellious tenants, who wanted God's vineyard for themselves. They would soon kill the Son. But they would be punished when the owner returned. The leaders knew Jesus had "spoken the parable against them" (v. 12). They might have taken it as a warning, and repented. Instead they tried even harder to find a way to be rid of Jesus.

We need to see all Scripture's warnings in this light. They are both invitation to repentance, and a stimulus to further sin. How we respond determines whether a warning will bring life, or kill.

Let's not follow the example of the Pharisees and teachers of the Law. If we but heed Scripture's warnings, they become channels of overflowing love and grace.

"The stone the builders rejected" Mark 12:10-12. Here Jesus applied Psalm 118:22-23 to Himself. Though rejected by the "builders," He Himself is the "capstone" of God's building.

The Greek word may mean "foundation-stone," which anchors a building, or "keystone," which completes an arch or building. The implication is the same in either case. Jesus is the foundation on which our understanding of Scripture must be constructed. He is the One who enables us to fit together Old and New Testaments in a harmonious whole. No one who approaches Scripture without faith in Jesus as the Son of God can hope to grasp its message, or use it successfully to build his or her own spiritual life.

"Is it right to pay taxes to Caesar?" Mark 12:13-17 There's more than a touch of irony in this story. Many Pharisees were well-to-do, and the Herodians especially had profited greatly from Rome's domination of Judea. Neither group felt Rome's taxation as a particular burden. It was the common folk who suffered. Note too that when Jesus answered the question, He had to ask for a denarius. And "they brought the coin."

Jesus' answer has rightly been understood to call on believers to live as loyal subjects in earthly kingdoms (see Matt. 22, Reading 207). But the interplay also makes it clear that Christ's accusers had failed to give "to God what is God's."

We are to be good citizens of both kingdoms. But loyalty to God's kingdom must have priority.

"I am the God of Abraham" Mark 12:18-27. How completely can we trust Scripture? Here Jesus bases His whole argument on the tense of a verb! When God spoke to Moses He said, "I am the God of Abraham." He did not say, "I was the God of Abraham." If He had said "was" then God would have confirmed Abraham's death. Since the Lord said "am," He confirmed the fact that Abraham still lived! You and I can have total confidence in the trustworthiness of the Word of God. And we can find comfort in the knowledge that our loved ones are not lost, but alive with and in our God.

"Not far from the kingdom of God" Mark 12:28-34. What is the Old Testament really about? How can its message be summed up? This question concerned the sages of Judaism, who attempted to sum up the 365 negative and 248 positive statutes they identified in the Old Testament. Hillel, challenged by a Gentile to make him a proselyte by teaching the whole Law while the Gentile stood on one foot, said, "What you hate for yourself, do not do to your neighbor: this is the whole law, the rest is commentary; go and learn."

Both the question and the answer reflect a works-righteousness understanding of the Old Testament, as did the common viewpoint that love and sacrifice (interpersonal duty and ritual duty) were the twin pillars on Old Testament thought.

But when Jesus was asked to sum up the message of the Old Testament, His answer was, love God supremely, and your neighbor as yourself. And one of the teachers of the Law who heard Him agreed!

What a lesson for us. No, not a lesson on the primacy of love, but a reminder that there were godly, spiritually sensitive men in first-century Judaism who were "not far from the kingdom of God." It's an error to stereotype all members of any group on the basis of the actions of a visible few. Let's not characterize anyone by group membership, but let's seek to know persons as individuals.

We may be surprised to find what folks today are also not far from God's kingdom.

"How is it?" Mark 12:35-38 The great claim to spiritual superiority made by the

"teachers of the Law" was that they had mastered both Scripture and the complex mass of traditional interpretations that had grown up around it. Ordinary folk, who lacked the time and resources needed to be devoted to study, were contemptuously dismissed as *am ha eretz,* just "people of the land." It's no wonder then that the crowds "listened to [Jesus] with delight" as He raised a question that the experts could not, or dared not, answer.

Somehow most people recognize hypocrisy and shame when they see it. The person who is proud of his knowledge of Scripture, but fails to live a righteous and loving life, fools no one but himself.

It is far more important for you and me to live what we learn than to be masters of Bible trivia, or even to be theologians of note.

"Watch out for the teachers of the Law" Mark 12:38-44. Most preachers today tend to be relatively poor. In the first century, most "teachers of the Law" were well off. For instance, we know of one wealthy rabbi, who not only owned vast lands but also ran a shipping business, who after the fall of Jerusalem was regularly given the tithe to be set aside for the Levites by his neighbors. He didn't need the money. But it was considered a good deed in early Judaism to contribute to a person who spent his life in study.

Jesus warned against those teachers of the Law who paraded themselves openly, whose prayers were a pious show, and whose greed was so great they would "devour widow's houses"—take money from those who were proverbially needy. Such men, Jesus said, "will be punished most severely." For contrast Mark immediately reported an incident in which Jesus praised a woman who freely placed her last coins in the treasury.

What a study in values. The greedy rich man, who always wanted more, and the poor widow willing to give all. The "great man" viewed with respect by society, and the insignificant woman, held in high regard only by God.

While you and I may be neither rich nor poor, our choices are likely to be governed by the values expressed by one of these two. Which of the two will we choose to be most like?

▶ DEVOTIONAL
Troubled Times
(Mark 13)

Sue said it yesterday. "I think the Lord must be coming soon." She'd been reading in the paper about drugs, and about students bringing guns to school. Then she got a letter from a friend of ours who counsels sexually abused children and does therapy with the abusers. In the letter our friend mentioned two especially terrible situations. One involved two gay mothers, Satan worshipers, who prostitute their six children for crack cocaine!

That was the last gloomy straw for Sue. The Lord must be coming soon, she felt, with our society becoming so corrupt.

Mark 13, a complex apocalyptic passage that draws a grim portrait of the future, tells us to expect tragedy and suffering in this world. We're not to be alarmed by wars or natural disasters (vv. 7-8), or by the corruption of society (v. 12). It's not these things, but the fulfillment of an ancient prophecy by Daniel, that signifies the end is near (v. 14). And after that, things will get even worse (vv. 15-23).

There are, however, three things in Mark 13 intended to encourage us. First, Jesus forewarned us. He knew the terrible things that would happen. God isn't surprised, and He retains control of history. Second, we're encouraged by the promise of God's presence. Even when Christians are actively persecuted for their faith, the Holy Spirit remains with us (v. 11), and will deliver those who endure (v. 13). Third, and most important, Jesus will come again "with great power and glory" (v. 26). In the end, God will set things right. And we're told to wait, and watch (vv. 33-35).

So in a way, Sue rightly interpreted current events. Not that they are predictors of when Jesus will come back. But the horrors we experience remind us that we cannot look to this world for our future. We must look up. And watch.

Personal Application

"What I say to you, I say to everyone: 'Watch!' " (Mark 13:37)

Quotable

"The truth of the second coming of Christ transformed my whole idea of life; it broke the power of the world and its ambition over me, and filled my life with the most radiant optimism even under the most discouraging of circumstances."—R.A. Torrey

AUGUST 5 *Reading 217*
CRUCIFIXION EVE
Mark 14

"The hour has come. Look, the Son of man is betrayed into the hands of sinners" (Mark 14:41).

The events of the night before Jesus was crucified are detailed in each Gospel. However familiar, each retelling speaks powerfully to our hearts.

Overview
Jesus was anointed with expensive perfume in Bethany (14:1-11). He shared a final supper with His disciples in Jerusalem (vv. 12-26). Afterward Jesus predicted Peter's denial (vv. 27-31), and prayed at Gethsemane (vv. 32-42) where He was arrested (vv. 43-52) and taken before the Sanhedrin (vv. 53-65). In the yard outside, Peter denied his Lord (vv. 66-72).

Understanding the Text
"She did what she could" Mark 14:1-11. While Mark is the shortest of the Gospels, it often provides more graphic eyewitness details than the others. That's the case here. Mark alone reported that some (another Gospel says the disciples!) were "indignant" and almost abusive.

Yet the woman's gift was both an act of love and an act of faith. In a sense, it was also a confession of futility. "She poured perfume on My body beforehand to prepare for My burial." Nothing could alter the tragic course events must now take. But, in love and faith, she did what she could for Jesus.

Often we feel deeply frustrated by our inability to help those we love. If we only could, we'd change so much. The agony of a loved one's divorce. The uncertainty of his unemployment. The anxiety of her illness. Perhaps one reason the "beautiful thing" this woman did for Jesus is to be remembered is to encourage us. Heartbroken, she could not do more; she did what she could. And it was a "beautiful thing."

Let's do whatever we can for others. Out of love, and though hurting for them and hurting that it cannot be more. Jesus' defense of the woman of Bethany assures us that when we do what we can, we do enough.

"And found things just as Jesus had told them" Mark 14:12-16. Some commentators have seen in this story evidence that Jesus had already made arrangements for the Last Supper room with its owner. Certainly at this time of year Jerusalem was overcrowded; many pilgrims at major festivals were forced to camp outside the city walls.

What we should see, however, is another indication that God was superintending the events that led to Jesus' crucifixion. Simply because bad things happen to good people, we should never assume God has withdrawn His sovereign hand.

So we take comfort in the "chance" meeting of the disciples with a man (rather than the usual woman) carrying a jar of water, and the empty upper room available in his house. From it we learn that "chance" has no place in the believer's experience. What we experience is not the result of circumstance, but a wise and good distribution from our loving Father's hand.

"One by one they said to Him, 'Surely not I?' " Mark 14:17-21 I like the hesitancy and doubt expressed in the shaken disciples' question. Each seems to have looked deep within himself, and despite his commitment to Jesus, sensed weakness enough to make him wonder. Could it be me?

It's much safer for us to ask this question than to make the kind of bold assertion these same disciples did later that night. When Jesus predicted Peter's denial, that apostle confidently cried, "I will never disown You." And Mark adds, "All the others said the same thing."

When we sense our weakness, you and I cling to the Lord for strength. But when we are victims of foolish self-confidence, we venture out on our own, and surely fail.

"Jesus took bread . . . and gave it to His disciples" Mark 14:22-26. John's Gospel tells us that before this simple ceremony, Judas slipped out to complete arrangements to betray Jesus. The gift of bread and wine then, was consumed only by the disciples, even as the broken body and blood of Jesus are appropriated only by those who have faith in Him as Saviour.

In this sense our celebration of the Lord's Supper is more than showing forth "the Lord's death until He comes" (1 Cor. 11:26). It is also an affirmation of a shared discipleship: the statement by a family of believers that in a unique way we belong to each other, for Christ belongs to each one of us. Perhaps this is why there is no hint in Scripture that the Lord's Supper is ever to be celebrated alone. He offered it to all of them. The sacred meal is to be shared, in affirmation that Jesus Christ unites us to all who trust in Him.

"Stay here and keep watch" Mark 14:32-42. Again Mark expanded an account found also in other Gospels (see Matt. 26:36-46, Reading 209). Mark too recorded Jesus' anguished prayer. But Mark seemed to emphasize the drowsy disciples.

Yes, it was late at night. They were tired. But Jesus had shared His heart with them, expressing His deep distress. "My soul is overwhelmed," Jesus said, choosing powerful terms. "Overwhelmed with sorrow to the point of death." And then Jesus made a simple request: "Stay here and keep watch."

The word for "watch" is *gregoreite,* an imperative. This was no mere request. It was an urgent command. And yet despite Jesus' poignant appeal and urgent command, the exhausted disciples fell asleep. When Jesus returned He found them there, apparently lying on the ground (v. 42).

Jesus did say, "The spirit is willing, but the body is weak" (v. 38). But this was no excuse made for the dozing disciples. It was a warning. Knowing that the flesh was weak, the disciples should never have laid down in the first place! Moved by the urgency of Jesus' appeal, they should have stood to watch and pray.

What a word for us. We too are weak. When we hear Jesus speak so passionately of His desires for us, we, His modern disciples, need to recognize our weakness, and avoid situations in which we are likely to fall. If we lie down, sleep may overcome us. Therefore we must be even more careful to stand.

"He broke down and wept" Mark 14:66-72. If you don't feel sorry for Peter at this point, I suspect you may be the judgmental type. After all, Peter truly did love his Lord. And, of all the disciples, Peter was apparently the only one with the courage to track the mob, and try to find out what was happening to Him. Peter didn't set out to disown Jesus: not at all. And when Peter finally realized what he'd done in swearing, "I don't know this Man," he was heartbroken. As Jesus later showed, folks who are heartbroken over doing wrong are to be comforted, not condemned.

But if we don't learn from Peter's betrayal, you and I miss the larger point of his experience. It's better not to disown Jesus, and have nothing to bemoan, than to shed the most heartfelt of tears afterward.

A little faith, a little courage, and we will have nothing to regret.

▶ DEVOTIONAL
No Justice
(Mark 14:43-65)

Our nine-year-old has three words we hear quite often. "It isn't fair."

Not that she's right. It's just her way of saying she doesn't like something she's asked to do, or supposed to do.

But in a larger sense, she is right. Life in this world isn't fair. And we shouldn't expect it to be. Life certainly wasn't fair in Jesus' case.

One of his closest friends betrayed Him. Together the "chief priests, elders and teachers of the Law" constituted the Sanhedrin, the supreme religious and legal court in Judea. Yet those responsible to administer law plotted to seize Jesus secretly, and dragged Him off to an illegal nighttime trial (vv. 43, 53). The same court, responsible to hear evidence, sought to manufacture it (v. 55), and even recruited false testimony (vv. 56-59). When Jesus affirmed His deity He was immediately condemned, even though the Law then called for a full day to pass in a capital case between a finding of guilt and sentencing (v. 64). No, there was nothing fair at all in the trial or conviction of Jesus Christ.

He came, He healed, He taught of God the Father's love, and after the mockery of a trial His enemies took delight in spitting on Him and striking Him with their fists.

It's something to remember when we feel life is unfair to us. Life in this sin-warped world has never been fair, even to the Son of God. The Apostle Peter, remembering that night and the following day, wrote, "If you suffer for doing good and you endure it, this is commendable before God. To this you were called, because Christ suffered for you, leaving you an example, that you should follow in His steps" (1 Peter 2:20-21).

Personal Application

If you too suffer for doing good, it will not be fair. But it will be a blessing.

Quotable

"Suffering is a short pain and a long joy."—Henry Suso

AUGUST 6 *Reading 218*
HE IS RISEN
Mark 15–16

"You are looking for Jesus the Nazarene, who was crucified. He has risen! He is not here. See the place where they laid Him" (Mark 16:6).

The ultimate act which proves the deity of Jesus, and the efficacy of His death, is the Resurrection that Mark and each of the Gospel writers report.

Overview

Pilate ordered Jesus crucified to satisfy a rioting crowd (15:1-15). Roman soldiers mocked (vv. 16-20) and then crucified Jesus (vv. 21-32). His death was witnessed by many (vv. 33-41), and He was buried (vv. 42-47). But later when women came to further anoint the body, they discovered an angel by an empty tomb (16:1-8). Later the risen Christ appeared (vv. 9-14), and commissioned His disciples to preach "everywhere" (vv. 15-20).

Understanding the Text

"The chief priests accused Him of many things" Mark 15:1-5. In most things the Romans were content to let subject peoples govern themselves. In Judea and several other provinces, the Romans at this time reserved the power of capital punishment for themselves. This caused a problem for the chief priests. Claiming to be the Son of God might be blasphemy and a capital offense to the Jews. But not to the Romans! So while they condemned Jesus for one crime, they had to manipulate Pilate into condemning Him for some other crime! They desperately tried to invent a capital crime—and when they could not, they relied on the threat of a riot to force Pilate's hand.

History tells us Pilate had no regard for the Jews he governed. But why ask for trouble at a time when Jerusalem was filled with fanatically religious pilgrims from all over the world?

Pilate's concern was simple. Not, is it right? But, is it expedient? Will it get me off the hook now?

Whenever we face any moral choice we weigh factors very much like those Pilate considered. He knew the priests were simply envious of Jesus (v. 10). But it was easier to give in to them than to have to report another bloody riot in a city he governed.

If we are repelled by Pilate, the man who ordered the crucifixion of our Lord, let us abhor his way of reaching a decision just as much. Let's commit ourselves to do what is right, whatever the cost may be.

"Barabbas" Mark 15:6-9. Pilate tried to manipulate the crowd by offering them either Jesus, the Teacher and Healer, or Barabbas, an insurrectionist "who had commit-

ted murder." Apparently Pilate was shocked when the crowds chose Barabbas.

He shouldn't have been.

One section of an 800-page report on youth suicide published in January 1989 by the U.S. Department of Health and Human Services blames Christian churches that condemn homosexuality for the suicides of gay youth. The report says churches must "reassess homosexuality in a positive context" and must "demand" a sympathetic attitude toward homosexual behavior.

As always, the world cries for the release of Barabbas, and the crucifixion of Christ. Unless Christians raise their voices for the truth as loudly as others cry out for the lie, legislators will, like Pilate, act to satisfy the crowd. And Barabbas will run rampant in our land.

"The whole company of soldiers" Mark 15:16-20. The soldiers stationed in Palestine at this time were not elite Roman troops, but auxiliaries recruited in some distant province. Today you can see in Jerusalem game boards many believe were carved in the stone floor of the ancient Praetorium, perhaps by the soldiers who mocked Jesus.

The soldiers meant no particular harm. They were just bored. And Jesus was to die soon, anyway. Why not have a little fun?

It may be hard for us to realize now, but beating Jesus was to them nothing more than a little entertainment.

Even if Jesus had not been the Son of God—even if He had not been a caring Healer and Teacher—such brutality is horrible, and was horribly wrong. Anytime any human being is brutalized in any way, the one really mocked is not that individual, but the God whose image that individual shares.

I've just seen a letter by the chairman of the Mennen company, targeted for a boycott by a group reacting against programs that emphasize violence and vulgar sex. The chairman decrys the boycott, and suggests offended viewers "simply stop watching the offending programs." After all, it's just entertainment. If it doesn't appeal to you, why deprive those who do enjoy it?

I suppose a soldier in the company that mocked and beat Jesus might have said much the same thing. "That bothers you? Well, just don't look." Let the mocking and the beating go on. Just look the other way.

But we can't. Christ's own suffering at the soldiers' hands reminds us that brutality is always horribly wrong. No one who truly cares for God or man can look the other way.

"A certain man from Cyrene, Simon . . . was passing by on his way" Mark 15:21-32. I suspect that at first Simon was frustrated and angry when forced to carry Jesus' cross. What he carried was actually the patibulum, or crossbar, that weighed only 30 or 40 pounds. It was nothing for a strong man, though for Christ, weakened by loss of blood from His beatings, even that was more than He could carry.

The problem for Simon was that carrying the cross, an instrument of death, might make him ritually unclean, and unable to take part in the festival he'd traveled all the way from Cyrene, in North Africa, to share.

How angry we feel when our plans go awry, or something we've struggled hard to attain is suddenly and unexpectedly lost.

Yet later how thankful Simon must have been. For the mention of his two sons, included most likely because those sons were known by the Roman church for whom Mark wrote (cf. Rom. 16:13), suggests that later Simon became a Christian, and had the privilege of knowing that he alone, of all mankind, had ministered to Christ on the way to Calvary.

When our plans are interrupted, we may feel the frustration and anger that almost always come. But when these feelings do come, let's remember Simon. And let's look around for someone whose burden we may be able to lighten. Just for a moment for them now, perhaps. But later on, for us a source of glory.

"He has risen! He is not here" Mark 16:1-20. For all of Christ's promises, His followers did not expect the Resurrection. It was a long time before the angel's words sunk home. Even then Jesus had to appear to many before the little company of His followers began to believe.

But when at last the disciples realized that Jesus was raised from the dead—that He was Lord—they shouted out a message of Good News that not only traveled like wildfire across the ancient world, but has kept on burning brightly for nearly 2,000 years.

The last verses of Mark's Gospel (vv. 9-20) are disputed. They are not in the best manuscripts, and some are fearful of the miracle-working power Jesus promised the disciples, even though Acts testifies of many a miracle in the early church. In any case, the words ring true. Jesus did show Himself, risen, to many.

And the conviction that Jesus lives has propelled His church to go out, and to preach Him confidently. Everywhere.

▶ DEVOTIONAL
Why?
(Mark 15:21-41)

As Jesus died, He cried out, "My God, My God, why have You forsaken Me?" (v. 34)

These words are undoubtedly the most mysterious in Scripture. It's not that we can't grasp what they mean. Some, of course, say the words reflect the pained surprise of a God-intoxicated man, who finally realized that God would not lift Him from the cross. But the New Testament gives us a better explanation. Paul said that Jesus was made "sin for us" (2 Cor. 5:21). In a moment of time, the dammed-up flood of human sin was released, and cascaded with awful force upon and into the Son of God.

In that moment, when the Son of God became sin for us, the Father looked away. For the first and only time in all eternity, within the matrix of the one God, Father and Son were brutally torn apart.

So we do know what the words mean. What we can never understand is what the experience they represent meant to Father and to Son. We can never plumb the depths of Jesus' anguish, or sense the waves of pain that echoed out through all eternity. We can never envision the corrosive scars that sin engraved on sinlessness.

All we can do is stand at the foot of the cross, hear that cry, and realize that what Jesus did for us cost Him more than we can begin to imagine.

And say, "Thank You, Lord."

Personal Application

The best thanks we can give is not framed in words, but in our lives.

Quotable

Thou has given so much to me,
Give me one more thing—a grateful heart,
Not thankful when it pleases me,
As if Thy blessings had spare days,
But such a heart
Whose pulse may be Thy praise.
—George Herbert

The Variety Reading Plan continues with PROVERBS

Luke

INTRODUCTION

This Gospel and the Book of Acts were written by the same person. Early tradition and internal evidence identifies the author as Luke, a physician and companion of Paul on many missionary journeys (2 Tim. 4:11).

Luke was a careful historian, who interviewed eyewitnesses to establish the factual basis of Christian faith (Luke 1:1-4; cf. Acts 10:39). Yet Luke's history is anything but dull. This Gospel is rich with sympathetic sketches of the people Jesus met and ministered to. Among them are more women, more children, and more poor, than are mentioned in the other Gospels.

This rich and complex work presents Jesus not only as a historic and admirable Person, but also as the Saviour come to "seek and to save what was lost" (Luke 19:10). Other themes that are emphasized by Luke are Jesus' prayer life and the ministry of the Holy Spirit. Appropriately, expressions of joy and praise abound in this Gospel of the glory of God as disclosed in His Son (1:46-55; 2:13-14; 7:16; 10:21; 18:43; 19:37-38).

OUTLINE OF CONTENTS

READING GUIDE (16 Days)

If hurried, you may read only the "core passage" in your Bible and the Devotional in each chapter of this Commentary.

Reading	*Chapters*	*Core passage*
219	1	1:26-55
220	2–3	3:1-20
221	4–5	5
222	6	6:27-42
223	7–8	7:36-50
224	9	9:28-36
225	10	10:25-37
226	11	11:1-10
227	12	12:22-34
228	13–14	14:15-24
229	15	15:11-32
230	16–17	17:1-10
231	18–19	19:28-48
232	20–21	21:5-36
233	22–23	22:66–23:25
234	24	24:13-35

Luke

AUGUST 7 *Reading 219*

IN GOD'S TIME

Luke 1

> *"You will be with child and give birth to a Son, and you are to give Him the name Jesus. He will be great and will be called the Son of the Most High" (Luke 1:31-32).*

God's Spirit is active whenever the Lord is about to do a work in and for His people.

Overview

Luke stated his purpose (1:1-4), and immediately launched his history. He reported angelic visitations before the birth of John the Baptist (vv. 5-25) and Jesus (vv. 26-38). He told of Mary's visit to John's mother (vv. 39-45) and recorded her "Magnificat," a hymn of praise (vv. 46-56). When John was born (vv. 57-66) his father, Zechariah, predicted his ministry as forerunner of Messiah (vv. 67-80).

Understanding the Text

"Eyewitnesses and servants of the Word" Luke 1:1-4. Many believe that Luke had the opportunity to travel in Palestine and interview Mary, Elizabeth, Zechariah, and others during the two years Paul was kept under arrest at Caesarea (cf. Acts 24:27). Luke himself said he "carefully investigated everything from the beginning," indicating he searched out many sources and compared their accounts before writing.

Luke wasn't interested in passing on rumors or twice-told tales. He offered a factual, carefully researched study of Jesus' life. Why? In sending this account on to Theophilus, to whom Acts is also addressed, Luke said he had written "so that you may know the certainty of the things you have been taught." Jesus did live; Jesus did teach and perform miracles; Jesus did die and rise again. Just as this and the other Gospels say.

So travel with Luke. Meet the people who actually knew Jesus, and hear their testimony about Him. As you do, you realize anew that our faith is rooted in reality, not in myths or legends.

"But they had no children" Luke 1:5-7. The pain of childlessness was particularly acute in Israel, where this condition was also a source of shame. But note that the text stresses the upright character of both Zechariah the priest and his wife Elizabeth. Only then does it say, "But they had no children."

By linking their character with her condition, Luke makes it clear that Elizabeth's barrenness was not a consequence of sin. He also reassures us. We too can experience suffering that has no relationship to personal sins.

God, who had only good in mind for Zechariah and Elizabeth, and ultimately blessed them, will ultimately bless you and me too.

"He was chosen by lot" Luke 1:9-12. The priests were divided into 24 groups, each of which served for a week twice a year at the Jerusalem temple. But the privilege of burning incense inside the temple was distributed by lot, and a priest might have this honor only once during his lifetime! Now, in Zechariah's old age, at last the lot fell on him.

Again we see that God's blessings are often delayed. Though it's hard, you and I too need to wait patiently for God's timing.

"He will be filled with the Holy Spirit even from birth" Luke 1:13-17. The angel that appeared to Zechariah conveyed God's promise of a son, who would be the forerunner of the promised Messiah (v. 17). The account contains the first mention of the Holy Spirit, whose activity dominates this chapter (vv. 35, 41, 67). God had chosen that particular moment in history to personally intervene, to bring salvation to humankind.

Note too the reference in each context to joy. John, filled with the Spirit, "will be a joy and delight to you" (v. 14). Elizabeth and her babe, also filled with the Spirit, "leaped for joy" when Mary "the mother of my Lord" came to visit. Neither Mary nor Zechariah could contain the overflow of praise as the Spirit worked in their lives (vv. 46-55; 67-79).

As we open ourselves to God's Spirit and surrender to Him, we too will discover a joy that bubbles over into praise.

"Because you did not believe my words" Luke 1:18-25. Asking God for a special sign of confirmation can be right—or wrong. In this case Zechariah's request for a sign grew out of unbelief, and therefore was wrong. But notice that Zechariah's unbelief did not cause God to go back on His word.

Sometimes true believers like Zechariah have difficulty taking hold of the promises of the Lord. Don't let others frighten you with the teaching that unless you believe, you will never benefit from God's promises or receive His gifts. Many promises are unconditional, and depend on the faithfulness of God rather than on the strength of the believer's faith. When you come across a promise in God's Word, deliberate on how trustworthy God is, and simply thank Him for His gift.

"Nothing is impossible with God" Luke 1:26-38. How fascinating to see a young girl, certainly not out of her teens, unhesitatingly accept Gabriel's promise of a Virgin Birth. Zechariah, a godly and aged priest, had doubted the same angel's promise of a far less wonder!

Mary is certainly one of Scripture's most appealing characters. She reminds us that finding favor with God and having faith in God do not depend on age, theological training, or high religious position. The youngest and the simplest of us can have a vital faith in God and be loved deeply by Him (see DEVOTIONAL).

"What then is this child going to be?" Luke 1:57-66 The story of John's unusual birth was told and retold for years in the hill country of Judea, where he was born. While Jesus grew up in obscurity, John was the focus of attention through childhood (v. 80). A Nazarite from birth, John wore his hair long and avoided wine, setting him apart from others (v. 15). This and the unusual events surrounding John's birth may have been one means God used to stimulate the attitude of expectancy that did grip many in the first century, who were eagerly looking for the appearance of the Messiah.

God not only prepared a place for His Son; He prepared the people who would be invited to trust Him.

It's helpful for us to remember this when we have an opportunity to witness. God will have already been at work, preparing the other person for what we have to share.

"His father Zechariah . . . prophesied" Luke 1:67-79. Zechariah's utterance is a prophecy: a prediction made by inspiration of the Holy Spirit. As such it sums up the implications of all the events that Luke described in this first chapter.

There's a pattern here, with each statement of God's action matched by praise for its benefits. God has come and redeemed His people (v. 68). God has raised up One of David's house, able to save and so kept His promise to rescue from all enemies (vv. 69-71). God has performed a covenant-keeping act of mercy (vv. 72-73) and not only rescued us, but enabled us to serve Him "in holiness and righteousness . . . all our days" (vv. 74-75).

As for John, he would be a prophet (v. 76), who went before the Messiah to give people "the knowledge of salvation through the forgiveness of their sins" (v. 77).

Earlier Gabriel had told Zechariah that John "will be a joy and delight to you" (v. 14). I know that nearly every child is a joy to its parents. But what a special joy, to know that our children will serve the Lord.

There has been only one John the Baptist. But many a Christian parent has shared the joy of Zechariah, and seen children trust God, and then mature in faith.

▶DEVOTIONAL
The Mother of My Lord (Luke 1:26-55)

There's a vast difference between calling Mary the "mother of my Lord," as Elizabeth did, and the "mother of God." In Jesus, God took on human nature, and that human nature was derived from His mother, Mary. God the Son, like God the Father, eternally existing, had no mother. In no way can His divine nature be attributed to Mary, who was merely a creature like you and me.

It's this that Luke seemed to emphasize in his lovely portrait of Mary. She was a creature, like you and me. But her unusual response to God sets us an example.

Mary is an example of submission. "I am the Lord's servant," she said. "May it be to me as you have said" (v. 38). Mary knew full well what she risked as an unmarried woman: rejection by Joseph, the scorn and contempt of her neighbors. Yet Mary did not hesitate. She committed herself totally to the Lord's plan for her life.

Mary is an example of humility. Twice in that poem known as Mary's "Magnificat," she mentions her "humble state" (vv. 48, 52). Though to Mary alone was granted the privilege of being mother of the Messiah, the "One desired by women" (Dan. 11:37), she never became proud. Many men of Scripture through whom God worked succumbed later to pride. Mary, who had more to boast of than any of them, never lost her spirit of selfless dependence on God.

Mary is an example of thankfulness. She responded to God's touch with her whole soul and spirit, praising and exalting the Lord. She saw in God's work in her own life evidence of His love for all His people, and was thrilled with God's might, grace, mercy, and faithfulness.

Today we should honor Mary, and thank God for her simple trust. But the best way to honor Mary is not to pray to her. Rather the best way to honor Mary is to model our own relationship with God on the traits she displayed. The acts of recognition of which Mary would approve remain the same: to readily submit to our Lord, to nurture a humble spirit, and to express our appreciation to God in praise, as Mary did so long ago.

Personal Application

Don't pray to Mary. But do honor her, by following her example.

Quotable

"Humility is like a pair of scales; the lower one side falls, the higher rises the other. Let us humble ourselves like the blessed virgin and we shall be exalted."—John Vianney

---

AUGUST 8 *Reading 220*
JESUS AND JOHN
Luke 2–3

> *"John answered them all, 'I baptize you with water. But One more powerful than I will come, the thongs of whose sandals I am not worthy to untie' " (Luke 3:16).*

Luke's written history draws attention to the special signs associated with Jesus' birth and His announcement by John. Truly, Luke is telling us, Jesus is the Son of man and the Son of God.

Overview

Luke dated Jesus' birth (2:1-7), and told of another angelic visitation (vv. 8-20). When presented at the temple, the Infant Jesus was identified as the Messiah by Simeon (vv. 21-32) and the Prophetess Anna (vv. 33-40). At age 12 Jesus visited the temple and called it "My Father's house" (vv. 41-52). Luke then dated and described John's ministry (3:1-20), reported Jesus' baptism (vv. 21-22) and gave Jesus' genealogy (vv. 23-38).

Understanding the Text

"Everyone went to his own town to register" Luke 2:1-7. Luke was careful to pinpoint

the date. But the passage of time has caused the reference points to be lost today, and the specific time of Christ's birth and the census continues to be debated. There is no doubt, however, that Roman practice required citizens of provinces to be enrolled in one's original home. Why is this important?

Micah had predicted the Christ would be born in Bethlehem. God used a census, called for by a pagan Roman emperor, to arrange for Mary and Joseph to travel to Bethlehem at just the right time. How wonderful our God is. He so shapes history that the decree of Augustus became a means of accomplishing His own divine decree. There is no circumstance beyond the power of our God to control—or to overcome.

"There was no room for them" Luke 2:7. This poignant phrase has touched Christians ever since Luke penned it. It may not have been an "inn" that turned the couple away: the Greek word is also used of guest rooms in private homes. As the crowds returned to Bethlehem for the registration, space was finally found for Mary in what tradition says was a cave used to stable animals. There, we're told, the Christ was born.

Contemplating the humble surroundings and the audience of animals, one hymn writer penned:

Thou didst leave Thy throne and Thy kingly crown,
When Thou camest to earth for me.
But in Bethlehem's home there was found no room
For Thy holy nativity.
O come to my heart, Lord Jesus;
There is room in my heart for Thee.—
Emily E.S. Elliott

"Good news of great joy that will be for all the people" Luke 2:8-18. A great company of angels appeared to shepherds in fields near Bethlehem, praising God. The meaning of their words, once translated: "Peace on earth to men of good will," is better captured in the NIV: "Peace to men on whom His favor rests." Rather than limit the promise of joy to men of good will, the angelic shout proclaims a grace of God that is Good News and the promise of joy to all! In Christ the Saviour, man's deepest need is met. Through Christ, God's favor is poured out on all who will but believe.

"But Mary treasured up all these things and pondered them in her heart" Luke 2:19. Despite all Mary had been shown, she could hardly grasp the full implication of her calling to be Jesus' mother. The Greek text draws a fascinating comparison. While shepherds and people who heard their report were amazed and excited, Mary in contrast ("but") chose to hold these things in mind and meditate on them.

Mary's course is the better one. Some of us respond with great, immediate emotion to almost any message. But the feelings quickly wear off, and with them our interest in the message disappears. Mary did not overreact to the amazing events. She chose to think about them, meditating on them for a long time.

It's true that God touches our emotions as well as our minds. But, like Mary's, our faith must be rooted in contemplation of what God has done and its meaning for us, not in feelings primarily—or alone.

"Moved by the Spirit" Luke 2:21-40. Luke related two more incidents that serve to demonstrate Jesus' identity. On the 40th day after His birth Jesus' mother came to the temple to offer the sacrifice required of the poor for purification after childbirth (v. 24; cf. Lev. 12:8). There the Holy Spirit caused two aged saints to identify Jesus as the promised Messiah.

While the incidents serve as historical evidence, they surely had special meaning to Joseph and Mary. Very shortly after this, Matthew tells us, the couple was forced to take the Baby Jesus and flee the country. How much the memory of every unusual word about their Child would serve to encourage Joseph and Mary then.

Many of God's most unusual works are performed more for the comfort of His own than for some great theological purpose. Here God comforted four: Simeon and Anna near the end of their lives; Joseph and Mary at the beginning of a difficult period in theirs. The very personal purposes seen here encourage us to expect the Lord to meet our needs as well.

"I had to be in My Father's house" Luke 2:41-

52. At age 12, when custom dictated a boy became responsible to the Law, Jesus' parents took Him to the temple at Passover. We might focus on Jesus' conversation with the sages who, during festival periods, taught publicly in the temple courts. Most significant, however, is Luke's mention of Jesus' attitude toward God.

The "theantropic person," a name theologians give to the bonding of Deity and humanity in Jesus, remains a great mystery. The incarnate Christ clearly did not exercise all of His attributes as Deity. As Luke says, He "grew in wisdom" as well as in stature. Yet there seems no question that Jesus was conscious at an early age of His unique relationship with God His Father. Yet at all times Jesus lived His life as a godly human being, even as a Child being "obedient to" His parents.

We will never unravel the mystery, or be able to isolate God from man in Jesus. And frequently, as here, we will be reminded by Luke of the mystery as well as history of our faith.

"As He was praying, heaven was opened" Luke 3:21-22. Luke is the only one of the Gospel writers to tell us that Jesus was praying as He was baptized and as the Spirit descended from heaven. Only Luke tells us Christ also prayed before choosing the Twelve (6:12) and on the Mount of Transfiguration (9:29). Other instances of Jesus praying are found in 5:16; 9:18; and 11:1.

Jesus did live His life on earth as a human being, but as a perfect Man. Christ's reliance on prayer reminds us how much we need to communicate constantly with our Heavenly Father.

"The son, so it was thought, of Joseph" Luke 3:23-37. The phrase "about thirty" in that culture is an approximate number. Christ may have been in His mid-30s when He began to minister. But while age was dealt with loosely, genealogy in ancient Israel was a serious issue, and records were meticulously kept. Luke would have had access to records that contained the data found in this chapter.

Luke's genealogy differed from the genealogy in Matthew. The places where the lines diverge have been explained by assuming Matthew traced the legal line through Joseph, while Luke traced the actual line of Jesus through Mary. Other explanations of the differences have also been suggested. We do not have enough information to know which explanation is the actual source of the variance.

What is most significant, however, is that while Luke made it clear that Joseph was only assumed to be Jesus' father (v. 23), Luke traces His ancestry not to David or Abraham but to Adam. Luke wants us to understand that Jesus was a true human being; one of us, as well as the Son of God.

▶ DEVOTIONAL
Kill to Make Alive
(Luke 3:1-20)

John was not a smooth, comfortable preacher. He was blunt, confrontive. He pulled no punches, and preached a message of coming wrath. He was one of those "sin" preachers that folks today seem to find so distasteful.

John's warning not to rely on descent from Abraham (v. 8) struck at a root of first-century Jewish faith. As the chosen people, the seed of Abraham, and possessors of God's Law, many felt their standing with God was secure. John attacked this favored doctrine, and demanded repentance matched by moral reform.

Perhaps it's surprising, but people often hunger for just this kind of preaching. Deep down everyone senses he is not what he could or should be. There's a sense of relief when pretenses are stripped away, and we're forced not only to face our need—but are given hope that we may somehow become better than we are.

It's this that kept crowds coming to hear John, and wondering in their hearts if John might be the Christ. And it's this that makes modern John-like messages of repentance and "unquenchable fire" messages of "good news" too (vv. 17-18). The Bible's "condemning" word about sin isn't condemning at all! In demanding that we face our guilt, Scripture brings rather than annihilates hope. Only when we face guilt do we seek forgiveness, and find the new life in the Jesus that John preached.

So while you and I rightly major on the grace of God when sharing Jesus with others, it's not wrong now and then to stand, like John, and fearlessly rebuke both sin and sinner. The word that condemns is at times the door of hope.

Personal Application
Let God guide you when to share the Good News in the guise of bad.

Quotable
"Ministers who can preach the Gospel of Jesus in our kind of civilization without making anyone uncomfortable deserve an automobile for the difficult feat. And they need one to compensate them for the lack of spiritual vitality which makes performance of the feat possible."—Reinhold Niebuhr

AUGUST 9 *Reading 221*
A HEALING MINISTRY
Luke 4–5

> *"The people brought to Jesus all who had various kinds of sickness, and laying His hands on each one, He healed them" (Luke 4:40).*

In describing the beginning of Jesus' ministry, Luke focuses our attention on Christ's healing and forgiving power. What Jesus did as well as what He said shows Him to be the Son of God.

Overview
After being tempted by Satan (4:1-13) Jesus began a ministry in Galilee (vv. 14-15). Jesus chose Nazareth to identify Himself as the Messiah (vv. 16-21), where He was angrily rejected (vv. 22-30). Moving on, Jesus drove out evil spirits (vv. 31-37) and healed (vv. 38-44). He also called His first disciples, typified by Peter (5:1-11). Jesus proved He has the power to forgive sins (vv. 12-26) and transform character (vv. 27-32), yet His hearers asked only trivial questions (vv. 33-39).

Understanding the Text
"Jesus, full of the Holy Spirit . . . was led by the Spirit" Luke 4:1. These chapters too emphasize the ministry of the Holy Spirit in Jesus' life on earth. The Spirit led Christ into the desert to be tempted (v. 1). Jesus began His ministry in the power of the Spirit (vv. 14-15), and announced that the Spirit of the Lord was on Him to preach the Good News and proclaim the year of the Lord's favor. All that Jesus did was infused with the dynamic of God's Spirit.

But there is something else to note. We realize that the Spirit enables us to serve the Lord. But we seldom think of Him leading us into trying times. Here Luke reminds us that the Spirit may even lead us into temptation! When life brings difficulties and challenges, let's not doubt the Spirit's leading—or His power to make us victorious.

"He was tempted by the devil" Luke 4:2-13. Reading 197 (Matt. 4) discusses the specific temptations Jesus overcame. Here we need to distinguish between three types of temptation. (1) When Satan tempts, he lures a person into doing evil. Satan was successful in tempting Adam and Eve (Gen. 3), but failed completely in his attempt to tempt Christ. (2) When we tempt God (cf. Deut. 6:16), we act contrary to faith and demand He prove Himself to us. (3) When God places us in a difficult situation, He does so to test us—in order that we might pass the test rather than fail it! James 1:13 assures us that "God cannot be tempted by evil, nor does He tempt anyone." God has given us His Spirit in order that we, like Jesus, may be victorious whenever we are tempted to sin.

"He went up to Nazareth" Luke 4:14-21. Jesus chose the synagogue at Nazareth to publicly announce Himself as Israel's expected Messiah. He did this by reading part of a well-known messianic passage from Isaiah. Both what Jesus read and what He left out are important. He focused on the Spirit's empowering to preach the Good News, especially announcing to the poor, the prisoner, the blind, and the oppressed—all who had no hope except for hope in God—that the moment of God's favor had arrived. The coming of Jesus meant, and still means,

there is hope for the hopeless.

What Jesus left out was a phrase found in the original Isaiah text: "the day of vengeance of our God." Christ's first coming was to pour out God's favor on humankind. Only at His second coming will vengeance and wrath overflow.

In this announcement Jesus set the agenda for the church as well. We are called to announce the grace of God today—and to display it as Jesus did, in acts of love and kindness.

"All the people in the synagogue were furious when they heard this" Luke 4:20-29. Why did Jesus' neighbors react as they did? The phrase "spoke well of Him" is probably an inaccurate interpretation of *emaryroun auto,* "bore Him witness." The people were already disturbed, first that a neighbor's Son should dare to make such a claim (v. 22), and second that Jesus had left out the day of vengenance to speak only of grace (e.g., "gracious words"). When Christ went on to suggest that His message would prove a blessing to Gentiles (vv. 25-27) and not be reserved for Israel alone, the people became furious enough to try to kill Him (v. 29).

Jesus had disappointed their fondest hopes, and rejected their claim to exclusive possession of the divine favor. The Jews wanted a Messiah to throw off the Roman yoke and exalt their nation. They did not want a Messiah who would merely heal and forgive sins. The thought that they would not be favored above the hated Gentiles drove the crowd wild.

Let's be warned by the reaction of Jesus' neighbors. We must be careful to come to God without conditions or expectations. We cannot dictate to Him what He will do. And we must realize that God's love is universal. While we are special to Him, others are just as special as we.

It takes true humility to relate to God in this age of grace. We must be humble in relation to the Lord, seeking only to do His will. And we must be humble in relation to others, and willing to put them first.

"A demon, an evil spirit" Luke 4:31-37. Luke, a physician, makes a careful distinction between normal sicknesses and demon possession. There is no "superstitious belief that all sickness is caused by the demonic" in Luke's Gospel!

What there is reminds us that Jesus is all-powerful. "With authority and power He [still] gives orders to evil spirits and they come out."

"When the sun was setting" Luke 4:38-44. The people waited until sunset, because it was considered unlawful to carry a burden on the Sabbath (cf. v. 38), even though the burden might be a sick person. Jesus, however, had healed Peter's mother-in-law on the Sabbath Day. You and I never have to wait to bring our burdens or needs to Christ.

"Go away from me, Lord; I am a sinful man" Luke 5:1-11. One of Luke's literary techniques was to tell his story through vignettes of individuals. Here he portrayed Christ's call of His disciples by focusing on Peter, the chief disciple.

The story is rich in psychological insight. Jesus acted in a way that Peter saw as miraculous. Even though what Jesus did was for Peter's benefit, Peter was suddenly stricken with a sense of guilt, and begged Jesus to go away. Like Adam and Eve in the Garden, Peter's first reaction when he became aware he was in the presence of the Lord was one of flight.

Jesus, however, was not put off. He had come to find sinners just like Peter—and to transform them into "fishers of men."

Some non-Christians, but not all, will feel much like Peter, uncomfortable at the thought of being in God's presence. It's up to us to reassure them. Jesus isn't worried about being contaminated by sinners. He came to save sinners, and has the spiritual power required to make even the most wicked good.

"Who had come from every village of Galilee and . . . were sitting there" Luke 5:17-26. Luke made it clear that the "Pharisees and teachers of the Law" present were an official delegation, come to check on the young Preacher and Teacher of Galilee.

In the first century a person could be recognized as a teacher of the Law—a rabbi, or sage—only after going through a lengthy period of training under an acknowledged master. Jesus had no such training, and so a skeptical ecclesiastical commission came down to observe Him.

Jesus could sense their condemnation when He forgave the paralytic's sin. He then announced He would heal the paralytic to prove that He had the power to forgive sin. If He failed, God had not heard Him, and His announcement of forgiveness was meaningless. But an actual healing would show that God was working through Him, and confirm His claim to be able to forgive.

Ecclesiastical commissions still have a tendency to stand in judgment on the working of the Holy Spirit through people who have no "official" recognition. Many a woman today with significant spiritual gifts is unable to exercise them in the church. But the key to effective ministry remains the same—God's gifts, and His calling. And evidence of God's call is still seen in the transforming results of an individual's ministry to others.

"Yours go on eating and drinking" Luke 5:33-39. I remain amazed at the mentality of people who can witness wonderful works performed by God and then argue about the insignificant. Good heavens! Jesus was casting out demons! He was healing the sick! He was claiming, and proving, His ability to forgive sins! And some folks asked Him a question about fasting!

Jesus' answer, basically, was this. Get rid of the old categories in which you've thought about religion and relationship with God. You must not try to fit what I say and do into your old ways of thinking, but you must put My "new wine" into "new wineskins."

How much we need to be open to what Jesus is doing in our world, and what He teaches in His Word. Our best theology cannot contain God's thoughts or purposes. If we become rigid in our thinking about God, we will fall into the trap of those who ignored Jesus' wonders to wonder about what might better have been ignored.

▶ DEVOTIONAL
That Three-Letter Word (Luke 5)

Most parents tend to watch out for four-letter words. But today many adults have at least as strong a dislike for a three-letter word: sin. It's certainly gone out of style today, and anyone who talks about it is likely to be accused of trying to "impose his (or her) morality on others." According to folks like Norman Lear and his People for the American Way, talking about sin is the biggest sin of all!

Actually, the Bible doesn't treat "sin" as such an awful word at all. In fact, sin is one thing Scripture is quite confident God is able to deal with. Why avoid it then, if it's really no longer a threat?

Luke 5 contains progressive stories about sin. Verses 1-11 tell how Peter came to realize that Jesus was truly Lord (note v. 5, and then v. 8), and that when He did Peter was suddenly aware he was a sinful man. He begged Jesus to leave, but Christ wouldn't go. Instead Jesus held out the prospect of a new life to Peter: "from now on you will catch men." Jesus isn't repelled by our sin either. He knows that He has power to change us, and to change our lives.

Verses 17-26 show us how Jesus deals with our sins. He forgives them. As He broke the power of the paralysis that kept the man immovable on his mat, so His forgiveness breaks the bonds that paralyze our ability to do good.

And verses 27-32 demonstrate just that power. For Levi, the tax collector and social outcast, was none other than Matthew, the disciple who wrote the Gospel that bears his name (cf. Matt. 9:9). Christ not only calls sinners to repentance, but those who do repent He transforms into servants of God.

So don't be put off by that word "sin," and don't apologize for it. Sin is still a reality that every human being needs to face. The good news we have to share is that sin isn't a problem . . . for God. In Jesus there is forgiveness and renewal.

Personal Application

Call a sin a sin to bless others, not to curse them.

Quotable

"Who does not know what it is to rise up from a fault—perceived, confessed, and forgiven—with an almost joyous sense of new energy, strength, and will to persevere?"—H.L. Sidney Lear

AUGUST 10 *Reading 222*
JESUS' TEACHINGS
Luke 6

> *"I tell you who hear Me: Love your enemies, do good to those who hate you, bless those who curse you, pray for those who mistreat you" (Luke 6:27-28).*

Jesus' "teaching on the plain" (v. 17) is a typical sermon of Christ from His Galilean ministry.

Overview
Luke summarized Jesus' Sabbath conflict with the Pharisees (6:1-11) and listed the Twelve Christ chose as Apostles (vv. 12-16). He also summed up common elements in Christ's preaching: His lists of blessings and woes (vv. 17-26), His call to love enemies (vv. 27-36), His prohibition of judging (vv. 37-42), His demand for evidence of righteousness (vv. 43-45), and His call to put His teachings into practice (vv. 46-49).

Understanding the Text
"What is unlawful on the Sabbath?" Luke 6:1-2 Each Gospel records Sabbath controversy between Jesus and the Pharisees. This focused on the multiplied rules of Sabbath observance that the rabbis had piled on during the preceding centuries. Sabbath controversies served as test cases, in that here the approach of rabbinic Judaism to the Scriptures was most clearly seen.

It is important to keep in mind that neither Jesus nor His disciples actually broke a biblical law, though the disciples did violate a rabbinical ruling.

In the Sabbath controversies Christ exercised His right as Lord to define authoritatively what the Sabbath was for—and not for. Essentially Christ taught (1) the Sabbath was instituted for man's benefit (cf. Mark 2:27) and therefore helpful deeds are permitted (Luke 6:9); (2) that Jesus Himself is Lord of the Sabbath (v. 5); and (3) that as God works on the Sabbath it is lawful for the Son to work also (John 5:17).

Human interpretations of Scripture must always be carefully scrutinized—particularly when they are in the form of rules and restrictions!

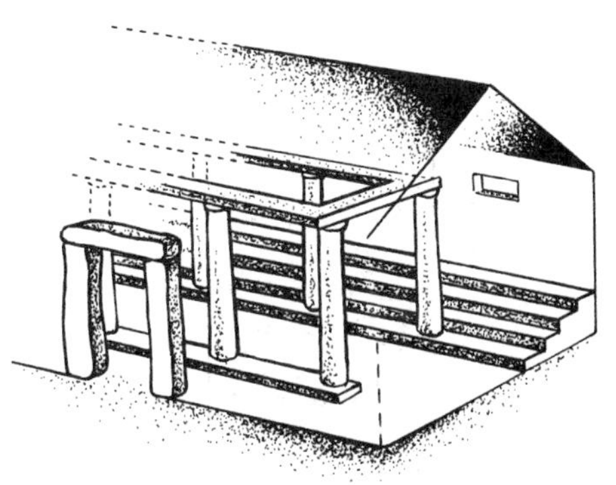

Luke frequently pictured Jesus in a synagogue on the Sabbath (4:16, 33; 6:6). Even small communities had synagogues, which served as houses of study as well as of worship. Archeologists have excavated this first-century synagogue, whose foundation was found underneath a fourth-century synagogue in Capernaum. The drawing shows the plans of the discovered synagogue, which is most probably the very Capernaum synagogue in which Jesus taught!

"Spent the night praying to God" Luke 6:12-16. Luke has described some of the pressures on Jesus. He was surrounded by milling crowds in search of healing. He was the center of controversy. And He had to make a critical decision, choosing 12 from among the many who followed Him to be "designated Apostles."

When the pressures are greatest and the decisions most significant, the best way to spend time is in prayer.

"He . . . stood on a level place" Luke 6:17-20. This summary of Jesus' teaching has been called the "sermon on the plain" in contrast to Matthew's "Sermon on the Mount" (Matt. 5–7). Luke may be describing the same event, but not necessarily. Most likely he reported standard features in the "keynote address" Christ likely repeated often when presenting His kingdom. The features we find here surely are basic elements in Christ's present kingdom, and foundational to our life as citizens in it. Jesus' focus on His disciples (v. 20) makes it clear this sermon is for us.

"Blessed are you" Luke 6:20-23. The blessing

Jesus referred to is the unique joy experienced only by those who participate in His kingdom. Note that Jesus used the present tense here: "Blessed are you." Out of what others call deprivation flows the unique joy of experiencing God's living presence. We who look beyond the material world not only have great reward in heaven, but even as we suffer we "rejoice in that day and leap for joy."

What a mistake to assume that joy and blessing depend on our bank balance, or well-stocked closets. Joy and blessing flow out of relationship with the Lord, and are dependent only on our closeness to Him.

"Woe to you who are rich" Luke 6:24-26. The woes stand in direct contrast to the blessings. The misery Luke associated with wealth is not rooted in riches themselves, but in the impact of riches on the individual. The wealthy are tempted to seek satisfaction in the things they can buy now, rather than giving priority to the world to come, and tend to ignore spiritual realities. And the wealthy seem to consider what others think of them more important than what God thinks. James 2:6-7 seems to assume, as Luke here may, that anyone in the first century who was wealthy had gained his or her riches at the expense of someone else. Whatever their source, Christ clearly taught that riches are deceitful. Rich or poor, we must learn to depend solely on the Lord.

"Love your enemies, do good to those who hate you" Luke 6:27-36. Sociologists call the pattern Jesus criticized the "norm of reciprocity." In any culture, people will tend to keep the social books balanced. If you invite the Joneses over for dinner, they'll feel they owe you an invitation. If you loan Mrs. Smith chocolate chips, she's likely to bring you a few of the cookies she makes.

Jesus didn't criticize this norm. He simply observed that even sinners live by it, so it is nothing special when we show love to those who love us. And He called us to live by the standard set, not by others in our society, but by God. Since God does good and loving things even for those who hate Him, we who are God's children and citizens in His kingdom are to do likewise.

We are not to live by the norm of reciprocity, but the norm of redemption.

"Do not judge" Luke 6:37-42. There is a great difference between using our ability to distinguish (judge) between right and wrong and what Jesus is speaking of here. Luke carefully ruled out any misunderstanding by using parallel repetition, common in Hebrew poetry and wisdom literature. We are to be morally discerning—but we may not use that discernment to condemn others. If we must be critical, let's turn a critical eye on our own behavior—and correct it!

"Each tree is recognized by its own fruit" Luke 6:43-45. Jesus' teaching here is no commission for you and me to become "fruit inspectors." It is, however, the statement of a principle that holds true in the spiritual realm as well as in nature. The fruit of a fig tree is figs. The fruit of a good heart is loving words and godly deeds.

Some take these words to be directed against the Pharisees, who stressed rigid obedience to hosts of man-devised as well as biblical regulations. Certainly Jesus' saying discounts the ritual in which they took such pride, and exalts ordinary goodness. Even more important, however, Jesus' words remind us that the quality of our life depends on our hearts. If your heart and mine overflow with love for God and a desire to please Him, our lives will be filled with an obvious and overflowing goodness. That's why Augustine could say, correctly, "Love God and do what you please." Augustine saw that if a person truly loves God, what that person wants will be to please God!

"Who comes to Me and hears My words and puts them into practice" Luke 6:46-49. There is no better foundation on which you and I can build our lives. We have come to Him. Now let us listen to His words—and go put them into practice. If we do, we will stand firm whatever the storms life may hold.

▶DEVOTIONAL
The Measure You Use (Luke 6:27-42)

Jesus' call to love enemies frightens us at first. If we love our enemies, surely they'll take advantage of us! If we love our enemies, we'll be more vulnerable to attack.

At first Jesus seemed to ignore this rather obvious objection. He simply reminded us that God is a lover of enemies, and that as God's children now we are expected to act as He does. Never mind the practicalities. Just do what is right.

But then Jesus went on to remind us that doing what is right is practical as well! "Give," He says, "and it will be given to you. . . . For with the measure you use, it will be measured to you" (vv. 37-38). You can break patterns of hostility and animosity! You can use the innate principle of reciprocity which God has planted in human nature by breaking the pattern of blow for blow, of pain given for pain received. You can initiate a new pattern by returning love for hate, good for evil, and in so doing establish the measure by which, in time, it will be measured back to you.

After all, didn't God do the same thing? We human beings were "enemies in our mind by wicked works" (see Col. 1:21). And God broke the pattern by one bold act of love, sending His Son to suffer and die for our sins. As we respond to that love, accepting the salvation Christ brings, our whole attitude toward God has changed, and we now love and want to please Him. God too has received in measure as He has given.

Oh, I know. It doesn't always work. Some who know of Christ remain as hostile to God as before. And, sometimes, the people we treat lovingly continue to do us harm. But the principle remains valid and true, whatever the individual exception. There is a way to break patterns of hostility in relationships. And that way is to take the initiative and begin, now, to give love where there is hate, compassion where there is hostility, and devotion where there is antagonism. When we do, we live out our calling as God's children. And we initiate transforming change.

Personal Application

The larger the measure of love you use, the greater the possibility of receiving love in return.

Quotable

"It is possible to have compassion without love, and it is possible to have kindness without love; but it is impossible for one who has put on love to be unkind and without compassion, for love itself is not just an accessory garment. Love is the complete garment that has all the others built into it, so that love is a total way of life."—Ray Anderson

---

AUGUST 11 *Reading 223*
JESUS' POWER
Luke 7–8

> *"Her many sins have been forgiven—for she loved much. But he who has been forgiven little loves little" (Luke 7:47).*

Christ's miracles showed His power over every natural and supernatural force, and frequently, the importance of faith.

Overview

Jesus healed a believing centurion's servant (7:1-10) and raised a widow's son (vv. 11-17). Jesus identified John as a prophet—and Himself as "Son of man" (vv. 18-35). He stunned a Pharisee by accepting the touch of, and forgiving, a sinful woman (vv. 36-50). "After this" Jesus began to teach in parables (8:1-15) and riddles (vv. 16-18). He continued to demonstrate His power, calming a storm (vv. 22-25), casting out a demon (vv. 26-39) and healing a chronically ill woman (vv. 40-48). He capped these miracles by raising a dead girl (vv. 49-56).

Understanding the Text

"Such great faith" Luke 7:1-10. "Faith" is a thread that runs through both of Luke's writings: this Gospel, and the Book of Acts. Here Luke introduced a Gentile, a centurion, who demonstrated "great faith" by expressing the conviction that Jesus was able to heal his critically ill servant by simply speaking a word—from a distance!

These career officers who led "hundreds" in the Roman army are presented in a positive light in the New Testament (cf. Acts 10–11). These well-trained, responsible, and intelligent men were often entrusted with special duties and sent on a variety of empire affairs. Several are mentioned in the New Testament as "God-fearers," Gentiles who worshiped God but did not convert to Judaism. In Luke's writings the believing centurions represent all Gentiles who come to trust in Jesus.

The centurion also showed great sensitivity. In saying he was "not worthy" to have Jesus enter his house, he showed a concern for Christ's reputation. The religious leaders would have been sure to criticize Christ if He had entered a Gentile's home!

May God give us similar gifts: great faith—and a deep concern that all we do contributes to the reputation of our Lord.

"He went up and touched the coffin" Luke 7:11-17. The use of "coffin" is an example of the NIV's tendency to seek modern equivalents for biblical terms. The Greek word indicates an open, stretcher-like bier, on which the dead were carried.

Christ's compassion for the widow who had lost her only son moved Him to help her. In doing so He touched the bier. This act would make the ordinary Jew "unclean," and unable to approach God at the temple. It did not affect Jesus, for immediately He called on God, and the dead returned to life! The dynamic power of life that infused Jesus could not be dampened by mere ritual rules.

Jesus' act convinced the onlookers that Christ was a Prophet. It undoubtedly reminded the crowd of Elijah, who had also brought a woman's only son back to life.

You and I now recognize Jesus as even more than a prophet. His touch is still able to make the dead live, and cleanse the unclean. We experience His life-giving power as we trust Him each day.

"Report to John what you have seen and heard" Luke 7:18-23. Even John seemed to have expected Jesus to set up an earthly kingdom. To settle his doubts, he sent his followers to put the question to Jesus directly: "Are You the One?"

Jesus listed specific healing works John's followers had seen, because the Old Testament declared that in the Messianic Age just such works would be performed! Isaiah 35 says, "Your God will come," and while the passage speaks of divine retribution, it also says, "Then will the eyes of the blind be opened and the ears of the deaf unstopped. Then will the lame leap like a deer, and the tongue of the dumb shout for joy" (vv. 4-6; cf. 61:1-2).

The evidence of Christ's works alone was sufficient to identify Him as the Messiah: as Israel's God, come at long last! The answer surely was enough for John.

He would set aside his preconceived ideas about how God must work, and simply trust.

The other day our Florida lottery reached 22 million dollars. "I'm praying about a ticket," a friend said. "God surely would want one of His own to have that money. Only a Christian could use it wisely." It seems logical, all right. Yet it's an idea of how God must work that is based on human reasoning. Like John of old, you and I must be willing to set aside all preconceived ideas. We have evidence of God's love in the Cross. Now we are to simply trust that what He chooses to do is what's best.

By the way. No lottery win for my friend. Yet.

"Like children . . . calling out to each other" Luke 7:24-35. Jesus identified John as a great prophet. While the sinful of society recognized him, and responded to his message, the "Pharisees and experts in the Law" had rejected John—and God's purpose for them! Why?

Jesus illustrates from the familiar scene of children, playing in the streets. They play "wedding" (v. 32b) and they play "funeral" (v. 32c). And they complain when other's won't play their game. And that, Jesus said, is what the religious leaders had done. They'd been playing games, and they whined because neither John, that gaunt and austere wilderness man, nor Jesus, a social, friendly Teacher, played their games with them! "If you won't play our way," Jesus pictured them saying, and we can clearly see the pout on petulant, childish faces, "we won't play at all. So there!"

But Jesus wasn't playing games. And if you and I are to have a meaningful relationship with Him, we can't play games either! In Jesus, our God has come. And we must now be fully committed to Him.

"She began to wet His feet with her tears" Luke 7:36-50. Don't think the woman was forgiven after she wet Jesus' feet with her tears. Oh, no. She was forgiven before. That was an act of love; an expression of gratitude. Her "many sins" had been purged, and her tears were tears of joy.

Jesus' later comments were explanation to Simon the Pharisee, and confirmation to the woman (vv. 48, 50). It's the same in our lives. Faith and forgiveness precede both joy and service.

"A farmer went out to sow his seed" Luke 8:1-15. This familiar parable is told in Matthew and Mark as well. In each telling the focus is on either the seed, or the ground on which it fell.

Sometimes you and I focus on the farmer—ourselves, as sowers of God's Word. We are essential. But results depend most of all on the inherent power of the Good News, and on the nature of the soil on which it falls. So you and I can sow freely. In its brief mention of the farmer, this parable helps set to rest such fears as "I don't know enough yet," or "I may say something wrong." All we need to do is scatter the seed. God will work in those who hear, according to their willingness to respond, to produce the crop.

"Your daughter is dead" Luke 8:26-56. These verses report how Jesus dealt with what must be considered "hopeless cases." The demon-possessed man had been chained "many times" but had always broken loose (v. 29). The woman who touched Jesus had been "subject to bleeding" for a dozen years, and "no one could heal her" (v. 43). And the daughter of Jairus was dead: all hope was gone, and friends advised, "Don't bother the Teacher any more" (v. 49). Yet Jesus cast out the demon, restored the health of the woman, and raised the little girl from the dead!

Strung together, as these stories are by Luke, they remind us of a wonderful truth. There are no "hopeless cases" with the Lord. And there are no "hopeless people" either. The power of Jesus Christ is great enough to meet every need, and to transform any sinner as well.

▶ DEVOTIONAL
Don't Talk to Yourself
(Luke 7:36-50)

G.K. Chesterton has pointed out that in every field except religion, people tend to come to an agreement. Scientists the world over agree on atomic structure. Nutritionists agree on what's best to eat. Common rules are developed for accounting, and all nations agree that the use of steroids in the Olympics is not right or fair. But there's no agreement on religion! And this despite thousands and thousands of years of searching and discussion.

Luke's report of a dinner Jesus had at a Pharisee's house helps us see why. A woman known to be a sinner—most likely a local prostitute—slipped into the dining room and began to anoint Jesus' feet, weeping as she did. The Pharisee observed what was happening and reasoned it out ("said to himself"). He was logical too. (1) A prophet would know she was a sinner. (2) A prophet wouldn't let a sinner touch him. (3) Ergo, Jesus was no prophet! (v. 39)

The only trouble was, the Pharisee was totally wrong in one of his premises. Jesus did know she was a sinner. But He knew she was a forgiven sinner, and that her love and tears flowed from faith in Him.

When Jesus explained, even the Pharisee had to grudgingly admit that a person who has been forgiven "much" will love more than a person who has been forgiven (what he considered!) little (vv. 41-43). Jesus then confirmed the message the woman had already heard: "Your sins are forgiven," and again, "Your faith has saved you" (vv. 48-50).

What's wrong with human efforts to construct religions? As with the Pharisee, each effort is merely "saying to oneself." The religious make statements that seem logical, but are faulty in one or more of the premises involved. Only when God speaks through Jesus can the truth be discerned. The only religious truth we can possibly have must come from God by revelation, for it can never be discovered by people who talk only with themselves.

So don't be disturbed when people have different beliefs and ideas about God than you do. Put your confidence in the Word of God. Let the others talk to themselves all they want. You talk—and listen—to God.

Personal Application

Have confidence in what God says, not in what other people think.

Quotable

"When you have read the Bible, you will know it is the Word of God, because you will have found in it the key to your own heart, your own happiness and your own duty."—Woodrow Wilson

AUGUST 12 *Reading 224*

JESUS, THE CHRIST

Luke 9

> *" 'But what about you?' He asked. 'Who do you say that I am?' " (Luke 9:20)*

In each Gospel, Peter's confession of Jesus as the Christ serves as a turning point. It is at this point that Jesus began to speak of His Cross.

Overview

Jesus intensified His impact by sending His disciples out to teach and heal (9:1-6), stirring more speculation about who He might be (vv. 7-9). Jesus fed 5,000 (vv. 10-17), and after Peter's confession that Jesus is the Christ (vv. 18-20), He spoke of His death (vv. 21-22) and the cost of discipleship (vv. 23-27). Eight days later Jesus was transfigured (vv. 28-36), drove out an evil spirit (vv. 37-45), and discussed greatness (vv. 46-50). On the way to Jerusalem He was unwelcome in Samaria (vv. 51-56), and He warned of difficulties to be faced by any who follow Him (vv. 57-62).

Understanding the Text

"He gave them power and authority" Luke 9:1-6. Miraculous powers were needed for healing. But authority was needed to cast out demons. As we see later in the same chapter, this authority was not retained by the disciples (v. 40). The power and authority were given to enable the disciples to perform the specific mission.

You and I can be confident that if we are called to any ministry or service, God will provide the strength and gifts we need to carry it out. We shouldn't expect to possess unusual gifts constantly, any more than the disciples were given power as a permanent possession. If we did possess special permanent powers, we would almost surely begin to think it was because of some special trait of our own.

No, God keeps us humble, so we will depend on Him. When He calls us, obedience is an act of faith, not self-confidence. Then, as we serve, and only as we serve, we discover that Christ has provided just the powers and authority we need to accomplish the appointed task.

"Who, then, is this?" Luke 9:7-9 The question that the intensified activity of Jesus and His disciples raised in Herod's mind was undoubtedly echoed everywhere. In reporting it, Luke was preparing his readers to answer this question for themselves—and preparing them for the answer that Peter would shortly provide.

I'm often surprised when I realize how much "witnessing" focuses on, "What church do you go to?" or "What do you believe about the Bible?" or even "What's your stand on abortion?" There is only one question that our witnessing should be designed to raise. We are to point others to Jesus, and raise the question on which each person's eternal destiny depends: "Who then is this?"

"You give them something to eat" Luke 9:10-17. The fact that each of the four Gospels tells of the feeding of the 5,000 suggests that it is important. And that we should look carefully in each Gospel account.

For now, though, note that when the disciples lamely suggested the crowd should disperse and try to find food, Christ put the responsibility back on the Twelve! "You give them something to eat."

What we may not have thought about is the fact that, in the end, the disciples did give the crowds food! They distributed the food that Jesus miraculously provided.

In this, the story is surely for us. We too are called by Jesus to meet the needs of others. Often we realize that we simply don't have the resources. Yet Jesus' words, "You give them something to eat," call us to our responsibility. Happily, the fact that Jesus miraculously provided food for the crowd reminds us that Christ still provides all that He asks us to share.

What a relief this is for us! We may be responsible to distribute. But Jesus remains responsible to provide the resources.

"The Christ of God" Luke 9:18-20. Earlier Jesus had identified Himself as the Messiah, by His acts (cf. 7:21-23) and references to Himself as "Son of man." This is the first time, however, a disciple had referred to Jesus as the Messiah (cf. 2:11, 26; 3:15; 4:41).

It's a healthy reminder for us. If men who had at this time spent years with Jesus, had heard His teaching, and witnessed His miracles, took so long to recognize Him, why should we expect friends or loved ones to become Christians after just a few hearings of the Gospel? Often saving faith grows on a person over time. We can nurture the growth of faith through consistent, loving witness by word and life.

We can also pull up a sprouting seed by pressing for a decision too soon.

"Take up his cross daily" Luke 9:23. There's a lot of misunderstanding about the Christian's cross.

One Christian mentioned his anger to a minister, and shrugged that "it's just the cross I have to bear." The preacher told him (kindly), "No. It may be the cross your wife has to bear, but for you it's just sin."

The Christian's cross isn't suffering, either. It is simply that, as Calvary's cross was God's will for Jesus, so our "cross" is whatever God's will for us is each day. That will may involve pain, but often involves joy. There may be tears, but our cross also carries shouts and singing. The one thing that we can be sure of, however, is that our cross calls us to daily choose God's will in preference to our own, and thus demands the most significant kind of self-denial.

"Whoever loses his life for Me will save it" Luke 9:24. The Greek word translated "life" is *psyche,* best understood here to refer to the essential person himself. The saying seems obscure until we think about it.

Satan is a good reverse example of what Jesus taught. The Old Testament pictures him as Lucifer, the "light bearer," a great and beauteous angel. But one day he made a choice, and determined to defy

God's will and exalt his own. In that choice he denied the beautiful self he was, and became the doomed and despicable enemy of God and humanity.

You and I, warped as we have been by sin, are given the choice of holding on to the old self, or by complete commitment to God, experiencing a transformation that will make us loving, beautiful, and new. If we choose to reject the will of God, and hang onto the old self, we lose. But if we choose to reject our old self, and do the will of God, we win. And our prize is the new self Jesus will help us become.

"Call fire down?" Luke 9:51-55 Can Jesus really provide us with a new self? The disciples were angry when a Samaritan village refused overnight hospitality to Jesus because He was traveling toward Jerusalem. James and John were so upset they asked Jesus, "Do You want us to call fire down from heaven to destroy them?"

What, John? John, the apostle whose letters and Gospel constantly emphasize love? Oh, yes. The old John. But never the new.

This self of fire and destruction is the self John lost. The self of light and love is the self John found in following Jesus.

You and I can find our new self too by following Jesus Christ.

▶ DEVOTIONAL
It's OK, Really
(Luke 9:28-36)

I know the Transfiguration was a unique and holy event. And I might be accused of trivializing it. But, after all, Luke wrote it down.

"He did not know what he was saying," Luke wrote of words that Peter blurted out. And our text, rightly, even encloses this aside in parentheses.

Luke wasn't putting Peter down here. Really, he was being kind. He was letting us know that the foolish thing Peter said when excited and exhilarated at seeing Christ's glory was not to be criticized. Yes, Peter blurted out the first thing that came to mind. He said it, and then probably felt utterly foolish. And though the historian in Luke was compelled to record this detail, he reported no rebuke by Christ, and he said in effect, "It's all right. Peter just didn't know what he was saying."

I remember as a new Christian a time we were counting members at church, and fell 1 short of the quorum needed to conduct business. I blurted out, "Hey! Where 2 or 3 are gathered in Jesus' name, He's there. So He makes our 50!"

As soon as I said it I felt pretty foolish. But nobody laughed. It was almost as if I could feel Luke's warm, caring remark flow from understanding hearts, and release me. "It's all right. He didn't know what he was saying." And no one ever mentioned that incident to me. Not one.

I suspect that sometimes in the practice of our faith we become a little insensitive to people. Not Luke. Even when describing one of the New Testament's most amazing and significant events, Luke had time to think of Peter's feelings and to make sure that no one might later accuse him of spiritual insensitivity. Yes, Peter said a foolish thing. We all do at times. How blessed we are when others let us babble, and then overlook our mistakes. And how wise we are, when we hear another blurt out some foolish thing, to remind ourselves that it's all right. To just say to ourselves that, like Peter, "He did not know what he was saying."

And then never even think of the incident again.

Personal Application

The words, "He did not know what he was saying" are often salve for two hurts: the other person's, and our own.

Quotable

"Keep a fair-sized cemetery in your backyard, in which to bury the faults of your friends."—Henry Ward Beecher

AUGUST 13 *Reading 225*
ON MISSION
Luke 10

> *"After this the Lord appointed seventy-two others and sent them two by two ahead of Him to every town and place where He was about to go" (Luke 10:1).*

If we are to serve Jesus, we must have a sense of mission as well as a message.

Background

Two by two. The Sanhedrin regularly sent pairs of representatives to Jewish communities throughout the Roman world. The messengers were typically rabbis or sages, whose mission was to communicate calendar dates set for the year's annual religious festivals. They also frequently served as judges to settle disputes that arose between fellow Jews.

One reason for sending such messengers out in pairs is found in Deuteronomy 17:6; 19:15. There had to be at least two witnesses to establish a fact in any court of Jewish law. Thus two witnesses to any official communication of the Sanhedrin were required.

Jesus also sent out His disciples in pairs. But there were three witnesses to the testimony that they bore to Him. There were the two disciples—and the miraculous power that Jesus gave them to cast out demons in His name.

God still provides supernatural witness to the authenticity of the Gospel. The Holy Spirit working in and through us confirms the truth to all who heed.

Overview

Jesus commissioned and empowered 72 (10:1-20), and praised God for His privilege of revealing the Father to men (vv. 21-24). He told the story of the Good Samaritan (vv. 25-37), and later rested at the Bethany home of Mary and Martha (vv. 38-42).

Understanding the Text

"Ask the Lord of the harvest, therefore, to send out workers" Luke 10:1-2. The goal of evangelism is multiplication. As the 72 ministered they were to pray not simply that those who heard would believe, but that they would become workers.

The world remains a harvest field. And our goal is not simply to bring others to faith, but to bring them to maturity so they might win others too.

"Do not take a purse or bag" Luke 10:3-5. These instructions are found in each Gospel's report of sending out any disciples as special messengers. Jesus' representatives called on others to depend on God. They had to demonstrate dependence on the Lord by their own lifestyle.

The principle remains the same today. We must practice what we preach. Our lives witness to the reliability of our words.

"The kingdom of God is near" Luke 10:8-16. "Good news, bad news" wasn't invented by a modern comedian. We have a classic case of it here. What's the good news? "The kingdom of God is near you" (v. 9). OK. What's the bad news? "The kingdom of God is near" (v. 11).

What makes the difference isn't the message, but whether or not the messengers were welcomed. Those who gladly received Jesus' messengers, and thus He Himself (v. 16), would have a place in Christ's kingdom and know His joy. But those who rejected the messengers, and thus the King (v. 16), could expect only judgment.

The other day Ted Turner, the builder of the cable TV empire that includes WTBS, CNN, and TNT, told an audience of cable system owners that he didn't need anyone to die on a cross for him. Sure, he'd had a few women and done some other things, but if God wanted to send him to hell for that, he'd go.

For Ted, the Gospel of Jesus is bad news. He's heard the message that millions have welcomed with joy, and rejected it. He now faces a judgment that is all the more severe (vv. 13-15).

We have an awesome responsibility to present the Gospel as clearly and lovingly as possible. For what is Good News to those who receive it is bad news indeed for those who scoff.

"Rejoice that your names are written in heav-

en" Luke 10:17-20. What gives a person joy is a measure of their values, and of their spiritual maturity. I can understand why the 72 were excited about power over evil spirits. That must be exhilarating! But Jesus suggested it was not an appropriate cause for rejoicing. It's like stuffing a pearl in your pocket and jumping up and down over an ordinary oyster shell.

What Jesus suggested is that while we appreciate our gifts and achievements, if we want to know real joy, we should reach into our spiritual pockets and pull out the pearl of salvation. As we gaze at it, and realize our names are written in heaven, we will know joy indeed.

"But he wanted to justify himself" Luke 10:25-29. Those "experts in the Law" we meet so frequently in Luke are rabbis, or sages, who devoted themselves to a study of the Old Testament and the massive body of interpretations which by this time had grown up around it.

The master interpreter of Judaism who now approached Jesus made the typical mistake of members of his class. He asked, "What must I do to inherit eternal life?"

When Jesus asked him his opinion, he rightly answered that Scripture calls us to love God supremely, and to love our neighbors as ourselves. These two requirements do sum up the religious and moral message of the Old Testament. But being "right" created a terrible problem. For Jesus then said, "Go and do it!"

"Go and do it" are words that confront everyone with the impossibility of earning salvation. Many of the world's religions have a high moral vision. But none provides believers with the ability they need to "go and do" the good that faith defines.

In telling this expert in the Law of God to "go and do" what he knew to be right, Jesus forced him to face the fact of his own inadequacy, and invited him to look at the Scripture with new eyes. What every person must seek is not more rules to follow in a vain attempt to earn salvation, but a forgiving and loving God, who has made a way for confessed sinners to come to Him.

"Only one thing is needed" Luke 10:38-42. People have speculated what the "one thing" in this story is. Was Jesus telling Martha, so flustered and upset as she rushed around preparing a meal for Christ and His disciples, that she was doing too much? "Just a casserole, Martha. Not a smorgasbord!"

Perhaps. Certainly we need to stop at times and ask, are we doing so much that we haven't time to sit at Christ's feet and learn? Too busy for Jesus is too busy—whatever we're about.

▶ DEVOTIONAL
Who Is My Neighbor?
(Luke 10:25-37)

Leviticus 19:18 says it: "Love your neighbor as yourself. I am the LORD." The expert in Old Testament Law who came to Jesus was right when he plucked this command out of a lengthy list of specific commandments, and held it up as one of the Old Testament's two foundational requirements for a righteous life.

Despite his motive (Luke 10:29), the question the legal expert asked, "Who is my neighbor?" is a good one. Just who is it you and I are to love "as ourselves"?

To answer, Jesus told of a man who was beaten and robbed on the 17-mile journey from Jerusalem to Jericho. Two fellow Jews, bound to the beaten man by race and religion, a priest and a Levite, saw him lying there—and left him! They were going away from Jerusalem, and by implication had just come from serving in the temple. They thus represented the "greatest" commandment, showing love for God. The fact that they were going away left them without excuse: if they had been going up to Jerusalem they might have claimed (wrongly) that worship of God had precedence.

The Samaritan, on the other hand, had no ties to the Jews. In fact, a long racial and religious hostility marked their relationship (cf. Luke 9:51-56). Yet the Samaritan "took pity on" the man, helped him, and even paid for his care while he recovered!

When asked, "Which . . . was a neighbor to the man?" the legal expert answered uncomfortably, "The one who had mercy." And he was right.

So then, who is our neighbor? What we learn from Christ's story is that being a neigbor has nothing to do with how near we live to others, or how similar our religion or race. Being a neighbor depends simply on our humanity—and on need.

Anyone you or I come in contact with who has a need is our neighbor. And to love our neighbor means to care enough to reach out, and help in any way we can.

Personal Application
"Jesus told him, 'Go and do likewise' " (10:37).

Quotable
"Because we cannot see Christ we cannot express our love to Him; but our neighbors we can always see, and we can do to them what, if we saw Him, we would like to do to Christ."—Mother Teresa

AUGUST 14 *Reading 226*
TEACHING ON PRAYER
Luke 11

> *"So I say to you: Ask and it will be given to you; seek and you will find; knock and the door will be opened to you" (Luke 11:9).*

Luke emphasized both Jesus' personal prayer life, and His teaching on how you and I should pray.

Overview
Jesus provided a model prayer (11:1-4). He taught confidence by contrast (vv. 5-8), by promise (vv. 9-10), and by reminder of God's Fatherness (vv. 11-13). Later Christ refuted a charge that He was in league with Satan (vv. 14-28), and refused to provide a "miraculous sign" (vv. 29-32) for those who were purposely blind (vv. 33-36). Jesus concluded by confronting the Pharisees and experts in the Law with faults calling for their judgment (vv. 37-53).

Understanding the Text
"Jesus was praying in a certain place" Luke 11:1. Luke frequently described Jesus at prayer (cf. 3:21; 6:12; 9:28). Now at last the disciples asked Jesus to teach them to pray. Christ's example motivated His disciples.

It's the same in our homes too. Mom and Dad's example is the most powerful tool available for motivating children toward godliness. If prayer is a natural and observed part of our lives, our children will learn to pray. If reading the Bible is a regular practice of ours, our boys and girls will be more likely to pick up the habit.

There is no suggestion in this Gospel that Jesus urged His disciples to pray. His example was much more powerful than any exhortation He might have given.

"Hallowed be Your name, Your kingdom come" Luke 11:2. The elements in this prayer are explored more thoroughly in the reading on Matthew 6 (see July 18, Reading 199). Here note that the first two "petitions" are not so much requests as worship.

When we pray, it's appropriate first of all to exalt God, praising Him for His holiness and the glory of His kingdom. In essence, prayer is talking to God, not necessarily asking Him for things. When we consider the greatness and love of our God, how appropriate if the first things we say to Him express our appreciation and praise.

"Lead us not into temptation" Luke 11:4. God never tempts a believer to sin (James 1:13). Yet the Holy Spirit did specifically lead Jesus into the wilderness where He was tempted by Satan (Luke 4:1).

Some people are uncomfortable with the notion of living by faith. They keep looking for tests, to prove to themselves that God is with them, that they are growing spiritually, that they are important, or for some other reason. Here Jesus teaches us to ask not to be led into temptation.

God will at times permit us to undergo temptation. When He does, He will provide a way for us to escape without sin

(1 Cor. 10:13). But it is both presumptuous and foolish for us to search out tests of our faith.

"Ask and it will be given to you" Luke 11:9-13. Several specific teachings are combined here to give us great confidence in prayer (see DEVOTIONAL). God, the good Father, gives good gifts to His children—including the best gift of all, the Holy Spirit (v. 13).

But note that we are told to "ask." We are to bring our requests to God, expressing our dependence on Him. The Apostle Paul exhorted, "In everything, by prayer and petition, with thanksgiving, present your requests to God." And he added this promise: "And the peace of God, which transcends all understanding, will guard your hearts and your minds in Christ Jesus" (Phil. 4:6-7).

"When someone stronger attacks" Luke 11:14-26. Maybe the Pharisees had been watching wrestling on TV. If so they surely noted that most of the audience couldn't see the obvious fact that the bouts were staged, and nearly every blow a sham. If folks are dumb enough to take a fake for real, maybe we can make them think that what's real is a fake!

Some reasoning like this must have led them to charge Jesus with being in league with Beelzebub (a common first-century name for Satan). Jesus blunted their attack simply and decisively and turned it around. He showed that since His work of casting out demons could not be with Satan's cooperation, it must have been done with God's. The Pharisees could only acknowledge that God's kingdom was present in Christ—or side with the evil one.

What's most fascinating is Jesus' final comment. He described an evil spirit that comes out (not "is driven out") of a man. After wandering awhile, it returns—and brings "seven other spirits more wicked than itself, and they go in and live there."

Jesus had power over evil spirits. But ordinary human beings are portrayed as helpless before them. Such spirits leave and return as they wish, apparently without even so much as a "by your leave."

How good to know that in Christ we have one "stronger" than every evil force; one who "overpowers" them all (v. 22) and sets us permanently free.

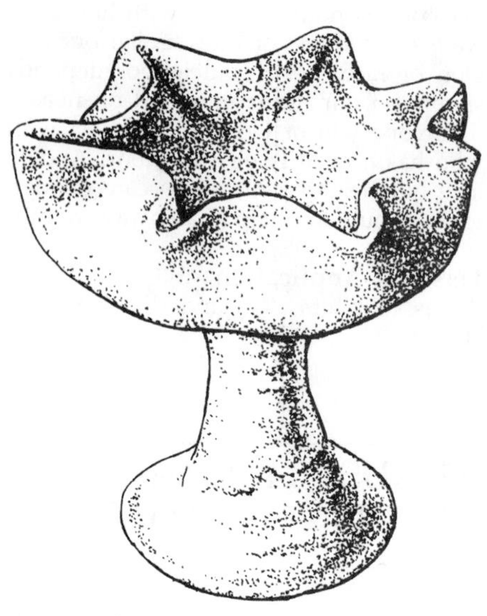

The wealthy might place olive-oil lamps on metal stands. In most homes, however, lamps burned in nitches along the wall or were set on pottery stands like this one. In Jesus' illustration, the "eye" is a lamp in that through it the body receives light. If Jesus' hearers were blind to the meaning of the works they had seen Him do, they were in darkness indeed!

"You Pharisees" Luke 11:37-54. When eating at the home of a Pharisee, Jesus identified six common sins of the "religious" of His day that kept them from seeing the light. The Pharisees and experts in the Law that Jesus indicted were furious. Instead of examining themselves, they reacted defensively and attacked Him.

Let's not read these verses so we can pile up more ammunition against the first-century Pharisees. Let's read them for criteria we can use in examining ourselves. If we do, we'll find—and hopefully use—a checklist like this:

___ Do I spend more time trying to look holy, or seeking to be holy? (vv. 39-41)

___ Do my priorities reflect God's? (v. 42)

___ Do I treasure the approval of others, or the approval of God? (vv. 43-44)

___ Do I make living a Christian life harder for people by my expectations, or do I encourage and help them? (v. 46)

___ Do I resist the Word of God brought to me by His ministers, or am I open and teachable? (vv. 47-51)

___ Do I distort the Gospel for myself and others by a legalistic attitude and approach to Christian faith? (v. 52)

If anyone should ever accuse you of one or more of these flaws, the way you react will be a good clue to your guilt or innocence.

▶DEVOTIONAL
Keep on Knocking? (Luke 11:1-10)

"Just keep on prayin' and prayin'. After while, God'll answer you if you keep on long enough."

I surely don't want to discourage persistence in prayer. But the "God'll hear you if you keep on long enough" school of thought definitely misunderstands something Jesus taught here in Luke 11, in the Parable of the Persistent Neighbor.

In New Testament times, hospitality was an obligation of the host family and of the entire village. So when a guest arrived late at night, it was all right for the host to go next door and ask for extra loaves of bread. It was all right. But it wasn't convenient. When the host in Jesus' story pounded on his friend's door late one night, it was a pain! It was common for the whole family to sleep together in a single room, often on a common mat unrolled on the floor. (Thus, "My children are with me in bed," v. 7.) For the father to get up, and stumble over the whole family, possibly awakening them too, wasn't convenient at all. But Jesus said that such a householder would get up anyway—if the neighbor made a pest of himself and kept on knocking.

Now, this story isn't intended to teach us persistence. In fact, it draws a series of contrasts between God and the best of neighbors. First, while the host and his neighbor had a duty of hospitality, the duty of a father (v. 2) to his children was far greater. Second, it's not inconvenient for God to answer our prayers. He doesn't have to wake from a sound sleep and stumble over dozing angels to groggily find us a few stale loaves of bread. And third, we don't have to make pests of ourselves to force an irritated Deity to respond. Our Father loves us. He provides what we need, not because we bother Him, but because He cares.

And so Jesus says to us today, "Ask and it will be given to you; seek and you will find; knock and the door will be opened to you."

When we understand who God is, and the nature of our relationship to Him, we can ask with confidence and with joy.

Personal Application

Don't rely on your persistence. Rely on God's pervasive love.

Quotable

No voice of prayer to Thee can rise,
But swift as light Thy Love replies;
Not always what we ask, indeed,
But, O most Kind! what we most need.
—H.M. Kimball

AUGUST 15 *Reading 227*
ON TREASURES
Luke 12

> *"Provide purses for yourselves that will not wear out, a treasure in heaven that will not be exhausted, where no thief comes near and no moth destroys. For where your treasure is there will your heart be also" (Luke 12:33-34).*

Our attitude toward material possessions is a good indicator of our spiritual depth.

Overview

Jesus warned against the hypocrisy of the Pharisees (12:1-12), and called on His hearers to be "rich toward God" (vv. 13-21). Knowing God as Father frees us from anxiety even over necessities (vv. 22-34), and enables us to concentrate on serving the Lord (vv. 35-48). People will be bitterly divided over Christ (vv. 49-53), yet every sign points to the fact that the day of decision has come (vv. 54-59).

Understanding the Text

"The yeast of the Pharisees, which is hypocrisy" Luke 12:1-3. Luke 16:14 explains the connection between the Pharisees' hypocrisy and the "treasures" theme of this chapter. There he identified this sanctimonious well-to-do group as men "who loved money." Pious outwardly, the majority were not motivated by a love of God.

Jesus' next words serve as a healthy reminder for you and me. Whatever our true motives are, they cannot be hidden. No mask can survive the scrutiny of God. One day what we whisper when we think no one can overhear will be "shouted from the housetops."

How blessed we are when what we think, what we say in secret, and what we say in public, all reflect our deep love for the Lord.

"The Son of man will also acknowledge . . . before the angels of God" Luke 12:4-9. These words also serve to introduce the theme of treasures—in two ways.

As Jesus continued to minister, it became increasingly clear that the religious establishment was hostile to Him. John 9:22 tells us that they agreed to "put out of the synagogue" (excommunicate) anyone who acknowledged Jesus as the Christ. This was a terrible threat, implying first of all isolation from one's family and the whole community, and second implying the threat of death. To "acknowledge [Jesus] before men," then, might mean the loss of all worldly possessions and even of life itself.

Yet Christ reminds us that the greatest of treasures is not life in this world, but life in the next! We must decide which world is most important to us—and commit.

The wonderful thing is that choosing Jesus and the world to come does not mean that we lose out now! On the contrary, Jesus reminds us that those who treasure Him are treasured by God! The very hairs of our head are "all" numbered (v. 7). God will guard us in this world, even though all this world's authorities be ranged against us.

What a joy. To surrender what we cannot keep, to gain what we cannot lose. And to live the rest of our lives here on earth cherished and protected by God!

"The Holy Spirit will teach you at that time what you should say" Luke 12:10-12. There's a neat contrast here. The Pharisees, who had just accused Jesus of performing His miracles by Satan's power, in so doing had spoken against and blasphemed the Holy Spirit (11:14-28). But Jesus' followers are assured that in times of need they will speak by the Holy Spirit.

In persecution, we have the direct support and guidance of the very Person who enabled Jesus to perform His miracles here on earth!

"You fool! . . . Then who will get what you have prepared for yourself?" Luke 12:13-21 Jewish rabbis were often called on to serve as judges and settle disputes. So the person in the crowd who asked Jesus to "tell my brother to divide the inheritance with me" was not acting out of line.

Jesus refused. He had not come to sit in judgment on such disputes, but to call us to judge our basic attitude toward earthly and heavenly treasures.

The story of the rich farmer has been grist for many a sermon, but remains a pointed challenge to each of us. Why pile up wealth here on earth? Why work to gather more than you will ever need? Christ's question, "Who will get what you have prepared for yourself?" recalls the words of Ecclesiastes 2:18-19:

> I hated all the things I had toiled for under the sun, because I must leave them to the one who comes after me. And who knows whether he will be a wise man or a fool? Yet he will have control over all the work into which I have poured my effort and skill under the sun. This too is meaningless.

The rich farmer had ignored these words of the ancient wisdom writer, and he was a fool: an *aphron,* one who rejects the precepts of God as a basis for life.

The familiar story still challenges us to reexamine our values. A recent survey of top business executives showed that over 70 percent would, if they had it to do over, abandon the "fast track" in favor of spending more time with their families. But no one has life to "do over." Each of us makes value decisions that necessarily shape our lives. What Jesus invites us to remember is that those decisions shape life here—and in eternity. Only the fool rejects the precepts of God and bases his life on the pursuit of earthly treasure.

"A treasure in heaven that will not be exhausted" Luke 12:22-34. The rich fool's treasures contrast with the treasures of Jesus' followers. The one is on earth. The other in heaven. The one can be exhausted as expenses drain what we save. The other keeps on growing as we add to it. The one brings anxiety, as security systems are installed against thieves, and accountants are hired to avoid taxes. The other frees from anxiety, for God Himself guarantees its safety. The one can't be taken with us. The other can never be left behind, for like ourselves, it is eternal.

But there's one respect in which earthly and heavenly treasures are similar. If we pile up treasures on earth, our hearts will bond with the earthly. If we pile up treasures in heaven, our hearts will be drawn toward God.

If your heart were a compass today, which way would it point?

"Be dressed ready for service" Luke 12:35-48. Jesus continued to explore the impact of treasure on our way of life. If we are committed to Him, and have psychologically abandoned material goals, we will actively serve others—and be looking expectantly for Christ's return.

The return of Christ is a frequent theme in each of the Gospels. Jesus is not gone; He has temporarily withdrawn. The wise believer expects His return, and lives accordingly.

"Fire on the earth" Luke 12:49-53. Jesus would soon suffer death (v. 50), and His resurrection would precipitate a personal crisis for each who heard Him. Each would be confronted with the utter necessity of a decision about who Jesus is—and that decision would divide families.

Again the contrast is drawn between commitments on earth and in heaven. However painful it may be, whatever the cost, the wisest choice one can make is for Jesus.

"How to interpret this present time" Luke 12:54-59. A person glances at the sky, and decides it's a good time to plant, or a good time to set out in his boat for fishing. Every one of His listeners could recognize the signs that predicted weather in Galilee and Judea.

Jesus called the crowd "hypocrites," implying that those who heard Him were insincere in claiming not to be able to interpret the signs that indicated who Jesus is. They knew. And now, in God's window of opportunity, each must make the critical decision and decide for "what is right"—before it is too late, and he or she must face God the Judge (vv. 58-59).

▶ DEVOTIONAL
Radical Christianity
(Luke 12:22-34)

Today those two words hardly seem comfortable, rubbing up against each other as they do here. "Radical" belongs with some weird group of students on a college campus. "Christianity" belongs with church bells, well-filled parking lots on Sunday morning, well-dressed women and respectable men sitting attentively in a pew. For most of us, Christianity isn't radical at all.

The trouble is, it's supposed to be. And that's what Jesus was pointing out here.

Oh, He didn't mean that each of us should sell everything and go live out of a backpack or in a commune. He did mean that Christians are to adopt a radical perspective on life—and to live by it. In this passage Jesus identified three aspects of the radical viewpoint that are to shape our lives.

First, we're not to live anxiously. Jesus pictured pagans as "running after" the necessities of life, panting in exhaustion as they wear themselves out trying to guarantee themselves food, clothing, and shelter. We, on the other hand, have a Heavenly Father, who knows our needs, and will supply them. This doesn't mean we stop working. But it does mean we stop worrying. We don't focus our energies on piling up possessions. And, in this world, that's radical.

Second, we're to live with abandon. "Sell your possessions" can be taken literally, and some have made just this response to Jesus' words. Even those who have not are still to abandon their possessions psychologically. We are not to care about mere things. They are not to get in the way of our readiness to respond to God or to others. And that's radical.

Third, we're to live with compassion. We're not just to "sell your possessions," but also to "give to the poor." Possessions aren't to be burned, as though they had no worth. They are to be used to minister to people. In essence, we are to value others more than we value things. And that's radical.

As I write this, the most recent San Francisco earthquake has just taken place. And in Los Angeles, a twenty-year-old who won a red sports car in a radio station's contest told the station, "Sell the car. And send the money to the folks who need it in San Francisco." I don't know if the young man is a Christian or not. But his act was certainly radical. And it sums up beautifully what Jesus says to you and me.

Don't become anxious about things, or spend your life accruing them. Abandon your possessions, breaking any hold they have on your life. And live with a deep concern for others. That's radical.

"Radical" and "Christianity." Right where they belong.

Together.

Personal Application

Only a fool is unwilling to live a radical Christian life.

Quotable

"In the year 1627, there was a wonderful outpouring of the Spirit in several parts of England as well as in Scotland and the north of Ireland. But riches and honor poured in upon them as well, and their hearts began to be estranged from God and started to cleave to this present world. As soon as persecution ceased, the Christians who were once poor and despised became invested with power, ease, and affluence. Riches and honor quickly produced the usual effects. Receiving the world, they quickly loved the world. They no longer panted after heaven, and lost all the life and power of religion."—Charles Wesley

AUGUST 16 *Reading 228*
URGENT MATTERS
Luke 13–14

"Make every effort to enter through the narrow door, because many, I tell you, will try to enter and will not be able to" (Luke 13:24).

The choices that we make in our todays affect our tomorrows—and our forever.

Overview

Jesus warned, "Repent, or perish" (13:1-5). All deserve punishment (vv. 6-9), but Jesus showed that this is the day of God's grace (vv. 10-17). Though Jesus' kingdom may seem insignificant (vv. 18-21), it is vital to enter now (vv. 22-30). Christ's warning rejected, He wept over Jerusalem (vv. 31-35).

At a Pharisee's dinner party Jesus healed (14:1-6), commented on guests' and host's behavior (vv. 7-14), and spoke of God's eschatological kingdom (vv. 15-24). Later He spoke to the crowds about the cost of discipleship (vv. 25-35).

Understanding the Text

"Do you think that these Galileans were worse sinners?" Luke 13:1-5 It was common belief that those who were cut off in the prime of life had been guilty of some great sin. When someone asked about some Galileans who were killed by Pilate's soldiers while coming to the temple to offer sacrifice, Jesus rejected the common view. In saying they were no more guilty than all others in Jerusalem, Jesus taught that all were worthy of death!

It's useless to compare ourselves with others and think, "I never do things like that." All have sinned. Unless we repent, we will all perish.

Here "repent" is used in its most basic meaning of a change of heart and mind. The listening crowd had to change its mind about Jesus, before it was too late.

"Leave it alone for one more year" Luke 13:6-9. The parable emphasizes how close judgment had come, and how little time was left for repentance and change. If repentance did not come soon, the verdict would be, "Cut it down."

"On the Sabbath Jesus was teaching" Luke 13:10-17. Though all were guilty and deserved punishment, Christ's healing of the crippled woman was an affirmation of grace.

The indignation of the ruler of the synagogue shows how little understood grace was. And how little desired. The woman who experienced grace praised God. But the president of the synagogue rebuked Jesus for helping her!

Many first-century rabbis held that it was valid to untie a farm animal to permit it to drink on the Sabbath, though the strict sect of the Essenes would not permit help to be given even to an injured animal. Christ's contemptuous dismissal of the charge as hypocrisy shamed His opponents. But it delighted the crowds.

How fascinating that no matter how the hypocrite postures and pretends, others see through him.

Or us.

"What is the kingdom of God like?" Luke 13:18-21 The details of Jesus' sayings are irrelevant to His point, which is simply this: Jesus' kingdom appeared insignificant to many onlookers. But ultimately Christ's kingdom will dominate all.

"Make every effort" Luke 13:22-30. Because Christ's kingdom is the ultimate reality, entry becomes an urgent matter. Mere familiarity with Jesus will not do. One must know Him intimately, and be known the same way.

A feast or banquet is a common prophetic image associated with the establishment of God's future and final kingdom. That meaning, clearly defined in verses 28-30, is carried through the next chapter's stories, which are set at or told about banquets.

This was why repentance and faith in Jesus are such urgent matters. Individuals who failed to turn to Him will be shut out of the future kingdom, where "there will be weeping . . . and gnashing of teeth."

"Leave this place and go somewhere else" Luke 13:31-35. The Pharisees' hypocritical warning symbolized the official rejection of

Jesus by the religious leaders. No doubt if Herod had intended to imprison Jesus, these same men would have done all they could to keep Jesus there!

Christ, rather than being angry, expressed anguish and sorrow over the city which must now face desolation and judgment. The house of Israel, having rejected Jesus, became an empty shell. It would remain a mere shell until that future day when God's people acknowledge Christ, and are restored (vv. 34-35; cf. Rom. 11:25-32).

"Is it lawful to heal on the Sabbath or not?" Luke 14:1-6 This is the fourth reference in Luke to the Sabbath issue, showing how serious it was in the conflict between Jesus and the religious elite (6:1-5, 9-11; 13:10-17). This time it took place at a meal in the home of a "prominent Pharisee." The Greek term is *archonton,* "ruling," and suggests he was a member of the Sanhedrin.

While Christ seemed to bring the issue up, Luke noted that the man with dropsy had been seated "in front of Him." And that all Jesus did was being "carefully watched." Again, no compassion was shown for the sick man, who was simply a pawn to be used against the Lord.

The rabbis had ruled that a person whose life was threatened might be taken to a doctor on the Sabbath, but one not suffering from a life-threatening disease should wait till the next day for treatment. Jesus healed the man anyway and then, arguing from the lesser to the greater, showed their hypocrisy. Any one of them would pull a son or an ox out of a hole on the Sabbath, even if their life was not in immediate danger. How then could they object to healing a man on God's holy day?

It must have been frustrating, to be an opponent of Jesus. Whenever they attempted to act against Him, they simply injured themselves!

As long as we live in the spirit of Jesus, maintaining His compassion for others, any who criticize us will also expose only their own hardness of heart.

"Do not take the place of honor" Luke 14:7-11. Still at the banquet, Jesus commented on the behavior of the guests, who competed with each other for "places of honor." In the first century banquet seating arrangements reflected the social status of guests. The closer to the host (the "higher" the seat), the greater the honor done a guest.

The scrambling for position Jesus observed reflected the heart attitude of the Pharisee's guests. As Jesus pointed out, it was also foolish, as it exposed a person to the danger of embarrassment if asked to go down lower.

You and I can afford to take the humblest of places here on earth. In time God Himself will say to us, "Move up to a better place."

"When you give a luncheon or dinner" Luke 14:12-14. Jesus also had advice for His host. Don't use your dinners for social advantage, or to seek a quid pro quo. Invite the homeless and hungry when you want to share a meal. Let God repay you.

The advice should not have been needed. Proverbs 19:17 says, "He who is kind to the poor lends to the LORD, and He will reward him for what he has done." The social life of the religious, who scorned both the poor and those ignorant of the Law's minutia, the *am ha eretz,* showed that they used religion as well as others for personal ends.

How challenging it is to truly let God's Word shape our lives. The most ordinary actions demand scrutiny. All we do reflects the values of this world—or of the next.

"If anyone comes to Me" Luke 14:25-35. Later, on the road with the same crowds that the Pharisees and teachers of the Law tended to despise, Jesus spoke of discipleship. One of the most urgent issues we must decide is whether we will follow Christ wholly.

What's involved? A commitment to Jesus that places Him even above family (vv. 26-27). A conscious commitment, that looks ahead and counts the cost, and determines to carry discipleship through to completion (vv. 28-33). A continuing commitment, that once begun maintains its fervor, even as salt to be useful must retain its savor (vv. 34-35).

Difficult? Certainly. But how wise we are to make that conscious, continuing commitment to Jesus Christ!

▶ DEVOTIONAL
The Streets and Alleys (Luke 14:15-24)

Banquets in the ancient world were eagerly looked forward to. Life was difficult at best, and festive meals were a time to cast off cares, and enjoy.

That's probably why the Old Testament prophets frequently picture the establishment of God's final kingdom as a great feast, overflowing with food and wine and shouts of joy. Here Jesus picked up the familiar Old Testament image, using it in a parable that every listener understood refers to the coming eschatological (future, and final!) kingdom of God on earth.

The parable makes several points that His hearers would understand, but that might escape a modern reader. First of all, the refusal of the invited guests was shocking. It was an honor to be invited. And an obligation to come. Besides, who would ever think of passing up a "great banquet"? All who heard would have understood Jesus to accuse the religious leaders of refusing God because they were consumed with earthly affairs.

A second impression would have been made by Jesus' reference to "streets and alleys."

First-century Jewish cities were bisected by a few broad streets (where the Pharisees liked to come and preen). But they were also warrens of alleys, twisting and turning back to little courts opening out on the hovels occupied by the poor. In Jesus' story, the host sent his servants everywhere, even to the obscure homes of the "poor, the crippled, the blind and the lame."

And when the banquet hall was still not filled, the servants were sent out, beyond the walls that kept outsiders from the city, to distant roads and country lanes, with a compelling invitation that would move even strangers to Israel's God to respond.

The parable, uniquely shaped to Jesus' hearers, still speaks to us. It is still incomprehensible that many who hear God's invitation are too caught up with the affairs of this life to heed. And it is still the glory of the Gospel that its message is for everyone, everywhere.

Personal Application

As servants of God, we are to probe the streets and alleys of our world for guests to God's banquet at history's end.

Quotable

"O merciful God, who hast made all men, and hatest nothing that Thou hast made, nor desirest the death of a sinner, but rather that he should be converted and live; have mercy upon all who know Thee not as Thou art revealed in the Gospel of Thy Son. Take from them all ignorance, hardness of heart, and contempt of Thy Word; and so fetch them home, blessed Lord, to Thy fold, that they may be made one flock under one Shepherd, Jesus Christ our Lord, who liveth and reigneth with Thee and the Holy Spirit, one God, world without end." —Book of Common Prayer

AUGUST 17 *Reading 229*
CONCERN FOR OUTCASTS
Luke 15

"Now the tax collectors and 'sinners' were all gathering around to hear Him. But the Pharisees and the teachers of the Law muttered, 'This Man welcomes sinners and eats with them' " (Luke 15:1-2).

It's not necessary to be like the people we associate with. That's good, because we must spend time with people if we are to say, "I care."

Overview
Criticism of Jesus' association with the outcasts of Jewish society (15:1-2) was answered by three parables: the Story of the Lost Sheep (vv. 3-7), the Lost Coin (vv. 8-10), and the Lost Son (vv. 11-32).

Understanding the Text
"Tax collectors and 'sinners' " Luke 15:1-2. The tax collectors, who worked on commission and were notorious for overcharging, were automatically considered dishonest or immoral in first-century Jewish society. "Sinners" is placed in quote marks in the NIV to show that the evaluation was made by Pharisees, not by Jesus or Luke.

The fact is that we are all "sinners." But in the eyes of the Pharisees, the title belonged exclusively to those who were less rigorous than they in keeping the rituals of law. The very idea of having table fellowship (eating) with such persons horrified the Pharisees, for to eat with sinners would contaminate them.

Yet throughout the Gospels "sinners"—including such real sinners as prostitutes—are constantly portrayed as "gathering around" Jesus! Somehow they felt comfortable with the holy Son of God. How do we explain that? Very simply. Jesus constantly showed that He cared.

The outcasts of society were comfortable with Jesus, because instead of dislike and condemnation, they sensed love.

The outcasts of society still need less of our judgmentalism, and more of our love. We need to remember that it was the outcasts who responded to Jesus, not the "respectable" Pharisees, and learn to express that nonjudgmental love that so attracted first-century social outcasts to Jesus.

"The Pharisees and the teachers of the Law muttered" Luke 15:1-2. It's impossible to leave these two pregnant verses without noting that anyone who feels comfortable with society's outcasts, and spends time with them, will be muttered about by folk like the Pharisees and teachers of the Law.

Two divergent views of people and of holiness come into conflict here. For Jesus, holiness was rooted in a dynamic, intimate fellowship with God. For the Pharisees, holiness was rooted in do's and don'ts. Jesus' kind of holiness was warm and attractive. The Pharisees' kind of holiness was austere and judgmental. Jesus, freed by the nature of His holiness, reached out to others to share God's love. The Pharisees, bound by the nature of their holiness, drew back from others in distaste, fearful of contamination.

Today if you and I maintain that warm, intimate relationship with God that is the source of true holiness, we too can reach out lovingly to the outcasts of our society and be welcomed by them. But if our "holiness" is a front, a pretense maintained by desperately following a modern rule of do's and don'ts, we too will fear and be repelled by the outcasts of society.

What a test of the quality of our relationship with God! Are we more like Jesus in our contacts with outcasts? Or more like the Pharisees and first-century teachers of the Law?

"And loses one of them" Luke 15:3-7. The three parables related in Luke 15 are each designed to reveal God's attitude toward the outcasts of society. The Pharisees muttered when Jesus ate with tax collectors and "sinners." But God rejoiced. These outcasts of society were precious to Him. And are still.

One hundred sheep was a typical flock in the first century. When even 1 was lost, Jesus reminded His audience, the shepherd went in search of it. "Open country" was a relatively safe place to leave the 99, so there is no question of abandoning the many to seek the one.

The impact of the story was felt as Jesus related the shepherd's joy as he carried the lost sheep home. "In the same way" rejoicing echoes in heaven when one sinner repents!

It's important to note that Jesus' purpose in associating so freely with sinners was redemptive. He was seeking God's lost sheep. We can't defend participating with sinners in their sin on the basis of Luke 15:1-2! But we need never apologize for associating with sinners with the redemptive intent that moved our Lord.

"Suppose a woman has ten silver coins and loses one" Luke 15:8-10. Both the story of the 1 lost sheep and the 1 lost coin were drawn from first-century Jewish daily life. All were familiar with shepherds. All felt the impact of Christ's story of the 10 coins.

These were 10 dowry coins, given the woman when she married. The chances are that she wore them constantly on her headdress. Ten coins were a small dowry, yet were an important symbol to her. They showed that she had worth and value to her father, who had sacrificed to give them to her. And that she came into the marriage as a partner, bringing resources of her own. If she were ever divorced, or widowed, the 10 coins at least were hers, a symbol of her identity as a person. The 10 coins, then, were vitally important to her, and the loss of even 1 had far greater significance than the coin's intrinsic worth might suggest.

Again Jesus emphasized the intensity with which the woman searched, and her joy at finding the coin. Ecstatic with delight at finding the precious object, she hurried and told her friends.

Again Jesus was affirming the importance of the outcast. Of little intrinsic worth, the coin was vitally important to the woman who lost it. In the same way, while human beings may discount the worth of the outcast, in God's sight every individual is of infinite value.

What a reminder to us to look at others with God's eyes, not society's. The mother on welfare, the teenage dropout, the convict behind bars, the jobless and homeless, the drunk sleeping in the doorway, are God's lost coins. They have value to Him.

"Quick! Bring the best robe and put it on him" Luke 15:11-27. The only possible rival to this parable for "best known of Jesus' sayings" is the Story of the Good Samaritan. Probably the Story of the Prodigal Son would top most people's list.

It has so much to say.

There's the vivid picture of the younger son, who wanted to go out on his own with his (one third) share of the father's estate. He left, made unwise and immoral choices, and found himself abandoned and starving. He realized what a mess he'd made of his life and decided to go home. Knowing he had no right to expect treatment as a son, he hoped to be treated as one of his father's hired servants. In earlier stories Jesus stressed the joy in heaven over a sinner's return. In this story we are invited to share the lost son's joy, as his father rushed out to welcome him and shower him with evidence of his love.

So is our welcome when we, like the lost son, come to our senses and appeal to God for mercy. We are treated like sons and showered with love. The "best robe" is none too good for God's lost who have been found.

Consider too the father. He gave his younger son freedom, and the resources to use that freedom. He knew the son would waste his inheritance, yet the father also knew that only through the free exercise of choice can the decision to return be made. And then the father waited.

We can imagine him, each day glancing frequently toward the road his son must travel to return. We can imagine his anxiety. And yet the father waited. The lost son had to make the choice.

And then one day the choice was made. While the boy was still a long way off, the father saw him, was filled with compassion, and "ran to his son, threw his arms around him and kissed him."

Oh, friend, you and I never need to fear turning to God, even after the most terrible of sins. We must make the choice. But as we make our first, penitent step back toward God He runs to us, and we can sense His loving, forgiving embrace.

"The older brother became angry" Luke 15:28-32. And so we turn to the older brother, who like the Pharisees stood by and mut-

tered angrily at the welcome given sinners. What gave the father and the lost son joy made the older brother resentful and angry.

How long he had lived with his father. Yet how little he understood him, or shared his capacity for love.

Perhaps this is the primary lesson you and I need to draw from this most famous of Jesus' tales. Those who live with and in God must adopt His values, and be moved by His love—or lose salvation's joy.

▶DEVOTIONAL
Which Lost Son? (Luke 15:11-32)

We all know the Story of the Prodigal Son. We know how foolish the younger brother was. And we wonder at the forgiving love of the father, who welcomed his lost son home even after all the boy had done. But the strange fact is, it is the older brother who had really lost his way!

When the younger son left he was given the equivalent of one third of the estate, for the eldest son in Judaism received a double portion. While the younger tasted both the delights and the devastation of sin, the older son stayed home and worked the land with his father. "You are always with me" was the greatest gift the father could provide. But the older son had even more. While he complained, "All these years I've been slaving for you," the father rightly pointed out, "Everything I have is yours."

The older son had enjoyed his father's fellowship, and all the work he had done had only enhanced his own inheritance. And yet when the younger son returned, and the father welcomed him, the older son became bitter and angry.

That bitterness and anger, that lack of love for his brother, tell us that it was really the older son and not the younger who had lost his way. It's not that his actions were open to criticism, but because his heart was so far out of harmony with the heart of the father. He had never strayed from the path of morality. But he had never found the highway of forgiving love.

He had worked for the father. But he had never valued his brother as the father had always valued him.

The younger brother is an encouragement for nonbelievers, and for Christians who are deeply aware of their sin. But the older brother is a constant challenge to you and me. As hard as we work for the Lord, and as moral a life as we may lead, unless we have God's heart for the outcast, we have truly lost our way.

Personal Application

God does not call us just to be good, but to be like Him.

Quotable

"Real love is the universal language—understood by all. You may have every accomplishment or give your body to be burned; but, if love is lacking, all this will profit you and the cause of Christ nothing."—Henry Drummond

AUGUST 18 *Reading 230*
WORLDLY WEALTH
Luke 16–17

"No servant can serve two masters. Either he will hate the one and love the other, or he will be devoted to the one and despise the other. You cannot serve both God and Money" (Luke 16:13).

Once again Jesus took up the topic of money and its relationship to the kingdom of God, and showed its relationship to faith.

Overview

A "shrewd" but dishonest manager used money to prepare for his future (16:1-12). Sneering Pharisees, who loved money, were told to repent and live the truth they claimed to honor (vv. 14-31). Jesus urged His disciples to guard against causing sin (17:1-4), and taught that His command required obedience rather than more "faith" (vv. 5-10). Those who have known Christ's healing touch are to praise God (vv. 11-19) and look for His coming kingdom (vv. 20-23), though others are entranced by this world's pleasures (vv. 24-37).

Understanding the Text

"The master commended the dishonest manager" Luke 16:1-13. Don't suppose that Jesus implied a tribute to dishonesty. The compliment is focused on one thing only. The dishonest manager ("unjust steward" in older versions) had realized that money is to be used to prepare for his future.

Jesus applied the story to us. We too are to view worldly wealth as nothing more than an instrument for gaining the true riches in heaven.

"You cannot serve both God and Money" Luke 16:13. The saying focuses on our choices. A person who serves another does what his master chooses. In this life God and Money compete for our allegiance. If our choices are motivated by a desire for money, we will not serve God. If we serve God, our choices will not be motivated by a desire for money.

The excuse that's sometimes offered, "I want to make money so I can serve God," is just that: an excuse, intended to mask the fact that love for money dominates our lives.

Yes, a rich person can love God. But if he does, the way he or she uses the money possessed will reveal it.

"The Pharisees . . . were sneering at Jesus" Luke 16:14-18. It's best to take these puzzling verses, along with the story of the rich man and Lazarus, as Jesus' response to the Pharisees. What do they mean?

Jesus identified the Pharisees as money lovers (vv. 14-15). They were well-to-do as well as pious men. Christ accused them of seeking to "justify yourselves in the eyes of men" rather than God. Anyone who cares more about what others think of him or her than what God thinks shares in this condemnation. Jesus affirmed the primacy of Scripture, and of His kingdom. The kingdom, not money, and not the accolades of others, both of which the Pharisees loved, has permanence. The difficult phrase rendered "everyone is forcing his way into it" is better taken "and enthusiastic men lay hold of it." Unlike the Pharisees, others were unwilling to settle for the tinsel of this tawdry world.

The reason for the insertion of the verse on divorce here is uncertain (v. 18), though it may suggest some of the sneering Pharisees had divorced their wives to marry more attractive, younger women.

"I am in agony in this fire" Luke 16:19-31. This pointed story underlines the failure of the Pharisees to truly believe the Scriptures in which they boasted. If they had believed, they would not have loved money, but the poor. They would not have built personal estates, but rather would have fed the hungry. Instead, like the rich man in the story, Jesus' money-loving critics "dressed in purple and fine linen and lived in luxury every day" while beggars lay outside their gates.

Many believe that this is not a parable but identifies actual people. In parables, people are identified as "servants," or as a "sower" or "master" or "guest." In no parable is any actor given a personal name, as Lazarus is here. Yet whether or not Lazarus and the rich man are real individuals, or merely representative, the story contains one of Scripture's clearest pictures of the after-death experience. There is blessing for God's own, and torment for those who refuse His grace. And between these two states lies an uncrossable gap.

The choices we make during this life do fix our destiny. Those who wish can scoff at Jesus' warnings of the corrupting influence of wealth. But many have pushed heaven away while grabbing greedily for this world's worthless gold.

"They will not be convinced even if someone rises from the dead" Luke 16:31. The teachers of the Law and Pharisees frequently demanded Jesus provide a "sign from heaven" to prove His messiahship (11:16; cf. Matt. 12:39; 16:4; Mark 8:11). Why didn't He provide it? Part of the answer lies in Scripture's emphasis on faith. We are to trust God and His Word to us. Yet part of the answer lies in unbelief. Whatever sign Jesus provided would not convince those determined not to believe.

Even when Jesus did rise from the dead, His opponents refused to believe. If a person will not hear and respond to the Word of God, "to Moses and the Prophets," they simply "will not be convinced."

It's good for us to remember this when we share the Gospel with others. The Word of God is living and vital. It reaches human hearts, and those who are open to God respond. Those who do not believe will not believe, and would not even if we could perform miracles before them in our own day.

So we witness without hesitation, confident that where the seed of the Word finds fertile soil, new life will sprout.

"Things that cause people to sin" Luke 17:1-10. Again one of Jesus' frequent teachings is found in a context different from that in which it appears in other Gospels. Here Christ shows us how we can help each other accept and live by values the Pharisees had rejected. We are to rebuke one another when one of us sins, but be quick to forgive when he or she repents.

How is this relevant to our theme? Simply that each of us is to accept responsibility to care about one another's walk with God. Other's may stumble often, but in the community of faith each is to find forgiveness and support to live a godly life.

The Apostles were right to see this as challenging and difficult. But Jesus leaves us no choice (see DEVOTIONAL).

"Have pity on us" Luke 17:11-19. The healing of the lepers is a case study in attitude. Ten were healed of a dread disease that isolated them from all the pleasures of life in this world. They were cut off from loved ones. They were cut off from work. They were cut off from their homes, and even from the worship of God.

But 10 lepers who appealed to Jesus were healed! And 9 of them couldn't wait to return to the world from which they had been cut off. Only 1, a Samaritan, after showing himself to a priest and being confirmed as clean, returned to thank the Lord.

We are in danger from the meshes of that love for money that ensnared the Pharisees. We are in danger, after being spiritually healed, of dashing back into the world, without acknowledging our debt to Jesus, and without putting praise first.

Only by valuing God supremely can we be protected from the love of money and ease.

"The kingdom of God is within you" Luke 17:20-21. It seems better to take Jesus' reference to the invisible form of His kingdom as "among" rather than "within" the Pharisees who questioned Him. The kingdom was already present, in the person of the King. It was not present in pomp or glory. It was not present in power. All the emblems of worldly rule had been discarded. And the Pharisees, deceived by the phantoms they pursued, simply could not recognize the kingdom when it came.

What a lesson for us. God's kingdom is among us too. Christ is here, hidden but present in His church and in His people. Christ is here, in the needy and the oppressed. Christ is here, in the hopeless and the weak. Let's never be deceived, as were the Pharisees, by worldly wealth, by buildings, or by pomp. God's kingdom is among us, as Christ expresses His love in the ministry of His people to all.

"As it was in the days of Noah" Luke 17:22-37. Christ's kingdom is among us—and

coming. What is hidden now will be revealed. But when Christ returns He will find the world as it was in the days of the Pharisees. As it was in Noah's day. As it was when fire rained down on Sodom. As it was when San Francisco quaked.

People are so caught up in eating and drinking, in marrying and being given in marriage—in the pleasures and pursuits of this world—that they cannot imagine that another world looms on the horizon, ready to break in on our reality and strip every illusion away.

The Pharisees, despite their religion, did not really believe, and so came to use their religious zeal as a cloak for money love. Yet one day, when Jesus comes or when death overtakes, wealth will at last be put in true perspective. It can be used by the wise believer to prepare for a better eternity. And it can destroy the fool, who ignores the Word of God, and reaches for the cash.

▶DEVOTIONAL
When Faith Doesn't Matter (Luke 17:1-10)

We Christians rightly put great emphasis on faith. So it's just next door to heresy to insist that in some things, faith doesn't matter. Not one little bit.

Still, that is what Jesus is saying here in Luke 17. It's like this. Jesus told His disciples to guard one another. When one sinned, another is to rebuke him. Then, if the sinning disciple repents, he's to be forgiven (vv. 1-4).

It seems simple enough, even though we don't like confrontation. But Jesus went on to make it even more difficult. He said if a brother sins against you he's to be forgiven. Even if he keeps on sinning against you, time and time again! That's right. Even if it happens over and over again, daily.

Each time the brother says, "I'm sorry," he's to be welcomed back. Even though by a sixth or seventh time even the most gullible of us would suspect he's putting us on.

At this point the dismayed disciples cried out, "Lord, increase our faith." Lord, they're saying, if You expect us to live this way, we're going to need a whale of a lot more faith than we have now!

Then Jesus used another illustration. He spoke of a slave (servant) and a master. Would a slave be praised for doing whatever duty the master assigned? Hardly. He'd only be doing what is expected of a slave.

But why this story? Simply because Jesus, the disciples' Lord and Master, commanded them to confront, to accept "I repent," and to forgive. Responding to a command isn't a matter of faith. It's a matter of obedience.

And so we have to examine our own lives carefully. How many times have we held back, wishing we had more faith so we could do something we knew God wanted us to do? How many times have we pleaded for more faith in our inadequacy? And how many times has the longing for more faith simply masked the fact that we have been unwilling to obey?

Personal Application

Don't deceive yourself. Much in the Christian life is not a matter of faith. It's a matter of obedience!

Quotable

"The accomplishment of the divine will is the sole end for which we are in the world."—John Eudes

AUGUST 19 *Reading 231*
PARABLES AND PEOPLE
Luke 18–19

"Today salvation has come to this house, because this man too is a son of Abraham. For the Son of man came to seek and to save what was lost" (Luke 19:9-10).

Luke's vivid sketches of people and his dramatic retelling of Jesus' parables leave a lasting impression.

Overview

Jesus contrasted an indifferent judge with God (18:1-8), and a proud Pharisee with a penitent sinner (vv. 9-14). He welcomed children (vv. 15-17) but discouraged a wealthy would-be follower (vv. 18-30). Jesus predicted His death (vv. 31-34), and illustrated its impact by restoring physical and spiritual sight (v. 35–19:10). The Parable of the Ten Minas taught delay of His earthly kingdom (vv. 11-27), but still the crowd saluted Him as Messiah as He approached Jerusalem (vv. 28-44). There, rather than proclaim a kingdom, Jesus purified the temple (vv. 45-48).

Understanding the Text

"Pray and not give up" Luke 18:1-8. There are times when we become discouraged about prayer. We claim the promises of Luke 11; we ask, seek, and knock. But we find no answer, and no doors seem to open to us.

The story of the unjust judge encourages us to keep on praying, and to keep expecting God to answer. Luke used a common literary device: contrast. The unjust judge just didn't care about the widow, but finally gave in because she kept on bothering him. Delay may be within the will and purpose of God. But answers to our prayers are assured, not because we're persistent, but because unlike the judge, God does care!

Even in the most extreme situations, which move us to cry out to God day and night, we can be assured of justice, though it be delayed till Jesus comes.

"I am not like all other men" Luke 18:9-14. This story is directed to all people everywhere who are "confident of their own righteousness and [look] down on everybody else" (v. 9). The Pharisee, who represented this group, thought his works were a ticket into God's kingdom. In contrast the tax collector, a representative "sinner," simply cried out for mercy.

Self-justification is still a fantasy. Those who pray as the Pharisee did have their eyes fixed only on themselves and not God. Only by taking our place beside the despised first-century tax collector, acknowledging our sinfulness, and relying solely on God's mercy, can we be justified before God.

"Receive the kingdom of God like a little child" Luke 18:15-17. The incident is purposely sandwiched between stories of two adults who sought entrance into God's kingdom, one by religious works and the other by good deeds. Here the significant aspect of little childness is dependence. No little child expects his own effort will provide him with even food or shelter. As a little child depends on his parents for everything, so we are to depend on God for entrance into His kingdom.

"What is impossible with man is possible with God" Luke 18:18-30. The rich young ruler represents those who rely on morality and decency to gain eternal life. In the first century the rich, who had the resources to be benevolent, were thought to have the inside track on pleasing God by helping others!

Jesus told the wealthy young man to abandon his wealth, and follow Him. This is not a universal command. It was given to a specific individual for a specific purpose: to help the young man see that he relied on his wealth rather than on God.

It is this that makes it hard for "the rich to enter the kingdom of God." A person with wealth comes to depend on it rather than on the Lord.

As a young Christian I feared possessions. I wanted a car, but worried that if I had one it might become too important to me. Finally, when at age 23 I bought an old Nash Rambler for $500, I enjoyed it, but I learned with delight that it meant nothing to me at all!

The Lord seldom requires we "leave all

we have" to follow Him (v. 28). But each of us does well to psychologically abandon all our possessions, that we might rely on God and respond freely to His will.

"Its meaning was hidden from them" Luke 18:31-34. Luke reported a number of sayings in which Jesus foreshadowed or specifically predicted His death (cf. 5:35; 12:50; 13:32; 17:25).

He also often mentioned the disciples' failure to grasp the meaning of this and other teachings, as do the other Gospel writers. Here Luke clearly implied that God Himself withheld understanding awaiting the right time.

What a helpful reminder! Often those we teach or minister to, including our own children, seem unwilling to grasp and apply truths we know are vital. Despite all we say, they make unwise or foolish choices. While the reason may lie in their own willfulness, we must remember that it may simply be that it isn't yet God's time for them to understand. God often hides the meaning of what we teach until the time is right to reveal it.

Let's deal graciously and patiently with others, as Jesus did with His disciples. If they seem slow or reluctant, let's consider the possibility that God has His own reasons for withholding understanding for a time.

"Jesus, Son of David, have mercy on me" Luke 18:35-43. The disciples didn't understand when Jesus spoke of His coming death. Yet the next incidents illustrate its meaning. Jesus healed a physically blind man who cried out for mercy (vv. 35-43), and then brought salvation to one who had been spiritually blind (19:1-10). Through His death Jesus would lay the foundation for the defeat of every force hostile to humankind.

The healing of the beggar illustrates the way in which human beings lay hold on all that Jesus provides. Jesus told him, "Receive your sight; your faith has healed you" (18:42). We need only come to Jesus, confident that He is able to save. That faith is the channel through which God's goodness flows.

Note, however, that faith is the beginning of a new life, not simply the end of the old. The blind man received his sight, ending his years in darkness. And he "followed Jesus, praising God." This is the essential nature of the new life faith launches. It is a life of following Jesus. And of praising God.

"He was a chief tax collector and was wealthy" Luke 19:1-10. Many tax collectors in first-century Judea were simply employees. But "chief tax collectors" were major contractors, who guaranteed a certain sum to Rome or Herod—and were free to extort more as they could. Thus Zaccheus would have been considered a far greater sinner than, for example, Levi, who simply manned a highway tax station (5:27-30).

Several of Luke's themes are united in this story. Jesus reached out to and associated with sinners. His contact is redemptive, bringing both salvation and transformation. The renewal of Zaccheus is evidenced by his repentance, and his change of attitude toward wealth.

Perhaps the most important lesson for you and me is reflected in the stunned look that must have covered Zaccheus' face, as Christ looked up in the tree where he was perched and said, "Zaccheus, come down immediately." The short tax collector had climbed a tree because he wanted to see Jesus. But he never imagined that Jesus would want to see him.

How we need to take the initiative in seeking out folks others may hold in contempt. Jesus did come "to seek and to save what was lost." Jesus is gone now. And He's committed His treasure hunt into our hands!

"To have himself appointed king and then to return" Luke 19:11-27. This parable is linked with the story of Zaccheus (v. 11). Salvation came "today," but final judgment would be delayed.

The story has a historical context. Would-be local rulers in Palestine had to go to Rome to be appointed by the emperor (v. 12). While the principle would be understood by Jesus' listeners, it is not to be applied in interpreting the parable, which makes one major point. Jesus will return, and when He does a day of judgment will occur.

His servants will then be evaluated on the basis of how they used the resources

He provided. And His enemies will be destroyed.

The story served as a clear warning to enthusiasts who had witnessed His healings and the transformation of Zaccheus. They were not to expect Jesus to set up an earthly kingdom at that time. The warning was ignored, and before Christ reached Jerusalem crowds gathered to acclaim Him Messiah and King (vv. 28-38).

It's important we do not forget His warning. Jesus will return, and each of us will give an account. If we have used our resources—of time, talent, and wealth—to promote God's kingdom, there will be praise from our Lord, and a responsible role to fulfill in eternity.

"Blessed is the king who comes" Luke 19:28-38. Zeal without knowledge. It's not unusual, but it's sad. Jesus had just warned that He was not yet coming as King: He had to return to heaven and be confirmed in that role by His Father (v. 12). So of course the crowds shouted all the louder, "Blessed is the King who comes!"

The crowds were right. Jesus is King. But He was not yet coming as King.

We may be zealous and enthusiastic. But unless we listen to God's Word far more carefully than the crowds listened to Jesus, we will be as unaware of God's present purposes in our lives.

▶ DEVOTIONAL
Dreams and Devastation (Luke 19:28-48)

As I write this, Jim Bakker is awaiting afternoon sentencing for fraud, for lying to the Christian public in order to bilk them of funds. In his defense, Jim told the jury about his vision—his dream of a playground for Christians, of Heritage, U.S.A. Whatever a person may think of Jim Bakker, I'm sure each of us would give him this. He had a dream. And he saw his dream lie, shattered, at his feet.

The people who welcomed Jesus so enthusiastically on Palm Sunday had a dream too. They dreamed of Israel restored to its ancient glory under God's

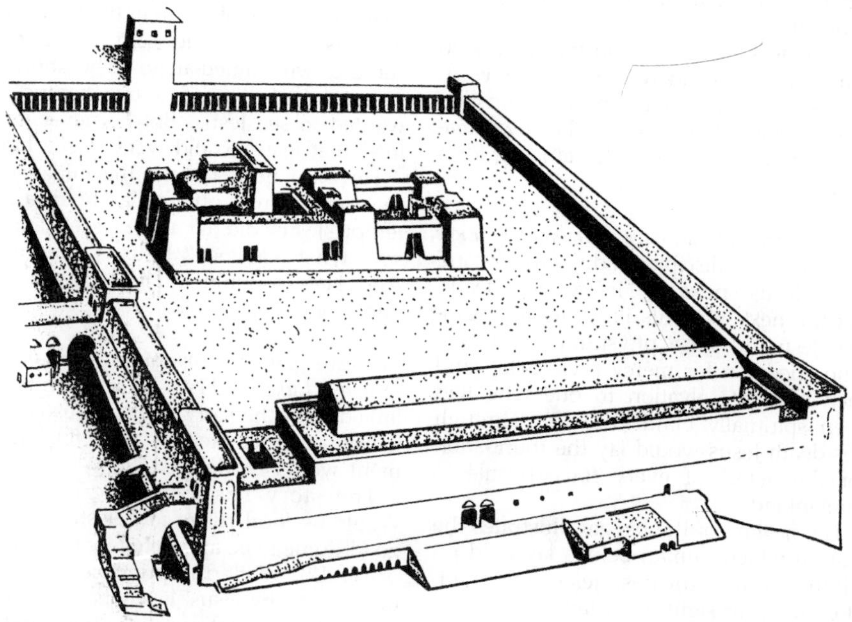

Herod the Great dedicated 40 years and untold wealth to beautify the Jerusalem temple. That temple was one of the wonders of the ancient world, and drew thousands of Gentile as well as Jewish visitors to Judea. Yet Christ's anger that its courts had become a "den of robbers" reminds us that the true significance of any house of worship is not found in how it looks but in what happens there.

Messiah, the promised Descendant of David. Their shouts, as Jesus rode slowly toward Jerusalem, revealed the dream that possessed them completely: "Blessed is the King who comes in the name of the Lord!"

As they drew near the city the shouting, elated crowd must have envisioned its walls heightened and expanded, sure it was destined to become the center of a theocratic kingdom that would replace Rome as ruler of the world.

But when Jesus saw the city, He wept. What Jesus saw was not towering new walls, but crumbled ruins. What Jesus heard was not the joy of misguided supporters entranced by their dreams, but the wailing and crying of the victims who would suffer there. And Jesus wept.

The next thing Luke tells us is that Jesus entered the temple area. There He found those who were selling; who had turned God's house from a house of prayer to a den where robbers lurked, eager to defraud the pilgrims who came to Jerusalem to worship. The dream was nothing. The reality was all.

I think that the sequence of these events serves as a parable of our times. So many Christians have dreams. So many are so zealous to build empires to God's glory; edifices they dream of proudly showing Jesus when He comes, saying (but humbly, of course), "See what we've done in Your name!"

Yet one by one such dreams, like the walls of ancient Jerusalem, fall into ruin. We have zeal. But are the dreams that possess us given by God, or are they like the shouts of the Palm Sunday crowd who insisted on welcoming Jesus as King despite what He had told them?

I suspect that what Jesus wants is revealed in His first action in Jerusalem. He cleansed the temple. He chased out the hucksters who had corrupted what was intended to be a house of prayer, and once again put worship first.

Personal Application

It is more important to cleanse our temple than to pursue our dreams.

Quotable

"It sounds terribly spiritual to say 'God led me,' but I am always suspicious of a person who implies that he has a personal pipeline to God. When no one else senses what the person suggests is the will of God, then we had better be careful. God has been blamed for the most outlandish things by people who have confused their own inverted pride with God's will."—Paul E. Little

---

AUGUST 20 *Reading 232*
LASTING LESSONS
Luke 20–21

"He is not the God of the dead, but of the living, for to Him all are alive" (Luke 20:38).

Jesus' last days in Jerusalem occasioned some of His most important teaching, conveying lasting lessons.

Overview

Jesus rebuked His critics (20:1-8), and told a parable that exposed their motives (vv. 9-19). He turned aside their attempts to trap Him, and used them to teach responsibility (vv. 20-26) and resurrection (vv. 27-40). Christ silenced His opponents with a riddle that had an obvious but rejected answer (vv. 41-44) and then openly condemned them (vv. 45-47), praising a widow, one of the oppressed they exploited (21:1-4). A last lengthy dialogue focused on Christ's return (vv. 5-38).

Understanding the Text

"By what authority You are doing these things" Luke 20:2. The chief priests and teachers of the Law were members of the Sanhedrin, Judaism's supreme religious and civil authority. How frustrated they must have been by Jesus, who bypassed them completely to teach, and performed miracles that proved He had been anointed by God.

Authority was extremely significant in the religion of the first century. As today in rabbinic Judaism, the opinions of earlier rabbis were eagerly searched and quoted as authority for contemporary decisions. But "authority" in the language of the New Testament is freedom of action. The person with authority can speak or act without fear his or her will will be thwarted by another.

Thus the irony in Jesus' question. He asked these leaders, who claimed authority, to give their opinion of John the Baptist. And they refused! They had no freedom, no true authority, at all! Their freedom to speak was taken from them by fear of what Jesus might say in rebuttal, or how the people they claimed to lead would react.

Today you and I have freedom in Christ. We are truly free to speak and act in accord with our convictions. We are free, because we trust God to guard us from those who might do us harm. Let's claim the authority that Jesus' critics surrendered, and always be ready to speak the truth in Jesus' name.

"May this never be!" Luke 20:9-19 It was clear to all who heard that the Parable of the Tenants, in which the dearly loved son of the owner was killed, was a veiled reference to the religious leaders and to Jesus Himself. At first glance the horrified reaction of the crowds seems to express the wish that the owner's son should escape (v. 16). But a closer look at the sayings just before and after correct the impression.

Jesus had warned that the furious father would appear and kill the wicked tenants, and give the vineyard to others. It was this that provoked the reaction, "May this never be!"

How like each of us. No one wants to be held accountable for his or her actions. Our nine-year-old wants to mess up her room—but not be forced to clean it up. The pregnant teen wanted experimentation or sought popularity—but doesn't want the baby. One of the most important things we can do for our children is to make sure they learn early that every choice has its consequences. "May this never be!" is a useless plea.

"Give to Caesar what is Caesar's" Luke 20:25. Throughout the last 2,000 years believer and unbeliever have paused in wonder over the profound simplicity of Jesus' saying.

We live in the world, but are not of it. Caesar can require worldly things from us, and we are to give them gladly. But nothing Caesar does can touch that which we owe to God: our love, our worship, and our concern for others for whom Jesus also died.

"Even Moses showed that the dead rise" Luke 20:27-40. This is a fascinating passage for any who are uncertain about the integrity and full authority of Scripture.

It's popular with some scholars to assume that the books attributed to Moses are a much later fiction: the name of a mythical Jewish hero, Moses, was attached in the 600 B.C.s to give the editors' invention credibility. With scissors and paste many modern scholars romp through the Old Testament, cut up the Pentateuch and Prophets, and assign this verse to one supposed set of authors, and that to another.

How different from the way Jesus viewed the Scriptures. According to Christ, it was Moses who spoke what is recorded in Exodus, and even a seemingly minor thing like the tense of a verb is authoritative. Do the dead really live again? They live now! The God of the Old Testament is the God of Abraham, Isaac, and Jacob, long after their biological deaths.

On this issue of Scripture, I suspect it's wiser to trust Jesus' pronouncement than to trust the theories of the self-proclaimed wise men of our day. When we do so, we rejoice in the confidence that we too will live forever with Abraham's and our God.

"How then can He be his Son?" Luke 20:41-44 The Jewish people loved riddles and word games. But the religious leaders who had set themselves against Jesus positively hated one riddle Christ put to them. It wasn't because they didn't know the answer. The riddle was objectionable because they did know the answer!

Simply put, the only way that David's Descendant could be his Lord was if the expected Messiah were somehow God Himself. And this is one thing the leaders of Christ's day could not and would not consider.

Sometimes we're like them when seeking God's will. "Lord," we say, "show me what You want"—when all along we know what God wants, and hope desperately He'll change His mind.

Let's learn from the Pharisees how not to approach our own relationship with God.

"Such men will be punished most severely" Luke 20:45-47. Each Gospel records something of Christ's final evaluation of the ultra religious men who were His most severe critics. Matthew 23 focuses on their hypocrisy. Luke drew attention to their affront in putting on religious airs while secretly "devouring widows' houses"—an expression which means taking financial advantage of those unable to defend themselves.

Again we see the terrible corrupting power of a love for wealth and a preoccupation with appearances. Judgment for such persons is sure and severe.

"She out of her poverty put in all" Luke 21:1-4. It's not how much we give, but our willingness to surrender all. Undoubtedly Luke purposely placed the ragged, humble widow beside the posturing, well-dressed politicians whose pretentions Jesus had just exposed. Luke wanted us to see others as God sees them. He wants us to realize that the mighty are seldom high on God's scale of values.

▶ DEVOTIONAL
Do's and Don'ts to Live By (Luke 21:5-36)

Ask a Christian to make up a list of "do's and don'ts believers should live by" and you probably won't get the Ten Commandments.

In the little church I joined after I was converted, our list had things like "don't smoke," "don't drink," "don't go to movies," "do be at church Sunday evening as well as morning," and a few other similar things. Our do's and don'ts list didn't keep us from loving the Lord and other people. And it didn't keep us from some of the most meaningful prayer and worship I've ever experienced. In fact, looking back, I doubt that the list had any great impact on my life at all—except to make me a little uncomfortable when some sailor friend lit up a cigarette in my "Christian" car.

A list of do's and don'ts that can really make a difference is buried in Luke's report of Jesus' teaching on the future. Among teachings that apply directly to us are:

- Don't follow false leaders (v. 8).
- Don't be frightened when natural and other disasters befall (vv. 9-11).
- Don't be anxious if persecuted because of your Christian witness (vv. 12-16).

And on the positive side:

- Do persevere and maintain a firm stand when others turn against you (vv. 17-19).
- Do take heart; full redemption will be yours when Jesus comes (vv. 25-28).
- Do watch and pray, that you might live a life the Son of man will approve (vv. 34-36).

Personal Application

God's do's and don'ts belong at the top of our lists.

Quotable

"Have thy tools ready; God will find thee work."—Charles Kingsley

AUGUST 21 *Reading 233*
THE FINAL HOURS
Luke 22–23

"With loud shouts they insistently demanded that He be crucified, and their shouts prevailed" (Luke 23:23).

Carefully Luke, like each of the evangelists, traced Jesus' final hours from betrayal to burial.

Overview

Judas agreed to betray Jesus for money (22:1-6). At the Last Supper Jesus spoke of a New Covenant in His blood (vv. 7-23), spoke again on greatness (vv. 24-30), and predicted Peter's denial (vv. 31-38). Events now moved quickly. Jesus prayed (vv. 39-46), was arrested (vv. 47-53), disowned by Peter (vv. 54-62), and mocked by His guards (vv. 63-65). He was taken before Pilate and Herod (v. 66–23:16), condemned (vv. 17-25), crucified (vv. 26-43), died (vv. 44-49), and was buried (vv. 50-56).

Understanding the Text

"They were afraid of the people" Luke 22:1-6. During major religious festivals Jerusalem overflowed with pilgrims. Excited and volatile during these times, both the Roman government and the Jewish leaders kept close watch, hoping to avoid a spontaneous riot. Luke pictured the religious leaders, desperate to get rid of Jesus, actively "looking for" some way to dispose of Him.

When Judas appeared to bargain for money they were delighted: What they feared to do openly they would gladly do in secret!

What a simple test this suggests for us to apply to our own lives. If afraid or ashamed to do anything openly—don't do it at all!

"Satan entered Judas, called Iscariot, one of the Twelve" Luke 22:1-6. The expression does not imply Satan entered against Judas' will. Instead it suggests that Judas' own openness to evil gave Satan an opportunity to work through him.

If you have ever feared Satan's power, this passage in Luke indicates how fallible the ruler of evil is. Satan inspired Jesus' betrayal. He eagerly choreographed Christ's steps to the cross. And all along Satan was ignorant of the fact that the cross would be the instrument of his own defeat!

Satan is powerful, yes. But he is not a god. His struggle against God is destined for utter defeat, and God is able to transform the most evil acts along the way into instruments of His good.

"This cup is the New Covenant in My blood" Luke 22:1-23. The term "covenant" is one of the most significant in Scripture. In Old Testament times a covenant was a binding legal agreement, whose nature was determined by the parties involved. Between two businessmen it was a contract. Between nations it was a treaty. Between ruler and people it was a constitution. But between God and human beings, the basic force of "covenant" is a commitment. God's ancient covenant with Abraham is marked by His statement of what "I will" do. God's temporary covenant with Israel established through Moses, the Law, specified what God would do if Israel obeyed—or disobeyed. The "New Covenant" Jesus spoke of at the Last Supper, instituted at His death and sealed by His own shed blood, is God's commitment to forgive the sins of those who believe in His Son, and to transform their character from within (cf. Jer. 31:31-34; Heb. 10:16-18).

As we read the chapters which trace Jesus' last day, we need to remember that Christ went to the cross knowing what His death would mean for you and me. Jesus suffered willingly. And He Himself is our guarantee: He is Himself the divine commitment to forgive us, and to make us new.

"Which of them was considered to be greatest?" Luke 22:24-30 Some, noting that Matthew's Gospel placed this dispute at a different time and place, cry "discrepancy," and so "prove" the Bible is not without error after all. Such folks have never had children.

I don't know how many dozens of times I've heard the same argument between Sarah and our Matthew. Or how many times Sarah has asked the same question, blithely forgetting or ignoring the answer she's been given again and again. The necessary assumption underlying the cry of "discrepancy," that any human being will talk about something important to him once, and only once, seems utterly amazing to me.

So I'm not surprised that the disciples, still unaware of Jesus' imminent death, went back to arguing about who would be greatest in Christ's kingdom. And I'm not surprised that Jesus once again contrasted the "greatness" of secular rulers with that servanthood which makes a man great in the eyes of the Lord.

A discrepancy in Scripture? No. A flaw in the disciples? Yes. And a flaw in us if, like the Twelve, we expend our energies in the pursuit of status—while a dying world cries out for help and hope.

"I confer on you a kingdom" Luke 22:28-30. Luke now added something not found in Matthew. At the Last Supper Jesus added these words, and the promise that one day the 12 disciples would sit on thrones to judge Israel's 12 tribes.

There's plenty of "greatness" ahead for us all. But that's for history's end, not for now. Today there's servanthood. And the greater our willingness to serve, the greater our future reward will be.

"That is enough" Luke 22:35-38. Earlier the Twelve and also 72 were sent out to minister, and told to take no money or extra clothing with them. Jesus mentioned this, and reminded His disciples that when they did go, they lacked nothing.

He then seemed to revise His instructions. Most take this unexpected reversal either as sarcasm, or as a way of emphasizing the seriousness of the immediate crisis. Surely His saying, "Buy a sword," suggests imminent danger. But when the disciples showed Him two blades, He said, "That is enough."

Today, two are still enough. They are enough to symbolize the dangers of this present world. Yet they are not enough to protect us from those dangers, any more than two swords in the hands of untrained disciples could protect Jesus from the approaching mob.

It's important for us to recognize the danger to be found in the world. But it is just as important, in our helplessness, to realize that we cannot rely on worldly means for our defense.

"He touched the man's ear and healed him" Luke 22:47-53. When the mob arrived, a disciple tried to use one of the two swords. He swung (wildly?) and succeeded in slicing off one man's ear!

Jesus, saying, "No more of this!" touched the man and restored his ear.

At the very beginning of Jesus' ministry He had said, "Love your enemies, and pray for those who persecute you" (Matt. 5:44). Now, about to go to the cross, He took love a step further. Even as your enemies seek to destroy you, make them whole.

"The Lord turned and looked straight at Peter" Luke 22:54-62. Only Luke added this detail. It was not the crowing of the cock that made Peter realize what he had done in disowning Jesus. It was the fact that, as the cock crowed a third time, Peter glanced up and met Christ's eye.

Later Peter wrote an epistle that quotes Psalm 34:14: "For the eyes of the Lord are on the righteous" (1 Peter 3:12). The meaning is that God is watching over His own, eager to do them good. God watches us, as Christ looked at Peter, with love! The guilt Peter suddenly felt was not in Christ's look, but reflected from Peter's own eyes.

Sin has a peculiar impact on us. It makes us look away from God, trying to forget that He always sees us. Thus sin keeps us away from the one Person we most need when we fail. Let's learn two things from Peter's experience. First, after doing wrong, look quickly to the Lord. The love you see in His eyes may move you too to weep bitterly. But in that process you will be healed. And second, look unceasingly to the Lord. If you never look away, the love in Christ's eyes will keep you from sin.

"Jesus, remember me when You come into Your kingdom" Luke 23:26-42. The thief on the cross is healthy corrective to the superficial treatment of Jesus by Pilate and Herod (see DEVOTIONAL). At first both thieves mocked Jesus. But in time one

asked Jesus, "Remember me."

There's no guarantee that facing death will bring a person to consider eternity. There were two thieves, but only one stopped his ridicule after a time. Only one said, "Remember me." Still, that one thief reminds us that as long as life lasts, it's not too late to appeal to God in Jesus' name. And that because the longest life is but a brief moment compared with eternity, we must call on Jesus while we can.

After all, He did die to save us. As the Crucifixion account reminds us, it's a matter of Jesus' death—and our eternal life.

"Wrapped it in a linen cloth" Luke 23:50-56. Jesus died. He was buried. And there these chapters—but not His story (or history) end.

▶ DEVOTIONAL
Hoping for a Miracle (Luke 22:66–23:25)

The trial of Jesus was a disappointment to everyone. Pilate kept on saying, "There's no basis for a charge against this Man" (23:4). The Jewish leaders kept on desperately trying to find something that would move Pilate to order Christ's execution (vv. 2, 5, 10, 14). The carefully recruited crowd got hoarse shouting out, "Crucify Him!" on cue. And poor Herod, who'd wanted to see Jesus for a long time, was upset because when Jesus was brought to him in chains, Christ wouldn't perform a miracle for his entertainment!

Barabbas, a convicted insurrectionist and murderer, was satisfied. He was released instead of Jesus and slipped away, never to be mentioned again.

But I'm sorriest of all for poor, superficial Herod. I imagine he sulked for hours. All those months hoping to see a miracle, and then—nothing! What in the world would Herod talk about at his next dinner party? How he finally saw Jesus, and Jesus wouldn't perform?

Actually, Herod reminds me of a lot of Christians. One recent survey suggests that people shop for churches as for a commodity. They check out agencies. They ask about the preaching. They find out who goes to the church. They listen critically to the choir. Are there enough activities for children? For teens?

Even then all too many come on Sunday and go away disappointed, because for some reason God or the preacher didn't perform well that day. Like Herod, they came to be entertained. They came "hoping for a miracle," and God wasn't putting on a special performance for them that day.

We can see clearly what was wrong with Herod's attitude. The Son of God was about to go to the cross, and all that Herod cared about was being entertained! But can we see this flaw in ourselves? Have we ever stopped to think that church isn't supposed to be entertaining?

Church is to be a gathering place for a community of faith; a company of men and women who worship the crucified Saviour, and who commit themselves to minister to a lost and suffering mankind.

Personal Application

What you come to church for determines what you take away.

Quotable

"It's hard to imagine—Paul having the gift of entertainment.—Barnabas being the minister of entertainment rather than the minister of encouragement.—Jesus selling tickets to the feeding of the 5,000.—Peter peddling his 'Feed My Sheep' seminars.

"Far too often, we've tried to bring ministry, music, and entertainment together, and in so doing we've lost the integrity and true meaning of the church. No one can honestly say they've been called by God to entertain."—Glenn W. Harrell

AUGUST 22 *Reading 234*
ALIVE AGAIN
Luke 24

> *"Did not the Christ have to suffer these things and then enter His glory?" (Luke 24:26)*

We share today the glory into which the resurrected Christ has entered.

Background

Resurrection. The Gospels report several incidents where Jesus brought the dead back to life. This was not resurrection, but resuscitation. In resuscitation biological life is restored. But the individual remains mortal, and must experience biological death again.

On the other hand resurrection is not a restoration of biological life. It is a transformation of the individual; a transmutation from mortality to immortality. The resurrected never again die, but live forever with the Lord. The resurrected are not subject to suffering or pain, or to the limitations that restrict mere men.

Christ entered into the glory of the resurrected life when He burst triumphant from His tomb.

Overview

The first day of the week angels told awed women that Jesus had risen (24:1-8). Peter and John hurried to view the empty tomb (vv. 9-12). Jesus revealed Himself to two followers He met on the road to Emmaus (vv. 13-35). He met with all the disciples and "opened their minds" to the Scriptures (vv. 36-49) before being taken up into heaven (vv. 50-53).

Understanding the Text

"On the first day of the week" Luke 24:1. From the very beginning of the church, Christians have held services on the first day of the week rather than the seventh. The Sabbath (Saturday) memorialized Creation and God's rest. The first day (Sunday) celebrates the resurrection of Jesus, and our victory over sin in Him.

Each Sunday as we worship let's commit ourselves to live in the newness of life that Jesus brings.

"Then they remembered" Luke 24:2-8. It was only when the women saw the angel and were reminded by him that Jesus had promised to rise again that they remembered.

If they had remembered earlier, how differently they would have felt during the nights and days Jesus' body lay in the grave. If they had remembered earlier, they would have come to the tomb with hope and expectation.

When a loved one dies, those who are left behind always grieve. But if we remember the empty tomb—and what it promises to us—we will come to the graveside of our believing dead weeping tears that glisten with the promise of joy.

Jesus arose. And so will we.

"You are witnesses of these things" Luke 24:36-49. Later Jesus appeared to the 11 disciples. Seeing His hands and His feet, hearing His familiar voice, every doubt was overcome, and His disciples believed.

It was then, after faith had come, that they were able to understand the Scriptures. Verses that had been familiar suddenly were filled with a meaning they had not grasped before.

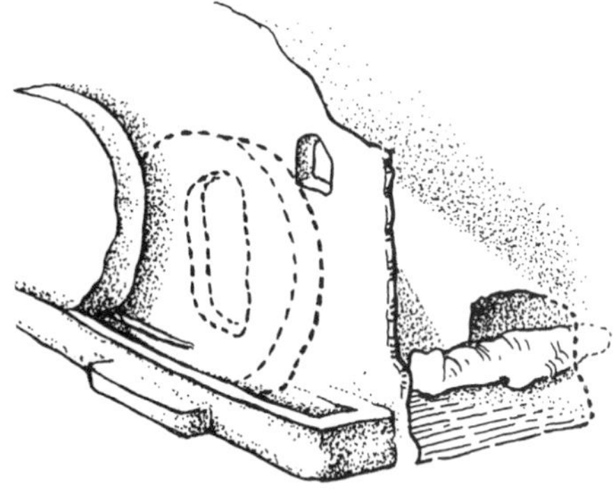

Many believe that the first-century tomb shown here is similar to that in which Jesus lay. The track in which a massive stone rolled (24:2); the low cut door at which Peter stooped (v. 12); the tiny window through which dawn's light fell on the empty graveclothes (v. 12); all fit the details of the Gospel account. And the Garden Tomb lies near a mount that some identify as Calvary. Whether or not this is like the actual tomb is unimportant. What is important is that Jesus arose!

And then Jesus said a strange thing. The disciples were to "be witnesses" to all the things the Scripture had predicted would happen. They were to confirm the Word of God by testifying to its truth!

In one sense, of course, nothing you or I can say can confirm or detract from the Word of God. God's Word is truth, whatever men say about it. Yet in another sense we do bear witness to its trustworthiness.

The 11 Jesus chose would preach the prophecies, and then would say, "I saw them fulfilled." Even as today you and I share the Gospel and say, "I know it's true. I have seen God's promises fulfilled in my own life. I have experienced God's forgiveness, and seen Jesus Christ change me."

▶ DEVOTIONAL
Downcast Disciples
(Luke 24:13-35)

That Resurrection morning, as two of Jesus' disciples trudged along the dusty road to Emmaus, a town about seven miles from Jerusalem, their faces were downcast. Mournful and gloomy, they undoubtedly made dreary companions that Easter morn.

Yet when Jesus joined them in the guise of a stranger, the two disciples revealed they had a host of Resurrection facts! They even told the friendly Stranger about the empty tomb.

Yes, some of their company had talked with angels, who said Jesus had risen from the dead.

Yes, two disciples had gone to the tomb, and found it empty. But they hadn't seen Him.

So as these disciples trudged along, their faces sad, their hearts burdened, mourning the triumph they thought a tragedy, Jesus traced the Old Testament passages which predicted the Messiah's death and foretold His resurrection. And even then the two disciples couldn't shake their gloom.

Downcast disciples.

Downcast disciples, walking along the road with Jesus by their side.

Downcast disciples, mourning as though their God really were dead rather than with them, and triumphantly alive.

If you think that this is strange, think for a moment about your own life. Have you forgotten what the two on the road to Emmaus didn't know? Do you find that you have a downcast mood that slips up on all of us now and then. But when it does, that's the time to remember the lesson of the road to Emmaus. Our feelings do not fit the facts! We're not alone anymore. Jesus lives, and our resurrected Lord walks our road with us.

When we focus our attention on Him, and realize how close beside us He is, that downcast mood will be replaced by joy.

Personal Application

Resurrection means the risen Christ is with you and me today.

Quotable

"The Lord who took on our life had to die to give us His divine life. But death could not keep Him, so He rose again on the third day. My deepest rejoicing is in the living Word of God assuring us of the victory of Jesus over death, for I know that the little Child who was born in Bethlehem had to suffer before I could be saved. I cannot therefore be grateful enough to Him. I pray that I daily may know Him more and more, that I do not harden my heart when He speaks to me, that when He clearly speaks to me, I may obey Him, and that above all I may adore Him as my God and Saviour.

"If we love Him above everything else in life, He will give us power to master our problems, overcome our fears and rise above every temptation and every sin. And then we shall be granted a foretaste of life eternal even in this mortal life."—Charles H. Malik

---

The Variety Reading Plan continues with SONG OF SONGS

John

INTRODUCTION

John is the fourth and last-written of the New Testament's portraits of Jesus Christ. Most believe it was composed between A.D. 70 and 100 by John, son of Zebedee, one of Jesus' 12 disciples. This is the most theological of the Gospels. It grew out of the need of second- and third-generation Christians for an authoritative answer to the questions about Christ's nature which then troubled the church. John said of his work, "These things are written that you may believe that Jesus is the Christ, the Son of God" (20:31).

Unlike the other Gospels, which follow a chronological sequence, John related separate incidents and teachings which help us better understand Jesus' universal mission. Much of what John shared is not found, or is only briefly mentioned, in Matthew, Mark, and Luke. Through John's clear portrayal of Jesus and His teaching, we do come to a much deeper appreciation of Jesus and what it means to have faith in Him.

OUTLINE OF CONTENTS

I. Prologue . . . . . John 1:1-18
II. Jesus, the Life Giver . . . . . John 1:19–4:42
III. Jesus, Healer and Judge . . . . . John 4:43–5:47
IV. Jesus, the Bread of Life . . . . . John 6
V. Jesus, Water and Light of Life . . . . . John 7–8
VI. Jesus, Shepherd of Mankind . . . . . John 9–10
VII. Jesus, Resurrection and Life . . . . . John 11:1-54
VIII. Jesus, the Triumphant King . . . . . John 11:55–12:50
IX. Jesus, Life of the Church . . . . . John 13–17
X. Jesus, Life from Death . . . . . John 18–21

READING GUIDE (20 Days)

If hurried, you may read only the "core passage" in your Bible and the Devotional in each chapter of this Commentary.

Reading	*Chapters*	*Core passage*
235	1:1-18	1:1-2
236	1:19–2:25	1:43-51
237	3	3:3-10
238	4	4:43-54
239	5	5:31-47
240	6	6:39-59
241	7	7:25-43
242	8	8:31-47
243	9	9:13-25
244	10	10:22-29
245	11	11:17-44
246	12	12:12-24
247	13	13:31-35

248	14	14:1-6
249	15	15:9-17
250	16	16:1-15
251	17	17:20-23
252	18	18:28-40
253	19–20	20
254	21	21:15-19

John

AUGUST 23 *Reading 235*
THE LIVING WORD
John 1:1-18

> *"No one has ever seen God, but God the only Son, who is at the Father's side, has made Him known" (John 1:18).*

John introduced the ultimate mystery. God had somehow taken on human nature and become flesh.

Background

The Word. In both Testaments "word" is a pivotal and complex concept. The Greek *logos* appears over 300 times in the New Testament, with a variety of meanings. Jesus' identification as the "Word" has great theological significance. As the Word, Jesus is the expression of God's person and character in the world: the One who reveals the Father. And as the Word, Jesus is also the powerful, active presence of God in the world: the One with ultimate authority over all natural and supernatural forces, able through infusions of grace not only to make alive but also to transform the inner nature of human beings to fit them for fellowship with God.

While theologians tend to wax eloquent over the philosophical implications of *logos,* as we read John's Gospel we can have a simpler, more direct meaning in mind. Jesus, the Word of God, is the One through whom we hear God's voice. He is the One in whom we meet God, and welcome God into our lives.

Overview

The "Word"—the Creator and source of our life—preexisted with and as God (1:1-5). John the Baptist announced His coming (vv. 6-9), yet when He arrived His own people rejected Him (vv. 10-11). But all who do receive Him become children of God (vv. 12-14). He is the source of grace, the Son who, being God, reveals the Father to mankind (vv. 15-18).

Understanding the Text

"In the beginning was the Word" John 1:1-2. Like the first verses of Genesis, John 1:1-2 catapult us back beyond the origins of time, into the mystery of God Himself.

Christians have affirmed the New Testament's teaching that the One God of the Old Testament exists in three Persons: God the Father, the Son, and the Holy Spirit. John launched his Gospel with a powerful statement that the Man Jesus is God the Son, the eternal Word through whom God has always expressed Himself (see DEVOTIONAL).

"In Him was life" John 1:3-5. In John's Gospel "life" sometimes indicates biological vitality, but more often indicates spiritual life. John often described the life he spoke of as "eternal." The life available to us in Christ has a supernatural quality and power, as well as endless extent. It is this eternal life which Christ offers that shines in our world as a bright light. Like a beacon to a lost traveler, the light shining in Jesus offers all men hope. Not only hope for life after death, but hope for a rich and meaningful life here and now.

"The darkness has not understood it" John 1:5. The specific intent of the Greek verb, *katelaben,* has been much debated. Is it simply saying that men in darkness haven't realized the nature of the shining light? Or does the word mean "overcome," as in other passages in John? (6:17; 8:3-4; 12:35)

Soon John would develop his theme of a basic conflict between good and evil, darkness and light. The world of men is not just ignorant of the character of the light, but hostile to it!

An invisible war rages on Planet Earth. God and Satan are in perpetual conflict, and knowingly or not every human being takes sides. The light shed by the Son's offer of eternal life makes the issues of the war more clear, and challenges everyone to take sides.

How good to know that no matter how hostile men and women may be, they can never overcome Christ's light.

"A man who was sent from God" John 1:6-9. Luke told the Baptist's background; John emphasized his mission. The fact that he was "sent from God" established his authority. His mission was summed up in the word "witness" (v. 8). Throughout this Gospel John would assemble evidence that established Jesus as the Son of God. The Baptist was the first witness, identifying Jesus for the Jewish men and women of the first century.

Today too God sends men and women to witness of His Son. While Jesus Himself is the light, you and I must give testimony about the benefits of coming to Him for eternal life.

"The right to become children of God" John 1:10-13. These verses, like much of John's writing, are packed full of information. The "world" in verse 10 is first earth itself as the environment for life, and second a sinful social order which refused to acknowledge the Creator. While Jesus' own people and nation would not receive Him, He continues to hold out the divine offer of eternal life to individuals. Those who do receive Him are given the right to become sons of God.

The verses clarify two issues. First, are all human beings God's children? While all human beings are His creations, and objects of His love, John reminds us that not all are spiritually related to God. Only the special gift of eternal life in Christ changes our nature, so that we become God's *tekna;* His "born ones" who by spiritual rebirth share His divine nature.

Second, what does it mean to "believe"? John began his explanation by equating "believe" with "receive." New life in Christ is offered as a gift. Just as one who reaches out and takes a gift shows by his accepting it that he believes in the reality of the gift and the trustworthiness of the person who offers it, so in receiving Christ as Saviour, we demonstrate belief in the gift and in the trustworthiness of God the Giver

How simple it is. We hear the Gospel's Good News, our heart welcomes Christ, and in a grand supernatural transaction we are forgiven and flooded with new life. We become God's children, born anew by an act of God Himself.

"Grace and truth came through Jesus Christ" John 1:15-17. The Law of Moses established a standard of righteousness for humankind. Jesus revealed God's gracious attitude toward all mankind. Looking at the Law we see what we should be, and feel ashamed. Looking at Jesus, we realize God loves us despite our sins, and rejoice.

"God the only Son" John 1:18. The essence of Deity is unseen because our eyes cannot detect Him. So God took on a form that we could see.

"Only" here has the essential meaning of "unique." Jesus is the Son of God in a way that we can never be, for He preexisted time itself. We become God's children. Jesus is and has always been God's only Son.

▶ DEVOTIONAL
No Greater Love
(John 1:1-2)

"Three gods! You've got three gods!"

That misunderstanding of Christian faith is common in both Muslim and Jewish circles. And yet Christians claim, "No. We have one God, the God of the Old Testament, who is shown in the New Testament to exist in three Persons."

It's nonsense to many, of course. And yet as we read John's first verses, we see that this is just what the Bible teaches. The Word, a few verses later on identified as the Son incarnate, Jesus Christ, was there in the beginning. He was with God. And He was God.

Many attempts have been made to find an analogy that will help us better grasp the mystery of the Trinity: the Three-in-

Oneness of Scripture's one God. All fall short. The Trinity remains a mystery. Perhaps the best suggestion though was made in the fourth century of our era by Saint Augustine. Augustine argued that God must be a Trinity, for God is love. Before the Creation of the world, God must have had someone to love, and some way to convey love. It follows, Augustine taught, that there must be Three within the oneness of God: a Father to love, a Son to be the object of that love, and a Holy Spirit to convey and express love.

What a thought. Before God created, God was a Person who loved. Because He existed as a Trinity, God has always been able to express that love fully within His own being. And yet God's love is so great that it overflowed beyond His own self. In love God created the world and populated it with persons in His own image. In love God gave those persons freedom of choice. And, in love, God sacrificed the Son He loved to preserve all who believe from the disastrous and eternal consequences of the choices they have made.

The Gospel of John is not only the Gospel of belief and faith, as most emphasize. John is the Gospel of unimaginable love.

Personal Application
Considering who Jesus is can deepen your love for Him.

Quotable
"Alexander, Caesar, Charlemagne, and myself founded empires; but on what foundation did we rest the creations of our genius? Upon force. Jesus Christ founded an empire upon love; and at this hour millions of men would die for Him."—Napoleon Bonaparte

AUGUST 24 *Reading 236*
THE LAMB OF GOD
John 1:19–2:25

"Then John gave this testimony: 'I saw the Spirit come down from heaven as a dove and remain on Him. . . . I have seen and I testify that this is the Son of God' " (John 1:32, 34).

Discipleship calls us to be ever aware of the power of God and to live confidently we are as in His presence.

Overview
John explained his mission (1:19-28) denying that he was the Christ and identified Jesus as the Son of God (vv. 29-34). Several future disciples, including Andrew and Peter, met Jesus for the first time (vv. 35-42) and returned with Him to Galilee (vv. 43-51). There Jesus prefigured His ministry of transformation by changing water into wine (2:1-11), and later His ministry of purification by driving money changers from the temple (vv. 12-17). At that time Jesus spoke of His coming death and resurrection (vv. 18-25).

Understanding the Text
"Who are you?" John 1:19-28 An official delegation questioned John the Baptist concerning his identity. Who did he claim to be? The Messiah? Elijah, returned from the dead? (cf. Mal. 4:5) The Prophet predicted by Moses? (cf. Deut. 18:18) John refused each of these important titles, and spoke of himself simply as a "road builder." His mission was to make it easier for folks to meet the "One who comes after me." And, John added, he himself was "not worthy" to untie the thongs of that One's sandals.

What's significant here is that the lowest servant in the house was given the task of stooping to untie a guest's sandals. John was saying, "I'm a nobody."

Yet later Jesus Himself said that John was greater than any of the mighty prophets of the Old Testament! (Matt. 11:11) John was a "nobody" only in comparison to the One he announced, who towered so much above him.

I can think of nothing more fulfilling than to be "road builders" today. The "nobody" who introduces somebody to Jesus has become important indeed.

"I myself did not know Him" John 1:29-34.

John's confession is one of the most interesting sidelights on Jesus to be found in the Bible. You see, John was Jesus' cousin, and undoubtedly knew Him well. In fact, the other Gospels tell us that when Christ came to be baptized, John didn't want to do it!

The reason is simple. John knew Jesus as a truly righteous and good Jew. John called on people to be baptized as a sign of repentance of sins and recommitment to God. John didn't think it was right for Jesus to "recommit," when He had been committed all along!

But why then didn't John recognize Him?

Probably because John, like all of us, had an image in his mind of what the Messiah would be like. And "a truly good man" wasn't a major element of that image.

Hopefully, folks around us will be surprised when they learn we're Christians. No, not because we've tried to hide the fact, or failed to speak of Jesus. But because we won't fit the image portrayed on TV and in the movies of narrow, bigoted, insensitive people who never have any fun, and hate to see others enjoy themselves either.

How delightful when someone says, "Oh, you're a born-again Christian? But you're so friendly!" Or, "You're such a good listener!" Or, "You're so understanding!" Or best of all, "But you really care!"

"I have seen and I testify that this is the Son of God" John 1:34. John fulfilled his mission in life by preparing folks to meet the Son of God, and then identifying Jesus as God's Son.

This also brings our ministry of road building into perspective. "I have seen," John said.

It's very little help to others to engage in arguments over their beliefs, or over the interpretation of a verse in the Bible. What we need to do is to testify, as John did, to our experience of God's truth.

I don't mean we shouldn't share Scripture. I simply mean we should share Scripture through our experience.

A good friend of mine, Dr. Paul Johnson of Seattle, had life-threatening cancer a few years ago. As he was going under the anesthetic before his operation, Paul felt himself falling, falling, falling. And then suddenly, he felt himself caught and held, and he realized he was being held in Jesus' arms. Paul tells the story today, not as some mystic experience, but as an illustration of Scripture's promise, "I will never leave you or forsake you" (Josh. 1:5), and especially of the phrase, "underneath are the everlasting arms" (Deut. 33:27). Paul's faith in Jesus provided peace and hope in the darkest time of his life.

You and I needn't argue about the Bible. All we need to do is to share it, and say with John, "I have seen and I testify."

"Come . . . and you will see" John 1:35-39. John could and did point his followers to Jesus. But as today, each person must find out who Jesus is for himself. Curiosity may lead some to approach Jesus; a sense of need or desperation may move others. Yet each person must then come, and see for himself if Christianity "works." Each person must meet Jesus for himself, listen to His teachings, observe His actions, and respond to His voice.

One of the most important things we can do to help any inquirer is to encourage him or her to read the Bible—especially a Gospel like Luke or John. We can do so confidently. As Christ told the questioning pair so long ago, "Come, and you will see!"

"The first thing Andrew did" John 1:40-42. This too follows a basic pattern. Evangelism is the spread, not just the sharing, of the Good News.

Often sharing our salvation is one of the first things that happens to us as new Christians. Too often the failure of others to respond surprises and hurts us. For all too many, a negative first experience stops witnessing altogether.

There's a special word here, however, that will encourage us to keep on sharing Christ. Andrew told his brother, Peter. And Peter later became the chief of the apostles; the outspoken, enthusiastic and especially human disciple whom God used to preach the first Christian sermon to the Jews (Acts 2) and to the Gentiles (Acts 10–11), and to write two of the epistles in our New Testament.

How is that encouraging? This way.

You never know when you share Christ with someone how important that person may become!

"He . . . drove all from the temple area" John 2:12-14. John's failure to follow chronology in his report of events makes it difficult to place this incident. The other Gospel writers report that a similiar incident took place the last week of Christ's life.

John, however, organized events out of sequence, to impress his readers with their significance. And this event truly is significant. Christ, who transformed water into wine, also purified the temple. He drove out corruption, and insisted that the worship of God be holy and clean.

He does this in our lives too. As He transforms He cleanses, until, purified, we exhibit a holiness which is appropriate to those who worship and honor God.

Perhaps this is why John also places a reference to the Cross in this passage. The transforming and purifying ministry of Christ is costly. There is no cheap salvation. The price of our renewal was the sacrificial death of God's unique and only Son.

▶DEVOTIONAL
I Saw You!
(John 1:43-51)

I've always liked this passage, ever since as a young seminary graduate working with preschoolers I wrote a lesson for three- and four-year-olds based on it. It illustrates how a simple story can convey the most profound theological concepts.

The lesson I wrote was called, "Jesus Always Sees Me." That's another way of talking about the doctrine of omnipresence, which states that God can be and is everywhere in the created universe at once. He is always present with us: He sees us at all times.

While Jesus did not exercise this attribute at all times, a number of biblical stories show that He was aware of events that took place beyond the range of sight. For instance, Jesus in Galilee knew that His friend Lazarus had died in Bethany, near Jerusalem in Judea (John 11). Nathanael, obviously accurate theologically, knew that there was no way Jesus could have seen him under that fig tree before Philip arrived, and came to the conclusion that Jesus was the Messiah, the Son of God. And of course Nathanael had reasoned correctly.

None of this, however, was important to the preschoolers for whom I wrote. They weren't interested in solving the mystery of the theantropic person (God/Man). They didn't care to debate to what extent Jesus surrendered exercise of the attributes of Deity when He took on humanity. But they did care that "Jesus always sees me." They did care that even when Mommy and Daddy were out of sight, Jesus was watching over them. They did care that whether they were riding in a car, sleeping in the dark, or playing outdoors, Jesus was there, and could see.

What a lesson for us today. Yes, theology is profound. But relationship with God is far greater than the most profound depiction of doctrine. And our relationship with God can be expressed in words just as simple as "I saw you." And can be understood in the comforting terms of "Jesus always sees me."

Personal Application

Let the assurance that Jesus is with you bring you peace.

Quotable

"In all thy actions think God sees thee; and in all His actions labor to see Him; that will make thee fear Him; this will move thee to love Him. The fear of God is the beginning of knowledge, and the knowledge of God is the perfection of love."—Francis Quarles

AUGUST 25 *Reading 237*
GOD SO LOVED
John 3

"God so loved the world that He gave His one and only Son, that whoever believes in Him shall not perish but have eternal life" (John 3:16).

John summed up Jesus' talk with Nicodemus in the most famous verse in the Bible: the "Gospel in a nutshell," John 3:16.

Overview

Jesus explained "born again" to a leading member of the Sanhedrin (3:1-14). John summed up the Gospel, and defined the critical role of faith (vv. 15-21). He reported the Baptist's delight in Jesus' growing popularity (vv. 22-30), and commented on the primacy of Jesus Christ (vv. 31-36).

Understanding the Text

"A man of the Pharisees named Nicodemus" John 3:1. Nicodemus reminds us that while the Pharisees were generally ranged against Jesus, there were good and godly men among them. Through this interview Nicodemus remained courteous, though obviously puzzled. Later references to Nicodemus suggest that he became one of Jesus' followers (7:45-52; 19:38-43).

It's a mistake to judge individuals by their class alone. In Jesus' time most people had intense respect for the Pharisees. Jesus showed that those of this class who opposed Him were hypocrites. Yet Nicodemus was honest in his desire to please God, as were many other Pharisees who later became Christians (cf. Acts 15:5; 23:6).

As John pointed out in this chapter, the great dividing line between human beings is not race or class, but whether or not they believe in Jesus Christ (John 3:18).

"He came to Jesus at night" John 3:2. We shouldn't make too much of this phrase, though some have suggested Nicodemus sneaked in to see Jesus for fear of criticism. Social visits often took place in the late evening: most folks in first-century Judea worked during the daylight hours.

What's important is Nicodemus' admission that "we know You are a Teacher who has come from God." Even the few miraculous healings Jesus performed in the early stages of His ministry were recognized by the ruling class as a divine authentication.

Jesus' miracles did not produce faith. Later, members of the ruling counsel condemned Jesus to death despite many more miracles! What the miracles did was to win Jesus a hearing. They produced a kind of "pre-faith": a realization that this Man must be heard.

There's a miracle that wins us a hearing today too. It's the miracle God works within us, making us loving, caring people who reflect Jesus' concern for others. This miracle will win a hearing for the Gospel. But don't be surprised if the message of Jesus provokes opposition as well as faith.

"Born of water and the Spirit" John 3:5. The meaning of this phrase has long been debated, with some insisting the "water" refers to water baptism. It does. But it refers to the baptism of John, in which water was a symbol of repentance.

God saves no one against his or her will. While the new birth is a work of God within us, God just doesn't grab folks around the neck and make them hold still while the Spirit inserts new life! No one can give themselves new life, but each person must acknowledge his or her sins, as John's baptism symbolized. By a change of heart and mind we must open ourselves to God's work within us.

And so we are born again, by water and the Spirit. We acknowledge our sins and turn to the Lord. And He works His miracle within us.

"As Moses lifted up the snake" John 3:11-14. Jesus told Nicodemus the source of His authority to promise a new birth: He had come down from heaven, and so He knew. To help Nicodemus understand what He had said, Jesus referred to an Old Testament incident. Once during the Exodus the Israelites disobeyed God, and were punished by an infestation of poisonous serpents whose bite was fatal. Moses made a bronze snake—a symbol of their judgment—and raised it on a pole. The people were then urged to simply

look at the serpent, and were promised life.

Soon Christ would Himself be lifted up on another pole, at Calvary. His death would symbolize the judgment all human beings deserve. And ever afterward, all people would be urged simply to look to Jesus, and receive new life. As the hymn writer says, "Jesus paid it all, all to Him I owe. Sin had left a crimson stain. He washed it white as snow!"

"Whoever believes in Him is not condemned" John 3:15-18. Here the Apostle John left off his report, and on his own commented. "God so loved the world that He gave His one and only Son, that whoever believes in Him shall not perish but have eternal life."

This, undoubtedly, is the most famous verse in Scripture. It links what God has done with what we must do. God has provided eternal life in Jesus. Our part is to believe.

In John 1:12 the apostle defined "believe" in terms of "receive." In John 3:15 "believe" is defined in terms of "repent."

Other images follow in this book that has been called the "Gospel of Belief." Both repenting and receiving are aspects of a true belief in God. Biblical belief is turning from ourselves and our old ways to God, and trusting God enough to open our hearts to the gift He wants to give us.

If you have turned to God and you trust His promise to give you new life in Jesus, you have eternal life, now!

"Whoever does not believe stands condemned already, because he has not believed" John 3:18. Don't suppose God condemns a person because he or she hasn't believed. That's not John's point. John said a person "stands condemned" because he hasn't believed.

Suppose you and a friend are standing on a train track, and the train is coming. You jump off and live. He doesn't move and is killed. In one sense he was killed because he didn't get off the track. That would have saved him. But in another sense he was killed because he stood on the track in the first place.

John wasn't saying that God punishes people for not believing. He says that people who deserve punishment can avoid it only by faith in Christ. Sin puts people on the track along which God's judgment is coming. Belief in Jesus gets them off the track and out of the way. If they are condemned it won't be for not believing. But it will be *because* they did not believe.

Don't let folks confuse you on this. Jesus didn't come to condemn anyone. He came that all who would believe might be saved.

"Men loved darkness instead of light" John 3:19-21. Why, when people hear the Good News of God's gift of eternal life, do so many of them not believe? John said that they love darkness. To come to Jesus means repentance: it means admitting that our deeds are evil and that we need to be born again. Some people are repelled by the Gospel because the evil within them dreads exposure.

How foolish. And how tragic. One day every man's deeds will be exposed anyway. And those who have not found forgiveness in Jesus will be condemned.

"He must become greater; I must become less" John 3:22-30. How great a protection John's attitude is from the Christian's greatest temptation: pride. Even the little man is tempted to be proud that he's so humble. And the Christian who knows success is in danger indeed!

John wasn't concerned about the smaller crowds that came to hear him when Jesus was preaching in the same district. His great joy was that Jesus become greater, and he himself less.

The person who is ready to accept a John-like role in life will, like John, find himself often "full of joy" (v. 29).

"Placed everything in His hands" John 3:31-36. Again the author broke off his report to comment. Why did Jesus deserve the priority that John the Baptist acknowledged?

What a list of reasons he gave! Jesus has priority because He is above all (v. 31). Because He comes from heaven (v. 31). Because He knows by experience what He is speaking about (v. 32)—and all who accept His words discover personally just how truthful He is (v. 33). Jesus has priority because He speaks the words of God (v. 34). Because God gives Him an unlimited supply of the Spirit (v. 34). Because the Father loves Him (v. 35) and has placed everything in His hands (v. 36). Because He is the source of eternal life for all who believe (v. 36), the only way to escape the coming wrath (v. 36).

This Jesus, who is preeminent, must have priority in our lives.

▶ DEVOTIONAL
You Must Be Born Again (John 3:3-10)

This passage is the source of what today is the prime evangelical catchphrase: "Born again." Most folks don't really understand, though polls show a large percentage of our population claims a "born-again experience." Running up against it for the first time, Nicodemus was totally confused.

Yet according to Jesus, he should have understood (v. 10). As "teacher of Israel" this member of the supreme Jewish council should have grasped the meaning of Old Testament prophecies about the new birth. Take for instance Ezekiel 36:26-27. There God said, "I will give you a new heart and put a new spirit in you; I will remove from you your heart of stone and give you a heart of flesh. And I will put My Spirit in you and move you to follow My decrees and be careful to keep My laws."

This is what it means to be "born again." It means to experience a spiritual rebirth: to know an inner transformation of the sin-hardened heart; a redirection of the life toward God.

Only a supernatural work by God the Holy Spirit within us can accomplish so dramatic a change.

And so when Jesus says, "You must be born again," He simply means that to enter His kingdom, you and I must let God into our lives, to work there as He pleases. When we do, eternal life will be ours—now—and through the miracle of the new birth our life on earth will become fresh and new.

Personal Application

Don't simply accept new life in Jesus. Live it!

Quotable

"The elect are the 'whosoever wills'; the nonelect are the 'whosoever won'ts.' "—D.L. Moody

AUGUST 26 *Reading 238*
WOMAN AT THE WELL
John 4

> *"We no longer believe just because of what you said; now we have heard for ourselves, and we know that this Man really is the Saviour of the world" (John 4:42).*

Testimony helps. But to "know," we have to come to Jesus for ourselves.

Overview

Jesus identified Himself to a Samaritan woman (4:1-26). He expressed satisfaction at doing God's will (vv. 27-34), and spoke of the harvest His disciples would share (vv. 35-38). Many Samaritans came to hear Him (vv. 39-42). Back in Galilee Jesus healed a nobleman's son (vv. 43-54).

Understanding the Text

"He left Judea and went back once more to Galilee" John 4:1-3. The other Gospel writers focused on Jesus' ministry in Galilee, and did not mention an early ministry in Judea. The early popularity of Jesus stirred up the Pharisees, leading Jesus to return to Galilee. John didn't explain why Jesus left.

"A Samaritan woman came to draw water" John 4:4-9. The Samaritans were descendants of pagan peoples settled by the Assyrians some 700 years before on land that had been part of the ancient Northern Kingdom of Israel. They had adopted Yahweh who was viewed as the god of that land, but maintained many of their pagan practices. The centuries-old hostility between the two peoples, whose religion the Jews viewed as apostate, was still intense in the first century.

This partly explains the woman's sur-

The Samaritan woman came to the well but was ignored by the other women. This was unusual, as drawing water at the community well was a time for socializing in the ancient East. Perhaps this woman, who was sexually promiscuous (4:16-18), was an outcast in her own village. Jesus knew who and what she was, and still took time to lead her to faith. Let's be guided in relationships with others by His example.

prise that a Jewish rabbi should ask her for a drink. Most religious Jews would view her as unclean, and would feel contaminated by any contact with her.

We need to surprise people today with our willingness to reach out to "sinners." Jesus here reminds us that God calls no person unclean, and that the godly person is not contaminated by ministering to sinners.

"Go call your husband and come back" John 4:16. The instruction was socially correct. In that culture no rabbi would speak with a woman without her husband present. But Jesus had another purpose in mind. He wanted to get beyond mere conversation (vv. 10-15) to touch her deepest emotions, and lead her to face her need for redemption.

While attending the University of Michigan I worked in a mental hospital. During that time I witnessed frequently to another ward attendant, who was in the Master's program there. After leaving to go to seminary, I wrote him a letter in which I spoke very personally—and insulted him to the extent that I never heard from him again.

Yet another person I witnessed to, a patient, responded to the personal approach. Though once a Sunday School superintendent in a conservative church, he shared his story of years of alcoholism and marital unfaithfulness, and turned back again to the Lord. I had the joy—against hospital policy—of contacting his wife, and helping the family build a new and different life together.

In one case the personal approach led to the slamming of a door; in another to the rebuilding of broken lives.

That's what is so powerful about being open and personal in our witnessing. As we build a relationship, becoming personal breaks through the barriers of superficiality that people erect to isolate themselves. We need wisdom from the Lord as to how and when to attempt a breakthrough. And at times the personal approach will be rebuffed. Yet we need to help people deal with the basic issue of life to which the Gospel so powerfully speaks.

"They are the kind of worshipers the Father seeks" John 4:19-26. The woman tried to change the subject by bringing up a theological red herring (v. 20). Be alert, for almost every time you are close to touching a person's heart, he or she will try to change the subject to theology!

Jesus was undeterred. The question was set aside, and the issue pressed. God is Spirit, and seeks worshipers who will come to Him in spirit and truth (v. 24). It's best to understand these words as a promise. God is looking for worshipers. All He asks is that we turn our hearts toward Him, and come to Him without pretense.

The woman at the well knew the truth about herself: she was a sinner. God knew too and still sought her as a worshiper! Would she face the truth about herself, and come to God as she was?

What a wonderful promise to share with others. God is looking for you! He's seeking worshipers! Come as you are, not trying to hide your flaws. Turn your hearts toward heaven, where God awaits.

"I know that Messiah" (called Christ) "is com-

ing" John 4:25-26. This woman, who claimed not to know the difference between Mount Zion where the Jews worshiped and Mount Gerazim, where her people went, did know one thing. God had promised to send a Saviour, and He would have all the answers!

That's all we need to know today. It's not our theological acuteness that saves us. It's not our mastery of obscure Old or New Testament texts. It's the simple belief that God has sent a Saviour, and He has the answers.

You and I want to study and grow in our faith. But all we must know as we start each day is that God has sent us our Saviour. And He has the answers we need in order to live our today in God.

"I have food to eat that you know nothing about" John 4:27-34. When the disciples returned, the woman was just leaving. They urged Jesus to eat something. And they didn't understand His reply.

What Jesus said shows us how to find what our constitution guarantees we can pursue: happiness. Jesus found His deepest satisfaction in doing the Father's will.

And so will we.

"They are ripe for harvest" John 4:35-38. God's field is perpetually ripe. Each day is the "today" when some will welcome the Gospel and find salvation.

Your part may be sowing the seed. Or encouraging its growth. Or perhaps gathering in a crop over which someone else has labored. No matter. Whenever a person is gathered into God's kingdom, all are filled with joy.

"We have heard for ourselves" John 4:39-42. As a college student I sold encyclopedias for a time. I was enthusiastic when I began, and sold 11 of my first 13 presentations.

But then I began to think about what I was saying as I followed the script for my presentation. And I realized that much of what I was saying just wasn't true. After that, though I kept on trying for a while, I could make no sale at all.

That's one thing that's so exciting about presenting Jesus to others, as the Samaritan woman did. We can share with enthusiasm, for God's promised benefits are assured. Whoever comes to see for himself or herself will be saved.

"A certain royal official" John 4:43-54. Historians note that Herod tended to recruit Gentiles as royal officials, and so suggest perhaps this man was one of them. If so, the three stories found in John 3 and 4 prefigure the spread of the Gospel: to Nicodemus the Pharisee, a Jew (Acts 2; 4)—to the woman at the well, a Samaritan (Acts 8)—and to the royal official, a Gentile, representing the whole world (Acts 10–11; 13ff).

If so, these three representative persons illustrate John's theme. God gave His Son that the whole world might know salvation. "Whosoever will" includes everyone (John 3:16).

▶ DEVOTIONAL
The Dilemma of Faith (John 4:43-54)

Nobody ever said having faith was easy. Certainly the Apostle John didn't say so. In fact, this story shows just how difficult it is.

Just glance through the story and you see first of all a frantic father hurrying to find Jesus. His son was close to death, and the only one who could possibly save him was Jesus!

When he finally did find Jesus, Christ didn't seem very sympathetic. "Unless you people see miraculous signs and wonders," He said, "you will never believe." The saying wasn't a rebuke. Jesus didn't question the frantic father's motives. In fact, the saying is intended to stimulate faith! For when the father begged Him again to come, Jesus simply said, "You may go. Your son will live" (v. 50).

This is the dilemma of faith.

God, in response to our desperate appeals, speaks to us and says, "You may go." In other words, "It's done. Go home and you'll find the sick healed." And what is there for us to do?

If we keep begging Jesus to come with us, we display unbelief. But to go means to head home with no evidence at all that the promised healing has taken place! How terrifying a choice. Do we keep asking after Jesus has said, "You may go"? Or do we leave, trembling, believing despite the lack of proof?

The royal official made the choice of faith. On the way excited messengers met him. His son was recovering. The fever had broken—at the exact hour Jesus had told him, "You may go."

Faith is still very much the same. We come to God desperate for salvation. And all He says is, "You may go." The work is done, your healing accomplished. And, though we lack evidence then, if we are wise we turn, in faith, and walk away as Jesus said.

But later we discover to our joy just how completely Jesus has performed His miracle within.

Personal Application

Believe. And go.

Quotable

"It is the heart that senses God, and not the reason. That is what faith is. God perceptible to the heart and not to reason."—Blaise Pascal

---

AUGUST 27 *Reading 239*
WITNESSES TO JESUS
John 5

"I have testimony weightier than that of John. For the very work that the Father has given Me to finish, and which I am doing, testifies that the Father has sent Me" John 5:36.

Those who reject Christ do so despite the evidence, not because of it.

Overview

Jesus healed a paralytic at the pool of Bethesda (5:1-15). Jesus responded to critics by claiming Deity (vv. 16-18) and explained His relationship with God the Father (vv. 19-30). And He identified five witnesses that supported His claim (vv. 31-47).

Understanding the Text

"Do you want to get well?" John 5:1-6 The pool of Bethesda was a gathering place for the infirm, hoping to benefit from its healing waters. John focused on a man who had been paralyzed for most of his life. While the story is not symbolic, the situation and dialogue between Jesus and the man are filled with implications for us.

Consider Jesus' question, "Do you want to get well?" We might answer for the man, "Of course!" But think about it. For some 38 years the paralyzed man had lived a dependent life. He'd lived by begging, for he could earn no wages. If he were healed, who would give him food? It was considered a good deed in Judaism to give alms to the disabled. But not to the able-bodied, who were expected to work!

Getting well would mean the man would have to take care of himself. So the question was a penetrating one.

It's a question we have to ask ourselves as Christians. Do we want Christ to heal the areas in our lives where we've been damaged? Or do we want to keep feeling anger and resentment, or bitterness, or hurt and betrayal? Too many Christians hold on tightly to the things that paralyze them spiritually. Christ can heal us of these things. But if He does, we'll be left without excuses for the choices we make in the future—and the choices we made in the past. We'll no longer be able to delude ourselves and cry, "My life isn't my fault: others are to blame."

And so Jesus' question echoes in our today: "Do you want to get well?"

"I have no one to help me" John 1:7-9. The man did not answer Jesus' question. Instead he offered an excuse. "I'm all alone. I have no one. There's no one here to help me."

We can certainly feel for the paralyzed man. Over the decades the family into which he'd been born had died. Friends had left him. If he'd ever had a wife or children, they were gone too. And somehow, paralyzed as he was, he'd never grown close to anyone.

Yet, while what the man said was true, this too was also an excuse. "There's no one to help me" means "I can't help myself." And it also means "God isn't here for me either."

Jesus paid no attention to the excuse. He told the man, "Get up and walk." At once the cure came, and he got up and walked.

It's like this with us today. Jesus doesn't come to us with a maudlin sympathy that accepts all our excuses, and moans "poor you" in harmony with us. He comes to us with a message of life and vitality. His message to us is, "Get up and walk!"

In Christ, the cure is ours.

In Christ, we do have Somebody.

Not someone to drag us here and there on our mats. But someone who can bring life to our own limbs, and who therefore commands, "Get up and walk."

The man obeyed. And in obeying, he experienced the healing that was his.

How many of us have in fact been healed by Jesus Christ, but because we have not obeyed His command, "Get up and walk," have never experienced the healing? God's work in our life is accomplished by God and grace alone. But it is experienced only as we obey.

"It is the Sabbath; the law forbids you to carry your mat" John 5:1-14. In John's Gospel "the Jews" is John's name for the Pharisees and those experts in the written and oral law of Israel who were Christ's primary opponents. While the term is a pejoritive, it is not anti-Semitic in any sense.

So it was "spiritual leaders" who jumped all over the restored paralytic for carrying his mat on the Sabbath. The act was not a violation of the Old Testament itself, but it was a violation of the rabbinic rulings which guided first-century Jewish practice.

The restored paralytic had an answer for his critics. "The Man who made me well said to me, 'Pick up your mat and walk.' " The ecclesiastical establishment had done nothing to restore the paralytic's health. He would obey the Man who had healed him.

When John Wesley began to preach an evangelical message in England, the established church was scandalized. Soon Wesley was denied access to church pulpits—and so he began to preach outdoors. For 50 years Wesley crisscrossed the British Isles, and hundreds of thousands came to know the Saviour. Wesley, like the paralytic, is an example of a person who was undeterred by the opposition of the ecclesiastical establishment. He too determined to obey the Man who had healed him.

So must we all.

"My Father is always at His work to this very day" John 5:16-17. When the Jewish leaders criticized Christ for healing on the Sabbath, He had a fascinating answer. God doesn't suspend His activities on the Sabbath!

Natural laws continue to operate. If a person cuts himself, healing begins at that moment. In healing the paralytic Jesus was acting in complete harmony with the way God, His Father, operates!

How often "religion" makes the simple complicated, and confuses human rulings with the gracious operations of God. Let's trust in Jesus, and respond spontaneously to the needs of others. In nearly every case any "religious rules" that would block such a response will be as opposed to godliness as were the first-century rabbinic rules governing Sabbath observance.

"Calling God His own Father, making Himself equal with God" John 5:18-30. Jesus' answer infuriated "the Jews" (i.e., the religious leaders). They understood Him to claim equality with God. And He did! In His next words Jesus went on to define His relationship with His Father!

Yesterday two Jehovah's Witnesses appeared at our door with an "Awake" tract. My wife called out from the living room, "We're Christians. We don't want it."

One of the two answered, "We're Christians too. We believe in Jesus Christ as our Saviour."

That's good. As far as it goes. But the next question that needs to be answered is, "Which Jesus?"

There are many Jesuses in vogue today. There's the "good man Jesus," who was misunderstood and killed, and whose teachings are still wonderful. There's the "liberation Jesus," who calls for the oppressed to take up weapons and kill their oppressors. There's the "Jewish rabbi Jesus," who never thought of himself as God and was later dubbed with a title he would have hated by his enthusiastic followers—especially Paul. There's the "a god" Jesus of several cults, who is either a sort of high angel, or a human being lifted to a higher spiritual plane. And then there is the God Jesus of John's Gospel, who is equal to God in nature, and who from the beginning was God and is God.

Here in these verses, in Christ's own words as reported by John, is the Jesus of Scripture. He is:

- vv. 17-18: the equal of God the Father
- v. 18: the Son, not identical with the Father, but unified with Him
- v. 19: in total harmony with the Father in all His works, and submissive to His will
- v. 20 loved by the Father, with full knowledge of His plans and purposes
- v. 21 empowered by the Father, and able to give life as the Father has and does
- v. 22 entrusted with authority to judge
- v. 23 equal in honor with the Father
- v. 24 determiner of human destiny: the object of a faith that transfers from the realm of death to that of life
- v. 25 able to raise the dead
- v. 26 one who like the Father is uncreated, having life in Himself
- v. 27 as Son of man, God enfleshed

It does make a difference which Jesus we believe in. How wonderful it is to know that the Jesus we believe in is the eternal Son of God. One of the earliest creeds of the church, the Nicene Creed, puts it this way:

> I believe in . . . one Lord Jesus Christ, the only-begotten Son of God, begotten of His Father before all worlds, God of God, Light of Light, very God of very God, begotten, not made, being of one substance with the Father, by whom all things were made; who for us men and for our salvation came down from heaven, and was incarnate by the Holy Spirit of the Virgin Mary, and was made man, and crucified also for us under Pontius Pilate; He suffered and was buried, and the third day He rose again according to the Scriptures, and ascended into heaven, and sitteth on the right hand of the Father; and He shall come again with glory to judge both the quick and the dead; whose kingdom shall have no end.

This is the Jesus of the Bible. This is the Jesus in whom we believe!

▶ DEVOTIONAL
Jesus on Trial
(John 5:31-47)

Every Christmas *Miracle on 34th Street* shows up on TV again. You know the story. A jolly little man goes to work as a department store Santa, and it turns out he's the real Santa Claus. Persecuted by nasty folks, he's put on trial, and the hero "proves" he is Santa by getting post office employees to deliver bags of "Santa" letters to him in the courtroom. Cute. But more a case of legal sleight of hand than hard evidence.

In a way, though, the story parallels Scripture. There a young Healer and Miracle worker appears. He comes in conflict with nasty religious leaders, is persecuted, and claims to be the "real" God of Israel! But this time there's no legal sleight of hand. He actually has witnesses to support His claim! In fact, in this passage in John, Jesus produced five witnesses to His deity!

The first witness (v. 31) was Jesus Himself. While self-witness was not valid in Jewish courts, Jesus' testimony counted, for He knew "where I came from and where I am going" (8:14).

The second witness (5:32-35) is John the Baptist. John had heard God's voice speak, and seen the Spirit descend. And John had told his disciples that Jesus was the Son of God (1:19-34).

The third witness (5:36) was that of the miracles Jesus performed (cf. 10:25–14:11). The Gospel of John lists seven, each of which shows Christ's power in a different arena of life (water to wine, 2:1-11; heal official's son, 4:43-54; heal paralytic, 5:1-15; feed multitude, 6:1-14; walk on water, vv. 16-21; cure blind man, 9:1-41; raise Lazarus, 11:1-44). Each was a sign demonstrating Jesus' power and His authority, and together they authenticated His claims of Deity.

The fourth witness (5:37-38) is the Father Himself, speaking through but distinguished from Jesus' miraculous works.

The fifth witness (vv. 39-41) is the Scripture, for the Law and the Prophets both predict Jesus' coming, and describe His ministry.

For those who actually heard Jesus speak, the fifth witness was the most telling. For if the Jews had only believed Moses, they would have recognized Jesus and believed in Him. Even as, today, we who believe the Word of God accept its testimony, and through the Scriptures have come to a saving knowledge of Jesus Christ.

Personal Application

We can trust the Word about the Word.

Quotable

"It were better to have no opinion of God at all than such a one as is unworthy of Him; for the one is only unbelief—the other contempt."—Plutarch

AUGUST 28 *Reading 240*
THE BREAD OF LIFE
John 6

"The bread of God is He who comes down from heaven and gives life to the world" (John 6:33).

Participation in Christ as source and sustainer of eternal life is our assurance of heaven.

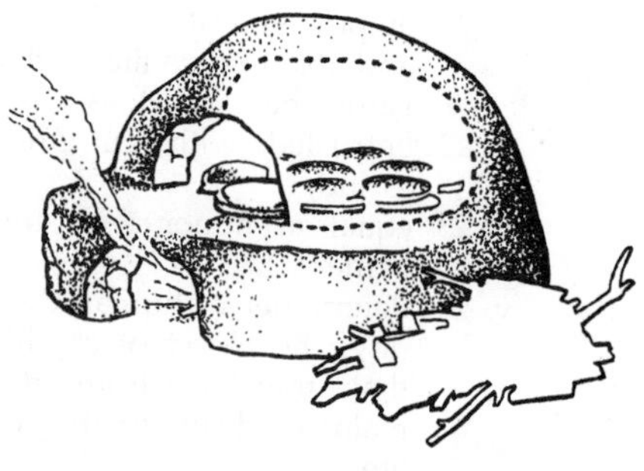

Background

Bread. Bread was the staple food in Palestine. It was so basic in the diet that "bread" is a synonym in Scripture for "food"; that which sustains physical life. The bread of the well-to-do was made of wheat; that of the poor, of barley. But rich and poor viewed bread as the basic element in the daily diet. It was the woman's task to grind grain daily, mix it with water and olive oil, and to cook the day's supply of bread. Bread was baked in a variety of ways: inside a hollow hivelike oven, or in flat cakes on its sides.

Jesus could have found no more powerful way to affirm that He was the source and sustainer of spiritual life than to compare Himself to the bread that sustained the physical life of all his listeners.

Overview

Jesus fed a multitude with a few loaves and fish (6:1-15). That evening the Twelve saw Him walk on water (vv. 16-24). When the crowds found Him they demanded a sign (vv. 25-31), but were exhorted to feed on Him as the "Bread of Life" (vv. 32-59). Many adherents deserted Him at this point, but the Twelve remained, convinced He is "the Holy One of God" (vv. 60-71).

Understanding the Text

"Where shall we buy bread for these people to eat?" John 6:1-7 Jesus' miracles drew large crowds to Him. John selected one occasion, near a Passover festival, when some 10,000 came. (John mentioned 5,000 "men," but Matthew tells us that there were also a great many women and children, so 10,000 is a conservative estimate: Matt. 14:21.)

Jesus drew Philip's attention to the crowd, and asked how they might be fed. Philip took a quick survey, and came back with statistics. "It'll take approximately eight months wages [200 denarii] to buy bread for this many!"

Philip reminds me of many folks in modern ministries. Let's take a survey. Let's gather data. And all too often, when the results are in, we end up saying, "Well, I guess it's impossible. It's surely too big a job for our little congregation!"

But John observes that Jesus "already had in mind what He was going to do" (6:6).

When we see a need, the thing we may need to do is not take a survey, but in prayer seek the way Jesus intends us to meet it.

"Here is a boy with five small barley loaves" John 6:7-15. Andrew took a different approach. He surveyed the available resources, and offered them to Jesus.

There wasn't much. Certainly not enough to feed 10,000 people! Or so it seemed.

The miracle of the feeding of the multitude, with 12 basketsful left over, reminds us that God is well able to multiply whatever resources we may have—as long as we offer them to Him.

It's not what we have. It's what God can and will do with what we have that counts!

"A strong wind was blowing" John 6:16-24. Evening breezes still whip up strong waves on the Sea of Galilee between Bethsaida and Capernaum. The disciples, heading into the wind, made slow progress: three and one half miles is only halfway there (cf. Mark 6:47).

The disciples saw a shape walking on the water toward them, and at first were frightened of what they took as a ghost. But they recognized Jesus' voice and took Him aboard. The text says, "Immediately the boat reached the shore where they were heading" (John 6:21).

This was a "private miracle" witnessed only by the disciples. As such it helped to build their growing faith in Christ, so that they remained faithful later, even though they did not understand everything He said. But there's a special reminder for us in the story. Like the disciples, we often find ourselves laboring hard, and making little progress. Yet Jesus is nearby, however strong the winds that buffet us. We need to recognize Him, and invite Him to become involved. We may not reach shore "immediately." But we will find strength to keep on.

"Because you ate the loaves and had your fill" John 6:25-29. The crowds Jesus had fed were surprised to find Him in Capernaum. They'd been looking. But for the wrong reason. Jesus had satisfied their physical hunger. They sought Him because of what He could do to meet material needs.

So much in our relationship with Jesus remains rooted in materialism. We trust Him, hoping He'll keep us healthy. Or get us a job. We even pray for the Lord to give us the numbers so we can win Lotto! Or we send in money to the media evangelist who promises that God will reward us a hundredfold. If $10 will get you $1,000, why not send in $1,000 and get $100,000—or at least a lifetime of free vacations!

It's not that God doesn't care about our material needs. God does. And He meets them, providing our "daily bread." The thing is that God cares most about our spiritual needs: the truly vital and important needs that every human being has.

As long as we seek to "use" relationship with God to gain material blessings, we'll miss the spiritual blessing that He so abundantly provides.

"The works God requires" John 6:28-29. The twin of materialism is seen in these verses. It is the foolish assumption that, whatever God may require, we can do.

Jesus had the definitive answer. The true work of God is simply to believe in the One God has sent. We cannot "do the works God requires" at all. Our only hope is to rely on what Christ has done.

"Our forefathers ate the manna in the desert" John 6:30-36. Earlier John reported that those Jesus fed began to speculate that Jesus was "the Prophet who is to come" (v. 14). The reference is to Deuteronomy 18, where Moses spoke of a Prophet like himself who would speak the words of God to Israel, and to whom the Jewish people must listen.

The reason for the identification was Jesus' feeding of the multitude. Moses provided Israel with manna during the

Exodus period. Jesus fed the crowds. Perhaps He was another Moses!

When Jesus called on the crowd to simply believe in Him, however, they demanded a "sign from heaven." I suspect this was more manipulation than doubt. Moses gave Israel bread from heaven—for 40 years! Jesus provided a miraculous meal, for one afternoon. Perhaps by demanding a sign the whole nation could "go on the dole" for decades!

But Jesus came to provide the "true" bread. The word, *alethinos,* means "genuine" or "original." Material bread sustains physical life. But human beings are not merely animals. True bread must sustain the inner life that exists when biological life ends. And Jesus is the one and only source of this life.

We will never find satisfaction if our life is focused on the material world alone. Jesus is the true bread, because He satisfies that aspect of human nature which transcends the material and is eternal. Jesus is not just "bread." He is the "Bread of Life." Our true selves are fed and sustained only by that faith in Him which appropriates what He supplies.

"Many of His disciples turned back and no longer followed Him" John 6:60-71. The word "disciple" is used in various ways in the Gospels. Here it simply means "adherent": someone who attached himself or herself loosely to Jesus and trailed along with Him.

When Jesus spoke of Himself as the Bread of heaven, and spoke symbolically of eating His flesh and drinking His blood, that "hard saying" made many such "disciples" turn away. They couldn't understand that Jesus meant accepting Him as a person accepts a meal: trusting its wholesomeness and value and taking it in, to be assimilated as part of one's very being.

The Twelve, Jesus' closest followers, undoubtedly didn't understand it all either. But when asked if they would leave too, Peter answered: "We believe and know that You are the Holy One of God."

We don't understand it all. But "we believe and know You."

This is Christianity in its essence. Believing and knowing Jesus Christ.

▶ DEVOTIONAL
Assurance: The Father's Will (John 6:39-59)

The sermon on the Bread of Life did confuse doubters. But it confirmed the faith of the believers. That sermon offers Jesus' own assurance that we possess, now, eternal life.

I've talked with folks who "hope" they have eternal life. I've talked with folks who "trust they will have" eternal life. And I've talked with folks who get angry and insist that it's presumptuous to claim to have eternal life now. "How can you know until you're dead?" some will say. Others will say, "What makes you think you're so much better than me?"

The fact is, though, that Jesus made an issue of assurance. He wants us to know, now, that eternal life is ours. Period.

"Whoever comes to Me I will never drive away," Jesus said (v. 37). In the same verse He reminds us that God's powerful invitation moved us to come in the first place. Having responded to God, He will keep us safe, forever.

Jesus went on to speak of the Father's express will. "I shall lose none of all that He has given Me," Jesus said, "but raise them up at the last day. For My Father's will is that everyone who looks to the Son and believes in Him shall have eternal life, and I will raise him up at the last day" (vv. 39-40).

A little later Jesus said, "I tell you the truth, he who believes has everlasting life" (v. 47). Not "will have." Not "may have." And not "maybe has." It's "does have."

And finally, "The one who feeds on Me will live because of Me" (v. 57).

So if you've come to Jesus and believe on Him, don't be an uncertain Christian. Jesus says you have eternal life. And you can take His Word for it.

Personal Application

Assurance isn't presumption; it's promise.

Quotable

"John Wesley, founder of Methodism, received this witness at a meeting on Aldersgate Street, London, as he listened to one reading Luther's Preface to the Book of Romans: 'About a quarter before nine, while he was describing the change which God works in the heart, through faith in Christ, I felt my heart strangely warmed. I felt I did trust Christ, Christ alone, for salvation: and an assurance was given to me that He had taken away my sins, even mine, and saved me from the law of sin and death' (Wesley's Journal, May 24, 1738).

"For some this confidence dawns gradually. For others, it is a sudden discovery at the moment of faith. EACH OF US CAN BE ASSURED OF OUR ACCEPTANCE WITH GOD!"—"Four Great Emphases of United Methodism"

AUGUST 29 *Reading 241*
UNCERTAINTY
John 7

> *"Among the crowds there was widespread whispering about Him. Some said, 'He is a good man.' Others replied, 'No, He deceives the people'' (John 7:12).*

Amid growing uncertainty one basic truth emerges. We each must listen to Jesus, and decide.

Overview

Jesus anonymously joined the crowds at the Feast of Tabernacles, where speculation about Him reached fever pitch (7:1-13). His public teaching aroused opposition (vv. 14-24) and debate over His true identity (vv. 25-44). The rulers, however, remained antagonistic and unbelieving (vv. 45-52).

Understanding the Text

"No one who wants to become a public figure" John 7:1-4. These words of Jesus' brothers drip with sarcasm. They impute contemptible motives to one who wanted only to do the Father's will. And they seem to cast doubt on Christ's miracles as well. Smirking, the brothers said Jesus ought to go up to Judea and join the festivities, so everyone can witness His miracles rather than simply hear rumors about them.

Unbelief has a habit of imputing the worst of motives to the best of acts. Christ's works of compassion—His healings and feeding a hungry crowd—were dismissed as the publicity-seeking acts of a man hungry for recognition. Jesus found only skepticism and raised eyebrows in His own family!

Don't be surprised if the things you do to serve the Lord are similarly misunderstood. And don't let the veiled attacks of those who should be supporters deter you. Like Jesus, you and I serve the Lord and seek to please Him. If what we do is motivated by a desire to serve the Lord, what others think is irrelevant. God knows our hearts.

"Even His own brothers did not believe in Him" John 7:5. There is a note of encouragement to be found here, in the fact that we can rightly add, "then." Later Christ's brothers did believe, and were with the little company of believers when the Spirit fell that first Day of Pentecost (Acts 1:14).

Keep on serving the Lord. In time even your critics will understand.

"The right time for Me has not yet come" John 7:6-13. Jesus' purposes were not political, but spiritual. The crowds had already tried once to "make Him King by force" (6:15). There was the distinct possibility that if Christ had gone to the festival publicly, with marching bands of disciples cheering Him along His way, that a populace hungry to throw off Rome's yoke would have burst into spontaneous rebellion.

This scenario is not mere speculation. The history of the time reveals that a number of rebellions and revolts led by pseudo-messiahs had already broken out!

Modern political figures realize that most of their supporters actually want to use them rather than follow them. That's why the reliance on polls. The candidate checks carefully on the strength of "pro-life" and "pro-choice" feelings in his district, or comes to the religious rally and announces his support of a bill guaranteeing the rights of Christian schools. The supporters cheer. They'll vote for him because he'll support their cause.

The honest politician supports a cause because he or she believes it is right. The rest cynically consult the polls, and sell themselves for votes.

Jesus sought no such supporters. Jesus leads, and calls us to follow. He sets the agenda, and His refusal to go up publicly to the feast was a refusal to let Himself be used for political purposes.

"Such learning, without having studied" John 7:14-16. This is one verse we had better not apply to ourselves!

Of course, in context "the Jews" (e.g., Christ's "opposition") were speaking of the well-established system by which one gained recognition as a rabbi, or teacher. This system called for the learner to attach himself to a recognized authority in Jewish Law, and study with him for years. Christ had not gone through this discipling process: yet Christ displayed an amazing mastery of Scripture.

Jesus explained that He received His teaching directly from "the One who sent Me." This was a dual claim: to have been "sent" from God meant to speak with His authority. To have been taught by Him meant that Jesus was a channel of revelation!

You and I must settle for study of what has been revealed. Christ had learning "without having studied," but you and I will never learn unless we apply ourselves to study the Word of God.

"If anyone chooses to do God's will" John 7:17. The word "chooses" here is a strong one. It represents a settled determination to do God's will. Only such a determination will lead to spiritual understanding and settled faith.

If you've ever wondered why so many intelligent people can know so much about the Bible, and still not believe in either Christ or the Scriptures, here is one explanation. Finding out that Jesus' teaching comes from God depends on our commitment to do God's will.

We discover the truth of Scripture not by intellect, but by obedience.

Man's approach to spiritual life has always been learn, that you may do. The divine formula is, "Do, that you may know."

"You are demon-possessed" John 7:18-20. Much in John relies on background found in the other three Gospels. As the last to write, it seems likely John felt no need to restate material in the other, widely distributed, works.

We see this reliance on background here. The accusation of the crowd, "You're demon-possessed," reflects the charge brought against Jesus by the Pharisees and rulers in an attempt to explain away His undeniable spiritual powers (cf. Matt. 9:34; 12:24; Mark 3:22; Luke 11:15). While Jesus knew the opposition was determined to kill Him, rumors to this effect had only begun to circulate among the people (cf. John 7:25).

If only folks would stop to think today, they would realize that they must make some decision about Jesus. In the first century His miracles demanded an explanation. Today 2,000 years of the persistent faith of millions that Jesus is the Son of God also demands explanation.

How can an obscure carpenter in a tiny, backward district of an empire long turned to dust continue to affect so many human lives? This is perhaps the greatest miracle of all, and any thinking person must be driven to find some explanation.

"I did one miracle" John 7:21-24. Jesus had done more than one miracle. But the one that stuck in the craw of the opposition involved the healing of the paralytic on the Sabbath.

John gives us another line of biblical reasoning that Christ used to show up the fallacy of strict Phariseeism. Sabbath observance was rooted in the Creation account, and thus was in effect long before the Mosaic Law was given. Yet a child was circumcised on the eighth day, even if that day was the Sabbath! And so, Jesus said, if a rite that marks a person's purification is permitted in one member of the body on the Sabbath, why should Jesus be criticized for making a sick man well on that day?

"Stop judging by mere appearances" is both a rejection of the rulers' right to stand in judgment on Jesus, and an expression of contempt for their superficial grasp of God's Word.

"The chief priests and the Pharisees sent temple guards to arrest Him" John 7:25-47. Jesus' teaching had its impact. While many remained uncertain, some "put their faith in Him" (v. 31). Afraid that the Jesus movement would gain momentum, the members of the Sanhedrin sent temple guards to arrest Him. These were Jewish rather than Roman soldiers: Levites, who were trained to keep order in the temple area and to guard its purity. Yet when the detail sent to arrest Jesus heard what Christ said, they "went back to the chief priests and Pharisees" without Him (v. 45).

It took courage for these soldiers to disobey orders. They may not have been sure who Jesus was. But their stand, and the Pharisees' furious response, implies some level of faith.

We need to honor these temple guards, and all military men like them, who through the ages have refused to obey orders that violated their beliefs and consciences. And we need to model ourselves on them.

Civil disobedience was praised in the '60s, when the issue was civil rights. The same folks who praised it then now condemn civil disobedience by pro-life forces who picket abortion clinics, and then willingly accept any penalties imposed by the law. The temple guards remind us that, whatever the issue, the believer is responsible to obey conscience first and legally constituted authorities second.

"The Pharisees retorted" John 7:47-52. The contempt the Pharisees felt for everyone but themselves comes through clearly. To the rulers, the temple guards, though recruited from the tribe of Levi, weren't smart enough to listen to Jesus and make up their own minds. The average Jewish person was part of a mob "that knows nothing of the Law—there is a curse on them" (v. 49). And when Nicodemus made a feeble attempt to bring up a point of law in defense of Jesus, the other Pharisees silenced him with ridicule.

Note well these characteristics of Christ's opposition. They still appear today in those who falsely claim spiritual authority. When you sense arrogance, contempt for the spiritual insight of others, dismissal of ordinary folks, and see the use of ridicule to silence others, you can be sure that such leaders do not represent Jesus Christ.

▶ DEVOTIONAL
Grab a Yellow Pad
(John 7:25-43)

One of my most important tools is a pad of yellow, lined paper. I use it to make lists of things I have to do each day. And I use it to help in making tough decisions—pros on one side, cons on the other. Listing on yellow pads helps me sort through almost any issue.

The folks who listened to Jesus speak at that Feast of Tabernacles seem to have needed one of my yellow pads. Or maybe they were using one mentally, totaling up pros and cons and options.

Pros? Well, Jesus was out there preaching, and the authorities had done nothing to stop Him. Maybe the rulers knew He is really the Christ (v. 26). And those miraculous signs: Jesus sure had performed a bunch (v. 31). And His teaching: what power and authority (vv. 40-41).

Cons? Some said the authorities were trying to kill Him. They wouldn't kill a real prophet, would they? (v. 25) Isn't the Christ supposed to appear suddenly, out of nowhere? (v. 27) And look, this Jesus is from Nazareth. Micah said the Christ was to be born in Bethlehem (v. 42).

Options? What choices do we have? Well, Jesus could be demon-possessed (cf. v. 20). He could be a charlatan; a deceiver who deserved death (v. 25, cf. v. 12). He could be nothing more than a good Man (cf. v. 12). He could be the prophet predicted by Moses (v. 40). He could be the Christ (vv. 31, 41).

And it really was just like this, as most people of Judea struggled with uncertainty that Tabernacles week, and endlessly discussed pros and cons.

But there were a few people who threw their yellow pads away. These folks listened to Jesus "and put their faith in Him."

I suspect this is the best pathway to faith, for us and for those we witness to. Put away the yellow pad. Abandon listing pros and cons and options. Instead, simply listen to Jesus. And let our hearts tell us who He is.

Personal Application
To find freedom from uncertainty, always listen to God's Word with your heart.

Quotable
"In all my perplexities and distresses, the Bible has never failed to give me light and strength."—Robert E. Lee

AUGUST 30 *Reading 242*
JESUS, THE "I AM"
John 8

" 'I tell you the truth,' " Jesus answered, 'before Abraham was born, I am!' At this, they picked up stones to stone Him, but Jesus hid Himself, slipping away from the temple grounds" (John 8:58-59).

Sometimes a blunt presentation of truth, even though it provokes angry opposition, is necessary.

Overview
Jesus forgave a woman caught in adultery (8:1-11). Jesus' continuing claims about Himself were rejected by the leaders (vv. 12-30), and He in turn rejected their claim of descent from Abraham (vv. 31-41). Their hatred of God's Son showed they were members of Satan's family, not God's (vv. 42-47). The angry confrontation reached a peak when Jesus claimed to be the I AM (*Yahweh*) of the Old Testament, and His opponents sought to stone Him for blasphemy (vv. 48-59).

Understanding the Text
"A woman caught in adultery" John 8:1-11. One of the most fascinating aspects of every trap Jesus' opponents devised is that each time they netted themselves. It's almost a cartoon: Elmer Fudd aims at Bugs Bunny, never noticing the gun barrel has been bent, and shoots himself in the foot.

Look at this incident. I'm sure the teachers of the Law and Pharisees were sure they had Jesus neatly trussed up when they brought Him a woman caught in the very act of adultery! If Jesus said, "Stone her!" He'd be sure to lose popularity. If He said, "Let her go," they could get Jesus for rejecting Moses' Law.

But think about it for a minute. In the first place, where would you go to catch some woman in the act of adultery? There may be someplace here in our town, but I sure don't know where it is. How did the religious leaders know the address?

And then, who was the man? Why did they let the guy go—and which one of them got him to volunteer?

The more you think about the scene, the more it raises serious questions, not about Jesus, but about the men who captured the adulteress!

It's helpful to remember this when someone attacks our faith, and we're momentarily off guard. Whatever the nature of their attack, it says more about them than about Christ.

"Neither do I condemn you" John 8:7-11. Some have suggested that when Jesus wrote on the ground He recorded the sins of the woman's accusers. They slipped away, not because of any shame or sympathy for the woman, but because they dared not risk exposure. Whether or not this is true, it is dangerous to condemn others. In so doing, we condemn ourselves, for none of us is without sin.

What's stunning in this account, however, are Jesus' words. As one who was without sin, and who had been appointed by the Father to judge humankind (cf. 5:22), Jesus refused to condemn the woman despite her real guilt.

The saying echoes John's words in 3:17. Jesus did not come into the world to condemn the world, but that the world through Him might be saved. And that salvation involves more than forgiveness. It involves a change of life: a change reflected in Christ's words, "Go now and leave your life of sin."

D.L. Moody was once met by a man who staggered out of a bar, gripped the evangelist's lapels, and announced with delight, "You're the man who saved me!" Moody replied, "I suspect I did. If Jesus had saved you, you wouldn't be here now."

When Jesus saves us, we really do leave our life of sin.

"I am the light of the world" John 8:12. John records several "I am" claims made by Jesus. This is one of the most significant. Jesus had said, "I am the Bread of Life" (John 6), and thus claimed to be the source and sustainer of spiritual life. His saying, "I am the light of the world," is a claim to be the genuine light by which truth and falsehood are distinguished.

Light and darkness are important images in John's Gospel and his epistles. Light reveals reality as God knows it. Darkness is the shadowy world of illusion cast by human notions of what constitutes reality: a world of delusion, deception, and fantasy.

Apart from relationship with and trust in Jesus no one has the slightest chance of knowing reality.

"The Pharisees challenged Him" John 8:13-30. The challenge was on a technical point of Old Testament Law. It required two witnesses to establish a fact in court (Deut. 17:6). The Pharisees' point was that they didn't have to believe anything Jesus said about Himself, because there was no one to corroborate His claims.

They were wrong! Standing beside and in Jesus Christ was God the Father Himself! As One sent by the Father (emphasized four times in this chapter: John 8:16, 18, 26, 29), Jesus spoke with the Father's voice, and the Father spoke through Him.

Several things follow from this truth. A person who was truly in touch with God would have recognized Jesus (v. 19). Failure to recognize Jesus for who He is meant that Israel's spiritual leaders did not know the God they claimed to represent, and that they surely would die in their sins.

We can understand why the Pharisees were so upset. No one likes to hear that their religion is meaningless, and that unless they turn to Jesus they are doomed. No one likes to hear it. But it's true! And it is a valid approach to evangelism. The Bible says that many who heard these blunt claims of Jesus put their faith in Him, even as He spoke (v. 30).

"We are Abraham's descendants and have never been slaves of anyone" John 8:31-41. The conflict and anger became even more intense as the religious leaders defended themselves. As biological descendants of Abraham, they had a claim on God who made a covenant with Abraham.

It's true that the Old Testament Covenant did give the Jewish people certain wonderful privileges. But no individual has ever had an automatic relationship with God based on biological descent. Growing up in a Christian home doesn't make a person a Christian, anymore than growing up in a university town makes a person intelligent. All either provides is an opportunity.

That's what Jesus was saying to these religious leaders. Descent from Abraham gave them a special opportunity to know God. But if they had really been like Abraham, they would have acted as Abraham did and responded to God rather than plot to kill God's Son.

Mere opportunity to know God doesn't count for any more today than it did then. We must seize the opportunity, and respond to Him, now as then (see DEVOTIONAL).

"Then you will know the truth, and the truth will set you free" John 8:31-32. The saying has nothing to do with its use on the banner of the New York *Times*. Jesus had already said, "If you hold to My teachings [keep My words] then you'll be My disciples." Only then did He speak of knowing the truth, and the truth making men free.

Jesus' teachings are "true." That is, they are accurate representations of reality. There is only one way to "know" reality, and that is to experience it. What Jesus said was that if we put His teaching into practice, we will actually experience moral and spiritual reality. And the experience of that reality will set us free.

In the words of a modern commercial, "Try it. You'll like it."

"Who do You think You are?" John 8:48-59 The words are laced with hostility and scorn. Jesus was making Himself out to be someone greater than Abraham, the father of the Jewish race! He was claiming He could give endless life through Abraham.

Jesus' claim that Abraham had "rejoiced at the thought of seeing My day" angered the leaders even more. How could Abraham, who lived some 2,000 years before, have known anything about Jesus of Nazareth, a Man not yet 50!

What followed is one of the clearest of Jesus' claims to Deity. "Before Abraham was born, I am!"

That "I am" is rooted in the Exodus revelation of the personal name of God, *Yahweh*. It was "I Am," *Yahweh*, who sent Moses to deliver Israel. And here Jesus claimed that before Abraham was born, He Himself existed as sacred history's "I Am."

The claim was understood, and the listeners picked up rocks to stone Jesus for blasphemy.

Ultimately every person's destiny depends on how he or she responds to Jesus' claim to be "I Am." What a blessing for us to acclaim, "He is!"

▶DEVOTIONAL
All God's Children?
(John 8:31-47)

I don't know any issue on which I've heard preachers fudge more often. Some minister's on a radio or TV talk show and is accused of believing that only Christians are God's children. The others there are incensed at the very thought of such raw prejudice, and the poor preacher stumbles and mutters. On the half dozen or so occasions I've heard such confrontations, the preacher has quickly backed off. If he did believe non-Christians aren't God's children, he wasn't about to admit it and take all that heat.

I honestly don't understand why. Of course non-Christians aren't God's children. No way!

This doesn't mean that every human being doesn't have great worth and value to God. Each of us is an object of His great love. After all, Christ died for those who were actively hostile toward Him because of sin and guilt. But none of that means non-Christians are in God's family.

John 8 reports how Jesus insulted a panel of Pharisees far more than anyone's been insulted on a TV talk show. Jesus not only said God wasn't their Father; He said straight out that they "belong to your father, the devil." And Jesus proved His accusation by showing that the leaders' lies and anger at Him mirror the lies and anger of Satan at God. Of course they were the devil's children. They acted just like him!

What bothers me about modern ecclesiastical fudging is that it prevents people from facing the most important issue anyone has to face in this life. Do we belong to God, or not? Are we members of God's family, or not? Will we spend eternity with God, or not?

There's no room for "maybe" here. There's no room for just being nice, and saying what will make people feel good. These questions demand a clear-cut yes or no. A person is either a member of God's family through faith in Jesus Christ, God's Son, or he or she is right there in the devil's camp, with the folks who murdered our Lord.

I know. It's not nice to say such things. It's not polite. It doesn't sound open-minded enough. It makes people angry when they hear us say it. I suspect many Christians fear that it will "turn people off" if they're told we don't think of them as children of God too.

But it's not true to suggest that those who do not know Jesus can have a relationship with God. And it's not loving to let people think that they're all right when in fact they are lost.

Personal Application

No one can choose between the truth and a lie unless they know what the truth is.

Quotable

"Apart from blunt truth, our lives sink decadently amid the perfume of hints and suggestions."—Alfred North Whitehead

AUGUST 31 *Reading 243*
THE GIFT OF SIGHT
John 9

"One thing I do know. I was blind but now I see!" (John 9:25)

Only the man who insists "I see" is doomed to remain spiritually blind.

Overview
Jesus, "the light of the world," gave sight to a man born blind (9:1-8). Stunned neighbors (vv. 9-12) took him to the Pharisees, who criticized Jesus for healing on the Sabbath (vv. 13-23). The healed man ridiculed the Pharisees' rejection of Jesus (vv. 24-34), and worshiped Christ as Lord (vv. 35-39). The Pharisees remained spiritually blind (vv. 40-41).

Understanding the Text
"Rabbi, who sinned . . . that he was born blind?" John 9:1-4 Popular first-century theology explained every disaster as a consequence of sin. Seeing a man born blind led the disciples to ask a puzzling theological question. Since the man was born blind, whose sin had caused his blindness? Did he somehow sin in the womb, as some rabbis argued? Or had a sin of his parents caused his condition?

This strange theology is still popular. When my wife lost a daughter in childbirth, her sister-in-law remarked, "I hope I don't do anything that will make God punish me like that!" Many a Christian friend, come to comfort a person who is suffering, has made a similarly thoughtless remark.

How callous of the disciples, and of us. The man born blind and the devastated mother aren't objects for theological speculation. They are hurting human beings, not riddles for which we have to offer some solution.

Jesus rejected both alternatives. The blind man's plight was an opportunity for God to relieve suffering. The cause was unimportant. This is still the case today. The cause of a person's suffering is not at issue. The reality of suffering is. All suffering is still an opportunity for God—and God's people—to express compassion.

"I am the light of the world" John 9:5. John first recorded this claim in 8:12. The present incident, again reported without regard to chronology, both demonstrates and illustrates the theme.

As Son of God, the Creator who called light and life into being at the beginning, Jesus performed a creative act to give the man sight. The man had been born blind. This miracle was no restoration of a damaged capacity, but the creation of a totally new capacity.

There is an analogy here to spiritual enlightenment. Human beings are born in sin, without the capacity to see the spiritual world or know spiritual reality. Only by a creative work of God in our hearts can we be given spiritual sight. The man born blind received both physical and spiritual sight as he gradually came to trust Jesus as Lord.

"The man went and washed, and came home seeing" John 9:6-12. While the restoration of physical or spiritual sight is possible only by a creative act of God, the recipient is not passive. Thus Jesus put clay on the blind man's eyes, and told him to find his way to the pool of Siloam and wash.

Without at least a hesitant faith, or some dawning hope, the blind man would have bitterly removed the clay and sulked at what seemed ridicule. This man, however, responded to Christ's words, and went to the pool as directed.

This and this alone is man's part in receiving spiritual sight. We hear Jesus speak and, however hesitantly, we respond. We take those first stumbling steps of faith, and in responding we suddenly discover that we truly can see.

Actually, this chapter traces the growth of the blind man's faith in Jesus, from first response to full discipleship. We notice the stages in the way the man speaks and thinks of Jesus: He was "the Man they call Jesus" (v. 11), then "He is a Prophet" (v. 17), then "from God" (v. 33), the "Son of man" (a messianic title) (v. 35), and finally, "Lord" (v. 38).

So our faith grows too. At first we fail to understand fully who Jesus is. But as our spiritual sight becomes more acute, we acknowledge Him as Lord, and worship Him.

"They brought [him] to the Pharisees" John 9:13-17. The stunned neighbors brought the now-sighted man to the Pharisees in hopes of an explanation. These men were regarded as religious experts. Perhaps they could explain what had happened.

The Pharisees struggled to force the square peg of this miracle into the round holes of their theology. It just wouldn't fit. Jesus had performed the miracle on the Sabbath, and in the process had made mud (vv. 6, 14). This was "work" according to earlier rabbinical rulings, and forbidden on the Sabbath. Theology demanded they classify Jesus a "sinner." But reality demanded they acknowledge a miracle that required the exercise of God's creative power.

There's an important lesson for us here. Christian experience will never violate the Scriptures. But it may run contrary to our interpretation of the Scriptures! When a person gives evidence of a work of God in his or her life, we need to reexamine our understanding of the Word of God.

John showed that some of the Pharisees considered Jesus' works on their own merit, without trying to explain them away because they didn't fit contemporary theology (v. 16). The blind man, who saw more clearly than the leaders, had the simplest explanation. Jesus was obviously a Prophet: one of those men called and empowered by God, who spoke and acted with God's own authority, and thus was above the leaders' jurisdiction.

It is both dangerous and foolish to claim the right to stand in judgment on a work performed by God.

"They sent for the man's parents" John 9:18-23. The opposition party (in John, "the Jews") refused to believe the man had been born blind until they called his parents. They insisted that the healed man was their son, and that he had been born blind. But they refused to be involved in the controversy over Jesus.

How desperately the Pharisees tried to avoid facing the reality of this miracle. They knew as well as the blind man that the only valid explanation was that God was working in and through Jesus. But they refused to admit this obvious fact even to themselves.

Later Jesus accused them of being blind, and observed that they would remain blind, since they insisted they saw. There is no one as blind as the person who sees the truth, and then shuts his eyes tight in a desperate effort to avoid admitting it.

"Anyone who acknowledged that Jesus was the Christ would be put out of the synagogue" John 9:20-23. There's often a terrible cost to discipleship. In the first century being "put out of the synagogue" meant being cut off from Jewish society. Friends would not speak to such a person; no one would buy from or sell to him. He could not participate in worship or ritual. By implication he was cut off not only from the covenant people but also from salvation itself.

The mother and father of the blind man were unwilling to risk such a penalty by stating their (implied) belief that Jesus was the Christ. The blind man himself was not so hesitant. He boldly affirmed his faith to the Pharisees, and even ridiculed their doubts. Awed by the miracle that had taken place in his own life, he was no longer in awe of mere human authorities.

The greater our focus on what the Lord is doing in our own lives, the less hesitant we'll be in speaking out for Him.

"Now that is remarkable!" John 9:26-34 The blind man finally tired of the inquisition. We catch both sarcasm and contempt in his words to the religious leaders as he stated the obvious. "We know that God does not listen to sinners. He listens to the godly man who does His will. Nobody has ever heard of opening the eyes of a man born blind. If this Man were not from God, He could do nothing" (vv. 31-33).

Unable to refute the blind man's logic, Jesus' opponents resorted to personal attack. When someone resorts to personal attacks on you, you know he or she is desperate, and cannot deny the truth of what you're saying.

"Do you believe in the Son of man?" John 9:35-39 Later Jesus looked for and found the man He had healed. The man undoubtedly recognized Jesus' voice, though he had not seen Him earlier. When Jesus identified Himself as the "Son of man," a messianic title that many believe implied Deity, the man fell on his knees and worshiped.

As our faith grows, we, like the blind man, are gradually given fuller and fuller revelations of Jesus and His will. Spiritual sight becomes more acute, and we acknowledge Jesus as Lord in every area of our lives.

"Are we blind too?" John 9:39-41 Some Pharisees who heard Jesus' remarks on blindness were highly insulted. Jesus answered them honestly and bluntly. Their conviction that they could "see" spiritually prevented them from confessing blindness, and becoming candidates for sight. Anyone who insists that he "sees" spiritually, but refuses to confess that Jesus is Lord, is both blind and guilty, lost in his or her sins.

▶DEVOTIONAL
One Thing We Know
(John 9:13-25)

People who are far more intelligent than we scoff at faith in Jesus. They speak with great superiority of comparative religions, of evolution, or of the latest scholarly reinterpretation of Bible history. Or they claim that Jesus never saw Himself as Son of God. That was just foisted off on the church by the Apostles.

In short, they take the role of the Pharisees of John 9, as Jesus' critics. There the Pharisees tried so hard to ignore Jesus, and discredit the blind man's story. But every time the man responded with a truth so obvious that the foolishness of the Pharisees' position was exposed.

"We know this Man is a sinner" (v. 24), the Pharisees announced. "We know."

The blind man just shrugged and refused to be drawn into that kind of argument. "One thing I do know. I was blind, but now I see."

The Pharisees could say whatever they wanted about Jesus. But they had to face the fact that He gave sight to a man born blind. Today too people can pass any judgment they wish on Jesus. But if they are honest they have to face the fact that millions testify to Jesus' transforming work in their lives. John Newton, once a slave trader, in personal bondage to the most vile practices, experienced a transformation expressed in this hymn he later wrote:

> Amazing grace! How sweet
> the sound—
> That saved a wretch like me!
> I once was lost but now am found,
> Was blind but now I see.
>
> 'Twas grace that taught my
> heart to fear,
> And grace my fears relieved;
> How precious did that grace appear
> The hour I first believed.

One thing we know. Once we were blind. Now we can see. Once we were in bondage to sin. Now we love and serve Jesus Christ.

No argument that the Pharisees or scholars of this world can marshall against our faith can stand before our experience of this reality.

Personal Application

We do not merely hope. We know.

Quotable

"I've never gotten over the wonder of it."—Gipsy Smith

SEPTEMBER 1 *Reading 244*
THE GOOD SHEPHERD
John 10

"I am the Good Shepherd. The Good Shepherd lays down His life for the sheep" (John 10:11).

The true spiritual leader still cares for the sheep, not for what he can get for their fleece.

Background

Sheep and shepherds. These images are some of the most powerful in the Old Testament. David's Psalm 23 picks up the warm and comforting image of the believer as a sheep in the personal care of God. Because "the Lord is my Shepherd" the psalmist is secure. He is convinced, "I shall lack nothing," for God Himself wields the staff of protection, and leads him to green pastures and beside still waters.

The shepherd is also a common image in the Prophets. There it stands for spiritual leaders: first describing rapacious spiritual leaders who profit by exploiting God's sheep (cf. Jer. 25; Ezek. 34), and then by promising the appearance of a Descendant of David who will shepherd God's sheep in His name (cf. Isa. 44:28; Ezek. 34:23-24). These images were so well known it is almost impossible to explain how first-century Jews could have missed the implications of Jesus' claim. Their demand to be told "plainly" if Jesus was the Christ brought an understandable response: "I did tell you, but you do not believe."

Today as then, relationship with God is not a matter of hearing the truth, but of believing it.

Overview

Jesus claimed to be the True Shepherd of God's sheep (10:1-6). As the "gate for the sheep" Jesus brings His sheep abundant life (vv. 7-10). As "Good Shepherd" He lays down His life for His sheep (vv. 11-13), and is recognized by them (vv. 14-21). Later Jesus told His enemies plainly that He is the Christ, and one with the Father (vv. 22-30). When they prepared to stone Him, Jesus challenged them to deny His miracles (vv. 31-42).

Understanding the Text

"The man who enters by the gate is the shepherd of his sheep" John 10:1-6. The contrast here is not between Jesus and the religious leaders, but between Jesus and false messiahs. Christ came to Israel through the gate identified by Old Testament prophets: "The LORD has anointed Me to preach good news to the poor. He has sent Me to bind up the brokenhearted, to proclaim freedom for the captives and release for the prisoners, to proclaim the day of the LORD's favor" (Isa. 61:1-2).

Others came preaching a fiery bloodbath of retribution against Israel's oppressors. They were false shepherds, climbing in another way.

History's false messiahs have retained this characteristic. They would bring in God's kingdom of peace by bloodshed, and "liberate" the oppressed by killing the oppressors. Watch out for such people. You'll not hear the voice of Jesus in their strident calls for revolution.

"His sheep follow him because they know his voice" John 10:4. This theme is repeated frequently by Jesus. The relationship of an Eastern shepherd with his sheep was personal. The shepherd knew each sheep by name, as an individual. He led, rather than herded, the sheep. The sheep also recognized their protector, and responded to his voice. Their hearing was acute enough that if another tried to mimic his voice, they became frightened.

There's another implication here too. At night typically four or five herds of sheep were gathered together in a protected area or sheepfold. In the morning, when a shepherd called, his sheep responded to his voice and separated themselves from the herd! It was response to the shepherd's voice that identified his sheep from hundreds of other sheep who might have looked just like them to the casual observer.

Today too those who hear the Gospel, and recognize in it the voice of God calling to them, respond. It is our response to Jesus that identifies us as His sheep.

"I am the gate for the sheep" John 10:7-10.

This is another of Jesus' great "I Am" statements in John's Gospel. Its meaning should have been familiar to Jesus' first hearers, who understood sheepherding.

At night sheep were kept in a "fold": an enclosure of stones, briars, or at times a cave. This sheepfold had only one opening, and at night the shepherd slept in it. No wild animal or robber could get at the sheep, because the shepherd was himself at the gate.

As the gate, Jesus presented Himself as the only means of entrance to His flock, and at the same time the avenue through which the flock within would pass to find pasture. No wonder Jesus said, "I have come that they may have life, and have it to the full" (v. 10).

"I am the Good Shepherd" John 10:1-16. The "good shepherd" is a unique designation, for it emphasizes the willingness of the shepherd to die for his sheep. A "hired man"—and here Jesus refers to Israel's religious leaders—will care for the sheep only so long as it is profitable or safe. The good shepherd who values the sheep for themselves will lay down his life for them. In fact, it is in this, the laying down of his life, that the goodness of the shepherd is established.

If it seems foolish to think of a man being willing to die for mere animals, however great his affection for them, remember this. There is a far greater gap between God and human beings than there is between human beings and sheep! The amazing goodness of God is fully displayed in this awesome wonder: Jesus loved us enough to lay down His life for us.

If you ever feel like a little lost sheep, alone and frightened in a dark and hostile world, remember the Good Shepherd. You can *know* He loves you because He laid down His life for you. He who loved you this much will never desert you. In Jesus you are never, ever, alone.

"They too will listen to My voice" John 10:15-16. The Jews had only contempt for the pagan Gentiles, though some actively sought them as converts. But the thought that any Gentile might have access to God without first becoming an adoptive member of the covenant people was foreign to Judaism. Jesus, however, made it clear that the great dividing line between God's own and all others was not to be Jewishness, but rather response to His own voice. Today none of the differences that exist between Christian communities have any real significance. All who respond to Jesus' voice, and have a true faith in Him, are members of Christ's "one flock."

Let's make less of the differences that set us apart from other Christians and more of the Person who unites us as the one people of God.

"I lay down my life—only to take it up again" John 10:17-21. There are two things here that thrill believers. First, Jesus laid down His life voluntarily. There was no way that the Sanhedrin or the Romans could have taken His life. His death was a voluntary self-offering. And it was "for the sheep": for our benefit.

Second, Jesus took up His life again! He submitted to death and emerged from it victorious, triumphantly alive! His resurrection proves His authority over all—and assures us that the voice we have heard calling us truly is the voice of God.

Never apologize for believing in Jesus, as though hearing His voice were somehow irrational. It is the person who does not believe the truth shining through the reality of Christ's resurrection whose reasoning is flawed.

"If you are the Christ, tell us plainly" John 10:22-30. Jesus *had* been telling everyone. Even though the questioners had not believed, He told them again—and reminded them that their unbelief was rooted in the fact that "you are not My sheep."

Again we see the great dividing line drawn. To those who respond to Jesus and believe in Him, Jesus "give[s] them eternal life, and they shall never perish; no one can snatch them out of My hand" (v. 29). In the great enterprise of salvation, Jesus and the Father are One, as They are in identity, as God.

There is no question about the clarity of this claim. The Jews understood it as a claim to "be God" (v. 33), and were ready to stone Jesus for blasphemy.

"You are gods" John 10:33-42. Jesus did not

deny their charge in any way. He did unmistakably claim to be the Son of God, and as evidence pointed to the miracles He had performed. Jesus also referred to an Old Testament passage that applied the word "gods" to mere mortals or to angels (cf. Ps. 82:6). If the reception by human beings of God's words lifted them to an exalted status, surely Christ's miracles proved He was justified in claiming to be the "Son of God."

The argument from miracles was futile, as Jesus knew it would be. The issue is never one of evidence. It is one of hearing God's voice as Jesus speaks to us. While the religious leaders stopped their ears, many others who heard Jesus speak recognized what they heard, "and in that place many believed in Jesus."

▶ DEVOTIONAL
Tug-of-War with God
(John 10:22-29)

I remember when my oldest son was about four. We used to play tug-of-war: him against my thumb. Not surprisingly, no matter how he heaved and pulled, and pulled and panted, my thumb always won.

At four, Paul, now in his mid-30s, just couldn't understand that my three-inch thumb was attached to a 230-pound man. Try as he would, his 40-pound body never could win.

The contests I remember are just about as unequal as one Jesus mentioned in John 10. "I give them eternal life," He said of those who have faith in Him. "And no one can snatch them out of My hand. My Father, who has given them to Me, is greater than all; no one can snatch them out of My Father's hand. I and the Father are One."

Yet Christians, standing secure in the palm of God's hand, often play "snatch." They find some 40-pound sin has a hold on them, and they're terrified that it will snatch them out of God's hand, and that they'll lose eternal life. Or they note some 40-pound doubt skipping around in their head, and they're frightened that it will snatch them away from salvation. Others worry about their own 40-pound will, anxious that it may run wild and catapult them from God's grip.

Well, Jesus has good news, "My Father . . . is greater than all; no one can snatch them out of My Father's hand."

Jesus has given us eternal life. And God the Father keeps us in the hollow of His almighty hand.

Personal Application

God wants us to build on the foundation of our salvation, not hold on desperately for fear we'll fall off.

Quotable

"Whatever troubles come on you, of mind, body, or estate, from within or from without, from chance or intent, from friends or foes—whatever your trouble be, though you be lonely, O children of a Heavenly Father, be not afraid!"—J.H. Newman

SEPTEMBER 2 *Reading 245*
POWER OVER DEATH
John 11

"I am the resurrection and the life. He who believes in Me will live, even though he dies; and whoever lives and believes in Me will never die. Do you believe this?" (John 11:25)

Death has no claim on those who believe in Jesus.

Overview

Jesus delayed response to Mary's appeal for her dying brother (11:1-6) until after Lazarus died (vv. 7-16). When Jesus arrived in Bethany, He called Himself "the resurrection and the life" (vv. 17-37) and raised Lazarus from the dead (vv. 38-44). This act confirmed faith but also hardened opposition. The leaders determined Jesus must be killed (vv. 45-53). Jesus withdrew, but both the crowds and the leaders expected Him to reappear in Jerusalem (vv. 54-57).

Understanding the Text

"Lord, the one You love is sick" John 11:1-3. Jesus had a long-standing and close relationship with Mary, Martha, and their brother, Lazarus. Verses 1 and 2 of this chapter are not evidence, as some suggest, that the story was inserted later into the Gospel narrative. These verses were penned by John to remind us of how close Jesus was to the little family in Bethany. And to help us realize that when Mary made her appeal to Jesus, she did so with absolute confidence that Jesus would respond immediately. After all, Lazarus was "the one You love": a close and precious friend.

Verses 1 and 2 of this chapter are also directed to us, for those times when we pray for some desperate, important need. A mom or dad or child is suffering from a fatal disease. Unemployment suddenly threatens us with the loss of our home. At such times we remind ourselves of Jesus' love, and launch prayers toward heaven that are desperate, and confident. Surely the Lord will deliver us. How could anything else possibly be His loving will?

But if the loved one dies, the divorce becomes final, the home is lost—we're torn by doubt. Why didn't God respond? Didn't we have enough faith? Or can it be He doesn't love us as much as we thought He did?

As John began the story of Lazarus, he wanted us to know how deeply Jesus did love the man and his sisters. Jesus delayed His response to Mary's prayer, and Lazarus did die. But in this case—as in ours—Jesus had a purpose no one was able to grasp until Lazarus was raised.

Don't let God's failure to give you what you ask shake your confidence in prayer or in God's love. He has something better in mind for you too.

"Lazarus is dead, and for your sake I am glad I was not there" John 11:7-15. The disciples misunderstood Jesus' reason for not going at once to Bethany. They supposed He was unwilling to return to Judea, where He had almost been stoned for His teaching (cf. 10:31). Only Jesus knew what He intended to do—and that the delay which led to Lazarus' death and caused Mary and Martha so much suffering had a beneficial purpose.

Let's be careful not to second-guess God. We have no way to gauge His motives, or to forecast His actions. What we can be sure of is that in everything God is working for the good of those who love Him (Rom. 8:28).

"Our friend Lazarus has fallen asleep" John 11:11. The word translated "sleep" here, *koimao,* is found 18 times in the New Testament, with all but three references being to biological death. This perspective on death does not imply the dead are unconscious (cf. Luke 16:19-31; 23:43; Phil. 1:23). It does, however, imply an awakening.

Sleeping Lazarus would soon hear the voice of Jesus, and his essential personality would be reunited with his revitalized body. Death for him was but a brief nap from which Jesus would awaken him. For us death may be a longer sleep for the body. But at history's end we too will hear the call of Jesus. Our bodies will rise from the dust and be transformed and, united with our resurrection forms, we will remain awake and alive forevermore.

"Let us also go, that we may die with Him" John 11:16. Thomas' pessimistic words help us sense how intense the opposition to Jesus had become, and how loyal the little band of true disciples was. Thinking that it would cost Jesus His life to return to Judea, the disciples were prepared to go with Him, even though it would probably cost them their lives too.

Few disciples are called to actually die for Christ and the Gospel. But all of us are to be willing to.

"If You had been here, my brother would not have died" John 11:17-27. The words express faith, and perhaps reproach. Jesus should have been there for His friend Lazarus. But He wasn't. And Lazarus died.

If we look back over our lives, we can all identify times when God could have intervened for us, but did not. He could have changed things. Yet for some reason we can't understand, He did not. At such times it's likely that we too mix a measure of faith with a measure of reproach.

Let's remember the rest of this story. Then let faith grow and reproach go.

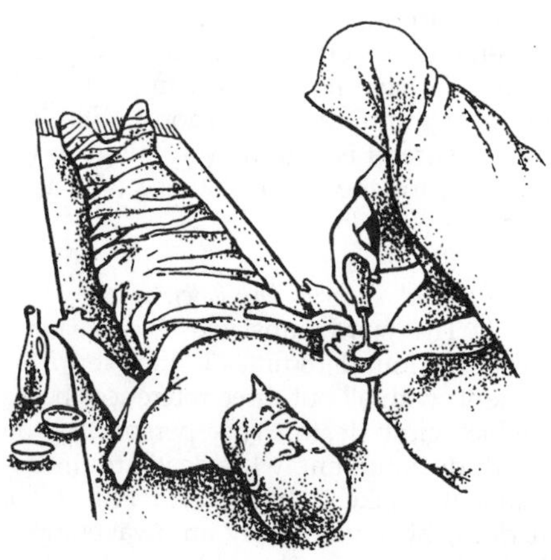

The Jews buried a corpse on the day of death, wrapping the body in strips of cloth or in a sheet. They did, however, return to the grave, to make sure the person was really dead and not in a coma. Lazarus had been in his tomb four days (v. 17) when Jesus arrived. When Lazarus responded to Jesus' call and came out from the grave, there was not the shadow of doubt that Christ had recalled a dead man to life.

"Jesus wept" John 11:35. This is the shortest verse in the Bible. It is also one of the most significant. Along with verses 33 and 38 it assures us that Jesus did not wait callously, intending to "use" Lazarus' death to His own advantage.

Jesus cared deeply about His friends, and their suffering "deeply moved Him in spirit" and "troubled Him." Even though Jesus knew what He was about to do, the sight of His friends' suffering caused Him to weep. What an insight into the heart of God. And what comfort for us when we suffer. God is not sitting back, indifferent on the throne of heaven, moving us here and there in accord with some great, complex plan. He is deeply troubled for us. He weeps with us in our pain. When God permits us to suffer we know that it *must* be because the experience is intended for our good.

"I am the resurrection and the life" John 11:25-44. This great "I Am" claim was vindicated in the raising of Lazarus. Jesus brought life into being. He conquered death itself. And it is the very glory of God to give human beings eternal life as a free gift in and through Jesus.

My wife remarked last night that most of the 11th-graders in her English classes seem to categorize religion as "superstition." To modern teens here in Florida, at least, belief in God ranks right alongside belief in Santa Claus and fear of black cats.

No such confusion existed that day in Bethany when Jesus claimed to *be* the resurrection and the life, and proved it by raising Lazarus from the dead.

"Many . . . put their faith in Him but some of them went to the Pharisees" John 11:45-53. The whole of Jesus' ministry led up to this culminating miracle. All He had done was intended to force a choice between belief and unbelief. Each of His "I Am" statements brought the issue into clearer focus. Now His claim to be the resurrection and the life, vindicated by the miracle of Lazarus' return to life, made it impossible to avoid a decision any longer.

John made it clear that a number of the Jews from Jerusalem who had come to comfort Mary and Martha saw the miracle, and were convinced. Others scurried away to report the miracle to the authorities, who called a meeting of the Sanhedrin to determine policy. No one suggested acknowledging Jesus as the Christ and worshiping Him. All admitted He performed miracles, but refused to take the logical step of faith.

What's fascinating is that the Sanhedrin argued that the "responsible" thing to do was to kill Jesus before everyone acknowledged Him as the Messiah and there was a general uprising. These "spiritual" leaders seemed to fear the force of Roman arms more than the supernatural powers demonstrated by Jesus. And "from that day on they plotted to take His life."

The materialist will always make this choice. Whatever the materialist witnesses, it will never dawn on him or her that the spiritual world is more significant than the physical, or that Christ is Lord of all. Whatever the evidence, the materialist will attempt to do away with Christ rather than to worship Him.

▶ DEVOTIONAL
At the Last Day
(John 11:17-44)

The words Martha blurted out put her in a category shared by many modern Christians.

Jesus had just said, "Your brother will rise again" (v. 23). And Martha said, "I know he will rise again in the resurrection at the last day" (v. 24).

But Jesus kept on probing. "I am the resurrection and the life," He said. "Do you believe this?" (vv. 25-26)

You can almost see Martha nod in puzzlement. " 'Yes, Lord,' she told Him, 'I believe that You are the Christ, the Son of God.' "

It was after this that Jesus went on down to the tomb where Lazarus had laid for four days, and gave the dead man back his life. And it is only in this event that we can understand the implications of Jesus' conversation with Martha.

You see, Martha did believe. She was convinced that Jesus was the Son of God. She was convinced that He could raise her brother—in the resurrection of the last day. But Martha never stopped to think that Jesus could also raise her brother *then!*

Like Martha, many modern Christians have a deep and abiding faith in Jesus. They are sure He has won eternal life for them, and believe in a resurrection which they will share. But, like Martha, many modern Christians *limit the power of Jesus to the future.* They fail to realize that Jesus brings life to the dead now.

He can take our dead hopes, and revive them. He can take our dormant relationships, and revitalize them. He can transform the spiritually indifferent, redirect the life of the sinner, and bring a vibrant newness to every dead area within our lives.

Martha limited Jesus by expecting Him to act only in the future. Jesus in raising Lazarus demonstrated that He is ready, willing, and able to act in our *now.*

Personal Application

Never limit Jesus. Expect Him to act, today!

Quotable

"The steps of faith fall on the seeming void and find rock beneath."—John Greenleaf Whittier

SEPTEMBER 3 *Reading 246*
THE CRISIS
John 12

"Even after Jesus had done all these miraculous signs in their presence, they still would not believe in Him" (John 12:37).

People can waver for a time. But a moment comes when a once-and-for-all decision must be made.

Overview
Jesus was anointed by Mary, Lazarus' sister (12:1-11). On the way to Jerusalem He was acclaimed King (vv. 12-19). Deeply troubled, Jesus predicted His death (vv. 20-28). He was reassured by God (vv. 29-30) and spoke of what His death would accomplish (vv. 31-36). John commented on the blindness of the leaders (vv. 37-43) and reported Jesus' final call to faith (vv. 44-50).

Understanding the Text
"The house was filled with the fragrance" John 12:1-3. The perfume that Mary used to anoint Jesus was worth some 300 denarii, equivalent to a year's wages. Perfume was imported into Palestine, and because of its value was often purchased as an investment. The nard Mary poured on Jesus' feet may well have represented her life savings.

From what we know of Mary—her eagerness to learn at Jesus' feet, and the genuine faith she exhibited when Lazarus died—it seems likely that she anticipated Christ's coming death. At the very least she sensed the increasing stress under which He lived, and sought to show her devotion. Her loving act "filled the house" with fragrance.

There is always something beautiful and fragrant about what we do out of love. No act performed out of a mere sense of duty, or out of obligation, can fill the air with that kind of fragrance.

"You will always have the poor among you" John 12:4-11. Judas' insincere concern for the poor earned a much misunderstood retort from Jesus. John tells us that Judas had a selfish reason for rebuking Mary. He was upset because he wanted cash in Christ's coffers—so he could steal some! The other Gospels report that Judas' remark led other disciples to be critical as well.

But what did Jesus mean when He said, "The poor you will always have among you"? Simply that any person who is truly concerned for the poor need not worry. There will always be opportunities to aid the poor!

Today the moment for pouring perfume on Jesus' feet is long past. But the poor are still with us. And we do have an opportunity to aid them, in Jesus' name.

"Many of the Jews were going over to Jesus and putting their faith in Him" John 12:9-10. The raising of Lazarus convinced many who had hesitated before. If John used "the Jews" here as he had earlier, even members of the opposition party were being converted.

These verses introduce us to the sharp divisions that now developed in Judean society. Some were "going over to Jesus and putting their faith in Him." The Jerusalem crowds, convinced by the ultimate miracle that Jesus must be the Messiah, wanted to make Him King. The religious leaders were intent on getting rid of Jesus. And Christ urged hesitating individuals to get off the fence; to not only hear but also to keep His words.

In the swirling turmoil of excitement that swept Jerusalem as Passover week arrived it was utterly clear that everyone must make *some* decision about who Jesus was.

One of Satan's favorite ploys is to keep people putting off that decision. Satan is delighted when days and nights are filled with ordinary activities that dull the soul to eternal issues. On the other hand, times marked by turmoil or suffering are especially tense for Satan and are opportunities for Christians to press the claims of Christ.

"Blessed is the King of Israel" John 12:12-19. The raising of Lazarus seems to have convinced the crowd that Jesus truly was the Messiah, the Ruler promised by the prophets. They greeted Him with shouts acclaiming Him Israel's King. Even "Ho-

sanna" suggests the thought, for it means "Save Now!"

While the Triumphal Entry did fulfill prophecy, it also showed that even the many who had come to "believe" in Jesus accepted on their terms, not His. They believed what they wanted to believe about Him—that He would free them from Rome and set up God's kingdom on earth.

It's not unusual for folks today to believe Jesus will act in ways they expect or want Him to. Not unusual, but still a mistake.

"Sir, we would like to see Jesus" John 12:20-26. The "Greeks" who wanted to see Jesus may have been Gentiles present to observe the spectacular Jewish festival of Passover, or perhaps Greek-speaking Jews. In either case, they had their own agenda in asking to see Jesus. Curiosity.

Christ seemed to ignore the request when it was passed on to Him. Instead He spoke of His coming death. Jesus had an agenda set by the Father, and nothing would distract Him from doing the Father's will.

"Now is the time for judgment on this world" John 12:28-33. The Gospels speak of a literal voice coming from heaven at three points in Jesus' ministry. At His baptism (the beginning), at His transfiguration (the midpoint) and now, just before His crucifixion (the end). Here it marks the time of decision. In saying, "Now is the time for judgment on this world," Jesus meant that with His death, God's ultimate self-revelation would be complete. From then on, belief and unbelief would mark a line that divides mankind into two groups, distinct in nature and in destiny.

"They still would not believe in Him" John 12:37-50. The final crisis had arrived, and still most held back from the full commitment of faith. Jesus made one last stunning statement about Himself. In quoting Isaiah 6 John says that he implicitly claimed that Isaiah "saw Jesus' glory and spoke about Him" (John 12:41). Turning to that chapter we realize that the person Isaiah describes is Yahweh Himself, seated on a heavenly throne (6:1) and acclaimed by angels who constantly cry out: "Holy, holy, holy is the LORD Almighty; the whole earth is full of His glory" (v. 3).

God Himself has come to earth, and displayed His power in miraculous signs. Yet men were more impressed with the puny power of other men than with the glory of their God (John 12:42-43).

When we grasp the glory of our God, we will be thoroughly *unimpressed* with men. Then we will acknowledge and obey Jesus Christ.

▶ DEVOTIONAL
Who's on First?
(John 12:12-24)

Abbott and Costello are credited with the baseball comedy routine, "Who's on First?" (What is on second base, Where plays third, and I think Why is shortstop.) If I'm confused about the players and their positions, well, this report in John shows a somewhat similar confusion existed in first-century Jerusalem as Jesus approached that city for the last time.

John tells us He was met by cheering crowds, who greeted Him as "the King of Israel." The raising of Lazarus had convinced the crowds: Jesus must be the expected Messiah after all. And so they shouted out praises and cried, "Hosanna," which means "Save Now!" At last, they thought, Jesus would get on with the Messiah's real business, throw out the Romans, and make Israel a world power.

A little later some Greeks approached one of Jesus' disciples, and politely expressed their interest in seeing Him. So Philip and Andrew passed on the message. "Some nice Greek folk would like to see You, Lord." Perhaps they were thinking it would be good politics for Jesus to establish relationships with foreigners. Maybe Philip or Andrew would do for a diplomatic posting to a major city, like Corinth or Philippi!

I can understand the crowds, the Greeks, and the disciples. They all had agendas that were important to them. And each had a big role for Jesus in his plans!

There was only one problem. Not one had stopped to ask the truly critical question: "Who's on first?"

Jesus cleared up the confusion, though, just as He clears up ours. After speaking of His death, Jesus said, "Whoever serves

Me must follow Me; and where I am, My servant will also be" (v. 26). You see, the mistake made by the cheering crowds, the Greeks, and even the disciples—the mistake still made by us, that causes so much confusion—is that all forgot who's on first. God's blunt and simple answer is, Jesus is on first.

We don't lead, and expect Jesus to follow. We let Jesus go first, and we follow Him.

If you and I keep this order in mind, it will clear most of our confusion about life. We'll seldom become depressed or anxious about why God doesn't do things our way. We won't expect Him to. And we'll seldom wonder why God hasn't blessed our plans, when we've gone to all the trouble of making them and then asking Him to bless. As Jesus' servants we'll have sought His will first—and then done our very best to follow closely where He leads.

So enjoy the Abbott and Costello routine when you hear it. But don't let yourself be confused about who's on first in the Christian life, and who follows.

Personal Application

Don't try to use Jesus. Follow Him.

Quotable

"Ideally, when Christians meet, as Christians, to take counsel together, their purpose is not—or should not be—to ascertain what is the mind of the majority but what is the mind of the Holy Spirit—something which may be quite different."—Margaret Thatcher

SEPTEMBER 4 *Reading 247*
A NEW COMMANDMENT
John 13

> *"A new command I give you: Love one another. As I have loved you, so you must love one another. All men will know that you are My disciples if you love one another" (John 13:34-35).*

Love isn't an option. It's a commandment, and the mark of Christ's new community.

Overview

Jesus shared a final meal with His disciples, at which He washed their feet (13:1-11). He required His disciples to follow His example of humble service (vv. 12-17). Jesus predicted His betrayal, and Judas left (vv. 18-30). Christ then gave His "new commandment" to love one another (vv. 31-35), and predicted Peter's betrayal (vv. 36-38).

Understanding the Text

"He now showed them the full extent of His love" John 13:1. This chapter begins John's treatment of Christ's final hours before His crucifixion. In one sense, it is the journey Jesus now took to the cross that unveiled the "full extent" of His love. But probably John has in mind here what Jesus did and said at the Last Supper. The act of foot-washing related in this chapter, Christ's teaching on the gift of the Holy Spirit (John 14; 16), His revelation of a Vine/branches relationship with Him (John 15), and His prayer for our sanctification (John 17), all uniquely unveil the extent of Christ's love in the great salvation His death has won for us.

This first-century basin features a raised footrest in the center. A guest placed his foot on the rest, as a slave poured water on it to wash away the dust of travel. The task was assigned to the lowest menial. That Jesus, their Lord and Master, should stoop to wash the disciples' feet, was a stunning example of humility (13:4-5).

"Jesus knew that the Father had put all things under His power" John 13:2-5. John added, Jesus knew that "He had come from God and was returning to God." And then John inserts a strange little word: "so."

"So" Jesus got up, wrapped a towel around His waist, poured water in a basin, and began to wash His disciples' feet.

Why the "so"? Because only a person who is truly secure in his identity can afford to take the role of a servant. Jesus knew who He was. He was the Son of God, and He could not be diminished by humbling Himself to serve His disciples.

It's true for us today too. In the world people struggle to gain every social advantage, and to appear great. Insecure and aware of their vulnerability, they prop themselves up by pride of accomplishment. Many Christians are like this—competing with others to appear important. But the Christian who realizes the significance of his sonship, and of being deeply loved by God, will have none of the insecurity that generates competition.

You and I can stoop to serve others. The humblest of roles cannot diminish us.

"You shall never wash my feet" John 13:6-11. Peter was shocked by the inappropriateness of it. The One he called Lord, serving *him!* It just wasn't right. Peter should serve Jesus, not the other way around.

John pointed out that Peter did not understand the symbolism of the act, or its power as an example of servanthood. Jesus must "wash" His followers, not just to make them *socially* acceptable, but to make them acceptable for the kingdom of God.

Many have suggested that here the "bath" (v. 10) represents the total cleansing of a person from sin that takes place when we put our trust in Jesus as Saviour. Foot-washing represents the cleansing of sins that we commit as believers—sins analogous to the dust a person would pick up after bathing, while walking home through a dusty Judean street.

We have been washed clean by faith in Jesus. But we stand in continual need of cleansing from the sins we still commit.

"You also should wash one another's feet" John 13:12-17. Luke 22:24 tells us that as the disciples entered the room where the Last Supper was to be held, they were arguing about who would be greatest in the kingdom of heaven.

This bit of background from Luke helps us sense the significance of Jesus' question, "Do you understand what I have done for you?" If Jesus, their Lord and Master, could stoop to serve, the disciples should not compete for greatness, but rather concentrate on servanthood. "I have set you an example, that you should do as I have done for you."

In a few Christian traditions literal foot-washing is practiced. But Christ's concern is not for the act, but for the attitude it displays. Humility and servanthood are necessary elements of Christian discipleship. If we are followers of Jesus, we must certainly follow this example.

"Jesus was troubled in spirit" John 13:18-30. It would be wrong to suppose that Jesus did not love Judas. The psalm Jesus quoted (v. 18) was a psalm of David, that laments the defection of a friend. A similar lament is found in Psalm 55:12-14, which captures the pain of a friend's betrayal:

> If an enemy were insulting me,
> I could endure it;
> if a foe were raising himself against me,
> I could hide from him.
> But it is you, a man like myself,
> my companion and close friend,
> with whom I once enjoyed sweet fellowship
> as we walked with the throng
> at the house of God.

If you have been abandoned by a friend, or betrayed by someone you loved, never doubt for a moment that Jesus understands.

"As soon as Judas took the bread Satan entered into him" John 13:27. The phrase does not mean that Satan took control of Judas against his will. Just the opposite! When Jesus offered Judas a bit of bread with meat from the main dish on it, Judas knew without a doubt that Christ knew Judas intended to betray Him. The other disciples did not understand, but Judas did.

This was the crucial moment. No one

knew but Jesus. At that moment Judas could have changed his mind. Instead he took the morsel that Christ held out to him, in effect announcing his intent to complete his bargain with the priests.

It was when Judas made his irrevocable commitment that "Satan entered him." In deciding to abandon Christ, Judas had opened wide the door of his personality to the control of an evil, spiritual force.

No one who makes such an irrevocable commitment against Christ finds freedom. He or she has simply exchanged submission to good for submission to evil. Submission to God for submission to Satan. And eternal life for eternal damnation.

"And it was night" John 13:30. Perhaps as Judas opened the door and went out John caught a glimpse of Jerusalem, lying in the deep shadows of Palestine's sudden nightfall. All we know is that darkness closes in at this point—and that a dark, somber hue colors the subsequent events that lead inexorably to the cross. The pale of night now lies over Jerusalem, and will not be dispelled until Resurrection Day.

"I will lay down my life for You" John 13:36-38. Peter must have been a comfort to Jesus. Judas plotted to betray Him. But faithful Peter, ever eager and willing, truly was committed to his Lord. Even though Jesus knew that before many hours passed Peter would deny Him, Peter's love still must have been a comfort.

It's hard for us to realize that the people who love us are often as weak as well-intentioned Peter. People who love us don't *want* to hurt us, any more than we want to hurt them. But we human beings are so weak.

I suspect that this is what we are to learn from Peter's betrayal. Each of us is weak. And motives, while important, are no guarantee that we will not fall. How good to know that Jesus understands our weakness, and accepts us anyway. How necessary that we understand each other's weaknesses, and be ready to forgive.

▶ DEVOTIONAL
So What's New?
(John 13:31-35)

That's the problem with Jesus' "new commandment." Love? What's *new* about *that?* The other Gospel writers inform us that Jesus identified love as the greatest of the Old Testament's commands: Love God with all your heart, He'd said, and love your neighbor as yourself (Matt. 19:19; 22:37-39; Mark 12:30-33; Luke 10:27). Whatever we can say about love, we can't say it's "new." Love for God and others is woven into the whole of the Old Testament revelation!

The answer lies in the Greek word here, *kainen.* It does not imply "recent," or even "different." What it suggests is that there is something fresh and new in the love that Jesus commanded. And, looking closely at the text, we can see what that is!

First, the freshness is found in the new relationships Jesus creates (John 13:34). The Old Testament said, "Love your neighbor" (Lev. 19:18). Jesus was about to establish a new community, in which believers will be brothers and sisters—family, not merely neighbors. Love takes on fresh new meaning in the intimacy possible for members of the family of God.

Second, the freshness is found in the new standard Jesus applies. The Old Testament said, "Love your neighbor as yourself." Jesus said to love "as I have loved you" (John 13:34). Just as Jesus' love was self-sacrificial, and put our benefit before His own well-being, so we now have the opportunity to express, and receive, truly selfless love.

The next verse adds one more dimension to the love Jesus commanded. There is a fresh, new impact on the world, worked by Jesus' kind of love. "All men will know that you are My disciples, if you love one another." The most compelling evidence we can present of the reality of Jesus Christ is our love for one another. When Christians love one another as Jesus loves us, all do know that we follow Him, and that He lives.

Personal Application

Love isn't Jesus' "new suggestion." It is His "new commandment."

Quotable

"People don't go where the action is, they go where the love is."—Jess Moody

SEPTEMBER 5 *Reading 248*
TROUBLED HEARTS
John 14

> *"Do not let your hearts be troubled. Trust in God; trust also in Me" (John 14:1).*

Jesus' words of comfort and encouragement continue to relieve our troubled hearts.

Background

The Holy Spirit. These chapters, which contain the Last-Supper dialogue of Jesus, are filled with teaching on the ministry of the Holy Spirit. Christians understand the Holy Spirit not as an influence or force, but as a Person, who with God the Father and the Son are united in Scripture's one God. Here in John 14 the Spirit is given a personal name: Counselor. What ministries does the Holy Spirit have in our day? (1) He is the Source of believers' spiritual power (John 14:16-17; 16:5-15; Acts 1:8). (2) He bonds us to Christ and to each other, making us one church and one family of God (1 Cor. 12:13). (3) He enables us to know God's will and to control our sinful natures (Rom. 8:5-11). (4) He transforms our character and makes us more Christlike (Gal. 5:22-23; 2 Cor. 3:18). (5) He equips us for ministry, distributing spiritual gifts that enable us to contribute to the salvation and growth of others (1 Cor. 12–14; Rom. 12).

In a very real sense, the vitality of our Christian lives depends on the Holy Spirit, whose ministries Christ introduces in this and the next few chapters of John's Gospel.

Overview

Jesus encouraged His disciples to trust (14:1-4), calling Himself the "way, the truth, and the life" (vv. 5-7). Jesus had fully revealed God the Father in His own person (vv. 8-11): He would enable believers (v. 12) and would answer prayer (vv. 13-14). He would also give the Holy Spirit (vv. 15-20), and those who obey Him out of love will experience God's presence (vv. 21-24). The Spirit, who would come after Jesus left, would bring believers peace (vv. 25-31).

Understanding the Text

"Do not let your hearts be troubled" John 14:1. The disciples seem to have had reason to be troubled! The leaders in Jerusalem were plotting Jesus' death (10:31; 11:45-53). Jesus Himself predicted He would die (12:23-28). Jesus had just said one of them would betray Him (13:21), and that Peter would disown Him (v. 38). It was undoubtedly a troubled group of disciples that huddled around Christ.

But Jesus had a solution for them—and for us. "Trust in God and in Me" (14:1).

However grim the circumstances that threaten us, trust in God and Jesus has the power to quiet the troubled heart, and bring us peace.

"In My Father's house are many rooms" John 14:2-3. The image is in stark contrast to the "many mansions" of the KJV translators, who pictured manor houses on a hilltop, where aristocratic landowners lived in splendid isolation. In the Oriental house there were instead many rooms, frequently constructed around a central courtyard. There the entire family—the father, all his sons and their wives and their children—lived together.

This is an image of the experience that awaits us when Jesus returns. Not splendid isolation, but the warmth of intimate fellowship, gathering together as a family to share endless joys. Whatever troubles us these days, Paul says, is "not worth comparing to the glory that will be revealed in us" (Rom. 8:18).

This is one defense of the troubled heart. We can look ahead, sense what lies beyond our experience in this world, and find comfort. Yet as Jesus went on, He showed His disciples other sources of comfort for the believer: comfort here and now.

"Lord, we don't know where You are going, so how can we know the way?" John 14:5-7 Thomas is the disciple we all recognize: the pessimist. He saw the dark side of everything, and was sure to point it out! Yet before we criticize Thomas, we need to remember that even when he was sure Jesus and all His disciples would be killed if they returned to Judea to help Lazarus, Thomas said to the rest, "Let us also go, that we may die with Him" (11:16).

One of my good friends, the pastor of a church I attended for many years, is very much like Thomas. He can always be counted on to see, and to feel deeply, the dark side of things. Yet he is one of the few men I know who despite premonitions of doom is always ready to "also go" in any direction God leads.

How I admire the pessimist who sees danger everywhere, yet loyally follows where Christ leads. If you've been dismissed as a pessimist—and the pessimist is often criticized in our churches—take comfort. Thomas, a pessimist who remained totally loyal, provides an example you can follow.

Seeing difficulties is not the measure of a man. Being obedient despite them, is.

"Lord, show us the Father" John 14:8-11. The remarks of both Thomas and Philip seem to be interruptions that cause Jesus to digress from His main line of teaching. Yet Jesus' answer to each disciple adds important truth. Jesus told Thomas that if he realized fully who Jesus was he would know the Father also (v. 7). Philip's question led Jesus to expand on this thought. "Anyone who has seen Me has seen the Father" (v. 9).

Jesus so perfectly expresses the very person of God that to know Jesus is to know the Father. The individual who wonders what God is "really like" need only to look at Jesus Christ, and he or she will know.

"He will do even greater things than these" John 14:12. This is another of those puzzling verses of Scripture. How can a mere human being, even though he or she believes in Jesus, do "greater things" than Jesus did here on earth?

One suggestion is rooted in the observation that Peter, in preaching just one sermon (Acts 2), won more converts than Jesus did in His years of ministry! I think, however, that something more significant is implied.

The works Jesus did here on earth were in accordance with the will of the Father, and in the power of the Holy Spirit. They were special—but not amazing. After all, Jesus is God the Son and as God, not only knows but is in full harmony with the Father's will, and is always receptive to the Spirit's leading. You and I on the other hand are mere creatures, and sinful creatures at that. It is a far more amazing and wonderful thing when we act in full harmony with the Father's will, and are receptive to the Spirit's leading and His power. Our "greater works" are greater in wonder—in the awesome realization that God can use weak, sinful creatures like us to accomplish His purposes in our world.

"Whatever you ask in My name" John 14:13-14. The Christian's power to do "greater works" is clearly rooted in prayer. We are not able to perform them: it is Christ in us who "will do" whatever we ask.

But note that we ask "in My name." This means more than tacking "in Jesus' name" to the end of every petition. In Hebrew thought the "name" expresses the essential character of the thing or person named. To pray "in Jesus' name" is to make requests that are in fullest harmony with Christ's character and His purposes. When we pray in this way, we can be sure our prayers will be answered, and that God's power will flow.

"Another Counselor to be with you forever" John 14:16. Jesus would soon leave His disciples. Yet He would not leave them *alone.*

The word translated "counselor," *parakletos,* means "a person summoned to one's aid." The word translated "another," *allos,* means "another of the same kind," in distinction to another of a different kind. Jesus would leave, but God the Father would send the Holy Spirit, who like the Son is God, to be present for our aid and comfort.

This Counselor is with us now, and forever.

"I too will love him and show Myself to him" John 14:21-24. These verses contain one of the most significant teachings on the Christian life. How do we experience the presence of Christ? No one can *see* Him, and yet in some mystic sense believers through the ages have known His real presence.

The principle Jesus laid down was: Love and obey. And the linkage between the two is that love stimulates obedience. In fact, the two are linked in an endless spiral. As love moves us to obey, obedience brings us closer to Jesus, which stimulates even more love. But a lack of love will lead to disobedience and a sense of unreality in our faith.

If Jesus seems unreal to you, look first to your love, then to your obedience.

"[He] will teach you all things" John 14:26. The Holy Spirit reminds us of what we have learned. The person who has made no effort to study and understand what Jesus has said will have nothing to be reminded of!

"My peace I give you" John 14:27. At best the world knows an uneasy peace, for the world's peace depends on circumstances. An earthquake, an outbreak of war, the loss of a job, a sickness—these are just a few of the things that destroy the world's peace.

In contrast Christ's peace is independent of circumstances. It is rooted in the knowledge that God is our Father, Christ our Saviour, and heaven our home. Nothing that happens in this world can affect these realities.

▶ DEVOTIONAL
Don't Miss the Way
(John 14:1-6)

As my dad got older, his eyesight began to betray him. It wasn't that he couldn't see. It was just that he didn't see as well—or respond as well to what he saw.

I'll never forget the reaction of my two sons, Paul and Tim, after they took a rather wild ride with Dad in northern Wisconsin. He drove his camper-equipped truck along a narrow dirt road, tree branches whipping at its sides, as my two teens gripped whatever they could hold on to in the cab. "I'm not going to ride with Grandpa again!" they later announced.

I could understand. Whenever I flew into Detroit, I always arranged to drive the car home when Dad picked me up. It really is dangerous when people can't see that way.

It's dangerous spiritually too when people assume that there are many roads to God, and set off blithely down one of them, confident that it will ultimately lead them to Him. Jesus made it unequivocally clear that there is just one way that leads to God, and that He is the way.

His words, "I am the way and the truth and the life. No one comes to the Father except through Me," stake out Christianity's most exclusive claim. Other religions offer paths to follow. Others exhibit moral insight. Others hint at a life after death. But only in the person of Jesus Christ can anyone find THE way to God, THE truth about the universe, and THE life that is eternal. Only through Jesus can anyone approach God.

My teens were right about not wanting to take a ride with my dad. And we're right in trusting ourselves to no one except Jesus. Everyone else has missed the way.

Life Application

The road to God really is marked with "One Way" signs.

Quotable

You, my son,
Have shown me God.
Your kiss upon my cheek
Has made me feel the gentle touch
of Him who leads us on.
The memory of your smile, when young,
Reveals His face,
As mellowing years come on apace.
And when you went before,
You left the gates of heaven ajar
That I might glimpse,
Approaching from afar,
The glories of His grace.
Hold, my son, my hand,
Guide me along the path,
That, coming,
I may stumble not,
Nor roam,
Nor fail to show the way
Which leads us home.—Grace Coolidge

SEPTEMBER 6 *Reading 249*
THREE RELATIONSHIPS
John 15

"Remain in Me, and I will remain in you. No branch can bear fruit by itself; it must remain in the vine. Neither can you bear fruit unless you remain in Me" (John 15:4).

Christianity is not just a religion of beliefs: it is a religion of relationships.

Overview

Jesus' people are branches, He is the Vine (15:1-4). As we remain in His love, we produce fruit (vv. 5-10). Jesus' people are to love one another (vv. 11-13), and serve Jesus as friends rather than servants (vv. 14-17). And Jesus' people are to expect persecution in a hostile world (vv. 18-25), but continue to testify about Him (vv. 26-27).

Understanding the Text

"I am the true vine" John 15:1. The vine is a frequent illustration in the Old Testament of God's people. Psalm 80:8 speaks of Israel as "a vine brought out of Egypt." The clearest use of the image is found in Isaiah 5. There the prophet says:

My loved one had a vineyard
  on a fertile hillside.
He dug it up and cleared it of stones
  and planted it with the choicest vines.
He built a watchtower in it
  and cut out a winepress as well.

And he explains,

The vineyard of the LORD Almighty
  is the house of Israel,
and the men of Judah
  are the garden of His delight.
(Isa. 5:1-2, 7)

But Israel failed to produce the fruit of righteousness and justice that God looked for. And so Christ came, as the "true Vine," that in and through Him believers might produce the fruit of true goodness (cf. Gal. 5:22-23).

Only through relationship with Jesus Christ, the "true [authentic] Vine," can the moral qualities that God seeks in human beings be produced. Personal relationship with Jesus is the essence of Christianity.

"He cuts off . . . he trims clean" John 15:2. The gardener who prunes his vine works with extreme care. There is no threat here in the picture of God as the gardener who prunes His vines. There is no warning to "produce, or else." Instead we're assured that God, the gardener, actively tending His vineyard, is fully committed to bring us to maximum fruitfulness.

God's pruning work benefits us; it doesn't threaten us.

"Remain in Me" John 15:4-9. The KJV says, "Abide in Me." The same point is made by both words: live in intimate union with Jesus.

The analogy itself tells us why. A branch draws its vital juices from the vine to which it is united. In the same way we draw the spiritual vitality that enables us to produce fruit from Jesus. Thus Jesus says clearly, "Apart from Me you can do nothing."

The Christian life is a supernatural life, flowing from Jesus to us. It can be experienced only as we live in intimate fellowship with our Lord.

"If you obey My commands" John 15:10. Jesus also made it clear how we "remain in" Him. Jesus kept close to the Father by being responsive to His will: by obeying Him. In the same way we keep close to Jesus by being responsive to Christ's will: by obeying our Lord (see DEVOTIONAL).

Jesus never abandons us. Any failure to abide in Him is our choice.

"He is like a branch that is thrown away" John 15:6. The wood of the grapevine is stringy and twisted. It can't be cut into lumber. It can't be shaped into furniture or utensils. It has value only when it lives in the vine, bearing fruit. So Jesus' picture of the branch, thrown away and burned, is intended to emphasize uselessness of a branch that is not producing fruit.

Note that Jesus did not say the believer

is thrown away and burned. He said that the believer who fails to produce fruit is like a discarded branch. You and I have been chosen by God, and called into relationship with Christ, that we might produce the fruit of true goodness, and display God's character in our world. If we fail to abide in Jesus, the penalty is an empty and useless life—not abandonment by the Lord.

"That your joy may be complete" John 15:7-11. God is glorified by the Christian's fruitfulness. But, as in all things, that which glorifies God benefits the disciple. Note the benefits you and I experience when we stay close to Jesus. We produce "much fruit," and thus find a sense of satisfaction in fulfilling our destiny (v. 5). We gain power in prayer, asking "whatever you wish" (v. 7). We demonstrate our discipleship, showing the reality of our link with Jesus (v. 8). We remain in Jesus' love, detecting a sense of closeness (v. 10). And, we experience a joy that bubbles up within us, despite difficult circumstances (v. 11).

Yes, God calls us to abide in His Son. But that calling is an expression of His great love; His desire that we might know fulfillment and joy.

"Love each other as I have loved you" John 15:12-17. The second great relationship that John 15 draws attention to is our relationship with one another. We are called to remain in Christ, and to live with each other in love.

Why the emphasis on community? Because how we relate to each other has such a tremendous impact on how we relate to Jesus. If our relationship with other Christians is marked by rivalry, suspicion, and selfishness, it will be hard to maintain an intimate, responsive relationship with the Lord. On the other hand, an experience of belonging, trust, and caring in the Christian community encourages our trust in and responsiveness to the Lord.

You and I can't be solely responsible for how others in Christ's church behave. But we can be responsible for our own relationships with our fellow Christians. We can set the tone of active love that Christ commands, and thus help others draw nearer to our Lord.

"If the world hates you" John 15:18-27. This is the third relationship explored in John 15. We have a relationship with "the world."

The "world" in John's writings is most often that complex of values, attitudes, and behaviors that shapes sinful human society. In his first letter John wrote that love of the Father and love of the world are in conflict: We cannot love both God's ways and the ways of sinful man (1 John 2:15-17).

Because the world is hostile to God we can expect to experience persecution in it. A world which has no understanding of God (John 15:21) hated Jesus, because His life and character rebuked it.

There was no real cause for antipathy to Jesus, for Christ came to cleanse mankind from sin. Yet in the process His very presence exposes sin. Those unwilling to acknowledge their sin and trust Christ for cleansing become hostile. They are angry at being exposed as sinners.

There are times when Christians who live truly good and loving lives are hated for exactly the same reason. Their very goodness exposes the wickedness of those around them, and creates hostility.

But don't stop doing and being good. The Holy Spirit is testifying through us—and our calling is to show others, as well as tell others, about Jesus.

▶ DEVOTIONAL
Friend Jesus
(John 15:9-17)

I haven't noticed it in any theology books. But that word, "friend," is one of the most significant in Scripture to help us understand the Christian life.

The significance is seen in Christ's analogy. A lord or master has the right to give his servants or slaves orders. It is none of their business why the master gives a command. Slaves are responsible only to obey—and they must obey, or else!

While Jesus is Lord, and thus has the right to give commands which must be obeyed, He has chosen to call His followers friends. This means first that He shares His purposes and motives with us when telling us His will. And it means, second, that we are given a choice not available to slaves. A friend may respond to a friend out of affection. But a friend does not have to obey!

Our Sarah is taking piano lessons. It's her first year, and all too often we hear, "I hate the piano!" Pouting and miserable, she heads off to practice, but only because we tell her she has to. My two nephews, Stephen and David, are accomplished violinists. And they love to practice! Even their summer vacations are dedicated to playing in some orchestra, or heading off to a succession of music camps. What a difference between having to practice and wanting to.

It's just this difference that Jesus implied—and that is the key to a successful Christian life. God doesn't want Christians to go out, pouting and miserable, to obey Jesus because they have to. God wants Christians to be Jesus' friends: to eagerly respond to His wishes and commands because we want to please Him.

We show that we are Jesus' friends when we do what He commands. For God will not force us. Instead Jesus invites us to respond to Him, out of love.

Personal Application

Love God and do what you please. Love God, and pleasing Him is what you'll want!

Quotable

"It is not a question of how much we know, how clever we are, nor even how good; it all depends upon the heart's love. External actions are the results of love, the fruit it bears; but the source, the root, is in the deep of the heart."—François Fénelon

---

SEPTEMBER 7 *Reading 250*
THE SPIRIT'S WORK
John 16

> *"It is for your good that I am going away. Unless I go away, the Counselor will not come to you; but if I go, I will send Him to you" (John 16:7).*

The Holy Spirit is alive and present with each believer today!

Overview

Jesus warned of the world's hostility (16:1-4), but promised to send the Holy Spirit to convict the world (vv. 5-11). The Holy Spirit will also guide believers into all truth (vv. 12-16). Jesus promised that soon after His departure (death) the disciples would see Him again (in resurrection), and know joy (vv. 17-24). God loves and hears the prayers of those who believe in Jesus (vv. 25-28). Even imperfect faith is an avenue to peace (vv. 29-33).

Understanding the Text

"You will remember that I warned you" John 16:1-4. The reason for the warning? "So that you will not go astray" (v. 1). We all have a powerful desire to be accepted by others. Sometimes the desire stimulates relatively harmless behavior: kids want to wear what other children wear, and to have the same kind of school notebook. And businessmen dress as clones.

But a need to fit in can be dangerous. A teen takes a drink, or tries a drug, because the gang urges him to. A teenage girl abandons her values in search of popularity. An adult violates his integrity for the approval of a boss or coworkers. Our need of acceptance is strong—and costly.

If you or I ever assume that our faith is compatible with acceptance from the world, we're in real danger of going astray. Jesus wants us to know ahead of time that when society asks, "Goin' my way?" it is not inviting us to go His!

The world lacks an accurate concept of God and of godliness (v. 3). Jesus said the world was hostile to and actually "hated" Him (15:18). To avoid the danger of being led astray by the world, we have to make a firm commitment to the Lord.

So don't make it your goal to please people. Love and serve others. But seek to please only the Lord.

"It is for your good that I am going away" John 16:7. We can understand why the disciples were filled with grief at the thought of losing Jesus. Why would He "go away" and desert them?

Christ tried to help His friends understand that His apparent desertion was for their benefit. Today we do understand: Christ left, but sent the Holy Spirit, who is a living presence within every believer. While Jesus was here on earth, He could only be present with a few of His own at a time.

Yet note Christ's sensitivity, and the disciples' mistaken grief. Jesus knew and cared about how the 11 felt, even though their feelings were based in part on a misunderstanding of the situation.

Sometimes you and I feel deserted and alone too. We wonder why God seems so far off, and why our prayers go unheeded. Jesus cares about our feelings of loneliness—even though such situations too are "for your good."

How close we can feel to Jesus when trials come. He is near, and He cares. He is at work even in our tragedies to bring us good.

"If I go, I will send Him to you" John 16:7. In God's wondrous plan, the Holy Spirit is the Person of the Godhead who bonds us to Jesus, and who lives within us as an endless source of spiritual strength and vitality. Christ took His bodily presence from earth for a time, and in return granted us His spiritual presence, in the person of the Holy Spirit.

This is one of the most exciting consequences of the Resurrection. A risen Jesus was free to pour out the Spirit on His followers. You and I aren't alone. The Holy Spirit of God is with us, always.

"He will convict the world" John 16:8-11. Jesus had warned of an essential conflict between Himself and the world. He went on to explore the ministry of the Holy Spirit to the world.

The word "convict" is *elencho,* a legal term that means to pronounce a guilty verdict, thus defining justice and fixing responsibility. While the Spirit convicts the world, He does so by working through us. We are the channels through which the guilty verdict is announced.

Earlier Jesus warned that the world is hostile to Christ and to believers. He told the disciples to expect animosity, and not to be "led astray" when the world demands we conform to its values and standards. Now Jesus tells us that the Holy Spirit will convict the world through us.

It is not enough to go quietly about our business. We are to make a stand, and by standing enable the Spirit of God to speak to the world.

"In regard to sin and righteousness and judgment" John 16:8-11. How are we to understand these three ministries of the Holy Spirit to the world? In regard to sin: the essence of sin is unbelief (v. 9). Our steadfast trust in Jesus stands in contrast to the world's rejection of Him, and confirms its guilt. In regard to righteousness: the ultimate standard of righteousness is God Himself, expressed in Jesus, whose claims have been vindicated by His return to the Father's side (v. 10). Though men see Jesus no longer, His character is displayed in believers' Christlike lives. We continually exhibit the gap that exists between sinners and the Lord.

In regard to judgment: the Cross and Resurrection—the reality of which are seen in the believer who lives his life in Jesus' resurrection power (Rom. 8:11), proves unequivocally that Satan is a defeated foe. Thus the world system he dominates is an empty sham.

There is nothing you and I can do to convict the world we live in. It is our lives, infused by the Spirit's power and displaying heaven's grace, that boldly proclaim the judgment of our God.

"He will guide you into all truth" John 16:12-13. The Spirit has a ministry to believers as well as to the world. The Holy Spirit helps us understand and apply God's truth to our lives as we grow in Him.

The primary application of this teaching is to the 11 disciples, who later came to new and deeper understanding of what Jesus said and did. This deeper understanding is reflected in the epistles and other writings of the New Testament. Even so, we can see something similar happening in us. As young Christians we struggle to understand what seems obscure and puzzling. Then as we grow in our Christian experience, what was hidden becomes clear.

When we are eager to know Jesus and to please Him, the Holy Spirit will surely guide us nearer and nearer to our Lord (see DEVOTIONAL).

"Now is your time of grief, but I will see you again, and you will rejoice" John 16:17-22. Jesus most probably was speaking of His resurrection and the sudden, joyous knowledge that He was alive that would drive away His disciples' tears. Yet there is again application to you and me. Life on earth isn't easy; in many ways this is our time of grief. But we too look forward to a return of Jesus Christ. When He comes, we will rejoice, and no one will ever take away that joy (v. 24).

"Ask and you will receive, and your joy will be complete" John 16:23-28. There are two meanings of "ask" in this passage. The first "ask" in verse 23, means to "ask a question." The disciples decided that there was no need to question Christ further. They thought they understood. Later, all He had taught would in fact become clear.

The second meaning of "ask" is to "ask a favor." Knowing Jesus lives, and that we are His, we now come freely to God to make our requests.

People have a saying, "It's not how much you know, it's who you know." All that means is that if you want to get an interview for a job, it sure helps if someone high in the company will give you a letter of recommendation! If the person is high enough—the boss himself, perhaps—then the endorsement almost certainly means you've got the job.

Some folks think that "asking in Jesus' name" is like asking for Jesus to endorse our request. It isn't. Asking in Jesus' name means we identify with Christ's values and goals so that what we ask reflects His will. *We don't need His endorsement!* "I am not saying I will ask the Father for you," He said. "No, the Father Himself loves you" (vv. 26-27). What an amazing thing! We don't need a go-between in our dealings with God, because God loves us for ourselves.

This is what's wrong with the notion in some Christian traditions that we should ask dead saints to intercede. God loves Mary so much, so the reasoning goes, that He would certainly honor her request. So let's ask Mary—or St. Francis, or whomever—to intercede for us.

But, wonder of wonders, we've no need to seek a go-between! God loves you so much He is eager to honor your request. To ask some saint to intercede for you is to question the reality of God's love—and Jesus' assurance of that love.

"That in Me you may have peace" John 16:29-33. Jesus' instruction satisfied His disciples' curiosity. And they thought they understood. They didn't—and within a few hours they would scatter and leave Jesus to His fate. But even their imperfect faith was enough to win peace.

Looking back the disciples would realize that there is no security, no basis for confidence, in themselves. But in Christ, and in Him alone, they would find peace. As the Resurrection demonstrates, Jesus is the Victor over this world. In Him and in His victory we have peace.

▶ DEVOTIONAL
He Will Guide You into All Truth (John 16:1-15)

Of all the ministries of the Holy Spirit, this may be the least understood.

We see the misunderstanding in the complaint that Christians are divided over doctrine. Some immerse for baptism, and some say sprinkling is enough. Some argue for predestination, others for free will. Some say Christians should speak in tongues today, others disagree. There are Baptists, Catholics, Methodists, Pentecostals, and multiplied other Christian brands. It seems that if the Holy Spirit were sent to guide us into all truth, He surely has fallen down on the job!

The problem is our view of "truth." To many folks, "truth" is "doctrine." It's beliefs or ideas about God. For these folk, the differences in Christian belief are deeply troubling.

But biblically "truth" is not found in a harmony of ideas, but in the harmony of experience with reality. Both Hebrew and Greek words translated "true" mean "in complete harmony with reality." Something is true because it penetrates the fog of human opinion and unveils reality as God alone knows it.

The mission of the Holy Spirit is to guide you and me into "all truth." His mission is to help us experience reality: to know Jesus as He is, to live a life in accord with true holiness, and to build relationships rooted in real love.

The Bible never guarantees Christians will agree on every belief or doctrine. But the Bible does promise that as you and I live in fellowship with our Lord, God the Holy Spirit will take our hand, and conduct us step by step. We will know God's truth, and our experience of that truth will set us free (8:32).

Personal Application

The Spirit doesn't supervise disputes. He guides our experience.

Quotable

"I find that doing the will of God leaves me no time for disputing about His plans."—George MacDonald

---

SEPTEMBER 8 *Reading 251*
JESUS' FINAL PRAYER
John 17

> *"I am not praying for the world, but for those You have given Me, for they are Yours" (John 17:9).*

Our prayers reveal our priorities. In Jesus' final prayer, He showed His concern was for all believers—present and future.

Definition of Key Terms

Glory. The words "glory" and "glorify" occur over and over in John 17. In the secular world of the first century, *glory* was "the high opinion of others." A person's glory thus was rooted in the assessment by others of his actions or accomplishments. In Scripture, however, "glory" is not linked with human assessment. It is instead linked with the revelation of God's majesty. God's qualities are glorious in and of themselves. Jesus glorified God simply by doing God's will, and thus revealing what the Father is like.

How then do we glorify God? In two ways. First, by recognizing His works and praising Him for the qualities His acts reveal. And second, by "bearing fruit" (15:8). The stunning thought here is that as you and I live in intimate relationship with the Lord, He acts in and through us, thus revealing Himself to others. Like Jesus, we can glorify God by being channels through which the Lord reveals His beauty to mankind.

Overview

Jesus asked God to glorify Him, now that His mission of glorifying the Father was complete (17:1-5). Christ asked the Father to preserve His 11 disciples (vv. 6-12). He then prayed for all future believers (vv. 13-26): that we might be one with Him (vv. 13-23), see Jesus' glory (v. 24), and love Him completely (vv. 25-26).

Understanding the Text

"Glorify Your Son, that Your Son may glorify You" John 17:1. The prayer recorded in John 17 has been called Christ's "High Priestly Prayer." It is the prayer of one about to offer Himself on the altar as a sacrifice for humankind, and it's filled with expressions of love. This prayer is also filled with expressions of Christ's purpose in permitting Calvary.

This verse states the first, and perhaps most important purpose. Jesus went to the cross to glorify the Father, and that the Father might glorify Him. In view of the New Testament meaning of "glorify" (see DEFINITION), what Jesus had in mind was the whole sequence of events that were about to take place. These events—the capture, the trial, the journey to the cross, Christ's death, burial, and resurrection—comprise the ultimate revelation of God's unimaginable love for lost humanity. In this, the ultimate revelation of God's love, grace, and power, these qualities of our God are fully displayed. In this ultimate revelation of the Father and the Son, Each glorified the Other, for Father and Son were united in the plan to save humankind.

Today anyone who wishes to know God need only look to Calvary. There, in the cross, the love, the grace, and the glory of God burn forever bright.

"This is eternal life: that they may know You, the only true God, and Jesus Christ, whom You have sent" John 17:2-3. Merrill Tenney suggests that "life is active involvement

with environment; death is the cessation of involvement with the environment." A worm has an earthly life, in that its environment is the dirt in which it lives. It has no capacity to interact with an environment of water or air.

Similarly human beings have biological life that enables them to interact with the biosphere: the realm of life on earth. But human beings have no native capacity to interact with the realm of the spiritual and eternal. Unless they have come to know God through Jesus Christ, and have been given eternal life by God.

What an insight into the nature of our "eternal life." It is not simply endless. It is the capacity now to be involved with God: to speak to Him, to be guided by Him, to be empowered by the Holy Spirit. We live with our feet on the ground. But our native environment now is eternity, and our primary relationship is with God.

"You gave them to Me and they have obeyed Your word" John 17:6-8. Jesus' prayer now focused on the 11 disciples who had been His companions through His years of ministry. What a beautiful picture John drew. The 11 were God's gift to Jesus. And they demonstrated that fact by obeying Jesus' word.

Some would see here an interplay between predestination and human responsibility. God gives individuals to Jesus. They reveal their election by obedience. But it's best not to be drawn into that debate. The 11 were God's gifts to Christ. What we need to ask is, what made them valuable and beautiful gifts?

The answer to that question is found in the text. To be a beautiful gift a person (1) obeys Jesus' words (v. 6), for he accepts Jesus' words as God's own (v. 8); and (2) knows with certainty Jesus came from God the Father (v. 8).

Jesus deserves the most beautiful gift we can possibly give Him. We can be that most beautiful of gifts ourselves, if we trust Jesus completely and obey His words.

"Protect them by the power of Your name" John 17:9-12. The Greek word, *tereo,* when applied to persons, has the general meaning of "preserve." Jesus was about to leave, and His disciples would seemingly be alone in a hostile world.

We may be alone. But we are not unprotected! God the Father has committed His name (which means "all that He is," and here emphasizes His omnipotence) to preserve us from harm.

This is no guarantee of protection from physical suffering. Jesus Himself suffered and died. No, God's protection is far more significant than that. What God is committed to do is to preserve the oneness relationship that exists between the believer and Jesus (v. 11). Nothing on earth can tear us away from our Lord. We are safe, for God has committed all that He is to protect and preserve our relationship with Christ.

"None has been lost except the one doomed to destruction" John 17:12. There is a slight difference in the word Jesus used when speaking of His own "protection" of the Twelve. God was committed by Jesus' prayer to preserve (*tereo*) the 11. Jesus when on earth defended (*phylasso*) them from external attack.

That defense operated while 11 of the Twelve gradually found their way to full faith in Jesus—and while Judas worked his way to rejection and betrayal.

While the shade of difference in the Greek words is slight, there is a vast difference between Christ's protection of His disciples from outside attack while they were making up their minds about Him, and God's preservation of the 11 who had achieved the certainty of their faith (cf. vv. 7-8).

Don't let Judas' loss frighten you. No one who has a settled faith in Jesus is in danger of losing his or her eternal life.

"They are not of the world, even as I am not of it" John 17:16. To be "of" the world is to have our roots in the complex of motives and passions that rules sinful human society. Because of union with Christ, the Christian's roots are in heaven. We live in the world, but our motives and our perspective on life is shaped by our relationship with God.

It's helpful to be clear on the nature of a "worldly" person. Worldliness is not a matter of do's and don'ts, but of attitudes and perspectives. If our priorities and values are like those of non-Christians in our society, we are worldly.

"Sanctify them by the truth; Your Word is truth" John 17:17. To be sanctified is to be set apart, or dedicated. It's not enough to "just believe." God calls all who believe to complete dedication to Him and His ways.

How does a believer become sanctified? By the working of God's Word in his or her life. Scripture is not just a statement of standards by which we are to live. It is a powerful, active agent God uses to call us closer to Him, and to guide our steps.

Don't expect your life to change if your Bible gathers dust on some shelf.

"For those who will believe in Me through their message" John 17:20-26. This is the third section of Jesus' prayer: a section whose focus is you and me. What does Jesus want most for you and me? He wants us to be one in Him (vv. 20-23, see DEVOTIONAL), He wants us to be with Him and see His glory (v. 24), and He wants us to be filled not only with love but with Christ Himself (vv. 25-26).

What does it mean that Jesus prayed these things for us? It means, simply, that we have what He prayed for! It is impossible to imagine that God the Father would not answer Christ's prayers. Thus we are sure that this prayer has been, is being, and will be answered. You and I are one with Jesus, and can experience this oneness. We will surely be with Jesus and see His glory. And Christ today is present with us, to fill our lives not only with love, but with a sense of His presence.

So claim the promises that Christ's prayer guarantees. And enjoy being a Christian.

▶DEVOTIONAL
Being One
(John 17:20-23)

I learned a new word the other day playing a game called Balderdash. The word was "Martext." It describes a preacher with poor delivery and fuzzy thought processes. When you think about it, it's easy to see where the word came from. Such a preacher would *mar* any *text* he preached from!

I suspect that John 17:22 has been marred by preachers as much as any text in the Bible. It records Jesus' prayer that all believers "may be one as We are One." Many preachers have taken this text as a call for Christian unity. I have no statistics on how often this text has been used when denominational groups meet to consider merger, but I'd bet it's served as a proof text about 99.9 percent of such times.

The only problem is, Jesus wasn't praying for Christians to be one with each other. He wasn't asking for organizational or even experiential unity in the body of Christ. What Jesus asked is that all believers be one with Him!

We know this from the passage itself. Jesus' relationship with the Father is the model of the oneness Christ prayed for. Jesus is in the Father, and the Father in Him (v. 21). They are bound together: by shared nature, by mutual love, by oneness of purpose, by a single, harmonious will. Jesus lived His life on earth in union with God the Father, and His actions here revealed God to us all.

And now, wonder of wonders, Jesus asked that we may have the kind of relationship with Him that He has had with the Father! Jesus asked that we might be bound to Him: given a new nature that is like His, a capacity to love that reflects His own, a place in God's plan and purpose, and knowledge of God's will.

Equipped with these gifts, found in Him in the same way He is in the Father, you and I like Jesus can display God's glory to the world. We can be channels through which God reveals Himself to other men.

What's wonderful is that this prayer has been answered. We are one with Jesus, our lives bound up in His. Christ's desire for us, now that we are one, is that we might "be brought to complete unity" experientially, that through us "the world [may] know" that Jesus is the Father's Son.

Personal Application

Being one with Christ means you and I can live our lives on earth in union with God.

Quotable

"Christ is my form, my furniture and perfection, adorning and beautifying my faith as the colour, the clear light, or the whiteness do garnish and beautify the wall. We cannot spiritually conceive that Christ is so nearly joined and united unto us, as the colour or whiteness are unto the wall. Christ therefore, saith He, thus joined and united unto me and abiding in me, liveth this life in me which I now live; yes Christ Himself is this life which now I live. Wherefore Christ and I in this behalf are both one."—Martin Luther

SEPTEMBER 9 *Reading 252*
ARREST AND TRIAL
John 18

> *"[Pilate] went out again to the Jews and said, 'I find no basis for a charge against Him' " (John 18:38).*

Knowing what is right, and doing what is right, are all too often different things.

Overview
Jesus was betrayed by Judas and arrested (18:1-11). He was taken to Annas and then to Caiaphas (vv. 12-14). While outside Peter disowned Jesus (18:15-18, 25-27), Christ was interrogated by the high priest (vv. 19-24). Early in the morning Jesus was taken to Pilate, the Roman governor, for preliminary questioning (vv. 28-40).

Understanding the Text
"Simon Peter, who had a sword, drew it and struck the high priest's servant" John 18:1-11. John gives us more details of Peter's attempt to defend Jesus. Disregarding the odds, Peter struck out at "the" high priest's servant. The definite article here suggests that this servant was an important official, perhaps even in charge of the mob that came out to arrest Jesus.

Peter's act, and the implied rebuke by Jesus, who quickly healed the injury Peter caused, remind us of a principle suggested several times in this passage: Loyalty may be commendable, but God's battles cannot be won with man's weapons!

The ultimate example is, of course, Christ's own death on the cross. The world tries to conquer with swords and spears, with bombs and machine guns. Christ conquers with a cross. Victory is not found in superiority, but in sacrifice. Conquest is not killing, but making alive.

We make a terrible mistake if we take up the world's weapons to fight our spiritual battles.

"Annas, who was the father-in-law of Caiaphas" John 18:12-14. The two men mentioned here were the respected leaders of Jewish religion and the chief arbiters of Jewish Law. They possessed political power. Again we see the contrast.

Two men standing at the pinnacle of worldly power looked down on a bound and apparently helpless Jesus. Yet Jesus was the Victor. In the end the two who judged Jesus did not condemn Him, but themselves.

"He replied, 'I am not!' " John 18:15-18 Peter illustrates the danger of reliance on force. Peter was brave to take up a sword and attack the mob that approached Jesus. But in doing so he committed himself to war with the world on its home ground. Later, when Peter was threatened, he realized his vulnerability and, in fear, disowned his Lord.

Paul says that "the weapons we fight with are not the weapons of the world" (2 Cor. 10:4). If we intend to battle the people of the world, let's do so on our own ground, not theirs.

"I have spoken openly to the world" John 18:19-24. The high priest and the Sanhedrin had already determined Jesus must die. But they had no charges that would stand examination in a Roman court. The interrogation by the high priest was intended to find some charge that could be brought against Jesus.

Christ didn't bother to answer. He had spoken openly, preaching publicly in the temple and synagogue. All He stood for was well known; many witnesses could be found to tell the court what He had said.

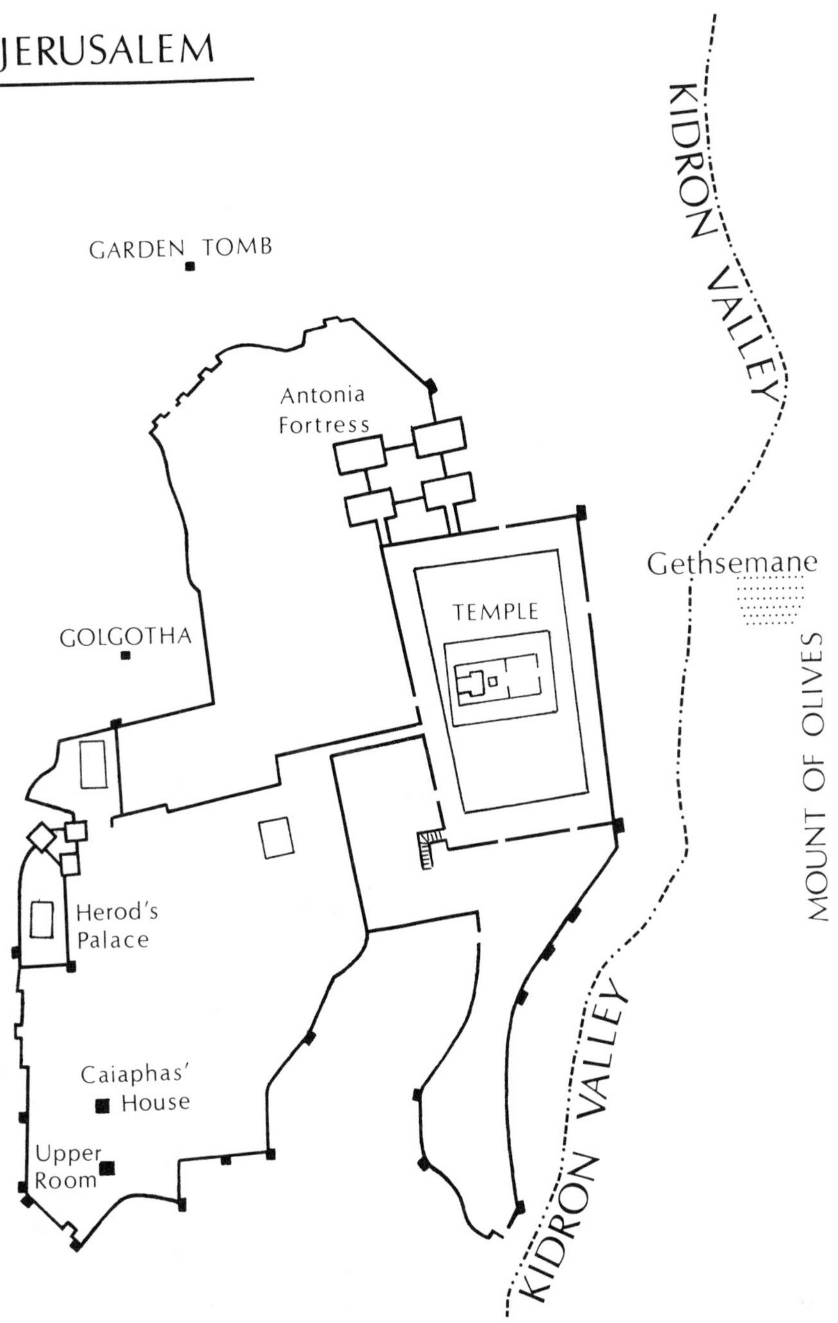

Use this map to locate the events of Jesus' last day, listed below.

1. Last Supper with disciples (John 13–16)
2. Arrested at Gethsemane (John 18:1-11)
3. Pretrial hearing by Annas (John 18:19-24)
4. Examination by Caiaphas (Matt. 26:57-68)
5. Official Sanhedrin trial (Matt. 27:1-2)
6. Examination by Pilate (John 18:28-40)
7. Sent to Herod, ruler of Galilee (Luke 23:6-12)
8. Returned to Pilate for sentence (John 19:1-16)
9. Taken to execution hill and crucified (John 19:17-37)
10. Buried in Joseph's new tomb (John 19:38-42)

Openness and utter honesty are the most powerful spiritual defenses we possess. If we are open and honest, the only charges others can bring against us will be false charges.

"The Jews led Jesus . . . to the palace of the Roman governor" John 18:28-40. John gives us the most thorough account of Jesus' trial before Pilate.

Again notice that Jesus refused to rely on any but spiritual resources. Christ admitted His kingship, but affirmed that "My kingdom is not of this world. If it were, My servants would fight" (v. 36). The real conflict was not between Jesus and the Jews who accused Him, but between the forces of evil and of God. Spiritual warfare only appears to be fought on earthly battlegrounds. And spiritual victories are never won using mankind's destructive weapons.

There was another battle taking place in Pilate's judgment hall: a battle between Pilate and his own conscience. Pilate shrewdly realized that the Jewish leaders were jealous of Christ's religious influence, and wanted to use him to get rid of One they saw as a rival. Pilate also knew that Jesus had committed no capital offense.

At the same time Pilate wanted to avoid trouble during the ever-volatile festival season. And research has shown that Pilate himself was politically vulnerable at this time.

So Pilate too fought a battle; a battle between his conscience and his political instincts. Not surprisingly, his political instincts won out. Being used to worldly ways of thinking, he made a worldly decision—and condemned Jesus to death.

The spiritual man ignores political considerations to follow his conscience as that conscience is informed by the Word of God. Let's not take Pilate's course, and let worldly concerns dictate our decisions. Moral weakness wins no spiritual battles.

"What is truth?" John 18:38 We have no way of knowing Pilate's tone of voice as he spoke these words. Was he scoffing? Or did he perhaps speak with longing, or despair?

We do know that truth is discovered only by those who abandon worldly moral compasses, and chart a course by the Word of God. Only those willing to do God's will can know it, and only those who do God's will discover truth.

Again the spiritual battlefield is defined. Let's set our course in life by the compass of God's Word, and ignore the advice and the "wisdom" of mere men.

▶DEVOTIONAL
"Free Barabbas!"
(John 18:28-40)

The word that John used to describe Barabbas is *lestes*. It does not mean thief, but outlaw: an insurrectionist. In our day we'd probably call Barabbas a "freedom fighter." He was one of those people who chafed under Roman rule, found a contributor or two, and with freshly armed companions set out to cause as much trouble as he could.

It would be a shame if a few innocent bystanders got killed. But the cause was just. What are a few lives measured against advancement of the cause?

So Pilate made a grave miscalculation when he asked the crowd to choose between Jesus, the miracle worker and healer, and Barabbas, the terrorist. The crowd shouted for Barabbas, and undoubtedly the TV cameras and reporters crowded around, and Barabbas was invited to speak to the United Nations, firmly gripping his swords and knives.

What amazes me is the number of Third World movements that pass themselves off as Christian—and are lauded by churchmen. Have you ever noticed that, when Christians cry out against injustice, all too many shout for the release of Barabbas rather than Jesus? They call for the sword and spear, the arming of the oppressed, rather than the spiritual armory of Jesus.

Real victories are never achieved by Barabbas, who mutilates and kills. Real victories, of the spirit over the flesh, of love over hate, of patient faith and goodness over brutality and evil, are won as Jesus won His victory over Satan. By taking up the cross; by bearing witness; by dying if need be. And by resurrection.

Personal Application

When faith adopts unbelief's weapons, evil has already won.

Quotable
"What will it profit a man if he gains his cause, and silences his adversary, if at the same time he loses that humble tender frame of spirit in which the Lord delights, and to which the promise of His presence is made!"—John Newton

SEPTEMBER 10 *Reading 253*
RAISED FROM THE DEAD
John 19–20

> *"Go . . . to my brothers and tell them 'I am returning to My Father and your Father, to My God and your God.' Mary of Magdala went to the disciples with the news, 'I have seen the Lord!' " (John 20:17-18)*

Because Jesus lives, God is our Father and our God.

Overview
Pilate permitted Jesus to be crucified (19:1-16). About noon Friday Jesus was nailed to a cross (vv. 17-21). His executioners gambled for His clothes (vv. 22-24), and Jesus committed His mother to John's care (vv. 25-27). Jesus' death (vv. 28-30) was confirmed by the soldiers (vv. 31-37), after which His body was placed in a tomb (vv. 38-42). But early Sunday Jesus' followers discovered the tomb was open—and empty (20:1-9). Jesus, alive, spoke with Mary of Magdala (vv. 10-18), and appeared to His disciples (vv. 19-31).

Understanding the Text
"He claimed to be the Son of God" John 19:1-16. The Jews viewed Jesus' claim to be the Son of God as blasphemy, and reacted either with faith or fury. Pilate reacted with fear. Already in some awe of Jesus, who had said He was ruler of a kingdom that is "not of this world," Pilate tried desperately to avoid having to make a personal decision. But there are some decisions no one can avoid. And this is one. Each individual must choose to believe or disbelieve the Bible's clear affirmation that Jesus Christ is the Son of God.

Pilate tried to set Jesus free without making that decision. But the Jewish leaders threatened to accuse him of supporting a rival to Caesar (v. 12), and Pilate turned Jesus over to be crucified.

It was the wrong choice. Perhaps we can sympathize with the vascillating Pilate, but the resurrection of Jesus shows just how wrong Pilate was. The Resurrection proves that Jesus is the Son of God, and, under pressure, Pilate chose not to believe. Let's remember the Resurrection, and make our daily choices for, rather than against, Jesus Christ.

"We have no king but Caesar" John 19:15. These words of the chief priests reveal their utter hypocrisy. The Jews supposedly had no king but God, who ruled from heaven through His Law. In their frenzy to see Jesus dead, the leaders of the Jewish people repudiated God Himself!

If we are to live as God's people, there are certain principles on which we can never compromise. One of the most important of these is that, always, our first allegiance must be to God.

"This happened that the Scripture might be fulfilled" John 19:17-24. John's report of the Crucifixion and Resurrection are intended to demonstrate that Jesus truly is the Son of God. How does the story of the soldiers' division of Christ's clothing at Calvary fit this theme?

John reports the event, and shows that over a thousand years before David had foreseen and predicted this event (Ps. 22:18). Even the "minor details" of Jesus' crucifixion were carefully superintended by God, and were elements of a carefully orchestrated plan.

The casual observer might think that death on the cross, so terrible and so unjust, proved that Jesus was not the Son of God. How could God allow His Son to suffer such a terrible death? So John links several "minor details" of the scene to Old Testament prophecy, to show that God not only knew but described beforehand just what would happen at Calvary (cf.

also John 19:36 with Ps. 34:20, and John 19:37 with Zech. 12:10). Fulfilled prophecy proves John's thesis. Jesus truly is the Son of God.

John's evidence that Christ's death was in accord with the fixed intention of God raises the question, "Why?" How wonderful the answer. Through death Jesus is able to offer us forgiveness and cleansing. He suffered gladly, knowing His suffering was for you and me.

"Here is your mother" John 19:25-27. All commentators agree that the disciple mentioned here is John himself. His closeness to Jesus made him Christ's choice as the one to care for His mother, Mary.

Some Christians reading this passage emphasize how precious Mary was to Jesus. She was most certainly dearly loved. But this only serves to emphasize the deep love of John for Jesus, and of Jesus for John. Christ was comforted knowing that His friend would care for His dearly loved mother.

The closer we are to the Lord, the more likely He is to commit precious things and precious people to our care. Let's love Him deeply, that we might be privileged to serve our Lord as John served Christ.

"Myrrh and aloes, about seventy-five pounds" John 19:38-42. Spices had to be imported, and were extremely expensive. The contribution of 75 pounds of spices was extravagant, indicating both the wealth and the love of the giver.

John tells us that the giver was Nicodemus—the important religious leader who years before had come to Jesus at night. At last Nicodemus was ready to declare his allegiance to Jesus, even though Jesus was dead.

It's one thing to jump on the bandwagon of a person or movement then at the height of popularity. It's another thing entirely to come out publicly in support of a leader who has been rejected and lies dead.

The test of our faith is faithfulness to Jesus when things go wrong, not when everything is going right.

"He saw the strips of linen lying there" John 20:1-9. The first reaction to the discovery that Jesus' tomb was empty was one of panic. Someone must have stolen His body!

John, the "other disciple," saw the linen in which Christ had been wrapped lying on a stone slab, and assumed Jesus' body was still there. Peter stooped and went inside, and discovered that the linen wrappings were empty and hollow! They were shaped like a human body. But there was no body within!

John entered then, and saw the wrappings and the napkin that had been placed over Jesus' face. The evidence was incontrovertible. The two did not understand, but they knew. Jesus had risen from the dead.

There is no more carefully documented event in ancient history than the death and resurrection of Jesus. The evidence is indisputable. People do not have to understand. But any careful examination of the testimony compels belief that Jesus is risen indeed.

"I have seen the Lord!" John 20:10-18 There's a difference between circumstantial and eyewitness testimony. The first may compel a verdict. The other confirms it.

Like Mary, Christians today believe in the Resurrection not only on the evidence offered in Scripture, but on the basis of personal experience. We know Jesus lives, because He has entered our hearts, and we experience His presence.

It's not enough to agree intellectually that Christ was raised. We need to open our hearts to Jesus, and to experience His presence by faith.

"I will not believe it" John 20:24-29. What a blessing Thomas is to Christians everywhere. He reminds us that the skeptic is not rejected by God—that doubts and uncertainty do not lose us a place in God's kingdom. He reminds us too that Jesus willingly comes to us, to show us His hands and side, that we might believe.

If you have any doubts—even as deep as Thomas' doubts—share them. Jesus will come to you, and when you recognize Him, you will bow down with Thomas and cry, "My Lord and my God!"

"These are written that you may believe" John 20:30-31. John didn't try to give a complete account of Christ's life. That would have been impossible. What John did was to carefully select material that would reveal Jesus as the Son of God, and so stimulate belief in Him.

Because you and I do believe, the purpose of John's Gospel has been fulfilled in us. We have, now, "life in His name."

▶DEVOTIONAL
"The Resurrection"/Jonathan Brooks (John 20)

His friends went off and left Him dead
In Joseph's subterranean bed,
Embalmed with myrrh and sweet aloes,
And wrapped in snow-white burial clothes.

Then shrewd men came and set a seal
Upon His grave, lest thieves should steal
His lifeless form away, and claim
For Him an undeserving fame.

"There is no use," the soldiers said,
"Of standing sentries by the dead."
Wherefore, they drew their cloaks around
Themselves, and fell upon the ground,
And slept like dead men, all night through,
In the pale moonlight and chilling dew.
A muffled whiff of sudden breath
Ruffled the passive air of death.

He woke, and raised Himself in bed;
Recalled how He was crucified;
Touched both hands' fingers to His head,
And lightly felt His fresh-healed side.

Then with a deep, triumphant sigh,
He coolly put His graveclothes by—
Folded the sweet, white winding sheet,
The toweling, the linen bands,
The napkin, all with careful hands—
And left the borrowed chamber neat.

His steps were like the breaking day;
So soft across the watch He stole,
He did not wake a single soul,
Nor spill one dewdrop by the way.

Now Calvary was loveliness;
Lilies that flowered thereupon
Pulled off the white moon's pallid dress,
And put the morning's vestures on.

"Why seek the living among the dead?
He is not here," the angel said.

The early winds took up the words,
And bore them to the lilting birds,
The leafing trees, and everything
That breathed the living breath of spring.

Personal Application
Rejoice! Christ is risen from the dead.

Quotable
"Christ is risen!" "He is risen indeed!"—Traditional Russian Orthodox Easter Greeting

SEPTEMBER 11 *Reading 254*
FEED MY LAMBS
John 21

" 'Simon son of John, do you truly love Me?' He answered, 'Yes, Lord, You know that I love You.' Jesus said, 'Take care of My sheep' " (John 21:16).

Those who love Jesus are still responsible to care for His sheep.

Overview
The disciples went fishing, and Jesus joined them on shore (21:1-4). When they recognized Jesus, Peter leaped overboard and swam in his eagerness to reach Him (vv. 5-14). Jesus recommissioned Peter, questioning his love the same number of times Peter had earlier disowned Him (vv. 15-17). Jesus predicted Peter's manner of death (vv. 18-19), but turned aside questions about John (vv. 20-23). John closed with an affirmation that his testimony about Jesus is true (vv. 24-25).

Understanding the Text
"I'm going out to fish" John 21:1-3. In New Testament times fishing wasn't a recreational activity. It was work. It was the profession followed by several of the disciples before Jesus called them.

So there's a question about Peter's decision to go fishing. Was this planned as just a day's activity? Or did he intend to return to his old profession?

Actually, since the Resurrection Jesus had only appeared to the disciples two times (cf. v. 14). The disciples were obviously uncertain about their future. Were they to just wait for Jesus' return in glory? If so, they had to do something in order to eat, didn't they?

The fact is that Jesus had very specific plans for the 11. They would never go back to live ordinary lives again.

It's like this for us too. When we meet Jesus, our lives change—forever. No, I don't mean we should quit our jobs, and take up professional evangelism. I simply mean that our relationship with Jesus becomes the most important thing in our lives. We'll keep on working, but work won't be "ordinary" anymore. We'll labor to the best of our ability, because we'll be aware that honest work honors our Lord. We'll continue to have the same relationships we had before. But those too will be changed. Now we'll be far more sensitive, more concerned and loving. We'll care about people who may not have been important to us as persons before.

I don't blame Peter for going back to his fishing. He wasn't yet sure just what he was supposed to do. How wonderful that you and I are sure: we're to serve Jesus and others in everything. And our lives will never be "ordinary" again.

"Throw your net on the right side of the boat and you will find some" John 21:4-14. What's the significance of the amazing catch of fish? John said both that the net was so full they couldn't drag it in, and later that he counted 153 "large fish." I suspect it served both as a sign of comfort, and as a promise.

It was a comfort, because Jesus displayed no anger that His disciples had returned to their old trade. The disciples might have felt a little peculiar about that, but the great catch of fish put them at ease.

Primarily, though, I think the net filled with fish was a promise. It was Jesus' way of saying, "Don't worry. I can and will continue to meet every material need." The disciples would soon set out on the most insecure of all lives: they would be traveling evangelists, dependent on others for their food and lodging. Though these skilled fishermen had practiced their trade all night, they had caught nothing. But a single word from Jesus filled their nets.

We can't depend on our own skills or abilities to meet our needs. But we surely can depend on Jesus!

"Large fish, 153" John 21:11. Why include the specific number? Why not just say, "there were a whole bunch of fish"? I suspect it was because we human beings are quite numbers oriented.

I know I am. For one thing, I have a retarded daughter, Joy, who lives in a special residential care center in Arizona. Joy's expenses run between $17,000 and $18,000 a year—and much of this is not even tax deductible. I have another responsibility that runs about $10,000 a year, so between these two and taxes, I need to earn some $40,000 a year before I have a single cent to dedicate to my own family's normal expenses.

Joy is 28 now, and all these years God has supplied whatever I've needed to care for her and the rest of the family. There's never been anything in the bank, and often piles of bills awaiting payment. But always, just in time, the nets have been filled. And when I've counted, as we numbers-oriented people tend to do, there have always been the 153 fish we need, and more.

"Do you truly love Me?" John 21:15-23 John tells us that Jesus asked Peter three times, "Do you love Me?" While the Greek text shows a fascinating use of different words for "love" and for "know" (see DEVOTIONAL), the overall purpose of the questioning was healing and restoration.

Peter had denied Jesus three times. His tears of anguish afterward show how great his grief was. Even though Peter was hurt that Christ asked him the same question three times, the triple affirmation of love was important to Peter. How do we know that the triple affirmation was for Peter rather than for Jesus? Because after the first expression of Peter's love, Jesus commissioned him to "feed My sheep."

Christ accepts our love immediately, and graciously permits us to serve Him. He asks us to reaffirm our love, so that we might examine ourselves, and be sure that our love for Him is real.

When you and I realize that we do love God, we are motivated and freed to serve Him without self-doubts.

"Do you truly love Me more than these?" John 21:15 There are three possible references in "these." Jesus might mean, do you love Me more than these other men do? He might mean, do you love Me more than you love these men? Or He might mean, do you love Me more than these things—his boats, nets, and the rugged life of a fisherman.

We don't know which was really intended. Actually, we don't need to know. All we really need to know is that we love Jesus as much as we can, without comparing ourselves with others. That we love Him more than the dearest of human companions. And that we love Him more than the occupation which we so completely enjoy.

Do we love Jesus "more than these"? Yes. Jesus means more to us than anything else in life.

"The kind of death by which Peter would glorify God" John 21:19. Peter was commissioned, and then called: "Follow Me."

Peter did follow. He followed for the rest of his life, taking the lead in the church's early evangelism and, reliable tradition tells us, ultimately ministering to the growing Christian community in Rome itself.

There, tradition also says, Peter followed Christ to death by crucifixion. But as a last request Peter begged to be crucified upside down, feeling unworthy to die in the same fashion as his Lord. This death is what Jesus refers to: a death that came by stretching out aged hands, to receive nails like those that pierced the hands of Christ. A triumphant death.

Peter once denied Jesus with his lips. But from that time on his every action was one that affirmed the authenticity of his trust in the Saviour. In life, and in death, Peter's faithfulness brought glory to God.

"Lord, what about Him?" John 21:20-25 Peter loved and revered Jesus. But Peter could still say foolish things.

One of the most foolish things a Christian can do is to ask, "What about him?" It's foolish, because Christ, not you or I—or even Peter—is Lord. We need to take Jesus' reply to Peter to heart: "What is that to you? You must follow Me."

Our responsibility is to keep our eyes fixed on Jesus, and follow Him closely. This is challenge enough. It's not our place to question God's leading of another disciple of our Lord.

"Jesus did not say that he would not die" John 21:22-25. John outlived all the other disciples, many by as much as 30 years! He was a very old man when he wrote this Gospel: some think in his 90s.

During the decades that had swept by after Jesus' resurrection, John had seen the church grow explosively. By the time he wrote, second- and even third-generation Christians were common. And so John penned the Gospel that bore his name as the last living witness to events he himself had seen, heard, and played such a vital part in.

"This is the disciple who testifies to these things and who wrote them down. We know that his testimony is true" (v. 24).

▶ DEVOTIONAL

You Know I Love You (John 21:15-19)

Jesus asked Peter three times, "Do you love Me?" The first two times that Jesus posed this question, John records the Greek word *agapao*. To capture its implications, the NIV translates it, "Do you truly love Me?" This Greek word is used in the New Testament to speak of God's great love for us in Christ. This is the word, for instance, in John 3:16 and 13:34-35. "Truly love" is probably a good English translation.

Each time Peter answered, "Lord, You know that I love [*phileo*] You." The third time Jesus also used the Greek word *phileo*, usually understood to emphasize friendship, fondness, or liking. Some Greek scholars believe the two are used interchangeably here: others are sure that Peter's answer shows hesitancy to respond to Jesus on the deeper level the question implies.

But perhaps more interesting is the shift in the words Peter used, when he said, "Lord, You know that I love You." The first two times Peter used *oida*, a word that indicates an intellectual acceptance of a fact. The third time Peter used the stronger *ginosko*, which indicates knowledge gained through experience.

You and I can and will love Jesus in many ways, on many different levels. But the love that counts, and that equips us to feed Christ's sheep, is a love that proves itself in experience.

Tell Jesus you love Him.

But also show Him you love Him in all that you do.

Personal Application

Spell out your love by your actions, and its reality will never be misunderstood.

Quotable

"O God, let the words of my mouth offer hope and confidence and give fresh assurance. But only when my life reflects Your Word."—Jack L. Moore

---

The Variety Reading Plan continues with ACTS

Acts

INTRODUCTION

Acts is Luke's report of the beginning and the explosive growth of Christianity. Its dominant theme is the Holy Spirit, whose coming after Christ returned to heaven launched the church as the living body of Christ.

Acts focuses on the ministry of two men. The Apostle Peter dominates the first 12 chapters, as the church is firmly established in Palestine and welcomes the first Gentile converts. The Apostle Paul is featured in the rest, as he launches an aggressive missionary campaign that within decades reached every part of the Roman Empire, and beyond.

Acts fascinates us today, with its vivid images of first-century life, its clear depiction of early Gospel preaching, and its testimony to the work of the Holy Spirit. A study of this book reminds us that the Spirit is still the source of spiritual power for Christ's church today.

OUTLINE OF CONTENTS

READING GUIDE (18 Days)

If hurried, you may read only the "core passage" in your Bible and the Devotional in each chapter of this Commentary.

Reading	*Chapters*	*Core passage*
255	1	1:1-8
256	2	2:22-47
257	3–4	4:23-37
258	5	5:1-11
259	6–7	6:1-7
260	8	8:26-40
261	9	9:1-19
262	10–11	11:1-18
263	12	12:1-19
264	13–14	14:8-29
265	15	15:36-41
266	16	16:1-10
267	17–18	18:18-28
268	19–20	20:13-37
269	21–22	21:1-36
270	23–24	24:1-27
271	25–26	25:23–26:32
272	27–28	27

Acts

SEPTEMBER 12 *Reading 255*
PREPARATION
Acts 1

> *"But you will receive power when the Holy Spirit comes on you; and you will be My witnesses in Jerusalem, and in all Judea and Samaria, and to the ends of the earth" (Acts 1:8).*

sense of mission can infuse any Christian's life with purpose.

Overview
Luke continued the story of Jesus begun in his Gospel (1:1-2). Christ gave His last words to the disciples and ascended into heaven (vv. 3-11). The disciples, while waiting in Jerusalem as Christ instructed, chose Matthias to replace Judas as a witness to the Lord's resurrection (vv. 12-26).

Understanding the Text
"All that Jesus began to do and to teach" Acts 1:1. Both Luke's Gospel and Acts are addressed to Theophilus. In Luke 1:3 he is addressed as "most excellent," a title that suggests Theophilus held high rank or social position. Some think that Theophilus, whose name means, "he who loves God," financed Luke's research.

At any rate Theophilus was eager to know all about Jesus. And Luke made it clear that to understand Jesus, the story must be continued beyond Christ's resurrection and return. The Gospel of Luke told us only what Jesus "began to do and teach." Acts tells us what Jesus continues to do and teach through the church, His living body here on earth (see DEVOTIONAL).

"Wait for the gift My Father promised" Acts 1:4-5. Earlier Peter and several of the disciples had gone back to Galilee, and back to fishing (cf. John 21:1-3). They didn't know what to do, and just waiting wasn't easy for these active, restless men.

Waiting is hard on all of us. Sometimes it hurts and we know we can't stand it for another moment. Sometimes it's uncertainty. We know we'd feel better doing something—anything—even the wrong thing. Anything would be better than waiting.

And then Jesus' words come to us, as they came to the disciples. "Wait." "Wait for the promise of the Father."

I know that these instructions were unique. It was the disciples who were told to wait for the coming of the Spirit on Pentecost. Nevertheless, Jesus often has the same instructions for us. Wait. Wait for God to act. Wait for God to fulfill His promise, and do you good.

I have no idea how many personal tragedies could have been avoided if believers would only have listened, and heard God say, "Wait." I do know, however, that until we sense His "Now!" the very best thing we can do is wait.

"Are You at this time going to restore the kingdom to Israel?" Acts 1:6-8 Even now the disciples remained "Old Testament believers." They knew the promises made by the prophets. They were convinced that Jesus, who had proved Himself the Messiah, would make Israel a nation again, and indeed the dominant world power. Their only question was, "When?" And so they asked, with a word order in the original that reflects the emphasis on time, "At this *time* are You going to restore the kingdom to Israel?"

Jesus certainly didn't rebuke His followers for believing that the promises of the Old Testament would be fulfilled literally. He didn't say, "Oh, don't take all that stuff literally. Didn't I say that My kingdom isn't of this world?"

The fact is that God's kingdom has far more facets than most are aware of, and a future earthly kingdom is one, but only one, of them.

What Jesus did say is, "It is not for you to know the times or dates." Believe that this will happen. But don't try to pin down the when.

This is a good principle for us to follow in our relationship with the Lord. Believe His promises. Even when you are asked to wait, trust that the good gifts God distributes will be yours.

But leave the when entirely up to God.

"But you will receive power . . . you will be My witnesses" Acts 1:8. It's not wrong to probe Scripture in an effort to understand the sweeping nature of God's grand plan for humankind. It's commendable.

But at the same time, it's often irrelevant. What is relevant is to know God's purpose for you and me, now.

This is the significance of what Jesus said to the disciples. They questioned Him about His kingdom. And He told them their specific role in what was to happen next.

I don't know when Jesus will return. I expect it in my lifetime—but so have believers through the ages. In a very real sense, when Jesus is to return is none of my business! What I need to know is what the Lord wants me to do with my life. I need to know how to make the decisions that affect next month and next year. I need to know what He wants me to do today.

That's what the disciples needed, and were given. Wait a few days. The Spirit will come. You will receive power. And then you will be My witnesses—next door, and throughout the world!

"This same Jesus . . . will come back" Acts 1:9-11. You and I don't need to know when Jesus will return. We do need to live with the conviction that He will return.

The fact that Jesus will come back means that life here is doubly temporary. It is temporary in that death stalks all of us after our few short years. It is temporary in that whether we remain on earth or not, the way of life represented in man's society is destined to disappear. When Jesus returns the injustice, the selfishness, every dark and unfair deed will all be purged, and true goodness will fill the land.

The certain knowledge that Jesus will return gives us the courage to fight on against present evils. Despite setbacks and defeats, in Jesus our victory is already won.

"They all joined together constantly in prayer" Acts 1:12-14. This verse marks the first appearance in Acts of a very special Greek word: *homothymadon.* In fact, 11 of 12 uses of the word are in Acts; the other is in Romans 15:6.

What does the word mean? It is a word which pictures the church gathered—praying, worshiping, reaching decisions—in a spirit of unity and harmony. In fact, harmony is perhaps the best description. It is as if a great orchestra assembles, with each instrument retaining its individuality, yet under the baton of a great conductor blending to produce a symphony.

This is what the church is intended to be. Not mass-produced tonettes, each with five holes punched in black plastic, but a gathering of distinctive, hand-made instruments. All different. Yet under the guiding hand of God united to play the masterpiece God has composed.

"Show us which of these two You have chosen" Acts 1:15-26. Two of the men who had followed Jesus from the beginning, and yet had not been numbered with the Twelve, were recommended by the little company of believers to take Judas' place. After prayer, the two drew lots and Matthias was selected.

This is the last recorded incident in the New Testament of believers seeking to know God's will "by chance," and it is significant that it took place just before the Holy Spirit came. From that time on, the Spirit would guide His people from within, and outward signs were no longer necessary.

But note that there were two good men, each with the necessary qualifications for leadership, and that only one was chosen. There are nearly always more men and women with leadership potential in the church than are needed.

So what about the man who was not chosen: Justus? Was he set aside, to mold on some shelf? Not at all.

Matthias was chosen to "become a witness with us of His resurrection" (v. 23). The implication, of course, is an official witness; one representing the church as a whole. But what's exciting to me is that Justus, while not "official," was nevertheless a witness still. And he, just as Matthias, could and undoubtedly did bear witness to his Lord.

I'm sometimes puzzled by the clamor of some to be "official" leaders. Being on a board or committee, or being ordained, adds nothing to your or my right to serve Jesus, or to witness to His love and grace. If you're one of those folks who feels some hurt because you've been denied some "official" position in the church, why not take Justus as your patron saint? The man who was not chosen to become one of the Twelve. But who had just as much freedom to witness to Christ's resurrection as they—because like them he had been with Jesus from the first.

Think about it. Isn't being with Jesus a far greater honor than being elected to an office in His church?

▶DEVOTIONAL
Keep on Doin'
Acts 1:1-8

The knock comes on the door, and the little child, left alone for a few hours and carefully instructed by Mom and Dad, leaves the door shut. The knock comes again. Finally, a little desperate, the child cries out, "Go away. There's nobody home."

Sometimes I think we Christians feel like that little child.

We feel all alone. When folks come knocking on our door, we hide inside, hoping they'll leave us alone. If only Jesus were here, He'd be able to respond. So, aware of our weakness, we finally cry out, "Go away, there's nobody home!"

That's why we need to read Acts more often. To remind ourselves that someone is home! That all that Jesus did while He was here on earth was just the beginning of His ministry. Today Jesus is still actively at work, in and through His body here on earth. The church. You, and me.

When Jesus left His disciples for the last time, He told them the secret. In a few days, He said, you'll be baptized with the Holy Spirit. I know that there's a lot of debate of the meaning of that baptism. But certainly everyone would agree with 1 Corinthians 12:13. That verse says that by the Spirit all we Christians were "baptized into one body." And that body is the body of Christ.

God the Holy Spirit has so bonded to Jesus that, though He is in heaven, we are His living body, a body of flesh and blood, present here on the earth. And in His body, Jesus is present too!

So the next time someone from the world knocks on your door, and you feel anxious and uncertain, don't shout, "Go away. There's nobody here."

Someone is here.

Jesus Christ is present, in you! And in your loving, caring response to the people who knock on your door, Jesus continues His loving, saving work in our world.

Personal Application

Trust, and let Jesus work through you.

Quotable

"Attempt great things FOR God and expect great things FROM God."—William Carey

SEPTEMBER 13 *Reading 256*
POWER
Acts 2

"All of them were filled with the Holy Spirit and began to speak in other tongues as the Spirit enabled them" (Acts 2:4).

The most important gift of the Spirit is not tongues, but enablement.

Overview

The Spirit suddenly and visibly came to the gathered believers on Pentecost (2:1-4). They began speaking in languages recognized by visitors to the great feast (vv. 5-13). Peter preached history's first evangelistic sermon to the crowd that gathered (vv. 14-39). Some 3,000 believed (vv. 40-41), and began to meet in house churches (vv. 42-47).

Understanding the Text

"The Day of Pentecost" Acts 2:1. Pentecost was a major religious festival. It was held just 50 days after Passover. On Pentecost the Jews celebrated God's goodness by offering firstfruits of the grain harvest to the Lord. In the first century it was also thought of as the anniversary of Moses' giving of the Law to Israel.

Each association is significant. Christ had died for sinners: on this Pentecost the first results of that harvest of souls was seen as the Spirit bundled the believers together, to form the living church. It also ushered in a new era. The Law had come by Moses, but grace and truth by Jesus Christ (John 1:17). Pentecost marked the full initiation of the age of grace, in which you and I now live.

"A sound like the blowing of a violent wind" Acts 2:2-4. While some Christians tend to focus on only one, there were in fact four visible signs of this unique work of the Holy Spirit by which the Church Age was launched. (1) There was the sound of rushing wind, heaven's hurricane. (2) There was the appearance of a fireball of leaping tongues of flame. (3) There was the separation of the fireball into individual flames, which came to rest on each of the assembled believers. (4) There was an outburst of sound, as all in the band of believers spoke in languages that were foreign to them.

This was a unique event: in no other passage in the New Testament is an exact parallel to be found. Yet often in Acts Luke speaks of the Spirit filling believers, and empowering them for ministry.

It would be wrong of us to dogmatically insist that the "gift of tongues" is not for today. But it would be just as wrong to single out this one of four Pentecost signs and insist that it remains the mark of the Spirit's presence among God's people. The exciting reality is that God the Holy Spirit still rests on "all of them" who belong to Jesus Christ, and that He is the source of supernatural power in our lives today.

"Each of us hears them in his own native language" Acts 2:5-13. In the first century Jews were scattered in every country of the Western and Eastern world. Many of these Jews spoke only the language of their homeland, and did not even know the Aramaic spoken in Jerusalem or the Hebrew of the Old Testament.

Yet *diaspora* (scattered) Jews were faithful to God's Law and to the temple. Each year many came as pilgrims to celebrate one or more of the annual religious festivals. Undoubtedly many who were present that Pentecost had been there for Passover as well, and had some knowledge of the events surrounding Christ's crucifixion.

What was the miracle of tongues? In this passage at least it's clear it must have been one of two things. The miracle was either in the speaking, as believers were enabled to speak in a foreign language they had never learned. Or the miracle was in the hearing, as members of the crowd each heard what the believers said in their mother tongue.

Whichever it was, one thing is plain. That first use of tongues was the gracious gift of a God who wants all men to understand who Jesus is, and what He has done for us.

"This is what was spoken by the Prophet Joel" Acts 2:14-21. One important characteristic

of biblical prophecy is temporal distortion. By that I simply mean that time, sequence, and all those other things we use to organize information, are lacking in much of the prophetic word. Events that are separated by hundreds or thousands of years of history, may be linked in a single prophecy and separated only by a comma.

So when Peter quoted Joel he expected his listeners to understand. Joel said God would pour out His Spirit on all peoples (vv. 17-18). This He has done. Joel said that God would show signs in the heaven just before the coming of Judgment Day (vv. 18-20). So the pouring out of God's Spirit is a warning that judgment will surely follow (but not an indication of when judgment will follow!). Joel went on, "Everyone who calls on the name of the Lord will be saved." Now, then, after the outpouring of the Spirit and before the day of judgment, is the moment to call on His name.

It's the same for us today. The sun stands still for us as it did for Joshua long ago. God is lengthening the day of opportunity, this time that all may be saved.

"Men of Israel, listen to this" Acts 2:22-39. I've known lots of Christians who have felt uncomfortable about witnessing to others. Often they just didn't know what to say. Or how to explain the Gospel.

Peter's sermon—the very first Christian sermon ever preached—is a good explanation of the basic elements of the Gospel. We could do a lot worse than to memorize these points, and draw on them when we're asked to share the Gospel with others.

1. Jesus was crucified and raised from the dead	2:23-24
2. Jesus' death was predicted and explained in the Bible	2:25-35
3. He is Lord and Christ	2:36
4. Repent and	2:38a
5. Your sins will be forgiven, and God will give you His Holy Spirit	2:38b-39

Effective evangelism is nothing more or less than telling who Jesus is and what He did, and inviting others to accept forgiveness.

The first Christians met in houses where they shared meals and "devoted themselves to the Apostles' teaching and to the fellowship, to the breaking of bread, and to prayer" (v. 42). Meeting in houses kept groupings small and intimate, encouraging the deep caring that characterized the early church.

"Those who accepted his message were baptized" Acts 2:41. Baptism here is water baptism—within the tradition established by John the Baptist, but slightly reoriented by Jesus. John preached baptism as a symbol of repentance: an indication that a person confessed his sins and was turning from them. Jesus was baptized over John's objection because it was "the right thing to do." Jesus had no sins to confess, but it was right for Him to publicly identify Himself with John and his message.

The baptism urged by Peter served both these functions. It was a confession of past failures. But more than that it was a public affirmation of faith: a step that forever identified the baptized person as one who identified himself with Jesus Christ. After that first sermon some 3,000 persons turned to Jesus, and publicly identified themselves as followers of the Lord by following His example of water baptism.

▶ DEVOTIONAL
Lost, or Loved?
(Acts 2:22-47)

"Oh, I slip out of church during the last hymn. I just come for the preaching."

Lots of Christians feel something like this. They want to attend on Sunday. After all, it's the right thing to do. But they want to remain anonymous.

I suspect that this is part of the appeal of some of the superchurches of our day. They're big enough for people to get lost in. You can go to church. But you don't have to get to know anyone.

Personally, I'm fascinated by the pattern I see here in Acts 2. Big? You bet. Some 3,000 people were converted by Peter's first sermon. That's a pretty good start on what you'd call a big church!

But lost in the crowd? Never! Because that big First Church of Jerusalem immediately divided those converts up into small groups, got them to meeting in houses, and before you knew it, each of these folks found he or she was loved—and loved others.

Luke described the result. They experienced unity in their house fellowships (v. 42). They expressed their love for each other in the most practical of ways (v. 44). They got together in larger groups to worship with enthusiasm (v. 46). They became such friends they spent a lot of time with each other's families (v. 46). They felt so glad that praise kept welling up out of their lives (v. 47). And, oh, yes, everyone was favorably impressed—and more people kept on being converted daily.

Of course, we're lucky in our day. We don't have to meet in homes. We just put up a church building on some corner, pack it with a few hundred (or thousand) people once or twice a week, and get on with our daily lives. It's not like first-century Jerusalem. Here you can get lost in the crowd—even in a small crowd. But if you're one of those folks who's been lost in a large church, you've also lost out on a vital ingredient of real Christianity. You've lost out on love—on being loved, and loving, in intimate, truly Chistian ways.

Personal Application

Go to a big church if you want. But please, not to get lost.

Quotable

"One thing about the New Testament church. There's a climate of loving relationships. A sense of warmth and care permeates the whole, and fondness for individuals breaks through repeatedly. People knew how to love and be loved by each other."—Norm Wakefield

SEPTEMBER 14 *Reading 257*

IN JESUS' NAME

Acts 3–4

> *"Silver or gold I do not have, but what I have I give you. In the name of Jesus Christ of Nazareth, walk" (Acts 3:6).*

We can have the utmost confidence today in the power of Jesus' name.

Background

Name. In our society a name is a label that identifies a person. In Hebrew culture the name indicated far more. The name expressed the essence of the person's being. Thus to preach or heal in the name of Jesus was to release the power of Jesus in that situation.

This concept of "name" lay behind magic practiced in the ancient world. People pronounced names in hopes that the power of the being would be activated.

What a difference in the use of Jesus' name by Peter, and by the church. As God, Jesus was actually present in power when Peter healed the cripple, even as Jesus is present in power with His people today. It was not magic that healed the cripple. It was the power of God, and Peter's use of Jesus' name was an expression of faith that Christ's essential power could meet the cripple's need.

Today too we are to pray, speak, and live in the utter confidence that the One on whose name we rely, Jesus, is present with us too. Jesus' power still flows, and we meet every challenge in His name.

Overview

Peter healed a cripple in Jesus' name (3:1-10), and called the crowd that gathered to repent and believe in Jesus (vv. 11-26). Peter and John were arrested (4:1-4). Peter boldly confronted the men who had condemned Jesus, and credited the resurrected Christ with the miraculous healing (vv. 5-12). The two disciples were threatened, beaten, and released: they were not to speak in Jesus' name again (vv. 13-22). The church joined Peter and John in prayer (vv. 23-31), and all were filled with the Spirit. Boldness in witness and a marvelous unity resulted (vv. 32-37).

Understanding the Text

"What I have I give you" Acts 3:1-7. Our society has a "throw money at it" philosophy. For Congress and many Christians, throwing money seems to be the first and last approach to solving social and/or spiritual problems. We throw money and then, feeling our duty is done, we hurry on about our own business.

Peter and John had a peculiar advantage. They had no money to throw! Instead, they gave what they had. In this case what they had was the power to heal in Jesus' name.

You or I may not have the power to heal. But we need to follow the two apostles' example, and give what we have. Perhaps a listening ear. Perhaps a helping hand. Certainly love and concern. These, offered in Jesus' name, have more power to lift others up than all the money in the world.

"Walking and jumping, and praising God" Acts 3:8-10. When the preaching of Wesley began to stir England, the religious establishment was disturbed. Those people had too much "enthusiasm." And "enthusiasm" seemed inappropriate to the staid churchmen of the era. But how appropriate it seemed to the cripple, who realized he was healed, to walk and jump and praise God! And how appropriate for us, who have experienced Christ's healing touch, to be excited about our Lord.

"Jesus' name and the faith that comes through Him" Acts 3:11-26. Peter's second sermon, while less polished than the first (Acts 2), emphasized the same themes. Jesus is the Christ. He died as the Scriptures predicted, and was raised again. Turn to Him for forgiveness.

Every generation or so, someone comes along and claims that for this new day, we need a fresh way to express the Christian message. Usually that "new" way deemphasizes Jesus, questions His deity, doubts His death and resurrection, and ignores the need for forgiveness of sins.

There is no "new" way to express the Gospel, for the Gospel of Jesus remains the same Good News it was when first preached by Peter, and believed on by thousands of Jerusalem Jews.

If you want to be an effective witness, don't worry about finding a new way to communicate. Just tell the old, old story of Jesus and His love.

"It is Jesus' name" Acts 3:11-26. A unique aspect of this sermon is Peter's use of a variety of names for Jesus. Jesus is God's Servant (vv. 13, 26), the Holy and Righteous One (v. 14), the Author of life (v. 15), the Christ (Messiah) (v. 18), and the foretold Prophet like Moses (v. 22).

Each of these names unveils more of Jesus' essential character, and each displays the harmony of the new revelation of Jesus with the Old Testament. God has fulfilled His ancient promises, and demonstrated this by raising Jesus from the dead.

Peter pressed these claims by insisting that his listeners "repent." The basic meaning of *repent* is to "change your heart and mind." Peter's sermon was designed to unveil the true nature of Jesus so that his listeners, who had hesitated to accept Christ's claims while He lived among them, would change their minds about Jesus.

Anyone who thinks of Jesus as anything less than God, and the Saviour of mankind, must change his or her mind about Jesus to be saved.

"By what power or what name did you do this?" Acts 4:1-7 I'm constantly amazed by the gall of those who see God do some great work through others—and then set up an ecclesiastical court to decide whether or not they should have done it. Still, it happens all the time.

It was arrogant of the Sanhedrin to arrest Peter and John. Oh, it was their official responsibility to supervise Jewish religious affairs. But when they asked, "By what power or what name did you do this?" they asked a foolish question. Only God had the power to heal a cripple from birth. They knew full well the miracle was from God—and that the apostles had healed in Jesus' name.

I remember in the early days of Billy Graham's ministry, our little congregation in Brooklyn, New York decided not to support his Madison Square Garden campaign—because he had a "liberal" on the sponsoring committee and sitting on the platform with him. How arrogant of us. God was using Billy and many were being converted. But our church's little court decided he wasn't dotting the right theological i's and crossing the correct doctrinal t's. So we wouldn't play.

Let's not deny what we see God doing through other Christians, just because they dot their i's and cross their t's differently than we do. It's far more appropriate if we join those who experience His grace, and are found walking, and jumping, and praising God.

"Whom you crucified but whom God raised" Acts 4:8-12. Peter pulled no punches in speaking to the Sanhedrin. They had engineered the murder of Jesus. And God in raising Christ from the dead made it clear that the One they rejected was the cornerstone of God's plan of salvation! Blunt and fearless, Peter announced, "There is no other name under heaven given to men by which we must be saved" (v. 12).

How gracious of God! The very men who murdered the Saviour now heard a clear and simple presentation of the Gospel. They had yet another chance to repent, and believe.

Let's be as gracious as God in our dealings with others. However bluntly or forcefully others reject Jesus, let's give them another chance.

"We cannot help speaking about what we have seen and heard" Acts 4:13-22. Peter and John were classed by the religious elite as "unschooled, ordinary men" (v. 13). I suspect that most people in our world fit pretty well into that category.

But Peter and John, ordinary though they were, had a personal relationship with Jesus that gave them the spiritual power to perform a miracle that not one of the elite could duplicate!

Don't worry about being ordinary. If you too have "been with Jesus" (v. 13), your relationship with Him lifts you far above the ordinary. Confident of your relationship with the Lord, you too like Peter and John will obey God rather than mere men, and speak boldly about what you have seen and heard.

"They were all filled with the Holy Spirit" Acts 4:32-37. Acts 4 suggests two results of filling with the Spirit. They "spoke the Word of God with boldness." And "all the believers were one in heart and mind."

The Holy Spirit is our living link with Jesus and the Father. It is through Him that Jesus' power flows. We are to be controlled—for "filled" implies—by the Spirit, clear channels filled to the full by His own dynamic power.

But how does a Spirit-filled people display that presence? Not by spectacular signs. But by boldness in sharing the Good News of Jesus, and by loving unity in the body of Christ.

▶ DEVOTIONAL
Prayer Power
(Acts 4:23-37)

It's one thing to be told what to do, another to be shown, and yet another to try it yourself.

I remember reading about how to drive. Then I carefully watched my dad drive. And then my dad let me try—in a very old 1920 Ford he picked up somewhere. The first time I tried to drive it I went too fast on a turn, bounced over a curb, and blundered up on a neighbor's yard. I ended up nestled in some bushes just a few feet from the house wall, with my dad tightly gripping the seat beside me.

I'd read all about it.

I'd seen him do it.

But somehow it was different when I tried. Still, I suspect if I hadn't been carefully watching Dad for some time, I probably would have gone through the neighbor's house instead of just her yard.

That's why I'm so attracted to this description of the early church at prayer. These Christians faced a crisis. They were in trouble, and needed help. Acts 4:23-37 doesn't just tell us that they prayed. It shows us how they prayed. Watching them carefully, you and I can learn how we should pray when we too face a personal or corporate crisis.

There are 141 words in the NIV version of this prayer. And 104 of them are in praise of God's sovereignty. They rehearse His greatness as Maker of heaven and earth; they review Scripture's affirmation of His power; they recall how His Sovereign power was expressed in turning the conspiracy against Jesus to His own purposes. Only then, after affirming God's sovereignty, do they make their request. And that request is specific, and to the point.

Think about it for a moment. Out of 141 words, 104 are in praise of who God is. That means that five sevenths, or 70 percent of the prayer, wasn't concerned with their needs at all. It was concerned with God. In remembrance and in praise, these Christians not only honored the Lord, but also strengthened their faith in Him. In response to that prayer God poured out His Spirit, and gave the Jerusalem church both boldness and love.

What an example for us. And what a challenge. Do I come to God hastily, a runaway Model T bouncing over someone's yard, so desperate to make my request that I have no time to remember who God is? Or do I come like the early church, affirming my faith and confidence in One who is Sovereign over all? And then making my request, sure that because God is God, He can and will respond.

Personal Application

For prayer power, praise.

Quotable

"We have to pray with our eyes on God and not the difficulties."—Oswald Chambers

---

SEPTEMBER 15 *Reading 258*
REVERENTIAL AWE
Acts 5

> *"Great fear seized the whole church and all who heard about these events" (Acts 5:11).*

Fear of God" is another way of saying that we take God seriously!

Overview

A husband and wife conspired to deceive the church—and were struck dead by God (5:1-11). An eruption of miracles polarized public opinion (vv. 12-16), and led the Sadducees to arrest the Apostles (vv. 17-18). Released from prison by an angel (vv. 19-20), they preached in the temple (vv. 21-25). Arrested and tried for contempt of court, the Apostles were flogged, warned, and released (vv. 26-40). Yet they "never stopped teaching" of Jesus (vv. 41-42).

Understanding the Text

"He . . . brought the rest and put it at the Apostles' feet" Acts 5:1-11. Peter has taken a beating by the critics over the story of Ananias and Sapphira. They've said he was completely brutal and unkind to cause the death of Ananias, and then Sapphira. Why, he didn't even give them a chance to repent.

Of course, the critics miss the point. Peter had nothing to do with the death of this pair. He did not act as judge. He didn't pass judgment. He simply stated the case against the two who had conspired to lie to the church, never realizing that they were really lying to God.

God passed judgment. Both Ananias and Sapphira dropped dead.

And the text says, "Great fear seized the whole church and all who heard about these events."

Here, as in most places in Scripture, fear of God is not terror, but a reverential awe. The church took even more seriously the fact that God was alive, active, and present with them! Living with God—and being honest with Him!—had a priority it had not had before.

I don't know about you, but I'm not about to pass judgment on God for condemning Ananias and Sapphira to biological death. If you or I were to debate the "morality" of God's act, we'd totally miss the point. The early church didn't miss it. And neither did the people living in Jerusalem. God is alive! God is active. And we had better take Him seriously if we are to live happy, healthy—and long—lives!

"At the Apostles' feet" Acts 5:2. There's so much to be mined in this story of Ananias and Sapphira (see DEVOTIONAL). But just one more thought now. Luke had just told how generous members of the early church were, and how some even sold houses and other property to feed the needy. Luke pointed out Barnabas as an example of generous giving (4:32-37).

Well, Ananias and Sapphira wanted to be thought of as examples too. They wanted folks to point them out, as Luke pointed out Barnabas, and say glowing words about what good and generous Christians they were.

But Ananias and Sapphira weren't comfortable giving all, so they kept part of the cash, and made the rest a down payment on the praise of men they hoped to buy.

The conspiracy reminds us how important motives are. If we give, let it be because we care about people in need, not money or the praise philanthropy so often buys.

"No one else dared join them" Acts 5:12-16. The sense of God's active presence that the judgment of Ananias and Sapphira produced was heightened by a flurry of miracles performed by the Apostles. Great crowds of country people brought their sick to Jerusalem to be healed—and they were.

Note the impact of this obvious moving of God on the people who observed. (1) The believers continued to meet together on "Solomon's Colonnade" (a long porch running the length of the temple's outer courtyard). The exercise of God's power drew the church closer together as a joyous, praying and witnessing people. (2) "No one else" is literally *hoi laipoi,* "the rest." Here it identifies unbelievers who did not dare to "join them." When God works, some people find it most uncomfortable, and draw back. (3) "The people" were responsive, and regarded the Christians "highly" (v. 13). Many of "the people" who remained open to the Apostles and their message, subsequently believed in the Lord and "were added to their [the Christians'] number."

In one sense there are only two groups of people in the world: those who have eternal life, and those who do not. But this second group can be further divided into those who are open and responsive, and those who are closed and antagonistic. While we want to witness to all, let's give special attention to folks who are willing to hear.

"The party of the Sadducees, were filled with jealousy" Acts 5:17-20. This faction in first-century Judaism controlled the higher offices of the priesthood. Its members were wealthy and aristocratic, and had profited from a close association with Herod and the Romans. The popularity of the Apostles and the miracles they performed were seen as a threat by the chief priests, who were also members of the Sanhedrin that had recently engineered the death of Jesus.

It's not surprising that they acted against the Apostles and had them arrested.

I'm sometimes surprised, when Christianity comes up on talk shows, that so many people are actively hostile. In just the past couple of weeks I've heard Christianity bashed by a popular radio talk-show host, by a best-selling author of advice on how to live successfully, by a "scientist," and by a pro-abortion advocate. At first I figured they just didn't understand the Gospel and the Christian message. But on second thought, I concluded several of them do understand—and don't like it one bit! After all, if they took a biblical view of how to discipline children, live a successful life, view Creation and an unborn child's right to life, what they promote would have to be abandoned. Like the Sadducees of the first century, some modern pundits would rather die than admit—even to themselves—that they might be wrong.

The sad thing is, they will.

"Go . . . tell the people the full message of this new life" Acts 5:19-26. What a beautiful way to put it. Peter and the others were not miraculously released from jail to publicly debate doctrine. They were sent by

God's angel to tell the people about "this new life."

That's what the Gospel of Jesus is. Not a call to join our church. Not an exhortation to subscribe to our doctrinal distinctives. It's an invitation to receive new life from Jesus, and to live that new life to the full!

Let's keep this focus when we share with others.

"They made them appear before the Sanhedrin" Acts 5:27-32. The account in Acts 4 of Peter and John's first appearance before the Jewish high court notes that the court adjudged them "unschooled, ordinary men" (v. 13). In first-century Judaism an ordinary man called before a court for violating some religious law was warned, and the offense carefully explained. A rabbi or biblical scholar would have been punished, for the court would assume that he knew better, while an ordinary man might not. If there were a second offense, the ordinary man, having been warned, might now be punished.

The Apostles had been warned not to speak in Jesus' name. They had kept on preaching. There was no need for an inquiry. "We gave you strict orders" was all the high priest needed to say.

The Apostles did not equivocate. "We must obey God rather than men."

As for the charge that the Apostles were determined "to make us guilty of this Man's blood," they were guilty. As Peter responded, "you had [Him] killed by hanging Him on a tree" (v. 30).

It's important for us to remember that we can sometimes do the right thing, be guilty before the law, and innocent before God. Martin Luther King, Jr., whatever his flaws, was willing to take a stand against the evil of racial prejudice and oppression. He broke man's laws, went to prison, and I suspect that in this he was innocent before God. Many who have chosen to take a stand against the evil of abortion do, in the process, break man's laws. But I suspect that most of them too are innocent before God.

It is never a light thing to break the laws of our nation. But there are times when as the Apostles "we must obey God rather than man." In this way we do show reverential awe of God.

"If their purpose or activity is of human origin . . . it will fail" Acts 5:33-42. Rabban [our rabbi, or teacher] Gamaliel the Elder, whom Luke mentioned here, is revered in Judaism as one of the wisest and most holy of its sages. In this instance Gamaliel's personal charisma and the respect he had earned in his own day prevented the Sanhedrin from attempting to do away with the Apostles, as they had done away with Jesus.

The principle Gamaliel stated shows another way we express reverence for God and the conviction that He is actively at work in our world. Gamaliel's advice: let history judge. Don't take too much into your own hands, because you are not able to perceive what God may be doing.

History has judged. The Christian movement not only flourished in the early decades of the first century, but matured into a faith that has sustained millions across some 2,000 years.

Yet today we may need to show a similar reverence for God in dealing with others. Parents all too often are sure they know just what's best for their mature children. But there comes a time when we have to back off, and say with Gamaliel, "If this purpose or activity is of human origin it will fail." If we truly trust and reverence God, at the right time we will let our maturing children be responsible to Him, and not to us.

▶ DEVOTIONAL
At Your Disposal
(Acts 5:1-11)

Some have argued that the early church practiced a form of "Christian communism." After all, doesn't Acts 4:34-35 say there were "no needy persons among them" because folks "who owned lands or houses sold them" and the money was "distributed to everyone as he had need"?

Anyone who thinks that should read on. He'd immediately be corrected by the story of Ananias and Sapphira.

This pair conspired to sell property, keep some of the cash, but pretend to give all by putting money at the Apostles' feet as others had. Their immediate deaths came not because they kept the money, but because their act was a lie: a deception to manipulate the Christian community and disguise their true motivations.

What's fascinating is that if they'd kept all the cash, invested it in a shipping venture, and turned into the Donald Trumps of their day, they'd probably have lived "happily ever after"! As Peter said, wasn't the property theirs in the first place? Wasn't the money at their disposal? (v. 4) That's not communism. That's capitalism! And what's more, according to Peter, it's all right!

Now, before you get the wrong impression, this isn't a devotional on the American way, or an exhortation to "invest your way to riches." It's simply an observation that whatever you or I have is ours. What we own, we own. When we have money, it is at our disposal.

Acts 4 and 5 don't raise the question of Christian communism at all. But these chapters do raise a question. The question is, are we at God's disposal or not?

You and I aren't likely to suffer the fate of Ananias and Sapphira, whatever we may do. We won't drop dead if we deal deceitfully with the church. But we can't deceive God. And one day, we will be judged.

Personal Application

Our money may be ours. But we are God's.

Quotable

"The genius of Christian spirituality is to integrate [the] spirit of possession with the spirit of dispossession. The spirit of dispossession implies that all the good and delightful things of this world are never allowed to own, possess, or shackle me. Dispossession implies that I am always free, my own person, liberated from the tyranny that possession can easily exercise over us."—John Powell

---

SEPTEMBER 16 *Reading 259*

THE FIRST MARTYR

Acts 6–7

> *"While they were stoning him, Stephen prayed, 'Lord Jesus, receive my spirit.' Then he fell on his knees and cried out, 'Lord, do not hold this sin against them' " (Acts 7:59-60).*

The good sometimes die young. But never unnoticed.

Overview

Conflict in the community was resolved by appointing seven deacons (6:1-7). One of them, Stephen, spoke so effectively that other Greek-speaking Jews attempted to have him done away with (vv. 8-15). In his defense, Stephen reviewed Israel's history (7:1-34) to demonstrate Israel's historic rejection of Moses and his Law (vv. 35-43) and its distortion of temple worship (vv. 44-50). Stephen charged that in the same rebellious spirit, this court betrayed and murdered Jesus, God's Messiah (vv. 50-56). The court became a mob and stoned Stephen (vv. 57-59).

Understanding the Text

"The Grecian Jews among them complained" Acts 6:1. The Grecian Jews were most likely Jews who had come to Judea from foreign lands, but spoke only Greek and no Semitic language. Documents reflecting the first century show that such Jews, whether converts or Jewish by birth, were looked down on by natives of the Holy Land.

Apparently the prejudice survived conversion. The dispute over neglect of Grecian Jewish widows may well reflect a sharper split in the Jerusalem church.

Most people try to maintain groups by keeping out those who differ, not by seeking to include them. Christian sociologists have noticed that local churches that appeal to a particular strata of society tend to grow more rapidly. Folks feel comfortable with others who are like them. Thus few American congregations have extremes of wealth and poverty, of low and high degree of education, or of mixed races.

Perhaps this is good from a sociological viewpoint. It isn't from a spiritual viewpoint. God sacrificed His Son to create a church that is one body, united in and around Jesus Christ. When differences of any kind isolate us from others, we distort that truth and violate one of God's great purposes in the Incarnation.

Acts 6 shows us that the Jerusalem church faced, and overcame, the threat raised by prejudice and differences. We need to face and overcome such threats too.

"The Twelve gathered all the disciples together" Acts 6:2. How fascinating. The "pastoral staff" didn't take responsibility for distributing the food. Instead the Apostles led the congregation to solve the problem themselves!

Note these principles. You can use them in church—and at home! First, there was no attempt to blame. We need to find solutions, not fault! Second, the leaders suggested a way the congregation might resolve the problem. Again, the leaders didn't take this responsibility on themselves. The solution could be found by the people involved. Third, the leaders gave the congregation full authority. The people involved, who knew the situation best, were given freedom to correct any injustice.

Each step here is important. In church, in families, and in society at large, we tend to be paternalistic. Appointed or elected leaders take on more and more responsibility, and give less and less authority to those affected by the social or personal problems. Acts 6 shows us a better way. That way may not work well in society. But it will work in the Christian church, and in the family where Christ dwells.

"Choose seven men" Acts 6:3-7. Did you notice? The NIV version of this passage which some churches refer to when proof texting the role of deacons, doesn't mention "deacon" at all? Why?

Because the title deacon (Gk., *diakonos)* is not in the Greek text. Why then do other versions have "deacon" in these verses? Because the verb *diakoneo,* "wait on" or "serve," and a similiar noun, *diakonia,* "distribution," are in the Greek text.

What does all this mean? Simply that the ministry of the "deacon" came into being long before the office was invented. And this is important. You and I don't have to hold an office to serve others. We don't have to carry a title to minister. What's more, the function is undoubtedly more important than the office in the sight of God. So let's not be concerned about holding office in the church. Let's simply be concerned about serving others for Jesus' sake.

"Full of the Spirit and wisdom" Acts 6:3. You need the Holy Spirit to be a driver for "meals on wheels"? You bet. Any ministry, however menial, must be performed in the Spirit's power if it is to be a means of grace.

Some of the most meaningful ministry I ever had came when I was a young Christian, in the Navy, serving as volunteer janitor at our little Baptist church. What a joyous time those Saturday mornings were, singing as I pushed my broom and arranged chairs in the church basement.

There's no service that's demeaning to a Christian. And there's no ministry that we are to perform in our own strength.

"Stephen, a man full of God's grace and power" Acts 6:8-15. The "meals on wheels" man, performing miraculous signs and preaching powerfully? You bet.

Again, what a false distinction we make in ranking some ministries as "higher" than others. The janitor who cleans the church and the preacher who speaks to the congregation both are God's servants. Both need to be good men, filled with God's Spirit.

Don't be surprised if one day the janitor becomes the preacher. Serve God well in small things. Remember, He promotes from within the company.

"Members of the Synagogue of the Freedmen" Acts 6:8-13. This synagogue was most likely composed of Jews like Stephen who spoke only Greek. One reason for its hostility may well have been the general feeling that Hellenistic (Grecian) Jews were not as "good" Jews as the native born. These Grecian Jews would have a powerful motive to refute Stephen, and thus show orthodoxy.

When they could not defeat Stephen by argument, they arranged for false witnesses to charge him with speaking "against Moses, and against God." That is, they said Stephen rejected the Mosaic Law, and that he showed contempt for the temple at which God was worshiped. Stephen's defense (Acts 7) is geared to refute these two charges.

Lying about someone to defend "orthodoxy" is the last resort of desperate men. And it's done by Christians today. One recent Christian bestseller roused righteous indignation by charging well-known believers with all sorts of heresies, and "proving" the charges by quoting them—out of context.

Just remember when you run across such things, or are tempted to defend the faith that way yourself, that in Acts 6 God is on the side of the victim. That kind of act puts a person right there beside those folks from the Synagogue of the Freedmen who were guilty of Stephen's death.

"Like the face of an angel" Acts 6:15. Don't take this to mean Stephen's face shone. In contemporary idiom, saying one's face was like that of an angel was a compliment given very devout men. Stephen, composed and serene, reflected a calm which could only be ascribed to the Spirit's presence and his own knowledge of his innocence.

"The God of glory appeared to our father Abraham" Acts 7:1-34. It was customary in Judaism to incorporate a review of God's work in history into any declaration of faith. Stephen followed this pattern here.

How important for us, as we face any modern test, to have our faith firmly anchored in a grasp of God's redemptive work in history. We stand in a millennia-old tradition of men and women of God, who have seen God act, and who know that He is totally trustworthy.

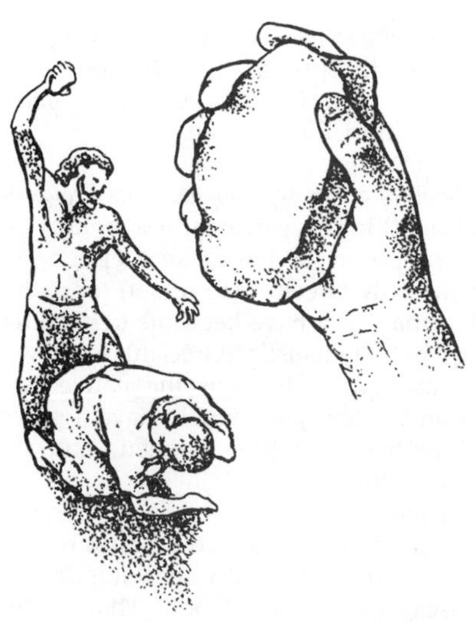

"The same Moses whom they had rejected" Acts 7:35-43. Stephen's review of history is more than an affirmation of his faith. It is a bold and courageous confrontation of his accusers. The history which showed God had acted for His people showed that God's people rejected Moses, and were so disobedient to Moses' Law that they finally were sent into Exile! Now Israel had compounded the sin by rejecting the "prophet like me [Moses]" whom God had sent!

Thus Stephen showed that the men who charged him with disrespect for the Law of Moses were the real culprits, for they rejected the source of a new revelation that that law itself predicted.

"What kind of house will you build for Me?" Acts 7:44-50 Disrespect for the Jerusalem temple was viewed by the Sanhedrin as disrespect for God Himself. Stephen showed that God, who fills the heavens and the earth, cannot be totally identified with any human construction. His accusers were the ones guilty of distorting God's truth.

"You stiff-necked people" Acts 7:51-58. With total boldness Stephen drove his point home. His accusers were in the line of those Israelites who persistently resisted God, not those who represented Him.

When Stephen had the temerity to shout that he saw Jesus, standing at God's right hand, the court became a mob and stoned him.

Don't look at Stephen's boldness as a mistake. The text reminds us that Stephen was "full of the Holy Spirit" as he spoke (v. 55). The martyrdom of Stephen was no more an unavoidable mistake than was the crucifixion of Jesus. Each was an element of the plan of God for His people.

It's a mistake too for us to say about our own lives, "That didn't turn out well, so it must not have been God's will." We can't judge God's will that way, for He has a habit of turning "bad" results into unexpected good.

"The Son of man standing" Acts 7:54-60. Stephen saw Jesus "standing" by God's right hand. Why standing? Perhaps because in Jewish courts a person giving testimony stood before the tribunal. As Stephen stood before the Sanhedrin testifying to Jesus, Christ stood before God, speaking for Stephen.

In a few moments Stephen, who died with a prayer for his murderers on his lips, was in the presence of the Lord.

It matters little what men say to us or do to us. What counts is what Christ says about us before the Father's throne.

▶ DEVOTIONAL

How to Put Down Troublemakers (Acts 6:1-7)

They could have handled it differently. I mean, when people complain, you've got to be firm. You tell 'em, "Listen. I'm in charge here. If you have a complaint, put it in writing. I'll get to it as soon as I can."

And then you drop the complaint in the circular file (wastebasket, to the uninitiated) and go on about your business.

I suppose that's one way to put down troublemakers. Or ignore them. Or lose their files. Or make promises you don't expect to keep. Or multiply forms, till it's too much work to fill them out.

The Jerusalem church, though, had a little different approach. When Grecian Jewish Christians complained that their widows weren't getting a fair share when food was distributed, the church listened to them. Then the Apostles got the whole church together, suggested they choose seven known "to be full of the Spirit and wisdom," and let the seven solve the problem. What's fascinating is that every one of the seven that the church chose had a Greek name. What does that mean? Simply, that the church, instead of slapping on the label "troublemakers," gave the people who experienced an injustice the power to correct it.

In the process the Hebrew Christians made themselves vulnerable. They surrendered their rights to those who had felt, and had been, victims of their injustice.

How did the Jerusalem church put down troublemakers? It didn't. It lifted the troublemakers up, and gave them the authority they needed to solve the problem they complained about.

Can this radical kind of solution work in Christianity today? Yes, if we keep three things in mind. (1) Don't view people with problems as troublemakers. Take their concerns seriously. (2) Don't be defensive, or try to fix blame for past failings. The past isn't the issue. The problem is. And (3), don't be paternalistic. Don't think that "leaders" are the only folks who can solve problems. Select wise, Spirit-filled folk who know the problem firsthand, and give them the authority they need to solve it.

The Holy Spirit really is resident in the church. We exhibit trust in God when we "put down" our troublemakers, by lifting them up.

Personal Application

The tighter folks hold on to the reins of spiritual power, the less trust they exhibit in God.

Quotable

"In order to obtain and hold power a man must love it. Thus the effort to get it is not likely to be coupled with goodness, but with the opposite qualities of pride, craft, and cruelty."—Leo Tolstoy

SEPTEMBER 17 *Reading 260*
BEYOND JUDEA
Acts 8

"A great persecution broke out against the church at Jerusalem, and all except the Apostles were scattered throughout Judea and Samaria" (Acts 8:1).

The church that prospers under persecution crumbles when comfortable.

Overview

Intense persecution scattered Christians through Judea and Samaria (8:1-3). Samaritans (vv. 4-7) and even a magician named Simon (vv. 9-13) were converted by Philip's preaching. Apostles came from Jerusalem to investigate, and gave the Holy Spirit in a way that established their authority and the unity of the church (vv. 14-17). Simon was rebuked for trying to buy spiritual power (vv. 18-25). An angel directed Philip to leave the revival to lead a lone individual to Christ (vv. 26-40).

Understanding the Text

"On that day a great persecution broke out" Acts 8:1-2. The Apostles had been told that God's purpose was to plant the Gospel first in Jerusalem, then "in all Judea and Samaria" and then to the "ends of the earth" (1:8). For a long time, however, the church remained a Jerusalem phenomenon. The thousands of converts came from that city—and stayed there. Why leave such a loving community of believers, such outstanding leaders?

We all have a tendency to "settle down" here on earth. As strange as it seems, God's blessings can sap our spiritual vitality. It took an outburst of persecution to scatter the Jerusalem believers—and the Gospel message—across Judea and Samaria. Let's not "settle down" too comfortably in this world. God has work for each of us to do.

"Saul began to destroy the church" Acts 8:3. We know Saul better as Paul the Apostle. But that story comes later. Now Saul, with authority from the Sanhedrin, zealously went about trying to stamp out the Christian movement.

After his conversion Paul had a key role in God's great plan for evangelizing the world. But even now, before his conversion, Paul played a key role in that same plan! It was Paul's active persecution that scattered believers—and thus spread the Gospel.

God is great enough that even His most active enemies actually promote His cause.

"Philip went down to a city in Samaria and proclaimed the Christ there" Acts 8:4-7. Philip was one of seven "deacons" chosen to distribute food to the needy (6:1-7). Here we see him preaching and performing miracles in Samaria. Another "meals on wheels" driver had been promoted in God's army!

What's really significant, however, is that Philip preached in Samaria. The Samaritan religion was a perverted form of Judaism, and Samaritans were viewed with hostility and contempt by the Jews. Philip, however, viewed them as human beings for whom Christ died, and preached Christ to them.

How we classify people determines to a large extent how we relate to them. We Christians are not to classify others by racial or socioeconomic group, or even by such categories as drug addict, homosexual, or convict. We are to look at other believers as brothers and sisters in the Lord. And we are to look at every non-Christian as a candidate for salvation—as a person God loves, and for whom Christ died.

"Peter and John placed their hands on them, and they received the Holy Spirit" Acts 8:14-17. Every now and then we need to be reminded that Acts is a book of history, not of doctrine. Some of the things that are reported there are not normative. That is, they are not patterns for all Christians to follow everywhere.

This is one of those incidents. God did not give the Holy Spirit to the Samaritans until two apostles came down from Jerusalem. Then the Spirit was given when and only when John and Peter laid hands on the new believers.

Remembering the ancient hostility and religious rivalry between the Jews and Samaritans, we can see why this was necessary. The church of Christ is one, and the ministry of the Apostles was foundational to its teaching and unity. Only such an obvious sign of unity and authority could keep the Samaritans from developing a separate church in the critical early Christian decades as they had developed a separate form of Judaism.

So don't build your doctrine of the Holy Spirit and His coming on the experiences reported in Acts. Look for the unusual reasons for God's unusual actions.

"Simon . . . offered them money" Acts 8:9-13, 18-25. Simon was one of those folks who made a good living promoting his or her supposed supernatural powers. Like the modern stage magician, Simon knew some mighty good tricks, and had deceived "high and low" into honoring him as "the Great Power." And then Simon got converted. But he brought some of his old attitudes into his new life.

Peter's rebuke is blunt and to the point. It is also directed to you and me. Like Simon we bring too many of our old attitudes and values with us when we become Christians. And we have to get rid of them, for they have no place in people who belong to Jesus.

"On his way he met an Ethiopian eunuch" Acts 8:26-35. Usually "eunuch" indicates a male who has been castrated. It was quite common in ancient times for rulers to castrate young boys and train them for administrative duties. The theory was that with no family to consider they would be more faithful to the ruler they served.

In time "eunuch" was used in some societies as a title for certain officials, whether they had been castrated or not. So we can't be sure if this high Ethiopian official was a true eunuch or not. It's tempting to think that he was, just because Old Testament Law forbade such persons to participate in temple worship. How exciting it must have been for the Ethiopian as Philip taught him to realize that in Christ, God would welcome even him.

Everyone is welcome in Christ. Whatever one's background, whatever he has done or not done, there is room for him or her. The Good News for every outcast is, come on in!

"How can I . . . unless someone explains it to me?" Acts 8:31-40 Most people do not really comprehend what they read. That's frustrating for those of us whose ministry is writing. But it's exciting for everyone else.

I communicate by computer. But you have the opportunity to explain to friends or neighbors or folks you meet on the plane, face-to-face, the wonderful message that led to the joyful conversion of the Ethiopian eunuch.

I've been told (by publishers) that authors are (or were, before TV evangelists came along) the "superstars" of Christianity. Having received little adulation, I'm not at all convinced. But I am convinced that the most effective and most exciting ministry there is is the simple one-on-one explaining of the Gospel to someone who wants to understand what he's read or heard.

Why not ask God to send you to someone like the Ethiopian eunuch today?

▶ DEVOTIONAL
Go South
(Acts 8:26-40)

I've learned over the years that God has a habit of asking us to change directions suddenly. The night of my seminary graduation, I had the privilege of speaking for the "future pastors." Three days later I was on a plane to interview for a position as an editor at a Christian publisher.

Several years later I spoke at a church that was looking for a pastor. I was expecting a call. Two weeks later I was an assistant professor at Wheaton College Graduate School.

I finally got my Ph.D. and tenure, and looked forward to a lifelong career in teaching. A few months later I moved to Phoenix, with no job, to launch a writing ministry.

It seemed that every time I was set on my direction in life, God interrupted, and said, "Go another way."

That's surely what happened to Philip. But Philip's change of direction was even more stunning. He was right in the middle of a great revival: hundreds of people were being saved. And God said to him, "Go south to the road—the desert road." What? Leave the city and the big tent meeting, where conversions were coming by the dozen. Go where? The desert!

Philip knew better than to question. He went out by the road, and there he met an Ethiopian official that he led to Christ. Undoubtedly that official then carried the Gospel back to his distant homeland.

I suppose that a Government Accounting Office official would argue that going south wasn't cost effective. I mean, stay where you can get the most for your money. Don't reserve all that time for just one person when it could be used to reach hundreds. But it's kind of nice to remember that God isn't a GAO accountant. To Him, the individual is still as important as the crowd.

So the next time God says, "Go south," to you, don't hesitate. It may not make much sense to you. But whatever God tells us to do makes a lot of sense to Him.

Personal Application

Be sensitive to God's change of direction.

Quotable

(Morning prayer): "Good morning, God, I love You! What are You up to today? I want to be a part of it."—Norman Grubb

SEPTEMBER 18 *Reading 261*

PAUL'S CONVERSION

Acts 9

> *"This man is My chosen instrument to carry My name before the Gentiles and their kings and before the people of Israel" (Acts 9:15).*

Salvation first: service second.

Overview

Saul set off to stamp out Christianity in Damascus (9:1-2) but was converted on the way (vv. 3-19). His bold preaching of Christ aroused deadly hostility in Damascus (vv. 20-25). Back in Jerusalem, his fearless witness again endangered him, and Saul was sent home to Tarsus (vv. 26-31). Meanwhile Peter, in Joppa, raised a beloved widow from the dead (vv. 32-43).

Understanding the Text

"Breathing out murderous threats" Acts 9:1-2. The Sanhedrin had the right to discipline any Jew living in the Empire. Letters from that body gave Saul legal authority to arrest Christian Jews in Damascus.

But why was Paul so adamantly opposed to the Christians? He undoubtedly saw faith in Jesus as a corruption and perversion of the Scriptures, and very possibly saw himself as a worthy successor of such ancient heroes as Moses or Phinehas, who killed immoral Israelites at Baal of Peor (Num. 25:1-15). There is no question that zealous first-century Jews viewed hatred of the wicked as a mark of righteousness.

Saul's absolute certainty serves to alert us to a common danger. It is always possible to apply Scripture wrongly. The Word is reliable, but we human beings have a tendency to proof text our actions. And the verse or principle we refer to may not apply to our situation! God has given us His Holy Spirit to guide our application of Scripture. We must remain sensitive to His leading, or risk running enthusiastically in the wrong direction, as Saul surely did!

"And heard a voice say" Acts 9:3-9. This is the first of three accounts of Saul's conversion that are found in the Book of Acts (cf. Acts 22; 26). Why three accounts? In part because the later two are reports of how Paul told his conversion story when speaking to different audiences. But mostly because Saul's conversion was the most significant event in his life.

You and I hardly have conversion stories to match Saul's for drama. But ours do match his for significance! The most important event in any human being's life is coming to know Jesus Christ as personal Saviour. (See DEVOTIONAL.)

"I have heard many reports about this man" Acts 9:10-19. We know little about Ananias of Damascus. What we do know is admirable. He was "a disciple" (a term which in Acts almost always is used with the

sense of "a Christian"). Ananias responded immediately to God's instructions and went to see Saul, despite Saul's reputation. And he accepted Saul as "Brother Saul."

Sometimes despite Christ's call to us to be witnesses, we hesitate to approach people about whom we've "heard reports." Often the reports aren't true. More often than not when I've gotten to know people that others criticized or gossiped about, I've found the reports totally wrong. But at times the reports we hear are true, as in the case of Saul. Even then, there's an unknown factor. God may have been working in their lives, as He worked in Saul's.

We should never let what people say about another person keep us from reaching out to him or her with God's Good News.

"He got up and was baptized" Acts 9:18. Even before Paul ate—and he had fasted the three days he remained blind—he was baptized. The act was a public confession of his faith in Jesus, and of his solidarity with the Christians of Damascus.

Too many Christians seem intent on keeping their allegiance to Christ a secret in the workplace. Not that believers should carry red-covered Bibles, pass out tracts, and buttonhole colleagues for a three-minute sermon every day. But in every relationship there are times when it is natural and necessary to affirm our relationship with Jesus. A Christian really has to work at being a secret believer. He or she must consciously choose not to speak of his faith many times.

We need to let Paul be our example here. One of his first acts as a believer was to publicly identify himself with Christ and with other Christians. If we're to serve God and other people effectively, we need to be publicly identified with Jesus too.

"At once he began to preach" Acts 9:20-25. Paul had been a committed and zealous persecutor of the church. The same dynamic qualities were now dedicated to promoting the faith he had once tried to destroy. The text says that Saul "grew more and more powerful." As he preached Jesus as the Son of God and the Old Testament's promised Messiah, he grew in his understanding of Scripture and his ability to communicate.

There's an important principle here. No one can wait until he is "powerful" to begin witnessing or preaching. We grow in the doing, not in the waiting.

If you want to develop in any area of your Christian life—be it in prayer, Bible study, witnessing, teaching, whatever—start.

"They were all afraid of him" Acts 9:26-27. Barnabas is undoubtedly one of the most attractive figures in Scripture. In Acts 4 we saw him sensitive to the needy, and willing to sell his property to meet others' needs. Here in Acts 9 we see him sensitive to Saul's loneliness, and willing to risk possible betrayal to the authorities by contacting him.

Some Christians care about others. And then, some Christians *care* about others. Members of the first group have honest emotions of concern or pity. Those in the second group are willing to *do something* to meet others' needs. Barnabas belonged to this second group. What group do you and I belong to? Those who care, or those who *care?*

"They tried to kill him" Acts 9:28-31. This is the second time in just a few verses that folks with whom Saul debated about Jesus were ready to kill him (cf. vv. 23-25). Somehow I get the impression that the fiery young Pharisee, so eager to attack error in the church, hadn't changed a great deal! I may be wrong, but I suspect that Saul wasn't at all worried about being diplomatic in his approach to evangelism. "Attack!" was Paul's watchword. And holy zeal made that attack even more enthusiastic.

Note that the brothers "took him" down to Caesarea and sent him off to Tarsus. At that point brother Saul was just stirring up trouble for the church, not winning converts! With Saul gone, "the church . . . enjoyed a time of peace" and "it grew in numbers" (v. 31).

Much later Saul, by then Paul and a veteran of decades of ministry, wrote, "The Lord's servant must not quarrel; instead, he must be kind to everyone, able to teach, not resentful. Those who oppose him he must gently instruct, in the hope that God will give them repentance leading them to a knowledge of the truth" (2 Tim. 2:24-25). That kind of wisdom comes to most of us later in life.

"In Joppa there was a disciple named Tabitha" Acts 9:32-43. The story of Dorcas is fascinating for two reasons. First, this is the only case in which a miracle worker was sent for after a person had died (vv. 37-38). Even Jesus was sent for while dying persons still breathed. Apparently the Christians at Joppa had such a firm faith that they expected God to bring Dorcas back from the dead.

Second, note the reason for the church's desire for Dorcas' resuscitation. She "was always doing good and helping the poor" (v. 36). This is perhaps even more important. Let's commit ourselves to being the kind of persons whose loss would be felt deeply, because we too are "always doing good."

▶DEVOTIONAL
The Mark of Saul
(Acts 9:1-19)

Every true Christian must bear the mark of Saul.

I don't mean that you or I have to have an exceptional conversion experience. Or even that we have to put a date and time to the moment we came to know Christ. I do mean that there are some things in the account of Saul's conversion that really are normative for Christians. Even though the story is found in Acts.

You know the story. Saul was stunned by the flash of light and the voice from heaven, which he recognized as a sign of divine revelation. But he was even more stunned to hear a voice say, "I am Jesus, whom you are persecuting." With those words everything Saul had believed with such fierce conviction, everything he had staked his life and being on, was shown to be utterly false.

Most people drift through life, with few strong religious convictions. Conversion seems a welcome or delightful thing. Some, as Saul, experience conversion as a total redirection of belief and life.

Yet there are certain things that are common to every Christian conversion. For each of us, becoming a Christian means (1) acknowledging the error of old beliefs and abandoning them, (2) revising our opinion of Jesus to acknowledge Him as Saviour and Lord, (3) gradually realizing that life must take on a new direction, with service given priority.

In Saul, these changes were instant and dramatic. In others the changes may take place more gradually, and certainly less dramatically. But Christian conversion must bear these marks. Many assume that they "believe" in God or in Jesus. But if the three indelible marks of conversion are lacking, that "belief" is superficial and not true Christian faith.

Personal Application

How does your life display the mark of Saul?

Quotable

"The mark of a saint is not perfection, but consecration. A saint is not a man without faults, but a man who has given himself without reserve to God."—Brooke Foss Westcott

SEPTEMBER 19 *Reading 262*
BREAKING THE BARRIER
Acts 10–11

"You are well aware that it is against our law for a Jew to associate with a Gentile or visit him. But God has shown me that I should not call any man impure or unclean" (Acts 10:28).

Social barriers to fellowship between Christians must be broken down.

Overview

An angel told a devout Roman centurion to send for Peter (10:1-8). God prepared Peter with an unusual vision (vv. 9-23), and he readily traveled to Cornelius' home (vv. 24-29). As Peter revealed God's promise of forgiveness (vv. 30-45) the Spirit fell on the Gentiles and they spoke in tongues (vv. 46-48). Back in Jerusalem Peter related what God had done, and the church realized Christ is for Gentiles as well as Jews (11:1-18). When a strong Gentile church developed in Antioch (vv. 19-24), Barnabas sought Saul in Tarsus to join him in leadership (vv. 25-30).

Understanding the Text

"He and all his family were devout" Acts 10:1-8. Cornelius is also described as "God-fearing." In the first century this served as a technical term for those who admired Israel's religion, and worshiped Israel's God, but had not converted to Judaism.

We can't be sure that "God-fearing" is used in this technical sense here. But certainly Cornelius did worship God as well as he was able, showing his devotion in regular prayer and by giving generously to those in need. God's stamp of approval is given in the angel's words: Cornelius' prayers and acts had "come up as a remembrance before God" (v. 4).

We can be sure that God will reveal Himself and the way of salvation to any person like Cornelius, who honestly seeks to know and to serve the Lord.

"Bring back a man named Simon who is called Peter" Acts 10:5. If Paul was the "apostle to the Gentiles," why was Peter chosen to open the door of Gentile conversion? In part to show that the church is one: there could be no schism between a "Gentile" and "Jewish" church. The leading Jewish apostle was selected to preach the first Gospel message to Gentiles.

There's probably another reason. First-century Jews looked down on Gentiles and carefully separated themselves from them. Just entering a Gentile home made a person ritually unclean, and it was unthinkable to eat a meal with a Gentile. Only testimony by a leader of Peter's standing would possibly be accepted by the Jewish believers. The barriers between Jew and Gentile were just too great.

But soon, through Peter's ministry in the house of Cornelius, those barriers would begin to go down.

"Do not call anything impure that God has made clean" Acts 10:9-23. Peter could not be called a "strict" Jew. We remember all too well how he and the other disciples were criticized by the Pharisees, to assume he was a strict legalist (cf. Matt. 12:1-2).

But like all Jews, Peter had a deep-seated awareness of Israel's call as God's people. He was firmly committed to the basic symbols of his people's separation to God.

That's why the command, "Kill and eat," was so traumatic for him. Peter realized that the voice in the vision was from heaven, and thus was God's. Yet the voice commanded him to eat animals which the Law of Moses identified as "unclean," and thus a violation of the principle of separation.

God's word to Peter was clear. Peter was not to call "unclean" what God had made clean. God, who established Israel's dietary laws, had the right to change them, or any other element of the ancient faith! Peter must change his outlook in order to be in step with God.

Sometimes we find ourselves in a similar situation. We meet someone with different convictions than our own, and feel terribly uncomfortable. Yet we discover he or she is a committed Christian! Something in our outlook must change, for our concept of separation has come in conflict with Scripture's teaching that all believers are brothers and sisters. If God calls them clean in Christ, how can we separate ourselves from them?

Peter was about to learn a lesson each of us must learn. We can keep our convictions about what is right and what is wrong for us to do. But we cannot let our convictions become a barrier to fellowship with believing brothers and sisters with whom we differ. (See DEVOTIONAL.)

"God has shown me I should not call any man impure or unclean" Acts 10:23-29. Peter openly acknowledged the divine correction. A few days before he would never have entered the house of Cornelius. But the vision showed him that "clean" and "unclean" were terms that should not apply to persons.

You and I can hold convictions about what actions are right or wrong. But we can never let our convictions spill over to shape our attitudes toward fellow Christians.

The other day I dropped a can of Diet Pepsi. When it hit, a tiny hole was opened in its side, and it spun round and round on the floor, with Pepsi spurting from the hole and staining the whole kitchen. I found drops on the cupboards, chairs, refrigerator, walls—even in the dining room. My wife had just one word for me: Clean.

Sometimes convictions are like that Pepsi—they spurt out and stain everyone around us, convincing us that others are unclean. And we impulsively grab for our rags, intent on cleaning them up!

Convictions, like Pepsi, are to be kept in the can except when in use. They're ours, and we should live by them. But we can't let them spurt out and taint our attitude toward other Christians whose convictions may differ.

"Peter was still speaking these words" Acts 10:39-48. Use of the Greek *rhemata* rather than the familiar *logos* here suggests that it was the specific words concerning forgiveness of sins through Jesus' name to which these Gentiles responded.

We can believe many things "about" God and still come short of salvation. That comes as we trust God's promise of forgiveness through Jesus Christ.

"The circumcised believers . . . were astonished" Acts 10:44–11:18. Peter had been accompanied by six Jewish Christians. Later their testimony that the Holy Spirit had indeed been given to Gentiles was crucial in convincing the Jerusalem church that Christ reached out to all.

Again we see special circumstances for an unusual event. The Gentiles gave evidence of the Spirit's presence by speaking in tongues. Later Peter related this to the Pentecost experience. As Gentiles had been given the same gift that was given the Jewish believers, they had obviously been accepted by God. So "who was I to think that I could oppose God?" (11:17)

When there was a need to convince a skeptical Jewish church that God intended to welcome Gentile converts, a special sign was given. We don't need to be convinced—or shouldn't need to be. We know from Scripture that all who profess Christ as Saviour, whatever their previous background, belong to Him. And belong with us.

"A great number of people believed and turned to the Lord" Acts 11:19-24. It was one thing to accept Gentile converts into a predominantly Jewish church. But now in Antioch, a major city of the Empire, a predominantly Gentile church was established!

Barnabas was sent from Jerusalem to find out what was happening. He was an excellent choice, for he was "a good man, full of the Holy Spirit and faith." He may have been one of the few Jewish Christian leaders sensitive enough to sense what God was about, and able to resist the temptation to impose a Jewish lifestyle on these Gentile converts.

What Barnabas did do is again a model for us to follow. He simply "encouraged them all to remain true to the Lord with all their hearts" (v. 23).

God doesn't need or want cookie-cutter Christians, all stamped out on the model you and I provide. He wants Christians who are true to Him with all their hearts. If we help others be true to Him, they will reject sin. And they will be responsive to God, who is better able to shape their convictions and their lifestyle than we are.

"The disciples . . . decided to provide help" Acts 11:25-30. When a severe famine was predicted and came, Judea was especially hard hit. The Gentile church in Antioch, led now by Saul as well as Barnabas and

its own elders, sent aid.

Again we see a principle at work. When barriers are let down, and Christian brothers and sisters released to work out their own way of expressing their commitment to the Lord, love and caring also flow. As an expression of that love the Gentile church of Antioch sent its gift to their Jewish brethren by Barnabas and Saul.

Love others and give them freedom in Christ. That kind of love will surely be returned.

▶ DEVOTIONAL
Broken Barriers
(Acts 11:1-18)

Thirty years ago I'd have bristled a bit, put up my defenses, and wondered if he was converted. But then, 30 years ago I erected all sorts of barriers to protect myself from having to consider that folks whose convictions and beliefs differed from mine might be Christians.

My list of convictions included such things as no smoking, drinking, or going to movies. And my list of essential beliefs ruled out Catholics and a goodly number of Protestants too.

I couldn't help smiling about this last weekend, as I stood just off the dance floor with Bob Dyksra. The band was blaring as he sipped his cocktail, and shouted just a bit to be heard. We were back in Michigan for my wife's niece's wedding, and Bob, a cousin, had come up from Indianapolis. We'd stayed in his home one weekend a few years before, and discovered that he was an active member in a large Catholic parish, heavily involved in small group Bible study. Among his more unusual claims to fame, Bob is one of the few persons, if not the only one, who's read all the articles in my 720-page *Expository Dictionary of Bible Words* (Zondervan, 1985).

Last weekend, though, Bob was telling me about a family he met in the Orlando airport. The dad was 64, wheeling a 42-year-old son in a wheelchair. The son had been stricken with a disease that gave him no control at all over his body, but left his mind sharp and unimpaired. Mom and Dad had cared for him for years, but as their lives were drawing to a close, they knew that they had to find someplace for their son to be cared for. They were going to Indianapolis, where Bob's parish sponsored just such a facility.

Bob looked at his watch as he told me the story. It was nearly 10 P.M., and he and his wife had to leave to drive back home from Grand Rapids. It seems he'd told the mom and dad that whenever they came to Indianapolis to visit their son, they could stay at his home. So he had to get back that night, to pick them up early next morning at the airport and take them out to see their boy.

Bob took one last swig of his drink, smiled, and left for the long drive home. And I felt a little bit like the Jerusalem church must have, when it praised the Lord that God had "even granted the Gentiles repentance unto life." This ol' Diet-Pepsi-drinking-Protestant is so glad the barriers are going down, and that I can feel comfortable calling a modern "Gentile" who loves Jesus, prays regularly, and gives generously to those in need, "Brother."

And love him in the Lord.

Personal Application

Keep your convictions. But don't let them keep you from others.

Quotable

"To pass judgment on another is to usurp shamelessly a prerogative of God, and to condemn is to ruin one's soul."—John Climacus

SEPTEMBER 20 *Reading 263*
GOD INTERVENES
Acts 12

"Now I know without a doubt that the Lord sent His angel and rescued me from Herod's clutches" (Acts 12:11).

God is involved with His people everywhere.

Overview
The Apostle James was executed by Herod Agrippa (12:1-2) and Peter was imprisoned, awaiting trial (vv. 3-5). An angel released Peter (vv. 6-11), who was welcomed by stunned Christians hardly able to believe their prayers had been answered (vv. 12-19). God struck Herod down (vv. 20-23) and the Judean church continued to grow (v. 24). Luke now returned to Paul, to begin the story of his mission to the Gentiles (v. 25).

Understanding the Text
"King Herod . . . had James, the brother of John, put to death" Acts 12:1-2. The king named here is Herod Agrippa I, the grandson of Herod the Great. Agrippa worked actively to win the loyalty of his Jewish subjects, and even resisted the mad Emperor Caligula's plan to put an idolatrous statue of himself in the Jerusalem temple. The Mishna, which includes rabbinical writings of this period, speaks favorably of Agrippa, and reports one incident in which the people shouted enthusiastically, "Our brother art thou!"

When Herod realized that persecution of Christians would enhance his popularity, he executed James the brother of John and arrested Peter. Agrippa intended to try and execute Peter just after the Passover, when that act would have maximum impact on the great crowds of Jewish pilgrims gathered for the festival.

The character of Herod Agrippa's actions remind us of how easy it is to fall into the trap of using others for our own ends. Herod made the mistake of all such "users." He neglected to consider the possibility that God might intervene.

Peter was given double the normal guards and kept in chains in an inner prison cell. Acts 12:3-11 tells the story of his miraculous release. The divine intervention reminds us that God kept on working actively in the original Jewish church, even though the rest of Acts will emphasize missionary expansion.

"Now I know without a doubt that the Lord . . . rescued me" Acts 12:11. Peter never doubted that the Lord could rescue him. But there was a question as to whether the Lord *would* rescue him. After all, James, the brother of John, was an apostle too, and he had been executed by Herod Agrippa.

You and I live with a similar tension between faith and uncertainty. We know that the Lord can deliver us from whatever danger we face. But we never know "without a doubt" that the Lord *will* deliver us.

It's important to remember that God loved both James and Peter. Both were important to Him. Yet one was permitted to die, and the other miraculously released from prison. Whether you and I have the role of James or of Peter in this life, let's rest assured that we are loved by God, and important to Him. Today both James and Peter are at home with the Lord, rejoicing in His presence. It is this, not the brevity or length of life on earth, that counts.

"Peter knocked at the outer entrance" Acts 12:12-19. The story is so delightful. We can see it now, Peter pounding on the door. The flustered and "overjoyed" Rhoda, running first to the door, then back

into the house, so excited she doesn't know what to do. And the folks inside, praying earnestly for Peter, all unaware that God has already answered their prayers (see DEVOTIONAL).

Answered prayer has a tendency to excite any Christian. We go to prayer sensing the terrible pressure of our need, and when the answer comes, and the pressure's relieved, we're buoyed up with joy.

One of the best ways to hold on to that joy is to keep a prayer record. All it takes is a simple notebook. You jot down what you pray for on one page, and on the facing page, you leave space to record God's answers.

As the list of answered prayers grows, read them over. You'll feel the same joy and excitement that filled the group meeting that night in Mary's house to pray so successfully for Peter's release.

"What could have happened to Peter?" Acts 12:18-19 Even Herod should have known better than some modern critics who, eager to rid the Scripture of the supernatural, suggest that some early Christian drugged the guards and bribed the jailer to let Peter go. In Roman times, a jailer who let a prisoner escape was subject to whatever punishment the escapee would have suffered. So Herod did nothing unusual when he marched the guards off and had them executed (v. 19).

What is amazing is the question everyone asked: "What could have happened to Peter?" Chained to his guards, locked inside a cell guarded by yet more sentries, inside a prison barred by a locked iron door, it should have been clear that Peter had not just picked his locks and hidden in some broom closet. The inescapable conclusion was that something supernatural had occurred. God had intervened, or Peter would not have been gone.

Herod apparently didn't even consider the supernatural option. He was as much a materialist as modern folks, who can look at a sunset, or examine some complexity of nature, and say, "Isn't evolution wonderful." Even today the evidence of God's intervention is everywhere. But only the eyes of faith seem able to see.

"He was eaten by worms and died" Acts 12:21-24. Both Luke and the first-century Jewish historian Josephus report Herod's death in A.D. 44, shortly after the release of Peter. Josephus tells us Agrippa died "exhausted after five straight days by the pain in his abdomen." Luke, the physician, describes symptoms that suggest an infection of intestinal roundworms. These grow up to 15 inches long, and when bunched can obstruct the intestine. The infested person experiences intense pain, and often vomits up worms before he dies.

Strikingly, both Luke and Josephus attribute Agrippa's death to the king's impiety, and see it as a judgment of God. God had intervened to remove a ruler who had proved to be a persecutor of His people, and a danger to His church.

With Herod gone, "the word of God continued to increase and spread" (v. 24).

"They returned from Jerusalem" Acts 12:25. Luke now left the Judean scene, and his report of Peter's ministry, to focus on Paul. Verse 25 is a transition statement that effectively shifts our attention to the coming mission to the whole world.

While Luke would say little more of events in the Jewish homeland, his vivid portrayal of Peter's release and the death of Agrippa reminds us of a vital truth. We may not be aware of what is happening in Judea. But God is there, active, still intervening on behalf of His own.

What a comfort this is for us, as our children grow up and move away. We're not there to watch out for them. But God is. He is actively, lovingly caring for His own everywhere. We can trust our own to His care.

▶DEVOTIONAL
Believe It or Not
(Acts 12:1-19)

God must have a sense of humor.

You and I can't read the account of Peter's release from prison, and the furor at the house of Mary in Jerusalem, without seeing how funny it all was.

There's Peter, pounding on the door, while inside the house a whole group of despondent Christians is praying desperately for his safety. And when the servant girl runs in the room, shouting that she's heard Peter's voice outside, nobody believes her. "You're out of your mind," they tell her. Peter was in prison, about to be executed. If the girl really heard his voice, "It must be his angel [ghost]."

If you ever thought that getting an answer to prayer depends on firmly believing the answer will come, well, this story ought to raise a few doubts. The gathered church certainly hoped that God would save Peter. But believe it? Why, they didn't even believe it when the prayer was answered!

I suspect that God must have been chuckling over the scene with something like delight.

"Surprise!" you can almost hear Him shout. And as the gathered Christians realized Peter really was free, and jumped for joy, the Lord may well have laughed an infectious, happy laugh, right out loud.

Oh, yes. God can answer prayer, even when our faith is weak and doubts are strong. So when you pray don't worry if you're not totally positive about what God will do. Just remember the folks in Acts 12, who told a servant girl, "You're out of your mind," when she reported that Peter stood at the door.

Just pray. And expect to be surprised.

Personal Application

Answers to prayer depend on our great God, not on our jumbo faith.

Quotable

"I never prayed earnestly for anything but it came sooner or later, and oftentimes in the way I least imagined. But it came."—Adoniram Judson

SEPTEMBER 21 *Reading 264*

THE MISSION BEGINS

Acts 13–14

> *" 'Set apart for Me Barnabas and Saul for the work to which I have called them.' So after they had fasted and prayed, they placed their hands on them and sent them off" (Acts 13:2-3).*

God still has a worldwide vision that He wants us to share.

Background

Missionary strategy. Paul is credited with developing the church's missionary strategy. He went to cities which were communication, transportation, and market centers. He went first to the Jewish synagogue, where he reached not only his own people but also the Gentiles who were attracted to Jewish faith and morality.

Paul's missionary team instructed the first converts as thoroughly as time permitted, and went on to the next city. The congregations they established served as the core for evangelizing the surrounding area as well as their own city (cf. 1 Thes. 1:4-8).

Later Paul might return to give further instruction and to confirm the local church's choice of elders. Paul also sent letters and representatives, like Timothy and Titus, to answer questions and help the congregation deal with any problems that developed.

The itinerant strategy of Paul placed great responsibility on each local church for its own life. And it showed the apostle's utter confidence in the Holy Spirit's ability to guide and sustain God's people. Modern missions has much to learn from Christianity's first great missionary, the Apostle Paul.

Overview

Barnabas and Paul were commissioned to spread the Gospel (13:1-3). Their first stop was in Cyprus (vv. 4-12). In Pisidian Antioch, success in reaching Gentiles created jealousy and opposition from the Jews (vv. 13-52). Conflict continued as they ministered in Iconium (14:1-7), Lystra, and Derbe (vv. 8-20) before they turned toward Antioch and home (vv. 21-28).

Understanding the Text

"Set apart for Me" Acts 13:1-3. Many have wondered how a person can tell if he or she is "called" to the ministry. We find a few hints here.

First, Saul and Barnabas were already deeply involved in ministry when set apart by God. It would be foolish to think that going to seminary could make a "minister" out of a person who has shown no inclination to serve and witness before his or her training. Second, the "call" was not given just to Saul and to Barnabas; it was sensed by all the leaders of the Antioch church. The congregation of which a person is a part should be able to confirm that person's call.

If you've ever wondered if God is calling you to full-time ministry, the experience of Paul and Barnabas is suggestive. If you are active in ministry now, and affirmed by your church, your sense of calling may be confirmed.

"The procounsul . . . sent for Barnabas and Saul" Acts 13:4-12. The invitation to preach before Sergius Paulus was official, motivated by the proconsul's responsibility to govern Cyprus and its mixed population of Gentiles and Jews. Rumors of the apostles' preaching, and very likely charges against them, would have quickly come to his attention. The proconsul, being "an intelligent man," would investigate carefully before taking any action.

The hostility of Bar-Jesus, whose alternate name Elymas means "sorcerer" or "magician," led to a confrontation. The outcome stunned Sergius Paulus, and led to his conversion.

Opposition to the Gospel often has an unexpected effect. God often uses it to open doors of opportunity. So don't be overly disturbed by opposition, and be alert for how God intends to use it for His own ends.

"Saul, who was also called Paul" Acts 13:9. The change of name here is significant. Saul was the apostle's Hebrew name. Paul is Greek, and the name by which the apostle went while ministering in the Gentile world. The shift of names alerts us to the fact that from now on, Paul's ministry will be largely to the non-Jewish population of the Roman Empire.

Later Paul wrote in one of his letters, "To the Jews I became like a Jew, to win the Jews," and "to those not having the Law I became like one not having the Law" (1 Cor. 9:20-21).

Paul did not compromise. Rather he looked for ways to identify with those he wanted to reach.

When I joined the Navy I found that at first I was shunned by other sailors. I finally discovered they thought I was stuck up because I used big words. I'd never realized it: I was brought up in a home where the way I spoke was normal. To fit in and have any chance of reaching my Navy buddies, I had to learn to speak as they did (though without the cuss words).

Later I worked in a state hospital, and taught a nightly Bible study. Each evening I thought about what to say, and how to make it as simple as possible. I found it paid big dividends. Many of the men told me, "If you ever get a church, let me know. You're the first preacher I ever heard I could understand."

Even little things in Scripture, like the shift here of a name, speak volumes to us. If you want to reach people, search out points of similarity, and try to be like them. Never emphasize your differences from those you hope to influence.

"On the Sabbath they entered the synagogue" Acts 13:13-15. Paul's habit of going first to the synagogue was rooted in conviction as well as strategy. It was good strategy because Jewish visitors were often invited to speak when they came to synagogue services. But Paul's habit also expressed a deep love for his people. Though his life had been threatened several times by his co-religionists, Paul held that the Gospel's salvation power is "first for the Jew, then for the Gentile" (Rom. 1:16).

Every Christian should recognize the great debt we owe to God's chosen people. We can begin to repay that debt only as Paul did as he carried the Gospel into the synagogue.

"Men of Israel and you Gentiles who worship God, listen to me" Acts 13:16-43. Luke now included a summary of the kind of sermon Paul preached in the synagogues. He began, as was typical, with a review of Hebrew history. This culminated with David, from whose descendants the Messiah would come. Paul then went on to show that Jesus fulfilled those promises. Christ's resurrection not only fits the Scripture, but those Scriptures He fulfills show Him to be the Holy One, the Son of God. Through Him God offers to all the forgiveness of sins.

Like the other sermons recorded in Acts, this one focuses attention directly on the person of Jesus Christ, and on Christ's offer of the forgiveness of sins.

Whatever you or I may do to identify with others, we do not change the Gospel message. That message alone can bring salvation and new life to all.

"They were filled with jealousy" Acts 13:44-52. The message of a salvation offered freely to all spread quickly, and the next Sabbath "almost the whole city" gathered to hear the two missionaries speak.

The "jealousy" of the Jews was not simply over numbers. It was a jealousy for their faith. Paul's message of salvation had, in effect, set aside the Law, and meant that a Gentile could relate to Israel's God without approaching Him through Judaism.

Paul bluntly told the now hostile Jewish population, "We now turn to the Gentiles." A great many people in Antioch were converted before official persecution drove the missionaries from the area.

This is the first hint of the great challenge about to face early Christianity—and modern Christians. What is the relationship between the Old and New Testaments, between Law and grace? Is Moses' Law binding on the believer in Christ? Or is the "new" faith the radical departure from Judaism that Paul seemed to suggest.

The question is important to you and me because we need to live in intimate fellowship with the Lord. Unless we are clear on the distinctions between the age of Law and of grace, this is a difficult task indeed (see Romans, Galatians).

"The people of the city were divided" Acts 14:1-6. Don't expect everyone to be open to the Gospel. Acts reminds us that the message of Christ divides people, even as it unites believers. If you are effective in sharing the Gospel, you can expect opposition as well as enthusiastic response.

"The gods have come down to us in human form" Acts 14:8-20. Don't be surprised when some who acclaim you one moment are ready to stone you the next. The people of Lystra were ready to worship Paul and Barnabas as gods. When the two failed to meet the crowd's expectations, the mob was easily persuaded to stone Paul.

Popularity is fleeting, a gossamer fabric that disappoints all who pursue it.

"They gathered the church together and reported all that God had done through them" Acts 14:21-28. Some share what God has done through them to glorify themselves. Others to glorify God.

▶ DEVOTIONAL
Truth or Fantasy?
(Acts 14:8-29)

A hundred years before the visit of Paul and Barnabas to Lystra, Ovid recounted an ancient legend native to that area. Zeus and Hermes once wandered that hill country in the guise of mortals. Though they asked at a thousand homes, no one would take them in. Finally a poor couple offered them lodging in their straw shack. As a reward the shack was transformed into a temple of marble and gold, and the couple became ever-living trees at its door. And the thousand inhospitable homes were destroyed.

It's likely that this legend stimulated the wild excitement at Lystra when Barnabas and Paul healed a cripple there. The gods Zeus and Hermes had returned! The enthusiastic populace was determined to do them honor.

When the crowd found out that Paul and Barnabas were messengers of the one true God, and not gods themselves, they became hostile, and were easily moved to stone Paul.

They had been so delighted with fiction that they resented hearing the truth.

What's even more fascinating is that archeologists have unearthed inscriptions near Lystra that date from the third century A.D., showing that Zeus and Hermes were still being worshiped there. Fiction's grip is strong.

Every now and then I speak with someone who has his or her own ideas about what God is like. "God isn't like that!" such a person is likely to say if punishment for sin, or the death of Christ for sinners, happens to come up. Such folks are a little like the men and women of Lystra. They have their own ideas about God. And they don't want to change them, thank you. To such folks it makes no difference if what you say is true. For fiction's grip is strong.

Personal Application
The truth is good news, whether people accept it or not.

Quotable
"With God a thing is never too good to be true; it is too good not to be true."—Oswald Chambers

SEPTEMBER 22 *Reading 265*
JERUSALEM COUNCIL
Acts 15

"Paul and Barnabas were appointed, along with some other believers, to go up to Jerusalem to see the Apostles and elders about this question" (Acts 15:2).

Differences must be faced and resolved.

Overview
A doctrinal dispute over whether Gentile believers must adopt Judaism (15:1) brought representatives of the Antioch church to Jerusalem (vv. 2-5). A council of leaders determined that Old Testament Law was not binding on Gentile Christians (vv. 6-19), but asked them to be sensitive to Jewish convictions (vv. 20-21). The Antioch delegation returned with a freeing letter from the Apostles (vv. 22-35). But a personal dispute between Paul and Barnabas could not be resolved, and the two separated (vv. 36-41).

Understanding the Text
"Unless you are circumcised . . . you cannot be saved" Acts 15:1. The earliest Jewish Christians lived as Jews, committed to the the Old Testament Law. As Gentile churches were established outside Judea, a critical question arose. Did these Gentiles have to abandon their own culture and adopt Jewish customs to enjoy the salvation offered by Israel's God?

The Old Testament frequently predicted that Gentiles would be saved. But most such references linked their salvation to Israel's resurgence under the Messiah. But now Gentiles were coming directly to God, apart from Jewish faith and practice! This many believing Jews did not understand—or appreciate! And so some Jews began to travel and teach that to really be saved, a person must convert to Judaism as well as to Christ.

Today we call this ethnocentrism: the idea that one's own customs and practices are right, and others' are wrong. It crops up in missions as it did in Antioch so long ago. Many a church service has been set in Africa or Asia for 11 A.M., in spite of local customs, just because the missionary's home church meets then. And many a hymn tune has been transferred from West to East, despite the fact that Eastern musical traditions are completely different from our own.

You and I too need to watch out for ethnocentrism. Let's not assume that folks who are different from us are either wrong or inferior. Faith in Christ and love for Jesus can be expressed in a variety of ways besides our own.

"To go up to Jerusalem to see the Apostles and elders" Acts 15:2-5. The attempt to impose Judaism challenged the validity of Gentile conversion, and questioned the nature of the Gospel itself. Was the Good News really that God forgives the sins of anyone who believes in Jesus or not?

To say, "You can be saved if you believe AND are circumcised AND keep Moses' Law" is not the Gospel Peter preached to Cornelius, or that Paul preached on his travels.

We need to be just as clear today that salvation is through our faith in Jesus Christ, with no ANDs at all. As the old hymn says, "Jesus paid it all." The new life of love and obedience that we adopt after salvation is a consequence, not a condition of salvation.

How freeing it is to realize that our salvation rests on what Jesus has done, not on what we must do. Like the early church, we need to be on guard against any teaching that would rob Christ of His preeminence, or faith of its centrality in Christian experience.

"God . . . showed that He accepted them" Acts 15:6-11. It was not easy for pious Christian Jews, dedicated to their traditional customs and still worshiping at the temple, to face this issue. But Peter had a compelling argument. God showed that He accepted Gentiles as well as Jews when He purified the house of Cornelius by faith and gave them the Holy Spirit. God thus "made no distinction between us and them." It was clear that all are saved "through the grace of God." Keeping Jewish Law was not at issue.

Let's keep the focus on grace today too. Salvation is by grace through faith, with no other condition. To insist that others conform to purely cultural standards to be welcomed into full fellowship is wrong.

The issue isn't as abstract as it may seem. Some of us resist fellowship with folks who raise their hands when praying, while others can't relate to those whose worship is liturgical. How irrelevant these things are! Let's affirm each other's freedom to differ, without a hint of criticism, knowing that the God who has accepted us in Christ also accepts our worship as an act of love.

"The words of the prophets are in agreement" Acts 15:12-19. Paul and Barnabas joined Peter in arguing from evangelistic experience that God accepted Gentiles "as is," without requiring them to adopt Judaism first (v. 12). James, the brother of Jesus, highly respected for his piety, showed that what Peter and Paul reported was in harmony with Old Testament Scripture. After all, Amos spoke of "all the Gentiles who bear My name." Clearly Gentiles as Gentiles were expected to bear God's name in the Messianic Age, which had now come in the person of Jesus.

Evidence from Christian experience is important. But we must always check to see that our experience is in harmony with the Word of God. When experience is confirmed by Scripture, we can act confidently, as did the Jerusalem church.

The council's decision was that Gentiles are not subject to the Law God gave to Israel, nor must they live like Jews to be acceptable to God.

"We should write to them, telling them to abstain" Acts 15:20-21. The three issues raised here have been much debated. Why these three? And what is their significance? If "from sexual immorality" is understood as referring to marriages between persons whose union is prohibited in the Old Testament, it seems that the Jerusalem Council asked Gentile converts to be sensitive to their Jewish brethren's convictions.

We certainly need to be sensitive to others today. Later Paul would write to the Romans and to the Corinthians, and encourage them not to misuse their freedom, but to avoid giving unnecessary offense to those whose convictions might differ from their own.

As the letter the council sent to Antioch and beyond said, "You will do well to avoid [such] things" (v. 29).

"They chose Judas (called Barsabbas) and Silas" Acts 15:22-29. It was customary in Judaism to send two sages with any official communication from the Sanhedrin to Jewish communities abroad. The early church adopted this wise custom, and sent two prophets along with the letter that explained the Council's decision.

The letter brought relief. The two messengers, who "said much to encourage and strengthen the brothers," communicated love. The personal touch is vital in our own relationships with others as well.

"It seemed good to the Holy Spirit" Acts 15:28. The Jerusalem Council seemed so sure that they had the mind of the Spirit. How did they know?

First, they had gathered the leaders together, being careful to communicate the process to the "whole church" (vv. 4, 22). Different viewpoints were openly expressed (v. 5). They went through a process of "much discussion" (v. 7). They tried to discern God's will by recognizing what God had taught them through His past working among them (vv. 8, 12). They compared this with Scripture (v. 15).

And they reached a consensus, expressed by James (v. 19). The achievement of a consensus after working through this careful process was the Spirit's stamp of approval.

Churches would do well to adopt the same approach to problem-solving. Our goal is the same as that of the first church Council: not to make the best decision we can, but to discern what God's will is.

▶ DEVOTIONAL
Differences That Divide
(Acts 15:36-41)

I don't know if you've ever noticed it. The doctrinal differences we seem to be able to handle. It's those interpersonal conflicts that really divide.

When I was a teen we visited one of my dad's friends, a retired man who had a cottage on a lake. On the way home Dad remarked that when his friend was a child, he'd been to a church supper and asked for a piece of a cake he'd seen earlier in the kitchen. The lady at the counter said the cake was gone. But a few minutes later, he'd seen her, sitting in the kitchen, eating a piece of that very cake. Dad's friend never went to church again!

It wasn't doctrine that turned him off. It was a woman's lie about a piece of cake.

The early church was able to work out the doctrinal conflict between Hebrew Christians who felt strongly that Gentile believers should be circumcised and those who felt strongly they should not. But when Barnabas wanted to take John Mark, his nephew, along on another missionary venture—oh, no. Paul just wouldn't have it. Mark had left them in the lurch on the first missionary trip (13:13), and Paul had no sympathy with quitters.

Luke said that "they had such a sharp disagreement that they parted company" (15:39). Barnabas took Mark and went off one way. Paul took Silas and headed off a different direction.

Doctrinal disputes they could handle. A personal conflict? No way. If I can't have my piece of cake, I'll quit, and go on home. So there!

Actually, there is a way to deal with interpersonal conflicts. Jesus spoke of remembering that we human beings are all like sheep, sure to go astray. We have to be brought home lovingly and with rejoicing (Matt. 18). Paul himself would one day write, "Do nothing out of selfish ambition or vain conceit, but in humility consider others better than yourselves. Each of you should look not only to your own interests, but also to the interests of others" (Phil. 2:3-4).

Interpersonal differences don't have to divide Christians. But the separation of Paul and Barnabas reminds us how vulnerable we all are. Disputes will certainly divide. Unless we are sensitive, and humble as well.

Personal Application

It's often more important to be loving than to be right.

Quotable

"I used to think that God's gifts were on shelves one above the other, and that the taller we grew in Christian character the easier we could reach them. I now find that God's gifts are on shelves one beneath the other. It is not a question of growing taller, but of stooping down, to get His best gifts."—F.B. Meyer

SEPTEMBER 23 *Reading 266*
ON TO EUROPE
Acts 16

"During the night Paul had a vision of a man of Macedonia standing and begging him, 'Come over to Macedonia and help us' " (*Acts 16:9*).

The course of history in many a region has been changed by the coming of the Gospel of Jesus Christ.

Background

Mission to Europe. Paul's second missionary journey penetrated Europe and many major cities of the Roman Empire. Many of his New Testament letters were later directed to the European churches of Thessalonica, Rome, Corinth, and Philippi. The foundation Paul laid led to the later Christianization of the Empire, and shaped the history of the West.

Overview

Timothy (16:1-5) and Luke (v. 11) joined Paul's missionary team and sailed for Europe (vv. 6-12). Paul's first convert in Europe was a woman named Lydia (vv. 13-15). He was later arrested, beaten, and thrown into prison (vv. 16-24). This led to the salvation of the Philippian jailer before Paul was released and left the area (vv. 25-40).

Understanding the Text

"Timothy . . . whose mother was a Jewess and a believer" Acts 16:1-5. The few details given here tell us much about young Timothy and his city. The Jewish community must have been small and weak there, for Timothy's mother was allowed to marry a Gentile. Its weakness—or laxness—is further emphasized by the fact that Timothy had not been circumcised. Any child of a Jewish mother was considered a Jew, and a strong Jewish community would have insisted on his circumcision. These few details enhance what Paul said in a later letter to Timothy: Timothy was taught the Scriptures by his grandmother and mother "from infancy" (2 Tim. 1:5; 3:15). It really is difficult for those who have to bring up children in a home where only one spouse is a believer. But Timothy serves as a beacon of hope. Despite difficulties, the sincere faith of his

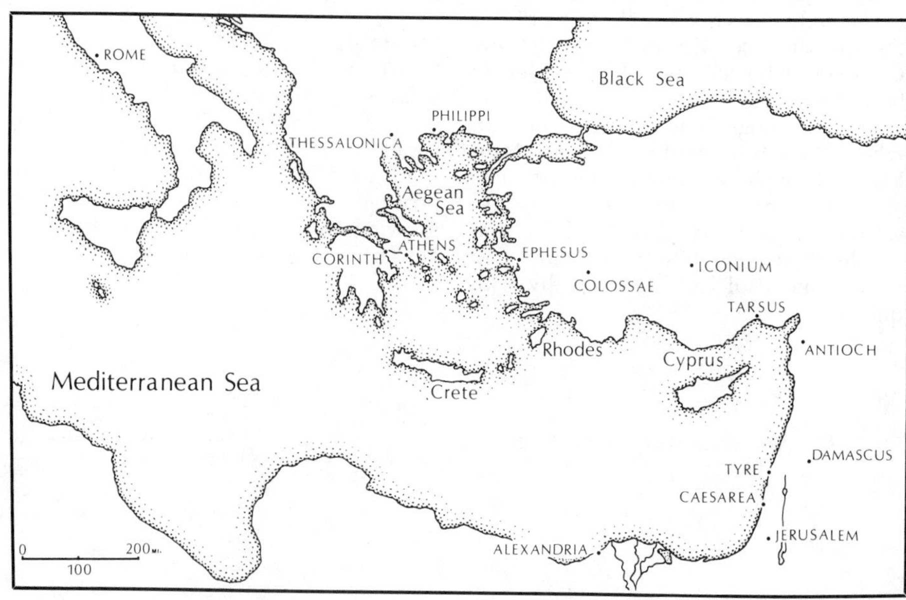

The Roman Empire in the First Century

believing mother was shared effectively with her son.

We will have to work "from infancy" at sharing our faith. But God can and will work in the children of divided homes.

"Paul . . . circumcised [Timothy] because of the Jews who lived in that area" Acts 16:3. Paul's decision to have Timothy circumcised was not, as some have thought, a compromise with his convictions. First-century Jewish believers did not abandon their heritage when they became Christians, but continued in it. As Timothy was known in the area as a Jew, it was appropriate for him to express his faith in Christ through his Jewishness. Paul had no quarrel with this. Paul's quarrel was with those who tried to identify their way of life as "the" Christian way, and to impose it on others.

Today messianic, or "completed," Jews often form synagogue/churches, and worship Jesus in the traditional forms of Judaism. Not the form, but the faith, counts.

"The Holy Spirit. . . . the Spirit of Jesus. . . . God" Acts 16:6-10. If you are ever challenged to prove that the early church really believed Jesus is God, here's a good passage to turn to. Luke wasn't teaching the doctrine. But in the most natural and unconscious way Luke used these names in the same paragraph, and so expressed the early church's trinitarian faith.

"We went outside the city gate to the river" Acts 16:11-15. It took 10 adult Jewish men for a *minyam,* the quorum needed to establish a synagogue. In cities where this was lacking, Jewish worship took place out under the open sky, often by a river's edge. When Paul found the local Jewish "place of prayer" he reached Europe's first convert: a woman named Lydia.

From this beginning the Lord developed one of the strongest churches in Europe, and one dearly loved by the apostle.

"These men are servants of the Most High God" Acts 16:17-18. The persistent shouting of the demon-possessed slave girl drew attention away from the message of the apostles to herself. Finally Paul, in the name of Jesus Christ, commanded the demon to leave.

The situation reminds me of the instant celebrity that the church sometimes creates of murderers and movie stars. After a sudden conversion, the famous individual appears on Sunday TV, to give a testimony that draws more attention to him or her than to Jesus. And all too often the convert's "faith" dissipates as soon as the appearances cease.

The credibility of a witness is as important when speaking up for Jesus as in speaking up in a court of law. Let's give new converts time to mature before pushing them forward, no matter how famous they may be.

"These men are Jews" Acts 16:19-21. When Paul cast a demon out of a slave girl who had earned money for her owners by fortune-telling, the owners were furious. Their subsequent attack on Paul reflects an anti-Semitism which was already deeply rooted in first-century society. That accusation was enough to cause an uproar, which the two missionaries were then blamed for starting! Add the charge that they were preaching a religion illegal for "us Romans" to practice, and we sense the strong racial antagonism the slave girl's owners consciously appealed to in order to get back at Paul.

Today a similar kind of hostility toward Christians is found in news stories, and in media portrayals of believers and pastors. Those who speak out of Christian conviction are often labeled pejoratively as "fundamentalists," in an attempt to have their views rejected before they are even heard. It's wrong to victimize anyone by an appeal to prejudice rather than to the facts.

"Sirs, what must I do to be saved?" Acts 16:23-34 After being beaten Paul and Silas were put in prison, only to be released from their chains by an earthquake. The jailer must have been somewhat familiar with Paul's message, probably through the persistent shouting of the slave girl before her demon was exorcised. But now his terror at finding his prison doors open, and his narrow escape from suicide, created a readiness for salvation.

Let's recognize the earthquakes God brings into our lives as His gracious gifts, intended to turn our thoughts toward Him.

"You and your household" Acts 16:31. In New Testament times the "house" or "household" of a person extended beyond spouse and children. Slaves, clients, and close friends were all part of one's household. We need to understand Paul's promise of salvation to "you and your household" not as blanket assurance that one's children will someday be saved, but as assurance that they, like us, can find salvation through faith in the Lord.

"Let them come themselves and escort us out" Acts 16:35-40. Roman citizens were under the protection of the Empire wherever they traveled. Even in a semi-independent colony like Philippi, no Roman citizen could legally be treated as Paul and Barnabas had been.

Paul was always quick to assert his rights, and not just for personal reasons. Those rights of citizenship were guarantees that he could not be stopped from preaching simply because some mob disliked what he was saying.

We Christians need to affirm our rights for the same reason. In demanding our rights we maintain the freedom of all to share the Gospel of Jesus without fear.

▶ DEVOTIONAL
Relying on the Spirit
(Acts 16:1-10)

When the great missionary pioneer and founder of the China Inland Mission, Hudson Taylor, came to Canada for a speaking tour, the first person he stayed with was excited. At last he was going to meet a true giant of the faith! He was also curious. How would this Spirit-led believer go about planning his itinerary?

The next afternoon he was shocked when Taylor asked for railroad timetables, and simply sat down at the kitchen table to work out his schedule. Where was the prayer and fasting the host had expected? Hudson was surprised. God had already provided Canada's railroads and the timetables. What more was there to ask?

Paul's approach to missions was similar. He had a strategy he used to select key cities, and to minister when he reached them. Like Hudson Taylor, Paul went about ministry in a practical way. But the lives of both men show that they also remained sensitive to the Spirit's leading, ready to change plans or direction at the Spirit's call, and relied on the Spirit fully.

We don't need to be mystical to rely on the Holy Spirit. We can rely on Him while using what God has provided for us—from timetables to our ability to plan and develop strategy. But relying on the Spirit also means remaining totally open to God, ready to change any plan when He says, "No," or "Go."

Personal Application

Mind and heart must cooperate as we rely on the Spirit to lead.

Quotable

"When we rely on organization, we get what organization can do. When we rely upon education, we get what education can do. When we rely on eloquence, we get what eloquence can do. But when we rely on the Holy Spirit, we get what God can do."—A.C. Dixon

SEPTEMBER 24 *Reading 267*
THE UNKNOWN GOD
Acts 17–18

"I even found an altar with this inscription: to an unknown god. Now what you worship as something unknown I am going to proclaim to you" (Acts 17:23).

We must be very wise when we begin to proclaim a God who is unknown.

Overview
Paul was driven from Thessalonica by Jewish hostility (17:1-9), but found the Jews of Berea more ready to listen (vv. 10-15). Paul preached to philosophers in Athens (vv. 16-34) before moving on to Corinth (18:1-5), where charges made by the Jews were rejected by the Roman proconsul (vv. 6-17). Paul traveled with friends through Ephesus on his way back to Antioch (vv. 18-23). In Ephesus these friends, Priscilla and Aquila, explained the Gospel to a powerful preacher named Apollos who had heard only of John the Baptist's preaching.

Understanding the Text
"A large number of God-fearing Greeks and not a few prominent women" Acts 17:1-9. Paul continued to preach the Gospel to his own people first. Even though only a few would respond, they deserved the opportunity to hear first.

We mustn't measure a person's or group's right to hear the Gospel by their response. Even if the response is as hostile as the Jewish reaction to the missionaries in Thessalonica, everyone has the right to hear.

"The Bereans were of more noble character" Acts 17:10-12. The "nobility" of the Jews in Berea was displayed not by their willingness to hear Paul out, but by their careful daily examination of the Scripture to make sure what he said was true.

It may be hard to grasp, but the "noble" Christian today listens to preachers skeptically. The minister who insists, "Trust me," whether from the local pulpit or on the airwaves, doesn't seem to realize that the Word of God, not his teaching, is our ultimate authority. So be noble. Listen, but then study the Bible to make sure what you hear from the pulpit is true.

"He reasoned . . . in the marketplace day by day" Acts 17:16-21. Paul was forced to leave Berea when a delegation of Thessalonian Jews came there to stir up trouble. As the other members of his team still had an opportunity to minister, Paul went on to Athens alone to wait for them.

The idolatry Paul saw in Athens upset him greatly. As well as minister in the synagogue on the Sabbath, he started a street ministry, talking daily with anyone who would listen.

I learned about street meetings as a young Christian in New York City. A man was standing on a short stepladder, preaching in Rockefeller Center, just opposite Saint Patrick's Cathedral. About a hundred folks were gathered around listening. I stopped for a while and then the man, hoarse from shouting, invited anyone who wanted to give a word of testimony to climb on his ladder. I certainly didn't plan it, but suddenly I found myself standing there in my Navy uniform, preaching away.

Street ministry isn't popular or easy. Yet I later learned that one of the deacons in my local church had been converted in a street meeting.

Paul showed us in Athens that it's all right to adopt unorthodox ways to reach

Acts 17:18-33: While in Athens Paul addressed its philosophers on Mars Hill, shown here. His message on the nature of God and the Resurrection seemed foolish to most. But some believed, including one Dionysius who was a member of the "Council of Ares," the local governing body.

people who might not otherwise hear.

"Something unknown I am going to proclaim to you" Acts 17:18-32. Paul's sermon on Mars Hill is a classic example of what today is called "contextualization." He did not begin with quotes from the Jewish Scripture, or a review of Hebrew history. Rather Paul drew on pagan Greek poets to establish a point of contact, and then went on to proclaim God's truth. Paul did not use pagan authors as authorities, and his use doesn't suggest that what they said is necessarily true. But his quotes did set the stage for his teaching.

That message directly confronted the worldview of his listeners. God is the Creator of the world and all in it. God is the Creator of all men, and all are responsible to Him. It is ignorant to think of the divine Being in terms of gold, silver, or stone idols. A day of judgment is coming, and the proof is that God has raised Jesus from the dead.

It's one thing to find a point of contact so we can tell them about a God they do not know. It is another thing entirely to abandon biblical truth so that what we say will be more "acceptable" to them.

"When they heard about the resurrection of the dead, some of them sneered" Acts 17:32-34. If Paul had spoken only of the immortality of the soul, many more might have listened. That belief had deep roots in Greek philosophy. Instead Paul spoke of resurrection, a keystone of Christian faith and biblical revelation.

Luke tells us that when this teaching was advanced some sneered—but others wanted to hear Paul again on the subject.

It's our task, as it was Paul's, to present the truth of God without apology to those who do not know Him. Today too some will ridicule and turn away. But some will keep coming back, and some of these will believe.

"A Jew named Aquila" Acts 18:1-3. This man and his wife Priscilla illustrate the mobility of people in the Roman Empire of the first century. The couple had been expelled from Rome. They settled in Corinth (v. 1), later moved to Ephesus (v. 19), and still later are found again in Rome (Rom. 16:3). They were tentmakers (leatherworkers) by trade, and very successful, for their home was large enough for church groups to meet there. This freedom to travel was a key to the spread of the Gospel in the first century, and the early Christians took full advantage of it.

Today we should take advantage of every opportunity society affords to spread the Gospel where God is unknown.

"Priscilla and Aquila" Acts 18:18. The first time Luke mentioned this couple, Aquila was named first. That's appropriate. In the world of the first century, men were head of the house. But every other mention of this pair in Scripture names Priscilla first. Apparently she made the strongest impression, and very possibly was the one who took the lead in ministry.

It's likely that Paul's relationship with women like Lydia of Philippi, the "prominent women" of Thessalonica, Damaris of Athens, and Priscilla of Corinth, helped shape the apostle's far more liberal view of women and their place in ministry than he is often credited with.

"Gallio was proconsul of Achaia" Acts 18:7-17. The response of the Corinthian Gentiles to the Gospel again aroused the hostility of unbelieving Jews. At this time Gallio, well-known in secular history, was proconsul. Gallio was the brother of Seneca, the philosopher and politician, and was an influential man in his own right. When the Jews tried to haul Paul into court on a charge of teaching an illicit religion, Gallio threw the case out. He was willing to hear civil and criminal cases, but not religious disputes.

This decision by a well-known and highly respected proconsul set a precedent, and for over a decade after Christianity was given the protection of a licit faith. During that time Paul preached freely in the provinces, without fear of coming in conflict with Roman law.

Again an attack by Paul's enemies was deflected by God, and even used to make the Christian community more secure.

▶DEVOTIONAL
Speak Up—Wisely
(Acts 18:18-28)

I always cringe a little when I hear folk speaking about "contending" for the faith.

I get this picture of the grim-faced fellow who on the way out of church tells the preacher (loudly) how his sermon twisted the morning's text. Or the young man who visited our congregation one Sunday morning, and ostentatiously walked out when Ruth Flood, who's been a speech teacher in several Christian colleges, read Scripture from the pulpit. He was letting us know that we were ignorant of the fact that womenfolk shouldn't get up on that platform. He was contending for the true faith.

Actually, there are times when any of us need to be informed or corrected. But how a person tries to clear up another's ignorance makes a big difference. There's a right way and a wrong way to go about it.

Priscilla and Aquila show us the right way. A fiery preacher named Apollos came into town, teaching the imminent coming of the Messiah. He had his Scriptures right. But he'd never heard about Jesus. All he knew was that John the Baptist had appeared in the homeland, and said the promised One was due to arrive. That was enough for Apollos, and he went out to preach the Good News as he knew it.

It would have been easy for Priscilla or Aquila to stand up in that meeting and bring Apollos up to date. Or to correct him as they shook hands on the way out the door. Instead the couple invited him over for dinner, complimented him on his speaking, and "explained to him the way of God more accurately."

What a model for us to follow. Sure we want to clear up misunderstandings, and enlighten folks who worship a God they don't really know. But let's do so wisely. Not in public, where someone might be embarrassed. But in the warmth of our home, or the privacy of a friendly chat.

Actually, I suspect that Apollos was too big a man, and far too sincere, to have been turned off even if Priscilla and Aquila had been as obnoxious as some of us Christians are. So perhaps Luke tells the story more as a reminder than anything else. The best way to present an unknown God is not to "contend" at all, but in a spirit of warmth and love to share our understanding of God's great and wonderful good news.

Personal Application

Sensitivity to others' feelings opens their ears.

Quotable

For me 'twas not the truth you taught,
To you so clear, to me so dim,
But when you came to me you brought
A sense of Him!
And from your eyes He beckons me,
And from your heart His love is shed,
Till I lose sight of you and see
The Christ instead.—Author unknown

SEPTEMBER 25 *Reading 268*
COMMITTED TO GOD
Acts 19–20

> *"Now I commit you to God and to the word of His grace, which can build you up and give you an inheritance" (Acts 20:32).*

Saying good-bye is made easier by knowing that God will be with our loved ones.

Background

Ephesus. The city of Ephesus had been a major commercial city as well as the Asian center of the religious cult of Artemis (Diana). Over the centuries area forests were denuded, and the Ephesus harbor gradually filled with silt. In Paul's day, the economy of Ephesus depended to a great extent on the massive temple of Artemis, which was considered one of the wonders of the ancient world. Paul's ministry was so effective that tradesmen who depended on the sale of religious medals saw their business fall off dramatically. The result was intense hostility toward Paul and his message.

Overview

In Ephesus Paul told disciples of John the Baptist about Christ (19:1-7). His two-year ministry there was supported by miracles (vv. 8-16). It yielded so many converts (vv. 17-22) it threatened the temple-based trade of the Ephesian silversmiths, who rioted (vv. 23-41). Paul revisited his Macedonian churches (20:1-6). In Troas Eutychus died and was restored to life (vv. 7-11). Paul stopped near Ephesus, and bade that church's elders a last goodbye (vv. 12-38).

Understanding the Text

"John's baptism" Acts 19:1-7. Even decades after the death of Jesus there were Jews in the Roman Empire who knew of John the Baptist and accepted his message, who had not heard of Jesus. There were no mass media: information came by word of mouth. The dozen Jews that Paul met when he arrived in Ephesus had been baptized by John years before, probably when on a pilgrimage to one of the great religious feasts in Jerusalem. Their commitment was real, however, and when they heard of Jesus they believed the Gospel.

This is the third "unusual" case in Acts of receiving the Holy Spirit. Here as in Samaria it was by laying on of hands. And here, as at the house of Cornelius, the Spirit's coming was marked by speaking in tongues. Why here? Perhaps for the same reason that Paul's ministry in Ephesus was marked by a number of "unusual" miracles. Ephesus was a center of evil supernatural activity. God through Paul was about to display true supernaturalism.

Every now and then the unusual does mark our Christian experience. But we're not to expect supernatural signs every day. If they happened every day, they would not be unusual. And soon we would be living by sight, not by faith.

"The lecture hall of Tyrannus" Acts 19:8-10. Most commentators believe that Tyrannus rented his lecture hall to itinerant teachers for public lectures. Paul's daily lectures and discussions there reached "all the Jews and Greeks who lived in the province of Asia" (v. 10).

Paul always found a way to reach people. We can too. As a new convert, I started a noon Bible study on my Navy base. Two civilian workers came, but none of my Navy friends. So I began putting a Bible "verse for the day" on the bulletin board by the office coffeepot. If we look around, God will always show us some way to share our faith.

"God did extraordinary miracles through Paul" Acts 19:11-20. The practice of magic was common in the first century, and especially in the cult center of Ephesus. The goal of magic was to manipulate supposed supernatural powers to protect oneself, or gain an advantage over another person. It is significant that the "extraordinary" miracles of Paul were performed there rather than, say, in Athens.

God often chooses to meet human beings where they are. In intellectual Athens, Paul gave a philosophical defense of the faith. In Ephesus, where the practice of magic and superstition ruled, miracles were performed. On whatever ground Satan chooses to do battle, his defeat is certain.

"Seven sons of Sceva, a Jewish chief priest" Acts 19:13-16. In the practice of ancient magic, knowing "names" was critical, for one who knew the name of a supernatural being was thought able to access his power.

For this reason Jewish magicians were thought of highly. Jewish priests especially were reputed to know the secret name of the most powerful God of all. This reputation stemmed in part from the Jew's reverence for the personal name of God, Yahweh, which was never spoken aloud by a pious Jew.

Apparently the family of Sceva, a Jewish priest, made a good living in Ephesus by the practice of magic. When Paul came along, and began to heal and cast out demons in the name of Jesus, the family decided to go with the more powerful "name."

It didn't work. Uttering the name of Jesus is no key to supernatural power. The key is having a personal relationship with Jesus, and being available to Him. We do not use Jesus' name. He uses us to accomplish His purposes.

"They calculated the value of the scrolls" Acts 19:17-22. In Ephesus the impact of the Jesus movement was demonstrated by

burning books on magic worth 50,000 days' labor! How do you tell if a conversion is real? One good way is to check the bottom line. People who cleanse their lives of what is evil, even when it costs them money, are likely to have a faith that's real.

"After all this had happened, Paul decided to go to Jerusalem" Acts 19:21-22. Paul's great passion was to preach the Gospel where it had never been heard. With evidence that a strong church was now established in Ephesus, Paul was ready to move on. Most of us have a tendency to settle down with success and enjoy it. Paul was always looking for new challenges.

I know some older Christians who share Paul's outlook. "Retirement" for them has meant more time for ministry. One retired carpenter takes regular trips to mission fields to help with building. One grandma has more time to spend with the retarded folks she ministers to. The best way to keep young is to keep active serving God and others.

"The temple of the great goddess Artemis will be discredited" Acts 19:23-34. The "great goddess Artemis" deserved to be discredited. This was not the Diana of Greek mythology, but a multibreasted "earth mother" goddess of the East. Her moral and spiritual qualities were reflected in the practice of magic that flourished in Ephesus.

Then as now the practice of magic was a desperate attempt to control supernatural forces. We live in a world over which we have little control, and are subject to seemingly impersonal forces. The present fascination with satanism in our culture reminds us that when materialism fails to satisfy, and there is a religious vacuum, people quickly fall prey to evil.

In Ephesus the coming of the Gospel so reversed this situation that not only were books on magic being burned, but a serious threat existed to worship at the temple of Artemis.

The Gospel and the Gospel alone is able to discredit evil and reverse the trends now seen in our society.

"They have neither robbed temples nor blasphemed our goddess" Acts 19:35-41. A city official silenced the rioters and sent them home. His review of the situation was fascinating, for it gave an insight into effective evangelism. The Christians did not speak against Artemis, but for Jesus.

The Christian has a positive message to share. But it will only be communicated if all Christians become involved.

A survey of 2,000 members of the United Church of Christ, from more than 200 congregations, revealed that members of that 1.6-million-member church are extremely uncomfortable when it comes to talking about their faith. Other mainline churches, concerned about a membership plunge that has continued since the 1960s, are now trying to emphasize evangelism.

It's easy to accuse liberal churches of failing to have a faith worth talking about. But this would miss the point. Every Christian, and there are many in every Christian tradition, is to witness.

Perhaps it would help if we all realized as the Ephesian Christians apparently did that witness is simply a positive presentation of Jesus, not an attack on others' beliefs. As people turn to Christ, not only magic but modern temples to false religions will automatically be discredited.

"Because he intended to leave the next day, he kept on talking until midnight" Acts 20:7-11. It's not the raising of Eutychus that fascinates me in this paragraph. It's Paul, talking first till midnight, then taking a break and going on till daylight.

I remember when I was dating in my Navy days in New York. I'd take my girlfriend out, then sit in the car in front of her home and talk for hours. Finally she'd go in and I'd drive back to my base, many times almost falling asleep on the way. Why keep talking till you're ready to fall asleep? Love. Somehow you can't tear yourself away, even for a brief parting.

I think that's what was happening here. Paul was leaving folks he loved. Yes, he had things he wanted to say. But what kept him talking till dawn, and what kept the people there to hear him, was love.

▶DEVOTIONAL
Fond Farewells
(Acts 20:13-37)

The scene is touching. When Paul said good-bye to the elders of Ephesus he knew they would never again meet in this life. Luke, watching, said, "They all wept as they embraced him and kissed him" (v. 37). It was a sad, but a fond farewell. Somehow in just two brief years an unbreakable bond had been forged between Paul and these converts.

Perhaps it seems strange to us, because we live in such an impersonal society. Few of us, saying farewell to friends made during a two-year stay anywhere, would be seen off with such emotion. Yet if we look closely at Paul's farewell remarks, we can see what made these people so fond of him. And we learn how to become close to others ourselves. How?

Paul let people know how he lived (v. 18). In our society we tend to keep people at arm's length. Paul opened up his life, and invited people to see and know the real him. Thus he said, "You know" several times as he reviewed his way of life in Ephesus. Being willing to share ourselves is a key to building intimacy.

Paul served the Lord with humility (v. 19). What gave Paul such integrity was that he maintained a close relationship with the Lord. An intimate walk with God gives our lives an authenticity which enables others to trust us.

Paul didn't hesitate to be helpful (vv. 20-21). This meant speaking up about Jesus as well as giving other assistance. If you and I really care about another person, we will offer any help we can in a spirit of love. And we will be loved in return.

Paul was an example of Christian values (vv. 33-35). Paul chose to earn his own living rather than be supported by the gifts of those he taught. While Paul had a right to such support, he chose to live as an example of Christian values in action.

These qualities combined to create a bond of deep love and affection between Paul and the Ephesians. And these same qualities can create bonds of affection between us and others today.

Let's not complain how difficult it is to make friends in our impersonal society. Let's invite others into our lives, serve the Lord with humility, never hestitate to be helpful, and live our Christian values.

Personal Application

Be a Christian friend, and you will make friends.

Quotable

"You can make more friends in two months by becoming interested in other people than you can in two years by trying to get other people interested in you."—Dale Carnegie

SEPTEMBER 26 *Reading 269*

TO JERUSALEM

Acts 21–22

> *"Through the Spirit they urged Paul not to go on to Jerusalem. But when our time was up, we left and continued on our way" (Acts 21:4-5).*

Sometimes we have to choose a course we know holds danger.

Overview

Paul set out for Jerusalem despite warnings (21:1-16). He was welcomed by Jerusalem Christians (vv. 17-20), but was asked to show his personal dedication to Old Testament Law by paying expenses for men discharging a Nazarite vow (vv. 21-26). Paul was accused by Asian Jews, and almost killed in the riot (vv. 27-32). Saved by the Roman army (vv. 33-40), Paul told the crowd of his conversion (22:1-20). When Paul mentioned his commission to go to the Gentiles, they cried for his death (vv. 21-24). Paul then asserted his rights as a Roman citizen (vv. 25-30).

Understanding the Text

"They urged Paul not to go on to Jerusalem" Acts 21:1-6. Luke seemed to draw a parallel between Jesus' determination to accept the Cross, and Paul's commitment to face danger in Jerusalem. Jesus knew what lay ahead. Paul too was shown by the Spirit what lay ahead for him. Like Christ, Paul refused to fear, but set out to do God's will whatever the cost.

Some have argued that Paul was willfully disobedient in going to Jerusalem. After all, wasn't it "through the Spirit" that the disciples near Tyre urged Paul not to go on? It seems best to take the phrase "through the Spirit" as referring to the agency by which these believers learned Paul would be in danger. Their conclusion, "then don't go on," was their own.

Let's remember that danger alone is not a sufficient reason to turn back. Let's also remember that each of us is responsible to determine God's special will for himself or herself. Others can advise us. But we must respond to the Holy Spirit who speaks in us.

"The Holy Spirit says" Acts 21:7-16. It's only natural that after hearing this message, Paul's Christian friends "pleaded with Paul not to go up to Jerusalem." That's what was wrong with their response! It was only "natural."

This was one of those times when the message was not intended to change Paul's mind, but to provoke intensified prayer support for him. Again there's a parallel with Christ's last days. When Jesus spoke of His coming death, His disciples were quick to say, "Never" (cf. Matt. 16:22).

When others make a difficult decision, let's not make it harder for them by urging them to take an easier course. Let's give them our support, promise our prayers, and say as the Caesarean Christians finally did, "The Lord's will be done."

"Thousands of Jews have believed, and all of them are zealous for the Law" Acts 21:17-28. Christian Jews were not expected to abandon Judaism, any more than Gentile Christians were to abandon their culture and heritage. But Paul's mission to the Gentiles had stimulated rumors that he was anti-Judaism. To reassure the Jewish Christian community, Paul paid the expenses of four persons who were completing a Nazarite vow. This was considered a "good deed" in Judaism, and would show that Paul was not anti-Judaism.

Some have condemned Paul for his act, holding that he compromised his convictions. Hardly. Instead the act shows that Paul was far more sensitive to the meaning of freedom than his critics! As the Gentiles were free to worship God apart from Jewish rituals, so Jewish Christians were free to worship within their heritage.

You and I are likely to be criticized by others if we maintain a truly Christian view of freedom. That's all right. Just as Paul was willing to suffer in Jerusalem under the Spirit's guidance, he was willing to be criticized. So should we be.

"He at once took some officers and soldiers and ran down to the crowd" Acts 21:27-36. Some Asian Jews visiting Jerusalem recognized Paul, and assumed he had brought a Gentile companion into a forbidden area of the temple. Their outcry started a riot and mob attack on an innocent Paul.

Some might today call the Roman Empire a tyranny. In many ways it was. But when the commander of Roman troops in Jerusalem heard the uproar, he immediately dashed into the crowd and rescued Paul. Later events showed he thought Paul was a notable revolutionary. Even so, the Roman officer was committed to the rule of law.

Our government, like that of ancient Rome, surely has flaws. But the rule of law is to be preferred to the mob rule that would certainly replace it. We can be especially grateful to those who take responsibility to maintain law and order today.

"Listen to my defense" Acts 22:1-20. The mob was as confused as the Romans about why Paul was being attacked. No one had stopped to get the facts. Paul's "defense," made in Aramaic, the everyday language of the Jews, was biographical. Paul established his identity with his listeners in a common commitment to the God of Israel, and told of his conversion. In Judaism orthopraxy (orthodox behavior; keeping the ritual law) was at least as important as orthodoxy (orthodox belief). Also first-century Jewish religious literature abounds with stories of visions, so Paul's report must have captured his listeners' interest. As Paul's hosts had said, there were "many thousands of Jews" who had believed in Jesus, "and all of them zealous for the Law" (21:20). In that society mention of Jesus was not enough to set the mob against Paul.

Paul was a master at identifying with those to whom he ministered. He used this gift to share Christ all over the world. Let's be sensitive to the beliefs and prejudices of others. They may take offense at the Gospel. But let it not be because we are offensive.

"I will send you far away to the Gentiles" Acts 22:21-23. Sometimes truth itself is offensive to people. Should we try to avoid offensive truths? When Paul reported his commission to go to the Gentiles, the mob again shouted for his death. The notion that God accepted Gentiles on the same basis He accepted Jews was totally repugnant to this people who had for centuries thought of themselves as God's chosen people.

It takes real wisdom to know how to share God's truth with others. The response to Paul's defense in Jerusalem reminds us that however wise we may be, the truth will sometimes be rejected—and we will be rejected with it.

"I was born a Roman citizen" Acts 22:22-30. When the Romans were unable to tell what the riot had been about, the commander ordered that Paul be examined under torture. This involved being beaten with a flagellum, a leather whip studded with sharp pieces of metal or bone. It was illegal to put a Roman citizen to this torture. When Paul claimed citizenship, the Roman commander hurried to release him. A verbal claim of citizenship was all that was needed in the first century: the penalty for lying about citizenship was death.

Paul did not hesitate to claim his legal rights as he traveled through Empire lands. We can be proud of our citizenship too and should actively assert our rights under the law to practice our faith.

Today these rights are in fact being challenged on many fronts. The American Legal Society has even begun to hold seminars on how to sue churches and religious organizations. The day may come soon when many legal challenges to our constitutional rights will be mounted, and all of us will be called on to make a stand.

Paul had followed God's leading and come to Jerusalem. He had been attacked. But God acted to protect His servant. God will protect us as we follow His leading today.

▶ DEVOTIONAL
God's Special Will
(Acts 21:1-36)

My old Christian education professor at Dallas Seminary told of the woman who, when he was a seminary student, passed on some exciting information. God had told her that Mr. Howard Hendricks was supposed to marry her daughter!

This exciting revelation was shared regularly, until Howie finally said, "Let's wait until God tells me."

God never did, and later Howie married his lovely wife of many years now, Jean.

The story illustrates some of the confusion that exists about knowing God's special will. By "special will," I mean His will for each of us as individuals, in contrast to His general will for all believers as revealed in Scripture. Guidance for who we marry, what occupation we pursue, when and whether to move on, are illustrations of that "special" guidance we want from God, but can't get by turning to a verse or passage in the Bible.

Several things in Acts 21 help us think more clearly about God's special will for us. And the first is that God's will for the individual is to be discerned by the individual himself or herself. Not by others. That was true for Howie Hendricks. Momma didn't have any right to tell him it was God's will for him to marry her daughter. It was true for the Apostle Paul. The believers at Tyre (vv. 1-6) and at Caesarea (vv. 8-12) didn't have any right to tell Paul it was God's will for him not to go up to Jerusalem. And it's true for you and me.

A second helpful principle is that God's will can't be determined by what seems wise or expedient. When Ella's daughter began to do visitation in inner-city Chicago, the suburban mother was terrified. She had been ready to see her daughter go to Africa as a missionary. But to Chicago? That was too dangerous! Yet during her months in Chicago God not only kept the daughter safe, but gave her an effective ministry.

Finally, even a "disastrous outcome" is no sure indication of God's will. We can't second-guess ourselves, or others. Paul was almost killed, and was arrested in Jerusalem. But God turned this disaster to

Paul's and His own advantage. In time the apostle was brought to Rome, and there won members of "Caesar's household" (Phil. 4:22).

We Christians believe in a God who is Sovereign, and in an indwelling Holy Spirit who guides us through life. Part of our responsibility is to be sensitive to the Spirit, and to seek His leading. To live a responsible Christian life means in part accepting responsibility for our own choices, and doing God's will as we understand it.

Personal Application

Listen to others' advice. But be led by God.

Quotable

"The surest method of arriving at a knowledge of God's eternal purposes about us is to be found in the right use of the present moment. God's will does not come to us in the whole, but in fragments, and generally in small fragments. It is our business to piece it together, and to live it as one orderly vocation."—F.W. Faber

SEPTEMBER 27 *Reading 270*

PAUL ON TRIAL
Acts 23–24

"Five days later the high priest Ananias went down to Caesarea . . . and they brought their charges against Paul before the governor" (Acts 24:1).

The best defense is the simple truth.

Overview

Paul's statement to the Sanhedrin divided that body along party lines (23:1-11). The chief priests then joined a conspiracy to assassinate Paul (vv. 12-15). Paul's nephew warned the Roman commander (vv. 16-25), who sent Paul under heavy guard to the Roman governor in Caesarea (vv. 26-35). On trial before Felix, Paul told the simple truth (24:1-21). Felix, hoping to be paid a bribe, delayed his decision for two whole years (vv. 22-27).

Understanding the Text

"The high priest Ananias" Acts 23:1-5. The order of Ananias to strike Paul was in character. This Ananias was high priest from A.D. 48 to 59, and is mentioned in first-century writings. Josephus says he stole tithes given ordinary priests and bribed Romans and Jews. He is ridiculed in the Talmud, and was hated for both his brutality and greed. He was killed by Jews in the Jewish uprising of A.D. 66.

Paul did not recognize Ananias as high priest because the meeting was called by the Roman commander, who would have been seated as presiding officer between the Sanhedrin on one side and Paul on the other. Paul's outrage at the order he be struck was justified (v. 3). Yet he apologized, because the office of high priest commanded respect even though the man filling the office did not.

In the secular world and in the church it's right to show respect for the office. But it's even better to see to it that secular and spiritual offices are held by those of high moral character and integrity.

"I stand on trial because of my hope in the resurrection of the dead" Acts 23:6-11. The Pharisees believed in the resurrection of the dead and in angels, while the Sadducees did not. Paul identified himself with the first group, and claimed that the real issue before the court was belief in resurrection. Paul has been criticized for this statement, which some take as nothing more than a trick used to obscure the issue of his Christian commitment. But the resurrection is the issue. It was by his resurrection from the dead, Paul wrote in his letter to the Romans, that Jesus was proven "with power to be the Son of God" (Rom. 1:4).

The uproar that broke out "when he said this" (Acts 23:7) prevented Paul from developing this theme. But clearly Paul was laying the foundation for another presentation of the claims of Christ, by finding common ground with a large segment of his listeners.

The accusation that Paul used a shoddy

trick reminds us of the danger of standing in judgment on others' motives. Christians are to agree with God's assessment that certain acts are sinful. But we are not to judge the motives or personal convictions of others.

"The dispute became so violent" Acts 23:10-11. Passionate belief is one thing. Doing violence to others is another. Paul may not have been surprised at the reaction of the Sanhedrin, but he was clearly endangered by it. God's reassurance and promise were especially welcome at that time.

God doesn't speak with us today as He did to Paul. But the Lord speaks to us through His words to the great apostle. That "take courage" is for us in our times of turmoil or danger. So is the sense of His promise. As God had a purpose for Paul to fulfill, so He has a purpose for you and me to fulfill as well.

"They went to the chief priests and elders" Acts 23:12-22. The "chief priests and elders" were members of the Sadducee party. They were also members of the Sanhedrin, the supreme court of Judaism, responsible to administer God's Law. All we can say about their willingness to join in a conspiracy to assassinate Paul is that it is a shocking revelation of their character.

But never mind their hypocrisy. We need to watch ourselves! You and I need to be on guard against professing Christian values, and then acting in a way that denies them.

"We have taken a solemn oath not to eat anything" Acts 23:14. Don't suppose the conspirators starved when they didn't kill Paul. Rabbinical rulings allowed any vow to be broken if it was incited by others, if it involved exaggeration, if made in error, or if unfulfillable. In other words, the vow to not eat until after murdering Paul was meaningless!

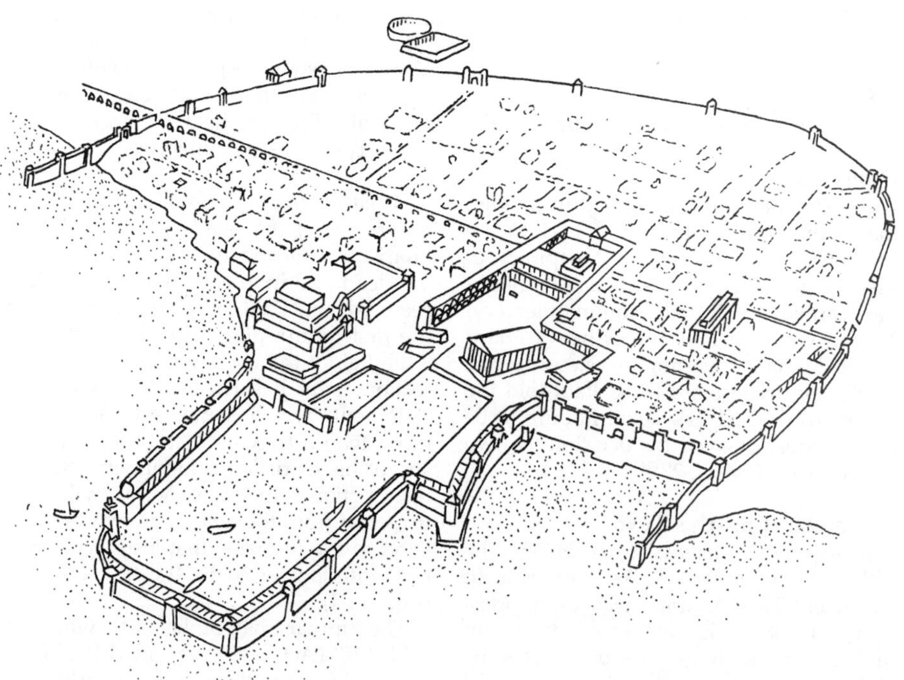

Caesarea Maritima ("by the sea") was so well designed by engineers that the action of the ocean itself kept the harbor clear of silt and drifting sand. The beautiful city, decorated by Herod the Great with many public buildings, was Palestine's major seaport and the Roman administrative center. Paul was held there under house arrest for two years before being sent on to Rome for trial (Acts 24–25).

No wonder Jesus once urged His followers to let your yes mean yes, and your no mean no. If we are not persons of our integrity, making a vow is meaningless.

"He wrote a letter as follows" Acts 23:23-35. When word of the conspiracy reached the Roman commander, he arranged to send Paul with a strong escort to the Roman governor at Caesarea. The original makes it clear that Luke did not have the specific letter, but that the commander's letter was similar to the summary Luke includes.

"Your foresight has brought about reforms in this nation" Acts 24:1-9. It was typical to launch a case in court with flattering remarks addressed to the judge. But the words addressed to Governor Felix by the orator hired by the chief priests to bring charges against Paul are so blatantly false as to be hypocritical.

Felix was born a slave, but later was freed by the mother of the Emperor Claudius. The Roman historian Tacitus called Felix "a master of cruelty and lust who exercised the powers of a king with the spirit of a slave." His years in Palestine saw numerous insurrections, and Felix used increasingly brutal methods to put them down. To speak of Felix's rule as a "period of peace" and to commend the governor for bringing about reforms was worse than ridiculous.

How strange it is that those who wish to be flattered lose perspective on reality. The greater the lie, the more welcome it seems. No wonder Scripture warns us, "Do not think of yourself more highly than you ought, but rather think of yourself with sober judgment" (Rom. 12:3).

"Paul replied" Acts 24:10-21. Paul's reply was quite different from the accusation. He used no flattery (v. 10). He identified himself as a Christian (vv. 14-16). And he stated simply the facts that refuted their charges. He had only come to Jerusalem 12 days earlier: how could he be a "ringleader" of anything? (v. 11) When he was taken he was alone: how could he "stir up riots" without talking to a crowd? (vv. 12, 18) As to why he was in Jerusalem, he came to worship, and to bring gifts from Christians to the (Christian) people of Jerusualem (vv. 17-18). If Paul were guilty of some other charge, where were his accusers? (v. 12)

This last question was significant, as Roman law penalized accusers who committed *destitutio,* abandoning charges made against another person. If no accusers appeared, the legal significance was that of withdrawing the charges. It was clear, then, that there was no legal basis to condemn or even to hold Paul. Was Paul acquitted? No. The governor decided it would be expedient to use judicial delay in hopes feelings would grow less intense—and in hopes that Paul might bribe him to obtain his release (v. 26).

Being in the right is no guarantee to either acquittal or justice. All you and I are guaranteed is that God is in full command of our situations, and that He intends to do us good.

▶ DEVOTIONAL
Having Our Say
(Acts 24:1-27)

On the one hand, Acts 24 seems to be a defeat or at least a setback for Paul. He made a compelling defense before the Roman governor Felix, and showed how weak the chief priest's case against him was. But Felix waffled, and refused to decide the case. Paul was put under house arrest, and kept there for two years! Later Felix and his third wife, Drusilla, a Jewess who abandoned her husband Azizus to marry Felix, heard Paul discourse on "righteousness, self-control and the judgment to come" (v. 25). Felix was frightened and sent Paul away. Only his hope that Paul would offer him a bribe moved Felix to talk with Paul from time to time. It looked like failure. But in fact it was success! For Paul, and the Gospel, had a hearing.

That's really what we Christians want. A hearing. We shouldn't expect to be popular. Or that the majority of folks will experience instant conversion. But at the least we must have a chance to be heard.

That's why it's significant that powerful media unions, the American Federation of TV and Radio Artists (AFTRA) and the Screen Actors Guild (SAG) want to censor a new publication called *TV*, designed to report information on networks, stars, and program content. The values reflected in *TV* are those espoused by Paul as he confronted Felix and Drusilla with the biblical teaching on "righteousness, self-control and the judgment to come." While AFTRA and SAG are both adamant against censorship of the movie and TV industries, actor John Randolph, who introduced a resolution at AFTRA's national convention condemning the *TV* newsletter, said, "I want this to be stopped before it really gets started."

If you want information on networks, sponsors, and groups which are actively anti-Christian, and on Christian organizations working to help Christians have our say in modern society, write the American Family Association, P.O. Drawer 2440, Tupelo, MS 38803.

Personal Application

Don't be discouraged if few respond to your witness. Having your say is success!

Quotable

"What the world expects of Christians is that Christians should speak out, loud and clear . . . in such a way that never a doubt, never the slightest doubt, could rise in the heart of the simplest man."—Albert Camus

SEPTEMBER 28 *Reading 271*

ON TRIAL AGAIN

Acts 25–26

> *"I have nothing definite to write his majesty about him. Therefore I have brought him before all of you, and especially before you, King Agrippa" (Acts 25:26).*

It is unwise to judge any situation by appearances alone.

Overview

The chief priests pressured the new Roman governor to let them try Paul, who then exercised his right to demand trial in Rome (25:1-13). Festus asked King Agrippa for advice (vv. 14-21). Agrippa asked to hear Paul for himself (v. 22), and was treated to Paul's most famous presentation of the Gospel (v. 23–26:32).

Understanding the Text

"Festus went up from Caesarea to Jerusalem" Acts 25:1-7. Festus, who began his rule in A.D. 60, was a fair-minded administrator far different from the governors of Judea before and after him. On arriving in Judea he immediately went up to Jerusalem to meet with the Jewish leaders. This was an unusual courtesy, for he might well have called them to appear in Caesarea.

The chief priests assumed this was the ideal time to press for resumption of Paul's case, before the new administrator understood the situation. Luke tells us their request that Paul be brought up to Jerusalem as a "favor" to them was part of another plot to ambush and kill Paul (v. 3). There's no way to tell if Festus was made suspicious by their urgency. At any rate, God overruled, and the new Roman governor decided to hear the case in Caesarea when he returned there.

The old saying "man proposes, but God disposes" remains true.

"I appeal to Caesar!" Acts 25:8-12 When Festus asked Paul if he would go voluntarily to Jerusalem, the apostle appealed to Caesar. In the first century the right of such an appeal was limited to extraordinary cases, where violent or capital punishment might be imposed.

The appeal resolved a major problem for Paul and for Festus. The danger to Paul was that Festus, as yet unaware of Jewish culture and beliefs, might make an unwise decision. The problem for Festus was how to get off to a good start in his relationships with the Jews, and still treat Paul fairly.

A fair-minded person can usually find a way to do the right thing—or at least to avoid doing wrong.

"Agrippa and Bernice" Acts 25:13-21. Agrippa was the great-grandson of Herod the Great. He ruled part of the ancient family territory to the north of Judea. Later he unsuccessfully tried to keep the Jews

in his area from rebelling against Rome. His loyalty was appreciated, and he was given most of the ancient family lands to rule.

Bernice was his sister, reputed also to be his mistress. She married twice, and became the mistress of the Roman general and later Emperor Titus, but spent most of her time in her brother's court.

When Agrippa made a courtesy visit to the new governor of Judea, Festus asked his advice. Festus had been unable to make heads or tails of the dispute between Paul and the chief priests. What could Festus report as the charges against Paul when he sent him to Rome for trial?

It was an enviable position for Paul to be in—or for any Christian. If we are imprisoned, let it be for our faith, and not because we have broken any law.

"I would like to hear this man myself" Acts 25:22. Agrippa was thoroughly acquainted with the Jewish faith and, according to Paul, was known to believe the prophets (26:27). His interest in hearing Paul may have been prompted simply by curiosity. But the Greek construction, "I myself also would like to hear this man," suggests a more personal interest.

We should be glad whatever motive people have for wanting to hear the Gospel.

"You have permission to speak for yourself" Acts 26:1-23. This is the third report in Acts of Paul's conversion. This time Paul emphasized his roots in Pharisaic Judaism, his persecution of Christians, and his discovery after his vision on the Damascus road that the resurrection of Jesus was in complete harmony with Moses and the Prophets.

This is less of a defense than a direct and powerful evangelistic appeal to a ruler who was intimately familiar with Judaism and the Old Testament. Again Paul had shown his mastery of gearing his presentation of the Gospel to the person he wanted most to hear.

"You are out of your mind, Paul!" Acts 26:24 Festus, completely out of his depth, interrupted Paul's talk about resurrection. To the Roman, whose viewpoint was limited to this world, talk of the dead coming to life was mad indeed.

Many moderns share Festus' view. Life is limited to our brief days on this earth. We live, we die, and death is the end. One day the universe itself will wink out, as the heat is drawn from the last flickering stars, and an endless dark will fall. To talk of resurrection, to speak of life after death, may be comforting. But it's mad.

Perhaps. But the Festuses of this world need to answer one question. If belief in a resurrection is mad, what have they to lose by trusting Christ? If belief in a resurrection is not mad, what have they to gain?

"Do you think that in such a short time you can persuade me to be a Christian?" Acts 26:28-32 Paul's message had been directed to Agrippa. Now Paul challenged the king directly. Since Agrippa believed the Prophets, he must know that what Paul said was true.

Agrippa equivocated. His reply, "Do you think that in such a short time you can persuade me to be a Christian?" was neither a yes nor a no. In modern slang, Agrippa "fudged."

I can sympathize with Agrippa. Here he was, on the spot. Festus had just called Paul mad. If Agrippa said he believed what Paul proclaimed, wouldn't the Roman ruler think him mad too?

How tragic when any of us are unwilling to look beyond appearances. How tragic when fear of what others may think seems more important to us than truth we are invited to embrace.

▶ DEVOTIONAL
Welcome to Oz
(Acts 25:23–26:32)

Who can forget the Wizard of Oz, that bumbling huckster who, hiding behind his curtain, manipulated an awesome figure that magnified his voice and pumped frightening puffs of smoke out at those seeking an audience. He was a fraud. But at least he was a lovable fraud.

I'm reminded of the Wizard as I read Luke's description of the pomp with which Festus, Agrippa, Bernice, and their "high ranking officers" filed into the courtroom. You can almost hear trumpets blare, see each in his or her finery. Here they come, proud, wealthy, powerful. Taking their raised seats as they looked down on the ordinary mortals below.

And then here came Paul. A small man, weighted down with chains, he shuffled into the room, stood for a moment, and when the investigation was formally handed over to Agrippa by Festus, Paul began his defense.

What's fascinating to realize is that the man in chains and not the finery-bedecked listeners had the real power. His talk, of a suffering Christ, of a resurrection from the dead, this is reality. The swords and spears of the guards, the chain mail worn by the officers standing beside governor and king, these are as gossamer and transitory as a butterfly's wings.

We need to remember Oz. And to remember Paul before Festus and Agrippa. Just as the Wizard of Oz was a fraud, so are the powers of this world. Look behind the curtain, see the reality, and they fade to meaninglessness. Look more closely, and you realize that the man in chains was free. And those who proclaimed their freedom by their pomp were bound. Eternally.

Personal Application

Don't fear the Wizard of Oz, whatever guise he wears.

Quotable

"The eyes of the world see no further than this life, as mine see no further than this wall when the church door is shut. The eyes of the Christian see deep into eternity."—John Vianney

SEPTEMBER 29 *Reading 272*
ON TO ROME
Acts 27–28

> *"When we got to Rome, Paul was allowed to live by himself, with a soldier to guard him" (Acts 28:16).*

Even a prisoner who knows God can influence others.

Overview

Paul joined a group of prisoners being transported under guard to Rome (27:1-8). He warned futilely against sailing from Crete (vv. 9-12), and their ship was caught in a severe storm (vv. 13-25). Though the ship was wrecked, all aboard survived (vv. 26-44). Paul healed the chief official on Malta, where they wintered (28:1-10). Arriving in Rome, Paul was allowed to live in a rented house (vv. 11-16), and to preach Christ to the Jewish community and his visitors (vv. 17-31).

Background

Beyond Acts. The Book of Acts closes with Paul in Rome awaiting trial. While there he wrote several of the letters found in the New Testament, including Colossians, Philippians, Ephesians, Philemon, and the first Letter to Timothy. Scholars believe that Paul was set free after his trial, and spent several more years as a missionary, probably in Spain. But the political climate was changing. Nero, whose first years were marked by excellent rule, gradually became more and more erratic. When a great fire struck Rome, Nero blamed the Christians in order to divert criticism from himself. As official hostility developed, Paul was arrested again and faced another trial. During this second imprisonment he wrote his second Letter to Timothy. As that letter implies, Paul did not survive his second trial, but was executed in Rome.

One of the purposes that Luke had in writing Acts was to demonstrate through his story of Paul's ministry that the Christian faith was no threat to the Empire. Paul had friends among the Asiarchs in Ephesus. When he was examined by Felix he was cleared of any criminal activity. King Agrippa, a close friend of the Emperor Claudius, agreed that Paul had done nothing to merit arrest or trial. Whenever the facts were examined by an impartial Roman administrator, Paul and the Christians he represented were cleared.

While the evidence Luke presented was compelling, it was not enough. Hostility to Christianity was not rooted in a knowledge of the facts of our faith, but in the prejudices and moral turpitude of its enemies. Despite the fact that some today who claim to be Christians have given the faith a bad name, it remains true that any hostility to our faith is not rooted in what Christ taught or what Christians believe. It is rooted in the fact that Christianity functions as a light shining in a dark world. The darker the society, the brighter that light must shine. And the more those who cower back into the darkness will hate and resent it.

Understanding the Text

"We boarded a ship" Acts 27:1-9. This is one of four "we" sections in Acts. Most scholars believe that Luke was with Paul, and described the events of these sections from eyewitness knowledge. Those who have studied Luke's account of the voyage find it a totally accurate portrayal of first-century ships, ports, and trade routes.

Even more important from Paul's point of view, the use of "we" here indicates that Paul was not alone. Friends went with him on the journey to Rome. Any time we face an uncertain future, having friends with us for support is vitally important. Are there people you know who would like you to serve as their Luke?

First-century cargo ships carried grain from the East to Rome. Some were large enough to also carry several hundred passengers. However, the passengers slept on deck and provided their own food for the journey. Thousands of tourists frequented such ships, though travel on the Mediterranean was dangerous.

"So Paul warned them" Acts 27:9-14. Paul had not yet had time to establish that "personal power" needed to influence the centurion who guarded them and the ship's captain. Now he would win their sudden respect. The two ignored his advice and set out to sea. Before they were out of sight of the island they were struck by winds of "hurricane force."

Perhaps as a prisoner Paul had no right to speak up. But he did express his convictions. His confidence, plus the fact that his advice was quickly shown to have been right, established a personal power he was able to use later to influence the centurion and save lives.

Don't hesitate to speak out for what is right. Ultimately your influence depends on you, not on your position.

"God whose I am and whom I serve" Acts 27:15-25. Paul spoke confidently out of the assurance rooted in his relationship with God. If we trust God, as Paul did, and are committed to Him, we too can speak out with confidence and be heard!

"Unless these men stay with the ship, you cannot be saved" Acts 27:27-44. People in panic are nearly uncontrollable. Yet by this time Paul's personal power and influence were so great that he was able to get the soldiers to cut away the ship's lifeboats and what seemed their best chance of escape.

Even more, he was able to quiet the terror of the sailors and passengers enough so that they actually took a little food.

Paul's own confidence in God's commitment to save the ship and crew were communicated by his voice and demeanor. If we have that God-based confidence, we will be able to influence others for their own good too.

"They changed their minds and said he was a god" Acts 28:1-10. People have a tendency to jump to extreme conclusions. Seeing Paul bitten by a poisonous snake, the people of Malta assumed he was a murderer. When he didn't die, they assumed he was a god. Paul was neither. He was just a human being committed to the Lord.

You and I can be comfortable being "just folks" too. God can and does take ordinary people and through them do extraordinary things.

"With a soldier to guard him" Acts 28:11-16. Soon after this Paul mentioned believers in Caesar's own household in his letter to the Philippians. The chances are that these believers were soldiers in the Praetorian Guard, the regiment assigned as the Emperor's. And most likely the soldiers detailed to guard Paul in his house!

How Paul must have looked forward to the changing of the guard, and another soldier to speak to about Jesus Christ.

"He explained and declared . . . and tried to convince them" Acts 28:17-29. As always Paul showed special concern for his brothers, the Jews. An intense effort to evangelize the local Jewish community saw some respond to the Gospel message, but the majority rejected it.

There are limits to what I've been calling "personal power." Those with personal power can influence others up to a point. But when we speak about Jesus, there is a point at which the other person will commit to Christ or reject Him. We have to respect the right of others to make that decision.

We should speak with confidence. But we must not manipulate others into a decision they are not ready to make.

"For two whole years Paul stayed there in his own rented house" Acts 28:30-31. Paul's life and ministry falls into periods of one or two years, but seldom more. He was probably in Corinth longer than two years. But he spent two years at Ephesus, two in Caesarea, and now two more years in Rome.

Didn't all that moving around bother Paul? Paul realized something that is true for each of us. We are soldiers, God is our Commander. We never know when we put down our tent how long we'll stay. Let's be good soldiers, ready to move or stay at God's command. And always ready to speak up for our Lord.

▶ DEVOTIONAL
Personal Power
(Acts 27)

My wife has it in her classroom. She has no problems maintaining order among her 11th-graders. She doesn't even raise her voice. But when she uses it, her quiet "power" voice creates dead silence.

I'm not planning to market a psychological seminar guaranteed to give those who pay some astronomical sum an edge in negotiating. Or a fast trip up the corporate ladder. I'm simply noting a reality that at least one critic of Acts overlooked.

The critic, a scholar named Haenchen, pooh-poohed the notion that a person who was a prisoner, being conveyed to Rome under guard, could possibly have been given special favors or listened to with respect by his captors. The details Luke gives of the voyage are undoubtedly accurate. But the idea that Paul played the role described is, to Haenchen, beyond belief.

I suspect this scholar, based on his reasoning, would also argue that Lech Walesa must be something of a fictional character too. After all, what pipe fitter from a Polish shipyard could form a union, be outlawed, and then silenced for years, and play a critical role in the fall of Poland's Communist government?

What Haenchen failed to realize was that the personal power of a human being is not related to his or her social position. People with position can be utterly ineffective. And others with no position at all can change the course of history.

Paul had an advantage—the confidence and the assurance that come with a personal relationship with Jesus Christ. Paul knew Jesus and lived in close fellowship with the Lord. When Paul spoke, that personal power rooted in his relationship with God shone through. Others sensed his personal power. And responded to him.

What excites me is that Paul's source of personal power is available to every Christian. If we know Jesus, and live close to Him, we too will have that calm assurance that translates into personal power.

Personal Application

Live close to Jesus, and when you speak, everybody will listen.

Quotable

"If you are a Christian in small things, you are not a small Christian."— Walter B. Knight

---

The Variety Reading Plan continues with ISAIAH

Romans

INTRODUCTION

This letter was written by the Apostle Paul to the church in Rome about A.D. 57. The theme of the letter is righteousness. Despite man's sin, Paul showed that God declares those who believe in Jesus both innocent and right with Him. Even more, through the Holy Spirit that Christ gives, God works within to enable believers to actually live righteous lives, individually and as a redeemed community.

Romans is perhaps the most powerful Christian document ever written. Towering figures like Luther and Wesley trace their conversions to this book. Any Christian can deepen his appreciation of all God has given us in Christ by a careful study of Romans. And every Christian can discover here the source of that spiritual power man needs to live a life that glorifies the Saviour.

OUTLINE OF CONTENTS

I. Introduction . . . . Rom. 1:1-17
II. Righteousness: Man's Great Need . . . . Rom. 1:18–3:20
III. Righteousness as God's Gift . . . . Rom. 3:21–5:21
IV. Righteous Living Today . . . . Rom. 6–8
V. Righteousness in History . . . . Rom. 9–11
VI. Righteousness in Community . . . . Rom. 12–16

READING GUIDE (14 Days)

If hurried, you may read only the "core passage" in your Bible and the Devotional in each chapter of this Commentary.

Reading	*Chapters*	*Core passage*
273	1	1:18-32
274	2–3	2:25–3:20
275	4	4:18-25
276	5	5:1-11
277	6	6:1-14
278	7	7:14-25
279	8	8:26-39
280	9–10	10:1-15
281	11	11:25-36
282	12	12:9-16
283	13	13
284	14	14:1-4
285	15	15:1-6
286	16	16:25-27

Romans

SEPTEMBER 30 *Reading 273*
THE POWER OF GOD
Romans 1

> *"I am not ashamed of the Gospel, because it is the power of God for the salvation of everyone who believes: first for the Jew, then for the Gentile" (Rom. 1:16).*

The power of God is displayed in those who believe. And the need for God's power in those who do not.

Overview
Paul greeted his Roman readers (1:1-7), and shared his longing to see them (vv. 8-13). He shared too his sense of obligation to bring to all a Gospel that revealed God's righteousness even as it brought salvation (vv. 14-17). Paul then began his exposition: all mankind is wicked, and under God's wrath (vv. 15-32).

Understanding the Text
"Set apart for the Gospel of God" Rom. 1:1-2. Paul first of all identified himself as a "servant" of Jesus Christ. The Greek word is *doulos,* and means a bondslave. Paul also identified himself as an apostle, a role that placed him at the top of the early church's hierarchy. But in Paul's thinking, being a slave of Jesus was a far greater honor than the high office he filled.

What an antidote to any jealousy that may appear among us today. What does it matter if I or someone else has a high church or secular office? The greatest honor you or I can have is to be a bondslave of Jesus Christ, and to serve Him with all our hearts.

"Regarding His Son" Rom. 1:3-5. In the ancient world a slave's status was determined not just by his position in a household, but by whose slave he was. Paul was proud to serve Jesus, because no greater master can be conceived of.

Just think who Jesus is. He is the fulfillment of the prophets' dreams, the subject of Old Testament revelation (v. 2). In His humanity He is royalty; a Descendant of David (v. 3). At the same time He is the Son of God (v. 4), and was so declared by His resurrection from the dead (v. 4). He is the ever-living source of grace, the Lord who called Paul to his apostleship (v. 5). In short, Jesus Christ is the focus of God's eternal plan, the heart and center of the believer's life.

Compare this with some of the masters men choose to serve. Some are slaves of drink or drugs. Some are slaves of their passion for political power. Some are slaves of a passion for wealth. Some are slaves of sex. Some sell themselves for popularity. As Paul points out later, each of us is the slave of whatever we choose to serve in life.

How wise then to choose to be slaves of Jesus Christ, the highest position to which we can aspire. How foolish to serve a lesser master.

"Who are loved by God and called to be saints" Rom. 1:7. Paul knew that we believers have other identities besides that of being slaves of Jesus Christ. He mentioned two here. We are God's loved ones. And we are His saints.

The word "saints" (*hagiois*) means "holy ones." The core meaning of "holy" is "set aside or apart for God." In the New Testament "saints" frequently has the ordinary meaning of "Christian" or "believer." But its significance is far from ordinary. God has set you and me apart as His precious possessions. He has chosen us, and marked us as His own. If we understand how precious we are to the Lord and how greatly we are loved, the "grace and peace" Paul wished for the Romans will surely be ours.

"I thank my God . . . for all of you" Rom. 1:8-10. One of the most impressive features of Paul's letters was his frequent affirmation that he prayed "constantly" for others. When Paul wrote this letter he had never been to Rome. He did know several individuals who were part of the Roman church (cf. Rom. 16). But most he had only heard of. Yet Paul was excited about them, and he cared enough to "remember you in my prayers at all times."

I confess that one of my own needs is for a greater involvement in prayer for others. I pray for folks when I think of them. But I don't think of them often enough. Paul's vision for others was worldwide. We need to maintain that worldwide vision too.

"That you and I may be mutually encouraged" Rom. 1:11-13. Paul's humble attitude is a model for modern ministry. All too often the person who is called and trained for "full-time Christian service" goes out, assuming that he or she will give out—and that others will passively receive. After all, the professional has the knowledge and the training in such esoteric skills as public speaking and counseling. Or at least that's what many assume.

The problem with this view is that God's Holy Spirit resides in every believer. Each of us has some spiritual gift that enables us to contribute to others. Ministry is a mutual, not a professional, undertaking. No one is simply a "giver." Each of us gives to others, and receives from others. Only the full-time minister with this attitude toward ministry will build a strong church or mission.

See how sensitively Paul approached the Romans. He yearned to be with them to "impart to you some spiritual gift to make you strong." He wanted to use his spiritual gifts to help them. But the exercise of his gift would not be one-way, him to them. He expected to receive as well as give. He sought a mutual relationship which would enable each to be encouraged by the other's faith.

How we need this perspective in our own ministry to others. And in Christ's superstar-studded church.

"I am obligated" Rom. 1:14-15. I was once challenged as to why I shared the Gospel with some non-Christian friends. "Why do you try to impose your faith on us?" was the rather hostile question.

I answered by asking another question. "If you were out on the highway on a stormy night, and discovered that a bridge across a deep ravine had been washed away, would you stand there with a flashlight and try to warn oncoming traffic, or not?"

Paul had a deep sense of obligation that grew out of his awareness that both Jew and Greek, apart from Jesus Christ, rushed headlong toward eternal disaster. The Christian doesn't try to "impose his faith" on others. The Christian warns others that the bridge has been washed away, in an honest effort to save them from disaster.

"It is the power of God for the salvation of everyone who believes" Rom. 1:16. I've heard the Gospel referred to as the "dynamite" of God. But the analogy really doesn't work, or reflect the concept of this text. A better analogy is to an appliance with an electric cord. Push your vacuum as hard as you can, and if it's not plugged in, it won't pick up dirt. Or stir egg whites with your electric mixer, and if it's not plugged in, no meringue. In the same way, work at saving yourself as hard as you want. But if you are not plugged into God's source of power for salvation, nothing will be gained.

The Gospel plugs us into the one and only source of salvation power. If you and I are plugged into Jesus, the power of God will save us for sure.

"The wrath of God is being revealed" Rom. 1:18. In the ancient world the familiar phrase, the "wrath of God," indicated God's indignant response to human impiety or transgression. In other New Testament passages God's wrath is His righteous and necessary response to sinners, expressed in His condemnation of their

Martin Luther and John Wesley, two of church history's towering figures, came to Christ through Romans 1:17. Through this verse each realized that God's righteousness is obtained by faith, not by human effort or merit. Through their influence millions have claimed God's righteousness, and made it their own "by faith from first to last."

acts. Here the emphasis is on moral corruption in society as the operation of a present divine judgment on sin.

We need look no farther than today's movies and newspapers to see what Paul meant. In our area the owner of a little restaurant was beaten and killed by a neighbor who stole frozen food. Just a few days before the owner had given the killer food for his hungry baby. In St. Petersburg a federal judge was arrested for drug use and committing sex acts with teenagers. The police found videos he had made. Every day seems to bring at least one story of child sexual or physical abuse. And every day TV or the movies advertise another feature glorifying sex and violence.

With no anchor of commitment to God and His laws, society becomes more and more corrupt. The media's "right" to corrupt and show corruption leads inexorably to the further breakdown of society. And no one understands what is happening or why.

What is happening is just what Paul described. A society which has turned its back on God is seeing "the wrath of God . . . being revealed from heaven against all the godlessness and wickedness of men."

"What may be known about God is plain to them" Rom. 1:18-20. Paul's point is that the universe is like a radio station, which from creation has sent out its message about God. What's more, God created human beings with a built-in radio receiver! We human beings actually hear the message. Only by "suppress[ing] the truth"—turning down our built-in radio till the message is only whisper loud—can man avoid the obvious truth that God exists, and that He is greater than the things He has made.

No human being ever born has been without a witness to the truth of God. The only explanation for man's failure to turn to God is sin (see DEVOTIONAL).

"God gave them over . . . to sexual impurity" Rom. 1:18-32. Commentators debate whether Paul was giving us a historical or psychological profile of our race. Yet the pattern is clear. Those who abandon God turn to false objects of worship and their society becomes more and more corrupt morally. In time, "Although they know God's righteous decree that those who do such things deserve death, they not only continue to do these very things but also approve of those who practice them" (v. 32).

It's significant that Paul devotes two of the eight verses describing moral corruption to homosexuality. Our society's present drive to validate homosexual behavior as an acceptable "alternate lifestyle" places modern America squarely in Romans 1:32.

▶ DEVOTIONAL
Holding Hands
(Rom. 1:18-32)

I must admit that I grinned Monday night as I watched my youngest son coming up the walk toward Capio's restaurant. He was holding hands with Liz, a 3rd-grade teacher he met at his church's youth group. Not that Tim's all that young. The occasion was his 27th birthday. It was just nice to see him, good-looking but very shy, walking hand-in-hand with an attractive and very nice girl.

Actually, holding hands is a pretty good image of the response God wants when He reveals Himself to us. When we catch a glimpse of God, we should be attracted to Him, and reach out. In Paul's words we should automatically find ourselves glorifying Him as God and being thankful.

But Romans 1 describes a totally different reaction. Instead of reaching for God's hand, as Tim did for Liz's, mankind reacted as if God were a hot iron. When brushing up against God, the natural man jerks away! Again in Paul's words, they supressed the truth. And rather than turn to God, they turned away, so that "their thinking became futile and their foolish hearts were darkened" (v. 21). What followed the rejection of God was idolatry, immorality, and wickedness of every kind.

Why does Paul launch his exploration of righteousness with this description of our race? For a very simple but important reason. He doesn't want anyone to think man lacks righteousness because God has been holding out on us, or even because of the wicked deeds men do. Mankind lacks righteousness because all men are sinners by nature. And the proof is that when God revealed Himself to man, man jerked his hand away.

Tim and Liz reach out naturally for each other's hand. They feel an affinity, a warmth of affection. Man's rejection of a loving and righteous God is unmistakable proof that human beings are lost and in sin. If they felt any affinity with God, they would respond to Him with warmth. Only the power of God flowing through the Gospel can change man's heart, and enable us to respond to God's great love.

Personal Application

Reach out your heart's hand to God today.

Quotable

"By nature I was too blind to know Him, too proud to trust Him, too obstinate to serve Him, too base-minded to love Him."—John Newton

---

OCTOBER 1 *Reading 274*
NO ONE RIGHTEOUS
Romans 2–3

> *"No one will be declared righteous in His sight by observing the Law; rather through the Law we become conscious of sin" (Rom. 3:20).*

All have sinned. So all are eligible for the salvation won by Jesus for sinners.

Background

Law. "Law" is one of the most complex concepts in Scripture. The Hebrew Torah may refer to the Pentateuch, to the entire Old Testament, to the Ten Commandments, to the whole body of God's requirements for Israel, and to the way of life adopted by the covenant community. The Greek *nomos,* used here by Paul, has these meanings and more. So as we approach each section of Romans it's important to ask what Paul meant when he spoke of the "law." In Romans 2 and 3 the basic meaning of "law" is "God's revealed requirements for righteous living." Later in Romans the meaning of "law" will shift subtly, and often. Here, however, we need only keep in mind the "revealed standards" aspect of God's moral law.

Overview

God alone is competent to judge (2:1-4), and He judges Jew and Gentile on the basis of truth (vv. 5-11). Gentiles sin against their conscience (vv. 12-16). Jews boasted of possessing God's Law (vv. 17-20), but law is of no value to those who break it (vv. 21-29). Those entrusted with the words of God must respond with faith (3:1-8). Yet Scripture shows that no human being is righteous (vv. 9-18). Thus the law's intent is to make man conscious of sin, not to be an instrument of salvation (vv. 19-20). Through faith in Christ's blood we are given a righteousness apart from the law (vv. 21-26). Jew and Gentile are saved by faith (vv. 27-31).

Understanding the Text

"You are condemning yourself" Rom. 2:1-3. One of the hardest things we have to learn is that when we point a finger at others, we point four at ourselves!

That's what Paul said here. We look at another person's actions, and we say, "That's wrong." And as soon as we do, we admit that moral standards exist. After all, we used some standard to determine he or she was "wrong"! So anyone who judges others, and we all do, says in effect, "It's right to judge. Standards do exist."

Of course, once judgment is introduced, our own actions become subject to examination. And when God measures our actions, He uses a more demanding standard than we possibly could: truth.

You might try that on a friend who pretends, as many do these days, that morality is personal and relative. Such folks will tell you, "What I do may be wrong for you, but it's all right for me." Well, if you ever hear a moral relativist condemn any action, say, "Gotcha! You just condemned yourself." And then explain. By admitting that moral standards exist, that person made himself subject to judgment. By God.

"God's kindness leads you toward repentance" Rom. 2:4-5. The next question folks are likely to ask is, if God judges sin, why doesn't He do something about the real bad guys? Paul's answer to this is a stunner.

If He did something about the child abusers and rapists right now, He'd have to do something right now about you! God is holding back Judgment Day to give people a chance to repent. God's failure to zap people when they sin isn't evidence of His disinterest. It's evidence of His kindness and love.

How glad you and I can be that the Lord waited for us. Judgment Day will come. Let's pray that before it does, many sinners will respond to the kindness of God and come to know the Lord.

"Persistence in doing good" Rom. 2:6-11. Paul isn't suggesting that doing good will get anyone to heaven. He's just making it clear that knowing good isn't enough. God judges what we do, without showing favoritism to the Jew or the Gentile.

The philosopher Plato assumed that if a person knew the good, he would be sure to do it. It doesn't take long to show how foolish that notion is. Just try for three days to do only what you know is good and right. And see how long before the gap between knowing and doing appears.

It's a fun challenge to pose to a person who claims he or she doesn't need salvation. After a couple of days of trying to do only what he judges to be right and good, suggest he read Romans 2:7-8.

"They are a law for themselves" Rom. 2:12-16. What if a person says, "God's not fair. There are people all over the world who don't even know what His standards are."

Paul's answer was that God bends over backward to be fair. Those who don't know God's standards "are a law for themselves." Every society and every individual has standards. They may not be God's standards. But they are standards—and they fall into the same categories as do the standards expressed in Moses' Law. There are sexual standards. There are standards governing how others should be treated. There are standards about work and payment. And so on.

So, just to be fair, God is willing to judge men by their own standards, not His! It's fair. But people still don't have a chance. Even using the lowest of human standards, all have sinned! Every person's conscience accuses him or her of falling short not just once, but many times. If we were completely honest with ourselves, and evaluated our own actions by truth, every one of us would confess, "I have sinned."

"You . . . brag about your relationship to

God" Rom. 2:17-29. Paul knew that any Jewish reader of his letter would argue that a distinction should be made between Jews and Gentiles. What Paul said about folks being sinners might fit the Romans and the Greeks and the Scythians, and citizens of the good old U.S.A. But it doesn't fit the chosen people!

So Paul took a look at the basis of the brag. Yes, Israel knew God's will and even approved of it. But the issue is, did the Jew do God's will?

Circumcision, that sign of membership in God's covenant people, doesn't help a person who breaks the Law. And uncircumcision doesn't hurt the person who keeps it. What God cares about is the heart, and a person's personal relationship not with the Law but with Him (see DEVOTIONAL).

"God's faithfulness" Rom. 3:1-8. God chose Israel, and generation after generation proved faithless. Did God fail? Not at all. God kept His promise and all who believed experienced His blessing. Don't think if someone fails to respond to the Gospel that God has failed. God faithfully keeps His promise and welcomes all who come to Him by Jesus.

"What shall we conclude then?" Rom. 3:9-18 Paul showed by argument that no one is righteous, and that all have sinned. Now he proved it, by quoting Scripture.

Like D.L. Moody, we should be ready to say, "God said it. I believe it. That settles it." When God has spoken, there is no more to say.

"Through the Law we become conscious of sin" Rom. 3:19-20. Some folks think of the Law as a ladder to climb, so we can approach God. It's not. The Law is a mirror to look in, so we can see ourselves, and realize how much we need God to approach us in Jesus.

"God presented Him as a sacrifice of atonement" Rom. 3:21-26. The NIV translation here is weak, for the Greek *hilaserion* means not atonement but a "sacrifice of propitiation." The sacrifice of Jesus satisfied the just requirements of our holy God. Jesus died not just to cover our sins, but to pay for them.

In that great act which satisfied the claims of justice once and for all, God Himself was shown to be righteous. He did not just "overlook" sin. He imposed the penalty sin demands. But He imposed it on His own Son instead of on you and me.

At last God is displayed as just in forgiving the sins of those who lived in the past—and in forgiving our sins. Even those we will commit in the future.

How great God is. And how beyond imagination His love.

"We uphold the Law" Rom. 3:27-31. How wonderful this principle of faith. It excludes boasting, for we are saved by God, not by anything we do. It opens the door of salvation to Gentile as well as Jew, for any human being who hears can believe. And it puts Law in its rightful place, not as a means of salvation, but as a revelation of the righteous standards of God.

We believe in Law, and in righteousness. But we do not believe that keeping God's Law can save, or make us righteous within. For that we look to Christ, and to Him alone.

▶DEVOTIONAL
Halfway Christians
(Rom. 2:25–3:20)

In early American colonies founded by religious groups, the vote was often reserved for believers. But as new generations came along, all too often grandsons and granddaughters were not converted. How could a way be found for these folks to vote—and thus keep the wealth and power in the hands of established families?

The answer was the "halfway covenant." God, the theologians proposed, was committed to save the children of believers someday. So they were halfway in the church anyway. So if your parents were Christians in good standing, you could vote, even if you didn't believe in Jesus yourself.

People always seem to be looking for a "halfway" religion. The Jews of Paul's time possessed the Law and circumcision. They were God's covenant people, His chosen nation. Wasn't that good enough? In this passage Paul said no. Not only isn't it good enough; it doesn't mean a thing (2:25-29). Jews had the advantage of circumcision and knowing the words of God. But that didn't save them.

Folks today too look for a halfway kind of Christianity. My parents were good Christians. Doesn't that count? I've belonged to my church, the "true church," since I was a child. Doesn't that count? I tithe. How about counting that?

Well, having Christian parents and being in church all our lives is certainly an advantage. But it doesn't take us even halfway to salvation.

Paul tells us why. Jews and Gentiles alike are all in the grip of sin (3:9). As the Scripture says, "There is no one righteous, not even one" (v. 10). The only thing that counts, the only thing that can save us, is breaking the grip of sin. And neither Mom and Dad, our racial heritage, or our church membership can do that.

How glad we can be that Jesus Christ takes us all the way, not just halfway, to God. By Jesus' death and resurrection, and through faith in Him, we become Chrstians indeed.

All the way Christians.

The only way.

Personal Application

Count on nothing but Jesus to save you.

Quotable

"The Gospel is Good News. But Jesus never said it was easy news. The central truth of the cross is death before life, repentance before reward. Before His Gospel can be the Good News of redemption, it must be the bad news of the conviction of sin."—Charles Colson

OCTOBER 2 *Reading 275*

ABRAHAM'S FAITH

Romans 4

> *"The words, 'It was credited to him,' were written not for him alone, but also for us, to whom God will credit righteousness—for us who believe in Him who raised Jesus our Lord from the dead" (Rom. 4:23).*

From the very beginning, righteousness has been a gift, received by faith.

Overview

Abraham serves as a test case, to prove Paul's thesis that righteousness is a gift received by faith (4:1-3). Neither works (vv. 4-8) nor circumcision (vv. 9-12) nor Law (vv. 13-15) have anything to do with forgiveness of sin (vv. 16-17). Righteousness is credited to all who have an Abrahamlike faith in the God who raised Jesus from the dead (vv. 18-25).

Understanding the Text

"Abraham, our forefather, discovered in this matter" Rom. 4:1-3. Paul turned to the towering figure of Abraham, and proposed he be used as a test case. Since the Jewish people acknowledged Abraham as the father (source) of their race, in Hebrew thought he would set the pattern for his descendants' relationship with God.

Abraham was an admirable man. He risked all in obedience to God. But the biblical text also reports his sins. So the Old Testament says God "credited" his faith to him "as righteousness." If Abraham had to be given a righteousness he did not possess, and if faith was credited to his account as righteousness, then from the very beginning the key to salvation has been faith—and nothing else. In their teaching on salvation Old and New Testaments are one.

You and I who depend solely on Jesus Christ for salvation are one with that unbroken line of saints extending back, even beyond the cross. We are members of history's grandest order: the order of those who have caught a glimpse of the goodness of God, and who believe Him completely worthy of our trust.

"Justified" Rom. 4:1. At God's Lighthouse Mission in Manhattan the men who attended services in the '50s were drilled nightly in Bible verses and in a particular definition of "justified." Justified, they were taught to repeat, means "just as if I had never sinned in the sight of God."

Actually the Greek verb, *dikaioo,* means to be acquitted, or to be pronounced righteous. It's not "just as if I had never sinned." It means "just as if I had lived as perfect a life as Jesus did!"

Once, when my normal green-tinted sunglasses were lost, I put on a rose-colored pair. And everything I saw through them was rose colored too. Justification is a little like this. God sees you and me through Christ-colored glasses. When God looks at the person who believes in His Son He sees Jesus Himself.

Never hesitate to come freely to God, whatever your need. As you approach, God sees you as His dearly beloved Son.

"Credited to him as righteousness" Rom. 4:3. This is another of several key theological terms in this chapter. The Greek word is *logizomai.* A common word in New Testament times, it meant "to make an entry in the account book."

The *Expository Dictionary of Bible Words* (Zondervan) says, "As sinners, you and I have no righteousness that would be acceptable to God. But God has given His Word of promise. When we respond to Him in faith, against our name in His account book He makes an entry that says in effect, 'This person is righteous in My sight!' Our faith has been credited to us as righteousness" (p. 203).

Some might complain that this concept of salvation is too crude. But that same person, if he went to his bank and found that someone had credited his account with the gift of 10 million dollars, wouldn't complain about "crude." He'd more likely shout for joy! As we do, knowing that in Christ God has credited to us something far more precious than worldly wealth.

"God who justifies the wicked" Rom. 4:4-8. There's so much packed in these few verses. But most important perhaps is a unique vision of God.

I remember a student of mine in grad school when I taught at Wheaton. He was always friendly and most ingratiating. Later he taught at Moody Bible Institute evening school—and his students were very upset. When he taught he was rude, always putting them down and ridiculing any idea that didn't match his own views. What a revelation of character. You can tell a lot about people by seeing how they treat those who are subordinate to them.

What a revelation of God's character, this teaching of justification by faith. We human beings are not only subordinate, but we've rebelled actively against Him. Yet God's response is to offer us a matchless gift: to justify the wicked, and credit sinners with righteousness.

How blessed we are to have, and to know, such a God!

"Is this blessedness only for the circumcised?" Rom. 4:9-13 The Jews claimed Abraham as the father of their race. Abraham had received the covenant promises which, transmitted from generation to generation, guaranteed Israel its place as God's chosen people. It would seem then, that Jesus and justification were Jewish by right. How could Paul defend his missionary work among the Gentiles?

In the Old Testament circumcision, the cutting off of the flap of skin which covers the tip of the male penis, was introduced as a sign of God's covenant with Abraham (Gen. 17). But, Paul said, this came after God announced Abraham was justified by faith (15:6). It followed, then, that justification by faith did not depend on a person having a previous covenant relationship with God. So justification by faith is available to all!

God doesn't set any preconditions on salvation. We don't have to clean up our act first. We don't have to join any particular church or group. We don't have to beg, or even pray. All we need to do is what Abraham did: trust God's promise. The blessedness of forgiveness of sins is ours, and righteousness is credited to our account.

"Where there is no law there is no transgression" Rom. 4:13-15. We have a new puppy, a miniature schnauzer named Mitzi. Like most pups, when Mitzi was young she had "accidents," and went to the bathroom on the floor. As soon as she got old enough, we began to train Mitzi. We made it very clear that going to the bathroom indoors is wrong.

This morning she slipped off into a bedroom and left a (thankfully dry!) pile on the floor. As soon as I saw her coming out of the room, her ears went back, and she began to slink—the image of guilt. She'd been taught not to do her jobs indoors. My few swats with a newspaper were accepted as just punishment.

That's about what Paul's saying here about law. Don't count on law to save you. Law introduces transgression. Mitzi was doing her jobs indoors with a perfectly clear conscience—before she was taught not to. Now that "no" has been introduced, she still does her jobs indoors sometimes. But now she's guilty of transgressing a rule, and she knows it! The law didn't change her behavior to any great extent. But it surely did make her realize her errors.

We can't look to law as a way of salvation. Law simply marks out the things we do by nature as sin—and makes us feel guilty when we realize that, even knowing the law, we still do wrong.

"That it may be by grace and may be guaranteed" Rom. 4:16-18. Why didn't God let us at least try to earn salvation? Why not, say, let us do 25 percent, and let Him supply the other 75 percent? Or, if that's too much, do 20 percent? Or 15 percent?

Paul had an important answer. Because if anything depended on you and me, there could be no guarantee. Even the Israelite descendants of Abraham, who were given a head start by receiving Moses' Law, would have no guarantee of salvation. The issue would remain forever in doubt—at least from a human point of view.

From God's point of view, of course, we have all sinned and fallen short. No one can contribute even 1 percent of that absolute goodness God's holiness demands He require. But that's irrelevant to Paul's point here. Salvation rests on God's gracious promise alone. Since it all depends on God, our salvation is guaranteed.

▶DEVOTIONAL
Abraham's Faith
(Rom. 4:18-25)

I once read a science fiction story in which the crew of a spaceship suddenly found itself behind windowless, doorless metal walls. Food was regularly passed in, seeming to slide through the walls themselves. Days and weeks went by, and the crew could find no way out.

Suddenly one of the crew laughed aloud, and explained. Their captivity must be a test devised by an alien civilization. The walls, which seemed so real to touch and sight, weren't there at all. They were illusions. If only the crew would believe—really believe—that the walls were unreal, they could walk out of their cage.

It was very much like this for Abraham. He was 100 years old. His wife, Sarah, was 90. She'd ceased menstruation long before. To every human sense, an impenetrable barrier existed between Abraham and the fulfillment of God's amazing promise that he and Sarah would soon have a son. Abraham examined these medical facts. He fully understood the impossibility. And he ignored it. He ignored the facts because he was "fully persuaded that God had power to do what He had promised." And it was this kind of faith, that saw God as the ultimate reality, that moved Abraham to trust God's promise despite its patent impossibility.

For you and me, faith is not really belief against all evidence. We have evidence that Scripture is trustworthy. We have the testimony of untold numbers of persons who have become Christians and tell of inner transformation and peace. We have proof of life after death in the resurrection of Jesus. But the basic nature of faith remains the same. We hear God's word of promise. And we are fully persuaded that He has power to do for us all that He says He will. Like Abraham, we commit ourselves to the Lord, and receive righteousness as the gift of our loving God.

Personal Application

"Faith" is committing ourselves completely to God.

Quotable

"Tell me Your name," I challenged Christ.
"Were You a prophet, saint supreme?
Did You wear true flesh and blood?
Are You that which we call God?
Or but a hope, a sigh,
A thing compacted of man's dream?"

"I will declare Myself," said Christ,
"When you confess your name and station."

Easy terms. I thought and thought
But still the sum of me as nought.
"A dying sinner, I."

And straight He told His name, "Salvation."—Anna Bunston de Bary

OCTOBER 3 *Reading 276*

LIFE IN CHRIST

Romans 5

> *"For if, by the trespass of the one man, death reigned through that one man, how much more will those who receive God's abundant provision of grace and of the gift of righteousness reign in life through the one Man, Jesus Christ" (Rom. 5:17).*

Life or death do not just lie at the end of two pathways. They are the two pathways.

Overview

Justified by faith, we have peace and joy (5:1-5). This is all because of Christ, who died for us sinners (vv. 6-8) and who lives to maintain our new harmony with God (vv. 9-11). As the sin of one man, Adam, doomed our race to death (vv. 12-14), so the gift of one Man, Jesus Christ, overflows to bring life to all who believe (vv. 15-19). In Christ grace reigns, and eternal life is ours (vv. 20-21).

Understanding the Text

"Peace with God" Rom. 5:1-2. The very first benefit of the believer's new relationship with God that Paul mentioned was "peace."

As I wrote this, the Berlin Wall that isolated East and West Germany began to go down. Hundreds of thousands of Germans crossed once impassable barriers to visit relatives in the West that they hadn't seen for nearly 30 years. But even as the wall began to go down, there was no guarantee of peace. No guarantee that complete harmony between the deeply divided East and West will ever be restored.

Paul exclaimed that we have "peace with God." Not only has the wall that sin created between us gone down, but we now pass freely into once forbidden territory, knowing that a permanent harmonious relationship between us and the Lord has been established. Paul said we "have gained access" (v. 2). We now stand securely within the circle of God's grace (v. 2). The two Germanys are uneasy and uncertain about the future; we are filled with joy, for our future is sure.

"We rejoice in the hope" Rom. 5:2. Don't let the word "hope" throw you. In our language "hope" is a word that suggests uncertainty. "I hope I'll be able to go with you," means I'd like to, but I don't know if I can. A young woman's "hope chest" was traditionally a place where she stored precious items she would use when—and if!—she married. "Hope" to us is a "maybe" kind of thing.

But it's not this way in the New Testament. In fact, it's just the opposite! Hope (*elpis*) is the settled and confident expectation that we will obtain a future good. Hope is being sure that what God has promised will be ours, even if today we only glimpse it from afar.

What a blessing to remember as we read the New Testament. Because of Jesus, we have hope. We know that we have a share in the glory of God.

"We also rejoice in our sufferings" Rom. 5:3-5. "Hope" is a word about our tomorrows. All too often "suffering" seems to be the word for our today. But Paul said that, because of our peace with God through Jesus, we even "rejoice in our sufferings."

Perspective provides the reason. A young woman experiencing the pains of childbirth still rejoices—because she knows that her suffering will give birth to a precious new life. She looks ahead, and the promise the future holds gives meaning to her present pain.

It's just this way with Christians. Knowing that we have peace with God, we are sure that our present is pregnant with promise. We experience joy in suffering because we know out of pain God will bring something good.

Paul even tells us one good our suffering will bring! Our pain will produce perseverance, and this will produce character, and character will produce hope. Through hope, that expectant gaze we fix on the future, we will find the true meaning of life.

This doesn't mean we'll have a grim life here, in exchange for a joyful future. Oh, no. It means we will have joy now as well as then. Learning to hope will save us from trying to anchor our souls on the slippery bottom of this world's riches or fame. As we put our hope in God, His Spirit will flood our hearts with a sense of His love. And this, the present experience of the love of God, will give us present joy.

"Christ died for the ungodly" Rom. 5:6-8. The unmistakable sense of God's love that floods our hearts even in suffering is a very personal, subjective kind of thing. We know we are loved. We can tell others. But how can they know that God's love is real?

Paul answered that there is objective as well as subjective evidence of the love of God. Christ's cross towers in history, casting its shadow in every century, vivid and unmistakable proof that God does love us indeed! While an unusual person might give his life to save a truly good man, Jesus Christ gave His life to save us despite the fact that we were sinners.

There may be times when you and I can't feel the love of God. But there need never be a time when we doubt it. We need only look to Calvary, and remember why Jesus died.

"We have now received reconciliation" Rom. 5:9-11. This is another of those important "theological" words of the Bible. As with most such terms, its meaning is actually quite simple. It is something like a man who wakes up, finds that his watch has stopped, and turns on the radio to learn the time. When he hears, he sets his watch by the radio time. What he's done is to "reconcile" his watch to the radio.

Through the death of Jesus, God "reset" our inner clock. Our hearts now ticking in time with His, our values match His own. We are "saved by His life," for the risen Christ lives within us, to enable us to actually live in harmony with God! Through Jesus we are saved from the wrath that spills over today as the consequences of sinful acts. Through Jesus we have this unutterable joy.

You've trusted Jesus to save you from the eternal consequences of your sins through His death. Have you trusted Him to save you in the present by His life? Trust Him, rely on the strength He provides, and you will be able at last to live a life that is truly in harmony with God.

"The gift of righteousness reign[s] in life through the one Man, Jesus Christ" Rom. 5:12-20. The whole passage contrasts Adam and Jesus, each of whom fixed the future of all living in the epoch he initiated. Adam initiated the epoch of sin, and all who descended from him have found themselves trapped in a morass of sin and death. Jesus initiated the epoch of grace, and all who trace their relationship to Christ are freed from sin, to be righteous and to live righteously.

Consider some of the differences brought out in this chapter, shown on the following chart. And rejoice. You have been adopted into the family of the Son whom God loves.

ADAM/CHRIST in Romans 5:11-21

v.	Adam	Christ	v.
12	Introduced sin, death	Introduced grace,	15
		righteousness,	17
		and life	17
16	Men condemned,	Men given righteousness	16
19	made sinners	and life, and justified	21
16	Judgment a consequence	Grace reigns as a consequence	21
17	All subject to death	Many brought to eternal life	19
19	Disobedient	Obedient	19

"Before the Law was given, sin was in the world" Rom. 5:13. When a friend of mine went through a stop sign, he got a ticket. Later he went to court and argued that the stop sign had been put up only the day before and was hard to see.

It was an interesting argument. The highway commission had determined that that particular intersection was dangerous, and that a sign should be there. My friend didn't argue about that. He even admitted going through the sign. He argued only that he wasn't guilty, because the sign was new and obscured.

Paul's point is something like this. Sin has been in the world since Adam. And because of sin, human beings have been dying since Adam, as a necessary consequence of sin is death. But people were not guilty of sin before there was a law that, "this is wrong." To be guilty of transgressing the law, law must exist, and be known.

The argument was important for reaching the Jews, who placed altogether too much importance on their possession of Moses' Law. In essence, Paul said the Jews were worse off than the Gentiles. Gentile and Jew had both suffered spiritual death as a consequence of sin. But the Jews, who had the Law and had broken it, were also guilty!

Thank God, neither death nor guilt is a problem for Christians. Jesus gives eternal life to all who believe in Him. Through Christ we are raised from death to life, freed from the present power of sin, and forgiven every violation. What a difference Jesus makes to those of us who know Him.

▶ DEVOTIONAL
Everywhere You Look
(Rom. 5:1-11)

There's an old riddle that says: What direction did the polar bear look when he turned his head to the right? To the left? And when he looked straight ahead? The answer in each case is south. He was standing on the North Pole.

It's something like this with a term we find in Romans 5:1-11. What does a Christian see if he looks back? If he looks ahead? If he looks around? Reconciliation!

Looking back, we realize that the death of Jesus has changed our condition and our heart. We have been reconciled to God, and He has transformed us from enemy to friend (v. 10). Looking ahead we see an endless future in which Christ stands by our side, till ultimately we stand by His throughout eternity (v. 9). Looking around us, we find that we experience joy in serving Jesus. We have a "now" experience of reconciliation as well.

Even the word "saved" is like this. Look back: you have been saved. Look ahead: you will be saved. Look around: you are being saved. Jesus is even now at work within to give you the power to live a holy life.

Our past, our present, and our future are all transformed because of Him. Wherever we look, everything is bright and new, and completely different, because of Jesus Christ, God's Son.

Personal Application

Let Jesus change your perspective on everything in life.

Quotable

"If you were to spend a month feeding on the precious promises of God, you would not be going about with your heads hanging down like bulrushes, complaining how poor you are; but you would lift up your heads with confidence, and proclaim the riches of His grace because you could not help it."—D.L. Moody

OCTOBER 4 *Reading 277*
FREED FROM SIN
Romans 6

> *"Count yourselves dead to sin but alive to God in Christ Jesus. Therefore do not let sin reign in your mortal body so that you obey its evil desires" (Rom. 6:11-12).*

The good news is we're no longer captives of sin. We have a choice.

Background

Sin. Romans 6–8 explores the impact of the Gospel on the individual. Paul portrayed this impact in respect to three vital issues, asking: What about sin? What about the Law? What about our mortality?

In this chapter Paul announced the believer's freedom from sin through union with Jesus. To understand Paul's teaching we need to realize that the Bible makes a distinction between sin and sins. On the one hand, sin is a state or condition. It is the corruption of human nature; the warping of the human will, emotions, and understanding. On the other hand, sins are specific acts that intentionally or unintentionally fall short of God's perfection because of our rebelliousness, our evil desires, or our failure to grasp what is right and good. The good news that Paul announced in this chapter is that through union with Jesus, we have within us the source of perfection! We no longer are limited to the choices, desires, or understanding of a corrupt nature! In Christ, we can at long last actually be, and do, good.

Paul did not teach that the old corrupt nature that expressed itself in acts of sins is gone. Not at all. Sin is still with us. But so is Jesus. And because Jesus is with us, we need no longer commit sins.

Overview

Salvation by grace through faith is no license to sin (6:1-2). By our union with Christ we died to sin and were raised to new life (vv. 3-10). We are not to permit sin to reign in our lives (vv. 11-14), but instead to offer ourselves to God as His slaves, to live holy and righteous lives (vv. 15-23).

Understanding the Text

"Shall we go on sinning so that grace may increase?" Rom. 6:1 The question was sarcastic. It was not the honest doubt of a person who wonders why, if a person knows he is going to heaven, he or she would want to live a good life. That person, with significant insight into human nature, asks, "If I didn't fear damnation, what would keep me from doing wrong?"

The questioner of verse 1 said, "If God gets so much glory out of freely forgiving sinners, then maybe you'd better keep on sinning, so God can get even more glory!" Paul's response was a shocked *me genito,* a phrase we might render "God forbid!" or "Unthinkable!" or "Never!"

Shock is an appropriate response. God has no affinity with sin at all. He forgives sinners. But with forgiveness He calls each believer to live a holy and righteous life. The ultimate evidence of God's grace is not seen in forgiveness of sin. It is displayed in the moral transformation of the sinner.

Christians are called "trophies of grace." God has won us in Christ. Up there, on His figurative shelf, we do bring Him glory. But no trophy if tarnished and dulled brings much glory to its owner. To truly reflect the glory of God's grace, we need to live lives that are polished and pure.

"[We] who were baptized into Christ" Rom. 6:2-4. Paul wasn't thinking of water baptism here. Instead he was using the word *baptizo* as a metaphor: we have been immersed in Jesus. Unlike a piece of cloth immersed in dye that it might take on its color, we have by faith plunged into Jesus and become so completely united to Him that the death He died was our death, and the resurrection life He possesses now is our life too.

Perhaps the closest modern analogy is found in "community property" states. Say a poverty-stricken young woman marries a multimillionaire. At the moment of marriage, the law considers half of all he owns hers. It is as if, legally, she had been a participant when he earned his millions. And now that they have been united in marriage she has his vast resources to draw on.

This is what Paul said about you and Jesus. When you believed in Jesus, you were united to Christ. It is as if, theologically, you hung there on the cross with Him. When Jesus died, you died. And when Jesus was raised from the dead, you too were raised! Now that you have been united by faith to Jesus, you have His vast spiritual resources to draw on. And the result? "We too may live a new life."

Next time you're tempted to sin, picture yourself immersed in Jesus. Draw freely on His resurrection power. Choose that new life that is yours!

"So that the body of sin might be rendered powerless" Rom. 6:6. Immersed in Jesus, our old self was crucified with Him. This is the basis of our ultimate freedom from sin's very presence at our resurrection. But until then, sin is all too present with us. We feel its pull; we sense it in thoughts that chase one another through our minds. But, thank God, sin though present is "rendered powerless." At last we can ignore sin's pull (see DEVOTIONAL).

As Martin Luther said, "We can't keep the birds from flying around our head. But we needn't let them build a nest in our hair!"

"Offer yourselves to God" Rom. 6:11-14. Freedom from sin has a price tag. The tag reads, "Offer yourselves to God."

From the beginning individuals have assumed that "freedom" is being able to do what a person wants to do, when he wants to do it, with no reference to anyone or anything. That idea has absolutely no correspondence with reality.

The fact is that we human beings are creatures, and as creatures we always serve some master. The master may be sin, expressing itself as a passion for wealth or power, or merely as a selfish passion for one's own way. Or the master may be God. But it is impossible for us to live without a master.

I can think of many reasons why God is a better master than sin. But one of them surely is the thing Paul mentioned in verse 23. "The wages of sin is death."

Personally, I'd much rather offer the parts of my body to God as "instruments of righteousness."

"You have been set free from sin and have become slaves to righteousness" Rom. 6:18. In a way, the Christian life is one of extreme simplicity. In every situation, ask yourself, What is the righteous thing to do?

Folks sometimes try to complicate this, and argue that they often don't know the righteous thing to do. That may be. But we nearly always know when something is the wrong thing to do!

What it boils down to is: Don't do what you know or suspect is wrong. You may not be positive a particular course of action is best. But you surely will recognize actions that are wrong.

"What benefit did you reap at that time from the things you are now ashamed of?" Rom. 6:19-23 This is a fair question. What does any person get out of sin? A momentary thrill? An instant of satisfaction? A mercurial sense of power? This is what sin offers at best—and with sin comes a sense of guilt and deep dissatisfaction. When you add endless death to the list, sin doesn't seem to pay well at all.

Righteousness pays off in holiness. That isn't highly valued by the world, but it can buy inner peace, freedom from guilt, joy, a sense of being right with God and yourself, and eternal life.

▶DEVOTIONAL
Just Don't Jump
(Rom. 6:1-14)

Donald Grey Barnhouse used to say about this passage, "When the old captain shouts, just don't jump!"

Dr. Barnhouse was a master at finding illustrations to make the most complex concepts simple and clear. We surely need that gift to help us with Romans 6. What's all this about "the body of sin" being "rendered powerless"? And "death no longer having mastery" over us? How do we explain "count yourselves dead to sin but alive to God"?

Barnhouse would say we're like the crew of a ship at sea. We took orders from our captain, body of sin. But then one day while we were still at sea, that captain was replaced, and authority passed to a new captain, God. So body of sin was rendered powerless, with no right of mastery over us at all. God is the only One we have to obey.

The trouble is, the old captain is still on board the ship, and even though he has no authority, he keeps on shouting orders. Because we're so familiar with his voice, we all too often find ourselves jumping to obey him. What we have to do, Barnhouse said, is to "count yourselves dead" to the old captain's orders, and just don't jump to obey his commands.

I always liked the illustration. Isn't it great that we don't have to jump when a sinful thought urges us on to sin? What fun to tell sin to go jump instead!

Personal Application

Resist the devil. And thumb your nose at sin.

Quotable

"We are too Christian really to enjoy sinning, and too fond of sinning really to enjoy Christianity. Most of us know perfectly well what we ought to do; our trouble is that we do not want to do it."—Peter Marshall

OCTOBER 5 *Reading 278*
FREE FROM LAW
Romans 7

> *"For when we were controlled by the sinful nature, the sin passions aroused by the Law were at work in our bodies, so that we bore fruit for death" (Rom. 7:5).*

Even Christians find God's Law hard to keep—for good reason!

Background

More on Law. Romans 7 explores the impact of the Gospel on the individual in his or her relation to "God's Law." This is one of the Bible's most difficult passages, but contains exciting truth! To understand it, we need to note that Paul uses "law" in more than one sense here.

We've earlier seen that "God's Law" is God's revelation of morally righteous standards. But here "law" is not only those standards, but also the impact of those standards on human nature. Paul is concerned not only with laws, but with the response God's commandments stimulate within us.

There's also another use of "law" in this chapter. When Paul speaks of a "law at work" within him, as in verse 21, or the "law of my mind" and the "law of sin at work in the members" (v. 23), he means not standard, but "fundamental principle." The "law of gravity" is a statement of a fundamental principle of our experience: things fall down toward earth. The "law of sin at work in my members" is also a statement of a fundamental principle of human experience: we do wrong, even when we don't want to.

In his talk about these "laws," Paul is making statements about how human nature works and does not work. What Paul says is that God's Law and human nature aren't compatible, any more than a car designed to run on gasoline is compatible with diesel fuel. God's Law may be great fuel for diesel engines. But human nature operates on gasoline.

And this leads to the issue that Paul explores in Romans 7. What is the relationship of the Gospel to a divinely given Law that, however "good" and "right" it may be, has never been able to produce righteousness in a single human heart?

Overview

Christians are free from man's obligation to keep the Law (7:1-3). We must be, if we are to live holy lives (vv. 4-6). To try to relate to God through His Law makes the Christian life a constant, losing struggle (vv. 7-20). But God in Christ rescues us from our native inability (vv. 21-25).

Understanding the Text

"The Law has authority over a man only as long as he lives" Rom. 7:1-4. The old Gospel hymn says,

> Free from the law, oh happy condition.
> Jesus has died, and there is remission.
> Cling to the cross, your burden will fall.

Christ has redeemed us, once for all.

But the Jewish reader of Romans is sure to object to that first line. How can a human being be "free from the law"?

Paul's argument was rooted in the fact of union with Christ, which he introduced in Romans 6. In a marriage the husband and wife are united as one, and as one are subject to the "law of marriage." But if one spouse dies, the other is free from the marriage law. He or she is no longer obligated to be faithful to the deceased spouse.

The Christian is united to Jesus, and as long as each lived, each was responsible to God's Law. But Jesus died on Calvary, and we "died" with Him! As a dead person is released from obligation to keep God's Law, so are we! Moreover, when Christ was raised, we became obligated to Him, not to the Law. Jesus is that "another" to whom we now belong.

Paul never suggested that we Christians aren't to live disciplined and righteous lives. He did, however, remind us that we respond, not to a written code, but to a Person. Our new and exciting obligation is to respond to Jesus, not to a list of do's and don'ts, however fitting that list may be.

"The sinful passions aroused by the Law" Rom. 7:5. This is a key to Paul's exploration of the Law and the believer, and explains why the New Testament teaches that the Christian must be freed from the Law. Law arouses man's sinful passions, and produces fruit unto death.

The idea isn't all that unfamiliar. Think of the mom who made chocolate chip cookies for a get-together with some friends. She says to her kids, "Don't touch the cookies. They're for my group, and I have just enough."

Now, any kid worth his salt is going to naturally want a chocolate chip cookie. The smell alone is enough to awaken the desire. But when Mom says, "Don't touch," somehow the odor becomes almost irresistible. Her law has even further aroused the children's cookie passion.

Law, Paul says, is like that. Somehow it stimulates man's sinful nature. And we all know it. That's why the old saying, "Forbidden fruit is sweeter," hangs on in our culture. We all realize that, somehow, the saying is true. You just can't motivate people to do what's right and good by saying, "You ought to!" or "You must!"

"We have been released from the Law so that we serve in the new way of the Spirit" Rom. 7:6. In saying that we have "died" to the Law that once bound us, Paul was saying first that we're legally free from obligation to the Law, and that Law is now irrelevant to our life in the Spirit.

My children have suffered over the years as I've used their doings in illustration after illustration. I suspect all preacher's kids have the same problem. But anyway, here I go again.

My youngest son is seeing a lovely gal named Liz. I've noticed that no one tells him, "You have to phone Liz this evening." Or, "You must take Liz out at least three times a week." Somehow their relationship isn't a matter of "have to's" or "musts" at all! What happens is that Tim wants to call and see Liz. His growing love makes rules for such things in their relationship totally irrelevant.

This is what Paul wants us to realize about our relationship with God. "Have to's" and "musts" have no relevance! We love Jesus. And love for God will move us to do willingly what no rules could compel.

"Fruit to God . . . fruit for death" Rom. 7:4-6. In a way, this paragraph is about horticulture. It describes two systems for growing fruit. And it says, you can't mix systems.

One system relies on the pronouncements of Law. But such pronouncements stimulate man's sinful nature, and the fruit produced is sin "unto death." The other relies on relationship, with the Spirit of Jesus taking the place of Law. The Spirit stimulates that resurrection life we received from Jesus, and produces fruit "to God." That fruit is exhibited in righteous acts and godly character (Gal. 5:22-23).

The sad thing is that all too many Christians try to fertilize their spiritual lives with liberal applications of Law. And then they can't understand why their Christian life seems such a burden, and failure a constant companion. What you and I

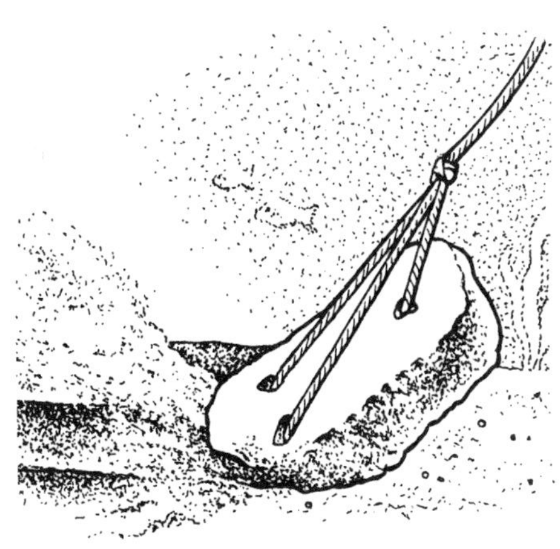

First-century seamen relied on heavy stone anchors like these to hold their vessels. These anchors were effective . . . except when the bottom was smooth and they could obtain no hold. This is what Paul said about God's Law in Romans 7. The Law in itself is holy, righteous, and good (v. 12). But human nature is so hard and smooth the anchor could not hold. The fault is not in God's Law, but in us!

need to do is to focus our heart's attention on our Lord, and hear what Scripture says to us as a loving invitation to walk with Him. When we do, our Christian life will seem exciting, and success will walk by our side.

"I would not have known what sin was except through the Law" Rom. 7:7-13. Paul talked principle and concept. Now he talked experience. How does the believer experience God's Law?

First, Law makes us aware of sin. It puts a bright, bold label on things that are wrong. That label isn't like the skull and crossbones on medicine bottles, which warns us away. It's more like the two punctures in the skin, that inform us the snake that just bit us is poisonous.

If you're struck suddenly by a hiding snake, the quick way to tell if the bite is venomous is to look at it closely. If there's a row of little marks, you're safe. But if there is the mark of two fangs, venom has already been introduced into your system. That's what God's Law did for Paul. In labeling acts sin, it caused the apostle to realize that death had already been introduced into his system.

The Law itself may be good. But it deals a fatal blow to our assumption that we are alive and well!

Don't be surprised if Law treats you this same way. It's supposed to. If you and I could make it by ourselves, we wouldn't need such reminders. By testifying to us of death, God's Law grips us firmly by the shoulders, turns us around, and points us to Jesus.

He is the source of life, for us, and for the world.

▶ DEVOTIONAL
One Too Many
(Rom. 7:14-25)

The other day I saw the TV interview of a woman who has multiple personalities. One personality is warm and loving, another childlike and petulant, a third angry and promiscuous. These personalities developed early in life and, as in all such cases, remained unaware of each other, though each controlled the woman's actions at different times.

In a way, Paul suggested that he too was a victim of multiple personalities. But he was all too aware of them! One "I" was his "sinful nature." There was nothing good about this "I." It not only kept on doing evil, it messed up the good Paul wanted and tried to do (vv. 19-20).

Then there was another "I," an "inner being" (v. 22) that passionately wanted to do good. This "I" delighted in God's Law, and responded to it. What troubled Paul was that every time the "inner being" acted, the "sinful nature" jumped right in to corrupt and spoil the good.

It's as if a person with multiple sclerosis were writing a letter. In his mind's eye he sees each word crisp and clear. But when he writes, the palsy in his hands forms almost unreadable letters, shaky and distorted. In just this way, Paul cried out in frustration; he as a believer wanted only to do good. But something inside kept spoiling his best efforts. The principle of sin and death was like another personality within him, at war with the personality that wanted honestly to serve God.

We all have one personality too many. But we do have a wonderful source of comfort. The words we form as we seek to make our very lives a love letter to God may be shaky, but God sees and welcomes our love. He knows it's not the "I" of the inner man that makes our offerings imperfect, but the "I" of the sinful nature. Just as a parent welcomes with delight the first efforts of a toddler to write his name, so God welcomes our every effort to please Him.

Someday that one personality too many will be gone. Only the "I" that delights in God and His Law will survive our resurrection. As Paul said, "Thanks be to God," for Jesus "will rescue me from this body of death" (vv. 24-25). But until then, thanks be to God for another wonderful gift.

God doesn't demand that we be perfect as we seek to please Him. He only asks that we love Him—and that we try.

Personal Application

Don't let failures dampen your love for God, or your eagerness to please Him.

Quotable

"God uses failure, sickness, breakdown, sin, personal tragedy, and sorrow to reduce His people to usefulness. Unless the servant of God learns to depend utterly on God and to forsake self-dependence of any kind, he or she remains too strong to be of much value."—Robert C. Girard

OCTOBER 6 *Reading 279*
FREED FROM MORTALITY
Romans 8

> *"And if the Spirit of Him who raised Jesus from the dead is living in you, He who raised Christ from the dead will also give life to your mortal bodies through His Spirit, who lives in you" (Rom. 8:11).*

Despite our weaknesses, with the Spirit's help we can live holy lives.

Background

Mortal bodies. Paul's exposition of the Gospel's impact on individuals examines three vital issues: sin, Law, and mortality ("flesh"). Union with Christ in His death frees us from the domination of our sinful nature, so that we can offer ourselves to God as "slaves to righteousness" (6:18). Union with Christ in His death also legally frees us from man's obligation to God's Law. This is important, as Law stimulates the sin nature and corrupts even the good we seek to do. We are to respond to Jesus out of love, not obligation (Rom. 7).

Now Paul explored the problem of our mortality. Human beings are but flesh, *sarx.* As a theological term *sarx* stands for all that is weak and corrupt in human nature. In effect Paul asked, how can a mere mortal, whose essential being is tainted by corruption, live a godly life? His joyful answer leaps from the pages of Romans 8. God has given us His Holy Spirit! If we respond to the Spirit within us rather than the *sarx* within, the righteous requirements of that Law we could not keep will be "fully met in us!" God's Spirit vitalizes us, even in our present mortal state, so that we can live righteous and holy lives!

Then Paul went on. We are bound to our mortality now. But in the resurrection we will be fully liberated, along with the whole creation! And, until then, we can be sure of one thing. No one, and nothing, can ever separate us from the love of Christ.

Overview

The dynamic principle of new life in Christ overwhelms the principle of indwelling sin, enabling us to live righteously (8:1-4). If we as sons of God choose to live in harmony with the Spirit, not the flesh, the Spirit's resurrection power vitalizes us even in our present mortal state (vv. 5-17). In the future our bodies, with all creation, will be transformed (vv. 18-25). Till then we live in the love of the Spirit who prays for us (vv. 26-27), the Father who provides for us (vv. 28-33), and Christ who guards us (vv. 34-39).

Understanding the Text

"In order that the righteous requirements of the Law might be fully met in us" Rom. 8:1-4. So many Christians feel condemned to fail-

ure. They try. But somehow they keep on failing. The life of many Christians is like the god in Greek mythology who was condemned to roll a giant stone up a mountainside—only to see it tumble down into the valley every time he got near the top. What a condemnation this would be. Always to try. And always to fail. But Paul's message was, "no condemnation!" Jesus didn't die that we might be left frustrated and hopeless. God has introduced a vital new principle of life into our personalities, which frees us from bondage to the "sin living in me" that Paul acknowledged with such agony in Romans 7. In Jesus, we are freed to live righteous lives.

That's what's so special about Romans 8. It gives us hope. And it tells us how to draw on God's own resources to experience spiritual success, not failure.

"Righteous requirements of the Law . . . fully met in us" Rom. 8:4. The little Quaker lady was complimented by a younger woman, who was amazed at her self-control when provoked. No matter what, the little lady seemed to remain sweet and patient. She received the compliment, nodded, and then said, "But thee should know I'm shouting inside."

When Paul said that the righteous requirements of the Law are "fully met" in the believer, he was making an amazing statement. Rightly understood, the Law does not just speak to what we do and say "outside." It calls for us to be changed "inside" as well. A sweet and patient voice while "shouting inside" has not "fully met" the righteousness God requires.

Law itself can never make us good. But God can! The death of Christ, and the gift of God's Spirit, are intended to make you and me different inside and out.

"Controlled not by the sinful nature but by the Spirit" Rom. 8:5-9a. So many illustrations have been offered to clarify what Paul was saying here. Some speak of a tug-of-war between the Spirit and the flesh. Whichever side you choose to pull with will win. Some suggest a teeter-totter. The sinful nature is on one end, the Holy Spirit on the other. And you tip the balance.

These, and other illustrations, make a common point. There's a competition between God and man's mortal, sinful nature. The Spirit urges us to go in one direction and the flesh urges us to go another. And, each of us can choose. We can choose to follow the Spirit's leading, to pull with the Spirit, to add our weight to His side of the teeter-totter. Or we can choose to go the way of the flesh.

How gracious God is. Even now, He does not say "You must." That would be Law. Instead He reminds us that, because of Christ, and in the power the Spirit gives, "You can!"

"He who raised Christ from the dead will also give life to your mortal bodies" Rom. 8:9b-11. "You can!" is one of the hardest things for a Christian to truly believe. We're so used to failure that down deep many of us are convinced, "Well, I can't!"

When that conviction overwhelms you, remember the nature of God's power. God's power, exercised by the Holy Spirit, raised Jesus from the dead. That same power, exercised by the Holy Spirit, is fully capable of taking your mortality—your deadness—and making you live! And, this same verse says, His Spirit "lives in you."

Of course "I can't." But because God's Spirit lives in every true believer (v. 9b), you can!

To approach any spiritual challenge with the confidence that "I can" isn't presumption, it's faith. Faith that God's Spirit living in you will give you the power you need, despite your mortality, to succeed rather than fail.

Actually, this is how you and I add our weight to that inner tug-of-war, or climb on the Spirit's side of that teeter-totter. We say, "I can," confident that the Spirit will act in and through us.

And then, we do!

"You received the Spirit of sonship" Rom. 8:12-17. Paul concluded with a paragraph that emphasized consequences, obligation, and resources. The consequences of a choice to respond to the prompting of the sin nature are to live in the realm of death and defeat (v. 13). Our obligation and our resources are rooted in our new relationship to God.

When a person was adopted under Roman law, all earlier obligations were broken, and he became responsible only to his new father. He owed the adoptive father complete obedience, and everything he possessed was under the adoptive father's control. But as a child, he was now an heir of his new father. And under Roman law, an heir was considered to possess his inheritance even before the father died. In other words, all the resources of the father were, through the father, available to the child.

When we received the "Spirit of sonship" (literally, of "adoption"), the authority of the old nature over us was broken completely. We became obligated to no one but God, our new Father. And, as His heirs now, all the resources of God Himself are available to you and me.

No wonder Paul shouted, "There is now no condemnation" (v. 1). Because Christ died for us, because the Father adopted us, because the Spirit is given to us, there is now no question. We can live a victorious Christian life!

All we need to do is to believe. And, acting on faith, to step out and to do.

"Creation waits in eager expectation" Rom. 8:18-25. Still working with the theme of mortality, Paul noted that the entire creation has been affected by man's sin and is subject to decay. One day, when our redemption is complete, and our bodies, like our spirits, have been renewed, creation itself will be fully redeemed.

Till then, mortality means suffering. For us, and for nature. We know that our sufferings are insignificant when compared to the glory that awaits us. But till then, we can only look ahead, confident and eager, waiting for Jesus to return.

"In all things God works for the good of those who love Him" Rom. 8:28. The verse doesn't say that everything that happens to us is good. There's far too much pain in the world for that to be true. What Paul said was that God is at work in all things. He redeems even our suffering, using it to do us good.

"He also predestined to be conformed to the likeness of His Son" Rom. 8:29. Christians have argued over predestination. Did God simply know ahead of time what individuals would do? Or did God cause individuals to act as they did? Are we saved because of our faith, or did we believe because we are chosen?

This passage won't resolve questions like these. Why? Because it says we who believe are "predestined to be conformed to the likeness of His Son." God has determined that believers will become like Jesus.

The great contribution of this verse is the perspective it provides on the teaching that God works in all things "for the good of those who love Him." It tells us what God's "good" is: Likeness to Jesus.

What a wonderful thought. And what an exciting destiny. God wants us to be like Jesus. And He is committed to transform us into Christ's likeness. Even suffering, if it helps me learn Christlikeness, is a blessing from the Lord.

▶ DEVOTIONAL
Until Then
(Rom. 8:26-39)

Waiting is so hard. I remember as a child, sitting on the front porch, waiting. We were going up to Cedar Lake, and I could hardly stand the thought that the trip was three whole days away. And there was nothing I could do to make the time pass faster.

Waiting for Jesus is especially hard as we sense our vulnerability and mortality. We may even feel there's nothing we can do until then. When we do feel that way, it's helpful to remember that, until then, God is active for us!

God the Holy Spirit, sensitive to our mortality, "helps us in our weakness." The Spirit prays urgently for us and with us (vv. 26-27).

God the Father, who has adopted us, in that act committed Himself to us totally. God is for us: He gives us all things now, and will give us the glory that is assured in His initial choice and call (vv. 28-33).

God the Son, who died for us, is praying for and loving us. We sense that love, whatever our hardships. In everything we know with Paul that "neither death nor life, neither angels nor demons, neither the present nor the future, nor any powers, neither height nor depth, nor anything else in all creation, will be able to separate us from the love of God that is in

Christ Jesus our Lord" (vv. 38-39).

So if waiting seems hard, and a little frustrating because there doesn't seem to be anything you can do, remember. Until then, God is active for you. Until then, the Spirit prays, the Father provides, and the Son protects you.

And, until then, you can live your life here on earth for God.

Personal Application

Until then, serve the One who loves you.

Quotable

"The strength for our conquering and our victory is drawn continually from Christ. The Bible does not teach that sin is completely eradicated from Christians in this life, but it does teach that sin shall no longer reign over you. The strength and power of sin have been broken. The Christian now has resources available to live above and beyond this world. The Bible teaches that whosoever is born of God does not practice sin. It is like the little girl who said that when the devil came knocking with a temptation, she just sent Jesus to the door."—Billy Graham

OCTOBER 7 *Reading 280*

HAS GOD FAILED?

Romans 9–10

> *"It is not as though God's Word had failed. For not all who are descended from Israel are Israel" (Rom. 9:6).*

God's choice leaves room for man to decide.

Background

God's sovereignty. Two things are involved in this concept, His freedom to act and the fulfillment of His purposes. Freedom to act means that God is able to do as He chooses, without His choices being limited in any way by the actions of other beings, or by circumstances. Nothing can thwart God's will.

The fulfillment of God's purposes means that what God decrees will come to pass. Again, no actions by other beings, and no circumstances, can thwart God's will.

The problem is, the rejection of Jesus by the Jewish people seems to do the unthinkable, and to actually thwart God's will, so that His purpose for Israel has not been achieved! It is this vast issue, not the question of individual predestination, that Paul took up in Romans 9–11. He argued that the Jewish rejection of Jesus had not thwarted God at all. Instead, that rejection fitted patterns found in the Old Testament, and revealed a purpose more complex than believers often suppose.

It's important to remember as we read these chapters that the issue is not one of individual predestination to salvation. Anyone tempted to read this issue into the text can find some comfort in Paul's observation that "not all the Israelites accepted the Good News." The absolute freedom of God to act need not limit man's freedom to accept or to reject the Good News about Jesus. Our freedom to choose does in no way limit God's sovereignty, for God has freely decided to extend the Gospel invitation to all—and to permit each to respond as he or she will.

Overview

Had God failed because His promises to Israel had not produced faith in Christ? (9:1-6) No, for sacred history shows only some in the family line had been chosen (vv. 7-13), though all are within the framework of God's purpose (vv. 14-23). As for Gentiles, God has always intended to show grace to them as well as to the Jews (vv. 24-29). Israel misunderstood God's righteousness (v. 30–10:4), which is gained by faith rather than by Law (vv. 5-13). The failure of Israel to believe is not God's failure, but Israel's own (vv. 14-21).

Understanding the Text

"I have great sorrow and unceasing anguish" Rom. 9:1-5. Paul, despite the view of some, was certainly not anti-Semitic. He identified strongly with his race, and he

loved his Jewish people intensely. Paul was fully aware that God had poured out many blessings on Israel, and that these were evidence of God's committed love (vv. 4-5).

While "Christian anti-Semitism" has often cropped up in history, and raises an ugly head in our own country today, to place "Christian" and "anti-Semitism" together is a contradiction in terms! How can a person who loves God not love the people loved by the Lord?

"It is not as though God's Word had failed" Rom. 9:6. This verse is the key to unlock the argument of Romans 9–11. It is also a key to our own peace of mind.

All too often we pray and witness to folks who simply don't seem to understand. Or who refuse to respond. That may make us feel like failures. What did we do wrong? Why didn't they hear?

Paul reminds us that God's Word does not fail. Ever. Isaiah 55:11 says, "So is My word that goes out from My mouth: It will not return to Me empty, but will accomplish what I desire and achieve the purpose for which I sent it." Even if a person willfully refuses to respond, the failure is not in the Word, but in him or her.

So share Christ with a sense of confidence. God's Word does, and will, succeed.

"Through Isaac that your offspring will be reckoned" Rom. 9:6-13. One of several basic mistakes made by first-century Jews was to assume that physical descent from Abraham guaranteed a person God's favor. How does history show this was a mistake? It records the fact that Isaac inherited the covenant promises, while Ishmael did not. Both were physical descendants of Abraham.

If one wanted to argue that Ishmael had a slave as a mother, Paul pointed to Jacob and Esau. They had the same mother and father. But only Jacob inherited the promise. Physical descent is no guarantee of divine favor. Thus the failure of first-century Israelites to believe in Jesus did not indicate that God's Word had failed.

One of my professors at the University of Michigan was a Christian who had an atheist son. He kept reminding the son that it didn't matter. God, my professor thought, was obligated to save the children of believers, so his son would believe in Christ one day, no matter what. The view may have brought my professor comfort. But it was wrong, nevertheless. God was not under obligation to all physical descendants of Abraham and Isaac, and no child of believers is guaranteed salvation today. That fact shouldn't discourage us, however. It should encourage us—to pray for our children, to share with them, to teach and love them while they're with us in the home. Through our love God's love can be made real.

"Jacob I loved, but Esau I hated" Rom. 9:13. Don't misunderstand Paul's point. He used the language of inheritance to drive home his lesson, that Jacob was chosen to inherit the covenant promise and any claim of Esau was decisively rejected. Here "love" and "hate" are legal terms, not expressions of emotion.

Why did Paul emphasize God's choice of Jacob even before the twins were born? To show those who relied on works that they have no basis to argue, "Well, Esau was rejected because he despised his birthright." God's choice was announced before either son did anything, either good or bad.

We're not to extend this principle, as if Paul were teaching the predestination of individuals to salvation. That's not what he was writing about. He was simply making the point that God was not obligated in any way when He chose Jacob to inherit the Covenant. God's word of salvation in Christ has not failed, simply because first-century Israel rejected Jesus. God didn't have to save Israel, any more than He had to bring Ishmael and Esau into the covenant line.

How great a need we have to remember God's freedom. He doesn't have to act as we expect, or even want Him to. God is God, and we are creatures. The awesome wonder is that God has freely chosen in Christ to offer us salvation. When we choose Jesus, God welcomes us into His family. Then, whatever God chooses to do will be for our good.

"Does not the potter have the right?" Rom. 9:14-23 The image of God the potter molding human clay seems to some a harsh

one. Yet we shouldn't soften it too much.

The fact is that even Pharaoh, who was raised up and "hardened" to display God's glory, was not mistreated. Paul knew the Old Testament, and the Exodus passage makes it clear that Pharaoh hardened his own heart, as well as it being hardened by God. Exodus also makes it clear how Pharaoh was hardened: not by God, forcing Pharaoh against his will to resist God, but simply by revealing more and more of His divine power. The same heat which melts wax hardens clay. The same revelation which creates love for God in the heart of the believer intensifies the resistance of the person who has chosen not to believe.

But this was not Paul's point. Paul's point was that even those who reject God's grace, bring God glory. One of God's purposes in creating the universe as it is was to display His wrath against sin, even as another is to display His love for sinners.

Israel's failure to turn to Jesus was not a failure of God. God's purposes will be accomplished in those who reject as well as those who accept Jesus as Lord.

Thank God, you and I will display the riches of His grace, rather than the majesty of His wrath.

"I will call them 'My people' who are not My people" Rom. 9:24-30. Had the Gentile response to Jesus surprised God? Not at all. The Old Testament makes it clear that God had always intended salvation to come to the Gentiles. And that always a remnant—a few rather than all—Israelites have maintained their trust in God. Again, God's purposes have not failed. Salvation history is on course. What is happening now is what God intended all along.

"A righteousness that is by faith" Rom. 9:30–10:4. How do we explain Israel's failure to respond to Jesus? The Jews took the Old Testament as a rule book, and expected to gain merit with God by trying to keep His Law. They were so busy trying to establish their own righteousness, that they completely missed the message of Scripture, that God gives man a righteousness based on faith.

In making this statement, Paul summed up all he had taught in Romans 1–8. There are only two ways to seek a relationship with God: man's way or God's. Man's way assumes God is satisfied with merely human righteousness. God's way abandons self-reliance, and trusts God's word of promise.

Today those two choices still loom before us. We must trust ourselves. Or trust God. And only trust in God can save.

"Their voice has gone out into all the earth" Rom. 10:16-21. Is it possible that Israel hadn't heard the Good News of God's grace? "Of course they did," Paul said.

We can say the same thing today. Is it possible that someone hasn't heard God's voice? No, all have heard. All the earth has heard God speak in the creation, if not in the Gospel (cf. Ps. 19; Rom. 1:18-20). The failure of any man or group to respond to God is not the fault of the Lord. It is because of man's obstinate disobedience when God's voice is heard.

▶ DEVOTIONAL
Inside and Out
(Rom. 10:1-15)

"Henry! Henry Aldrich!"

When I was a kid, that call introduced one of my favorite radio programs. And always Henry's quavering voice replied, "Coming, Mother!"

Henry wasn't the greatest of sons. But you could still count on him to respond when Mom called.

As the Apostle Paul went through his explanation of Israel's failure to heed the Gospel, he made something perfectly clear. We need a righteousness that God is eager to give. We must claim it by faith. And faith is an "inside and out" response to God's promise.

What's the inside? "Believe in your heart that God raised [Jesus] from the dead." And the out? "Confess with your mouth, Jesus is Lord" (v. 9).

Why are both inside and out stressed here? When I ask nine-year-old Sarah to do something, I expect her to at least let me know she's heard. I admit I sometimes get irritated when Sarah, engrossed in play or in some TV show, never even looks up or in my direction when I speak to her. Somehow words addressed to another person not only have to be heard, but also need to be acknowledged.

It's the same with God's Word to us. Yes, God knows our hearts, and He knows when we've believed with our hearts. Yet God's Word is dynamic, and in a sense demanding. If we truly hear, we will, and must, respond. And so Paul said that salvation comes to those who believe in their hearts, and confess with their mouths. The Word has found a home in our hearts, and is acknowledged in our lives.

I have a hard time imagining that old radio show, opening with Mother crying out, "Henry! Henry Aldrich!" And not hearing Henry respond. It's almost as hard as it is to imagine a human being hearing and truly believing God's voice in his heart, and giving no evidence by his life that he has heard. As the old chorus says, "If you're saved and you know it, shout 'Amen.' If you're saved and you know it, shout 'Amen.' If you're saved and you know it, then your life ought to show it. If you're saved and you know it, shout 'Amen!' "

Personal Application

God knows your heart. Let the world hear your "Amen."

Quotable

"He that believes in the heart will not be ashamed to confess with the mouth."—Matthew Henry

OCTOBER 8 *Reading 281*

ISRAEL TO BE SAVED

Romans 11

> *"And so all Israel will be saved, as it is written: 'The Deliverer will come from Zion; He will turn godlessness away from Jacob. And this is My covenant with them when I take away their sins' " (Rom. 11:26-27).*

God doesn't break any of His promises.

Background

The remnant. The concept of a "remnant" is consistently emphasized in the Old Testament prophets. The word means "survivors." It is used of those Israelites who survived the various devastating judgments that God brought on His Old Testament people when they sinned. The 6,000 who refused to worship Baal in the time of Elijah were a spiritual remnant, whose faith survived the efforts of Ahab and Jezebel to impose Baal worship on Israel. Those who were carried to Captivity in Babylon when Judah fell and Jerusalem was destroyed were a physical remnant. From them God chose a spiritual remnant to return and rebuild the Jewish homeland some 70 years later.

Paul argued that those Jews who became Christians were the remnant. As always, God preserves some of His people, even though the majority turn away.

Picking up the argument from Romans 9 and 10, then, Paul showed that God's Word had not failed. The vital, living Word of the Gospel was heard and believed by those within Israel who, as the remnant throughout sacred history, displayed the matchless grace of God.

Overview

Some Israelites are among those chosen by grace (11:1-6), though not all (vv. 7-10). The fall of Israel permitted Gentiles to be grafted as branches on the Jewish root (vv. 11-24). Yet the fall of Israel is temporary. One day all Israel will be saved, and all God's ancient promises will be fulfilled (vv. 25-32). In view of the beauty and complexity of God's plan, all we can do is praise (vv. 33-36).

Understanding the Text

"There is a remnant chosen by grace" Rom. 11:1-6. This first paragraph reminds us that we're never alone in our commitment to Christ. Sometimes it may seem like it. Many a teen complains he or she is the only one who maintains moral convictions. Many an adult feels just as lonely when trying to do what he or she believes is right. God wants us to know at such

times that there is a remnant. Always. The grace that gave us a vision of Jesus and snatched us out of the world has been poured out on thousands more.

The fact that it's grace reassures us. If salvation depended on human effort, we might well be all alone. But salvation is an expression of divine grace, and God brims over with grace. Surely His grace has overflowed and showered others with the kindness we've experienced in Christ.

"God gave them a spirit of stupor" Rom. 11:7-10. Does this passage teach that God kept the majority of Israel from responding to the Gospel? Not at all. Paul said that Israel's earnest search for a works-righteousness caused that spiritual deafness and blindness which God "gave" as a consequence.

Last night I burst into Sarah's room and, shouting to be heard, told her to turn down her cassette player. She was listening to her "New Kids on the Block" tape—turned up as loud as possible. I told her to turn it down, because if she didn't she was going to lose her hearing for sure. Muttering unhappily, she turned the music down.

It's the same with a solar eclipse. People are warned not to look directly into the sun. Yet they do and lose their sight.

Too-loud music dulls the hearing; too-bright sunlight darkens the sight. And earnestly searching for works-righteousness in God's Word creates a spirit of stupor, so man can neither see nor hear the Gospel.

"Salvation has come to the Gentiles to make Israel envious" Rom. 11:11-16. Israel's fall is temporary. For a time Israel has been set to one side, and the salvation of the Gentiles has become central to God's activity in the world. But, Paul said, this is only for a time. One day Israel will again be showcased, as a dead people brought to life. And that restoration will bring riches to the world.

Some Christians, recognizing the Jews as God's chosen people, insist that our nation support the present Jewish state, whether that state's actions are right or wrong. We need to make a distinction between the people of God, and the modern state of Israel. The restoration that Paul predicted in Romans 11 will come. But it is not here yet.

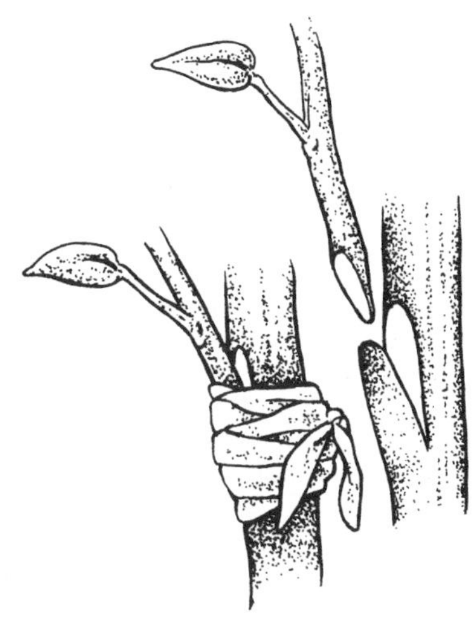

Farmers in Bible times grafted branches from cultivated olive trees onto wild stock, to improve the quality of the fruit. Paul pictured God, grafting wild Gentile branches onto cultivated Israel's roots—an act of amazing grace. The image is also a reminder. The natural branches lost their place because they failed to understand grace. We dare not lose sight of the fact that salvation is a gift of God, a demonstration of pure grace (vv. 17-24).

"Do not be arrogant, but be afraid" Rom. 11:20. Arrogance is always an enemy of grace. The arrogant person assumes that there is some virtue or quality in himself that wins God's approval. The fact is that there is nothing in any man or woman that merits praise. We are all sinners. We all fall so short that all we can rightly do is fall humbly to our knees.

If you catch the slightest hint of arrogance in any attitude, be afraid. You are rushing headlong away from grace. You are rushing headlong away from God.

"Grafted into their own olive tree!" Rom. 11:24 Paul wanted us to realize the great debt we owe to Israel. The roots of our faith are sunk deep into the history of the Jewish people, and their pilgrimage with God. The roots and trunk of Christianity are Jewish: we are but branches grafted on a mighty, living tree God has tended lovingly for thousands of years.

One day the Jewish people, cut off now because of unbelief (v. 23), will be grafted into their tree again. And every true Christian will shout for joy.

"God's gifts and His call are irrevocable" Rom. 11:25-32. Paul looked back into history, and reviewed in his mind the many promises that God gave to Abraham and the patriarchs. He heard again the thundering voices of the prophets, shouting stridently against sin, yet growing warm and loving as they looked ahead to a future filled with blessings for Israel.

There was no doubt in Paul's mind about the future. Those promises will be kept. Not as the "spiritual" experience of the church but as God's plan for the future of Planet Earth.

"All Israel will be saved."

"A Deliverer will come from Zion."

"God's gifts, and His call are irrevocable." There is a future for Israel as Israel, when "the full number of the Gentiles has come in" (v. 25).

Why is this important to us? In one sense it isn't. We live in today, not in tomorrow. God's future plan for Israel is less important to us than His will for our present. Yet there is a sense in which Paul's statements about Israel truly are important to us today. That importance is summed up in Paul's saying, "God's gifts and His call are irrevocable."

It's important to us that God be a Person of His Word. If He took back His promises to Israel, or if the promises were deceitful, not saying what they meant, then we might doubt the promises God has given to you and me. Thank God this is not the case. God is a Person of His Word. He doesn't change His mind. He doesn't take back His promises. He doesn't try to fool us with words that fail to say what He means.

We can count on God. We can trust His promises. His Word to us too is irrevocable. He will never go back on His Word.

▶ DEVOTIONAL
Doxology
(Rom. 11:25-36)

"Doxology" is a compound term, from *doxa*, glory, and *logos*, word. Together they mean a "glorifying word"; an expression of praise that glorifies God.

The doxology that concluded Paul's survey of Israel's relationship with God and the Gospel expressed praise for the complexity and beauty of God's plan. It was as if Paul had picked up a diamond cut by a master craftsman, and saw brilliant lights reflected from a multitude of facets. And suddenly he would find his heart filled with praise of the variegated wisdom, the vast knowledge, the intricate matrix of God's plan.

Theologians argue over Israel. Is there a future for Israel as Israel? Or is Israel today integrated within the church, which has inherited the ancient promises of the prophets? Personally I think the church and Israel are separate facets of a single, beautiful, complex divine plan. I think that this is exactly what Paul taught in Romans 11:25-32, with his reminder that "all Israel will be saved" and that God's "gifts and His call are irrevocable."

Perhaps verses 35-36 have an even more direct application to you and me. From my perspective I can only see a tiny facet of what God is doing in the world. I see my tiny circle of brothers and sisters. I know the prayers He answers for us, the little daily miracles He performs. But all too often I forget that there are literally millions in this world who experience God as I do. Who see Him at work. And who rejoice in His goodness.

If you or I could travel out in space, we'd see a globe inhabited now by over 5 billion human beings! And, if we had the spiritual sight, and each work God performed gave off an instantaneous flash, this globe would be alight with millions of points of brilliant light!

Perhaps then we would catch a glimpse of the qualities of God that Paul praised here. And we would say with him, in awe, "Oh, the depth of the riches of the wisdom and knowledge of God!" And, in renewed love, we would cry, "To Him be the glory forever! Amen!"

Personal Application

Consider the complex kindness of God. And offer Him your praise.

Quotable

"Though we speak much we cannot reach the end, and the sum of our words is, 'He is the all.' "—Ben Sira

OCTOBER 9 *Reading 282*
LIFE IN COMMUNITY
Romans 12

> *"Just as each of us has one body with many members, and these members do not all have the same function, so in Christ we who are many form one body, and each member belongs to all the others" (Rom. 12:4-5).*

Love binds the members of Christ's one body to Him, and to one another.

Background

A righteous community. Romans 12 opens the fifth major section of Paul's exploration of righteousness. Romans 1–3 demonstrated that no one is righteous in God's sight. Romans 4–5 showed that God credits righteousness to sinners who have faith in Jesus Christ. Romans 6–8 showed that union with Christ frees believers from the Law and, in the Holy Spirit, supplies the power needed to enable us to live righteously now. Romans 9–11 showed that Israel's temporary fall was due to its failure to seek righteousness from God, and that God Himself was righteous in His dealings with Israel. Now, in Romans 12–15, Paul is about to describe the righteous lifestyle of the new, Christian community.

This description is especially important for a church made up of Jews and Greeks, from different cultures, with diverse traditions. How could the two groups avoid conflict, and together form a just, moral community that would display God's righteousness in man's dark world? The question is just as vital today as in the first century. Jesus commanded His disciples to love one another, and said, "By this shall all men know that you are My disciples" (John 13:34). Only as our modern churches live in community, as community is portrayed in Romans 12–15, will the world know that we are Christ's. And that Christ is real.

Overview

The Christian's new motive for righteous living is worship, not Law (12:1-2). By nature the New Covenant community is an organism, the body of Christ (vv. 3-8), called to live together in love (vv. 9-21).

Understanding the Text

"I urge you, brothers, in view of God's mercy" Rom. 12:1. The Law demanded. Grace invites us to consider God's love, and respond to Him.

By implication Romans 12:1-2 lays out a principle that replaces Law in the Christian's life. We do not look to the Law, and respond because we must. We look at all God has done in showing us mercy, and respond to Him freely out of grateful love.

If you ever find it hard to do what you know is the right thing, don't say, "I ought to do this or that." "Ought" won't help. Instead, think of God's mercy to you, and of Christ's great love. In view of God's mercy, you will want to do right.

"Your spiritual worship" Rom. 12:1. The Old Testament worshiper brought animals to the temple, to be killed and laid on the altar. Paul reversed the imagery. Bring yourself to the altar. But do not die for God: live for Him!

This is one of the wonderful things about worship. We do worship God when we go to church, when we pray, when we raise our voices in song. But we also worship God every day whenever we do anything that pleases Him. Our hand on the arm of a hurting brother can be worship. Our effort to do our job honestly and well can be worship. Stopping to listen to an upset child, even though we're tired, can be worship. Everything we do, when done with a desire to please our Lord, is worship.

How gracious of God, in view of His mercy to us, to provide us with so many opportunities to worship Him.

"Be transformed by the renewing of your mind" Rom. 12:2. I'm sure hundreds of sermons have been preached on the Greek words in this verse. Each tells listeners that the idea behind being "conformed" is that of being squeezed into a mold. And each tells listeners that the idea behind "transformed" is metamorphosis—that passage which converts a creeping caterpillar into a beautiful, airborne butterfly. What a goal for the believ-

er: to become beautiful and new.

Paul also tells us how: by the "renewing of your mind." "Mind" here is *nous*, not so much the organ of intellect as the organ of perception. What is to be transformed is the way we look at life: the values, the thoughts, the motives, the viewpoint from which we evaluate choices. Simply put, we need to see everything from God's point of view.

What a clue to meaningful Bible study. We don't read Scripture simply to learn doctrine and know what we believe. We read to understand how God thinks and feels about issues we face in our daily lives. How does God view my responsibilities as an employee? How does God want me to respond to this person who seems to dislike me? How does God want me to deal with the hurt of my recent rejection?

If you come to God's Word with questions like these, He will give you His answer. And you will experience that renewing of your mind that transforms.

"Then you will be able to test and approve what God's will is" Rom. 12:2. If you and I don't learn to look at life from God's point of view, we will never know His will. And we'll never make the grand discovery that God's will is best—"good, pleasing, and perfect."

So come to Scripture with your questions and uncertainties. Ask God to speak. And then do what He tells you.

Try it. You'll like it.

"In Christ we who are many form one body" Rom. 12:3-5. What's the basis for fellowship in our churches? Is it common doctrine? A common preference for our particular traditions or ways of worship? Is it the conviction that our particular denomination best reflects New Testament principles, or that it is "the" church that traces its origin to the Apostles? Not according to Paul.

The basis for fellowship is the simple fact that we Christians are bound together with others in a living organism: the body of Jesus Christ. Because we are united to Him, we are necessarily united to each other. And therefore, Paul says, "Each member belongs to all the others."

Oh, it's not wrong for some to prefer the Episcopal high church to charismatic enthusiasm. And it's not wrong for some to believe in irresistible grace, while others emphasize free will. But it would be wrong for you or me to look at another believer in Jesus, and draw back because he or she raises his hands, or speaks in tongues, or baptizes infants rather than believers only. Or to draw back because one's skin is lighter and the other's darker, or because one's home is a hovel and the other's is a mansion.

Christ is the great leveler, not by bringing anyone down, but by bringing all up. And so we gladly welcome anyone who confesses Jesus Christ, affirming with Paul that "each member belongs to all the others."

"We have different gifts, according to the grace given us" Rom. 12:6-8. Unity doesn't mean sameness. The church in some ways is like a casserole. My mother used to make a delicious tuna casserole, using mushroom soup, fresh peas, tuna, and several other ingredients. Blended together the taste was delicious: each ingredient seemed to bring out the best in the others.

This is the real secret of Christ's body, the church. God blends together persons who are different, each with a different gift, so that each ingredient can bring out the best in the others.

Only as we live together in love, serving one another with the spiritual gifts God has provided, can we as individuals be all we were meant to be in Christ.

"Be devoted to one another in brotherly love" Rom. 12:9-16. Three themes are always found together in New Testament passages. The body of Christ, spiritual gifts, and love.

There are important reasons why these three themes are inseparable. Our relationship with other Christians is defined by participation together in a single body. Our service to other Christians is defined as using our gifts and abilities to serve them. Our attitude toward other Christians is one of active, caring love. Unity, service, and love are never separated in Scripture. Without unity, there can be no experience of service. Without service, there can be no experience of love. Without love, there can be no experience of unity. Each depends on the other.

If you love and serve others, you will begin to experience the unity of the body of Christ (see DEVOTIONAL).

"Leave room for God's wrath" Rom. 12:17-20. My wife, Sue, was deserted by her first husband when she was three months pregnant with Sarah, and trying to care for two-and-one-half-year-old Matthew. There was no seeming reason for the desertion: he simply left.

Over the years, this passage's reminder, "Do not take revenge," has been a constant challenge for Sue. Her ex-husband has wanted to keep in contact with the children. After we met and married, about three years after Sue's divorce, her ex visited us in Florida, staying in our home. What a challenge for her to live an "on the contrary" life, and "if your enemy is hungry, feed him." In every way Sue has tried to show kindness and concern for the man who shattered her world and burdened her with bringing up their little ones alone.

But how exciting it has been to see the fulfillment of God's Word. For Paul said, "Do not be overcome by evil, but overcome evil with good" (v. 21). He didn't mean that our good will overcome the evil in others. What he meant was that by doing good, we can overcome the evil in us!

The ugly things that we might have justified in anyone treated so wrongly—anger, hatred, hostility, revenge—have been overcome in Sue, and her life has instead displayed a love, forgiveness, and kindness that could come only from God.

I have no idea what Sue's obedience to this passage has done for her ex-husband. But I know what it has done for her. And to glorify the Lord.

▶DEVOTIONAL
Meat and Potatoes Love
(Rom. 12:9-16)

Love, Paul said, must be sincere (v. 9). But "love" is such an amorphous term in our society. Why, folks often use it to cover the basest of motives or actions. Like the person who uses "I love you" to manipulate another into satisfying mere sexual passion.

But "love" isn't an indistinct or slippery term in the New Testament. Love is practical, blunt, ordinary. It's the meat and potatoes of the Christian life.

What is meat and potatoes love? That dish we're to serve up daily, and live on within the Christian community? Here's the checklist Paul provided in Romans 12. Use it, not to measure how others perform, but how you're doing as Christ's disciple:
* I show real devotion to others.
* I honor others, and am more eager for their advancement than my own.
* I share with others when they are in need.
* I welcome others into my home, and into my life.
* I rejoice with those who rejoice.
* I mourn with those who mourn.
* I live in harmony with others.
* I associate as an equal with those who are socially or in other ways "beneath" me.

There are other passages that further define love, such as 1 Corinthians 13. But this passage gives us the meat and potatoes of Christian love. If you actively love other Christians in these ways, you're doing your part to bring vitality and life to the body of Christ on earth.

Personal Application

The most important thing you can do for others is to love them.

Quotable

"There are two ways of being united—frozen together, and melted together. What Christians most need is to be united in brotherly love."—D.L. Moody

OCTOBER 10 *Reading 283*
CLOTHED WITH JESUS
Romans 13

"Clothe yourselves with the Lord Jesus Christ, and do not think about how to gratify the desires of the sinful nature" (Rom. 13:14).

The Christian lives as Jesus did, in self-chosen submission and love.

Overview
Christians are to submit to governing authorities (13:1-7). We are always to display love (vv. 8-10) and holiness (vv. 11-14).

Understanding the Text
"Everyone must submit himself to the governing authorities" Rom. 13:1. For some, "submission" calls up the image of someone being dragged off in chains and forced to slave in some dark, underground mine. Not for the Christian. For us "submission" is a choice we make freely, gladly. We live as good citizens of our nation, because we are citizens of Jesus' kingdom, and represent Him here on earth.

"There is no authority except that which God has established" Rom. 13:1-2. It's not that God puts His stamp of approval on every government, whether it is just or unjust, democratic or tyrannical, capitalist or Communist. Paul's point was that God established the principle of human government, and thus existing governments derive their authority from Him. In honoring our government, whether good or bad, we honor God.

"He is God's servant to do you good" Rom. 13:3-4. Why did God ordain human government? Because government restrains sin, and serves as an "agent of wrath to bring punishment on wrongdoers." Life is safer for the individual under even bad government than under no government at all.

It's not that governments consciously see themselves as God's agents. Not at all. It is simply that to survive, any government must provide its citizens with some measure of tranquility. Citizens must be able to work, to produce the food and goods that government can tax. Laws that protect life and property must be enacted. It is in government's self-interest to see that citizens are prosperous and multiply, for a strong citizenry guarantees the survival of the state.

How wise God is. In creating human government, as flawed as governments may be, God ordained a system that can only survive by serving God's own gracious purpose of doing good.

"Because of conscience" Rom. 13:5-7. We Christians freely choose to keep our country's laws, to pay the taxes government is due, and to show respect to our nation's leaders and institutions. In this we're not motivated by fear of punishment. Instead it's a matter of conscience for us. We do these things because it's right to do them. In supporting our government, we support something which God has instituted for the good of all, even when we support government by disobeying unjust laws (see DEVOTIONAL).

"The continuing debt to love one another" Rom. 13:8. The Christian is obligated to support his government. And we have one further obligation. We are to love our fellowmen. Whether Christians or not, we are to love.

In explaining this, Paul said something that should open the eyes of those who see their primary obligation as keeping God's Law. The Law, said Paul, has always been a matter of love! Those commandments that define how we are to treat each other outline the way that real love finds expression in personal relationships. If you really love someone, you won't covet their possessions. If you love, you won't commit adultery, or murder, or steal. So in effect, "Love is the fulfillment of the Law."

Concentrate on loving. And you won't need to constantly refer back to the Law. True love will move you to do spontaneously what the Law requires.

"Love is the fulfillment of the Law" Rom. 13:10. Let's not make the mistake that "situation ethics" makes. That approach to

ethics suggests a person compute the consequences of his or her acts, and then do the "loving thing." That is, the thing that he believes will turn out best for the other person. In essence this approach to moral choice says, "Love instead of the Law."

But Scripture says that "love is the fulfillment of the Law," and this is a very different thing indeed. The Bible teaches that God's commandments are loving. Thus the loving thing to do is always to act in harmony with God's revealed will.

Law is something like the landing system used in commercial and military airplanes. As a plane approaches the runway, a repeating beep tells the pilot he is on course. If he drifts off course to either side, the pitch and frequency of the beep changes, warning him to make a correction before it's too late. This is how Law serves the Christian. Law never produces right action: love does that. But as we act in love, we need to glance frequently at what the Law says. If our loving acts do not fulfill the Law, we know we're off course, and need correction.

There is such a thing as "dumb love"—really caring and wanting to help, but doing something that harms instead of heals. What we need is "intelligent love." Really caring and wanting to help, and being guided by Scripture to actions which are right and good.

"Let us put aside the deeds of darkness" Rom. 13:11-13. For us, as J.B. Phillips translates verse 11, "The present time is of the utmost importance."

Yes, we look forward to the soon coming of Jesus. But until then, we are on a mission for our Lord. That mission requires us to "put on the armor of light" and live decent, holy lives here and now.

What an image that "armor of light" is. It's as if Paul envisions an army approaching as the sun rises and the darkness begins to fade. There, on the ridge across from us, the sun touches the armor the soldiers wear, and they glisten with a thousand points of light.

That's how the Christian is to appear to all in this world. We are the vanguard of Christ's coming invasion of man's sin darkened world. We are to live such holy lives that His beauty will glisten in the darkness. By your complete commitment to God's moral vision for mankind, you put on, and proudly wear, God's armor of light.

"Clothe yourselves with the Lord Jesus Christ" Rom. 13:14. We watched the remake of *Ivanhoe* on the Disney channel last night. That was unusual. We don't usually stay up that late, because Sue and I get up at 5 A.M., she to go to her teaching, and me to my computer. But it was a fun movie, and very well done.

In one sequence a Saxon noble's court jester entered the castle where the noble was being held prisoner. The jester wore a friar's brown robe. Inside, he exchanged it with the noble he served. When the "friar" left, it was the noble in disguise. No one even noticed the difference.

That's what Paul was telling us here when he said, "Clothe yourselves with the Lord Jesus Christ." We're to slip into Jesus, and wear Him everywhere we go. We're to look like Him. Walk like Him. Talk like Him. Act like Him. In fact, we're to be Jesus to others.

What a challenge. To wear Jesus so well that no one will notice the difference. To be in Him. And to let Him be fully in me.

▶ DEVOTIONAL
Civil Disobedience
(Rom. 13)

How can we obey God's command to submit to human government, if a government asks us to violate a divine law? That has happened more than once. It even happened at the beginning of the Church Age. Remember how the Sanhedrin commanded Peter and John not to preach Jesus? They disobeyed, saying, "Judge for yourselves whether it is right in God's sight to obey you rather than God."

In the case of direct conflict, the Christian must of course obey God.

But we can still submit to government's powers even when we disobey! You see, there are two ways that a person can uphold law and order. One way is to obey the law. The other is to accept the punishment the law requires. Each course of action upholds the law.

Those who in the '60s chose civil disobedience to protest discrimination against blacks were often jailed. Going quietly to jail, as Martin Luther King, Jr.

did, upheld the principle of law, even as laws were broken. But there were those in the late '60s who ran to Canada to escape the draft. They protested what they thought was an unjust war. But rather than uphold law and order by accepting punishment, their flight was a refusal to submit to the law of man and of God.

In the '90s there are other issues that may well demand Christians of conscience to break the laws of our land. But any who do must also submit willingly to any punishment the law decrees. If they do, they will honor their cause and show that Christian respect for the government that God commands.

Personal Application

We can obey God by breaking the law only if we are willing to accept the punishment law decrees.

Quotable

"A Christian man is the most free lord of all, and subject to none; a Christian man is the most dutiful servant of all, and subject to everyone."—Martin Luther

OCTOBER 11 *Reading 284*
CHRIST'S LORDSHIP
Romans 14

> *"For this very reason, Christ died and returned to life so that He might be Lord of both the dead and the living" (Rom. 14:9).*

We are to hold our convictions between ourselves and the Lord.

Background

Convictions. Some things are clearly labeled "sin" in Scripture. We Christians agree with God, and not only give up those things, but also seek to purge them from our fellowships (cf. 1 Cor. 5).

Yet there is a whole range of practices which don't bear that biblical label. And, at various times various groups of Christians have considered practices not called "sin" to be inappropriate for those who honor Jesus Christ. The congregation I joined as a new Christian in 1956 had convictions against smoking, drinking alcohol, going to movies, dancing, and other things I probably wasn't aware of. Since everyone in our congregation shared these convictions, no conflicts arose.

But folks in the first-century congregation in Rome did have conflicts over convictions. Some thought it wasn't appropriate for believers to eat meat. Some thought Sunday ought to be kept as a special day, much as the Jews kept the Sabbath. And others simply did not agree.

Soon the harmony and unity of the church was in jeopardy, as believers judged, criticized, and looked down on one another.

If you've ever wondered how to handle those differences that drive wedges between Christians, Romans 14 will be an especially exciting chapter for you.

Overview

Warmly welcome others without judging their convictions (14:1-8), thus affirming Christ's lordship in each life (vv. 9-12). Yet be sensitive to others' convictions (vv. 13-18), and do what promotes peace and growth (vv. 19-21). Personal convictions should be kept to oneself, as a matter between the individual and his Lord (vv. 22-23).

Understanding the Text

"Accept him whose faith is weak" Rom. 14:1. In this chapter Paul spoke of the "strong" and the "weak." What did he mean by these terms? Simply put, the strong are those who have a mature Christian perspective on what Paul called "disputable things." The weak are those who do not yet have a mature or an accurate grasp of such issues.

The striking thing is that Paul didn't side with the strong against the weak, or with the weak against the strong! Instead he modeled exactly what he called for in Romans 14: acceptance. Without looking down on either, or criticizing either, he shows that each believer is a valued member of the local body of Christ. Each is welcome. Each is loved. Each belongs.

What an important wonderful thing for every believer to know. Wherever you or I may be on the journey of faith, we are one with those before us, and behind. In the fellowship of Jesus, we are one.

"Passing judgment on disputable matters" Rom. 14:1. A "disputable matter" is any practice which God has not labeled "sin" that some Christians feel is all right, and others feel is wrong. We may use a biblical principle as basis for feeling that a particular practice isn't appropriate for Christians. But unless God has clearly stated a practice is sin, our opinion is "disputable."

That word, "disputable," reminds us to stay humble. We may be right in our opinions about disputable matters. But we may also be wrong. So while we follow our consciences and do what we believe is right, we also free others to reach their own conclusions. You and I must surely do what we believe will be most pleasing to the Lord. But in "disputable matters" we have no right to try to impose our beliefs on others.

"One man's faith allows him to eat anything" Rom. 14:2-3. You can easily generate your own list of "disputable matters." Here's how. First, start with Paul's two cases: eating meat vs. vegetarianism, and strict vs. lax observance of "holy days." Add to your list everything you can think of that are like these two.

Then note how disputes over such issues affect relationships. Some folks start judging others. They are critical and condemning. Others ridicule. They treat people with differing convictions with contempt. Now add to your list any issues that seem to have such effects on Christians you know.

When you have your list complete, post it. And remember. These are the things that you're to pay no attention to at all as you build Christian friendships. God has accepted those who differ with us on all issues like these. Since God has welcomed them, we surely must welcome them too (see DEVOTIONAL).

"Each one should be fully convinced in his own mind" Rom. 14:5-8. If you look over that list of convictions you just made out, you'll undoubtedly have an opinion about most items there. How can you tell what position you should take on each matter, not publicly, but for yourself?

You should study each issue to convince yourself: (1) That you can or cannot do this "to the Lord." (2) That you can or cannot do it giving thanks to God.

When you're "fully convinced in your own mind," do what you believe is right without fear of what others might think.

"That He might be the Lord of both the dead and the living" Rom. 14:9-12. What does Christ's lordship in disputable matters mean? First, that you and I are responsible to Jesus to do only that which we honestly believe will please the Lord. And second, that our Christian brothers and sisters are not responsible to us!

If Jesus is Lord, then judging is His job. And I am free forever from the burden of determining what is right and wrong for others.

How good that freedom feels. I don't have to condemn others. I don't have to try to argue them over to my point of view. All I have to do is love others, accept them, and share the joy of our common faith in Jesus Christ.

It's a terrible burden for a church, a pastor, or for you and me to play God. How freeing it is to let Jesus be Lord, and focus all my attention on serving Him.

"Make up your mind not to put any stumbling block or obstacle in your brother's way" Rom. 14:13-21. Have you ever noticed how some people flaunt their freedom? They make it a point to do things that shock others, or even offend them, just to show they can.

Paul was used to overreaction from the young Christians he'd nurtured over the decades. So he guarded against overreaction now. We're free to live according to our convictions. We're not free to use our convictions to club a brother to death!

This is an overriding concern felt by every mature believer. We really are to care about others and their welfare. Since flaunting my freedom might provoke someone to judge, or encourage a young believer to act against his conscience, I must exercise my freedom with restraint.

Sometimes this principle is misapplied, and we let those with the least maturity in disputable matters impose their views on the whole church. That's not what Paul asked. Paul was talking relationships, not church rules. He was telling you and me that when we suspect something we are free to do might harm a less mature brother or sister, then for Jesus' sake we should freely choose not to do it!

What a joyous freedom this is. It's the freedom we really want. Not a freedom to do what we like, or what we know is lawful for us. But a freedom to do what is loving. To do what expresses the warmth, the wonder, the joy of putting the welfare of others before even our own "rights."

"Whatever you believe about these things keep between yourself and God" Rom. 14:22-23. The best way to handle "disputable matters" is simply not to talk about them. To discuss and argue, to try to convince others we're correct, does nothing to promote harmony in the body of Christ. And it does nothing to build up a brother or sister in his or her faith.

All that disputing is likely to do is to create doubts and uncertainty.

That's why Paul reminds us that whatever "does not come from faith is sin." Whatever we do, we must do it in the conviction that we are pleasing Jesus Christ.

So be convinced in your own mind before you act. When you are convinced, feel free to do what you believe is pleasing to the Lord. But at the same time, be sensitive to the convictions of others, and how your actions affect them. Value your brother's well-being even more highly than your rights. And never, never make personal convictions the subject of debate.

▶DEVOTIONAL
There's a Welcome Here
(Rom. 14:1-4)

Paul immediately launched into the very heart of the issue. "Accept him whose faith is weak, without passing judgment on disputable matters."

That's really what it's all about. Not who's wrong and who's right. Just acceptance.

The Greek word translated "accept," *proslambano,* is one of the most powerful relational terms in the New Testament. It means to actively welcome. It's a glad smile, arms reached out to hug, a hand on an arm drawing a newcomer into a circle of close and loving friends.

Psychologists tell us how important acceptance is. If a child fails to feel acceptance from his parents, he's likely to grow up ridden with doubt and a sense of unworthiness. If an adult fails to feel acceptance from others, she will always be uncertain, fearful, isolated, and alone.

Paul reminds us that the church of Jesus Christ is God's family. Here every child of God is to experience welcome, and so feel the great value God places on him or her. The church of Jesus is home: it's where we can relax and be ourselves, knowing that here we belong. And here we are loved.

Acceptance is one of the most important gifts you can give another person. And one of the most valuable gifts you will ever receive. No wonder Paul began his discussion of disputable matters with the command, "Accept him."

However we may differ from others about issues the Bible does not label as "sin," and however passionately our convictions are held, our brother or sister in Christ has been accepted by God. And we are to welcome him or her too.

Personal Application

Give the gift that costs nothing, but means everything.

Quotable

"On Sunday they come from the town and stand in the doorway and so keep out the cold. One is not cold among his brothers and sisters. What if there is less fire on the hearth, if there is more in the heart!"—Henry David Thoreau

OCTOBER 12 *Reading 285*
ONE HEART AND MOUTH
Romans 15

> *"May the God who gives endurance and encouragement give you a spirit of unity among yourselves as you follow Christ Jesus, so that with one heart and mouth you may glorify the God and Father of our Lord Jesus Christ" (Rom. 15:5-6).*

"How good and how pleasant it is when brothers live together in unity!" (Ps. 133:1)

Overview

Christ modeled an attitude which leads to unity and glorifies God (15:1-6). Christ's acceptance of us sets the pattern for all believers' relationships with each other, and opens the door to joy and peace (vv. 7-13). As for Paul, he found fulfillment in serving God (vv. 14-22), and hoped soon to visit Rome (vv. 23-29). He urged the Romans to pray with and for him (vv. 30-33).

Understanding the Text

"Bear with . . . and not to please ourselves" Rom. 15:1-7. These verses belong with chapter 14. Paul had shown that in "disputable matters" each Christian must accept responsibility for his own convictions, and give others the same freedom to be responsible to Christ as Lord. Matters not clearly defined as sin in Scripture are disputable, but not debatable.

Now Paul reminds us of the attitude we must have if the unity of the body of Christ is to be preserved.

It's never enough to just leave others alone. "Do what you think is best," we may say. But what we may mean is, "Don't bother me. I don't really care what you do."

That's not what it means to let Christ be Lord in another believer's life. Paul says we "bear with" the "failings of the weak." For Jesus' sake, and for the sake of our fellow believer, we "please [our] neighbor for his good, to build him up." We live to serve, even as Jesus lived, and died, to serve us.

"Accept one another, then, just as Christ accepted you in order to bring praise to God" Rom. 15:7. Here's that word again. "Accept."

In Romans 14 we saw that it means to welcome: to open our arms and hearts to each other. To value the individual so much that he or she experiences warmth and belonging.

Here Paul shows us the standard by which acceptance is to be measured. We are to welcome others as Christ has welcomed us.

Did Jesus open His heart to us because we were such beautiful people? Because we had so much to offer to the group? Because we were well dressed, or wealthy? No, Jesus opened His heart and welcomed us when we were sinners, hostile toward God, clothed in the filthy rags of our own pretentions of righteousness, without a cent of heavenly currency. Jesus accepted us freely, with no preconditions, and despite our flaws.

That's how you and I are to relate to others. As Jesus has related to us.

And just as Jesus' redeeming love has begun to transform our lives, so in the fellowship of a loving, accepting congregation, the sinful and the weak will also be transformed.

"A servant . . . on behalf of God's truth" Rom. 15:8-12. What is the truth that Jesus served so well? That God loves both Jew and Gentile. That He has been faithful in keeping His covenant promises to Israel, and at the same time has opened the door of salvation to the rest of humankind.

The result of Jesus' servanthood? He gathers up and brings all mankind's praise to God. No less than five different Greek words for praise are used in three brief Old Testament quotes, reminding us how significant praise is in God's sight.

It reminds us of something else as well. Others may not appreciate what you do for them. That's actually good! The goal of Christian servanthood isn't to be praised. It is to gather up the praise of others and direct it toward God. When others are praising us, we intercept what really belongs to our Lord.

"The God of hope" Rom. 15:13. This is the second of two very special descriptions of

God in this chapter. Verse 5 portrays God as the "God who gives" (see DEVOTIONAL). Verse 13 pictures Him as "the God of hope."

"Hope" is a unique word in Scripture, where it indicates "confident expectation." The person with hope has complete assurance about the future. And the overflow of the hope we have as we trust in God fills us with joy and peace.

So give yourself up to serve. And let God fill you with that hope which overflows with joy and peace.

"Competent to instruct one another" Rom. 15:14-20. There's nothing that stunts spiritual growth quite so much as paternalism. That idea that big Daddy has to be there, or poor little you will be sure to make some horrible mistake or do something unutterably dumb.

Paternalism is a terrible temptation to anyone in ministry. If big Pastor isn't there, that small group Bible study will probably wander off into false doctrine. If big Preacher doesn't preach, nothing of value will happen in the service. If big Reverend doesn't do the counseling, how will those terribly messed up folks ever find the way out of their dilemma?

Well, big Apostle Paul didn't share that attitude at all! He'd said earlier, very plainly, that believers are united to Jesus and given the Holy Spirit (Rom. 6–8). He'd said that every believer has a gift that equips him or her to minister (Rom. 12). He'd shown that growth can take place when believers accept one another warmly, serve one another, and let Christ exercise His lordship in each life (Rom. 14–15). So Paul backed off, not only from paternalism, but from even the hint of paternalism!

Paul wanted to visit Rome to enjoy "your company for a while" (v. 24). He wasn't driven to visit Rome from the neurotic fear that the church there would go down the tubes without him. In fact, Paul was "convinced" that the church in Rome was "competent to instruct one another." The Romans had the Word, the Holy Spirit, and each other. Paul would bring a blessing. In the last analysis any church grows because of its relationship with God, not with God's servants.

How desperately both pulpit and pew need to hear this word from Paul. The pulpit needs to rid itself of paternalistic attitudes and actions, and nurture ministry by the laity. The pew needs to stop mistaking God's servant for God, and trust the Lord rather than the leader.

"A contribution for the poor among the saints in Jerusalem" Rom. 15:26-28. Judea was heavily dependent on income from the temple and from pilgrims who came to visit it. In time, as the little Christian community became more and more isolated from the rest of Judaism, Christians suffered more during times of depression or famine.

One of Paul's ministries was that of famine relief: raising funds from believers throughout the Gentile world to bring relief to the poor believers in Jerusalem.

To Paul, who developed a theology of giving in 2 Corinthians 8–9, seeing to the material needs of those Jewish believers from which the church sprang was an obligation and a joy. Spiritual and material needs were not kept in separate compartments, as we sometimes do. Any known need of a believer was an opportunity to serve.

How wonderful when we are able to see fulfilling our obligation to help one another as a joy and a priority. Paul was eager to go to Spain to open that land for the Gospel. But he saw no conflict in setting aside that mission for a time, to carry funds and food to those in need.

▶DEVOTIONAL
Giving Till It Hurts
(Rom. 15:1-6)

I sometimes hear a "Talknet" host on our local 620 AM station, whose major premise is that people ought to live more selfish lives. "You are important," he tells those who call in. "Think of yourself for once. Put you and your own needs first, because if you don't, no one else will."

It's a popular philosophy, and I'm sure there are folks who need to hear it. Folks who think of themselves as worthless, and so have lived doormat lives, walked on by petty tyrants from Mom and Dad to their own kids.

But for mature Christians, confident of their value and worth in Christ, the "let's live selfish lives" message is totally wrong. Paul even went so far as to say, "Each of us should please his neighbor for his good, to build him up."

To our talk show host, Paul's advice is utter nonsense. Even many Christians find it a little hard to swallow. We may very well think, "Why should I always have to be the one to give up what I want for the sake of someone else?" Many a time we think, "I'm tired of putting myself out for others, who don't even appreciate what I do for them."

If you ever feel that way, that you've been giving till it hurts, remember this little phrase from Romans 15:5: "The God who gives."

What you and I give up in following Christ's example of selflessness is nothing compared to what God gives us in return. He gives us endurance. Encouragement. And a "spirit of unity among yourselves."

When we give of ourselves to others, God gives us all the privilege of glorifying Him together with "one heart and mouth."

So next time you feel a little put upon, or unappreciated for the sacrifices you make for others, remember. God knows. And He gives you far more precious gifts in return than anything you have given up for Him.

Personal Application

It would be a privilege to follow Jesus' example, even if there were no rewards.

Quotable

"My mind was faced with choosing between my pleasure and God's, and since my mind saw the glaring inequality between the two, even in the slightest matter, I would be forced to choose what then seemed more pleasing to God."—Anthony Mary Claret

---

OCTOBER 13 *Reading 286*

SISTERS AND BROTHERS

Romans 16

> *"I commend to you our sister Phoebe, a servant of the church in Cenchrea" (Rom. 16:1).*

Lists of names mean little to us. But each name represents a person who is important to God.

Overview

Paul closed with personal greetings to close friends in Rome (16:1-16), with an exhortation (vv. 17-20), and with greetings from fellow workers who were with him (vv. 21-23). And he capped it all with praise to God (vv. 24-27).

Understanding the Text

"Greet" Rom. 16:3-16. The Bible's penchant for including long lists of names sometimes irritates readers. But there are always reasons. In the Old Testament, most listings of names are genealogical: they display the faithfulness of God to the people of Israel, with whom He maintained a covenant relationship over long and often stormy centuries. Those lists of names establish not only the identity of the people of God, but His faithfulness.

Here in Romans 16 is a list of names that has another purpose. It displays something of the network of warm and loving relationships which bound the early church together. Paul was not just a theologian, he was a friend. He did not just count up converts, he cared for people as individuals.

So let's not be put off by the list of names here. Let it remind us that in the eyes of God and in the church of Jesus, each person is important enough to be known by name.

"I commend to you our sister Phoebe, a servant of the church in Cenchrea" Rom. 16:1. The way translators have handled this verse makes Christian feminists see red. That word "servant" in the Greek is *diakonos.* More than one commentator has noted that the use of this form, rather than *diakoneo* or *diakonia,* suggests something more than casual service. It's likely that Phoebe held the leadership position of a deacon in her congregation, though at the time Romans was written it's impossible to say what this position involved.

I can understand why some Christian women are eager for Phoebe to gain greater recognition. The ministry of women hasn't been overly welcomed in the church. But probably the highest honor we can do Phoebe or any other believer is to note, as Paul does, that "she has been a great help to many people, including me."

After all, this is what our faith is all about. Not the office we may hold. But the help we can be to each other as we seek together to follow Jesus Christ.

"Priscilla and Aquila, my fellow workers in Christ Jesus" Rom. 16:3-4. It should give those folks who think of Paul as a male chauvinist a moment's pause at least. The first two folks that Paul mentioned in this greeting section of Romans 16 are women. And Priscilla was mentioned even before her husband, Aquila.

Both Priscilla and Aquila are acknowledged as Paul's "fellow workers," even as Phoebe was acknowledged as a church deacon. While Phoebe's ministry of help seems focused in her local house church, the word *sunergos,* "fellow worker," suggests this couple shared Paul's commission to serve as missionary evangelists.

There really is a place for women. At home. And abroad. In local churches. And in missions.

"Outstanding among the apostles" Rom. 16:7. The word "apostle" is used in a restrictive sense when applied to any of the Twelve and to Paul. These men were the divinely commissioned leaders of the church, and spoke with a unique authority. But many others earned the title "apostle," among them Andronicus and Junias. After all, the word "apostle" literally means one who is sent on a mission.

Paul's word about these relatives who were "outstanding among the apostles" reminds us that early Christians felt the missionary call to share their faith with others in the Roman world. Don't ever suppose that Paul and his little team of missionaries was responsible for the explosive spread of the Gospel in the first century. They didn't do it alone! Nor today can the Christian's commission to spread the Gospel be fulfilled by a few "full-time" missionaries.

Let's be sure that we are numbered "among the apostles." Let's even try to be outstanding.

"Ampliatus. . . . Urbanus . . . Stachys" Rom. 16:8-9. What was the church in Rome like? One hint comes from the names Paul mentioned in Romans 16. These names, for instance, along with many of the others, were most common among slaves, freedmen, and freedwomen in Roman society. It's quite clear that the church in Rome was not an upper crust phenomenon. The Christians there were mostly ordinary folk, and probably drawn from the lower strata of Roman society.

But notice how Paul spoke of "low class" Roman believers. Ampliatus was one "whom I love in the Lord." Urbanus was "our fellow worker in Christ." Stachys was "my dear friend." We can feel the love overflow as Paul wrote, surrounding each person with affection.

Class isn't to matter in Christ's church. It surely didn't matter to Paul. He loved these men and women for their own sakes, and because they were deeply loved by Jesus Christ. In this too let's follow Paul's example. Let's love people for themselves, not their positions. And let's let them know how much.

"Persis, another woman who has worked very hard in the Lord" Rom. 16:12. In another two generations Clement of Rome would report rulings severely restricting women's roles in church leadership. His words, in 1 Clement 20:7, are sometimes quoted to support modern restrictions on female participation in leadership in our own local churches. Whatever authority one may wish to concede to Clement, it must be significant that the Apostle Paul in this listing credits four women with significant service in their own congregations (Mary, Tryphena and Tryphosa, and Persis). In fact, he says this of four women—and no men—at least on this list.

In making this observation, I am not mounting a campaign for women's ordination, or claiming female superiority in local church leadership. I'm simply pointing out what the text says. And suggesting that perhaps—just perhaps—Clement of Rome overreacted to the freedom first-generation Christian women found through the Gospel to use their gifts in Christ's church.

Perhaps—just perhaps—some men today have overreacted too.

"Watch out for those who cause divisions" Rom. 16:17-19. If we are truly devoted to one another, there will be unity in Christ's church. That bond that Paul himself displayed with those now in Rome that he had come to know and love holds us together in intimate fellowship.

But beware if devotion flags, and the church becomes an impersonal gathering of strangers. Then the door is thrown open wide for "those who cause divisions." Their smooth talk and flattery is designed to deceive. They want to build their own little kingdom, with their own handful of followers. They are not serving Jesus, but their own pride, or need for adulation.

Paul had a simple prescription to deal with such people. Half of it is stated in verse 17: "Keep away from them." The other half is implied in his letter as a whole, and in the first 16 verses of this chapter: "Grow close to your brothers and sisters in the Lord. If you come to know the people in your local church family well, and if you love them deeply, then no smooth-talking stranger will be able to shatter the unity that Christ gives."

"Erastus, who is the city's director of public works" Rom. 16:23. I once worked for a Christian organization whose chapels one year featured Christian "success stories." The wealthy and respected of our community trooped one by one to the chapel pulpit, and each told how faith in Christ contributed to his rise. How I wished we'd find some poor, uneducated failure, who could tell us how faith in Jesus sustained him in his rush toward ruin.

It didn't happen of course. We get so excited over the converted movie star, the reformed criminal, the Miss World. Apparently the NIV translators share that failing, for Erastus the *oikonomos* may well have been a financial officer in the Corinthian government, but there's no way today to tell how high a rank he held. Was he really the "director of public works"? Well, maybe. But not likely.

Anyway, it really doesn't matter, does it? As James so wisely says, "The brother in humble circumstances ought to take pride in his high position [in Christ]. But the one who is rich should take pride in his low position [as a mere sinner saved by grace]" (James 1:9-10).

What really counts about Erastus wasn't his position in the Corinthian hierarchy. All that really counts is, he was one of Jesus' own.

And so are you.

▶ DEVOTIONAL
I Love a Mystery
(Rom. 16:25-27)

It was one of my favorite radio programs. I can hear the announcer now, his voice quavering with feigned excitement: "And now" (he'd begin, in hushed tones), "I" (pause), "Love" (a little louder) "A MYSTERY!"

I'd hurry into our little living room, flop down on my stomach in front of the radio, intent and ready to hear the next fascinating chapter in the current adventure.

Paul loved a mystery too. No, not the imaginary adventure of my radio days. The biblical mystery of Jesus Christ.

In Scripture "mystery" is a technical theological term. It identifies some previously hidden or only hinted at facet of God's eternal plan, which has only recently been revealed. Christ, Paul realized with wonder, is the greatest of all the mysteries of God. How could God forgive the sins of past saints? How could God not simply declare human beings righteous in His sight, but actually make them righteous? How could God, committed as He was to the Jews, open wide His arms to the Gentiles too? How could Jew and Gentile ever find common ground, enabling the race to be drawn back together into one? How could God's love for all the human race be so stunningly displayed that hardened sinners would suddenly halt, reconsider, and kneel, broken, before God?

These and all of history's unanswered questions are, for Paul, answered in Jesus Christ. He is the mystery hidden for long ages past. He is the One glimpsed in prophetic writings. He is the One who has come and stands fully revealed today that all nations might believe and obey Him.

He is the One who has at last enabled us to sense not only the love but also the wisdom of God. He is the One through whom God receives glory, forever and ever.

Christians can differ honestly about many doctrines. They can dispute about practices. But on one thing we all agree. We all love the One whose coming explained the mystery of God's plan, and revealed once and for all the full extent of His mysterious, wonderful love.

Personal Application

To see clearly, look at everything through Jesus Christ.

Quotable

"A God on the cross! That is all my theology."—Jean LaCordaire

---

The Variety Reading Plan continues with 1 SAMUEL

---

1 Corinthians

INTRODUCTION

Paul wrote his letter to Christians in the wealthy seaport city of Corinth in A.D. 55, some four years after he founded the church there. After Paul left, a number of problems developed in the church, and the Corinthians sent for advice. So 1 Corinthians is a practical, problem-solving letter. In it Paul explains how Christians are to deal with many issues, including divisions, immorality, and doctrinal disputes.

Paul's letter gives us fascinating insights into difficulties first-century congregations faced as they tried to live out their lives in Christ. First Corinthians remains one of the New Testament's most valuable letters. The principles Paul developed here serve as trustworthy guides to resolving interpersonal problems in today's church.

OUTLINE OF CONTENTS

I. Introduction . . . . 1 Cor. 1:1-9
II. Divisions in the Church . . . . 1 Cor. 1:10–4:21
III. Discipline of the Immoral . . . . 1 Cor. 5–6
IV. Divorce and Marriage . . . . 1 Cor. 7
V. Doctrinal Disputes . . . . 1 Cor. 8:1–11:1
VI. Conducting Worship . . . . 1 Cor. 11:2-34
VII. Defining Spirituality . . . . 1 Cor. 12–14
VIII. Understanding Resurrection . . . . 1 Cor. 15
IX. Conclusion . . . . 1 Cor. 16

READING GUIDE (9 Days)

If hurried, you may read only the "core passage" in your Bible and the Devotional in each chapter of this Commentary.

Reading	*Chapters*	*Core passage*
287	1	1:4-17
288	2–4	4
289	5–6	6:12-20
290	7	7:25-40
291	8–10	8:1-13
292	11	11:23-32
293	12–13	13
294	14	14:26-40
295	15–16	15:42-57

1 Corinthians

OCTOBER 14 *Reading 287*
THE DIVIDED CHURCH
1 Corinthians 1

> *"I appeal to you, brothers, in the name of our Lord Jesus Christ, that all of you agree with one another so that there may be no divisions among you and that you may be perfectly united in mind and thought" (1 Cor. 1:10).*

Divisiveness denies the truth that Christ's church is one.

Overview
Paul expressed thanks for his Corinthian brethren (1:1-9), but warned against divisions within the church (vv. 10-17) which reflect human foolishness rather than the wisdom of the Cross (vv. 18-31).

Understanding the Text
"Sanctified in Christ Jesus and called to be holy" 1 Cor. 1:1-3. Paul wished the very best for his readers: "Grace and peace to you from God" (v. 3). But he reminded them and us that to experience God's best, we must become what we are.

What are we? We are persons "sanctified in Christ Jesus." The word *sanctified* means "set apart to God." In Old Testament times sanctified persons, places, and things were never used for profane or ordinary purposes. They could only be used in God's service. The sanctuary table dedicated to God held loaves of bread. But not even the priests of Israel could put a meal on that table, pull up their chairs, and eat from it.

Paul said the Corinthians, "together with all those everywhere who call on the name of our Lord Jesus," are "sanctified in Christ Jesus." Jesus has set us apart to be God's own, and God's only. As God's people now, we are to live holy lives, not ordinary ones. That's why it is so important for believers to solve the kind of problems that emerged in the Corinthian church. Only as we live the holy life fitting for those sanctified by Jesus will we glorify God or experience His grace and peace.

"You have been enriched in every way" 1 Cor. 1:4-9. The Corinthian church had problems. But it had matchless resources too. Sometimes you and I focus so much on our problems that we forget the spiritual reserves that God has provided for us.

What resources did Paul remind us of? We have God's grace to enrich us, for it was poured out on us when we responded to the message about Jesus (vv. 4-5). We have spiritual gifts to enable us to grow and serve (v. 7). We have Christ's commitment to encourage us, for we know that He will keep us strong and safe until He returns (v. 8). We have God's faithfulness to ensure that none of these resources will be taken from us (v. 9).

It's all too easy for us to focus on our problems, and be overwhelmed. What God wants us to do is focus on His resources, and overcome! (See DEVOTIONAL.)

"Agree with one another" 1 Cor. 1:10-12. This earnest appeal for outward harmony is matched in verse 10 by an appeal for inward unity of "mind and thought." The divisions Paul spoke of are *schismata,* cracks that have appeared in the walls of the church, and threaten to cause the building to tumble. Paul wasn't asking the Corinthians to plaster over the cracks by

pretending to agree. He was asking everyone in Corinth to consider the issues carefully, so that there could be a real rather than false unity in the local body.

Plastering over differences never resolves them. Only when we face common problems together, determined to find a basis for unity, will things get better. This is true in the church. It's true in the family. It's true in all of life.

"Quarrels among you" 1 Cor. 1:11-12. Some folks get upset over the fact that Christendom has so many different denominations. "See!" they shout as they point to these verses in 1 Corinthians. "It's wrong for believers to say, 'I'm a Presbyterian,' or 'I'm a Baptist.' There should only be one grand Christian church, with no divisions."

But Paul here was dealing with quarrels. He was dealing with factions that not only competed, but were actively hostile to each other. The believers who made up the "party of Paul" and those in the "party of Apollos" fought and argued over who was best, right, and most Christian.

All Christian communities in first-century cities divided up and met in a number of different house-churches. Paul doesn't hesitate to identify one such congregation as folks "from Chloe's household" (v. 11). I don't expect he'd have any serious problem identifying modern Christians as folks "from the Baptist Church on 5th and Main," or from the "Presbyterian Church on Little Road."

So lets not make too much of such distinctions. Let's remember that Baptist or Presbyterian, Christ's church is one church. But, if the Baptists and Presbyterians start to quarrel over which group is right, or who are the best Christians, then we need to be concerned.

"Is Christ divided?" 1 Cor. 1:13-16 The basis for Christian unity is Jesus, who died for all who believe. Our union is with Jesus, and He is the source of our identity.

One of my wife's girlhood friends, a devout Catholic Christian, says bluntly that she is a Christian and a Catholic, but that she's a Catholic first. I appreciate her loyalty to her church as well as her sincere dedication to the Lord. But her approach to faith is too much like that of those in Corinth, whose allegiance to Paul or Peter or Apollos drove them to debate. In truth, our allegiance is to Jesus, and is not divided. He is One, and because He is the Head of every believer, the church is one.

My friend Bob Girard put it best when he moved to the Verde Valley in Arizona and wrote on the visitor's card his first Sunday in a new church. Where the card asked, Would you like to become a member of this church? Bob wrote, "I already am a member of the body of Christ. So naturally I want to become involved in any way I can with my brothers and sisters here."

If we nurture this attitude, the church of Jesus, which is one, will be one here on earth.

"Words of human wisdom" 1 Cor. 1:17-24. The word "wisdom" is one of the most significant words in Scripture. In both Testaments it involves the application of knowledge to guide daily life. The "wise" must have truth, and be able to apply it.

Mere human wisdom breaks down at both these points. Though all have smatterings of truth, human cultures and societies are flooded with lies and half-truths. And human wisdom is unable to either separate truth from fiction, or to correctly apply truth even when it is discerned.

Paul offered proof. When the message of the Cross is proclaimed, how does the self-proclaimed "wise man" respond? Those with roots in Jewish culture insisted on miracles to prove it. Those with roots in Greek culture insisted that it be "intellectually respectable." Neither realized that the preaching of the Cross is "the power of God and the wisdom of God" (v. 24).

Why this critique of wisdom here? Because those who quarreled over which splinter group of Christians was closer to God were relying on mere human wisdom. They marshalled their arguments, completely missing the central fact that in Christianity everything must be related to Christ.

Don't be surprised if non-Christians laugh at our faith. Carl Sagan publicly ridicules Creation. Ted Turner scoffed at the Cross in a speech to media executives. But never mind. "Has not God made foolish the wisdom of the world?" (v. 20)

Never mind. Just don't go taking a worldly approach to solving problems in Christ's church!

"God chose the foolish things of the world to shame the wise" 1 Cor. 1:26-31. The intelligentsia and the wealthy and the politically powerful are the shakers and movers in human society. They're the people who count: the people to see if you want to get something done. But, Paul pointed out, their intelligence, wealth, and power were absolutely useless when it came to winning salvation.

To bring salvation to the world God's Son became a poor Man, a Carpenter. He lived in a backward corner of the world, died a criminal's death, and even after His resurrection there were "not many . . . wise . . . not many were influential . . . not many were of noble birth" who responded to the Gospel's Good News. It follows that we Christians have nothing of which to boast, except of Jesus. Jesus Himself is our righteousness, our holiness, and our redemption.

What a rebuke for those who quarreled over mere human leaders. They not only argued like men of the world, they turned away from Jesus.

Jesus is the unifying center of our Christian faith. As we contemplate Jesus, we are so humbled that boasting in some supposed superiority of our little group seems to be the foolishness it is.

▶ DEVOTIONAL
Out, Damned Spot
(1 Cor. 1:4-17)

Shakespeare portrays Lady MacBeth, a conspirator in the murder of her king, compulsively washing her hands again and again. She feels that a spot of the king's blood has been splashed on her hand, and it rivets her attention.

Often we Christians respond a little like Lady MacBeth when we discover problems in our church or home. We almost compulsively focus on the problem, talking about it constantly, going over each detail again and again. Like the dear lady, we feel deep frustration, and the more we talk, the more serious the problem appears.

I'm not suggesting that you or I should avoid facing problems. Not at all. We should look honestly at things that need to be corrected, in our personal lives, in our families, and in our churches. But we should look at them positively. We should look at them confidently, in the full assurance that we can resolve them successfully.

In his Letter to the Corinthians Paul expressed confidence before he even mentioned the first problem. The Corinthians had been enriched by God's grace (vv. 4-6). They had been enabled with a full complement of spiritual gifts (v. 7). They had been strengthened by fellowship with Jesus Christ (vv. 8-9). Because of these matchless resources Paul was sure that the Corinthians could face and overcome their many problems.

Think about it. Only after the Corinthians had been reminded of their resources in Christ (vv. 4-9), did Paul go on to discuss the problem (vv. 10-17).

What a pattern for us to follow. Let's count up our spiritual assets in Christ. Then let's face our problems honestly, in the complete confidence that together we can resolve them in His strength.

Personal Application

Looking to Jesus first gives perspective on our problems.

Quotable

"It is called the community of the saints because they have fellowship in holy things, yea, in those things whereby they are sanctified, that is in the Father and the Son, who Himself sanctifieth them with all that He had given them. Thus everything serveth to the betterment and building up of one's neighbor and to the praise and glory of God the Father."—Menno Simmons

OCTOBER 15 *Reading 288*
SERVANTS OF JESUS
1 Corinthians 2–4

"What, after all, is Apollos? And what is Paul? Only servants through whom you came to believe—as the Lord has assigned each his task" (1 Cor. 3:5).

Only servants" is good for leaders to remember. And followers too.

Overview

In Corinth, Paul depended on God's Spirit (2:1-5), who makes the wisdom of God's message plain to believers (vv. 6-16). Divisions showed the Corinthians were still spiritual infants (3:1-4): the mature would realize leaders were merely servants of God and of the church (vv. 5-17). "Boasting about men" is worldly foolishness (vv. 18-23). So honor all God's servants—including Paul!—(4:1-13) and respond to instruction (vv. 14-21).

Understanding the Text

"I came to you in weakness and fear" 1 Cor. 2:1-5. My son Tim gave his first "devotional" the other night. He doesn't enjoy speaking, and was a little more than nervous. I suspect most of us feel "weakness and fear" when opportunities to minister come. But did you realize this puts us right there beside the Apostle Paul? What's most important, of course, is to remember that our impact doesn't rest on our brilliant or persuasive presentation, but on the Spirit's power.

We may have Paul's fears. But we also have the Spirit who made his ministry so effective.

"God's secret wisdom" 1 Cor. 2:6-10. The "wisdom of this age" relies on human senses to gather information, and the "rulers of this age" rely on the human intellect to put the gathered data together. "Rulers" was used by Paul of both religious and secular leaders, none of whom understood what they were doing when they crucified Jesus. The human senses (the eye and ear of v. 9) and intellect (the mind of v. 9) simply cannot grasp what God is doing in the world.

Paul offered proof. If human beings had the barest notion of what God was about, they would never have crucified Jesus.

So don't be overwhelmed by the eloquent or the intellectual of this world. And don't let them make you feel impotent. You know the "secret wisdom" of God.

"Expressing spiritual truths in spiritual words" 1 Cor. 2:13-14. Translators have struggled with the meaning of the Greek word *synkrinontes,* translated "expressing" in the NIV. It's better to take it as "bringing together." The Holy Spirit, who inspired the words of Scripture, lives in us, and enables us to accept and apply spiritual truth. He "brings together" the words and their meaning in ways that those without the Spirit simply cannot grasp. For they do not "accept the things that come from the Spirit of God, for they are foolishness to him" (v. 14).

I remember going once to a general assembly meeting of the United Nations in New York. Each seat had its earphones, with several channels. A speaker could use his own language, and if I turned to the English language channel, I could hear a running translation. This is what Paul was saying here. Scripture speaks a language that is foreign to humankind. Only a person with the Spirit, God's translator, can understand what is really being said.

When you read Scripture, be sure to ask God's Spirit to "bring together" its meaning for your life.

"The spiritual man makes judgments" 1 Cor. 2:15-16. The word for "makes judgment" is *anakrino.* It is used 10 times in 1 Corinthians, and means to examine, scrutinize, to investigate. The Scripture gives us an objective standard by which to evaluate "all things." But even more, the Holy Spirit confirms, and communicates to us the very "mind of Christ."

Don't make the mistake of thinking that Paul was concerned here with doctrinal systems or theological speculation. This verse does not guarantee that spiritual people will dot every theological "i" and cross every doctrinal "t" the same way. What Paul meant is that as you live your life all you need is Scripture and the Spirit to make wise and godly choices. In the Spirit you have access to the very "mind of Christ," and can know God's will!

Don't waver back and forth with every breeze of well-intended advice. Listen. But rely on the Spirit to show you what the Lord wants you to do.

"Mere infants in Christ" 1 Cor. 3:1-9. Even a child knows what infants are like. They're those tiny people who cry and scream, who kick their arms and legs without going anywhere, and who mess their diapers. No, it's not hard to tell a baby when you see—or hear—one.

It's the same spiritually. There's one unmistakable sign of spiritual babyhood: worldliness. Thinking, and behaving, just like the people of this world who lack the Spirit (v. 3). Here adulation of leaders, and the "jealousy and quarreling among you," are characteristic of the way "mere men" think and act.

How utterly foolish to exalt those who are "only servants," when God is the source of all spiritual growth, no matter who ministers (v. 6). And then, to quarrel over which leader is better.

Watch out for spiritual babies. As they kick and yell, they all too often bruise folks who come too near. And some spiritual babies never grow up.

"His work will be shown for what it is" 1 Cor. 3:10-15. True servants of God aren't motivated by adulation or a large following. They honestly want to build Christ's church. And they build on the one true foundation, Jesus Christ. They keep the focus of their followers on Jesus, not on themselves. Not even on their vision of a Christian Disneyland, or of the largest church building in the U.S., or of the biggest radio or TV following.

Paul knew that his accomplishments would be evaluated one day on just this basis. Was he working to promote Jesus or himself? When Judgment Day comes, the "quality of each man's work" will be revealed (v. 13).

Knowing this, what do we care how other people evaluate our service for Jesus? What do we care even for "success," or the praise of others? The only true success is in serving Jesus and His people well. The only reward we seek is Christ's, when our service for Him is judged at the last day (v. 13).

"You yourselves are God's temple" 1 Cor. 3:16-17. The Corinthians thought of leaders as the really important folks in the church, and argued, with a tad too much enthusiasm, over which leader was best.

That was foolish because, as Paul had said, leaders are only servants of Christ. God is the source of all spiritual growth and accomplishment, whichever leader He may work through. So focus on God, not your leader.

There's another reason the Corinthians were foolish. Paul said, "You yourselves are God's temple and . . . God's Spirit dwells in you" (v. 16). Who is really important? The temple of God? Or the servant who mops, polishes, and works to beautify it?

Next time you're tempted to glorify some human leader, picture him with a rag and polish. And picture yourself as a beautiful golden panel that leader has been assigned to polish. Honor him or her for the work. But remember that his job is to bring out the beauty in you, to the glory of God.

"So then, no more boasting about men!" 1 Cor. 3:18-23 What's left to boast about if we can't tell others how interesting our preacher is? Or how beautifully our choir sings. How aesthetically the building is designed. How worshipful the atmosphere when the organ begins to play. How active our young people's group. How dedicated to service the women's club.

Paul had a suggestion. Remember that "all things are yours" in Jesus Christ. Because you are His, and He is yours, glory in this world, life, death, the present, the future—are all within your grasp. So if you feel like boasting, boast about Jesus.

Boast about your pastor, someone might come to hear him, and be impressed. Boast about your church building, someone might come to see, and compliment you. Boast about Jesus, and someone might realize his need, and be saved.

"I do not even judge myself" 1 Cor. 4:1-5.

Paul honestly didn't care if the Corinthians "cross-examined" him. The image is of a preliminary hearing, held before a legal case goes to court. What human beings say is irrelevant. God was the sole Judge of Paul's motives and ministry.

To drive his point home, Paul said he did not even "cross-examine" himself. He didn't agonize over his motives, or pry into every dark recess of his mind to find out if his service was totally pure.

Paul wasn't competent even to judge his own motives. How could he be critical of others?

Paul had drawn two conclusions from the fact that Jesus will one day judge His own servants. Each promotes our mental and spiritual health. We don't judge others, and thus are freed from a critical spirit. We don't judge ourselves, and thus are freed from constant, agonizing self-doubt.

Accept Paul's conclusions, and get rid of both these weights. They simply drag you down. Then get on with serving Jesus and others with enthusiasm and joy.

"What do you have that you did not receive?" 1 Cor. 4:6-7 Don't you love the arrogance of the "self-made man"? "I did it all myself," he says. "I worked three jobs for two years. Then I saw an opportunity, took the risk, and now I'm a multimillionaire."

Of course, God gave him the health he needed to work three jobs. And the sharp mind, able to see the opportunity. And God saw that he was born in a country where a person could take risks, and succeed. But, other than the fact that every ability the self-made man used was a gift from God, he did it "all himself."

Paul wasn't trying here to steal credit from those who use their God-given abilities. He was just reminding arrogant Christians that it's God who "makes you different from anyone else." Anything we have we received as His gift. In that case, "Why do you boast as though you did not" receive it?

Pride is one of the most unspiritual attitudes of all. It reveals a total failure to credit God as the source of all our accomplishments.

"Already you have become rich!" 1 Cor. 4:8-21 Quarreling over leaders in Corinth was an expression of pride. The parties didn't really care whether Apollos or Cephas or Paul were superior leaders. They wanted to feel superior, so they claimed to follow the more polished and powerful preacher!

Paul contrasted his own way of life with theirs in verses 8-13. The Corinthian Christians (in their own eyes) were rich, self-satisfied, wise, strong, honored. Paul was viewed by the whole world as a poor fool, poverty-stricken, weak, dishonored. Paul didn't drive his point home. But he might have.

Even the unspiritual Corinthians had to realize that in service to Christ, Paul towered above them all. They even owed their faith to the apostle, who "became your father through the Gospel." As a first-century father had the right to set the pattern for his sons' way of life, Paul urged his spiritual children to discard their pride, grow out of spiritual infancy, and "imitate me" (v. 16).

We all imitate others. Let's be wise in the choice of those we choose as our examples.

▶DEVOTIONAL
A Popgun for Christmas? (1 Cor. 4)

I wanted a BB gun so badly. I was only six or seven. When Grandpa Zeluff grinned, and showed me the gun-shaped package under the Christmas tree, I was so excited I could hardly wait.

Everyone seemed to smile at me as the presents were passed out, one by one, till only that gun-shaped present remained. Then I had it in my hands! I tore off the paper—and almost burst into tears. It was a popgun. A toy for a toddler. It didn't shoot BBs. It fired a cork, all of two to three feet.

I choked out a "thank-you" to Grandpa Zeluff, and went outside. And then I did cry.

I suspect that many Christians have looked under the Christmas tree and seen a Christ-shaped package. They've opened it with great excitement, but somehow the power they expected to find just hasn't been there. In their life, Jesus has seemed about as effective as that popgun of mine, able only to poof out a cork or two.

Why? Why should our faith fizzle, and

become a popgun experience? In 1 Corinthians 4, Paul gave a number of reasons. First, we get sidetracked (vv. 1-7). We either criticize or rely on ourselves and our leaders, forgetting that the source of all success and the focus of our faith is God. Try relying on mere men for a while—on any mere man—and your faith will never generate more than popgun power.

Second, we get comfortable (vv. 8-17). We assume that Christianity is a matter of soft pews, dressing up on Sundays, and maintaining the respect of outsiders. We forget that the Apostles, who displayed dynamic spiritual power, saw Christianity as a calling to selfless service. Paul suffered to serve others. Concentrate on comfort rather than service, and you have all the popgun power of a popgun religion.

Finally, we get arrogant. We know the right words, and we treat Christianity as if it were just a matter of words rather than a matter of living as citizens of a heavenly kingdom. When faith is a matter of talk rather than a daily walk with Jesus, the power simply is not there.

I wept when I got my popgun that Christmas. What a disappointment. But how much more terrible to become a Christian expecting to experience God's power, and then to settle for a popgun religion.

You don't need to.

Keep your focus on Jesus. Concentrate on service. And walk daily with the Lord.

Personal Application

Find out for yourself that the kingdom of God is a matter of power.

Quotable

"Shortly before Christmas, John Sung [later the great evangelist of China] accompanied some fellow students to a special evangelistic campaign at the First Baptist Church. He expected to hear Dr. Haldeman, an eloquent and learned preacher, but instead, the speaker was a 15-year-old girl! She spoke simply and yet powerfully. The proud, skeptical heart of the Ph.D. scientist was moved to the depths. He determined to discover for himself the secret of such spiritual power. He began reading Christian biographies 'to investigate the secret of the effective ministry of great Christians of the past' and 'soon discovered that in each case it was the power of the Holy Spirit that made the difference.' Turning down opportunities to teach science in America and China, he decided rather to give his life to preaching the Gospel."—John T. Seamands

---

OCTOBER 16 *Reading 289*
CHURCH DISCIPLINE
1 Corinthians 5–6

> *"What business is it of mine to judge those outside the church? Are you not to judge those inside? God will judge those outside. 'Expel the wicked man from among you'" (1 Cor. 5:12-13).*

It is the responsibility of believers to keep the church morally pure.

Background

Church discipline. Christ's church represents Him on earth. Thus it is vital that the church be pure, holy, and self-cleansing. First Corinthians 5 makes it clear that persistent immorality requires discipline by the local congregation, and that if a believer fails to respond to discipline, he or she is to be cut off from fellowship.

It's important to note several things about discipline. First, it is NOT exercised over differences in doctrine. It is NOT exercised over differences in conviction. It is NOT exercised over divergent opinion on procedure, or questions about motives. Church discipline IS exercised only in cases where a believer openly and persistently engages in practices which Scripture identifies as sin. In such cases, the church is not judging so much as agreeing with God's verdict that certain behavior is sinful.

Church discipline is not to be vindictive, nor an attempt to punish a wrongdoer. It is to be a loving attempt to restore a sinning brother by acting out on earth the interruption sin causes in our fellowship with God. It is an obedient response to the Lord, who calls us to maintain a pure and blameless reputation as we represent Him.

Overview
Paul called for expulsion of an immoral brother (5:1-8), but not isolation from immoral non-Christians (vv. 9-13). Legal cases should be settled within church (6:1-8), as befits saints (vv. 9-11). Sexual immorality is unthinkable because of the believer's union with Christ (vv. 12-20).

Understanding the Text
"Put out of your fellowship the man who did this" 1 Cor. 5:1-3. Who is responsible for church discipline? You are. I am. The "you" in Paul's directive is plural, indicating that members of a congregation are accountable for the purity of the local body.

Matthew 18:15-17 is usually understood to give a pattern we can follow. First go to a brother alone. If he repents (stops doing what was wrong), drop the issue. If not, bring along another person and confront him again. If he repents, drop it. If not, bring in the leaders of the church. If he will not listen to them, inform the church as a whole, and "expel the wicked man from among you" (v. 13).

This process isn't an easy one to follow; many Christians would rather just look the other way. That happened in Corinth. And it happens in modern churches too. Yet through Paul the Lord tells us that, even though it hurts, church discipline must be enforced.

"Hand this man over to Satan" 1 Cor. 5:4-5. Long ago God told the serpent who had hosted Satan, "You will eat dust all the days of your life" (Gen. 3:14). Some commentators have observed that while Satan eagerly seeks the believer's life, all he ever gets is the dust of our bodies. Our souls—our essential self—is safe with God (1 Cor. 5:5).

Many see a reflection of this thought here. Expelled from the church, with the protection of believers' prayers withdrawn, the person under discipline is handed over to Satan "so that the *sarx* [the body, the flesh, not 'sinful nature' here] may be destroyed" (v. 5).

The sinning believer is out of fellowship, yes. But not out of Christ! Dust is still all the devil gets. "His spirit [is] saved on the Day of the Lord."

"A little yeast works through the whole batch of dough" 1 Cor. 5:6-8. Like yeast, malice and wickedness can quickly infiltrate and corrupt the spiritual life of a local congregation. Church discipline isn't an option. It's a necessity.

"Not at all meaning the people of this world who are immoral" 1 Cor. 5:9-13. Christians aren't party-poopers, always going around with a disapproving glare, pointing out the sins of others. Christians are partygoers, meeting others with a happy smile, always ready to lend a helping hand.

Somehow many Christians have the idea that unless they jump all over non-Christians and condemn their sins, they imply approval. Not at all. Everyone who gets to know us soon becomes aware of what we don't do, and would not do. But we don't judge non-Christians. We let the Holy Spirit convict. What we do is to associate with wicked folks when in good conscience we can, to show by our holy and happily lives that there's an alternative.

We need to be the kind of persons unsaved folks turn to as an alternative, not turn away from as an aggravation.

"You must not associate with anyone who calls himself a brother but is. . . . " 1 Cor. 5:9-13. "Must" is a pretty strong word. But it's the word Paul used. Don't worry about making the world holy by criticizing unbelievers. The world is simply being itself. Do worry about keeping the church holy by disciplining fellow believers. The church needs to be itself too!

"Take it before the ungodly for judgment instead of before the saints?" 1 Cor. 6:1-6 Paul wasn't asking Christians to accept the role of victim. In New Testament times, ethnic communities had a significant amount of self-government, including the right to settle disputes by applying their national law even if they weren't living in their homeland. So Paul implied here that

Christians, who are citizens of Christ's heavenly kingdom, ought to settle their legal disputes among themselves, applying the laws of Christ's heavenly kingdom rather than relying on earthly courts.

The shame was that the folks in Corinth either did not think of appointing a panel of fellow believers to settle disputes, or else were unwilling to.

I do watch one TV program each day when I can. It's "The People's Court," which comes on here at 10 A.M., about when I finish half my day's writing. The program concludes with a line we Christians ought to modify. The host says, "So, if you have a dispute you can't resolve, don't take the law into your own hands. Take it to court." Paul said, "Take it to church."

"You yourselves cheat and do wrong, and you do this to your brothers" 1 Cor. 6:7-11. I got a letter the other day from "Peacemakers International," a Christian ministry that seeks to help Christians resolve disputes in a biblical manner. It urged those who received it to get involved in a dispute between a well-known Christian and a believer who worked for him for some time, and finally has been taken to court. Not that it's over one of those "trivial cases" Paul mentioned in verse 2. Some serious charges are involved. The problem is, the "victim" has been willing to take it to a panel of Christian lawyers to settle out of court. But the other person has not—and has used verse 7 to condemn the brother who finally brought the suit!

What if the victim is willing to use a biblical procedure, and the perpetrator is not? "Peacemakers" says, "Treat him as you would a pagan or a tax collector" (Matt. 18:17). And there's no injunction in Scripture about taking one of them to court!

"The wicked will not inherit the kingdom of God" 1 Cor. 6:9-11. An apt paraphrase is, "The wicked are headed for hell." And Paul then went on to list behavior that requires such punishment: adultery, homosexuality, criminal behavior, alcoholism.

Don't think though that even such acts cut one off from the possibility of grace. Paul said, "That is what some of you were" (v. 11). That's *were.* What a Christian becomes, after he has been washed, sanctified, and justified in the name of Jesus, and is an ex-adulterer, an ex-homosexual, an ex-criminal, an ex-alcoholic. Don't let anyone who practices such sins deceive you by claims that he or she is a citizen of God's kingdom now.

▶ DEVOTIONAL
Sex and Sandwiches
(1 Cor. 6:12-20)

He was young. Good-looking. And he ardently challenged Billy Graham in a question/answer period after the evangelist's televised talk to college students. Why all this fuss about sex? If a person is hungry, he eats a ham sandwich, doesn't he? If he feels the urge, why not have sex and satisfy that hunger?

The question, though I saw the program about 15 years ago, reflects our society's blatant move toward pagan sexual standards. It also reflects the attitude of some Christians in Corinth, whom Paul quoted as he returned in these verses to the question of immorality. "Everything is permissible for me," Paul himself said of food choices (v. 12; cf. Rom. 14:14). And "God will destroy" this sinful body and replace it in the resurrection (1 Cor. 6:13). Why make such a big deal about what a person does with this meaningless ol' body anyway?

Paul's threefold response answered the question about sex and sandwiches as well as the Corinthians'. That casual pagan attitude toward sex fails to see that the body is important. The body is meant for the Lord, as a tool through which He performs righteous acts (v. 13; cf. Rom. 6:16-18). The body is important enough that God has determined to resurrect it (1 Cor. 6:13-14). The body is even now joined to Jesus Christ through our spiritual union with Him. Can we take Christ to visit a prostitute? (vv. 15-17)

In paganism, sex really is trivial. The casual attitude, the adolescent snickers, even the heated passion that constantly leers from movie screen and TV tube, all suggest that sex and sandwiches are on a par. Only Christianity affirms that life here on earth has more significance, and that our bodies were created for higher purposes.

Our bodies are temples of God's Spirit. Our bodies are instruments for His use. Our bodies—all we are and have—were bought with a price. We Christians are determined to use our bodies only to glorify Him.

Personal Application

Sex isn't trivial, because you and your body are special to the Lord.

Quotable

"Sex has become one of the most discussed subjects of modern times. The Victorians pretended it did not exist: the moderns pretend nothing else exists."—Fulton J. Sheen

OCTOBER 17 *Reading 290*
MARRIAGE MORALITY
1 Corinthians 7

"But since there is so much immorality, each man should have his own wife, and each woman her own husband" (1 Cor. 7:2).

Marriage is intended to be a joy—and a lifelong commitment.

Background

Confusion in Corinth. Paul didn't spell out the background when he discussed problems in Corinth. He didn't need to. He and the Corinthians knew the situation well. We, however, have to re-create the situation from clues in Paul's advice.

Most scholars draw this picture. Corinth was proverbial for sexual looseness. Paul taught a strict morality, but after he left, the church became confused about how to apply his teachings. Some opted for celibate marriage, assuming sex even in marriage was sinful. Some believed Christians shouldn't marry. Some thought they should divorce unconverted spouses. Others, who had been deserted by pagan spouses, wondered if they were somehow guilty of violating Christ's command, and if they were still bound in a now-empty relationship. In this brief chapter Paul clarified all these vital issues, and answered questions many ask today.

Overview

Husbands and wives are to meet each other's sexual needs (7:1-7). The unmarried with overpowering needs should wed (vv. 8-9). Christians should not seek a divorce, even from unbelieving spouses (vv. 10-14). But if one's partner leaves, the believing spouse is not bound (vv. 15-16). Paul advised retaining the place held when converted (vv. 17-24). He advised celibacy, but didn't restrict the virgin or the widow who wished to marry (vv. 25-40).

Understanding the Text

"It is good for a man not to marry" 1 Cor. 7:1-7. Paul frequently began by quoting what folks in Corinth had been saying. He did this here. And Paul agreed with the quote, insofar as it expressed his personal opinion. He did not agree that it expressed his official teaching (cf. v. 7).

We need to be as careful as Paul in making this distinction. It's one thing to tell someone, "Here's what I think best." It's another entirely to say, "Here's what all Christians must think or feel or do."

We shouldn't impose our personal preferences on others. And we shouldn't let others con us into believing their preferences are binding on us.

"The husband should fulfill his marital duty to his wife, and likewise the wife to her husband" 1 Cor. 7:2-5. The Bible identifies three functions of sex in marriage. Sex is a means of procreation of children, and the seal of marital intimacy (Gen. 2). And sex meets a legitimate human need.

It isn't "spiritual" to dislike sex. It isn't "spiritual" to have celibate marriages. What's spiritual is to realize that as a husband you are privileged not only to love your wife, but also to be God's gift to meet her sexual as well as other needs. What is spiritual is to realize that as a wife you are privileged not only to love your husband, but are also privileged to be God's gift to meet his sexual as well as other needs.

If you want a spiritually intimate marriage, giving your body gladly and lovingly to your partner plays an important part.

"It is better to marry than to burn with passion" 1 Cor. 7:6-9. Paul was not a supporter of the "anti-sex" clique in Corinth. While he himself had gladly chosen the celibate life, he realized that "each man has his own gift from God."

Today we recognize that hormones play a key role in the sexual drive of both men and women. Some, in Paul's terms, "burn." And some do not. Don't make the mistake of viewing one condition as better, or more spiritual, than the other. Paul didn't. The structure of our bodies, including the heat our hormones generate, is part of our gift from God. So don't look down on those whose physical nature is different from your own.

And don't envy them, either.

"I give this command (not I, but the Lord)" 1 Cor. 7:10-11. Paul spoke very bluntly when he shifted from giving personal advice to passing on Christ's command. Those folks who thought of sex as dirty and wrong, and were proceeding to divorce their spouses for "spiritual" reasons, must stop!

Immediately after stating a wife "must not," Paul added an "if she does" condition. Why? Quite likely because some in Corinth, in their eagerness to do what they thought God wanted, had already obtained divorces! Now Paul told them to remain single or be reunited with their spouses, and live together as man and wife.

There are valid reasons for divorce and separation (cf. Matt. 19:9). But there are no frivolous reasons for divorce. God's goal is a real marriage, that lasts a lifetime.

"The unbelieving husband has been sanctified through his wife" 1 Cor. 7:12-15. The next question the Corinthians were sure to ask was, "What about those of us married to non-Christians? How can we have a 'spiritual' relationship with an unbeliever?"

Paul's answer was surprising. When just one partner is a believer, the family is "set apart" to God through His relationship with the believing person. This is no guarantee that spouse or children will be converted. It is a guarantee that God's power flows from the believer, rather than Satan's power flowing from the unbeliever. The Christian radiates Christ, and all within the circle of his or her influence are affected by the divine magnetism. Rather than break contact by divorce, the Christian who already has an unsaved spouse who is willing to stay married to him or her should seek to deepen the relationship, not break it.

Let Christ touch your spouse and your children through you.

"If the unbeliever leaves" 1 Cor. 7:15-16. Sometimes a person can't help a divorce. Are we still bound to a relationship our spouse has abandoned? Paul's reassuring answer was, "A believing man or woman is not bound in such circumstances" (v. 15).

I've just contributed to an InterVarsity Press book that presents four views on divorce. There may be no more hotly argued question in many churches. There certainly is no issue that causes greater pain and anguish for anyone personally affected. It seems to me that Paul here takes a stand with grace. When a marriage simply cannot be maintained, and the relationship has in effect ended, let it go. The believer is "not bound" in such circumstances. He or she is unmarried in fact, and thus free.

In debates of this kind, where strong arguments exist for various interpretations of the biblical text, it's generally best to find yourself on the side of grace. That's where God usually is.

"Retain the place in life that the Lord assigned" 1 Cor. 7:17-24. Paul summed up his teaching with a general principle that is applicable to many different situations. Did God call you as a married person? Then stay married. Were you a slave? Then don't feel you have to be free, though you can take the opportunity for freedom if it comes.

A tremendously exciting concept underlies this principle. God can use us wherever, and whomever, we may be! You don't have to be free to be spiritually significant. You don't have to be married. Or celibate. The chances are that God can and will use you just where you are.

So don't fall into that awful "if only" trap. If only I were a college grad, we think, God could use me. If only I had a million dollars. If only I'd gone on to seminary. If only I didn't have a wife and 11 kids.

The devil loves to have us play "if only." It keeps our eyes on fantasy, and off reality. If we open our eyes to what's around us, we might be used by God where we are.

"What I mean, brothers, is that the time is short" 1 Cor. 7:25-35. Paul applied his "retain place" principle to marrieds and singles. But he also made an important point. It's so easy to get caught up by concern for the welfare of a spouse. It's so easy that we may become "engrossed in" the things of this world, in our attempt to make a better life for him or her.

We should love our husband or wife. But we Christians most of all should put God first—together.

▶ DEVOTIONAL
Undivided Devotion
(1 Cor. 7:25-40)

"June! Can you come over tonight? We've just met the nicest young man!" Ever notice the matchmaking that goes on in a church? Or how we pressure people to marry? A single person starts coming to church, and within a month everyone's busy trying to arrange a meeting with this or that prospect. It's the same with widows and widowers. "Would you like to come over this evening. We've met the nicest woman, and she's just your age!"

Well, it's not fair. Especially to those with a gift that Paul values highly: the gift of celibacy. We can make it really hard for men and women who, for their own reasons, choose not to marry. Instead of respecting their choice, we assume that there must be something wrong with them—and we mount campaigns to correct it!

Paul made it clear that virgins and widows are free to marry if they wish. But he wanted us to give brothers and sisters the freedom not to marry if they wish—and not to be harassed about their choice.

It may help us back off if we consider Paul's reasons. He said (and every married person knows it's true) that "those who marry will face many troubles in this life" (v. 28). The married become responsible for spouse and children, and thus have a powerful motive to be "engrossed in" the things of the world (v. 31). After all, we've got to provide a house to live in. And with the costs of a college education these days, we need to work harder and save more money than ever before!

Now, it's right to be concerned with "pleasing" our spouse. But the responsibilities that come with marriage mean we have less time, less money, and less energy to devote to pleasing God. Our choices are, rightly, shaped by considering the welfare of our families.

The unmarried, however, are free from all such restrictions, able to give "undivided devotion to the Lord." And this, the gift of undivided devotion, is something that God is certainly pleased to receive.

So the next time a single person comes into your fellowship, welcome him or her gladly. And forego the matchmaking. You may have one of those special people who has decided to follow Paul's advice, and live a life of undivided devotion to the Lord.

Personal Application

Welcome and honor singles in your church family.

Quotable

"This is self-renunciation—to unlock the chains of this earthly life which passeth away and to set oneself free from the business of men, and thus to make ourselves fitter to enter on that path that leads to God and to free our spirit to gain and use those things which are far more precious than gold or precious stones."—Basil the Great

OCTOBER 18 *Reading 291*
GOD AND IDOLS
1 Corinthians 8–10

"Be careful, however, that the exercise of your freedom does not become a stumbling block to the weak" (1 Cor. 8:9).

A person can be right about doctrine, and yet very, very wrong.

Background

Meat offered to idols. These chapters consider two separate but related issues. In Corinth most fresh meat was purchased at temple markets, which sold carcasses of animals offered to the deity they honored. Some Christians in Corinth argued that to buy a steak at such a market was participation in idolatry. Others thought this view foolish. After all, the gods represented by the idols weren't real. Paul affirmed the right of the Corinthians to eat such meat, but urged those who feel free to do so to consider surrendering this "right" in any situation where a weaker brother's conscience might be harmed.

The other issue concerned participation in banquets, which in the Roman world were typically dedicated to some god or goddess. Here Paul warned against participation, on the basis that though idols are not real, real demonic forces as well as immorality were associated with such feasts. A final note dealt with an ordinary supper invitation to the home of a pagan friend. Paul suggested the guest make no fuss about the meat, but if the host made a point of saying it had been offered to some pagan deity, then don't eat.

Overview

Eating meat purchased from a temple meat market is not wrong, but harming a weaker brother is (8:1-13). The Corinthians should follow Paul's example, for he had surrendered many apostolic "rights" to better serve others (9:1-27). Idolatry and associated immorality were to be avoided (10:1-13), so it was wrong to participate in banquets held in honor of some pagan deity (vv. 14-22). But a Christian could eat meat at an unconverted friend's house, unless the friend specifically said the meat had been dedicated to a pagan god (vv. 23-33).

Understanding the Text

"Since their conscience is weak, it is defiled" 1 Cor. 8:4-12. It's nice to be right. Those folks in Corinth who scoffed at pagan idols and held tight to the one true God probably felt a glow of self-satisfaction when Paul confirmed their view (vv. 4-6). They could pull up their chairs to a steak every night if they wished, and do so with a clear conscience.

The glow may have faded quickly, though. Paul reminded them, and us, that there's something more important than being right. And that's caring about the spiritual well-being of others.

Paul didn't ask folks who are right to surrender their doctrinal insights. He didn't even ask them to surrender a steak dinner now and then. He just asked them to care enough about others to be more concerned with their well-being than with either being right, or exercising personal rights.

Eating that steak at the church social doesn't improve or harm spirituality. Meat has nothing to do with that. But sin has a lot to do with spirituality. And it is sinful to knowingly wound the conscience of a weaker brother or sister in the Lord.

So be glad if you have a mature grasp of theological issues. But take pride in your mature surrender of personal rights out of love for a less mature Christian brother or sister.

"Am I not an apostle?" 1 Cor. 9:1-27 Paul presented himself as one who had surrendered many personal rights for the benefit of others. This was not bragging. It was sharing. As such, it was a powerful revelation of the motives that not only drove Paul, but also can energize us as we seek to serve the Lord.

Note first the rights Paul surrendered—and then his motives. He gave up the right to marry and travel with a "believing wife" (v. 5). He gave up the right to be financially supported by those he ministered to (vv. 6-12). And he gave up the right to live as he pleased in order to meet the expectations of those he ministered to (vv. 19-23).

Why? Paul wanted to make preaching the Gospel a gift, not a purchase (v. 18). He wanted to fit in with others, so as not to personally offend anyone who needed to hear the Gospel (vv. 22-23). He placed such a high value on the rewards Christ will give in the future that mere earthly pleasures held little attraction (vv. 24-27).

If you and I are as eager to serve God, as sensitive to others, and as focused on eternity, our "rights" will seem unimportant to us as well.

"These things occurred as examples" 1 Cor. 10:1-11. Paul turned again to the question of idolatry. This time he made an important point. The Bible isn't just a book of doctrine. It's a book of human experience as well. The experiences recorded in Scripture are intended to serve as examples for us.

Here Paul's argument from experience was that though the Old Testament community like the New participated in Christ (vv. 1-6), this was not enough. Some turned to idolatry and the immorality associated with it—and were destroyed (vv. 7-9). Some complained bitterly about their lot—and these too were destroyed (v. 10).

These experiences should serve as a warning to those Corinthians who are so sure of their doctrinal correctness. Those who "think you are standing firm, be careful that you do not fall!"

Being "right" is no guarantee we won't sin!

"God is faithful; He will not let you be tempted beyond what you can bear" 1 Cor. 10:13. Being right is no guarantee against sinning. But God does make us a promise. We are able to successfully overcome every temptation—if we take God's way out of it.

Don't think that God's way out is all that hard to find, either. Paul summed it up in the next verse when he said, "Flee from idolatry."

That word "flee" occurs several times in Paul's writings. The Greek word, *pheugo,* is found here, in 6:18; 1 Timothy 6:11; and in 2 Timothy 2:22. We're not only told to flee idolatry, but to flee fornication, flee love of money, and to flee youthful lusts. We may have to stand and fight Satan (James 4:7), but when it comes to temptation, Scripture's "way to escape" is just that: escape!

"Eat whatever is put before you without raising questions of conscience" 1 Cor. 10:23-33. It's not necessary to parade your faith. It's not even necessary, when eating lunch with non-Christian business associates, to bow your head and fold your hands in

First-century banquets like the one pictured above were commonly dedicated to a pagan god or goddess, and all were expected to offer a libation as part of the festivities. Paul urged Christians not to attend. Demonic forces lay behind paganism. One who participates in Christ can hardly join in the worship of demons (vv. 14-27).

obvious prayer. You can say, "Thank You" to God as you lift that first spoonful of soup.

That's essentially what Paul was telling the Corinthians here. You don't have to make a big show of being a Christian. Go on out to supper, and if your host makes no big deal out of the meat having been offered to an idol, enjoy it!

There's another side to this issue, though. Sometimes non-Christians have their own ideas about what a believer ought and ought not to do. So the host might feel uncomfortable offering a believer a dish made from dedicated meat. In that case, Paul said, don't eat, for the sake of his conscience! And, if your associates ask if you want to "say grace" before the meal, do it. Again, for the sake of their conscience, not yours.

What a sensitive way for Christians to live with others. Free, because we know the truth in Christ. But willing always to surrender any freedom that will benefit believer or unbeliever alike.

▶ DEVOTIONAL
When Doctrine Divides
(1 Cor. 8:1-13)

At first glance it looks like a fight over roast beef. One group said, "Don't eat it! It's polluted!" The other said, "Looks all right to me. Mmmm. Tastes good too!"

Actually it's a doctrinal battle, set in the kitchen. The folks who cried, "Polluted" were saying that any animal offered to a pagan deity bears the taint of idolatry. The folks who said, "Tastes good. And less filling," were saying that pagan deities aren't real! So whatever was offered to an idol can't be polluted by the act!

What fascinates me here is that Paul showed us a fascinating approach to resolving our doctrinal disputes. He didn't say, "Well, this group is right." Instead he said, "Knowledge puffs up, but love builds up. The man who thinks he knows something does not yet know as he ought to know. But the man who loves is known by God" (vv. 1-3).

What in the world was he saying? Simply that those arguments about "who's right" won't help settle doctrinal disputes! The claim of superior knowledge just leads to pride. And that pride was ill-founded. Whatever we know, we know it imperfectly. So those fights about who is right about doctrine can only isolate us from one another. In view of our human limitations, we can't even be sure the winner of the argument is more than half right!

What Paul suggested is that we approach doctrinal disputes on the basis of love, rather than of knowledge. Love doesn't puff people up, it builds them up. And love opens up our hearts to the ministry of the Spirit of God, who is able then to instruct both parties in the debate (implied by v. 3, "is known by God").

What about while we're waiting to learn? Why then, each group needs to be sensitive to the other's convictions and conscience. We can exercise our freedom and live by our personal beliefs. But we also need to be "careful, however, that the exercise of your freedom does not become a stumbling block to the weak" (v. 9).

Is it wrong to dispute over doctrine? Not at all. It's only wrong if dialogue becomes a dispute, and dispute dissension. We need to hammer out our understanding of God's truth. But we need to do it together, so we can learn from each other. And we need to do it in a spirit of love, so that both parties can grow spiritually through the experience.

Personal Application

Hold on to your doctrines, but hold on even tighter to your brothers and sisters in Christ.

Quotable

"It has not pleased God to save His people by dialectic."—Ambrose of Milan

OCTOBER 19 *Reading 292*
WOMEN AND WORSHIP
1 Corinthians 11

"In the Lord, however, woman is not independent of man, nor is man independent of woman" (1 Cor. 11:11).

Worship is still too significant to be conducted in an unworthy manner.

Background

Women and social customs. First Corinthians 11 is one of the most difficult biblical passages to interpret—and one of the easiest to twist. This is due in part to a tradition of interpretation that misunderstands several key terms, but mostly to our ignorance about certain first-century social customs and their meanings. Yet as we read carefully, it is clear that Paul carefully guarded against one major misinterpretation of his teaching. He did not want us to misuse this passage to justify the subordination of women to men in the church. He did not want us to think women are somehow less significant, or less able to contribute to mutual ministry, in the local community of faith. Women did "pray and prophesy" in first-century Corinth, and Paul clearly affirmed their right to do so (11:5, 10). So must we.

Overview

Men and women should preserve cultural distinctions between the sexes as both participate in worship (11:2-16). Fellowship meals should exemplify rather than deny Christian unity (vv. 17-22), and a distinction maintained between such meals and the Lord's Supper (vv. 23-34).

Understanding the Text

"The head of the woman is man" 1 Cor. 11:3. Most modern commentators agree that Paul was not establishing a hierarchy here. He was instead affirming that a distinction exists between men and women, man and Christ, Christ and God. The distinction is proven by the headship of one in relation to the other. "Head" here is not used in the modern sense of "head of state." It is used in the first-century and biblical sense of "source." Yes, women and men are different. Genesis 2 pictures Adam as the source of Eve, even as Christ as Creator is the source of mankind, and God as Father, the source of the Son.

But note. Woman is no more inferior to man in their differences than Christ is inferior to God! Difference, and even headship, is no basis for discrimination against one of the sexes.

"Every woman who prays or prophesies" 1 Cor. 11:4-10. Paul assumed that women, like men, should pray and prophesy in meetings of the local church. That was not a problem for Paul. The problem was that in Corinth the women did this with their "head uncovered."

The Greek word may suggest a head covering, as the NIV. But many believe it indicates loosed or unbraided hair. Just why this was a problem in the first century is something no one can imagine. First-century art showing men and women gives no hint. First-century pagan and Christian literature alike are silent. But clearly something about head covering or hairstyle was significant in that culture. To preserve the reputation of the church, Christian women were not to adopt styles the culture defined as appropriate to men.

Don't be distracted by what we don't know. What we do know is that women did "pray and prophesy" along with men in church meetings. And that Paul did not forbid, or even criticize, this practice.

"A sign of authority on her head" 1 Cor. 11:10-16. Please note. Paul didn't say a "sign of submission." He said a "sign of authority." Some, impelled by a misuse of "head" and a tad of male chauvinism, have added words lacking in the Greek. They say the hairdo is a "sign of [the man's] authority on her head." In fact, it's just the opposite!

As best as we can reconstruct the situation, some of the Christian women in Corinth were so excited at the freedom they had in Christ to participate in worship that they overreacted. If they could speak out, as men had always been able to, then they were now like men! And they would look and act like men!

Paul's reaction was one of horror. Didn't these women realize that God created the race male and female? That He made a distinction that was to be preserved? Even more, didn't they realize that now, in Christ, women have God's own authorization to participate as women in the life of the church?

By rejecting female headdress, the women of Corinth were denying the very truth that excited them in the first place! By trying to look and act like men, they obscured the fact that they now had authority to participate in worship as women!

What a wonderful truth this reminds us of. In Christ, none of us have to deny who we are. In Christ, every person counts! Each of us has significance; each has a gift and the authority to use it, and so contribute to others in the body of Christ. Just as we are.

"Woman is not independent of man, nor is man independent of woman" 1 Cor. 11:11-16. Paul added this, to make sure his earlier words would not be twisted. Yes, men and women are different. Yes, man (Adam) was the source of woman (Eve). It's even true that Eve was created to fill a need in Adam, rather than the other way around (v. 9). But some have drawn from this the notion that women are subordinate creatures.

To make sure that no one so twists his meaning, Paul added this section on interdependence. Life itself tells us that both men and women are necessary to the continuation of the race. Thus the drawing of Eve from Adam does not imply that women as women are subordinate. It implies they are necessary!

What a counterbalance to the teaching of some that women have no significant ministry to perform in the church. Men and women may be different. But as far as praying and prophesying are concerned, the ministry of both sexes isn't optional. It's required.

"It is not the Lord's Supper you eat" 1 Cor. 11:17-22. Social clubs were popular in the first century. These clubs held regular dinners, usually in a sponsor's home. Within these clubs clear social distinctions were maintained. The host or hostess would not only seat upper-class members above those in the lower classes, but also upper-class members would be given better wines and food, and sometimes would be served two or three times as much to eat as others!

Apparently the Corinthians imported the club dinner into the church, and dubbed it the "Lord's Supper." And the hosts and hostesses in Corinth followed normal practice and fed upper-class members well, while giving the poor only scraps!

Two great sins were involved. The one was to deny the unity of the body of Christ by making such distinctions (v. 22). What an opportunity such a meal would have been to affirm the truth that all are equal in Jesus Christ (cf. Gal. 3:26-29).

The other sin was to completely miss the significance of the Lord's Supper (see DEVOTIONAL). What is intended as one of the Christian's most solemn acts of worship became a rowdy party. And Paul was not amused.

You and I too need to approach worship with respect and great care. The God we come to honor is worthy of our best. Anything less is unacceptable to Him. And should be to us.

"That is why many among you are weak and sick" 1 Cor. 11:27-32. Worship in Corinth had become so lax that God intervened with judgment. Let's not let this happen to us.

What Paul called for was self-examination. Let's examine our hearts as we come to God, renounce any evil we find, and let the service of worship lift our hearts up to God.

▶ DEVOTIONAL
In Remembrance
(1 Cor. 11:23-32)

The Communion service is a unique expression of our faith. And the word "remembrance" is the key to understanding its significance.

The parallel word in the Old Testament is *zikkaron,* usually translated "memorial." Passover was a memorial feast. The pillar of stones that marked Israel's passage through the Jordan River was a memorial too. Like the others, these memorials were a witness to the past—and a call to each believer to enter into his heritage. As the Israelites ate the Passover meal, each family relived the experience of its ancestors. As an Israelite passed the heap of stones by the Jordan, and touched their rough surface, he or she was led back in time, and realized afresh that he was there when God parted the waters.

Communion too is a memorial. It is remembrance. Not of an event covered with the dust of centuries, but of an event that is ever fresh and new. Not of an experience witnessed by men and women long dead, but of an experience we share today as we return, through the elements that represent the body and blood of Jesus, to the foot of the cross.

In the Communion service we stand there again as, united with Christ through faith, we share His death even as we share in His resurrection. "Do this in remembrance" is an invitation to experience the awesome moment when our salvation was won.

"Do this in remembrance" is an invitation to experience the holy and, by coming into the very presence of God, to offer Him our thanks, our worship, and our praise.

Personal Application

Take Communion "in remembrance" of Jesus and His sacrificial love.

Quotable

"The effect of our Communion in the body and blood of Christ is that we are transformed into what we consume, and that He in whom we have died and in whom we have risen from the dead lives and is manifested in every movement of our body and of our spirit."— Pope Leo I

OCTOBER 20 *Reading 293*
TRUE SPIRITUALITY
1 Corinthians 12–13

> *"Love is patient, love is kind. . . . It always protects, always trusts, always hopes, always perseveres" (1 Cor. 13:4, 7).*

Love is the true test of spirituality.

Background

Tongues in Corinth. In first-century pagan culture, ecstatic expression and trances had long been associated with religion. Oracles, such as the famous one at Delphi, featured young women who breathed fumes, and whose mutterings were then interpreted by priests. Epilepsy, which threw its victims into seizures, was called the "divine disease," and a god was thought to struggle for control of the individual at such times.

It's not surprising that the spiritual gift of tongues, here speaking by the Holy Spirit in an unknown, spiritual language, was highly valued by believers saved out of paganism. In Corinth tongues was viewed as the true test of one's spirituality, and those with the gift were considered special.

So in 1 Corinthians 12–14 Paul addressed this issue. He never denied that tongues were a valid spiritual gift. In fact, Paul claimed the gift for himself (14:18). Instead Paul affirmed all the gifts of the Holy Spirit as vital to the body of Christ, held up love as the test of true spirituality, and then went on to correct abuses of the gift of tongues by the Corinthians.

Overview

The Holy Spirit's gifts enable each believer to minister to others (12:1-11). As a human body's parts differ, so do members of the body of Christ, which we are (vv. 12-31). Yet the truest expression of the Spirit's work in our life is love (13:1-13).

Understanding the Text

"Now about spiritual gifts" 1 Cor. 12:1. The Greek text simply says, "Now about the spiritual." Translators have supplied "gifts" because Paul went on to speak about them in verse 4. But it's best to understand Paul's subject as the broader issue of spirituality, not just spiritual gifts.

Most Christians are concerned about spirituality. How do I know when I'm living close to the Lord? What makes a person really spiritual? Is it that he or she prays a lot? Is it mastery of Scripture, or power in preaching? Who should be the spiritual leaders in our congregation? How can we recognize them? Can even I live a truly spiritual life? If so, how?

All these questions, and more like them, are answered by Paul in 1 Corinthians 12–14. If you're hungry for true spirituality, this passage will feed your soul.

"Jesus is Lord" 1 Cor. 12:2-3. Apparently some in Corinth so confused the ecstatic utterance with divine revelation that when such a speaker denied Jesus, some believers began to doubt. Paul said there's no doubt at all. Only one who affirms Jesus as Lord can be speaking by the Holy Spirit.

The utterance of anyone who denies Jesus as Lord comes from another source.

True spirituality is impossible for anyone who is unwilling to go beyond his or her salvation experience. You can receive God's gift of life in Jesus, and be saved. But for spiritual growth you must surrender your life to Jesus. Affirming "Jesus is Lord" involves more than uttering words. It involves committing yourself entirely to Him.

"There are different kinds of gifts, but the same spirit" 1 Cor. 12:4-6. What is important to true spirituality isn't possession of a particular spiritual gift. It's possessing the Spirit!

Paul made a vital point here. God's Spirit works in different ways through different persons. Rather than exalt certain gifts, we should exalt the God who expresses Himself in different ways through all His gifts.

One thing is sure. It is not "spiritual" to focus on the gifts. We are to focus on the Giver!

"To each one the manifestation of the Spirit is given for the common good" 1 Cor. 12:7. You have a spiritual gift. So does every other Christian. And those gifts were given by the Holy Spirit for a specific purpose: "the common good."

This tells us three things. (1) You and I need to use whatever gifts we may have to contribute to the welfare of others. (2) You and I need to be intimately involved with others so that we can minister to them, and receive their ministry. (3) Whatever spiritual gift I may have, it has not been given to set me apart, but to build others up!

As I write it's near Christmas, and the decorations have gone up on houses along our street. How bright and beautiful they look. Spiritual gifts are not like a string of Christmas lights, something to decorate and beautify. Spiritual gifts are much more like a hoe, something that serves as a tool to be used while working in a garden.

We're not to compare spiritual gifts, as if they were given to beautify us. We're to exercise them, as we work in God's field.

"There is given through the Spirit" 1 Cor. 12:8-11. Some of these gifts of the Spirit are visible and spectacular—"miraculous powers," "healing," even "tongues." Others seem almost pedestrian. Who gets excited when someone gives a "message of wisdom" or exercises exceptional "faith"?

This list of gifts isn't meant to be exhaustive. Paul purposely left off many of the more "ordinary" gifts he named in Romans 12:5-8. Why? Because his point was that both the ordinary and the spectacular gifts are given "through the same Spirit." Any spiritual gift is miraculous in its operation, for the work performed is a work that can only be done by God.

If your gift seems ordinary, don't be disturbed. And don't envy those with more visible expressions of the Spirit of God. The contribution you make to the good of others is as completely miraculous, and as much a work of God, as the contribution of anyone else.

"The body is a unit, though it is made up of many parts" 1 Cor. 12:12-31. Paul's powerful analogy was vivid and clear. The church, the body of Christ, is like a human body. Each part is different, yet each part is necessary to create a harmonious whole. Paul even went on to say that "those parts of the body that seem to be weaker are indispensable" (v. 22).

Whoever you are, and whatever your spiritual gift, you are "indispensable" to the others in your church, and in *the* church. So be an active participant in your local congregation.

After all, your left arm wouldn't do you much good if you were in Toledo, and it was in Detroit. The only way you can function as a part of Christ's body is to live in close relationship with them. When you're close to others, you can be their left arm.

And they can be your eyes, ears, and feet!

"Eagerly desire the greater gifts" 1 Cor. 12:31. This verse has been misunderstood by many, who have "tarried" after church to beg God for one of the more spectacular spiritual gifts. But Paul had just spent all of 1 Corinthians 12 arguing that all spiritual gifts are "great," for each is an expression of the Holy Spirit's divine power, and each is indispensable in the body.

At the back of the stage in the theater in Corinth were empty brass vases. The hollow vases were the first "sound system" used to amplify the voices of actors! Paul's "resounding gong" (13:1) is literally "sounding brass"—one of the hollow amplifying vases of first-century theater! And what an image! A person may serve as a channel for the Spirit. But without love, that person is himself a spiritual void, a hollow man. Don't confuse a person's gifts with his spirituality. First Corinthians 13 teaches that the truly spiritual person is filled with love.

It seems best to take this verse as an introduction to a theme developed in chapter 12, and interrupted by chapter 13. Paul would say to the Corinthian congregation, "If you want to emphasize any gifts, emphasize those that involve intelligible speech" (cf. 14:1-7).

But should you as an individual desire "the greater gifts"? Yes, if your motivations and understanding are in harmony with the Lord. Yes, if you passionately want a greater spiritual gift so you can better serve others. No, if you passionately want a spiritual gift so you can appear "special" or "spiritual."

"Love is" 1 Cor. 13:4-13. At last we come to Paul's description of the marks of true spirituality. And we make the amazing discovery that spirituality has nothing to do with one's gifts. It has nothing to do with training. It has nothing to do with platform skills. The truly spiritual person is the individual whose attitude and actions express love.

Verses 4-7 are well worth posting on the bathroom mirror, above the kitchen sink, and by your bed. And well worth memorizing. They remind us what we are to value in others. And what others will value most in us. And, above all, what God values in us.

▶ DEVOTIONAL
Without Love
(1 Cor. 13)

One of the most frustrating experiences a Christian can have is to serve faithfully, and feel totally empty inside.

It's happened to most of us at times. Some Christians live their whole lives feeling that crushing void. And wondering why.

Paul had an answer, in a little phrase found in verse 3. A person can serve selflessly, and if he or she "has not love," Paul said, "I gain nothing."

The text doesn't say that a person who serves "but has not love" is ineffective. Not at all. He or she may have spectacular gifts, and build a giant church where thousands are saved. In Paul's analogy, "If I give all I possess to the poor," the poor will certainly benefit. What Paul said was that while others may benefit from service rendered without love, whatever I do "I gain nothing."

If you've been one of those many Christians who work hard at serving, but still are empty, his reminder may be for you. If you or I serve in order to gain recognition, or because we fear we won't otherwise be accepted, or even because we feel it's our duty, our service will help others. But not us. We'll still struggle with dissatisfaction and loneliness. We'll still feel empty and unfulfilled.

But if we serve others out of love—ah, then we truly are filled! We gain satisfaction. We gain joy. We gain future rewards. And we gain the inner serenity that comes with knowing we have pleased the Lord.

Personal Application

If you lack love, ask Jesus to love others through you.

Quotable

"Tell me how much you know of the sufferings of your fellowmen and I will tell you how much you have loved them."—Helmut Thielicke

OCTOBER 21 *Reading 294*
CHURCH PRIORITIES
1 Corinthians 14

> *"I would rather have you prophesy. He who prophesies is greater than one who speaks in tongues, unless he interprets, so that the church may be edified" (1 Cor. 14:5-6).*

We gather to worship and build one another up.

Background

More about tongues. Modern exercise of the gift of "speaking in tongues" has become a divisive issue in many churches. A careful study of 1 Corinthians 14 should correct excesses of those on both sides of this issue. On the one hand, the validity of the gift of tongues was not challenged by Paul, nor was its exercise. On the other hand, Paul offered no support to those who held that this gift is "the" test of having received the Holy Spirit. In fact, Paul's argument hinged on intelligibility. Whatever happens when Christians gather as Christ's church must be for the building up of believers. Speaking in tongues does not make this contribution, unless the speaker interprets what he or she said.

But perhaps the greatest contribution to settling the controversy was made earlier, in 1 Corinthians 8. There Paul taught that doctrinal disputes do not need to divide Christians if those on each side consider the possibility that they may not have all the answers. Those on each side should constantly express their love for those with whom they differ, seeking to build them up rather than tear them down (8:1-4, see DEVOTIONAL).

Overview

Intelligible speech is to have priority in church meetings (14:1-19), where "tongues" has limited value (vv. 20-25). Participation during services is to be orderly (vv. 26-40).

Understanding the Text

"Especially the gift of prophecy" 1 Cor. 14:1-5. The exact nature of the gift of prophecy as exercised in the first-century church is much debated. Some take 13:8, "prophecies . . . will cease," to mean that after the New Testament writings were complete, special revelations given through members of local congregations were no longer needed. The original "gift of prophecy" has been transmuted into a gift of preaching the Word.

Others hold that this is a gift of revelation. Not that prophecy replaces the Word of God, but that it somehow supplements, while remaining subordinate to, Scripture.

Paul's view was clear. "Prophecy" is instruction uttered in plain, ordinary speech so everyone can understand, that builds up believers. Whatever prophecy was, it did the same thing for the church that a mother does when talking about God as she tucks her child in bed at night. It did the same thing for the church that a family does in reading a devotional book and talking about its meaning. It did the same thing for the church that a Sunday School teacher does when explaining how a passage of the Bible applies to daily life.

You may not think of yourself as a prophet. But you can have a prophet's ministry—and reward—as you share your faith with your family and friends.

"Speak intelligible words with your tongue" 1 Cor. 14:6-19. What we do when Christians gather is minister to each other. We need this perspective, not just for setting the gift of tongues in proper perspective, but for everything we do in our services. In prayer, praise, teaching, and sharing, God can and does use what we say to build up His church.

"Tongues, then, are a sign, not for believers but for unbelievers" 1 Cor. 14:20-25. Here as elsewhere, a "sign" is a visible mark of God's presence or activity. In saying tongues are not a sign for believers, Paul underlined an earlier point. We're not to look to this or any spiritual gift as a gauge of spirituality.

Tongues might have served, in first-century culture, as a sign to unbelievers who associated such phenomenon with a work of God (see 1 Cor. 12–13). But even then intelligible speech has priority in church. As Paul noted, if an unbeliever visits a church meeting and finds everyone speaking in tongues, he'll say, "You are out of your mind" (14:23). But an unbeliever who comes and understands what is being said will be convicted of sin, and converted (vv. 24-25).

Tongues are a valid spiritual gift. But they really weren't anything for the Corinthians to get so excited about.

"Women should remain silent" 1 Cor. 14:34-36. This is one of the most debated passages in the New Testament. Why? Because: (1) It doesn't seem to fit the context of Paul's argument. (2) It doesn't seem to reflect the attitude toward women that Paul displays in other passages, such as Romans 16. (3) It seems to directly contradict what Paul had said in 11:5, 13 about the right of women to "prophesy and pray" in congregational gatherings.

Some have argued, and on strong grounds, that these verses were not written by Paul, but were incorporated from a "gloss"—notes that someone made on an early manuscript. This may be the solution, as surely Scripture does not contradict Scripture, and earlier Paul argued powerfully for the right of women to take an active part in church meetings.

There's another possibility that some have suggested. Perhaps those who upset the orderliness of church meetings in Corinth were women, whose obsessive emphasis on tongues led to outbursts and loud demands. In that case, Paul might not contradict himself at all. First Corinthians 11 would teach that women can participate with men, while 1 Corinthians 14 would correct the abuse of that participation.

I don't think anyone really knows the answer. But we do know, for sure, that when the text says, "It is disgraceful for a woman to speak in the church," it is not saying, "Shut up!" to women who have a testimony to share, a prayer to offer, or a truth to relate.

Women have spiritual gifts too. And a church needs the exercise of those gifts to be healthy and whole.

▶DEVOTIONAL
Come on In!
(1 Cor. 14:26-40)

We knock. The door's thrown open wide, and we're welcomed by a smiling slave. One of the brothers. This is "going to church" in the first century, and we know it's going to be, well, different.

Inside we sit down in the largest room with some 15 or 20 others. The meeting starts with singing, and everybody seems to want to start a hymn. The singing is interrupted now and then as one person or another speaks—contributing "a word of instruction, a revelation, a tongue or an interpretation." We can't make out just who the pastor is. No one gets up in front and talks 30 or 40 minutes. Instead, almost everyone speaks; some just a word or two, others saying more. There's prayer too. And, even though we can't understand the Greek they speak, we sense their warmth and sincerity.

This is the picture Paul gives us of a church meeting in 1 Corinthians 14. One that fits perfectly with other New Testament references to Christian gatherings, found in Colossians 3:15-16 and Hebrews 10:24-25. What strikes us most of all is the informality, and the fact that everyone participates. These folks seem to take the teaching that everyone has a spiritual gift seriously! So everyone is given the opportunity to share.

Somehow in the nearly 2,000 years that have passed since Paul wrote these words, church meetings have changed. They're more formal now. Usually only one person, a professional, selects the hymns, prays, and speaks. The rest of us sit there, dressed up, worshiping. Even learning. But not using our gift, and not being ministered to by others.

I don't suppose any of us seriously imagine that we can go back to the first-century church. Or even that we should. But somewhere in your Christian experience and in mine we have to make room for that same kind of quiet gathering of believers who know, love, and minister to each other.

Maybe this is happening in your Sunday School class. Maybe in a prayer cell. Maybe even in your own living room, in a home Bible study. But it does need to be happening somewhere. You do have a spiritual gift. Others need your ministry to them. And you need theirs.

Personal Application

You don't have to go *to* church to be *in* church.

Quotable

"What matters in the church is not religion but the form of Christ, and its taking form amidst a band of men."—Dietrich Bonhoeffer

---

OCTOBER 22 *Reading 295*
RESURRECTION AHEAD
1 Corinthians 15–16

> *"So it will be with the resurrection of the dead. The body that is sown is perishable, it is raised imperishable; it is sown in dishonor, it is raised in glory; it is sown in weakness, it is raised in power; it is sown a natural body, it is raised a spiritual body" (1 Cor. 15:42-44).*

Life for the Christian never ends. New and endless life lies ahead.

Background

Resurrection. A number of Old Testament passages suggest that God intends to resurrect His saints (cf. Job 14:14; Pss. 17:15; 73:23-26; Isa. 25:8; Dan. 12:2). Yet the doctrine takes clear and definite form only in the New Testament, where the resurrection of Jesus serves as history's great example, and 1 Corinthians 15 provides the exhaustive teaching.

It's important to realize that incidents in the Old and New Testaments of bringing the dead back to life are not resurrections. They were simply restorations to earthly life, and the persons so restored were doomed to die again.

On the other hand, resurrection involves a transformation of the believer's body; an infusion of immortality that renders the believer forever free from the powers of sin and death. It is this transformation, which awaits us at Christ's return, that Paul deals with in 1 Corinthians 15.

Overview

Jesus' resurrection is a thoroughly attested historical event (15:1-11), essential to Christian faith (vv. 12-34). And the bodily resurrection that awaits us is God's final victory over death! (vv. 35-58) Paul closed with an exhortation to give (16:1-4), personal remarks (vv. 5-18), and greetings (vv. 19-24).

Understanding the Text

"This is what we preach, and this is what you believed" 1 Cor. 15:1-11. Ancient mystery religions featured mythical stories of gods who died and were restored to life. These represented the seasons of the year; the deadness of winter, followed by the revitalization of plant life in the spring, in the never-ending, repeated cycles of nature. But such folklore offered no hope to the

individual, who when fallen was planted in the ground, never to rise again.

And then God broke into history in the person of Jesus Christ. It is no myth that Jesus died for our sins, was buried, and was raised on the third day as predicted in the Scriptures. It is no myth that the risen Jesus, who appeared to many witnesses, dies no more. And this, Paul says, is "of first importance" (v. 3). The endless, hopeless cycle represented in ancient nature and mystery religions was broken by a real, historical event: an event that displays the power of the true God—and offers mankind hope.

The literal, bodily resurrection of Jesus is central to the Christian faith. It took place in history—in real space and time. And as Jesus was raised from the dead in this fashion, you and I will be too!

"If Christ has not been raised" 1 Cor. 15:12-19. The notion that the soul persists after death was common in Greek thought. But the idea of a bodily resurrection was not. So some in Corinth spiritualized the resurrection, as some do even today. It was Jesus' "spiritual presence" that the disciples sensed after the Crucifixion. And it was the awareness that what Jesus stood for would never die that transformed the disciples into bold missionaries of a new, positive faith.

To Paul, this was utter nonsense. "If Christ has not been raised, our preaching is useless and so is your faith" (v. 14). "If Christ has not been raised, your faith is futile; you are still in your sins" (v. 17).

What God did for us in Jesus was real. Christ became a real human being, lived a real human life, died a real human death. He was actually raised from the dead in a transformed body, and now lives an endless life. Because the historical Jesus experienced a historical death and resurrection, and only because of this, our salvation is secure.

"So in Christ all will be made alive" 1 Cor. 15:20-29. I enjoy science fiction. The imagination that creates new worlds and strange beings delights me. But when I read I'm always aware of the difference between science fiction and truth. One exists only in the realm of the mind. The other exists in the realm of space and time. The one is fantasy, the other historical, solid, real.

True Christianity is firmly rooted in history. It is touchable stuff. Jesus told Thomas to: "Put your finger here; see My hands. Reach out your hand and put it into My side" (John 20:27). This reminds us all that what we believe is historical, solid, real.

If the past that Scripture describes is real, so is the future! We can look forward to the flowering of the new era Christ introduced in His resurrection. We can know that the day is coming when it will be our turn to rise. To rise, and share in the ultimate reign of God over all.

"Baptized for the dead" 1 Cor. 15:29-34. This is the only reference in Scripture to this practice. Apparently some in Corinth were baptized for dead loved ones, assuming that somehow this rite, that symbolized participation in the death and resurrection of Jesus, might assure their resurrection too. Paul didn't cite the practice because he approved. He cited it only to show that it is inconsistent to both deny resurrection, and then be baptized for the dead in hopes of winning resurrection for them.

Paul believed totally in resurrection, and his life demonstrated it. Knowing and valuing what lies ahead more than present pain or pleasure, Paul "endangers" himself "every hour."

What Paul said makes sense. Our lives should be consistent with our beliefs. How is your life different from that of others because you know resurrection lies ahead?

"The body that is sown is perishable, it is raised imperishable" 1 Cor. 15:35-39. We can't know what our resurrection bodies will be like. Paul himself could only draw analogies.

Our present body is like a seed. When placed in the ground a seed is transformed and becomes a vital, living plant. Resurrection is something like this.

Adam and Christ provide another analogy. The body we inherit from Adam is flesh and blood, driven by its material ("earthy") character. The body we will receive through our relationship with Jesus is spiritual, and like His, will be driven by its spiritual character.

The analogies are insufficient. One thing we do know, however. We who die in weakness will be raised in power, to be forever like our Lord (see DEVOTIONAL).

"Your labor in the Lord is not in vain" 1 Cor. 15:50-58. The author of Ecclesiastes looked back over a busy and successful life, and declared it meaningless. All he had accomplished meant nothing, he complained, for he would die. And what he had built would be left to another (Ecc. 2:17-23).

Paul, however, shouted out in triumph. What we accomplish for Jesus is never in vain. Death is not the end! Death is a defeated enemy, to be swallowed up in victory when God clothes us with immortality. All that we accomplish for the Lord will reflect His glory for eternity.

"Now about the collection" 1 Cor. 16:1-4. After the theological "high" of chapter 15 Paul now brings us down to earth with talk about money. Right?

Not at all. There's a logical bridge here. Because resurrection lies ahead, and what we do for the Lord on earth is not in vain, money has heavenly significance. We use it now with eternity in view.

Paul suggested we give systematically, weekly, "in keeping" with our income. (He had more to say on this in 2 Cor.)

Do keep resurrection in mind as you reconsider your giving. What you spend is gone. What you give is yours forever.

"Do everything in love" 1 Cor. 16:5-24. The close of this letter is warm with love. Here as at the end of Romans Paul mentions person after person—people he knew and cared about—people he wanted the Corinthians to care about too.

"Love" can't be an abstract concept for us Christians. It's a people concept, and only becomes real as we spend time with others.

▶DEVOTIONAL
Sown Perishable
(1 Cor. 15:42-57)

Dad didn't want to go with my sister and me to meet with the doctor. We all knew what the verdict would be. Cancer.

Later Eunice and I told Dad what the doctor had said. The cancer was all through his body. It was just a matter of months.

I moved into my childhood home to take care of Dad those last weeks. At first he sat out in the living room with me and talked or watched TV. As a fighter, Dad overcame many a physical adversary during his 86 years. Now he felt frustrated. This was something he couldn't fight.

Soon he was unable to sit up, and he stayed in bed. As the pain got worse, I gave him regular shots of morphine. I listened as he ranged over his life in his delirium. And I watched his body shrink.

When the men from the funeral home took his body away, he seemed no larger than a small child, curled up on his side. This wasn't the father I'd known in my childhood, so big and so strong. It wasn't my fishing companion of our later years. It couldn't be. And yet it was. As Paul says, the body is sown perishable. Sown in dishonor. Sown in weakness.

But the glorious message of the Gospel is that the shriveled body that returns to the earth is nothing like the body that will be raised! I'll see my father again. I'll share with him in the coming resurrection. And when I do, the body in which he dwells will be imperishable, glorious, bearing no mark of man's weakness, but only the mark of God's power.

That's the vision I have of my dad today. Not the withered frame that lay dead on the bed in my boyhood home. But the vibrant form of the man I knew, vitalized by God's transforming power.

Personal Application

Thanks be to God who gives us this victory through our Lord Jesus Christ.

Quotable

"Taking all the evidence together, it is not too much to say that there is no single historic incident better or more variously supported than the resurrection of Christ."—B.F. Westcott

---

The Variety Reading Plan continues with 2 CORINTHIANS

2 Corinthians

INTRODUCTION

Paul's second Letter to the Corinthians was written a short time after the first. Though some of his instructions were followed, many in Corinth still seem to have rejected the apostle's authority. This most open and revealing of Paul's letters is an "apology": a defense of his apostleship and a compelling revelation of his motives in ministry.

Highlights include Paul's explanation of New Covenant ministry, his expression of confidence in God's transforming power, his teaching on giving, and his clarification of apostolic authority.

OUTLINE OF CONTENTS

I. Personal Items . . . . 2 Cor. 1–2
II. New Covenant Ministry . . . . 2 Cor. 3–13
  A. Principles . . . . 2 Cor. 3–5
  B. Practice . . . . 2 Cor. 6–7
  C. Giving . . . . 2 Cor. 8–9
  D. Authority . . . . 2 Cor. 10–13

READING GUIDE (7 Days)

If hurried, you may read only the "core passage" in your Bible and the Devotional in each chapter of this Commentary.

Reading	*Chapters*	*Core passage*
296	1:1–2:4	2:1-4
297	2:5–3:18	3:12-18
298	4–5	5:15-21
299	6–7	6:14–7:1
300	8–9	9:6-14
301	10–11	11:16-32
302	12–13	12:1-10

2 Corinthians

OCTOBER 23 *Reading 296*
GOD AND COMFORT
2 Corinthians 1:1–2:4

> *"God . . . who comforts us in all our troubles, so that we can comfort those in any trouble with the comfort we ourselves have received from God" (2 Cor. 1:3-4).*

Only the hurting know what it means to be comforted by God.

Overview
Paul praised his God of Comfort (1:1-7), and shared a personal experience (vv. 8-11). He explained his failure to visit, which had been misunderstood (v. 12–2:2), and the reason for his earlier, blunt letter (vv. 3-4).

Understanding the Text
"Paul, an apostle of Christ Jesus by the will of God" 2 Cor. 1:1. This unusual greeting reflects on the background of this letter. Paul's ministry had been challenged, and the apostle rejected, by many of the Corinthian Christians. This had to hurt Paul. But it did not shake him. His appointment as an apostle did not come from the Corinthians, but from God. It's not what they wanted, but what God willed that counted.

I've known many people who have suffered rejection. I've heard pastors weep over being considered—and treated—as nothing more than an employee of the church rather than a minister called by God. I've heard moms and dads with rebellious children weep too.

Paul would understand. And his response to the Corinthians' reaction serves as a guide to all of us in similar situations. Remember first who has appointed you to your role, whether it be pastor or parent, and serve Him. As the rest of this letter shows, keep on loving. Keep on sharing.

"The Father of compassion and the God of all comfort" 2 Cor. 1:3-5. God is not only the source of His servants' authority, He is the source of our comfort as well.

Paul was sure that God understands. He suffers along with us, for as members of Christ's body we are experiencing the overflow of His suffering.

It's all right to weep when the pain is great. But never imagine yourself alone. The God of compassion and comfort is right there with you, and if you will, you can sense His loving arm around you.

"If we are distressed, it is for your comfort and salvation" 2 Cor. 1:3-6. This is one of the most powerful ministry principles to be found in the entire Bible. Paul explained in verse 4: God "comforts us in all our troubles, so that we can comfort those in any trouble with the comfort we ourselves have received from God."

What Paul was saying is that people can identify with those who share the same pain. Have you lost a baby? Then those who have lost a child will understand. Have you known the anguish of a divorce? Then those whose marriages have crumbled know you understand them!

Why is this so important? Because the first reaction to any words of comfort is likely to be, "But you don't understand what I'm going through." Talk to such folks about God's comfort, and anything you say will seem empty and foolish. But listen to their pain, share enough so they know you do understand, and then share the comfort God has given you. This the sufferer can hear.

If you've ever anguished over the pain in your life, and cried out, "Why?" here is one possible answer. The pain has equipped you to minister to others who suffer now as you have. Without experiencing their pain there is nothing you could say that would be heard.

It is only because you hurt that you can help others heal.

"Just as you share in our sufferings, so also you share in our comfort" 2 Cor. 1:7. We parents have this terrible weakness. We don't want our children to go through all the troubles we have had. I find I don't care about winning Lotto for myself. But I sometimes daydream about what it would mean for my boys.

It's foolish, I know. God, lacking this kind of weakness, knows what Paul also understood. Only by going through the painful experiences as Paul himself, would the Corinthians become strong in their faith and commitment to God.

We parents need desperately to understand this principle. The overprotective mom and dad, who try to isolate their children from the troubles of life, do them terrible harm.

"We despaired even of life" 2 Cor. 1:8-11. Paul had that most unusual of qualities: moral courage.

What I mean is this. Most of us, if our authority were challenged, would rise to meet the challenge. We'd ready ourselves for war, gather all our strength, and march out to meet the rebels on the field of battle.

But not Paul. He actually humbled himself to meet the challenge! He put off his weapons, and exposed his weaknesses!

Is an apostle supposed to feel at the end of his strength, unable to endure a day longer? (v. 8) Is an apostle supposed to feel despair? (v. 8) Isn't the dark valley of depression something that only pagans experience, while believers dance on sunlit mountaintops for joy? Some may think so. But Paul knew better. And Paul knew something else too. Only as we minister from weakness, in transparent honesty, will we win others to commitment to Jesus Christ, and to trust in us.

Paul was an apostle. But he was also a human being. Because he suffered, he came to know God's comfort as a reality in his life. In this letter Paul was about to share all, and expose his humanness. Yet in the process he would reveal something else. God was, and had been, at work in his life.

If we want to touch others' hearts, we must take the path the apostle trod.

"In the holiness and sincerity that are from God" 2 Cor. 1:12-14. Today we call it transparency and honesty. Or we say, so and so is "real." Paul used theological terms instead of psychological and ethical ones. But the essential meaning is the same. The holy and sincere among us live without masks. They let us know them and their hearts. They are not perfect, but they are growing. We come to understand them even as we understand what they teach.

In a world when men and women wear masks, the person who wears his real face is often misunderstood. The face he presents is assumed to be a mask too. But keep on living that life of holiness and sincerity. In time everyone will know who you are.

And through you they will come to know God.

"It was in order to spare you that I did not return" 2 Cor. 1:15–2:4. Paul had heard that some in Corinth scoffed at the idea that Paul loved them. And they pointed to the fact that instead of coming himself, Paul wrote them a blunt and (to them) insensitive epistle. "Holy and sincere? Paul? Ha!"

Holiness and sincerity do imply being a person of one's word. Paul fully intended to carry out his promise to visit Corinth again. So he explained why he hadn't been able to do so yet—and why he hadn't wanted to! Rather than hurt his beloved Corinthians, he wrote so they would have an opportunity to correct what was wrong in their fellowship! It's not unusual for a "holy and sincere" individual to be misunderstood. People are likely to impute shameful motives to the best intended actions. People are also likely to criticize actions they don't understand. When that happens to you, it's best to follow Paul's example. Keep on affirming your love. Explain the motives and feelings that lie behind what you have done. Don't take personal offense. And don't quit.

Most of all, don't quit living that holy and sincere life.

You and I can't help what others say about us. But we can make sure that what they say isn't true.

▶ DEVOTIONAL
Caring Enough
(2 Cor. 2:1-4)

Sometime ago David Augsburger wrote an excellent book called *Caring Enough to Confront*. In it he showed that if we really care about others, we will be willing to confront them when their actions call for it.

Paul, who cared enough to confront the Corinthians in his first letter, shows us here just how to go about confronting.

First, he confronted to avoid a greater grief that would otherwise distort their relationship (v. 1). Confronting is a way to keep relationships strong and warm, for things left unmentioned can bring grief.

Second, his goal was not to hurt but to heal (v. 2). Confrontation works only when your motive is to help the other person. Don't think you can confront in anger or antagonism. Your hostility will come through more strongly than any of your words.

Third, he expected a positive response. It takes a large dose of trust in others to free us to confront. Paul's trust had solid roots in his faith in God. He knew God was at work in his brothers and sisters. God would use his blunt words to help them and to heal.

Finally, Paul hurt with the Corinthians as he confronted them. He wrote "out of great distress and anguish of heart and with many tears" (v. 4). Confrontation must grow out of and be an expression of love. You need to hurt along with the person you confront. Your pain will prove your love, and move the other person to respond.

Do you care enough to confront others when they go wrong? If you do, be sure your confrontation is marked by a desire to deepen the relationship, by love, by positive expections—and by personal grief and pain.

Personal Application

Confronting is one of those gifts we only give if we care enough.

Quotable

"The better friends you are, the straighter you can talk, but while you are only on nodding terms, be slow to scold."—Francis Xavier

---

OCTOBER 24 *Reading 297*
TRANSFORMATION
2 Corinthians 2:5–3:18

> *"And we, who with unveiled faces all reflect the Lord's glory, are being transformed into His likeness with ever-increasing glory, which comes from the Lord, who is the Spirit" (2 Cor. 3:18).*

It's not what we are, but what we are becoming, that communicates Christ.

Overview

Paul urged restoration of the penitent sinner (2:5-11). He spoke of his motives (vv. 12-17) and explained implications of the Spirit's New Covenant ministry (3:1-18).

Understanding the Text

"Reaffirm your love for him" 2 Cor. 2:5-11. In 1 Corinthians 5 Paul demanded that a brother living in open immorality be expelled. A majority (2 Cor. 2:6) did as Paul commanded, and the brother repented and broke off the illicit relationship.

While the Corinthians may not have known how to handle repentance, I suspect many felt the sinner deserved to be punished anyway. It seems too easy to let folks who have done wrong off the hook, just because they say, "I'm sorry," and promise not to do it again. It goes against our human sense of justice. A person who does wrong ought to pay.

But the purpose of Christian discipline isn't to punish! It's to restore. We're not out to make a person suffer for his sins. Christ has already suffered for those. What we're out to do is to bring a sinner back to righteousness and to fellowship with the Lord. Repentance—turning away from the sin and back to God—is everything.

How we need to remember this in our families, with our spouses, with our children. We punish to restore, not to make a person pay. Afterward, as Paul said, "You ought to forgive and comfort him, so that he will not be overwhelmed by excessive sorrow" (v. 7).

Love without discipline encourages a self-indulgent life. But discipline without love encourages bitterness and rebellion.

"We are not unaware of his schemes" 2 Cor. 2:11. Satan is much too clever to incite us to do open violence to others. We'd realize how wrong this is, and draw back from our hostile, angry feelings. So Satan encourages us to do destructive things that we can feel holy about.

That's what was happening in Corinth. The penitent sinner was left hanging, even after he renounced his sin, and most of the Corinthians felt self-righteously that justice was being done!

Watch out for self-righteousness. "Well, they deserve it" is true. But it isn't a Christian attitude. We all "deserve it." Yet what God poured out on us so richly was forgiveness, not punishment.

Forgiveness is a gift that has the power to transform. No wonder Satan schemes and struggles to convince us that we should punish instead.

"The aroma of Christ" 2 Cor. 2:12-16. The Gospel message stimulates conflicting reactions. Some who hear respond like a child who smells his mother's chocolate chip cookies baking. Some who hear react with wrinkled noses and expressions of disgust, as though a skunk had just passed by.

People's reactions to the Gospel tell us nothing about Jesus. Their reactions tell us everything about them.

"We do not peddle the Word of God for profit" 2 Cor. 2:17. The reaction of the hearer to the Gospel reveals their character. The motive of the preacher reveals his. Even in the first century, traveling evangelists could draw crowds and make a good living off offerings!

We have no right to judge the motives of anyone in ministry. If you should give, and later discover the ministry was run by a peddler who was only interested in his own profit, don't condemn yourself. God may even lead us to give to a religious huckster, for the Word of God is powerful even when preached with twisted motives. The peddler, who is paid in cash for his services, is the real loser. You still win, for you'll be rewarded in heaven for yours.

"Written not with ink but with the Spirit of the living God" 2 Cor. 3:1-3. With this chapter Paul began his exposition of New Covenant ministry.

The "New Covenant" is that special way in which God relates to human beings now that Jesus has died and been raised again. The "Old Covenant" refers to Mosaic Law, which defined the way God related to human beings from the time of Moses till Christ came.

In the earlier age "ministry" involved teaching the commandments and lifestyle God ordained for the Jews. In the present age "ministry" involves sharing the Good News of Jesus, and opening hearts to the transforming work of the Holy Spirit.

Paul tells us that there is one unmistakable mark of New Covenant ministry. People are transformed, so that what was written in stone is written now on the heart. The world knows of righteousness, not because it is recorded on stone tablets, but because it is engraved on the hearts of Christian men and women around them, and seen in their lives.

"Competent as ministers of a New Covenant" 2 Cor. 3:4-6. What an idea for the church's search committee. Next time you send out a questionnaire, don't ask folks to say how well the candidate preaches, or how often he visits. Simply ask, Has he helped the members of your church be like Jesus Christ?

"Since we have such a hope, we are very bold"

Moses' face shone with glory after each visit he had with God. But that glory faded after a time, and the veil Moses wore was intended to disguise that fact. Paul used this Old Testament incident to contrast Old and New Covenants. The glory of the Old, in which Moses went to God, faded as Moses left His presence. The glory of the New shines ever brighter, for God's Spirit has come to us never to depart, and He is transforming us from within (vv. 7-18).

2 Cor. 3:12-18. New Covenant ministry calls for transparency and honesty. It calls for taking off our masks, and being our real selves with others. It requires us to let others know us as we are. Warts and all.

That's the message of this important passage. It's not a message most are comfortable with. But it's one Paul desperately wanted us to understand.

To help us, he looked back to Moses and the incident of the veil (v. 13). Whenever Moses met with God, his face shone with an awe-inspiring splendor. But the brightness faded in time. Since Moses wanted the people of Israel to see only the splendor, he began putting on a veil to hide his face. Maybe then the people would assume he was still bright with glory. With us, Paul said, it's just the opposite. We're not like Moses. We're bold! We meet others with "unveiled" faces (v. 18).

The reason is a basic difference in our relationship with God. We don't go to meet Him. He has come into our hearts! His Holy Spirit is present within us, and is in the process of transforming us "into His [Jesus'] likeness with ever-increasing glory."

The glory seen on Moses' face was marred by deterioration. The glory that shines out through our faces is magnified by ever-increasing transformation! Thus we take the veils off our faces, convinced that as others are allowed to see the work that God is doing in our lives, they will be convinced that Jesus is real.

I know. It goes against everything most of us have been taught. After all, people say we have to try to present our best face as a "testimony" to Jesus.

But people are wrong. If we pretend, if we try to act holy, all that others will see is our posturing. But if we are real with others—if we don't hide our fears, our doubts, our weaknesses, our struggles—they will know that we are real. And because the Holy Spirit is in our lives, they will sense the reality of Jesus as our transformation continues to take place.

Let's be bold.

Let's believe the Good News of the New Covenant. Trust the Holy Spirit to do His transforming work in your life. And be honest with others, so they can see that Christ is really in you (see DEVOTIONAL).

▶ DEVOTIONAL
"Norm, Meet Jesus"
(2 Cor. 3:12-18)

Dwight buttonholed me as soon as we came out of church. "Larry, I want to talk to you," he said. And for 10 minutes he proceeded to recount the sermon I'd just preached. Later my friend Norm grinned. "He didn't want to talk to you," Norm said. "He wanted to talk at you." I smiled. If Norm had only known.

Eighteen months before two members of our church picked Dwight up off the street. He'd just been released from a local mental hospital, but still was unable to speak a sentence. They took him into their home, where he spent most of the time curled up in a dark closet. They brought him to church, but often Dwight would get up in the middle of the service and run out into the yard.

Then they started bringing Dwight over to my house each Wednesday evening. We'd play basketball, eat hot dogs, and talk together about Dwight's progress and how the couple could best help him.

In time we learned Dwight's story. He'd

been a successful young businessman, with a wife and two kids, a nice home, two cars, a boat. But then he'd become obsessed with illicit sex. Gradually his world fell apart. He lost his job, his home, his family, his cars and boat. Finally he even lost the capacity to talk in sentences. He was below rock bottom when the couple from our church found him and took him into their home.

The morning Norm made his joking remark I thought back over the months since Dwight had come to us. As he experienced the love of his new friends, he'd gradually calmed. As he participated with us in church, he'd found the Saviour. And then, not suddenly but surely, he'd begun to heal. That very week Dwight had begun to work again—he'd started a lawn service. And that morning he'd been able to tell me, in great detail, exactly what my sermon was about, and what it meant to him.

I had the overwhelming realization as I looked that morning at Dwight, that the Person I saw was Jesus. It was Jesus, looking out through the unveiled face of Dwight, revealed clearly through the transformation His Holy Spirit had worked in Dwight's life.

Each Sunday that I came to our little church and looked around, I saw Jesus everywhere. For each of us, like Dwight, had shared our lives with the others. We were an imperfect people. The warts and blemishes of our humanity were all too visible. But we were growing and changing too. In the ever-increasing glory of the transformations taking place, we recognized and knew our Lord.

Personal Application

Let the glory of Jesus be seen in you.

Quotable

"The Christian is a person who makes it easy for others to believe in God."—Robert M. McCheyne

OCTOBER 25 *Reading 298*

RECONCILIATION

2 Corinthians 4–5

> *"God was reconciling the world to Himself in Christ, not counting men's sins against them" (2 Cor. 5:19).*

Counted sins stunt other's growth.

Overview

Paul ministered the New Covenant in honesty (4:1-6), aware of his mortal weaknesses (vv. 7-15) yet confident of the unseen (vv. 16-18). Heaven is assured (5:1-10), as is the love of God which works transformation within the believer (vv. 11-15), assuring the success of the New Covenant ministry of reconciliation (vv. 16-21).

Understanding the Text

"We have renounced secret and shameful ways" 2 Cor. 4:1-6. Paul used no tricks in presenting the Gospel. He set "forth the truth plainly" (v. 2). Some will believe, others will reject. Paul trusted the outcome of his ministry to Christ.

Donald Barnhouse wrote a book called *The Invisible War.* In it he pictured spiritual armies of good and evil conducting their warfare on the battleground of history. This warfare is being conducted yet today, with Satan struggling to blind man's eyes to the Gospel, as God cries out, through the proclamation of Jesus, "Let there be light!"

How foolish we are to rely on our skill to make a material difference in the invisible war. Yet God has in fact entrusted to us the most powerful weapon of all, the simple message of Jesus and His love.

We can rely on the simple story. As Paul wrote to the Romans, it is "the power of God for the salvation of everyone who believes" (Rom. 1:16).

"We have this treasure in jars of clay" 2 Cor. 4:7-15. Paul wasn't being critical of the mortal body. He was simply contrasting the weak and ordinary character of the messenger with the overwhelming power of the message. Paul found himself under

pressure, perplexed, persecuted, knocked to the ground. Everything in his experience reminded him that the dynamic power that had marked his ministry had no source in him. He credited Jesus, who saves all who believe in Him, with the fact that despite his weaknesses he had not been crushed, nor drowned in despair, nor abandoned or destroyed.

Don't let a sense of personal weakness keep you from serving God. The fact that you and I are weak is the backdrop against which the incomparable power of God is revealed.

"We fix our eyes not on what is seen, but on what is unseen" 2 Cor. 4:16-18. This verse is the key to understanding New Covenant ministry. We don't rely on the evidence of our senses. We rely instead on the utter reality of what has been revealed to us by God.

Paul said, "Therefore we do not lose heart" (v. 16). Setback after setback can occur. People we minister to—our children, our friends—can fail again and again. But we remain confident that God's Spirit does transform those who know Jesus, and will work in the lives of those we serve.

Paul said that there is only one thing certain about things we can see and touch and feel. They are temporary: they can and will change (v. 18). And there is one thing certain about the unseen world. God will not change! What He has said is fixed for all eternity.

How much better then to rely on what we cannot see than to rely on what we can see. Never mind discouraging setbacks. Never mind disappointments. These can and will change. Simply count on God, who can't change. And who won't.

"If the earthly tent we live in is destroyed" 2 Cor. 5:1. We know only too well that one of those things which changes is our body. We grow old. We develop wrinkles. Our eyesight dims, our stride shortens, our back bends. One day the body, our "earthly tent," will be destroyed.

The seen is temporary, changeable. How wonderful to be able to look beyond our own decaying frames, and know that "we have a building from God, an eternal house in heaven" (v. 1).

Some ridicule Christians for confidently looking for life beyond death. How ridiculous instead to pin all one's hope on an earthly body that every passing year brings closer to the grave.

"Clothed with our heavenly dwelling" 2 Cor. 5:4-9. Christians earnestly debate Paul's meaning here. Was he speaking about the

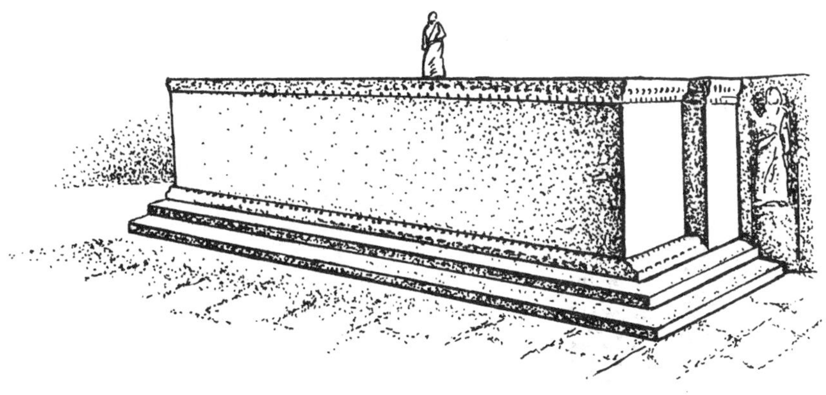

The "judgment seat" (*bema*) at Corinth was a large platform from which official announcements were made, and special honors given citizens were proclaimed. Paul's teaching that "we must all appear before the judgment seat of Christ" (v. 10) is no threat suggesting punishment. It is a promise implying reward!

resurrection body? Or, as the text seems to suggest, was he teaching that an intermediate body is worn by those who die until the time of resurrection comes? No one is really sure. But we can be sure that after death "what is mortal" will be "swallowed up by life."

How can we be sure? The Holy Spirit is a down payment God has made, His guarantee of what lies ahead. The Spirit is unseen, but real. His presence makes it possible for us to say "we are always confident" and that we "know" (v. 6).

"What is seen rather than what is in the heart" 2 Cor. 5:11-14. Anyone other than Paul might have been discouraged at the unresponsiveness and unspirituality displayed by the Corinthians. Many a pastor has despaired over people like them. And many a parent has felt grief and remorse over a rebellious child. But Paul placed no confidence in what is seen (4:18). He was not one of those folks who viewed statistics as the bottom line in ministry.

Yes, it's nice to be able to report 39 folks joined the church, giving is up 18 percent, 7 young people went off to help construct a building in South America, and to bask in the envy of fellow pastors at the annual district meeting.

But Paul took no pride in statistics (in "what is seen"). What counted for Paul was what was in the heart. However discouraging things may be, if Christ is in the heart, believers will be compelled by love to grow. And growth will transform the stumbling, unspiritual men and women of today into tomorrow's saints.

"Christ's love compels us" 2 Cor. 5:14. One of the worst things desperate pastors and parents do is turn to inadequate motivators of spiritual growth. Some say "you must" and try to force growth. Some say "you should" in hope that guilt will move the reluctant. Some say "you can," and try to create a willingness to try.

Paul said, "Jesus loves you." And he counted on an awakening response of love for Jesus to move others to want to grow and change.

Keep on telling others, "Jesus loves you, and I love you too." Love is the unseen reality that motivates spiritual growth and change.

"He died for all" 2 Cor. 5:15. How could Paul have such confidence in the Corinthians, whose unspirituality he admitted in his first letter? (1 Cor. 3:1) Despite the evidence of all those problems in the church?

Paul tells us that Christ died not just to forgive our sins, but to transform us. He died, "that those who live should no longer live for themselves but for Him who died for them." It is unthinkable that God's grand purpose in the sacrifice of His Son should fail. It is unthinkable that the Cross should have no impact on those who believe.

Our progress may be slow. But God is committed to bring all who believe to the place where they gladly live for him!

"We regard no one from a worldly point of view" 2 Cor. 5:16-17. Paul developed the thought of verse 15. Judged from a worldly point of view—by what we can see and observe—some might throw up their hands and give up on the Corinthians. Sometimes we feel that way about our fellow Christians too.

But Paul said that's not the way to look at people. Why, if we looked at Christ from that point of view, even He would seem a failure: a preacher of love, who awakened so much hatred that He was unjustly slaughtered by His enemies.

But if we look at Jesus from God's point of view, we see in the Cross the triumph and not the defeat of God. And if we look at our fellow believers from God's point of view, we see Christ in the heart. And we know, whatever a believer may be now, he is one of God's new creations, and one day he will become a living example of the triumph of God's saving grace.

▶ DEVOTIONAL
Reconciled
(2 Cor. 5:15-21)

Mom and Dad looked at each other in fresh despair. No matter what they did, Jimmy didn't seem to respond. Try to develop responsibility with regular chores, and Jimmy "forgot." Insist he pick up his room before playing, and somehow or other he slipped out of the house before either of them could ask if he'd finished.

Not just once. Not just twice. Dozens of times.

Mom's and Dad's frustration mirrors that of many who come after a time to expect their children—or their charges—to misbehave. Ready to give up, their attitude says loud and clear that they don't really expect their children to change. And that makes change even more difficult.

Paul, on the other hand, exuded confidence in the Corinthians. Even though they challenged his authority. Even though they'd failed time and again. How can we have his confidence in others, and communicate that confidence as well?

Paul understood the nature of reconciliation. This biblical term means, essentially, "to bring into harmony with." Paul was sure that God, who in Christ has reconciled the world to Himself, will work in the believer's life until he is experientially reconciled, and lives that life of righteousness that reveals our harmonious relationship with the Lord.

Paul understood reconciliation. "God was reconciling the world to himself in Christ, not counting men's sins against them" (v. 19). Paul understood, and he modeled his ministry on God. Like God, Paul didn't hold the Corinthians' sins against them. He didn't even count their sins! Instead Paul communicated total confidence. The purpose for which Christ died will be accomplished, and the lives of believers will be brought into harmony with the righteousness of God.

With this assurance, you and I are freed too. We're freed not to count the sins of those who are young in our family or our faith. We're freed not to hold their failures against them. And we're free to communicate our confidence that, though they stumble, they will rise again.

Personal Application

Expect God to work in others, and they will believe that He can.

Quotable

"It is the Christian's business to believe in others until they learn to believe in themselves."—Gilbert R. Martin

OCTOBER 26 *Reading 299*
CARING IN MINISTRY
2 Corinthians 6–7

> *"We have spoken freely to you, Corinthians, and opened wide our hearts to you. . . . As a fair exchange—I speak as to my children—open wide your hearts also"* (2 Cor. 6:11, 13).

To minister effectively, we must do so in love.

Overview

Paul expressed his love for the Corinthians by facing hardships (6:1-10), by personal openness (vv. 11-13), by confrontation (v. 14–7:1), by expressing confidence (vv. 2-4), by joy (vv. 5-7), by rebuke (vv. 8-12), and by delight at Titus' affection for them (vv. 13-16).

Understanding the Text

"Now is the time of God's favor" 2 Cor. 6:1-2. Most feel these verses belong at the end of chapter 5. Yet they also fit here. Paul was about to express his feelings for the members of the church in Corinth. These feelings were intense, because he was gripped by a sense of urgency. "Now," Paul was convinced, "is the day of salvation."

Driven by this conviction and by love for others, Paul gave his all to win them to Christ and lead them to a full present experience of salvation.

Both a sense of urgency and love are vital if we are to have an impact for Christ on those around us. We must be convinced that "now" is vital for them. And we must care.

"As servants of God we commend ourselves in every way" 2 Cor. 6:3-10. Real love is expensive. And Paul had spent himself without holding anything back.

Some might think the physical hardships Paul listed—beatings, imprisonments, sleepless nights, hunger—are the greatest evidences of his love (vv. 3-5). Yet we all know that it's much harder to always show "purity, understanding, patience and kindness" to our loved ones than to suffer hardships for them. You or I might give our lives for a loved one. Yet we find ourselves snapping at him or her in irritation, being critical, or uttering some cutting word we'd never think of saying to a stranger.

Let's remember, as Paul did, that we are "servants of God." As God's servants we have been assigned the task of showing His love to others. We may never have to show that love by braving the kind of hardships Paul faced. But we daily have the opportunity to show love by our purity, patience, understanding, and kindness.

"We have spoken freely to you" 2 Cor. 6:11-13. When I first read 2 Corinthians as a young Christian, I was embarrassed for Paul. He seemed so, well, emotional. I much preferred the reasoned argument of Romans and Galatians, or the visionary images of Ephesians. Only much later did I realize that while Romans and Galatians represent the head, or the intellectual content of the Gospel, 2 Corinthians represents the heart, or the emotional drive of ministry.

Actually, the heart is at least as important as the head. And in this book Paul "opened wide" his heart, for us to see. His emotions spilled out freely, touching us almost against our will. His feelings are so strong that we either draw back, as I once did, or we respond to the warmth.

Why did Paul share himself so freely with the Corinthians, where many were already critical of him? Paul realized that human beings are whole. People are not computers who output programmed information, but sentient beings whose feelings play a vital part in every significant choice.

Emotions play such a large part in every life. If we truly wish to influence others, we must love them, and let the love show.

"Do not be yoked together with unbelievers" 2 Cor. 6:14-18. Paul wasn't speaking here about casual friendships (cf. 1 Cor. 5:9-11). We're not asked or encouraged to cut off all contact with non-Christians.

The image of "yoked together" draws an analogy from an Old Testament law which forbade the Israelites to hitch animals of different kinds to the same plow. Two oxen might work a field together. Or two donkeys. But not an ox and a donkey. Thus partnership in a cooperative endeavor is what Paul forbids. Don't go into a business partnership with a non-Christian and expect that you'll pull together. Don't marry an unbeliever, and expect to walk through life in harmony, matching stride for stride.

There's no guarantee that a professing Christian will make a perfect partner or spouse. But you will have Christ in common, and God will "live with them and walk among them." A common commitment to Jesus is the foundation on which we can build harmonious relationships in our significant personal relationships (see DEVOTIONAL).

"You have such a place in our hearts that we would live or die with you" 2 Cor. 7:2-7. People we care deeply about can have a powerful effect on us. Paul's relationship with the Corinthians had been rocky: they'd given him many an hour of anguish and worry. Yet at the same time that love makes us vulnerable to hurt, it opens up our lives to unexpected joys.

It's this that buoys up the apostle. Despite the troubles that had marked the relationship, Paul had great pride in the Corinthians, and word of their continued affection for him stimulated great joy.

Caring may make us vulnerable. But it also expands our lives and gives us deep and abiding joys. Don't hold back for fear of pain. Press on to deepen your relationships with other Christians in expectation of joy.

"Your sorrow led you to repentance" 2 Cor. 7:8-9. Scholars believe the letter mentioned here is not 1 Corinthians, but another, lost epistle. Paul must have spoken very bluntly: so bluntly he regretted rebuking his beloved friends. But the letter had its desired result, and the Corinthians responded.

Bluntness and rebuke are an important element in love. An acquaintance of ours brought up a son without ever rebuking him. Even worse, whenever the son was in trouble, the mother protected him from harmful consequences. Today the son is married with three children, is in constant trouble with drugs and alcohol, has permanently lost his driver's license, and only holds a job because he works in his father's factory. Misplaced love, unwilling to rebuke, contributed to his situation.

If you really love another person, you will rebuke him or her when you see wrong.

"Godly sorrow brings repentance" 2 Cor. 7:11-13. The world's sorrow is an "I'm sorry I got caught" kind of sorrow. The individual is sorry for himself, and the consequences he now has to pay. Godly sorrow is grief about the original act, and repentance—a commitment to turn from wrongdoing.

We need to be careful when someone says with tears, "I'm sorry." If they're crying because they're sorry for themselves, don't expect a change. If they're weeping because they feel grief over what they did, there's hope.

"I had boasted to him about you" 2 Cor. 7:13-16. Tim brought his new girlfriend, Liz, along to meet Sue and me the other day. He'd told her, "Don't worry. They won't be critical."

It would have been hard to be critical of this girl even if we'd tried. And of course we didn't. Later Tim told us Liz had been worried, and felt so relieved afterward. Tim hadn't been worried. He knew we'd welcome her.

It was so nice to hear that Tim had been confident in introducing us to his currently constant date. That's just what Paul was telling the Corinthians. "Titus really appreciated you. I told him he would, and he did." It makes others feel good when we can tell them honestly, "I am glad I can have complete confidence in you."

Along with infrequent rebukes, true love offers frequent reassurance and praise.

▶ DEVOTIONAL
Be a Father
(2 Cor. 6:14–7:1)

Most of God's promises are claimed simply by faith. Here's a promise, however, that's contingent. "Touch no unclean thing" the Old Testament says (Isa. 52:11), and "I will be a Father to you" (2 Cor. 6:17).

At first this seems a strange promise. After all, God is our Father through faith in Christ. But He is able to be a Father to us only as we live holy lives.

My wife's oldest, Matthew, lives in Michigan with his father. For five years he lived with us, and while he was here, I was able to be a father to him. I disciplined him, took him on fishing trips, got him to bed on time, and did all the other things that are part of parenting. But when he moved to Michigan, I could no longer be a father to him. The distance between us is just too great. That's what Paul is telling us here. God, who is a Father to us, *wants* to be a Father to us. But it's our responsibility to see there's no distance between us.

Usually when you and I read Paul's warning in 6:14-16 about being yoked together with unbelievers, we think of disasters that can result if we disobey. We think of the partner we can't trust; of the spouse whose values and commitments are so different from ours. But Paul wants us to consider first the impact of being unequally yoked in our walk with God.

You see, we Christians are to be completely separated unto the Lord, with that separation as sharp as the dividing line between light and darkness, between Christ and Satan, and between the temple of God and a shrine where idols are worshiped. In short, we are to "purify ourselves from everything that contaminates body and spirit."

Why? Because sin's contamination separates us from God. He is our Father even then, but when we isolate ourselves from Him by bad choices, He is not able to be a Father to us in the same, intimate way He would if we were in close fellowship with Him.

What a joy it is to have God be a Father to us. To walk hand in hand with Him. To be disciplined, yes. But then to be caught up in His arms and comforted as well. No wonder Paul urges us to purify ourselves from everything that contaminates out of reverence for God. There is no greater experience here on earth than to walk with the Lord, and have God be a Father to us.

Personal Application

Each step away from sin is a step closer to our Heavenly Father.

Quotable
"My Lord and my God, take from me all that separates me from Thee! My Lord and my God, give me everything that will bring me closer to Thee! My Lord and my God, protect me from myself, and grant that I may belong entirely to Thee!"—Nicholas of Flue

OCTOBER 27 *Reading 300*
NEW COVENANT GIVING
2 Corinthians 8–9

> *"Each man should give what he has decided in his heart to give, not reluctantly or under compulsion, for God loves a cheerful giver" (2 Cor. 9:7).*

God wants the giver, then the gift.

Overview
Paul reminded the Corinthians of the Macedonians' generosity (8:1-7), and urged them to give (vv. 8-13). Giving is sharing (vv. 14-15): a proof of love (vv. 16-24), and a service to the saints (9:1-5). God will supply those who give (vv. 6-11), for giving stimulates praise and thanksgiving to the Lord (vv. 12-15).

Understanding the Text
"Their overflowing joy and their extreme poverty welled up in rich generosity" 2 Cor. 8:1-5. The poor still tend to be more generous than the rich. Perhaps it is just that those who are needy can better identify with others in need. Or perhaps it's that those with little have learned to trust the Lord so much that they do not fear giving.

When I was in seminary my Uncle Al sent us $20 a month. I was very concerned, because I knew something of the financial burden my uncle labored under. I even (foolishly and most ungraciously) wrote and said that if it was a burden for them, we could get along. They were hurt, but like the Macedonians in Paul's time, "they urgently pleaded with us for the privilege of sharing in this service to the saints." I was relieved, because that $20 was often all we had for food the last week of the month! And I hope I learned then that giving is a joy of which no one should be deprived.

"I am not commanding you" 2 Cor. 8:6-9. Paul brought up the subject of giving because he had sent Titus to Corinth, and one of his tasks was to receive the funds that had been collected there for the needy. Yet Paul maintained a delicate balance in dealing with the topic, and was very careful not to "command" giving.

The Old Testament did command giving. The Law required that a tenth of the produce of the land be contributed for the support of the Levites and priests who led the community in worship. An additional tenth was gathered every third year and placed in local storehouses, for distribution to the poor and needy. Later in Israel's history additional amounts were collected as taxes by Jewish kings, and then by the Gentile emperors who dominated Syria-Palestine. Each of these contributions was required: one had to pay.

Now Paul introduced another principle. No one has to give. And no fixed percentage of income was set as the "right" amount! Moreover, while some giving did go to the support of missionaries (cf. Phil. 4:14-19), most collections mentioned in the New Testment were in the nature of disaster relief, and sent to saints in parts of the world stricken by drought or devastated by war.

No one was commanded to give to meet such needs. But, as Paul reminds us, giving is (1) a grace to be developed (2 Cor. 8:7), (2) an evidence of sincere love (v. 9), and (3) an appropriate response to Jesus, who "though He was rich, yet for your sakes He became poor, so that you through His poverty might become rich" (v. 9).

"If the willingness is there, the gift is acceptable" 2 Cor. 8:10-12. It's easy to daydream about how generous we'd be if we suddenly inherited millions of dollars. But giving is a matter of "what one has, not . . . what he does not have."

God isn't as interested in the amount as

He is in our willingness. Ten dollars from a poor widow may mean more than $10,000 from a wealthy man—and that $10 may have a greater spiritual impact on others.

"That there might be equality" 2 Cor. 8:13-15. The giving we see in the New Testament is sharing, not giving. In fact, the word "share" (*koinonia*) is used more often by Paul in these chapters than the word "give" (*doron*).

What Paul pictured for us is Christ's living body, extended over the entire earth. Money in this analogy is the sustenance carried by the blood supply. It needs to reach every cell, so that each will be able to carry out its function.

Paul did not want one part of the body bloated and fat, while another is starved to helplessness. Instead the part of the body that has shares with that which lacks, aware that one day positions may be reversed. If such sharing does take place, the whole body of Christ on earth will be strong, able to carry out God's will for humankind.

We moderns have a tendency to lose sight of Paul's worldwide vision. We give to pad our own pews, or enlarge our church buildings. Such giving may be valid. But it is not that sharing that Paul or the New Testament envisions in 2 Corinthians 8–9 and similar passages.

"We are taking pains to do what is right, not only in the eyes of the Lord but also in the eyes of men" 2 Cor. 8:16-24. What a principle for modern media ministries to remember. And for the local church as well.

We're all vulnerable to money; if not to cash itself, to the power money represents. This is one reason why every Christian ministry must be protected by establishing financial controls, and establishing a policy of absolute openness concerning its books.

Don't be insulted if someone asks to check on your receipts and expenditures. Thank him. He's doing you the service of holding you accountable to man as well as God.

"Then it will be ready as a generous gift" 2 Cor. 9:1-5. I know some folks think that church budgets are at best unspiritual, and a pledge drive is close to satanic. These can be, if they're manipulative. Any approach to raising money for Christian work is wrong if it operates by producing guilt or twisting arms.

But Paul reminds us that it's not wrong for giving to be organized and systematic. If you pledge, and set apart a certain amount each week, you're more likely to be able to give what you intend to than if you wait till the last moment, and find you're short on cash.

Lack of planning and organization can transform what was intended to be spontaneous and joyful into grudged giving.

▶ DEVOTIONAL
Joyful Giving
(2 Cor. 9:6-14)

Emphasize the benefits! According to my friends in marketing, this is the key to good advertising. Make sure folks see the benefits that accrue if they buy your product.

I imagine that makes it tough for an ad agency trying to sell cigarettes. And for a preacher trying to sell giving! Paul, however, was a master salesman. He stuck strictly to the truth. He didn't push. And yet he made it clear that joyful giving has tremendous spiritual benefits.

No one has to give. In fact, Paul didn't want any reluctant givers. A person who feels he has to give, or gives grudgingly, shouldn't drop a single coin in the collection plate. God doesn't need the money. And that kind of giving won't bring the giver any blessings at all! But if we want to give—ah, then we reap tremendous blessings.

So Paul reminded the Corinthians and us of the blessings that make Christian giving such a joy.

First, giving benefits you materially and spiritually. You see, it's impossible for us to outgive God (vv. 6-11). God is able to pour so much grace into our lives, that having been "made rich in every way" we "can be generous on every occasion."

This isn't a "send in 10 dollars and God will send you 100" kind of promise. It is simply a reminder that God is the source of bread as well as the inner joy we experience in Christ. We give only money. God meets our material needs, and gives us spiritual riches as well.

Second, giving permits us to bless others. What you give supplies "the needs of God's people." Even more, our giving deepens the relationship of others with the Lord. As they realize God prompted us to give, they "will praise God for the obedience that accompanies your confession of the Gospel."

Third, giving stimulates others to pray for us. As others identify us as the means God used to meet their needs, they will respond with gratitude and appreciation. And each of us needs all the prayers we can get!

God doesn't really care about our money. After all, His resources are infinite. But He does care about the spiritual benefits that generosity brings the giver and the recipient of this unusual grace.

Personal Application
Give joyfully, for you will be blessed.

Quotable
"The New Testament does not teach us simply to give away possessions for the sake of giving them away or appearing virtuous. Nor does it encourage us to adopt a 'simple lifestyle' because simplicity has merit in itself. Rather, all of these commands are put in the context of glorifying God and furthering the work of His kingdom, and of laying up treasures in heaven and increasing our heavenly reward."—Wayne Gruden

---

OCTOBER 28 *Reading 301*
PAUL'S APOSTLESHIP
2 Corinthians 10–11

> *" 'Let him who boasts boast in the Lord.' For it is not the one who commends himself who is approved, but the one whom the Lord commends" (2 Cor. 10:17-18).*

The differences between true and false servants of God are surprising.

Overview
Paul further explained his New Covenant ministry, touching on its resources (10:1-6), its essential character (vv. 7-18), its counterfeits (11:1-15), and its costs (vv. 16-33).

Understanding the Text
" 'Timid' when face to face" 2 Cor. 10:1. These words reflect charges made against Paul by those in Corinth who shrugged and tried to dismiss the apostle as an insignificant man.

They surely had their reasons. Paul wasn't much of an orator (cf. 1 Cor. 2:4). He wasn't a dominating personality: "timid" fit far better than "bold." If we can believe early descriptions Paul was unimpressive physically. The earliest account we have describes Paul as a wizened little man, with a large hooked nose, peering up through eyebrows that met in the center of his forehead. Only his bright, twinkling eyes reflected the force of his personality.

It's all too easy for us to dismiss others on the basis of appearances. Or to be overly impressed. The last four chapters of 1 Corinthians serve as an important corrective, as Paul helps us better understand the qualities that make for spiritual power.

Judging by appearances is neither right nor safe!

"We do not wage war as the world does" 2 Cor. 10:2-6. Paul had been dismissed as spiritually irrelevant. He was not. Christians do not "live by the standards of this world" and there is a vast difference between spiritual and worldly power.

Paul relied not on weapons of the world but on "divine power to demolish strongholds." The image here is of an ancient fortified city set to resist a conqueror by taking refuge behind strong walls. Paul knew that those who resisted his authority resisted Christ, who appointed him an apostle. Paul was absolutely confident that God's "divine power" would "demolish" the arguments of those who resisted his authority, for Paul's sole goal was to bring every thought of the Corinthians into harmony with Christ's will.

Three things here lie at the root of spiritual power. To be called by Christ. To have confidence in spiritual rather than worldly power. To desire only to bring others to obedience to Jesus.

Too many try to rest ministries on a two-legged rather than three-legged stool, and thus fall. Some are called and confident, but desire personal power over others. Some are called and seek to bring others into obedience to Jesus, but rely on worldly styles of "leadership." But effective ministry must rest on all three legs for spiritual power.

"Once your obedience is complete" 2 Cor. 10:6. Paul was sure that God's power would work within the Corinthians, to change the minds and hearts of the majority and reestablish their obedience. Any who then continued to resist would be disciplined.

Let's be among the first to respond when called back to Christ. It's dangerous to be among the last.

"Building you up rather than pulling you down" 2 Cor. 10:7-11. Paul used this same phrase again in 13:10 to describe his authority.

This is a critical difference between spiritual and worldly authority. Spiritual authority builds up others. Worldly authority builds up leaders. Watch a parade in Russia, and you see gigantic pictures of Marx and Lenin, with the current Chairman. In a land supposedly dedicated to equality, the fluttering portraits bear witness to the fact that in this world, leaders exalt themselves, not others.

Christians become so used to worldly leadership that unless Christian leaders behave in the same way, we assume they are weak. We want "strong leaders." Leaders the world will look at as "great" because they exalt themselves. It makes us feel good to be the followers of an acknowledged "great man."

But Paul, and mature believers today, knew that spiritual authority is given leaders to build others up. The test of spiritual leaders is not how "weighty and forceful" they appear to the world, but whether they are effective in helping others follow Jesus more closely.

Don't be taken in by the world's fascination with "great men." Choose instead the "timid," unimpressive man or woman who sees authority as the privilege of building others up.

"When they . . . compare themselves with themselves, they are not wise" 2 Cor. 10:12-18. Paul was picturing the yearly denominational get-together. One pastor in Chattanooga is on five radio stations. His friend in Nashville is on six. One candidate for the "fastest growing church" has increased in membership 89 percent. Another candidate claims 89.5 percent. There's a hot debate over baptisms. Seven churches have baptized 38 folks since the last annual meeting. But three of them counted people who were rebaptized, and some of the brethren think this shouldn't count.

Paul looked at this kind of thing and simply said, "They are not wise." Numbers do count. But comparing numbers—measuring ourselves by ourselves—isn't wise.

Paul didn't say exactly why, but I suspect there are several reasons. It makes us unduly proud. It makes us self-satisfied. It shifts our focus from Christ to ourselves. It shifts our focus from the people leaders are called to serve to the leaders themselves. It makes us look to others for approval rather than to Jesus.

Paul avoided all these traps, and simply said he wanted to reach out as far as he could with the Gospel of Christ. And that his hope was the Corinthian's faith would continue to grow.

I suspect if our whole motivation is to share Christ and see Christians grow, the numbers will take care of themselves. And our commendation will come from the Lord rather than from ourselves.

"Sincere and pure devotion to Christ" 2 Cor. 11:1-6. Paul's great frustration was to see the Corinthians showing devotion to human leaders—some even to him!—rather than to Christ. How baffling when modern "super apostles" appear, and our friends seem more committed to them than to Jesus.

"Preaching the Gospel of God to you free of charge" 2 Cor. 11:7-12. We recently had a

TV "exposé" of a tent evangelist in St. Petersburg. They took him to task for the usual things—an emphasis on money, a lavish lifestyle, a million-dollar home. We're so used to such things that it's almost stunning to realize that Paul was being criticized in Corinth for not taking money!

There is one thing anyone in ministry can count on. Whatever you do, someone will be there to criticize you.

Paul was not one of those hard shell types, able to shrug off criticism. It hurt Paul. Just as it hurts most of us. When we do something out of love for others, to have that act twisted and used as a club against us is painful indeed.

In this case, Paul reacted strongly. He explained why he acted as he did, expressed the love that motivated his action, and said he would "keep on doing what I am doing." There are times it may be best to suffer in silence. But there are times when we need to confront criticism, and make our motives clear.

"Satan himself masquerades as an angel of light" 2 Cor. 11:13-15. Don't expect the spiritual fraud or pseudo-apostle to appear wicked. In fact, such people "masquerade as servants of righteousness."

Paul's point was that we must be rigorous in testing those who announce themselves as heaven's great gift to the church! If we stick to the context of these two chapters, we have several tests we can apply. Are our leaders concerned with building us up—or themselves? Do they rely on worldly leadership practices, or the spiritual armory of Paul? Are they eager for personal wealth, or indifferent to it?

If we move to other passages on false teachers we find more specific tests. Is their teaching true to the Word? And do they live what they teach?

Let's not be fooled by the masks people wear, or their pious talk. It doesn't take too much wisdom to distinguish those who want to exploit you from those who wish to serve.

▶DEVOTIONAL
Hire This Man!
(2 Cor. 11:16-32)

The ad said "Résumés Professionally Prepared." It went on to say how important it is to make a good first impression. And how the professional résumé service would help emphasize strengths, and even shape the presentation to the specific job you were looking for. What would happen if the Apostle Paul walked hesitantly into such an office, and diffidently held out the handwritten list of accomplishments that are found in 2 Corinthians 11:16-33? Well, let's listen to the résumé writer.

"A Jew? That's one strike against you, Paul, if you really want to work in Gentile society.

"Ummm. Let's see. In prison. Flogged. Beaten five times by the Jews, three times with rods by the Gentiles. Stoned by a mob. It seems, Paul, you have a hard time getting along with people.

"And this. In danger a lot. From bandits? At sea? In the city? The country? I guess your judgment isn't too good, eh? Always getting yourself in these difficult situations.

"Worked hard, gone without sleep. Often gone without food? I'm afraid your only experience is in the unskilled, low-pay labor market, Paul. You can't expect to get an important job with this your only experience.

"This mention of 'pressure' and 'feeling weak' has got to go. Makes you sound emotionally unstable, you know.

"Oh, no. Fled arrest in Damascus?

"Paul, there's nothing we can do for you. Your résumé reveals far too many weaknesses for you to succeed at anything.

"Oh? The job you're applying for requires weaknesses? What in the world could that job be? Oh, the ministry.

"I see. It's so whatever you accomplish will clearly be through Christ's power, not your own? And so you won't rely on your own strengths or talents?

"Let me make a phone call. 'God, I've got an . . . What? Oh, sure.'

"Paul. You're hired."

Personal Application

God still looks for weak people in whom to display His strength. Want the job?

Quotable

"When God delivered Israel out of Egypt, He didn't send an army. We would have sent an army or an orator. But God sent a man who had been in the desert for 40 years, and had an impediment in his speech. It is weakness that God wants! Nothing is small when God handles it."—D.L. Moody

OCTOBER 29 *Reading 302*
CHRIST IN US
2 Corinthians 12–13

"He is not weak in dealing with you, but is powerful among you. For to be sure, He was crucified in weakness, yet He lives in God's power. Likewise, we are weak in Him, yet by God's power we will live with Him to serve you" (2 Cor. 13:3-4).

Christ in us remains the source of our strength.

Overview

Paul's chronic illness exhibited Christ's power at work through weakness (12:1-10). Paul's "defense" had been motivated by a desire to help the Corinthians understand and repent (vv. 11-21). Christ will surely discipline those who do not test themselves (13:1-10). Paul closed abruptly, with very brief greetings (vv. 11-14).

Understanding the Text

"Visions and revelations" 2 Cor. 12:1-6. Anyone other than Paul would have quickly broadcast reports of the stunning vision of paradise he alluded to here. Paul, however, preferred to highlight his weaknesses. Why? In part perhaps because the revelation Paul mentioned may have been personal: an encouragement from God strengthening Paul for the hardships ahead.

But Paul had another reason. He knew that no one's faith can rest on secondhand experiences. The conversion and growth of the Corinthians must be a response to the Word Paul had been called to teach, not to Paul's report of a personal supernatural experience.

Paul wanted the Corinthians to base their belief on what Paul said (his teaching of truth) and did (his modeling of truth). In this way the Corinthians' faith would be rooted in their own experience of God, not Paul's.

You and I can testify to what God is doing in our lives, and so bless others. But no one can have our experience "secondhand." At best such testimonies encourage others to step out in personal response to God's Word, and experience Him for themselves.

"There was given me a thorn in my flesh" 2 Cor. 12:7-10. Scholars still debate the nature of Paul's "thorn in the flesh." Most often mentioned is a disfiguring eye disease that made it difficult for Paul to read and write (cf. Gal. 6:11). All we really know is that it troubled Paul greatly. So greatly that he prayed futilely for its removal and that he finally came to appreciate his thorn as a weakness through which Christ's power might be more clearly displayed (see DEVOTIONAL).

The lesson Paul learned can encourage us all. That sense of weakness we feel need not keep us from ministering confidently. In fact, it is a source of confidence. The more clearly I realize that God's power is best expressed in weak human beings, the more freedom I will have to serve. And the more Christ will use me.

"I will boast all the more gladly about my weaknesses" 2 Cor. 12:9. In a significant little book on ministry (*When the Vision Has Vanished*), Bob Girard reviews the weaknesses that Paul mentioned in 2 Corinthians 11–12. He notes that Paul admits:

- he was not a skillful speaker (11:6)
- he was seen as a "weak" leader (11:21)
- he had a prison record (11:23)
- he was wracked by internal conflict (11:28-29)
- his prayers had gone unanswered (12:8-9)
- he had been insulted (12:10)
- he had been in distress (12:10)
- he had experienced persecution (12:10)
- he had been afraid of disappointments (12:20)

he had been afraid of rejection (12:20)
he had been afraid of facing difficult situations (12:20)
he had feared public humiliation (12:21)
he had feared he would break down and cry publicly (12:21)
he had been afraid people would not listen, but keep on being rebellious (12:21).

Yet all these things which might make us stamp "failure" on Paul's forehead were actually turned by God into strengths. Paul faced his weaknesses, accepted them, and in complete confidence that God would work through a weak—and thus humble—man, set out to serve with all his might.

When we catalog Paul's successes, the churches he planted, the letters he wrote, the clarification he brought to the nature of Christian faith, we might well stand amazed. All this done by an admittedly weak man? Yes. Because in his weakness this man trusted himself completely to Jesus, so that Christ's power might rest on him.

What an exciting prospect for you and me. Let's not conceal our weaknesses, or deny them. Let's learn to use them, to turn our hearts to Christ that we might know His power.

"The things that mark an apostle" 2 Cor. 12:11-18. The Corinthians were unwilling to take weakness as a mark of apostleship. Or even Paul's failure to demand money! So Paul reminded them that God "persistently" performed miracles among them while he was there.

Paul became a bit sarcastic now. What a crafty fellow! He tricked them into following him by not demanding money! And the only explanation he had was love!

How strange that some Christians are totally loyal to those who exploit them for money. More than one minister has said, and truthfully, "My people want me to drive a Mercedes. They expect me to have a half-million dollar home." And more than one congregation has been contemptuous of those who serve them out of love.

The things you and I see as marks of apostleship are often the measure, not of the man we evaluate, but of our own spiritual maturity and insight.

"Everything we do . . . is for your strengthening" 2 Cor. 12:19-21. When I first read 2 Corinthians, I was embarrassed for Paul. I misunderstood what he was doing in sharing so openly. Only later did I understand how a careful study of 2 Corinthians is not only a course in Christian leadership, but a guidebook for congregations. If the Corinthians would only understand the implications of Paul's sharing in this deeply personal book, their view of ministering and ministry would be transformed.

Then they would respond, not to the exploitative "super-apostle," but to the "weak" Paul. And following him rather than other divisive leaders would bring an end to the "quarreling, jealousy, outbursts of anger, factions, slander, gossip, arrogance and disorder" that marked the church.

Have you learned the lessons Paul was so eager to teach? Does your church understand? Look around. The existence in any church of these sins of Corinth suggests that leaders and people alike have missed Paul's point.

"He is not weak in dealing with you" 2 Cor. 13:1-10. Paul now warned the Corinthians. If they did not respond, he would use the authority he had been given by God to discipline them.

The issue of authority has troubled the church in every age. Too often authority has meant power, and power the ability to punish. Thus some leaders have assumed a worldly kind of authority, and ruled over God's people. Paul rejected worldly authority in all its forms. Yet he warned the Corinthians of the danger of resisting the authority he had received from Christ.

What is this authority Paul had, and how was it exercised? Paul said simply "He [Christ] is not weak in dealing with you, but is powerful among you" (v. 3). Paul's authority was from Christ, and rested entirely on Christ's work among His people. He, Paul, didn't have to do anything to discipline the Corinthians. Jesus, living in His church, "is powerful among you."

When Suzie began living with a married man, we elders went to see her. We encouraged her to see that what she was doing was sin, and to break off the relationship. When she refused, we followed the biblical pattern for discipline laid down by Paul in 1 Corinthians. But we also rebuked Suzie. God does not permit His own to ruin their lives by habitually practicing sin. Exercising our authority, we sternly warned her.

What were we elders going to do? Put her in jail? Fine her? Burn down her house? Of course not. We had no worldly power. But we knew that Christ lives, and is powerful in His church. Our warning simply meant that unless she repented and turned back to the Lord, Christ Himself would act.

And He did.

True spiritual leadership relies on God for spiritual results. And relies on Him to exercise authority over the church which is Christ's body.

"Aim for perfection" 2 Cor. 13:11-14. It's not enough to be an "average church." It's not enough to wait patiently for Jesus to return. God calls us all to aim for perfection: to work toward the goal of fulfilling Christ's purpose in our individual and corporate lives. For this we too must hear Paul's appeal to the Corinthians, to be of one mind, and to live with one another in peace.

▶DEVOTIONAL
Unexpected Gifts
(2 Cor. 12:1-10)

"Why has this happened to me?" She was a young woman, with two children. An aerobics instructor, and a teacher. She'd hurt her back, and been told an operation would solve the problem. But something terrible went wrong. Nerves were cut, and suddenly she found herself able to walk only with the aid of a walker and, most awful of all, without bowel or bladder control.

Some Christians give peculiar answers to the question of "why?" "You didn't have enough faith," some will say. And they are likely to add, "Claim the promises of God and even now He'll heal you." Another person will say, "You sinned in going to a doctor. You should have relied on God only."

I suppose that Paul offered the strangest answer of all. It's found in verse 7. "Your back injury and the operation were a gift from God."

That's what pops out if you look at this verse in the Greek. *Edothe moi skolops te sarki,* it says. "THERE WAS GIVEN ME a thorn in the flesh." And that word "was given" is a word used to denote special favors given by the Lord to His saints (cf. Gal. 3:21; Eph. 3:8; 1 Tim. 4:14).

God gave Paul a terrifying weakness, a chronic illness, and though Paul prayed desperately for relief, God caused Paul to live with it the rest of his life.

As a gift.

You and I do others no favor when we tell them that God guarantees His children health and wealth in this life. That simply is not true. We do them no favor when we tell them if they only have enough faith, they'll be healed. That's not true either. Paul prayed with total confidence, only to learn that the answer was no.

He learned in time that the weakness which devastated him was truly a gift from God. A gift that enabled him to experience God's grace, presence, and power, in ways he would never have experienced them otherwise.

Perhaps this is what we need to tell others, or remind ourselves of, when tragedy strikes and disaster comes. God gives His own strange gifts. But gifts they are. As we seek His strength, we'll discover a depth to our relationship with the Lord that we would otherwise never have known. And a strength that makes weakness a triumph and a joy.

Personal Application

God's best gifts are often wrapped in tragedy and suffering.

Quotable

"I do not believe that sheer suffering teaches. If suffering alone taught, then all the world would be wise. To suffering must be added mourning, understanding, patience, love, openness and the willingness to remain vulnerable."—Anne Morrow Lindbergh

---

The Variety Reading Plan continues with JOSHUA

Galatians

INTRODUCTION

Paul's letter was directed to churches in the Roman province of Galatia, founded during his first missionary journey. These churches were soon visited by men from Jerusalem who denied Paul's apostolic authority. The "Judaizers" insisted that to be saved a Christian must be subject to Jewish Law and adopt a Jewish lifestyle. Grace, they charged, led to loose living. Paul answered each charge in turn in this little letter, proving that believers are saved and enabled to live holy lives by faith, not by Law.

This epistle continues to bring joy to Christians who experience the freeing relationship with the Holy Spirit which Paul explained here.

OUTLINE OF CONTENTS

READING GUIDE (3 Days)

If hurried, you may read only the "core passage" in your Bible and the Devotional in each chapter of this Commentary.

Reading	*Chapters*	*Core passage*
303	1–2	2:11-21
304	3–4	3:26–4:7
305	5–6	5:12-26

Galatians

OCTOBER 30 *Reading 303*

PAUL'S GOSPEL

Galatians 1–2

> *"The Gospel I preached is not something that man made up. I did not receive it from any man, nor was I taught it; rather, I received it by revelation from Jesus Christ" (Gal. 1:11-12).*

God validates the Gospel, not the church or any group of men.

Background

Judaizers. The first Christians were Jews who acknowledged Christ as Saviour. These Jewish Christians continued to express their faith within Judaism, all of them "zealous for the Law" (Acts 21:20). But as the church expanded beyond Judea and Galilee, and Gentiles were saved, tensions developed. Jewish and Gentile Christians had vastly different cultural heritages. And many Jews understandably felt that since God had ordained the Law of Moses, they should continue to express their faith within Judaism's traditions. Some went further, and held that Gentiles must also show their faith by adopting Jewish ways. To be saved, they must keep the Laws given to Israel, be circumcised, and in essence become Jews.

When Paul heard that men representing themselves as messengers from the Apostles in Jerusalem were teaching legalism in the Galatian churches, he was incensed. He immediately wrote this powerful though brief circular letter.

Galatians played a central role in the Protestant Reformation's recovery of the doctrine of salvation by faith alone. Martin Luther playfully called it by the name of his wife, for he said of Galatians, "I am wedded to it." Millions since then have found in this book joy, freedom, and the liberty to live a victorious Christian life.

Overview

Paul greeted the Galatians (1:1-5) and immediately launched a defense of his Gospel (vv. 6-10). He received this Gospel directly from God (1:11-23), his call was confirmed by the original Apostles (2:1-10), and he defended his Gospel against Judaizing tendencies by rebuking Peter himself (vv. 11-21).

Understanding the Text

"Sent not from men nor by man" Gal. 1:1-2. The polemic nature of Paul's letter bursts from its very first line. Paul did not come representing men, nor did he depend on any human commission for his authority. Paul was an apostle—a royal emissary—who spoke authoritatively for the Person who did send him, Jesus Christ.

Paul was not acting like a maverick here. He was not one of those folks who couldn't get along with denominational leaders and so started up his own splinter movement. Paul was stating the facts. His conversion was by a direct confrontation of the risen Christ, and his commission to go to the Gentiles also came from Jesus (cf. Acts 9). Paul was in harmony with the Jerusalem Apostles, but in no way dependent on them or the Jerusalem church for his authority.

Many young persons chafe under leaders they feel hold them back, lack vision, or simply resent them. Let's not be too quick to take the maverick solution, and set out on our own. Unless we have as clear and certain a calling as did the Apostle Paul! In most cases it's far better to accept waiting as a discipline from God, and be patient until He opens doors.

"Who gave Himself for our sins to rescue us from the present evil age" Gal. 1:3-5. Paul had affirmed his own direct call as an apostle. Now he affirmed grace. Jesus gave Himself not only that we might be forgiven, but that we might be rescued from the present evil age. The power that will free us from sin, and enable us to live righteous lives, is found in Jesus. Not, by implication, in the Law!

Salvation is received as a grace gift, and brings peace. Any "gospel" which fails to rely on Christ's sacrifice of Himself for our sins, which fails to rescue us from the evil within and around us, and which fails to rest on grace rather than self-effort, is not the Gospel of Jesus.

"A different gospel" Gal. 1:6-10. In Greek *allos* means another of the same kind. *Heteros* means another of a different kind. The gospel these Judaizers had introduced to the Galatians was a *heteros* gospel: it was a gospel that was essentially different from the Gospel of God. It was, Paul said, "No gospel at all."

Why? Because the Gospel is "Good News." Any message that tells us "try harder," even if we're provided with a rule book, is no good news at all. No matter how hard you or I may try, we can never be good enough to escape the chains of "the present evil age." Only God's grace, bursting into history in the person of Jesus Christ, and doing for us what we could never do for ourselves, is truly Gospel, "Good News."

"Am I now trying to win the approval?" Gal. 1:10 One of the arguments the Judaizers had against Paul was that he emphasized salvation by grace alone to make salvation easy, and so "win approval" from men. Salvation by faith alone still seems to some to be an "easy" or "cheap" religious philosophy.

But it wasn't cheap at all. Jesus paid the ultimate price that we might enter heaven free of charge.

"I received it by revelation from Jesus Christ" Gal. 1:11-23. The Judaizers claimed to represent Christ's original Apostles. Paul answered in two ways. Jesus Himself revealed the Gospel to Paul, so he was not dependent on the Twelve, nor did his authority come from them (vv. 11-17). Then, after Paul had worked out the implications of the Gospel through years of prayer and study, when he did visit Jerusalem, the Apostles added nothing to his message but instead praised God for his conversion (vv. 18-24).

Don't get the impression that Paul was a loner. Acts shows us that even during these early stages of his Christian life Paul was actively involved in preaching the Gospel and in fellowship with Christian brothers and sisters (9:19-31). We may not derive spiritual authority from others. This comes as a gift from God. But we do need to fellowship with other believers if we are to mature spiritually.

"I . . . set before them the Gospel that I preach among the Gentiles" Gal. 2:1-7. Paul continued with the story of his relationship with the Apostles. He explained the Gospel he preached to the Apostles, and did so just because "false brothers" like those that have disturbed the Galatian believers "infiltrated our ranks" in order "to make us slaves" (of the Law). The Apostles not only added nothing to Paul's message, they also acknowledged his call to minister to the Gentiles. They didn't even ask that Titus, a Greek Christian who accompanied Paul, be circumcised!

Paul's point was that the Judaizers, who claimed to represent the Jerusalem church, did not in fact have the approval of the original Apostles. And Paul—though he did not depend on this—did!

Have you ever noticed that it's often the least-mature or least-taught believer who is most eager to set up rules and impose them on others? This is what happened in the first century. The Apostles, who truly grasped the Gospel, affirmed Gentile freedom from Jewish Law. It was others, still unaware of the Gospel's implications, who tried to tie the Gentiles down with Jewish laws and customs. Watch out when young believers tell you how you should or must live your Christian life. Especially when they claim that the authority for their rules is someone you respect. Don't accept their word for it. Go to the source.

"Those reputed to be pillars, gave me and Barnabas the right hand of fellowship" Gal. 2:8-10. Do you remember an incident reported in Mark 9:38-41? The disciples of Jesus, who were now Apostles, saw someone driving out demons in Jesus' name and "we told him to stop, because he was not one of us."

What a difference now! Paul and Barnabas report their ministry among the Gentiles, and now the Apostles "recognized the grace given to me." They even agreed that Paul should concentrate on a Gentile ministry, while Peter, who also traveled at this time, focused on a ministry to Jews.

Let's not be put off when other Christians have a different emphasis than we do, or come from a different tradition. Let's recognize the grace given to them, and gladly extend the "right hand of fellowship."

"I have been crucified with Christ" Gal. 2:20. The Christian's hope and joy is our union with Jesus Christ. We share in His death, and thus the bonds of sin are broken. We share in His resurrection, and thus receive power for a new life. It is Christ living in me, not any attempts of mine to keep a law given to men of a different race in a different age, that is the secret of spiritual life and vitality. Jesus, not the Law, must remain the beating heart, the sole center of our lives, the key to our personal relationship with God.

▶ DEVOTIONAL
Setting Aside God's Grace (Gal. 2:11-21)

For Paul, this was the decisive argument. He had been accused of preaching a distorted Gospel: one not sanctioned by Jerusalem.

So he told of a time when Peter himself acted the hypocrite. When Peter was alone with Gentile believers in Antioch, he sat right down with them and ate Gentile food. But when some Jewish Christians arrived from Jerusalem, Peter was fearful of what they might think, and wouldn't eat with the Gentiles anymore.

Paul saw this not merely as hypocrisy, but also as setting aside the grace of God in favor of a Law which had never and could never produce righteousness. So Paul confronted Peter openly. He argued that the principle of justification by faith had set aside observance of the Law. Peter's pandering to Judaizers "rebuilt" a way which the Gospel had destroyed.

What's important to us here isn't the confrontation. We might admire Paul for standing up to Peter, and Peter for bowing to the truth Paul spoke. But what we learn is we can, by our actions, "set aside God's grace." We can act in ways that obscure, or even deny, grace.

One of the most deceptive ways to deny grace is to confront non-Christians with their sins. "Don't you know that's wrong?" we ask. Or we suggest, "What you're doing is harmful as well as sinful." Our motive may be good. We may expect exposure of sin to lead to conviction and this to salvation. But by drawing disapproving attention to another's sin, we draw attention away from Jesus and the grace of God.

Our message isn't that all men are sinners. Deep down others know their flaws. Our message is that God loves sinners. We must display the love of God, or we will surely obscure the message of His grace.

Personal Application

Let God's love shine through everything you do and say.

Quotable

"Men may not read the Gospel in sealskin, or the Gospel in morocco, or the Gospel in cloth covers, but they can't get away from the Gospel in shoe leather."—Donald Grey Barnhouse

OCTOBER 31 *Reading 304*
FAITH AND LAW
Galatians 3–4

"If a law had been given that could impart life, then righteousness would certainly have come by the law. But the Scripture declares that the whole world is a prisoner of sin, so that what was promised, being given through faith in Jesus Christ, might be given to those who believe" (Gal. 3:21-22).

Faith and law live at opposite ends of town.

Overview

The Galatians' own experience (3:1-5) and Abraham's example demonstrate that salvation is by faith and not Law (vv. 6-14). Law never abrogated promise as the key to God's dealings with man (vv. 15-25), and in Christ believers become sons of God (v. 26–4:7). The Galatians' perplexing return to "religion" (vv. 8-20) was abandonment of freedom for spiritual slavery (vv. 21-31).

Understanding the Text

"You foolish Galatians!" Gal. 3:1-5 The word Paul used here does not mean mentally deficient. It means inept! These folks had normal intelligence and plenty of evidence, but for some inexplicable reason they didn't put two and two together!

Don't think that the Bible is as "hard to understand" as some claim. The Bible isn't a puzzle that people have to struggle to solve. It is a clear, unmistakable revelation of God's will, purposes, and gifts. Only if we fail to apply ourselves to study, or to think about what we read, will we find ourselves in the position of those "foolish Galatians."

"Before your very eyes" Gal. 3:1-5. Paul listed three facts that should have enabled the Galatians to see through the Judaizers' false gospel. First, Christ has been "clearly portrayed as crucified." Paul stripped the Gospel of inessentials, and focused on Jesus. Failure of the Judaizers to give Christ the same place in their system should have alerted the Galatians at once.

This is still the test of any teaching. What place does Jesus crucified have? If there is no central role for the Saviour on a cross, then the teaching is false.

Second, the Galatians' own experience should have alerted them. They were given the Spirit when they believed—not for keeping the Law. Why, when their initial experience with God was rooted in faith, would they expect Him to change now? Politicians seeking reelection used to argue against "changing horses in midstream." Paul does too. If faith has got you this far, why get off faith and try a different mount now?

Third, God's present work among the Galatians was in response to faith, not to their obedience to Law. God works among us today through faith, not through legalism.

What Paul was really doing is expressing shock and amazement. Yet throughout church history there have always been those who try to remake Christianity into a religion of works and Law rather than of faith and grace. Don't be surprised when you come across it today. But don't be taken in, no matter how pious its proponents may seem.

Believing, or observing?

The Gospel	*Legalism*
Faith (Abraham) 3:6-9	Law (Curse) 3:10-14
Faith (Covenant) 3:15-18	Law (Transgression) 3:19-22
Faith (Sonship) 3:23-29	Law (Slavery) 4:1-7

Paul contrasted his Gospel of a grace that comes through faith with the Judaizer's demand for a return to Law. In a carefully reasoned argument Paul showed why Gospel and Mosaic Law are contrary to each other, and why the Galatians must opt for the Gospel of a salvation won and experienced by faith alone.

"Consider Abraham" Gal. 3:6-9. From the very beginning God has related to men by faith. Abraham, the father and prototype of the chosen race, was justified by faith. Those in his line must have a relationship with God which rests on faith.

Paul quoted Old Testament references to Gentile salvation (v. 8) to show that God always intended to bring Gentiles into Abraham's family line. Since Gentiles can't go back and be born again as Jews, this could only be done through a faith like Abraham's own.

God did make Israel His chosen people. But even as He selected Abraham, He was thinking of you and me!

"Cursed is everyone who does not continue to do everything" Gal. 3:10-14. Faith is inclusive, and brings everyone with Abraham into relationship with God. Law is exclusive. It rules everyone out!

Take a balloon, blow it up, and use a felt-tipped pen to write on it the 633 precepts of Old Testament Law identified by the rabbis. Then take a pin, and prick just one of those precepts. You've not broken just one commandment, you've broken the whole thing!

This is the point of Deuteronomy 27:26, which Paul quoted here. Keep the Law, and yes, you'll be blessed. But break even one command, just once, and you come under the Law's curse! If you turn to legalism, you must accept the Law's obligation to keep it perfectly. All the time.

How glad we can be that Christ "redeemed us from the curse of the Law." Jesus paid the price that frees us from the penalty Law-breaking entailed. And He also freed us from legalism, which continues to curse mankind with its demand for perfection.

"Law, introduced 430 years later" Gal. 3:15-19. God's promise to Abraham was made centuries before Moses gave the Law to Israel. That promise was confirmed by covenant: a legally binding instrument. Adding the Law didn't invalidate the covenant, or nullify the promise.

To suppose that Law replaced faith as God's way of relating to His own is to suppose that God doesn't keep His Word! The Law, which casts a searchlight on our sins, makes us realize how desperately we need the salvation that God makes available through faith.

"But God is One" Gal. 3:20-21. There's a beautiful truth here. Moses served as a mediator in giving the Law, for he stood between God and mankind, representing both. But this wasn't good enough for God. So in Christ God Himself became the Mediator. Through Jesus we deal directly with God, and are welcomed into His presence.

"No longer under the supervision of the Law" Gal. 3:23-25. All English transcriptions obscure what was a powerful image in the first century. The Law, Paul said, was a *paidagogos*. This was a slave employed by wealthy Greeks as a "child-attendant" who supervised underage children. While underage, even though a child might be heir to the family estate, he had to obey the orders of his attendant.

Law was just such a *paidagogos* for Israel before Jesus came. The Jews were "locked up" by the Law, not as prisoners, but so they would be kept out of trouble! While the Law was unable to keep Israel from sinning, it did keep that people together and preserve their identity until Jesus, the Seed of Abraham through whom the promises to all humanity would be kept, arrived.

Paul's point was that, now that Jesus had come, we no longer need to be locked up! We can be set free! For, brought into intimate relationship with God through Christ, we can now be trusted to live truly godly lives!

One reason Christians sometimes feel a need for restrictive laws is that we recognize and fear our potential for sin. But God wants you and me to recognize the potential we now have in Christ to live dynamic, godly lives! When we rebuild the cage of Law, we don't lock up our old nature. We lock up the new self God wants us to become.

"Until Christ is formed in you" Gal. 4:8-20. American Indians used to wind infants tightly in cloths, and strap them to a carrying board. But when the children grew, they were released. Only release from the binding wraps of legalism can enable us to grow—and Christ to grow in us.

"The women represent two covenants" Gal. 4:24-25. Paul's extended analogy continues to the way of Christ with a religion of works and Law. The correspondences here are:

Hagar, the bond-woman	Sarah, the free
Ishmael, a natural birth	Isaac, a supernatural birth
The Old Covenant	The New Covenant
Earthly Jerusalem	Heavenly Jerusalem
Judaism	Christianity

The point of the analogy remains the same. Christ brings us freedom. And it is freedom that we must claim.

▶ DEVOTIONAL
Sons of God
(Gal. 3:26–4:7)

Jewish, Greek, and Roman cultures all marked a specific time when a child entered fully into adult responsibility. The Jews fixed the time at age 12, the Greeks at 18, and the Romans permitted the father to fix the time.

Even in Rome though, the formal ceremony in which the child became an adult, was marked by a sacred family festival, the *Liberalia.* The father presented his son and acknowledged heir with the *toga virilis,* and the proud son put off the clothing that had marked him as a mere child. How moving the ceremony was: the father proudly embracing his son, the boy both triumphant and a little frightened at his new responsibilities.

A minor child, in the eyes of the law, was no different than a slave. He made no significant decisions. He had no freedom. But with formal acceptance as an adult, all that changed. He was now responsible. He was now free.

To Paul, salvation is God's *Liberalia.* It is a joyous festival of freedom. It is the moment when God puts His arms around us, acknowledging us as His sons and heirs. And, in place of the Law, God puts around our shoulders the cloak of His Holy Spirit, the *toga virilis* which we wear constantly as a symbol not only of our freedom, but of our allegiance to our Father above. No longer limited by law to a slavelike existence, we are ushered into a freedom that demands we take responsibility for our choices. A freedom that means that as an adult member of the family of God whatever we choose to do will bring honor to the family name.

Don't be afraid of the freedom God has given you. Rejoice in it! And use it, to bring honor to Him.

Personal Application

Don't fear freedom. Use it to serve God.

Quotable

"There are two freedoms—the false, where a man is free to do what he likes; the true, where a man is free to do what he ought."—Charles Kingsley

NOVEMBER 1 *Reading 305*
CHRISTIAN FREEDOM
Galatians 5–6

> *"It is for freedom that Christ has set us free. Stand firm, then, and do not let yourselves be burdened again by a yoke of slavery" (Gal. 5:1).*

The Christian is freed from the Law in order to become righteous through Christ.

Overview

Law and grace are conflicting principles (5:1-12). Christians are freed from the Law in order to live a life of love, led by God's transforming Spirit (vv. 13-25). We must be committed to doing good (6:1-10), as God's new creations (vv. 11-18).

Understanding the Text

"It is for freedom that Christ has set us free" Gal. 5:1. The Judaizers argued that by rejecting Mosaic Law, Paul rejected righteousness. And this could not be of God! Casting off the Law must lead to licentiousness: man uncaged would have no reason not to sin!

Galatians 5 and 6 give Paul's response. There are two ways to handle the beast in man. The approach of Law was to cage the beast, though it eagerly tried to break out. The approach of grace is to change the beast! Removing the bars is safe if the man's nature can be transformed.

This, Paul tells us, is exactly what God

has done! Through Christ God has given us a new nature that can be controlled by the Spirit of God. As we yield to the Spirit, we live righteous lives and we experience a gradual transformation. Christian freedom is no license to live according to our sinful nature. Christian freedom is stepping out beyond the bars, to live a life of love in the Holy Spirit's power. So freedom from Mosaic Law does not imply a retreat from righteousness. Through grace God has done what Law was never able to do. He has changed us within, and by making us righteous He enables us to live good and holy lives.

Don't be afraid of freedom. Trust Jesus, respond to the Holy Spirit, and use your freedom to live a life of love.

"Christ will be of no value to you at all" Gal. 5:2-6. Paul was looking here at the Christian life, not at salvation. If any Christian turns to legalism, represented here by circumcision, and struggles to live a good life by self-effort, his union with Jesus "will be of no value." Paul made his position very clear by going on. The Galatians who decided to follow the Judaizers and were circumcised alienated themselves from Christ. They fell "away from grace."

What do these frightening verses mean? It's as if a man with a power lawnmower decided to push the mower back and forth over his yard without ever starting it. He would work harder at mowing than if the motor was on, and would get absolutely nothing done! Paul was saying that when we rely on self-effort, guided by Law, to live the Christian life, Christ, though present within us, is "turned off." We work so hard. And we get nothing done at all!

Don't fall away from grace. Fall back on it! Rely completely on Jesus, for "the only thing that counts is faith expressing itself through love."

"Rather, serve one another in love" Gal. 5:12-15. We Christians truly are free. Free to indulge the sinful nature. Free to serve one another in love. Each choice has consequences, of course. But this does not disguise the stunning fact that God now stands back and says, "You choose."

Maybe before, you and I had excuses. We blamed our parents, our poverty, our bad luck, or our temptations for our failures. When Christ made us free, however, all those things became irrelevant. Never mind the poor self-image. Never mind your weaknesses. All those things are in the past. In Christ you and I can choose to live a life of love!

"Live by the Spirit, and you will not gratify the desires of the sinful nature" Gal. 5:16-18. The reason that we are truly free isn't that our past has been changed, or our present feelings have changed. We may still feel inadequate, unsure, hesitant, afraid. We are free because God has given us His Holy Spirit. The Spirit of God within enables us.

Freedom doesn't mean life without conflict. It does mean the possibility of life without defeat! Our weaknesses need not drag us down, our past no longer cripples us. The Holy Spirit is on our side in the war against the desires of our sinful nature. We no longer look to Law, and struggle. We look to the Holy Spirit, trust in Him, and do what is right.

"Those who live like this will not inherit the kingdom of God" Gal. 5:19-21. Paul listed activities that characterized man's sinful nature. Those marked by them are, if we paraphrase, "on the road to hell."

There's an implied warning to Christians here. In Colossians 1:13 Paul says that believers have been rescued from the kingdom of Satan, and transferred to the kingdom of the Son He loves. We believers have already inherited the kingdom. We live and breathe its richly scented air, and in our spirit we walk with the angels as we talk with God. But never suppose that believers who choose to gratify the desires of the sinful nature will possess this inheritance now!

We really can choose between living by the sinful nature and by the Spirit. But we can't choose the consequences. Those are fixed. And the consequence of the wrong choice is a present life choked with petty miseries.

"The fruit of the Spirit" Gal. 5:22-24. We can't choose the consequences that follow our decision to serve one another in love either. God has already chosen them. What if we make this choice, and live in

the power of the Spirit? Then God fills us to overflowing with love, joy, peace, patience, kindness, goodness, faithfulness, gentleness, and self-control.

Have you ever noticed that along the banks of a stream the vegetation is always abundant and luxurious? This is what the Bible says about us. As the Holy Spirit flows freely in our lives, a rich and beautiful character grows. We are filled with love, with joy, with peace. In every relationship we exhibit that patience, kindness, goodness, faithfulness, gentleness, and self-control that mark us as God's own.

There is no way, however much we plow and harrow, or cultivate and hoe our character, to produce this crop by ourselves. This crop is produced only by God the Holy Spirit, and only in those who live by Him (see DEVOTIONAL).

"Against such things there is no law" Gal. 5:23. The Judaizers insisted that man needs the Law in order to affirm righteousness. Paul has given several answers. (1) Law and grace are opposing principles: you must choose one or the other. (2) Law can be summed up in the call to love one's neighbor: Christ has freed us to serve one another in love, so Law is no longer necessary. (3) Law cannot release us from bondage to our sinful nature: the Spirit can and so, if we are led by Him, Law is irrelevant.

Now Paul made a final point. Laws are passed against sinful acts. No one would think of passing a law against love, joy, kindness, goodness, or patience. It follows then that Law is irrelevant to Christians who live by the Spirit. What need is there for Law in a heart where love, kindness, and goodness reign?

Commit yourself to Jesus, actively love others, and trust the Spirit to express Himself through you. Do this, and you need not worry about the Law.

"You who are spiritual should restore him" Gal. 6:1-5. What a joy to realize that we aren't expected to step out into this risky world of freedom alone. God has given us brothers and sisters to walk in the Spirit with us—to restore us when we fall, to hold us up when the load becomes too heavy.

There's a beautiful interplay between verses 2 and 5 in the Greek. The burden we help others bear is a *bare,* a heavy load. The load we are to carry on our own is a *phortion,* the normal load for which we were designed. How wonderful that with the aid of God's Spirit we are now not only able to meet life successfully, but even to help others for whom the burden is too great.

"A man reaps what he sows" Gal. 6:7-9. Again Paul expressed a basic truth. We can now choose our way of life. But God has chosen the consequences. Let's follow the path that leads to abundant life!

"What large letters" Gal. 6:11-18. Letters in New Testament times were typically dictated to secretaries, who wrote down the words. The author might pen a few words at the end, as Paul did here. Some see in the "large letters" a suggestion of the eye trouble Paul mentioned in 2 Corinthians 12. Others take it as emphatic: see, I'm underlining this!

What did Paul underline? His decisive rejection of the legalistic approach to the Christian life represented by the Judaizers, and his own changeless focus on Christ and His cross. Those who wanted the Galatians to cut their bodies as a sign of submission to Law should go the whole way, and castrate themselves! To impose Law on the Christian Gospel of grace would make the Gospel impotent and void of power.

What counts is that we are new creations in Christ. And because of that renewal, we are free!

▶ DEVOTIONAL
In Step with the Spirit (Gal. 5:12-26)

It's such a dazzling prospect! To be free to serve one another in love. To be free from the crushing demands of our sinful nature. To be free to experience love, joy, peace, patience—all those things Paul said the Holy Spirit produces in the believer.

But how disappointed many Christians are as they catch a vision of what can be—and tremble to realize that as far as they are concerned, it is not. How disappointing to want the kind of life Paul described here, fail to find it, and never realize why.

I suspect for many of us the reason why is given in the little phrase in verse 25: "Keep in step with the Spirit." If you were in the army, you might hear a sergeant shouting it at you. "Keep in step, Recruit! Move it!"

Some folks interpret a legalistic life as a life of trying, and the Spirit-filled life as a life of resting. They wait for the Holy Spirit to direct them. And, all too often, if they don't feel the Spirit moving, they just sit.

Paul said, "Keep in step with the Spirit." Don't sit down. Don't wait for the Spirit to tap you on the shoulder and point. Move it!

Paul told the same thing in other ways. We're to "use" our freedom to serve one another (v. 13). Right there we have the Spirit's marching orders. We don't need to wait for further instructions. We simply need to get out and start serving! "The only thing that counts," Paul said earlier, "is faith expressing itself through love" (v. 6).

Again we see the same emphasis. Faith must express itself. Faith is active. It moves! Faith doesn't sit around waiting. God has work for us to do, and if we really trust God to work in us, we naturally get up and get at it!

It seems so simple. And yet so many of us miss it. Do you believe God's Spirit lives in you? Do you believe He is able to work through you? Then show your faith by stepping out to serve others in love, and in the serving you will experience the Spirit's power. And in the serving you will find your own character transformed.

Personal Application

God's Spirit is at work in the world today. Keep in step with Him.

Quotable

"Every time we say, 'I believe in the Holy Spirit,' we mean that we believe there is a living God able and willing to enter human personality and change it."—J.B. Phillips

---

The Variety Reading Plan continues with JUDE

Ephesians

INTRODUCTION

Paul's letter to the Ephesians was written during his two-year imprisonment in Rome, about A.D. 61. It shares Paul's vision of a Christian community united by love and a common purpose under the headship of Christ. Each believer, linked to Jesus by faith, is linked to every other believer as cells in a living organism. By living together in love, the whole body and its individual members grow to spiritual maturity.

This is both one of the most theological and most practical of Paul's letters. It exalts Jesus as Head of the living church, and it exhorts each of us to "live a life of love" in all our personal relationships. Ephesians also includes a number of moving prayers, and passages which many view as elements in the liturgy of the early church.

OUTLINE OF CONTENTS

READING GUIDE (5 Days)

If hurried, you may read only the "core passage" in your Bible and the Devotional in each chapter of this Commentary.

Reading	*Chapters*	*Core passage*
306	1	1:3-14
307	2	2:11-22
308	3–4	3:14-21
309	5	5:22-33
310	6	6:1-9

Ephesians

INTRODUCTION

Paul's letter to the Ephesians was written during his [illegible] imprisonment in Rome, about A.D. 61. [illegible] [illegible] united by love and a common purpose [illegible] Head [illegible] each believer [illegible] a living organism [illegible] individual [illegible] grow [illegible] maturity.

This is [illegible] one of the [illegible] letters. It calls [illegible] the living church, and [illegible] to "live a life of love" in all [illegible] relationships. Ephesians also includes [illegible] passages [illegible] in the early church.

OUTLINE OF CONTENTS

I. [illegible]

II. The Church as Body and Family [illegible]

III. The Christian's Life of Love [illegible]

READING GUIDE (7 Days)

If [illegible] you may read only the [illegible] Devotional in each chapter of this Commentary.

[illegible]

[illegible] 3:14-21

[illegible] 4:1-16

[illegible]

[illegible] 5:21-6:4

[illegible] 6:10-20

Ephesians

NOVEMBER 2 *Reading 306*
THE TRUE CHURCH
Ephesians 1

> *"You also were included in Christ when you heard the Word of truth, the Gospel of your salvation. Having believed, you were marked in Him with a seal, the promised Holy Spirit" (Eph. 1:13).*

Christ's church is people, not buildings.

Background

Ephesus. When Paul wrote his letter the harbor of the aging city of Ephesus was nearly filled with silt, and its boast as the "landing place" of Asia was empty indeed. Yet Ephesus had one claim to fame. It was the site of the magnificent temple of Artemis (Diana), four times the size of the Parthenon of Athens, and held in reverence throughout "Asia and the world" (Acts 19:27). Tourists and worshipers flocked to Ephesus to visit the splendid shrine, which also served as a bank in which cities and kings deposited funds—and from which they drew loans.

Innkeepers, restauranteers, and tradesmen depended on the tourist trade that made pagan religion such an economic success in Ephesus.

So to the believers in this city founded on institutional religion, Paul wrote a letter conveying a vastly different vision. The church of Christ is a body, not a building. It is constructed of living, breathing human beings, not marble. And its vitality is seen not in the cash it contributes to a city's economy, but in the love and purity that shine through its members' lives.

In reading Ephesians we too are called to catch Paul's vision of Christ's church. Beside that vision even our greatest cathe-

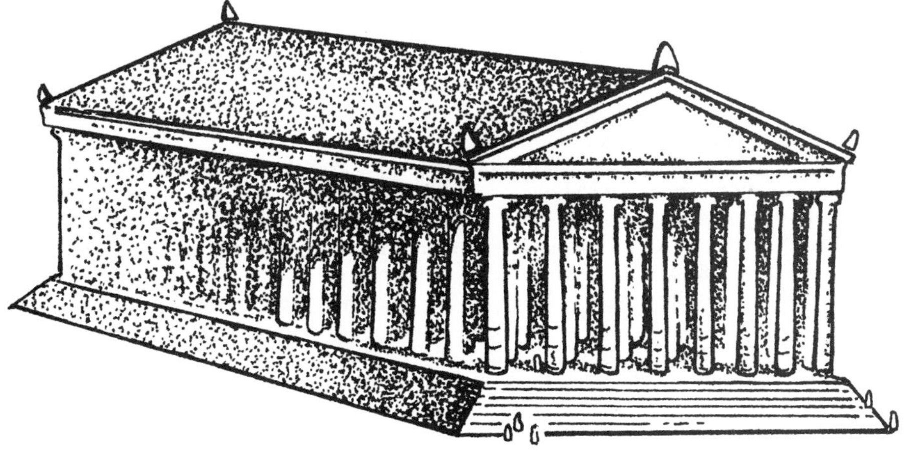

TEMPLE OF ARTEMIS

drals fade to insignificance, as we realize that the building which thrills our God is the reconstruction of our lives to bear the image of His Son.

Overview

Paul greeted the saints (1:1-2) and then reviewed the role in their salvation of the Father (vv. 3-6), Son (vv. 7-13a), and Holy Spirit (vv. 13b-14). Paul praised God (vv. 15-16) and prayed for the Ephesians (vv. 17-19), as he exalted Jesus, the Head of His church (vv. 20-23).

Understanding the Text

"To the saints in Ephesus" Eph. 1:1-2. The word "saints" means "holy ones" or "set apart ones." In the Old Testament, the Jerusalem temple and all utensils used in the service of God were holy, set apart to the Lord. Paul commonly greeted believers as saints. Here there is even more meaning, for Paul was about to display the great truth that today we ourselves are temple and utensil in one.

God doesn't look for beauty in church buildings. He looks for beauty in church members.

"Praise be to the God and Father of our Lord" Eph. 1:3-6. The Ephesians looked back in history and spoke of a meteorite that fell from the heavens, and was shaped into the form of the idol that stood in their temple. Paul looked back beyond history, into the very origins of the universe. There he saw God the Father, the Architect of our salvation, drawing up plans for the living church!

Like any architect would, the Father specified the materials that would go into His construction: He "chose us in Him before the Creation of the world." God also specified how the materials would be worked: He chose us "to be holy and blameless in His sight," to be "adopted as His sons." The beauty to be displayed in our worked and polished lives will reflect through eternity "to the praise of His glorious grace" (see DEVOTIONAL).

People wondered at the great temple that graced Ephesus: at its design, at its pillars of marble, at its columns carved in the Doric style. Paul wants us to wonder at the church which God the Father Himself designed, carefully specifying its materials and defining just how they would be shaped to glorify Him.

Always remember, you and I have been chosen by God to display His grace and wisdom. Let's gladly dedicate our lives to exhibit the beauty of holiness.

"In Him we have redemption through His blood" Eph. 1:7-13a. If God the Father was the Architect of our salvation, Christ was the Builder. He was the One who slipped into history as a Babe, grew up in dusty Palestine, taught amid noisy crowds, and bled on Calvary's cross. In that great act you and I have "redemption through His blood, the forgiveness of sins, in accordance with the riches of God's grace."

That awful work complete, Christ today has a right to stand back and look at the building He has erected. And He has the right to expect us to be to "the praise of His glory." We are a costly building indeed, and Jesus has a right to expect us to be beautiful.

"Marked in Him with a seal, the promised Holy Spirit" Eph. 1:13b-14. The Holy Spirit has moved into the building that the Father planned and the Son built.

In New Testament times a "seal" was often placed on goods to be shipped or on a completed product, as a mark of ownership. That which bore the seal was protected, its future guaranteed. The owner would take full possession in his own time.

You and I, Christ's living church, have in the Holy Spirit the mark of divine ownership. The Spirit is the sure guarantee of our future in God. And the Spirit in us enables us to live, today, to "the praise of His glory."

"I keep asking that the God of our Lord Jesus Christ" Eph. 1:15-19a. Paul praised God for the Ephesians, living stones in the church built by God. And he offered a very specific prayer.

One way to build our own prayer lives, and to direct our intercession for others, is to model our prayers on those found in Scripture. Here we see a prayer Paul offered with the intention of strengthening Christ's church. What did Paul ask? That we might know God better (v. 17). That we might look beyond appearances, to see the church as God does—a people transformed to display His glory, unspeakably precious to Him (v. 18). That we might sense and experience the working of "His incomparably great power for us who believe" (v. 19a). I suppose it's all right to pray for that addition to a new Sunday School wing. Or the funds to go on the radio. But if we want our church to truly be the church, the things Paul prayed for here are vastly more important.

"Far above all rule and authority" Eph. 1:19b-23. If we measure the church by the members of the body seen here on earth, we might well be discouraged. We're weak. We're undisciplined. We squint desperately with our spiritual eyes, and our spiritual ears are dull.

But the church isn't to be measured by its members. We're to measure by the Head. We're to see Christ, exalted above every "rule and authority, power and dominion." We're to acknowledge Him as our living Head, respond to His guidance. And in His name, conquer.

▶ DEVOTIONAL
Predestination and Praise (Eph. 1:3-14)

Twin themes are repeated three times in these 12 verses, which tell the story of the construction of God's living temple, the church.

The first of these themes is predestination: the idea that God marked out ahead of time those who would serve as living stones in His glorious temple. Paul said the Father "chose us in Him before the Creation" (v. 4). That "in love He predestined us to be adopted as His sons" (vv. 4-5). And that "in Him [Christ] we were also chosen, having been predestined according to the plan of Him who works out everything in conformity with the purpose of His will" (v. 11).

Some resent this emphasis, and some fear it. But if we look at it in the framework of Paul's imagery, as he pictured God the great Architect planning construction of the church and specifying materials, there's nothing sinister here. And there is nothing that contradicts the broadest application of the Gospel. As one preacher succinctly put it, " 'Whosoever will' is elect. 'Whosoever won't,' ain't."

What's usually lost in the debate over predestination is the other theme that is restated three times here. God the Father planned our adoption as sons "to the praise of His glorious grace" (v. 6). He drew us to Christ that we "might be for the praise of His glory" (v. 12). And His Spirit marks us as God's own possession—"to the praise of His glory" (v. 14).

You and I can't resolve the long debate over predestination. We probably shouldn't even try. But as living stones in a building that God intends to reflect His beauty, we can make sure that we live "to the praise of His glory."

I'm satisfied to let God resolve the paradox of predestination and free will. All I'm really concerned about is, is God satisfied with me?

Personal Application

Glorifying God beats debating predestination any day!

Quotable

"The church of Christ is not an institution; it is a new life with Christ and in Christ, guided by the Holy Spirit."—Sergius Bulgakov

NOVEMBER 3 *Reading 307*
GOD'S WORKMANSHIP
Ephesians 2

"Like the rest, we were by nature objects of wrath. But because of His great love for us, God, who is rich in mercy, made us alive with Christ" (Eph. 2:3-5).

Considering what God had to work with, He's done an amazing job!

Overview

God selected sinful, spiritually dead human beings as materials for His church (2:1-3). He gave us life and called us to good works, that His grace might be displayed (vv. 4-10). United now, Jew and Gentile form one building, with Christ the Cornerstone (vv. 11-22).

Understanding the Text

"Dead in your transgressions and sins" Eph. 2:1-3. "Death" is one of the most awesome and complex of biblical concepts. We understand biological death, and to a certain extent spiritual death is modeled on it. As the dead body cannot sense or respond to the material world, the dead spirit cannot sense or respond to God.

But spiritual death moves beyond this to imply corruption. As the physical body decays, so the spiritually dead become infested with all sorts of corruption. The spiritually dead "followed the ways of this world and of the ruler of the kingdom of the air [Satan]." The rotten flesh of the spiritually dead gasps and heaves in the grip of "the cravings of our sinful nature," whose desires and thoughts the lost blindly follow.

Paul's graphic portrait is horrible, and we may well draw back. But Paul wanted us to understand that this is the raw material from which God constructs His church! This mass of corruption is what God intends to use to display His glory and the beauty of His holiness.

It's not nice. But it is important for us to be totally honest with ourselves and with God. Paul drew this portrait, and he said, "This was you." He went on. "All of us also lived among them at one time, gratifying the cravings of our sinful nature."

Thank God this is what we were, not what we are! And thank God that He saw fit to make me His own anyway.

I once worked with a man, not a Christian, who had chosen to marry a woman who had been a prostitute. I remember one of my coworkers telling me, "She'd do anything for Jim. He always treats her like a lady."

We Christians are not to deny our past. We're to remember, and to realize that in spite of what we were, God has loved us and made us His own. And He always treats us "like a lady."

What a motivation to do anything for Him!

"Because of His great love for us" Eph. 2:4-7. The old song rightly says, "I'm not what I wanta' be, I'm not what I will be, but thank God I'm not what I was." Paul has reminded us of what we were. Now he tells us what we are, and will be.

What we are is persons who have been given the gift of life. He has "made us alive with Christ." The Gospel message brought us to life, raised us up, and even seated us with Him in the heavenly realms! This last image is one of power. God, seated on heaven's throne, is Sovereign over all. In Christ we are not only alive, but conquerors.

Never forget who you were. But never imagine you are still the same old man or woman. Addiction, depression, depravity, despair, low self-esteem, inconsistency, lack of self-discipline—whatever troubled you, was an expression of the old life that had established a grip on your personality. Now you have been raised with Christ to a vital, new life capable of breaking out of any bondage. Don't look back. Look ahead, and realize that God has destined you to display "the incomparable riches of His grace."

"By grace you have been saved, through faith—and this not from yourselves, it is the gift of God" Eph. 2:8-9. Many debate whether the gift of God here is the faith, the salvation, or the grace. In a sense, it makes no difference. Paul simply wants us to understand that our life in Christ is a miracle. We didn't earn it; God gave it.

The TV last night reported on "sweat

equity," a new approach to home ownership. People who have no money for a down payment on a new home can contribute labor, while the bank or government finances materials. The work they put in on building their own homes is their "sweat equity."

Well, verses 8-9 state that you and I don't even have "sweat equity" in our salvation. We had no cash for the down payment. And there was not a single thing we could do to contribute to the work. God did it all, so that for all eternity you and I will stand as trophies of His grace, saved through no merit of our own.

"We are God's workmanship, created in Christ Jesus to do good works" Eph. 2:10. Good works can't contribute to our salvation. But good works are an outcome of salvation.

We have been given life to glorify God. And one way we glorify God is by performing good works.

What are "good works"? The Greek word here is *agathois,* which means "useful, helpful." God has saved us and set us on a path filled with opportunities to be helpful to others, and useful in accomplishing His own purposes.

Again we sense the contrast between what we were, and what we are. Corrupted by sin, we could do nothing for God, for ourselves, or for others. Made alive by God in Christ, we are different. And we make a difference!

Never put yourself down. God has prepared useful works for you to do.

"In Christ Jesus you who were once far away" Eph. 2:11-13. Paul directed these remarks to Gentiles, who were isolated from the promises and covenants given to Israel. Christ, however, has changed their situations as well as changed them! In Christ God brings believers to Himself, and to each other.

The image of a living temple helps us here. A building is a construction: formed by fitting different kinds of material together. The cement foundation is laid, a wood frame is put up, plywood sheeting and plaster board are added. God's church is also a construction, and this too requires that different kinds of material be fitted together.

What God has done in Christ is to draw all believers to Himself, and thus draw us into intimate relationship with each other as well. If you or I isolate ourselves from any of God's other building materials, some beautiful aspect of His living temple may be marred.

"He put to death their hostility" Eph. 2:14-18. In New Testament times the Old Testament Law was a "barrier" between Gentile and Jew. And that barrier did create hostility: anti-Semitism led to frequent riots in ancient cities, and ancient Jews did look with contempt on Gentile neighbors.

Then Jesus died, and made Law irrelevant. Jew and Gentile alike approached God by faith, and through faith each had direct access to God the Father. Suddenly it became clear that the church is one, and that out of the two hostile groups God formed "one new man" which was called to live at peace.

How we need to learn that lesson today. Whatever there may be in any society that creates barriers, and arouses hostility, is irrelevant now. Blackness and whiteness are irrelevant now. Each approach God through faith in Christ, and from the two God is at work forming His "one new man." Think of any groups who have inherited a tradition of hostility, and the Christ of the Gospel cries, "Peace." Christ has brought you near to God through faith, and in bringing you near God He has brought you near each other.

Let's realize what God is doing in His church. And let's make peace.

"In Him the whole building is joined together and rises to become a holy temple in the Lord" Eph. 2:19-23. Whatever may divide us, Christ brings us together. Whatever fears or suspicions arouse hostility, Christ brings peace. And we must let Him. For the "holy temple in the Lord" that Jesus is building today rises only as we, His people, are "joined together."

Don't let the partisan divide you. Don't let the strident preacher of doctrinal distinctives isolate you from brothers and sisters whose faith is one with you, but whose beliefs may differ. And don't let race, or age, or social status, or education, or wealth or poverty, drive you apart.

Reach out for others, and hand-in-hand be built, "together to become a dwelling in which God lives by His Spirit."

▶ DEVOTIONAL
Were, Are, and Will Be (Eph. 2:11-22)

Christianity is a faith of contrasts. Often the contrast we emphasize lies between past and future. We were lost sinners. But we will be raised in Christ's own image.

The "were" and "will be" of Christianity are exciting. But Ephesians 2 reminds us that there should also be a contrast right now, between what we "were" and what we "are." Being a follower of Jesus is to make a dramatic difference in our present. What we "are" is to stand out as clearly as what we "will be" against what we "were"!

Here in Ephesians the "were" and "are" contrast is seen in our relationships. Human beings by nature are separate from Christ and, as strangers and aliens, are isolated from His people. In fact, sinful human beings find all sorts of reasons to separate themselves from others. We turn away from others because of race, of looks, of clothing, of customs, of wealth, of language. And we look down on others, supposing ourselves better than they. This is a "were" dimension of human beings separated from Jesus Christ.

How different those who know Jesus are to be. The cross has reconciled us to God, and brought us near to Him. And, in Christ, God has brought us near to all humanity, and especially those of the household of faith. We "are" one now with all believers. One in the Spirit. And by God's grace, one in love, one in caring, one in honoring and respecting each other. We "are" being "built together to become a dwelling in which God lives by His Spirit."

When you and I ignore those things that divide mere human beings, and because of Jesus reach out to others who are different from us, the contrast of what we "are" with what we "were" gives vivid witness to our relationship with Jesus Christ.

Personal Application

Real love for those who are different is evidence of God's work within.

Quotable

"And they'll know we are Christians by our love, by our love. Yes, they'll know we are Christians by our love."—Peter Scholtes

---

NOVEMBER 4 *Reading 308*
BECOMING MATURE
Ephesians 3–4

> *"So that the body of Christ may be built up until we all reach unity in the faith and in the knowledge of the Son of God and become mature, attaining to the whole measure of the fullness of Christ" (Eph. 4:12-13).*

Love is essential to mutual ministry, and mutual ministry to spiritual growth.

Overview

The unity of Jew and Gentile in one body is an unexpected revelation (3:1-13). Yet, one family now, unified by love, Christ's people experience His power at work in us (vv. 14-21). We are to maintain this unity and mature in Christ (4:1-16), as new men and women living together in love and holiness (vv. 17-32).

Understanding the Text

"The mystery made known to me by revelation" Eph. 3:1-9. A "mystery" in Scripture is a facet of God's plan previously unknown, but now revealed. The Old Testament made it clear from the very beginning of the Jewish people that God intended to bless Gentiles (Gen. 12:1-3). The unexpected aspect of God's plan was that Jew and Gentile would be united in Christ's church, with each welcomed alike on the basis of faith (Eph. 3:6).

This feature of the Gospel antagonized many Jews, who thought of themselves alone as God's chosen. If we're not alert, we can fall into the same trap, and resent others who unexpectedly receive the grace of God. Let's remember that the Gospel is God's great equalizer. Scripture marks everyone as a sinner, so that anyone can be lifted up by grace.

"The manifold wisdom of God should be made known" Eph. 3:10-13. The word "manifold" might be translated "multifaceted." God's plan seems so straightforward when we read the Old Testament. He chose a people, promised them redemption, a Saviour King, and ultimate triumph. And history moved toward this fulfillment. Then, suddenly, the Son of God appeared as the promised King, was rejected by His people, crucified, and resurrected, and we realize that all along God intended far more for humankind than was previously revealed.

Don't put God in a box, or try to squeeze Him into limiting categories. God's plans and purposes are multifaceted, and each facet reflects His complex wisdom and love. The more we glimpse of that complexity, the more we should be moved to worship and to praise.

"I kneel before the Father, from whom His whole family . . . derives its name" Eph. 3:14. Paul immediately gives us an example of God's complex wisdom. The church is the body of Christ: each believer is united to Him as Head, and thus to one another. But, Paul said, the church is also family. We derive that name, family, from the fact that we are also related to God the Father. And, if we are sons of the same Father, we must by virtue of our relationship with Him be brothers and sisters—family.

How complex the wisdom God displays in the church. No single image is capable of expressing what we have in Christ, or who we are (see DEVOTIONAL).

"Immeasurably more than all we ask or imagine" Eph. 3:20-21. This benediction may well have been drawn from early church liturgy. If not, it must soon have become part of the Christian church's affirmation of Christ's great power.

These verses surely challenge us today. Sit down, and list the greatest work you can imagine that God might do in your life or the life of a loved one. Then ask Him, in complete confidence, to do it. You can have complete confidence, for our God is "able to do immeasurably more than all we ask or imagine."

"There is one body and one Spirit" Eph. 4:1-6. Everything Paul wrote in this letter was based on the conviction that the body of Christ is one. "One Lord, one faith, one [Spirit] baptism, one God and Father of all" (vv. 5-6). Our lives also must express this conviction. And the way we express it is by affirming our love for other believers—even for those with whom we differ.

Paul reminds us, "Be completely humble and gentle." Christians do differ, and differ on important matters. If we focus on our differences, convinced as we are that we are right and the others are wrong, we will become proud and judgmental. Only a humble spirit will free us to love without feeling the need to debate our differences. Only a humble spirit will maintain the bond of peace.

Don't be proud. No matter how doctrinally correct you may be, if your attitude denies the oneness of the body of Christ, you are wrong.

"He led captives in his train" Eph. 4:7-16. The image is of the return of a conquering general, who liberally distributes the spoil he took from a defeated enemy.

Christ triumphant distributes gifted individuals to the church, not to do the ministry, but "to prepare God's people for works of service" (v. 12).

Here's another expression of the complex wisdom of God expressed in His design of Christ's church. Growth toward maturity doesn't depend on the ministry of leaders, but on the ministry of the laity, whom leaders are to equip! Here too we see an echo of Paul's prayer in 3:14-19 (see DEVOTIONAL). Growth toward maturity takes place as the whole body "grows and builds itself up in love, as each part does its work."

The spiritual vitality of your congregation depends on becoming a loving, serving community of saints.

"Put off your old self . . . put on the new self" Eph. 4:17-24. In Ephesians 2 Paul led us to look at the raw material from which God

has constructed Christ's church. He showed us our deadness: the corruption of our original nature, and the futility of self-effort. And Paul reminded us that God "raised us up with Christ and seated us with Him in the heavenly realms."

This imagery is picked up here in Ephesians 4. The "old self" is that person we were when ruled by "deceitful desires." The "new self" is the astounding capacity God has given us to love others, to love God, and to set our hearts on service. The "old self" is selfish and self-centered. The "new self" is selfless and "like God in true righteousness and holiness."

Many different illustrations have been used to capture the implication of having an "old self" to put off, and a "new self" to put on. Some say it's like a teeter-totter: when one side is up, the other must be down. Some say it's like a path that forks in opposite directions, and each person decides down which he will turn. An old Indian is supposed to have said there were two horses inside him, one black, one white, pulling against each other. Which one won? The one he decided to ride.

Paul himself used an analogy. The old and the new are like cloaks a person wears. You put off one, and put the other on. This analogy has surprising force. Teens have always adopted clothing styles as symbols of how they see themselves. Research has shown that these symbols have great power in shaping adolescent behavior. Change the hairstyle, replace that pale, white makeup and the clothes that don't match, and you change the way a teenage girl sees herself, and thus the way she behaves.

This is what Paul is saying here. Don't see yourself in the old way anymore. Take off the old man, and hang it up like a suit of discarded clothes. Put on the new man, look at yourself in God's mirror, and when you see yourself clearly, go out and behave like the person you now really are.

"Be kind and compassionate" Eph. 4:25-32. Just so there'll be no mistake, Paul held up a mirror for us to look into. Here, he said, is the new man. He doesn't lie. He gets angry now and then, but not enough to lose control and sin. Once a thief, he's now hard at work on an assembly line. Once foul-mouthed, he now concentrates on saying loving, positive things that build others up. Instead of bitterness and rage, the new man is marked by kindness and compassion. Instead of brawling, the new man forgives others just as Christ forgave him—freely, generously.

Look closely in this mirror. The person you see—the honest, decent, loving, forgiving individual—is you! This is who you are in Christ!

So put this new man on. And take him with you wherever you go.

▶ DEVOTIONAL
Knowing Christ's Love (Eph. 3:14-21)

I've recently been made aware again of how few people really know love. No, not love as something they give. Love as something they get. So many of us have never really been loved: loved for ourselves, loved unconditionally, completely.

I thought of that again as I reread this prayer of Paul's for the Ephesians, and sensed his earnest desire that God's people be "rooted and established in love." The "love" Paul spoke of here isn't the love of God, or love for God. His theme was family love—love for one another in Christ. And it's vital that we understand why Paul prayed so fervently that God's family members root and establish their relationship with each other in love.

Paul said that so rooted, we have power "together with all the saints" to grasp and know the love of Christ (vv. 18-19). So family love is a key to spiritual growth—"that you may be filled to the measure of all the fullness of God."

Why is this? Partly at least because "love" is such an abstract, confusing term. All too often it's a selfish term: "I love you" means nothing more than I want to use you to meet some physical or psychological need of my own. How different the love of Christ! Christ's love is totally unselfish: His "I love you" means He was willing to give Himself to meet our own most desperate need.

How can we ever grasp or understand such love? God, in His wisdom, drew Christ's people together and made us family. In the context of the family, a family that loves and cherishes, that nurtures and supports, that cares and shares, we are to learn by experience the width and length and height and depth of the love of Christ.

The first great calling of any congregation is not to build a larger building, to raise more money for missions, or even to evangelize its neighborhood. The first great calling of any congregation is to be family. Nurtured by the warmth of Christ's love as this is expressed through brothers and sisters who care, God's people are "filled to the measure of all the fullness of God." And Christ, filling our lives, will then reach out through us to win not just our neighborhood but the world.

Personal Application

The mark of a truly spiritual church is still, "See how they love one another."

Quotable

Christ has no body now on earth but yours;
yours are the only hands with which He can do His work,
yours are the only feet with which He can go about the world,
yours are the only eyes through which His compassion can shine forth upon a troubled world.
Christ has no body now on earth but yours.—Teresa of Avila

NOVEMBER 5 *Reading 309*
IMITATORS OF GOD
Ephesians 5

> *"Be imitators of God, therefore, as dearly loved children and live a life of love, just as Christ loved us and gave Himself up for us" (Eph. 5:1-2).*

There's nothing flattering in a poor imitation.

Overview

Christians are to follow God's example and live loving (5:1), holy lives (vv. 2-14), responsive to the Spirit (vv. 15-18) and to one another (vv. 19-20). Christlikeness is especially to be demonstrated by mutual submission in the Christian home (vv. 21-33).

Understanding the Text

"Be imitators of God" Eph. 5:1. The New Testament often encourages Christians to follow the example set by other believers. Here though we're exhorted to follow the example set by God Himself. This would be impossible if it were not for one thing. We are His "dearly loved children."

As God's children we have a new heredity. His own life is planted deep within us. Because of this new life, it is now possible for us to actually be like God.

The verb is best translated "become" rather than "be." It reminds us that the potential in us has to become actual. You and I have to decide if we will become what we are in Christ, or if we will settle back down into living a mere human life. God has given us all we need to become like Him. The choice is ours.

"Live a life of love" Eph. 5:2. Paul went on to define the decision we have to make. We can choose to live a life of love, and give ourselves to others as a sacrifice to God, or to live a selfish life.

It's really a simple question. Will I set my heart to ask, "What can I do for others?" or will I set my heart to ask, "What can others do for me?" Will I be a giver? Or a getter?

The wonderful truth is that in giving we receive the most wonderful gift of all: the privilege of being like God, and bringing praise to His name.

"Not be even a hint" Eph. 5:3-7. God is characterized by holiness as well as by love. It's because we represent Him that no hint of sexual immorality, greed, obscenity—any kind of impurity—are to be associated with Christians.

Some may laugh at the Christian as a prude. We're not. Sex within marriage is rich, beautiful, exciting, and free. The off-color joke and sly innuendo that the world thinks of as so clever aren't witty at all.

They reflect a warped view of life and goodness, lie under the judgment and wrath of God.

Don't, however, get the impression that the Christian goes around with a sour face, looking daggers at passing sinners. That's why Paul mentioned love first (v. 1). If you live a life of love, you can be holy without being self-righteous. If your holiness isn't beautified by love, holiness itself distorts the image of God.

"Live as children of light" Eph. 5:8-14. Light and dark are symbols John used more often than Paul. But Paul had a special reason for using them here.

I remember fishing once on Lake Saguaro near Phoenix, Arizona. My boys and I got on the lake when it was still dark. We motored up the familiar shore—and suddenly I was completely lost. Strange shapes that appeared to be unknown islands loomed out of the darkness. What could they be? Where was I?

Then, as the sun peeked over eastern cliffs, I saw what had happened. In the dark I'd missed a point and turned into a different arm of the lake than I intended. In the growing brightness I knew where I was, and where I should go.

That's what Paul is telling us here. In the darkness it's so easy to become lost. Wander into the realms of darkness, and we'll lose all sense of reality, and not even know what to do. But if we choose that life of love and holiness that keeps us in God's light, we'll expose "the fruitless deeds of darkness." We will know them for what they are, and we will also "find out what pleases the Lord."

Walk in the light. Where you are and where you want to go will be clear.

"The fruitless deeds of darkness" Eph. 5:11. Some take this exhortation to mean Christians are supposed to run around busily pointing out others' sins. Not at all. Paul explained what he meant by saying that we Christians are now "light in the Lord."

What does a light do when it's carried into a dark place? Why it exposes what's there. In the light, you can see the true shape of things that without light are distorted shadows.

This is how we Christians expose the deeds of darkness. We walk into the room, living expressions of God's love and holiness, and suddenly the true nature of immorality, impurity, greed, obscenity, and all other sins are exposed. People can't pretend that "bad" is "good" when true goodness is present in the room.

Live as a child of light, and let the beauty of your life expose all that is ugly in this world.

"Be filled with the Spirit" Eph. 5:17-18. People of the world try to escape from the dreariness of their everyday existence by seeking an alcoholic high. Paul said find that escape through the Spirit. Let Him lift you. Let Him make life fresh and new.

You won't even have a hangover!

"Speak to one another with psalms, hymns and spiritual songs" Eph. 5:19-20. This is one of only a few passages in the New Testament that pictures Christians gathering as the church. Each time the Scriptures suggest closeness and warmth, a rich participation with one another in a common life.

Picture yourself in the setting Paul knew so well. The family has gathered. Brothers and sisters, glad to see each other, crowd together in the room. Soon one starts a hymn. Then another contributes a song. Everyone's heart is lifted and soon the room is filled with spontaneous prayer.

We don't have many actual descriptions of such gatherings in the New Testament. But from this book alone we know meetings must have been just like this. We're to be "rooted and established in love" (3:17). We're to grow and build ourselves "up in love, as each part does its work" (4:16). How else could this happen if we did not draw close, sharing as a family, loving and praising together.

Don't think such descriptions of Christ's church are ideal, even in our age of sitting passively in the Sunday pew. Somewhere in your church there are brothers and sisters who meet, or would be willing to meet, as family. In a Sunday School class. A women's circle. A home Bible study. Perhaps in your own home. The church still is the church. Really. And in the church, God has family for you.

"Submit to one another out of reverence for

Christ" Eph. 5:21. Somehow the designers of our English versions decided that verse 21 shouldn't be attached to verse 22. These are carefully separated in most versions—even in the NIV!

I can't imagine why. "Submit" (*hypotasso*) simply means to subordinate yourself to those considered worthy of respect. If we take seriously verses like Romans 12:10 ("honor one another above yourselves") and Philippians 2:3 ("in humility consider others better than yourselves"), we'd all be quick to submit—not only to leaders, but to other brothers and sisters as well. Not only wives to husbands, but husbands to wives.

In fact, it's only in the context of a body in which mutual submission is practiced by all that we can really understand what Paul said about husbands and wives in the rest of this chapter.

But never mind. It's enough here to note that in Christ submitting isn't an admission of inferiority. It's simply an affirmation that others are valued and important enough to be heard, loved, and their needs responded to. In God's peculiar way it is submission that makes us great.

▶ DEVOTIONAL
Head of the Wife
(Eph. 5:22-33)

Paul said it quite plainly. The wife sets the example of submission. The husband sets the example of loving. Each makes it easier for the other by taking the lead in his or her own unique contribution to the Christian home.

I don't know whether to be angry at the way some Christians twist this passage, or to weep. I've done each at times. Angry, when a husband misuses this passage as a club in an attempt to dominate his wife. Weeping, when a wife has surrendered her hopes and talents and even her identity in an effort to be obedient to what she thought Scripture taught.

Putting it most simply, Paul told us husbands that we are the heads of our wives "as Christ is the Head of the church" (v. 23). Paul went on to show that what this meant to Christ was that He "loved the church and gave Himself up for her to make her holy" (vv. 25-26). Headship to Christ didn't mean domination. It meant self-sacrifice. Headship didn't mean "I'm boss." It meant, "How can I meet your needs?"

That's what it must mean for a husband who wants to be a Christlike head of his home. It means putting his wife's needs before his own. It means doing everything he can to help her reach her full potential as a person and as a Christian. It means loving, self-sacrificially, as Christ loved.

So preach me no sermons demanding wives "submit." Instead, preach me sermons calling on Christian men to love as Christ loved. If a husband gives this kind of love, submission will be joyous and free.

Personal Application

Being head of the home means accepting your responsibility to take the lead in love.

Quotable

"The most important thing a father can do for his children is to love their mother."—Theodore M. Hesburgh

NOVEMBER 6 *Reading 310*
THE ARMOR OF GOD
Ephesians 6

> *"Be strong in the Lord and in His mighty power. Put on the full armor of God so that you can take your stand against the devil's schemes" (Eph. 6:10-11).*

Use every resource God has provided to wage spiritual warfare.

Overview

Paul examines mutual responsibilities of children and parents (6:1-4), and of slaves and masters (vv. 5-9). Paul reviewed the teaching of this letter, picturing the resources God has provided as a soldier's armor (vv. 10-20), and closes with brief greetings (vv. 21-24).

Understanding the Text

"Honor your father and mother" Eph. 6:1-3. Paul further developed the thought of mutual submission introduced in 5:21, and applied to husband/wife relationships in verses 22-33. A child's submission is expressed by obedience to his or her parents.

We might well place a comma in the saying, "Which is the first commandment, with a promise." Psychologically this is the first commandment that a person experiences: We learn to obey our parents long before we learn about stealing, or murder, or adultery. If we learn to obey our parents as they try to bring us up in the Lord, then the rest will be so much easier. If we are rebellious all the others will be more difficult, even as it will be more difficult to submit to God.

No wonder this commandment has a promise attached. The child who learns to respond to parental guidance will avoid those destructive and harmful behaviors that tend to shorten life.

"That it may go well with you" reminds us again. God gives us His commandments for our benefit. As we live in harmony with what God says is right, we truly are blessed.

"Fathers, do not exasperate your children" Eph. 6:4. One English version has it, "Don't overcontrol your children." The thought is expressed in a number of enlightening synonyms: aggravate, provoke, hassle, rile. As children submit to parents by obeying, so parents must submit to children by being sensitive, by listening to their point of view, by being fair.

The important thing to remember in any relationship is that the person with the greatest social power—here, Mom and Dad—have the greatest responsibility to use that power lovingly and wisely.

"Slaves, obey your earthly masters" Eph. 6:5-8. In the Roman Empire slaves were property with no right to direct their own lives. As the Gospel spread, many slaves became Christians. Several of the epistles give guidance to slaves, in each case counseling submission to their masters.

Paul went beyond the other passages here, for he emphasized an inner attitude with which the slaves' service is to be rendered. For slaves "submission" was not grudging compliance, but wholehearted commitment to doing the master's will.

Today I suppose Paul's words would be directed to employee/employer relationships. Surely the advice would be the same. We are to do our work honestly, "with sincerity of heart" at all times. We may not have a supervisor's eye on us. But God's eye is. Ultimately the reward for an honest day's work isn't to be found in our paycheck, but in God's "well done."

"Masters, treat your slaves in the same way" Eph. 6:9. Again "submission" is reciprocal for Christians. The employee submits by giving an honest day's work. The employer submits by treating employees fairly, with an honest concern for their well-being.

Reciprocal submission is one of the most important principles of Christian living. In every relationship we have, whether personal or professional, you and I are to consider the welfare of others, and act accordingly.

"Take your stand against the devil's schemes" Eph. 6:10-11. Ephesians is a book about the church. In it Paul presented Christ's church as a body, a family, and a holy

The heavily armed Roman legionnaire stands in full armor, equipped for battle. Paul summed up his teaching in Ephesians by linking major themes to different parts of the infantryman's equipment.

temple. Each of these images calls for Christians to live together in love and unity. It is this dominant theme of the book that helps us understand the nature of the devil's schemes, and the armor God has provided us to use in withstanding them. Simply, the devil's schemes in Ephesians are his strategies for disrupting the unity of the church. And the armor of God is God's resource for maintaining unity.

Living together in love as the living church of Jesus Christ isn't optional. It's essential!

"The belt of truth buckled around your waist" Eph. 6:14. Paul had written, "Each of you must put off falsehood and speak truthfully to his neighbor, for we are all members of one body" (4:25). Openness and honesty will ultimately create a climate of trust and unity. Attempts to hide our motives, or deceive others, will create a climate of misunderstanding that makes unity impossible.

That "little white lie" that seems so innocent is one of the devil's messengers intended to disrupt fellowship in Christ's church.

"The breastplate of righteousness" Eph. 6:14. Paul had written, "Among you there must not be even a hint of sexual immorality, or of any kind of impurity, or of greed, because these are improper for God's holy people" (5:3). Personal holiness and purity are essential to unity, and to corporate holiness in Christ's church.

"Your feet fitted with the readiness that comes from the Gospel of peace" Eph. 6:15. Paul had frequently stressed the fact that the Gospel brings peace, not only reconciling us to God but also to one another (cf. 2:11-22). In Ephesians, "peace" is that quality of full acceptance which maintains the bond of unity created by the Spirit, enabling the church to move, responsively, to the marching orders of Christ our Head. Without peace, the work of Christ on earth is crippled.

"Take up the shield of faith" Eph. 6:16. Paul has shown us a God who is "able to do immeasurably more than all we can ask or imagine, according to His power that is at work within us" (3:20). If we keep our eyes on this God, all Satan's fiery darts of doubt will be extinguished.

"Take the helmet of salvation" Eph. 6:17. Paul described who we were in Ephesians 2. And there too he affirmed who we are: persons who are alive in Christ, who are God's workmanship. Together we Christians need to keep this identity foremost in our thoughts.

Let's not see others in the church in the light of what they were, or even what they are now. Let's see them in all their potential, in what we are together becoming. If this perception of our fellow Christians shapes our attitude toward them, one of Satan's most effective schemes—to make us critical, hostile, or rejecting—will be defeated indeed.

"The sword of the Spirit, which is the Word of God" Eph. 6:17. This is the only piece of armor that Paul explained. Why? Because the themes represented by the other parts of the soldier's equipment were explored in Ephesians, but Paul had not earlier touched on the Word of God.

The other parts of the armor are for our defense against the devil's disruptive schemes. This, the Word of God, enables us to take the offensive. When we teach and live God's Word, Satan will increasingly be revealed to be a defeated foe.

"And pray in the Spirit on all occasions" Eph. 6:18-20. God has provided us with the resources we need to fight our spiritual battles. But we cannot use them without prayer. For these are spiritual resources, and we must rely on God as we use them.

▶ DEVOTIONAL
Workplace Imitation
(Eph. 6:1-9)

Paul's challenging call, "Be imitators of God" (Eph. 5:1), has long captured the fancy of Christians. From Thomas à Kempis' *The Imitation of Christ* to Sheldon's *In His Steps,* believers have tried to imagine what it would be like to truly imitate God in daily life.

What many miss is that Paul went on in Ephesians to describe the life of imitation as a life of mutual submission in every relationship. Husbands love their wives and put their needs first, and wives gladly respond to husbands. Children obey parents, and parents are sensitive to their children's feelings and needs. Slaves serve their masters wholeheartedly, and masters consider the needs of their slaves.

It's perhaps a little pedestrian, but the fact is that the imitation of Christ is perhaps most clearly seen where an employee arrives on time, works hard during the day, and does his best to contribute to the profitability of his boss' business. And where an employer pays a fair wage, makes sure his employees have medical insurance, makes sure working conditions are safe, and is satisfied with a reasonable profit, even though he could make more by taking advantage of his employees.

But then again, maybe the mundane and commonplace expressions of Christian faith are the most important. After all, we're to imitate God, and God in Christ entered the world as a human being. He lived with ordinary people, did ordinary work, and only during the last tenth of His 30-year life on earth taught or performed miracles.

You and I may not be able to imitate Christ in the last, spectacular 10 percent of His life on earth. But we surely can imitate Him in the 90 percent He lived as an ordinary man. And, in the ordinary things of our life—in the home, in the workplace—we can display in our submission to others something of the hidden glory of our God.

Personal Application

Imitate God tomorrow. Do an honest day's work!

Quotable

"He became what we are that He might make us what He is."—Athanasius of Alexandria

---

The Variety Reading Plan continues with PHILEMON

Philippians

INTRODUCTION

This warm and upbeat letter was written while Paul was imprisoned in Rome around A.D. 61. Despite this circumstance, the key word in Philippians is "joy" or "rejoice," which occurs 14 times. While the letter is personal, rather than a theological treatise like Romans or Galatians, it contains one of Scriptures' most powerful affirmations of the Incarnation and exaltation of Christ (2:1-11). The Book of Philippians is also a beautiful expression of the values and motives of Paul himself, and thus an example for Christians of every era.

OUTLINE OF CONTENTS

I. Introduction .... Phil. 1:1-11
II. Paul's Imprisonment .... Phil. 1:12-30
III. Imitating Christ's Humility .... Phil. 2:1-18
IV. News of Epaphroditus .... Phil. 2:19-30
V. Warnings .... Phil. 3:1–4:1
VI. Personal Exhortations .... Phil. 4:2-9
VII. Thanks and Farewell .... Phil. 4:10-23

READING GUIDE (4 Days)

If hurried, you may read only the "core passage" in your Bible and the Devotional in each chapter of this Commentary.

Reading	*Chapters*	*Core passage*
311	1	1:12-19
312	2	2:6-11
313	3	3:4-11
314	4	4:6

Philippians

NOVEMBER 7 *Reading 311*
PAUL IN CHAINS
Philippians 1

> *"What has happened to me has really served to advance the Gospel" (Phil. 1:12).*

In Christ, even bad news can be good news in disguise.

Background
The church in Philippi. Paul founded the church in the Roman colony city of Philippi about A.D. 50, some 10 years before this letter was written. He visited there again about A.D. 55, and kept in contact with the believers through letters and helpers like Timothy. The Philippians were apparently very upset when they heard that Paul had been sent to Rome after his arrest in Jerusalem (Acts 21–28). They sent a gift of money with Epaphroditus to help Paul with his expenses. This messenger became extremely ill, but recovered, and Paul sent this letter to the Philippians by him when he recovered. Paul touched on many different topics in Philippians, from his own imprisonment to a feud between two leading women in the church there. Despite his own uncertain circumstances and indications of problems in the Philippian congregation, Paul's letter is vibrant with a joy that exists independent of circumstances. In Philippians, we find the sources of joy available to Christians who walk through dark places with the Lord.

Overview
Paul thanked God and prayed for his partners in the Gospel (1:1-11). He assured them that his imprisonment had been a good thing (vv. 12-26), and exhorted them to stand firm together (vv. 27-30).

Understanding the Text
"I always pray with joy" Phil. 1:4. Prayer for others isn't a duty. It is a joy: a special opportunity to caress and be close to people we love.

This fresh approach to intercession marks the opening words of Paul's letter to the Philippians. No special, desperate need drove Paul to prayer. Instead Paul had cultivated the habit, whenever he thought of his dear friends in Philippi, of expressing the joyful feelings remembrance brings by offering up a prayer for them.

What a simple, yet meaningful way for us to enrich our prayer lives. We can cultivate the habit, whenever we think of others, to give thanks and pray for them "with joy."

"He who began a good work in you will carry it on to completion" Phil. 1:3-6. My first week in college in Ohio I had an appendix attack, and an emergency operation. My mom and dad drove down to see me, and Mother brought me a Bible. Trying to joke, I took it and said, "I'm not that sick!"

Sometimes even we Christians think of prayer or other religious exercises as a last resort kind of thing. We pray when we're desperate, or when we are fearful for others. But Paul prayed out of joy, and with supreme confidence. There was no clear and present danger to the Philippian church. These believers had worked in partnership with Paul in spreading the Gospel from the first. And Paul had total confidence that the work God began in their lives would be carried on to completion, "until the day of Christ Jesus."

We can have this same confidence when we pray for one another. God won't abandon any of His own. Our prayers aren't a last-ditch effort to keep them from sliding over the edge of some spiritual precipice. We pray for other Christians with joy, and with total confidence that God is at work in their lives.

Why then do we pray? We pray as an expression of love. And we pray because we believe that God in some mysterious way uses our prayers to enrich that good work He is committed to do in His children's lives.

"And this is my prayer" Phil. 1:9-11. Romans 8:26 notes that we do not really know what we ought to pray for others. Yet Paul's prayers for other believers, like the one recorded here, and like prayers in Ephesians 3 and Colossians 1, can guide us. These prayers are well worth committing to memory. Then, when we think of a friend, we can ask "that your love may abound more and more in knowledge and depth of insight, so that you may be able to discern what is best and may be pure and blameless until the day of Christ, filled with the fruit of righteousness that comes from Jesus Christ—to the glory and praise of God."

"What has happened to me has really served to advance the Gospel" Phil. 1:12-18. The Philippians were deeply upset at Paul's imprisonment. For one thing, if Paul were convicted, the Christian movement might be threatened. The Roman government had declared certain religions licit, giving them the legal right to be practiced. Other religions had no legal standing. As the Christian movement emerged from Judaism, and Judaism was a legal religion, early Christianity was protected. If Paul were convicted of some religious crime, the movement he represented might be officially proscribed.

Even if this didn't happen, the great apostle and evangelist seemed "put on the shelf." He had been under arrest for two years in Caesarea. Now he was under house arrest in Rome. What would happen to the Gospel without Paul?

I read in today's paper an account of the explosive growth of evangelical Christianity in Guatemala. That land, torn by bloodshed, its economy destroyed and its people destitute, now is about one third evangelical Christian, and the number is growing at approximately 10 percent a year! We must hurt for those experiencing the terrors of poverty and civil strife. Yet we also need to realize that God is using their suffering on earth to open their hearts to the Gospel.

How often we are shaken by circumstances that are admittedly terrible, but in God's providence "serve to advance the Gospel." The lesson Paul was trying to teach the Philippians is that God takes apparent tragedies and molds them into triumphs (see DEVOTIONAL).

"For to me, to live is Christ and to die is gain" Phil. 1:21. Paul stated the one attitude which enables us to discover good in ills that would otherwise mar our lives. If we look at circumstances merely from a human point of view, and think first of our own comfort or our situation in this life, we might have good reason for despair. But Paul didn't look at life this way at all. He was concerned only with serving Jesus and glorifying Him.

If this is our primary motivation, our circumstances here will be relatively unimportant. We can live for Jesus in a hovel or a palace. We can share our pennies or our millions. We can give thanks for our rags or for our riches.

Make pleasing Jesus your sole desire, and you declare independence from all the circumstances that can ruin the lives of others who struggle on without Him.

"Whatever happens, conduct yourselves in a manner worthy of the Gospel" Phil. 1:27-30. This paragraph sums up Paul's theme in a simple exhortation. "Whatever happens." Whether you prosper or go bankrupt. Whether you become popular or an object of scorn. Whatever comes, live as a Christian who is worthy of the great gift God has given in the Gospel.

What marks the "worthy" Christian life? Maintaining unity. Contending for the Gospel. Remaining confident rather than fearful.

The exhortation is important for us as well as for the first-century Philippians. In this life we too may be given an unusual gift. The gift, "on the behalf of Christ, not only to believe on Him, but also to suffer for Him."

By using any circumstances He sends as opportunities to serve God, we can make our suffering not only a gift from God, but a gift to Him.

▶ DEVOTIONAL
Circumstantial Evidence (Phil. 1:12-19)

In our courts of law the best evidence is direct evidence: there are witnesses to an event who can testify to who did what and when. Next best is circumstantial evidence: facts and information that when interpreted make who, what, and when likely. The problem with circumstantial evidence is always in that little phrase, "when interpreted."

For instance, take a beautiful, vibrant, athletic young woman. She has an accident that permanently paralyzes her from the neck down. "Terrible," we say. And we're right. "Her life is ruined," we think. And we're wrong! Through that accident Joni Eareckson Tada became a great gift to the church, and found a new and fulfilling life for herself.

This is essentially what Paul was trying to teach the Philippians when he wrote, "I want you to know, brothers, that what has happened to me has really served to advance the Gospel" (v. 12). Circumstances are deceiving. Yes, Paul, the early church's premier evangelist and church planter, had been put on the shelf. Yes, he'd spent two years locked up in Caesarea, and now he was under house arrest in Rome. It looked like a terrible setback for the church, and a terrible waste of Paul's few remaining years. But that is only how it looked. That is not how it was.

Look, Paul said. Everyone in the palace guard knows I'm here because of Jesus. And most of the brothers have been "encouraged to speak the Word of God more courageously." Like a football team whose star quarterback is out of the game, the rest try harder! Even those who resented Paul were out preaching more vigorously, and though their motives were questionable, Christ was being preached! So Paul didn't see his imprisonment as a tragedy at all. He looked beyond the circumstances, and interpreted them with a clear understanding of God's goal of getting out the Gospel. As for Paul himself, well, through the Philippians' prayers, he would surely be delivered.

Let's learn to interpret circumstantial evidence as Paul did, taking into account the fact that God works all things together for good for those who love the Lord. What looks like a tragedy may lead to one of history's greatest spiritual triumphs. What looks like defeat may be turning into victory. What looks like suffering may be the harbinger of joy.

Personal Application

Face the worst, and expect the best.

Quotable

"Suffering, though a burden, is a useful burden, like the splints used in orthopedic treatment."—Sören Kierkegaard

NOVEMBER 8 *Reading 312*
HUMILITY INCARNATE
Philippians 2

"Your attitude should be the same as that of Christ Jesus: Who being in very nature God, did not consider equality with God something to be grasped, but made Himself nothing" (Phil. 2:5-7).

The way to be exalted is still, be humble.

Overview

A humble concern for others (2:1-4) mimics the humility displayed by Christ (vv. 5-11), which leads to blameless and pure lives (vv. 12-18). Paul commended two men he was about to send to Philippi (2:19-30).

Understanding the Text

"If you have any encouragement" Phil. 2:1. The Greek language has several different words and constructions that we render "if" in English. The "if" in Philippians 2:1 assumes the condition is already fulfilled, and means "since."

So what Paul was saying is, since you are united with Christ, and since you find comfort in His love, and since you share in God's Spirit.

How well Paul understood God. Paul was about to appeal to his friends in Philippi to commit to a more humble, caring lifestyle. In the world, people trying to influence others might say, "If you will do this, then I will do something for you." But not God, and not Paul! Instead Paul reminded his readers of how God had poured out His grace on them, and then said, "Since you have been so blessed, take the step of obedience."

There's no hint of threat in our relationship with God. There's no hint of bribery. God won't take our blessings away, and there is no need to add to them! Paul simply reminds us of what God has already done for us, and asks us, out of gratitude, to respond appropriately to God.

The next time you face a difficult choice, remember all God has given you so freely. As an expression of thanks, choose just as freely to do what will please Him.

"Like-minded, having the same love" Phil. 2:2-4. Two themes found throughout the New Testament letters are woven together here. One is unity: that common life shared by those who constitute Christ's church, and who achieve spirituality only when the bond between members is close and warm. The other is humility: that basic attitude toward ourselves and others that is required for unity to exist.

Every once in a while I see a magazine on a newsstand featuring a new self-test: "How well do you understand your spouse?" "What kind of a lover are you?" "Check your parenting skills!" Well, the Apostle Paul has given us a simple self-test here on an even more important question. "How do you rate in your relationship with other Christians?"

Part of the test measures the community of which you're a part. Are you "like-minded, having the same love, being one in spirit and purpose"? (v. 2) Part of the test measures your personal attitudes. "Do nothing out of selfish ambition or vain conceit, but in humility consider others better than yourselves. . . . Look not only to your interests, but also to the interests of others" (vv. 3-4).

If the church you belong to fails the first part of the test, don't be discouraged. If you pass the second part, God can use you to change your church!

"Your attitude should be the same as that of Christ Jesus" Phil. 2:5. Christ is our Saviour, plus. There are many words we might tack on behind that "plus." He is our Saviour, plus our Lord. He is our Saviour, plus our High Priest. But here, as in Ephesians 5:1 and other passages, Paul reminds us that Jesus is our Saviour, plus our example. We are to be like Jesus, not just in the way we act, but in our innermost values and attitudes toward life.

This is why Paul stressed humility. It's not enough to *act* interested in others. We must *be* interested in others. It's not enough to act unselfishly. We must be free of "selfishness and vain conceit."

This would be an impossible task if it weren't for one wonderful reality. God has already acted to make possible everything He asks of us! No wonder Paul began by saying, "Since you are united with

Christ . . . since you have fellowship with the Spirit." Christ and His Spirit live within us, and through their presence we can develop "the same" attitude "as that of Christ Jesus."

"Therefore God exalted Him to the highest place" Phil. 2:9-11. Our Christian faith is filled with paradoxes. This is one of the most powerful. Because Christ humbled Himself, God exalted Him. The way up, is down. The key to mastery is servanthood. The greatest among us are the servants of all.

It is a paradox, but it is also reality. We who choose humility now will be raised higher than the proud. We who give ourselves to others gain. We who lose ourselves find our true and better selves.

There is no other way to succeed in the Christian life than to walk the road Jesus traveled.

"The name that is above every name" Phil. 2:9-11. The name "Lord" has significance in both Testaments. In the Old Testament it is the personal name of God, Yahweh, and means "the One Who Is Always Present." It was by this name that Israel was to remember God, and to experience Him as reality in every setting of life.

In the New Testament "Lord" is the name of honor. It captures the spirit of the Old Testament name, and fills it with fresh new meaning through Jesus' suffering and exaltation. The ever-present God came into the world in a human body, and the God-Man Jesus was raised triumphant. One day all mankind will worship Jesus as Lord—the eternal, personal God of history and Scripture.

There is a note of finality here. "Every knee shall bow" is not a Gospel promise. It is a blunt statement that those who are now unwilling to acknowledge Jesus will be forced to do so at history's end. How glad we can be to acknowledge Him now, freely, and with joy.

Let's not make our acknowledgment of Christ as Lord mere lip service, though. In view of who Jesus is, and what He suffered for us, let's pledge ourselves to render Him full obedience, now and evermore.

"Work out your salvation" Phil. 2:12-18. As the old preacher said, "Oh, salvation's in him. It just hasn't worked its way out yet!"

But it will. For God is at work in His own, and by His grace we will display the blamelessness and purity of the sons of God.

"Who takes a genuine interest in your welfare" Phil. 2:19-24. Paul commended Timothy for the very quality he had been exhorting: a humility that lets us put others first. How important it is for churches to have leaders who demonstrate the attitudes they exhort.

"Welcome him in the Lord with great joy" Phil. 2:25-30. Some feel Paul went out of his way to commend Epaphroditus and explain his dangerous illness. They suggest that some in Epaphroditus' home church of Philippi were critical of this messenger of theirs. Paul countered the criticism by reminding the Philippians twice that Epaproditus "almost died for the work of Christ."

The role of "critic of the brethren" is one we want to avoid at all costs. It expresses the exact opposite of the attitude of humility that is appropriate for you and me.

▶DEVOTIONAL
Make Yourself Nothing
(Phil. 2:6-11)

The affirmation of Paul, in this hymn to Christ as God incarnate, is thought to be one of the church's earliest confessional statements, used in first-century worship. It is surely one of Scripture's most profound statements of Jesus' full deity. It portrays Christ as "in very nature God," but emptying Himself to take on human nature and suffer a shameful death. It affirms not only Jesus' resurrection but His ultimate exaltation over all.

Yet Paul applied this most profound of the mysteries of our faith in such a simple, practical way! We are to look at the attitude of humility Jesus displayed, and adopt it in our relationships with others.

It's no wonder, with talk like this, that Christianity has been accused of being the religion of wimps. Ted Turner, for one, has publicly described Christians as people who can't make it in this world, and so turn to the next. Christians are weak, dull, too scrupulous or too cowardly, to make it big in this world.

The stereotype has been around a long time, and the accusation is nothing new. The arrogant of this world understandably look down on people who talk more about love than success, and who seem to prize humility more than headlines.

What the world doesn't understand is that Christians choose humility not out of weakness, but out of strength. We choose humility, because our vision of Jesus deals a death blow to all man's pride. Whatever basis we might have for believing ourselves better than others—intelligence, looks, wealth, education, breeding—all pale to utter insignificance when we see Jesus, willing to abandon His rightful claim of full equality with God, to not only become a human being, but even to die on a cross.

Seeing Jesus, we realize that all those claims we might make to superiority must also be nailed to Jesus' cross. We must give them up; put them to death once and for all. For only when our pride has been put to death will we begin to care for others as Christ has cared for us. And to the true Christian, as to Christ, the interests of others are more important than his own.

Personal Application

We climb to glory on the down escalator.

Quotable

"Humility is the garment of the Deity. The incarnate Word was clothed in it, and through it, conversed with us in our bodies, covering the radiance of His greatness and His glory by this humility lest the creature be scorched by the sight of Him. The creature could not have looked at Him, had He not taken on some part of it and thus conversed with it. Therefore every man who clothes himself in garments of humility becomes clothed in Christ Himself."—Isaak of Syria

NOVEMBER 9 *Reading 313*
TO KNOW CHRIST
Philippians 3

> *"I consider everything a loss compared to the surpassing greatness of knowing Christ Jesus my Lord" (Phil. 3:8).*

Power for living as well as salvation is to be found in Christ alone.

Overview

Paul had abandoned confidence in his own works (3:1-6) to trust Christ completely (vv. 7-9) and spiritual enablement (vv. 10-11). All mature believers will follow Paul's example and press toward this goal (vv. 12-17), eagerly awaiting Christ's return and our transformation (vv. 18-21).

Understanding the Text

"Finally, my brothers, rejoice in the Lord!" Phil. 3:1 This is not the last thought Paul intended to share. It is instead the ultimate thought.

Paul had already noted many sources of joy for the Christian life. We find joy in fellowship with others whom we love (1:4). We find joy in sharing the Gospel (v. 18). We find joy in our unity with other believers (2:2). Yet the final, the ultimate joy, which Paul expressed in Philippians 3, is found in Christ Himself.

It is this joy, which is available to you and me always, that Paul explored in this very personal chapter of Philippians.

"Put no confidence in the flesh" Phil. 3:2-4. Paul began by warning against the Judaizers. These men of Jewish extraction and pharisaical tendency visited all the churches Paul founded, and tried to convince the believers that they must become Jews to be Christians. They must accept circumcision, and keep the many regulations of the Old Testament, as interpreted by tradition.

Paul angrily called these men evil, mere "mutilators of the flesh." In focusing the attention of believers on works, they drew attention away from Christ.

This is the first clue to finding the Christian's ultimate source of joy. Don't count on what you have done, are doing, or will do. Count only on what Christ did.

Watchman Nee, the great Chinese evangelist and writer on the spiritual life, has rightly said, "Christianity is a queer business. If at the outset we try to do anything, we get nothing; if we seek to attain something, we miss everything. For Christianity begins not with a big DO, but with a big DONE."

Only by continuing to rely on Christ and what He has done, only by abandoning all reliance on our own works, can we go on in the Christian life or experience joy. (See DEVOTIONAL.)

"Somehow, to attain to the resurrection of the dead" Phil. 3:10-11. Verse 11 has confused some, who assume Paul was speaking about the future resurrection of his own body. But verse 10 makes it clear Paul was speaking about knowing Christ now, and experiencing now the power of His resurrection.

Paul spoke in the same vein in Romans 8:11: "If the Spirit of Him who raised Jesus from the dead is living in you, He who raised Christ from the dead will also give life to your mortal bodies through His Spirit, who lives in you." Thus Romans identifies the source of power for Christian living. Philippians 3:10-11 now goes on to tell us how to tap this source of power. Paul's explanation? Become "like Christ in His death."

The prescription is explained in the verses above. We abandon any confidence we had in the flesh. We confess our lifeless state, and the utter impossibility of any spiritual achievement. As the dead body of Christ was buried, so we bury the rubbish we once considered our righteousness.

Then, standing by the grave of self, we hear Christ's invitation to share His sufferings and experience the power of His resurrection.

"I press on toward the goal" Phil. 3:12-14. Don't get the idea that the Christian life is passive. We do stop trying. But we do not stop pressing on.

This may be a paradox, but it is not a contradiction. What we put behind us is self-effort, and the notion that anything we can do in ourselves can possibly please or be of service to the Lord. What we hold out before us is the fact that, here on earth, we are Christ's hands and feet. We are His body now, the presence He still maintains in the world of men. It is that "for which Christ Jesus took hold of me." It is that that you and I prize most as we journey heavenward.

It's not that we will ever perfectly express Christ to others. But as we rely completely on Him to work through us, and as we commit ourselves to do God's will, we will experience something of resurrection power and joy today.

"Our citizenship is in heaven" Phil. 3:17-20a. A citizen owes allegiance to the laws and rulers of his nation. Paul closed this section of Philippians by calling on us to remember what it means to be united to Jesus in His death and resurrection. We owe no allegiance to our old way of life. Those who even try to be good and so merit God's favor are enemies of the Cross, which stands stark and bare as a symbol of man's utter sinfulness.

We who have heard the message of the Cross, are to keep on hearing it in each of our todays. It tells us that what man cannot do, God has done. And God will continue to do, in you and in me.

"We eagerly await a Saviour from there, the Lord Jesus Christ" Phil. 3:20b-21. Earlier Paul wrote, "Not that I have already obtained all this, or have already been made perfect" (v. 12). Those who expect the spiritual life to be one of sudden transformation, or instantaneous perfection, are sure to be disappointed. God still has only our mortal bodies to work with, and all too often lacks even our cooperation! But despite our imperfection, God's power does flow in us and through us. In our weakness we know something of His strengthening power.

No wonder Paul said we wait eagerly for Jesus to return. Then, what we experience imperfectly now will be fully ours. When Jesus returns, "He will transform our lowly bodies so that they will be like His glorious body" (v. 21). Then at last we will realize to the full "the surpassing greatness of knowing Christ Jesus" our Lord (v. 8).

▶ DEVOTIONAL

A Vote of No Confidence (Phil. 3:4-11)

She was an older lady, well-dressed, clearly upper class. She'd stopped to watch as I stood on a street evangelist's stepladder outside St. Patrick's Cathedral in New York to give my "word of testimony." Perhaps it was the novelty of seeing one of Uncle Sam's sailors, in uniform, preaching on the street. Perhaps it was just curiosity.

After I got down I talked with her. She thought that Jesus was all right for some people. Certainly the bums on the bowery needed something. But she was not only religious, she was a truly good person. She had never done anything mean or petty, and while others might need Jesus, she most assuredly did not.

Often the hardest people to reach with the Gospel are those who truly have tried to live good lives, and by all appearances have succeeded! Paul was one of those people, and his credentials were far superior to any you or I might muster. Or even that lady I met so briefly on the street over 35 years ago.

But Paul did something with his credentials that you and I must do with ours. We have to recognize them not as advantages, but liabilities! If we for a moment rely on them, or think that they commend us to God, they replace to that extent our confidence in Christ, and thus weaken us spiritually.

It may seem strange, but the truly wicked have a great advantage over the good when they become Christians. John Newton, for instance, had a great advantage over you and me. He went to sea early in life, and quickly became a vile, drunken, blasphemous, and violent man. And a slave trader. Later, when Newton was converted, he never lost his sense of the dark pit from which he had been rescued, or an awareness of his own corrupt nature.

So don't take comfort in the "good" life you may have lived before your conversion. Or even in your honest efforts to do well since. Like the Apostle Paul, consider such advantages to be liabilities. Let your heart be filled with the "surpassing greatness of knowing Christ Jesus." Cloak yourself in the righteousness that comes from Him by faith, and rely on His resurrection power to express itself through you and your life.

Personal Application

The Christian life is resurrection life. But before you can rise again, you must die to self.

Quotable

"This Christ life is simply turning the little shop of life, so woefully perplexing, over to another. Christ becomes owner, manager, overseer; His is the responsibility, the upkeep. Your part is to be a faithful clerk, steward of the grace of God. You are to trust the management to Him and obey orders; take off the shelves anything displeasing, add anything He commands. But He is also your elder brother and His love takes out all the worry, fever, and tension. And one day, if you have been faithful over a few things, He will give you a heavenly shop in the city of the King!"—Charles H. Robinson

NOVEMBER 10 *Reading 314*
CONTENT WITH CHRIST
Philippians 4

"I have learned to be content whatever the circumstances" (Phil. 4:11).

When you have it all, more means little.

Overview
Paul exhorted his friends (4:1-9), put their gift to him in unique perspective (vv. 10-20), and added final greetings (vv. 21-23).

Understanding the Text
"Therefore . . . stand firm in the Lord" Phil. 4:1. Most connect this exhortation with the teaching in chapter 3. The reason is the "therefore." As the old preacher observed, "Whenever you see a 'therefore,' you gotta look back to see what it's there for."

What is this "therefore" there for? Paul had just explained the futility of trying to relate to God through works, and reminded the Philippians of the resurrection power available to those who rely completely on Christ, and who "press on toward the goal" Christ sets for His own. In view of the supernatural character of the Christian life, believers are to "stand firm in the Lord," and resist every effort to shift the focus of their faith from Jesus Himself.

The verse contains another of those 14 occurrences of "joy" or "rejoice" found in Philippians. Here Paul called the Philippians "my joy and crown." In this he reflected a theme found in 3 John 4: "I have no greater joy than to hear that my children are walking in the truth."

When you and I stand firm in the Lord we do give our leaders joy. More important, we give God Himself joy, for we fulfill His purposes for us.

"I plead with Euodia and I plead with Syntyche" Phil. 4:2-3. Paul knew the hurt caused by misunderstandings and sharp disagreement. His own stubbornness had caused a break with his dear friend Barnabas (Acts 15:36-41). Paul didn't condemn these women who for some reason found themselves at odds. He instead pleaded, "Help these women."

There's a vital lesson here. In Philippians 2 Paul described the attitude of humility which alone is capable of melding believers together (2:1-4). Paul might very well have bluntly accused each of these women of abandoning this attitude, and bluntly demanded they get right with God and then get right with each other.

But Paul did not! Instead he was sensitive, caring, and—please note, respectful! He pleaded, not ordered. He asked others in Philippi to help, not demand or discipline. And he showed respect for these two women by praising them for contending "at my side" for the Gospel. He carefully numbered them along with the "rest of my fellow workers."

We make a great mistake if in trying to cure we condemn, or in trying to help we disparage. Belittle a person whom you hope to help respond positively, and you're almost sure to harden him or her in his position. But appeal with respect, as Paul did, to the better self others have displayed, and you free others to make right choices.

Really, having faith in God's people to do the right thing is having faith in God. As Paul has said, "It is God who works in you to will and to act according to His good purpose" (v. 13).

"Rejoice in the Lord always" Phil. 4:4. It is significant that Paul burst out with another expression of joy just after mentioning the conflict between two good women in Philippi.

Charles L. Allen tells about the manager who took a pen and put a black dot in the center of a large sheet of white cardboard. "Your trouble is," the manager told his employees, "that the moment one black spot appears you fix your attention on that, and fail to see all the clean white space." We Christians are like that too. When a black spot, or a dozen black spots, appear, we spend all our energy thinking about them rather than on the vast white space that represents what we have in Christ.

Paul wasn't going to let conflict between Euodia and Syntyche pull his eyes away from Christ! And so he tells us, when the black spots appear in our lives, as they surely will, to "rejoice in the Lord always. I will say it again: Rejoice."

"Do not be anxious about anything" Phil. 4:6-7. Psychologists have defined anxiety as a feeling of apprehension, cued by a threat to something we hold essential. Some, however, are chronically anxious: fearful and nervous even when there is no apparent threat. Whatever the source of anxious feelings, they're no fun to have.

I suspect that the real cause of anxiety is a sense of powerlessness. We feel threatened, but don't know what to do about the threat. Paul reminds us that we can not only do something—we can do the most effective thing! We can place the problem squarely in the hands of the one Person in the universe who can deal with every threat.

So Paul said, "In everything, by prayer and petition, with thanksgiving, present your requests to God." The thanksgiving is important. It is our affirmation of faith that God will surely deal with the situation we have just handed over to Him.

"The peace of God, which transcends all understanding" Phil. 4:7. Why does the peace of God "transcend understanding"? Simply because, on the surface, our circumstances will not have changed. Something we hold dear will still be threatened. We'll still be out of work. Or our child will still be bullied on the school bus. Or our spouse will still face a battle with cancer. We could explain the peace we feel to others if we could announce, "I have a new job!" Or if the bully was kicked off the bus, or the doctor announced the cancer cured.

The thing that's special about the peace God gives, and the thing we can never explain to those who have never had the experience, is that we experience peace before the situation changes in any way. God's Spirit calms us, and whispers in our hearts, "It's all right now. God will provide."

"Think about such things" Phil. 4:8-9. The word translated "think" here (*logizesthai*) means to "continually focus your mind." But more is implied than considering. We are to concentrate on expressing these qualities in our lives, so that as we dwell on them, they in turn dwell in us.

Paul's list includes:

* the true—meaning the truthful in thought as well as every aspect of life.

* the noble—meaning that which wins respect; the honest, honorable, worthy.

* the right—meaning that which fulfills all our obligation to God and to other men.

* the pure—meaning that which fits us for fellowship with and service to God, including but more than freedom from bodily sins.

* the lovely—meaning that which is attractive and winsome.

* the admirable—meaning that which is kind and likely to win others.

These were considered excellent and praiseworthy qualities in Greek culture as well as among Christians. The Christian is not to be the "odd" man in society, but the ideal man (see DEVOTIONAL).

"I have learned to be content" Phil. 4:10-20. Paul had received a money gift from the Philippians, which he appreciated. It revealed their continuing love for him, and this was important to Paul. And as an expression of love for God, the gifts are "a fragrant offering, an acceptable sacrifice." Paul also shared his own unique perspective on money. During his 25 years of ministry Paul had known times when money was plentiful, and times he was "in need." And Paul had learned that neither condition made any real difference: "whether well-fed or hungry, whether living in plenty or in want" Paul had learned to be content.

His independence from circumstances grew out of the conviction that his God meets all our needs "according to His glorious riches in Christ Jesus" (v. 19), and the conviction that "I can do everything through Him who gives me strength" (v. 13).

This is one of the greatest gifts that is ours through our relationship with Jesus. We have a God whose endless resources will be used to meet our needs. And a God who will give us strength to meet every challenge. If we constantly remember who our God is, we too will grasp the secret of being content, whatever our circumstances.

▶ **DEVOTIONAL**

Hear, See, Do
(Phil. 4:6)

My wife is one of those naturally good cooks. I say naturally, but I don't really know whether it's a gift, or the result of practice. On the other hand, I have a hard time trying to cook, largely because I don't have the patience to follow a recipe's instructions. I look at a list of ingredients, throw them all together, and somehow don't notice that the shortening wasn't supposed to be melted before being mixed in. Or if I'm making the gravy, I plop the flour and milk I've mixed so carefully into the broth in one great glop, creating some of those wonderful lumps that my mom's gravy—or Sue's—never has.

Sometimes we Christians make a similar mistake with the Bible. We read it and get all the ingredients straight. But then we don't notice just how they are supposed to be blended together. And what we sometimes get is a disaster instead of a tasty dessert.

Philippians 4 is like this. Paul gives us ingredients for a vital and joy-filled Christian life. He writes about bringing our anxieties to God (vv. 6-7). He reminds us of the qualities we're to nurture (vv. 8-9). He even tells of the contentment that comes as we rely on God rather than our current bank balance (vv. 10-20). And there, right in the middle, he tells us how these ingredients are to be combined!

Paul said, "Whatever you have learned or received or heard from me, or seen in me—put into practice" (v. 9).

It's dangerous to leave out any of these steps. If you're a parent or a teacher or preacher, it's not enough to speak the truth. To translate what is heard, most people need to see it put into practice by others. So those of us who teach in any setting need to open our lives to others, so they can see how the truths we share find living expression in our thoughts, attitudes, and actions. Preachers can't just proclaim the truth and expect their people to go out and practice it. God's recipe calls for a vital intermediate step.

If you and I are learners, there's a reminder for us here too. We can't just "learn and receive and hear" the truth from our teachers, or just see it in other's lives. We have to go on to personally "put it into practice." Truth we don't practice is about as useful as a tire without air. We won't get very far on either!

So let's remember as we try to put together the ingredients God gives us for a truly Christian life that we have to follow His recipe carefully. We have to hear, see, and then do.

Then, and only then, will we experience what Paul knew so well: the joy of knowing that "the God of peace" is with us.

Personal Application

What you don't know, you can't do. But what you don't do, you cannot truly know.

Quotable

"There is only one golden rule for spiritual discernment, and that is obedience. We learn more by five minutes' obedience than by ten years' study."—Oswald Chambers

---

The Variety Reading Plan continues with PSALMS 85–150

Colossians

INTRODUCTION

Colossians is one of four letters Paul wrote from prison in Rome, about A.D. 61. This letter has a sharp focus: Paul wrote to combat a peculiar heresy that seemed to blend occult superstition with a "hollow and deceptive philosophy" (2:8). The effect of the heresy was to rob Christ of His central role in Christian faith. To oppose it, Paul provided one of Scripture's clearest and most powerful statements of who Jesus is and what He has done.

Paul then went on to describe the way of life that is appropriate for those who know the real Jesus, and shows us that true spirituality is living a godly life in this present world.

OUTLINE OF CONTENTS

READING GUIDE (3 Days)

If hurried, you may read only the "core passage" in your Bible and the Devotional in each chapter of this Commentary.

Reading	*Chapters*	*Core passage*
315	1	1:15-28
316	2	2:16-23
317	3–4	3:16-17

Colossians

NOVEMBER 11 *Reading 315*
CHRIST SUPREME
Colossians 1

> *"He is the beginning and the firstborn from among the dead, so that in everything He might have the supremacy" (Col. 1:18).*

Without Christ, Christianity is nothing.

Background

The Colossian heresy. Features of the heresy that was corrupting the church at Colosse have been deduced from Paul's letter, and seem to match a movement later known as Gnosticism. The Gnostics held a strict dualism: all matter was evil. Thus God, who is good, could never have really become a man. This directly challenged Christian doctrine of the Incarnation, and relegated Jesus Christ to a minor role in salvation history. To replace faith as a way of salvation the Gnostics offered a hidden knowledge (*gnosis*). To replace the living of a holy life in this world, the Gnostics might either try to subdue their fleshly body by asceticism, or they might live profligate lives, arguing that the "evil" body was simply following its nature, while the inner "I" was unaffected.

While the Gnostic movement dissolved long ago, Colossians remains a vital book for Christians who want to let Christ rule supreme, and to know true spirituality.

Overview

Paul reported two prayers he offered for the Colossians (1:3-14), and immediately made a profound affirmation of Christ's supremacy (vv. 15-23) and His living presence in the believer (vv. 24-29).

Understanding the Text

"To the holy and faithful brothers" Col. 1:1-3. Paul's greeting shows characteristic gentleness. He did not attack them, even though many had apparently been sucked into a heretical group that neither lived a holy life nor was faithful to the doctrine of Christ. Paul was convinced that the truth he presented would correct their misunderstandings and rescue them.

Doctrinal dispute can become so vitriolic that those in error are driven from the truth by those who know it. If you know others who are currently trapped in misunderstanding, don't attack them. Trust them to respond to truth when it is clearly and gently presented.

"When we pray for you" Col. 1:3-8. Paul continued his loving approach by telling how he thanked God each time he prayed for them. Pray for an "opponent" and thank God for him or her, and it will change your attitude for the better!

"All over the world this Gospel is producing fruit" Col. 1:6. This is a gentle reminder. The Gospel the Colossians originally heard was the one that was being preached so effectively all over the world. The Gnostics were like the mother who saw her son marching with the high school band and said, "Look, they're all out of step except my Bernie!"

When everyone else is out of step, it's time to reexamine your position!

"We have not stopped praying for you and asking God" Col. 1:9-11. This prayer for the Colossians is one of the most significant in the New Testament, for it depicts the pro-

cess of spiritual growth. Simply, the prayer describes a growth cycle, one which spirals ever upward to maturity. If you want to grow spiritually, let this prayer of Paul's be your constant guide.

You begin with "the knowledge of [God's] will" (v. 9a). This is the kind of information about Himself and His will that God has revealed in Scripture. But you hold this knowledge in "all spiritual wisdom and understanding" (v. 9b). Both "spiritual wisdom" and "insight" describe seeing implications: seeing how to respond in every life situation by applying your knowledge of God.

You then respond according to God's Word, "that you may live a life worthy of the Lord and may please Him" (v. 10a). And, in the process of living out God's known will, you bear "fruit in every good work" (v. 10b) and you also come to know God Himself better (v. 10b). In this whole process you are "being strengthened with all power" by God Himself, and so share in all that you have inherited through your relationship with Jesus.

What is exciting about this to me is that it clearly defines our part in the spiritual life, and God's part. You and I must (1) seek to know God's revealed will and (2) seek to apply it in daily life. As we do, God supernaturally (1) strengthens us with His power, (2) produces fruit in and through us, and (3) makes Himself ever more real to us.

There's no great mystery about living the Christian life. And no overwhelming difficulties. We need simply to study and apply God's Word as best we can—and trust God to do the rest!

"The image of the invisible God" Col. 1:15-19. In its essence idolatry is putting anything less than God in God's place.

The Gnostics did this by honoring imagined ranks of angels, each a little less material and more spirit, standing between the universe and God. And they placed Jesus below these angels, very distant from God!

One of the magazines I take and enjoy very much is the *Catholic Digest*. It is a warm and often enriching magazine. But every now and then I'm troubled by references to Mary that make her, in effect, the focus of a Christian's prayers and faith. "Ask Mary, and she'll get her Son to do it for you," is an all too frequent theme. To the extent that Mary is given Christ's role, the respect rightly won by the young Jewish woman so long ago is transformed into idolatry too.

Paul wants us to put nothing in place of Christ. He is supreme. He is all. In Christ the invisible is revealed. Christ has the "firstborn's" right to inherit all things. His claim is doubly established, for "by Him all things were created." Visible and invisible—including the ranks of angels that the Gnostics superstitiously honored (v. 16b)—were created by Christ.

And the resurrected Jesus, as Head of His body the church, is to be supreme in our lives. God in all His fullness, all that God is, exists and finds its expression in Jesus Christ (v. 20).

It is this Jesus, the exalted God, who bled and died for us, who now represents us before the throne of grace. How foolish, when He who is God Himself is on our side, to put anyone or anything in Jesus' rightful place.

"To reconcile to Himself all things" Col. 1:20. The Gnostics proposed a great gap between earth and heaven. Paul rejected the notion. Christ proves that God can and does act in the material universe. In becoming man and dying, Christ made peace. He is the bridge, not just over troubled waters, but between heaven and earth.

"Enemies in your minds because of your evil behavior" Col. 1:21. The Gnostics had the peculiar idea that the mind, as man's immaterial part, could be in tune with God no matter what the body, the material and thus "evil" element of a person, might do.

The idea hasn't died out yet. Folks still go to church and assume they can think good thoughts on Sunday, and live like the devil during the week. Research has shown that many a wife beater spends a pious Sunday in church, or even serves as a church officer!

To be really in tune with God, all that we are must be in harmony with Him. A "faith" that is not expressed in a godly life is not "faith" at all, and the mind of such a person remains hostile to the God revealed in Jesus.

"Not moved from the hope held out in the Gospel" Col. 1:21-23. The warning is directed to the Colossian church, not to individuals. The church must never exchange the hope held out in the Gospel for the false hope offered by mere human philosophies. And, again, Jesus Christ as God in the flesh is the focus of our hope! Because He died for us we stand before God holy, without blemish, and free from accusation.

"Christ in you, the hope of glory" Col. 1:24-29. J.B. Phillips translates this phrase, "Christ in you, the hope of all the glorious things to come." Because Jesus is in His body now on earth, you and I as part of that body have hope for the future. Not just the hope of resurrection glory, but hope for glorious things now! The living presence of Christ in us, of God still present in the world of here and now, opens up our future to glorious possibilities.

We are not yet all we could be. But because Christ is in us, we are becoming.

As we go on in full commitment to Christ, we will become "perfect [mature] in Christ."

▶DEVOTIONAL
Christ in You
(Col. 1:15-28)

The French have a phrase, *Le Bon Dieu.* It means "the good God," and is used almost with fond contempt. It suggests a grandfatherly figure in his dotage, vaguely but fondly nodding when visited briefly by one of his many offspring. *Le Bon Dieu* may not be pleased at everything one does, but if he should notice, he's much too mild to take any action. A person can feel comfortable with *Le Bon Dieu*—and safely ignore him.

What a different image of the invisible God from that portrayed in Christ! Here in Colossians we meet a dominant God, Master of Creation, who boldly stepped into the physical universe. He took on a body to deal with those sins that seem trivial to those who worship *Le Bon Dieu.* He endured the cross with fierce dedication. He triumphed in a resurrection that lifted Him above power. Looking at Christ we find no *Le Bon Dieu* who is dead, but the all-powerful Ruler of heaven and of earth.

For the patrons of *Le Bon Dieu,* the real Christ is a disquieting figure. For the Christian, however, Christ preeminent, Christ incarnate, is recognized with a surge of hope and excitement. For Paul tells us that this Christ who brought God to earth is "in you"!

The Incarnation meant that God expressed His supreme power in this world of space and time in the person of Jesus. "Christ in you" means that God still expresses His supreme power in this world—through us!

Because this Christ is in us, we do have hope for glorious things ahead. We will triumph today, and tomorrow will join Christ in glory!

Personal Application
Don't give up. Christ in you cannot fail.

Quotable
"Jesus is not to us as Christmas is to the world, here today and gone tomorrow."—Rick Mylander

NOVEMBER 12 *Reading 316*
LIFE IN CHRIST
Colossians 2

"So then, just as you received Christ Jesus as Lord, continue to live in Him, rooted and built up in Him, strengthened in the faith as you were taught, and overflowing with thankfulness" (Col. 2:6-7).

Understand life in Christ and we won't be taken in by substitutes for true spirituality.

Overview

It is essential to know Christ (2:1-5) and live in Him (vv. 6-7). Christianity offers union with Christ, and this brings life (vv. 8-13) and releases from the burden of Law (vv. 14-15). Disciplined submission to rituals and rules may make a person look pious but is no route to spiritual reality (vv. 16-23).

Understanding the Text

"For all who have not met me personally" Col. 2:1. The spirit of prayer breathes through all of Paul's letters. Yet perhaps we sense his commitment to prayer most clearly here. Paul prayed not only for churches he founded, but for groups of Christians "who have not met me personally."

Actually, this habit is an easy one for us to develop! Every night on the news we hear of people in tragic situations. How easy it would be to turn to God, and ask Him to bless or comfort them. We read Christian magazines, and listen to Christian radio. Again and again we hear of believers who face great difficulties. How simple it would be to bear them up, and ask God to be with them in power. We talk to a friend on the phone, or chat over a Coke. How easy to pray briefly for that person as we hang up or walk away.

Paul cultivated the habit of praying for others as he heard about them. A week of serious effort to cultivate just such a habit might very well transform our prayer lives!

"Encouraged in heart and united in love" Col. 2:2. If you want to know Christ better, get to know your brothers and sisters better. Paul said this before (cf. Eph. 3:15-18). If we are to have a complete understanding of Christ, we need to deepen our relationships with others.

Perhaps one reason is suggested in the phrase "encouraged in heart." As we draw close to others, we sense God at work in their lives, and become more and more confident that He can work in us. Faith grows stronger as we see the reality of Jesus through His impact in those we love.

The most important thing you can do to encourage another believer may be to share what Christ is doing in your own life.

"All the treasures of wisdom and knowledge" Col. 2:3-5. The promoters of the heresy corrupting the Colossian church claimed to have access to a "hidden" or special wisdom through a series of angels who were supposed to exist in ordered ranks between Christ and God. Paul said that all the treasures of wisdom and knowledge are "hidden" in Christ.

Here "hidden" does not mean concealed. It means stored up. God has a warehouse full of riches—and He has given us the key! Christ. In Him, we have access to all God has and is.

Many Christians are honestly hungry for deeper spiritual experiences. Some are so hungry that they will follow any seemingly pious route that others suggest.

"All you need to do is pray an hour daily—preferably at 4 A.M., to show God you're really serious."

"Meditation techniques will make all the difference."

"Just fast until God gives you a special filling of the Spirit."

"Follow this list of do's and don'ts, and be in church three times a week."

Paul dismissed all such prescriptions as deceptive. God has stored everything we could possibly need in Christ. We will find spiritual fulfillment in Him, and in Him alone.

"Continue to live in Him" Col. 2:6-10. To say that Christ is the warehouse in which all God's treasures of wisdom and knowledge are stored sounds right. But it also sounds mystical, or obscure. How do we

obtain these riches? If Christ is the key, how do we use it to open the door?

Paul tells us. "Just as you received Christ Jesus as Lord," he said, "continue to live in Him." How did we receive Christ? By faith. We rested the full weight of our hope on what Christ has done for us, and trusted Him completely. This, Paul tells us, is the way we unlock the treasures of the Christian life. Live in Christ just as you received Him. Rest the full weight of your hopes on what Christ will do in you, and trust Him completely.

We can't count on early morning prayer, on meditation techniques, on fasting, on keeping lists of do's and don'ts. We can't rely on anything we do. We must rest our full weight on Christ, and trust Him to work as we live our lives in Him.

Live each day for Jesus, and because you live in Jesus, His wisdom and power will express themselves through you.

"Hollow and deceptive philosophy" Col. 2:8. Paul's approach to spirituality is deceptively simple. In contrast, the rigorous approach of the Gnostics sounded both "religious" and reasonable to the folks at Colosse. But it was hollow and deceptive for three reasons. It depended on "human tradition," the various pagan philosophies current during that day. It depended on the "basic principles" of the world. The Greek word may mean "the ABCs," and thus an elementary rather than an advanced understanding of the universe. But it may mean "elemental power," and refer to demonic evil forces. Most decisively, however, it does not depend on Christ.

Any system promising spiritual advancement that replaces complete dependence on Christ with anything at all is "hollow and deceptive."

"All the fullness of the Deity lives in bodily form" Col. 2:9-12. The safest thing you or I can do is set out to live godly lives, and rely completely on Christ to make it possible.

Why is this so safe? Because all Christ is flows into us as we live for Him. This is the implication of Paul's statement, "You have been given fullness in Christ, who is the Head over every power and authority."

The Christian life isn't like the pump that stood on the back porch of my uncle's cottage on Cedar Lake. I had to run down to the lake, get a can of water, prime the pump, and then pump the handle up and down endlessly until a trickle of water flowed. The Christian life is more like a fireman who connects his hose to a city hydrant, turns it on, and struggles to hold on as the water surges powerfully out!

You and I are connected to Jesus, who is Himself a reservoir of endless power. Simply open yourself to God by total reliance on Jesus, and His power will flow into and through you.

"In Him you were also circumcised" Col. 2:11-13. The circumcision promoted by the corrupters of the faith in Colosse physically cut away the flap which covered the end of the male penis. It was a symbol in Old Testament times of covenant relationship with God. Paul reminded his readers that the New Testament symbol of covenant relationship with God is spiritual circumcision. God, not man, cuts away and discards not a mere flap of skin, but man's sinful, bodily nature itself!

How was this done? Through our union with Christ in His death and resurrection! We who were dead in sins and the "uncircumcision of your sinful nature" have been made alive in Christ.

That is how Christ's power can flow through us. We are alive in Him now. We are united to Him. No wonder we can rely completely on Him. We are channels through which the vibrant, surging life of Christ is now ready to flow.

"Canceled the written code" Col. 2:14-15. The word translated "written code" was used in ancient times of an indictment drawn up against a prisoner. Paul, clearly referring here to the Mosaic Law and its regulations, viewed the written code as a devastating charge list, signed and entered in court, proving us guilty. Yet in Christ all our sins have been forgiven, and the code that condemned us has itself been canceled.

Again, Law in itself is holy, just, and good. But in terms of its impact on a sinful humanity, Law was "against us" and "stood opposed to us." Any demand that we "do" is an instrument of condemnation. That is why our life in Christ is not weighted down by Law or demands.

Understanding this, every New Testament call to obedience, and every New Testament exhortation to live a holy life, is transformed. New Testament commands are not laws, demanding that we "do." They are promises, explaining what Christ will do in us as we respond in faith.

"Having disarmed the powers and authorities" Col. 2:15. The Cross freed us from Law. And it marked Christ's triumph over hostile spiritual forces. Like a conquering general who displays his defeated enemies to all, Christ has made a public spectacle of every enemy.

What possible reason should you and I have not to rely on Christ the Victor? We live our Christian life not by self-effort, but by faith in Him.

▶ DEVOTIONAL
Find Reality
(Col. 2:16-23)

How do we find reality in our spiritual lives? Folks at Colosse had answers that still appeal to those who see a need for strict and rigorous self-discipline. Follow dietary laws (v. 16). Keep holy days (v. 16). Submit to various rituals and regulations (v. 17). Concentrate on mystical experiences (v. 18). Live an ascetic life of self-denial (vv. 21-23). Follow rules designed to make you a disciplined person.

We can almost see Paul shake his head as he completed this list. These aren't avenues to spiritual reality. They are detours away from reality in our spiritual lives. A life marked by rigorous self-discipline may "have an appearance of wisdom," Paul said. But such "false humility" and "harsh treatment of the body" has no value at all in "restraining sensual indulgence."

Paul was saying that rules that measure spirituality by externals look holy, but tend to make a person contemptuous of others internally! And inner sins are just as much "sensual indulgence" as gluttony or sexual promiscuity.

Paul wants us to experience spiritual reality. He didn't want us to just appear holy but to be holy. And we find the secret of being holy only in Christ, not in trying to follow lists of do's and don'ts.

In fact, Christ is reality. We experience reality only as we experience Him. So let's rest every hope in Him, and trust Christ to live out His life in us as we take daily steps of obedience to His Word.

Personal Application

Don't rely on self-effort. Let Christ make something of you.

Quotable

"If you make a great deal of Christ, He will make a great deal of you; but if you make but little of Christ, Christ will make but little of you."—R.A. Torrey

---

NOVEMBER 13 *Reading 317*
CHRIST IN THE LIFE
Colossians 3–4

> *"As God's chosen people, holy and dearly loved, clothe yourselves with compassion, kindness, humility, gentleness and patience" (Col. 3:12).*

It's easy to recognize Christ in another person's life—and even easier to recognize Him in your own.

Background

Review and preview. Paul began his letter by affirming the superiority of Christ. He then showed that our union with Christ is the key to a vital Christian experience. Because we are "in Christ," His power can flow through us. We were saved by faith in Christ, and we must live by faith in Him. Alone.

Now Paul went on to describe Christ in the Christian's life. How do we recognize His presence? Paul earlier rejected the notion that spiritual reality is found or displayed by following religious rules or self-discipline's "harsh treatment of the body." Now he showed that spiritual reality is experienced and expressed in rejection of evil and a transformed character. We recognize Christ in the Christian's life by the love and mutual submission expressed in every relationship.

What a thrilling book Colossians is. And what wonderful assurance it provides. Christ is supreme. We are in Christ. And Christ now lives out His own holy and dynamic life through us.

Overview

Christ makes us new persons, who reject evil (3:1-11), live holy, loving lives (vv. 12-17), and express our faith in relationships rather than by keeping rules (v. 18–4:1). Paul concluded with several instructions (vv. 2-6) and lengthy greetings (vv. 7-18).

Understanding the Text

"You have been raised with Christ" Col. 3:1-4. It's easy for us to feel down. When we do, Paul has a suggestion. Look up. Look up, and see Christ seated at the right hand of God. And then realize that you are up there too for "your life is now hidden with Christ in God."

In Tarpon Springs, a little city about 10 miles from where we live, one of the major occupations is sponge diving. The sponge diver puts a helmet on his head, drops into the water, and as he gathers sponges he breathes through air lines fed by pumps in a boat far above him. Without that connection to a source of life far above him, the diver would be unable to survive.

Paul is telling us that we too live this life in a dangerous and deadly environment. But we too are connected to a source of life far above us. Whenever we feel down, or get discouraged, or feel endangered, we're to fix our minds not on what surrounds us, but on what sustains us. The very life force of Jesus flows into and through us. Because we are connected to Him, we will not only survive. We will triumph.

"Put to death, therefore, whatever belongs to your earthly nature" Col. 3:5-11. The Christian's greatest enemy is not outside, but inside. It is the "earthly nature" which struggles to express itself in our attitudes and actions. We need to be alert, recognize that nature for what it is, and deal with its appearance immediately. How can you recognize the earthly nature? It's that nature that has crept out whenever you sense yourself feeling anger or malice, whenever your thoughts wander to the impure, or your imagination to what you would do if you had a million dollars. And the time to deal with it is as soon as the first thoughts and feelings drift across your consciousness.

How? Paul said, "Put [it] to death" (v. 5), and he further explained with the image of "taking off" the old self and "putting on" the new.

My wife likes to try on clothes. She prides herself as a teacher in looking professional, and is very conscious of how she dresses. And she's very critical of what she tries on. What looks good on the rack may not hang just right, or be cut just right, to fit her well. This is a picture of what Paul is telling us here in Colossians. Take a good look in the mirror, and when you sense anger or impurity or evil desires in yourself, decisively reject them. Such things simply don't fit the Christian!

God has a much better looking set of clothing for us, one that fits and flatters us. And also honors Him.

"As God's chosen people, holy and dearly loved" Col. 3:12-14. How does Christ express Himself in the believer's life? First, He clothes us in His own character, filling us with compassion, kindness, humility, gentleness, and patience. He gives us grace to forgive as we have been forgiven, and fills us with love. Then He calls us to live out His character in our relationships with others.

This is true spirituality. It is not found in rules that we follow, or in rigorous self-discipline. It is found instead in simple and pure expressions of compassion and love for others (see DEVOTIONAL).

"Let the peace of Christ rule" Col. 3:15-16. In the Old Testament peace is *shalom,* which conveys a sense of well-being, of harmony within and without. When Christ has drained us of our selfishness and competitiveness and given us His own deep love for others, peace will rule in our hearts, and in our congregations. Then we will be able to "teach and admonish one another with all wisdom" and will worship together with joy.

True spirituality is Christ living out His life through the individual believer, and through a united Christian community.

"Whatever you do" Col. 3:17. The false teachers at Colosse had impressed everyone with their rigor and the many rules they proposed for spiritual advancement. Paul shrugged all that aside, and replaced every do and don't with one instruction. "Whatever you do . . . do it all in the name of the Lord Jesus, giving thanks to God the Father through Him."

This is really the only rule required by those who wear the new man, and in whom Christ is being formed. "Lord, can I do this in Your name, rejoicing and thanking God for the opportunity?" If you have put off the old man, and the answer to this question is "Yes," rules and regulations are irrelevant.

"Wives, submit" Col. 3:18–4:1. If Christians don't need rules, why did Paul go on immediately to instruct wives and husbands, children and parents, slaves and masters?

We see a similar pattern in the Old Testament. In Exodus 20 God gave Israel Ten Commandments expressed as principles: do not do this, or that, or the other. Then in chapters 21–23 a number of specific cases are discussed. This "case law" illustrates how the general principles are to be applied.

In the same way Paul now illustrated how the qualities he had described, and the general principle of acting in Christ's name, will be expressed in the most intimate personal relationships of the first-century world.

Paul's choice of illustrations brings home a telling point. Those who will really know if Christ is in our lives are those who know us best—our families, and people we work with every day. A spirituality which does not find expression in these relationships is empty indeed.

"Pray that I may proclaim it clearly" Col. 4:2-6. Expressing Christ in our lives is vital to an effective witness. But it is not enough. The Gospel is a message delivered in words, and authenticated by life. Both word and life must be shared.

▶ DEVOTIONAL
The Emperor's New Clothes (Col. 3:6-17)

You remember the story. The fast-talking tailor convinced the emperor he was preparing a magnificent suit from cloth so special that only an honest man could see it. The emperor couldn't see it, but he was too embarrassed to say so. His courtiers couldn't see it, but since they didn't dare appear dishonest, they loudly praised it at every fitting. And so when the special occasion came for which the suit was being made, the emperor proudly marched down the avenue—in his underwear. Only the snicker of a little child, the only one truly honest, brought the fraud all knew about into the open.

Colossians has been something like this story. Paul had taken an honest look at the "superior" religion of false humility, ritual, and rigorous self-discipline promoted by some at Colosse, and exposed it. Folks who struggle to put on this suit find that, like the emperor, they have nothing on at all! All they have done has no spiritual value at all.

But Paul did go on to describe clothing fit for an emperor—clothing you and I are to wear. It is not the cloaking of ourselves in pious appearing actions. It's putting on the new self we have in Christ and reflecting His image. Our new clothes are not seen in the rules we keep, but the love we express. The marks of reality in the Christian life are a warm compassion, a responsive kindness, an unself-conscious humility, a gentleness and patience, that well up in our lives as we love, worship, and respond to Jesus. The mark of reality in the Christian life is Christ's likeness, as Jesus expresses Himself through us in every relationship.

Don't worry about looking pious, or even feeling pious. That's as useless as the emperor's invisible suit of clothes. Love Jesus, let His love fill your life, and "whatever you do" do it thankfully, in Jesus' name. Then you'll find that you are clothed with a compassion and kindness fit for a child of the King of kings.

Personal Application

Let Christ show Himself to the world in your life.

Quotable

"The person who has the abundance of life Christ came to bring us can spend virtue lavishly because his resources are plentiful. He can care for people unreservedly, the people near him and all over the earth, people of his own creed, color, and nationality and those of other faiths, races, and nations, because his resources of care are attached to the limitless reservoirs of God's care.

"He can afford to be slighted, shunned, hurt, because he has enough forgiveness in his heart for any crisis that comes his way. He can squander love upon the undeserving and the unresponsive because he knows there will always be more love where the last love came from."—Harold E. Kohn

The Variety Reading Plan continues with EXODUS

1 Thessalonians

INTRODUCTION

The young church at Thessalonica suffered immediate persecution, and Paul was driven from the city (Acts 17:1-9). This early letter, written about A.D. 50, was intended to encourage and further instruct very new believers.

This and a second letter pick up themes found in all Paul's letters, such as the inspiration of Scripture, the deity of Christ, salvation based on Jesus' death, personal purity, love, and especially emphasizes teaching about Jesus' second coming. Paul clearly felt it was important to ground new converts in basic Christian doctrines.

OUTLINE OF CONTENTS

READING GUIDE (2 Days)

If hurried, you may read only the "core passage" in your Bible and the Devotional in each chapter of this Commentary.

Reading	*Chapters*	*Core passage*
318	1–3	2:1-12
319	4–5	5:1-11

1 Thessalonians

NOVEMBER 14 *Reading 318*
EFFECTIVE MINISTRY
1 Thessalonians 1–3

> *"We were gentle among you, like a mother caring for her little children. We loved you so much that we were delighted to share with you not only the Gospel of God but our lives as well, because you had become so dear to us" (1 Thes. 2:7-8).*

The way we relate to others authenticates the Gospel's message of love.

Overview

Paul praised God for the Thessalonians' steadfastness (1:1-3) and evidences of their true conversion (vv. 4-10). He reminded them of his very personal ministry there (2:1-12) and encouraged them in their suffering (vv. 13-16). He spoke of the love which moved him to send Timothy to visit them (v. 17–3:7) and his own joy at Timothy's good report (vv. 8-13).

Understanding the Text

"Work produced by faith" 1 Thes. 1:1-3. The Thessalonians were remarkable as a truly committed church. They not only received the Gospel—they acted on it!

What is so surprising is that Acts 17 seems to suggest Paul's missionary team was in this city of 200,000 only a few weeks or at most a couple of months before riots and rumors forced them to flee to Berea. Even so they left behind the nucleus of a strong, vital church, which remained faithful despite persecution. What a challenge to us, who may have known the Gospel much longer, but may display less evidence of its grip on our lives.

What was the Thessalonians' secret? They had faith that produced work, love that prompted labor, and hope that inspired endurance (v. 3). No one who truly lays hold of the Gospel's message of faith, love, and hope can remain the same.

"You welcomed the message" 1 Thes. 1:4-6. Verses 4-10 describe a total response to the Gospel message: a response that preachers everywhere yearn to see in their congregations, and we yearn to see in those we love.

The very first element in that response is, "You welcomed the message." God's people in Thessalonica did not hesitate, or hold back, or cluck critically. They were excited and enthusiastic when they heard the Word of God.

Some years ago Joe Bayly wrote a classic little book called *The Gospel Blimp.* It told of some enthusiastic Christians who decided to bombard their town with tracts, and figured that a blimp would be great. They could drift over backyards and drop tracts on everyone! It's hard to imagine that folks would really "welcome" Gospel bombs detonating in their yards. Certainly Paul had a better way. He shared the Gospel personally "with deep conviction" and relied on the power of the Holy Spirit, not the Gospel Blimp. And Paul "lived among" the people he tried to reach, so that they knew him and his way of life.

If you and I want others to welcome the Gospel, Paul's approach is essential.

"The Lord's message rang out from you" 1 Thes. 1:7-9a. The old saying is still true. Shepherds don't have lambs. Sheep do.

It certainly was true in Thessalonica. Paul was forced to leave the city after riots were stirred up by Jewish opponents. But the church kept on growing, spiritually and numerically. Awhile ago I was talking with a Chinese friend just back from mainland China, who was telling me about the quiet revival going on there. In the '70s when religion was proscribed, the church was forced underground, and leaders were stifled or imprisoned. Yet now, just 15 years later, Christmas church services are swamped as millions openly profess their faith in Christ, and many more millions take part in a dynamic house-church movement. The shepherds were taken away by the state. But it didn't matter. It is sheep who have lambs, not shepherds, and the ranks of Chinese Christians continue to swell.

Wherever average Christians are willing to become imitators of the Lord, to serve as models for others, and to sound forth the Word, the Gospel will continue to thrive.

"You turned to God from idols" 1 Thes. 1:9b-10. The sequence here can never be reversed. Some try to reform a person before or without conversion. Some say, "I'd like to come to church, but I have this habit. As soon as I break it, then."

What's wrong is that we don't turn from idols to God. We turn to God from idols. We have to turn to God first, because only God's power will enable us to break the chains that bind us.

So don't think, "As soon as I get my life straightened around, I'll come to God." Come to God, and let Him straighten your life around for you.

"You know that we never" 1 Thes. 2:1-6. Paul had two gifts to offer the Thessalonians. These are the same two gifts that you and I have to offer others. The Gospel and ourselves.

Both the gifts can and often will be misunderstood. But you and I as persons are the most vulnerable to criticism. What a grand way to attack the Gospel. Ignore its message of God's love, and suggest that the messenger is greedy, or deceitful, or is trying to trick people. It really does hurt the Gospel when something like this proves to be true, as in several celebrated televangelists' cases.

But think what a great opportunity you and I have to adorn the Gospel by being honest and loving! Paul said, "You know we never used flattery, nor did we put on a mask to cover up greed." The really significant words here are "you know." Paul developed a close enough relationship with the Thessalonians, even in the brief time he knew them, that he was sure they knew his inmost motives and self.

By living openly and honestly with others we guard not only our own reputation but the integrity of the Gospel as well.

"Like a mother caring for her little children" 1 Thes. 2:7-9. When Paul tried to describe the relationship he developed with others as he shared the Gospel, only family images would do.

It would have seemed funny to strangers, to hear Paul, described in early documents as a wizened little man whose large nose almost met his chin, speak of himself as a "mother caring for her little children [infants]." But it wouldn't seem funny to the Thessalonians, for they would have felt just that quality of tender, protective love, flowing from the great apostle.

Love isn't a matter of how we look, or how much money we have, or how much education. Love is simply the overflow of a deep concern for the welfare of others. If you have that love, nothing else matters. If you do not, nothing else counts.

"We dealt with each of you as a father deals with his own children" 1 Thes. 2:10-12. Paul continued to use family imagery. Again, nothing else quite conveys the kind of relationship that fits the Gospel (see DEVOTIONAL). This time the key words are "each of you."

My sons, Paul and Tim, had the same parents, grew up in the same house, went to the same schools—but are very different from each other. Each needed to be treated as an individual. That's what is so impressive about Paul's reminder here that, like a father with adolescent children, he dealt with "each" of the Thessalonians as an individual. Those who needed encouraging, he encouraged. Those who needed comfort, he comforted. Those who needed urging—what we might call a good kick in the pants—Paul urged. His goal was the same in every case: to help them "live lives worthy of God." But how he worked with others toward that goal took individual differences into account.

If we're to minister effectively to others—even members of our own families, we must come to know them as individuals and respond to each according to his or her characteristics and needs.

Loving doesn't just mean letting others know us and our motives. It means getting to know others, individually, and well.

"The Word of God, which is at work in you" 1 Thes. 2:13-16. Frank was a young convert in our Brooklyn congregation. The jolly, heavy-set 20-year-old paid a high price for his faith. His mom and dad, traditional '50s Catholics, saw his conversion as apostasy. They tried to bribe him with a set of drums he'd longed for. Finally they threw him out of the house. Frank suffered intensely, but he kept faith with what he thought was right. And all of us young people in our church hurt for him.

Paul knew the ambivalence that must come when someone becomes a believer and suffers persecution as a result. But Paul reminded himself and the Thessalonians that you "became imitators of God's churches in Judea." There's a long tradition of suffering linked with Christian commitment. Things don't automatically get better. They may get worse!

When those we love suffer for their faith, we can hurt with them. But we must remember that suffering is nothing new. What is new is the fact that God's Word is at work in us. And in this we can rejoice.

"Our hope, our joy, or the crown in which we will glory" 1 Thes. 2:17–3:13. When the very elements that make up this universe dissolve in fervent heat, only human beings will remain. Paul had chosen to love people, rather than things. When Christ comes again, Paul's hope, joy, and crown of rejoicing will be present with him, preserved for all eternity.

Paul was forced to leave these very precious people when the rioting began in Thessalonica. No wonder he sent Timothy to visit them as soon as he could (3:1-5), and was filled with joy when he brought back a good report (vv. 6-13).

Let's make others the focus of our concern, and the touchstone of our values, so that they become our joy.

▶ DEVOTIONAL
Home, Sweet Home
(1 Thes. 2:1-12)

I suppose I had many reasons for taking the bus home from college so many weekends. I did bring back bags of dirty laundry, like most college guys. But the real reason was that nothing felt quite like home. Nothing was quite as comfortable as Mom baking bread in the tiny kitchen, or Dad smoking his pipe on the front porch. Nothing felt quite so "right" as watching Dad wash the dishes while Mom dried, or sprawling in an easy chair while Mom read aloud stories and articles from the *Saturday Evening Post.*

Home was warm, comfortable, a place where I was welcomed and loved even if I was a college man now, and out on my own. Home had a climate all its own.

Paul understood this as well as anyone. He knew that home is the one really effective climate for evangelism and for spiritual growth. So Paul not only brought others the Gospel in word, he created a sense of family by the way he loved every member of the Thessalonian church.

What people need today, perhaps even more than in other times, is that climate of warmth, intimacy, and caring that marks a loving home. The church that provides this climate will be sure to grow. And its members will become mature.

Personal Application

Build your church as birds build nests—one tiny twig of love at a time.

Quotable

WE EXIST TO PROVIDE LOVE AND CARE FOR ONE ANOTHER . . .

through sharing each other's needs, burdens, and joys

through serving each other in a sacrificial way

through learning how to love and be loved.

God in His grace, has given us to each other. An integral part of our life as His body is caring for and supporting each other.—From the Mission Statement, Crossroads Community Church

NOVEMBER 15 *Reading 319*
THE LORD WILL COME
1 Thessalonians 4–5

"The Lord Himself will come down from heaven, with a loud command . . . and the dead in Christ will rise first" (1 Thes. 4:16).

Christ's coming is both comfort and challenge.

Background

Eschatology in the Thessalonian letters. It is clear from reading these letters that during the few short weeks or months Paul was with the Thessalonians, he gave them a rather detailed picture of the end times. These letters speak of Christ's return for His saints, the appearance of the Antichrist, final judgment, and other aspects of the end time. Yet the exact sequence of events, and how elements of the whole eschatological picture fit together, is a matter of debate by earnest Christians.

Perhaps the most important thing to remember as we read these letters is that, as Christ's "first coming" encompassed a period of more than 30 years, His "second coming" also embraces a period of years. Much of the confusion about the end times comes from assuming that the "Second Coming" is a single event, rather than a series of world-shaking events spread over a period of years.

This does not necessarily help in determining how the events mentioned in the Thessalonian letters relate to each other or other Old and New Testament passages. Even so, we can accept each as describing some aspect of future history.

What seemed most important to Paul was not to provide a chart, but to provide a challenge. Paul called on the Thessalonians and on us to see what God intends to do, and then to apply that vision of the future to guide current choices and adjust present attitudes. It is the application of prophecy that we need to focus on as we read these letters devotionally.

Overview

Pleasing God calls for holiness (4:1-9) and brotherly love (vv. 10-12). Christ's own will be raised at His imminent return (v. 13–5:3). Till then we are to live expectant, self-controlled lives, encouraging one another (vv. 4-11). Paul closed with various specific instructions (vv. 12-28).

Understanding the Text

"How to live in order to please God" 1 Thes. 4:1. The verb rendered "please" here had a broad meaning in the New Testament era. It spoke of action which not only won approval, but which constituted active and actual service. We are God's servants as well as His sons. We are to dedicate our lives to serving Him.

Paul said that the Thessalonians knew how to live to please/serve God. But he went on to remind them anyway. If we are not constantly reminded of what we know, we are all too prone to forget. So let Paul's words of exhortation remind us too of the persons we are called to be, and the service we are called to render.

"It is God's will that you should be holy" 1 Thes. 4:3-8. Paul specifically mentioned avoiding sexual immorality. But Paul's broader concern was for controlling all "passionate lust." Paul used this phrase not just of sexual appetite but of overpowering desire of any kind. A passion for power, a passion for money, a passion for food, a passion for approval and popularity can have just as destructive an impact on holiness as sexual passion.

We are not to be mastered by our desires, but are to let God master us. We must keep a tight reign on any desires whose grip might keep us from serving Him and others.

"You yourselves have been taught by God to love each other" 1 Thes. 4:9-10. One of the most powerful motivations for that service which pleases God is Christian love. Note that such love is reciprocal: Christians love "each other."

There is something deadly about an unrequited sacrificial love. The daughter who gives up marriage to care for her invalid mother may do so out of love. But if the mother remains critical, bitter, and demanding, even the purest love is likely to sour. The husband who keeps on loving his unfaithful wife may be admirable.

But in time that home is sure to shatter from her sheer selfishness. Any love which is constantly rejected must ultimately fail.

This is one reason why God created His church to be family. God gave us brothers and sisters in Christ so we can experience as well as extend love. In the mutuality possible in the body of Christ, our ability to love can grow, and we can find the resources we need to enable us to love others who do not love in return.

If you are in a situation where your love is met only with bitterness or rejection, seek Christian friends who will support and love you. Even in the best of situations we need an intimate relationship with other believers where we can give and receive love.

If you're looking for a church, don't look first at programs and activities. Look to see if the people of the church truly love each other.

"Make it your ambition" 1 Thes. 4:11-12. We're used to parents being ambitious for their children. Usually what Mom and Dad are ambitious for is that the kids get ahead—a bigger job, a higher salary, more status. And often we nod approval when young people show "drive and ambition." Again what we mean is that they work hard, find a good job, and are on their way "up in the world."

Paul had a different slant on ambition. In essence, Paul said make it your ambition to be as ordinary as possible. Lead a quiet life. Mind your own business. Work hard, earning your own living with your own hands. Be a good, but rather ordinary, citizen.

I rather like Paul's emphasis. Ordinary folks, living good, honest, hardworking, ordinary lives, have a habit of winning the respect of those who know them. For God's people, winning respect is a much higher goal than getting to the top!

"About those who fall asleep" 1 Thes. 4:13-18. One of the most powerful of Paul's eschatological statements emerged from a very practical concern. Some of the Christians in Thessalonica had died. Friends and family were terribly upset. Would these folks miss out on Jesus' return?

In compelling language, Paul reassured them. When Jesus appears, believers who are "asleep" will be raised from the dead, and then, together with still-living saints, all Christians will soar together into the clouds to meet Jesus, and be with Him forever.

Paul then applied this dramatic vision simply: "Encourage one another with these words." When a loved one dies, we can look ahead, catch a glimpse of Jesus' triumphant appearance, and rejoice.

"About times and dates" 1 Thes. 5:1-3. The early church expected Jesus to return at any moment. They didn't know when. They just knew that, at a moment the world did not expect Him, Jesus would appear to execute final judgment.

What Paul was talking about is the doctrine of "imminence." All that this means is that Jesus could return at any moment. There are no conditions to be met that would hinder Him from coming today, tonight, or tomorrow. We know that Halley's comet won't return until the late 21st century. But Christians through the ages have been aware that Jesus could return at any moment.

Wouldn't it be grand if Jesus should come November 16th? Or even today? (See DEVOTIONAL.)

"Hold them in highest regard" 1 Thes. 5:12-13. I suffer from a terrible disease. The Sunday service snoozies.

It goes back to my days in seminary, when I worked from 11 P.M. to 7 A.M. seven nights a week and carried a full 19 semester-hour-load of classes. Every day at chapel I'd find a seat near the wall, lean my head against it, and sleep. Now, even when I preach, it's hard to keep awake as the service proceeds. And when others preach—well, it's been nearly impossible. Till we came to our present church and the excellent preaching of our pastor, Richard Schmidt, a warm and delightful brother. I suddenly realized that my wife's elbow hadn't been buried in my ribs for several months, and that I was actually staying awake most Sundays! I called Richard and told him how much I appreciated his sermons. They were even worth staying awake to hear!

He laughed and said "thanks." And added, he wished the other retired preachers in the congregation had the same attitude. It seems they persistently gave him a hard time.

If God has used your minister to speak to you, to bless you, to encourage or strengthen you, why not give him or her a call? Such folk need more than our respect. They need our encouragement.

"Do not put out the Spirit's fire" 1 Thes. 5:19. Older versions say, "Don't quench the Spirit." The meaning isn't mysterious at all. Have you ever had a youngster come to you, full of enthusiasm over an idea or project? And watched his or her face fall when you said no?

Well, the Holy Spirit is enthusiastically committed to ideas and projects by which you can serve God and experience great blessing. And every time you say no to His prompting, it's like throwing a bucket of cold water.

The Spirit won't force you or me to follow His promptings. We can quench His ministry to us by a simple no. But when we do, it is to our great loss.

▶ DEVOTIONAL
Sons of Light
(1 Thes. 5:1-11)

I remember very well playing down in the basement as my mother washed clothes. I was 4 or 5, so it was well over 50 years ago that I dressed up as Pecos Pete, and rode down the steps to rescue her from rustlers. That was pretend. But I also remember very well my mother telling me she expected Jesus to return in her lifetime. That wasn't pretend. That was very real to my mom. She was wrong. She died in a car accident in the 1960s. But awareness that Jesus' return was just around the corner was a cornerstone of my mother's life.

What Mom told me as a child is still very real to me. My wife and I often speak of it, and expect Jesus to return before either of us joins Him through death. We don't know when He will come. The "times and the seasons" are a mystery. But the reality of Jesus' return looms large in our thoughts.

Paul pictured those who live with that awareness as "sons of the light and sons of the day." We're not in the dark about the future—or about how to live our lives here and now.

Jesus is coming! And so we exercise self-control, and keep our values in harmony with His. Jesus is coming! And so set faith and love as a guard over our hearts. Jesus is coming! And so our perspective is shaped by the certain hope of His appearance, not to judge us, but to rescue us from the wrath about to fall on our lost world. Jesus is coming! And so we encourage each other, and build each other up, placing a higher premium on persons than on things. As God does.

My mother wasn't wrong to expect Jesus. We're not wrong either. And as long as His coming is real to us, our choices, and our lives, are sure to be transformed.

Personal Application

Look for Jesus, and brighten the eastern horizon of your life.

Quotable

"I have felt like working three times as hard since I came to understand that my Lord is coming again."—D.L. Moody

---

The Variety Reading Plan continues with PHILIPPIANS

2 Thessalonians

INTRODUCTION

Paul's second Letter to Thessalonica was sent a few months after his first. Some had assumed Jesus' second coming was so near they could quit work. Paul corrected this misunderstanding, and emphasized the importance of using the present time wisely.

OUTLINE OF CONTENTS

READING GUIDE (2 Days)

If hurried, you may read only the "core passage" in your Bible and the Devotional in each chapter of this Commentary.

Reading	*Chapters*	*Core passage*
320	1	1:5-10
321	2–3	3:6-15

2 Thessalonians

NOVEMBER 16 *Reading 320*
GOD IS JUST
2 Thessalonians 1

> *"God is just: He will pay back trouble to those who trouble you and give relief to you who are troubled, and to us as well" (2 Thes. 1:6-7).*

A wishy-washy God is a fiction that appeals to the guilty, not the godly.

Overview
Paul praised perseverance (1:1-4), and promised that those who persecute believers will be punished when Jesus returns (vv. 5-10). Paul prayed that till then the Thessalonians would live to glorify God (vv. 11-12).

Understanding the Text
"Your faith is growing more and more" 2 Thes. 1:3. "Faith" seems to be a rather hard thing to measure in normal circumstances. It remains quite invisible—quite "inside." Even when others are living by faith, what they say and do may seem quite ordinary to us. Only if we could look deep inside would we see what it costs them to maintain an ordinary life.

Don't be discouraged if others don't realize how much of your life is lived by faith. God knows and will reward you.

"Love . . . is increasing" 2 Thes. 1:3. Unlike faith, love is visible in the most ordinary of situations. When Paul said, "The love every one of you has for each other is increasing," he was talking about something that can be seen and measured.

We see love in the smile of welcome when friends meet. We see it in the phone call, just to say, "I'm thinking about you. How are you doing?" We see love when a friend says to the harried mom of preschoolers, "Let me stay with your kids today. You need a break." We see love when the snow is shoveled from an older person's walk, and in the time spent with a shut-in. We see love in listening, in reaching out a hand to touch, in a comforting hug, a heartfelt prayer.

While faith is hidden in ordinary life, it is through the ordinary things of life that love is most clearly revealed.

"Perseverance and faith in all the persecutions and trials you are enduring" 2 Thes. 1:4. Faith, invisible in ordinary life, is clearly revealed in persecutions and trials. The Christian family in rural Colombia that refuses to grow plants that the cartel will turn into drugs—and suffers not only economic loss but also threats of death from the drug lords, displays faith. The Protestant pastor in Rumania, who defied an order to be silent and stimulated the revolt that overthrew the Communist regime in December of 1989, displayed faith. The Christian in the mental institution in Russia, who refuses to stop witnessing, or the parents there who see their children's hope of higher education lost because they stand fast in their commitment to Christ, display faith.

When trials come, and Christians remain committed to Christ, then the invisible becomes visible, and the world sees that Christian faith is real.

When your turn comes, through personal tragedy or national disaster, stand firm, and hold the banner of your faith high.

"Evidence that God's judgment is right"

2 Thes. 1:5. God has declared all who believe in Jesus righteous in His sight. He has declared us citizens of His kingdom, brothers and sisters of His Son. When we persevere in our faith, despite persecutions, we vindicate God's declaration of innocence. We show that knowing Christ does make a difference; that God has made us "new creations" indeed (2 Cor. 5:17).

Our suffering for His kingdom's sake is evidence, not to God, but to the world. And throughout church history, the willingness of believers to suffer and even die painful deaths for Jesus' sake has moved many to believe in Him. It has been said, and often proven, "The blood of martyrs is the seed of the church."

"God is just: He will pay back trouble to those who trouble you" 2 Thes. 1:6-7. The justice of God is displayed in two ways. One is in His balancing of the moral books by "paying back" those who do evil. This, Paul said, will happen when Jesus returns. The other is in His balancing the moral books by taking on Himself the punishment due those who do evil. This has already happened, and God's willingness to suffer for us has been displayed on Calvary.

Whether an individual is in the group to whom payment is due, or in the group for whom payment has already been made, is not up to God. It's up to the individual.

In Christ, God has been more than fair to the wicked. Now it is up to each man or woman to choose to take advantage of God's unfair provision of salvation, or to demand fair treatment—and be condemned (see DEVOTIONAL).

"To be glorified in His holy people" 2 Thes. 1:10. While punishment of sin is associated with Christ's second coming, Paul did not say Jesus will return in order to punish. Instead, Jesus will return "to be glorified in His holy people."

One peculiar feature of diamonds is that, in the rough, they look like dull, ordinary stones. One might pick them up, look at them, and throw them away as valueless. But when cut by a master jeweler, a brilliant stone is revealed. Held to the light, it reflects splendor from every facet.

The world places very little value on Christians. To others we often seem dull, ordinary, valueless. In fact, the more committed to Christ we are, the less we seem to fit into the world's scheme of things, and the less value we seem to have to people of the world. But when Jesus returns, He will hold us up to His light, and suddenly the facets that trials and persecution have carved will flash with scintillating light. This is why Jesus will return: to hold us up and "be glorified in His holy people." And to be "marveled at among all those who have believed."

"We pray constantly for you" 2 Thes. 1:11-12. This is another of those prayers of Paul which teach us how to pray for others. This prayer focuses on "follow-through."

Christians often have good intentions. We're often moved by a desire to help, to act, to accomplish something special for Jesus or His people. But that desire often fades just as quickly, and our good intentions are forgotten. Paul asked, and we can pray, that God may fulfill "every good purpose of yours and every act prompted by your faith."

Just think. If every Christian's good intentions were translated into action, how greatly God would be glorified in our lives.

▶ DEVOTIONAL
God Is (Not) Nice
(2 Thes. 1:5-10)

You won't find it in the Bible. I don't know of a single text that says, "God is nice." Particularly when we define "nice" in terms of its synonyms—agreeable, congenial, favorable, and pleasant. God is gracious, yes. And compassionate. But nice? Never.

Some folks, however, want to think of God as being nice. Much too nice to get angry or upset at people. Much too nice to punish sin. Maybe the "God of the Old Testament" was harsh. But, they say, the "God of the New Testament" is loving. And what they mean by loving is "nice." He's candy-sweet, and all too innocuous to fear.

Second Thessalonians 1:5-10 must come as a shock to the proponents of "God is nice" theology. What's this about Jesus coming "in blazing fire and with His powerful angels" to "punish those who do not know God"? What's this about being "punished with everlasting destruction and shut out from the presence of the Lord"? Why, that doesn't sound nice at all!

It isn't nice. But it is just, and it is right. And most of all, it's coming. God the loving is also God the Judge. God the tender is God the tough. God the compassionate is God the severe. And when Jesus comes, those who have accepted the Gospel and those who have not will display these desperate aspects of the character of our God.

Then we will shout that God is gracious. And others will confess that God is just.

But no one will assume that "God is nice."

Personal Application

Maintain your respect for God: don't fall into the trap of dismissing Him as "nice."

Quotable

"The demand that God should forgive such a [sinful] man while he remains what he is, is based on a confusion between condoning and forgiving. To condone an evil is simply to ignore it, to treat it as if it were good. But forgiveness needs to be accepted as well as offered if it is to be complete: and a man who admits no guilt can accept no forgiveness.

"In the long run the answer to all those who object to the doctrine of hell, is itself a question: 'What are you asking God to do?' To wipe out their past sins and, at all costs, to give them a fresh start, smoothing every difficulty and offering every miraculous help? But He has done so, on Calvary. To forgive them? They will not be forgiven. To leave them alone? Alas, I am afraid that is what He does."—C.S. Lewis

---

NOVEMBER 17 *Reading 321*
THE DAY OF THE LORD
2 Thessalonians 2–3

> *"For that day will not come until the rebellion occurs and the man of lawlessness is revealed" (2 Thes. 2:3).*

Holding to Christian teachings involves remembering what lies ahead.

Background

The Day of the Lord. This phrase, that was picked up from the Old Testament has great theological significance. In its broad sense, it identifies any period of time in which God actively rather than providentially intervenes to shape the flow of history.

Most often in prophetic passages, however, it is used of the end times, that final period associated with the return of Christ, the crushing of man's final rebellion by God, the restoration of Israel and universal peace, the last judgment, and the establishment of a new heaven and earth as the dwelling place of the saved. As noted earlier, these events fit in a span of time, not in a point of time. A number of years, not simply a 24-hour day, is intended when "Day of the Lord" is used. And any Old or New Testament passage mentioning the Day of the Lord is likely to focus on any one of these major aspects of that period.

We must then interpret Paul's references to the "man of lawlessness" as a marker indicating that the Day of the Lord has come in total context. Some folks at Thessalonica interpreted the persecutions they experienced as evidence that the Day of the Lord had arrived. Paul said simply, "Look around. Do you see counterfeit miracles? Do you see the Man of Lawlessness in control? This is not the Day of Lord."

Many Christians throughout the ages have experienced persecution even sharper than that suffered by the Thessalonians, and have wondered if what they experienced might be a sign of the end. Paul's teaching reminds us that in this world, we can expect suffering. But, because in Christ we fix our eyes in a future beyond this world, even in suffering we have hope.

Overview

The Day of the Lord will be marked by the appearance of a "lawless" one and counterfeit miracles (2:1-12). Till then believers are to engage in "every good deed" (vv. 13-17), sure of protection from the evil one (3:1-5). The church is to discipline those who will not work (vv. 8-18).

Understanding the Text

"And our being gathered to Him" 2 Thes. 2:1. There's nothing like persecution (1:4) to make people eager for Jesus' return. And there's nothing like momentary prosperity to drain our sense of urgency. Then when troubles come—a job is lost, a serious illness strikes, an accident takes a loved one—we remember again how vulnerable we are.

In one of his psalms David prayed that God would help him to "know his end," and remember "how frail I am." The prayer isn't morbid at all. It reflects a vital need that each of us has to keep life on earth in perspective. When you and I do this, we look eagerly for Jesus to return, whatever the state of our health or our bank account.

"The man of lawlessness is revealed" 2 Thes. 2:1-4. The reference here is clearly to a person commonly referred to as the Antichrist. He is introduced in Daniel 9:25-27, and his introduction of an abominable image in a Jerusalem temple plays a key role in Jesus' prophetic teaching (cf. Matt. 24; Mark 13). He appears again in Revelation 13, and is discussed here by Paul, and mentioned by John in 1 John 2:18.

Here Paul picked up the emphasis seen in Daniel and in Christ's utterances: the Antichrist arrogantly "opposes and exalts himself over everything that is called God or is worshiped, and even sets himself up in God's temple."

I've been fascinated to notice in recent Evolution/Creationism debates how some scientists oppose and exalt themselves over everything called God—pushing Him into the realm of the "merely religious" and thus irrelevant. And then such people set themselves up in God's place, announcing their own answers to the mystery of origins and their own predictions about the future of the universe. What is most fascinating, of course, is their insistence that only they have the right to make such "scientific" pronouncements, and that the Creationist point of view must not even be permitted a hearing. The arrogant spirit of antichrist is deeply rooted in mankind, even though the individual called the Antichrist has not yet appeared.

It is good to remember that the Antichrist, and all who act as he will, are "doomed to destruction." God will be victorious in the end.

"The secret power of lawlessness is already at work" 2 Thes. 2:5-7. When terrible things happen to God's people, it is important to remember one thing. When persecution comes—when the courts decided that permitting a group of Christian young people to meet in a classroom after school hours for Bible study must not be permitted, but that it's all right for a gay and lesbian teen organization to meet—when a major network determines that it is against their policy to show any program rooted in Christian values—when we see the "spirit of lawlessness" at work—we can take comfort. Paul knew that even then there was one who held back the full expression of that spirit in society (v. 7).

Nearly all commentators agree that the restraining power is exercised by the Holy Spirit. And many suggest that the Spirit's power is exercised through His church. If this is true, then you and I need to be involved in social issues that affect our faith. We need to take a stand, lovingly and graciously, but firmly, and let the Holy Spirit exercise His restraining influence through us.

"In accordance with the work of Satan" 2 Thes. 2:8-12. The end times will be marked by the sudden emergence of the supernatural into the realm of nature. Miracles will be performed. But this time, by the Antichrist, through power provided by Satan.

It's strange. People who scoff at the supernatural when we Christians speak of it will be entranced by the counterfeit miracles performed by the Antichrist. Paul said God will send them "a powerful delusion so that they will believe the lie." But note. The delusion is sent only to those who have previously "refused to love the truth and so be saved."

Our only protection against Satan is found in Christ. But in Christ, our protection is guaranteed. The Lord Jesus will overthrow the Antichrist and Satan as well "by the splendor of His coming."

"Through belief in the truth" 2 Thes. 2:13-17. The willing victims of the Antichrist's campaign refused to believe the truth. What about those of us who do believe?

Paul says we are loved by the Lord. We are chosen by Him. We experience salvation through the Spirit's sanctifying work. We have been given hope and encouragement by God, and one day we will even share Christ's glory. We Christians are the new humanity: God's new breed of mankind.

You and I as God's new breed are to demonstrate our nature to all in a most simple way. We are to give ourselves to "every good deed and word."

This is undoubtedly the real miracle that God performs daily. He snatches men and women from Satan's realm, human beings who have lived selfishly, driven by personal passions, and through Christ makes us truly good. He transforms us, until we are moved to do good in every deed, and every word. No miracle Satan can empower can match the miracle that is taking place in you and me.

"Not everyone has faith" 2 Thes. 3:1-5. It's important to pray, as we wait for Jesus to return and the end to come, that we will be delivered from "wicked and evil men." God will guard us from Satan. But we may experience persecution from those who are in his camp. When we do, Paul has a simple prescription. Keep on loving God. Keep on persevering for Christ's sake. And keep on living the kind of good life that Paul's letters exhort.

▶ DEVOTIONAL

Take This Job (2 Thes. 3:6-15)

The country song must have reflected the frustration many felt with their jobs. "Take This Job and Shove It," the husky voice echoed from stations all over the land. "I ain't working here no more."

Many in Thessalonica felt that way. Jesus coming back? Great! "I quit."

They did quit. And, since they had to eat, they just sponged off other Christians. And passed their time gossiping.

Paul had a simple response. They won't work? Then don't feed them. Each person should earn his own bread. Warn each idler lovingly, as a brother. But don't feed him.

I intended, when I started this devotional, to write about the sanctity and the fulfilling nature of work. But I think Paul is making another vital point here. That point? If we fail to practice real love, we hurt rather than help those we love.

The real culprits in Thessalonica may not have been the folks who quit work, but the people who fed them! If no one fed the hungry slacker, I suspect they would have gone back to work mighty quickly!

It's the same with so many things in our lives. We complain about what our kids eat. But then we make them a cheese sandwich instead of saying, "Eat the roast I'm serving tonight or go hungry."

Rather than set a policy, no TV till after the homework is done, we let a child watch "my very favorite show" first—and then are upset the next morning when somehow homework was forgotten.

Paul's instructions to the church at Thessalonica remind us. If someone in the family has bad habits, just don't contribute to them. Unless you or I take a stand that forces others to suffer the consequences of their own bad choices, they'll keep on making those choices. And, at least in part, it will be our fault.

Personal Application

Don't feed other's bad habits by contributing to them.

Quotable

"Did I but live nearer to God, I could be of so much more help."—George Hodges

The Variety Reading Plan continues with HABAKKUK

1 Timothy

INTRODUCTION

Paul's two personal letters to Timothy and one letter to Titus are called the "Pastoral Epistles." Each gives advice to younger coworkers of Paul who served as his representatives, visiting and giving guidance to churches in various cities of the Roman Empire.

First Timothy was written some time between Paul's release from prison about A.D. 62 and his execution under Nero in A.D. 68. The letter warned against false teachers, gave qualifications for local church leaders, and dealt with a variety of other practical issues related to healthy, vital congregational life. This book is especially helpful to those in any leadership position.

OUTLINE OF CONTENTS

I. Timothy's Task .... 1 Tim. 1
II. Guiding the Church .... 1 Tim. 2–3
III. Personal Encouragement .... 1 Tim. 4
IV. Relationships in Church .... 1 Tim. 5–6

READING GUIDE (4 Days)

If hurried, you may read only the "core passage" in your Bible and the Devotional in each chapter of this Commentary.

Reading	*Chapters*	*Core passage*
322	1	1:12-16
323	2–3	3:1-7
324	4–5	5:3-16
325	6	6:6-11

1 Timothy

NOVEMBER 18 *Reading 322*
TRANSFORMING TRUTH
1 Timothy 1

> *"Here is a trustworthy saying that deserves full acceptance: Christ Jesus came into the world to save sinners—of whom I am the worst" (1 Tim. 1:15).*

God's truth transforms.

Background

Itinerancy in the first century. It's popular to speak of Timothy and Titus as "pastors" of local churches. In fact neither Timothy nor Titus settled down into a pastoral role. Each of these younger companions of Paul served as a trouble-shooter, sent by Paul to correct abuses or give additional instruction to congregations the apostle had founded. Timothy and Titus were much more like the modern "bishop" or "district superintendent" than like local church pastors.

It's difficult for us to recapture the role of the itinerant Christian leader of the Apostolic Age. Letters of Polycarp, dating to about A.D. 115, show that significant changes in church structure had already taken place by his time. Many, many more changes have taken place since. However, the basic framework of first-century church life and ministry are relatively clear.

Christians met in houses in smaller groups, which may infrequently have met together. Local elders guided the church in the wider community, and the terms "elder" and "bishop" were used interchangeably to identify them. The churches also developed the office of "deacon." Their function seems to have centered on charity and on those administrative tasks required in any organized group.

The life of these early churches was enriched by many itinerant teachers and preachers, who traveled from city to city visiting the house-churches. The itinerant teacher would stay for a while with a Christian family, share his special teaching, and then move on—often helped along his way with a gift of funds or food. But one problem with itinerants was that false teachers could and did pose as Christians. Some, particularly those with a Jewish background who argued that Old Testament Law was binding on Christians, succeeded in subverting the faith of young congregations.

The Apostles followed the itinerant pattern, though they and their representatives were rightly viewed as having special divine authority. Timothy and Titus were two of these "sub-apostles," by whom Paul sent special messages to the churches he founded. Paul also sent them to correct doctrinal errors introduced by false teachers, and to call believers back to a dedicated Christian lifestyle.

In reading the Pastoral Epistles, then, we are reminded of the needs of all Christian churches, not just the situation in a single church pastored by Timothy, or by Titus. What we read here applies to the church of Jesus Christ everywhere, at all times. Thus it applies, not just to leaders, but to you and to me as well, and the congregations of which we are a part.

Overview

Paul warned Timothy (1:1-2) against false teachers (vv. 3-7) who misunderstood the nature of the Law (vv. 8-11). The Gospel emphasizes transforming grace (vv. 12-17) and calls for commitment (vv. 18-20).

Understanding the Text

"Timothy my true son in the faith" 1 Tim. 1:1-2. The word translated "true" here means "genuine." It was frequently used in first-century letters to indicate affection and appreciation.

Timothy was the young son of a Jewish mother and Greek father whom Paul met on his second missionary journey (Acts 16:1-3). Paul invited Timothy to join his missionary team, and within a few years Timothy was trusted as an emissary Paul could send to visit churches in his stead. Paul said of the faithful Timothy in Philippians 2:20: "I have no one else like him, who takes a genuine interest in your welfare."

This letter was written to Timothy to give him special instruction and encouragement while he was on a mission for Paul in Ephesus.

"Myths and endless genealogies" 1 Tim. 1:3-7. This phrase, with the observation that many in Ephesus were devoting themselves to "empty chatter," suggests that some in the church there had begun to follow Jewish teachers who used an allegorical method of interpreting the Old Testament.

It was not uncommon in late Judaism or in early Christianity to look for "spiritual" meanings assumed to be hidden in the literal words and narratives of Scripture. The great Jewish philosopher, Philo, and the second-century Christian theologian, Origen, are both examples of this tendency. But the great problem with speculative approaches to Scripture is that there is no check on a person's interpretation—and that such approaches fail to promote faith.

The meaning of the events of Scripture, as of the teaching of the Prophets and Apostles, is found in the plain intent of the words of the Bible, not in some hidden meaning discovered by supposedly gifted interpreters. Those who ignore the plain meaning of God's Word show that "they do not know that they are talking about or what they so confidently affirm."

"The goal of this command is love" 1 Tim. 1:5. In the Pastoral Epistles Paul often emphasized the importance of teaching "sound doctrine" (cf. v. 10) as well as of silencing those who teach "false doctrines." His reason was not just that sound doctrine is true, and false doctrine is not. Paul noted that teaching sound doctrine produces a distinctive lifestyle—and that teaching false doctrine does not!

The product of sound doctrinal teaching is "love, which comes from a pure heart and a good conscience and a sincere faith" (v. 5). This conviction was the foundation of Paul's ministry. Teaching the truth will transform human beings. God's truth has the power to stimulate faith, to cleanse the conscience, and purify the heart. A person touched by truth will become a loving, caring individual.

We're not to fight for God's truth. We are to open our hearts to the truth, and let it transform us.

"Law is made not for good men" 1 Tim. 1:8-10a. The allegorical approach of the teachers Timothy was to silence emphasized Law, not faith (cf. v. 4). Paul was not anti-Law. But he insisted Law be given only its rightful place.

Law is something like the iron bars that make a tiger's cage. The bars are there to keep the tiger in. Thus Paul said, "law is made" for "lawbreakers and rebels, the ungodly and sinful," and went on to list their terrible crimes. You need a cage for people like this. The cage is there to protect others from the harm the loose tiger would do.

But what if the tiger has been transformed into a puppy dog? You don't need a cage for a friendly puppy. A friendly puppy barks and wags his tail in welcome, and leaps up to lick your face. No one puts a puppy behind iron bars, because the puppy will do them no harm.

This was Paul's point. The non-Christian needs the Law: it provides some restraint against harmful behavior. But why would Christians need Law? The Christian has been made good by Christ: our tiger has been tamed! What you do with a Christian is throw the cage away, and let him or her love you!

It may sound religious, holy, and dedicated to speak up for the Law. But the Law, which says, "Thou shalt not," is irrelevant for Christians, who "will not" anyway!

"The glorious Gospel of God" 1 Tim. 1:10b-11. How glorious the Gospel of God is! God has given us a truth that transforms human nature itself.

"Holding on to faith and a good conscience" 1 Tim. 1:18-20. Paul had discussed, and illustrated (see DEVOTIONAL) the revolutionizing power of the Gospel. Now he urged Timothy, and us, to "fight the good fight" for God's transforming truth.

Two things are necessary if we are to serve God effectively. We must "hold on to faith," that sound doctrine Paul affirmed. And we must hold to "a good conscience." Simply put, we must hold sound doctrine—and let it get a hold on us.

Being doctrinally correct has no value to us or to others unless we are also doctrinally corrected: unless the lives we lead are as pure as the truth we embrace.

▶DEVOTIONAL
Was . . . and Am
(1 Tim. 1:12-16)

I love those diet ads on TV and in the newspapers that feature "before" and "after" pictures. Sometimes they are obviously staged. The fatter "before" person slouches and thrusts out the tummy. The leaner, meaner "after" shows a side view, with his chest stuck out, his tummy tucked in.

In other diet ads the young woman featured (it's almost always young, very attractive women), looks like she never had a "before." She's like our 98-pound friend, Carol, who's always moaning she's 2 pounds overweight, and claiming with a straight face that 2 pounds on her tiny frame are as bad as 60 extra on my six foot two.

The Gospel makes "before" and "after" claims too. And here Paul presented himself as an example. Before he was "a blasphemer and a persecutor and a violent man." After, having met Christ and experienced the overflow of His grace, Paul became a different man.

This is what is unique about the truth of the Gospel. It isn't just a collection of true facts, or a compilation of doctrinal data. The truth of the Gospel is vital, transforming, dynamic. It is the living, active Word of God that when welcomed into our hearts works an inner alchemy.

Violence is transmuted into compassion. Blasphemy is altered to praise. Persecution is commuted into brotherly love.

Paul said, "Jesus Christ came into the world to save sinners—of whom I am the worst." You and I may not be able to pose with Paul for the "before" picture. But let's make sure we're right there with him for the "after."

Personal Application

What you were isn't as important to God or others as what you are.

Quotable

"He that gives good admonition and bad example builds with one hand and pulls down with the other."—Francis Bacon

NOVEMBER 19 *Reading 323*
GOD'S HOUSEHOLD
1 Timothy 2–3

"I am writing you these instructions so that. . . you will know how people ought to conduct themselves in God's household, which is the church of the living God" (1 Tim. 3:14-15).

The Christian community as well as the individual Christian represents Jesus to the world.

Overview

Christians are to pray for rulers and peace (2:1-8). Women are to be adorned with good deeds (vv. 9-10), but are not to exerise authority in the church (vv. 11-15). Overseers and deacons must be of exemplary reputation (3:1-13). All are to conduct themselves wisely in the church of Jesus Christ (vv. 14-16).

Understanding the Text

"Requests, prayers, intercession and thanksgiving" 1 Tim. 2:1-4. Paul wanted us to make no mistake, so he piled up synonyms. We

Christians have a vital stake in what happens in our society, and we can influence rulers through prayer.

"Quiet lives" 1 Tim. 2:1-4. We pray for peace, that others may find peace in Christ. This is the reason Paul advanced for offering prayers for secular rulers. Someone said, "There are no atheists in foxholes." The idea is that intense danger forces people to turn to God. This may be true, but "deathbed conversions" are notorious for their brevity. When the danger is past, all too often God is forgotten.

The most effective evangelism is supported by the evidence of "quiet lives" lived "in all godliness and holiness." The most powerful aid to the Gospel is not sudden fear created by danger, but a growing hunger for the peace and goodness observed in the lives of ordinary Christians.

"God our Saviour, who wants all men to be saved" 1 Tim. 2:3-4. This is an important verse if you've prayed for unsaved loved ones, and been discouraged by their lack of response. We know from Scripture that not everyone will be saved. But we also know that God wants—in the sense of desires—all to come to know Christ. This means that when you pray for any individual's salvation, you can have great confidence. What you are praying for is definitely in harmony with God's wishes and desires.

It's different if you pray for success in robbing a bank, or even that you win the latest Publishers' Clearing House contest. You know that robbing a bank is against God's will, and you have no basis to suppose the Lord wants to drop several hundred thousand dollars a year in your lap. But when it comes to praying for a loved one's salvation, you're on solid ground! That's something God wants too.

"One God and one Mediator between God and men" 1 Tim. 2:5-7. A mediator, a *mesites* in Greek, is someone who steps in between two persons, to make or to restore peace and friendship. Paul reminds us that only Jesus can possibly fulfill this role.

A good image of a mediator is found in the great bridge that ties the state of Michigan together. One side is anchored in the Lower Peninsula, and the other is anchored in the Upper. We can cross from one to the other only because the gap between them has been thus bridged.

Jesus, being fully God, has an anchor in heaven, and being truly man, has an anchor in humanity. He is the one and only Person able to bridge the gap between us and God: the one and only Saviour able to carry us from one side to the other.

"Appropriate for women who profess to worship God" 1 Tim. 2:9-10. I've known some women who have taken this passage as a condemnation of makeup, and so have struggled to look as severe and plain as possible. That was not Paul's point. His point was that Christian women should not rely on an artifice that is able only to decorate the outside—and that when overdone marks them as superficial.

What makes a woman really beautiful is a love and goodness that glows within, and is revealed in good deeds rather than strings of pearls.

Women should feel free to make themselves look attractive. But they should spend more time on beautifying the inner person than on decorating the outside.

"To teach or to have authority over a man" 1 Tim. 2:11-14. This is one of the most controversial passages in the New Testament, primarily because we are not sure exactly what it means—but quote it anyway to "keep women in their place."

There certainly is a place for women in active church ministry. Paul spoke approvingly of women praying and prophesying in church (1 Cor. 11:5). He praised the mother and grandmother who trained Timothy (2 Tim. 1:5; 3:15). And Paul outlined specific teaching responsibilities for older women in his Letter to Titus (2:3-4).

What seems to be involved here is "authoritative teaching"—that is, an authoritative statement by church leaders concerning Christian truth or lifestyle.

In some traditions this is understood to mean that women, welcome in every other role, are not to serve as "elders" or members of the "board" responsible for spiritual oversight of the church.

I know this understanding upsets some. But perhaps it shouldn't. After all, most men are excluded from this particular church leadership role too! And serving as an elder is only one of many, many opportunities to minister within and beyond the walls of the local church.

Perhaps each of us ought to focus on the things we can do, and do them to the glory of God, rather than resent being excluded from things we cannot do. Resentment can only deepen our hurt, while serving others in any way can bring us joy—and glorify our Lord.

"Full submission" 1 Tim. 2:11. Vine suggests that "the injunction is not directed toward a surrender of mind and conscience, or the abandonment of the duty of private judgment; the phrase 'with all subjection' is a warning against usurpation of authority" (Vine's *Expository Dictionary).*

Those who twist verses like 11-12 to suggest women are inferior, or to demand subservience, violate the spirit of God's Word, as well as do violence to sound interpretation.

"Women will be kept safe through childbirth" 1 Tim. 2:15. This puzzling verse has spawned a variety of interpretations. Some think "childbirth" refers to the birth of Jesus. Some connect the verse to Genesis 3:15, and the promise of a Seed who will crush Satan and bring mankind salvation. Others see the verse as a continuation of Paul's discussion of women's roles. Women will find physical health and spiritual fulfillment through accepting the mother role, viewed by society as proper for women. Here "saved" is not the theological deliverance of the soul, but the very practical release of the woman from a felt need to deny her sex in search of a more "significant" role in life or in the church.

You and I have no need to deny our sex, our race, our heritage, or characterizing marks, to be significant as a Christian. We can find fulfillment in serving Christ where, and as, we are.

"On being an overseer" 1 Tim. 3:1-7. The traditional translation of *episcopos* is "bishop." The word seems to be used interchangeably with *presbuteros,* "elder" (cf. Titus 1:6-7). The fact that there were several bishop/elders in first-century churches (cf. Acts 20:17) makes it clear that the title meant something different then than it means in contemporary denominations.

Our best understanding is that bishop/elders were responsible for the spiritual oversight of local churches, or perhaps of several house-churches. Their mission was to teach both sound doctrine and a holy lifestyle, and to equip believers for active participation in ministry. One who "sets his heart on" being an overseer surely "desires a noble task."

But church leadership is a heavy responsibility, not an honorary office to be listed on one's résumé. Christian leaders sacrifice to serve.

"Deacons, likewise" 1 Tim. 3:8-16. While the specific role of first-century deacons is also a mystery, it's clear from these verses that anyone officially representing a local Christian congregation must have an exemplary life.

How fascinating that, while Paul did not define the duties of any church leaders, he was more than careful in describing their character! We may call our leaders by any name we wish, and assign any duties to them. These things have always shifted and changed from age to age, and from society to society. What can never change is the high standard of Christian character and conduct required of those who guide the people of God (see DEVOTIONAL).

▶ DEVOTIONAL
Love Is Blind
(1 Tim. 3:1-7)

When my wife was praying for a husband to nurture her two preschoolers, she made up a list of qualities, and showed it to a counselor friend. He was shocked. "There may be one or two people like this," he told her, "but the chances of your finding one is almost zero! Lower your expectations."

Today, when telling the story, Sue says the counselor was wrong. And I say (quite truthfully) that love is blind!

God has His own challenging list of qualifications for church leaders. And we Christians are to look closely at candidates for spiritual leadership, and choose our leaders with our eyes wide open!

Here are 15 things on God's list for

bishop/elders, those local church leaders who are charged with spiritual oversight of a local congregation. Consult them carefully, and check candidates carefully when it comes time to choose the leaders of your church.

1. "Above reproach." If someone laid charges against this person, everyone would laugh at him!

2. "The husband of but one wife." Not "married only once," but totally faithful.

3. "Temperate." This clear-headed individual doesn't make snap decisions.

4. "Self-controlled." Watch out for the person who gets carried away with wild ideas!

5. "Respectable." You can count on a man who behaves in an orderly, honorable manner.

6. "Hospitable." A person who loves strangers and always welcomes friends is right for a faith that emphasizes love!

7. "Able to teach." The good leader may not be the most talkative. He's the one who exhibits the deepest understanding of Scripture and its application to life.

8. "Not given to much wine." Watch out for the tipsy or rowdy person described by this suggested phrase.

9. "Not violent." The competitive person always out to win isn't fit for church leadership.

10. "Gentle." String together these qualities, and you catch a glimpse of the quality the Greek word was getting at: gracious, kindly, forebearing, considerate, genial. In other words, not the football coach determined to win an any cost!

11. "Not quarrelsome." Here's another person to avoid: the contentious individual always ready to fight, or to pick one.

12. "Not a lover of money." Love for possessions ultimately destroys love for people. And people must be the Christian leader's priority.

13. "Manage his own family well." Our ability to influence others for good is seen first in the family. If it is not seen there, it won't show up in the church.

14. "Not be a recent convert." You can only tell the kind of fruit a plant produces after it has matured.

15. "A good reputation with outsiders." Non-Christians are quick to recognize phonies!

The list is long. And it may be hard to find folks who fit. But the most important leadership qualification a Christian can have is a godly character.

Personal Application

Don't ache for leadership. Ache to be the kind of person leaders are to be.

Quotable

"The man most fit for high station is not the man who demands it."—Moses Ibn Ezra

---

NOVEMBER 20 *Reading 324*
LIFE TOGETHER
1 Timothy 4–5

> *"I charge you, in the sight of God and Christ Jesus and the elect angels, to keep these instructions without partiality, and to do nothing out of favoritism" (1 Tim. 5:21).*

What we do for God, we do to others.

Overview

Paul warned Timothy again against false teachers (4:1-8), and exhorted him to minister confidently (vv. 9-16). He stated general principles for relating to others (5:1-2), and gave specific advice concerning widows (vv. 3-16), elders (vv. 17-20), and other matters (vv. 21-25).

Understanding the Text

"Things taught by demons" 1 Tim. 4:1-5. Paul described one of Satan's most persistent avenues of attack on Christians. He illustrated two forms—an appeal to asceticism that rejects marriage, or forbids eating "certain foods." Underlying such regulations is the notion that the Christian life is advanced by some legalistic discipline.

In fact, the Christian life is to be lived as an expression of personal relationship with Jesus: a relationship that rests on faith, and is expressed by a faith response to His Spirit's promptings. Anything less is a doctrine of demons.

"Train yourselves to be godly" 1 Tim. 4:6-8. Rejection of demon-inspired demands for rigid self-discipline does not mean that the Christian is to live an undisciplined life. Paul drew a sports analogy: people work out to develop themselves physically. Christians are to "work out" to develop spiritually.

What is the difference between this and the devil's counterfeits? We "work out" at being godly.

A weight lifter develops his ability to lift weights by lifting them. A Christian develops his ability to live a godly life by making godly choices. What you eat, and whether or not you abstain from marriage, have nothing to do with godliness, and so discipline in these areas is irrelevant to spiritual growth. If you want to grow spiritually, concentrate on those acts which show your love for God and for others.

"And especially of those who believe" 1 Tim. 4:9-10. Jesus has offered Himself as Saviour to all men. But He in fact saves only those who respond to His offer and believe.

Again we're reminded of the freedom we have to share salvation with others. Christ did die for all. Not one person has been excluded by God. The only one who can keep a person out of heaven—is the person himself!

"Because you are young" 1 Tim. 4:11-14. In the ancient world, age was respected and equated with wisdom. The older individual was thought to have gained insight with his years. Thus it was sometimes difficult for Timothy, who lacked the wrinkles and white hair associated with authority, to assert himself.

Every society has such cues. In our culture, the tall person tends to get ahead more rapidly than the short one. The person with that magic piece of paper, the "college degree," gets the promotion, while the high school graduate who may be better qualified gets passed over. And the woman who holds down a responsible job is almost sure to be paid less than a man in the same position.

What Paul was saying was, don't let society's expectations cramp your style as a Christian. Look confident, act confident, be confident! Spiritual significance does not depend on one's height, education, or sex.

If you want to be used by God, "set an example for the believers in speech, in life, in love, in faith and in purity." Anyone who sets such an example will be used mightily by the Lord.

"Watch your life and doctrine" 1 Tim. 4:15-16. Again we see twin themes that Paul linked in the Pastoral Epistles (cf. 1 Tim. 1:5; 2 Tim. 1:13; 3:10; Titus 2) as in his other letters (cf. Phil. 4:9). Doctrine is to find expression in life, and life is to be conformed to doctrine. Christian faith and life are woven so tightly together that neither can stand alone.

But what did Paul mean when he told Timothy that if he "persevere[s]" in Christian doctrine and life he will "save both yourself and your hearers"?

Most likely Paul was thinking of "present tense" salvation. We were saved from the guilt of sin when we believed, we will be saved from the very presence of sin when Jesus returns. And, until then, we are being saved from the grip of sin on our lives. If you want to free yourself from sin's grip—and be influential in the salvation of others—persevere in Christian life and doctrine.

"Father . . . brothers . . . mothers . . . sisters" 1 Tim. 5:1-2. Here as in 1 Thessalonians 2, Paul resorted to the image of the family to describe relationships in the church. But here there is a special emphasis: Paul was telling Timothy, a young leader, how to relate to those for whom he was responsible.

Earlier Paul told Timothy to "command and teach" truths Paul had just outlined. Here he helps us see that "command" in the Christian context is not the "demand" of the secular world. The authority behind the command comes from God. The Christian leader does not seek a relationship "over" others—but a relationship of intimacy among them.

How clearly this comes through in

Paul's guidelines. The leader treats older men with the respect due their own fathers, and older women with the respect due their mothers. The younger men are treated as brothers, and the younger women as sisters. Respect and affection shape the attitude of the Christian leader toward others, and there is no hint of domination over them.

You and I, whether leaders or not, need to nurture just such relationships with other believers. Respect and affection create the context in which we can have a beneficial impact on each other's lives.

"Those widows who are really in need" 1 Tim. 5:3-16. While the early church showed a consistent concern for needy members (cf. also Acts 6:1-6), it also showed a great respect for them. Christian widows were not just pensioned off. They were organized for ministry!

"Charity" can be so demeaning. And, whatever else it may have done, the early church was not into demeaning anyone. Instead all were expected to participate as they were able in enriching the life of the body of Christ (see DEVOTIONAL).

"Do not muzzle the ox" 1 Tim. 5:17-20. Paul warned against taking advantage of leaders in two distinct ways. First, those in full-time ministry deserve to be supported financially—and not grudgingly so. And second, unsubstantiated rumors and accusations against leaders are to be ignored. Leaders are particularly vulnerable to rumor and to false accusation.

Paul's next saying, "Those who sin are to be rebuked publicly," has a double reference. A leader who sins must not be allowed to hide behind his or her position. And a person who brings a false accusation must also be publicly rebuked. Only by such absolute fairness can the purity of the church be maintained.

"The sins of some men are obvious" 1 Tim. 5:22-25. It's a big mistake to quickly set up a new convert, or a newcomer to the local congregation, as a leader. Paul made the reason very clear. Some folk's sins are obvious, but the sins of others "trail behind them." We don't recognize their flaws until they've been around awhile.

In the same way, the good deeds of some are obvious—but many outstanding qualities of others are only recognized after long acquaintance.

Paul's principle can be applied in any relationship where some sort of commitment is involved. For instance, don't go into partnership with someone you don't know very well. And, don't get married in a hurry. The flaws in that guy or gal who looks so good now may trail so far after him it will take time for them to catch up. And given time, you may find that some pleasant but unspectacular person has just the qualities you want in a spouse.

▶ DEVOTIONAL
Retire—or Inspire?
(1 Tim. 5:3-16)

It's fascinating to read between the lines of Paul's instructions to Timothy about widows. Several things are obvious. The early church cared about its widows and, if there were no family to help them, it made sure they had food and lodging. It's also clear that widows were valued members of the congregation. They didn't just fold Sunday bulletins, or fill Communion cups. They were kept busy and active and, according to the Letter to Titus, were involved in training "the younger women to love their husbands and children, to be self-controlled and pure, to be busy at home, to be kind, and to be subject to their husbands, so that no one will malign the Word of God" (Titus 2:4-5).

Reading between the lines, we sense that the first-century widows Paul commended had reached a third stage in their Christian experience, and had made a definite choice.

The first stage was that of new convert and learner of the faith. The second stage, represented in 1 Timothy 5:9-10, was that of personal maturity: the commended widow "has been faithful to her husband, and is well known for good deeds, such as bringing up children, showing hospitality, washing the feet of the saints, helping those in trouble and devoting herself to all kinds of good deeds." And, now that her family was gone, and her personal responsibilities had been fulfilled, she had reached the third stage. She was ready to become a servant and trainer of the next generation of Christian adults. Out of her rich fund of personal experience with

Christ, she shared now with others.

Paul suggested that this was not her only choice. Some widows "live for pleasure." These women thought, as many do today, that they've done their share. They taught Sunday School, led the circles, and served on the committees. Now they choose to start looking out for number one, and looking for personal pleasure. They've earned a rest—and they are going to take it.

As a church, we today fail to use the vast resource of wisdom and maturity that exists in Christian brothers and sisters who have retired. We tend to put them in an old folks class, send them on bus trips, and make sure they have an activity day together once a week or so. We so seldom realize these are third-stage Christians—Christians with vital gifts to give other believers.

But then too, all too many retirees look at the 60s and 70s as a time to sit back, or travel, or just relax after years of carrying too much of the load. I suspect that only when we show that we value the retired Christian will most retirees realize that their later years may be the most spiritually significant years of all.

Personal Application

Retire—to inspiring others to live more committed lives.

Quotable

"What great things some men have done in the later years of their life. Michelangelo painted the ceiling of the Sistine Chapel lying on his back on a scaffold when almost 90; Paderewski at 79 played the piano superbly; at 88 John Wesley preached every day; Tennyson, when 88, wrote 'Crossing the Bar.' Booth Tarkington wrote sixteen novels after 60, some of them when he was almost totally blind."—Walter B. Knight

---

NOVEMBER 21 *Reading 325*

CONTENTMENT

1 Timothy 6

> *"Godliness with contentment is great gain. For we brought nothing into the world, and we can take nothing out of it" (1 Tim. 6:6-7).*

It's fine to have money as long as money doesn't have you.

Overview

Even servitude provides opportunities to minister (6:1-2). A love of money characterizes false teachers (vv. 3-5) and is a trap believers are wise to avoid (vv. 6-10). Godly people pursue righteousness (vv. 11-16), and view their wealth as providing opportunities to do good (vv. 17-21).

Understanding the Text

"Those who benefit from their service" 1 Tim. 6:1-2. The New Testament has a unique outlook on relationships. There is no shame in being a slave, because servitude provides a person with an opportunity to benefit others. The thought is reflected in other passages. Whatever role God gives us in life provides some opportunity to do others good.

The husband who loves his wife shows the same concern for her needs that Christ showed for the church. Thus "headship" is transformed by Jesus' example from a grab for power to a commitment to servanthood. In the same way the wife's "in subjection" position is not demeaning, but a description of one way she takes the lead in serving her husband.

You and I need to adopt this biblical perspective in all that we do. Are you an employee? Then work hard, to help your employer make a profit. Are you an employer? Then make sure you pay your workers a fair wage, and that you have a real concern for each one's welfare.

When we see each relationship as a God-given opportunity to minister, all of our relationships with others will be fulfilling. And we will glorify God in them.

"Who think that godliness is a means to financial gain" 1 Tim. 6:3-5. One attribute of the false teacher, mentioned in nearly every New and Old Testament passage on the

subject, is a love for money. They slip on a cloak of religion, not because they love God, but because they see it as a way to make a buck.

Paul noted other attributes: they invent distinctive and false doctrines to set themselves off from others (v. 3). They have an unhealthy interest in controversy—often encouraging suspicion of or antagonism toward others (v. 4). And those who follow their teachings are characterized by envy and malice rather than by Christian love (v. 5).

We need to be alert for such signs when popular new teachers appear. But more than that, we need to be alert for an unhealthy interest in money arising in our own hearts. Godliness often costs us opportunities to pile up earthly riches, and seldom pays material dividends. But it sure pays off in the end!

"Godliness with contentment" 1 Tim. 6:6-8. When Jesus taught His disciples to pray, "Give us this day our daily bread," He didn't use the wrong word. Sometimes I know I'd feel more comfortable if I had my "10 years bread" socked away in CDs or a money market fund. But if I did, I wouldn't have the same motivation to rely on God for tomorrow's, or this week's, or this month's needed income.

What God wants me to cultivate is an attitude of contentment with what I have now. Having "food and clothing," Paul said, "we will be content with that." God provides the necessities—and I don't need the luxuries.

How do I know? Why, when I die, nothing material I've gained will be taken with me. But the essential "me"—all that I am as an individual, all that I have or will become, is carried on into eternity. In the last analysis, nothing else counts.

So if you're not rich, count it a blessing. The opportunity to deepen your faith in God as you trust Him for daily bread is a great blessing. For the more godly person that you are becoming will enter God's presence, and every material possession will be left behind.

"The love of money is a root of all kinds of evil" 1 Tim. 6:9-10. The common misquote of this verse says, "Money is the root of all evil." This is a double misunderstanding. Money isn't bad in itself, and having money doesn't automatically make you a bad person. And, every evil does not find its roots in money. Much good is done by money given by Christians and used to help others.

What Paul warned against is a love for money, for that passion for wealth can motivate a person to any and every sort of evil deed. Love for money can lead a person to lie, to defraud others, to betray friends, to steal, cheat, slander, and murder. A person whose goal is to get rich is sure to be betrayed by that passion.

If riches come, it's all right to welcome them. But it is a "temptation and a trap" to desire them (see DEVOTIONAL).

"Flee from all this" 1 Tim. 6:11. The Christian life isn't one of negatives. Wherever there is a "don't," we find implied a "do."

It's the same with a desire for money. Paul said flee this kind of thing. And then he listed values to hold in money's place. What are we to love and pursue if we don't love and pursue money? Why, righteousness, godliness, faith, love, endurance, and gentleness.

So when it comes to making decisions, we have some pretty clear guidelines. Which choice accords with righteousness? Which will help me grow in godliness? Which will help me develop and express faith, love, endurance, and gentleness?

Try using these guidelines when you make the significant decisions in your life. You'll find true contentment. And you'll spare yourself a lot of grief!

"In the sight of God" 1 Tim. 6:13-16. Sometimes we can fool ourselves about the motives for our actions. But we can never deceive God. And, deep down, you and I usually know when what we are doing is out of God's will.

Paul used powerful words to remind us that we live "in the sight of God" when he urged Timothy, and us as well, to "take hold of the eternal life to which you were called."

Ordinary people "take hold of" earthly life, and understandably pursue earthly goals. We can't criticize the non-Christian for being motivated by money and the power or security he thinks it will bring. But you and I have been called to eternal life! We've been called to live here on earth in the constant awareness that our destiny is eternity. We know that life here flickers but for a brief moment, and then as we pass into the presence of God will burn brightly forever and ever. You and I, then, should never be deceived, or take the empty goals of earthlings as our own.

So let's live "in the sight of God," not only aware that He sees us, but seeing Him. If God is ever before us, the vision of His glory will release us from the inferior desires.

"Those who are rich" 1 Tim. 6:17-21. Earlier Paul asked us to view slavery as an opportunity to serve. Now he reminded the rich that their wealth gave them a unique opportunity to serve others.

But again, attitude is important. The rich are not to count on their riches, nor to guard their wealth jealously. Instead the rich are to "put their hope in God," and "be rich in good deeds." A generous rich man is a bright jewel in God's crown. And, in being generous, the rich will find a meaning in life that they would otherwise never know (v. 19).

▶ DEVOTIONAL
Eager for Money
(1 Tim. 6:6-11)

"I want a college major that will prepare me to make a lot of money."

"I want to marry a millionaire."

"I need to take this transfer if I'm going to advance in the company."

I suppose each of these statements expresses a pretty common viewpoint. Each, however, also expresses something else. Each makes it clear that eagerness for money is a value that determines the speaker's decisions.

Paul had a lot of sympathy for such folks, because they've missed something vital in Christian faith, and have set out on a course that's likely to "pierce themselves with many griefs."

Why? Well, for one thing, we Christians are placed here on earth to serve others and to glorify God. Looking at college as a ticket to some high-paying job means that the person is not looking at his life-work in a Christian perspective. All too many fast-track businessmen over 40 look back, and realize that in their pursuit of money they've sacrificed their families, health, and their own higher ideals. The grief they feel when it's too late can never be assuaged by a six-figure salary, even with bonuses.

The girl who wants to marry a millionaire is being totally unrealistic about marriage. The qualities that make for a happy, successful, and lasting marriage can't be measured by one's bank account. If such women are unfortunate enough to find their millionaire, they all too often pay a high price in loneliness, lovelessness, and unhappiness.

The person who evaluates a transfer only in terms of financial benefit is also ignoring more important values. Is the family settled down in the present community, with a circle of good Christian friends, and a significant church life? How will the spouse and children be affected by a move just for the sake of the career? Again, moves motivated by a desire for money have often proven disastrous, and created many griefs for the individual and his or her family.

What Paul is saying to us isn't that we should ignore the economics of our decisions. He is warning us that if we find an eagerness for money pushing out consideration of other, more important values, we're in serious personal and spiritual danger. We can be sure of one thing. That desire for money was not given to us by God.

Personal Application

Keep "money" last on your list of reasons for making any significant decision in your life.

Quotable

"Of all temptations, none so struck at the whole work of God as the deceitfulness of riches, a thousand melancholy proofs of which I have seen during my fifty-year ministry. How deceitful indeed are riches! Only a few—perhaps sixty, maybe not even half that—of the rich people I have known during my fifty years of ministry, as far as I can judge, were as holy being rich as they would have been had they been poor."—Charles Wesley

The Variety Reading Plan continues with 2 TIMOTHY

2 Timothy

INTRODUCTION

This last letter of Paul was written during a second imprisonment in Rome, about A.D. 67 or 68. Paul was fully aware he was soon to be executed, and he both encouraged Timothy, who would carry on his work, and warned against the growing corruption of true Christian teaching. The letter throbs with evidence of the great apostle's triumphant faith, and his confidence in the Lord whom he would soon join.

OUTLINE OF CONTENTS

READING GUIDE (2 Days)

If hurried, you may read only the "core passage" in your Bible and the Devotional in each chapter of this Commentary.

Reading	*Chapters*	*Core passage*
326	1–2	2:20-26
327	3–4	4:10-17

2 Timothy

NOVEMBER 22 *Reading 326*
STRONG IN GRACE
2 Timothy 1–2

> *"You then, my son, be strong in the grace that is in Christ Jesus" (2 Tim. 2:1).*

Paul exhibited a strength of commitment that Timothy—and we—are expected to imitate.

Background

The setting. Most believe that Paul won release from the imprisonment mentioned at the end of Acts about A.D. 62. He continued to minister, perhaps in Spain, but was rearrested in the mid-60s. A strong tradition indicates that Paul was executed in Rome during Nero's reign, about A.D. 68.

Paul's conviction that "the time has come for my departure" (4:6) suggests this letter was written during that final imprisonment. If so, what we have here are the last words of Paul: a "deathbed" blessing and exhortation directed to Timothy, but just as applicable to you and to me. All the wisdom and experience of Paul's long life with his Lord are shared here for our profit and encouragement. So let's take Paul's words of advice to heart, and so live that when our time of departure nears, we too will be satisfied that we have "fought the good fight" (v. 7).

Overview

Paul expressed confidence in Timothy (1:1-7). He called on Timothy to be faithful to the Gospel (vv. 8-18) and transmit it accurately (2:1-2). Soldier (vv. 3-4), athlete (v. 5), and farmer (vv. 6-7) illustrate faithfulness to a faithful Lord (vv. 8-13). Ministry demands that one rightly handle God's Word (vv. 14-19) and pursue righteousness (vv. 20-26).

Understanding the Text

"To Timothy, my dear son" 2 Tim. 1:1-2. It is significant that Paul called Timothy his beloved son. Paul would soon exhort this younger coworker to face and endure great hardships—something we hardly ever want for our children. Yet Paul knew the rewards of suffering for Christ's sake. He wanted the best for Timothy—and he knew that the path to glory is often marked by hardship and suffering.

We need to remember this in dealing with our own beloveds. We do them no favor by smoothing their way so much that they come to trust us rather than God.

"Your sincere faith" 2 Tim. 1:3-7. Paul kept the delicate balance here between what others can do for us, and what we must do for ourselves. The spark of a parent's faith can ignite our own. But we must fan it into flame (v. 6).

"Join with me in suffering for the Gospel" 2 Tim. 1:8-11. It is amazing to me what people are willing to suffer for. Some are willing to suffer to reach a mountaintop. Some are willing to suffer to finish an "iron man" competition, that demands they swim 5 miles, bike over 100, and then run a full marathon. Others sacrifice home and family to make more money on a job that takes them constantly on the road.

Paul asks us to suffer for something far more worthwhile. The Gospel is that stunning expression of God's grace, revealed in Christ's appearance, that announces

God's victory over death and invites every man to come to Him for "life and immortality." Now that is something worth suffering for. No wonder Paul said he was "not ashamed" to testify about our Lord!

"I know whom I have believed" 2 Tim. 1:12. Paul didn't say, "I know what I have believed." He said, "I know whom." Our faith does have content, and that content is to be believed. But the foundation of faith is a personal relationship with God through Jesus.

When we can say, with Paul, "I know Him," we have the same complete confidence that Paul expressed: I "am convinced that He is able to guard what I have entrusted to Him [my very self!] for that day."

"The pattern of sound teaching" 2 Tim. 1:13-14. "Sound" here is *hygiainonton,* "healthy." The teaching Paul gave had unique vitality: it is able to produce a spiritual healthiness that projects "faith and love in Christ Jesus."

There are two tests for sound doctrine. One is its correspondence with the teaching of the Apostles that is recorded in the Scriptures. The other is its power to produce faith and love in the one who holds it. We may hold orthodox doctrines without being loving persons. But if we are not loving, those doctrines clearly do not have a hold on us.

"Everyone in the province of Asia has deserted me" 2 Tim. 1:15-18. "Asia" here means the Roman province, in what is now part of Turkey. Ephesus, where Paul spent some three years, was its leading city. How tragic then that "everyone" there turned away from Paul, even though perhaps we can understand why.

Nero focused the existing hostility of the general populace against the Jews on the Christians. The arrest of both Peter and Paul, and their execution in A.D. 68, suggests that it had become dangerous to be associated in the official mind with these Christian leaders. So perhaps fear motivated many to abandon Paul.

But fear did not deter one man Paul had known in Ephesus: Onesiphorus. Rather than distance himself from Paul, Onesiphorus came to Rome and searched until he found Paul. He must have asked dozens of minor officials where Paul was—and been firmly linked to Paul in their minds. How fortunate Paul was to have at least one loyal and faithful friend.

Such loyalty might bring us into danger in this world. But Paul was sure that Onesiphorus will "find mercy from the Lord on that day!"

"Entrust to reliable men" 2 Tim. 2:1-2. Verse 2 is inscribed on the seal of the seminary that I attended. Truth is passed on from generation to generation by those gifted by God to instruct others in the meaning of what is now recorded in Scripture.

Yet each of us is a transmitter, not only of truth, but of life. As Lois and Eunice, the grandmother and mother of Timothy, shared the spark of their faith with him, so each of us communicates the reality of our faith to those closest to us.

"Endure hardship with us like a good soldier" 2 Tim. 2:3-4. Paul now gives us three images of Christian ministry. This ministry he wrote of is not just for the full-time Christian worker. These images fit the ministries of each of us—to family, to friends, to neighbors.

The first image is military, and emphasizes disciplined commitment. We try to please our commanding officer. An easy life, distractions from our goal, these are all to be rejected. We're to pick up our packs, and march through life as men and women on a mission.

"If anyone competes as an athlete" 2 Tim. 2:5. In swimming, the course is carefully laid out. Stray from your lane, and you will be disqualified.

The image of the athlete competing within the rules is another picture of full dedication. The soldier who wants to please his commander doesn't get involved in civilian affairs (v. 4), and the athelete who wants to win doesn't wander from his lane.

"The hardworking farmer" 2 Tim. 2:6-7. The last image adds a new dimension to Paul's analogies. The "hardworking farmer" has to be patient and wait to enjoy the fruit of his labor. He deserves a share of the crop. But the crop isn't available when he plows

the ground. The crop isn't there when he plants the seed, or hoes the weeds, or even when he shoos birds away from the ripening grain.

Like the soldier and athlete, we discipline ourselves to serve. And like the hardworking farmer, we discipline ourselves to wait patiently until the crop of righteousness we have planted ripens. But we wait confidently, for we know God is faithful. He will give us a larger share of the crop than our labors deserve.

"Remember Jesus Christ" 2 Tim. 2:8-13. Remembering Jesus is what sustains us as we serve Him, waiting expectantly for rewards that seldom are granted here and now.

The "trustworthy saying" Paul shares with us is likely drawn from the liturgy of the early church. It is a hymn or confession encouraging the faithful to look ahead, and take heart at the thought of Christ's faithfulness. The faith even of the true believer may wane. But even "if we are faithless, He will remain faithful."

It is this absolute confidence in Jesus' commitment to us that gives us the strength to live and die with Him, and to endure whatever comes.

"Who correctly handles the Word of truth" 2 Tim. 2:14-19. Context helps us understand Paul's intent. Scripture is not something to be debated. It is to be applied to deepen our faith in God, and to produce righteousness.

This is God's "solid foundation," that no twisting of His Word can shake. While only the Lord can look into hearts, and know who belongs to Him, those who do belong will "turn away from wickedness" (v. 19).

"Along with those who call on the Lord out of a pure heart" 2 Tim. 2:22. Human beings have always been vulnerable to the influence of others. This is why Paul calls on us to "pursue righteousness, faith, love and peace along with" others who share our commitment to Christ.

We express concern over the peer group's influence on our teens. But what we need to realize is that God's plan is to use every person's peer group in a positive way! This is why we have such a deep need for Christian fellowship. The encouragement of others is vital for our own pursuit of righteousness.

"He must gently instruct" 2 Tim. 2:23-26. Other's may "oppose" us. But in ministering to others we must always remember that we are on their side! We are not trying to win an argument, but to win a person who desperately needs to "come to [his] senses and escape from the trap of the devil."

Heated argument is the worst possible way to accomplish this task, and so Paul said that God's servant "must not quarrel," but "be kind to everyone" and "gently instruct." We rely on love, and on the Spirit of God who is at work through us in others' lives.

If this is our outlook, we'll be freed from that terrible urge to compete, and to "win" arguments at the cost of losing others' souls.

▶ DEVOTIONAL
Noble Purposes
(2 Tim. 2:20-26)

The most common archeological find in biblical lands are pieces of broken pottery. When Paul spoke of many "articles" (KJV, "vessels") found in every household, he meant the ceramic and wooden as well as the metal pots, bowls, and dishes that furnished first-century homes. But his reference to a "large house" and to gold and silver made it clear that he had in mind the home of a very wealthy person indeed.

Of course, even the wealthy used the more common clay vessels for ordinary ("ignoble") things. But, even as today we bring out the best china and the silver when guests come, the householder reserved his best vessels to use when an opportunity for "noble" use presented itself.

Paul's point was that in the church of Jesus everyone is a useful vessel. But some, perhaps because they have not dedicated themselves to a pursuit of righteousness (v. 22), or have not cleansed themselves of a hostile attitude (vv. 24-25), are fit only for the most ordinary tasks.

What is exciting is that Paul suggested each us can become vessels suitable for

God to use for the most noble purposes of all. If we will cleanse ourselves, and commit ourselves to holiness, you and I can be "useful to the Master and prepared to do any good work."

Personal Application
To be used, we must be useable.

Quotable
"Behold, Lord, an empty vessel that needs to be filled. My Lord, fill it. I am weak in the faith, strengthen me. I am cold in love; warm me and make me fervent, that my love may go out to my neighbor. I do not have a strong and firm faith; at times I doubt and am unable to trust You altogether. O Lord, help me. In you I have sealed the treasure of all I have. Therefore I will remain with You, of whom I can receive, but to whom I may not give."—Martin Luther

NOVEMBER 23 *Reading 327*
THE GOOD FIGHT
2 Timothy 3–4

> *"I have fought the good fight, I have finished the race, I have kept the faith" (2 Tim. 4:7).*

How good to look back at the end of life and be satisfied with the way you lived.

Overview
Paul warned of growing godlessness (3:1-9) and of persecution awaiting those who live godly lives (vv. 10-13). Timothy was to trust the Scriptures (vv. 14-17) and fulfill his calling (4:1-5). Paul had lived this life, and was ready for his reward (vv. 6-8). Paul closed with personal remarks (vv. 9-22).

Understanding the Text
"A form of godliness but denying its power" 2 Tim. 3:1-5. The phrase "the last days" need not, but may, focus on the years just preceding Christ's return. Here it seems better to see Paul's remarks as directed to our own age, which has now extended over 1,900 years.

Our times are perilous because of the distortion of true religion by those who have the outward form of religion, but who deny its power. What is the power of godliness that they deny? Why, it is the power to take sinful people and purge their character of the sins that Paul lists here!

The power of true religion is seen in its transformation of the character of those who truly believe.

"Have nothing to do with them" 2 Tim. 3:1-5. Paul listed 18 traits that mark individuals off as strangers to true religion. Look at the list, not to see how others measure up, but to see what God has done to transform you—and what He is committed to do for you in the future. Here is the list:

1. Selfish—a "lover of yourself."
2. Materialistic—a lover of money.
3. Boastful.
4. Arrogant—contemptuous of others.
5. Abusive—slandering others.
6. Disobedient to parents.
7. Ungrateful.
8. Unholy—without relationship to God and living a purely secular life.
9. Unloving—lacking even normal affection for family.
10. Unforgiving—resisting reconciliation with others.
11. Slanderous—prone to falsely accusing others.
12. Without self-control—living in the grip of physical passions.
13. Brutal—savage and fierce.
14. Indifferent to good and drawn to evil.
15. Treacherous—without loyalty.
16. Rash, reckless.
17. Conceited.
18. Lovers of pleasure—putting themselves in the place of God as the center of their affections.

"Their folly will be clear to everyone" 2 Tim. 3:6-9. It's easy to appear religious. But when folks get to know us, they quickly

realize whether our faith is a facade or real.

Think how hard it is for an arrogant, ungrateful, unloving, treacherous, selfish individual to disguise those traits for long. And think how long before others learn whether we are responsive, grateful, loving, trustworthy, and caring persons. Only the complete fool can be long deceived.

There's a comforting thought here for us. As we experience God's inner transformation, our character becomes more and more clear to those who know us. The very persons we are brings glory to God, and demonstrates the power of the Gospel.

"Everyone who wants to live a godly life in Christ Jesus will be persecuted" 2 Tim. 3:10-17. It's strange, perhaps, but the world isn't really eager to welcome godly persons. We make it too uncomfortable for others.

A young Christian friend, convinced that as a Christian he should work hard on his job, was persecuted unmercifully by his coworkers, who insisted he slack off as they did. His commitment to do an honest day's work for his pay showed up their own laziness and indifference!

When "evil men and impostors" become worse, the believer whose life exposes their character, becomes less and less popular. So what are we to do? Just what Paul told Timothy. "Continue in what you have learned and have become convinced of."

"You know those from whom you learned" 2 Tim. 3:13. We can picture the church as a long line of men and women holding hands, reaching from our own time back to the day of the Apostles. That "hand in hand" is important.

I have often asked members of Christian groups to think of a person who had a strong, positive influence on their life. Then I've described opposing aspects of relationships. Was the relationship you had with the influential other more close, or distant? Was it more warm, or cool? Was communication one-way, or two-way? Did you feel that person knew you, or not? Did you know him or her, or not?

Invariably over 90 percent of the group say they had a warm, close, relationship with the influential others, in which each talked and listened, and in which enough sharing took place that the two seemed to know each other. No wonder Paul said, "You know those from whom you learned."

Don't be surprised at persecution from strangers. Just concentrate on building the intimate kind of relationship with others through which faith is most effectively shared.

"All Scripture is God-breathed" 2 Tim. 3:16-17. I'm one of those old-fashioned types who is convinced that the Bible is God's inspired Word: accurate, trustworthy, reliable in every sense. Perhaps you are too. But Paul merely introduced his theme by affirming Scripture's inspiration. His point was that Scripture is useful!

The more firmly you and I believe the Bible is the Word of God, the more faithfully we ought to apply it, relate its teachings to our lives, hear its rebukes, heed its correction, and thus let the Scripture equip us "for every good work."

"Keep your head in all situations" 2 Tim. 4:1-5. It's not easy to be rejected and ignored. Right now one of my closest friends, who has pastored one church for over 25 years, is feeling the frustration Paul alluded to. Somehow his leadership now seems unwelcome. It's not that the people have turned "their ears away from the truth." Its just that, somehow, he seems much less effective than before.

The work of ministry, whether engaged in as a profession, or as an expression of every believer's faith, is both rewarding and discouraging. When discouragement comes it's so easy to lose heart—and to fail to keep our heads.

How do we respond? We do the work God has called us to do. For Timothy this was preaching the Word, in and out of season, correcting and rebuking and encouraging—and all with great patience and care. For us, ministry is exactly the same. We have the same Word to share, the same concern for others, that any professional pastor has.

It isn't necessary that everyone respond favorably to us as we serve them for Jesus' sake. It is only necessary to "discharge all the duties of your ministry."

"To all who have longed for His appearing" 2 Tim. 4:6-8. Paul had known plenty of discouragement, and abundant persecution. But he looked back over his life with a sense of satisfaction. Through it all, Paul kept on serving. He fought a good fight. He ran a good race. He kept the faith. And now he looked forward to his reward.

Paul wanted you and me to know that God has the same reward for you and me. We haven't been turned aside by any rewards this world might offer, or by any threats men of the world might make. We have lived our life here aware that this earth is temporary, and all its pleasures are passing. We have yearned not for the things of earth, but for Jesus to return. And this longing has kept us, as it kept Paul, faithfully committed to whatever ministry God has given us.

Don't be downhearted, whatever discouragement may come. Even now the bands are gathering in heaven, and the parade is forming. Soon you'll take your place in the open limo that leads the parade down heaven's streets to the grandstand where rewards will be distributed. And then you'll know, with Paul, that it was worth it all.

"The Lord stood at my side and gave me strength" 2 Tim. 4:9-18. We do need the support and encouragement of others. But sometimes we simply do not receive it.

When others fail us, we have been given a great opportunity to experience the faithfulness of our God. He will stand by our side. He will give us strength. And He will rescue us "from every evil attack and will bring us safely to His heavenly kingdom."

▶ DEVOTIONAL
From Infancy
(2 Tim. 4:10-17)

Our acceptance and nurture in the Scripture usually takes place in the context of some close, intimate relationship. That was definitely the case with Timothy, who came to know and love God's Word early in life. We have no indication of just how Lois and Eunice shaped young Timothy's faith. But we do have a list of rules followed by Susannah Wesley, mother of 19 children, including hymn writer Charles Wesley and the founder of Methodism, John Wesley. Here are her "bylaws."

(1) Cowardness and fear of punishment often lead children into lying. To prevent this, a law was made, that whoever was charged with a fault, of which they were guilty, if they would ingenuously confess it, and promise to amend, should not be beaten.

(2) That no sinful action, as lying, pilfering, playing at church, or on the Lord's Day, disobedience, quarreling, etc., should ever pass unpunished.

(3) That no child should ever be chided, or beat twice, for the same fault; and that if they amended, they should never be unbraided with it afterward.

(4) That every . . . act of obedience should always be commended, and frequently rewarded, according to the merits of the cause.

(5) That if any child performed an act of obedience, or did anything with an intention to please, though the performance was not well, yet the intention should be kindly accepted; and the child with sweetness directed how to do better in the future.

(6) That propriety be inviolably preserved, and none suffered to invade the property of another in the smallest matter.

(7) That promises be strictly observed; and a gift once bestowed, and so the right passed away from the donor not to be restored, but left to the disposal of him to whom it was given.

Personal Application
The best way to teach the Word to our children is to live it—and to see that it is lived.

Quotable
"The religion of a child depends upon what its mother and its father are, and not on what they say."—Henri Frederic Amiel

---

The Variety Reading Plan continues with ECCLESIASTES

Titus

INTRODUCTION

This brief letter to one of Paul's young associates was probably written shortly after Paul's release from prison in Rome, in A.D. 62 or 63. It was intended to guide Titus on his mission to correct faults in the churches of Crete. The letter is practical, and emphasizes the essential link between doctrine and moral purity.

OUTLINE OF CONTENTS

READING GUIDE (1 Day)

If hurried, you may read only the "core passage" in your Bible and the Devotional in this Commentary.

Reading	*Chapters*	*Core passage*
328	1–3	2

Titus

NOVEMBER 24 *Reading 328*

UNFINISHED BUSINESS
Titus 1–3

> *"I left you in Crete . . . that you might straighten out what was left unfinished and appoint elders in every town" (Titus 1:5).*

Titus summarized the things that we too should teach—and must learn.

Biography: Titus
Little is known of Titus. He is mentioned in Galatians 2:1-3 as a companion of Paul. Shortly before writing 2 Corinthians, Paul sent Titus on a mission to that church, which was quite successful (2 Cor. 2:12-13; 7:6-13). When Paul wrote this letter, Titus was working in Crete to "straighten out" the disorganized and somewhat corrupt churches there. A last mention of Titus is found in 2 Timothy 4:10, which shows him off on another mission as Paul faced execution in Rome.

Commentators agree that the few references to Titus which exist depict him as a forceful, resourceful, and yet tactful young Christian leader, who was successful in dealing with a variety of sensitive problems in the early church.

Overview
Paul greeted Titus (1:1-4) and reviewed his mission on Crete (vv. 5-16). Titus' teaching was to focus on a lifestyle appropriate to sound doctrine (2:1-15). In view of Christ's kindness (3:1-7), believers are to devote themselves to doing good (vv. 8-11). Paul closed with personal remarks (vv. 12-15).

Understanding the Text
"The preaching entrusted to me" Titus 1:1-3. Paul's introductory remarks are exceptionally long, matched only in his much lengthier Letter to the Romans. Paul underlined his high calling, possibly as a reminder and as an encouragement to Titus. God had entrusted the apostle with a mission. He was to bring to God's people life-giving truth that leads to godliness. The eternal commitment of God to provide eternal life has been fulfilled in Christ, and this Paul had been commissioned to proclaim.

Titus, Paul's son in their "common faith," was on a difficult mission. He may well have needed the reminder. However difficult our task, when we serve God and His elect we engage in the highest calling of all.

"Appoint elders in every town" Titus 1:5-9. One of Titus' tasks was to strengthen the organization of Crete's churches. This was done by appointing leadership teams in each congregation.

The word "appoint" or "ordain" does nothing to help us understand how leaders were selected in the apostolic church. Certainly Titus supervised the process, and established guidelines to be followed. As in his first Letter to Timothy, Paul emphasized character in specifying a leader's qualifications.

We may use a variety of means to select our spiritual leaders. But we cannot afford to ignore the New Testament's emphasis on character.

"Rebuke them sharply" Titus 1:10-14. I learned long ago that, when teaching a Sunday School or Bible class, it's better to simply overlook dumb things people say. If you say, "You're wrong," and make a

big issue of the error, what usually happens is that people remember the error rather than the correction! And after a few embarrassing lectures on their mistakes, folks in your class aren't likely to risk speaking up and being wrong again. In such cases it's better to find some small point to agree with—and then go on to state the truth that corrects the error in a simple, positive way.

But Paul doesn't suggest my approach to Titus. Why? I suspect because the folks that Titus dealt with were like Joe, a Ph.D. I had in one of my Sunday School classes. Joe didn't say dumb things. He said wrong things. On purpose, and just to stir up trouble. That's what was happening in Crete. People were teaching error on purpose, and in the process "ruining whole households." In this case, Paul said, don't be so gentle. Confront such people openly, and rebuke them publicly.

The Cretans, like some modern Christians, just weren't taking the faith seriously, and were playing games. Perhaps this is another reason for Paul's lengthy greeting. We need to remember that the words in the vocabulary of our faith are God's words, and the issues they deal with are matters of life and death.

"To the pure, all things are pure" Titus 1:15-16. Paul was undoubtedly thinking of the Jewish legalists who played a disruptive role in Crete's congregations (cf. v. 10). Legalism located "purity" in such things as the foods one ate. Christianity locates purity in the heart. It is not what we eat, but what we think and feel and do that marks us as pure.

The contrary is also true. If a person is corrupt within, whatever regulations he observes are corrupt as well, tainted by their association with him (v. 15).

While this is the interpretation of the passage, there is an interesting application. The pure in heart tend to see things in a pure light. The pure see others as persons God loves—the impure see them as sex objects. The pure ascribe the best of intentions to others, and so are seldom hurt by remarks the impure see as slights or attacks. The pure rejoice over another's success, the impure feel jealous.

The purity of your heart will shape the way you look at all things. A heart purified by God protects from much hurt and harm.

"Teach what is in accord with sound doctrine" Titus 2:1-15. Here as in Timothy "sound" doctrine is "healthy" doctrine. God's truth has a vitality, that is not only healthy itself but that produces health and well-being in the believer.

In a way, Christian truth is a wonder drug. Kept in the laboratory, or the theologian's dissertation, truth may be fascinating and worthy of study. But the real value of truth is when it is given to suffering human beings, and makes us well.

When Paul said, "Teach what is in accord with sound doctrine," he put the emphasis on truth's application to life. He did not say, "Teach sound doctrine," as though truth were to be examined only in the classroom. He said, "Teach what is *in accord with* sound doctrine" (italics added). Christian teaching is to emphasize the healthy lifestyle that is produced in believers by God's health-giving Word (see DEVOTIONAL).

"We too were" Titus 3:1-3. The "before and after" snapshot is as applicable to Christian faith as to diet clinics. In fact, the approach is much more reliable in faith than diet ads. Christ in the life makes life different. And makes us different too.

"The kindness and love of God our Saviour appeared" Titus 3:4-7. These verses are one of Scriptures' most beautiful and clear expressions of the Gospel. Salvation: not because of who we were, but because of who God is. Not to keep us as we are, but to make us new.

"Devote themselves to doing what is good" Titus 3:8. Sarah and her friend Vanessa are currently devotees of the New Kids, a singing group that might well be forgotten by the time this is published. Yesterday afternoon Vanessa brought over a New Kids video tape—so my wife and I retreated to my office, closing the door against the ecstatic little-girl screams that found their way even through two sets of closed doors. I suppose it's cute. I'm sure its typical. After all, little girls act like little girls.

We all realize that it's appropriate for

people to act in character. This was Paul's point here. We Christians have experienced the kindness and love of God. He has saved us, and with salvation poured out on us the Spirit of rebirth and renewal. We are new persons now, and so it is appropriate that we act in character. It is important that we Christians be what we are.

And "in character" for a Christian is to "devote [ourselves] to doing what is good." Let's do it with the all the enthusiasm and energy of Sarah and Vanessa. If we do, the reverberations of our good works will penetrate the closed doors of many a heart, and open those doors for Jesus.

"Our people must learn to devote themselves to doing what is good" Titus 3:12-15. Perhaps this sums up the message Paul wanted Titus and the Cretans to hear. Being and doing good is not optional for Christians. It's a "must." In the same way that birds must fly, and fish swim to live in harmony with their nature, so Christians must be devoted to doing good to live in harmony with the new nature God has given us.

▶ DEVOTIONAL

Teaching Is . . .
(Titus 2)

If you've thought of "teaching" and of "learning" as something that happens in a classroom, where rows of students sit to listen as a teacher gives them important information, Titus 2 holds some surprises. In the first place, "teaching" here isn't about information. Teaching is about life. It's not "sound doctrine" but "what is in accord with sound doctrine" that Paul urged Titus to teach (v. 1). Paul didn't insist Titus make sure each believer can proof-text the Trinity. But he did insist believers learn to be reverent, self-controlled, pure, upright, and godly.

Next, teaching isn't a classroom kind of thing! The teacher of Titus 2 is so involved in life with the learners that he or she is able to "set them an example by doing what is good" (v. 7).

Finally, Christian "teaching" is such a broad concept that no single word can describe the activity. This chapter says "teach" (vv. 1-4, 7, 9-10, 12, 15), "train" (v. 4), "encourage" (vv. 6, 15), "set an example" (v. 7), and "rebuke" (v. 15). If we were to include all the ideas conveyed by the Greek words, teaching would be: speaking, communicating, asserting, encouraging, advising, urging, providing a pattern or example to follow, instructing, guiding, correcting, bringing to light, exposing, pointing out, convincing, and reproving when necessary to convict—and all to help another live a life that fits the truth we believe, and the relationship we have with Jesus Christ.

Personal Application

More real teaching takes place outside the church building than in it—and you and I are the teachers!

Quotable

"I am convinced if I asked any one of you suddenly to recall five sermons you have listened to, you would be hard put to answer. But if I should ask you to name five persons through whom God has put His hand on your life, you would not hesitate a moment."—Halford E. Luccock

---

The Variety Reading Plan continues with COLOSSIANS

Philemon

INTRODUCTION

This brief, intensely personal letter was written to Philemon, a wealthy Christian slave-owner in Asia Minor's Lycus Valley. In it Paul appealed to Philemon to welcome back Onesimus, a runaway slave who had been converted under Paul's ministry. The letter is a dramatic example of how the Gospel unites people of every social class in Christ.

OUTLINE OF CONTENTS

I. Thanksgiving and Prayer . . . . Phile. 1-7
II. Plea for Onesimus . . . . Phile. 8-22
III. Greetings, Benediction . . . . Phile. 23-25

READING GUIDE (1 Day)

If hurried, you may read only the "core passage" in your Bible and the Devotional in this Commentary.

Reading	*Chapter*	*Core passage*
329	1	vv. 8-21

Philemon

NOVEMBER 25 *Reading 329*
DEAR BROTHER SLAVE
Philemon

"No longer as a slave, but better than a slave, as a dear brother" (Phile. 16).

Hearts must change before institutions can.

Background
Slavery. A high percentage of the inhabitants of the Roman Empire were slaves. Slaves were viewed as property, and had few personal rights in the Roman world. Several of the New Testament epistles encourage Christian slaves to serve their masters wholeheartedly, as if serving Christ (Eph. 6:5-9; Col. 3:22-25; 1 Peter 2:13-21). These same letters urge masters to treat their slaves well.

There was a movement in the Roman Empire in the first century that saw many masters free their slaves. Other slaves purchased their own freedom with income they earned on the side. It is striking that the Christian community did not become involved in this social issue, even though slavery seems to violate the biblical view of the value of every person. Paul even told Christian slaves not to be troubled by their state, but to accept freedom if the opportunity came (1 Cor. 7:21-23).

The underlying reason seems to be that the early church emphasized the opportunity that any social role gave an individual to serve others. Service, not social status, was given priority. A slave could minister in his servitude; a slave owner could minister by caring for his slaves; a rich man could serve by generously sharing his wealth; a poor man could serve by using his gifts to contribute to the body of believers. What really counted was not the position a person filled in society, but how he served God and others in that role.

Overview
Paul greeted and expressed thanks for Philemon (vv. 1-7), and appealed to him to welcome back his runaway slave Onesimus as a brother (vv. 8-22). He closed with greetings (vv. 23-25).

Understanding the Text
"A prisoner of Christ Jesus" Phile. 1:1. Most believe Paul wrote this letter while in prison in Rome, about A.D. 60–61. If so, the letter is an illustration of something Paul wrote at the same time to the church in Philippi: "What has happened to me has really served to advance the Gospel" (Phil. 1:12). Even in prison Paul found opportunities to share Christ—and reached at least one person, Onesimus, he would never otherwise have met.

We need to have a similar perspective on our downs, as well as our ups. God remains in charge even when we suffer reverses. Indeed, our reverses might be more important than our successes in fulfilling God's plan for our lives!

"The church that meets in your home" Phile. 1:2. The "home" was that of Philemon, and the fact that it was large enough for him to host a church, as well as the fact that he owned slaves, suggests that he was relatively wealthy.

How fascinating this is. A zealous, Pharisaic Jew wrote a warm personal letter to a wealthy Asiatic Gentile, appealing to him to welcome back a runaway slave as a brother! No greater social gaps can be imagined than between these three groups in the first century. And yet these people had become one in a common commitment to Jesus, and in the fellowship of His church.

How good it is to become blind to social distinctions, and to see acutely the bond that makes us one with others who know and love our Lord.

"You, brother, have refreshed the hearts of the saints" Phile. 1:4-7. We can appreciate Philemon as a genuine Christian. Sometimes folks like to invite the traveling evangelist or missionary home—but won't have anything to do with ordinary folks. This is not the impression we receive of Philemon. According to Paul, he was a man marked by love, who expressed love by welcoming and refreshing "the hearts of" all the saints.

Even so Paul prayed that Philemon would "have a full understanding of every good thing." Paul was about to stretch Philemon's capacity to love by asking him to welcome back his runaway slave.

The quality of our love and understanding will be shown when we too are challenged to love someone we might have reason to despise! It's going the extra mile that shows the great depth of Christian love—and reveals a mature understanding of what is good.

"I appeal to you on the basis of love" Phile. 1:8. Influence, not power, is the secret of Christian leadership. What is the difference? Power coerces others, forcing them to do what we wish whether they want to or not. Influence respects the rights of others to choose, and makes it clear that others have the freedom to make up their own minds.

Paul did marshal a variety of strong arguments, that made very clear what he thought Philemon should do. He exerted a kind of pressure that only a close friend, whose love is well known, would be comfortable in exerting. In fact Paul was confident that Philemon would respond as a Christian should. How wonderful when we can have confidence that our loved ones will do what is right.

"Formerly he was useless to you, but now he has become useful" Phile. 1:11. There is a play on words here in the Greek, for the name Onesimus means "useful." As a runaway slave, Onesimus "stole" from his master—even though he may have taken nothing away but himself.

In the first century an ordinary slave cost about 500 denarii, equivalent to some 500 days pay for a common laborer. Slaves with special skills might cost hundreds of times as much. By running away, Onesimus was not only "useless" but deprived his master of his rightful capital.

It is understandable, then, why runaway slaves were not very popular in the Roman Empire. When caught they were often put to hard labor in mines, or other settings where they quickly died.

Paul reassured Philemon that Onesimus would now be an asset to him. In doing so he implicitly asked Philemon not to punish the runaway severely.

"Better than a slave, as a dear brother" Phile. 1:16. Paul did not ask Philemon to free the slave Onesimus. Indeed, he implied that the once-useless slave would now be an asset. What he asked was that Philemon now see and treat Onesimus as a "dear brother."

Ultimately this transformation of perspective undercut the institution of slavery itself. Slavery can only be maintained when some people are viewed as property rather than human beings. The Christian Gospel has not only lifted up repressed classes by acknowledging their human rights, but often has led to the recognition of outcasts as brothers and sisters to be loved.

"I will pay it back" Phile. 1:17-21. Paul here used the language of business. His "personal note" constitutes an IOU. If Philemon had lost money on Onesimus, Paul was willing to repay it personally if Philemon should so demand.

Martin Luther saw this as a picture of what Christ has done for us. Luther wrote, "Here we see how Paul lays himself out for poor Onesimus, and with all his means pleads his cause with his master, and so sets himself as if he were Onesimus, and had himself done wrong to Philemon. Even as Christ did for us with God the Father, so does Paul for Onesimus with Philemon. We are all his Onesimi, to my thinking."

▶ DEVOTIONAL

The Eye of the Beholder (Phile. 8-21)

We have a new game. You have folks look at some weird inkblots, write their interpretations, and then you guess who wrote which interpretation.

Everyone knows that inkblot interpretations depend more on what a person thinks than on what he sees. The average person might see a butterfly—and a disturbed person a giant with outstretched arms, about to grab and crush him. What a person sees says more about him than about the inkblot.

The Letter to Philemon reminds us that how we see others is also "in the eye of the beholder." Paul asked Philemon to stop seeing Onesimus as a "runaway slave," and to begin seeing him as a "dear brother."

The Gospel makes the same request of each of us. We're to stop seeing others as "that dumb blond," or "that sloppy dresser," or "that dreamboat," or "that Very Important Person," and start seeing them in totally different ways. Non-Christians we're to see as individuals of infinite worth and value, for whom Christ died. And Christians we're to see as "dear brothers," and to love them as members of our family.

Perhaps this is the great contribution to modern believers of Paul's Letter to Philemon. It asks us pointedly, "What is in your eye when you look at others?"

Personal Application

See others as God sees them, and you will be able to love them.

Quotable

"Man becomes a holy thing, a neighbor, only if we realize that he is the property of God and that Jesus Christ died for him."—Helmut Thielecke

---

The Variety Reading Plan continues with HOSEA

Hebrews

INTRODUCTION

The author of this unique New Testament letter is not identified. It is thought he wrote to Christian Jews a few years before the temple in Jerusalem was destroyed in A.D. 70. The Book of Hebrews carefully compares Old and New Testament faiths. It shows how Christianity grew out of and fulfilled Judaism, by relating Jesus to key Old Testament institutions. On each point, Jesus is shown to be superior: He brings a better revelation, serves as a better High Priest, institutes a better Covenant, and offers a better sacrifice than the old system could provide.

The Book of Hebrews helps us understand the foundations of Old Testament faith, but most importantly helps us to appreciate the work of Jesus Christ. Its warnings encourage full commitment to Him, and the vivid image of Jesus as our ever-living High Priest, who understands our weaknesses, encourages us to come boldly to God's throne for grace to help us in our times of need.

OUTLINE OF CONTENTS

READING GUIDE (10 Days)

If hurried, you may read only the "core passage" in your Bible and the Devotional in each chapter of this Commentary.

Reading	*Chapters*	*Core passage*
330	1	1:1-4
331	2	2:14-18
332	3:1–4:13	4:1-13
333	4:14–6:20	6:13-20
334	7–8	8:7-13
335	9	9:23-28
336	10	10:19-39
337	11	11:1-7
338	12	12:5-11
339	13	13:17

Hebrews

NOVEMBER 26 *Reading 330*
CHRIST, THE SON
Hebrews 1

> *"The Son is the radiance of God's glory and the exact representation of His being, sustaining all things by His powerful word" (Heb. 1:3).*

Christian faith rests on the conviction that Jesus Christ is God the Son.

Background

The Book of Hebrews. Like the other letters that have found a place in our New Testament, Hebrews was circulated among congregations of the early church, and quickly acknowledged as authoritative. Both the name—"to the Hebrews"—and the content of this letter have led most to suppose the intended readers were Jewish Christians, whose commitment to Christ wavered as they remembered the richness of their heritage. How could they abandon a faith and lifestyle which generations of their forefathers had been firmly convinced was revealed to them by God?

Recently modern scholars have questioned the belief that Hebrews was originally directed to Jewish Christians. In the first century many active "Judaizers" sought to draw Gentile believers into Judaism by superimposing their Law and religious practices atop Christianity. Some think that Hebrews is directed to Gentiles, to counter Jewish corrupters of early Christian faith.

Whichever theory is correct, the writer of this epistle showed his readers that faith in Christ is not abandonment of Jewish hopes. Christianity is the fulfillment of all that Old Testament faith and life promised. All that was so dear to Jewish believers—the revelation of God's will through Moses, the priesthood, the covenant, the sacrifices, the temple worship—were but shadows that dimly revealed the Son. The Son of God, not the shadows, represents spiritual reality. Thus the Jew who turns to Jesus does not abandon his heritage: he discovers the reality to which that heritage has pointed all along!

The Book of Hebrews remains a rich vein of truth to be mined by modern Christians. While the modern church is not threatened by Judaizers, we do need to sense the essential harmony between the Testaments. And we need to examine carefully the person of Jesus and His impact on our lives. For these two purposes—to understand Jesus better, and to experience Him more fully—Hebrews remains an unmatched spiritual resource.

Overview

The source of the new revelation is God's own Son (1:1-3), demonstrably superior to the angels thought by Israel to have mediated Old Testament revelation (vv. 4-14).

Understanding the Text

"God spoke to our forefathers" Heb. 1:1. The Old Testament faith is a revealed religion. Moses didn't invent it. The priests of Josiah's day did not—as some modern skeptical scholars have suggested—rewrite Jewish history, inventing the bulk of the documents we ascribe to Moses. No, God spoke—and what He said was accurately reported by the prophets of a hundred different times and places. What's more, what God said is accurately recorded in the books of the Old Testament.

That of course is what gave some early Christians pause. If God ordained the faith of Israel, how could He overturn or abandon that Word? How could He reject His chosen people in favor of Gentiles?

As we read on in Hebrews we'll see that the Old Testament word to Israel was neither overturned nor abandoned, but fulfilled. But first the writer of Hebrews makes a vital point. We can trust the Old Testament, for God spoke to man through the prophets of old. But we can trust the New Testament even more, for the Agent of that revelation was no mere man! The Agent of New Testament revelation was God the Son! God did not merely speak to us through men, He became a man, and as a man spoke to us directly.

What an awesome thought. God bridged the vast gap between Himself and humanity by becoming a human being. Only in this way could He clearly, and with unmistakable authority, communicate the Good News to us. Let us approach the Scriptures, and especially the New Testament, with great reverence and awe. We are not just reading words. We are listening to the voice of God, and hearing the words of Jesus Christ.

"By His Son" Heb. 1:2-3. Christianity, the saying goes, is Christ. And the saying is exactly right. Everything hinges on Jesus and who Jesus is.

And so the author of Hebrews tells us, clearly and unmistakably. Jesus, the Son, is the "Heir of all things." Jesus, the Son, is the Creator of the universe. Jesus, the Son, is the visible expression (the radiance) of God's glory. Jesus, the Son, is an exact representation of God. Jesus, the Son, maintains the universe, His word alone enabling it to exist. Jesus, the Son, having dealt decisively with the problem of sin, is seated at the right hand of God, the place of power and authority.

After membership class yesterday our pastor mentioned his frustration when two Mormons tried to join the church. He had tried to be gracious in speaking with them privately. He listened to their protests that they were "Christians too." He agreed that there were some beliefs we hold in common. But there was also a critical difference: Who is Jesus? Only when a person confesses joyously that Jesus is the Son of God, the Heir, Creator, and Sustainer of all things, one with God in His

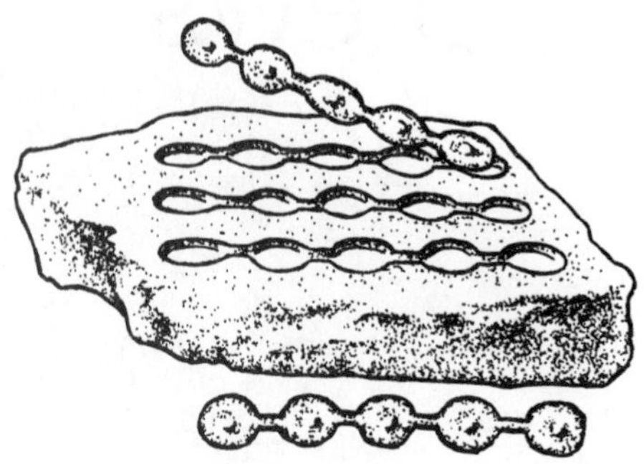

In New Testament times coins were made stamped in a die, leaving an exact impression of the original. The word for the impress of a die was *charakter,* the word translated "exact representation" in Hebrews 1:3. Jesus is identical with God. His very being—His essence, His *hypostaseos,* is an exact representation of the essence of Scripture's God!

essential being and the radiant expression of God's own glory, can he or she claim the name "Christian."

"Superior to the angels" Heb. 1:4. The writer of Hebrews used the word translated "superior" or "better" 13 times. Only 1 Corinthians, with 3 occurrences, has it more than once!

In Hebrews 1:4 the emphasis is on Jesus' personal superiority to angels. Often though the emphasis is on the superiority Jesus brings to you and me. Because of who Jesus is and what He has done, you and I have a better hope (7:19), a better covenant (v. 22; 8:6), better possessions (10:34), a better country (11:16), and a better resurrection (v. 35).

Jesus always was superior to angels, for His "name" (identity) as Son of God is better than that of any created being. How then is Jesus superior to angels?

The most likely answer seems to be that Jesus became superior to angels as a Mediator of revelation. Hebrews 2:2 suggests that angels mediated transmission of God's Word to Moses and the Prophets. Jesus, in fulfilling His mission as God's Spokesman, became superior to angels in this aspect of ministry.

Angels are at the present superior to human beings. But Jesus, in His nature and in His mission, is far superior to them. We need neither fear demons, nor reverence angels. Jesus is above all.

"You are My Son" Heb. 1:5-13. Drawing on the Old Testament to prove his point, the writer of Hebrews showed that the Son is superior to angels in His relationship with God (v. 5), His claim to worship (vv. 6-7), His authority (vv. 8-9), His eternality (vv. 10-12), and His destiny (v. 13). Jesus is superior to all!

"Sent to serve those who will inherit salvation" Heb. 1:14. This verse indicates that believers do have "guardian angels." We may be powerless in ourselves. Yet God has put His Spirit in us, and His angels stand guard around us.

▶ DEVOTIONAL
Son of God
(Heb. 1:1-4)
It's hard sometimes to know just how to think about Jesus. He alone is both a true human being, and at the same time truly God. Sometimes we're comforted by concentrating on the humanity of Jesus. We know He understands us and sympathizes with our weakness. We remember His compassionate involvement in the lives of so many, and feel close to Him.

On the other hand, it's hard to feel close and comfortable with the God who created the universe and whose elemental power sustains it even now. What accord can we finite, short-lived beings have with one whose existence stretches unbroken from and to eternity itself?

Perhaps the best answer for us is to think "Jesus" when we need to sense the loving character of God, and to think "God" when we need to trust the ability of Jesus to meet our every need.

Personal Application
To deepen your faith, meditate on who Jesus is.

Quotable
"Something fiery and star-like gleamed from His eyes and the majesty of Godhead shown from His countenance."—St. Jerome

---

NOVEMBER 27 *Reading 331*
A MAN LIKE US
Hebrews 2

> *"Since the children have flesh and blood, He too shared in their humanity so that by His death He might destroy him who holds the power of death . . . and free those who all their lives were held in slavery by their fear of death" (Heb. 2:14-15).*

Jesus fully understands us and our needs.

Overview
We must heed Jesus' message (2:1-4). It reveals the destiny God gives us through Jesus (vv. 5-13), who took on humanity to break the enslaving grip of death and Satan on our race (vv. 14-18).

Understanding the Text
"We must pay more careful attention" Heb. 2:1. The warning found in verses 1-5 seems to fit best with chapter 1. God's Son Himself has delivered the message of salvation, making that message even more binding than the earlier binding revelation given through angels.

The image of "drift away" is significant. It pictures an ancient sailing ship, anchored near shore. As the sailors sleep, the wind picks up, and the anchor begins to drag slowly across the sandy bottom. By the time the sailors awake, the ship is pitching dangerously in heavy seas.

You and I aren't likely to consciously pull up the anchor of our faith and abandon the shelter Jesus provides. But unless we give constant heed to Christ's word, we can drift unaware from our moorings.

"How shall we escape if we ignore such a great salvation?" Heb. 2:2-4 This is the first of several warnings found in Hebrews. These warnings are addressed to believers, and generally deal with our experience of the superior salvation provided in Christ.

Here the theme is Jesus as the Living Word.

Those warned have heard the Gospel. They are urged to hold to what was heard, for if they do not they will drift from life's moorings and fail to experience the benefits of God's great salvation.

What a blessing God's Word is to us. It is a sure message, confirmed by witnesses who heard Jesus teach and saw His miracles, and confirmed by the continuing work of the Holy Spirit in our lives. Yet it is so easy for us to drift. What we need to do is to give Scripture our constant attention—and make sure we respond to God's Word by putting it into practice.

"What is man that You are mindful of him?" Heb. 2:6-7 How do we explain the wonder of God's appearance in the flesh? The writer quoted Psalm 8, which displays the amazing fact that God cares about human beings. God has chosen not to ignore us, but has concentrated His attention on us that He might lift us up.

He "made him [man] a little lower than the angels." But what we were is not what we will be! We are destined for glory and honor and dominion at God's side.

"But we see Jesus" Heb. 2:8-9. The idea that humanity has been crowned with glory and honor seems laughable to some. Look at the mess we're in—and have been in throughout recorded history. How does the human condition speak of glory, or of sovereignty?

God has "put everything under his [man's] feet." How about sickness? How about suffering? How about wars, and crime, and drunk driving, and child abuse?

Hebrews answers, "At present we do not see everything subject to" man. But what we do see is God, becoming incarnate in Jesus, suffering death for us, and "now crowned with glory and honor."

In the resurrection and exaltation of Jesus you and I see our own destiny. The glorified Jesus is proof positive that glory lies ahead for you and me.

While a skeptical world looks at the ruin man has made of our earth, confident believers look at the triumph of Jesus, and find peace.

"Perfect through suffering" Heb. 2:10. Again we have a seeming contradiction. How could God, who by definition is perfect, have been "made" perfect through suffering?

The idea of perfection is expressed in the Greek word, *teleios*. This root is used nine times by the author of Hebrews, and it means "completed, mature, with every potential realized." Suffering did nothing to add to Jesus character or nature. Yet it did equip Him for His saving work. In suffering as human beings suffer, Jesus shared all that it means to be human. As the writer added in verse 18, "Because He Himself suffered when He was tempted, He is able to help those who are being tempted."

In His incarnation Jesus experienced humanness in a way never possible for the preincarnate Son. His suffering as a man was necessary for His complete identification with us.

What this means is twofold. It means that Jesus understands you and me in our pain and suffering. And it means that God loves us more than we imagine, for Christ's exposure of Himself to mankind's vulnerability was more costly than we can ever know.

"I will declare Your name to My brothers" Heb. 2:12. Mark is a missionary to inner-city street people. He works with the addicts, the pimps, the prostitutes, the alcoholics, the homeless that inhabit the night. He lives on the streets with the members of his parish, because he is convinced that only by sharing the life they lead will he gain the credibility required to reach them for Jesus. Hudson Taylor, like Mark, adopted this principle of identification. When Taylor ministered in China he put off his Western dress, adopted Chinese garb, and grew his hair so it might be put in a cue. To reach the Chinese, he became Chinese in his ways.

This is what Jesus did for us. He came, became one with us, and called us "My brothers." By identifying Himself fully with us, He made it possible for us to put our trust in Him.

If you want to reach others, don't consider how different you are from them. Instead consider all the ways you are one with them.

The more closely you can identify with others, the more clearly they will see the

Lord Jesus in your life.

"Him who holds the power of death" Heb. 2:14. Scripture speaks of two realms: a realm of darkness and a realm of light; a realm of death and a realm of life. While God is the ultimate authority in the material and spiritual universe, Satan is the present ruler of darkness. Where Satan reigns death, as spiritual insensitivity, selfishness, and guilt, hold sway. Human beings who live in Satan's realm are captives of their own sin natures—and of the fear of death. It is the terror of the unknown, and the fear of extinction or of final judgment, that keeps humanity enslaved.

The writer does not explain this imagery. But we can understand it. We know how fear petrifies and inhibits. Like the tiny animal held motionless by the gaze of the cobra, the terror of death keeps man from seeking God. No man aware of committing a crime is likely to search out the sheriff. No person fearing punishment for sin is likely to set out to find God, the Judge, and risk the death he knows he deserves.

What Good News then the Gospel is. The Gospel trumpets Satan's defeat, and announces a pardon available to all. Because Jesus lived and died as a man, and so defeated Satan, we no longer fear death. The paralysis caused by fear is broken, and we run, exulting, into God's presence, eager to live the rest of our lives in His presence.

▶DEVOTIONAL
Merciful and Faithful
(Heb. 2:14-18)

Nobody likes "have to" very well. Around our house, "You have to practice your music lesson now" meets with almost as many squeals of protest as, "You have to go to bed."

Actually, I'm not all that wild about "have to" myself. I often find myself saying or thinking, "I have to get my day's work done first," when I'd rather go fishing or just take off and play some tennis. But "have to" takes precedence. If the more important goals are to be reached, discipline is required.

That's what Hebrews 2:14-18 tells us about Jesus. His goals were so important that He did whatever He had to in order to reach them. And what Jesus had to do really hurt.

First, He had to become a real human being, and suffer the pressure of all those temptations that trouble humanity, if He was to be a merciful High Priest. Philo, the first-century Jewish philosopher, held that the high priest must not show his feelings, but "have his feeling of pity under control." But Jesus endured the human condition just so that He might display the depth of God's compassion for us. If we were to know for sure that God loves us, we had to be shown a Saviour who was willing to suffer. Because Jesus did what He had to, you and I know that our High Priest is merciful.

But Jesus also had to endure the ultimate suffering of the Cross to "make atonement for the sins of the people." The Greek word here, *hilastekesthai*, means to make a propitiation—to satisfy and thus turn aside the wrath of God. He was faithful in this obligation which He as High Priest had to God. If Jesus was to accomplish the purpose for which He was sent, He had to offer up His own life. And, faithful in His commitment to God's will, He did exactly that.

For Jesus, the goal of satisfying God's justice and showing mercy to mankind was so important that "have to" was transformed into "want to." He chose freely to suffer for us. And we can learn from the voluntary suffering of Jesus. Let's make the goal of doing God's will so central in our lives that when you or I "have to" suffer in order to obey, we will want to respond, no matter what the cost.

Personal Application

When you truly "want to" please God, the things you "have to" do will become a joy.

Quotable

"I will be Christian. Like a crimson line running through my life, let the covenant bind me to the will and way of Jesus.

"I will be Christian. My body, mind, and spirit Christ-centered, that I may learn His will; that I may walk His way; that I may win my associates; and that 'in all things He might have the preeminence.'

"I will be Christian. My voice of passion

in an age grown cold and cynical because of faltering faith and shrinking deeds; my answer to the Macedonian call of spiritual continents unpossessed and unexplored.

"I will be Christian. In my heart, in my home, in my group, in my country—now, to help save America that America may serve the world.

"I will be Christian. Across all lines of color and class, into every human relationship, without respect for temporal circumstance, in spite of threat and with no thought of reward.

"I will be Christian. That Christianity may become as militant as Fascism; as terrible toward wrong as God's hatred of sin; as tender with the weak as His love for little children; as powerful as the prayer of the righteous, and as sacrificial as Calvary's Cross.

"I will be Christian . . . So help me God."—Daniel A. Poling

NOVEMBER 28 *Reading 332*

GREATER THAN MOSES

Hebrews 3:1–4:13

> *"Jesus has been found worthy of greater honor than Moses, just as the builder of a house has greater honor than the house itself" (Heb. 3:3).*

Heeding the Word of Jesus is our key to rest.

Overview

Jesus is superior to Moses the Law-giver (3:1-6). The generation Moses led failed to respond to God's voice, and as a result was unable to enter God's rest (vv. 7-19). The promise of entering God's rest still stands, as it did in the time of Moses, Joshua, and David (4:1-8). We enter that rest through a faith expressed in obedience to God's living and active Word (vv. 9-13).

Understanding the Text

"Just as Moses was faithful in all God's house" Heb. 3:1-6. Angels might be superior to men. But one human being dominated the history of Israel. This man, Moses, was THE spokesman of God, and while his brother Aaron served as high priest, it was Moses who in prayer faithfully represented the people to God. To the pious Jew even the angels seemed hardly superior to Moses, the Law-giver.

And so the writer of Hebrews met this challenge. The "Apostle and High Priest" of our faith, whose role corresponds to that of Moses, is Jesus Christ. And He is greater than Moses. Jesus is Builder of the house of God, of which Moses is a part. Moses was faithful as a servant, Christ is faithful as a Son. It follows that the revelation Jesus brought is superior to that brought by Moses!

When the writer said, "Fix your thoughts on Jesus," he was calling the reader to compare Christ to Moses, not to put Moses down, but to see how much greater Jesus is than this greatest of men. For us, "fix your thoughts" has another implication. If Moses was held in such high regard that the average Israelite was zealous to keep his commands, how much more dedicated should Christians be to doing all that Jesus commands?

"Today, if you hear His voice" Heb. 3:7-11. This quote from Psalm 95:7-11 sets the theme for this second "warning" passage in Hebrews. The central thought is that when the Word of God was communicated by Moses to the Exodus generation, what they heard was the very voice of God, addressing them in their today.

That generation hardened its hearts against God's Word. They would not trust God, and refused to obey Him. As a result the generation that Moses led from Egypt wandered for decades in the wilderness, never able to enter the Promised Land.

Unbelief and disobedience have tragic consequences. Whenever we hear God's voice, it is essential that we trust Him, and obey.

"As long as it is called Today" Heb. 3:12-15. What is "Today"? It is now, this moment, and every moment of our future, as long

as you and I live on this earth.

The wonderful message of Hebrews 3 and 4 is that God still has a today voice! He is ever here, ever speaking to us, ever inviting us to respond to His direction and guidance.

One of the most important purposes of the church is to provide a fellowship in which we encourage one another to respond to God's voice when He speaks. As long as you live it will be today for you. In each of your todays you need to be listening for God's word of guidance, direction, or command. Active participation in a local church, and building relationships with others who love the Lord, can help keep you sensitive to His voice, and ready to respond.

"Because of their unbelief" Heb. 3:16-19. Another key word in these chapters is "rest." The specific "rest" in view shifts as the argument develops. At first there is rest for the wandering Israelites awaiting in Canaan (v. 19). Later there is total victory over enemies in Canaan (4:8). But these are only illustrations, to help us sense what the rest promised believers today is like. Everyone who has heard and responded to the message of Jesus is invited to experience a rest of complete inner peace. Only one thing holds us back. The same thing that condemned the Exodus generation to years of unfulfilled wandering. And that is a failure to trust God completely; a failure exhibited in our refusal to respond to His voice.

You can be saved and miserable. You can a Christian and anxious. You can be converted, and totally unfulfilled. And you most surely will be if you harden your heart, and fail to respond when you hear God's voice in your today.

"The promise of entering His rest still stands" Heb. 4:1-2. What a tremendous message of hope this is. Perhaps you've been a disobedient Christian. Perhaps you can look back on wasted years and lost opportunities. Perhaps you grieve over relationships so tangled and distorted that they are beyond healing. Yet whatever happened to you yesterday, "the promise of entering His rest still stands."

You still have today. And God says, "Today, if you hear His voice." God does not say, "Yesterday, if you had heard it." Every today gives us a fresh start, another opportunity. If you hear His voice today, and respond in faith and obedience, you can still experience His rest! You can still know peace, and a tomorrow that will be filled with joy.

"His work has been finished since the Creation of the world" Heb. 4:3-4. The Jewish rabbis noted that in the Genesis Creation account the description of each creative day concludes with, "there was evening, and there was morning." But no such closing phrase is found in the description of the seventh day. The rabbis wisely concluded that the seventh day had no end: God is active, but He is at rest.

What's the significance of this comment? Simply that in the six days of Creation God set in motion a universe whose ages He had already determined. God rested on the seventh day, as there is no contingency for which He has not planned. There is no problem for which He has not already worked out the solution. There is no need He has not already arranged to meet.

Have you ever noticed that what drains us is the stress of work, and not work itself? It is the uncertainty, the doubts, the unexpected setbacks, the awareness that no matter how hard we try, so many things are beyond our control. The Sabbath reminds us that there is no such stress for God. He is active, at work in us and in our world, but in His work He is at rest, sustained by perfect peace and certainty.

What a God we have! And what an invitation—that we should enter "His rest."

"There remains, then, a Sabbath-rest for the people of God" Heb. 4:5-11. The writer mentioned Joshua and David to show that God's ancient promise of "rest" was not totally fulfilled when Israel at last possessed the Holy Land. Entrance into Canaan, victory over the Canaanites, and even David's successful campaigns to expand Israel's kingdom, were merely metaphores—symbolic of a reality far more significant than even these key historic events.

The fact that each of these periods in sacred history is identified as a "Today" also serves to remind us that "Today" is here and now for you and me. When we hear God's voice, we can respond, and in responding find the Sabbath rest that God Himself enjoys!

But why does the writer tell us to "make every effort to enter that rest"? What is that rest, and how do we experience it?

It is God's own rest. It is the realm in which the future is assured, for every contingency has been planned for. We enter that rest by responding to God's voice with faith and obedience. He who knows the future can and will guide us safely through our today. The voice of Him who has solved every problem will lead us to His solutions. The voice of the One who knows every need will guide us to the place where our needs will be met. Our struggle is not to find our way into tomorrow, but to submit to His will, so that He can guide us to where we must be.

The result of total submission to God and obedience to His Word is rest. We suddenly, inexplicably, find ourselves at peace. Dangers abound. Difficult decisions must be made. Circumstances remain beyond our control. But by submitting to Jesus we have rested from our own works, to rely completely on Him.

And so we find the Sabbath rest that is promised to us by our God.

▶ DEVOTIONAL
The Word of God
(Heb. 4:1-13)

Have you ever noticed that when you read the Bible, you tend to imagine a tone of voice? Reading some passages, like Psalm 23, we imagine a warm, loving tone. Reading other passages we can almost hear disapproval or anger. Actually, the tone of voice we imagine is most helpful—or harmful—when it comes to really understanding God's Word.

Take for instance those verses that conclude this fascinating passage on God's rest. I suspect that most folks tend to hear a grim, threatening tone when they read that God's Word is sharper than a sword. That it judges the thoughts and attitudes of the heart, and that "nothing in all creation is hidden from God's sight."

But if you do imagine a threatening tone as you read, you'll miss the message completely!

You see, the writer has been telling us that God has a wonderful gift for us—an inner rest and peace that you and I experience as we respond to His voice when He speaks to us in our today.

It sounds grand. Until we ask, where are we to hear that voice? How will we recognize it? Does God speak to me, personally, and not to everyone?

The simple answer is in the Bible. That book, which is rich in truth revealed for all mankind, is also God's living and active Word to the individual believer. How can that be? Very simply, God's Word, while written by men, is a supernatural channel through which He speaks personally to the individual.

The Word of God is so sharp a scalpel that it is able to surgically dissect our inmost being. The living, active Word of God assesses even our thoughts and attitudes. Nothing is hidden from God, and through the Word He has given us He penetrates our consciousness, to speak to each of us as an individual.

The voice of God is heard in the Word of God. And the Word that is His voice echoes in sermons and classes and in Christians' conversations. As we are sensitive to God and seek His guidance, we hear His voice speaking directly to our hearts. As we respond to the voice we hear, we find the promise fulfilled in our hearts. Today, we experience His rest and find inner peace.

Personal Application

Today, if you hear His voice, do not harden your heart and miss promised peace.

Quotable

"Starting afresh patiently and in good cheer and hope is the mark of the Christian. One of the helpful definitions of Christianity is this: the Christian life is a series of new beginnings."—John B. Coburn

NOVEMBER 29 *Reading 333*
OUR HIGH PRIEST
Hebrews 4:14–6:20

> *"Every high priest is selected from among men and is appointed to represent them in matters related to God, to offer gifts and sacrifices for sins" (Heb. 5:1).*

With Jesus as our High Priest, we can approach God's throne with confidence.

Overview

Having Jesus as High Priest guarantees our welcome by God (4:14-16), for Jesus, who God appointed to represent us (5:1-6), is also the source of our salvation (vv. 7-10). To reach maturity we must build on this foundation (v. 11–6:3), which cannot be laid again (vv. 4-6). Rooted in faith, we will produce the fruit that accompanies salvation (vv. 7-12), resting on the unbreakable promises God has made to us in Jesus Christ (vv. 13-20).

Understanding the Text

"Tempted in every way, just as we are—yet was without sin" Heb. 4:14-16. "But you don't understand," are perhaps the most common words a pastor or Christian counselor is likely to hear. Each of us has a tendency to think that our troubles, our temptations, are unique. They're not. Each human being is tempted through the same avenues—through relationships with others, through vulnerability to pain, through pressures beyond his or her control, etc. It's true that not everyone knows the pain of rejection by a spouse bent on divorce. But even our nine-year-old knows the pain of rejection by a best friend, who over a misunderstanding takes off her half of their "best friend's necklace," covers her ears with her hands, and says, "I'll never talk to you again."

That's what the writer tells us about Jesus. In His humanity Christ experienced every kind of temptation—every vulnerability of mankind. He felt the pain of rejection, the pangs of hunger, the hostility of the crowds, the fear of His coming death. And because He knows exactly how painful it is to be a human being, He is able to "sympathize with our weaknesses."

Think about this next time you're hurting. Think about Jesus the Man; remember how completely He understands. Then, without hesitation, come confidently to the throne, where God dispenses grace, and receive the mercy and help He is so eager to pour out on you.

"Every high priest" Heb. 5:1-10. The writer continued to develop the theme of Jesus' humanity, to show how it relates to His priesthood.

No angel could serve as high priest, for no angel could understand our weaknesses and "deal gently with those who are ignorant and are going astray" (v. 2). It takes a human being, aware of human weaknesses, to be sensitive to humanity's needs and so represent us before God.

What a wonder this is. Jesus came to know the anguish of vulnerability. Jesus, approaching the cross, "offered up prayers and petitions with loud cries and tears." One of the Gospel writers tells us that His agony was so great He sweat drops of blood. Oh, yes. Jesus understands us, far better than we understand our own weakness. He resisted every temptation, and so experienced man's weakness to the full.

The thought here is important. Suppose two friends go on a diet. The first day each becomes hungry, and one says, "I've got to have a candy bar!" And he eats. The other says, "I've got to have some candy too—but I won't." Instead he stays faithful to the diet for six weeks. Which one, do you suppose, really understands hunger and a yearning for food? The one who surrendered to his hunger the first day, or the one who lived with his hunger for six weeks?

This is what the text is saying about Jesus. He understands our weaknesses, because He never gave in to them! Jesus lived, day after day, week after week, month after month, year after year, with all our vulnerabilities, and never once surrendered to them. And in this process He was "made perfect" as our Saviour. Not that there was any change in His essential nature as God. He was "made perfect" in the sense of being fully equipped by suffering to sympathize with us, for by suffering He learned what it means to be human. Because our High Priest became a man and lived as a man among us, He is able to "deal gently" with us who are so ignorant and so prone to go astray.

Jesus understands our weakness.
He does not condemn. He saves.
And Jesus cares.

"By constant use have trained themselves to distinguish" Heb. 5:11-14. The writer seemed more than a little upset that his readers had not realized what a wonderful High Priest we have in Jesus, and gone on to maturity. He expressed his annoyance. But he also shared the key to maturity. We become mature by constantly using the truth God has revealed to distinguish good from evil.

Don't mistake possessing information for maturity. The ability to quote long passages of Scripture or to argue theology is meaningless. What brings a believer to maturity is the conscious effort to distinguish between good and evil on criterion established by God's Word. The difference between "milk" and "meat" is not a difference between a superficial and comprehensive knowledge of Christian doctrine. It is not a difference between a little knowledge and a lot. The difference is found in the way we process Scripture. To those who hear but do not apply Scripture, the truths they know are milk. But to those who hear and do apply the Word of God, the same truths become solid, sustaining meat.

"Let us go on to maturity" Heb. 6:1-6. It's important to notice that this famous warning passage in Hebrews is concerned with maturity rather than salvation. Some have become deeply concerned that they might "fall away" from salvation, and be unable to be "brought back to repentance."

However, as the whole section from 5:11–6:12 deals with maturity, it's best not to assume the writer suddenly shifted in mid-thought to a different topic.

What then is the passage saying? First, that the foundation on which we build our lives has already been laid in Christ. When we trust Him, our great High Priest, we are already on the foundation. Now we need to build on it—not lay it again.

The image that I keep seeing is that of a terrified person stretched out on a solid cement slab laid on solid rock. He's digging in his fingernails and holding on for dear life, terrified that he'll fall off the foundation. The problem is, since he's just laying there holding on, the rest of the house isn't going up! The wood for the frame and the trusses for the roof are sitting there on the ground, but nothing can be done as long as the man lies there, clutching the foundation as if his life depended on it.

Our relationship with God through Jesus is not like that! In Christ God has laid a foundation on which we are secure. Rather than devoting all our energy to holding on, we're to devote our energy to building on the foundation God has laid. Once we realize how safe we are, we can step out in joyous faith and go on to maturity.

"Crucifying the Son of God all over again" Heb. 6:4-6. The issues of death, faith, and resurrection have all been resolved in the death of Christ. The problem with the panicky people the author addressed here was that they hadn't thought through what uncertainty about their relationship with God implied. So the writer, with more than a hint of sarcasm, asked a hypothetical question. We can see it clearly in this paraphrase of these critical verses.

What would you want to do? View your failure as a falling away of God, so access is lost? How then would you ever be restored—you who have been enlightened, tasted the heavenly gift, shared in the Holy Spirit, and known the flow of resurrection power? Do you want to crucify Jesus all over again, and through a new sacrifice be brought back to repentance? How impossible! What a disgrace, this hint that Jesus' work for you was not enough.

Thank God, Jesus' work as our High Priest was enough. And we are secure in Him.

"We are confident of better things in your case" Heb. 6:7-12. The writer shifted images from construction to agriculture. God wants us to produce a useful crop. And, because of our relationship with Jesus, we will! Good things do accompany salvation:

things like work and love shown toward God, and help offered to His people.

These are the things we should concentrate on. We need not be anxious about our salvation. We can put all our energy into serving God and others.

▶ DEVOTIONAL
God Doesn't Lie
(Heb. 6:13-20)

I like the familiar saying. I've even seen it on bumper stickers. "God Said It. I Believe It. That Settles It."

Of course, for some people, that doesn't settle it. That was the problem with some of the folks the Letter of Hebrews is addressed to. And so the writer invented his own bumper sticker.

God promised.

God swore He'd keep His promise.

And that settles it for sure.

It's not just that God, who doesn't lie, has promised to bless us. God sealed His promise with an oath, executed in the blood of His one and only Son. God wouldn't lie in the first place. But God would never, ever, consider violating an oath that He made at such unimaginable cost.

Why did God take such pains to confirm His promise? Because He knew how vulnerable we are to fear and doubt. He knew how weak our faith becomes at times. And so, not because He needed to, but as an anchor for the hope we have in Christ, God promised, and He swore His oath—to reassure us.

What a gracious God we have. And how little cause we have to doubt Him. What God has promised us in Christ is ours. In Jesus we have "an anchor for the soul, firm and secure."

Personal Application

Don't rely on your ability to keep on believing. Rely on God's ability to keep His promises.

Quotable

"Faith is a living, daring confidence in God's grace. It is so sure and certain that a man could stake his life on it a thousand times."—Martin Luther

---

NOVEMBER 30 *Reading 334*
A BETTER COVENANT
Hebrews 7–8

> *"The ministry Jesus has received is as superior to theirs as the covenant of which He is made Mediator is superior to the old one, and it is founded on better promises" (Heb. 8:6).*

Because of Jesus, God remembers our sins no more.

Overview

Christ is no levitical priest; His priesthood is of a totally different order (7:1-11). Thus every element of the Mosaic system is also replaced: its ineffective Law (vv. 12-19), its mortal priesthood (vv. 21-28), its inadequate gifts and sacrifices (8:1-6). Christ has instituted the promised New Covenant, which brings forgiveness and renewal to all who believe (vv. 7-13).

Understanding the Text

"This Melchizedek was king of Salem and priest of God Most High" Heb. 7:1. Hebrews 6:20 says Jesus is a High Priest in the "order of Melchizedek." His priesthood was traced to Melchizedek, not to Aaron.

Even before explaining the implications, the writer took pains to show the Melchizedekian priesthood is greater than Aaronic. This man, who appears briefly in the Old Testament account of Abraham's life (Gen. 14:18-21), was a king (Heb. 7:2). Since no mention is made of his birth or death in the Old Testament, he appears in Scripture as a "priest forever" (v. 3). Since Abraham, the ancestor of Aaron, paid tithes to Melchizedek, the implication is that Aaron, in the person of his forefather, conceded his superiority (vv. 4-10).

Even today a person's family name has significance. That's one reason why a Japanese firm recently bought a controlling interest in a Rockefeller holding company. With it, they purchased the right to use the name "Rockefeller" in their marketing!

The family line—the name of the person to whom one's identity can be traced—was particularly significant in Judaism. And thus the writer took great pains to show that Jesus' priesthood is not Aaronic, but can be traced back to a more ancient and honorable name.

For us the name to which we trace our identity is Jesus Christ. We hold up that name whenever we identify ourselves as Christians. Because Christ's name is so honorable, it is vital that everything we do makes it shine even brighter. And that nothing we do tarnishes a single letter.

"When there is a change of the priesthood, there must also be a change of the law" Heb. 7:11-17. The argument may seem obscure to us, but was very clear to the first-century Jewish reader. The Law given by Moses was a carefully designed system that governed the whole of the believer's relationship with God and with others. The priesthood was an integral part of that system: it was designed for the system, and the system was designed for it. If the priesthood changed, then everything else in the Old Testament system was affected.

Compare the motor of your car. If the transmission is a certain size, it is because it was made to fit the size and the engine of the model car you drive. If you change the transmission size, it's clear you have to change vehicles if it is to fit.

Hebrews tells us that God has provided a whole new vehicle in which we who believe in Christ travel now with Him. The old model, that of Old Testament Law, is obsolete. With the change in priesthood, everything has changed.

This is to be true of our lives as well. When Jesus enters our lives, everything changes—and is to change. We can't go on the way we have been. Jesus' own "indestructible life" is ours. We must learn to make everything harmonize with Jesus, who has entered our life to make us fresh, holy, and new.

"The Law made nothing perfect" Heb. 7:18-19. The loss of the Law was no disaster, for it was "weak and useless." Here again the writer included the whole system, with its code of conduct, its priesthood, its sacrifices, and its worship. The Old Testament system did not succeed in making men better, or bringing them closer to God.

This is something for us to remember. Rules and regulations are no help if we want to draw near to God. What counts is the work Jesus has done for us on the cross. And the work Christ is still doing as High Priest, dispensing both mercy and grace to help us in our time of need (4:16).

"Jesus lives forever" Heb. 7:20-25. The quote from Psalm 110:4 makes a vital point. God provided us a Priest who could guarantee us salvation, for He made an oath that "You are a Priest forever."

Only in someone who lives forever could this promise be realized. And only God the Son, Jesus, who does live on, could have a permanent priesthood.

What does the permanent priesthood mean to us? The other day I read of a legal battle going on to break a will. There's a good chance that the deceased's plans to disburse his estate will not be carried out. The resurrection of Jesus to the role of High Priest tells us that God guarantees that the purposes He had in mind in Christ's death will be fulfilled. Jesus died to make heaven's riches ours. And He rose from the dead to supervise the distribution of those riches Himself!

No wonder the writer said that "He is able to save completely those who come to God through Him." His living presence certifies that all we need to guarantee our salvation will be provided by Him.

And note that "save completely." We are not just saved by Jesus from punishment for our sins. We are being saved from sin's insidious control of our thoughts and actions daily. Jesus is the source of our forgiveness, and the source of our transformation as well.

"He sacrificed for their sins once for all when He offered Himself" Heb. 7:26-28. With the change in the priesthood all the elements of the Old Testament system were replaced. The inadequate sacrifices of the old system were replaced by Jesus' sacrifice of Himself for our sins.

▶ DEVOTIONAL
New!
(Heb. 8:7-13)

Advertising Age pointed out long ago that the two most attractive things a seller can

Hebrews 8:1-6 reminds us that everything in the Old Testament system had significance, but that the significance was primarily symbolic. The gifts and offerings made by Old Testament priests were vivid illustrations of what Jesus would do in the heavenly sanctuary of which the earthly tabernacle and temple were merely "copies and shadows." Christ is the reality, and His work has won us a full salvation.

say about his product are "New!" and "Free!"

But that's not always the case. I have a six-year-old van, with about 70,000 miles on it. I don't want a new one. I plan to keep this one till it runs up at least 300,000 miles. Why get something new if what you have works perfectly well?

Yet that's just the point the writer was making in Hebrews 8. The old system of Law didn't work (vv. 7, 9, 13). The covenant made by Moses, called the Old Covenant here, was "obsolete and aging" almost before it was given.

What makes the New Covenant God has made with us in Christ superior? Two things. It provides complete and full forgiveness for all our wicked acts (v. 12). Because Christ has paid for our sins, God is no longer obligated to "remember"—in the sense of punish—our sins.

And, the New Covenant operates to "put My laws in their minds, and write them on their hearts." The Old Covenant engraved standards that human beings proved unable to meet on tablets of stone. The New Covenent engraves the desire to please God in our inmost being, and moves us to do the very things Law demanded, but could not produce.

When it comes to faith, "New!" truly is a sell word. Those who have tried everything else, and failed to become the kind of person they, and God, want them to be, can turn to Jesus and find themselves forgiven and renewed.

And, in case you didn't notice, the other sell word applies too. The salvation offered us in Christ, costs us nothing.

Personal Application

The best advertisement for Christianity is the new and improved Christian.

Quotable

"We ought to be Christians in large type, so that it would not be necessary for others to be long in our society, or to regard us through spectacles, in order to detect our true discipleship. The message of our lives should resemble the big advertisements which can be read on the street by all who pass by."—F.B. Meyer

DECEMBER 1 *Reading 335*
THE BLOOD OF CHRIST
Hebrews 9

"How much more, then, will the blood of Christ, who through the eternal Spirit offered Himself unblemished to God, cleanse our consciences from acts that lead to death, so that we may serve the living God" (Heb. 9:14).

Once cleansed, we can serve.

Overview
The focus of Old Testament worship was the blood sacrifice offered on the Day of Atonement (9:1-7), though that repeated sacrifice was unable to cleanse worshipers (vv. 8-10). Christ's blood, however, cleanses us and brings us forgiveness (vv. 11-22). His one sacrifice brings full salvation (vv. 23-28).

Understanding the Text
"An earthly sanctuary" Heb. 9:1-6. Earlier the writer noted that the tabernacle on earth was a "copy and shadow" of heavenly realities (8:5). Here he suggested that the whole thing was designed with a single focus. The tabernacle was a setting in which the priests might perform their ministries.

The most important thing in life is our relationship with God. Establishing and maintaining relationship with God is to be the focus of our efforts as well.

"Only the high priest entered the inner room" Heb. 9:7-10. The tabernacle and temple were designed to portray a staged approach to God. An Israelite might enter the outer court, bringing an offering for a priest to sacrifice. An ordinary priest might enter the first room of the structure inside the court. But only the high priest, and that once a year, could enter the inner room of the house of worship, where God's presence was deemed to rest.

This staged entry conveyed a significant message. Though the people of Israel were God's chosen people, they were not yet cleansed from sin. They had no direct, personal access to God. Even the high priest could not enter the inner room without sacrificial blood, which provided a temporary and symbolic cleansing for him as well as for the people.

How different it is for you and me. Through Christ, our High Priest, we have direct access to God—at any time! At any moment in your life you can tune your heart to the Lord, and know that in that moment He is giving full and immediate attention to your need. Hebrews 4:16 assures us that we can come to the throne of grace with confidence—even if we need mercy because we have slipped and sinned! And surely we can come to find grace to help and strengthen us when we feel pressure or have any need.

What a privilege it is, to rush unhesitatingly into the presence of God, absolutely sure that He welcomes us!

"By His own blood" Heb. 9:11-12. Throughout Scripture blood has unique significance. Blood was shed to provide the animal skins that covered the nakedness of Adam and Eve, for the sacrifices mentioned in Genesis, and in the sacrifices ordained in Old Testament Law. Blood was so significant that God's people were forbidden to eat or drink it, for Leviticus 17:11 said, "The life of a creature is in the blood, and I have given it to you to make atonement for yourselves on the altar; it is the blood that makes atonement." Blood not only represents life, but life poured out in sacrifice.

Even more significantly, the blood of Old Testament sacrifices prefigured the ultimate sacrifice to come. The blood that permitted the Israelite to approach God was a vivid metaphor of the blood that would one day be poured out on Calvary; a picture promise of the full redemption to come. Blood. Life, poured out in sacrifice.

This is the source, and the promise, of the eternal redemption obtained for us by Jesus Christ.

"The blood of Christ [will] cleanse our consciences from acts that lead to death" Heb. 9:14. Each of us, if we look back into our pasts, can easily locate incidents over which we feel both guilt and shame. Such incidents lodge themselves in the human conscience. Lodged there, they have a ter-

Hebrews reminds us that Old Testament Law required "that nearly everything be cleansed with blood, and that without the shedding of blood there is no forgiveness" (vv. 16-22). Here an Old Testament priest sprinkles the blood of a sacrificial animal on the horns and at the base of the altar.

rible impact on our present. They remind us of our failures, and so keep us from stepping out to try again. They create a sense of dread and fear of God, who we feel must punish us. At best they lead to frantic self-effort as we try to make up for our past by doing better in the future—effort which can only lead us farther away from a God who insists we abandon self-effort in favor of faith.

But the writer of Hebrews tells us that the blood of Christ cleanses the conscience. All the guilt, all the shame, all the scars caused by our sins, is washed away by the forgiveness that flowed with the blood which poured from our Lord. In the blood of Christ we hear the message, "I will forgive their wickedness and will remember their sins no more" (8:12).

When we claim forgiveness by faith, our conscience is purged and cleansed. And with a cleansed conscience, we are at last enabled to "serve the living God." Perhaps you've seen a child's motorized toy, with its steering wheel fixed, going round and round in a circle. It cannot break out of that circular path. Its direction is fixed. We were like this before Jesus cleansed us. Sin and guilt had fixed the pattern of our lives. Then forgiveness came and filled in the rut which guilt had worn in our personalities. With that cleansing also comes enablement. Our lives change direction. We begin to move toward the goal of righteousness, and as we move, we experience freedom and joy.

Don't live on in the grip of past guilt. Accept God's Word that the blood of Christ has wiped out your past, and let the Holy Spirit make this real to you. Freed from the grip of your past, you can look ahead with joy, confident that God will enable you to serve Him well.

▶ DEVOTIONAL
Once, for All
(Heb. 9:23-28)

"Back on the machine, dearie." The nurse's voice was cheerful. But even though it was only the machine that kept him alive, he dreaded going into the white, antiseptic-smelling room again. The kidney dialysis machine that kept him alive also reminded him of his fatal illness. He was not free, but bound to return to the machine that purified his blood again and again. Away from it, his sickness quickly took grim hold on his body, and sapped all his strength.

That's just what Hebrews 9 says about the Old Testament system (vv. 6-9). The fact that the sacrifices of atonement had to be constantly repeated meant that the patients were not cured! Sin kept its grip on them, and they were only maintained in fellowship with God by repeated applications of sacrificial blood.

The writer of Hebrews shouted the news. Christ "appeared once for all at the end the ages to do away with sin." In Christ and by His one sacrifice, we are cured. We stand forgiven, cleansed. Possessors of a new and endless life, we are equipped to love and serve our God.

The repeated sacrifices of the Old Testament system reminded worshipers of their continuing desperate condition. The one sacrifice of Christ reminds us of His total victory. Don't let yourself be dragged back into sin by the weight of your past. Because of Jesus, the past has no hold on you anymore!

Consider: The blood of Christ has cleansed you from all sin! By one sacrifice Jesus has made you well, and guaranteed victory! We are the lame, called to leap and dance. We are the blind, called to see. We are the deaf who now hear. By the once for all sacrifice of Jesus, we are forgiven, made well, and called to face life rejoicing in the assurance that the victory we need has already been won!

Personal Application

Let Christ's one sacrifice free you to live confidently, and joyously.

Quotable

"One Sunday it happened that St. John could not be at church with his friends, for like Elisha, like Jesus, he was taken by the armed men, and held in prison. But God consoled him with a vision: he saw the Christian sacrament that morning not as men see it, but as it is seen in heaven. His spirit went up; he saw the throne of Glory, and the four Cherubim full of eyes in every part, who sleep not, saying Holy, Holy, Holy. And he saw the sacrifice, the Lamb of God: a Lamb standing as though slaughtered; a Lamb alone worthy to open for mankind the blessed promises of God. He saw the Lamb, and then the angels. I saw, he says, and heard the voice of many angels around about the Throne, the number of them ten thousand times ten thousand, and thousands of thousands: saying with a loud voice, Worthy is the Lamb who was slain to receive the power and riches and wisdom and might and honor and glory and blessing. That is the Christian eucharist. Certainly when we gather here, those that are with us are more than those who stand upon the opposing side. For all heaven is with us when once we lift our hearts up to the Lord, and praise the everlasting Love, the One God in three Persons. Father, Son, and Holy Ghost: to whom is ascribed, as is most justly due, all might, dominion, majesty and power, henceforth and forever."—Austin Farrer

DECEMBER 2 *Reading 336*

A PERFECT SACRIFICE

Hebrews 10

> *"When this priest had offered for all time one sacrifice for sins, He sat down at the right hand of God" (Heb. 10:13).*

Christ's work is completed in heaven. But it continues in you and me.

Overview

Repeated Old Testament sacrifices could not perfect worshipers (10:1-7), but we are made holy by the completed sacrifice of Jesus (vv. 8-18). We must hold firmly to our hope in Christ (vv. 19-25), resist deliberate sin (vv. 26-31), and persevere in doing good till Jesus comes (vv. 32-39).

Understanding the Text

"Make perfect those who draw near to worship" Heb. 10:1-7. A critical question for any religion is not what it asks you to do, but what it does in you.

Even Old Testament faith, with all its required sacrifices, only covered the sins of worshipers. The repeated sacrifices of the Old Testament could not make anyone perfect. This was the one, devastating flaw in that system. And so Christ came, to do God's will, and offer up Himself as a perfecting sacrifice.

My youngest son was remarking yesterday that the Sunday School teacher of his singles' class has the notion that if a person is a true Christian, he'll stop sinning, and never even slip. To him any deviation from the ideal is evidence the person was never saved. That is an oversimplification. Any living, growing thing requires time to mature. The spiritually immature, like the physically immature, have a tendency to do things that a mature adult never would. And even the mature make choices at times that are not just unwise, but wrong.

Even so, Christ came to make a specific

difference within worshipers. His was a perfecting sacrifice, for He came to perfect us: to make us suitable within and without to worship the holy God.

There is nothing we can do to repay God for the gift of His Son. But the least we can do is open our hearts to His Spirit, and live that changed life which is appropriate for worshipers of Jesus Christ.

"We have been made holy through the sacrifice . . . of Jesus Christ once for all" Heb. 10:8-10. Holiness is a somewhat frightening concept. Until we remember that "holy" has the basic meaning of being set apart to God, and that holiness has two primary aspects. The ceremonial aspect, so important in Old Testament worship, has now been dismissed as irrelevant. What is left is the personal dimension of holiness: a dynamic moral quality of active goodness that characterizes God Himself.

What the writer of Hebrews tells us is that God in Christ has acted to set us apart as His own. But if we are to be God's, we must be holy too. And so God has infused something of Himself within us. Jesus died that we, like God, might be energetically good.

Not passively good, in the sense of just refraining from evil. But actively good, in the sense of expressing in this world the compassion and love that marked Jesus in His incarnation.

The most important thing that you or I can do in life, recognizing that we are holy, is to be holy.

"He sat down at the right hand of God" Heb. 10:11-14. The Old Testament priest always stood as he ministered. The fact that Jesus sat down after He offered Himself as a sacrifice indicates that His work was done. There were no more sacrifices to offer. Jesus "made perfect forever those who are being made holy."

Through Christ's death you and I have been perfected. And we are being made holy. We are in the process of becoming what we are.

This is an exciting truth. You can pick up an acorn, hold it in your hand, and know for sure that if it is planted a mighty oak will grow. That acorn won't become a reed, or a stalk of corn, or a geranium. It will become an oak, for though it looks very different from a mature tree, it *is* an oak, and in time will become one.

You and I may look very different from Jesus today. Yet God has placed Christ's own nature in us. We are Christian now, and in time we will be Christian. We are holy now, and in time we will be holy.

Some fat folks post pictures of themselves on the refrigerator, to remind themselves of how they look. It usually just makes them feel bad, and doesn't help at all. How much better God's way is. He posts His portrait of the ideal "you" in your heart, and tells you to act like the person you are. As we act in harmony with the vision of our ideal self, that is what you and I become.

Never let yourself be discouraged about the slowness of your spiritual growth. God sees you perfected, standing in His presence with a character like that of His own Son. This is who you are—and it is who you most certainly will become.

No wonder the passage says that those "He has made perfect forever" are even now "being made holy."

"This is the covenant" Heb. 10:15-16. Use any word you want. Use pledge, promise, bond, compact, contract, agreement, deal, pact, pledge, treaty, or oath. Use any of these words, or any other, to convince yourself that you truly have been forgiven, and that God no longer remembers your sins or lawless acts. Convince yourself that your past no longer stands between you and God.

Once you are convinced, you'll be able to stop worrying about your past, and dedicate your future to serving God as the holy person you are.

"He who promised is faithful" Heb. 10:19-23. When I was a young teen I plowed with a handheld plow pulled by a team of horses. At first I made ragged, twisting furrows as I struggled to hold the plow steady. Then my dad showed me that to plow a straight furrow, I needed to stop looking at the ground ahead of me, to fix my eyes on a pair of landmarks, and keep them lined up as I moved across the field.

We have landmarks to guide us as we approach God. We see Jesus, our cleansing sacrifice. And we see Jesus standing before God's throne, our High Priest.

When we hold unswervingly to the hope this provides, we will "have confidence to enter the most holy place" at any time.

"Spur one another on to love and good deeds" Heb. 10:24-25. The classic American is John Wayne as Rooster Cogburn, riding alone toward his foes, guns blazing. The rugged individualist attracts us, and serves as a cultural ideal.

It may be American, but it's not Christian. We don't achieve holiness alone, rushing in rugged defiance toward our enemies of sin, Satan, and temptation. We achieve holiness as we share our lives with others, give and receive encouragement, spurring one another on to love and to good deeds.

Don't try it alone. God has given us Christ's church for support and assistance. And He intends us to keep on meeting with others throughout our whole life.

"If we deliberately keep on sinning" Heb. 10:26-31. This part of the third major warning found in Hebrews (vv. 19-39) is based on the writer's presentation of Jesus as the perfect sacrifice. It is a warning addressed to those considering a return to Judaism. Under the old system, individual sacrifices could be made for unintentional sins, but the only sacrifice for deliberate sins was that offered on the Day of Atonement by the high priest. But the writer has shown that even those sacrifices were ineffective, while the one sacrifice by Jesus of His own blood perfected His worshippers, and thus never needs repeating.

If those who rejected Moses' Law were stoned, the writer asked, what do you think a person who treats the blood of God's own Son with contempt (v. 29) deserves?

There's a thought in this for us. Whenever we feel uncertain, or inclined to doubt our ability to live a holy life, let's remember that Christ died to make just this possible. Surely He did not shed His blood in vain. Surely you and I will find the strength to live as God desires.

▶ DEVOTIONAL
How Do Holy People Live? (Heb. 10:19-39)

That word "holy" keeps popping up in Hebrews. Christ has cleansed us from sin, and made us holy. His sacrifice has perfected us forever, and we "are being made holy" (v. 14). That's great. But it doesn't help unless we can visualize how holy people live.

Here's a checklist with some characteristics of holy people, drawn from verses 19-39.

* Holy people draw near to God in full assurance of faith (v. 19).

* Holy people hold unswervingly to the hope Christians profess (v. 23).

* Holy people spur each other on to love and good deeds (v. 24).

* Holy people meet together regularly to encourage one another in the faith (v. 25).

* Holy people don't sin deliberately (v. 26).

* Holy people are willing to suffer insult and persecution when these are offered (v. 33).

* Holy people stand by those who are mistreated (v. 33).

* Holy people accept confiscation of their property, without throwing away their confidence (vv. 34-35).

* Holy people simply try to do the will of God, deeming this the most important thing in this present life (v. 36).

* Holy people joyfully expect Jesus to come in just a little while, and are satisfied to wait for rewards until then (vv. 36-39).

That doesn't seem so hard, does it? Not for those cleansed by the blood of Jesus Christ.

Personal Application

Set out to be holy because you are holy.

Quotable

"Practical holiness is the only holiness of any value in this world, and the only kind the Holy Spirit of God will endorse."—Oswald Chambers

DECEMBER 3 *Reading 337*
TRIUMPHS OF FAITH
Hebrews 11

"These were all commended for their faith" (Heb. 11:39).

Faith is more clearly expressed in the way people live than in what they claim to believe.

Overview
The nature and value of faith are revealed (11:1-3) and illustrated in this honor roll of Old Testament saints (vv. 4-40).

Understanding the Text
"Faith is being sure of what we hope for" Heb. 11:1-3. To our society "faith" seems insubstantial: it is persistently holding on to notions that can't be proven and thus are flimsy and unreal. In Scripture, the reverse is true. Faith is confident expectation that what we cannot see is more solid and real than the material universe.

The root of this kind of faith is our conviction that "the universe was formed at God's command." God has priority over things we can taste and touch and see and feel. God is more real than they are, because God is the source of their existence.

The ancients, and believers today, are commended for such faith. When you and I realize that God is the ultimate reality, and act on this conviction, we have a faith which makes a difference in our life, and will enable us to triumph.

Anything less than conviction translated into action falls short of biblical faith.

"By faith Abel offered God a better sacrifice" Heb. 11:4. Genesis 4 indicates that both Cain and Abel knew God required animal sacrifice. Why else would God speak to Cain after rejecting his sacrifice of fruits and vegetables, saying if he "did well" he could still be accepted? The difference between the two is that Abel responded to God's word. Only Abel did as the Lord required.

This is the first evidence of a true faith. We respond to God's Word, and choose to do the things that please Him.

It's striking that Abel's act of faith led directly to his death. His brother's jealous anger was stimulated by Abel's obedience. But it is even more striking when Hebrews tells us that by faith Abel "still speaks." Abel is dead as far is this world is concerned; his body dust. Cain too is long dead. But Abel, pronounced righteous by God on the basis of his faith, "still speaks." Abel's faith brought him the gift that faith brings you and me: eternal life.

"By faith Enoch was taken from this life" Heb. 11:5-6. Abel exhibited saving faith; and Enoch a faith that holds the believer close to Lord.

We know little of Enoch from the Old Testament except that he "walked with God" and after a time "he was no more, because God took him away" (Gen. 5:24). How does the writer know so much about Enoch from such brief mention? Simply by virtue of the fact that Enoch did please God, and "without faith it is impossible to please God."

No one can approach God without faith. It takes faith to believe that God exists when He cannot be seen. And it takes even more faith to believe that God rewards those who seek Him, when rewards so often are delayed.

Anyone who walks with God will find his faith tested. When you and I flip a light switch, the light goes on. When you turn the faucet, water flows. Push the "on" button, and your TV screen is filled with flickering pictures. The reward of our actions is immediate, and invariable. But many times you and I pray, and it seems no answer comes. We cry out to God, but our troubles persist. It takes very little faith to expect a light to go on when it always does. It takes much more faith to walk with God. For your belief that He is a rewarder of those who seek Him will be sorely tested again and again.

But don't be discouraged. As each hero in this hall of fame demonstrates, your faith will make a difference in the way you live your life. And in the blessings you enjoy.

"By faith Abraham . . . obeyed and went" Heb. 11:8-10. Some people find it almost impossible to take risks. "I'd like to try," they think, "but what if I failed?" Abra-

ham reminds us that faith frees us to venture confidently into the unknown.

Too fearful to pray aloud? Too unsure to express your opinion? Like to try a new job, but frightened to leave the old? Want to share a word of witness, but anxious about how others might react? Faith frees us to step out even when, like Abraham, we don't know where we are going.

How does faith help? Faith reminds us that God, who guides and directs us, also goes with us. We need not fear risks when faith tells us that the Lord is by our side.

"They were longing for a better country" Heb. 11:13-16. There is such a thing as heavenly dissatisfaction. The Old Testament saints on this honor roll experienced it. They just didn't feel at home in this world. Somehow something was lacking.

Archeologists have shown that Abraham lived in Ur during a vital and prosperous age. Ur offered luxuries and wealth, and Abraham possessed both. But Abraham wasn't satisfied, and so set out in search of something better. This is one evidence of a growing faith: we become dissatisfied with the things of the world. We can be thankful for all the good things God has given us. But faith makes us aware that nothing we have is enough to satisfy our deepest needs.

The text says that these people were "living by faith when they died." They never found the completion or fulfillment they searched for. You and I won't either, for we were created for heaven, not for earth. We too may spend our lives "longing for a better country." But, through faith, we will spend eternity enjoying it!

"By faith Abraham, when God tested him" Heb. 11:17-19. There comes a time in each of our lives when God will test us. And the test will be like that of Abraham, when God demanded he sacrifice his son, Isaac.

This is the test of full surrender. It is the test that calls on us to give up our heart's desire, because God asks us to. Only a unique faith will enable us to do this, and to surrender all.

What is that unique faith? The Old Testament text tells us that when Abraham went up to Mount Moriah to offer Isaac, he told his servants to wait, saying that "the lad and I" will return. Hebrews explains. Abraham had been promised descendants through Isaac. Abraham was so thoroughly convinced God would keep His promise that he believed God would raise Isaac from the dead if that was necessary.

God has promised us His very best. He has assured us that all things work together for the good of those who love Him. We are able to surrender all when we have the faith to believe that, if God asks it, renouncing our heart's desire is both right and good.

How close Abraham must have been to God, to trust Him so. Let us stay close to the Lord too, that we too might have a faith that surrenders all.

"By faith Moses" Heb. 11:24-28. Moses' life too exhibits faith. As the "son of Pharaoh's daughter" Moses was in line for the throne of Egypt, or at the least high position in that affluent land. No pleasure would have been denied him. Yet Moses spurned the "pleasures of sin" and chose to identify himself with God's people, even though they were then a race of slaves.

Let's identify ourselves with God's people too, no matter how popular it may be to ridicule the "born again." Disgrace for the sake of Christ still has higher value than all the treasures of this world.

"By faith the prostitute Rahab" Heb. 11:31. Faith rules no one out, but draws a great circle that encompasses all. Whatever our past, faith opens the door to relationship with God and a new, righteous life.

"God had planned something better for us" Heb. 11:32-40. Faith does not guarantee anyone a life free of stress or pain. Many over the millennia have suffered and even died for their faith. Yet faith won for each the commendation of God.

Faith wins even more for you and me. The Old Testament saints looked forward to a salvation they could not understand. We look back to a salvation assured by Calvary. And through the Spirit of God we enjoy a relationship with the Lord which can be more real to us than to the Old Testament saints.

▶ DEVOTIONAL
Earthquake Zone
(Heb. 11:1-7)

A sports columnist, reporting from San Fransisco on an upcoming football game between the 49ers and another team, wrote of the silence. That city, usually bursting with tourists, was all but deserted. The earthquake that struck in October 1989 frightened visitors away.

What's surprising was that it seemingly hadn't shaken many residents. Throughout California millions continue to live along earthquake fault lines, with never a thought of moving to avoid the devasting tremors that they must know will certainly come.

This was what made Noah such an unusual person, and a rightful recipient of God's commendation. Noah had never even seen rain, for in his day springs watered the earth (Gen. 2:6). But when God announced that a great Flood would destroy life on earth, Noah built the ark in which his family and animal life were preserved.

The Hebrews 11 honor roll has helped us define faith. Faith views God as more real than the material universe He created (vv. 1-3). Faith saves, for Abel "still speaks" even though his body is long dead (v. 4). Faith enables us to walk with God, even when visible rewards of seeking Him are delayed (vv. 5-6). But now the writer contrasts the wisdom of faith with the foolishness of unbelief.

Noah took God's warning of an utterly unknown danger seriously. In "holy fear" he acted on it. Noah had never experienced floods or rainfall. But he believed God when he was warned. His response "condemned the world," in that his faith exposed the utter unbelief of those whom Noah continually warned while he and his family labored on the ark (cf. 1 Peter 3:20).

What a stunning portrait of today. The Gospel shouts out the Good News that in Christ we can be saved from coming judgment. Those with faith respond with "holy fear," and hurry to Christ for refuge. But the unbeliever scoffs, and continues to ignore warning of imminent disaster.

The fact that so many choose to stay on in California's earthquake zones reminds us how unreal the future is for most human beings. Most of us live as though today were everything, and tomorrow unreal. But Scripture tells us that there, just over the horizon of tomorrow, a juggernaught of judgment waits. It is unwise to live on a fault line in an earthquake zone. But it is utterly foolish to remain outside of Christ, exposed to the judgment that most surely will come.

Personal Application

Tomorrow is real. Take it into account as you live today.

Quotable

"We should all be concerned about the future because we will have to spend the rest of our lives there."—Charles F. Kettering

DECEMBER 4 *Reading 338*
DIVINE DISCIPLINE
Hebrews 12

> *"No discipline seems pleasant at the time, but painful. Later on, however, it produces a harvest of righteousness and peace for those who have been trained by it" (Heb. 12:11).*

To benefit from discipline we must respond to it.

Overview

The example of Jesus stimulates us to struggle against sin (12:1-4). We are to view hardship as God's discipline of dearly loved sons (vv. 5-11), and strengthen our resolve to live holy lives (vv. 12-17). For God has not spoken to us in a distant law, but in a nearby Christ (vv. 18-24), whose kingdom is not to be despised (vv. 25-29).

Understanding the Text

"A great cloud of witnesses" Heb. 12:1-3. Some consider this a reference to saints and angels observing us, as the crowd in a great stadium cheers on those on the playing field. Others see us observing the saints of ages past, taking heart from their consistent testimony (witness) to God's faithfulness.

Either understanding motivates us to "throw off everything that hinders and the sin that so easily entangles."

What a great responsibility, to know that what we do impacts others' commitment to Jesus Christ.

"Let us fix our eyes on Jesus, the author and perfecter of our faith" Heb. 12:2-3. Jesus is the "pioneer" (author) of our faith, in that He followed the path of faith all the way to its end. He trusted all the way to death, and then broke out of the grave to open the way to glory.

Jesus is also the perfecter of faith. In Jesus we see faith's ultimate nature perfectly expressed. Perfect faith is complete trust in God, however awesomely death and destruction crowd in around us.

No wonder the writer said, "Let us fix our eyes on Jesus." When we are frightened, seeing Jesus will enourage us to keep on trusting. When we are tired, seeing Jesus will give us strength to go on. When we want to turn back, focusing on Jesus will reassure us that the glory ahead is well worth the present pain.

"In your struggle against sin" Heb. 12:4. One of history's great saints, John Chrysostom, whose exile in A.D. 403 was caused by his denunciation of powerful churchmen for their pretentions and lack of charity, wrote from exile: "there is only one thing to be feared, Olympias, only one trial, and that is sin."

Jesus as faith's pioneer and perfecter reminds us that we are better off to choose suffering rather than to choose sin. Christ resisted choosing sin "to the point of shedding His blood." You and I are most unlikely to have so grim a choice to make.

So let's not feel sorry for ourselves when suffering comes. Let's rejoice that whatever our suffering, we have not and will not choose sin in order to avoid it.

"The Lord's discipline" Heb. 12:7. As the early decades of the Church Age passed, Christians found themselves under increasing pressure. There was often hostility from neighbors. In some localities there was unofficial persecution. In others there was official persecution by Roman authorities. So the Book of Hebrews, written as it seems to have been toward the end of the 60s, speaks as do other later New Testament epistles, of suffering and pain.

Here the writer of Hebrews asks us to view hardship and suffering as discipline. God has not abandoned Christ's followers. God is simply treating them as any wise father treats dearly loved sons.

It may seem strange, but this perspective makes any hardship we face so much easier. We no longer have to cringe away, wondering what we've done that God should punish us so. Instead we reach up in our pain, convinced that even our suffering is an expression of the love of God.

If you know God loves you, you can endure almost anything.

And if you ever doubt that God could permit His loved ones to suffer, consider Jesus. The pioneer and perfecter of our faith suffered the ultimate anguish, though He is God's dearly beloved Son.

"God disciplines us for our good, that we may share in His holiness" Heb. 12:7-13. Two things reassure us when God disciplines. We remember that Jesus suffered first. And we remember that God has graciously explained His motive for discipline.

One thing that bothers us is not knowing "why." We lose our job, and in our fears about the future cry out, "Why?" We lose a loved one, and agonize, "Why him, and why not me?" We suffer from a lingering illness and, try as we may, we can find nothing "good" in it. We begin to doubt Romans 8:28, and again we ask, "Why?"

God doesn't give us reasons for specific hardships. But He does explain, carefully, what He is doing. God is treating us as any good parent treats his own children. God is disciplining us "for our good, that we may share in His holiness."

Don't expect an economic benefit from the loss of a job, an emotional benefit from the loss of a loved one, or a health benefit from a serious illness. But do expect a spiritual benefit from any hardship. If you and I submit to God (v. 9), He will work in our lives, and through suffering we will grow in holiness. Even more, we will reap a rich "harvest of righteousness and peace" from the training hardship is intended to provide.

"See to it that no one misses the grace of God" Heb. 12:14-17. The very hardship which is intended to bless can ruin us.

Whether suffering strengthens or weakens us depends on our response to it. If we look at suffering only as an evil, and become bitter, the discipline God intended as a love gift will become a burden and a thorn.

Such people miss the grace of God. No, not the grace expressed in bringing the specific trial. But the grace that marks our entire relationship with God, and the grace that is available to strengthen us in our difficulties. A focus on God's grace will lead to an experience of God's grace in our situation, and that will free us from bitterness, and we will grow.

"You have not come to a mountain that can be touched" Heb. 12:18-24. When the people of Israel gathered at Mount Sinai to receive the Law, lightning flashed and thunder grumbled threateningly. The people drew back in fear, and Moses alone approached the Lord. It was hard to sense the grace of God there.

But we Christians come not to Sinai but to Zion. There we meet Jesus Himself, as thousands of angels sing for joy. We come to God through Jesus, and experience an intimacy that was only dreamed of in Old Testament times.

Let's be careful that we do not refuse the God we know so well when He speaks. If those who knew Him less well suffered for ignoring His Word, how much more will we lose; we who know Him so intimately?

"A kingdom that cannot be shaken" Heb. 12:25-28. God shakes the earth. The image reminds us how insubstantial and unstable the material universe is. Out of all that is, only human beings will exist out beyond time and into eternity. Everything else will disappear.

How good God is, then, to permit us to suffer in this world, if the benefits of holiness and righteousness that divine discipline develops will persist long beyond time.

God is good. And when He disciplines us, it is for our good as well.

▶DEVOTIONAL
Child Abuse!
(Heb. 12:5-11)

Kids pick up on things so quickly. I suspect that's why one parent we know was threatened by her 11-year-old. "Make me do it," he said to his mother, "and I'll call 911 and tell them child abuse."

Mom kept cool. "Go ahead. I may spend a couple of days in jail. But they'll put you in a foster home. No Nintendo. No color TV in your room. No stereo. No tapes or CDs. No room of your own." The boy thought for a moment and then said, "OK, Mom."

It wasn't like that when I was a boy. I suspect some of the things that happened to me would have raised cries of concern today. Like the time Dad took me out in the garage and whipped me with a leather belt. Or the time I ran away, again, and my disgusted father took the collar off my dog Ezra and put it around my neck! "I can trust Ezra more than I can trust you," he told me, and drove away.

I sat outside that warm summer morning, totally crushed, until Dad returned from his mail route and let me go. But even then I would never have cried, "child abuse." Even then I was perfectly aware that Dad loved me, and that what he did was not so much an expression of his anger as it was an expression of his concern. Dad disciplined me, not for his pleasure, but for my benefit. And somehow I knew.

How wonderful it is for you and me, when tragedy strikes, to be able in our misery to look up and know that we are loved. How wonderful it is, when we can't understand "why," to know we're not the victims of child abuse, but the recipients of love.

Children today who shout "child abuse" when loving parents discipline them reject one of Mom's and Dad's greatest love gifts. They will surely be the poorer for it. And Christians today, who utter that same shout when troubles come, have forgotten the depths of God's love, and miss out on one of life's greatest gifts: the certainty that God is with us, always. And that He cares.

Personal Application

Let God's discipline of believers serve as a model for your nurture of your boys and girls.

Quotable

"Troubles are often the tools by which God fashions us for better things."—Henry Ward Beecher

DECEMBER 5 *Reading 339*
HONORABLE LIVES
Hebrews 13

> *"We are sure that we have a clear conscience and a desire to live honorably in every way" (Heb. 13:18).*

Exhortations to honorable living grow naturally out of the most exalted doctrine.

Overview

The writer closes with exhortations (13:1-19), with one of the most powerful doxologies in Scripture (vv. 20-21), and with personal greetings (vv. 22-25).

Understanding the Text

"Keep on loving each other as brothers" Heb. 13:1. Nearly every New Testament letter contains an exhortation to love. This is only appropriate, as the night before His crucifixion Jesus emphasized his "new commandment" (John 13:33-34). Christ's followers are to love one another as Jesus loved them.

This verse, however, has a distinctive emphasis. "Keep on" loving. The emphasis is important. As we come to know others better and better, more and more of their flaws are likely to appear. How many a gal has come home, excited over meeting "the" man, only to become disenchanted a few weeks or months later.

We Christians, however, don't have the liberty of disenchantment. Or of disengagement. Someone born to my parents is my sister or my brother, not by my choice, but by virtue of shared parentage. We may choose our mates, but we don't choose brothers and sisters. And somehow, despite everything, in most families siblings learn not only to get along, but to love each other as well.

It's like this in God's family. We are family, not by our choice, but by God's. We have the same Father, and so we all belong. Period. We can become disenchanted. But we can't withdraw, or reject someone whom God has accepted.

And so Hebrews 13:1 sets a distinctive challenge before us. "Keep on" loving.

How good to know that, as we keep on loving, love will find a way. Through love we will be a blessing, and find blessing.

"Do not forget to entertain strangers" Heb. 13:2-3. Hospitality was one of the most

important of ancient virtues. No hotels or motels dotted the first-century countryside. Tired and hungry people often appeared in town or at one's door, hoping for a place to stay.

There are distinct aspects to the Christian's relationships with others. We are to keep on loving Christian brothers. And we are to entertain strangers. Whether the people we meet are in or out of God's family, we are to show loving concern.

The writer went even further. The believer is to "remember those in prison." A person in prison isn't free to come to your church. He's not free to knock on your door. You have to take the initiative and search out the person in jail.

What's more, it is uncomfortable to take that initiative. When someone comes to your house, you're on your own turf. You are relatively secure. When you go beyond the places you normally frequent, you feel uncertain and unsure. There you can't insulate yourself from others' suffering. It's unpleasant at the very least.

But if we remember all that Hebrews tells about what God has done for us in Christ, we understand why we need to relate to brothers, strangers, and prisoners. Christ's gift of redemption is a love gift offered to every man. Christ's blood was shed for the stranger and the outcast as well as the brother. We need to go where Christ would go if He were here.

"Keep your lives free from the love of money" Heb. 13:4-6. It's easy to say. But how do we find contentment, when everything in our society shouts at us, insisting that we desire more?

The answer is, remember that in God you already possess everything.

The stock market can fall, and you will lose everything. Thieves can break in, and your possessions will disappear. The economy can crash and interest rates rise. In this world there simply is no security in wealth, or the things that money can buy. But when God is with you, and when you have His promise, "Never will I leave you," you enjoy the ultimate security.

God, the Creator of heaven and earth, the Owner of the cattle on a thousand hills, is your helper. There is nothing that can threaten the man or woman who walks hand in hand with the Lord.

"Remember your leaders" Heb. 13:7. What a fascinating way to put this. The writer didn't say, "Remember what your leaders taught." He didn't say "Remember what your leaders told you to do," even though they "spoke the Word of God to you." What the writer said was, "Consider the outcome of their way of life and imitate their faith."

We are to remember them, for their example teaches us something that their words cannot. As we consider the faith they live by, we learn to live by faith.

"Our hearts to be strengthened by grace" Heb. 13:9-14. The ceremonial foods on Old Testament altars symbolized God's sustaining grace. You and I, however, have no need of symbols. We have Christ Himself, who suffered to make us holy.

Going "outside the camp" indicates breaking out of Old Testament faith and ritual. There is nothing left for us inside them, for with their symbolism fulfilled in Christ, they are now empty shells. And so the author said, "Let us then go to Him."

If you want your heart to be strengthened by grace, follow this prescription. Go directly to Him.

"A sacrifice of praise" Heb. 13:15. Let's not come empty-handed to the Lord. And let's not rush into His presence, shouting out our needs and demanding attention without first paying attention to Him.

What we bring Christ as our sacrifice today is praise. And He is worthy to be praised.

Perhaps it's not surprising, but even in this we find that God thinks of us, even as He asks us to consider Him. When we do focus our attention on the Lord, and praise Him for His great attributes, we pray with much greater confidence. Rehearsing His praises strengthens our faith, and faith is essential to answered prayer.

"We have a clear conscience and desire to live honorably in every way" Heb. 13:18. If this is true of us, and reflects our heart's desire, we will do more than praise God. Our lives will bring Him praises.

"The God of peace" Heb. 13:20-21. These verses contain one of the most beautiful benedictions in the Old or New Testa-

ments. It is a "must memorize": a passage that can bring confidence as well as focus to your life.

▶DEVOTIONAL
Let Yourself Be Led
(Heb. 13:17)
It's almost hidden, tucked in with a number of other exhortations that the writer of Hebrews hurried to add as he closed his epistle. Most who do notice it seem to take it wrongly, as if the writer were encouraging a hierarchy of leaders, who had the right to demand obedience.

I don't believe the first readers had that impression for several reasons. In the Greek the phrase reads *peithesthe tois hegoumenois hyman kain hypeikete*. The Greek work *peithesthe* means, "Let yourselves be persuaded, or convinced." A fair English paraphrase would be, "Open your hearts to the persuasion of your leaders."

The word translated "leaders" here is used for rulers and princes, but originally meant "to lead or guide." The idea seems to be that spiritual leaders are to be those who have traveled the road of faith (see v. 7), and thus can serve as guides for others.

The single word *hypeikete* is rendered by the English phrase, "Submit to their authority." Originally it was used in classical Greek to describe soft and yielding substances. The root idea is not "give in," but "be disposed to yielding."

Putting this together the instruction focuses on the attitude that you and I are to maintain as we travel the Jesus road, led by others who have traveled on farther than we. What the first readers would have understood is this charge: "In your relationship with those who are your leaders and guides to godliness, be sure you maintain a yielding disposition, and remain open to their persuasion."

It's an approprirate exhortation here at the close of Hebrews. In Jesus we have a superior revelation, a superior High Priest, a better covenant, and a better faith. And we are called by God to experience, through faith, every blessing provided by the Son of God. How important, as we travel the Jesus road with others, to choose as leaders those who have gone on ahead—and to let ourselves be led.

Personal Application
Though responsible for your own choices in life, remain open, and let yourself be led by godly men and women.

Quotable
"The question, 'Who ought to be the boss?' is like asking, 'Who ought to be the tenor in the quartet?' Obviously, the man who can sing tenor."—Henry Ford

---

The Variety Reading Plan continues with JOB

James

INTRODUCTION

This letter was written by James, the brother of Jesus, who was a leader of the Jerusalem church (cf. Acts 15:13-29; Gal. 2:12). It may date from the late A.D. 40s, just after persecution scattered the members of the new movement (James 1:1; cf. Acts 8:1-3). If so, James would be the earliest of the New Testament letters.

James' focus was on how faith is to be expressed in a believer's life. He concentrated on such issues as facing trials, dealing with temptation, showing favoritism, taming the tongue, patience, and prayer. The book continues to serve as a reminder that our faith is also a way of life, and as a guide to putting our faith into practice.

OUTLINE OF CONTENTS

I. Practicing Faith . . . . James 1:1–2:13
II. Principles of Faith . . . . James 2:14-26
III. Problems for Faith . . . . James 3–4
IV. Prospects for Faith . . . . James 5

READING GUIDE (4 Days)

If hurried, you may read only the "core passage" in your Bible and the Devotional in each chapter of this Commentary.

Reading	*Chapters*	*Core passage*
340	1	1:13-18
341	2	2:14-26
342	3	3:1-6
343	4–5	4:1-10

James

DECEMBER 6 *Reading 340*
FACING TRIALS
James 1

> *"Blessed is the man who perseveres under trial, because when he has stood the test, he will receive the crown of life that God has promised to those who love Him" (James 1:12).*

Trials and temptations are God's invitation to overcome.

Biography: James, the brother of Jesus
The Gospels tell us that at first Jesus' brothers were skeptics (cf. John 7:5). After the Resurrection James, one of the brothers, became a leading figure in the Jerusalem church (cf. Acts 15:13-29; 21:17-25; Gal. 2:12). Church history calls him "James the Just," and also gives him the nickname "Camel knees," because the skin on his knees is supposed to have become calloused from spending so much time in prayer. According to Josephus, James was martyred in A.D. 62.

Overview
God provides the wisdom we need to face trials (1:1-8), and perspective on poverty (vv. 9-11). God does not tempt us to do evil; He gives only good gifts (vv. 12-18). God's Word can save us from anger and moral filth (vv. 19-22), but only if we practice it (vv. 23-25). The truly religious person cares for those in distress (vv. 26-27).

Understanding the Text
"To the twelve tribes scattered among the nations" James 1:1. The greeting helps us grasp the historical setting. James wrote when the church was young, composed of Jewish believers. He wrote after the stoning of Stephen (Acts 7), when severe persecution in Judea forced Christians to leave Jerusalem (8:1-3).

Understanding this setting helps us see why James is one of the least theological of the New Testament letters. Early Jewish Christians knew who Jesus is! They had heard Him teaching in the temple courts. They knew Lazarus, whom Jesus raised from the dead, personally. They might even have visited the empty tomb, and most likely were acquainted with 1 of the 500 witnesses who saw Christ after His resurrection (1 Cor. 15:6).

These scattered members of the Jerusalem church did not need to be taught who Jesus is: they knew the promised Messiah, the very Son of God!

And so James rightly assumed that his readers have faith in Christ, and moved immediately to his purpose for writing. In blunt, compelling prose James spoke about the lifestyle appropriate to those who know Jesus. And about the unique understanding faith brings to issues that are faced by all men, everywhere.

When we read this little book we can hear James—and the Holy Spirit through him—speak to us. For the lifestyle of faith is essentially the same for you and me as it was for those who first believed in Christ, nearly 2,000 years ago.

"Consider it pure joy, my brothers" James 1:2-4. The last thing we usually do when trials come is rejoice. The Greek word here, *peirasmos,* suggests a difficult situation; a painful pressure. We can understand why the Jerusalem Christians, forced to leave their homes and flee to foreign lands, would face "trials of many kinds." But to

"consider it pure joy"?

James explained. God uses trials to develop our character. The process may be painful, but the product, maturity, is worth it!

This is one of the unique things about faith. It shapes our perspective. It lets us look at even painful experiences in a new light. And when we look at trials from the perspective of Christian faith, and see the product God intends to produce in us, we truly will be able to rejoice.

"Ask God, who gives generously to all without finding fault" James 1:5-8. In Scripture "wisdom" is invariably the ability to apply knowledge in a real-life situation, and so make godly and right choices. The trouble is, some of us don't really know what the wise thing to do is. That may have been the complaint of these early Christians, who were frustrated in the face of their "many kinds of trials."

James' advice was, "Ask God." After all, God knows what's best for us to do. And, James said, unlike some human beings, God gives generously to all without finding fault. Our Sarah would understand how important that is. She came in the office yesterday and asked for help with a fourth-grade English exercise. I looked at it, and rather than tell her the answers, asked questions to help her figure out the answers for herself. Soon she flounced out in a huff. I'm sure she was quite disgusted with a daddy who wasn't at all generous in his answers, and seemed to her to find fault.

There's no need to worry about that kind of response when we ask God for guidance and direction. He gives it to us—generously. And without finding fault.

But there is one condition. We must "believe and not doubt." James, in going on to draw his picture of the "double-minded man," helps us understand just what he meant. If we ask God for wisdom, we must be prepared to act on what He shows us. We can't go to God and say, "Maybe I'd like to do it Your way, and maybe not." We must go in faith, and ask without any hesitation or mental reservation.

If you and I are willing to do God's will, He will show us what to do. But we can expect guidance only when we are ready to respond.

"Take pride in his high position" James 1:9-11. Christian faith also brings perspective to the inequities of life. In this world great gaps exist between rich and poor. And people evaluate themselves and others by the criterion of wealth. James suggested a way to balance things out. The poor man can take comfort in his high position in Christ. And the rich in his "low position."

The thought seems to be that present trials serve to remind the rich man how fleeting and transitory life is—and thus guard him against the pride and self-confidence that insulate so many wealthy people from reality and from God.

"When tempted" James 1:13. The word for "temptation" is also *peirasmos,* the same word we met as "trial" in verse 2. Its use in Scripture is shaped by an Old Testament concept expressed in the Hebrew word *nasah.* Pressure exerted on an individual brings a reaction, through which the character or commitment of the believer is demonstrated. Temptations are intended to reveal the quality of one's faith—not to trip a person up.

This is something we need to remember always. Our temptations are not evil. They are opportunities to display the beauty of Jesus and the reality of our faith (see DEVOTIONAL).

"Humbly accept the Word" James 1:19-21. When temptations arise we can surrender to our inner urge to react sinfully. Or we can surrender to the guidance of God's Word. James promises us that when we "humbly accept the Word" that Word will "save" us—from ourselves!

"Do not merely listen to the Word" James 1:22-25. There was another of those stories in the newspaper just last month. An older woman, alone, living in squalor, starved to death. And in her bedroom the police found hundreds of thousands of dollars stuffed in pillowcases.

What an image of the Christian, who has in Scripture all the resources needed for spiritual prosperity. But those resources will do us no good at all if we merely "listen" to the words of Scripture.

To be of any value, we must look "intently into the perfect law that gives freedom, and continues to do this, not forgetting what he has heard, but doing it."

Scripture blesses us. But only in doing it!

"Religion that God our Father accepts" James 1:26-27. Three of the five occurrences of the Greek word translated "religion" or "religious" are found here in these verses. The word portrays someone who performs the external acts of religion: who does what a religious person is expected to do.

On the one hand, James said that the religion of a person who acts religious but does not control his tongue is a sham. On the other, he said that true religion is not measured by attendance at church or ritual piety, but by acts of compassion intended to help those in distress. True religion, which expresses outwardly an honest inner faith, serves people in need.

▶DEVOTIONAL
Temptations Welcome
(James 1:13-18)

I remember my first visit to a fun house. It was on Coney Island, in New York. Inside, mirror after mirror reflected a distorted image of me and my date. In one mirror we looked short and squat, in another we were thin above the waist, and lumpy below. And though I rather liked the one that made me look slender, I wasn't sorry to leave.

Christians sometimes have a fun house view of temptations. Situations in which we feel tempted are looked at as hulking and dangerous, or as wildly appealing. Sometimes such a situation even seems like a trap, set by God to trip us up.

James wants us to leave our house of mirrors, and see temptations for what they are. In themselves, the situations we find ourselves in are neither evil, nor dangerous, nor appealing, nor traps. What transforms a situation into a temptation comes from within us: we are tempted by our thoughts and reactions, our feelings and desires. While the situation we find ourselves in may be from God, the temptation we feel in them is not.

James reminds us of something utterly important. God gives only "good and perfect gift[s]." God cannot be tempted by evil, nor does He tempt anyone. This means that the situation in which we feel temptation is itself good—even though the evil in us wants to twist it into something evil. In saying "every good and perfect gift is from above" James calls on us to radically change our perspective, and look at the situation we see as an evil as something wonderful and good.

But how can this be? Again, James explained. God, the Giver of good gifts, "Chose to give us birth through the Word of truth." There's more than "evil desire" in our hearts! There is a new and wonderful life, the very life of God, flowing through us now. And the same situation that as a temptation provides an opportunity for our evil desires to trip us up, provides an opportunity for the new life from God to enable us to stand! We don't have to give in to the evil impulses that entice us and would drag us into sin. God's new creation frees us to bring forth beauty, and good. In this wonderful sense, every situation and every trial, and even every temptation, is a good and perfect gift from our loving God.

Personal Application

Transform your temptations into triumphs by choosing to do good.

Quotable

"Why comes temptation but for man to meet
And master and make crouch beneath his feet,
And so be pedestaled in triumph?"
—Robert Browning

DECEMBER 7 *Reading 341*
FAITH DISPLAYED
James 2

> *"As the body without the spirit is dead, so faith without deeds is dead" (James 2:26).*

Biblical faith is alive and active.

Overview

Favoritism does not fit with love of neighbors (2:1-13). By its very nature faith must express itself in works: a faith without works is dead and useless (vv. 14-26).

Understanding the Text

"Don't show favoritism" James 2:1. The original says, "Stop showing favoritism!" James was dealing with a problem that already existed in believers' fellowships.

It's fascinating that James spoke of "our glorious Lord Jesus Christ." "Glory" in biblical times indicated a person's "weight" or "importance." In comparison with the overwhelming glory of Jesus, any differences in importance society assigns to one human being over another are insignificant indeed. Placing importance on people because of their wealth or social position, rather than to love each individual equally, is out of harmony with the nature of our faith.

We have to be as careful of showing favoritism today as in the first century. We sin if we elect the "successful" to church office, without consideration of spiritual qualities. We sin if we ignore the poor man who comes into our church, and fawn over the well-to-do. The church of Christ is a family of brothers. We are to live together as a family, freed of the discrimination and pride of position that corrupts society.

"A gold ring and fine clothes" James 2:2-4. Clothes make the man, the saying goes. It's true that clothing does symbolize social status in nearly every society. But symbols of status shouldn't determine the way you and I evaluate others.

That's what James was so upset about. The Christian community saw people with fine clothing as more important than the poor. In making this distinction, they became "judges with evil thoughts."

How are we to evaluate others? First of all as persons for whom Christ died, and thus important. No one is to be shunted aside or asked to "sit on the floor by my feet."

But other Christians are also vital members of the body of Christ, for each is gifted by the Spirit of God to minister to the rest. The poor may not add to our church budget. But the less able financially contribute just as much, and sometimes more, to our spiritual vitality.

"Chosen those who are poor . . . to be rich in faith" James 2:5. We've seen it over and over again throughout church history. The poor, with no hope but in God, seem far more rich in faith than the wealthy. You don't have to be poor to love God and look eagerly for Jesus to return. But there are times when it helps.

There's another thought here that is important. God has "chosen" the poor. He has looked at the neediest among the human family, and poured out His grace on them. What the poor lack now will be more than made up when we inherit the kingdom of God.

"Is it not the rich who are exploiting you?" James 2:6-7 In biblical times one major reason for the desperate condition of the poor was their exploitation by the rich. Those with social power could easily take advantage of the powerless—and they did.

How wrong it is for the church to find itself lining up against the powerless by showing favoritism to the wealthy. What God's people should do is to remind the wealthy of their obligation to the poor, not side with the rich.

"If you show favoritism, you sin" James 2:8-9. The Law that Jewish Christians rightly venerated commanded, "Love your neighbor." In no place was "neighbor" defined either as your friends, or as the rich among you. Neighbors are simply people: any and every person you may come in contact with. To show favoritism violated the ancient Law, for it redefined

"neighbor" and ruled out the poor.

Actually Old Testament Law carefully guarded against showing partiality to either the rich or poor. James didn't mention bias against the rich, simply because the people he wrote to would never discriminate against them!

The sins we don't commit do not require correction. It's the sins we do commit that are the problem.

"Is guilty of breaking all of it" James 2:10-11. I suppose that showing favoritism to the wealthy in our chruches seems like a "little" sin. After all, it's hardly in a class with adultery or robbery or murder.

But this wasn't James' view. To him, sin is sin. Breaking the Law is breaking the Law.

Imagine a woman who has made a special cake for her women's group, and warned the family, "Don't touch." Do you suppose, if she came home and found one tiny piece cut from the cake, that she wouldn't be upset? Of course she would be! The cake would no longer be whole.

We tend to divide up the Law into small pieces, and label one slice "adultery" and another slice "theft" and another slice "favoritism." We tend to see "favoritism" as a much smaller slice than most of the others. But James, like the woman who baked the party cake, saw the Law as a whole. When just one tiny slice has been cut out, the party cake was ruined. And when even one commandment of God has been violated, Law has been broken.

Never comfort yourself by saying, "Well, I've only committed a few little sins." Any sin violates the Law, and condemns us as lawbreakers. How important then that we seek to be holy in all that we do.

"Judged by the law that gives freedom" James 1:12-13. The "law that gives freedom" is the Christian law of love, which sums up in a single principle the rationale behind the rules and regulations of the Old Covenant. This law gives us freedom, because it helps us focus on the true meaning of all we do. We are not boxed in by rules, but released to live dynamic lives of love.

How serious then that early Christians were already violating that law, and showing favoritism to the rich. Rather than display the mercy they received when Christ welcomed them as they were, they withheld mercy from the poor in order to play up to the rich!

The judgment of Christians, here as elsewhere, carries no threat of hell. But the threat is real. In the day you and I stand before Christ to receive our rewards, if we have failed to display mercy, the record will be scoured clean, and we will have nothing to show for our years here on earth.

"The demons believe that—and shudder" James 2:14-19. We all know that there is faith, and then there is faith. One kind of faith says "I believe," and means, "I suppose it is true." The other kind of faith says, "I believe," and means, "I commit myself heart and soul to God." The devils believe in the first sense. Christians believe in the second.

It's easy for folks to get confused about which faith is meant when someone says "I believe." What James said was that there is a way to tell the difference. Faith that says, "I suppose" has no transforming power. This kind of faith produces no works. Faith that says, "I commit myself, heart and soul," is transforming faith. This kind of faith will always produce good works in the life of the man or woman who believes.

What kind of faith do you and I have in Christ? A look at our lives ought to tell.

"A person is justified by what he does and not by faith alone" James 2:20-26. The word "justified" is a legal term that can mean declared innocent, or proven innocent. We are justified by faith, in that on the basis of our faith God declares us innocent. But we are also justified by works, in that it is on the basis of our works that we are proven innocent. The proof of the pudding, the old saying goes, is in the eating. The proof of justification is in the good works that a true faith in Jesus Christ produces in our lives.

That's why James concluded, "Faith without deeds is dead." If your faith in Christ has made no difference in your way of life, then you have a dead and not a living faith in our Lord.

▶ **DEVOTIONAL**
That Kind of Faith
(James 2:14-26)
Luther called James an "epistle of straw," and was upset by what he viewed as its works/righteousness teaching. Really though, this critical segment of James does not teach works/righteousness, but asks a vitally important question. And that question is—what kind of faith do you have?

Abraham had a very real faith. We know that Scripture says, "Abraham believed God, and it was counted to him as righteousness" (v. 23). In one sense of that legal term "justified," Abraham was justified at that moment, declared innocent in the sight of God.

But Abraham was not proven righteous until he subsequently obeyed God's command and came to Mount Moriah, ready and willing to sacrifice his beloved son, Isaac. In that act he was justified in another vital legal sense: his innocence was displayed!

What James tells us is that the kind of faith that makes us righteous before God will also make us righteous before men. A true faith in God will transform us within, and the new person we have become will act out a relationship with God.

Even as Rahab showed that she had a true and saving faith in God by hiding the spies that had entered Jericho.

Even as you have shown that you have a true and saving faith in God by many of the choices you have made since you became a Christian.

What a joy it is to know that our faith is real. What a joy it is to have a faith that works.

Personal Application
Consider some of the ways your faith has expressed itself in your deeds.

Quotable
"You can say you are a Christian, but that doesn't make you one. The true Christian will give evidence of faith by a transformed life. The kind of faith that will take you to heaven is the kind of faith that will produce godliness in your life here and now."—Charles H. Robinson

DECEMBER 8 *Reading 342*
TAMING THE TONGUE
James 3

> *"If anyone is never at fault in what he says, he is a perfect man, able to keep his whole body in check" (James 3:2).*

What we say about others says more about us than about them.

Overview
Even teachers must watch their tongues (3:1-2), which must be tamed and harnessed (vv. 3-12). True wisdom is not ambitious but pure and peace-loving (vv. 13-18).

Understanding the Text
"We who teach will be judged more strictly" James 3:1. James wasn't thrilled and happy that so many Christians present themselves as authorities on the faith. It's certain that some who covet the title of "teacher" are spiritually immature, not realizing that a teacher bears a heavy responsiblity. Because teaching is such a responsibility, teachers will be judged "more strictly,"—that is, their lives will be more closely scrutinized.

Note that it is the teacher's life that is given close scrutiny. Why? Because Christianity is not just a set of beliefs, but life-changing truth. A person who communicates the Christian message must model what he or she teaches.

In some ways Christianity is like a style show. A new line of clothes is being introduced, and the designer parades models wearing that new line for potential customers to see. After all, you can't really tell how clothes will look, if they're just hanging on the rack.

Through the Gospel, God is introducing His new line to humanity. And folks can't tell how Christianity looks on the rack either.

Every believer is to model the faith in

daily life, and teachers have the greatest responsibility of all.

"We all stumble in many ways" James 3:2. James, possibly the most respected person in the Jerusalem church, included himself with the stumblers. From Scripture and early Christian literature we know that "stumble" indicates commission of sin. As we know from the stories of saints like King David, and from modern televangelisms' scandals, the great as well as ordinary believers remain vulnerable to sin.

One of the great mistakes you and I can make is to suppose that our faith is so strong we are invulnerable to temptation. We need to remain humble, and rely completely on the Lord. It's when we think that we stand that we are most likely to fall.

"He is a perfect man" James 3:2. The word "perfect" is again used in the sense of maturity, not sinlessness. To James, one mark of maturity was the wisdom to overcome our tendency to keep our mouths active when it would be best to keep them closed! A person who can control his or her tongue is well along the way to Christian maturity (see DEVOTIONAL).

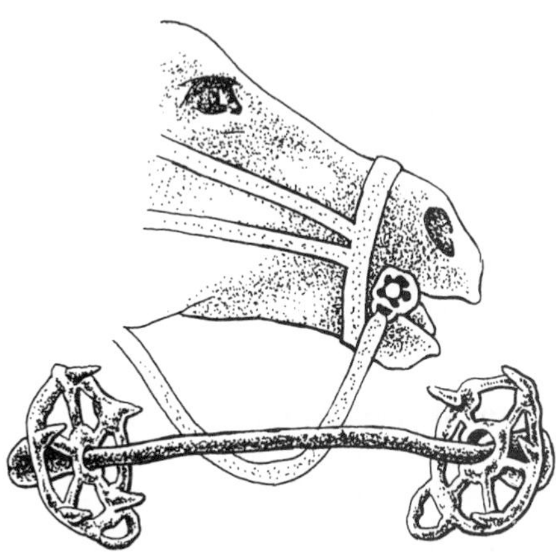

James 3:3-6 says that as the bit in a horse's mouth is used to guide it, so our tongue has a powerful influence on us—and on others! We Christians must be especially careful in our talk, because words have such great impact for good and for ill.

"The tongue also is a fire" James 3:6. James spoke of the tongue earlier. In 1:19 he wrote, "Everyone should be quick to listen, slow to speak, and slow to become angry." And in verse 26 he wrote, "If anyone considers himself religious and yet does not keep a tight rein on his tongue, he deceives himself and his religion is worthless." Talking without reflecting on what we say is not just foolish, it's harmful, to ourselves and to others.

As I frequently say to Sarah—without making much impression—"God gave us two ears and just one mouth. So we ought to listen at least twice as much as we talk."

"This should not be" James 3:7-12. James didn't get into theology the way Paul did in his letters. But James' comments reflect a deep understanding of both theology and our personal dilemma.

James was well aware that Christians have divided hearts. We want to please God. But there is always a twisted delight in sin that churns within us too. The divided nature of our hearts is shown most clearly in what we say, one moment expressing a godly thought, and the next a sinful sentiment.

You and I will never gain complete control over our tongues (v. 8). But let's remember that the new life God has given us is a pure spring, from which refreshing waters flow. Let's commit ourselves to refresh others with everything we say, and keep mean and hateful thoughts unsaid.

"Who is wise and understanding?" James 3:13 The word translated wise, *sophos,* was the technical Jewish term for a teacher or rabbi. James thus picked up the theme of verse 1 and reinforced it. A person who is qualified to be a teacher must "show it by his good life."

In an earlier time, Robert Ingersol traveled our country giving lectures that ridiculed Christianity. While on a train a well-meaning Christian spoke to Ingersol, sure that if he only understood the Gospel, he would be converted. Ingersol interrupted the Christian's rather halting explanation, and asked, "Is this what you mean?" He went on to explain the way of salvation with perfect clarity. The great unbeliever had the ability to explain Christian beliefs.

Let's not be impressed with how well another person can speak. God is impressed only with how well we live what we believe and teach.

"The wisdom that comes from heaven" James 3:14-18. So many Christians seem to delight in partisan defense of the truth. The more anger and selfish zeal, the better. Perhaps that's why so many appeals for contributions picture the sender as the one existing barrier to corruption of the faith by other Christians, who are cast as conscious or unwitting enemies of Christ.

It's nice to get appeal letters like this. I don't even have to pray about whether to give or not. I just toss them in the wastebasket. "Such 'wisdom,' " James tells us, "does not come down from heaven but is earthly, unspiritual, of the devil."

"The wisdom that comes from heaven" James 3:17-19. James' comments on wisdom are intended to promote self-examination. I may use the principles to evaluate appeals for contributions. But the really important use of these principles is to help me evaluate my own attitude in various situations.

If I sense "bitter envy" or "selfish ambition" in my heart, I'm in no condition spiritually to make a wise or godly decision. And I am definitely in no condition to teach others! But if my understanding and application of Scripture has led me to a grasp of truth that makes me "pure; then peace loving, considerate, submissive, full of mercy and good fruit, impartial and sincere," then—perhaps—God intends to use me to teach.

▶ DEVOTIONAL
Whip-Cracking Time
(James 3:1-6)

He walks confidently into the cage. Nervous lions and tigers perched on stools watch him with veiled eyes, now and then roaring, or slapping at him with outstretched paws. Then, when the lion tamer seems about to lose control, he cracks his whip, and the beasts settle back or perform their tricks on command. One of the most important things we need to learn as Christians is to recognize situations in which you and I need to crack the whip, and keep that wild and unruly tongue of ours under control. Here are a few typical ones.

One of your friends comes up and says breathlessly, "Did you hear about Sally Price? I understand she. . . . " You open your mouth, about to tell what you've heard—and it's whip-cracking time! Gossip is definitely a no-no.

A young friend comes to you for advice. You try to help him think the issue through, and give him some biblical perspective. You're not sure he's going to do what you think is wise, and you're about to tell him what he's got to decide—and realize it's whip-cracking time. You know he has to be responsible for his own decisions, and that you need to give him room to make them.

Your spouse has put the dishes in the wrong space in the cupboard, again! You know he's trying to help, but this is the umpteenth time he's gotten it wrong. You feel yourself getting angry, and you open your mouth—when you realize, it's whip-cracking time. Men! You smile, glad you've got a husband who's willing to at least try, and remember that men are constitutionally incapable of figuring out where dishes belong.

Everyone's so enthusiastic, you get carried away too. You're just about to commit yourself to going along with the gang when you stop. It's whip-cracking time. You'd better not make a decision till you have time to think about it!

These are just a few of the situations where that wild and unruly tongue is likely to carry us away before we even stop to think! Learning to recognize such situations, and taming our tongue, is vital for our growth toward Christian maturity.

Personal Application

Learn the value of remaining silent when you most want to talk.

Quotable

"The best time for you to hold your tongue is the time you feel you must say something or bust."—Josh Billings

DECEMBER 9 *Reading 343*
PROSPECTS OF FAITH
James 4–5

"Be patient, then, brothers, until the Lord's coming" (James 5:7).

Patience and prayer are resources that make present sufferings bearable.

Overview
Motives and attitudes affect prayer (4:1-6). Humility (vv. 7-10), nonjudgmentalism (vv. 11-12), and trust (vv. 13-17) in the face of injustice (5:1-6) are fitting for believers, as are patience (vv. 7-11) and simple honesty (v. 12). Till Jesus comes we have prayer (vv. 13-18), and each other (vv. 19-20).

Understanding the Text
"What causes fights and quarrels?" James 4:1-4 It's easy to blame circumstances and other people for conflicts. Sometimes others really are to blame: some folks are simply hostile, always looking for a chance to harm or to fight. But the first place to look when we feel hostility is within ourselves.

James' point is that we become hostile and quarrel with others when they seem a threat to something we want. You're more likely to fight with a rival for that promotion you want than with another coworker. Jealousy of another person will color the way you act toward them, and how you interpret their actions.

There's not much you or I can do if another person is determined to be hostile. But there's a lot we can do when we locate the reason for strife within ourselves. First, we can examine our motives, to see if they are in harmony with godliness. Second, we can determine not to use sinful means to reach even a good goal. Third, we can pray for the person(s) with whom we have problems, asking God to help them—and to help us care about them.

Finally, we can commit ourselves to the Lord, asking Him to give not what we want, but what we need.

"Friendship with the world is hatred toward God" James 4:4. Here as in John, the "world" (*kosmos*) is sinful human culture, with its complex web of motives, desires, and perceptions that are focused selfishly on life in the present universe. James says that we can't develop an affinity for the world's outlook on life and expect to stay friends with God, whose outlook is entirely different.

The warning reflects something James just said about prayer. Often our prayers go unanswered "because you ask with wrong motives, that you may spend what you get on your pleasures" (v. 3). It's not that God begrudges us a good time, or relaxation. But a self-centered attitude, in which a desire for personal gratification shoves concern for God and others aside, will not stimulate prayers that God is willing to answer.

This world isn't a toy shop. And God isn't an indulgent daddy who buys us anything we want. Especially when the toys that worldly people clamor for are hateful to God!

"God opposes the proud but gives grace to the humble" James 4:5-6. "Envy" is a bitter feeling aroused by another's possession of something we want, whether wealth, popularity, or success. James warns us that "the [human] spirit he caused to live in us tends toward envy." All those desires that battle in us and cause "fights and quarrels" are rooted in fallen human nature itself. Don't be surprised if you find yourself oriented to the world that is God's enemy!

But verse 4 emphasizes "chooses." Desire in itself is not sin. Sin is a choice motivated by the desire. How wonderful that God "gives us more grace," and so enables us to overcome our natural tendencies. And how important to humble ourselves before Him, and ask for that grace.

"Who are you to judge your neighbor?" James 4:11-12 James has called on us to live humble lives. Now he goes on to illustrate it. A person who is quick to judge another's actions is not humble. He or she has clambered up on the Judge's bench, grabbed God's gavel, and pushed Him aside. There is only one Lawgiver and Judge. Remember that when you feel tempted to judge others. You and I aren't

on the bench. We're standing before the bar, beside the very person whose case we've arrogantly determined to try!

"You are a mist that appears for a little while and then vanishes" James 4:13-17. The old school teacher always closed her letters to ex-students with "d.v." Finally one asked her what the initials meant. The answer was, *"dio volente"*—if God wills.

That's what James was saying here. Be sure to add d.v. to every plan you make, every intention you express. Arrogance looks ahead and assumes that the future is secure; that the business will prosper, that the body will remain healthy, that loved ones will always be there. The humble person lives with an awareness of man's frailty, and d.v. is the postscript wisely added to every plan.

"Your gold and silver are corroded" James 5:1-6. This powerful condemnation of rich exploiters of the poor seems almost out of place. Yet those who trust in riches, and who trample on the rights of others to pile up wealth, are the antithesis of the humble persons God calls on believers to become. These rich men epitomize the world system which James says is hostile to God. They value material things, which have no lasting worth. And they disdain human beings, whom God says have ultimate value. Their life on earth, which is one of "luxury and self-indulgence," serves only to prepare them for the "day of slaughter" (divine judgment).

Don't envy the rich and famous. They've got it much harder than you and I!

"The farmer waits for the land to yield its valuable crop" James 5:7. Humility does not pay immediate dividends. James was realistic about it. We might as well be realistic too. If you want to get ahead in this world, maybe the "fight and quarrel" approach will work better.

But Christians are like farmers. We plant in this life. And we expect to harvest in the next. And like farmers, the only thing we can do till harvesttime comes is to wait. Hopefully, with patience.

"The Lord's coming is near" James 5:8-11. To help us develop patience James said two things. First, "the Lord's coming is near." The wait won't be as long as it sometimes seems. And second, look back in Scripture for examples of those who bore suffering patiently, and in the end were more than repaid by God. You and I will be richly repaid too.

"Call the elders of the church to pray over him" James 5:13-18. The Old Testament tells of one king of Judah who became ill and died, in part because he relied "only" on physicians.

The particular word used of "oil" here indicates that James did recommend a medicinal use of olive oil in treating the sick. But he expected Christians to rely on God for healing, and to confidently anticipate prayer to be answered. Part of the healing process is confession of sins: the loss of fellowship with God eats at us and makes us more vulnerable to illness. Part of the healing process is prayer by church elders. In combining medical and spiritual treatment we express that dependence on God which is in accord with humility.

"Turns a sinner from the error of his ways" James 5:19-20. James closed with this final illustration of humility. The one who has sins needs to be humble, in order to confess his fault when confronted. And the one who confronts needs to be humble as well, lest an attitude of pride drive his brother farther away from the Lord.

What wonderful resources God has given us in each other as we wait, together, for the coming of our Lord.

▶DEVOTIONAL
Good Old American "How To" (James 4:1-10)

After years of ministering in churches and seminaries, I've noticed a peculiar thing. The first question we Americans ask is, "How?" Whether I'm teaching on Christian education or church leadership, whenever I introduce a concept, someone is bound to ask, "But how can we do that?" Not, "Is this right?" Not, "Is this biblical?" But, "How can we ever do THAT?"

It may be this is a human rather than just an American trait. I suspect that James was aware of the "how?" questions in his audience too. Certainly few passages of Scripture have as many active verbs strung together in such a few brief verses as 7-10, the "how to" section that caps James' discussion of conflict, unanswered prayers, and the need of grace to overcome our innate tendency to envy.

The first two verbs suggest general principles. We are to submit to God. And we are to resist the devil. Just HOW we do this is explained by the other verbs in these verses.

(1) We "come near" to God. Consciously fix your thoughts on the Lord, and approach Him in prayer. James promises us that when we do, God will bend down close to listen to us. This is always the first step in submission.

(2) We "wash . . . hands" and "purify . . . hearts." Approaching God as sinners, we confess our faults. And though we have been "double-minded" (cf. 1:8), we make a firm commitment to respond, whatever God may ask us to do.

(3) We change our "laughter to mourning." We reject the world system, with its false values. We realize that most of the things the world laughs about actually call for mourning, and most of the things the world finds joy in cast a pall of gloom over God's universe. Changing our laughter to mourning is exchanging lost man's perspective on life for God's, and evaluating all things by His standards.

(4) "And He will lift you up." When we humble ourselves in these ways before God, we sense His loving hands grip us, and lift us up. In humbling ourselves before God, more than our outlook on life is changed. We ourselves are changed! We are raised to newness of life.

Personal Application

Kneel, to be at, as well as on, God's side.

Quotable

"A meek man is not a human mouse with a sense of his own inferiority. Rather he may be in his mortal life as bold as a lion and as strong as Samson; but he has stopped being fooled about himself. He has accepted God's estimate of his own life. He knows he is as weak and helpless as God declared him to be, but paradoxically, he knows at the same time that he is in the sight of God of more importance than angels. In himself, nothing; in God, everything. That is his motto."—A.W. Tozer

The Variety Reading Plan continues with MATTHEW

1 Peter

INTRODUCTION

First Peter was written by the Apostle Peter from Rome, in the early A.D. 60s, to Christians in northern Asia Minor. This is a pastoral letter, written to encourage Christians who were already suffering persecution to live godly lives marked by submission and good works. Jesus is prominent in 1 Peter as our example of innocent suffering, and as the one whose resurrection to glory confirms our own hope. This powerful letter continues to inspire believers who suffer persecution for our common faith.

OUTLINE OF CONTENTS

READING GUIDE (3 Days)

If hurried, you may read only the "core passage" in your Bible and the Devotional in each chapter of this Commentary.

Reading	*Chapters*	*Core passage*
344	1	1:17-25
345	2–3	3:8-18
346	4–5	4:12-19

INTRODUCTION

[illegible]

OUTLINE OF CONTENTS

I. The Gift of Salvation ... 1 Peter 1:1-[illegible]
II. The Call to Submission ... [illegible]
III. [illegible] and Suffering ... 1 Peter [illegible]
IV. [illegible] ... [illegible]

READING GUIDE [illegible]

[illegible]

1 Peter

DECEMBER 10 *Reading 344*
SAVED FOR HOLINESS
1 Peter 1

"Just as He who called you is holy, so be holy in all you do; for it is written, 'Be holy, because I am holy'" (1 Peter 1:15).

After all, children are expected to resemble parents.

Biography: Peter
Peter was the acknowledged leader of the 12 disciples during Jesus' life on earth. He continued in that role in the earliest days of the church. We know more of Paul's later ministry: Paul's mission work is reported by Luke in the Book of Acts, and Paul contributed some 13 letters to our New Testament. Yet Peter continued to be a driving force in the Christian movement. Early tradition tells us that Mark was the "interpreter of Peter," and two of Peter's circulating letters of instruction are found in the New Testament. A firm tradition reports that Peter and Paul both died in Rome in the late A.D. 60s, victims of an outburst of persecution.

Overview
After a brief greeting (1:1-2), Peter praised God for the salvation of those who now suffered persecution (vv. 3-12). He urged them to remember the price of redemption and to live holy lives (vv. 13-25).

Understanding the Text
"Chosen according to the foreknowledge of God the Father" 1 Peter 1:1-2. By all accounts the first Christians in the Roman Empire were drawn from the lower, powerless classes. They were vulnerable to persecution; indeed, within 50 years of the writing of this letter Pliny, a Roman governor of Bythinia and Pontus, would summarily execute believers for merely admitting they were Christians! How vital then this greeting, which reminded the Christians of Asia Minor that they were "God's elect."

It makes little difference how people in our society view Christians. What counts is that we have worth and value in God's sight.

Remember that the Father chose you, the Spirit set you apart, and the Son cleansed you with His own blood. These reminders of God's love can comfort and support when any suffering comes.

"Through the resurrection of Jesus Christ" 1 Peter 1:3-4. In the first century many lower class citizens banded together in small associations or clubs, generally of some 50 to 200 members. The clubs provided an opportunity to socialize and a chance to gain recognition by holding office. Perhaps most important, club dues were used to meet burial expenses of members who died. Thus membership in a first-century *hataeria* offered benefits to its members in this life.

How different the church, the *ecclesia!* In God's great mercy He instilled life and hope into Christian believers, promising us life after death through Jesus' resurrection from the dead! The pagan club stored up treasure so funds would be available to bury its members. God stores up an eternal treasure that we inherit beyond death—and enjoy forevermore.

When suffering comes to us, as it surely must, what a joy to look ahead! For us, death is not an end, but a new beginning.

"Shielded by God's power until the coming of

the salvation" 1 Peter 1:5. Notice the double lock God has provided to ensure our future? He guards the treasures laid up for us by preserving them in heaven. And He guards us, by preserving us here on earth. Faith in Christ is the guarantee that God will keep us as His own till Christ comes back to take possession of us.

"You may have had to suffer grief in all kinds of trials" 1 Peter 1:6-9. Peter was particularly sensitive to the suffering Christians in many parts of the empire were already beginning to experience. In this brief letter *pascho,* the basic Greek word for suffering, is used 12 times. And several other Greek synonyms are also found. Peter hurt with the sufferers. But he also had words of encouragement for them—words that encourage us as well.

First, our suffering on earth is "for a little while." Even years, which seem so long to us, are less than an instant when compared to eternity.

Second, trials have great value in proving faith genuine. When Pliny questioned Christians, he released any who denied the faith by burning incense to statues of pagan gods. The "faith" of some has proven to be unreal under much less pressure. Yet the faith of millions more has proven real despite intense suffering, and this brings God "praise, glory and honor."

Third, trials give us a unique opportunity to experience our own salvation. When we take our stand for Jesus, we find ourselves "filled with an inexpressible and glorious joy" despite suffering and pain. This joy, a gift of the Holy Spirit, is evidence within that we are "receiving the goal of your faith, the salvation of your souls."

Those who suffer for Jesus' sake, and who remain true to Him, find an inner certainty that God is real, and that they are saved!

"The sufferings of Christ and the glories that would follow" 1 Peter 1:10-12. We Christians believe that glory follows and grows out of suffering. In the Old Testament era the prophets foresaw both the suffering and the glory of God's promised Messiah. But the "time and circumstances" involved remained a mystery.

The death and resurrection of Jesus resolved that mystery once and for all. Today we know that Christ came to suffer for us, returned to heaven, and that He will come again in glory. The "time" is suffering first, glory later.

This is also true for you and me. Suffering precedes glory. So if suffering comes, you and I can look beyond it and rejoice in what we know will follow.

Christ's coming even clarified the "circumstances." Suffering is to be expected as we live our lives on earth. And glory is to be expected when Jesus returns.

There is much in Old Testament prophecy that remains a mystery. But the link between suffering and glory, with the "time" and "circumstances," are revealed to us in Christ. Because we now understand them, we can't be devastated by suffering, as though something strange were happening to us. Instead we look beyond our suffering, and take comfort in the glory that will be ours when Jesus comes.

"Prepare your minds for action" 1 Peter 1:13-16. Knowing the pattern of suffering followed later by glory, you and I prepare to live godly lives. Peter tells us to get ready, to be self-controlled, to be obedient children, to be "holy in all you do." And he tells us one more vital thing. "Set your hope fully on the grace to be given you when Jesus Christ is revealed."

So often we "set our hope" on some near, immediate grace. "Lord, I'd like this new job." "Lord, heal my illness." "Lord, if only You'll let us get this home of our own." "Father, I know this marriage is just what I need to make me happy!" We may indeed get what we ask and hope for in this life. But any earthly prospect can disappoint, and every earthly possession be torn from our grasp. Only when we set our hope "fully" on the grace that will be ours when Jesus comes will we be immune to life's losses.

"Live your lives as strangers here in reverent fear" 1 Peter 1:17. When you and I take God seriously, we realize how fleeting our life on earth is. We enjoy God's good gifts. We feel the pain of our losses and our reverses of fortune. But somehow we're always aware that we are strangers

here. We don't quite belong. And we yearn for home.

This may be one of the most important values of suffering. If life on earth were a constant joy, why would we fix our hope fully on the grace to be brought to us at Jesus' return? If life on earth were without difficulty, how would we remain sensitive to our need for God? If life on earth were without trials or persecution, how would we be forced to choose between commitment to Christ and comfort or ease?

As Peter said, suffering does have value. It reveals the genuineness of our faith, and so brings praise to the Lord. And our experience of unexplained joy in our suffering assures us. We "are receiving the goal of your faith, the salvation of your souls" (v. 9).

▶DEVOTIONAL
Born Again
(1 Peter 1:17-25)

Jesus said it first: "You must be born again" (John 3:7). But Peter may give us the best explanation of the impact of being born again found in Scripture. In a brief, forceful passage he spoke of the cost of our new life, of its nature, and of the difference it makes.

The cost is "the precious blood of Christ," the price paid that we might have new life. By nature our new life is imperishable. And the difference it makes is as great as the difference between night and day.

J.B. Phillips helps us understand the nature of our new life in his paraphrase of 1 Peter 1:23: "God has given us His own indestructible heredity." Our new life is God's own life, fused permanently to our human personality. All flesh is like grass, perishable. Our new life from God is permanent, a source of endless existence and spiritual vitality.

You and I can't have God's life within us and be unchanged. Peter spoke of the difference as a purifying one. In obeying the truth (a phrase that simply means, in responding with faith to the Gospel message) we have "purified" ourselves. The old, selfish motives and desires that once ruled us no longer are our master. They have been replaced by that quality which most clearly revealed the heart of God Himself: love. Now, being born again "so that you have a sincere love for your brothers" we go on to "love one another deeply, from the heart."

Have you ever wondered if you really are born again? If you have God's heredity, you will begin to be like your Heavenly Father. And the mark of our family resemblance to Him is our growing capacity to love.

Personal Application

Do those who know you see the family resemblance to God?

Quotable

"By brothers, Christ made love the stairway that would enable all Christians to climb to heaven. Hold fast to it, therefore, in all sincerity, give one another practical proof of it, and by your progress in it, make your ascent together."—Fulgentius of Ruspe

DECEMBER 11 *Reading 345*
GOD LIVES
1 Peter 2–3

"Live such good lives among the pagans that, though they accuse you of doing wrong, they may see your good deeds and glorify God on the day He visits us" (1 Peter 2:12).

Christ is our model, who suffered for doing good.

Overview

Peter encouraged growth (2:1-3) in view of the believers' calling as God's chosen and holy people (vv. 4-10). Believers are to live good lives (vv. 11-12), and to submit to civil authorities (vv. 13-17), and masters (vv. 18-19), even when this involves suffering as Christ suffered (vv. 20-25).

Submission is appropriate in the home (3:1-7), and in the church (vv. 8-9). If a person should suffer for doing good, he should remember Christ's suffering (vv. 10-18) which led to our salvation (vv. 19-22).

Understanding the Text

"Crave pure spiritual milk" 1 Peter 2:1-3. In chapter 1 Peter reminded us that we have been born again and given God's own heredity. That first taste of grace should inspire us to grow! Our religious experience does not end when we are saved. It begins.

"Rejected by men but chosen by God and precious" 1 Peter 2:4-8. The values of God and of sinful man are in constant conflict. Pagan writers of the first centuries of our era, when they did mention Christ, scoffed at Him and His followers. Modern pagans have a similar attitude, though the name of Jesus is at least familiar. But to those of us who believe, the name of Jesus is precious.

These opposite reactions to Jesus have implications for what Peter was about to say concerning submission and suffering. The pagan, who disobeys the message of Jesus, will never sense the wisdom of submission, or the praiseworthiness of suffering. Only our faith in Jesus, with complete acceptance of the values affirmed by God, enables us to choose the path that Jesus Himself trod.

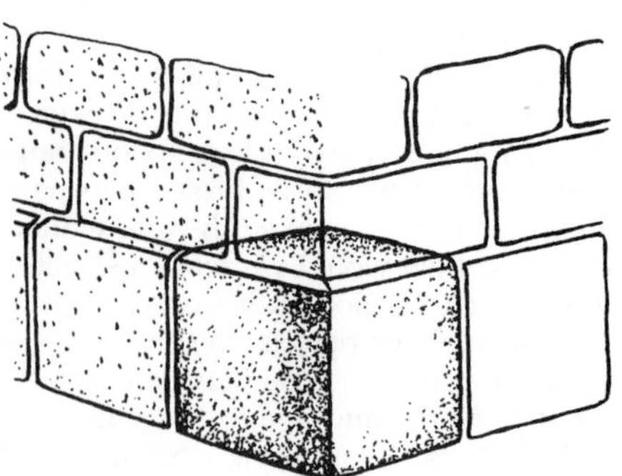

In ancient times the cornerstone was the anchor of a building's foundation. Psalm 118:22 and Isaiah 28:16 which refer to cornerstones were understood by Israel's rabbis to have messianic implications, and are applied to Jesus in the Gospels (Matt. 21:42; Mark 12:10; Luke 20:17), by Paul (Rom. 9:33; Eph. 2:20) and by Peter. Jesus is the foundation of our faith, and also of the church in which believers are living stones (1 Peter 2:4-7).

"A chosen people, a royal priesthood" 1 Peter 2:9-10. It is only right that we choose to live by God's values, for He has chosen us. In the Old Testament, priests officiated at sacrifices and led the worship of God. In first-century Roman culture, pagan priests also led worshipers in offering sacrifices and praises to the gods. In both contexts, it was considered a high honor to serve as a priest. So the imagery of a Christian royal priesthood was clear, and powerful. We who because of sin were not even a people of God have been called out of darkness, and given the highest position of all!

It is only appropriate then that we serve as priests, and "declare the praises" of Him who called us from darkness to light.

"Abstain from sinful desires" 1 Peter 2:11. Peter devoted the rest of this chapter and the beginning of the next to explaining how you and I "declare the praises" of God. Essentially, we declare God's praises more by the way we live than by what we say.

The first declaration of praise Peter mentioned was to "abstain from sinful desires." A better rendering suggests the

Christian is to make a clean break with the "natural impulses" which dominated us in the past. The adjective *sarkikon* found in this Greek phrase suggests that the impulses Peter had in mind are not impulses to gross sin so much as every person's natural inclination to preserve self and his material well-being. Peter warned that concern for the things of this world "war against your soul." The more we care about the material universe, the less we will care about the spiritual. The things of this life are to be of slight value to the Christian, whose hopes are fixed on Christ's return.

"Live such good lives among the pagans" 1 Peter 2:12. Freedom from care about those things which quite naturally concern pagans does not mean withdrawal from the world. Instead it means freedom to live good lives here and now. We can understand why. If you are primarily concerned about making your commission on a sale, you won't consider whether or not you treat your customer fairly. But if you are freed from "sinful desires," you will make your decisions solely on the basis of what is right and good.

Freed by our concern to please God only, we will be able to live such good lives that even those who slander us will be forced to acknowledge God's work in our lives, and thus glorify God when Jesus returns. "Every man has his price." Peter said that integrity is priceless—and Christians are to have it!

"Submit . . . to every authority instituted among men" 1 Peter 2:13-17. Early Christians were at times criticized as misfits who hated society, because they did not take part in worship at social events honoring the Emperor or state deities. Yet even pagan writers who mention early Christians confess that they were not rabble-rousers or political revolutionaries. In fact, the earliest description of Christians by Roman authorities reports an investigation which found that in Christian meetings they bound themselves by oath to live good lives, to pray for the Emperor, and to obey the authorities.

A life of submission to authorities will not prevent you from being slandered as a lawbreaker. But using your freedom to live as God's servant in human society will win you, and God, praise forevermore.

"Not only to those who are good and considerate" 1 Peter 2:18-21. It's easy to submit in a nation where laws are basically fair and rulers are honest men. Submission becomes difficult, however, when you are treated unfairly.

Yet Christians are called to submit even when treated unfairly. This is one of those areas of direct conflict: our "natural tendency" to shout out against submitting.

Peter remained adamant. The believer is to submit and bear "up under the pain of unjust suffering because he is conscious of God." Jesus walked the way of submission, and we are to follow in His steps.

Being a Christian is more challenging than it might seem. We discard the values of our society to adopt values that conflict with those things that come most naturally to us.

"He entrusted Himself to Him who judges justly" 1 Peter 2:22-25. Unfair treatment is most frustrating when we can't do anything about it. If we can take it to court—even "The People's Court" on TV—we may not win, but at least we will have done something. We will have tried to strike back.

But Peter called for submission even when we are treated unfairly. The slave with a harsh master isn't to run away, or land an uppercut to the master's jaw. He or she is simply to endure, and keep on doing what is good and right. It's fine to say this "is commendable before God" (v. 20). But that doesn't relieve the frustration of our helplessness.

Yet there is one thing we can do. And Peter tells us what. We can do what Jesus did when He suffered unjustly. Jesus didn't retaliate, or hurl insults back at those who insulted Him. What Jesus did was to entrust "Himself to Him who judges justly."

What a release this is. To simply trust ourselves to God, to remember that He judges justly, and leave our case in His hands.

Was Jesus wise to do so? Yes, for out of the innocent suffering of the Saviour God worked our salvation. The suffering of

Jesus was not meaningless; it was permitted that through it good might come. If we but commit ourselves into God's hands, we can be sure that not only justice will be done for us, but also that our suffering will serve the cause of grace.

"Your inner self, the unfading beauty of a gentle and quiet spirit" 1 Peter 3:1-6. The principle of submission, as a willingness to respond to others, applies in marriage as well as social and public life. Peter's call for wives to submit is not demeaning. He had uttered the same call to all believers, and shown that submission was the road chosen by Jesus. What Peter asked, and what the wise man will value, is the beautiful attitude of a woman willing to be responsive to her husband. Outward appearance fades. Inner beauty increases with the years.

"So that nothing will hinder your prayers" 1 Peter 3:7. A man with a responsive wife is greatly blessed—and responsible! Failure to be considerate and treat one's wife with respect, as a partner, blocks God's answers to our prayers.

"This water symbolizes baptism that now saves you also" 1 Peter 3:19-22. These verses have troubled Christians as much as any in the New Testament.

But all Peter was doing was drawing an analogy between the experience of Noah in the great Flood (Gen. 6–8), and the experience of the Christian. The floodwaters of judgment in that ancient day purged the old world of sin, and deposited Noah and his family on a fresh, new earth. This is like the baptism by which the Christian is united to Jesus (cf. 1 Cor. 12:13). In the judgment that Jesus experienced for us on the cross, all that was corrupt in us was cleansed. And in Jesus' resurrection, we were carried with Him into a new world. In the old world, Peter said, we lived our earthly life "for evil human desires" (1 Peter 4:2). Now, carried through the judgment in Christ, our ark of safety, we are to live the rest of our lives on earth for the will of God.

What an image of the Christian's experience. After our conversion we look around us, and realize that while the world remains the same, we ourselves are fresh and new! And we are called to live in newness of life!

▶DEVOTIONAL
When Bad Things Happen to Good People
(1 Peter 3:8-18)

The popular book with this title can be summed up in just a few words. Don't blame God. He's upset about it too!

Peter had a much more satisfying answer for us. He reminds us that God's eyes are on the righteous, so that in the normal course of affairs good things do happen to good people (vv. 8-13). But there are unusual cases when you do good, and suffer for it (v. 14). What's surprising is Peter's statement that if this happens to you, "you are blessed."

Before Peter explained, he told us how to react if something bad happens to us if we have been doing good (vv. 14b-17). Peter said: (1) don't be terrified or frightened; (2) remember that Jesus is Lord, and thus sovereign over all circumstances; (3) be ready to explain your positive outlook to those who are shocked you haven't crumbled; (4) keep a clear conscience; and (5) remember that if God chooses to let you suffer, it's much better to suffer for something you didn't do than to suffer for committing some sin!

It's nice to know how to react when something bad happens to us. But it doesn't explain why bad things happen. So Peter gave an answer; a reason why if this happens to you, "you are blessed." Peter reminds us that Jesus suffered innocently too. The evil men who deserved punishment unjustly caused Christ's death, and He suffered instead of them. Surely this is the greatest injustice, the clearest example of bad things happening to someone good, that history has ever known. And yet all this happened according to God's will. And through the injustice of Christ's suffering, our Lord brought us to God (v. 18).

Our amazingly wonderful and gracious God turned injustice into a means of grace and of blessing for all mankind.

This is God's Word to you and me when we suffer unjustly. The Lord hasn't forgotten or forsaken us. When bad things happen to God's good people we can be certain that He is personally involved!

And we can be sure that out of the evil God will bring some very real good.

Personal Application
Remember: bad things happen to good people that through suffering blessing may come.

Quotable
"O God, give us patience when the wicked hurt us. O how impatient and angry we are when we think ourselves unjustly slandered, reviled and hurt! Christ suffers strokes upon His cheek, the innocent for the guilty; yet we may not abide one rough word for His sake. O Lord, grant us virtue and patience, power and strength, that we may take all adversity with good will, and with a gentle mind overcome it. And if necessity and Your honour require us to speak, grant that we may do so with meekness and patience, that the truth and Your glory may be defended, and our patience and steadfast countinuance perceived."—Miles Coverdale

DECEMBER 12 *Reading 346*
LIFE IN GOD'S WILL
1 Peter 4–5

> *"Do not be surprised at the painful trial you are suffering, as though something strange were happening to you. But rejoice that you participate in the sufferings of Christ" (1 Peter 4:12-13).*

There is meaning in the suffering of the Christian.

Overview
Live for the will of God (4:1-6). Love and serve each other (vv. 7-11), and find joy in suffering as a Christian (vv. 12-19). Elders are to shepherd God's flock (5:1-4). All are to be humble and self-controlled (vv. 5-9), and look confidently to God (vv. 10-14).

Understanding the Text
"They think it strange that you do not plunge into the same flood of dissipation" 1 Peter 4:1-6. "But what do you do for fun?" is something we Christians hear quite often. At school teens ridicule Christian young people for not being involved in drinking and premarital sex. Coworkers can't understand why we don't stop off at the local bar after work to get drunk on Friday night. Manufacturers shout "censorship!" when Christians band together and pledge not to purchase products advertised on TV programs that exploit sex and violence. Just the other day I heard a radio ad for a TV daytime soap, which promised to provide "all of the sin, and none of the guilt" that listeners desire!

And yet so many non-Christians quite sincerely ask, "What do you do for fun?" They think it strange that we don't plunge with them into the same flood of dissipation. And, as Peter warned, they do more. They "heap abuse on you."

When that happens, remember that the world remains the same. But you are different. Adopt Christ's attitude and determine to be done with sin. No matter what the cost.

"They will have to give account" 1 Peter 4:5-6. Peter described Christ preaching through the Spirit to the "spirits in prison" who "disobeyed long ago" in the days of Noah (3:19-20). Genesis tells us that it took Noah 120 years to build the ark. All during that time the curious gathered, and Christ, speaking through Noah, preached to them. They paid no attention, however, and when the great Flood came, only Noah and his family entered the ark and were carried to safety.

Today too the Gospel is being preached "to those who are now [spiritually] dead." Their very failure to hear and respond demonstrates that God is right to judge and to condemn them.

The heart that is open to God will respond to the Gospel. Failure to trust in Jesus is evidence of a hardened heart, and of divine judgment to come.

"Above all, love each other deeply" 1 Peter 4:7-10. The more hostile the world is to us, the greater our need for support and en-

couragement. The antagonism of outsiders has the effect of bringing us closer and closer to others who think and feel as we do.

Peter pictured the Christian community as a close, warm, and supportive fellowship, where we can find encouragement and strength to get on with life in the grim outside world. While we may not appreciate the importance of Christian fellowship until persecution or suffering comes, support from other believers is important at all times. We need each other's love to reassure us of our worth and of God's forgiveness. We need each other's gifts to help us grow. And we need to exercise our gifts in ministry to others.

If you are missing the warmth of fellowship with other Christians, you lack something essential to your growth and wellbeing.

"Do it with the strength God provides" 1 Peter 4:11. It's not easy, this living by "the will of God" (v. 2). When Pete's mother called Marti, and asked her to come over, Marti hesitated. At the Bible study that week Pete's mom had stayed behind and talked to her, pouring out the pain caused by her husband, who said he wanted to stay married but insisted on keeping a mistress too. The talk had helped. But now Pete's mom was feeling desperate again, and wanted Marti to come over to talk and pray with her.

Marti put down the phone. She wanted to help. But she was afraid to go too. She had always been like that: honestly wanting to help, but fearful of taking any initiative. Like the time she'd taught the women's Bible study. Afterward she was asked to teach again and again. But she never would do it. She wanted to. But the thought of taking responsibility made her anxious and upset.

We may feel fearful when opportunities to minister come. But we can't make Marti's choice, and draw back. We have to "do it with the strength God provides."

That verse is not only a challenge, but also a promise. When you and I do step out to minister, God will provide the strength we need.

Don't expect the strength while you're standing there, struggling to decide. Decide to do God's will, and expect the strength to be provided when you need it.

"Not lording it over those entrusted to you" 1 Peter 5:1-4. Leaders are servants, not masters. This New Testament theme is reaffirmed here, with a word about leaders' motives. Leaders must want to serve; indeed, they must be willing, and even "eager to serve." People have many different motives for wanting to be leaders. But a passionate desire to serve others is a basic qualification for Christian leadership.

"Humble yourselves" 1 Peter 5:5-6. Here as earlier in this letter submission is viewed as a virtue. But never mistake either submission or humility as a weakness. Only the truly strong can control their natural desire to dominate rather than to submit; to appear powerful rather than pliant.

"Cast all your anxiety on Him" 1 Peter 5:7. Old and New Testaments both have much to say about anxiety. But this brief verse effectively sums it all up. Let God worry about you, because after all, He does care for you.

If you and I know that God is watching out for us, we have nothing left to worry about, and can get on with the business of living by the will of God.

"After you have suffered a little while" 1 Peter 5:10-11. It's hard not to be anxious when we're suffering. Leaving everything to God then seems difficult indeed. But Peter has a promise that will help. Suffering lasts only for a little while. God will restore you, and make you strong. And in His time will call you up to heaven to share in His own eternal glory. Whatever today's pain, we have the promise of strength, and the prospect of glory—forever.

▶ DEVOTIONAL
We Share
(1 Peter 4:12-19)

Remember the story of the little red hen? She wanted to bake bread, but none of the barnyard animals would help. So she did it herself. Of course, when the bread was baked, they all gathered around wanting a piece. But the little red hen ate it all herself.

The children's story is a commentary on

human rather than animal nature. We're not enthusiastic about the work. But we sure like to reap the benefits!

In a way, this is true of Christians. We tend to look foward to heaven, and plan to enjoy eternity there. But we're not too wild about experiencing any suffering down here. Yet Peter reminds us that suffering and glory are bound together inseparably. It was Jesus' total dedication to doing the will of God, even though that will led Him to Calvary, that vaulted Him to glory. The Resurrection was made possible by the Cross.

So Peter tells us not to be surprised if we too suffer painful things. Suffering isn't strange. It's natural for the person who participates in Christ's suffering. Jesus' commitment to do God's will brought Him into conflict with this world. If we share that commitment, we will come into conflict with the world and suffer too.

You and I aren't to go out of our way to find suffering. We are simply to commit ourselves fully to God, and continue to do good. Then, if suffering comes, we can praise God indeed! Suffering as Christians, and for Christ, will mean glory for us when His glory is fully revealed.

Personal Application

Bearing Christ's name may mean carrying His cross.

Quotable

"The worst part of martyrdom is not the last agonizing moment; it is the wearing, daily steadfastness. Men who can make up their minds to hold out against the torture of an hour have sunk under the weariness and the harassment of small prolonged vexations. There are many a Christian bereaved and stricken in the best hopes of life. For such a one to say quietly, 'Father, not as I will, but as Thou wilt,' is to be a martyr."—F.W. Robertson

---

The Variety Reading Plan continues with 2 PETER

2 Peter

INTRODUCTION

Peter's first letter dealt with persecution from outsiders. This second letter concerns dangers within the church itself, from false teachers and those who fail to take the Scriptures seriously.

The great value of 2 Peter is found in the apostle's call to resist false teaching by growth in godliness, while we await the promised return of Jesus Christ.

OUTLINE OF CONTENTS

READING GUIDE (3 Days)

If hurried, you may read only the "core passage" in your Bible and the Devotional in each chapter of this Commentary.

Reading	*Chapters*	*Core passage*
347	1	1:12-21
348	2	2:1-3, 17-22
349	3	3:10-18

2 Peter

DECEMBER 13 *Reading 347*
CHRISTIAN QUALITIES
2 Peter 1

> *"If you possess these qualities in increasing measure, they will keep you from being ineffective and unproductive in your knowledge of our Lord Jesus Christ" (2 Peter 1:8).*

It is more important to live the faith than to defend it.

Overview
God gives grace and peace through Christ (1:1-2). His gift of the divine nature (vv. 3-4) makes it possible for us to grow—which we must do (vv. 5-11). We remain confident because of the eyewitness testimony of the Apostles (vv. 12-18), and of God's prophetic Word (vv. 19-21).

Understanding the Text
"Through the righteousness of our God" 2 Peter 1:1. Usually we think of being saved by God's grace. Peter, like Paul in Romans 1, invites us to think of salvation in light of the righteousness of God.

Saving us was the right thing for God to do, not because He was obligated to us, but because He was true to Himself in expressing saving love. But God had to save us in the right way. There could be no cheap redemption. So God paid the price to set us free and give us new life. We can thank the fact that God is righteous as well as the fact that He is gracious for the salvation we now enjoy.

This is a good thing for us to remember. There are times when we want to do the right thing, but may draw back from paying the price. Remembering what God has done for us may free us to act righteously toward others.

"Grace and peace . . . in abundance" 2 Peter 1:2. When Peter expressed this desire he specified the source: grace and peace come "through the knowledge of God and of Jesus our Lord." Peter didn't mean knowing about God. The Greek word indicates "full knowledge": a knowledge of God personally, experientially. Staying close to the Lord brings each of us grace and peace.

"Everything we need for life and godliness" 2 Peter 1:3-4. Through believing the promise of the Gospel, God implants His own divine nature in us, and we experience a flood of spiritual power. In knowing Christ, we have everything we need to "escape the corruption in the world" that is caused by "evil desires."

The one thing a Christian is not is powerless. But we may not realize the nature of God's power, or why it is given to us. We are not given power to succeed in business, or power to become popular. We are given power to live godly lives.

If you and I concentrate on living godly lives, we will find we have power aplenty.

"Make every effort" 2 Peter 1:5-9. God provides the power that enables us to live a victorious Christian life. But you and I must make every effort.

We have an exercise bicycle in our family room. It's not for me—I only enjoy competitive exercise, like tennis or basketball. It belongs to Sue. And that exercise bike really helps. It helps her build stamina, and slims her thighs. But it does no good at all unless she puts in her daily effort.

Our relationship with God is something like this. The resource we need is always there for us. But to profit from what God has provided, you and I have to put in the effort.

"Add to your faith" 2 Peter 1:5-8. The word translated "add" means to make abundant provision for. Making every effort to live a Christian life means we begin with faith—but we do not stop there. We go on, and concentrate on developing the following Christian virtues:

Goodness. The Greek word is *arete,* not one of the more familiar words, rendered "good." *Arete* is usually translated excellence. It refers to the full development of our potential; to achievement in a chosen sphere of action. We are called to excel as Christians, not to live "average" lives.

Knowledge. The knowledge that we add to faith is a knowledge of God's will. The "superior knowledge" claimed by the false teachers Peter was about to discuss was empty and meaningless. What counts is understanding what God wants from us, and doing it.

Self-control. In Scripture this virtue is contrasted to excesses—to greed, to surrender to sexual passions. The Christian who understands the will of God is to discipline himself or herself to do it.

Perseverance. The word in Scripture suggests a distinctive view of time. The Christian takes the long view, and realizes that God does not work by man's timetable. However discouraging the circumstances, the Christian is able to keep on, faithfully doing the Lord's will.

Godliness. This Greek word for piety suggests a constant awareness of God and a commitment to doing things that are appropriate to one devoted to Him.

Brotherly kindness and love. The two words denote affection, and self-sacrifice. We learn to care about others and their welfare. And we are willing to help them, even at personal cost.

These qualities "in increasing measure" will keep us from being "ineffective and unproductive."

"If anyone does not have them" 2 Peter 1:9. My daughter, Joy, now 28, was brain damaged at birth. She has developed into a tall, attractive girl, physically. But mentally she'll never grow beyond a first- or second-grade level. All her life she will have to be cared for in a community like the one she now lives in, in Arizona.

Some Christians are like Joy. They remain "ineffective and unproductive." The placental separation that left my daughter without oxygen near the moment of birth, and damaged her irreparably, was a tragedy that only eternity will undo. But how much greater a tragedy it is when Christians, who have the potential to become mature, continue in spiritual babyhood.

You and I don't need to remain in spiritual infancy. All we need to do is to "make every effort" to live the quality Christian life Peter described.

"Make your calling and election sure" 2 Peter 1:10-11. The Emperor Trajan instructed governor Pliny to give Christians a chance to repent. If they denied Christ, and burned incense to statues of the ancient Roman gods, they were to go free.

In the early centuries of Christianity some did associate with the new faith only for a time, and then wandered away. Others denied the faith under persecution. Just associating with Christians, and even calling oneself a Christian, was no guarantee a person was one of the elect.

Even though the whole notion of election remains a mystery, there is a way you and I can make sure we are numbered among God's chosen people. That is to "do these things" that Peter has described. As we grow in grace, and in effectiveness as Christians, we "will never fall," and will "receive a rich welcome into the eternal kingdom" of Jesus.

▶DEVOTIONAL
Make Sure
(2 Peter 1:12-21)

Before you toss an anchor overboard, you'd better make sure of two things. Is the rope secured to the anchor? And is the other end of the line secured to your boat?

Peter's first chapter is something like this. His first 11 verses encourage us to make sure that our own lives are tightly entwined with Christian faith. And then verses 12 through 21 remind us how trustworthy the faith itself is.

Peter himself had no doubts at all. He spent years with Jesus. He was one of the "eyewitnesses of His majesty" when that was displayed on the Mount of Transfiguration (vv. 16-18). Even more, the words of the ancient prophets of Israel are in harmony with the vision of Jesus glorified (v. 19). Together the ancient words, given by God Himself, and the Transformation event, are irrefutable proof that a new day will dawn. Jesus will return for us, and all our hopes and dreams will surely be fulfilled.

Personal Application

There is more reason to doubt that dawn will come tomorrow than to question Jesus' return.

Quotable

People: Lamb of God, holy Lord God, hear our prayer of need; have mercy on us.
Leader: From the sin of not believing in you,
From all sins of flesh and spirit,
From all self-righteousness,
From all lukewarmness and drunkenness,
From all indifference to your wounds and death.
People: Defend us, dear Lord God. There is nothing in us but poverty. By your blood, death, and suffering give us a warm, completely submissive heart.
Leader: O Immanuel, Savior of the World
People: Make yourself known to us!
Leader: By your holy incarnation and birth
People: Make us love our humanity!
Leader: By your poverty and servanthood,
People: Teach us to be lowly in this world!
Leader: By your correct understanding of the Scripture
People: Make firm the word of truth in us.
—Nickolaus von Zinzendorf

DECEMBER 14 *Reading 348*
FALSE TEACHERS
2 Peter 2

"Many will follow their shameful ways and will bring the way of truth into disrepute" (2 Peter 2:2).

False doctrine produces a perverted lifestlye.

Background

False teachers. The later epistles of the New Testament, 2 Peter, 2 Timothy, and Jude, all describe and warn against false teachers. In the early decades the church was threatened by Judaizers, who attempted to bring Christians under the yoke of Mosaic Law. But by the mid 60s a different breed of false teacher emerged. These men treated the faith as a "philosophy."

In the first century a number of philosophies competed for popularity. Each had its own doctrines, and each emphasized a lifestyle in keeping with its basic tenents. Street teachers sought to attract adherents by giving lectures on how to live one's life, solve personal problems, and find meaning in life. From descriptions in 2 Peter and Jude particularly, it seems that the false teachers that threatened the church from within were the cultural equivalent of these traveling philosophers. But they twisted Christian doctrine, and taught a way of life that was antagonistic to godliness.

It may well be that some of the gross descriptions of Christian practices found in second century Roman writers reflects the actual behavior of some who falsely called themselves Christians, and followed false teachers like those Peter described here!

False teachers remain a threat to the Christian church. And 2 Peter 2 remains a source of insight into their teaching, their character, and their appeal.

Overview

False teachers who exploit believers (2:1-3) face certain judgment (vv. 4-10). They are marked by arrogance (vv. 11-12) and immorality (vv. 13-17), and by teaching that appeals to man's sinful desires (vv. 18-22).

Understanding the Text

"There will be false teachers among you" 2 Peter 2:1. It's not, "there may be." It's "there will be."

We can count on it today as well as in Peter's time. Within the broad framework of what is called Christendom, there are cults and churches whose doctrines are anti-Christian. Some who stand in the pulpits of churches which were historically Christian are false teachers too. Peter said false teachers introduce "destructive heresies," meaning that they lead adherents to destruction.

This first verse gives us a simple doctrinal test. The false teacher leads followers to destruction because he denies "the sovereign Lord who bought them." The earliest heresies redefined Jesus. In some systems He was a lower angel. In some He was a man raised to Deity at His baptism, or at His resurrection. In some systems Jesus only appeared to be human, but was in fact a spiritual "projection." But Scripture clearly presents Jesus Christ as God the Son, the sovereign Lord of the universe come in the flesh, born a human being that through the union of God and man He might purchase our redemption.

Most modern heresies still stumble over Jesus. Any who deny the full deity and actual humanity of Jesus Christ are false teachers. And what they teach is destructive heresy.

"Many will follow their shameful ways" 2 Peter 2:2. This is a second basic characteristic of false teachers and false teaching. It produces "shameful ways." It's a familiar saying now, that you can tell a tree by its fruit. You can tell false teaching from sound doctrine by its fruit too (see DEVOTIONAL).

"In their greed these teachers will exploit you" 2 Peter 2:3. The third characteristic of false teachers is greed. Peter had described godly leaders in his first letter: they are shepherds caring for God's flock, not greedy for money but eager to serve (1 Peter 5:1-4). In contrast false teachers serve for money, and are motivated by it.

We ought not be too quick to label someone a "false teacher" on the basis of his or her income. The issue here is one of motive and exploitation. The false teacher is greedy. A false teacher exploits, lies, and diverts money given for ministry to personal use.

While the greed of a few notorious Christian leaders is regularly exposed by the media, we can thank God for the many thousands who minister today, despite low pay and poor benefits, out of love for God and His people.

"If God did not spare" 2 Peter 2:4-10. Peter looked back into sacred history and found examples that drove home his point. False teachers will surely creep in to corrupt the church. But God knows how to save the godly, and "hold the unrighteous for the day of judgment."

Peter carefully selected his illustrations. The presence of false teachers in the church is serious. But it is not disastrous! So we need not panic. God will protect the righteous man. And God will punish the false teacher.

Peter's comments direct us to the best way that we can protect ourselves and others from false teachers. We focus, as did Noah and Lot, on preaching and living righteousness. Commitment to live a godly life, even when others live "filthy lives" around us, will guard us from going astray.

"Creatures of instinct" 2 Peter 2:11-12. Both Testaments use the metaphor of "brute beasts" and "creatures of instinct" to describe unbelievers who are actively hostile to God. They have completely abandoned the spiritual quest, and chosen to live like animals, in that this present world alone exists for them.

We human beings can choose to live like animals. We can seek to satisfy every craving, without standing in judgment on whether our desires or actions are morally right. But those who choose to live like mere animals by that choice determine their fate. They doom themselves to perish.

"Reveling in their pleasures" 2 Peter 2:13-16. Peter went on to describe the beast-like life that some human beings live. Man's present instincts reflect the corruption of

our nature by sin, and thus are no trustworthy guide to godly living. Man's corrupt instincts call for pleasures that stimulate and deaden, as modern drugs and alcohol (v. 13). Man's corrupt instincts lead to adultery (v. 14), and are expressed in a greed that wrongfully deprives others (v. 14). Peter's reference to Balaam was sarcastic. That prophet, moved by a passion for money, acted on instinct—when a mere animal, his donkey, knew better!

Don't listen to folks who tell you that since certain desires are "natural" they must be all right. What most men do by instinct is wrong. As Christians, we're called to judge our instincts, and to choose what is right.

"They promise them freedom, while they themselves are slaves of depravity" 2 Peter 2:17-29. The greatest slavery we can experience is slavery to our passions. "I can't help it!" has been the cry of those addicted to drink, drugs, and sexual depravities down through the ages. The surest road to misery is to do just what you want, whenever you want to do it. Soon you find that you no longer want what you do—but you are unable to help yourself. That, slavery to one's own depravity, is the most terrible slavery of all.

"It would have been better" 2 Peter 2:20-22. The two proverbs quoted in verse 22 explain Peter's comment. Each describes an animal which behaves according to its nature. Just so the individual who is introduced into the Christian community and makes a profession without experiencing regeneration. He sees in the holiness of God's people what it means to escape the corruption that is in the world through lust. But his unconverted nature causes him to revert to his old ways. Such a person might better never have been exposed to godliness. In turning his back on God his condemnation will be greater than before.

You can't be a "halfway" Christian, or a "social believer." Ulimately you will choose to go all the way, in full commitment to Jesus. Or your natural instincts will win out, and you'll turn away from the faith entirely. If you're in that halfway state, go the whole way, quickly. It's better to never have known the way, than to know it and turn back.

▶ DEVOTIONAL
The Way of the Cross
(2 Peter 2:1-3, 17-22)

One early Roman commentator on Christianity, Galen (born around A.D. 130) had no use for Christian doctrine. In one of his medical treatises he took time out to discuss, and reject, Moses' treatment of the Creation. But Galen was impressed that Christians, "in self-discipline and self-control in matters of food and drink, and in their keen pursuit of justice, have attained a pitch not inferior to that of genuine philosophers."

This may have been the most impressive thing about the early Christians to the pagans of their day. Certainly the educated pagan was put off by the Christian emphasis on faith. The Christian doctrine of Creation and especially of Resurrection seemed utter nonsense to those brought up on the idea that matter was eternal, and that God was subject to and not above natural law. And the pagans fiercely resented the Christian's refusal to participate in public religious observance. Such exclusiveness seemed tantamount to hatred of mankind itself, for the welfare of the state depended on expressing piety toward the gods.

But then, there was that virtuous life. How could such ordinary, mostly uneducated people attain the self-discipline and virtue thought to be reachable only by the philosopher who dedicated his life to study and self-mastery?

False teaching has no such power to help its adherents attain godliness. In fact, one of the characteristics of false teaching is that it appeals to man's lower nature. It promises freedom rather than demanding self-control. It offers pleasures rather than calling for commitment. And many a true Christian has, through the de-emphasis of godliness, been led astray by teachers whose emphasis is utterly, tragically false.

So watch out if a teacher promises you "freedom"—and means that you will be able to do whatever you want. And watch out if a teacher promises riches and ease! Jesus has never led His followers to Disneyland. The Jesus road winds off, over the hills, and there, ahead, you can glimpse Calvary.

Personal Application
Christ brings us both comfort and cross.

Quotable
"Almighty God, whose most dear Son went not up to joy but first He suffered pain, and entered not into glory before He was crucified; mercifully grant that we, walking in the way of the cross, may find it none other than the way of life and peace; through the same Jesus Christ our Lord."—Book of Common Prayer

DECEMBER 15 *Reading 349*
THE DAY OF THE LORD
2 Peter 3

"The heavens will disappear with a roar; the elements will be destroyed by fire, and the earth and everything in it will be laid bare" (2 Peter 3:10).

Seek solid joys and lasting pleasures.

Background
History's end. Both Testaments speak of a final judgment when this present heaven and earth will be destroyed. Isaiah said this present universe will wear out like a garment and vanish like smoke (51:6). Paul pictured Christ returning "in blazing fire" (2 Thes. 1:7). And Peter in this chapter gave a powerful description of the universe being reduced to its constituent atoms.

The biblical picture of a universe with a distinct beginning, and a distinct ending, was absolutely strange in the first century. The philosophers believed that matter was eternal, shaped by a craftsman god who was himself subject to natural law. A God who could create the universe from nothing, and dissolve it at will, was beyond their comprehension. The world was, always had been, and always would be. And human beings once dead were gone.

The spirit of our age is not all that different. Scientists speak of a beginning of our universe, but deny a Creator. All that exists is explained by evolution. And whatever the future holds, no God will intrude in the orderly process of the ages to put an end to matter, and then to raise the dead and judge them. First-century intellectuals scoffed in the name of philosophy. Two thousand years later our intellectuals scoff in the name of science. But both are wrong. For God is. And the material universe is not eternal, but destined for destruction. Soon.

This is the message of 2 Peter 3. This, and the kind of life to be lived by believers who know that they, and every other human being, will continue to exist long after our world comes to an end.

Overview
Trust the Prophets and Apostles (3:1-2) despite scoffers who ridicule the Second Coming (vv. 3-4) and deliberately ignore past divine judgment (vv. 5-7). God's timing differs from ours (vv. 8-9), but this present world will surely be destroyed (vv. 10-13). So be godly and grow in grace (vv. 14-18).

Understanding the Text
"Wholesome thinking" 2 Peter 3:1-2. Peter's two letters are designed to stimulate the reader to a "pure disposition"—an "uncontaminated understanding" of faith and life.

This is particularly important because false teachers attack the faith from within, and scoffers from without. Each, if their doctrines are followed, lead to immorality and undisciplined living. The false teachers appeal to sinful desires, and justify license as freedom. The scoffers, by removing the threat of judgment, drain away that awe of God which promotes godliness.

There is really only one antidote that can protect us from error within and outside the faith. That is the words spoken in the past by prophets and by Christ, as faithfully reported by His Apostles. Complete trust in the Word of God, and an intimate familiarity with it, can guard us against every kind of error.

"Scoffers will come" 2 Peter 3:3. There is a

fascinating parallel between scoffers and false teachers. Each follows "their own evil desires." Each resists truth, not so much out of intellectual conviction, but to guard against conviction of sin.

One of my books is on Creationism. *It Couldn't Just Happen* (Word, Inc.) explores fallacies in the popular notion of evolution, and explains some of the ways in which scientific discoveries point toward Creation of the universe, and of animal and human life. When my wife offered to contribute a copy to the library in the high school where she teaches, it was rejected. Creationism isn't "scientific" and might confuse students. Yet the same library contains books that ridicule Creationism, novels that vividly describe illicit sex, and books that present abortion and homosexuality in a positive light. How fascinating that to complain about such books would raise immediate cries of "Censorship!" But rejecting a book that supports a biblical position—a book which, by the way, won a Gold Medallion at Christian Booksellers as the best book for young people of 1988—is fine, because it would be "confusing" and "unscientific."

Scoffers will continue to scoff. But the underlying reason is not the respectability of our beliefs, but bias against a faith that calls men to take God seriously, and to curb sinful human desires.

"Everything goes on as it has from the beginning of Creation" 2 Peter 3:4. In science this concept is called "uniformitarianism." It assumes that everything that currently exists can be explained by processes now taking place. Given enough time, the shape of continents, the height of mountains, the depths of the sea, can be explained by erosion, volcanism, earthquakes, etc.

In essence this view says that God not only isn't necessary now (though He may have begun the process). It also implies that God can't become involved: even He is bound by natural law.

We Christians believe that Jesus will invade earth and, on His return, will shatter sinful human culture as well as shake the material universe. How ridiculous, the scoffer says. Why, from the beginning nothing has changed.

When you think about that argument, it seems more and more ridiculous itself. Nothing's changed? Oh? Who has been around "from the beginning" to see it? Nothing has changed? Why, purely secular scientists claim that earth has changed radically. At best we can only say little has changed in our lifetime, or that little has changed since history began to be recorded. We live so briefly, history is known so few thousands of years back, that it is utterly foolish to argue that Jesus will not come because "nothing has changed."

It will change.

Because Jesus WILL come.

"They deliberately forget" 2 Peter 2:5-7. One radical change that has taken place during mankind's residence on earth is described in Genesis 6–8. God brought a great Flood on the earth as a judgment on sin, and wiped out human civilization.

The biblical record of the Genesis Flood is supported by traditions reported by various peoples worldwide. And that Flood demonstrates God's ability to intervene in this present world—and His commitment to do so. Modern man doubts the historicity of the Flood. But the believer does not. And we find in the record of God's historic act of judgment proof that God is mankind's Judge, and that He will judge again.

"Not wanting anyone to perish" 2 Peter 3:8-9. Peter gave two insights into the lengthy delay between the promise of Jesus' return and its fulfillment. First, God doesn't view time as we do. What we might refer casually to as "a couple of days" He might think of just as casually as "a few thousand years." So we can't impose our time sense on God.

Second, God has good reason for what we experience as delay. Christ hasn't returned yet, because the Lord does not want "anyone to perish." As long as Jesus is absent, the door to salvation remains open. But when Jesus comes, that door will slam shut. And then it will be too late.

"As they do the other Scriptures" 2 Peter 3:16-18. Peter's reference to Paul's letters, equating them with the "other Scriptures," indicates how early the writings now in our Bible were recognized as

Scripture by the early church.

Every once in a while I see an ad urging me to send for the rest of the Bible—for lost gospels, or lost letters, or newly recovered apocalypses. Actually all these writings have been known for untold years. They are early Christian or heretical writings that circulated much as do books from the modern Christian bookstore. Some were propaganda for cults. Some were devotional writings intended to strengthen the believer. But none of them were ever considered Scripture—as the books in our New Testament quickly were.

No wonder Peter urges us to recall the words of prophet and apostle. And to ignore false teacher and scoffer alike. As we keep our hearts fixed on the inspired Word of God, we will grow in grace and be ready when Jesus comes.

▶ DEVOTIONAL
All Gone
(2 Peter 3:10-18)

Someone has said there is only one real difference between a man and a boy. A man's toys are more expensive.

There's probably more truth in that saying than we'd like to admit. It's really amazing how much time and money people spend on newer clothes, sportier cars, bigger screen TVs, and faster boats. Especially when one morning we're going to wake up, and find that everything we have is all gone.

That's the point Peter wanted to make here. He didn't really care that he'd provided insight into how the world will end. He just wants us to know that, when "the heavens will disappear with a roar; the [very] elements will be destroyed by fire," those material playthings we love so much will be all gone.

Of course, once we understand this, Peter wants us to act appropriately. "What kind of people ought we to be?" he asks. And he answers. "You ought to live holy and godly lives," as you look "forward to a new heaven and a new earth, the home of righteousness." Why clutch your playthings to you, when tomorrow morning they'll be gone anyway? And all you'll have left, is you. Why not invest that time, that enthusiasm, in building the new you?

A holy and godly life, marked by growth in the grace and knowledge of Jesus, will secure eternal rewards. How much better a focus that provides for our life than toys that, very very soon, will be all gone.

Personal Application

When time shall be no more, you will.

Quotable

Since I am coming to that holy room,
Where with thy choir of saints forevermore,
I shall be made thy music; as I come
I tune the instrument here at the door
And what I must do then, think here before.—John Donne

The Variety Reading Plan continues with EZEKIEL

1 John

INTRODUCTION

First John was written by the Apostle John, probably about A.D. 85–90. John also wrote two other brief letters, the Gospel of John, and the Book of Revelation.

This letter was written to reaffirm core Christian truths then being denied by false teachers. Using the familiar images of light, righteousness, and love, John showed that Jesus is the Son of God, that He did come in the flesh, and that salvation is ours only through Him. John also insisted that Christians do sin and must confess their sins. Cleansed, believers are to live as Christ lived, obedient to God and showing love toward all, and especially toward others in the community of faith.

OUTLINE OF CONTENTS

READING GUIDE (3 Days)

If hurried, you may read only the "core passage" in your Bible and the Devotional in each chapter of this Commentary.

Reading	*Chapters*	*Core passage*
350	1:1–2:2	1:5-10
351	2:3–3:24	3:4-10
352	4–5	5:11-15

1 John

1 John

DECEMBER 16 *Reading 350*
LIVING IN LIGHT
1 John 1:1–2:2

"If we walk in the light, as He is in the light, we have fellowship with one another, and the blood of Jesus, His Son, purifies us from all sin" (1 John 1:7).

God cleanses us that we may live Christlike lives.

Background
Traditional religion. In the first century, religions were generally evaluated by their antiquity. A faith that was ancient was assumed to be true. Those in the upper classes generally thought that there was one great God. They believed that this great God, along with lesser gods, was worshiped by different peoples under different names and by differing rites. As long as the worship practices of a nation or people had roots that could be traced back to antiquity, that religion was considered true.

It was not unnatural in such a society for some to view Jesus as a great and wise man, a worshiper of the great God. But Jesus could not be God Himself, for no religion introduced into the world a hundred or so years earlier could possibly be true. It did not pass the test of antiquity. The soul of Jesus might, upon His death, have attained the status of a lesser divinity. But He could not be God, as orthodox Christians claimed.

This issue, with others, was addressed by John in this brief but powerful letter to the churches of Asia Minor, where John lived out the last decades of his long life. As the Christian movement spread through the Roman world, false teachers did corrupt Christian teaching in an effort to make the new faith fit in with contemporary ideas on religion. But, as John showed, Christian belief is radical, and calls for a complete change of mind about religion, about one's condition as a sinner, about salvation, about godliness, and about the person of Jesus Christ.

Overview
John based his teaching on personal knowledge of Jesus and continuing fellowship with God (1:1-4). One who claims to be without sin is in darkness (vv. 5-8). Confession of sins brings forgiveness and purification by Christ, our atoning sacrifice (1:9–2:2).

Understanding the Text
"That which was from the beginning" 1 John 1:1. John's Gospel begins, "In the beginning was the Word, and the Word was with God, and the Word was God." The same thought is expressed here. Having faith in Jesus is not worshiping a newcomer on the scene of religion. Jesus existed from the very beginning, for Jesus is God: the source of earthly and eternal life.

"We have seen with our eyes" 1 John 1:1-3. John emphasized his role as an eyewitness to the Incarnation. God isn't someone far off, distant, unknowable. In the person of Jesus, John had seen God with his own eyes, touched God with his own hands, walked beside God on Palestine's rugged trails. When false teachers trot out philosophical arguments to prove that God could not become man, and that no human being could share substance with the great God, John had a simple answer. "I'm not talking arguments. I was there.

I'm talking what I've seen and heard."

You and I need to have this same kind of confidence. Not that we see and touch Jesus as John did, in the flesh. But today you and I can experience Jesus too. We can know the peace He brings when we are overcome with anxiety. We can sense His leading. We can feel conviction and know a joy that only the Holy Spirit brings. When we know Jesus in this deep, personal sense—when we experience Christ—we KNOW. The most logical-sounding arguments of scoffers have no compelling force when we know, by personal experience, that Jesus is God.

"So that you also may have fellowship with us" 1 John 1:3-4. The word translated fellowship appears over 60 times in the New Testament. The root concept is that of sharing; of having something in common. English versions have translated the Greek root by fellowship, communion, participation, partnership, and by sharing a common life.

Two thoughts are important here. First, "fellowship with us" precedes "fellowship with the Father" in these verses. Perhaps John was saying that we best experience God in and through the community of faith, not on our own. If you want to experience God at work in your life, become part of a church in which God is presently at work.

But John was saying more. He was saying that a person must experience Jesus for himself to have the assurance that possessed John. Knowing about God isn't enough. Believing that God exists isn't enough. You must commit yourself to Jesus, and in faith's link with Christ, that common life you will share with Him, you will experience Him for yourself. And then, you too will know.

What a wonderful thing to be able to say to scoffers, or those who doubt and hold back: I can tell you what I have seen and heard; I can tell you of my experiences. But why not try Jesus for yourself? Why not touch, and see, and hear the truth, as Jesus works in your life today?

"If we walk in the light" 1 John 1:5-7. John frequently contrasted light and dark in his writings. At times the emphasis is moral: darkness represents moral corruption, and light holiness. Here, however, light and darkness are reflections of reality. Those who walk in darkness can't grasp the true state of affairs. Those who walk in the light see, and are able to deal with, reality.

John was saying something that modern counselors have come to realize is basic to all human relationships. Unless you are willing to be honest with yourself and others, no basis for a close personal relationship exists. You can't say you have fellowship with God if you're not honest with Him and yourself. And you can't say you have fellowship with others. You may think that you have things in common. You may assume that your relationship is intimate and close. But if you're not in touch with reality, you are fooling yourself.

God can handle anything in our relationship with Him, except deceit. He can even deal with sins! John said that if we walk in the light as God is in the light—if we're honest with ourselves and with God about our sins—the blood of Christ will keep on purifying us from all sins.

Don't pretend with God, or yourself. When you do something wrong, face up to it. Admit it, and let God forgive and purify (see DEVOTIONAL).

"If we confess our sins" 1 John 1:9. The word "confess" is *homologeo*. It means to do an about face concerning a sinful act: to recognize it as sin, and to acknowledge it as sin to God. When we acknowledge our sins for what they are, God is able to act in us. He not only forgives us, but He keeps on cleansing us from all iniquity. Augustine wrote, "He who confesses and condemns his sins already acts with God. God condemns thy sins; if thou also dost condemn them, thou art linked to God."

"That you will not sin" 1 John 2:1-2. Lots of people don't understand how God does business. Tell us ahead of time that if we confess our sins we'll be forgiven? (1:9) Not even mention punishment, penance, remorse, or repayment? Just, confess and be forgiven? Why, if it's all that easy, why not just go out and sin all you please? All you'd have to do is drop in on God, say, "I did it," and go on home scott free!

I can understand why they're puzzled by this. In essence John was saying, I want you to know that Jesus completely satisfied the wrath of God against sinners, and that Jesus is there now, pleading His blood whenever you are accused of any sin. Jesus is saying, "That one's paid for, Father." And it is, so you go free.

John understands though. "I'm writing this," John wrote, "so that you will not sin." The thing that keeps Christians from sinning is not fear of punishment. It's love for Jesus. The more we realize the depths of our sin, and how much we've been forgiven, the more love we have for the Lord. The love that assures us forgiveness awakens our love, and we freely choose not to sin, for our lover's sake.

▶ DEVOTIONAL
"Not Me, Lord"
(1 John 1:5-10)

One of the characters that appears regularly in Family Circus cartoons is "Not Me." He's a ghostly figure, and every time Mom asks who broke the lamp, or who got into the cookies, the kids quickly blame "Not Me."

He was a familiar figure even in the first century. John pictured him in these verses of his first letter. "Anyone around here sin?" he asked. And everyone pipes up, "Not me."

To John, this is serious and not at all funny. "If we claim to be without sin," John writes, "we deceive ourselves and the truth is not in us" (v. 8). We've stepped out of the light, and lost that intimate contact with God that we maintain only by being honest with ourselves and with Him. There's even more. If we refuse to acknowledge our sin, our sins will go unconfessed. We'll miss experiencing the flood of forgiveness that deepens our love for the Lord. And we'll cut ourselves off from the cleansing work of God's Holy Spirit: a work that can only take place in those who are honest with themselves and honest with God.

So next time you get angry and strike out at a loved one, don't pass it off as "righteous indignation."

Next time you fudge on your income taxes don't think, "Everyone's doing it," and excuse yourself.

Next time your spouse says he or she needs to talk, don't turn your back in bitterness or indifference.

And never, never claim—even in your dreams—to be without sin. Take your place with the rest of us: weak, vulnerable, trying, and at times failing, but walking honestly with God and with others, and by God's grace growing better than we have been, and better than we are.

Personal Application

If you deceive yourself, you are in darkness indeed.

Quotable

There may be virtue in the man
  Who's always sure he's right,
Who'll never hear another's plan
  And seek no further light;
But I like more the chap who sings
  A somewhat different song;
Who says, when he has messed things up,
  "I'm sorry; I was wrong."

It's hard for anyone to say
  That failure's due to him—
That he has lost the fight or way
  Because his lights burned dim.
It takes a man aside to throw
  The vanity that's strong,
Confessing, "Twas my fault, I know;
  "I'm sorry; I was wrong."

And so, I figure, those who use
  This honest, manly phrase,
Hate it too much their way to lose
  On many future days.
They'll keep the path and make the fight,
  Because they do not long
To have to say—when they're not right—
  "I'm sorry. I was wrong."—*Herald of Light*

DECEMBER 17 *Reading 351*
TESTS OF FAITH
1 John 2:3–3:24

"Dear children, let us not love with words or tongue but with actions and in truth. This then is how we know that we belong to the truth, and how we set our hearts at rest in His presence" (1 John 3:18-19).

Love and obedience are inner and outer tests of a personal relationship with God.

Overview

John identified three tests of knowing God (2:3-11), and expressed confidence in his readers (vv. 12-14). He urged us not to love the world (vv. 15-17), and warned against antichrists (vv. 18-27). We are to live as children of God (v. 28–3:3), doing what is right (vv. 4-10), and loving one another (vv. 11-15) as God in Christ has loved us (vv. 16-20), assured by our lives and by the Spirit that we live in Him (vv. 21-24).

Understanding the Text

"We know that we have come to know Him" 1 John 2:3-11. Somehow the young woman in Canada got my Phoenix phone number. She began to call me, sometimes several times a day. She was anxious and afraid. She didn't know if she was a Christian, though she believed in Jesus. When the fears came flooding back, she dialed my number.

She was an extreme case, but many Christians have moments of uncertainty. How can we know that we've come to know Him? John gave three tests. First, we obey His commands (v. 5). A person wearing the uniform of the U.S. Army obeys the orders of officers over him. That's part of being a soldier. Obeying Jesus is part of being a Christian, and shows that we acknowlege His authority.

Second, we "walk as Jesus did" (v. 6). If we belong to Jesus we become more and more like Him. So when we respond to others and to life situations as Jesus did when He was here on earth, we show that we belong to Him.

Third, we love our brothers (v. 9). You can't hate others and belong to Jesus, because Christ loves others. People can say they belong to Christ, and be hateful and hating. But their actions deny their words.

So take a look at yourself. Do you find you keep Jesus' commands? Do you try to act as you think He would? Do you love your fellow Christians, and enjoy being with them? Then relax! You know Him. And others know you know Him as well!

"I write to you" 1 John 2:12-14. John's letter wasn't intended to convict, or to create anxiety. It was intended to encourage. It was written to those John knew were true believers, who showed the mark of Jesus in their lives. How good it is when others let us know they have confidence in us.

It can mean a lot to your family and friends if you give them the same kind of praise.

"Do not love the world" 1 John 2:15-17. In this famous paragraph "the world" is the total system of values and perceptions that together are expressed in the culture of sinful human beings. John revealed the nature of this system, saying that the roots of every human society are anchored deeply in the selfish cravings of sinful man, in man's tendency to greedily desire the materialistic things he sees, and in man's drive for ostentatious self-importance. Each of these is antagonistic to God, and a culture that weaves society from these values is corrupt.

We have to abandon the values of human society and adopt the values of God the Father. Man's culture is not ours, and we should not be comfortable in it.

"Many antichrists have come" 1 John 2:18-25. John did believe that in the future a specific individiual, the Antichrist, would appear. John also believed that false Christians who even then were seeking to lead believers astray were antichrists: enemies of Jesus and the Father.

We know two things about antichrists from this passage. We know that they were once members of the church, but "went out from us." They set up their own splinter movements. And we know that they revealed themselves by denying that Jesus is the Christ, the Son of God.

John said flatly that no one who denies the Son as God has any knowledge of the Father.

Not everyone who calls himself a Christian is one. In time, however, such folks reveal themselves, by causing schism in the church, and by denying the deity of Jesus.

"His anointing teaches you about all things" 1 John 2:24-27. What protects us from false teachers? Objectively, we make sure that "what you have heard from the beginning remains in you." The doctrine of the early church and the Apostles is preserved in the inspired Word of God; we study and stand on it. But there is a subjective source of security as well. This is the Holy Spirit, that "anointing you received from Him," who "teaches you about all things."

The inner voice of the Spirit and the objective Word combine to witness to the truth. We don't need any human authority to tell us what is true and what is false. If we listen to the Word, and to the Spirit, we will know.

"And that is what we are!" 1 John 2:28–3:10 Our dog Mitzi has this fixed idea that she's a member of the family, and ought to have a place at the dinner table. If we don't watch out, she jumps up on a chair, rests her chin on a place mat, and waits for the opportunity to grab a bite to eat. We have a hard time convincing her that she's a dog, and dogs don't eat people food at the dinner table.

John wants us to develop a fixed idea too. He wants us to understand that, even now, we ARE the children of God. We can't tell what that means ultimately, other than the fact that when Jesus comes we'll be like Him. But, knowing that we are God's children and that we will be like Jesus, has a tremendous impact. Mitzi's wrong when she thinks she's a person and tries to act like one. But we're right if we think we are God's children. If we are totally convinced we're God's own, John says we'll begin to act like God here and now.

If you ever wonder how to act in a particular situation, just remember that you're a child of God. And act as you believe a child of God should.

"Do not be surprised . . . if the world hates you" 1 John 3:11-15. In the first and second century of our era the world did hate Christians. The Christians refused to take part in public life because sacrifices offered to gods and goddesses were a traditional element in political and social gatherings. Christians were condemned as atheists and as haters of humanity, for to the pagan those who did not shoulder their civic responsibilities seemed to attack the social order.

Otherwise Christians were good citizens: honest, moral, responsible, but still hated. So these words of John were important. Hatred comes from sin, and if Christians were hated and killed, the persecution revealed the sin that infected society. But the obverse must also true. If hatred is the mark of evil, love is the indelible sign of good and godliness.

Some, even in America, are hated because their stand strips away the cloak that hides the basic immorality of such things in our society as abortion, exploitation of sex, and media corruption. They feel the hostility John wrote of. But all of us are to show love, the unmistakable evidence that God has touched, and entered, our hearts.

"If our hearts do not condemn us" 1 John 3:21-24. Deep down, you and I do know what's right. And we know when we do wrong. We may try to hide it, but even if we attempt to deceive ourselves, there remains a nagging certainty that we've done wrong.

What a powerful motive for choosing what is right and good! When our conscience is clear, when we know we've done our best, John says we "have confidence before God." We have confidence to pray, and confidence to claim the answer to our prayers. And most important of all, we have confidence that He does live in us.

Only Jesus within can motivate us to gladly choose what is right and good.

▶DEVOTIONAL
Toward the Light
(1 John 3:4-10)

I remember when I was in grade school I had to do an experiment growing a lima bean. I guess education hasn't advanced all that much, because now, 50 years later, the nine-year-old in our house has grown a lima been too. But what's interesting is that, the sprouting plant will always grow toward the sun. Somehow the life of the bean is drawn toward the light. You can turn the plant around, even lay it on its side. Whatever you do, the sprout will orient toward the sun.

That's what John was saying about us when he wrote, "No one who lives in Him keeps on sinning" (v. 6). The NIV captures the vital tense of the verb. It's not that a Christian never sins. It's that believers will not "keep on sinning." John said the reason is that God's seed—the principle of divine life —has been planted in our personalities. God's life within us grows in the direction of godliness. His life is oriented toward purity. And if God's life really is in us, there will be a definite tilt toward what is right, and away from sin.

Anyone may sin at times, and in all likelihood will. But you can still tell the DIRECTION in which a person is growing. And so can everyone else!

Personal Application

The direction of your life is more important than where you are now.

Quotable

"Glorious God, give me grace to amend my life, and to have an eye to my end without begrudging death, which to those who die in You, good Lord, is the gate of a wealthy life.

"And give me, good Lord, a humble, lowly, quiet, peaceable, patient, charitable, kind, tender and pitiful mind, in all my works and in all my words and all my thoughts, to have a taste of Your holy, blessed Spirit.

"Give me, good Lord, a full faith, a firm hope, and a fervent charity, a love of You incomparably above the love of myself.

"And give me, good Lord, Your love and favour, which my love of You, however great it might be, could not deserve were it not for Your great goodness.

"These things, good Lord, I pray for, give me Your grace to labour for."—Thomas More

DECEMBER 18 *Reading 352*

GOD'S GREAT LOVE

1 John 4–5

> *"This is how God showed His love among us: He sent His one and only Son into the world that we might live through Him" (1 John 4:9).*

We are to rest in the assurance of God's great love.

Overview

False prophets deny Jesus Christ is God and man (4:1-6). Love is the external mark of spiritual birth (vv. 7-21). The believer loves and obeys God, overcoming the world (5:1-5). The person who trusts Jesus has God's life within him (vv. 6-12). God wants us to know we have eternal life; to pray with confidence (vv. 13-15), to pray for those who sin (vv. 16-17), and to abandon sin (vv. 18-21).

Understanding the Text

"Test the spirits" 1 John 4:1-3. In the first century, itinerant teachers traveled the Roman world. Second Peter 2 tells us that many false teachers were among them; men who saw teaching the new religion as a way to make money. This fit a well-established pattern, as teachers of philosophy and other religions also traveled, gathered little groups of followers, and charged whatever the market would bear. All these traveling teachers were trained in rhetoric, and were skilled hucksters. So John warned the gullible. Don't be taken in by smooth-talking teachers.

The critical test then and now is, does this teacher present Jesus Christ as God in the flesh? Any who honor Jesus with less than full Deity express the "spirit of the antichrist" rather than the Spirit of God.

"The One who is in you is greater than the one who is in the world" 1 John 4:4-6. Every now and then I run across someone who is anxious about possible demon possession.

This verse can be a great comfort. The spirit that animates the antichrist, Satan himself, operates freely in this world. But the Christian is not part of the world! We have within us One who is far greater than Satan—the Holy Spirit of God.

Let the Spirit fill your life, and you are in no danger of demon possession. Satan can manipulate the circumstances around you. But he cannot touch your heart or spirit as long as God's Spirit lives within you.

"Whoever knows God listens to us" 1 John 4:4-6. Don't be defensive if others think your faith in Christ is foolish or peculiar. We Christians speak in the language of our land, yet what we say can't be "heard" by those who do not know God. The viewpoint of the world has always been blind to Scripture's God.

Instead of being defensive, keep on loving and doing good. Every day God calls more men and women out of the world to Him. Some you speak to will suddenly begin to hear—and you'll know that God is at work in their lives.

"Whoever does not love does not know God" 1 John 4:7-12. Non-Christians frequently ask believers to "prove" God. You can't see Him, or touch Him, they may say. How can you know God exists?

On the one hand, you and I might argue from history. Jesus lived. He died. And His resurrection is the most thoroughly attested event in the ancient world! Those events demonstrate God's existence, and His active love.

But there's an even better way to answer. God revealed Himself in the love Jesus showed in giving Himself for us. And God creates a Jesus kind of love in the hearts of those who know Him. Others can know that God is real by seeing Jesus' kind of love expressed by Christians.

It's sometimes possible to reason another person into faith. But it is usually easier to love them to a personal trust in Jesus.

"God lives in him and he in God" 1 John 4:13-16. The theme of "assurance" is strong in these last two chapters of 1 John. I've known folks who actually get angry if a Christian suggests he or she "knows" he is going to heaven. To some that's presumption. To others it's an insult—a sign that the believer thinks he or she is better than they. But John makes it clear that God wants us to know, for sure, that we are saved, and that God lives in us, as we live in God.

It is not presumption to take God at His word, or to rely on the love God has for us. It would be presumption NOT to trust God's promises.

"Perfect love drives out fear" 1 John 4:17-18. I suspect that most people feel a twinge of anxiety, and glance at their speedometer, if they see a police car while on the road. We appreciate police as guardians of the public good. But most of us are a little nervous around one.

It's similar for most folks with God. The idea that God is over there in the next car, watching us, makes a person feel a bit edgy.

John, however, said that we need have no fear or anxiety in our relationship with God. Any more than if the policeman we recognized in the next car was our dad. Then we'd just wave to him and smile. There would be no fear, because his presence near us offered no threat of punishment.

Love does just this in our relationship with the Lord. On the one hand, we know He loves us. So He will do nothing to harm us. On the other, as we respond to Him with love, there's no room left for fear. Terror of someone and love for him or her cannot exist at the same time. Real love drives out fear.

So don't fear God. Remember He loves you. And love Him in return.

"He first loved us" 1 John 4:19-21. In God's relationship with us, He is the initiator. He loves first. And His love makes a difference.

It's as if we were soaking wet kindling. We have no spark of love for God in us; no way to ignite a flame. But God's love encompasses us. It warms and dries us, and finally kindles love's fire in our own hearts. In our relationship with God love drives out fear. In our relationship with others, love creates true caring.

What John was saying here is very important. If God's love hasn't warmed, dried, and kindled our own love for others, then we have not yet learned to love God. The same fire that warms God's hearts warms our brothers and sisters.

"His commands are not burdensome" 1 John 5:1-5. Again John insisted that God stimulates one love in our heart; a love that expresses itself both toward God and toward others. We can't be warm toward God and cold toward our fellowman at the same time.

There's another exciting thing about love for God. It makes obeying easy. "Want to" is always easier than "have to." As long as we feel that we are forced against our will to do certain things that God demands, those things will be burdensome to us. But if we eagerly want to do those same things, they seem to us to be a delight.

You can easily check the state of your love for the Lord using this principle. If you find you want to do those things that you know please Him, you can be sure that your love for God is alive and well.

"There are three that testify" 1 John 5:6-9. The meaning of the "water and blood" here is much debated. Perhaps the best way to understand them is to identify the "water" as Christ's baptism, which introduced His public ministry here on earth, and the "blood" as His death, which ended it. Everything Jesus said and did in public, as well as His death, witness to His nature as the Son of God. The stories of Jesus' life and death, confirmed in us today by the Holy Spirit, continue to identify Jesus as God's Son and our Saviour. Anyone who rejects the record of Jesus' life and death for us, as that record was inspired by the Spirit and is authenticated by the Spirit today, makes God out to be a liar (v. 10).

How clearly this passage draws the issue for all mankind. We either believe God's Word in and about Jesus, or we call God a liar. There is no middle ground.

"God has given us eternal life" 1 John 5:10-11. Once again we have words of assurance. If you believe God's words about Jesus, you have been given eternal life. That life is yours, now. "He who has the Son has life."

Since you believe, enjoy! Be assured of your acceptance by God, and revel in the love God has for you. That love is far more wonderful than all the riches of the world.

"Ask anything according to His will" 1 John 5:14. It's not that we have to guess at God's will. This is a promise! As we live close to the Lord, He will guide our prayers, so that what we ask is what He wishes us to have.

"Sin that does not lead to death" 1 John 5:16-20. "Death" here is biological, not spiritual. We see a parallel in 1 Corinthians 5, where Paul demanded that a brother who lived in open, persistent sin be expelled from the church, and also be handed over to Satan "so that the sinful nature may be destroyed" and his spirit "saved on the Day of the Lord."

It is persistent, determined continuation in known sin that puts a person beyond the reach of prayer, and exposes him or her to judgment in this life.

But John wants us to realize true believers can sin, and should be the object of our prayers. And he wants us to be encouraged when we fall. God's life in us will call us back to holiness, and we will "not continue in sin."

Don't treat sin lightly. But don't be overwhelmed when you fail. Draw on God's strength, and stand again.

▶ DEVOTIONAL
Blessed Assurance
(1 John 5:11-15)

There are very few things in this world that we can be sure about.

Becky Schmidt, our friend and our pastor's wife went to the doctor for a regular checkup—and discovered she had cancer. She's responding well to treatment. But suddenly the whole world of Richard and their three boys was shaken.

Karl Klammer left the north to take a job here in Florida. The family sold their home, loaded their possessions in a U-Haul truck, and headed south. The day after he got here, the company he was to work for declared bankruptcy, and shut down operations.

Last Saturday night a junior in our local high school was on her way to work. Another car went through a stop sign, struck her vehicle, and killed her.

Assurance—that confident assurance about ourselves and our future—is something that this world simply does not offer.

Yet, right now, you and I can be absolutely sure, if we believe in Jesus, that we have eternal life. We can be completely confident that God listens to our prayers, and that as we ask according to His will, the answer is assured.

The circumstances of our life on earth will always remain uncertain. We can be assured only of the reality, and the wonder, of our relationship with God.

Personal Application

Claim the blessings of assurance, that are your heritage through faith in Jesus Christ.

Quotable

"To be assured of our salvation is no arrogant stoutness. It is faith. It is devotion. It is not presumption. It is God's promise." —St. Augustine

The Variety Reading Plan continues with 2–3 JOHN

2–3 John

INTRODUCTION

The Apostle John wrote these two brief letters. The first is addressed to an unknown Christian woman and her family; the second to a Christian leader and a friend named Gaius. These warm, personal letters emphasize themes found in 1 John: the doctrine of Christ's deity, and the call to love and do good works.

OUTLINE OF CONTENTS

READING GUIDE (1 Day)

If hurried, you may read only the "core passage" in your Bible and the Devotional in this Commentary.

Reading	*Chapters*	*Core passage*
353	2–3 John	3 John 3-19

2–3 John

DECEMBER 19 *Reading 353*
WALKING IN LOVE
2–3 John

> *"As you have heard from the beginning, His command is that you walk in love" (2 John 6).*

There can never be too many reminders to love and keep Jesus' commandments.

Background

John's later years. John outlived the other disciples of Jesus. If he died in the late 90s, as most believe, he outlived Peter and Paul by some three decades!

During these decades more and more hostility developed toward Christians. There was both official persecution, and many nonviolent expressions of discrimination. In addition, the false teachers Peter, Jude, and Paul had predicted did emerge, and corrupted the faith of many.

What then seemed most important for John to communicate as he neared the end of his life? These two brief letters help us understand, for they pick up themes we are familiar with from 1 John. John emphasized the full deity of Jesus, and love as the mark of an obedient community.

How important these twin pillars of faith are today. We worship Jesus the Son of God. And we love one another as brothers and sisters in the family of God.

Overview

John greeted an "elect lady" (2 John 1-3), to encourage continuing love (vv. 4-6) and warn against those who deny Christ's deity (vv. 7-13). John wrote Gaius (3 John 1-4), to encourage him to keep on ministering (vv. 5-8), to warn against Diotrephes (vv. 9-10) and to commend Demetrius (vv. 11-14).

Understanding the Text

"The elder . . . the elect lady" 2 John 1. John's reference may have been to his own age, but more likely to his position in the church. He was one whose maturity and wisdom had made him worthy of trust.

The name "elect" was used in the first century in the way we use "born again Christian"—to identify individuals as believers who have a personal relationship with Jesus Christ. The term need not be understood to imply predestination. But it does affirm that we who have chosen to believe in Christ have been chosen by God.

We want Him as a our God. But God wanted us first, as His children.

"Walking in the truth" 2 John 4. Here as in 1 John, "truth" is linked to reality. A person who walks "in the truth" lives in harmony with spiritual and moral reality, as these are known to us in Christ. You and I walk "in the truth" if our lives are marked by holiness and by love.

"His command is that you walk in love" 2 John 2:5-6. John emphasized a particular reality all Christians are to experience. We show our obedience to Jesus, and our harmony with Him, by loving fellow believers. I suspect that John may have thought the people he ministered to may have tired of his message. He did say the command wasn't new. And that the elect lady and her family had had it from the beginning. But John was not apologizing. He is

simply saying, love is so important, we must be reminded of it all the time.

John was like the old preacher who explained his philosophy of ministry. First, I tell 'em what I'm going to tell 'em. Then I tell 'em. And then I tell 'em what I told 'em." That's the way we need to be in reminding one another to keep on loving, for Jesus' sake.

"Jesus Christ as coming in the flesh" 2 John 7-11. There are many doctrines that are important to Christians. But none are as pivotal as this one. Jesus Christ, the Son of God, existed with God and as God from the beginning. And God the Son was born into our race, lived here on earth as true man, and after dying for us was raised from the dead. It was God the Son who died for us on the cross: God, come in the flesh to redeem us.

People can be Christian and have doubts about verbal, plenary inspiration. People can be Christian and be absolutely wrong in eschatology. But no one who denies that Jesus Christ is God come in the flesh can be Christian in any biblical sense.

We're not to run around ruling this or that person out of the faith because he or she differs from us on points of doctrine. But we are to have nothing to do with any who call themselves "Christian" but deny the full deity of Jesus Christ (v. 11).

"Your faithfulness to the truth" 3 John 1-4. John, in his 90s now, had developed a clear view of what is truly important in life. The things most of us focus our attention on—scrambling to advance in our careers, working out misunderstandings in our relationships, important things all—have receded in significance to the last apostle.

What thrilled him now? He wrote, "I have no greater joy than to hear that my children are walking in the truth" (v. 4).

We need to develop the same attitude when it comes to our children. I'm glad for the mom or dad who tells with obvious pride about the great job Joey's got, or the house with its own swimming pool that Suzie's husband bought in Houston at $40,000 less than it cost to build. But we need to remember that the one truly important thing in life is that our children walk in the truth, and walk with God.

"We ought therefore to show hospitality" 3 John 5-8. These few verses reflect the itinerant ministry of many in the first century who traveled from city to city, staying with one Christian group and then another, to share a special teaching or spiritual gift.

We saw in 2 Timothy, and in 2 Peter, how many of the itinerant teachers were false: they were insincere, seeking to gain a following only that they might win money from them. Here we see the other side. We see hundreds of believers who went on the road "for the sake of the Name," and who received "no help" from any source. These men gave up any personal ambitions to travel and nurture Christians throughout the empire, usually receiving nothing but food and lodging from those with whom they briefly stayed.

We still have folks like this today. Missionaries, preachers, school teachers, social workers, who for the sake of Jesus give up the prospect of lucrative careers to work in an area where they can serve others, and better share Christ. Such folk should be honored by their fellow Christians, and encouraged in practical ways.

▶DEVOTIONAL
Epitaphs
(3 John 9-13)

Ever read one of those books of humorous epitaphs? Like the one in England, that tells all:

> Mary Picket,
> Lies silent and fast,
> Her husband's ears
> Have peace at last.

Or the one from our own old West, that simply says:

> Flicker was quicker.

Actually, the thing about even humorous epitaphs is that most do say something about the character of the person they memorialize.

Something that stands out; something that folks remember.

In a sense John suggested a theme for the epitaphs of two leading individuals in the first-century Christian community of Asia. One, Diotrephes, was marked off as loving first place. He gossiped, trying to make others look small so he'd look bigger by comparison. And he tried to dominate his little group by cutting off any contact they may have with others. Someone might have written something like this on his tombstone:

> Diotrephes, who cut others down,
> Things are better
> Now he's not around.

On the other hand, we have Demetrius who was "well spoken of" by everyone, apparently because he was dedicated to doing good. I suspect a very different epitaph would have marked his memory.

You might try your hand at creating an epitaph for Demetrius. But it's more important to create an epitaph for yourself. But by how you live, not with words.

Personal Application

How do you want others to remember you?

Quotable

In heart a Lydia, and in tongue a Hanna,
In zeal a Ruth, in wedlock a Susanna,
Prudently simple, providentially wary,
To the world a Martha, and to heaven a Mary.—Epitaph of Dame Dorthy Selby

---

The Variety Reading Plan continues with NAHUM

Jude

INTRODUCTION

Jude is thought to be the brother of James and half-brother of Jesus. His short book is an urgent warning against those who were already introducing false teaching into the churches. God will punish those who turn from Christ and godliness, but preserve those who keep themselves in His love.

OUTLINE OF CONTENTS

READING GUIDE (1 Day)

If hurried, you may read only the "core passage" in your Bible and the Devotional in this Commentary.

Reading	*Chapter*	*Core passage*
354	1	vv. 17-25

Jude

DECEMBER 20 *Reading 354*

FALSE TEACHERS
Jude

> *"They are godless men, who change the grace of our God into a license for immorality and deny Jesus Christ our only Sovereign and Lord" (Jude 4).*

Hold fast to Jesus and godliness, and God will surely hold fast to you.

Biography: Jude
Jude's identification of himself as the brother of James, and a very early tradition, has led to his likely identification as a half-brother of Jesus Himself (cf. Matt. 13:55; Mark 6:3). James' humility in introducing himself only as a servant of Jesus may reflect his early rejection of his half-Brother as the Messiah (cf. John 7:5; Acts 1:14). While the letter is undated, if the author is Jude the brother of Jesus, its date probably falls somewhere between A.D. 60 and 80, as it reflects a concern for false teachers that is characteristic of the later letters of Paul and Peter, as well as John.

Overview
Jude wrote to warn of false teachers in the church (vv. 1-4), who will surely be judged by God (vv. 5-16). But believers who hold fast to Jesus and godliness (vv. 17-23) will be upheld by God, who merits our praise (vv. 24-25).

Understanding the Text
"Mercy, peace and love be yours in abundance" Jude 1-2. References in the Gospels to Jesus' half-brothers suggests that some hostility existed on their part. They weren't at all happy at the notoriety Jesus gained as He began His preaching and healing ministry in Galilee. No doubt, like siblings everywhere, they thought to themselves, "What's so special about HIM?"

Yet after Jesus' resurrection we find the brothers, with Mary and the disciples, praying in an upper room (Acts 1:14). The Baby born to their mother, the older Brother who roughhoused with them and took care of them as they grew up, was at last known by them as the Son of God.

It's one thing to know Jesus in the flesh. Today millions celebrate Christmas with no more insight into who Jesus really is than His brothers had. But when anyone comes to know Him as Son of God and Saviour, they like Jude find in Him mercy, peace, and grace in abundance.

"Contend for the faith that was once for all entrusted to the saints" Jude 3. Some things in life are relative. I prefer green, someone else prefers blue. I like popcorn. Someone else likes potato chips. With preferences, it doesn't make any real difference.

Truth is different. It is absolute, in the sense that truth remains fixed and sure despite human preferences. And so Jude reminds us that when someone says, "I prefer to think of Jesus as just a good man," we can't respond, "OK. But I prefer to think of Him as God."

Contending for truth doesn't mean being hostile, or shouting at those who do not believe. But it does mean making sure people realize that truth isn't a matter of preference. Someone may well say, "I prefer to think of Jesus as just a good man." But when they do, that's our cue to answer, "I'm really sorry about that. You see, the Bible says Jesus is God the Son, and your whole future depends on whether or know you accept the truth of of that claim."

"Have secretly slipped in among you" Jude 4. Yesterday our Sarah came home from Sunday School, wearing a large paper medallion around her neck, that said in letters two inches high, "I am forgiven."

False teachers don't wear medallions around their necks, announcing, "I am a false teacher." Instead they slip in secretly. They pretend to be believers, and only after being accepted do they begin to smuggle their heresies into the congregation.

Jude, as did Peter and Paul, reminds us that try as they will, false teachers can't hide two identifying marks. They deny Jesus Christ, making Him out to be less than God. And they twist that grace which frees us from the grip of sin into a license for sin.

Christmas is our great reaffirmation that Jesus Christ is God, come in the flesh. In remembrance of God's great gift, let's rededicate ourselves to live holy and godly lives.

"I want to remind you" Jude 5-7. Jude pointed to three groups whose experience reminds us that God does punish sin. The three groups are linked first in that each rebelled against God, and second, in that each when rebelling turned to immorality.

The most unusual group here is that of "angels who did not keep their position of authority." Comparing Jude's reference to first- and second-century B.C. Jewish works, he appears to refer to the "sons of God" of Genesis 6:4 who assumed bodies to mingle with the "daughters of men." This radical violation of the creation order led to the guilty angels being "kept in darkness, bound with everlasting chains for judgment."

Jude's point is clear. God will most certainly punish the false teachers who share the spiritual and moral depravity exhibited by the Exodus generation, by fallen angels, and by the homosexual communities of Sodom and Gomorrah.

Let's not hesitate to affirm this truth too. Sin merits punishment. And punishment will surely be meted out.

"These dreamers" Jude 8-10. I read science fiction now and then. Flights of the imagination that create new worlds and new cultures intrigue me. But I never mistake the imaginary world of some author for reality.

That's the problem with false religious teaching. It abandons the reality unveiled in Scripture, and substitutes man's imagination. "These dreamers" act like "unreasoning animals" in that they ignore spiritual truths and imagine a world in which they can give full reign to their natural baser passions.

This is the utmost arrogance, and Jude alluded to a popular story of his day in which the archangel Michael is portrayed struggling with Satan for the body of Moses after his death. Even in our fiction, Jude seemed to say, the greatest of the angels hestitates to rebuke a being of higher rank! How arrogant for mere men to speak of spiritual realities that are far beyond their capacity to grasp.

Watch out for those who ridicule spiritual things. What they say tells us nothing about God or angels. But it surely tells us a lot about them!

"Woe to them" Jude 11-13. Jude emotionally piled up images that characterize the false teacher. The way of Cain is to strike out at those who do good. The error of Balaam is to trade spiritual services for worldly wealth. And the destruction of Korah is direct, divine intervention to punish those who rebel against him.

The next series of images are powerful and poetic. Each pictures a phenomenon which promises much, but delivers nothing but harm. To be a shepherd is to promise to care for the sheep, but these shepherds take care of themselves! A dark cloud promises rain, but these false teachers bring only shrieking winds and no water. What a contrast to the thousands upon thousands of faithful pastors who give rather than receive, and who enrich our lives.

"Enoch, the seventh from Adam" Jude 14-20. Jude quoted here from a second century B.C. religious book called "The Book of Enoch." Jude's quotation did not mean he saw this book as Scripture, but does indicate he believed the sentiment expressed to be true. The Lord is coming, and with

thousands upon thousands of holy angels (cf. 2 Thes. 1:5-10). When He returns, He will judge. And then the false teachers will receive the punishment they deserve.

Until then, we should expect to find scoffers in the church, who will try to divide us (vv. 17-19). So let's be doubly careful not to fall into their grasp.

"But you, dear friends" Jude 20-21. The angels sang it on that first Christmas. "On earth peace to men on whom His favor rests" (Luke 2:14).

The strident calls of scoffers have no appeal to us, who know Jesus as God-sent Babe and risen Saviour. We experience peace, as we concentrate on building ourselves up in "your most holy faith," on prayer, and on keeping ourselves in love as we wait for Jesus to return. If you and I focus on these things we will experience a peace that certainty no one outside of Christ can possibly know.

"Be merciful to those who doubt" Jude 22. Don't classify those who doubt with false teachers. There's a vast difference between honest uncertainty and arrogant unbelief. Jude reminds us to "be merciful" to doubters. Show that you care, try to encourage and help, never condemn. By love and mercy you can take a doubter by the hand and lead him or her to Christ.

"Mixed with fear" Jude 23. Love for the lost must always be tempered by a hatred of sin. Jude warns us against identifying so closely with a sinner that we find ourselves drawn into his or her sin. The fear we feel in reaching out to others is not fear of them, but awareness of our own vulnerability.

▶DEVOTIONAL
Born a King
(Jude 17-25)

There's a strange correlation between the Christmas season and Jude's letter. Christmas brings us vivid images of Baby Jesus, lying in a manger, a helpless Infant, watched over by Mary and Joseph and farm animals. Jude's powerful warnings against false teachers contain vivid images too: images that make us sense our own vulnerability.

But Jude ended his letter with a paean of praise to One he at last came to recognized as God our Saviour, resplendent in "glory, majesty, power and authority." Jesus was born a helpless Babe. But He was born a King, and as King He now rules over all.

It's because of who Jesus is, "before all ages, now and forevermore," that despite our weaknesses we have complete confidence that whatever schisms tear at the church, we will remain safe and secure. We are secure, not because of the strength of faith in Him, but because of the strength of Him in whom we believe. As Jude says, He "is able to keep you from falling and to present you before His glorious presence without fault, and with great joy."

Personal Application

Trust in Jesus, not in your faith in Jesus.

Quotable

"Be persuaded, timid soul, that He has loved you too much to cease loving you."
—François de la Mothe Pennelon

The Variety Reading Plan continues with MARK

Revelation

INTRODUCTION

Revelation reports a vision seen by the Apostle John while exiled to the island of Patmos, in the mid A.D. 90s. At the time the church was undergoing persecution, and the book was intended to encourage believers suffering for their faith.

A variety of schemes for interpreting Revelation have been developed. It has been treated as pure prophecy, but also as a book whose symbols deal primarily with the situation in John's own lifetime. In any interpretive framework, however, it is clear that John presents us with an exalted vision of Jesus, and unmistakable images of the divine judgments to be executed on rebellious mankind. Even when the symbolism is most difficult to understand, we are shown with overpowering clarity a God who is in sovereign control of history and of His universe. And we are assured that this God will deal with evil, and one day rule a cleansed and purified new world, populated by His saints.

OUTLINE OF CONTENTS

I. The Glorified Jesus . . . . Rev. 1
II. Letters to Seven Churches . . . . Rev. 2–3
III. Visions from the Unsealed Scroll . . . . Rev. 4:1–19:10
IV. Visions of Christ's Return . . . . Rev. 19:11–20:15
V. Visions of the New Earth . . . . Rev. 21–22

READING GUIDE (11 Days)

If hurried, you may read only the "core passage" in your Bible and the Devotional in each chapter of this Commentary.

Reading	*Chapters*	*Core passage*
355	1	1:9-18
356	2–3	2:1-7
357	4–5	5:6-14
358	6–7	7:9-17
359	8–9	9:12-21
360	10–11	11:15-19
361	12–14	14:6-20
362	15–17	17
363	18–19	18:1-13
364	20	20:7-15
365	21–22	21:22–22:5

Revelation

DECEMBER 21 *Reading 355*

THE LIVING ONE
Revelation 1

> *"I am the living One; I was dead, and behold I am alive forever and ever!" (Rev. 1:18)*

To truly understand Christmas we must see Jesus in all His glory.

Background

Revelation. Revelation is a stunning and powerful affirmation of God's sovereignty in all things. Through John's vision we are taken into heaven, to observe from that viewpoint as God pours out devastating judgments on a rebellious earth.

Many commentators view the book as predictive prophecy, depicting events which will take place at history's end. Others view it as a metaphorical affirmation of God's control over all, while still others see in it veiled allusions to John's own time, intended to encourage persecuted believers by symbolic representations of God's spiritual warfare. While it is important to commit to a framework when one's object is to interpret a book, this is less important when treating a book like Revelation devotionally. Believers from each interpretive school agree that Revelation is a towering affirmation of the sovereignty of God, of the primacy of Jesus, and of the certain judgment God will bring on all evil—including the evil one, Satan, himself. We can profit greatly this season of the year as we meditate on the glory of God revealed in Jesus, and the ultimate triumph of God, which Christ's birth as a Babe portends.

Overview

John had a prophecy given him by direct revelation (1:1-3), which he sent to seven churches in Asia (vv. 4-6a) and dedicated to Christ as God (vv. 6b-8). John described the setting and his stunning vison of the resurrected Christ (vv. 9-20).

Understanding the Text

"The revelation of Jesus Christ" Rev. 1:1-3. This is both a revelation of Jesus, and from Jesus. John was stunned as he saw the glorified Christ, still, and yet no longer, the Master that John loved so well during Christ's years on earth. It is helpful for us too to remember. The Jesus of Bethlehem shines brighter than the most brilliant galaxy. The Babe in the manger created and sustains the world He entered. We who honor Jesus in His humility as a man must also hold fast to the conviction that He is now exalted in glory, ruling over all.

John's language also suggests that what he was about to describe is a vision from Jesus: a direct revelation from the risen Lord to all mankind. For this reason a special blessing is associated with the "words of this prophecy," and is granted to all who take to heart the truths and images conveyed.

What an exciting book then for us to read. Especially at this time of year, when we look back to Christ's birth, and ahead to a bright new year.

"The seven churches in the province of Asia" Rev. 1:4. Seven is a number with great symbolic significance in Scripture, speaking of perfection or completion. Thus many have taken the churches John wrote to as symbolic of the church universal, even as the "seven spirits" (or "sevenfold spirit") is symbolic of the Holy Spirit.

Clearly John drew together the persons of the Godhead, showing that each is fully involved in what he was about to share. And that all Christians, the church universal, is intended to pay close heed.

"To Him who loves us and has freed us from our sins by His blood" Rev. 1:5-8. Revelation is rich in the language of worship and praise. Perhaps these exalted sayings were part of the worship language of the church when John wrote. Certainly they now deserve to be woven into our prayers, and fixed securely in our minds.

Jesus, in His love and sacrifice, has indeed "made us to be a kingdom of priests to serve His God and Father." Let us dedicate ourselves to serve.

"I am the Alpha and the Omega" Rev. 1:8. Alpha is the first letter of the Greek alphabet, and Omega the last. Christ is the beginning and end, not only of our faith, but of history itself. The Creation owes its existence to Him, and when at last time shall be no more, Christ will be the One who brings all things to completion.

It's easier for us to conceive of a Babe in a manger than One who overflows the vastness of the universe around us. Yet Jesus truly is Alpha and Omega, the beginning and the end, the fountainhead and climax of existence itself.

"Because of the Word of God and the testimony of Jesus" Rev. 1:9-11. Early church tradition suggests that John was exiled to Patmos near the end of the reign of the Emperor Domitian (A.D. 81–96). The church was experiencing official persecution for a refusal to worship the emperor as a god. It's no wonder that John identified himself as a

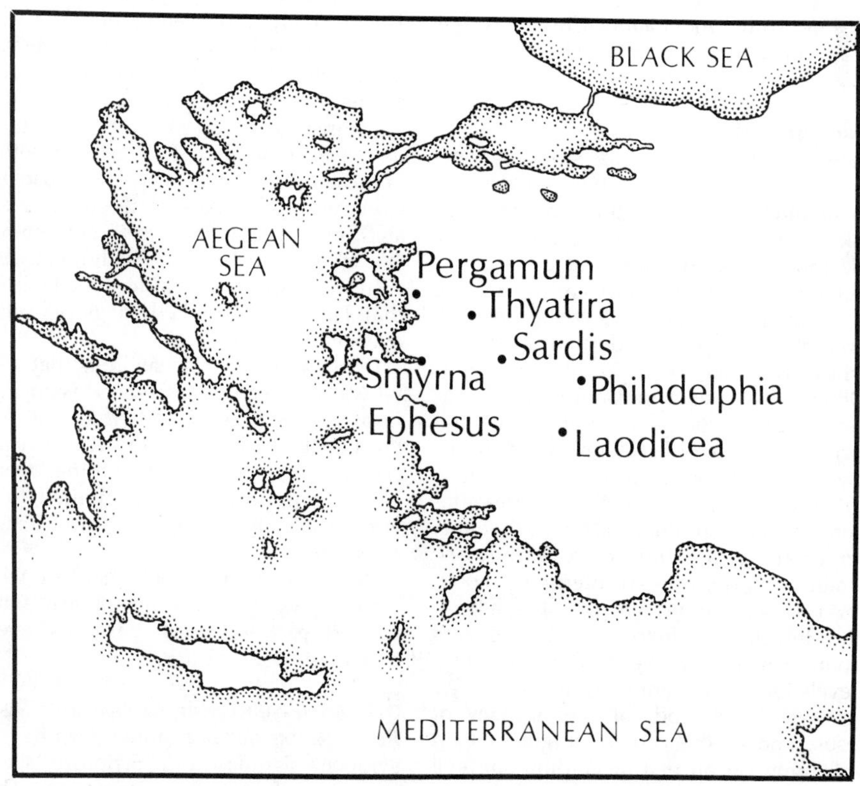

The seven cities to which John wrote (Rev 1:11; cf. 2–3) are sometimes taken to represent different periods in church history. What is clear is that they do represent the church universal. The messages John had for them are for us as well, and show us how to remain faithful till the glorious Lord of Revelation 1 returns triumphant.

companion "in the suffering and kingdom and patient endurance that are ours in Jesus."

It's important that we remember these three are often linked in Christian experience. We are citizens of Jesus' kingdom. Yet here on earth we often suffer, and must commit ourselves to endure until Christ returns and His rule is established over all. It is particularly important during times of suffering that we see the Jesus that John saw in his vision, and described in this powerful New Testament book. For the Jesus of Revelation is God, exalted in power, about to triumph over every foe. Though we suffer now, when His kingdom comes, we will rule with Him. Sustained by this hope, we patiently endure.

"When I saw Him, I fell at His feet as though dead" Rev. 1:12-18. At first John heard only a voice. When he turned to look, he saw a figure whose radiant appearance literally stunned him. The description John gave is filled with symbolism from the Old Testament (see DEVOTIONAL). But what is significant is the impact on John.

John was that disciple whom Jesus loved. John rested his head on Jesus' shoulder at the Last Supper. John was probably closest to Christ on a personal level. And through the last decades of John's life he preached and wrote about love for Jesus and love for brothers and sisters in Christ. Yet John, so close to Jesus while our Lord was on earth, and so near to Him in heart for over 50 years beyond the Resurrection, was shaken to his very core when he saw Jesus in His essential splendor.

We love Jesus, and feel close to Him. And this is right. But may we never become so casual in our thoughts of Him. For the Lord we love is Lord indeed, and were we to glimpse Him in His fundamental glory, we too would fall, stunned, at His feet.

"Write" Rev. 1:19. This verse is viewed by many as the key to interpreting Revelation. "What you have seen" corresponds to chapter 1, "what is now" to chapters 2–3, and "what will take place later" to the rest of the book. If we take this approach the bulk of Revelation is predictive prophecy, and deals with what will happen on earth as history draws to God's intended end.

"The seven stars are the angels of the seven churches" Rev. 1:20. Some of the symbols in Revelation are explained in the text itself, as here. Others are clearly derived from the Old Testament, and so can be explained by reference to earlier Scriptures. But some of the most powerful symbols cannot be easily explained at all. In most cases, it's best not to try. Linking disasters that Revelation describes to atomic holocausts, or germ warfare, is simply too speculative to help. What we need to seek is not some modern match to Revelation's imagery, but the trust of the passage itself: the broad impact of the passage on our view of God, of judgment, and of earth's future. The details remain open to debate. But the impact of most passages is unmistakably clear.

▶ DEVOTIONAL
Picture Perfect
(Rev. 1:9-18)

The famous German artist Albrecht Dürer did a woodcut of Jesus as portrayed here by John. For all the artist's skill, the figure looks awkward and stiff. Somehow none of the awe John felt is conveyed by the carved figure, with rays representing the brilliance around His head, and a literal sword protruding from His mouth.

That's one of the advantages of verbal symbolism over representational art. Somehow the images drawn by words can express with overwhelming power the most abstract ideas.

That's what we find here in Revelation 1. The utter glory of Jesus stunned John, and he struggled for words to express what he felt and saw. The robe was a common piece of clothing, and though the sash was golden, it was not unusual in itself. What stunned John was Jesus. And all he could do to describe the glorified Jesus to us was resort to Old Testament symbolism. Though human in form, His hair was "white like wool, as white as snow." The image calls to mind Daniel's vision of the Ancient of Days (Dan. 7:9; 10:5), about to exercise judgment. His eyes "like flaming torches" (cf. v. 6) indicate the fierceness of the judgment He metes out.

Bronze feet, the metal heated until it glows, also represents judgment. The Old Testament image is one of treading or trampling enemies, and bronze is the metal from which the altar of burnt offering was constructed. There sins were purged by sacrificing a substitute. Now Jesus is about to judge sinners themselves.

The voice is overpowering, a rushing Niagara of sound, and the "sharp doubled-edged sword" issuing from His mouth indicates both the war He will wage against sinners, and the means of His triumph. That simple spoken word by which Christ initially called all things into being will not be directed against the creation, and crush it to dust.

Dürer's figure remains a curiosity. It is almost laughable. Not so the vision of Jesus that John had, and not the words he used to describe our Lord. Those words remind us that the One who lay in a cradle, and hung from a cross, will fill the whole universe when He comes again. And He will crush evil under His feet.

Personal Application

Look at the Christmas crèche—but look beyond it too.

Quotable

"Looking unto Jesus and thinking about Him is a better way to meet and overcome sin than any physical austerities or spiritual self-reproaches. It is by looking at Him that we are changed."—Harriet Beecher Stowe

---

DECEMBER 22 *Reading 356*
SEVEN CHURCHES
Revelation 2–3

> *"These are the words of Him who holds the seven stars in His right hand and walks among the seven golden lampstands" (Rev. 2:1).*

Today too Jesus walks in our churches.

Background

The seven churches. Tradition says that John moved to Ephesus some 40 years before the Book of Revelation was written. He maintained close contact with believing communities in the seven major cities of the area to which he now transmitted Christ's message.

The seven churches were historical and symbolic congregations. Undoubtedly the issues each letter touched on were real at the time John wrote. Yet commentators through the ages have noted that these churches are also representative of churches of every place and time. It is helpful to look at each church, to see how its characteristics fit our own experience, and apply the words of commendation and corrections that John conveyed.

Each letter follows a pattern. Jesus identifies Himself, assesses the church's condition, and offers both commendation and criticism. With the criticism comes correction, and then a final promise.

In the words Jesus addresses to these seven first-century churches, we can still hear Him speak to you and me.

Overview

John recorded brief messages to the seven churches of Asia: Ephesus (2:1-7), Smyrna (vv. 8-11), Pergamum (vv. 12-17), Thyatira (vv. 18-29), Sardis (3:1-6), Philadelphia (vv. 7-13), and Laodicea (vv. 14-22).

Understanding the Text

"The church in Ephesus" Rev. 2:1-7. (See DEVOTIONAL.)

"The church in Smyrna" Rev. 2:8-11. Smyrna was a beautiful city of some 200,000 when John wrote. It was also the center of emperor worship, which was more a symbol of political allegiance than of religious devotion. Even so, Christians refused to perform the act, holding that Christ alone is to be honored as God. This created prejudice and persecution, and cost many not only their possessions but even imprisonment and death.

But persecution only strengthened the resolve of these Christians. And from

Jesus they—and we—hear words of encouragement. We may suffer loss of wealth, but we are rich in Christ. We may suffer death. But we will receive a crown of everlasting life.

"The church in Pergamum" Rev. 2:12-17. Pergamum was the provincial capital of Roman Asia. It was known for its wealth, but also for shrines to gods of healing, and many made pilgrimages to the city. This active center of paganism might rightly be called a city where Satan resided!

While holding fast to Christ, the believers in Pergamum were affected by their surroundings. The reference to the teaching of Balaam suggests a relaxing of moral standards in the church. While little is known of the "Nicolaitans," the meaning of the words, "conquer the people," suggests that the church permitted false teachers to establish some authority among them.

We too live in a society where moral standards are lax. It is all too easy for us, bombarded as we are by the attitudes of the world, to relax our standards as well. Christ sternly warned Pergamum, and us, against this course. But we are also given a promise. If we refuse the sweets of the world, Christ will provide "hidden manna." We will be fed a diet of goodness which will sustain life forever, while the moral "junk food" of this world destroys.

"The church in Thyatira" Rev. 2:18-29. This city was a commercial center when John wrote. Christ's description of Himself, with burning eyes and feet of burnished bronze, creates a setting of aura for this letter. Though the church was active and faithful in many respects, it had accepted the leadership of a woman characterized as "Jezebel." The first Jezebel introduced idolatry and gross immorality into ancient Israel, and we must assume the name signified the Thyatiran woman who did the same.

Thus what was known as "the church" was divided into faithful and corrupted segments.

The apostate and the genuine still exist within Christendom. The continued existence of the apostate reflects God's grace: He has "given her time to repent of her immorality." But the day of grace is drawing to a close. God will surely bring judgment on Jezebel and her followers.

The spirit of Jezebel still stalks the churches, and settles in wherever she can find room. Don't expect to purge Christendom, or even your denomination, of her influence. What Jesus says to those who do not accept her teaching is, "Hold on to what you have until I come."

We who hold fast to Christ and the authentic Gospel are to concentrate on good deeds, love, faith, service, and perseverance (v. 19). In doing Christ's will, we will find the spiritual authority we need to overcome (vv. 26-29).

"The church in Sardis" Rev. 3:1-6. Sardis was a prosperous and strategic city, known for its successful defense against invaders. It was also known for burial mounds, raised like a thousand hills on the skyline some seven miles from the city.

Sardis, with a reputation for vitality, was as dead spiritually as the nearby necropolis ("city of the dead"). Orthodoxy is never a substitute for spiritual life and vitality. And mere orthodoxy, like this church, receives and hears God's Word, but does not obey it.

What a challenge for us today. It's not enough to be doctrinally correct. We must be spiritually erect. It's not enough to know the Word. We must do it. Righteousness is not a shroud, but working clothes.

If you and I should find ourselves in a dead church, let's remember that even in Sardis there were saints dressed in white, the symbol not only of purity but of overcoming. The deader the faith of those around us, the more alive and active our faith must be.

"The church in Philadelphia" Rev. 3:7-13. This city of "brotherly love" lay on a major highway, and was also a major fortress. But the district in which Philadelphia was sited was earthquake-prone. Devastating quakes had made the people fearful, so at the slightest tremor crowds rushed out from behind the city walls.

The weakness of the earth beneath this city is reflected in the weakness of the church. But Christ spoke words of encouragement rather than rebuke. "I know that you have little strength," He said, "yet you have kept My Word and not denied My name."

Jesus is never contemptuous of our weaknesses. He understands our vulnerabilities only too well. So don't cringe from the Lord when you feel overwhelmed and ashamed. Jesus understands and praises you for what you have done rather than rail at you for what you have been unable to accomplish.

Christ does even more for the weak. The letter to Philadelphia says that Jesus holds the key. He opens doors, and no one can shut them. Christ goes with us, and before us. He opens doors and keeps them open. Even those most hostile to the claims of Christ will in time be forced to acknowledge that He has loved us. And each day we will find strength in the assurance of His continuing love.

"The church in Laodicea" Rev. 3:14-22. Laodicea was a wealthy city. The district around it also produced famous black wool. It was also a center for the production and distribution of "Phrygian powder," a famed cure for eye diseases.

The church at Laodicea apparently shared in the prosperity. Self-satisfied and comfortable, the Christians fit in with the rest of the population, just another of the many private clubs that characterized first-century social life.

Christ's church can thrive under persecution, and triumphantly survive all sorts of suffering. But material prosperity and social acceptability have consistently threatened the vitality of the church. When Christians fail to stand for something, they end up standing for nothing. The lukewarm church is the most pitiful church of all.

Christ's word to the lukewarm church, and the lukewarm Christian, is one of rebuke. He stands at the door and knocks, and asks us to exchange fellowship with the world for a more intimate, challenging walk with Him.

▶DEVOTIONAL
First Loves
(Rev. 2:1-7)

Just now several of the comic strips I glance at in the mornings are on the topic of divorce. I don't know how it happens, but it always seems that when one strip launches a particular theme, all the others quickly follow.

At any rate, Sally Forth and Gasoline Alley both are exploring the painful loss of first loves. Not that they have any answers. But painful topics have their humor, and the cartoonists are working hard to dig it out.

Actually, while the cartoonists have no answers for us, Christ's letter to the Ephesians has a great one. It's applicable to relationship with our spouses, and to relationship with God! And it may come as a surprise.

Ephesus was the site of the great temple of Artemis, famous in all of Asia. It was to this congregation Paul addressed a letter exploring the spiritual nature of the church as the body of Christ. Now, some 40 years after Paul's ministry, the church was commended for hard work, perseverance, and its commitment to holiness. Despite opposition this congregation has not tired of expressing a firm faith in Jesus as God's Christ (vv. 1-3).

But the church had a fault of which many of us are guilty. We keep on serving. But somehow in the struggle we lose the glowing love for Jesus that motivated us at first. It's good to be faithful. But faithfulness is no substitute for passion.

What can we do when we lose our first love? The text says, repent, and recapture it. And here's the surprising instruction: "Do the things you did at first" (v. 5).

We have the notion today that feelings and actions aren't tied as tightly together as they really are. Are you "falling out of love" with your wife? Don't try to change your feelings. Instead, begin to "do the things you did at first." Bring her flowers. Call her up, just to say "Hi!" and hear her voice. Tell her how much you love her. Write her little poems or notes. The wonder is that as you do these things that express love, the emotion of love returns.

It's just the same in our relationship with God. Are you faithful, but somehow unfulfilled as a Christian? Then look back, and remember some of the things you did as a young believer, just because you wanted to and not because they were religious duties. Do them again. And watch your feelings follow.

Personal Application
Love shown stays alive and vital.

Quotable
"God is Truth. To be true, to hate every form of falsehood, to live a brave, true, real life—that is to love God."—F.W. Robertson

DECEMBER 23 *Reading 357*

PRAISE IN HEAVEN
Revelation 4–5

> *"Worthy is the Lamb, who was slain, to receive power and wealth and wisdom and strength and honor and glory and praise" (Rev. 5:12).*

All in heaven praise Jesus. Praise Him here on earth!

Background
The Jews were scandalized that Jesus should be identified as equal with God (cf. John 8:48-58). The sophisticated first-century pagan believed in one "great God," with many subordinate deities. Jesus might possibly be granted the status of a hero or subordinate deity. But it was shocking to the pagan that Christians would claim that this crucified Galilean was in fact the great God come in the flesh.

Against this background of hostility and resentment, John's vision of the scene now unfolding in heaven is especially powerful. John was granted a vision of the great God Almighty, identified as the Creator. And then, standing on the very throne of the High God, John saw Jesus! And the inhabitants of heaven fell down and worshiped Jesus, granting Him the same praise and honor offered to God Himself.

Whatever else Revelation may teach us this Christmas season, it begins with the exaltation of Jesus. The Babe of Bethlehem, despite the skeptics' sneers, is the eternal God come in the flesh. All heaven joins us today in worshiping Him. And, when history draws to a close, and John's vision of the future is fulfilled, the universe will join in honoring Jesus Christ as Lord.

Overview
John was raised to heaven, and saw God on His throne, surrounded and praised by living creatures (4:1-11). A call went out for one worthy to open a sealed scroll (5:1-4). Jesus was then introduced as a Lamb slain (vv. 5-6), standing on the very throne of God and receiving worship as God (vv. 7-14).

Understanding the Text
"I will show you what must take place after this" Rev. 4:1. Some understand Revelation as a symbolic statement of God's sovereignty. Others see it as apocalyptic, meaning that it is a powerful but again symbolic description of the writer's impressions of events to take place at the end of time. The angel who called John up to heaven seemed to identify the rest of this powerful book as prophecy.

From this verse on John will watch future history unfold, not from man's viewpoint on earth, but from the viewpoint of a an observer in heaven.

What a privilege this is. And what a reminder for us. You and I are limited to physical eyes that see only what is taking place in the material universe. John's vision reminds us that all around us God and His angels are active, struggling with Satan's hosts in an invisible war. You and I are part of this warfare. Though we cannot now understand how the part we play contributes to final victory, through John we know that God will surely triumph in the end.

"A throne in heaven" Rev. 4:2-9. The vision of the throne, of the Person seated on it, and of the "living creatures" who constantly cry, "Holy, holy holy," recalls the vision of God granted to both Isaiah (Isa. 6) and to Ezekiel (Ezek. 1; 10).

This identification of the God John worshiped with the God of the Old Testament is vitally important. One of the early criticisms of Christianity was that while the church claimed to be a development from and a fulfillment of Judaism, Christians departed from worship of the Old Testament's God to worship a mere man. But the vision that John had of God in heaven is unmistakably that of the very God who revealed Himself in similar visions to Isaiah and to Ezekiel!

Here, in the last book of the New Testament, we have final reassurance that the God we know in Jesus is the one God who has revealed Himself in sacred history. Our faith is secure, rooted in a revelation that spans the millennia, a fulfillment of promises made to Abraham over 4,000 years ago.

"Twenty-four elders" Rev. 4:4. Those who study Revelation look for meaning in every detail. Thus the faces on the "living creatures," which we know from Ezekiel and Isaiah as a special order of angels called cherubim, are taken to represent the highest representative of each order of warm-blooded animal creation: the lion for predators, the ox for domesticated animals, the eagle for birds of the air, and above all, man.

What might the meaning of the 24 elders be? Most take them to represent the 12 tribes of Israel, and the 12 Apostles introduced by Christ. Thus the elders, like the vision of God Himself, tie together Old Testament and New, reaffirming the unity of God's plan, and the glorious truth that saints of every age have been saved by faith, through the salvation won for us all by Jesus Christ.

"You are worthy, our Lord and God" Rev. 4:9-11. The figure on the throne, "our Lord and God," receives perpetual praise from the living creatures and the elders. Inhabitants of both the spiritual and material universe unite to praise His name.

This first paean of praise focuses on God's worth as Creator. He created "all things." Again we see a sharp departure from first-century culture, where God was viewed as a craftsman who shaped preexisting matter into its present shape. The God of the Bible, however, created all things. All things material, all things spiritual, owe their existence to Him.

We too owe our existence to Him. As our very being is a gift from God, how fitting it is to join the heavenly throng, and offer Him our own perpetual praise:

> You are worthy, our Lord and God,
> to receive glory and honor and power,
> for You created all things,
> and by Your will they were created
> and have their being.

"A scroll with writing on it" Rev. 5:1-5. John's attention was drawn to a sealed scroll held in the hand of God, and he heard an angel calling for someone "worthy to break the seals and open the scroll." While the nature of the scroll was then a mystery to John, he was overwhelmed with a sense of urgency. When no one was found "in heaven or on earth or under the earth" who was worthy to break the seals, John was overcome and weeped uncontrollably.

Later we learn the significance of the scroll. It is the book of history's end, and contains all the judgments that God must pour out on the earth to satisfy justice, and to bring in everlasting righteousness. Now we can understand John's emotional outburst. He wept for all who experience injustice now. He wept for all who endure suffering and pain. He wept for all who are in anguish because of the sin that warps and twists every human society, crushing the hopes and the spirit of the individual. John wept, and his tears expressed all our yearnings for a world purified and purged of sin; a world made forever new.

We can search all of heaven and earth, we can search time past and time to come, and none worthy to bring history to God's intended end can be found. None—but One. The Jesus of history. Born a Babe. Born to die. But born to be raised up, and to come again.

"I saw a Lamb" Rev. 5:5-14. The stunning aspect of John's description is found in these words: "standing in the center of the throne." John had seen God seated on heaven's throne, and suddenly, there on the throne beside God, Jesus stood.

He took the scroll, and as He held it the living creatures and the elders fell down and worshiped Him.

What clearer affirmation could there be that Jesus and God the Father are One God? Distinct Persons, yes. But One in essential being, both equally worthy of our worship and our praise.

And suddenly heaven *is* filled with praises. Praises for the Lamb. Praises for One born in order to die, to purchase with His own blood "men for God from every tribe and language and people and nation."

You.

And me.

Men and women for God, to be a kingdom and priests, to serve our God and reign in Jesus Christ, forever and forever and ever. Amen.

No wonder we join this wonderous season with the crowds of heaven, and in a loud voice sing,

> Worthy is the Lamb, who was slain,
> to receive power and wealth and wisdom and strength
> and honor and glory and praise!

▶ DEVOTIONAL
Praise to the Lord
(Rev. 5:6-14)

In the A.D. 406 a 16-year-old English boy named Patrick was captured by Irish pirates and sold as a slave in Ireland. Later he escaped, trained for the priesthood, and returned to Ireland as a missionary, where he played a central role in converting the Irish to Christianity. This prayer, developed from Patrick's original version, helps us sense what it can mean for us to be ever aware of Jesus, triumphant with the Father on heaven's throne.

> I bind unto myself today
> The power of God to hold and lead,
> His eye to watch, His might to stay,
> His ear to harken to my need.
> The wisdom of my God to teach,
> His hand to guide, His shield to ward;
> The word of God to give me speech,
> His heavenly host to be my guard.
>
> Christ be with me, Christ within me,
> Christ behind me, Christ before me,
> Christ beside me, Christ to win me,
> Christ to comfort and restore me,
> Christ beneath me, Christ above me,
> Christ in quiet, Christ in danger,
> Christ in mouth of friend or stranger.
>
> I bind unto myself the name,
> The strong name of the Trinity;
> By invocation of the same,
> The Three in One, the One in Three,
> Of whom all nature hath creation;
> Eternal Father, Spirit, Word,
> Praise to the Lord of my salvation,
> Salvation is of Christ the Lord.

Personal Application

Take the enthroned Christ with you, within you.

Quotable

"He who has not Christmas in his heart will never find it under a tree."—Roy L. Smith

DECEMBER 24 *Reading 358*
WASHED IN THE BLOOD
Revelation 6–7

> *"They are before the throne of God and serve Him day and night in His temple; and He who sits on the throne will spread His tent over them. Never again will they hunger; never again will they thirst" (Rev. 7:15-16).*

Beyond the judgment lies blessing for God's own.

Background

Apocalyptic language. In these and future chapters we find language that may puzzle us. Take, for instance, Revelation 6:12-14. There John speaks of the sun turning black like sackcloth. He mentions a blood red moon; stars falling to earth from the sky. He sees the sky itself recede "like a scroll, rolling up." Mountains and islands are "removed from [their] place."

Many reading these descriptions have struggled to understand them in modern terms. The black sky and red moon might be explained by massive dust clouds filling the air. Perhaps this suggests atomic warfare, with mushroom clouds hurling ton upon ton of dirt and dust into the air. Are the falling stars meteorites? Or are they laser beams shot from satellites? What exactly does John see?

The difficulty with such visions lies in a simple feature of language. The words available for use are limited to concepts existing in the writer's time. If you lived in the United States just 300 hundred years ago, and suddenly were given a vision of giant planes landing and taking off from Chicago's O'Hare field, and saw expressways filled with speeding cars, how could you begin to describe what you saw? You have no terms for planes, cars, airports, superhighways. These would all be so strange you would have no way to talk about them—except to speak perhaps of giant shining birds that roar, of horseless carts that hurtle toward each other with astounding speed. And even then, your listeners would be unable to grasp what it really was that you saw.

It's the same with much of the language of Revelation. John saw something. He used the words available in his culture to describe them. But those words are inadequate. If John had seen an atomic explosion, he would not know what it was, much less be able to tell others about it. Perhaps all he could say would be, "the sky receded like a scroll."

Given then the limitations of language, we shouldn't expect to explain every scene described in Revelation. Yet even when we can't grasp the "how" or "why," what is happening is still relatively clear. The awesome and terrible nature of the events we are about to witness is unmistakable. And, when they do occur, we'll say, "Of course! I see now what John was talking about."

And, if we know Jesus, we will survive judgment's final, awesome storm.

Overview

The Lamb begins to open the seals, and awesome judgments are poured out on the earth (6:1-8). Slain saints cry out for Christ to judge (vv. 9-11), as further devastation strikes earth's terrified population (vv. 12-17). A sudden halt is called to the judgment as 144,000 Jewish witnesses are sealed (7:1-8). In heaven the saved and angelic hosts praise God, who deals mercifully with those who have suffered for His name (vv. 9-17).

Understanding the Text

"The Lamb opened the first of the seven seals" Rev. 6:1-8. The first four seals that are opened by the Lamb unleash on earth what are known as the "four horsemen of the apocalypse." These four are conquest (v. 2), warfare (vv. 3-4), famine—represented by the inflated price of grain—(vv. 5-6), and death-dealing plague (vv. 7-8).

None of these scourges are unknown in any generation. The thing that makes the judgments of the seals so terrible is that they strike the whole world, killing a fourth of earth's population. Always before wars, famine, and plague have been localized. It was terrible in Europe during the era of the Black Plague. It was terrible in Poland when the panzers rolled in, and the SS rounded up and killed that land's elite as well as its Jewish population. But what John pictures is worldwide terror.

Always before there was someplace to flee; someplace safe. But as God's final judgments begin, all hope is stripped away.

It's difficult, gathered at church for a candlelight celebration of the birth of Jesus, to imagine the future John portrays. Gathered together to celebrate, we feel safe, secure. And we are! For in the Babe of Bethlehem, God has provided a hiding place. We find our peace in Christ. Yet a most terrible fate awaits the world outside of Him.

"The souls of those who had been slain" Rev. 6:9-11. In this world we are subject to persecution. Over the centuries many believers have given their lives for the cause of Christ. Every indication is that as history draws to a close, and God's judgments are poured out on a terrified earth, intense persecution will resume.

Now John is shown the souls of many slain "because of the Word of God," and he hears them cry out for vengeance. These slain saints are told to wait, for others will be added to their number. But it is totally clear that God will not hold back judgment for long.

As we hear the victims cry, let's remember that it is right for God, who is "holy and true," to judge the inhabitants of earth and to avenge His murdered own. The offer of salvation has been extended to all for many thousands of years. Each Christmas, despite tinsel and commercialism, the world is reminded that God has come in the flesh to bring salvation. Those who reject the gift of God, who continue willfully in sin, and who then persecute God's people, deserve to be—and must be—judged by God.

Christ's birthday is a promise, and a threat. To those who believe, the birth promises salvation. To those who will not believe, it is a dreadful reminder that God can and will act in our world of space and time. But when He comes again, it will be to judge.

"Fall on us and hide us" Rev. 6:12-17. As the next onslaught of judgments crash on the earth, it becomes clear to all that "the great day of [God's] wrath has come." Those who have refused to take God seriously, and scoffed at the promise of salvation, are now certain that God is, and that the dreadful day of His judgment has come.

What strikes us is their reaction. There is no suggestion of repentance. All men seem able to do is try, futilely, to hide.

If we will not respond to grace, we will surely not respond to punishment. If God's love has not drawn us to Him, His anger most certainly will not either.

"Holding back the four winds of the earth" Rev. 7:1-8. There is an unexpected interlude, like the eye of judgment's awesome hurricane. The pause comes that God might place a protective seal on 144,000 individuals, 12,000 from each of the 12 tribes of Israel.

Many see in this listing of Israel's tribes a rejoining of the stream that separated over Jesus. In the first century the faith of some of the Jewish people flowed to the right. They accepted Jesus as the Messiah and Saviour predicted in the Old Testament, and became the first members of the Christian church. The faith of others flowed left, turning away from our Lord and holding fast to the old traditions as if He had never come. Yet Paul in Romans 11 looks foward to a day when the streams will meet again, and all Israel recognizes Christ as the Messiah for which the Jewish people continue to yearn. As the Prophet Zechariah says, "They will look on . . . the One they have pierced, and they will mourn for Him as one mourns for an only child, and grieve bitterly for Him as one grieves for a firstborn child" (Zech. 12:10).

If this passage is linked with the restoration of Israel, it describes 144,000 newly converted missionaries, who amid the terrible Tribulation that marks the end of history, witness joyfully to one who is Messiah, Saviour, and Judge.

"From every nation, tribe, people and language" Rev. 7:9-17. Now John's eye is drawn back to heaven, and he sees the innumerable company of the saved. Drawn from every people and tribe, dressed in the white robes of salvation, they join in offering praise and glory to God.

Some have drawn from this verse the notion that before Christ can return, every people must hear the Gospel. How else, they ask, can there be those from every nation, tribe, people, and language in heaven?

A better answer displays even more fully the love and grace of God. Uncounted millions of babes, some unborn, some barely entering childhood, have died since time began. All these, gone before old enough to make any personal response to God, will join us before the throne of God. No tribe, no nation, no people of history, will be unrepresented. God's salvation has already overflowed, to encompass all. Christ can come at any moment. Every precondition has already been fulfilled.

How good to know, as we celebrate the meaning of Christ's birth, that the overflow of God's love has surged around us. How good to know that we are guaranteed a place with the multitude that will praise Him in that day.

▶ DEVOTIONAL
Were You There?
(Rev. 7:9-17)

The angels and elders fall down and worship God. The joy they feel is shared and expressed by all of heaven's multitude.

> Amen!
> Praise and glory
> and wisdom and thanks and honor
> and power and strength
> be to our God forever and ever.
> Amen!

The words of praise echo throughout the unseen universe, as all join in.

But then a new song is begun. The angels fall silent. They can speak the words, but never sing them. They can observe, but never join in this chorus. For this is the song of salvation. To join in one must be a man. One must have known the anguish of sin, the painful grip of evil. To sing this song, one must know what it means to have been soiled—and then cleansed. To have fallen to the depths—and then been lifted up.

The song of salvation found in verses 15-17 is only for those who "have washed their robes and made them white in the blood of the Lamb" (v. 14).

And so there is another song we need to sing at Christmastime. Not "Joy to the World," not "O Little Town of Bethlehem," but "Were You There When They Crucified My Lord?"

Were you there?

Not as an observer, but as a participant. Not as a scoffer, but as one who was so perfectly united with our Lord through faith that His death was yours, His blood payment for your sins, His suffering your passport to eternal joy?

If you were there, at Calvary, you can be sure. One day you will stand with the white-robed throng before God's throne, and know the joy of the redeemed.

Never again to hunger.
Never again to thirst.
Never again to weep a tear.

For then the Lamb, at the center of God's throne, will be your Shepherd and your joy.

Personal Application

The Christ of Christmas, the Christ of Calvary, and the Christ of Glory, are one. And all are yours.

Quotable

Praise God for Christmas.
Praise Him for the Incarnation
for the Word made flesh.
I will not sing
of shepherds watching
flocks
on frosty night
or angel choristers.
I will not sing of stable bare
in Bethlehem
or lowing oxen
wise men
trailing distant star
with gold and frankincense
and myrrh.
Tonight I will sing
praise to the Father
who stood on heaven's
threshold
and said farewell to His Son
as He stepped across the
stars
to Bethlehem
and Jerusalem.
And I will sing praise to the
infinite eternal Son
who became most fine
a Baby

who would one day be
executed
for my crimes.

Praise Him in the heavens.
Praise Him in the stable.
Praise Him in my heart.—Joseph Bayly

DECEMBER 25 *Reading 359*
TRUMPET CALL
Revelation 8–9

> *"Woe! Woe! Woe to the inhabitants of the earth, because of the trumpet blasts about to be sounded" (Rev. 8:13).*

The certainty of judgment brings home the full meaning of Christmas.

Overview

The opening of the seventh seal reveals seven trumpets, representing even more severe judgments that are released on the earth (8:1–9:19). But even these crushing blows fail to bring mankind's survivors to repentance (vv. 20-21).

Understanding the Text

"He opened the seventh seal" Rev. 8:1-2. My wife has a set of nesting canisters. Each one, a bit smaller than the other, fits neatly inside its larger companion. The judgments of Revelation are something like this. The seventh seal is opened, to reveal seven trumpets. When the seventh trumpet finally sounds, watching eyes will discover within seven bowls filled with God's wrath. As we read Revelation, it seems that the judgments never stop, but roll on and on in an unending series of terrifying events.

As we look at each one, it seems these chapters are hardly suited for Christmas reading. Where is the Babe of Bethlehem in these awful descriptions of blazing mountains, a smoking abyss, and demonic tormentors of mankind? But He is here.

He is here, for in the description of the judgments that mark history's anguished end, we sense the reason for the Incarnation. Jesus was born, lived, died, and rose again, that you and I might escape the punishments described here.

He was born that all who believe might pass from the darkness into the light, from death to life, from anguish into joy.

"With the prayers of all the saints" Rev. 8:3-5. This is a stunning image. Suddenly the censor that contains the prayers of the saints is taken from a golden altar, filled with burning coals, and hurled out on the earth below. That which held the praise, the thanksgiving, the joys of Jesus' own, becomes a tool of judgment, convulsing earth itself.

How can this be? Perhaps because God's judgment is the vindication of His saints. His punishments are meted out on those who have persecuted and murdered godly men and women. But there seems to be even more than this. The prayers of those who have come to know the Lamb express a holiness to which all men are called, but many refuse. In the very contrast between the righteous and the evil, the worshiper and the rebel, the doom of the lost is sealed.

Why don't all see the real meaning of Christmas? Why don't all look beyond the wrapped packages, the laden tables, the holiday songs and the repeated portrayals of the Grinch who almost stole Christmas, or the *Miracle on 34th Street*? Why don't all see Christ, born to die, an Infant destined to be offered up for us all?

Why do not men realize that, if they will not have the Christ Child now, they will most certainly receive judgment from His mighty hand?

"Hail and fire mixed with blood" Rev. 8:6-12. The limitations of language make it impossible for us to know just what John describes. The images of the blazing mountain and the fiery star hurtling on earth are terrifying enough. The darkening of familiar heavenly bodies is even worse. Whatever these images used by John may really be, their effect is clear enough. A third of earth's vegetation, seas, and waters are destroyed, and millions die.

What a contrast, this, with brightly lit

houses with sparkling trees set prominently in front of living room windows. What a reminder that the choice God sets before is one of joy, or endless loss.

"The key to the shaft of the Abyss" Rev. 8:13–9:12. The former judgments might be classified as natural catastrophes. Despite their impact on the earth, materials from the physical universe were used to achieve them.

Now, however, hordes of hostile spiritual beings are unleashed. Demons, in the form of something like locusts, torment the remaining inhabitants of earth.

Even today there are those who choose to worship Satan, expecting some protection or gain. How foolish such people now are seen to be. Satan and his hordes have always hated humankind. Given the opportunity, the released demons cause such agony that men crave death. And death is denied.

Today there is a choice all men may make. And each Christmastime everyone, everywhere, is reminded of a Child who became a Man—and waits to welcome them home to heaven.

"The number of the mounted troops was two hundred million" Rev. 9:12-21. Yet another supernatural horde is unleashed against mankind. And this swarm kills. There is no skepticism now. The supernatural is known by all to be real.

Many today scoff or shrug at the supernatural, and believe, with the ancients, that the material universe is all that exists. Many demand proof or they will not believe. But if they had the proof, would they believe then?

Verses 20 and 21 tell us. Despite the evident nature of the judgment, the rest of mankind "did not stop worshiping demons, and idols of gold. . . . Nor did they repent of their murders, their magic arts, their sexual immorality or their thefts."

It is not proof mankind needs.

It is to heed the Word of God, and let God work a change within their hearts.

▶DEVOTIONAL
"Give Me Love"
(Rev. 9:12-21)

Every now and then Sarah crawls up in her mother's lap and says, "Give me love." They hug and pat each other, coo and smile, and feel especially close. Mom and daughter.

Christmas is just such a time for us. "Give me love," is Jesus' way. We gather around Him, eager to hug and be hugged. Eager to be reminded of His love, and eager to affirm ours as well.

There's something about love that draws us. And there's something about punishment that repels.

We see that in our home too. Even when punishment is well deserved, and Sarah knows it, the lower lip sullenly protrudes. She looks accusingly out of angry eyes, and sometimes even shouts out her feelings that it's all unfair.

This is a contrast we need to see this Christmastime, as we read of God's terrible judgments on a sinful human race—and feel shocked that Revelation reports, they "still did not repent." They did not change their minds or change their ways.

That's why Christmas is such an appropriate expression of our faith. It's God reminding us that He has heard our cry of "give me love." And He has given love in the Christ Child whose birth we celebrate.

As long as the world has Christmas, God reaches out to give us love, and the door of salvation is open wide. Oh, let us speak to others of this love, before the judgment comes, and hardened hearts are frozen in a rebellion that will lock them away from love for all eternity.

Personal Application

Share the love of God with others this Christmastime.

Quotable

"The innkeeper who gave Mary and Joseph a Christmas Eve cave should be a holiday model for Christians as they celebrate the birth of the Messiah. That's because that Middle Eastern Howard Johnson had the simple consideration to think beyond the 'no' that could have easily been his complete conversation with the visiting strangers who came to his door.

"In contrast, many Christians who honor the child born that night say no all the time to strangers during the very time of year when they should be opening their doors to the lonely, forgotten, and alienated."—James Greig

DECEMBER 26 *Reading 360*
NO MORE DELAY
Revelation 10–11

"In the days when the seventh angel is about to sound his trumpet, the mystery of God will be accomplished, just as He announced to His servants the prophets" (Rev. 10:7).

The fast-approaching new year may hold the events described in the rest of Revelation!

Background

Interpretation. From this point the Book of Revelation becomes even more difficult to interpret, and here commentators are most clearly divided.

The earliest interpretive school, current in the first two centuries, viewed Revelation as predictive prophecy, a literal though often obscure description of what is to happen in the future. In the third century Christians began to emphasize supposed allegorical meanings. Much later other Christians began to treat Revelation as a review of church history. For instance, depending on the commentator's view, they saw the "beasts" of the book as Pope and bishops, or the leaders of the Protestant Reformation.

A more sophisticated modern view suggests that each section of Revelation is a symbolic treatment of history, with each segment looking at God's working throughout the ages from a slightly different perspective.

And so any reader of Revelation has certain choices to make. Is the book predictive prophecy? Allegory? Or symbolic treatment of issues of John's day, of church history, or of history's end? Does the use of many terms found in Old Testament prophecy mean Revelation may be harmonized with Old Testament visions of history's end that feature Israel? Or does the use of Old Testament elements mean that Old Testament prophecy too must be treated symbolically rather than literally? Is there a future for Israel as a chosen people of God? Or does Israel, which still exists as a people, have no such future, and the ancient promises given to the Jews are in fact spiritual promises fulfilled in the church?

Even when reading the bulk of Revelation devotionally, and particularly chapters 10–14, some framework must be adopted for our reading.

While recognizing that difficulties exist for any interpretive school, it seems to me that to be most consistent with the nature of Scripture and the character of God we should take Revelation as a narrative of future history, with its images rooted in Old Testament prophecy, and its constant references to Israel evidence that God intends to keep the prophets' promises to His ancient people. Even given this framework, much in Revelation must remain a mystery. But much is also far more clear—and applicable to our lives.

Overview

John is told that history's predicted end will now unfold (10:1-7). He is given a scroll to eat and told to prophesy (vv. 8-11). Two terrible prophets testify against mankind for a time period predicted in Daniel (11:1-6). They are killed, but raised again and taken to heaven (vv. 7-14). There all rejoice, for God has begun to reign (vv. 15-19).

Understanding the Text

"Seal up what the seven thunders have said" Rev. 10:1-4. John is not able, even in the powerful symbolism of Revelation, to report all that he saw in his vision. It may be the seven thunders are yet another nested series of judgments. Or perhaps not. In either case, it's well for us to remember that it is God's grace which keeps many aspects of the future hidden from us.

Think how terrible it would be if you or I knew years ahead the tragedies we would experience. Then present joys would always be dimmed by our foreknowledge of darkness ahead. Or suppose we knew ahead of time that great prosperity and success were assured? Where would the struggle be? Where the satisfaction, as each effort received its reward?

God leaves us uncertain, to guard us from premature sorrow, to surprise us by joy, and most of all, so that each and every day we will sense our need to walk with our hand in His.

"There will be no more delay!" Rev. 10:5-7 One of the most powerful reasons to take Revelation as predictive prophecy is found in this verse. John tells us that the "mystery of God will be accomplished, just as He announced to His servants the prophets." What John now sees is what Old Testament prophets foretold.

In Scripture a "mystery" is something which has been for all time an element in God's eternal plan, but has been revealed to humankind only recently. The church itself is such a mystery: no one living before Christ imagined that God intended to bond Jew and Gentile together into one body through faith in the crucified Son of God.

Perhaps we can think of "mystery" as God, joyfully crying out, "Surprise!" as He unveils yet another stunning aspect of His complex plan for His creation.

Judgment too will come as a surprise, even though dark warnings abound in Scripture. Elements of what John tells us are new, though they fit into an Old Testament framework. Even now the certainty of punishment for sin, and of an end to evil, rings throughout the Word of God.

Let's never become so lost in trying to interpret the details of Revelation that we lose sight of the crushing impression it is intended to make. Judgment is coming. Doom awaits. One day soon all the terrors predicted by the prophets of every age will be realized here on earth. How important that we be ready, and not be surprised!

"Take it and eat it" Rev. 10:9-11. There is an obvious analogy here to Ezekiel, who was also told to take a scroll and eat it, and speak to the people of Israel (Ezek. 3). While that scroll too tasted like honey, it plunged the prophet into a ministry of condemnation, speaking against rebellious Israel until after the destruction of Jerusalem, and only then becoming a message of hope.

Revelation follows a similar pattern. John first describes terrible judgments that will strike the earth (11–18). But he concludes with the triumph of God, and the welcome of the saints to a new and purified heaven and earth.

In a way, even the Gospel is sweet and bitter. When we eat it, welcoming Christ into our hearts, we rejoice in its sweetness. But then, suddenly, we realize that the promise of salvation implies that all men are lost. We face that bitter truth, and realize that like Ezekiel and John, we are to witness to many who may not hear, and in refusing to listen, doom themselves to judgment.

"But exclude the outer court" Rev. 11:1-6. The focus of the vision now shifts to Jerusalem. The city lies under the control of Gentiles, and numbers found in Daniel's predictions concerning history's end make the link between Old Testament prophecy and Revelation unmistakably clear. There is no doubt that Jewish commentators, and early Christians as well, understood the visions of Daniel to predict or at least foreshadow the last years of world history and the career of the Antichrist.

But here more mystery is unveiled, and two unexpected figures appear. These are two witnesses, who are given supernatural powers reminiscent of Moses and Elijah. Interestingly, Jewish tradition foretold a return of Moses and Elijah at the time of the end.

Perhaps the most significant aspect of the vision of the two witnesses for us, however, is a reminder. Even in the most desperate of times, God's people are to take a stand against sin. And if such a stand provokes hostility, so be it.

"The beast that comes up from the Abyss" Rev. 11:7-14. John sees the two witnesses killed by an individual commonly identified as the Antichrist. But after three and a half days their exposed bodies return to life, and are visibly taken up into heaven, to the consternation of their enemies.

One phrase here says that people from "every people, tribe, language and nation" will gaze on the dead bodies of the two witnesses. It's likely that this phrase is a symbolic expression meaning little more than "all mankind." Still, it is fascinating to speculate. Ours is the only generation in history where events in any part of the world can be witnessed everywhere, as they take place. TV cameras, linked to satellites, simultaneously transmit pictures worldwide. How easy it would be today for people from every nation to see the dramatic events John portrays. Or to see them tomorrow!

▶ DEVOTIONAL
Begun to Reign
(Rev. 11:15-19)

A woman began the grand tradition. It was the first time she had heard Handel's *Messiah*. It happened when the great piece reached its triumphant culmination, and the choir sang out, "And He shall reign, for ever and ever!" Victoria, the Queen of England, deeply moved, stood in honor of her great King, Jesus, Ruler of the universe itself.

And ever since, as the "Hallelujah Chorus" is played, audiences have stood in awed respect.

Here in Revelation 11, we see the source of that great piece of music. As the seventh trumpet sounds, and judgments continue to dash themselves against an unrepentant earth, the choir of heaven shouts:

> The kingdom of this world
> has become the kingdom
> of our Lord and of His Christ,
> and He will reign forever and ever.

When the choir shouts out its joy, Christ does not yet stand on a subdued earth. Evil is not yet purged. The Antichrist continues to exalt himself, and Satan struggles mightily. Mankind spits out its hostility against God, and displays that hatred by killing God's servants. Yet in heaven, the hymns of praise reach a loud crescendo. All heaven knows that "You have taken up Your great power and have begun to reign."

We live in a day when God has set aside the open exercise of His mighty power. He works now through providence, so subtly that the lost laugh at the notion of divine sovereignty, and pass all things off as chance or happenstance. One day God will openly take up His mighty power, and then His rule will be unmistakable. And that day is coming, soon.

Until then, we must remember that when things look darkest on the earth, the songs of heaven are the most triumphant. You and I, limited to our physical eyes, may not see what is so clear in heaven. But we can still rise up, and shout it out with the angels.

God reigns!

Personal Application

Show reverence for God's name by trusting in His sovereignty.

Quotable

"Brethren, be great believers. Little faith will bring your souls to heaven, but great faith will bring heaven to your souls."—Charles Spurgeon

DECEMBER 27 *Reading 361*
THE BEASTS
Revelation 12–14

"Men worshiped . . . the beast, and asked, 'Who is like the beast? Who can make war against him?'" (Rev. 13:4)

Human beings are often deceived by those who appear to be powerful.

Background

Symbols in Revelation 12–14. We are naturally curious as to who is represented by the figures that make such an overwhelming impression in these powerful chapters of Revelation. One figure, that of the dragon, is interpreted in the text. The great red dragon is Satan himself, "who leads the whole world astray."

While the woman of chapter 12 has been variously interpreted as humanity, the church, and Mary, it is best to understand her as representing Israel. This is the people from whom Christ came; the people whose tragic journey over the past 2,000 years indicates Satan's continuing hostility.

The "sea" in Scripture generally is a symbol of humanity. The "beast out of the sea" is the Antichrist, who is clearly linked by details in the text to the Antichrist of Daniel's prophecies. The "beast out of the earth" is usually called the "false prophet." Together the devil, the Antichrist, and false prophet compose an unholy trinity, a distorted reflection of Father, Son, and Holy Spirit. They achieve great power on earth, and win the allegiance of what remains of humanity. They seem to triumph over God's saints. But the triumph is only apparent. After a final warning is conveyed to all on earth, a new, intensified level of judgment begins.

Overview

Signs in heaven review events: the hostility of Satan for God's chosen people (12:1-3), the birth from Israel of the Saviour (vv. 4-5), and an attack on Israel inspired by Satan during the Tribulation period (vv. 6-9). Satan's influence is now limited to earth (12:10-17), where he energizes the Antichrist (13:1-10) and false prophet (vv. 11-18) to rally mankind against God. The 144,000 witnesses of Revelation 7 remain faithful (14:1-8) as angels assist in warning humanity (vv. 6-13), and heaven itself joins in the destruction of sinful mankind (vv. 14-20).

Understanding the Text

"A male child, who will rule all the nations with an iron scepter" Rev. 12:1-5. The language of the text is messianic (cf. Ps. 2; Isa. 9:6-7). The woman is Israel, from whom the Christ was born. And the dragon is Satan.

How fascinating it is to see Satan crouched, ready to pounce on the Child as He enters this world in weakness. And what a reminder. Satan failed to thwart God when Jesus walked here as a man. Despite Satan's own considerable powers, how futile all his efforts are! He could not defeat a weakened Jesus. He is helpless against the Lamb, slain but now alive and powerful on God's own throne!

Don't worry about Satan. For all his posturing, he is a defeated enemy. Lost mankind may one day be enraptured by his appearance of power. But you and I know that there is more power in Jesus' appearance of weakness on the cross, than in all the armies Satan will be able to hurl against God.

"To a place prepared for her by God" Rev. 12:6. Some have linked this with Jesus' warning in Matthew 24:20-21, and concluded that during the Tribulation God will shelter the Jewish remnant in Mount Seir. One group has even gone so far as to store New Testaments, printed in Hebrew, in Seir's caves.

Perhaps they were too precise in their preparations. But they did not go too far in their faith. One day soon all that John describes will come to pass. History will culminate in scorching judgments. And we are wise if we too prepare for that day.

"He is filled with fury, because he knows that his time is short" Rev. 12:7-12. The one thing that opposing generals dread is that the enemy may learn their plans, and find some way to counter them. How fascinating that, in prophecy, God not only tells us what lies ahead, but also makes the

same information available to Satan!

But how significant this is as well. Satan may know what lies ahead. But there is nothing he can do to change the outcome of his rebellion! His frantic efforts, his raging hostility toward God's own, express frustration rather than confidence. He knows his time is short.

And we know that Satan has been, and will be, overcome by the blood of the Lamb.

"He pursued the woman who had given birth to the male child" Rev. 12:13-17. There really must be a place in our understanding of prophecy for Israel. God chose the Jewish people, and loved them consistently from the days of Abraham to the birth of Christ. Paul assures us that God has not rejected this people whom He foreknew, but that a day is coming when "all Israel will be saved" (Rom. 11:26). God's people still are precious to Him.

When, at history's end, the focus returns to Israel, and the prophet's visions take solid form, Satan's hatred of God will burn against the people that God so loves.

Whatever else this may say to us, one thing is clear. Satan hates what God loves. Those who have antagonism toward the Jews are most surely on the wrong side.

"Men worshiped the dragon because he had given authority to the beast" Rev. 13:1-10. Note the number of times that "power" is mentioned or alluded to in these verses. It's there in verses 2, 4, and 7.

Isn't it strange that "power to make war" is so attractive to humanity? We'll follow anyone who has power, and who promises to make us powerful. No wonder the dictators of history were able to win the allegiance of their people so easily. "Power to make war" attracts us, and we want to be on the winning side.

But note the word God has for His saints. As the Antichrist wins victory after victory, believers are told "this calls for patient endurance." Some of us will go into captivity. Some to the sword. And to all around us we will appear the weakest of all. And yet, the weak win. And the powerful of the earth lose.

May we learn to see the victory implicit in weakness, and the defeat inherent in power to make war, and live accordingly.

"He deceived the inhabitants of the earth" Rev. 13:11-18. I can't help being amused at those who take Uri Geller seriously. Bend nails by mind power? I'm sure! It's a lot like the "Christian" couple who amazed Christian congregations by the messages the Spirit gave about details of people's lives—until someone recorded the radio messages being transmitted to the speaker by his wife through a "hearing aid."

If we're so gullible when tricksters are involved, think how easily deceived folks will be when real supernatural powers are openly exercised!

The picture given of the future here contains a vital reminder. No matter what one claims to be able to do, don't desert the Word of God. No matter what economic sanctions exist, locking believers out of opportunities to work, or even to buy food, don't abandon the Word of God. Fix your confidence in Christ and His written Word, and do not be deceived.

"They follow the Lamb wherever He goes" Rev. 14:1-5. We met the 144,000 in Revelation 7. They were identified there as Jews, sealed and sent out by God to witness about Him during the terrible times associated with history's end. Here we see them, redeemed, standing before God's throne and praising Him with a song that is uniquely their own. And here we hear God's commendation. "They follow the Lamb wherever He goes."

You and I are not numbered with the 144,000. But we can be among those of every age, of whom it can be said, "They follow the Lamb wherever He goes."

"He had the eternal Gospel to proclaim" Rev. 14:6-13. Throughout the Christian era, sharing the Gospel has been the responsibility of human beings. But now, with humanity deceived by Satan, God demonstrates His grace in a unique way. Powerful angels call on mankind to worship God, and make the nature of the impending judgment absolutely clear.

This last expression of grace is rejected, and the saints are encouraged to endure. "Blessed are the dead who die in the Lord from now on," a voice from heaven says. "They will rest from their labor, for their deeds will follow them."

No matter how hard life here may be, or how unrewarding it seems to remain faithful to the Lord, remember. We are promised rest. And our deeds will not be forgotten, but will follow us to glory.

▶ DEVOTIONAL

Battle Hymn (Rev. 14:6-20)

Our American Civil War was undoubtedly the bloodiest of that era. Some 600,000 young men perished, 300,000 of them from disease and exposure associated with their military service.

As the terrible cost in lives became more and more clear, the imagery of Revelation 14 captured the imagination of Julia Ward Howe. How like a farmer harvesting a crop, gathering great armloads of grapes, and trampling on them till blood-red juices flow. How like John's terrible vision, in which the blood pours from the winepress of God's wrath, gushing down ravines surrounding the Holy City and spreading out for 180 miles!

And so the great "Battle Hymn of the Republic" was born. God, Howe said, is "trampling out the vintage where the grapes of wrath are stored. He has loosed the fateful lightning of His terrible swift sword." Somehow, in that terrible, costly struggle, Julia Ward Howe sensed the triumph of God's truth.

And she was right. Decades before, when the Constitution was being hammered out, the founding fathers shied away from the issue of slavery. The South was too wedded to the institution, and all the colonies must unite in declaring independence. And so the evil was ignored. It festered deep in the body politic year after year, until finally it could no longer be ignored. By then it was so deeply entrenched that it could only be excised at the cost of blood. The grapes of wrath were trampled out, and 600,000 young men died.

Every evil is like slavery. Undealt with, it festers in the soul. Christ purges those who turn to Him. But those who will not must be trampled, as God's truth goes marching on.

Personal Application

The vision of judgment teaches us the momentous nature of our sins.

Quotable

He has sounded forth the trumpet
  that shall never call retreat,
He is sifting out the hearts of men
  before His judgment seat;
O be swift my soul to answer Him!
  be jubilant, my feet!
Our God is marching on.

In the beauty of the lilies
  Christ was born across the sea,
With a glory in His bosom
  that transfigures you and me;
As He died to make men holy,
  let us live to make men free,
While God is marching on.

Glory! glory, hallelujah!
Glory! glory, hallelujah!
Glory! glory, halleluhah!
His truth is marching on.—Julia Ward Howe

DECEMBER 28 *Reading 362*
WRATH POURED OUT
Revelation 15–17

"Then one of the four living creatures gave to the seven angels seven golden bowls filled with the wrath of God, who lives forever and ever" (Rev. 15:7).

God is just in His judgments, however terrible they may appear to you and me.

Background

Mystery Babylon. After describing further judgments that are poured out on earth, John introduces something called Mystery Babylon. In symbolic form this is a woman, drunk on the blood of the saints, who is herself done away with by the Antichrist.

Identification of the Antichrist rests again on language found in Daniel's later chapters; language which suggests leadership of a consortium of political powers. The woman is often interpreted to represent a single, false, worldwide religion which featured worship of the beast and persecution of those who believe in God. The image of her riding the beast (17:3) suggests that religion is a tool used by the Antichrist in his rise to power—but discarded when power is achieved (see v. 17).

Certainly some of this is speculative. At the same time, within this context, explanations are given that make one thing sure. The beast of Revelation is the evil ruler and enemy of Israel whom Daniel describes in chapters 11 and 12. And the events here fit that prophecy so closely that we must assume Daniel and John share a common vision of things to come.

Overview

John sees seven angels, who are given bowls filled with the wrath of God (15:1-8). These are now poured out on the earth, but mankind's only response is to curse God (16:1-21). John also witnesses the destruction of a woman generally taken to represent false religion (17:1-6), which is done away with by the Antichrist, who demands the total allegiance of all (vv. 7-18).

Understanding the Text

"Last, because with them God's wrath is completed" Rev. 15:1. The judgments described in Revelation 15 and 16 are the last in the series of punishments to be experienced by earth's unrepentant population. These are terrible indeed. Yet we should remember that whatever happens on earth, to believer or unbeliever, is but a prelude to eternity. Some comfort themselves with the notion that a loving God would have no use for hell. The horrors which now take place on earth are evidence that God will deal most harshly with sin here and hereafter.

"Those who had been victorious over the beast and his image" Rev. 15:2-4. What a strange description: "Those who have been victorious." Victorious? When the context makes it clear that those so praised have died in the beast's vicious persecution of believers?

Yet they are victorious. Their victory consisted in resisting every pressure to join the powers of evil. The fact that they suffered is irrelevant. The fact that they were killed is of no account. What matters is that they remained true to God, and in that, they triumphed.

What a principle to remember as we enter another year. It is no matter what we may lose on earth, or how weak we may appear. In doing what is right, and remaining true to God despite the cost, we triumph.

"Out of the temple" Rev. 15:6–16:1. The seven angels that John now sees receive seven bowls filled with the dregs of God's wrath. When the content of these bowls is poured out on the earth, the temporal phase of God's judgment will be complete. But note that these angels appear from the temple.

In Israel's religion, the temple was the place God's people came to meet with Him. They worshiped God there. They brought their sacrifices and their offerings, and sang their praises on the temple steps.

There, hidden beyond the curtain that sheltered the temple's inmost room, God's presence rested. The wall and curtains that shielded Him from profane gaze also shielded the worshipers. The essential holiness of God, the blazing glory of His righteousness, was too overwhelming for any man to see and live.

But now we see seven angels, who have been within the temple and who are themselves afire with smoke and glory. They emerge to accept the bowls that bring God's judgments to a fiery close.

Let's remember, as we approach God, confident of our welcome, that His temple is a place of worship, but a holy place as well. We must approach Him in holiness and purity, for our God is a consuming fire (Heb. 12:29).

"And they cursed God on account of the plague of hail" Rev. 16:2-21. This chapter summarizes the series of judgments that are poured on the earth from the angel's golden bowls. It also reemphasizes a theme we've seen expressed before.

After the first series of judgments, John says that men tried to hide from God (6:15-17). After the next series he reports that mankind "still did not repent" of their idolatry or immorality (9:20-21). Now, after this series, John says, "They cursed God on account of the plague of hail, because the plague was so terrible."

These responses must be contrasted with the enthusiastic welcome given the Antichrist when he exhibited supernatural powers. The basic difference is that the judgments from God reveal His power—and man's sin. The wonders worked by the Antichrist reveal his powers—but appeal to man's sinful nature.

I've been interested in a new school of evangelism which argues that "signs and wonders" are and have been a key to winning people to Jesus. I doubt it. A person who will not respond to God's Word about Jesus will not be moved by signs and wonders. The issue lies in the heart of a man, and nowhere else.

"The great prostitute" Rev. 17:1-6. All through Scripture false religion has been identified with adultery and prostitution. This is in part because the pagan religions we meet in the Old Testament were nature faiths, and sexual orgies intended to stimulate nature gods to send rain were essential elements. Even more significantly, however, idolatry is associated in the Old Testament with immorality because the worship of false gods is a violation of covenant relationship with the Lord. There is only one God. To abandon Him in favor of another spiritual relationship is nothing less that adultery on a cosmic scale.

Thus interpreters of Revelation agree that in this chapter, Mystery Babylon, the great prostitute, the woman drunk with the blood of God's saints, is false religion. Even more, it is false religion developed to the nth degree: religion for its own sake, religion that hates the true God, religion that actively persecutes faith.

The reformers loved to identify the woman's purple and scarlet clothing with dress adopted in the Catholic church, and delighted in the fact that Rome is a city set on seven hills. As corrupt as 16th- and 17th-century Catholicism became, that identification is unlikely. What is sure, however, is that "religion" often is the enemy of God, and of His people. Cults today, and the possible future world religion portrayed here, are not friendly to true Christianity, which calls us simply to love Jesus and one another, and to be zealous of doing good.

▶ DEVOTIONAL
Riding the Beast
(Rev. 17)

Whatever else we may draw from Revelation 17, it seems quite clear that it's dangerous for religion to hitch a ride on politics.

Granted that the imagery is obscure. Even so, if we take the scarlet-clad woman as religion, the beast she rides (v. 7) fits Daniel's and Revelation's description of the Antichrist.

It's such a natural marriage. Religion, eager to gain adherents, unites with the current political power. But religion, which planned to use the marriage to gain her ends, suddenly discovers that she is herself being used! And when there is no more use for religion, she is cast aside.

I don't want to identify American Christianity with Mystery Babylon, or the beast with any political party. But it is worthwhile to observe that no marriage between faith and politics is secure. What is even worse, a marriage between an authentic Christianity committed to spiritual warfare and any political party, committed to maintaining political power, is disastrous for faith. The weapons of our warfare, Paul once wrote, are not carnal, but are spiritual.

Why then would we ever abandon the source of our power, to ride the beast?

Personal Application
Prayer and witness overcome the world.

Quotable
"Politics is the art of the possible, not the art of the ideal."—Russell Kirk

DECEMBER 29 *Reading 363*
BABYLON'S FALL
Revelation 18–19

> *"Woe! Woe, O great city, O Babylon, city of power! In one hour your doom has come!" (Rev. 18:10)*

When Christ intervenes, all the world holds to be important will be and mean nothing at all.

Background
Babylon. Babylon has both historic and symbolic significance throughout Scripture. Babel was the site of man's first banding together to build a city, and a tower, "that we might make a name for ourselves" (Gen. 11:1-5). Later the Babylon of Nebuchadnezzar served as the symbol of ultimate worldly power and wealth, and the temporary conqueror of God's people. The prophets rail against the pride and arrogance of Babylon; a pride rooted in military success and wealth. It is little wonder that here in Revelation the name "Babylon the Great" is given to human civilization itself. Mankind bands together, not to serve God and neighbor, but to make a profit, and enjoy luxuries which all too often are exacted from the poor and the oppressed.

In Revelation's picture of the fall of Babylon the Great at history's end, we read God's evaluation of worldly society itself. We read His contempt for the greed that motivates us, for the avarice that makes us passionately desire luxuries over justice, and for all our craving for power.

As we read of Babylon the Great, and observe its fall, we remember the verdict expressed in John's first letter:

> Do not love the world or anything in the world. If anyone loves the world, the love of the Father is not in him. For everything that is in the world—the cravings of sinful man, the lust of his eyes and the boasting of what he has and does—comes not from the Father but from the world. The world and its desires pass away, but the man who does the will of God lives forever (1 John 1:15-17).

Overview
An angel announces the end of human civilization, "Babylon the Great" (18:1-20). The judgment is carried out (vv. 21-24), to heavenly Hallelujah's (19:1-10). At last the heavens open, and Christ is revealed at the head of heaven's armies, as King of kings and Lord of lords (vv. 11-16). Earth's armies gather for a last desperate stand, only to be crushed by Christ Himself (vv. 17-21).

Understanding the Text
"A home for demons" Rev. 18:1-3. Babylon is a place where demons feel comfortable, because the values expressed in the society Babylon represents are at such odds with the values of our God. We must be careful, lest in valuing the wrong things, we find ourselves at home with evil (see DEVOTIONAL).

"Come out of her, My people" Rev. 18:4-8. The power and luxuries enjoyed by the men and women of this world are real enough. But they are devastating to the spiritual life. The greatest danger in having many possessions is that in time they begin to possess you.

God has given us all things richly to enjoy. But nothing must become more important to us than God. And no thing must become more important than a brother in need. Babylon is condemned because her people value material possession so much that they willingly commit crimes against their fellow man.

One of the greatest discoveries of my life came when I realized, after purchasing my first car, that I did not really care whether I had it or not. Since then I have lived alone in a single room, and been the owner of a fine, large house. And learned that there is no real difference to being with and being without.

Enjoy the things God gives you. But in your heart surrender them so perfectly to God that if He should take them all, you would suffer not one moment's grief.

"They will weep and mourn" Rev. 18:9-17. In 1929, as the stock market crashed, many a New Yorker opened his windows, and jumped. They would understand completely the grief expressed in Revelation 18, for they too cried out, "All your riches and splendor have vanished, never to be recovered."

Because they mistook the shadow for reality, the passing scene for stability, and the temporal for the eternal, they were unable to withstand the sense of loss.

How terrible to be a citizen of Babylon. How much better to fix our gaze and hopes on heaven.

"All who earn their living from the sea" Rev. 18:17-20. Again, the sea represents mankind. Those who earn their living from the sea are those whose whole grasp of life's meaning is bound up in society's material values. As civilization, with its wealth and splendor, comes crashing down at history's ends, such men will weep. But the saints, apostles, and prophets of God will rejoice.

Perhaps we should rejoice even now when we experience reverses. To lose what we cannot keep, that your desires may again be fixed on what we cannot lose, is great profit indeed.

"The light of a lamp will never shine in you again" Rev. 18:21-24. The world created by lost humanity is doomed to endless destruction. In biblical times a light was always kept burning in a family's home at night. Even the poor kept a single lamp lit. For one's "lamp to go out" symbolized an empty and abandoned home.

And so it is with Babylon. When with great violence God overthrows Babylon, that city of the lost will never be built again. Remember that, as you watch the endless stream of commercials that try to convince you that you must possess more and more. Babylon's light will soon go out, never to shine again. The spells that led all the names astray will crumble into dust. And those who resisted Babylon's allure will know an endless joy.

"Hallelujah!" Rev. 19:1-10 The scene again shifts to heaven. There the fall of Babylon is a cause for rejoicing. God now reigns. And all the saints will celebrate at the wedding supper of the Lamb.

The symbolism here is powerful too. In the Old Testament God is pictured as the Husband of Israel. In the New Testament Christ is the Bridegroom, the church His chosen bride. In biblical times the joining of the betrothed occasioned a week-long celebration. Friends and neighbors feasted, danced, and sang as they shared the newly married couple's joy.

The wedding supper thus joyously marked the inauguration of the rest of life: a life in which two who had been separate would now be one.

Just so with us. Earth's tragic tale is ended. Babylon lies in ruins. And at last Bridegroom and bride sit down together at the nuptial feast. For all eternity ahead life will be new. And they will at last be one.

"Kings of kings and Lord of lords" Rev. 19:11-21. Christ now and at last leads armies of angels that snuff out mankind's last resistance to His rule. Satan is bound. The beast and false prophet are summarily condemned to the lake of fire. And as for the rest, "the rest of them were killed with the sword that comes out of the mouth of the rider on the horse, and all the birds gorge themselves on their flesh."

▶ DEVOTIONAL
O Babylon!
(Rev. 18:1-13)

Babylon. The city of man.

John writes, "She has become a home for demons." If you wonder why, and want a standard against which to compare Babylon, choose Eden. In Eden man lived in harmony with nature. An intimate relationship existed between Adam and Eve, and the first pair and God. The scene is pastoral; the dominant impression is one of harmony and simple joys. In the quiet of Eden there is time to contemplate; time to discover; time to grow and to become.

In contrast the clamor of construction echoes throughout Babylon. The city rumbles with activity. Bustling crowds rush here and there, eager for success, zealous to gain some new luxury. God's gentle rule is replaced by an authoritarian government that maintains its power by serving the passions of its citizens, and carelessly crushing those who oppose. Shops filled with unnecessary goods stimulate citizens to greater effort to gain more. Everywhere in Babylon there is luxury without satisfaction, achievement without delight, success without fulfillment.

In the mad rush of Babylon mankind is caught up in the pursuit of the meaningless. In the lights of the city mankind's eyes are blinded to the real issues of life, even as a moth is drawn to the flame that snuffs out its life.

Babylon is a trap, crafted by Satan, populated by the foolish, filled with the detestable, rich in material wealth but utterly poverty-striken in the coin of heaven. Babylon is a home for demons, a snare for humankind.

In the coming year, guard your motives, and keep watch over your desires. Babylon is here around us. Do not let her seduce you.

Personal Application

Learn to see the demonic in what to others seems to give life meaning.

Quotable

"The final chapter of human history is solely God's decision, and even now He is everywhere active in grace or judgment. Never in all history have men spoken so much of end-time, yet been so shrouded in ignorance of God's impending doomsday."—Carl F.H. Henry

---

DECEMBER 30 *Reading 364*

THE LAKE OF FIRE

Revelation 20

> *"Then death and hades were thrown into the lake of fire. The lake of fire is the second death" (Rev. 20:14).*

Heaven and hell are the ultimate realities.

Background

The thousand-year-reign. This is the only mention in Bible of a thousand-year period during which Christ rules on our present earth. Yet many of the themes seen in this puzzling chapter are developed quite fully in the Old Testament and in Christ's own eschatological teaching. One scenario, which may not be correct, but which is most fascinating, explains the chapter in this way.

After the armies of earth are crushed at Christ's return, the surviving population experiences the judgment described in Matthew 24. Many who enter the kingdom Christ will rule are thus unconverted individuals; if you will, Germans, but not Nazis. Christians, members of the body of Christ, have already met Christ in the air, as 1 Thessalonians 4 describes. The martyrs who experience the "first resurrection" are Old Testament saints or believers of the Tribulation era, as Daniel 12:4 indicates. These reign with Christ on earth for the thousand years, fulfilling the prophets' predictions of an era of peace under the Messiah.

Despite the ideal environment established by Christ in the Millennium, when Satan is released at the end of the era he finds willing followers among the descendants of the survivors, eager to rebel against the Lord. This final rebellion is quickly put down, Satan is assigned to the lake of fire, and at this point the universe itself dissolves, as described by Isaiah and in 2 Peter 3.

Now final judgment takes place. The dead appear before God, and all who are not written in the Book of Life—that is, who have not during one of history's eras put their trust in God—are consigned to the lake of fire.

One thing fascinates me about this interpretation of Revelation 20 and the many Old Testament and New Testament passages integrated with it. When God warned Adam in the Garden of Eden not to disobey, He said, "When you eat of it you will surely die" (Gen. 2:17). When Adam sinned death struck: first a spiritual death, and out of that a biological deterioration. No matter what man accomplishes in the physical universe, humanity remains spiritually dead, the grip of sin tragic and unbreakable.

One way to look at sacred history is to see it as a demonstration of this fact, and of the utter necessity of salvation. Human beings can and do blame crime and corruption on environment, on heredity, on Satan's influence, and on a host of other factors beyond individual control. But the fact remains that it is because of sin and spiritual death that pain and evil stalk us still.

God first gave man utter freedom—and the world became so evil the race had to be destroyed in the Genesis Flood (Gen. 6–8). Then God instituted human government by making man responsible to correct evils (9:6). And ancient empires emerged, whose rulers' pride and greed was expressed in terrible wars and torture. Then God chose a single family, the Jewish race, and covenanted to be their God. Even though He gave them a law that showed how to love Him and one's fellow man, Israel rebelled again and again, turning aside to idolatry. So God sent a Saviour, and proclaimed a Gospel of forgiveness and transformation for all. And the world ignored the invitation, preferring the pursuit of sinful desires. So at the last Christ institutes a kingdom where righteousness is enforced: a golden age of peace and plenty, with Satan's influence removed. Even then, when Satan is released, mankind gladly throws off the bondage of goodness to rebel yet again against God. In this all the awfulness of sin is finally, fully, revealed. And man apart from God's redeeming grace is shown to be a sinner indeed.

In this historic demonstration of the sinfulness of humankind, the necessity for a lake of fire is found. Each human being is too significant to simply perish, as if he or she had never been. And yet because sin is sin, and unredeemed men truly are spiritually dead, the unredeemed must be forever isolated from eternity's holy state.

Overview

The last battle over, Satan is chained (20:1-3) and martyrs are raised from the dead to reign with Christ (vv. 4-7). After a thousand years, Satan is released and again deceives the nations, but is then thrown into the lake of fire (vv. 8-10). This universe is then dissolved, and all the dead judged. Those not in the Book of Life are thrown into the lake of fire (vv. 11-15).

Understanding the Text

"He seized the dragon" Rev. 20:1-3. "I don't know why I did it," some Christians say. "I guess the devil must have made me do it." At best it's a poor excuse. The devil may tempt and encourage us to sin. But Satan can't "make" us do anything. Why, even God doesn't "make" us do things. He simply gives us the freedom to choose.

It would be nice if Satan were bound today. I suspect some of the corruption we see in our society would disappear. But even if he were bound, you and I would remain responsible to choose between evil and good; between God's will, and our own.

"They came to life and reigned with Christ a thousand years" Rev. 20:4. The members of this group are carefully identified. The fact that they had not worshiped the beast or received his mark indicates they must have lived and died during the terrible final years when the Antichrist held sway.

Even so there is a vital lesson here for us. Participation in evil may seem the easy or even the necessary choice at times. Many an employee has remained quiet, despite being aware of illegalities in his company's practices. Many an engineer has remained silent despite doubts about the safety of the product his employer produces. Many an accounting firm has been aware of sharp practices covered up in creative annual reports—and by taking refuge behind "accepted accounting standards" perpetuated fraud rather than lose an account. The martyrs of Revelation remind us that it may cost to take a stand for what is right. But that in the end, the rewards of righteousness are great.

"The first resurrection" Rev. 20:5-6. Some have objected strenuously to the notion that there might be more than one resurrection of the believing dead. A Rapture for Christians? A special resurrection for Tribulation martyrs? Another for Old Testament saints? How confusing! "Why," they say, "God wouldn't do anything like THAT."

Perhaps not. But I'm always fascinated by folks who are utterly certain about what God would and wouldn't, or could and couldn't, do. It must be wonderful to have such a secure grasp of God's intentions.

Personally, while I'm not ready to be dogmatic, I have the impression that God's plans are far more complex and multifaceted than even the most creative of us can imagine. Why, even the good cooks I've known haven't been satisfied to serve meat and potatoes at every meal. I suspect the future God will place before us will outdo the most lavish spread ever conceived for a royal court or luxury cruise.

"The devil . . . was thrown into the lake of burning sulfur" Rev. 20:7-10. Jesus tells us that the lake of fire was "prepared for the devil and his angels" (Matt. 25:41). Hell wasn't formed with mankind in mind. Heaven was.

This is an important truth for us to hold on to. God has done everything possible to keep human beings out of that eternal lake of fire. Including experiencing on Calvary a fate more awful for Him than the lake of fire could be for any man. On Calvary He who knew no sin was made sin for us, and the crushing weight of all of history's evil seared the holy Son of God.

If anyone goes to the lake of fire it will be because he has not responded to the love of a God who reveals Himself to all men through creation's universal Word, and through His incarnation (see DEVOTIONAL).

"The Book of Life" Rev. 20:11-15. It's in the Old Testament as well as here. This image of a book in which a record of those who know and love God is maintained. Malachi 3:16 calls is a "scroll of remembrance" which "was written in His presence concerning those who feared the LORD and honored His name." Here it is the Book of Life. And how appropriate a name!

Being found here is the difference between eternal life and eternal death. Between endless life in heaven, and unending existence in the lake of fire. How good it is to know that when we trusted Jesus as Saviour, our names were recorded there.

▶ DEVOTIONAL
The Lake of Fire
(Rev. 20:7-15)

There are many images of eternal punishment in Scripture. But the one that recurs most often is that of a vast, dark, and smoldering pool of burning sulfur, whose fumes rise sullenly into a leaden sky. Jesus Himself used language like this. He spoke of a place "outside." A place of "darkness, where there will be weeping and gnashing of teeth" (Matt. 25:30). A moment later He called it "the eternal fire prepared for the devil and his angels" (v. 41). The striking fact is that in His teaching Jesus spoke far more often of hellfire than of heaven!

You and I can't begin to grasp what the lake of fire is like, or fully understand the necessity for its eternal existence. There are no words that soften the impression given in Scripture, no arguments that make the terrible fate so many face palatable. All we can do is to confess that Scripture teaches that the lake of fire smolders there at history's end. And confess that God is love, and by love's eternal sacrifice, God has offered each human being a way of escape.

Personal Application

Let Scripture's images of the lake of fire deepen your awareness of what it means to be saved.

Quotable

"I cannot preach on hell unless I preach with tears."—D.L. Moody

DECEMBER 31 *Reading 365*
"I AM COMING SOON"
Revelation 21–22

> *"The Spirit and the bride say, 'Come!' And let him who hears say, 'Come!' Whoever is thirsty, let him come; and whoever wishes, let him take the free gift of the water of life" (Rev. 22:17).*

God's final message to us is an invitation to heaven.

Overview

God creates a new heaven and earth where He will dwell with men (21:1-5), from which the ungodly will be excluded (vv. 6-8). A heavenly Jerusalem will serve as the capital of the recreated earth (vv. 9-21), and God Himself will be there (vv. 22-27). There will be no more curse or night, but we will serve God and see His face (22:1-6). The vision ends with a warning (vv. 7-11), an open invitation (vv. 12-17), and the assurance that Jesus is coming soon (vv. 18-21).

Understanding the Text

"A new heaven and a new earth" Rev. 21:1. Both Isaiah and Peter graphically describe the dissolution of the material universe. Second Peter 3:10 says that "the heavens will disappear with a roar; the elements will be destroyed by fire, and the earth and everything in it will be laid bare." There is no place in eternity for a universe which has been corrupted by sin.

What a reminder for us. If it is necessary for God to replace a thousand million galaxies, untold millions of light years removed from earth, and all because of human sin, how awful must sin be. And how swiftly we should draw back from temptation!

"The New Jerusalem" Rev. 21:2-4. The real significance of Jerusalem in history is that it is the one place on earth where God chose to be uniquely present with men. The story of the temple's dedication reports that God's glory filled the temple: He settled there to be accessible to those of Israel who worshiped Him. Thus earthly Jerusalem serves as a metaphor for the heavenly city, destined to be the capital of the new heaven and earth.

God was present in earthly Jerusalem, but insulated from His people by the curtains and walls of the temple. The New Jerusalem is heaven, because there will be no more insulation of God from men. He will be with us, and "He will wipe every tear from [our] eyes."

"To him who is thirsty I will give to drink" Rev. 21:6-8. Isaiah used this same imagery, crying out:

> Come, all you who are thirsty,
> come to the waters;
> and you who have no money,
> come, buy and eat!
> Come, buy wine and milk
> without money and without cost
> (Isa. 55:1).

Just so, here God says, "I will give to drink without cost."

Heaven is ours at no cost to us. But hell is earned, by the vile, unbelieving acts that men perform.

"It shone with the glory of God" Rev. 21:9-21. The New Jerusalem is the most carefully described of anything in these chapters. Possibly this is because the city is the residence of God, who is Himself the focus of eternity to come.

Some scoffers have had a field day with the Holy City. Even though it is a 1,400 mile square, one man calculated that it could hardly hold a fraction of the people who must have lived from Adam's distant day to ours.

"Heaven isn't big enough!" he announced. And newspapers actually picked up his words, and ran them as the heading of a story on his findings!

Of course, even a careless reading of the text of Revelation 21 shows that the city rests on a restored earth, in the center of a renewed universe, and that the city is NOT "heaven" at all. But no one bothered to check the Bible's text. Not the scoffer with the slide rule. And certainly not the editors of the papers that printed his findings.

How sad when people fasten on to some detail of the text, distort it, and announce once again that the Bible's credibility has been disproved. How sad when reading of an eternity we each must face, that what is overlooked is the promise, "I will give to drink without cost from the spring of the water of life."

This is the real story in Revelation 21. Not the details of what life may be like when time has come to an end. But the invitation to make God our God; God's promise that "he will be My son" (v. 7).

"The Lord God Almighty and the Lamb are its temple" Rev. 21:22-27. In the Book of Psalms there is a sequence of poems known as "songs of ascent" (Pss. 120–134). These songs were either sung by pilgrims as they approached Jerusalem to worship or, as some commentators believe, sung by Levites as they stood on one of the 15 steps that tradition says led up to the temple from the court below. These were songs of joy; songs of praise. Songs that expressed the worshipers' sense of grand privilege as they approached the dwelling place of God on earth.

Just think what it means for heaven to have no temple. And think of the songs of joy that we will sing. For when in eternity we enter the New Jerusalem, we will be coming not to a building that represents God's presence, but to God Himself. And our whole being will overflow with praises and delight.

"No longer will there be any curse" Rev. 22:1-5. This, with God's personal presence, is the most wonderful thing about heaven. There will be no more curse. We will at last be unfettered. The potential that God planted in the human soul when He created mankind in His own image will at last be released from the cancer that eats at us now. We do not yet know what we will be, John says, "when He appears, we shall be like Him, for we shall see Him as He is" (1 John 3:2).

We shall serve Him, the text says. We will see His face. And we will reign forever and ever. We can't imagine everything that serving God and reigning implies (see DEVOTIONAL).

But if you wish to dream, dream of freedom from sin's curse; of becoming the person God has always intended you to be. And dream of seeing God face-to-face.

"The time is near" Rev. 22:10-17. It seems strange to read, "Let him who does wrong continue to do wrong" and "let him who does right continue to do right." At least, it seems strange until we sense the immediacy in the context. Jesus has cried, "I am coming soon!" (v. 7) and will immediately utter the same cry again (v. 12).

When Jesus comes, our destiny will be fixed. Today there is still time for the one who does wrong to repent. When Jesus returns, the door of opportunity will close.

Jesus is coming soon. Every man needs to heed that warning cry, and respond while the Spirit and the bride still say, "Come!"

"Amen! Come, Lord Jesus" Rev. 22:18-21. The more we know of life on earth, the more attractive heaven is.

The young dream dreams of next year, of marriage, of promotions on the job. The middle aged dream of retirement. And the aged dream of yesteryear. How sad if all our dreams are of life on this earth, of fleeting days and nights, and passing joys.

The Christian who has gazed on earth and found it a void has a different dream. We look up, and in our reverie imagine a loud trumpet blast. And with the saints of every time and place, we cry "Amen! Come, Lord Jesus."

▶ DEVOTIONAL
Heaven
(Rev. 21:22–22:5)

Donald Grey Barnhouse used to speculate in his Monday night New York Bible Class. What would heaven be like? He didn't know, of course. But he was quite sure that God had wonders beyond description in mind.

"I expect that one day God will tell me, 'Donald, go create a world and people it and govern it for Me,' " Barnhouse would say. Somehow he felt that the whole recreated universe, with it myriads of galaxies and uncounted stars, should be filled with beings who loved and worshiped God, and found great joy in Him. To Barnhouse this earth, and our race, was but a seed. And when that seed sprouted, and history had run its course, a redeemed humanity would be the agency through which God spread the knowledge of Himself through an endless multitude of possible worlds.

Perhaps. God's purposes undoubtedly have a scope that exceeds our most exalted imaginings.

But these concluding chapters of Revelation do make one glory exceedingly clear. When this world ends, we will know God. We will walk in His light, freed forever from the curse of sin. Free to serve Him, to see His face, and to love Him as we ought to love.

And for us, this is enough. For the true definition of "heaven" is, "heaven is where God is."

And that is where we will be.

No wonder John, who has seen it all, cries "Amen! Come, Lord Jesus."

Personal Application

The greatest blessing the new year could possibly hold would be the return of Christ.

Quotable

"Will He not give us all things when we are with Him? What shall our life and our nature not be when His promises unto us shall have been fulfilled! What will the spirit of man be like when it is placed above every vice that masters and subdues—when, its warfare ended, it is wholly at peace."—St. Augustine

---

The Variety Reading Plan continues with 1 JOHN

INDEX